Thailand's
Islands & Beaches

Steven Martin
Joe Cummings

LONELY PLANET PUBLICATIONS
Melbourne • Oakland • London • Paris

KO CHANG NMP
Peaceful waterfalls set in undisturbed rainforest, wilderness walks, spectacular diving & snorkelling

KO SAMET
Fine white-sand beaches, coral gardens & uninhabited islands

HUA HIN
Only a half day's journey from Bangkok, enjoy sensational seafood & sublime boulder-strewn beaches

KHAO SAM ROI YOT NATIONAL PARK
Superb views, exotic bird & wildlife, explore intricate caves

KO TAO
Diverse & abundant dive sites

BANGKOK
Bustling streetscapes, fascinating temples, famous nightlife, outstanding restaurants

CAMBODIA

MYANMAR (BURMA)

Sihanoukville

Battambang

Sisophon

Aranya Prathet

Sa Kaew

Phanom Kung Historical Park

Thap Lan National Park

Khao Yai National Park

Nakhon Nayok

Prachinburi

Chachoengsao

Chonburi

Si Racha

Sattahip

Ko Si Chang

Ko Phai

Ko Larn

Ko Man Wichai

Ko Kham Yai

Ko Samaesan

Ko Chuang

Rayong

Ko Samet

Chanthaburi

Khao Chamao/ Khao Wong National Park

Khao Khitchakut National Park

Laem Ya/ Ko Samet National Park

Ko Chang National Marine Park

Ko Chang

Ko Mak

Ko Kut

Hat Lek

Trat

Saraburi

Ayuthaya

Pathum Thani

Nonthaburi

BANGKOK

Bangkok International

Samut Prakan

Samut Sakhon

Samut Songkhram

Nakhon Pathom

Suphanburi

Ratchaburi

Kanchanaburi

Nam Tok

To Mae Wong National Park

Kaeng Krachan National Park

Phetchaburi

Cha-am

Hua Hin

Khao Sam Roi Yot National Park

Prachuap Khiri Khan

Hat Wanakon National Marine Park

Thap Sakae

Bang Saphan

Ko Tao

Chumphon

Dawei

Myeik

Pran Buri Dam

ANDAMAN SEA

Isthmus of

14° N

12° N

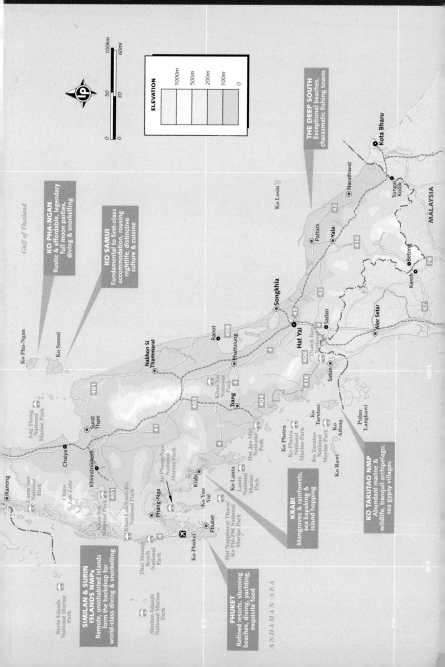

ELEVATION

1000m
500m
200m
100m
0

THE DEEP SOUTH
Exceptional beaches, charasmatic fishing towns

KO PHA-NGAN
Rustic & affordable, legendary full moon parties, diving & snorkelling

KO SAMUI
Fundamental to first-class accommodation, rousing nightlife, distinctive culture & cuisine

Gulf of Thailand

Kota Bharu

Ko Losin

Narathiwat

Sungai Kolok

MALAYSIA

Pattani

Yala

Betong

Keroh

Ko Pha-Ngan

Ko Samui

Songkhla

Alor Setar

Nakhon Si Thammaraat

Ranot

Phattalung

Hat Yai

Thaleh Ban National Park

Sadao

Satun

Khao Luang National Park

Trang

Pulau Langkawi

Ang Thong National Marine Park

Surat Thani

Chaiya

Khiriratnikhom

Ko Phetra National Marine Park

Ko Tarutao National Marine Park

Ko Adang

Ko Rawi

KO TARUTAO NMP
Abundant marine & wildlife, tranquil archipelago, sea gypsy villages

Hat Jao Mai National Park

Ko Lanta

Lanta National Marine Park

KRABI
Mangroves & rainforests, sea kayaking & island hopping

Ranong

Ngao Son National Park

Chiaw Lan Lake

Khao Sok National Park

Khao Lak/Lam Ru National Park

Ao Phang-Nga National Marine Park

Krabi

Phang-Nga

Ko Yao Yai

Thai Muang Beach National Park

Ko Phuket

Phuket

Hat Noppharat Thara Ko Phi-Phi National Marine Park

SIMILAN & SURIN ISLANDS NMPs
Remote, uninhabited islands form the backdrop for world-class diving & snorkelling

Surin Islands National Marine Park

Similan Islands National Marine Park

PHUKET
Refined resorts, stunning beaches, diving, yachting, exquisite food

ANDAMAN SEA

100m
50m
0

60mi
30
0

Thailand's Islands & Beaches
3rd edition – March 2002
First published – January 1998

Published by
Lonely Planet Publications Pty Ltd ABN 36 005 607 983
90 Maribyrnong St, Footscray, Victoria 3011, Australia

Lonely Planet offices
Australia Locked Bag 1, Footscray, Victoria 3011
USA 150 Linden St, Oakland, CA 94607
UK 10a Spring Place, London NW5 3BH
France 1 rue du Dahomey, 75011 Paris

Photographs
Many of the images in this guide are available for licensing from
Lonely Planet Images.
email: lpi@lonelyplanet.com.au
Web site: www.lonelyplanetimages.com

Front cover photograph
A fiery tropical sunset at Laem Phromthep, Phuket Province
(Anders Blomqvist)

ISBN 1 74059 063 5

text & maps © Lonely Planet Publications Pty Ltd 2002
photos © photographers as indicated 2002

Printed by The Bookmaker International Ltd
Printed in China

Contents – Text

Contents – Maps

GETTING AROUND

BANGKOK

EASTERN GULF COAST

NORTH-WESTERN GULF COAST (PHETCHABURI TO CHUMPHON)

SOUTH-WESTERN GULF COAST (SURAT THANI TO NARATHIWAT)

NORTHERN ANDAMAN COAST (RANONG TO PHUKET)

SOUTHERN ANDAMAN COAST (KRABI TO SATUN)

MAP LEGEND

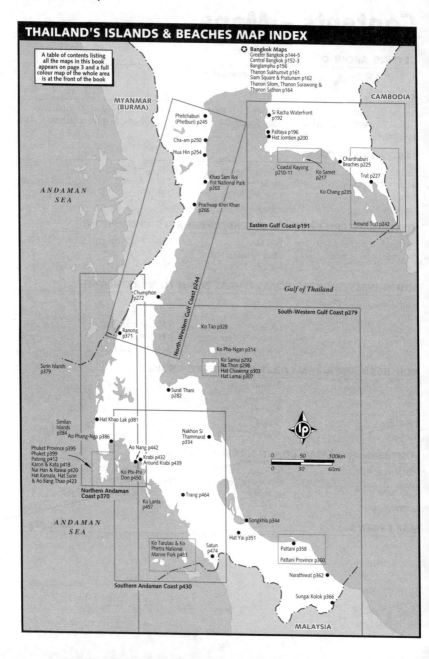

THAILAND'S ISLANDS & BEACHES MAP INDEX

A table of contents listing all the maps in this book appears on page 3 and a full colour map of the whole area is at the front of the book

Bangkok Maps
Greater Bangkok p144-5
Central Bangkok p152-3
Banglamphu p156
Thanon Sukhumvit p161
Siam Square & Pratunam p162
Thanon Silom, Thanon Surawong & Thanon Sathon p164

MYANMAR (BURMA)

CAMBODIA

Phetchaburi (Phetburi) p245

Cha-am p250

Hua Hin p254

Khao Sam Roi Yot National Park p263

Prachuap Khiri Khan p266

Si Racha Waterfront p192

Pattaya p196
Hat Jomtien p200

Coastal Rayong p210-11

Ko Samet p217

Chanthaburi Beaches p225

Trat p227

Ko Chang p235

Eastern Gulf Coast p191

Around Trat p242

ANDAMAN SEA

Gulf of Thailand

Chumphon p272

Ko Tao p328

South-Western Gulf Coast p279

Ranong p371

North-Western Gulf Coast p244

Ko Pha-Ngan p314

Ko Samui p292
Na Thon p298
Hat Chaweng p303
Hat Lamai p307

Surin Islands p379

Surat Thani p282

Similan Islands p384
Ao Phang-Nga p386

Hat Khao Lak p381

Nakhon Si Thammarat p334

0   50   100km
0   30   60mi

Phuket Province p395
Phuket p399
Patong p412
Karon & Kata p418
Nai Han & Rawai p420
Hat Kamala, Hat Surin & Ao Bang Thao p423

Ao Nang p442

Krabi p432
Around Krabi p439

Ko Phi-Phi Don p450

Northern Andaman Coast p370

Trang p464

Ko Lanta p457

ANDAMAN SEA

Songkhla p344

Ko Tarutao & Ko Phetra National Marine Park p483

Satun p474

Hat Yai p351

Pattani p358
Pattani Province p360

Narathiwat p362

Southern Andaman Coast p430

Sungai Kolok p366

MALAYSIA

The Authors

Steven Martin

Primed by frequent trips to Tijuana made during a wayward adolescence in San Diego, and inspired by the scenery in Francis Ford Coppola's *Apocalypse Now*, Steven squandered his parents' high school graduation gift of $1000 on a trip to the Philippines. This led to a stint on board a US Navy nuclear-powered attack submarine, and countless hours spent drunk or hungover in various ports of call along the Pacific Rim. Honourably discharged in 1988, Steven stayed on in the Philippines until a particularly violent coup attempt convinced him to relocate to Thailand in 1989. Since then Steven has taught English and Spanish, acted in a John Woo film, edited a now-defunct magazine and co-written a guidebook to Laos. He has also updated Lonely Planet's *Thailand* and *South-East Asia* guidebooks.

Joe Cummings

Joe began travelling in South-East Asia shortly after finishing university. Before writing became a full-time job, he was a Peace Corps volunteer in Thailand, a movie extra in *The Deer Hunter*, a graduate student of Thai language and Asian art history at the University of California in Berkeley, an East-West Center scholar in Hawaii, a university lecturer in Malaysia and a Lao bilingual studies consultant in the USA.

For Lonely Planet and other publishers he has written over 30 original guidebooks, photographic books, phrasebooks and atlases for countries in Asia and North America. For Lonely Planet he has authored the *Thai* and *Lao* phrasebooks as well as guides to *Thailand*, *Laos* and *Myanmar*, plus *World Food Thailand*, part of Lonely Planet's new culinary guide series. Joe has also published articles on culture, politics and travel in many print and online periodicals, including *Ambassador*, *Asia Magazine*, *Asian Wall Street Journal*, *Bangkok Post*, *Expedia*, *Fables*, *Geographical*, *Mexico Connect*, the *Nation*, *Outside*, *San Francisco Examiner* and *South China Morning Post*.

Joe has been covering South-East Asia for over 20 years and is fluent in Thai and Lao. He has twice been a finalist for London's Thomas Cook Guidebook of the Year Award for Lonely Planet's *Thailand* (1984) and *Vietnam, Laos & Cambodia* (1991) guidebooks. In 1995 he earned the Lowell Thomas Travel Journalism Gold Award for Lonely Planet's *Thailand*, an honour he also shared as a contributor and anonymous editor for *Travelers Tales Thailand* in 1993.

This Book

The 1st edition of *Thailand's Islands & Beaches* was co-authored by Joe Cummings and Nicko Goncharoff, and Joe updated the 2nd edition. This 3rd edition has been updated by Steven Martin.

FROM THE PUBLISHER

The 3rd edition of *Thailand's Islands & Beaches* was produced in Lonely Planet's Melbourne office. Mapping and design were co-ordinated by Jack Gavran, with additional mapping by Chris Love, Meredith Mail, Nick Stebbing and Chris Thomas. Matt King co-ordinated the illustrations, which were drawn by Mick Weldon, Jenny Bowman and Simon Borg. Photographic images were supplied by LPI, with special thanks to Valerie Tellini who went out of her way to organise the images for the special section. Pablo Gastar drew the chapter end, and Kusnandar created the climate chart. Simone Egger coordinated the editing with much assistance from Kristin Odijk (and the little one we look forward to meeting soon!), Errol Hunt, Jane Thompson and Rebecca Hobbs. Bruce Evans provided limitless stellar advice. The Language chapter was done by Quentin Frayne. Leonie Mugavin provided updated air travel information and library resources. Mark Germanchis assisted with layout, and artwork checks were done by Kristin, Chris, Bruce and Tim Fitzgerald. Thanks to the design department, in particular Jenny Jones for the cover. A special thanks to Lindsay Brown for writing the 'Thailand's Marine Environment' special section.

Thanks

Many thanks to the travellers who used the last edition and wrote to us with helpful hints, useful advice and interesting anecdotes:

Wayne Adams, Cat Adler, Martin Alvheim, Paula Anderson, Walter Andrea, Axel Aylwen, Hirokazu Azuma, Eric Bacci, Michael & Rosemary Bartlett, Guenther Beckermann, Maria & Tony Benfield, Edward A Berkovich, Kees Beukelman, Darin Bielby, Susan Blick, Sue Bollans, Philip Borrell, Stephanie Bourgeois-Fend, Sarah Budd, Peter Callaghan, Tony Carey, Maria Carrion, Lyle Cassard, Donna Clarke, Thierry Clerc, Roy Clogstoun, Marilyn Cook, Chris Courtheyn, Sally Cross, Carla Cudini, Patrick Cuff, Jon Curry, Eleena Darlow, Nichola Davenport, Sandy Denize, Katie Dobson, Daniel Donnelly, Kev & Dot Drinnen, Sheila Dunning, Mark Dwyer.

Per Edstrom, Bo Edvinsson, Honor Fallon, Stale Fedgaard, Filippo Fenara, Elisa Helena Fernandes, Tom Ferrington, Ray Field, Ryan Forsythe, Mickael Gaupillat, Tristan-Daniel Gavran, Evelyn Gerson, Stephen Gill, Sidsel Graae, Sally Graham, Joseph G Gschwendtner, James Harmen, IW Harris, Patrick Harris, Tye Hartall, Tracy Hay, Janos Hee, Sabine Heijman, Melanie Hill, Megan Ho, Neal Hollands, Kieran Howe, Matt Huddleston, Leclaire James, Nigel Johnson, David Joy, Tony Kelava, Domnal Kidney, Jochen Klaschka, Estelle Koh, Gerhard Kratz, Thomas Krogh, SK Lanter, Silvija Lapadatovic, Hanna Lasson, Shoham Latz, Kathrin Leaver, Jamie Lee, Annabel Lewis, V Liu, Marta Llorente, Joanne Lumb.

Tony Macvean, Elizabeth Madden, Claire May, Kevin May, Sara Mayes, Ian McLeod, Michael McWhirter, Mark Mellor, Wesley Mezzone, Steve Miller, Zoe Moore, Sauro Morganti, Marjorie Morkham, Nicki Mulhall, Michal Nis, Suzanne O'Brien, James Oehlcke, Peter Paal, Mary Page, Walter Paoli, John Pasley, Huong Lam Pham, Pedro Pinto, Inesa Pleskacheuskaya, Marga Pool, Samantha Pooley, Katherine Potter, Daniel & Catherine Price, Shahreen Quazi, Nipon Ratana-Arporn, Titti Ravaid, Sofia Rehn, Shannon Reid, Frances Runnalls, Angie Russell, Jim Ryan.

Jeremy & Sara Sampson, David Scarry, Martin Schmidt, Peter Scott, Katz Shoham, Don Silver, Ken Silver, Mark Slade, Margot Smith, Natasha Smith, Todd Sorel, James Sorrell, Rachael Stead, Andrew Stillman, Marie Sule, Helena Swan, Nick Talwar, Leslie Tan, Stephane Taulaigo, Joanne Terry, Dave Thompson, Arthur Torrence, Chris Torrens, Monica Ueltschi, Lele & Tom Uhl, Jacob Valdez, Mario van Hecke, Vincent van Rijn, Frank Visakay, Jessica Watson, Rosie Watson, Barney West, Frank Wheby, Peter White, Dave Williams, Steve Wilson, Max Wiman, Erwin Wisman, Andy Wong, Suyin Wong, Christian Woodyatt, Stephen Yarnold, Ante Zilic, Tom Zilic.

Foreword

ABOUT LONELY PLANET GUIDEBOOKS

The story begins with a classic travel adventure: Tony and Maureen Wheeler's 1972 journey across Europe and Asia to Australia. There was no useful information about the overland trail then, so Tony and Maureen published the first Lonely Planet guidebook to meet a growing need.

From a kitchen table, Lonely Planet has grown to become the largest independent travel publisher in the world, with offices in Melbourne (Australia), Oakland (USA) and Paris (France).

Today Lonely Planet guidebooks cover the globe. There is an ever-growing list of books and information in a variety of media. Some things haven't changed. The main aim is still to make it possible for adventurous travellers to get out there – to explore and better understand the world.

At Lonely Planet we believe travellers can make a positive contribution to the countries they visit – if they respect their host communities and spend their money wisely. Since 1986 a percentage of the income from each book has been donated to aid projects and human rights campaigns, and, more recently, to wildlife conservation.

> Although inclusion in a guidebook usually implies a recommendation we cannot list every good place. Exclusion does not necessarily imply criticism. In fact there are a number of reasons why we might exclude a place – sometimes it is simply inappropriate to encourage an influx of travellers.

UPDATES & READER FEEDBACK

Things change – prices go up, schedules change, good places go bad and bad places go bankrupt. Nothing stays the same. So, if you find things better or worse, recently opened or long-since closed, please tell us and help make the next edition even more accurate and useful.

Lonely Planet thoroughly updates each guidebook as often as possible – usually every two years, although for some destinations the gap can be longer. Between editions, up-to-date information is available in our free, quarterly *Planet Talk* newsletter and monthly email bulletin *Comet*. The *Upgrades* section of our website (W www.lonelyplanet.com) is also regularly updated by Lonely Planet authors, and the site's *Scoop* section covers news and current affairs relevant to travellers. Lastly, the *Thorn Tree* bulletin board and *Postcards* section carry unverified, but fascinating, reports from travellers.

Tell us about it! We genuinely value your feedback. A well-travelled team at Lonely Planet reads and acknowledges every email and letter we receive and ensures that every morsel of information finds its way to the relevant authors, editors and cartographers.

Everyone who writes to us will find their name listed in the next edition of the appropriate guidebook, and will receive the latest issue of *Comet* or *Planet Talk*. The very best contributions will be rewarded with a free guidebook.

We may edit, reproduce and incorporate your comments in Lonely Planet products such as guidebooks, websites and digital products, so let us know if you don't want your comments reproduced or your name acknowledged.

How to contact Lonely Planet:
Online: e talk2us@lonelyplanet.com.au, w www.lonelyplanet.com
Australia: Locked Bag 1, Footscray, Victoria 3011
UK: 10a Spring Place, London NW5 3BH
USA: 150 Linden St, Oakland, CA 94607

Introduction

Once known only to a trickle of backpacking hedonists plying the beach circuit between Crete and Bali, the beauty and bargains of Thailand's seaside resorts are now enjoyed by visitors of every ilk. In terms of variety and sheer attractiveness, and in many cases, cost, Thailand's islands and beaches more than hold their own against sun-and-sand offerings anywhere in the world.

Tropical Thailand offers the gentlest introduction to the Orient, combining images of the exotic – sparkling temple spires, sarong-clad farmers bending over rice shoots – with high standards of hygiene (including the best medical facilities in mainland South-East Asia) and most of the comforts of home. The country's 2710km dual coastline, lapped by the Andaman Sea and Gulf of Thailand, includes many of Asia's finest stretches of sand and marine recreation spots. The friendly and relaxed nature of the Thai people is also infectious: it doesn't take long for most visitors to slow their pace and move to the calmer rhythms of tropical Thai life.

Only a relatively small portion of coastline has been seriously developed for tourism. Travellers to these areas can choose from a variety of environments, from very casual palm-thatch and bamboo beach huts to luxurious Mediterranean-style idylls perched on sea cliffs. Seafood feasts, prepared as only the Thais know how, form a major part of coastal Thai culture and are available for every budget. Away from the tourist resorts and beach huts, a lesser known world of sand, rock, palm and salt water awaits discovery. Among the country's innumerable

THAILAND'S ISLANDS & BEACHES

coastal islands are many that few foreigners have yet stepped upon. Other beaches and islands – including several marine areas that enjoy national park status – receive only the occasional beachcomber, scuba diver, rock-climber or kayaker.

Whatever your style, whatever type of marine experience you may enjoy, Thailand's islands and beaches should fit the bill.

Facts about Thailand

HISTORY
Prehistory

The Mekong River Valley and Khorat Plateau areas of what today encompasses much of Thailand were inhabited as far back as 10,000 years ago. Modern linguistic theory and recent archaeological finds in Thailand show a culture that was among the world's earliest agrarian societies.

The ancestors of today's Thai were a diverse group scattered over a vast area including the South-East Asian mainland, Indonesia and south-west China. Many individual migrations brought these diverse peoples together in Northern Thailand.

Early Kingdoms

With no surviving written records or chronologies, it is difficult to say what kind of cultures lived in Thailand before the middle of the first millennium AD. However, by the 6th century an important network of agricultural communities was thriving as far south as modern-day Pattani and Yala, and as far north and north-east as Lamphun and Muang Fa Daet (near Khon Kaen).

Khmer conquests of the 7th to 11th centuries brought their cultural influence in the form of art, language and religion. A number of Thais became mercenaries for the Khmer armies in the early 12th century, as depicted on the walls of Angkor Wat. The Khmer called the Thais 'Syam', possibly from the Sanskrit *shyama* meaning 'golden' or 'swarthy', because of their relatively deeper skin colour at the time. Another theory claims the word means 'free'. Whatever the meaning, this was how the Thai kingdom came to be called Sayam or Syam. In north-western Thailand and Myanmar (Burma) the pronunciation of Syam became 'Shan'. English trader James Lancaster penned the first known English transliteration of the name as 'Siam' in 1592.

Meanwhile Southern Thailand – the upper Malay peninsula – was under the control of the Srivijaya empire, the headquarters of which may have been in Palembang, Sumatra, between the 8th and 13th centuries. The regional centre for Srivijaya was Chaiya, near the modern town of Surat Thani. Srivijaya art remains can still be seen in Chaiya and its environs.

Several Thai principalities in the Mekong Valley united in the 13th and 14th centuries, when Thai princes wrested the lower

A view of 19th-century Bangkok

10

north from the Khmer – whose Angkor government was fast declining – and created Sukhothai (Rising of Happiness). Thais consider Sukhothai the first true Thai kingdom. They later took Hariphunchai from the Mon to form Lan Na Thai (literally, one million Thai rice fields).

The Sukhothai kingdom declared its independence in 1238 under King Si Intharathit and quickly expanded its sphere of influence, taking advantage not only of the declining Khmer power but the weakening Srivijaya domain in the South. Although it was annexed by Ayuthaya in 1376, a national identity of sorts had already been forged. Many Thais today view the Sukhothai period sentimentally, seeing it as a golden age of politics, religion and culture – an egalitarian, noble period when everyone had enough to eat and the kingdom was unconquerable.

Among other accomplishments, the third Sukhothai king, Ram Khamhaeng, sponsored a fledgling Thai writing system that became the basis for modern Thai; he also codified the Thai form of Theravada Buddhism, as borrowed from the Sinhalese. Under Ram Khamhaeng, the Sukhothai kingdom extended as far as Nakhon Si Thammarat in the South, to the upper Mekong River Valley in Laos and to Bago (Pegu) in southern Myanmar. For a short time (1448–86), the Sukhothai capital was moved to Phitsanulok.

The Thai kings of Ayuthaya grew very powerful in the 14th and 15th centuries, taking over U Thong and Lopburi, former Khmer strongholds, and moving east until Angkor was defeated in 1431. Even though the Khmer were their adversaries in battle, the Ayuthaya kings incorporated large portions of Khmer court customs and language.

Ayuthaya was one of the greatest and wealthiest cities in Asia, a thriving seaport envied not only by the Burmese but by the Europeans who were in great awe of the city. It has been said that London, at the time, was a mere village in comparison. The kingdom sustained an unbroken monarchical succession through 34 reigns, from King U Thong (1350–69) to King Ekathat (1758–67), over a period of 400 years.

By the early 16th century Ayuthaya was receiving European visitors, and a Portuguese embassy was established in 1511. The Portuguese were followed by the Dutch in 1605, the English in 1612, the Danes in 1621 and the French in 1662. In the mid-16th century Ayuthaya and the independent kingdom of Lanna came under the control of the Burmese, but the Thais regained rule of both by the end of the century. In 1690 Londoner Engelbert Campfer proclaimed, 'Among the Asian nations, the kingdom of Siam is the greatest. The magnificence of the Ayuthaya Court is incomparable'.

The Burmese again invaded Ayuthaya in 1765 and the capital fell after two years of fierce battle. This time the Burmese destroyed everything sacred to the Thais, including manuscripts, temples and religious sculpture. The Burmese, despite their effectiveness in sacking Ayuthaya, could not maintain a foothold in the kingdom, and Phaya Taksin, a half-Chinese, half-Thai general, made himself king in 1769. He ruled from the new capital of Thonburi on the banks of Mae Nam Chao Phraya (Chao Phraya River), opposite present-day Bangkok. The Thais regained control of their country and further united the disparate provinces to the north with central Siam.

Taksin eventually came to regard himself as the next Buddha. His ministers, who did not approve of his religious fantasies, deposed and then executed him in the custom reserved for royalty: Taksin was beaten to death with sandalwood clubs while enveloped in a velvet sack – so that no royal blood would touch the ground.

Bangkok Rule

Another general, Chao Phaya Chakri, came to power and was crowned in 1782 under the title Phraphutthayotfa Chulalok. He moved the royal capital across the river to Bangkok and ruled as the first king of the Chakri dynasty. He and his heir, Loet La (1809–24), assumed the task of restoring the culture, so severely damaged decades earlier by the Burmese.

The third Chakri king, Phra Nang Klao (1824–51), went beyond reviving tradition

Rama V (1868-1910). Considered a champion of the common person, and now venerated as a demi-god within contemporary Thai culture.

and developed trade with China while increasing domestic agricultural production. He also established a new royal title system, posthumously conferring 'Rama I' and 'Rama II' upon his predecessors and taking the title 'Rama III' for himself.

Rama IV, commonly known as King Mongkut (Phra Chom Klao to the Thais), was one of the more colourful and innovative of the early Chakri kings. He originally missed out on the throne in deference to his half-brother Rama III and lived as a Buddhist monk for 27 years. During his long monastic term he became adept in Sanskrit, Pali, Latin and English, studied Western sciences and adopted the strict discipline of local Mon monks. He kept an eye on the outside world and when he took the throne in 1851 he immediately courted diplomatic relations with European nations, while avoiding colonialisation.

Thai trade restrictions were loosened and many Western powers signed trade agreements with the monarch. Mongkut also established Siam's first printing press and instituted educational reforms, developing a school system along European lines. Although the king courted the West, he did so with caution and warned his subjects: 'Whatever they have invented or done which we should know of and do, we can imitate and learn from them, but do not wholeheartedly believe in them'. Mongkut was the first monarch to show Thai commoners his face in public; he died of malaria in 1868.

His son, King Chulalongkorn (known to the Thais as Chulachomklao or Rama V, 1868–1910), continued Mongkut's tradition of reform, especially in the legal and administrative realm. Educated by European tutors, Chulalongkorn abolished prostration before the king as well as slavery and corvée (state labour). Thailand further benefited from relations with European nations and the USA – railways were built, a civil service established and the legal code restructured. Though Siam still managed to avoid colonialisation, the king was compelled to concede territory to French Indochina (Laos in 1893, Cambodia in 1907) and British Burma (three Malayan states in 1909) during his reign.

In 1912 a group of Thai military officers unsuccessfully attempted to overthrow the monarchy – the first in a series of coup attempts that continues to the present day.

Revolution & Succession

While King Prajadhipok (Pokklao or Rama VII, 1925–35) ruled, a group of Thai students living in Paris became so enamoured of democratic ideology that they mounted a coup d'état, successfully, against absolute monarchy in Siam. This bloodless revolution led to the development of a constitutional monarchy along British lines, with a mixed military-civilian group in power.

In 1935 the king abdicated without naming a successor and retired to Britain. The cabinet named his nephew, 10-year-old Ananda Mahidol, to the throne as Rama VIII, though Ananda didn't return to Thailand from school in Switzerland until 1945. Phibul (Phibun) Songkhram, a key military leader in the 1932 coup, maintained a position of effective power from 1938 until the end of WWII.

Under the influence of Phibul's government, the country's name was officially changed in 1939 from 'Siam' to 'Thailand' – rendered in Thai as 'Prathêht Thai'. 'Prathêht' is derived from the Sanskrit *pradesha* (country). 'Thai' is considered to have the connotation of 'free', though in actual usage it simply refers to the Thai, Tai or T'ai peoples, who are found as far east as Tonkin, as far west as Assam, and from southern China to northern Malaysia.

Ananda Mahidol ascended the throne in 1945, but was shot dead in his bedroom under mysterious circumstances in 1946. His brother, Bhumibol Adulyadej, succeeded him as Rama IX. Nowadays no-one ever speaks or writes publicly about Ananda's death. Even as recently as 1993, a chapter in David Wyatt's *A Short History of Thailand* chronicling the known circumstances surrounding the event had to be excised before the Thai publisher would print and distribute the title in Thailand.

WWII & Postwar Periods

During their invasion of South-East Asia in 1941, the Japanese outflanked Allied troops in Malaya and Myanmar. The Phibul government complied with the Japanese in this action by allowing them into the Gulf of Thailand; consequently the Japanese troops occupied a portion of Thailand itself. Phibul declared war on the USA and Great Britain in 1942 but Seni Pramoj, the Thai ambassador in Washington, refused to deliver the declaration. Phibul resigned in 1944 under pressure from the Thai underground resistance (Thai Seri) and, after V-J Day in 1945, Seni became premier.

In 1946, the year King Ananda was shot dead, Seni and his brother Kukrit were unseated in a general election and a democratic civilian group took power under Pridi Phanomyong, a law professor who had been instrumental in the 1932 revolution. Pridi's civilian government, which changed the country's name back to Siam, ruled for a short time, only to be overthrown by Phibul in 1947. Two years later Phibul suspended the constitution and reinstated 'Thailand' as the country's official name. Under Phibul the government took an extreme anti-communist stance, refused to recognise the People's Republic of China and became a loyal supporter of French and US foreign policy in South-East Asia.

In 1951 power was wrested from Phibul by General Sarit Thanarat, who continued the tradition of military dictatorship. However, Phibul somehow retained the actual title of premier until 1957 when Sarit finally had him exiled. Elections that same year forced Sarit to resign and go abroad for 'medical treatment'; he returned in 1958 to launch another coup. This time he abolished the constitution, dissolved the parliament and banned all political parties, maintaining effective power until he died of cirrhosis in 1963. From 1964 to 1973 the Thai nation was ruled by army officers, Thanom Kittikachorn and Praphat Charusathien, during which time Thailand allowed the USA to develop several military bases within its borders in support of the US campaign in Vietnam.

Reacting to political repression, 10,000 students publicly demanded a real constitution in June 1973. In October that year the military brutally suppressed a large demonstration at Thammasat University in Bangkok, but General Krit Sivara and King Bhumibol refused to support further bloodshed, forcing Thanom and Praphat to leave Thailand. Oxford-educated Kukrit Pramoj took charge of a 14-party coalition government and steered a leftist agenda past a conservative parliament. Among his lasting successes were a national minimum wage, the repeal of anticommunist laws and the ejection of US forces from Thailand.

Polarisation & Stabilisation

Kukrit's elected, constitutional government ruled until October 1976 when students demonstrated again, this time protesting Thanom's return to Thailand as a monk. Thammasat University again became a battlefield as border patrol police, along with right-wing, paramilitary civilian groups, assaulted a group of 2000 students holding a sit-in. Hundreds of students were killed and injured; more than a thousand were arrested.

To get an idea of the ruthless brutality of this event, have a look at the punk-band Dead Kennedys' album *Holiday in Cambodia*. The graphic cover photo wasn't shot in Khmer Rouge-controlled Cambodia, but at Thammasat University. Using public disorder as an excuse, the military stepped in and installed a new right-wing government with Thanin Kraivichien as premier.

This bloody incident disillusioned many Thai students and older intellectuals not directly involved with the demonstrations. As a result, numerous idealists 'dropped out' of Thai society and joined the People's Liberation Army of Thailand (PLAT) – armed communist insurgents, based in the hills of Northern and Southern Thailand, who had been active since the 1930s.

In October 1977 the military replaced Thanin with the more moderate General Kriangsak Chomanand in an effort to conciliate anti-government factions. When this failed, the military-backed position changed hands again in 1980, leaving Prem Tinsulanonda at the helm. By this time the PLAT had reached a peak force of around 10,000.

Prem served as prime minister until 1988 and is credited with the political and economic stabilisation of Thailand in the post-Indochina War years (there was 'only' one coup attempt in the 1980s). The major accomplishment of the Prem years was a complete dismantling of the Communist Party of Thailand and PLAT through an effective combination of amnesty programs (which brought the students back from the forests) and military action. His administration is also considered responsible for the gradual democratisation of Thailand, culminating in the 1988 election of his successor, Chatichai Choonhavan.

Approximately 60% of Chatichai's cabinet were former business executives rather than ex-military officers, compared to 38% in the previous cabinet. Thailand seemed to be entering a new era during which the country's economic boom coincided with democratisation. Critics praised the political maturation of Thailand, even if they grumbled that corruption seemed as rife as ever. By the end of the 1980s, however, certain high-ranking military officers had become increasingly dissatisfied, complaining that Thailand was being governed by a plutocracy.

February 1991 Coup

On 23 February 1991, in a move that shocked Thailand observers around the world, the military overthrew the Chatichai administration in a bloodless coup *(pàtìwát)* and handed power to the newly formed National Peace-Keeping Council (NPKC), led by General Suchinda Kraprayoon. It was Thailand's 19th coup attempt and one of 10 successful coups since 1932; however, it was only the second coup to overthrow a democratically elected civilian government. Charging Chatichai's civilian government with corruption and vote-buying, the NPKC abolished the 1978 constitution and dissolved the parliament. Rights of public assembly were curtailed but the press was closed down for only one day.

Following the coup, the NPKC handpicked the civilian prime minister, Anand Panyarachun, a former ambassador to the USA, Germany, Canada and the UN, to dispel public fears that the junta was planning a return to 100% military rule. Anand claimed to be his own man, but like his predecessors – elected or not – he was allowed the freedom to make his own decisions only insofar as they didn't affect the military. In spite of obvious constraints, many observers felt Anand's temporary premiership and cabinet were the best Thailand had ever had.

In December 1991 Thailand's national assembly passed a new constitution that guaranteed an NPKC-biased parliament. Under this constitution, regardless of who was chosen as the next prime minister or which political parties filled the lower house, the government would remain largely in the hands of the military. The new charter included a provisional clause allowing for a 'four-year transitional period' to full democracy.

Elections & Demonstrations

A general election in March 1992 ushered in a five-party coalition government with

Narong Wongwan, whose Samakkhitham (Justice Unity) Party received the most votes, as premier. But amid allegations that Narong was involved in Thailand's drug trade, the military exercised its constitutional prerogative and immediately replaced Narong with (surprise, surprise) General Suchinda in April.

Back in power again, the NPKC promised to eradicate corruption and build democracy, a claim that was difficult to accept since they had previously done little on either score. In many ways, it was like letting the proverbial fox guard the henhouse, as the military is perhaps the most corrupt institution in the country – always claiming to be free of politics and yet forever meddling in it. Thailand's independent political pundits agreed there was more oppression under the NPKC than under any administration since 1980.

In May 1992 several huge demonstrations demanding Suchinda's resignation – led by charismatic Bangkok governor Chamlong Srimuang – rocked Bangkok and larger provincial capitals. Chamlong won the 1992 Magsaysay Award (a humanitarian service award issued by a foundation in the Philippines) for his role in galvanising the public to reject Suchinda. After street confrontations between protesters and the military near Bangkok's Democracy Monument resulted in nearly 50 deaths and hundreds of injuries, Suchinda resigned after less than six weeks as premier. The military-backed government also agreed to institute a constitutional amendment requiring that Thailand's prime minister come from the ranks of elected MPs. Anand Panyarachun was reinstated as interim premier for a four-month term, once again winning praise from several circles for his even-handed and efficient administration.

The September 1992 elections squeezed in veteran Democrat Party leader Chuan Leekpai with a five-seat majority. Chuan led a coalition government consisting of the Democrat, New Aspiration, Palang Dharma and Solidarity parties. A food vendor's son and native of Trang Province, the new premier didn't fit the usual Thai prime minister mould since he was neither general nor tycoon nor academic. Though well regarded for his honesty and high morals, Chuan accomplished little in the areas of concern to the majority of Thais – most pointedly Bangkok traffic, national infrastructure and the undemocratic NPKC constitution. By the end of 1993 the opposition was calling for parliamentary dissolution and a royal command appointed a new cabinet for Chuan in December 1994.

Chuan never completed his four-year term, and a new general election ushered in a seven-party coalition led by the Chart Thai (Thai Nationality) Party. At the helm was 63-year-old billionaire Banharn Silapaarcha, whom the Thai press called a 'walking ATM'. Two of the largest partners in the coalition, the Palang Dharma and New Aspiration parties, were former participants from the Chuan coalition. Barnharn wasn't very popular with the Thai media, who immediately attacked his tendency to fill senior government positions from a pool of rural politicians known to be heavily involved in money-politics. In September 1996 the Barnharn government collapsed amid a spate of corruption scandals and a crisis of confidence. The November national election, marked by violence and accusations of vote-buying, saw former deputy prime minister and army commander Chavalit Yongchaiyudh of the New Aspiration Party secure the premiership with a dubious mix of coalition parties.

In July 1997, following several months of warning signs that almost everyone in Thailand and in the international community chose to ignore (see the Economy section of this chapter for details), the Thai currency fell into a deflationary tailspin and the national economy crashed to a virtual halt. In September 1997 the Thai parliament voted-in a new constitution that guaranteed – at least on paper – more human and civil rights than had hitherto been codified in Thailand. As the first national charter to be prepared under civilian auspices, the 'people's constitution' fostered great hope in a people emotionally battered by the ongoing economic crisis.

Hope faded as Chavalit, living up to everyone's low expectations, failed to deal effectively with the economy and was forced to resign in November 1997. An election brought Chuan Leekpai back into office, where he seemed to be doing a slow but steady job in righting the listing economy under the guidance of the International Monetary Fund (IMF). Yet for poor and rural constituents who suffered greatly from the economic downturn, Chuan's IMF-tutored policies seemed painfully ineffective. When Thaksin Shinawatra, a telecommunications tycoon from Chiang Mai, began promising a suspension on farmers' debt payments and a million *baht* in development funds for each and every village in Thailand, it spelt the end for Chuan. Despite charges that Thaksin was deceitful about his personal worth, he overwhelmingly defeated Chuan in elections in January 2001.

While over a decade has passed without a military-led coup, Thai cynics will tell you that things *never* change and that the democratic Chatichai, Banharn, Chavalit, Chuan and Thaksin governments may merely be short-lived deviations from the norm of military rule. Hardened cynics hold the view that Thailand's 20th-century coups and counter-coups are a mere extension of the warlordism of early Thai *jâo meuangs.*

Optimists on the other hand, see Suchinda's hasty resignation as a sign that the military coup, as an instrument of change in Thailand, was only a minor detour on the country's road towards a more responsive and democratic national government. Corruption remains a problem, though the Berlin-based watchdog Transparency International recently dropped Thailand from its top 10 list in the annual Corruption Perception Index. Without question, Thailand's revised and amended constitution strengthens the nation's future claim to democratic status and political stability, even while the economy remains shaky.

GEOGRAPHY

Thailand has an area of 517,000 sq km, making it slightly smaller than the US state of Texas, or about the size of France. Its shape on the map has been compared to the head of an elephant, with its trunk extending down the Malay peninsula. The centre of Thailand, Bangkok, is at about 14° north of the equator, putting it level with Madras, Manila, Guatemala and Khartoum.

The country's longest north-to-south distance is about 1860km, but its shape makes distances in any other direction 1000km or less. Because the north-south reach spans roughly 16 latitudinal degrees, Thailand has perhaps the most diverse climate in South-East Asia. The topography varies from high mountains in the north – the southernmost extreme of a series of ranges that extends across northern Myanmar and south-west China to the south-eastern edges of the Tibetan Plateau – to the limestone-encrusted tropical islands in the South that are part of the Malay archipelago. The rivers and tributaries of Northern and Central Thailand drain into the Gulf of Thailand via the Chao Phraya delta near Bangkok; those of the Mun River and other north-eastern waterways exit into the South China Sea via the Mekong River.

These broad geographic characteristics divide the country into four main zones: the fertile centre region, dominated by the Chao Phraya River; the north-east plateau, the kingdom's poorest region (with thin soil and occasional droughts and floods), rising some 300m above the central plain; Northern Thailand, a region of mountains and fertile valleys; and the southern peninsular region, which extends to the Malaysian frontier and is predominantly rainforest. The southern region receives the most annual rainfall and the North-East the least, although the North is less humid.

Seacoasts & Islands

Extending from the east coast of peninsular Malaysia to Vietnam, the Sunda Shelf separates the Gulf of Thailand from the South China Sea. The Gulf is relatively shallow, with an average depth of 30m, reaching down to 85m at its deepest points. Most of Thailand's major rivers drain into the Gulf, tempering the water's surface salinity significantly.

On the opposite side of the Thai-Malay peninsula, the Andaman Sea – over 100m deep in offshore areas – encompasses that part of the Indian Ocean east of India's Andaman and Nicobar Islands. Together Thailand's Andaman Sea and Gulf of Thailand coastlines form 2710km of beaches, hard shores and wetlands.

Hundreds of oceanic and continental islands are found on both sides. Those with tourist facilities constitute only a fraction. The two broad types of island geography in Thai waters are gently sloped, granitic islands, such as those of the Surin and Similan Groups, and the more dramatic limestone islands that characterise marine karst topography – often with steep cliffs, overhangs, and caverns above and below the tideline. Abundant examples of such limestone islands can be found in Ao Phang-Nga (Phang-Nga Bay, also known as the Sea of Phuket).

CLIMATE
Rainfall
Thailand's climate is ruled by monsoons that produce three seasons in Northern, North-Eastern and Central Thailand, and two in Southern Thailand. The three-season zone, which extends roughly from the country's northernmost reaches to Phetchaburi Province on the southern peninsula, experiences a 'dry and wet' monsoon climate, with the south-west monsoon arriving between May and July and lasting into November. This is followed by a dry period from November to May, a period that begins with lower relative temperatures until mid-February (because of the influences of the north-east monsoon, which bypasses this part of Thailand but results in cool breezes), followed by much higher relative temperatures from March to May.

It rains more and longer along the Thai-Malay peninsula south of Phetchaburi, an area subject to the north-east monsoon from November to January, as well as the countrywide south-west monsoon. Because of this dual monsoon pattern, and because it is located closer to the equator, most of Southern Thailand has only two seasons, a

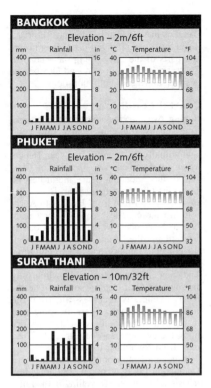

wet and a dry, with smaller temperature differences between the two.

Although the rains officially begin in July (according to the Thai agricultural calendar), they actually depend on the monsoons in any given year. As a rule of thumb, the dry season is shorter the farther south you go. From Chiang Mai north, the dry season may last six months (mid-November to May); in most of Central and North-East Thailand five months (December to May); on the upper peninsula three months (February to May); and below Surat Thani only two months (March and April). Occasional rains in the dry season are known as 'mango showers' (as they arrive with the onset of the mango season).

In Central Thailand it rains most during August and September, though there may be floods in October since the ground has reached full saturation by then. If you are in Bangkok in early October don't be surprised if you find yourself in hip-deep water in certain parts of the city. Along the Andaman Coast it rains most in May and October, as this area undergoes both monsoons.

Coastal Conditions

Having two curving coastlines to choose from means you can usually find good beach or island weather somewhere in Thailand virtually any month of the year. Hence, which coast you choose – the Gulf of Thailand or the Andaman Sea – might best be determined by the time of year. Both sides are mostly rain-free from January to April, both are more or less equally rainy from June to November, while the Gulf Coast is drier than the Andaman Coast from November to January, and in May and June. The south-west monsoon affects the Andaman Sea coast the most, while only the southern Gulf Coast – south of Phetchaburi – generally receives rain from the north-east monsoon. There is some rain year-round in the south, while it's very dry along the northern and eastern Gulf Coast areas from November to May.

In general, monsoon rains in Southern Thailand last only a couple of hours a day, occasionally longer. Travelling in the rainy season is usually not unpleasant, but unpaved roads may become impassable. 'Monsoon' comes from the Arabic *mausim*, which means 'season', and is not a reference to any type of tropical storm as is mistakenly believed by many outside tropical Asia. In the last 50 years only one typhoon has entered the Gulf of Thailand, though some generated along the Vietnamese coast may produce heavier than usual wind and rain conditions in the Gulf of Thailand from time to time. For climate detail as it affects divers, see Dive Seasons under Activities in the Facts for the Visitor chapter. See also When to Go under Planning in the same chapter for more climate information.

Temperature

Most of Thailand is very humid, with an overall average humidity of 66% to 82%,

depending on the season and time of day. The dry season reaches its hottest along the north-east plain, and temperatures easily reach 39°C in the daytime, dropping only a few degrees at night.

Temperatures south of Phetchaburi are more stable year-round. When it is 35°C in Bangkok, it may be only 30°C to 32°C on Ko Phuket or Ko Samui.

The eastern Gulf Coast, stretching from Bangkok to Trat, can be uncomfortably warm (over 35°C) during the months of March, April and May, although sea breezes tend to moderate inland temperatures.

ECOLOGY & ENVIRONMENT
Environmental Policy

Like all densely populated countries, Thailand has put enormous pressure on its fragile ecosystems. Fifty years ago the countryside was around 70% forest; as of 2000 an estimated 20% of the natural forest cover remained. The loss of forest cover has been accompanied by a similar reduction in wildlife populations. Logging and agriculture are mainly to blame for the decline.

In response to environmental degradation, the Thai government has created a large number of protected lands since the 1970s, and has enacted legislation to protect specific plant and animal species. The government hopes to raise total forest cover to 40% by the middle of this century. Thailand has also become a signatory to the UN Convention on International Trade in Endangered Species (Cites).

In 1989 logging was banned following a 1988 disaster in which hundreds of tonnes of cut timber washed down deforested slopes in Surat Thani Province, killing more than a hundred people and burying a number of villages. It is now illegal to sell timber felled in the country, and all imported timber is theoretically accounted for before going on the market. The illegal timber trade further diminished with Cambodia's ban on all timber exports, along with the termination of all Thai contracts by the Burmese. Laos is now the number one source for imported timber in Thailand, both legal and illegal.

These days builders even need government permission to use timber salvaged from old houses. This has helped curb illegal logging in the interior although corruption remains a problem. Unfortunately, Thai timber brokers are now turning their attention to Laos and Myanmar.

Corruption also impedes government attempts to shelter 'exotic' species from the illicit global wildlife trade and to preserve Thailand's sensitive coastal areas. The Royal Forestry Department is currently under pressure to take immediate action where preservation laws have not been enforced, including coastal zones where illegal tourist accommodation has flourished. There has also been a crackdown on restaurants serving 'jungle food' *(aahǎan pàa)*, which consists of exotic and often endangered wildlife species like barking deer, bear, pangolin, civet and gaur.

The tiger is one of the most endangered of Thailand's large mammals. Although tiger hunting and trapping is illegal, poachers continue to kill them for the lucrative Chinese pharmaceutical market; among the Chinese, the ingestion of tiger penis and bone is thought to have curative effects. In Taipei, the world centre for Thai tiger consumption, at least two-thirds of the pharmacies deal in tiger parts (in spite of the fact that such trade is forbidden by Taiwanese law). Around 200 to 300 wild tigers are thought to be hanging on in the national parks of Khao Yai, Kaeng Krachan and Khao Sok.

Forestry department efforts are limited by lack of personnel and funds. The average ranger is paid only 100B a day – some aren't paid at all but receive food and lodging – to take on armed poachers backed by the rich and powerful godfathers who control illicit timber and wildlife businesses. Increasing unemployment since the economic crisis of 1997 has also made wildlife poaching more attractive to those with dwindling livelihood options. This may be balanced by the countrywide decrease in land development and construction, as habitat loss is far more threatening to wildlife than poaching.

Marine resources are also threatened by a lack of long-term conservation goals. The upper portion of the Gulf of Thailand between Rayong and Prachuap Khiri Khan was once one of the most fertile marine areas in the world. Now it is virtually dead due to overfishing and the release of mainland pollutants.

Experts say it's not too late to rehabilitate the upper Gulf by reducing pollution and the number of trawlers, and by restricting commercial fishing to certain zones. A ban on the harvest of *plaa thuu* (mackerel) at the spawning stage has brought stocks of this fish back from the brink of destruction. The Bangkok Metropolitan Administration (BMA) is currently developing a system of sewage treatment plants in the Chao Phraya delta area, with the intention of halting all large-scale dumping of sewage into Gulf waters. Similar action needs to be taken along the entire eastern seaboard, which is rapidly becoming Thailand's new industrial centre.

Overdevelopment on Ko Phi-Phi is starving the surrounding coral reefs by blocking nutrient-rich run-off from the islands' interior, as well as smothering the reefs with pollutants. Ko Samui and Ko Samet face a similar fate if development isn't controlled and waste-disposal standards aren't improved.

One encouraging sign was the passing of the 1992 Environmental Act, which sets environmental quality standards and designates conservation and pollution control areas. Pattaya and Phuket were the first locales decreed pollution-control areas, making them eligible for government cleanup funds. With such assistance, officials in Pattaya claimed they'd be able to restore Ao Pattaya – exposed to improper waste disposal for at least the past 20 years – to its original state by the year 2000. A look at the bay tells another story. While Ao Pattaya may be cleaner than it was when the project began, anyone who remembers what the bay looked like in the 1970s can tell you that turning back the clock on environmental damage is easier said than done.

A large number of Thais remain unaware of the value of taking a pro-environment stance in everyday life or in encouraging ecologically sound tourism. The director of a certain regional Tourism Authority of Thailand (TAT) office was once heard to complain that eco-tourism was *lambàak* (inconvenient or bothersome) for Thai people but there was little she could do about it because 'that's national policy'. Fortunately such attitudes are steadily changing, especially among the young, who have grown up in relative affluence but who have begun to perceive the dangers of environmental neglect.

Even though environmentalism is national policy, only with strong popular support can protective laws, which are already plentiful but often ignored, be enforced. Current examples of 'people power' include the hundreds of forest monasteries that voluntarily protect chunks of forest. When one such *wát* (temple) was forcibly removed by the military in Buriram Province, thousands of Thais around the country rallied behind the abbot, Phra Prachak, and the wát's protectorship was re-established. On the other hand, wát with less ecologically minded trustees have sold off virgin land to developers.

Nongovernment organisations play a large role surveying and designating threatened areas and educating the public about the environment. In 1983 Wildlife Fund Thailand (WFT) was created under Queen Sirikit's patronage as an affiliate of the World Wide Fund for Nature (WWF). The main function of the WFT is to raise consciousness about the illegal trade in endangered wildlife. A list of several other groups is included in the following section. Citing the country's free press as a major incentive, the international watchdog organisation Greenpeace has a regional office in Bangkok.

Tourism & the Environment

In some instances tourism has had positive effects on environmental conservation in Thailand. Conscious that the country's natural beauty is a major tourist attraction for both residents and foreigners, and that tourism is one of Thailand's major revenue earners, the government has stepped up

efforts to protect wilderness areas and to add more acreage to the park system. In Khao Yai National Park, for example, all hotel and golf-course facilities were removed to reduce damage to the park environment and upgrade the wilderness. As a result of government and private sector pressure on the fishing industry, coral dynamiting has been all but eliminated in the Similan and Surin Islands, to preserve the area for tourist visitation.

According to *National Parks of Thailand* by Denis Gray, Colin Piprell & Mark Graham:

A growing number of conservationists, development experts and government officials believe that boundary markers and even guns do little to halt encroachment. The surrounding communities must somehow be allowed to share in whatever economic benefits a park can offer. Some sanctuaries, like Huay Kha Khaeng, recruit employees from local villages. In Thaleh Noi Wildlife Preserve, local fishermen are hired to take visitors around the lake in their boats to view the rich bird life. Rangers at Laem Son National Park encourage local fishermen to take visitors to outlying islands rather than over-fish the sea. Phu Kradung National Park takes on several hundred locals as porters to carry hikers' gear up the mountain. Some have become so protective of their park that they report violations of regulations to the rangers.

Of course, tourism has also caused environmental damage. Eager to make fist-fulls of cash, hotel developers and tour operators have rushed to provide ecologically inappropriate services in areas that are unable to sustain high-profile tourism. Concerns about this have prompted the government to look more closely at Ko Phi-Phi and Ko Samet – two national park islands notorious for overdevelopment. Part of the problem is that it's not always clear which lands are protected and which are privately owned.

Common problems in marine areas include the anchoring of tour boats on coral reefs and the dumping of rubbish into the sea. Coral and seashells are also illegally collected and sold in tourist shops. 'Jungle food' restaurants – with endangered species on the menu – flourish near inland national parks. Perhaps the most visible abuses occur in areas without basic garbage and sewage services, where there are piles of rotting garbage, mountains of plastic and open sewage run-off.

One of the saddest sights is the piles of discarded plastic water bottles on popular beaches. Many of these bottles are washed into the sea and waterways during the monsoon season. They are then sometimes ingested by marine or riverbank wildlife with fatal results.

What can the average visitor to Thailand do to minimise the impact of tourism on the environment? Firstly, avoid all restaurants serving exotic wildlife species. Visitors should also consider taking down the names of any restaurants serving or advertising such fare and filing a letter of complaint with the TAT, the WFT and the Royal Forestry Department (addresses are listed later in this section). The main patrons of this type of cuisine are the Thais themselves, along with visiting Chinese from Hong Kong and Taiwan; fortunately such restaurants are becoming increasingly rare as people come to understand the importance of preserving biological diversity.

When using hired boats near coral reefs, urge boat operators not to lower anchors onto coral formations. This is becoming less of a problem with established boating outfits – some of whom mark off sensitive areas with blue-flagged buoys – but is common among small-time pilots. Also volunteer to collect (and later dispose of) rubbish if it's obvious that the usual mode is to throw everything overboard.

Obviously, you shouldn't buy coral or shell products. Thai law forbids the collection of coral or seashells anywhere in the country, yet handicrafts made from coral or seashells are not hard to come by – Thai merchants simply import them from the Philippines.

See the boxed texts 'Trouble Underfoot' and 'Considerations for Responsible Diving' in the Facts for the Visitor chapter.

One of the difficulties in dealing with rubbish and sewage problems in tourist areas is that many Thais don't understand why tourists should expect different methods of disposal than are used elsewhere in the country. In urban and populated rural areas, piles of rotting rubbish and open sewage lines are frequently the norm – after all, Thailand is still a 'developing' country. Thais sensitive to Western paternalism are quick to point out that on a global scale the so-called 'developed' countries cause far more environmental damage than does Thailand (eg, per capita greenhouse emissions for Australia, Canada or the USA average over five tonnes each, while Asean countries contribute less than 0.5 tonnes per capita).

Hence, when making environmental complaints or suggestions to Thais in the tourist industry, it's important to emphasise that you want to work *with* them rather than against them in improving environmental standards.

Whether on land or at sea, refrain from purchasing or accepting drinking water offered in plastic bottles wherever possible. When there's a choice, request glass water bottles, which are recyclable in Thailand. The deposit is refundable when you return the bottle to any vendor who sells drinking water in glass bottles. When water is only available in plastic bottles, consider transferring the water to your own reusable container and leave the plastic bottle with the vendor if this is a more suitable disposal point than your eventual destination. If not, take the bottle with you and dispose of it yourself later at a legitimate rubbish collection site.

A few guesthouses offer drinking water from large, reusable plastic containers as an alternative to the individual disposable containers. This service is available in most areas of Thailand (even relatively remote areas like Ko Chang). Encourage hotel and guesthouse staff to switch from disposable plastic to either glass or reusable plastic.

In outdoor areas where rubbish has accumulated, consider organising an impromptu clean-up crew to collect plastic, polystyrene and other non-biodegradables for delivery to a rubbish pick-up point.

By expressing your desire to use environmentally friendly materials – and by taking direct action to avoid the use and indiscriminate disposal of plastic – you can provide an example of environmental consciousness not only for the Thais but for other international visitors.

Visitors should consider filing letters of complaint regarding any questionable environmental practices with TAT, the WFT and the Royal Forestry Department (addresses follow). Any municipal markets where endangered species are on sale should also be duly noted – consider enclosing photographs to support your complaints. For a list of endangered species in Thailand contact the WFT.

Write to the following organisations to offer your support for stricter environmental policies or to air specific complaints or suggestions:

Asian Society for Environmental Protection c/o CDG-SEAPO, Asian Institute of Technology, GPO 2754, Bangkok 10501

Bird Conservation Society of Thailand 69/12 Ramintra Soi 24, Jarakhe-Bua, Lat Phrao, Bangkok 10230

Friends of Nature 670/437 Th Charansavatwong, Bangkok 10700

Magic Eyes 15th floor, Bangkok Bank Bldg, 333 Th Silom, Bangkok 10400

Office of the National Environment Board 60/1 Soi Prachasamphan 4, Th Rama IV, Bangkok 10400

Project for Ecological Recovery 77/3 Soi Nomjit, Th Naret, Bangkok 10500

Raindrop Association 105–7 Th Ban Pho, Thapthiang, Trang 92000

Royal Forestry Department 61 Th Phahonyothin, Bangkhen, Bangkok 10900

Siam Environmental Club Chulalongkorn University, Th Phayathai, Bangkok 10330

The Siam Society 131 Soi Asoke, Th Sukhumvit, Bangkok 10110

Tourism Authority of Thailand (TAT) Le Concorde Bldg, 202 Th Ratchadapisek, Huay Khwang, Bangkok 10310

Wildlife Fund Thailand (WFT; ☎ 025 213 435, fax 025 526 083, e pisitnp@mozart.inet.co.th) 251/88–90 Th Phahonyothin, Bangkhen, Bangkok 10220; 255 Soi Asoke, Th Sukhumvit 21, Bangkok 10110

World Wild Fund For Nature, Thailand (WWF; ☎ 025 246 128, e wwfthai@ait.ac.th, w www.wwfthai.ait.ac.th) WWF Project Office, Asian Institute of Technology, PO Box 4, Khlong Luang, Pathum Thani 12120

FLORA & FAUNA

Unique in the region because its north-south axis extends some 1800km from mainland to peninsular South-East Asia, Thailand provides potential habitats for an astounding variety of flora and fauna.

Flora

As in the rest of tropical Asia, most indigenous vegetation in Thailand is associated with two basic types of tropical forest: monsoon forest (with a distinct dry season of three months or more) and rainforest (where rain falls during more than nine months of each year). Natural forest area – defined as having crowns of trees covering over 20% of the land – covers about 20% of Thailand's land mass. According to the UN World Development Report, Thailand ranks 44th in natural forest cover worldwide, ahead of Cambodia but behind Laos regionally, and equivalent to Mexico globally.

Monsoon forests constitute about a quarter of all the remaining natural forest cover in the country; they are characterised by deciduous tree varieties that shed their leaves during the dry season in order to conserve water. Rainforests, constituting about half of all forest cover in Thailand, are typically evergreen. The Central, Northern, Eastern and North-Eastern regions of Thailand mainly contain monsoon forests, while Southern Thailand is predominantly a rainforest zone. There is much overlap of the two – some forest zones support a mix of monsoon forest and rainforest vegetation.

The country's most famous flora includes an incredible array of fruit trees, bamboo (more species than any country outside China), tropical hardwoods and over 27,000 flowering species, including Thailand's national floral symbol, the orchid.

Fauna

As with plant life, the variation in the animal kingdom is closely affiliated with geographic and climatic differences. Hence, the indigenous animals of Thailand's northern half are mostly of Indochinese origin, while those of the South are generally Sundaic (ie, typical of Peninsular Malaysia,

Sumatra, Borneo and Java). The invisible dividing line between the two zoogeographical zones runs across the Isthmus of Kra, about halfway down the southern peninsula. The large overlap area between zoogeographical and vegetative zones – extending from Uthai Thani in the lower north to around Prachuap Khiri Khan on the southern peninsula – means that much of Thailand is a potential habitat for plants and animals from both zones.

Thailand is particularly rich in bird life, with more than 1000 recorded resident and migratory species – approximately 10% of the world's bird species. Coastal and inland waterways of the southern peninsula are especially important habitats for South-East Asian waterfowl.

Loss of habitat due to human intervention remains the greatest threat to birdlife; shrimp farms along the coast are robbing waterfowl of their rich intertidal diets, while in the South the over-harvesting of swiftlet nests for bird's nest soup may threaten the continued survival of the nests' creators.

Marine Life

Thailand's marine world falls within two major oceanic spheres. The Gulf of Thailand is itself an extension of the South China Sea, which is part of the Pacific Ocean, while the Andaman Sea is the section of the Indian Ocean east of the Andaman-Nicobar Ridge.

Coelenterates – a class of marine fauna characterised by the presence of a tentacle-rimmed mouth – are among the most exotic of Thailand's underwater life. They are appreciated by divers from all over the world, and include jellyfish, sea anemones and colourful corals. Among the most commonly seen are gorgonians, sea fans and sea whips.

Coral reefs may contain hundreds of thousands of species of flora and fauna; after tropical rainforests they are the most productive life habitat on the planet. A true coral reef develops on a substratum made up of the calcified 'skeletons' of hard coral. Most coral formations in Thai waters have established themselves on clusters of rock or on artificial structures such as shipwrecks. Over 200 hard coral species have been identified in the Andaman Sea, and around 60 in the Gulf. Coral generally isn't found below 30m, as its survival requires sufficient sunlight for photosynthesis.

Although they have not yet been properly catalogued, there are hundreds of species of fish in Thailand, from tiny gobies, the world's smallest fish (only around 20mm long), to gargantuan whale sharks, the world's largest fish (up to 18m and 3600kg). Reef fish, camouflaged among the colourful corals, provide endless hours of underwater entertainment for human observers. They include clownfish, parrotfish, wrasses, angelfish, soldierfish, rabbitfish, sweetlip, cardinalfish, triggerfish, tang, butterflyfish and lionfish. Deeper waters are home to larger species like snapper, jack, grouper, barracuda, mackerel, shark, marlin, sailfish, tuna and wahoo.

Four of the world's six species of sea turtle can be found in the Andaman Sea and the Gulf of Thailand: the Pacific ridley, green turtle, leatherback turtle and hawksbill turtle. All are endangered because their eggs, meat and shells are highly valued among coastal Thais. The loggerhead turtle once brought the list to five but has now been hunted to extinction in Thai waters. Turtle hunting and turtle-egg collecting are now illegal and the destruction of the turtle population has slowed considerably, but has not yet stopped. The main culprit in recent times has been Japan, the world's largest importer of sea turtles (including the endangered ridley and hawksbill). The Japanese use both of these for meat, leather and turtle-shell fashion accessories.

Thailand's warm waters attract whales and dolphins, around 25 species of which are known to frequent either or both the Andaman Sea and the Gulf of Thailand. Another marine mammal of note, the endangered dugong (also called manatee or sea cow), is occasionally spotted off the coast of Trang Province in Southern Thailand. The dugong is sacred to *pàk tâi* (Southern Thais) and is now protected by law.

National Parks & Wildlife Sanctuaries

Despite Thailand's rich diversity of flora and fauna, only in recent years have most of the 96 national parks (only around half of which receive an annual budget), 100 'non-hunting areas' and wildlife sanctuaries, and 65 forest reserves been established.

A number of the national parks are marine parks that protect coastal, insular and open-sea areas. The majority of these are well maintained by the Royal Forestry Department, but a few have allowed rampant tourism to threaten the natural environment, most notably on the islands of Ko Samet and Ko Phi-Phi. Poaching, illegal logging and shifting cultivation have also taken their toll on protected lands, but since 1990 the government has cracked down with some success.

Marine national parks offer very basic visitor facilities. There is usually somewhere to stay for a reasonable fee, and sometimes meals are provided, but it's a good idea to take your own sleeping bag or mat; basic camping gear is useful for parks without fixed accommodation. You should also take a torch (flashlight), rain gear, insect repellent, a water container and a small medical kit.

Most of the national parks are easily accessible, yet only around 5% of the annual number of visitors are non-Thai. Most parks charge a fee to visit (typically 200B) and there is usually somewhere to stay for a reasonable cost. For more information about staying in national parks, see Accommodation in the Facts for the Visitor chapter.

If you are interested in a more in-depth description of Thailand's protected areas, the well-researched *National Parks of Thailand* by Denis Gray, Colin Piprell & Mark Graham is highly recommended reading.

For a true appreciation of Thailand's geography and natural history, a visit to at least one national park is a must. In Bangkok the reservations office is at the national parks division of the forestry department (☎ 025 614 292), Thanon (Th) Phahonyothin, Bangkhen (north Bangkok). It's a good idea to get a Thai speaker to help with making this call or you'll have trouble navigating the Thai-language phone tree. Bookings from Bangkok must be paid in advance.

GOVERNMENT & POLITICS

The Kingdom of Thailand (to use its official English name) has been an independent nation since AD 1238, and is the only country in south or South-East Asia never colonised by a foreign power.

Since 1932, the government of Thailand has nominally been a constitutional monarchy inspired by the bicameral British model but with myriad subtle differences. National polls elect the 500-member lower house (Sapha Phu Thaen Ratsadon or House of Representatives, with four-year terms) and prime minister; until recently the 200 senators of the upper house (Wuthisaphaa or Senate, six-year terms) were appointed by the prime minister. In Thailand the Senate is not as powerful as the House of Representatives; the latter writes and approves legislation, while the Senate votes on constitutional changes.

Around ten political parties field candidates in national elections, of which only about half receive the bulk of the votes: Thai Nation Party, Democrat Party, New Aspiration Party, National Development Party and Thai Rak Thai Party.

The 1997 Constitution

Thailand's 15th constitution, enacted on 9 December 1991 by the military-controlled and now-defunct National Peace-Keeping Council (NPKC) limited public participation in the choosing of government officials. The 1991 constitution replaced one promulgated in December 1978.

On 27 September 1997, the Thai parliament voted in a new charter, Thailand's 16th such document since 1932 and the first to be decreed by a civilian government. Known as the *rátthàthamanun pràchaachon* (people's constitution) it puts new mechanisms in place to monitor the conduct of elected officials and political candidates and to protect civil rights. In many ways the new charter constitutes a bloodless popular revolution, as pro-democracy groups had been fighting for more than 10 years to reform the constitution. These groups were initially opposed by many in power, including the king, whose birthday speech in 1991 suggested leaving the military constitution in place. Such opposition to amendment of the military constitution led directly to the violence of May 1992 (see History, earlier in this chapter).

The document makes voting in elections compulsory, allows public access to information from state agencies, provides free public education for 12 years, permits local communities to manage, maintain, and use natural resources in their areas and forces Parliament to consider new laws upon receipt of 50,000 or more signatures in a public referendum. It also established several watchdog entities, including a constitution court, administrative court, national anti-corruption commission, national election commission, human rights commission and parliamentary ombudsmen to support constitutional enforcement. Other amendments include requirements for election candidates to hold at least a bachelor's degree, and for legislators who become prime minister or members of the premier's cabinet to relinquish their MP status.

As the pro-democracy newspaper the *Nation* pointed out when the new charter was passed, the document is not a panacea, but merely the start of a political reform process. Much depends on the will of Thailand's politicians to see that the charter guides new legislation and that such legislation is enforced.

Administrative Divisions

For administrative purposes, Thailand is divided into 76 *jangwàt* (provinces). Each province is subdivided into *amphoe* (districts), which are further subdivided to another five levels. Urban areas with more than 50,000 inhabitants and a population density of over 3000 per square kilometre are designated *nákhon*; those with populations of 10,000 to 50,000 with not less than 3000 per square kilometre are *meuang* (usually spelt 'muang' on roman-script highway signs). The term 'meuang' is also used loosely to mean metropolitan area (as opposed to an area within strict municipal limits).

A provincial capital is an *amphoe meuang*. An amphoe meuang takes the same name as the province of which it is capital, eg, amphoe meuang Surat Thani (often abbreviated as 'meuang Surat Thani') means the city of Surat Thani, capital of Surat Thani Province.

Except for Krungthep Mahanakhon (metropolitan Bangkok) provincial governors *(phûu wâa râatchakaan)* are appointed to their four-year terms by the Ministry of the Interior – a system that leaves much potential for corruption. Bangkok's governor and provincial assembly were elected for the first time in November 1985, when Chamlong Srimuang, a strict Buddhist and a former major general, won by a landslide. The mid-1996 elections saw independent Dr Pichit Ruttakul take over as Bangkok governor. By the end of 2000 the position had been overwhelmingly won by veteran politico Samak Sundaravej who promised to make Bangkok more livable by creating more parks and planting thousands of trees.

District officers *(nai amphoe)* are also appointed by the Ministry of the Interior but are responsible to their provincial governors. The cities are headed by elected mayors *(naayók thêtsàmontrii)*, tambon (precincts) by elected commune heads *(kamnan)* and villages by elected village chiefs *(phûu yài bâan)*.

The Monarchy

His Majesty Bhumibol Adulyadej (pronounced 'phumíphon adunyádèt') is the ninth king of the Chakri dynasty (founded in 1782) and the longest reigning king in Thai history (1988–). In fact, his Majesty is the world's longest reigning, living monarch.

Born in the USA in 1927 and schooled in Bangkok and Switzerland, King Bhumibol was a nephew of King Rama VII as well as the younger brother of King Rama VIII. His full name – including royal title – is Phrabaatsomdet Boramintaramahaphumiphonadunyadet.

His Majesty ascended the throne in 1946 following the death of Rama VIII, who had reigned as king for only one year (see History, earlier in this chapter). In 1996 Thailand celebrated the 50th year of the king's reign. He is fluent in English, French, German and Thai, as well as being a jazz composer and saxophonist. His royal motorcade is occasionally seen passing along Th Ratchadamnoen (Royal Promenade) in Bangkok's Banglamphu district; the king is usually seated in a vintage yellow Rolls Royce or a 1950s Cadillac.

The king has his own privy council comprising up to 14 royal appointees who assist with his formal duties; the president of the privy council serves as interim regent until an heir is throned.

The king and Queen Sirikit, have four children: Princess Ubol Ratana (born 1951), Crown Prince Maha Vajiralongkorn (1952), Princess Mahachakri Sirindhorn (1955) and Princess Chulabhorn (1957). A royal decree issued by King Trailok (reigned 1448–88) to standardise succession in a polygamous dynasty makes the king's senior son or full brother his *uparaja* (heir apparent). Thus Prince Maha Vajiralongkorn was officially designated as crown prince and heir when he reached 20 years of age in 1972; if he were to decline the crown or be unable to ascend the throne due to incurable illness or death, Ubol Ratana would be next in line.

Princess Ubol Ratana married American Peter Jensen in 1972 against palace wishes, thus forfeiting her royal rank, but was reinstated as Princess several years ago. The Crown Prince has married twice, most recently to an ex-actress. She has fallen from grace and is no longer living in Thailand.

Though Thailand's political system is officially classified as a constitutional monarchy, the constitution stipulates that the king be 'enthroned in a position of revered worship' and not be exposed 'to any sort of accusation or action'. With or without legal writ, the vast majority of Thai citizens regard King Bhumibol as a sort of demigod, partly in deference to tradition but also because of his impressive public-works record.

Neither the constitution nor the monarchy's high status prevent Thai people from gossiping about the royal family in private, however. Gathered together, the various whisperings and speculations with regard to royal intrigue would make a fine medieval fable. Many Thais, for example, favour the Princess Sirindhorn for succession to the Thai throne, though none would say this publicly, nor would this popular sentiment appear in the Thai media. Among the nation's soothsayers, it has long been prophesied that the Chakri dynasty will end with Rama IX; current political conditions, however, suggest the contrary.

It is often repeated that the Thai king has no political power (by law his position is strictly titular and ceremonial) but in times of national political crisis, Thais have often looked to the king for leadership. Two attempted coups d'état in the 1980s may have failed because they received tacit royal disapproval. By implication, the successful military coup of February 1991 must have had palace approval, whether *post facto* or *a priori*.

Along with nation and religion, the monarchy is very highly regarded in Thai society – negative comment about the king or any member of the royal family is a social as well as legal taboo. See Society & Conduct in this chapter for details.

ECONOMY

During the 1980s, Thailand maintained a steady GNP growth rate that by 1988 had reached 13% per annum. Thailand in the early and mid 1990s found itself on the threshold of attaining the exclusive rank of newly industrialised country (NIC). Soon, economic experts said, Thailand would be joining Asia's 'little dragons', also known as the Four Tigers – South Korea, Taiwan, Hong Kong and Singapore – in becoming a leader in the Pacific Rim economic boom.

The Bubble Bursts

In mid 1997 the 20-year boom went bust throughout South-East and East Asia, with Thailand leading the way. The economies worst affected by the financial turmoil – Thailand, Indonesia, Malaysia, the Philippines and South Korea – displayed certain common pre-crisis characteristics, including wide current-account deficits, lack of government transparency, high levels of external debt and relatively low foreign-exchange reserves. For the most part, the crisis stemmed from investor panic, with the rush to buy dollars to pay off debts creating a self-fulfilling collapse. Between 30 June and 31 October the baht depreciated roughly 40% against the US dollar, and dollar-backed external debt rose to 52.4% of the country's GDP. Such currency problems echoed the European currency crisis of 1992–93 when sudden, unforeseen drops in the pound, lira and other currencies sounded the death knell for a long period of steady growth and economic stability.

By January 1998 the Bank of Thailand stated that worsening economic conditions in the latter half of 1997 resulted in a doubling in the number of bad loans in the banking sector – about 18% of the total. Many banks and finance companies were forced to close in 1998, as the government made valiant efforts to restructure the economy and most especially the financial and property sectors. The International Monetary Fund (IMF) provided US$17.2 billion in loans, with the stipulation that the Thai government follow the IMF's prescriptions for recapitalisation and restructuring. The plan worked: The economy grew 4% to 5% in 1999 and 2000 after shrinking 10% in 1998. The weak baht helped to make Thai products more attractive overseas, and in 1999 Thailand's exports grew 13% over that of the previous year. These encouraging developments allowed Thailand to take an 'early out' from the IMF's loan package in 2000. Some observers have concluded that this forced cooling off was the best thing that could have happened to the overheated economy, giving the nation time to focus on infrastructure priorities and offering the Thai citizenry an opportunity to reassess cultural change.

What tends to get lost in discussions of Thai economic woes since 1997 is a long-term assessment of the journey the nation has travelled over the last three decades. Except for Malaysia and South Korea, no other country in the world has produced more rapid economic growth or seen such a dramatic reduction in poverty during that period. Per-capita income in Thailand increased 19-fold between 1963 and 1997. Even accounting for the recent baht devaluation, this means most Thais today are economically better off than they were in the 1960s. See Money in the Facts for the Visitor chapter for an account of the opportunities the baht devaluation has created for many foreign visitors.

The Big Picture

Around 14% of Thailand's exports are agricultural; the country ranks first in the world for rice (followed by the USA and Vietnam) and natural rubber, second in tapioca (after Brazil) and fifth in coconut (following Indonesia, the Philippines, India and Sri Lanka).

Other important agricultural exports include sugar, maize, pineapple, cotton, jute, green beans, soybeans and palm oil. Processed food and beverages – especially canned shrimp, tuna and pineapple – also account for significant export earnings. Thailand's top export markets include the USA, Japan and Singapore.

About 57% of the Thai labour force is engaged in agriculture, 17% in industry (including manufacturing), 15% in services and 11% in commerce. Manufactured goods have become an increasingly important source of foreign-exchange revenue and now account for at least 40% of Thailand's exports. Cement, textiles and electronics lead the way, with car and truck manufacture coming up fast. The country also has substantial natural resources, including tin, petroleum and natural gas.

Since 1987 tourism has become a major earner of foreign exchange, occasionally outdistancing Thailand's largest single export, textiles, with receipts as high as US$6 billion per annum. The government's economic strategy remains focussed, however, on export-led growth through the continued development of textiles and other industries such as electronics, backed by ample natural resources and a large, inexpensive labour force. Observers predict that such a broad-based economy will continue to make Thailand a major economic competitor in Asia in the long-term.

Raw, average, per-capita income at the time of writing was US$1949 per year; if measured using the 'purchasing power parity' method (which allows for price differences between countries), the Thais average US$6020 per capita annually. With an average net escalation of 11.2% per annum between 1985 and 1995, Thailand ranked highest in Asia in terms of real GDP growth per employee during that decade. Regional inequities, however, mean that annual income averages range from US$400 in the North-East to US$3000 in Bangkok. An estimated 20% of Thai citizens – mostly from Bangkok or Phuket – control over 60% of the wealth. The minimum wage in Phuket, Bangkok and its surrounding provinces is 165B (US$3.60) per day; in the outer provinces it falls to between 143B and 133B.

At the time of writing, the inflation rate had dropped to 1.5% per annum. Unemployment had risen to over 7%, over double what it was four years ago but still less than in many so-called industrialised countries.

Regional Economies

Southern Thailand is the richest region outside Bangkok, due to abundant agricultural (fruit, rubber, rice), fishing and mineral (tin and oil) resources, along with burgeoning beach tourism. Central Thailand, including the eastern Gulf Coast, grows fruit (especially pineapples), sugar cane and rice for export, and supports most of the ever-growing industries (textiles, food processing and cement).

North-Eastern Thailand has the lowest inflation rate and cost of living. Hand-woven textiles and farming remain the primary means of livelihood, though Nakhon Ratchasima (Khorat) is an emerging centre for metals and the automotive industry. Northern Thailand produces mountain or dry rice (as opposed to water rice, the bulk of the crop produced in Thailand) for domestic use, maize, tea, various fruits and flowers, and is very dependent on tourism.

Tourism

According to statistics from the TAT, Thailand received over 9.5 million tourists in 2000 – a 70-fold increase since 1960 when the government first began keeping statistics. Of these 57.9% of all visitors (5.5 million of the total) came from East and South-East Asia, with Japanese leading the way at 1.2 million, followed by Malaysians (1.1 million). Europeans as a whole made up approximately 2.3 million of the total, with Britons at the top (619,659), followed by Germans (390,030). American visitors accounted for 518,053 of the total (12,416 of whom were Thai-Americans), and Australians 314,531. Other major markets include China (753,781), Taiwan (706,482) and South Korea (451,347). With regard to per-day expenditures, Asians spent the most, Europeans the least.

Tourist revenue amounts to between US$5 billion and US$6 billion a year. A recent study carried out by the Thailand Development Research Institute confirms that:

Although the average daily expenditure of typical guesthouse tourists may not be as high as that of hotel dwellers, they...normally spend more because they usually stay in the country much longer. Income generated by these tourists is thought to penetrate more deeply and widely to the poorer segments of the industry.

The biggest growth in tourism since 1990 has been among the Thais themselves. Spurred by steady economic growth earlier this decade, and by the general lack of funds for international travel in their present economic situation, an estimated 40 million Thais per year are now taking domestic leisure trips. Ten or 15 years ago Western tourists often outnumbered Thais at some of the nation's most famous tourist attractions. Now the opposite is true; except at major international beach destinations like Phuket and Ko Samui, Thai tourists tend to outnumber foreign tourists in most places at a rate of more than five to one.

POPULATION & PEOPLE

The population of Thailand is about 62 million and currently growing at a rate of 1%

to 1.5% per annum (as opposed to 2.5% in 1979), thanks to a vigorous nationwide family-planning campaign.

Over a third of all Thais live in urban areas. Bangkok is by far the largest city in the kingdom, with a population of over six million (more than 10% of the total population) – too many for the scope of its public services and what little 'city planning' exists. Ranking the nation's other cities by population depends on whether you look at *thêtsàbaan* (municipal district) limits or at *meuang* (metropolitan district) limits. By the former measure, the four most populated cities in descending order (not counting the densely populated 'suburb' provinces of Samut Prakan and Nonthaburi, which would rank second and third if considered separately from Bangkok) are Nakhon Ratchasima (Khorat), Chiang Mai, Hat Yai and Khon Kaen. Using the rather misleading meuang measure, the ranking runs Udon Thani, Lopburi, Nakhon Ratchasima and Khon Kaen. Most of the other towns in Thailand have populations of well below 100,000.

The average life expectancy in Thailand is 69 years, the highest in mainland South-East Asia. Yet only an estimated 59% of people have access to local health services; in this the nation ranks 75th worldwide, behind countries with lower national incomes such as Sudan and Guatemala. There is only one doctor per 4166 people, and infant mortality figures are 31 per 1000 births (figures for neighbouring countries vary from 110 per 1000 in Cambodia to 12 in Malaysia). Thailand has a relatively youthful population; only about 12% are older than 50 years and 6% over 65 years.

The Thai Majority

About 75% of the citizenry are ethnic Thais, who can be divided into the central Thais or Siamese of the Chao Phraya Delta (the most densely populated region of the country); the Thai Lao of North-Eastern Thailand; the Thai Yuan of northern Thailand and the Thai Pak Tai of Southern Thailand. Each group speaks its own Thai dialect and to a certain extent practises customs unique to

Faràng Forever?

Visitors of European descent travelling in Thailand may sometimes hear themselves referred to as *faràng*. Although there's some debate as to the true historical derivation of the term, most linguists who understand Thai orthography agree it comes from the Thai word for 'French', *faràng-sèht*, which is the Thai pronunciation of the French word *français*. A few amateur linguists argue that the Thais derived faràng from the Arabic 'ferringi' or other terms used by Middle Eastern traders in South-East Asia, but this seems unlikely since the Thai spelling – not the romanised version, but the way the word is written in Thai script – makes it obvious it's simply the shortened version of the Thai word for 'French'; furthermore historical Thai phonology would not naturally transfigure 'ferringi' as 'faràng'. At any rate the argument is somewhat a moot point since 'ferringi' comes from the northern Indo-European 'frank', which simply means 'French'! It has even been suggested that the English word 'foreign' originally meant 'French'.

Wherever the word originated, nowadays faràng is used more broadly to refer to any and all foreigners who appear to have European features. Most Thais would say the term has a neutral, non-pejorative connotation, but there is recognition that some faràng take offence at being racially identified. Thus the more polite Thai will say *khon tàang châat* (person of a different birth), which is of course equally racial! A very, very few will say *khon tàang prathêht* (person of a different country). However most Thais will only use either of the latter two terms in front of faràng or on radio or TV. In private conversation it's back to faràng.

Most faràng living in Thailand do not take umbrage at the term. Like the word 'gringo' in Latin America and perhaps 'gaijin' in Japan, much depends on how it is used. I've heard Thais mutter 'faràng' under their breath after a particularly unpleasant encounter with some boorish tourist, leaving little doubt as to the intended pejorative sense.

Joe Cummings

its region. Politically and economically the central Thais are the dominant group, although they barely outnumber the Thai Lao in the North-East.

Smaller groups with their own Thai dialects include the Thai Yai or Shan (Mae Hong Son), the Thai Lü (Nan, Chiang Rai), the Lao Song (Phetchaburi and Ratchaburi), the Phuan (Chaiyaphum, Phetchaburi, Prachinburi), the Thai Khorat or Sawoei (Nakhon Ratchasima), the Phu Thai (Mukdahan, Sakon Nakhon), the Yaw (Nakhon Phanom, Sakon Nakhon) and the Thai-Malay (Satun, Trang, Krabi).

The Chinese

People of Chinese ancestry make up 11% of the population. They are mostly second- or third-generation Hokkien (Hakka), Tae Jiu (Chao Zhou/Chiu Chao) or Cantonese.

Ethnic Chinese probably enjoy better relations with the majority population here than in any other country in South-East Asia, due partly to historical reasons and partly to traditional Thai tolerance of other cultures (although there was a brief spell of anti-Chinese sentiment during the reign of Rama VI). King Rama V used Chinese businesspeople to infiltrate European trading houses, a move that helped defeat European colonial designs on Siam. Wealthy Chinese also introduced their daughters to the royal court as consorts, developing royal connections and adding a Chinese bloodline that extends to the current king.

Minorities

The second-largest ethnic minority group living in Thailand is the Malays (3.5%), most of whom reside in the southern Thai provinces of Songkhla, Yala, Pattani and Narathiwat. The remaining 10.5% of the population is divided among smaller non-Thai-speaking groups like the Vietnamese, Khmer, Mon, Semang (Sakai), Moken (*chao leh* or 'sea gypsies'), Htin, Mabri, Khamu and a variety of hill tribes in the North. There are also a small number of Europeans and other non-Asians living in Bangkok and the provinces.

EDUCATION

The literacy rate in Thailand runs at 93.8%, one of the highest rates in mainland South-East Asia. In 1993 the government raised compulsory schooling from six to nine years, and in 1997 it decreed that all citizens were entitled to free public schooling for 12 years. Although a high social value is placed on education as a way to achieve material success, the system itself favours rote learning over independent thinking at most levels.

Thailand's public-school system is organised around six years at the *pràthŏm* (primary) level beginning at age six, followed by six years of *mátháyom* (secondary) school and *udom* (tertiary) education. In reality less than nine years of formal education is the national norm. These statistics don't take into account the education provided by Buddhist monks at *wát* (temple monasteries) in remote rural areas, where monastic schooling may be the only formal education available.

Private and international schools for the foreign and local elite are found in Bangkok and Chiang Mai, and in some other larger cities. The country boasts 12 public and five private universities, as well as numerous trade schools and technical colleges.

A teaching certificate may be obtained after attending a two-year, post-mátháyom program at one of the many teachers colleges scattered throughout the country. Two of Thailand's universities, Thammasat and Chulalongkorn, are considered to be among the top 50 universities in Asia.

ARTS
Theatre & Dance

Traditional Thai theatre consists of six dramatic forms: *khŏn,* formal masked dance-drama depicting scenes from the *Ramakian* (the Thai version of India's *Ramayana*) and originally performed only for the royal court; *lákhon,* a general term covering several types of dance-dramas (usually for non-royal occasions) as well as Western theatre; *lí-keh* (likay), a partly improvised, often bawdy folk play featuring dancing, comedy, melodrama and music; and *hùn lŭang* or *lákhon lék* – puppet theatre.

Mánohraa Also known simply as *nora*, this is Southern Thailand's equivalent to lí-keh and the oldest surviving Thai dance-drama. The basic story line bears some similarities to the 2000-year-old *Ramayana*. In this case the protagonist, Prince Suthon (Sudhana in Pali), sets off to rescue the kidnapped Mánohraa, a *kinnarii* (woman-bird princess). As in lí-keh, performers add extemporaneous comic rhymed commentary – famed nora masters sometimes compete at local festivals to determine who's the best rapper.

Năng Shadow-puppet theatre – in which two-dimensional figures are manipulated between a cloth screen and light source at night-time performances – has been a South-East Asian tradition for perhaps five centuries. Originally brought to the Malay peninsula by Middle Eastern traders, the technique eventually spread to all parts of mainland and peninsular South-East Asia. As in Malaysia and Indonesia, shadow puppets in Thailand are carved from dried buffalo or cow hides (*năng* in Thai).

Two distinct shadow-play traditions survive in Thailand. The most common, *năng tálung*, is named after Phattalung Province, where it developed from Malay models. Like their Malay-Indonesian counterparts, Thai shadow puppets represent an array of characters from classical and folk drama, principally the *Ramakian* and *Phra Aphaimani* in Thailand. A single puppetmaster manipulates the cut outs, which are bound to the ends of buffalo-horn handles. Năng tálung is still occasionally seen at temple fairs, mostly in Songkhla and Nakhon Si Thammarat Provinces. Performances are also held periodically for tour groups or visiting dignitaries from Bangkok.

The second tradition, *năng yài* (literally, big hide), uses much larger cut outs, each bound to two wooden poles held by a puppetmaster; several masters (almost always male) may participate in a single performance. Năng yài is rarely performed nowadays because of the lack of trained năng masters and the expense of the shadow puppets. Most năng yài made today are sold to interior decorators or tourists – a well-crafted hide puppet may cost as much as 5000B.

In 1994, in order to celebrate the King's 50th year on the throne, the Fine Arts Department initiated a project to restore the original 180-year-old set of năng yài figures used by the Thai royal court. The project required the refurbishing of 352 puppets along with the creation of 100 new ones to complete the royal set, known as Phra Nakhon Wai (City-Shaking) – a tribute to the impact they had on audiences nearly two centuries ago. In addition to the occasional performance in Nakhon Si Thammarat or Bangkok, năng yài can be seen at Wat Khanon in Ratburi Province, where năng yài master Khru Chalat is passing the art on to younger men.

Music

Traditional Music The classical, central Thai music is spicy, like Thai food, and features an incredible array of textures and subtleties, hair-raising tempos and pastoral melodies.

The classical orchestra is called the *pìi-phâat* and can include as few as five players or more than 20. Among the more common instruments is the *pìi*, a woodwind instrument that has a reed mouthpiece; it is heard prominently at Thai boxing matches. The *pìi* is a relative of a similar Indian instrument, while the *phin*, a stringed instrument plucked like a guitar whose name comes from the Indian *vina*, is considered native to Thailand. A bowed instrument similar to ones played in China and Japan is aptly called the *saw*. The *ranâat èk* is a bamboo-keyed percussion instrument resembling the xylophone, while the *khlui* is a wooden flute.

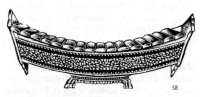

The ranâat èk, a type of xylophone with bamboo keys.

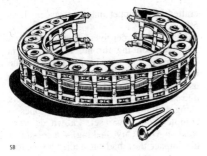
SB

The kháwng wong yài consists of tuned gongs arranged in a circular shape.

One of the more amazing Thai instruments is the *kháwng wong yài*, tuned gongs arranged in a semicircle. There are also several different kinds of drums, some played with the hands, some with sticks. The most important Thai percussion instrument is the *tà-phon* (or *thon*), a double-headed hand drum that sets the tempo for the ensemble. Prior to a performance, the players make offerings of incense and flowers to the tà-phon, which is considered to be the 'conductor' of the music's spiritual content.

The pìi-phâat ensemble was originally developed to accompany classical dance-drama and shadow theatre but can be heard in straightforward performance these days, at temple fairs as well as concerts.

One reason classical Thai music may sound strange to visitors is that it does not use the tempered scale. The standard Thai scale does feature an eight-note octave but it is arranged in seven full-tone intervals, with no semi-tones. Thai scales were first transcribed by Thai-German composer Phra Chen Duriyanga (Peter Feit), who also composed Thailand's national anthem in 1932.

Recommended books include *The Traditional Music of Thailand* by David Morton and *Thai Music* by Phra Chen Duriyanga (Peter Feit).

Modern Music Popular Thai music has borrowed much from Western music, particularly its instruments, but still retains a distinct flavour of its own. Although Bangkok bar bands can play fair imitations of every-

thing from Hank Williams to Madonna, there is a growing preference among Thais for a blend of Thai and international styles.

The best example of this is Thailand's famous rock group Carabao. Recording and performing for over 20 years now, Carabao is by far the most popular musical group in Thailand, and has even scored hits in Malaysia, Singapore, Indonesia and the Philippines with songs like 'Made in Thailand' (the chorus is in English). This band and others have crafted an exciting fusion of Thai classical and *lûuk thûng* (very rhythmic popular music from North-East Thailand) forms with heavy metal. These days almost every other Thai pop group sounds like a Carabao clone, and individual members of the original band are putting out solo albums using the now-classic Carabao sound.

Another major influence on Thai pop was a 1970s group called Caravan, which created a modern Thai folk style known as *phleng phêua chii-wít* (songs for life). Songs of this nature have political and environmental topics rather than the usual moonstruck love themes; during the authoritarian dictatorships of the 1970s many of Caravan's songs were officially banned. Though they dissolved in the early 1980s, Caravan re-formed for the occasional live concert. The group's most gifted songwriter, Surachai, continues to record and release solo efforts.

Yet another inspiring movement in modern Thai music is the fusion of international jazz with Thai classical and folk motifs. The leading exponent of this newer genre is the composer and instrumentalist Tewan Sapsanyakorn (also known as Tong Tewan), whose performances use a mix of both Western and Thai instruments. The melodies of his compositions are often Thai-based but the improvisations and rhythms are drawn from such heady sources as Sonny Rollins and Jean-Luc Ponty. Tewan plays soprano and alto sax, violin and khlui with equal virtuosity.

continued on page 33

MARK STRICKLAND

Thailand's underwater wonders can be conveniently accessed from island and beach resorts – there is easy snorkelling and, for those who wish to venture deeper, scuba courses and beginner dives, as well as adventurous liveaboard charters for the hardcore diver. Even the relatively shallow and busy Gulf of Thailand offers coral gardens around its offshore islands, but across the Isthmus of Kra the Andaman Sea beckons divers from around the world with its first-class diving. The Similan and Surin Islands, the Burma Banks and numerous deserted limestone islands can be accessed from popular resort centres such as Phuket and Krabi.

Soft corals and their relatives the gorgonians and sea whips do not develop the limestone skeleton of the reef-building, and more familiar, hard corals. Also unlike their hard cousins, soft corals do not contain light-dependent algae within their tissues and so are free to grow at greater depths away from sunlight. These graceful corals develop an amazing variety of forms in order to strain their microscopic food from the currents, and because the individual polyps of soft corals are not encased in a limestone cup, they are more visible, giving the colony its vivid colour.

MARK STRICKLAND

MARK STRICKLAND

Title Page: A seahorse perches among the coral, sponges and weed using its prehensile tail – a rare and rewarding sight in Thailand's famous coral reefs. (Photograph by Robert Halstead)

Top, middle & bottom left: Delicate soft corals and sea whips dominate the reef bottom at the Similan Islands. A diver must exercise buoyancy control and great care not to damage these habitats.

Molluscs, in their immense variety of form, inhabit all parts of the coral reef; among the most dramatic are the nudibranchs, or sea-slugs, unrivalled in the animal kingdom for elaborate shape and vibrant colour. Other molluscs of the reef include the snails, which encompass cowries and cone shells; bivalves, such as clams and oysters; and perhaps the most interesting of all, the cephalopods – octopus, squid and cuttlefish. The octopus is the master of stealth and camouflage, squeezing and contorting its colour-coded body and arms through impossible crevices to pounce on unwary crustaceans, particularly crabs. Squid and cuttlefish are superb swimming carnivores and can often be seen in schools. Along with the octopus, they possess unrivalled intelligence in the invertebrate world.

MARK STRICKLAND

MICHAEL AW

Top Right: Many species of nudibranch are bad tasting or poisonous – concentrating in their own tissues the stinging cells from their coral prey – and it pays to advertise such traits with vibrant colours (Similan Islands).

Bottom Right: Rapid colour changes enable the cuttlefish to blend with its immediate surroundings and to communicate mood swings or alarm. The diver may be left watching a pool of ink and a rapidly retreating cuttlefish.

Crabs, shrimps and other crustaceans abound on the coral reef, but it will take more than a cursory glance to spot them. Many are minute, spindly, almost transparent, others are masters of disguise – some crabs paste weeds and reef debris onto their carapace. Many of the small shrimps and crabs play a vital role in the reef ecosystem, removing detritus, dead tissue and parasites from their hosts, which may be a coral, sponge, fish or other reef creature.

ROBERT HALSTEAD

MARK STRICKLAND

Top Left: Concealed beneath the mantis shrimp's head are two praying mantis-like appendages used to catch prey. Spearer mantis shrimps impale their soft-bodied prey while smashers (pictured) hit their armoured prey repeatedly with a blunt, hammer-like heel.

Bottom Left: A twin-pronged spider crab, a slow-moving scavenger, crawls over a brilliant red gorgonian coral (Similan Islands).

MARK STRICKLAND

Looking more like a plant than an animal, the featherstar, or crinoid, is a primitive echinoderm, a group which also includes starfish, brittlestars, sea urchins and sea cucumbers. Featherstars, sometimes seen in 'rainbow' clusters of different species, grip onto coral outcrops with their claw-like cirri, and wave their brightly coloured arms in the current to trap water-borne food. Of the many starfish species, the most easy to recognise is the crown-of-thorns. Notorious for destroying large areas of reef when their populations periodically boom, the crown-of-thorns is, nevertheless, an integral part of the reef ecosystem.

Top Right: A featherstar nestles among soft coral in the Andaman Sea. Although appearing to have numerous arms, these are actually branches of just five arms – the five–part body plan is common to all echinoderms.

Bottom Right: The crown-of-thorns starfish feeds at night, everting its stomach over hard coral, digesting the polyps to leave behind a bleached white coral skeleton (Burma Banks, Andaman Sea).

MARK STRICKLAND

Shark encounters in Thailand are usually limited to the passive leopard and nurse shark, which shelter during the day in gutters and crevices, and the whitetip reef shark – these are easily excited predators, often baited to 'perform' for visiting divers. Along with the leopard shark, stingrays inhabit the sand and mud bottom adjacent to the reefs, feeding on molluscs and echinoderms that they find with acute senses of touch and taste. Stingrays mostly rest during the day, partially burying themselves in the substrate, and therefore posing a potential danger to unwary divers. Should a stingray be stepped on, its reflex action is to strike upwards with its poison-barbed tail. See Hazardous Marine Life later in this section for more information about sharks, stingrays and other scary things.

MICHAEL AW

MICHAEL AW

Top Left: A marbled stingray glides to the reef floor where it will partially bury its mottled form and all but disappear.

Bottom Left: The leopard shark is large (up to 3m) docile and lives on the sea floor. Its sluggish nature and size has made it a target for harassment by divers. Such behaviour is now actively discouraged by conscientious dive operators (Ko Tachai, Andaman Sea).

MARK STRICKLAND

Morays and other eels usually hunt at night, when they can be seen sliding in and around coral cavities and crevices searching for food which, for them, is virtually any animal, dead or alive. Morays must swallow their food quickly to re-establish sufficient water flow through the mouth and over the gills for breathing. During the day, morays retire to a coral grotto, their large heads and fang-filled mouths are all that is visible as they gape and 'pant' water. At a few popular dive sites in the Andaman Sea, morays have been accustomed to hand feeding to the point where they will leave their protective lairs at the first sign of an approaching diver and beg for hand-outs.

Top Right: A gaping moray eel in its coral cave – a common sight on day trips from Phuket. Lacking a swimbladder, and thus much in the way of buoyancy control, morays must rest among the reef crevices during the day after spending the night hunting and scavenging.

Bottom Right: Growing to over 1m long, though more usually seen at half that size, the blue ribbon eel starts life as a mostly black male, changing later into the blue-and-yellow female form (Similan Islands).

CASEY & ASTRID WITTE MAHANEY

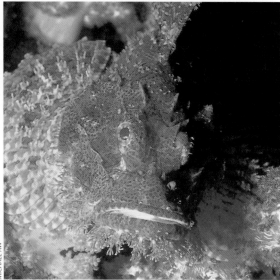

MICHAEL AW

To live among the riot of colour and shapes of the coral reef, many animals have evolved elaborate camouflage for protection and to aid hunting. Scorpionfish, stonefish and lionfish are related masters of camouflage, hunting by stealth and ambush. The scorpionfish lies motionless in the coral and reef rubble awaiting the approach of small fish; after a few small adjustments in position the strike will be a lightening-swift gulp. The lionfish uses a different tactic, slowly sneaking up on its prey before rapidly opening a cavernous mouth, sucking in a great volume of water and, if successful, a meal.

Top Left: Festooned with fleshy fringes, protrusions and mottled skin, the scorpionfish ingeniously blends into its surroundings (Richelieu Rock, Andaman Sea).

Bottom Left: Spotfin lionfish (also known as firefish) hunt by stealth. Their elaborate, elongated spines and contrasting markings confuse their prey; the familiar body shape of a predator does not register – until it is too late (Similan Islands).

MICHAEL AW

Relentless competition for food and a place to shelter has led to the amazing variety of shape, size, colour and behaviour of coral-reef fish. There are algal grazers, coral grinders and large-mouthed gulpers and sievers. There are countless ecological niches in the reef ecosystem, and often when a species rests, either during the day or night, another species will start its shift in that same niche.

GAVIN ANDERSON

MARK STRICKLAND

MARK STRICKLAND

Top Right: This splendid coral grouper, normally a voracious and opportunistic feeder, patiently waits at a cleaning station for a wrasse or shrimp to attend to its gills.

Middle Right: The regal anglefish is capable of producing a thumping noise that is loud enough to be heard by a diver.

Bottom Right: This ember parrotfish retreats to a small cave at night, after a day of scraping and grazing coral surfaces. Occasionally parrotfish secrete a clear mucous membrane in which they become encased while sleeping – perhaps as protection against predators that hunt using smell.

CASEY & ASTRID WITTE MAHANEY

In Thailand and all over the tropics, certain fish species have developed a close relationship with sea anemones. These fish are able to move freely among the stinging tentacles that would quickly paralyse other fish on contact. Although the anemone fish gains protection, and indeed is always found in proximity to an anemone, the anemone does not need the anemone fish and probably gains very little out of the deal.

MICHAEL AW

Top Left: Clown anemone fish never venture far from their host anemone. A typical group consists of a large dominant female, a single mature male and several immature males. When the female dies, the largest male will change sex and one of the smaller males will mature (Phuket).

Bottom Left: Anemone fish, such as this red and black one, are not born immune to the anemone's stinging tentacles. The fish acquire immunity by gradually covering themselves in the anemone's own mucous. Chemicals in the mucous stop the anemone from stinging itself and this feature is put to use by the anemone fish.

Many fish choose to feed at the edge of the reef where the plankton-rich waters of the open sea meet the reef. But away from the confines of the reef there is the increased danger of being eaten, so often fish will feed in tightly packed schools for protection. Along with common reef sharks and the occasional visit from larger oceanic sharks, other predators of the reef edge include turtles. Not great migrators like other turtles, hawksbill turtles are usually seen close to their feeding and breeding grounds, the coral reefs and tropical islands.

ASHLEY J BOYD

MARK STRICKLAND

Top Right: Fusiliers are among the most common schooling fish in Thailand's tropical waters. At night they disband and individuals find shelter in the nooks and crannies of the reef (Similan Islands).

Bottom Right: The hawksbill turtle is losing the battle for survival in South-East Asia. Not only is it still hunted for its 'tortoiseshell', but the quiet, sandy beaches it requires for nesting are disappearing under human encroachment (Ko Surin National Park).

THAILAND'S MARINE ENVIRONMENT

The largest animals likely to be encountered at Thailand's offshore dive locations are the magnificent whale shark, which is the largest living species of fish, and the manta ray, probably one of the most graceful and majestic of fishes. These docile plankton feeders are both entirely harmless and amazingly patient in the presence of over-friendly divers, but their true wonder is best appreciated from a respectful distance.

LAWSON WOOD

NIGEL MARSH

Top Left: The immense bulk of a whale shark is an unforgettable sight. Such encounters, though rare, can be had on day trips from Phuket.

Bottom Left: Dwarfing a diver, manta rays are a relatively common sight in the reef waters of Thailand. This manta is using its 'horns', modified from part of the pectoral fins, to feed by directing plankton-carrying water through its cavernous mouth.

MICHAEL AW

Hazardous Marine Life

Several marine organisms can cause physical pain to humans who come into contact with them. Although such occurrences are largely a matter of bad luck, it helps if you're aware of the hazards and ways to avoid contact. Don't touch anything underwater except rocks or sand, and never reach beneath rocks or into holes or crevices where marine life may be.

Jellyfish stings are the most common source of marine mishaps after sunburn. The presence of jellyfish at a beach is largely seasonal or storm related; a beach may be jellyfish free one day and seemingly full of them the next. Small ones without dangling tentacles (some may be almost invisible) usually cause only transitory discomfort. Larger jellyfish, especially those with long tentacles, can cause more severe and lasting pain.

For the latter, treat by removing any tentacles that may have become detached from the jellyfish. Don't use your bare hands but rather paper, leaves or some other object. Smaller more clinging tentacles or tentacle particles may require removal with soap and razor. Once all the stinging bits have been removed, wash the affected area with salt water, then rinse thoroughly with vinegar to deactivate any stingers that have not 'fired'. When vinegar isn't available, urine reputedly has the same effect. Calamine lotion, antihistamines and analgesics may reduce the reaction and relieve the pain.

Fire coral, found among reefs and other coral sites, is a branching hydroid (not actually a coral) that looks harmlessly fernlike but

Top Right: Schooling bannerfish patrol reef outcrops where these conspicuous reef dwellers actively feed on plankton during the daylight hours.

Far Right: Fire coral is often found encrusting the skeletons of dead coral. Contact with the stinging white hairs that protrude from its mustard-coloured surface will cause painful irritation that can last several days.

Right: Large conspicuous jellyfish pose little danger to divers and swimmers but the long trailing arms that carry innumerable stinging cells can be dislodged in rough seas and these almost invisible tentacles can still cause harm.

MICHAEL AW

MICHAEL AW

packs a distinctly uncomfortable – sometimes quite intense – prickle if exposed skin brushes against it. Treat as for jellyfish.

Coral cuts acquired by brushing against dead coral can easily become infected as tiny pieces of bacteria-infested coral can work themselves deep into the cuts. Wash thoroughly with soap and hot water, disinfect with alcohol or hydrogen peroxide, apply antibiotic ointment and bandage.

Sea urchins are found in sandy spots near rocks and coral, often in popular snorkelling areas. They are easily spotted – look for dark spheres radiating thin spines. Take care when wading or snorkelling not to be knocked over by waves or tidal surges. Contact with sea urchins may leave their spines embedded in your skin. Treat minor punctures by extracting the spines, if possible. Once the spines have been dealt with, the painful venom can be neutralised by immersing the infected area in very hot water (recommended 43°C to 45°C, or as hot as you can stand) for 30 to 90 minutes. The venoms of marine organisms are protein based and broken down by intense heat.

Scorpionfish, lionfish and **zebrafish** are very colourful and interesting but their dorsal spines can pack a painful wallop – don't touch! Stings from these bizarre beauties are uncommon, but they can be treated with hot water as described for sea urchins.

MICHAEL AW

MICHAEL AW

Top Left: Sea urchins often gather in large numbers – the sea floor being a mass of spiny balls. In some species light-sensitive cells scattered over the body help the urchin direct the thin, hollow spines towards any potential attacker.

Bottom Left: The elaborately decorated zebra lionfish seems to forewarn would-be predators and divers of its painfully poisonous spines, which it will raise while manoeuvring into a defensive posture.

Cone shells are cone shaped sea snails with a venomous proboscis that darts from the narrow end of the shell to ward off aggressors. Never touch or even get close to a cone shaped shell in the sea. For emergency treatment, immobilise the affected limb if possible and keep it at a lower level than the victim's heart. Dress the wound with an elastic bandage to prevent the spread of venom and seek medical help. If help is unavailable, immerse the affected area in nonscalding hot water.

Stonefish, which as their name suggests, may resemble stones lying in the sand, have a rather potent venom. If approached by unwary divers or a carelessly placed foot of a reef fossicker it will maintain its stand among the reef rubble or mud bottom and simply raise its lethal dorsal spines. Treat as for cone shell stings.

MICHAEL AW

Top Right: The various species of beautiful cone shells are sought after by collectors, although their bite is potentially lethal. The poison is injected by a highly modified radula or mouth part.

Bottom Right: Expertly camouflaged, the potentially deadly stonefish lies in wait for its next meal to swim by.

MICHAEL AW

ROBERT HALSTEAD

Sea snakes, all of which produce some venom, are common but tend to avoid humans. At any rate their mouths are so small that it's very difficult for them to bite humans except between the fingers and toes. In the highly unlikely event of a bite, wrap the site with an elastic bandage, immobilise the affected limb and seek medical help for an injection of commonly available antivenin.

Stingrays have barbed tail spines that can inflict painful wounds. Experienced beach-goers perform the 'stingray shuffle' when walking on sandy bottoms. If you bump into a ray resting on the bottom, it will usually swim away; if you step on one, it's likely to give you a flick of the barb. Treat with very hot water as previously described, but first be sure to remove the barb sac from the wound, or it will continue to release venom.

Sharks have a bad reputation, but are not a significant danger in Thailand. In fact, there has never been a single report of a shark attack on humans in Thai waters, which favours the propagation of smaller species such as the leopard shark, nurse shark and whitetip or blacktip reef shark – all of which tend to be quite timid. One exception to the 'small sharks' rule is the Burma Banks area of the Andaman Sea (and possibly other as yet unexplored areas far west of the mainland), where there are some large hammerheads and tiger sharks with the potential to inflict serious bites on humans.

Nevertheless, handing food to sharks underwater – an activity practised and promoted by a few recreational dive operations in Thailand – is never a good idea. Besides the potential risk it poses (long-term studies suggest hand-feeding makes sharks more aggressive around humans), such practices habituate wildlife to getting human hand–outs. This interrupts the natural marine food chain and disrupts the undersea ecological balance.

MICHAEL AW

MICHAEL AW

Top Left: Sea snakes are reptiles that have evolved from land-dwelling ancestors to live a totally aquatic life. They can hold their breath for up to an hour while hunting for small eels and other fish before replenishing their lungs at the surface.

Far Left: The whitetip reef shark is a territorial, bottom-dwelling shark sometimes seen resting under ledges or in caves. Its curiosity aroused, this shark will approach divers but it is rarely aggressive and is not considered dangerous.

Left: Gregarious and inquisitive, grey reef sharks investigate the slightest disturbance or unusual object in their territory. These skittish sharks can be aggressive if approached and are easily excited by baiting.

continued from page 32

Other notable groups fusing jazz and Thai music include Kangsadarn and Boy Thai; the latter adds Brazilian *samba* to the mix. Thai instrumentation in world music settings are specialities of Todd Lavelle and Nupap Savantrachas, each of whom scored hits in Thailand during the late 1990s. Fong Nam, a Thai orchestra led by American composer Bruce Gaston, performs an inspiring blend of Western and Thai classical motifs.

The discerning listener will have to make an effort to find the aforementioned artists. Thai pop music, much like Western pop, is dominated by the tastes of teens and preteens. Boy bands cooing sappy love songs and bouncy girl groups chirping along to maddening dance ditties proliferate.

Cassette tapes of Thai music are readily available in department stores, cassette shops and from street vendors. The average price for a Thai or licensed Western music tape is 100B. Bootlegged Western tapes are cheaper (about 40B each) and while Thailand pays lip service to international copyright laws, bootlegs are numerous on Th Khao San (Khao San Road) in Bangkok.

Music CDs are more expensive, averaging 450B for a licensed version, and about 100B for a pirated one.

Literature

The most pervasive and influential of all classical Thai literature is the *Ramakian*. The Indian source – the *Ramayana* – came to Thailand with the Khmer 900 years ago, first appearing as stone reliefs on Prasat Hin Phimai and other Angkor-period temples in the North-East. Eventually, the Thais developed their own version, first recorded during the reign of Rama I (1782–1809). This version contained 60,000 stanzas, about 25% longer than the Sanskrit original.

Although the main theme remains the same, the Thais embroidered the *Ramayana* by providing much more biographical detail on arch-villain Ravana (Dasakantha, called Thótsàkan or '10-necked' in the *Ramakian*) and his wife Montho. The monkey-god, Hanuman, differs substantially in the Thai version insofar as he is very flirtatious with females, whereas in the Hindu version he follows a strict vow of chastity. One of the classic *Ramakian* reliefs at Bangkok's Wat Pho depicts Hanuman clasping a maiden's bared breast as if it were an apple.

Also passed on from Indian tradition are the many *jataka* (life stories) of the Buddha (*chaa-tòk* in Thai). Of the 547 jataka tales in the Pali *Tripitaka* (Buddhist canon) – each one chronicling a different past life – most appear in Thailand almost word-for-word as they were first written down in Sri Lanka. A group of 50 'extra' stories, based on Thai folk tales of the time, were added by Pali scholars in Chiang Mai 300 to 400 years ago. The most popular jataka in Thailand is one of the Pali originals known as the *Mahajati* or *Mahavessandara* (Mahaa-Wetsandon in Thai), the story of the Buddha's penultimate life. Interior murals in the *bòt* (ordination chapel) of Thai wát typically depict this jataka and nine others: *Temiya, Mahaachanaka, Suwannasama, Nemiraja, Mahaasotha, Bhuritat, Chantakumara, Nartha* and *Vithura*.

The epic *Phra Aphaimani*, composed by poet Sunthorn Phu in the late 18th century and set on the island of Ko Samet, is Thailand's most famous classical literary work. It tells the story of an exiled prince who must complete an odyssey of love and war before returning to his kingdom in victory.

Architecture & Sculpture

The scheme outlined in the 'Thai Art Styles' boxed table is the latest one used by Thai art historians to categorise historical styles of Thai art, principally sculpture and architecture (since very little painting prior to the 19th century has survived).

A good way to acquaint yourself with the various styles is to visit Bangkok's National Museum, in Banglamphu, where works from each period are on display. Then, as you travel and view old monuments and sculpture, you'll know what you're seeing, as well as what to look for.

Areas of historical interest for art and architecture in coastal Thailand include

Thai Art Styles

Mon Art (formerly Dvaravati, 6th to 11th century, & Hariphunchai, 11th to 13th century)

Originating in Central, Northern and North-Eastern Thailand, Mon Art is an adaptation of Indian styles, principally Gupta.

Khmer Art (7th to 13th century)

Centred in the Central and North-Eastern areas of Thailand, this style is characterised by post-classic Khmer styles accompanying the spread of Khmer empires.

Peninsular Art (formerly Srivijaya, 3rd to 14th century)

Centred in Chaiya and Nakhon Si Thammarat, this style exhibits Indian influences from the 3rd to 5th century, Mon; 5th to 13th century local influences; and Khmer influences from the 11th to 14th century.

Lanna (formerly Chiang Saen, 13th to 15th century)

Centred in Chiang Mai, Chiang Rai, Phayao, Lamphun and Lampang, Lanna is influenced by Shan/Burmese and Lao traditions, mixed with local styles.

Sukhothai (13th to 15th century)

Centred in Sukhothai, Si Satchanalai, Kamphaeng Phet and Phitsanulok, this style is unique to Thailand.

Lopburi (10th to 13th century)

This Central Thailand style is characterised by a mixture of Khmer, Pali and local styles.

Suphanburi-Sangkhlaburi (formerly U Thong, 13th to 15th century)

A Central Thailand style combining Mon, Khmer and local styles. A prototype for the later Ayuthaya style.

Ayuthaya A (1350 to 1488)

Central Thailand style characterised by Khmer influences and gradually replaced by revived Sukhothai influences.

Ayuthaya B (1488 to 1630)

Central Thailand style with characteristic ornamentation distinctive of Ayuthaya style, eg, crowns and jewels on Buddhas.

Ayuthaya C (1630 to 1767)

This Central Thailand style heralded a baroque stage followed by a decline.

Ratanakosin (19th century to the present)

This is a Bangkok style that heralds a return to simpler designs and marks the beginning of European influences.

Thonburi, Phetchaburi, Chaiya and Nakhon Si Thammarat. Some of the monuments at these sites have been restored by the Fine Arts Department and/or by local interests. For more detail on historical sites, see the relevant regional sections in this book.

Recommended books on Thai art and architecture include AB Griswold's classic *Arts of Thailand*; the similarly titled *The Arts of Thailand* by Steve Van Beek; *A Concise History of Buddhist Art in Siam* by Reginald Le May; and *Naga: Cultural Origins in Siam and the West Pacific* by Sumet Jumsai. There are several decent English-language books on various aspects of Thai art for sale at the national museums around Thailand (particularly at the National Museum in Bangkok) and at the Ancient City (Muang Boran) office on Th Ratchadamnoen Klang in Bangkok.

For information about the export of antiques or objects of art from Thailand see Antiques & Art under Customs in the Facts for the Visitor chapter.

Traditional Architecture Traditional home and temple architecture followed relatively strict rules of design that dictated proportion, placement, materials and ornamentation. With the modernisation of Thailand in the 19th and 20th centuries, stylistic codification gave way, firstly to European functionalism, and then to stylistic innovation in more recent times.

Traditional Thai residential architecture consists either of single-room wood houses raised on stilts, or more elaborate structures of interlocking rooms with both indoor and shaded outdoor spaces, all supported at least 2m above the ground by stilts. All Thai settlements were originally founded along river or canal banks. The use of stilts protected the house and its inhabitants from flooding during the annual monsoon. Even in areas where flooding wasn't common, Thais continued to raise their houses on stilts until relatively recently, using the space beneath the house as a cooking area, for tethering animals, or for parking their bicycles and motor vehicles. Teak has always been the material of choice for wood structures, although with the shortage of teak in Thailand nowadays few houses less than 50 years old are constructed from it.

Rooflines in Central Thailand are steeply pitched and often decorated at the corners or along the gables with motifs related to the *naga* (mythical sea serpent), long believed to be a spiritual protector of Thai cultures throughout Asia. In Southern Thailand, bamboo and palm thatch have always been more common building materials than wood, and even today these renewable plant sources remain important construction elements. In certain areas of the South you'll also see thick-walled structures of stuccoed brick, architecture introduced by Chinese, Portuguese, French and British settlements along the Malay peninsula.

In Thailand's four southern-most provinces, it's not unusual to come upon houses of entirely Malay design in which high masonry pediments or foundations, rather than wooden stilts, lift the living areas above the surrounding ground. Roofs of tile or thatch tend to be less steeply pitched, and hipped gables – almost entirely absent in traditional Thai architecture farther north – are common in these Malay-influenced buildings.

Contemporary Architecture Modern Thai architects are among the most daring in South-East Asia, as even a short visit to Bangkok will confirm. Thais began mixing traditional Thai and European architectural forms in the late 19th and early 20th centuries, as exemplified by Bangkok's Vimanmek Teak Mansion, the Author's Wing of the Oriental Hotel, the Chakri Mahaprasat (part of the Grand Palace) next to Wat Phra Kaew, the Thai-Chinese Chamber of Commerce on Th Sathon Tai and any number of older residences and shophouses in Bangkok or provincial capitals throughout Thailand. This style is usually referred to as 'old Bangkok' or 'Ratanakosin'.

Buildings of mixed design in the South typically show Portuguese influence. Shophouses throughout the country, whether 100 years or 100 days old, share the basic Chinese shophouse (*hâwng thǎew* in Thai) design in which the ground floor is reserved for trading purposes while the upper floors contain offices or residences.

During most of the post-WWII era, the trend in modern Thai architecture – inspired by the European Bauhaus movement – was towards a boring functionalism in which the average building looked like a giant egg carton turned on its side. The Thai aesthetic, so vibrant in prewar eras, almost entirely disappeared in this characterless style of architecture. About the only saving grace of this period was the use of decorative sunscreens on the facades of some buildings in the 1960s and early 1970s. The eclectic shapes and patterns of these screens served to protect Bangkok's first tall buildings from sun and rain. The idea spread to Saigon during the same period – reinforced versions of these sunscreens were used to shield important buildings from rocket attacks. The AUA building on Th Ratchadamri and the Krung Thai Bank head office on Th Yukhon 2 sport outstanding examples of decorative sunscreens.

When Thai architects began experimenting again during the building boom of the mid-1980s, it was to provide high-tech designs like Sumet Jumsai's famous robot-shaped Bank of Asia on Th Sathon Tai in Bangkok. Few people seemed to find the space-age look endearing, but at least it was different. Another trend was to affix gaudy Roman- and Greek-style columns to rectangular Art Deco structures in what was almost a parody of Western classical architecture. One of the outcomes of this fashion has been the widespread use of curvilinear banisters on the balconies of almost every new shophouse, apartment or condominium throughout Thailand, often with visually disturbing results.

A good book on Thai residential design, interior or exterior, is William Warren's *Thai Style*, a coffee-table tome with excellent photography by Luca Invernizzi Tettoni.

Painting

Except for prehistoric and historic cave or rock-wall murals found throughout the country, not much formal painting predating the 18th century exists in Thailand. Presumably there were a great number of temple murals in Ayuthaya that were destroyed by the Burmese invasion of 1767. The earliest surviving temple examples are found at Ayuthaya's Wat Ratburana (1424), Wat Chong Nonsii near the river in southern Bangkok (1657–1707) and Phetchaburi's Wat Yai Suwannaram (late 17th century).

Nineteenth-century religious painting has fared better. Ratanakosin-style temple art is in fact more highly esteemed for painting than for sculpture or architecture. Typical temple murals feature rich colours and lively detail. Some of the finest are found in Wat Phra Kaew's Wihan Buddhaisawan (Phutthaisawan) Chapel in Bangkok and at Wat Suwannaram in Thonburi.

SOCIETY & CONDUCT

Citizens of the only South-East Asian country never to be colonised by a foreign power, the Thais are independent-minded yet steeped in a tradition of friendliness towards visitors. Although the pressures of modern development (Thailand enjoyed double-digit economic growth throughout the 80s) have brought a changing set of national values – not always for the better – the travel-poster epithet 'Land of Smiles' still applies to the treatment most visitors receive. The influence of Buddhism, arguably the most tolerant of the world's major religions, is said to be largely responsible for the Thais' easy friendliness.

Traditional Culture

When outsiders speak of 'Thai culture' they're referring to a complex of behavioural modes rooted in the history of Thai migration throughout South-East Asia, with many commonalities shared by the Lao of neighbouring Laos, the Shan of north-eastern Myanmar and the numerous tribal Thais found in isolated pockets from Dien Bien Phu (Vietnam) all the way to Assam (India). Nowhere are such norms more generalised than in Thailand, the largest of the Thai homelands.

Practically every ethnicity represented in Thailand, whether of Thai ancestry or not, has to a greater or lesser degree been assimilated into the Thai mainstream. Although Thailand is the most 'modernised' of the existing Thai (more precisely, Austro-Thai) societies, the cultural underpinnings are evident in virtually every facet of everyday life. Those aspects that might be deemed 'Westernisation' – eg, the wearing of trousers instead of *phâakhamáa* (wrap around), the presence of cars, cinemas and 7-Eleven stores – show how Thailand has adopted and adapted tools originating from elsewhere.

Such adaptations do not necessarily represent a cultural loss. Ekawit Na Talang, a scholar of Thai culture and head of the government's National Culture Commission, defines culture as 'the system of thought and behaviour of a particular society – something which is dynamic and never static'. Talang and other world-culture experts agree that it's paradoxical to try to protect a culture from foreign influences as cultures cannot exist in a vacuum. Culture evolves naturally as outside influences undergo processes of naturalisation. From this perspective, cultures that don't change, die. As Talang has said, 'Anything obsolete, people will reject and anything that has a relevant role in life, people will adopt and make it part of their culture'.

Nevertheless there are certain aspects of Thai society that virtually everyone recognises as 'Thai' cultural markers. The Thais themselves don't really have a word that corresponds to the term 'culture'. The nearest equivalent, *wátánátham*, emphasises fine arts and ceremonies over other aspects usually covered by the concept. So if you ask Thais to define their culture, they'll often talk about architecture, food, dance, festivals and the like. Religion – obviously a big influence on culture as defined in the Western sense – is considered more or less separate from wátánátham.

Sànùk

The Thai word *sànùk* means 'fun'. In Thailand anything worth doing – even work – should have an element of sànùk, otherwise it becomes drudgery. This doesn't mean Thais don't want to work or strive, they just tend to approach tasks with a sense of playfulness. Nothing condemns an activity more than the description *mâi sànùk*, 'not fun'. Sit down beside a rice field and watch workers planting, transplanting or harvesting rice; it's obviously back-breaking work, but participants generally inject the activity with lots of sànùk – flirtation, singing, trading insults and cracking jokes. The same goes in an office or a bank, or other white-collar work situations – at least when the office is predominantly Thai (businesses run by non-Thais don't necessarily exhibit sànùk). The famous Thai smile comes partially out of this desire to make sànùk.

Face

Thais believe strongly in the concept of saving face, that is, avoiding confrontation and trying not to embarrass themselves or other people (except when it's sànùk to do so). The ideal face-saver doesn't bring up negative topics in everyday conversation, and when they notice stress in another's life, they usually won't say anything unless that person complains or asks for help. Laughing at minor accidents – like when someone trips and falls – may seem callous to outsiders but it's really just an attempt to save face on behalf of the person suffering the mishap. This is another source of the Thai smile – it's the best possible face to put on in almost any situation.

Status & Obligation

All relationships in traditional Thai society – and virtually all relationships in the modern Thai milieu as well – are governed by connections between *phûu yài* (big person) and *phûu náwy* (little person). Phûu náwy are supposed to defer to phûu yài following simple lines of social rank defined by age, wealth, status, and personal and political power. Examples of 'automatic' phûu yài status include adults (vs children), bosses (vs employees), elder classmates (vs younger classmates), elder siblings (vs younger siblings), teachers (vs pupils), military (vs civilian), Thai (vs non-Thai) and so on.

While this tendency towards social ranking is to some degree shared by many societies around the world, the Thai twist lies in the set of mutual obligations linking phûu yài to phûu náwy. Some sociologists have referred to this phenomenon as the 'patron-client relationship'. Phûu náwy are supposed to show a degree of obedience and respect (together these concepts are covered by the term *kreng jai*) towards phûu yài, but in return phûu yài are obligated to care for or 'sponsor' the phûu náwy they have frequent contact with. In such relationships phûu náwy can, for example, ask phûu yài for favours involving money or job opportunities. Phûu yài reaffirm their rank by granting requests when possible; to refuse would be to risk loss of face and status.

Age is a large determinant where other factors are absent or weak. In such cases the terms *phîi* (elder sibling) and *náwng* (younger sibling) apply more than phûu yài and phûu náwy, although the intertwined obligations remain the same. Even people unrelated by blood quickly establish who's phîi and who's náwng; this is why one of the first questions Thais ask new acquaintances is 'How old are you?'.

When dining, touring or entertaining, the phûu yài always picks up the tab; if a group is involved, the person with most social rank pays the check for everyone, even if it empties his or her wallet. For a phûu náwy to try and pay would risk loss of face. Money plays a large role in defining phûu yài status in most situations. A person who turned out to be successful in his or her post-school career would never think of allowing an ex-classmate of lesser success – even if they were once on an equal social footing – to pay the bill. Likewise a young, successful executive will pay an older person's way in spite of the age difference.

The implication is that whatever wealth you come into is to be shared – at least partially – with those less fortunate. This doesn't apply to strangers – the average Thai isn't big on charity – but always applies with friends and relatives.

Foreigners often feel offended when they encounter such phenomena as two-tiered pricing for hotels or sightseeing attractions – one price for Thais, a higher price for foreigners. But this is simply another expression of the traditional patron-client relationship. On the one hand foreigners who can afford to travel to Thailand from abroad are seen to have more wealth than Thai citizens (on average this is self-evident), hence they're expected to help subsidise Thais' enjoyment of these commodities; and at the same time, paradoxically, the Thais feel they are due certain special privileges as locals – what might be termed the 'home-town discount'. Another example: in a post office line, Thais get served first as part of their national privilege.

Comportment

Personal power (*baará-mii*, sometimes mistranslated as 'charisma') also has a bearing on one's social status, and can be gained by cleaving as close as possible to the ideal 'Thai' behaviour. 'Thai-ness' is first and foremost defined, as might be expected, by the ability to speak Thai. It doesn't matter which dialect, although Southern Thai – with its Malay and Yawi influences – is slightly suspect, mainly due to the region's association with the 'foreign' religion of Islam.

Other hallmarks of the Thai ideal – heavily influenced by Thai Buddhism – include discretion towards the opposite sex, modest dress, a neat and clean appearance, and modes of expression and comportment that value the quiet, subtle and indirect rather than the loud, obvious and direct.

The degree to which Thais conform to these ideals matches the degree of respect they receive from most of their associates. Although high rank – based on age or civil, military or clerical roles – will exempt certain individuals from chastisement by their social 'inferiors', it doesn't exempt them from the way they are perceived by other Thais. This goes for foreigners as well, even though most first-time visitors can hardly be expected to speak idiomatic Thai. But if you do learn some Thai, and you make an effort to respect Thai social ideals, you'll come closer to enjoying some of the perks awarded for Thai-ness.

Dos & Don'ts

Monarchy and religion are the two sacred cows in Thailand. Thais are tolerant of most kinds of behaviour as long as it doesn't insult one of these.

King & Country The monarchy is held in considerable respect in Thailand and visitors should be respectful too – avoid making disparaging remarks about the king, queen or anyone in the royal family. One of Thailand's more outspoken intellectuals, Sulak Sivaraksa, was arrested in the 1980s for lese-majesty because of a passing reference to the king's fondness for yachting (referring to His Majesty as 'the skipper') and again in 1991 when he referred to the royal family as 'ordinary people'. Although on the first occasion he received a royal pardon, in 1991 Sulak had to flee the country to avoid prosecution again for alleged remarks made at Thammasat University about the ruling military junta, with reference to the king (Sulak has since returned under a suspended sentence). The penalty for lese-majesty is seven years' imprisonment.

While it's OK to criticise the Thai government and even Thai culture openly, it's considered a grave insult to Thai nationhood, as well as to the monarchy, not to stand when you hear the national or royal anthems. Radio and TV stations in Thailand broadcast the national anthem daily at 8am and 6pm. In towns and villages (and even in some Bangkok neighbourhoods) the anthem is broadcast over public loudspeakers in the streets. The Thais stop whatever they're doing to stand during the anthem (except in Bangkok where nobody can hear above the din of the street) and visitors are expected to do likewise. The royal anthem is played just before films are shown in cinemas; again, the audience always stands until it's over.

Objects with a picture or image of the king should also be treated with respect. If you drop a coin or banknote, do not stomp on it to keep it from rolling or blowing away. Always pick it up with your hands.

Religion Correct behaviour in temples entails several considerations, the most important of which is to dress neatly and take your shoes off when you enter any building that contains a Buddha image. Buddha images are sacred, so don't pose in front of them for pictures and definitely do not clamber upon them.

Shorts or sleeveless shirts are considered improper for both men and women when visiting temples. Locals wearing either would be turned away by monastic authorities, but except for the most sacred temples in the country (eg, Wat Phra Kaew in Bangkok), Thais are often too polite to refuse entry to improperly clad foreigners. Some wát hire trousers or long sarongs so that tourists wearing shorts can enter the compound.

Monks are not supposed to touch or be touched by women. If a woman wants to hand something to a monk, the object should be placed within reach of the monk, not handed directly to him.

When sitting in a religious edifice, keep your feet pointed away from any Buddha images. The usual way to do this is to sit in the 'mermaid' pose in which your legs are folded to the side, with the feet pointing backwards.

A few of the larger wát in Bangkok charge entry fees. In other temples, offering a small donation before leaving the compound is appropriate. Usually there are donation boxes near the entry of the *bòt* (central sanctuary) or next to the central Buddha image at the rear.

Show respect for religious symbols and rituals. Avoid touching spirit houses, household altars, village totems and other religious symbols, as this often 'pollutes' them spiritually and may require the villagers to perform purification rituals after you have moved on. Keep your distance from ceremonies being performed unless you're asked to participate.

Social Gestures & Attitudes Traditionally, Thais greet each other with a prayer-like palms-together gesture known as a *wâi*. If someone wais you, you should wâi back (unless wai-ed by a child). Most urban Thais are familiar with the international-style handshake and will offer that to a foreigner, although a wâi is always appreciated.

Thais are often addressed by their first name with the honorific *khun* or other title preceding it. Other formal terms of address include *Nai* (Mr) and *Naang* (Miss or Mrs).

Friends often use nicknames or kinship terms like *phîi* (elder sibling), *náwng* (younger sibling), *mâe* (mother) or *lung* (uncle), depending on the age difference.

A smile and *sawàt-dii khráp* or *sawàt-dii khâ* (the all-purpose Thai greetings) goes a long way towards calming the trepidation locals may initially feel upon seeing a foreigner, whether in the city or the countryside.

When handing things to other people you should use both hands or your right hand only, never the left hand (reserved for toilet ablutions). Books and other written material are given a special status over other secular objects. Hence you shouldn't slide books or documents across a table or counter-top, and never place them on the floor – use a chair instead if table space isn't available.

When encounters take a turn for the worse, don't get angry – losing one's temper means loss of face for everyone present. Remember that this is Asia, where keeping your cool is paramount. Talking loudly is seen as rude by cultured Thais, whatever the situation. Remember, the pushy foreigner often gets served last.

Feet & Head The feet are the lowest part of the body (spiritually as well as physically) so don't point them at people or point at things with your feet. Even when sitting crossed-legged, for example, it's good to make sure you're not inadvertently aiming your lowliest body part at your neighbour. Don't prop your feet on chairs or tables while sitting. Never touch any part of someone else's body with your foot.

In the same context, the head is regarded as the highest part of the body, so don't touch Thais on the head – or ruffle their hair – either. If you touch someone's head accidentally, offer an immediate apology or you'll be perceived as very rude.

Don't sit on pillows meant for sleeping – this represents a variant of the taboo against head-touching. Hats should also be treated with respect. If you take your hat off indoors, place it on a table or hang it someplace high – never put it on the floor. And we really shouldn't have to say that using your toes to pick up a hat that has

blown off someone's head would be extremely insulting!

Never step over someone, even on a crowded 3rd-class train where people are sitting or lying on the floor. Instead squeeze around them or ask them to move.

Dress & Nudity Shorts (except knee-length walking shorts), sleeveless shirts, tank tops (singlets) and other beach-style attire are not considered appropriate dress in Thailand for anything other than sporting events. Such dress is especially counter productive if worn to government offices (eg, when applying for a visa extension). Having an attitude of 'This is how I dress at home and no-one is going to stop me' gains nothing but contempt or disrespect from the Thais.

Sandals or slip-on shoes are OK for all but the most formal occasions. Short-sleeved shirts and blouses with capped sleeves are also quite acceptable.

Thais would never dream of wearing dirty clothes while abroad, so they are often shocked to see Westerners travelling around Thailand in clothes that apparently haven't been washed in weeks. Keep up with your laundry and you'll receive far more respect everywhere you go.

Regardless of what the Thais may or may not have been accustomed to centuries ago, they are quite offended by public nudity today. According to Thailand's National Parks Act, any woman who goes topless on a national park beach (eg, Ko Chang, Ko Phi-Phi, Ko Samet) is breaking the law. If you are at a truly deserted beach and are sure no Thais may come along, there's nothing stopping you; however, at most beaches travellers should wear suitable attire. Topless bathing for females is frowned upon in most places except on heavily-touristed islands like Phuket, Samui, Samet and Pha-Ngan. Likewise, except when on the beach, men should keep a shirt on; entering a shop or (particularly) a restaurant half naked looks barbaric to the Thais. Many Thais say nudity on the beach is what bothers them most about foreign travellers. Thais often take nudity as a sign of disrespect for the locals, rather than as a libertarian symbol or modern custom. Thais are extremely modest in this respect (Patpong-style go-go bars are cultural aberrations, hidden from public view and designed for foreign consumption) and visitors who have any respect for their hosts won't try to 'reform' them.

Shoes As in temples, shoes are not worn inside people's homes, nor in some guest-houses and shops. If you see a pile of shoes at or near the entrance, you should respect the house custom and remove your shoes before entry. Several Thais have confided to us that they can't believe how oblivious some foreigners appear to be of this simple and obvious custom. To them, wearing shoes indoors is disgusting and the be-haviour of those who ignore the custom is nothing short of boorish.

Visiting Homes Thais can be very hos-pitable and it's not unusual to be invited home for a meal or a sociable drink. Even if your visit is very brief, you will be of-fered something to eat or drink, probably both – a glass of water, a cup of tea, a piece of fruit, a shot of rice liquor, or whatever they have on hand. You are expected to par-take of whatever is offered, whether you're thirsty or hungry or not; to refuse at least a taste is considered impolite.

Message From a Reader As a final com-ment on avoiding offence, here is a plea from a reader who wrote following an ex-tended visit to Thailand:

Please do whatever you can to impress on trav-ellers the importance of treating the Thai people, who are so generous and unassuming, with the re-spect they deserve. If people sunbathe topless, take snapshots of the people like animals in a zoo and demand Western standards, then they are both offending the Thai people and contributing to the opinion many of them have of us as being rich, demanding and promiscuous.

Treatment of Animals
Thailand is a signatory to the UN Conven-tion on International Trade in Endangered Species (Cites). Educational levels have risen to the point that many international watchdog groups, such as the World Wild Fund for Nature and Wildlife Conservation Society, receive much local support. An il-licit trade in endangered and threatened wildlife continues but appears to be much smaller than even 12 years ago.

In less-developed rural regions of the country, particularly in the North and North-East, and among Thailand's hill tribes, hunting remains a norm for obtaining animal protein. Over-fishing of lakes, rivers and oceans poses a danger to certain fish species.

Harder to understand, at least for some of us, is the taking of monkeys, birds and other animals from the jungle to be kept as pets – usually tied by a rope or chain to a tree, or confined to cages. Several non-government organisations (NGOs), such as the Phuket Gibbon Rehabilitation Centre, are working to educate the public about the cruelty of such practices, and have initiated wildlife rescue and rehabilitation projects.

In any case wildlife experts agree that the greatest threat to Thai fauna is neither hunting nor the illegal wildlife trade, but loss of habitat – as is true for most of the rest of the world. Protect the forests, mang-roves, marshes and grasslands, and they will protect the animals.

For further comment on this topic, see Ecology & Environment, earlier in this chapter.

Prostitution
As throughout most of south and South-East Asia, men in Thailand have greater freedom in their sexual activities than women – who are expected to arrive at the marriage altar as virgins and to refrain from extramarital affairs. This attitude creates a sexual imbalance in which large numbers of males are seeking casual sexual contact, but few females are available. The resulting commercial sex industry, catering largely to indigenous demand, thus maintains an ongoing reservoir of sex workers and clients. In Bangkok (and to a much lesser degree in other large urban centres), the im-balance is righting itself as premarital and

extramarital sex between non-paying consenting Thais becomes more common.

Among foreigners it's a common perception that Thai women become sex workers because they don't have recourse to similar or better-paying employment in other areas, but employment statistics don't support this notion. Thailand's work force is 44% female, ranking it 27th on a world scale, just ahead of China and the USA. On a purely economic level there is no compelling reason to choose prostitution over weaving, rice-milling or office work. Thai women who participate in prostitution either do so unwillingly – in the case of bonded or forced service – or willingly in hopes of obtaining luxuries in excess of mere livelihood. In either case it's the demand side of the equation – caused by the lack of available female sex partners – that appears to drive the industry.

RELIGION
Buddhism

Approximately 95% of Thais are Theravada Buddhists. The Theravada (literally, teaching of the elders) school is an earlier and, according to its followers, less corrupted form of Buddhism than the Mahayana schools founded in East Asia or in the Himalayan lands. Also called the 'southern' school, it took a southern route from India, its place of origin, through South-East Asia (Myanmar, Thailand, Laos and Cambodia), while the 'northern' school proceeded north into Nepal, Tibet, China, Korea, Mongolia, Vietnam and Japan. Because the Theravada school tried to preserve or limit the Buddhist doctrines to only those canons codified in the early Buddhist era, the Mahayana school gave Theravada Buddhism the name Hinayana (lesser vehicle). It is claimed the Mahayana school was the 'great vehicle', because it built upon the earlier teachings, 'expanding' the doctrine in such a way as to respond more to the needs of lay people.

The ultimate end of Theravada Buddhism is to reach *nibbana* (Sanskrit: *nirvana*), which literally means the 'blowing out' or extinction of all desire and thus of all suffering (dukkha). Effectively, it is also an end to the cycle of rebirths (both moment to moment and life to life) that is existence. In reality, most Thai Buddhists aim for rebirth in a 'better' existence rather than the supramundane goal of nibbana, which is highly misunderstood by Asians as well as Westerners.

Many Thais express the feeling that they are somehow unworthy of nibbana. By feeding monks, giving donations to temples and performing regular worship at the local wát they hope to improve their lot, acquiring enough merit (Pali: *puñña*; Thai: *bun*) to prevent or at least lessen the number of rebirths. The making of merit *(tham bun)* is an important social and religious activity in Thailand. The concept of reincarnation is almost universally accepted, even by non-Buddhists, and the Buddhist theory of karma is well expressed in the Thai proverb *tham dii, dâi dii; tham chûa, dâi chûa* – 'do good and receive good; do evil and receive evil'.

Thai Buddhism has no particular day of the week to make temple visits. Nor is there anything corresponding to a liturgy or mass over which a priest presides. Instead Thai Buddhists visit the wát whenever they feel like it, most often on *wan phrá* (literally, excellent days), which occur every full and new moon, ie, every 15 days. On such a visit lotus buds, incense and candles are offered at various altars, and bone reliquaries are placed around the wát compound. Other activities include offering food to the temple Sangha (monks, nuns and lay residents – monks always eat first), meditating (individually or in groups), listening to monks chanting *suttas* (Buddhist discourses) and attending a *thêt* or *dhamma* talk by the abbot or other respected teacher. Visitors may also seek counsel from monks or nuns regarding new or ongoing life problems.

Monks & Nuns Socially, every Thai male is expected to become a monk for a short period, optimally between the time he finishes school and the time he starts a career or marries. Men or boys under 20 may enter the Sangha as novices – this is not unusual since a family earns great merit when one of its sons takes robe and bowl. Traditionally, three months is spent in the wát during the

Buddhist lent *(phansǎa)*, which begins in July and coincides with the rainy season. However, nowadays men may spend as little as a week or 15 days to accrue merit as a monk. There are about 32,000 monasteries in Thailand and 200,000 monks; many of them ordain for life. Of these, a large percentage become scholars and teachers, while some specialise in healing and/or folk magic.

At one time the Theravada Buddhist world had a separate monastic lineage for females, who called themselves *bhikkhuni* and observed more vows than monks did – 311 precepts as opposed to the 227 followed by monks. Started in Sri Lanka around two centuries after the Buddha's lifetime by the daughter of King Asoka (a Buddhist king in India), the bhikkhuni tradition in Sri Lanka eventually died out and was unfortunately never restored.

In Thailand, the modern equivalent is the *mâe chii* (Thai for 'nun'; literally, mother priest) – women who live the monastic life as *atthasila* (eight-precept) nuns. Thai nuns shave their heads, wear white robes and take vows in an ordination procedure similar to that undergone by monks. Generally speaking, nunhood in Thailand isn't considered as 'prestigious' as monkhood. The average Thai Buddhist makes a great show of offering new robes and household items to the monks at their local wát but pay much less attention to the nuns. This is mainly due to the fact that nuns generally don't perform ceremonies on behalf of laypeople, so there is less incentive to make offerings to them. Furthermore, many Thais equate the number of precepts observed with the total Buddhist merit achieved, hence nunhood is seen as less 'meritorious' than monkhood since mâe chii keep only eight precepts.

This difference in prestige represents social Buddhism, however, and is not how those with a serious interest regard the mâe chii. Nuns engage in the same fundamental activities – meditation and dhamma study – as monks do. In fact wát that have sizeable contingents of mâe chii are highly respected, since women don't choose temples for reasons of clerical status. When more than a few nuns reside at one temple, it's usually a sign that the teachings there are particularly strong.

An increasing number of foreigners are coming to Thailand to ordain as Buddhist monks or nuns, especially to study with the famed meditation masters of the forest wát in Southern and North-Eastern Thailand.

Further Information If you wish to find out more about Buddhism you can contact the World Fellowship of Buddhists (☎ 026 611 248, e wfb_hq@asianet.co.th), 616 Soi 24, Th Sukhumvit, Bangkok. Senior faràng monks hold English-language dhamma and meditation classes there on the first Sunday of each month from 2pm to 6pm; all are welcome.

A Buddhist bookshop opposite the north entrance to Wat Bovornives (Bowonniwet) in the Banglamphu district of Bangkok sells a variety of English-language books on Buddhism. Asia Books and DK Book House also stock Buddhist literature. See Bookshops under Information in the Bangkok chapter for locations.

For more information about studying meditation in Southern Thailand see the sections on Chaiya's Wat Suan Mokkhaphalaram and also Wat Khao Tham on Ko Pha-Ngan. Both are in the South-Western Gulf Coast chapter.

Recommended books about Buddhism include:

Buddhism Explained by Phra Khantipalo
Heartwood of the Bodhi Tree by Buddhadasa Bhikku
In This Very Life: The Liberation Teachings of the Buddha by Sayadaw U Pandita
Living Dharma: Teachings of Twelve Buddhist Masters edited by Jack Kornfield
The Long View: An Excursion into Buddhist Perspectives by Suratano Bhikku (T Magness)
The Mind and the Way by Ajaan Sumedho
Phra Faràng: An English Monk in Thailand by Phra Peter Pannapadipo
A Still Forest Pool: the Teaching of Ajaan Chaa at Wát Paa Pong compiled by Jack Kornfield & Paul Breiter
Thai Women in Buddhism by Chatsumarn Kabilsingh
What the Buddha Taught by Walpola Rahula

Two good sources of publications on Theravada Buddhism are the Buddhist Publication Society, PO Box 61 54, Sangharaja Mawatha, Kandy, Sri Lanka, and the Barre Center for Buddhist Studies, Lockwood Rd, Barre, MA 01005, USA.

The Internet is an excellent source from which you can freely download many publications, including the complete English version of the Pali canon. The Access to Insight: Readings in Theravada Buddhism Web site (**W** world.std.com/~metta) is cross-indexed by subject, title, author, proper names and even Buddhist similes. Two other recommended Web sites with lots of material on Theravada Buddhism, as well as links to other sites, include DharmaNet Electronic Files Archive (**W** www.dharmanet.org) and Buddha Net (**W** www.buddhanet.net).

Other Religions

A small percentage of Thais and most of the Malays in the South, amounting to about 4% of the population, are followers of Islam. Half a percent of the population – primarily missionised hill tribes and Viet-namese immigrants – are Christians, while the remaining half percent are Confucianists, Taoists, Mahayana Buddhists and Hindus. Mosques (in the South) and Chinese temples are both common enough that you will probably come across some in your travels in Thailand. Before entering *any* temple, sanctuary or mosque you must remove your shoes, and in a mosque your head must be covered.

LANGUAGE

The language of Central Thailand, referred to simply as 'Thai' is the official language of Thailand. There are, however, three other major dialects and many subdialects as well as the languages of ethnic minorities such as Malay and Min Nan Chinese – over 70 different languages are spoken in Thailand!

Although most travellers get by without learning a word of Thai, any efforts to learn the language will be enormously appreciated by locals and will open up whole new experiences. See the Language chapter later in this book for useful terms and a food glossary.

Facts for the Visitor

HIGHLIGHTS

Thailand's unique geography offers three starkly different coastal settings.

The eastern Gulf Coast, stretching south-east from Bangkok to the Cambodian border, is a succession of beaches and offshore islands that face south-west and thus escape one of the two major monsoons that sweep across mainland South-East Asia each year. The oldest and most well established of the resorts along this coast is densely developed Pattaya, although nearby alternatives are expanding with each passing season. The main advantage of the eastern Gulf resorts is their proximity to Bangkok; except for some of the islands, such as Ko Samet and Ko Chang (in Thai, *ko* means 'island'), the beaches aren't all that spectacular.

The Malay peninsula extends 1600km south from Bangkok, creating a slender land barrier between the South China Sea and the Indian Ocean. Lined on either side by sandy bays, lagoons, mangroves, islands and islets, over half the length of this peninsula falls within Thailand's borders.

The western side of the peninsula, referred to in this book as the Andaman Coast, faces the Andaman Sea (the part of the Indian Ocean that lies between the Andaman Islands and Thailand's west coast). This coastline is characterised by karst topography: craggy cliffs and islands composed of a chalky limestone that dissolves to impart a deep turquoise hue to coastal shallows. Diving among the coral reefs in this area can be superb.

Phuket, Thailand's largest island, is the Andaman Coast's most popular resort, followed by Ko Phi-Phi and Ko Lanta to the south, and Hat Khao Lak to the north. Travel to the more remote island groups is seasonal, since during the height of the south-western monsoon (May to October) the Andaman Sea becomes too rough for offshore navigation.

Waters along the Gulf Coast of the Malay peninsula are calmer year-round. This coast remains the most undeveloped, with the bulk of the tourist activity focussed on Ko Samui, Thailand's third-largest island. The opening of Samui's airport in the late 1980s spurred the island's already rapid development, while other islands nearby remain favoured destinations for those with more time than money.

Which side of the peninsula you choose – the Gulf of Thailand (for Prachuap Khiri Khan, Ko Samui, Songkhla) or the Andaman Sea (Phuket, Krabi, Trang) – might be determined by the time of year. See When to Go under Planning later in this chapter and Climate in the previous chapter for more information on seasonal considerations.

If time is limited, check out the beaches and islands along the eastern Gulf Coast of Central Thailand (Pattaya, Ko Samet, Ko Chang) or the northern part of the peninsula (Cha-am, Hua Hin) for shorter beach excursions. Head to Southern Thailand if you have a week or more and will be using ground transport. Or fly to one of the airports in the southern beach-resort areas (eg, Ko Samui, Phuket, Krabi).

One of the main highlights of Thai travel is soaking up the general cultural ambience, which can be done just about anywhere away from the resorts. You won't experience much of that if you spend most of your time sitting around in guesthouse cafes, hanging out on the beach or diving with your own kind. At least once during your trip, try going to a small to medium-sized town well off the main tourist circuit, staying at a local hotel, and eating in Thai curry shops and noodle stands. It's not as easy as going with the crowd but you'll learn a lot more about Thailand, and these experiences will likely be the most enduring.

Resorts & Convenient Escapes

Ko Samet Off the eastern Gulf Coast and only three hours from Bangkok by a combination of road and boat, this island can be quite overrun on weekends and holidays.

The fine white sand and clear waters attract a cross-section of expats, Thais and tourists. There's some decent snorkelling at nearby islets. Prices: inexpensive to moderate. Accessible by boat only.

Hua Hin & Prachuap Khiri Khan The upper-peninsula province of Prachuap Khiri Khan, facing the Gulf, has sandy beaches of medium quality along much of its length, from the well-touristed Hua Hin in the north to little-known Thai resorts near Ao Manao and Bang Saphan farther south. Most accommodation is in medium-priced hotels. There is not much in the way of diving, but seafood is superb and economical. It can be crowded on holidays. Prices: inexpensive to moderate. Accessible by air (Hua Hin only), rail and road.

Ko Samui Off the coast of Surat Thani, in the Gulf of Thailand, this is the third-largest island in the country and quite heavily developed. Once a haven for backpackers on the Asia Trail, it is for the most part now given over to middle-class hotels and guesthouses, though dirt-cheap digs can still be found. Snorkelling and diving are fair, beaches superb. Prices: inexpensive to moderate, with a few luxury resorts. Accessible by ferry from Surat Thani, air from Bangkok or by train/bus/ferry combo from Bangkok.

Phuket In the Andaman Sea, Thailand's largest and most geographically varied island was the first to develop a tourist industry. Phuket has become a fairly sophisticated international resort, albeit one with the highest number of 'green' hotel developments as well as two well-respected national parks. There's good diving at nearby islands and reefs of the Andaman Sea and Ao Phang-Nga (Sea of Phuket) and the best Thai cuisine of any of the islands. Prices: moderate to expensive. Accessible by air and road (via a causeway).

More-Remote Beach & Island Areas

Ko Chang & Ko Kut Near the Cambodian border, in the Gulf of Thailand, these islands are relatively untouristed. Though part of a national park, both islands have coastal zones where development is permitted, but so far high-profile development has been kept at bay by the islands' distance from Bangkok and mountainous geography. They attract those looking for quiet, economical beach stays, and have some spill over from Ko Pha-Ngan. Waterfalls and hiking trails on Ko Chang add to its attraction. Prices: inexpensive, except for a couple of moderate to expensive beach resorts. Accessible by boat only from Trat.

Songkhla, Pattani & Narathiwat These deep south Gulf of Thailand provinces near Malaysia offer hundreds of kilometres of deserted beach. During the north-east monsoon (November to March), the water tends to be murky due to cross-currents. Culturally these are some of the most interesting coastal areas in the country due to Islamic-Malay influences. Good for regional handicrafts, including cotton prints, sarongs and batik. Very little is available in the way of beach accommodation, though village housing is a possibility for those with initiative and who can speak some Thai. Prices: inexpensive. Accessible by rail (parts of Narathiwat and Songkhla only) and road. Hat Yai is the nearest air hub.

Ko Similan, Ko Surin & Ko Tarutao National Marine Parks These Andaman Island groups enjoy some of the best park protection in Thailand. There is fantastic diving and snorkelling at all three; Similan and Surin are rated among the world's top 10 dive destinations. Accommodation is mostly limited to park bungalows and camping. Prices: inexpensive. Accessible by boat only, and only during the non-monsoon months (November to April), from Phuket and the mainland.

Krabi This province, facing Ao Phang-Nga, opposite Phuket, offers a range of beaches and islands ringed with striking limestone formations. Rock climbing, snorkelling, diving, boating and fishing provide opportunities for active holidays. Generally quiet, although accommodation tends to book out from December to February, while during May, June, September and October it can be nearly deserted. Prices: inexpensive to moderate, with a handful of luxurious resorts. Provincial capital accessible by half-day boat or bus trip from Phuket, an overnight bus trip from Bangkok. Islands, and some beaches, accessible by boat only.

Ko Lanta Actually part of Krabi Province, this slender island is a perennial favourite among low-budget travellers. It is however, practically deserted from April to November when lashed by south-western monsoon rains and the beach becomes covered with rubbish and other floating debris. It has some snorkelling and diving, and good seafood. It can be crowded on holidays. Prices: inexpensive. Accessible by boat from Krabi and Ko Phi-Phi, by road and ferry from nearby coastal towns.

Trang The next province south of Krabi, facing the Andaman Sea, Trang is largely undiscovered, but the beaches and islands aren't as pretty as Krabi's. It has good diving but you'll have to bring your own gear. Prices: inexpensive to moderate. Islands accessible by boat only, mainland by road and air.

National Parks in Coastal Areas

Thailand boasts nearly 80 national parks. See National Parks & Wildlife Sanctuaries under Flora & Fauna in the Facts about Thailand chapter for general information about the country's protected areas, and the destination chapters for complete details on each of the parks covered in this book. The book *National Parks of Thailand* by Denis Gray, Collin Piprell & Mark Graham is the most comprehensive source of English-language material on the parklands.

Ko Chang National Marine Park, Trat Province

The mountainous Ko Chang archipelago encompasses around 50 islands, all but three of which are almost completely undeveloped. Beaches and interiors tend to be pristine, though transport among them can be problematic (except for Ko Chang, where boat transport is regular). It's good any time of year, although the June to October south-western monsoon strikes here with more force than elsewhere on the Gulf Coast.

Khao Sam Roi Yot National Park, Prachuap Khiri Khan Province

This 98-sq-km park on the coast near Hua Hin is one of the country's most scenic due to a blend of mountains and coast. It has good trails and camping and is best visited from November to July – though it's relatively protected from the south-western monsoon so don't rule out other months.

Khao Sok National Park, Surat Thani Province

Limestone crags, rainforests and jungle streams provide the perfect environment for the remnants of Thailand's threatened tiger and clouded leopard populations, as well as two species of rafflesia. Tree-house accommodation protects the forest floor and gives visitors an opportunity to experience one of the country's most important ecosystems. Best visited December to February.

Khao Lak/Lam Ru National Park, Phang-Nga Province

This 125-sq-km park combines sea cliffs (with 1000m peaks) with beaches, virgin rainforest and mangroves. There is good hiking and the chance to see wildlife, including gibbons and (less likely) the Asiatic black bear. Bungalow accommodation is available at the visitors centre and private resorts nearby. Best visited November to April.

Ao Phang-Nga National Marine Park, Phang-Nga Province

The coastline is marked by stunning karst topography, with steep-sided, verdant limestone islets dropping straight into deep, turquoise waters. Over 40 islands are included in this park near Phuket. Best visited November to April.

Hat Noppharat Thara/Ko Phi-Phi National Marine Park, Krabi Province

Although this huge marine park in the southern half of Ao Phang-Nga is unevenly protected, many designated park islands are still pristine. Ko Phi-Phi is the glaring exception as it is crowded with illegal beach accommodation and is probably a lost cause (as a parkland). Great opportunities exist for kayaking, diving and snorkelling. There is no park accommodation, though there is private accommodation on Ko Phi-Phi. Typical marine karst topography as elsewhere in Ao Phang-Nga. Best visited November to April.

Sirinat National Marine Park, Phuket Province This park in the north-western corner of Phuket, comprising two smaller, formerly separate national parks and Thailand's longest beach, covers a total of 22km of shoreline. Sea turtles nest here, and there is a coral reef offshore. A visitors centre, toilets and picnic tables are the only facilities provided. Best visited from November to April.

Cultural Pursuits
Those who would like to temper beach time with cultural and spiritual diversions can do so in Southern Thailand, though less so along the eastern Gulf Coast. Following are a few recommended sights; greater detail can be found in the relevant destination chapters.

Historic Temples Although the eastern Gulf Coast is predominantly Buddhist, there are virtually no temples of particular historic value in the region. Southern Thailand, despite its heavily Muslim character (predominantly so in the deep South), does have several Buddhist centres with significant temple sites.

The provincial capital of Phetchaburi on the north-western Gulf Coast contains numerous older *wát* (temples), including a few with some of the best preserved Ayuthaya-period temple murals in the country.

In Chaiya, Surat Thani Province, a highly venerated stupa at Wat Phra Boromathat dates from the Srivijaya era (8th to 13th centuries).

Nakhon Si Thammarat boasts Wat Phra Mahathat, one of the oldest Buddhist temples in Thailand, in a large 13th-century

compound, which also contains an exhibit of antique religious objects.

Museums Coastal Thailand isn't known for the outstanding quality of its museums, but there are a few worth looking out for. Nakhon Si Thammarat's National Museum features a room dedicated to works of religious art and handicrafts that originated in Southern Thailand, as well as the country's best collection of southern Thai religious art, plus Dong-Son bronze drums, Dvaravati Buddha images and Pallava (south Indian) Hindu sculpture.

The Songkhla National Museum is a work of art in itself, an old Sino-Portuguese mansion converted into exhibition space for historic artefacts from around the South.

The Satun National Museum is also housed in a historic mansion and gives an interesting introduction to the Muslim folkways and traditions of Southern Thailand.

The Southern Thai Folklore Museum on Ko Yo, near Songkhla, contains an impressive array of southern Thai religious and folk art.

If you're coming through Bangkok, a visit to the National Museum, Vimanmek Teak Mansion and Jim Thompson's House can be recommended for their displays of art and artefacts from centuries past.

SUGGESTED ITINERARIES
Most visitors to Thailand's beaches pick one beach or island and spend their entire holiday there, whether it's one week or one month. Those with more ambitious beach-hopping ideas might sample one or more of the following coastal routes.

One Week
Temples & Gulf Beaches For a short Thailand sampler, start with a two-day taste of Bangkok's heavily gilded temples and urban intensity, then flee towards the former royal capital of Ayuthaya to take in the 400-year-old temple and palace ruins, right in the centre of the city. A day in Ayuthaya is enough for most people with limited time. Transit back through Bangkok and head south-east to Ko Samet off the eastern

Gulf of Thailand coast for two or three nights on this all-season island before saying farewell to Thailand. Substitute Hat Jomtien near Pattaya for Samet if your tastes run towards international-class hotels rather than simpler beach bungalows.

Two Weeks

Bangkok to Ko Chang As above, start with Bangkok, then hopscotch along the north-eastern Gulf to coastal Rayong, Ko Samet and the islands in the Ko Chang archipelago, spending more or less time at each according to your tastes.

Bangkok to the Malaysian Border

After you've had enough of Bangkok – three or four days does the trick for most people who have only two weeks in the country – start rolling down the Malay peninsula with a day and two nights in Phetchaburi, a city of venerable late-Ayuthaya-period temples and a hill-top royal palace.

After Phetchaburi, take your pick among the beaches at Cha-am, Hua Hin or in the vicinity of Prachuap Khiri Khan – all places where middle-class Thais like to vacation. For good coastal and hillside hiking visit Khao Sam Roi Yot National Park.

For some serious beach time, zero in on one or more of the three major islands off the coast of Chumphon and Surat Thani Provinces – Ko Tao, Ko Pha-Ngan and Ko Samui – depending on your tastes.

If you're ready for a little culture, sail back to the mainland and visit Chaiya (Srivijaya-era ruins and a world-famous meditation monastery) or Songkhla (Sino-Portuguese architecture and a national museum).

Follow with a night or two in Hat Yai to sample some of Thailand's best Chinese food outside Bangkok and to shop for Southern Thai or Malay textiles. For your entry into Malaysia, take the east-coast route via Narathiwat for the best natural scenery, the west coast if you're in a rush to reach Penang or Kuala Lumpur.

Three Weeks

Choose one of the two-week itineraries outlined previously, and tack on a week roaming the northern Andaman Coast from Ranong to Phang-Nga. Consider taking at least a day for a sea-canoe trip in Ao Phang-Nga or a jungle walk at Khao Sok National Park.

Four Weeks

With a month of beach and island hopping you can easily add the southern Andaman Coast, sampling Krabi's rugged karst topography as well as the virtually untouched Surin, Similan, Phetra or Tarutao archipelagos.

PLANNING
When to Go

The best time to visit coastal Thailand vis-a-vis climate is between November and March – during these months it rains least and is not so hot. Temperatures are more steady in the South, making it a good refuge when the heat peaks in the rest of Thailand (April to June).

Both the Gulf of Thailand and Andaman Sea coastlines are mostly rain-free from March to May, both are somewhat rainy from June to November, while the Gulf side is drier than the Andaman side from November to January. See Climate in the Facts about Thailand chapter for more detail on seasons, which can vary significantly from one part of the country to another.

The peak tourist months are November, December, February, March and August, with secondary peaks in January and July. Consider travelling during the least crowded months of April, May, June, September and October if you want to avoid crowds and take advantage of discounted rooms and other low-season rates.

Who Goes Where

These days in Thailand you're liable to meet people from all walks of life and from just about any country in the world, but when it comes to beaches and islands, certain types of visitors tend to favour certain areas.

Phuket and nearby Hat Khao Lak attract a well-heeled, middle-aged singles-and-couples crowd of Australians and Europeans who are most numerous in August,

Finding Addresses

Any city as large and unplanned as Bangkok can be tough to get around. Street names often seem unpronounceable to begin with, compounded by the inconsistency of romanised Thai spellings. For example, the street often spelt as Rajadamri is pronounced Ratchadamri (with the appropriate tones), or abbreviated as Rat'damri. The 'v' in Sukhumvit should be pronounced like a 'w'. The most popular location for foreign embassies is known as Wireless Rd and Th Withayu (*wítháyú* is Thai for radio). New Rd, which was Bangkok's first paved road and is far from new, is also known as Th Charoen Krung (Thai for Prosperous City).

Many street addresses show a string of numbers divided by slashes and dashes; for example, 48/3–5 Soi 1, Th Sukhumvit. This is because undeveloped property in Bangkok was originally bought and sold in lots. The number before the slash refers to the original lot number; the numbers following the slash indicate buildings (or entrances to buildings) constructed within that lot. The pre-slash numbers appear in the order in which they were added to city plans, while the post-slash numbers are arbitrarily assigned by developers. As a result, numbers along a given street don't always run consecutively.

The Thai word *thànǒn* means road, street or avenue (it's shortened to Th in this book). Hence Ratchadamnoen Rd (sometimes referred to as Ratchadamnoen Ave) is always called Thanon (Th) Ratchadamnoen in Thai.

A *soi* is a small street or lane that runs off a larger street. In our example, the address referred to as 48/3–5 Soi 1, Th Sukhumvit will be located off Th Sukhumvit on Soi 1. Alternative ways of writing the same address include 48/3–5 Th Sukhumvit Soi 1, or even just 48/3–5 Sukhumvit 1. Some Bangkok sois have become so large that they can be referred to both as thànǒn and soi, eg, Soi Sarasin/Th Sarasin and Soi Asoke/Th Asoke.

Smaller than a soi is a *tràwk* (usually spelt *trok*) or alley. Well-known alleys in Bangkok include Chinatown's Trok Itsanuraphap and Banglamphu's Trok Rong Mai.

In rural areas, along beaches and on most islands, addresses sometimes consist of a house number followed by a village number. For example, 34 Muu 7, would be house number 34 in village number 7 (the 'Muu' is short for *mùu bâan,* Thai for 'village'). Villagers almost never display this address anywhere on their houses, as it is really only used by postal workers and other officials. Places such as guesthouses do sometimes display such an address, though you're more likely to spot a sign with the name of the guesthouse before you see the address. In most cases we've left out this kind of address, unless we've noticed cases in which it might actually help travellers with locating the place in question.

December and January. They tend to stay for a week or less.

Older Europeans, Russians and families on short-stay budget packages tend to frequent Pattaya and, increasingly, Hua Hin and Cha-am. Since these areas are within an easy afternoon's drive from Bangkok, both resort areas tend to be more crowded on weekends and holidays than at other times.

Despite the gentrification of tourist facilities in recent years, Ko Samui continues to attract a younger, more-wealthy group of international beach-goers who like to party.

Peak seasons on Ko Samui are July to August and November to February.

Krabi, Ko Lanta and other Ao Phang-Nga beach areas draw a younger, more adventurous bunch, who are typically on an extended search for low-cost, less-discovered Asian beaches. The winter tourist season is a bit longer here, from mid-November to early March.

Rustic Ko Pha-Ngan and Ko Chang are favoured by backpackers who spend less and stay longer than any of the aforementioned groups. The high season on these islands more or less corresponds with that in Ao Phang-Nga.

Maps

Lonely Planet recently published the completely redesigned and updated, 112-page *Thailand, Vietnam, Laos & Cambodia travel atlas*. It has full colour maps at a scale of 1:1,000,000, a full index of all features and is compact and sturdy. The atlas is available at many Bangkok bookshops, as well as overseas. The comprehensive information in the atlas has been fully cross referenced with Lonely Planet's guidebooks.

Periplus Travel Maps publishes a series of five folding sheet maps covering Thailand: one each on Thailand, Bangkok, Chiang Mai, Phuket and Ko Samui. The 1:2,000,000 Thailand map is quite useful, as are the Phuket and Ko Samui maps. Several Thai map publishers issue various regional maps of Thailand, but none of them can be recommended except for Window Group/Book Athens *Thailand Highway Map* series.

The Roads Association of Thailand annually publishes a large format, 48-page, bilingual road atlas called *Thailand Highway Map* (same name as the Window Group/Book Athens publications, but not the same maps). The atlas has cut the Highway Department maps to a more manageable size and includes dozens of city maps, driving distances and lots of travel and sightseeing information. It costs around 120B, but beware of inferior knock-offs. A big advantage of the Thailand Highway Maps is that the town and city names are printed in Thai as well as roman script.

Real map aficionados should head down to the Army Map Department (Krom Phaen Thi Tahan; ☎ 022 228 844), also known as the Royal Survey Department. Although the 1:250,000 maps are rather old (1984), they show details beyond Thai borders (Myanmar and Malaysia) and are nicely coloured and suitable for framing. The Army Map Department is located on Th Kanlayana Maitri, next to the Defence Ministry (the building with a collection of antique cannons in front of it), just east of the Grand Palace.

The Lonely Planet atlas, or the maps from either the Highway Department or Periplus, are more than adequate for most people.

Regional Maps Several companies in Thailand publish 'guide maps' to Phuket, Krabi and the Samui archipelago. Most accurate and current are those published by V Hongsombud, such as the *Guide Map of Krabi*. Periplus Editions' *Ko Samui Southern Thailand Travel Map* contains maps of the Samui archipelago, Southern Thailand, the Tarutao archipelago and a city plan for Hat Yai.

The beaches and islands of the eastern Gulf coast, save for the area around Pattaya, have so far been neglected by regional map publishers.

Prannok Witthaya publishes individual maps of most of the provinces along the coast. These include English and Thai script, and can be found in most bookshops in Thailand. The maps are often a little out of date and are therefore not always accurate, but are of a larger scale than the regional and country maps.

What to Bring

Pack light, tropical-weight clothes, along with a light parka or windbreaker for occasional breezy or rainy evenings. Natural fibres can be cool and comfortable, except when they get soaked with sweat or rain, in which case they quickly become heavy and block air flow. Some of the newer, lightweight synthetics breathe much better than natural fibres, keep sweat away rather than holding it in, and may be more suitable for the beach and the rainy season. Sunglasses are important, and slip-on shoes or sandals are highly recommended – besides being cooler than lace-up shoes, they are easily removed before entering a Thai home or temple.

You might also think about picking up a *phâakhamáa* (short Thai-style sarong for men) or a *phâasîn* (a longer sarong for women) to wear in your room, on the beach or when bathing outdoors. These can be bought at any local market (different patterns/colours in different parts of the country) and the vendors will show you how to tie them.

The sarong is a very handy item; it can be used to sleep on or as a light bedspread, as a makeshift 'shopping bag', as a turban/scarf to keep off the sun and absorb perspiration, as a towel, as a small hammock and as a device with which to climb coconut palms – to name just a few of its many functions. It is not considered proper street attire, however.

A small torch (flashlight) is a good idea, as it makes it easier to find your way back to your bungalow at night if you are staying at the beach or at a remote guesthouse. Other handy items include a compass, a plastic lighter for lighting candles and mosquito coils, and foam ear plugs for noisy nights.

Toothpaste, soap and most other toiletries can be purchased anywhere in Thailand. Sun block and mosquito repellent are widely available in beach areas. If you want to wash your own clothes, bring a universal sink plug, a few plastic clothes pegs and 3m of plastic cord, or plastic hangers for hanging wet clothes out to dry.

If you're a keen snorkeller, you might want to bring your own equipment (see Diving & Snorkelling in the Activities section of this chapter). This will save you having to rent gear and assure a proper fit. Shoes designed for water sports, eg, aquasocks, are great for wearing in the water whether you're diving or not. They protect your feet from coral cuts, which easily become infected.

If you require computer modem communications in Thailand, see the Email & Internet Access section later in this chapter for items you might need to bring with you.

TOURIST OFFICES

The Tourism Authority of Thailand (TAT), a government-operated tourist information and promotion service, attached to the prime minister's office, maintains 22 offices within the country and 16 overseas. TAT has regulatory powers to monitor tourism-related businesses throughout Thailand, including hotels, tour operators, travel agencies and transport companies, in an effort to improve these services and prosecute unscrupulous operators.

The quality of the printed information that TAT produces is second to none among South-East Asian countries, including copious pamphlets describing sightseeing, accommodation and transport options for each province. The staff is huge; the main office in Bangkok occupies 10 floors of a new office building in the Ratchada area of Huay Khwang.

In Bangkok you can get tourist information in English and French by calling ☎ 022 829 773 from 8.30am to 4.30pm daily.

In addition to the following offices, you'll also find TAT information counters in the international and domestic terminals of Bangkok's Don Muang Airport.

Local TAT Offices
Bangkok
Central Bangkok: (☎ 022 829 773) 4 Th Ratchadamnoen Nok, Bangkok 10100
Huay Khwang: (☎ 026 941 222, fax 026 941 220–1, ℮ info1@tat.or.th) Le Concorde Bldg, 202 Th Ratchadaphisek, Huay Khwang, Bangkok 10310
Cha-am
(☎ 032 471 005–8, fax 032 471 502, ℮ tatphet@tat.or.th) 500/51 Thang Luang Phetkasem, Amphoe Cha-am, Phetchaburi 76120
Hat Yai
(☎ 074 243 747, fax 074 245 986, ℮ tathatyai@hatyai.inet.co.th) 1/1 Soi 2, Th Niphat Uthit 3, Hat Yai, Songkhla 90110
Nakhon Si Thammarat
(☎ 075 346 515–6, fax 075 346 517, ℮ tatnakhon@nrt.csoms.com) Sanam Na Meuang, Th Ratchadamnoen Klang, Nakhon Si Thammarat 80000
Narathiwat
(☎ 073 516 144, fax 073 522 412, ℮ tatnara@cscoms.com) 102/3 Th Narathiwat-Tak Bai, Narathiwat 96000
Pattaya
(☎ 038 427 667, fax 038 429 113, ℮ tatpty@chonburi.ksc.co.th) 609 Mu 10, Th Phatamnak, Pattaya 20260
Phuket
(☎ 076 217 138, 076 211 036, fax 076 213 582, ℮ tathkt@phuket.ksc.co.th) 73-75 Th Phuket, Phuket 83000
Rayong
(☎ 038 655 420–1, fax 038 655 422, ℮ tatry@infonews.co.th) 153/4 Th Sukhumvit, Rayong 21000

Surat Thani
(☎ 077 288 818–9, fax 077 282 828,
e tatsurat@samart.co.th) 5 Th Talaat Mai,
Ban Don, Surat Thani 84000

Trat
(☎/fax 038 597 255) 100 Muu 1, Th Trat-
Laem Ngop, Laem Ngop, Trat 23120

TAT Offices Abroad

Australia (☎ 02-9247 7549, fax 9251 2465,
e info@thailand.net.au) Level 2, 75 Pitt
Street, Sydney, NSW 2000
France (☎ 01 53 53 47 00, fax 01 45 63 78 88,
e tatpar@wanadoo.fr) 90 Avenue des
Champs Elysées, 75008 Paris
Germany (☎ 069-138 1390, e tatfra@
t-online.de) Bethmannstrasse 58, 60311
Frankfurt/Main
Hong Kong (☎ 02-2868 0732, fax 2868 4585,
e tathkg@hk.super.net) Room 401, Fairmont
House, 8 Cotton Tree Drive, Central
Japan (☎ 03-3218 0337, fax 3218 0655,
e tattky@crisscross.com) Room 259, 2nd
floor, South Tower, Yurakucho Denki Bldg,
1-7-1 Yurakucho, Chiyoda-ku, Tokyo 100
Laos (☎ 21-217157, fax 217158) 79/9 Th Lan
Xang, Vientiane, Lao PDR, or PO Box 12,
Nong Khai 43000
Malaysia (☎ 093-262 3480, fax 262 3486,
e sawatdi@po.jaring.my) C/o Royal Thai
embassy, suite 22.01, level 22, Menara Lion,
165, Jalan Ampang, Kuala Lumpur, 50450
Singapore (☎ 65-235 7694, fax 733 5653,
e tatsin@mbox5.singnet.com.sg) C/o Royal
Thai embassy, 370 Orchard Rd, 238870
UK (☎ 020-7499 7679, fax 7629 5519,
e info@tat-uk.demon.co.uk) 49 Albemarle St,
London W1X 3FE
USA (☎ 213-461 9814, fax 461 9834, e tatla@
ix.netcom.com) 1st floor, 611 North Larch-
mont Blvd, LA, CA 90004

VISAS & DOCUMENTS
Passport

Entry into Thailand requires a passport
that is valid for at least six months from
the time of entry. If you anticipate your
passport may expire while you're in Thailand, you should obtain a new one before
arrival or inquire from your government
whether your embassy in Thailand (if one
exists – see Embassies & Consulates later
in this chapter) can issue a new one after
arrival.

Visas

Whichever type of visa you have, be sure to
check your passport immediately after
stamping. Overworked officials sometimes
stamp 30 days on arrival even when you
hold a longer visa; if you point out the error
before you've left the immigration area at
your port of entry, officials will make the
necessary corrections. If you don't notice
this until you've left the port of entry, go to
Bangkok and plead your case at the central
immigration office.

Similarly, if you plan to come back to
Thailand at some point, make sure your visa
is stamped when you leave the country. One
poor fellow, who had last left Thailand via
an unstaffed checkpoint at the Malaysian
border, flew in from London for a return
visit only to be refused entry and put on the
next flight back home! All because he
didn't have the proper exit stamp.

Once a visa is issued, it must be used (ie,
you must enter Thailand) within 90 days.
The Thai embassy in Washington, DC,
maintains one of the best Web sites for
information about visas for Thailand
(w www.thaiembdc.org/consular/visa/
visa.htm).

Transit & Tourist Visas The Thai government allows 57 different nationalities to
enter the country without a visa for 30 days
at no charge. Seventy-eight other nationalities – those from smaller European countries like Andorra or Liechtenstein, or from
West Africa, South Asia or Latin America
– can obtain a 15-day Transit Visa on arrival for a 300B fee. Some visitors, such as
those from eastern European countries,
have found that on-arrival visas can only be
obtained if they fly into Bangkok, and can't
be arranged at land border crossings.

A few nationalities (eg, Hungarians)
must obtain a visa before arriving or
they'll be turned back. Check with a Thai
embassy or consulate if you plan to arrive
without a visa.

Without proof of an onward ticket and
sufficient funds for one's projected stay,
any visitor can be denied entry, but in practice your ticket and funds are rarely checked

if you're dressed neatly for the immigration check. See Exchange Control in the Money section later in this chapter for the amount of funds required per visa type.

Next in its length of validity is the Tourist Visa, which is good for 60 days and costs US$15. Three passport photos must accompany all applications.

Non-Immigrant Visas You must apply for a Non-Immigrant Visa in your home country. It is good for 90 days, costs US$20 and is not difficult to obtain if you can offer a good reason for your visit. Business, study, retirement and extended family visits are among the purposes considered valid. If you want to stay longer than six months, this is the one to get.

Another type, the Non-Immigrant Business Visa (usually abbreviated by Thai immigration officials as 'Non-B') allows unlimited entries in and out of Thailand for one year. The only hitch is that you must leave the country at least once every 90 days to keep the visa valid.

Re-Entry Permits & Multiple-Entry Visas If you need to leave and re-enter the kingdom before your visa expires, say for a return trip to Laos or the like, you may need to apply for a Re-Entry Permit at a Thai immigration office. The cost is 500B and you'll need to supply one passport photo. There is no limit to the number of Re-Entry Permits you can apply for and use during the validity of your visa.

Other than the Non-Immigrant Business Visa, Thailand does not issue multiple-entry visas. If you want a visa that enables you to leave the country and then return, the best you can do is to obtain a visa permitting two entries; this will cost double the single-entry visa. For example, a two-entry, 90-day Non-Immigrant Visa will cost US$40 and will allow you six months in the country, as long as you cross a border with immigration facilities by the end of your first three months. The second half of your visa is validated as soon as you re-cross the Thai border, so there is no need to go to a Thai embassy/consulate abroad.

An alternative is to apply for a Re-Entry Permit (or the Multiple Re-Entry Permit, if established as proposed by Thai immigration) after you're already in Thailand, as described previously.

See Non-Immigrant Visas earlier in this section for a description of the multiple-entry Non-Immigrant Business Visa.

Visa Extensions Sixty-day Tourist Visas may be extended by up to 30 days at the discretion of Thai immigration authorities. The Bangkok office (☎ 022 873 101) is on Soi Suan Phlu, Thanon (Th) Sathon Tai, but you can apply at any immigration office in the country – every province bordering a neighbouring country has at least one. The usual fee for extension of a Tourist Visa is 500B. Bring along one photo and one copy each of the photo and visa pages of your passport. Normally only one 30-day extension is granted.

The 30-day, no-visa stay can be extended by 7 to 10 days (depending on the immigration office) for 500B. You can also leave the country and return immediately to obtain another 30-day stay. There is no limit on the number of times you can do this, nor is there a minimum interval you must spend outside the country.

Extension of the 15-day, on-arrival Transit Visa is only allowed if you hold a passport from a country that has no Thai embassy.

If you overstay your visa, the usual penalty is a fine of 200B per day of your overstay, with a 20,000B limit; fines can be paid at the airport or in advance at the Investigation Unit (☎ 022 873 101–10), Immigration Bureau, Room 416, 4th floor, Old Building, Soi Suan Phlu, Th Sathon Tai in Bangkok.

Extending a Non-Immigrant Visa very much depends on how the officials feel about you – if they like you then they will extend it. Other than the 500B extension fee, money doesn't usually come into it; neat appearance and polite behaviour count for more. You must collect a number of signatures and go through various interviews, which may result in a 'provisional' extension. You would then have to report to a local immigration office every 10 to 14 days for the next three months until the extension comes through.

Retirees 55 years of age or older can extend the 90-day Non-Immigrant Visa to a yearly visa. To do this you will need to bring the following documents to the Immigration Bureau: a copy of your passport's personal details pages, one photo, 500B extension fee, proof of your financial status or pension. The requirement for the latter is that foreigners aged 60 or older must show proof of an income of not less than 200,000B per year (or 20,000B per month for extensions of less than a year); for those aged 55 to 59 the minimum is raised to 500,000B/50,000B. According to immigration regulations, however: 'If the alien is ill, or has weak health and is sensitive to colder climates, or has resided in Thailand for a long period, and is 55-59 years of age, special considerations will be granted'.

Foreigners with Non-Immigrant Visas who have resided in Thailand continuously for three years – on one-year extensions – may apply for permanent residency at Section 1, Subdivision 1, Immigration Division 1, Room 301, 3rd floor, Immigration Bureau, Soi Suan Phlu, Th Sathon Tai (☎ 022 873 117–01). Foreigners who receive permanent residence must carry an 'alien identification card' at all times.

The Thai government maintains the One-Stop Visa Centre (☎ 026 939 333, fax 026 939 340) Krisda Plaza, 207 Th Ratchadaphisek, where Non-Immigrant Visas for investors, businesspeople and foreign correspondents only can be renewed in less than three hours.

Various law offices in Thailand, especially in Bangkok, Chiang Mai and Hat Yai, can assist with visa extensions, renewals and applications – for a fee of course. One in Bangkok that has been around for a while is Siam Visa (☎ 022 382 989, fax 022 382 987, e siamvisa@loxinfo.co.th), 7th floor, Kasemkit Bldg, Th Silom. This does not constitute an endorsement for the agency – be cautious and ask plenty of questions before plunking down your money.

Onward Tickets

Thai immigration does not seem very concerned that you arrive with proof of onward travel. Legally speaking all holders of Tourist Visas or the no-visa 30-day stay permit are *supposed* to carry such proof. In many years of frequent travel in and out of the kingdom, our documents haven't been checked a single time.

Travel Insurance

A travel-insurance policy to cover theft, loss and medical problems is strongly recommended. Though Thailand is generally a safe country to travel in, sickness, accidents and theft do happen. There are a wide variety of policies and travel agents can advise you. Check to see if the policy covers any potentially dangerous sporting activities you may do, such as diving, trekking and riding motorbikes, and make sure that it adequately covers your valuables. You may prefer a policy that pays doctors or hospitals directly rather than having to pay on the spot and claim later. If you have to claim later, make sure you keep all documentation. Some policies ask you to call back (reverse charges) to a centre in your home country, where an immediate assessment of your problem is made.

Check that the policy covers ambulances or an emergency flight home.

Driving Licence & Permits

An International Driving Permit is necessary for any visitor who intends to drive a motorised vehicle while in Thailand. These are usually available from motoring organisations, such as AAA (USA) or BAA (UK), in your home country. If you'd like to obtain a Thai driving licence, see the Driving Permits section of the Getting Around chapter for details.

Hostel Cards

Hostelling International (HI; formerly International Youth Hostel Federation) issues a membership card that will allow you to stay at Thailand's member hostels. Without such a card or the purchase of a temporary membership you won't be admitted to stay at associated hostels.

For further information on hostelling in Thailand, check HI's Web site (W www .tyha.org).

Student Cards

The International Student Identity Card (ISIC) can be used for the student discount offered rarely at some museums in Thailand. It's probably not worth getting just for a visit to Thailand, but if you already have one, or plan to use one elsewhere in Asia, bring it along. For a list of agents that issue ISIC cards, visit the International Student Travelling Confederation's Web site (W www.istc.org).

Copies

Important documents (passport personal-details and visa pages, credit cards, travel-insurance policy, air/bus/train tickets, driving licence etc) should be photocopied before you leave home. Leave one copy with someone at home and keep another with you, separate from the originals.

You can also store details of your vital travel documents in Lonely Planet's free online travel vault. See eKno Communication Service under Post & Communications later in this chapter.

EMBASSIES & CONSULATES
Thai Embassies & Consulates

To apply for a visa, contact the Royal Thai embassy (or consulate) in any of the following countries. In many cases, if you apply in person you may receive a tourist or Non-Immigrant Visa on the day of application; by mail it takes anywhere from two to six weeks.

Australia (☎ 02-6273 1149, 6273 2937) 111 Empire Circuit, Yarralumla, Canberra, ACT 2600

Cambodia (☎ 855-2336 3869–70) 196 MV Preah Norodom Blvd, Songkat Tonle Bassac, Chamkar Mon, Phnom Penh

Canada (☎ 613-722 4444) 180 Island Park Drive, Ottawa, Ontario K1Y OA2

China (☎ 010-6532 1749) 40 Guanghua Lu, Beijing 100600

France (☎ 01-56 26 50 50, 01 56 26 50 54) 8 Rue Greuze, 75116 Paris

Germany (☎ 30-794810) Lepsiusstrasse 64–66, 12162 Berlin

Hong Kong (☎ 02-2521 6481, 2521 6485) 8th floor, Fairmont House, 8 Cotton Tree Drive, Central

India (☎ 11-611 8103, 611 5678) 56-N Nyaya Marg, Chanakyapuri, New Delhi, 110021

Indonesia (☎ 021-390 4052/3) Jalan Imam Bonjol 74, Jakarta, Pusat 10310

Japan (☎ 03-3441 1386, 3447 2247) 3-14-6 Kami-Osaki, Shinagawa-ku, Tokyo 141-0021

Laos (☎ 21-21 4582–3) Th Phonkheng, Vientiane Poste 128

Malaysia (☎ 03-2148 8222, 2148 8350) 206 Jalan Ampang, Kuala Lumpur

Myanmar (Burma; ☎ 01-51 2017–8) 437 Pyay Lan, Yangon

Nepal (☎ 71-371410–1) Ward No 3, Bansabar, Kathmandu

Netherlands (☎ 070-345 0632) Laan Copes van Cattenburch 123, 2585 E2, The Hague

New Zealand (☎ 04-476 8618–9) 2 Cook St, Karori, Wellington 5

Philippines (☎ 02-810 3833, 815 4219) 107 Rada St, Legaspi Village, Makati, Metro Manila

Singapore (☎ 65-737 2158, 737 2644) 370 Orchard Rd, 238870

Sweden (☎ 08-791 7340) Floragatan 3, 5-11431, Stockholm

UK & Northern Ireland (☎ 020-7589 2944) 29–30 Queen's Gate, London SW7 5JB

USA (☎ 202-944 3600) Suite 101, 1024 Wisconsin Ave NW, Washington, DC 20007

Vietnam (☎ 04-823 5092) 63-65 Hoang Dieu St, Hanoi

Embassies & Consulates in Thailand

Bangkok is a good place to collect visas for onward travel, and most countries have diplomatic representation there. The visa sections of most embassies and consulates are open from around 8.30am to 11.30am Monday to Friday only (but call first to be sure).

Countries with diplomatic representation in Bangkok include:

Australia
(☎ 022 872 680) 37 Th Sathon Tai

Cambodia
(☎ 022 546 630) 185 Th Ratchadamri, Lumphini, Pathumwan

Canada
(☎ 026 360 540) 15th floor, Abdulrahim Place, 990 Th Rama IV, Bangrak

China
(☎ 022 457 043) 57 Th Ratchadaphisek
France
Th Charoen Krung: (☎ 022 668 250) 35 Soi Customs House (Soi 36), Th Charoen Krung
Th Sathon Tai: (☎ 022 872 585) Consular section (visas), 29 Th Sathon Tai
Germany
(☎ 022 879 000) 9 Th Sathon Tai
India
(☎ 022 580 300) 46 Soi Prasanmit (Soi 23), Th Sukhumvit
Indonesia
(☎ 022 523 135) 600–602 Th Phetchaburi
Ireland
(☎ 022 230 876) 205 United Flour Mill Bldg, Th Ratchawong
Japan
(☎ 022 526 151) 1674 Th Phetchaburi Tat Mai
Laos
(☎ 025 396 667) 520/1–3 Soi 39, Th Ramkhamhaeng
Malaysia
(☎ 026 792 190) 33–35 Th Sathon Tai
Myanmar
(Burma; ☎ 022 332 237, 022 344 698) 132 Th Sathon Neua
Nepal
(☎ 023 917 240) 189 Soi Phuengsuk (Soi 71), Th Sukhumvit
Netherlands
(☎ 022 547 701, 022 526 103) 106 Th Withayu
New Zealand
(☎ 022 542 530) 87 Th Withayu
Philippines
(☎ 022 590 139) 760 Th Sukhumvit

Singapore
(☎ 022 862 111) 129 Th Sathon Tai
Sweden
(☎ 022 544 954) 20th floor, Pacific Place, 140 Th Sukhumvit
UK
(☎ 023 058 333) 1031 Th Withayu
USA
(☎ 022 054 000) 120–122 Th Withayu
Vietnam
(☎ 022 515 836) 83/1 Th Withayu

CUSTOMS

Like most countries, Thailand prohibits the importation of illegal drugs, firearms and ammunition (unless registered in advance with the Police Department) and pornographic media. A reasonable amount of clothing for personal use, toiletries and professional instruments are allowed in duty-free, as is one still or one movie/video camera with five rolls of still film or three rolls of movie film or videotape. Up to 200 cigarettes can be brought into the country without paying duty, or up to 250g of loose tobacco. One litre of wine or spirits is allowed in duty-free.

Electronic goods such as stereos, calculators and computers can be a problem if the customs officials have reason to believe you're bringing them in for re-sale. As long as you don't carry more than one of each, you should be OK.

For information on currency importation or export, see Exchange Control in the Money section of this chapter.

Your Own Embassy

It's important to realise what your own embassy – the embassy of the country of which you are a citizen – can and can't do to help you if you get into trouble. Generally speaking, it won't be much help in emergencies if the trouble you're in is remotely your own fault. Remember that you are bound by the laws of the country you are in. Your embassy will not be sympathetic if you end up in jail after committing a crime locally, even if such actions are legal in your own country.

In genuine emergencies you might get some assistance, but only if other channels have been exhausted. For example, if you need to get home urgently, a free ticket home is exceedingly unlikely – the embassy would expect you to have insurance. If you have all your money and documents stolen, it might assist with getting a new passport, but a loan for onward travel is out of the question.

Some embassies used to keep letters for travellers or have a small reading room with home newspapers, but these days the mail holding service has usually been stopped and even newspapers tend to be out of date.

Antiques & Art

Upon leaving Thailand, you must obtain an export licence for any antiques or objects of art you want to take with you. An antique is any 'archaic movable property, whether produced by man or by nature, any part of ancient structure, human skeleton or animal carcass, which by its age or characteristic of production or historical evidence is useful in the field of art, history or archaeology'. An art object is a 'thing produced by craftsmanship and appreciated as being valuable in the field of art'. Obviously these are sweeping definitions, so if in doubt go to the Fine Arts Department for inspection and licensing.

Applications can be made by submitting two front-view photos of the object(s) (no more than five objects to a photo) and a photocopy of your passport, along with the object(s) in question, to one of three national museums: Bangkok, Chiang Mai or Songkhla. Allow three to five days for the process to be completed.

Thailand has special regulations for taking a Buddha or other deity image (or any part thereof) out of the country. These require not only a licence from the Fine Arts Department but a permit from the Ministry of Commerce as well. The one exception to this are the small Buddha images (*phrá phim* or *phrá khrêuang*) that are meant to be worn on a chain around the neck; these may be exported without a licence as long as the reported purpose is religious.

Temporary Vehicle Importation

A passenger vehicle (car, van, truck or motorcycle) can be brought into Thailand for tourist purposes for up to six months. Documents needed for the crossing are a valid International Driving Permit, passport, vehicle registration papers (in the case of a borrowed or hired vehicle, authorisation from the owner) and a cash or bank guarantee equal to the value of the vehicle plus 20%. (For entry through Khlong Toey port or Bangkok international airport, this means a letter of bank credit; for overland crossings via Malaysia a 'self-guarantee' filled in at the border is sufficient.)

Home Country Customs

Be sure to check the import regulations in your home country before bringing in or sending back a large quantity (or high value) of Thai goods. The limit varies from country to country; the USA, for example, allows US$400 worth of foreign-purchased goods to enter without duty (with no limit on handicrafts and unset gems), while in Australia the total value is limited to A$400.

MONEY

Currency

The basic unit of Thai currency is the *baht*. There are 100 *satang* in one baht; coin denominations include 25-satang and 50-satang pieces, and baht in 1B, 5B and 10B. Older coins exhibit Thai numerals only, while newer coins have Thai and Arabic numerals. Twenty-five satang equals one *saleung* in colloquial Thai, so if you're quoted a price of six saleung in the market, say, for a banana or a bag of peanuts, this means 1.50B. The term is becoming increasingly rare as inflation makes purchases of less than 1B or 2B almost obsolete.

Paper currency comes in denominations of 10B (brown), 20B (green), 50B (blue), 100B (red), 500B (purple) and 1000B (beige). A 10,000B bill is on the way. The 10B bills are being phased out in favour of the 10B coin and have become rather uncommon. Notes are scaled according to the amount; the larger the denomination, the larger the note. Large denominations – 500B and especially 1000B bills – can be hard to change in small towns, but banks will always change them.

Exchange Rates

Exchange rates at the time of writing include:

country	unit		baht
Australia	A$1	=	23.21B
Canada	C$1	=	29.01B
Euro	€1	=	38.70B
France	FF1	=	5.80B
Germany	DM1	=	19.53B
Japan	¥100	=	35.98B

Malaysia	M$1	=	9.57B
New Zealand	NZ$1	=	18.19B
Singapore	S$1	=	24.60B
UK	UK£1	=	62.53B
USA	US$1	=	44.50B

Prior to June 1997 the baht was pegged to a basket of currencies heavily weighted towards the US dollar, and for over 20 years it hardly varied beyond 20B to 26B to the dollar. A year after flotation, in June 1998, the baht had slipped approximately 30% against the dollar.

Lately exchange rates seem to have stabilised, but there's always the chance the Thai currency will go for another roller-coaster ride. Hence it's a good idea to stay abreast of exchange rates during your stay in Thailand – changing currencies at the right time could extend your budget significantly. Exchange rates are printed in the *Bangkok Post* and the *Nation* every day, or you can walk into any Thai bank and ask to see its daily rate sheet. A good place to check the exchange rate for the baht against kangaroo currencies such as the Lao kip, Myanmar kyat and Cambodian riel is W www.oanda.com.

Exchanging Money

There is no black market for baht. Banks or legal moneychangers offer the best exchange rate within the country. US dollars are the most readily acceptable currency and travellers cheques get better exchange rates than cash. Since banks charge up to 23B commission and duty for each travellers cheque cashed, you will save on commissions if you use larger cheque denominations (eg, a US$50 cheque will only cost 23B while five US$10 cheques will cost 115B). British pounds are second to the US dollar in general acceptability.

Note that you can't exchange Malaysian ringgit, Indonesian rupiah, Nepali rupees, Cambodian riel, Lao kip, Vietnamese dong or Myanmar kyat into Thai currency at banks, though some Bangkok moneychangers along Th Charoen Krung and Th Silom in Bangkok carry these currencies. These moneychangers can, in fact, be good

places to buy these currencies if you're going to any of these countries. Rates are comparable with black-market rates in countries with discrepancies between the 'official' and free-market currency values.

Visa and MasterCard credit card holders can get cash advances of up to US$500 (in baht only) per day through some branches of the Thai Farmers Bank, Bangkok Bank and Siam Commercial Bank (and also at the night-time exchange windows in well-touristed spots like Banglamphu, Chiang Mai, Ko Samui and so on).

American Express (AmEx) card holders can also get advances, but only in travellers cheques, and the maximum amount depends on the status of your card. The AmEx agent is SEA Tours (☎ 022 165 759), Suite 88–92, Payathai Plaza, 8th floor, 128 Th Phayathai, Bangkok.

See the Business Hours section later in this chapter for information on bank opening hours.

Exchange Control Legally, any traveller arriving in Thailand must have at least the following amounts of money in cash, travellers cheques, bank draft or letter of credit, according to visa category: Non-Immigrant Visa, US$500 per person or US$1000 per family; Tourist Visa, US$250 per person or US$500 per family; and Transit Visa or no visa US$125 per person, or US$250 per family. Your funds may be checked by authorities if you arrive on a one-way ticket or if you look as if you're at 'the end of the road'.

There is no limit to the amount of Thai or foreign currency you can bring into the country. Upon leaving Thailand, you're permitted to take no more than 50,000B per person without special authorisation. If you're going to one of Thailand's neighbouring countries, you are allowed to take as much as 500,000B per person. The exportation of foreign currencies is unrestricted.

It's legal, though a bit of a hassle, to open a US-dollar account at any commercial bank in Thailand. As long as the funds originate from abroad, there are no restrictions on their maintenance or withdrawal. (Thai nationals are prohibited from opening US-dollar accounts.)

International Transfers If you have a reliable place to receive mail in Thailand, one of the safest and cheapest ways to receive money from overseas is to have an international cashier's cheque (or international money order) sent by courier. It usually takes no more than four days for courier mail to reach Thailand from anywhere in the world.

If you have a bank account in Thailand or your home bank has a branch in Bangkok, you can have money wired direct via a telegraphic transfer. This costs a bit more than having a cheque sent; telegraphic transfers take anywhere from two days to a week to arrive. International banks with branches in Bangkok include Hong Kong Bank, Standard Chartered Bank, Sakura Bank, Bank of America, Banque Indosuez, Citibank, Banque Nationale de Paris, Chase Manhattan Bank, Bank of Tokyo, Deutsche Bank, Merrill Lynch International Bank, United Malayan Bank and many others.

ATM & Credit/Debit Cards An alternative to carrying around large amounts of cash or travellers cheques is to open an account at a Thai bank and request an automatic-teller-machine (ATM) card. Major banks in Thailand now have ATMs in provincial capitals, and in many smaller towns as well, open 24 hours. Once you have a card you'll be able to withdraw cash at machines throughout Thailand, whether those machines belong to your bank or another Thai bank. ATM cards issued by Thai Farmers Bank or Bangkok Bank can be used with the ATMs of 14 major banks – there are over 3000 machines nationwide. A 10B transaction charge is usually deducted for using an ATM belonging to a bank with whom you don't have an account.

Debit cards (also known as cash cards or cheque cards) issued by a bank in your own country can also be used at several Thai banks to withdraw cash (in Thai baht only) directly from your cheque or savings account back home, thus avoiding all commissions and finance charges. You can use MasterCard debit cards to buy baht at foreign-exchange booths or desks at either Bangkok Bank or Siam Commercial Bank. Visa debit cards can buy cash through Thai Farmers Bank exchange services.

These cards can also be used at many Thai ATMs, though a surcharge of around US$1 is usually subtracted from your home account each time you complete a machine transaction. Some travellers now use debit or ATM cards in lieu of travellers cheques because they're quicker and more convenient, although it's a good idea to bring along an emergency travellers cheque fund in case you lose your card. One disadvantage of debit-card accounts, as opposed to credit-card accounts, is that you can't arrange a 'charge back' for unsatisfactory purchases after the transaction is completed – once the money's drawn from your account it's gone.

Credit cards and debit cards can be used for purchases at many shops, hotels and restaurants. The most commonly accepted cards are Visa and MasterCard, followed by AmEx and Japan Card Bureau (JCB). Diners Club and Carte Blanche are of much more limited use.

Card Problems Occasionally when you try to use a Visa or MasterCard at rural hotels or shops, the staff may try to tell you that only cards issued by Thai Farmers Bank or Siam Commercial Bank are acceptable. With a little patience, you should be able to make them understand that the Thai Farmers Bank will pay the merchant and that your bank will pay the Thai Farmers Bank – and that any Visa or MasterCard issued anywhere in the world is indeed acceptable.

Another problem concerns illegal surcharges on credit-card purchases. It's against Thai law to pass on to the customer the 3% merchant fee charged by banks, but almost all merchants in Thailand do it anyway. Some even ask 4% or 5%! The only exception seems to be hotels (although even a few hotels will hit you with a credit-card surcharge). If you don't agree to the surcharge they'll simply refuse to accept your card. Begging and pleading or pointing out the law doesn't seem to help. The best way to get around the illegal surcharge is to politely ask that the credit-card receipt be itemised with cost of product or service and the surcharge listed separately. Then when you pay your bill back home, photocopy all receipts showing the surcharge and request a 'charge back'. If a hotel or shop refuses to itemise the surcharge, you could take down the vendor's name and address and report them to TAT's Tourist Police – they may be able to arrange a refund. Not all banks in all countries will offer refunds – banks in the UK, for example, refuse to issue such refunds, while banks in the USA often will.

To report a lost or stolen credit/debit card, call the following telephone hotlines in Bangkok:

AmEx	☎ 022 730 022–44
Diners Club	☎ 022 383 660
MasterCard	☎ 022 608 572
Visa	☎ 022 731 199/7449

See Dangers & Annoyances in this chapter for important warnings on credit-card theft and fraud.

Security

Give some thought in advance to how you're going to carry your financial resources – whether travellers cheques, cash, credit and debit cards, or some combination of these. Many travellers favour hidden pouches that can be worn beneath clothing. Hip-pocket wallets are easy marks for thieves. Pickpockets work markets and crowded buses throughout the country, so it pays to keep your money concealed. See Dangers & Annoyances later in this chapter for more on petty crime.

It's a good idea not to keep all your money in one place; keep an 'emergency' stash well concealed in a piece of luggage separate from other money. Long-term travellers might even consider renting a safety deposit box at a bank in Bangkok or other major cities – although nowadays most banks require that you open a savings account with them before they'll rent you a safety deposit box. Keep your onward tickets, a copy of your passport, a list of all credit-card numbers and some money in the box just in case all your belongings are stolen while you're on the road. It's not common, but it does happen.

Costs

For most visitors the major expense of a Thai beach holiday is getting there. Comfortable beach-or-island accommodation is inexpensive by international standards, and a full day's worth of world-class Thai cuisine usually costs less than a standard lunch back home. An overnight train journey costs about the same as a short taxi ride in many Western cities, and long-distance buses are even cheaper.

Outside major beach resorts, budget-squeezers should be able to get by on 250B per day if you really keep watch on your expenses, especially if you share rooms with other travellers. This estimate includes basic guesthouse accommodation, food, nonalcoholic beverages and local transport, but not film, souvenirs, tours, long-distance transport or vehicle hire. Add another 60B to 90B per day for every large beer (30B to 60B for small bottles) you drink.

Expenses vary from place to place; where there are high concentrations of budget travellers, for example, accommodation tends to be cheaper and food more expensive. With experience, you can travel in Thailand for even less if you live like a Thai of modest means and learn to speak some of the language.

Someone with more money to spend will find that for around 400B to 500B per day, life can be quite comfortable; cleaner and quieter accommodation is easier to find once you pass the 250B-a-night zone in room rates. Of course, a 100B guesthouse room with a mattress on the floor and responsive management is better than a poorly maintained 500B room with air-con that won't turn off and a noisy all-night card game next door.

In Bangkok, Phuket and Ko Samui there's almost no limit to the amount you

Sample Prices

item	approximate price
1L petrol	13B
average meter-taxi ride, central Bangkok	60B
average bus fare, Bangkok	3.50B
sǎwngthǎew ride in a provincial city	10B per person, or 40B to 50B charter
3rd-class train fare, Bangkok to Surat Thani	107B
one day's 100cc motorcycle rental, Hua Hin	150B
dorm bed in a guesthouse or youth hostel	80B
mid-range hotel double, Bangkok	1600B
beach hut – single, Ko Pha-Ngan	100B to 150B
budget beach hotel – single, Phuket	500B
bowl of kǔaytǐaw, Prachuap Khiri Khan	20B
10 eggs from a market	22B
can of Campbell's Vegetarian Vegetable soup	45B
substantial lunch for two at an average Thai vegetarian restaurant	50B
five-dish dinner for three at an ordinary Thai-Chinese khâo tôm restaurant, no booze	245B
small New Orleans BBQ Chicken pizza, Pizza Hut	145B
large dinner for four at a good non-hotel Thai restaurant, including two large bottles of beer	1000B
dinner for two, with wine, at Lord Jim's, Oriental Hotel	3000B
one copy of the Bangkok Post or the Nation	20B
monthly rent for an economical two-bedroom apartment or house, Rayong Province	4000B to 10,000B

could spend, but if you live frugally, avoid the tourist ghettos and ride the public bus system you can get by on only slightly more than you would spend in more remote areas. Where you stay, at the resort beaches and in Bangkok, is of primary concern as accommodation will cost 300B to 400B per day when it includes air-con (in a twin room).

Those seeking international-class accommodation and food will spend at least 1500B to 2000B per night for a room with all the modern amenities – IDD phone, 24-hour hot water and air-con, carpeting, fitness centre and all-night room service. Such hotels are found only in the major cities and resort areas.

Food, is somewhat more expensive in Bangkok and resort beaches than elsewhere. Western food (especially beef) costs significantly more than Thai and Chinese food. Seafood – particularly shrimp and lobster –

also increases the tab. Still, when you consider that Thailand has possibly the best seafood cuisine in the world, it's often a bargain.

Tipping & Bargaining

Tipping is not normal practice in Thailand, although staff are getting used to it in expensive hotels and restaurants. Elsewhere don't bother. The exception is loose change left from a large Thai restaurant bill; for example if a meal costs 288B and you pay with a 500B note, some Thais and foreign residents will leave the 12B coin change on the change tray. It's not so much a tip as a way of saying 'I'm not so money-grubbing as to grab every last baht'. On the other hand, change from a 50B note for a 44B bill will usually not be left behind.

Good bargaining, which takes practice, is a good way to cut costs. Anything bought in a market should be bargained for; prices in department stores and most non-tourist shops are fixed. Sometimes accommodation rates can be bargained down. One may need to bargain hard in heavily touristed areas since the one-week, all air-con type of visitor often pays whatever's asked, creating an artificial price zone between the local and tourist market that the budgeter must deal with.

On the other hand the Thais aren't *always* trying to rip you off, so use some discretion when going for the bone on a price. There's a fine line between bargaining and niggling – getting hot under the collar over 5B makes both seller and buyer lose face. Likewise a frown is a poor bargaining tool. Some more specific suggestions concerning costs can be found in the Accommodation and Shopping sections later in this chapter.

Value-Added Tax

Thailand has a 7% value-added tax (VAT). The tax applies only to certain goods and services, but unfortunately no one seems to know what's subject to VAT and what's not, so the whole situation can be rather confusing. Legally, the tax is supposed to be applied to a retailer's cost for the product. For example, if a merchant's wholesale price is 100B for an item that retails at 200B, the maximum adjusted retail including VAT should be 207B, not 214B. But this doesn't always stop Thai merchants from trying to add 'VAT' surcharges to their sales.

VAT refunds are given at some department stores to visitors holding a tourist visa. It can be worth asking for details if you're buying something expensive, say over 10,000B. The actual refund isn't given until the visitor leaves the country, and then only if one leaves via one of Thailand's international airports.

Tourist hotels will usually add a 7% hotel tax, and sometimes a 10% service charge as well, to your room bill.

POST & COMMUNICATIONS

Thailand has an efficient postal service and postage is very cheap within the country.

Bangkok's main post office on Th Charoen Krung (New Rd) is open from 8am to 8pm Monday to Friday, and until 1pm weekends and holidays. A 24-hour international telecommunications service (including telephone and fax) is in a separate building to the right and slightly in front of the main post office building.

Outside Bangkok the typical main provincial post office is open from 8.30am to 4.30pm Monday to Friday, and from 9am to noon on Saturday. Larger main post offices in provincial capitals may also be open for a half day on Sunday.

Postal Rates

Airmail letters weighing 10g or less cost 14B to anywhere in Asia (Zone 1 in Thai postal parlance), 17B to Europe, Africa, Australia and New Zealand (Zone 2), and 19B to the Americas (Zone 3). Aerograms cost 15B regardless of the destination, while postcards are 12B to 15B depending on size.

Letters sent by registered mail cost 25B in addition to regular airmail postage. International express mail (EMS) fees vary according to 15 zones of destination radiating out from Thailand, from 310B for a document sent to zone 1 to 2050B for a document sent to zone 15. EMS packages range from 460B to 2400B. Within Thailand, this service costs only 25B (100g to 250g) in addition to regular postage.

Sample air rates include: Singapore, 560B for the first kilogram, then 100B for each additional kilogram; Europe 1100B and 350B; USA 775B and 300B. A service called Economy Air SAL (for Sea, Air, Land) uses a combination of surface and airmail modes with rates beginning at 20B for the first 50g, plus 7B for each 25g after that. As a comparison, a 2kg parcel sent to the USA by regular airmail would cost 1810B, while the same parcel sent via Economy Air SAL would cost only 888B. There are a few other wrinkles to all this depending on what's in the package. Printed matter, for example, can travel by air more cheaply than other goods.

Parcels sent domestically cost 15B for the first kilogram, then 10B for each additional kilogram.

You can insure a package's contents for 7B per US$20 of the goods' value, plus a 25B surcharge.

Sending Mail

Couriers The following companies will pick up mail or parcels anywhere in Bangkok for overnight delivery to other towns in Thailand, or to most places in the world within three to four days. Be sure to allow plenty of time between your call and the expected pick-up time for traffic jams.

DHL World Wide Express (☎ 026 588 000)
1st floor, Grand Amarin Tower, Th
Phetchaburi Tat Mai
Federal Express (☎ 023 673 222) 8th floor,
Green Tower, Th Rama IV
UPS (☎ 027 123 300) 16/1 Soi 44/1, Th
Sukhumvit

Two international courier services also have offices in Phuket:

DHL World Wide Express (☎ 076 258 500)
61/4 Th Thepkasatri
UPS (☎ 076 263 989) 64/53 Th Chao Fa

Packaging In Bangkok there's an efficient and inexpensive packaging service at the main post office where you can have parcels wrapped, or you can simply buy the materials at the counter and do it yourself. The packaging counter is open weekdays from 8am to 4.30pm and Saturday from 9am to noon. Branch post offices throughout the city also offer parcel services.

Most provincial post offices sell do-it-yourself packing boxes (11 sizes) costing 5B to 35B; tape and string are provided free. Some offices even have packing services, which cost 4B to 10B per parcel depending on size. Private packing services may also be available near large provincial post offices.

Receiving Mail

Thailand's poste-restante service is reliable, although during high tourist months (December to February, July, August) you may have to wait in line at post offices in Bangkok and on Ko Samui. There is a fee of 1B for every piece of mail collected, 2B for each parcel. As with many Asian countries, confusion in poste-restante offices is most likely to arise over given (first) names and surnames. Ask people writing to you to print your surname clearly and to underline it. If you're certain a letter should be waiting for you and it cannot be found, check if it has been filed under your given name. You can collect poste restante at almost any post office in Thailand.

Telephone

The telephone system in Thailand, operated by the government-subsidised Telephone Organization of Thailand (TOT) under the Communications Authority of Thailand (CAT), is quite efficient and from Bangkok you can usually direct dial most major centres with little difficulty.

The country code for Thailand is ☎ 66. See the Thai Area Codes table in this section for listings of domestic area codes.

In 2001 the TOT instituted a new system of nine-digit telephone numbers throughout the country. This was done by combining the area code with the old number. In Bangkok, all phone numbers are now prefaced with the old area code (02) for Bangkok. Provincial telephone numbers used to have only six digits prefaced by a three-digit area code. These have also been combined to make nine-digit phone numbers.

Some businesses, such as upscale hotels, have a range of telephone numbers; we've indicated the range with a dash. Thus, ☎ 022 373 385–7, means that there are three possible numbers in the range, the last digit being either 5,6 or 7.

Telephone Office Hours Main post-office phone centres in most provincial capitals are open daily from 7am to 11pm; smaller provincial phone offices may be open from 8am to either 8pm or 10pm. Bangkok's CAT phone office (renamed the Public Telecommunications Service Center) at the Th Charoen Krung main post office, is open 24 hours.

eKno Communication Service Lonely Planet's eKno global-communication service provides low-cost international calls – for local calls you're usually better off with a local phonecard. It also offers free messaging services, email, travel information and an online travel vault, where you can securely store all your important documents' details. You can join online (**W** www.ekno.lonelyplanet.com) where you will find the local access numbers for the 24-hour customer-service centre. Once you have joined, always check the eKno Web site for the latest access numbers for each country and updates on new features.

Domestic Calls There are two kinds of public pay phones: coin-operated blue phones and card-operated green phones. Both can be used for making local and long-distance calls within Thailand. Local calls from coin-operated blue phones cost 1B for about two and a half minutes (add more coins for more time). Local calls from private phones cost 3B; no time limit. Some hotels and guesthouses have private pay phones that cost 5B per call. Note that it is not possible to call a cellular phone from a private pay phone.

Card phones can be found at most Thai airports as well as major shopping centres and other public areas throughout urban Thailand. Phonecards come in 25B, 50B, 100B, 200B and 240B denominations, all roughly the same size as a credit card; they can be purchased at any TOT office or 7-Eleven store. In airports you can usually buy them at the airport information counter or at one of the gift shops.

Another way to pay for domestic calls is to use the Pin Phone 108 system, which

Thai Area Codes

The area codes for Thailand's major cities are presented below. See the relevant destination chapters for the area codes of smaller towns not listed here. Note that zeros aren't needed in area codes when dialling from overseas but they must be included when dialling domestically. To dial a long-distance, domestic phone number use the full area code (eg, to call the THAI office in Bangkok from Chiang Mai), dial ☎ 02-513 0121.

The country code for Thailand is ☎ 66, but omit the 0 from the domestic area code if calling from outside Thailand. To call Bangkok from overseas, dial ☎ 66 2-513 0121.

Bangkok, Nonthaburi, Pathum Thani, Samut Prakan, Thonburi	☎ 02
Cha-am, Phetchaburi, Prachuap Khiri Khan, Pranburi, Ratchaburi	☎ 032
Kanchanaburi, Nakhon Pathom, Samut Sakhon, Samut Songkhram	☎ 034
Ang Thong, Ayuthaya, Suphanburi	☎ 035
Lopburi, Saraburi, Singburi	☎ 036
Aranya Prathet, Nakhon Nayok, Prachinburi	☎ 037
Chachoengsao, Chonburi, Pattaya, Rayong, Si Racha	☎ 038
Chanthaburi, Trat	☎ 039
Chiang Khan, Loei, Mukdahan, Nakhon Phanom, Nong Khai, Sakon Nakhon, Udon Thani	☎ 042
Kalasin, Khon Kaen, Mahasarakham, Roi Et	☎ 043
Buriram, Chaiyaphum, Nakhon Ratchasima (Khorat)	☎ 044
Si Saket, Surin, Ubon Ratchathani, Yasothon	☎ 045
Chiang Mai, Chiang Rai, Lamphun, Mae Hong Son	☎ 053
Lampang, Nan, Phayao, Phrae	☎ 054
Kamphaeng Phet, Mae Sot, Phitsanulok, Sukhothai, Tak, Utaradit	☎ 055
Nakhon Sawan, Phetchabun, Phichit, Uthai Thani	☎ 056
Narathiwat, Pattani, Sungai Kolok, Yala	☎ 073
Hat Yai, Phattalung, Satun, Songkhla	☎ 074
Krabi, Nakhon Si Thammarat, Trang	☎ 075
Phang-Nga, Phuket	☎ 076
Chaiya, Chumphon, Ko Samui, Ranong, Surat Thani	☎ 077

allows you to dial ☎ 108 from any phone – including cellular phones and public pay phones, then enter a PIN code to call any number in Thailand. To use this system, however, you must have your own phone number in Thailand.

Mobile Phones TOT authorises use of private mobile phones using two systems, NMT 900MHz (Cellular 900) and GSM, and the older NMT 470MHz. The former system is more common.

It costs 1000B to register a phone and 500B per month for 'number rental' with the 900MHz and GSM, or 300B per month for 470MHz. Rates are 3B per minute within the same area code, 8B per minute to adjacent area codes and 12B per minute to other area codes. Mobile-phone users must pay for incoming as well as outgoing calls. Keep this in mind whenever you consider calling a number that begins with the code ☎ 01 – this means you're calling a mobile number and will be charged accordingly. (Note: the zero in '01' must be dialled).

Directory Assistance If you're trying to find a phone number within Thailand, you can try ringing English-language directory assistance (☎ 1133) for any part of the country. Tell the operator the name of the province in which the number is listed before giving the name of the person or business you wish to contact. The operators aren't always exactly fluent in English, so be patient – speak slowly and clearly.

International Calls To direct dial an international number (except those in Malaysia and Laos, see later this section) from a private phone, simply dial ☎ 001 before the number. For operator-assisted international calls, dial ☎ 100.

A service called Home Country Direct is available at Bangkok's main post office (Th Charoen Krung), at airports in Bangkok, Chiang Mai, Phuket, Hat Yai and Surat Thani, and at post office CAT centres in Bangkok, Hat Yai, Phuket, Surat Thani, Pattaya, Hua Hin and Kanchanaburi. Home Country Direct phones offer easy one-button connection with international operators in 40-odd countries around the world. You can also direct dial Home Country Direct numbers from any private phone (but not most hotel phones) in Thailand.

For Home Country Direct service, dial ☎ 001-999 followed by:

Australia (Optus)	☎ 61-2000
Australia (OTC)	☎ 61-1000
Canada	☎ 15-1000
Canada (AT&T)	☎ 15-2000
Denmark	☎ 45-1000
Finland	☎ 358-1000
France	☎ 33-1000
Germany	☎ 49-1000
Japan	☎ 81-0051
Korea	☎ 82-1000
Netherlands	☎ 31-1035
New Zealand	☎ 64-1066
Norway	☎ 47-1000
Singapore	☎ 65-0000
UK(BT)	☎ 44-1066
UK(MCL)	☎ 44-2000
USA (AT&T)	☎ 11-1111
USA(MCI)	☎ 12001
USA(Hawaii)	☎ 14424
USA(Sprint)	☎ 13877

Hotels generally add surcharges (sometimes as much as 30% over and above the CAT rate) for international calls; it's always cheaper to call abroad from a CAT telephone office. These offices are almost always attached to a city's main post office, often on the building's 2nd floor, around the side or just behind the main post office. There may also be a separate TOT office down the road, used only for residential or business services (eg, billing or installation), not public calls. Even when public-phone services are offered, TOT offices accept only cash payments – reverse-charge and credit-card calls aren't permitted. Hence the CAT office is generally your best choice.

To make an international call (*thorásàp ráwàang pràthêt*) at a CAT office you must fill out a bilingual form with your name and details of the call's destination. Except for reverse-charge calls (*kèp plai thaang*), you must estimate in advance the time you'll be on the phone and pay a deposit equal to the time/distance rate. There is always a minimum three-minute charge, refunded if your call doesn't go through.

Usually, only cash or international phone credit cards are acceptable for payment at CAT offices; some provincial CAT offices also accept AmEx and a few take Visa or MasterCard.

If the call doesn't go through you must pay a 30B service charge anyway – except for reverse-charge calls, for which you pay the 30B charge only if the call goes through. Depending on where you're calling, reimbursing someone later for a reverse-charge call to your home country may be less expensive than paying CAT/TOT rates – it pays to compare rates at the source and destination. For calls between the USA and Thailand, for example, AT&T collect rates are less than TOT's direct rates.

Private long-distance telephone offices operate in most towns, but sometimes these are only for calls within Thailand. Often they're just a desk or a couple of booths in the rear of a shop. These private offices typically collect a 10B surcharge for long-distance domestic calls, 50B for international calls. The vast majority accept cash only.

Whichever type of phone service you use, the least expensive time of day to make calls is from midnight to 5am (30% discount), followed by 5am to 7am and 9pm to midnight (20% discount). You pay full price from 7am to 6pm (except on Sunday when a 20% discount applies). Some sample rates for a three-minute call during the daytime include: North America 30B, UK 42B, Asia 40B, Australia 34B, Europe 46B.

International Phonecards Yellow international phones use Lenso phonecards in denominations of 250B and 500B, which can usually be purchased in 7-Eleven stores. Some major credit cards can also be used with Lenso phones when dialling AT&T direct-access numbers.

A CAT-issued international calling card, called Thai Card, comes in 300B and 500B denominations and allows calls both to and from many countries (including the USA, the UK, Hong Kong, Japan, Macau, Korea, New Zealand, Belgium, Singapore, Philip-

pines, Indonesia, Australia, Taiwan and Italy) at standard CAT rates.

Malaysia & Laos CAT does not offer long-distance service to Malaysia or Laos. To call these countries you must go through TOT. For Laos, you can direct dial ☎ 007 and country code ☎ 856, followed by the area code and number you want to reach. Malaysia can be dialled direct by prefixing the Malaysian number (including area code) with the code ☎ 09.

Fax

Telephone offices, in main post offices throughout the country, offer fax services. There's no need to bring your own paper, as the post offices supply their own forms. A few TOT offices also offer fax services. International faxes typically cost a steep 100B to 130B for the first page, and 70B to 100B per page for the remaining pages, depending on paper size and the destination.

Larger hotels with business centres offer the same services but always at higher rates.

Email & Internet Access

The Internet continues to expand in Thailand, especially as an increasing number of local, Thai-language pages go online and folks get Thai-language software installed. The scene is changing rapidly and nowadays Thailand's better Internet service providers (ISPs) offer dial-in nodes in a dozen or more towns and cities around the country, which means if you are travelling with a laptop you won't necessarily have to pay long-distance charges to Bangkok.

The major limitation in email and Internet access continues to be CAT, which connects all ISPs via the Thailand Internet Exchange (THIX) at speeds that are relatively slow by international standards. CAT also collects a hefty access charge from local ISPs, which keeps rates high relative to the local economy.

Nevertheless, Thailand is more advanced in the cybernautic world than any other country in South-East Asia at the moment and rates continue to drop from year to year. Many guesthouses and bars/cafes in

Bangkok, Chiang Mai, Ko Samui and Phuket offer email and Internet log-ons at house terminals. For the visitor who only needs to log on once in a while, these are a less expensive alternative to getting your own account – and it certainly beats lugging around a laptop. The going rate is 1B offline/2B online per minute, although we've seen a few places where slower connections are available at 0.5B per minute. If past experience is any measure, rates will continue to drop.

Due to the high number of cybercafes, and the frequency with which they come and go out of business, we've not attempted to list them in this guide except in places where they're a rarity, or where the services offered are especially extensive.

Nowadays most ISPs worldwide offer the option of Web-based email, so if you already have an Internet account at home you can check your email anywhere in Thailand simply by logging onto your ISP's Web site (using an Internet browser such as Internet Explorer or Netscape). If you have any doubts about whether your home ISP offers Web-based email, check before you leave home. You may want to register with one of the many free Web-based email services, such as MS Hotmail, Yahoo!, Juno or Lonely Planet's eKno. You can log onto these services at any cybercafe in Thailand.

Plugging in Your Own Machine In older hotels and guesthouses the phones may still be hard-wired, but RJ11 phone jacks are the standard in new hotels. For hard-wired phones you'll need to bring along an acoustic coupler.

Long-term visitors may want to consider opening a monthly Internet account. Local ISPs – of which there were 18 at last count – typically charge around 400B to 500B per month for 20 hours of Internet access. Low-grade, text-only services are available for as little as 200B a month. With any of these accounts additional per-hour charges are incurred if you exceed your online time.

Loxinfo (**W** www.loxinfo.co.th), one of the better ISPs in Thailand, offers temporary accounts. You can buy a block of 25 hours for 500B, or 45 hours for 700B –

good for up to one year. Purchasers are provided with a user ID, password, Web browser software, local phone access numbers and log-on procedures, all (except the Web browser software) available via email. You'll be able to navigate the Internet, check email at your online home address and access any online services you subscribe to.

INTERNET RESOURCES

The World Wide Web is a rich resource for travellers. You can research your trip, hunt down bargain air fares, book hotels, check weather conditions or chat with locals and other travellers about the best places to visit (or avoid).

There's no better place to start your Web explorations than the Lonely Planet Web site (**W** www.lonelyplanet.com). Here you'll find succinct summaries on travelling to most places on earth, postcards from other travellers and the Thorn Tree bulletin board, where you can ask questions before you go or dispense advice when you get back. You can also find travel news and updates to many of our most popular guidebooks, and the SubWWWay section links you to the most useful travel resources elsewhere on the Web.

A growing number of online entities offer information on Thailand. Many of these Web sites are commercial ones established by tour operators or hotels; the ratio of commercial to noncommercial sites is liable to increase over time if current Internet trends continue. Remember that all URL's (universal resource locaters) mentioned are subject to change without notice. There's a lot of information out there: a quick search on Yahoo at the time of writing yielded a list of over 800 Web sites devoted to Thailand.

TAT maintains a well-designed Web site (**W** www.tat.or.th) containing a province guide, numerous and up-to-date press releases, tourism statistics, TAT contact info and trip planning hints. The well-tuned National Electronics and Computer Technology Center (Nectc; **W** www.nectec.or.th) site exhibits great depth and breadth; it contains links on everything from a list of all

Thai embassies and consulates abroad and details of visa requirements to weather updates. Another Web site is ThaiIndex (W www.thaiindex.com). Pages include general information, government office listings, travel listings, a hotel directory and other links. Most hotel lists on the Internet appear to be sorely incomplete.

Mahidol University in Bangkok maintains a very useful site (W www.mahidol .ac.th/Thailand) with a keyword search system.

The *Bangkok Post* Web site (W www .bangkokpost.net) runs around 60 pages of stories as well as photos. Aside from Web sites, another Internet resource is the usenet group soc.culture.thai – it's very uneven, basically a chat outlet for anyone who thinks they have something to say about Thailand, but it's not a bad place to start if you have a burning question that you haven't found an answer to elsewhere.

BOOKS

Most books are published in different editions by different publishers in different countries. As a result, a book might be a hardcover rarity in one country while it's readily available in paperback somewhere else. Fortunately, bookshops and libraries search by title or author, so your local bookshop or library is best placed to advise you on the availability of the following recommendations.

For books on Buddhism and Buddhism in Thailand, see Religion in the Facts about Thailand chapter.

Lonely Planet

Lonely Planet publishes several other guides to Thailand: *Thailand; Bangkok; Thailand, Vietnam, Laos & Cambodia travel atlas*; *Thai phrasebook;* and *Thai Hill Tribes phrasebook*. For diving books, see Diving & Snorkelling under Activities in this chapter.

Finally there's Lonely Planet's new *World Food Thailand*, an intimate guide to exploring the country and its cuisine. This full-colour book covers every food and drink situation the traveller could encounter and plots the evolution of what we know as Thai cuisine. It also includes an extremely useful language section.

Description & Travel

The earliest Western literature of note on Thailand, Guy Tachard's *A Relation of the Voyage to Siam*, recounts a 1680s French expedition through parts of the country with little literary flair. Shortly thereafter, Simon de la Loubére's 1693 *New Historical Relation of the Kingdom of Siam* chronicled the French mission to the Ayuthaya court in great detail. Maurice Collis novelised this period with a focus on the unusual political relationship between King Narai and his Greek minister, Constantin Phaulkon, in *Siamese White*.

Joseph Conrad evoked Thailand in several of his pre-WWII novels and short stories, most notably in his 1920s *The Secret Sharer* and *Falk: A Reminiscence*.

Pico Iyer, Robert Anson Hall and several other well-known and not-so-well-known authors have contributed travel essays of varying styles to *Travelers' Tales Thailand* (edited by James O'Reilly & Larry Habegger). It was the first title in a series that assembles travel articles and chapters from various sources into a single anthology devoted to a particular country. Savvy travel tips are sprinkled through the text.

A more serious collection of literature is available in *Traveller's Literary Companion: South-East Asia*, edited by Alastair Dingwall. The Thailand chapter, edited by scholar Thomas John Hudak, is packed with information on the history of literature in Thailand and includes extracts from various works by Thai as well as foreign authors.

Culture & Society

Naga: Cultural Origins in Siam & the Western Pacific by Sumet Jumsai is an inspired theory on the supposed oceanic origins of Thai people and culture. With direct inspiration from the late R Buckminster Fuller, who collaborated with the author/ architect/Cambridge lecturer Sumet to a degree, the book outlines in prose and carefully collected illustrations how the myths, symbols and architecture common to Thailand and other mainland South-East Asian civilisations – in particular the *naga* (sea dragon motif) – stem from an earlier phase in Asian-Western Pacific history, when most of the peoples of the region inhabited islands and lived largely seafaring lives.

Culture Shock! Thailand by Robert & Nanthapa Cooper is an interesting book about adapting to the Thai way of life, although it's heavily oriented towards Bangkok life. *Letters from Thailand* by Botan (translated by Susan Fulop Kepner), and Carol Hollinger's *Mai Pen Rai Means Never Mind* can also be recommended for their insights into traditional Thai culture. *Bangkok Post* reporter Denis Segaller's *Thai Ways* and *More Thai Ways* present further expat insights into Thai culture.

Behind the Smile: Voices of Thailand by Sanitsuda Ekachai is a very enlightening collection of interviews with Thai peasants from all over the country. *In the Mirror* is an excellent collection of translated modern Thai short stories from the 1960s and 70s. The Siam Society's *Culture & Environment in Thailand* is a collection of scholarly papers by Thai and foreign authors delivered at a 1988 symposium that examined the relationship between Thai culture and the natural world; topics range from the oceanic origins of the Thai race and nature motifs in Thai art to evolving Thai attitudes towards the environment.

Siam in Crisis by Sulak Sivaraksa, one of Thailand's leading intellectuals, analyses modern Thai politics from his Buddhist-nationalist perspective. Sivaraksa has written several other worthwhile titles on Thai culture that have been translated into English. Essays by this contrary and contradictory character posit an ideal that neither Thailand nor any other country will likely ever achieve, and his attempts to use Western-style academic argument to discredit Western thinking can be both exasperating and inspiring.

History & Politics

George Coedes' classic pre-war work on South-East Asian history, *The Indianised States of South-East Asia*, contains groundbreaking historical material on early Thai history, as does WAR Wood's *A History of Siam*, published in the same era. One of the more readable general histories written in the latter half of the 20th century is David Wyatt's *Thailand: A Short History*.

Concentrating on post-revolutionary Thailand, *The Balancing Act: A History of Modern Thailand* by Joseph Wright Jr, starts with the 1932 revolution and ends with the February 1991 coup. Wright's semi-academic chronicle concludes that Thai history demonstrates a continuous circulation of elites governed by certain 'natural laws' and that, despite the 1932 revolution, democracy has never gained a firm foothold in Thai society.

Axel Aylwen's novel *The Falcon of Siam* and its sequel *The Falcon Takes Wing* capture the feel and historical detail of 17th-century Siam, including several locales in southern Thailand; Aylwen obviously read Collis, Loubére and Tachard closely (see the earlier Description & Travel entry in this section).

Fiction

The Lioness in Bloom, translated by Susan Fulop Kepner, is an eye-opening collection of 11 short stories written by or about Thai women. Jack Reynolds' 1950s *A Woman of Bangkok* (republished in 1985), a well-written and poignant story of a young Englishman's descent into the world of Thai brothels, remains the best novel yet published with this theme. Expat writer Christopher G Moore covers the Thai underworld in his 1990s novels *A Killing Smile*, *Spirit House*, *A Bewitching Smile*, and a raft of others, with an anchor firmly hooked into the go-go bar scene. His description of Bangkok's meta-sleazy Thermae Coffee House (called 'Zeno' in *A Killing Smile*) is the closest literature comes to evoking the perpetual male adolescence such places cater to. If you're going to spend some time lounging on a Thai beach, you might as well pick up a copy of Alex Garland's 1997 novel *The Beach* and judge for yourself how apt the descriptions are.

Natural History

Complete with sketches, photos and maps, *The Mammals of Thailand*, by Boonsong Lekagul & Jeffrey McNeely, remains the classic on Thai wildlife in spite of a few out-of-date references (it was first published in 1977). Bird lovers should seek out the *Bird Guide of Thailand* by Boonsong Lekagul & EW Cronin for comprehensive descriptions of Thailand's birdlife.

Detailed summaries of 77 of Thailand's national parks, along with an objective assessment of current park conditions, are available in *National Parks of Thailand* by Gray, Piprell & Graham.

FILMS

A number of classic international films have used Thailand either as a subject or as a location – more often the latter. In fact nowadays location shooting in Thailand has become something of a boom industry as Thailand's jungles, rice fields and islands find themselves backdrops for all manner of scripts set in 'exotic' tropical countries.

The first film to come out of Thailand was *Chang*, a 1927 silent picture shot entirely in Nan Province (then still a semi-independent principality with Siamese protection). Produced by American film impresarios Copper and Schoedsack – who later produced several major Hollywood hits – *Chang* contains some of the best jungle and wildlife sequences filmed in Asia to date. *Chang* is available on film or video from speciality houses. Around 1930 a movie called *I Am from Siam*, produced and narrated by *Bangkok Post* founder Don Gardner and starring none other than King Rama VII, emerged. It's virtually impossible to find this film today outside Thailand's National Film Archives.

Next came *Anna & the King of Siam*, a 1946 American production (filmed on Hollywood sets) starring Rex Harrison and based on the book *The English Governess at the Siamese Court* by Anna Leonowens, who cared for Rama IV's children in the 19th century. *The King & I*, grew from a very successful Broadway stage production starring Yul Brynner (who earned an Oscar for the film). Both films, as well as the musical, are banned in Thailand because they are seen to compromise the dignity of the monarchy.

Probably the most famous movie associated with Thailand is *The Bridge on the River Kwai*, a 1957 Academy Award-winning production stemming from Pierre Boulle's book of the same name and starring Alec Guinness. Although based on WWII events in Thailand, much of the film was shot on location in Sri Lanka (then Ceylon).

The Man with the Golden Gun, a pedestrian 1974 James Bond vehicle starring Roger Moore and Christopher Lee, brought the karst islands of Ao Phang-Nga to international attention for the first time. A year later the French soft-porn movie *Emmanuelle* ('Much hazy, soft-focus coupling in downtown Bangkok', wrote the *Illustrated London News)* added to the myth of Thailand as sexual idyll and set an all-time box-office record in France.

Virtually every film produced with a Vietnam War theme has been shot either in the Philippines or in Thailand, with the latter ahead by a long shot as the location of choice due to relative logistical ease. The first Vietnam-themed movie to use Thailand as a location was *The Deer Hunter*, which won the 1978 Academy Award for best picture. The dramatic Russian-roulette scene was shot in an old neighbourhood on Th Charoen Krung, while the Saigon bar scenes were shot in Bangkok's Patpong district. Oliver Stone's *Heaven and Earth* (1993) is one of the more recent pictures to paint Vietnam on a Thai canvas.

The Killing Fields (1984) skilfully used Thailand as a stand-in for Cambodia. In a 1987 spin-off of this movie, *Swimming to Cambodia*, monologist Spalding Gray recounts behind-the-scenes anecdotes of the Thailand shooting of the film.

Jean-Claude Van Damme's *The Kickboxer* brought *muay thai* (Thai boxing) to the big screen with a bit more class than the average martial-arts flick; more than a few foreign pugilists have packed their bags for Bangkok after viewing the movie's exotic mix of ring violence and Thai Buddhist atmospherics. Sly Stallone's 1980s *Rambo* movies (*Rambos II* and *III* used Thailand locations) did little for Thailand, but the success of *Good Morning Vietnam* (1988), a Robin Williams comedy widely publicised as having been shot in Bangkok and Phuket, helped generate a tourism boom for the country.

Trainspotting's Danny Boyle directed teenage heart-throb Leonardo DiCaprio in a film adaptation of Alex Garland's novel *The Beach* in early 1999. The shooting of this film on Ko Phi-Phi caused some controversy, see the boxed text 'Notes on *The Beach*' in the South-West Gulf Coast chapter for more.

Thailand now maintains a substantial contingent of trained production assistants and casting advisers who work continuously with foreign companies on location shoots – many of them from Japan, Hong Kong and Singapore.

NEWSPAPERS

Thailand's 1997 constitution guarantees freedom of the press, though the National Police Department reserves power to suspend publishing licences for national security reasons. Editors nevertheless exercise self-censorship in certain realms, particularly with regard to the monarchy. Monarchical issues aside, Thailand is widely considered to have the freest print media in South-East Asia. In a survey conducted by the Singapore-based Political and Economic Risk Consultancy, 180 expatriate managers in 10 Asian countries ranked Thailand's English-language press the highest in Asia. Surprisingly, these expats cited the *Bangkok Post* and the *Nation* more frequently as their source of regional and global news than either the *Asian Wall Street Journal* or the *Far Eastern Economic Review*.

These two English-language newspapers are published daily in Thailand and distributed in most provincial capitals throughout the country – the *Bangkok Post* in the morning and the *Nation* in the afternoon. The *Nation* is almost entirely staffed by Thais and presents, obviously, a Thai perspective, while the *Post*, which was Thailand's first English-language daily (established 1946),

has a mixed Thai and international staff and represents a more international view. For international news, the *Post* is the better of the two papers and is in fact regarded by many journalists as the best English daily in the region. On the other hand, the *Nation* has better regional coverage – particularly with regard to Myanmar and former Indochina, and the paper is to be commended for taking a harder anti-NPKC stance during the 1991 coup.

The *International Herald Tribune* is widely available in Bangkok, Chiang Mai and heavily touristed areas like Pattaya and Phuket.

The most popular Thai-language newspapers are *Thai Rath* and *Daily News*, but they're mostly full of blood-and-guts stories. The best Thai journalism is found in the somewhat less popular *Matichon* and *Siam Rath* dailies. Many Thais read the English-language dailies as they consider them better news sources. The *Bangkok Post* also publishes a Thai-language version.

MAGAZINES

English-language magazine publishing has faltered with the economic slowdown in Thailand, and several mags failed after 1996. Now Thailand's biggest selling English-language magazine, *Bangkok Metro* continues to inject urban sophistication into the publishing scene with extensive listings concerned with art, culture, cuisine, film and music in Bangkok, along with less extensive Pattaya, Phuket and Chiang Mai pages.

Le Gavroche offers monthly news and features on Thailand for the Francophone community.

Many popular magazines from the UK, USA, Australia and Europe – particularly those concerned with computer technology, cars, fashion, music and business – are available in bookshops that specialise in English-language publications (see Bookshops under Shopping later in this chapter).

RADIO

Thailand has more than 400 radio stations, with 41 FM and 35 AM stations in Bangkok alone. Radio station 107 FM, affiliated with

Radio Thailand and Channel 9 on Thai public television, broadcasts CNN news coverage of the Asia region almost every hour between 5pm and 2am daily, and features some surprisingly good music programs with British, Thai and American DJs. Bilingual DJs at Star FM 102.5 present R&B, pop, rock and alternative music 24 hours a day. Another station with international pop and English-speaking DJs is Radio Bangkok (Gold FMX), 95.5 FM, which plays contemporary hits as well as oldies 24 hours a day.

If you're looking for Thai music, Station 87.5 FM broadcasts classic Thai pop, including old *lûuk thûng* (very-rhythmic popular music from North-Eastern Thailand) styles played on accordion.

Chulalongkorn University broadcasts classical music at 101.5 FM from 10.30pm to 1am nightly, and 'light classical, popular golden oldies and jazz' from 4pm to 6.30pm. A schedule of the evening's programs can be found in the *Nation* and *Bangkok Post* newspapers.

The Voice of America (VOA), BBC World Service, Radio Canada, Radio New Zealand, Singapore Broadcasting Company, Radio Japan and Radio Australia all have English and Thai-language broadcasts over short-wave radio. The radio frequencies and schedules, which change hourly, also appear in the *Post* and the *Nation*. BBC, Radio Australia and VOA are the most easily received by the average short-wave radio.

Radio France Internationale and Deutsche Welle carry short-wave programs in French and German respectively. Deutsche Welle also broadcasts 50 minutes of English programming three times daily.

TV

Thailand has five VHF TV networks based in Bangkok. Following the 1991 coup the Thai government authorised an extension of telecast time to 24 hours and networks have been scrambling to fill air time ever since. As a result, there has been a substantial increase in English-language telecasts – mostly in the morning hours when Thais aren't used to watching TV.

Upcountry cities will generally receive only two networks – Channel 9 and a local private network with restricted hours.

Satellite & Cable TV

As elsewhere in Asia, satellite and cable TV services are swiftly multiplying in Thailand, and competition for the largely untapped market is keen. The most successful cable company in Thailand is UBC, available in CaTV, MMDS and DTH systems. Among the many satellite transmissions carried by UBC are six English-language movie channels (including HBO and Cinemax, both censored in Asia for language, nudity and violence), two to four international sports channels, imported TV series, MTV Asia, Channel V (a Hong Kong-based music video telecast), CNN International, CNBC, NHK, BBC World Service Television, the Discovery Channel and all the standard Thai networks. For further information see UBC's Web site (W www.ubctv.com) or obtain a copy of its free monthly *UBC Magazine*.

Thailand has its own ThaiCom 1 and 2 as uplinks for AsiaSat and as carriers for the standard Thai networks and Thai Sky (TST). The latter includes five channels offering news and documentaries, Thai music videos and Thai variety programs. Other satellites tracked by dishes in Thailand include China's Apstar 1 and Apstar 2. Additional transmissions from these and from Vietnam, Myanmar and Malaysia are available with a satellite dish.

VIDEO SYSTEMS

The predominant video format in Thailand is PAL, a system compatible with that used in most of Europe (France's SECAM format is a notable exception) as well as in Australia and New Zealand. This means if you're bringing video tapes from the USA or Japan, which use the NTSC format, you'll have to bring your own VCR to play them. Some video shops (especially those that carry pirated or unlicensed tapes) sell NTSC as well as PAL and SECAM tapes. A 'multisystem' VCR has the capacity to play both NTSC and PAL, but not SECAM (except in black and white).

PHOTOGRAPHY & VIDEO
Film

Print film is fairly inexpensive and widely available throughout Thailand. Japanese print film costs around 100B per 36 exposures, US print film a bit more. Fujichrome Velvia and Provia slide films cost around 265B per roll, Kodak Ektachrome Elite is 230B and Ektachrome 200 about 280B. Slide film, especially Kodachrome, can be hard to find outside Bangkok and Chiang Mai, so be sure to stock up before heading upcountry.

VHS video cassettes of all sizes are readily available in Bangkok, Chiang Mai, Hat Yai and Phuket.

Processing

Film processing is generally quite good in the larger cities and also quite inexpensive. Dependable E6 processing is available at several labs in Bangkok and Chiang Mai. Kodachrome must be sent out of the country for processing, so it can take up to two weeks to get it back.

Pros will find a number of labs in Bangkok that offer same-day pick up and delivery at no extra cost within the city. IQ Lab offers the widest range of services, including all types of processing (except Kodachrome), slide duping, scanning, digital prints, OutPut slides, photo CDs and custom printing.

Technical Tips

Pack some silica gel with your camera to prevent mould growing on the inside of your lenses. A polarising filter could be useful to cut down on tropical glare at certain times of day, particularly around water or highly polished glazed-tile work. Tripods are a must for shooting interiors in natural light.

Video

Properly used, a video camera can give a fascinating record of your holiday. As well as videoing the obvious things – sunsets, spectacular views – remember to record some of the ordinary everyday details of life. Often the most interesting things occur when you're actually intent on filming something else. Remember too that, unlike still photography, video 'flows' – so, for example, you can shoot scenes of countryside rolling past the train window to give an overall impression that isn't possible with still photos.

Video cameras often have amazingly sensitive microphones, and you might be surprised how much sound will be picked up. This can also be a problem if there is a lot of ambient noise – filming by the side of a busy road might seem fine while you are doing it, but viewing it back home might simply give you a deafening cacophony of traffic noise. One good rule to follow for beginners is to try to film in long takes, and don't move the camera around too much. Otherwise, your video could well make your viewers seasick! If your camera has a stabiliser, you can use it to obtain good footage while travelling on various means of transport, even on bumpy roads. And remember that you're on holiday – don't let the video take over your life and turn your trip into a Cecil B de Mille production.

Make sure you keep the batteries charged, and have the necessary charger, plugs and transformer.

Finally, remember to follow the same rules regarding people's sensitivities as for still photography – having a video camera shoved in their face is probably even more annoying and offensive for locals than a still camera. Always ask permission first.

Airport Security

The X-ray baggage-inspection machines at Thailand's airports are all deemed film safe. Nevertheless if you're travelling with high-speed film (ISO 400 or above), you may want to have your film hand-inspected rather than X-rayed. Security inspectors are usually happy to comply. Packing your film in see-through plastic bags generally speeds up the hand inspection process. Some photographers pack their film in lead-lined bags to ward off potentially harmful rays.

TIME
Time Zone
Thailand's time zone is seven hours ahead of GMT/UTC (London). Thus, noon in Bangkok is 10pm the previous day in Los Angeles, 1am in New York, 5am in London, 6am in Paris and 3pm in Sydney.

Thai Calendar
The official year in Thailand is reckoned from 543 BC, the beginning of the Buddhist Era (BE), so AD 2002 is BE 2545.

ELECTRICITY
Electric current is 220V AC, 50Hz (cycles). Electrical wall outlets are usually of the round, two-pole type; some outlets also accept flat, two-bladed terminals, and some will accept either flat or round terminals. Any electrical-supply shop in Thailand will carry adapters for any international plug shape, as well as voltage converters.

WEIGHTS & MEASURES
Dimensions and weight are usually expressed using the metric system in Thailand. The exception is land measure, which is often quoted using the traditional Thai system of *waa*, *ngaan* and *râi*. Old-timers in the provinces will occasionally use the traditional Thai system of weights and measures in speech, as will boat-builders, carpenters and other craftspeople when talking about their work. Here are some conversions to use for such occasions:

Thai units	metric conversion
1 sq *waa*	= 4 sq m
1 *ngaan*	= 400 sq m
	(100 sq waa)
1 *râi* (4 ngaan)	= 1600 sq m
1 *bàht*	= 15g
1 *taleung* or *tamleung*	
(4 bàht)	= 60g
1 *châng* (20 taleung)	= 1.2kg
1 *hàap* (50 châng)	= 60kg
1 *níu*	= about 2cm
1 *khêup* (12 níu)	= 25cm
1 *sàwk* (2 khêup)	= 50cm
1 waa (4 sàwk)	= 2m
1 *sén* (20 waa)	= 40m
1 *yôht* (400 sén)	= 16km

LAUNDRY
Virtually every hotel and guesthouse in Thailand offers a laundry service. Rates are generally geared to room rates; the cheaper the accommodation, the cheaper the washing and ironing. Cheapest of all are public laundries, where you pay by the kilogram.

Many Thai hotels and guesthouses also have laundry areas where you can wash your clothes at no charge; sometimes there's even a hanging area for drying. Laundry detergent is readily available in general mercantile shops and supermarkets.

Laundries that advertise dry-cleaning often don't really dry-clean (they just boil everything!) or they do it badly. Most luxury hotels have dependable dry-cleaning services.

TOILETS
In rural Thailand the 'squat toilet' is still the norm – except in hotels and guesthouses geared towards tourists and international business travellers. Instead of trying to approximate a chair or stool like a Western sit-down toilet, a traditional Thai toilet sits more or less flush with the surface of the floor, with a footpad on either side of the porcelain abyss. For travellers who have never used a squat toilet it takes a bit of getting used to. If you find yourself feeling awkward the first couple of times you use one, you can console yourself with the knowledge that, according to those who study such matters, people who use squat toilets are much less likely to develop haemorrhoids than people who use sit-down toilets.

Next to the typical squat toilet is a bucket or cement reservoir filled with water. A plastic bowl usually floats on the water's surface or sits nearby. This water supply has a two-fold function; toilet-goers scoop water from the reservoir with the plastic bowl and use it to clean their nether regions while still squatting over the toilet. Since there is usually no mechanical flushing device attached to a squat toilet, a few extra scoops must be poured into the toilet basin to flush waste into the septic system.

In larger towns, mechanical flushing systems are becoming increasingly common, even with squat toilets. More-rustic toilets in rural areas may simply consist of a few planks over a hole in the ground.

Even in places where sit-down toilets are installed, the plumbing may not be designed to take toilet paper. In such cases the usual washing bucket will be standing nearby or there will be a waste basket where you're supposed to place used toilet paper.

Public toilets are common in cinema houses, department stores, bus and train stations, larger hotel lobbies, petrol stations and airports. While on the road between towns and villages it is perfectly acceptable to go behind a tree or bush, or even to use the roadside when nature calls.

BATHING

Some hotels and most guesthouses in the country do not have hot water, though places in the larger cities will usually offer small electric shower heaters in their more expensive rooms. Very few boiler-style water heaters are available outside larger international-style hotels.

Some rural Thais still bathe in rivers or streams, or around village wells. Those living in towns or cities may have washrooms where a large jar or cement trough is filled with water for bathing. A plastic or metal bowl is used to sluice water from the jar or trough over the body. Even in homes where showers are installed, heated water is uncommon. Most Thais bathe at least twice a day, and never use hot water.

If ever you find yourself having to bathe in a public place you should wear a phâakhamáa or phâasîn (the cotton wraparounds); except for young children, bathing nude will cause offence.

HEALTH

Travel health depends on your predeparture preparations, your daily health care while travelling and how you handle any medical problem that may develop. While the potential dangers can seem quite frightening, in reality few travellers experience anything more than an upset stomach.

Predeparture Planning

Health Insurance Make sure that you have adequate health insurance. See Travel Insurance under Visas & Documents earlier in this chapter for details.

Travel-Health Guides If you are planning to be away or travelling in remote areas for a long period of time, you may like to consider taking a more detailed health guide.

Lonely Planet's *Healthy Travel Asia & India* is a handy pocket size and packed with useful information including pretrip planning, emergency first aid, immunisation and disease information and what to do if you get sick on the road. *Travel with Children* from Lonely Planet also includes advice on travel health for younger children.

Guide to Healthy Living in Thailand, published jointly by the Thai Red Cross Society and US embassy, is available in Bangkok from the 'Snake Farm' (Queen Saovabha Memorial Institute; ☎ 022 520 161) for 100B. This booklet is rich in practical health advice on safe eating, child care, tropical heat, immunisations and local hospitals. It contains wise tidbits with a literary flair, including 'Bangkok is a stopping point for many travellers and restless souls. Acute psychiatric emergencies, including alcoholism and drug abuse, are, unfortunately, not rare' and 'Bangkok's traffic poses a far greater danger than snakes and tropical diseases combined'.

There are also a number of excellent travel health sites on the Internet. From the Lonely Planet home page there are links (at Ⓦ www.lonelyplanet.com/weblinks/wlheal.htm) to the World Health Organization and the US Centers for Disease Control & Prevention (CDC).

Other Preparations Make sure you're healthy before you start travelling. If you are going on a long trip make sure your teeth are OK. If you wear glasses take a spare pair and your prescription.

If you require a particular medication take an adequate supply, as it may not be available locally. Take part of the packaging showing the generic name, rather than the brand, which will make getting replacements easier. It's a good idea to have a *legible* prescription or letter from your doctor to show that you legally use the medication to avoid any problems with customs on arrival.

Immunisations

Plan ahead for getting your vaccinations: some of them require more than one injection, while some vaccinations should not be given together with others. Note that some vaccinations should not be given during pregnancy or to people with allergies – discuss with your doctor.

It is recommended that you seek medical advice at least six weeks before travel. There is often a greater risk of children contracting disease. There's also increased risks during pregnancy.

There are currently no immunisation requirements for entry into Thailand except for yellow fever if you come from an infected zone. Discuss your requirements with your doctor, but vaccinations you should consider for this trip include the following (for more details about the diseases themselves, see the individual disease entries later in this section). Carry proof of your vaccinations, especially yellow fever, as this is sometimes needed to enter some countries.

Cholera The current injectable vaccine against cholera gives poor protection and has many side effects, so it is not generally recommended for travellers.

Diphtheria & Tetanus Vaccinations for these two diseases are usually combined and are recommended for everyone. After an initial course of three injections (usually given in childhood), boosters are necessary every 10 years.

Hepatitis A Hepatitis A vaccine (eg, Avaxim, Havrix 1440 or VAQTA) provides long-term immunity (possibly more than 10 years) after an initial injection and a booster at 6 to 12 months.

Alternatively, an injection of gamma globulin can provide short-term protection against hepatitis A – two to six months – depending on the dose given. It is not a vaccine, but a ready-made antibody collected from blood donations. It is reasonably effective and, unlike the vaccine, it is protective immediately, but because it is a blood product, there are concerns about its long-term safety.

Hepatitis A vaccine is also available in a combined form, Twinrix, with hepatitis B vaccine. Three injections over a six-month period are required, the first two providing substantial protection against hepatitis A.

Hepatitis B Travellers who should consider vaccination against hepatitis B include those undertaking a long trip, as well as those visiting countries where there are high levels of hepatitis B infection, where blood transfusions may not be adequately screened or where sexual contact or needle sharing is a possibility. Vaccination involves three injections, with a booster at 12 months. More rapid courses are available if necessary.

Japanese B Encephalitis Consider vaccination against this disease if spending a month or longer in rural Northern Thailand, making repeated trips to a risk area or visiting during an epidemic. It involves three injections over 30 days.

Polio Everyone should keep up to date with this vaccination, normally given in childhood. A booster every 10 years maintains immunity.

Rabies Vaccination should be considered by those who will spend a month or longer in Thailand, especially if cycling, handling animals, caving or travelling to remote areas, and for children (who may not report a bite). Pretravel rabies vaccination involves having three injections over 21 to 28 days. If someone who has been vaccinated is bitten or scratched by an animal, they will require two booster injections of vaccine; those not vaccinated require more. Rabies vaccinations are available at nearly every public clinic or hospital in Thailand.

Tuberculosis The risk of TB to travellers in Thailand is usually very low.

Typhoid Vaccination against typhoid may be required if you are travelling for more than a couple of weeks in most parts of Asia. It is now available either as an injection or as capsules to be taken orally. A combined hepatitis A/typhoid vaccine was launched recently but its availability is still limited. Check with your doctor to find out its status in your country.

Malaria Medication
Antimalarial drugs do not prevent you from being infected, but kill the malaria parasites during their development and significantly reduce the risk of becoming very ill or dying. Expert advice on medication should be sought, as there are many factors to consider, including the area to be visited, the risk of exposure to malaria-carrying mosquitoes, the side effects of medication, your medical history and whether you are a child or an adult or are pregnant. Travellers to isolated areas in high-risk countries may like to carry a treatment dose of medication for use if symptoms occur. See Malaria under Insect-Borne diseases later in this section for information on the prevalence of malaria in Thailand.

Basic Rules
Food There is a colonial adage that says: 'If you can cook it, boil it or peel it you can eat it, otherwise forget it'. Vegetables and fruit should be washed with purified water, or peeled where possible. Beware of ice cream that is sold in the street or anywhere it might have been melted and re-frozen; if there's any doubt (eg, a power cut in the last day or two), steer well clear. Shellfish, such as mussels, oysters and clams, should be avoided, as well as undercooked meat, particularly in the form of mince. Steaming does not make shellfish safe for eating.

If a place looks clean and well run and the vendor also looks clean and healthy, then the food is probably safe. In general, places that are packed with travellers or locals will be fine, while empty restaurants are questionable. The food in busy restaurants is cooked and eaten quite quickly with little standing around and is probably not reheated.

Water If you don't know for certain that the water is safe always assume the worst. Reputable brands of Thai bottled water or soft drinks are generally fine. In some cheap hotels the freebie bottles of water found in rooms may be refilled with tap water. Only use water from containers with a serrated seal – not tops or corks. Tea or coffee should be OK, since the water should have been boiled.

Ice is produced from purified water under hygienic conditions and is therefore theoretically safe in Thailand. During transit to the local restaurant, however, conditions are not so hygienic (you may see blocks of ice being dragged along the street), but it's very difficult to resist in the hot season. The rule of thumb is that if it's crushed or chipped ice, it probably came from an ice block (which may not have been handled well) but if it's ice cubes or 'tubes', it was delivered from the ice factory in sealed plastic. In rural areas, villagers mostly drink collected rainwater during the rainy season and well-water during the dry season. Some travellers can drink this without problems, but other people can't tolerate it. It's best to bring your own water if there's any doubt.

In Thailand, virtually no-one bothers with filters, tablets or iodine since bottled water is so cheap and readily available. If you are unable to find bottled water, the simplest way of purifying water is to boil it thoroughly. Vigorous boiling should be satisfactory; however, at high altitude water boils at a lower temperature, so germs are less likely to be killed. Boil it for longer in these environments.

Consider purchasing a water filter for a long trip. There are two main kinds of filter. Total filters take out all parasites, bacteria and viruses and make water safe to drink. They are often expensive, but they can be more cost effective than buying bottled water. Simple filters (which can even be a nylon mesh bag) take out dirt and larger foreign bodies from the water so that chemical solutions work much more effectively; if water is dirty, chemical solutions may not work at all. It's very important when buying a filter to read the specifications, so that you know exactly what it removes from the water and what it doesn't. Simple filtering will not remove all dangerous organisms, so if you cannot boil water it should be treated chemically. Chlorine tablets will kill many pathogens, but not some parasites like giardia and amoebic cysts. Iodine is more effective in purifying water and is available in tablet form. Follow the directions carefully and remember that too much iodine can be harmful.

Medical Problems & Treatment

Self-diagnosis and treatment can be risky, so you should always seek medical help. Although we give drug dosages in this section, they are for emergency use only. Correct diagnosis is vital. An embassy, consulate or five-star hotel can usually recommend a local doctor or clinic.

In Thailand just about any kind of medication is available over the counter and prices are cheaper than in the West. Many Thais routinely go to the pharmacy and let the pharmacist diagnose them to save money – it's cheaper than going to a clinic or hospital. Needless to say, rare is the pharmacist who is actually qualified to be giving medical advice. When buying medicine be sure to check the expiration date, and try to be familiar with what it is you are buying. Some drugs that have been discredited – even banned – in the West are still being dispensed in Thailand.

Antibiotics should ideally be administered only under medical supervision. Take only the recommended dose at the prescribed intervals and use the whole course, even if the illness seems to be cured earlier. Stop immediately if there are any serious reactions and don't use the antibiotic at all if you are unsure that you have the correct one. Some people are allergic to commonly prescribed antibiotics such as penicillin; carry this information (eg, on a bracelet) when travelling.

Environmental Hazards

Air Pollution Pollution is something you'll become very aware of in urban Thailand, especially Bangkok, where heat, dust and motor fumes combine to form a powerful brew of potentially toxic air. Air pollution can be a health hazard, especially if you suffer from lung diseases such as asthma. It can also aggravate coughs, colds and sinus problems and cause eye irritation or even infections. Avoid walking or riding *túk-túk* through badly polluted areas if you think it might jeopardise your health, especially if you have asthma, or invest in an air filter.

Heat Exhaustion Dehydration and salt deficiency can cause heat exhaustion. Take time to acclimatise to high temperatures, drink sufficient liquids and do not do anything too physically demanding.

Salt deficiency is characterised by fatigue, lethargy, headaches, giddiness and muscle cramps; salt tablets may help, but adding extra salt to your food is better.

Anhidrotic heat exhaustion is a rare form of heat exhaustion that is caused by an inability to sweat. It tends to affect people who have been in a hot climate for some time, rather than newcomers. It can progress to heatstroke. Treatment involves removal to a cooler climate.

Heatstroke This serious, occasionally fatal, condition can occur if the body's heat-regulating mechanism breaks down and the body temperature rises to dangerous levels. Long, continuous periods of exposure to high temperatures and insufficient fluids can leave you vulnerable to heatstroke.

The symptoms are feeling unwell, not sweating very much (or at all) and a high body temperature (39°C to 41°C or 102°F to 106°F). Where sweating has ceased, the skin becomes flushed and red. Severe, throbbing headaches and lack of coordination will also occur, and the sufferer may be confused or aggressive. Eventually the victim will become delirious or convulse. Hospitalisation is essential, but in the interim get victims out of the sun, remove their clothing, cover them with a wet sheet or towel and fan continually. Give fluids if they are conscious.

Jet Lag Jet lag is often experienced when a person travels by air across more than three time zones (each time zone usually represents a one-hour time difference). It occurs because many of the functions of the human body (such as temperature, pulse rate and emptying of the bladder and bowels) are regulated by internal 24-hour cycles. When we travel long distances rapidly, our bodies take time to adjust to the 'new time' of our destination, and we may experience fatigue, disorientation, insomnia, anxiety, impaired concentration and loss of appetite. These effects will usually be gone within three days of arrival, but to minimise the impact of jet lag:

• Rest for a couple of days prior to departure.
• Try to select flight schedules that minimise sleep deprivation; arriving late in the day means you can go to sleep soon after you arrive. For very long flights, try to organise a stopover.
• Avoid excessive eating (which bloats the stomach) and alcohol (which causes dehydration) during the flight. Instead, drink plenty of non-carbonated, nonalcoholic drinks such as fruit juice or water.
• Avoid smoking.
• Make yourself comfortable by wearing loose-fitting clothes and perhaps bringing an eye mask and ear plugs to help you sleep.
• Try to sleep at the appropriate time for the time zone you are travelling to.

Motion Sickness Eating lightly before and during a trip will reduce the chances of motion sickness. If you are prone to motion sickness try to find a place that minimises movement – near the wing on aircraft, close to midship on boats, near the centre on buses. Fresh air usually helps; reading and cigarette smoke don't. Commercial motion-sickness preparations, which can cause drowsiness, have to be taken before the trip commences. Ginger (available in capsule form) and peppermint (including mint-flavoured sweets) are natural preventatives.

Prickly Heat Prickly heat is an itchy rash caused by excessive perspiration trapped

under the skin. It usually strikes people who have just arrived in a hot climate. Keeping cool, bathing often, drying the skin and using a mild talcum or prickly heat powder or resorting to air-con may help.

Sunburn In the tropics, the desert or at high altitude you can get sunburnt surprisingly quickly, even through cloud. Use a sunscreen, a hat, and a barrier cream for your nose and lips. Calamine lotion and aloe vera are good for mild sunburn. Protect your eyes with good-quality sunglasses, particularly if you will be near water or sand.

Infectious Diseases
Diarrhoea Simple things like a change of water, food or climate can all cause a mild bout of diarrhoea, but a few rushed toilet trips with no other symptoms is not indicative of a major problem.

Dehydration is the main danger with any diarrhoea, particularly in children or the elderly as dehydration can occur quite quickly. Under all circumstances *fluid replacement* (at least equal to the volume being lost) is the most important thing to remember. Weak black tea with a little sugar, soda water, or soft drinks allowed to go flat and diluted 50% with clean water are all good. With severe diarrhoea a rehydrating solution is preferable to replace minerals and salts lost. Commercially available oral rehydration salts (ORS) are very useful; add them to boiled or bottled water. In an emergency you can make up a solution of six teaspoons of sugar and a half teaspoon of salt to a litre of boiled or bottled water. You need to drink at least the same volume of fluid that you are losing in bowel movements and vomiting. Urine is the best guide to the adequacy of replacement – if you have small amounts of concentrated urine, you need to drink more. Keep drinking small amounts often. Stick to a bland diet as you recover.

Gut-paralysing drugs such as loperamide or diphenoxylate can be used to bring relief from the symptoms, although they do not actually cure the problem. Only use these drugs if you do not have access to toilets, eg, if you *must* travel. Note that these drugs are not recommended for children under 12 years. Do not use these drugs if the person has a high fever or is severely dehydrated.

In certain situations antibiotics may be required: diarrhoea with blood or mucus (dysentery), any diarrhoea experienced along with fever, profuse watery diarrhoea, persistent diarrhoea not improving after 48 hours and severe diarrhoea. These suggest a more serious cause of diarrhoea and in these situations gut-paralysing drugs should be avoided.

In these situations, a stool test may be necessary to diagnose what bug is causing your diarrhoea, so you should seek medical help urgently. Where this is not possible the recommended drugs for bacterial diarrhoea (the most likely cause of severe diarrhoea in travellers) are norfloxacin 400mg twice daily for three days or ciprofloxacin 500mg twice daily for five days. These are not recommended for children or pregnant women. The drug of choice for children would be co-trimoxazole with dosage dependent on weight. A five-day course is given. Ampicillin or amoxycillin may be given in pregnancy, but medical care is necessary.

Two other causes of persistent diarrhoea in travellers are giardiasis and amoebic dysentery.

Giardiasis is caused by a common parasite, *Giardia lamblia*. Symptoms include stomach cramps, nausea, a bloated stomach, watery, foul-smelling diarrhoea and frequent gas. Giardiasis can appear several weeks after you have been exposed to the parasite. The symptoms may disappear for a few days and then return; this can go on for several weeks.

Amoebic dysentery, caused by the protozoan *Entamoeba histolytica*, is characterised by a gradual onset of low-grade diarrhoea, often with blood and mucus. Cramping, abdominal pain and vomiting are less likely than in other types of diarrhoea, and fever may not be present. It will persist until treated and can recur and cause other health problems.

You should seek medical advice if you think you have giardiasis or amoebic dysentery, but where this is not possible, tinidazole or metronidazole are the recommended drugs. Treatment is a 2g single dose of tinidazole or 250mg of metronidazole three times daily for 5 to 10 days.

Fungal Infections Fungal infections occur more commonly in hot weather and are usually found on the scalp, between the toes (athlete's foot) or fingers, in the groin and on the body (ringworm). You get ringworm (which is a fungal infection, not a worm) from infected animals or other people. Moisture encourages these infections.

To prevent fungal infections wear loose, comfortable clothes, avoid artificial fibres, wash frequently and dry yourself carefully. If you do get an infection, wash the infected area at least daily with a disinfectant or medicated soap and water, and rinse and dry well. Apply an antifungal cream or powder like tolnaftate. Try to expose the infected area to air or sunlight as much as possible and wash all towels and underwear in hot water, change them often and let them dry in the sun.

Hepatitis Hepatitis is a general term for inflammation of the liver. It is a common disease worldwide. There are several different viruses that cause hepatitis, and they differ in the way that they are transmitted. The symptoms are similar in all forms of the illness, and include fever, chills, headache, fatigue, feeling weak, aches and pains, followed by loss of appetite, nausea, vomiting, abdominal pain, dark urine, light-coloured faeces, jaundiced (yellow) skin and yellowing of the whites of the eyes. People who have had hepatitis should avoid alcohol for some time after the illness, as the liver needs time to recover.

Hepatitis A is transmitted by contaminated food and drinking water. You should seek medical advice, but there is not much you can do apart from resting, drinking lots of fluids, eating lightly and avoiding fatty foods. **Hepatitis E** is transmitted in the same way as hepatitis A; it can be particularly serious in pregnant women.

There are almost 300 million chronic carriers of **Hepatitis B** in the world. It is spread through contact with infected blood, blood products or body fluids, for example through sexual contact, unsterilised needles and blood transfusions, or contact with blood via small breaks in the skin. Other risk situations include having a shave, tattooing or body piercing with contaminated equipment. The symptoms of hepatitis B may be more severe than type A and the disease can lead to long-term problems such as chronic liver damage, liver cancer or a long-term carrier state. **Hepatitis C and D** are spread in the same way as hepatitis B and can also lead to long-term complications.

There are vaccines against hepatitis A and B, but there are currently no vaccines against the other types of hepatitis. Following the basic rules about food and water (hepatitis A and E) and avoiding risk situations (hepatitis B, C and D) are important preventative measures.

HIV & AIDS Infection with the human immunodeficiency virus (HIV) may lead to acquired immune deficiency syndrome (AIDS), which is a fatal disease. Any exposure to blood, blood products or body fluids may put the individual at risk. HIV is a major health problem in Thailand although the overall incidence of infection has slowed. In Thailand transmission is predominantly through heterosexual sexual activity (over 80%); the second most common source of HIV infection is intravenous injection with used needles (about 6%). The disease is often transmitted through sexual contact or dirty needles – vaccinations, acupuncture, tattooing and body piercing can be as dangerous as intravenous drug use. HIV/AIDS can also be spread through infected blood transfusions, although in Thailand this risk is minimal due to vigorous blood-screening procedures.

The Thai phrase for 'condom' is *thŭng yaang ànaamai*. Good-quality latex condoms are distributed free by offices of the Ministry of Public Health throughout the country, or they can easily be purchased at pharmacies or 7-Eleven stores (where they're conveniently displayed on the counter near the cashier – simply point and

smile). One of the better commercial brands available in Thailand is Durex.

If you should need an injection, ask to see the syringe unwrapped in front of you, or take a needle and syringe pack with you.

Intestinal Worms These parasites are most common in rural, tropical areas. The different worms have different ways of infecting people. Some may be ingested on food such as undercooked meat (eg, tapeworms) and some enter through your skin (eg, hookworms). Infestations may not show up for some time, and although they are generally not serious, if left untreated some can cause severe health problems later. Consider having a stool test when you return home to check for these and determine the appropriate treatment.

Sexually Transmitted Diseases (STDs)
Gonorrhoea, herpes and syphilis are among these diseases; sores, blisters or rashes around the genitals and discharges or pain when urinating are common symptoms. In Thailand gonorrhoea, nonspecific urethritis (NSU) and syphilis are the most common of these diseases. In some STDs, such as wart virus or chlamydia, symptoms may be less marked or not observed at all, especially in women. Syphilis symptoms eventually disappear completely but the disease continues and can cause severe problems in later years. While abstinence from sexual contact is the only 100% effective prevention, using condoms is also effective. The treatment of gonorrhoea and syphilis is with antibiotics. The different sexually transmitted diseases each require specific antibiotics. There is no cure for herpes or AIDS.

Typhoid Typhoid fever is a dangerous gut infection caused by contaminated water and food. Medical help must be sought.

In its early stages sufferers may feel they have a bad cold or flu on the way, as early symptoms are a headache, body aches and a fever that rises a little each day until it is around 40°C (104°F) or more. The victim's pulse is often slow relative to the degree of fever present – unlike a normal fever where the pulse increases. There may also be vomiting, abdominal pain, diarrhoea or constipation.

In the second week the high fever and slow pulse continue and a few pink spots may appear on the body; trembling, delirium, weakness, weight loss and dehydration may occur. Complications such as pneumonia, perforated bowel or meningitis may present.

Insect-Borne Diseases

Filariasis, Lyme disease and typhus are insect-borne diseases, but they do not pose a great risk to travellers. For more information on them see Less Common Diseases later in this section.

Malaria This potentially fatal disease is spread by mosquito bites. Malaria risk exists throughout the year in rural Thailand, especially in forested and hilly areas. Thailand's high-risk areas include northern Kanchanaburi Province (especially Thung Yai Naresuan National Park) and parts of Trat Province along the Cambodian border (including Ko Chang).

According to the CDC and to Thailand's Ministry of Public Health, there is virtually no risk of malaria in urban areas or the main tourist areas (eg, Bangkok, Phuket and Pattaya).

If you are travelling in endemic areas it is extremely important to avoid mosquito bites and to take tablets to prevent the onset of this disease. The most recommended malarial preventive for Thailand travel is 100mg of doxycycline taken daily. Western doctors who know the situation in Thailand no longer recommend either chloroquine or mefloquine (Lariam) for Thailand, due to the malaria parasite's near-total resistance to these drugs. Side effects of doxycycline include photosensitivity, ie, your skin will be more easily affected by the sun.

On the other hand the Malaria Division of Thailand's Ministry of Public Health, which is better acquainted with malaria in Thailand than any other health agency in the world, has issued an unequivocal announcement stating 'Malaria chemophro-

phylaxis is not recommended'. For more information contact the Hospital for Tropical Diseases (☎ 022 469 000), 420/6 Th Ratwithi, Bangkok.

Symptoms of malaria vary widely, ranging from fever, chills and sweating, headache, diarrhoea and abdominal pains, to a vague feeling of ill-health. One of the tell-tale long-term signs is the cyclic nature of the symptoms, coming on every 24 hours or every three days for example. Seek medical help immediately if malaria is suspected. Without treatment malaria can rapidly become more serious and is sometimes fatal.

Every medical clinic or hospital in Thailand can easily test for malaria and treat the disease. If for some reason medical care is not available, certain malaria tablets can be used for treatment. If you took anti-malarial tablets before contracting malaria, you'll need to use a different malaria tablet for treatment as obviously the first one didn't work.

For Fansidar the treatment dose is three tablets. If you cannot obtain Fansidar, then other alternatives are Malarone (atovaquone-proguanil; four tablets once daily for three days), halofantrine (three doses of two 250mg tablets every six hours) or quinine sulphate (600mg every six hours). Be aware also that halofantrine is no longer recommended by the WHO as emergency stand-by treatment, because of side effects, and should only be used if no other drugs are available.

Travellers are advised to prevent mosquito bites at all times. The main messages are:

- Wear long trousers and long-sleeved shirts.
- Wear light-coloured clothing.
- Use mosquito repellents containing the compound DEET on exposed areas (prolonged overuse of DEET may be harmful, especially to children, but its use is considered preferable to being bitten by disease-transmitting mosquitoes).
- Avoid perfumes or aftershave.
- Use a mosquito net impregnated with mosquito repellent (permethrin); it may be worth taking your own.
- Impregnating clothes with permethrin effectively deters mosquitoes and other insects.

For those with an allergy or aversion to synthetic repellents, citronella makes a good substitute. Mosquito coils *(yaa kan yung bàep jùt)* do an excellent job of repelling mosquitoes in your room and are readily available in Thailand. Day mosquitoes do not carry malaria, but do carry dengue.

Dengue Fever This viral disease is also transmitted by mosquitoes, and occurs mainly in tropical and subtropical areas of the world. Generally, there is only a small risk to travellers except during epidemics, which are usually seasonal (during and just after the rainy season).

The *Aedes aegypti* mosquito, which transmits the dengue virus, is most active during the day, unlike the malaria mosquito, and is found mainly in urban areas, in and around human dwellings.

Signs and symptoms of dengue fever include sudden onset of high fever, headache, joint and muscle pains (hence its old name, 'breakbone fever') and nausea and vomiting. A rash of small red spots appears three to four days after the onset of fever. Dengue is commonly mistaken for other infectious diseases, including influenza.

You should seek medical attention if you think you may be infected. Infection can be diagnosed by a blood test. There is no specific treatment for dengue. Aspirin should be avoided, as it increases the risk of haemorrhaging.

Recovery may be prolonged, with tiredness lasting for several weeks. Severe complications are rare in travellers but include dengue haemorrhagic fever (DHF), which can be fatal without prompt medical treatment. DHF is thought to be a result of secondary infection due to a different strain (there are four major strains) and usually affects residents of the country rather than travellers.

In 2000 Thailand's Mahidol University announced the development of a vaccine for all serotypes of dengue. Human trials for the vaccine began late that year, and if successful should be available in 2003 or 2004. As with malaria, the best precaution is to avoid being bitten by mosquitoes.

Japanese B Encephalitis This viral infection of the brain is transmitted by mosquitoes. Most cases occur in rural areas as the virus exists in pigs and wading birds. Symptoms include fever, headache and alteration in consciousness. Hospitalisation is needed for correct diagnosis and treatment. There is a high mortality rate among those who have symptoms; of those who survive many are intellectually disabled.

Cuts, Bites & Stings
See Less Common Diseases for details of rabies, which is passed on through animal bites.

Cuts & Scratches Skin punctures can easily become infected in hot climates and may be difficult to heal. Wash well and treat any cut with an antiseptic such as povidone-iodine. Where possible avoid bandages and Band-Aids, which can keep wounds wet. Coral cuts are notoriously slow to heal and if they are not adequately cleaned, small pieces of coral can become embedded in the wound. Avoid walking on and touching fragile coral reefs in the first place, but if you are near coral reefs, wear shoes and clean any cut thoroughly.

Bedbugs & Lice Bedbugs live in various places, but particularly in dirty mattresses and bedding, evidenced by spots of blood on bedclothes or on the wall. Bedbugs leave itchy bites in neat rows. Calamine lotion or sting-relief spray may help.

All lice cause itching and discomfort. They make themselves at home in your hair (head lice), your clothing (body lice) or in your pubic hair (crabs). You catch lice through direct contact with infected people or by sharing combs, clothing and the like. Powder or shampoo treatment will kill the lice and infected clothing should then be washed in very hot, soapy water and left in the sun to dry.

Bites & Stings Bee and wasp stings are usually painful rather than dangerous. However, in people who are allergic to them, severe breathing difficulties may occur and urgent medical care is required. Calamine lotion or Stingose spray as well as ice packs will reduce the pain and swelling. There are some spiders with dangerous bites but antivenins are usually available in local hospitals. Scorpions often shelter in shoes, clothing or damp towels.

There are various fish and other sea creatures that can sting or bite dangerously or which are dangerous to eat – seek local advice. See Hazardous Marine Life in the colour section 'Thailand's Marine Environment' for information about dealing with these bites and stings.

Leeches & Ticks Leeches may be present in damp rainforest conditions; they attach themselves to your skin to suck your blood. Trekkers often get them on their legs or in their boots. An insect repellent may keep them away.

You should always check all over your body if you have been walking through a potentially tick-infested area as ticks can cause skin infections and other more serious diseases. If a tick is found attached, press down around the tick's head with tweezers, grab the head and gently pull upwards. Avoid pulling the rear of the body as this may squeeze the tick's gut contents through the attached mouth parts into the skin, increasing the risk of infection and disease. Salt or a lighted match or cigarette end will make them fall off. Clean and apply pressure if the point of attachment is bleeding. Smearing chemicals on the tick will not make it let go.

Snakes To minimise your chances of being bitten always wear boots, socks and long trousers when walking through undergrowth where snakes may be present. Don't put your hands into holes and crevices, and be careful when collecting firewood.

Snake bites do not cause instantaneous death and antivenin is available at hospitals throughout Thailand and in pharmacies in larger towns and cities. Immediately wrap the bitten limb tightly, as you would for a sprained ankle, and then attach a splint to immobilise it. Keep the victim still and seek medical help, if possible with the dead snake for identification. Don't attempt to catch the snake if there is a possibility of being bitten again. Tourniquets and sucking out the poison are now comprehensively discredited.

Women's Health
Gynaecological Problems Antibiotic use, synthetic underwear, sweating and contraceptive pills can lead to fungal vaginal infections, especially when travelling in hot climates. Thrush (yeast infection) or vaginal candidiasis is characterised by a rash, itch and discharge. Nystatin, miconazole or clotrimazole pessaries are the usual treatment, but some people use a more traditional remedy involving vinegar or lemon-juice douches, or yoghurt. Maintaining good personal hygiene and wearing loose-fitting clothes and cotton underwear may help prevent these infections.

Sexually transmitted diseases are a major cause of vaginal problems. Symptoms include a smelly discharge, painful intercourse and sometimes a burning sensation when urinating. Medical attention should be sought and male sexual partners must also be treated. Remember that in addition to these diseases, HIV or hepatitis B may also be acquired; besides abstinence, the best prevention is to practise safe sex using condoms.

Pregnancy It is not advisable to travel to some places while pregnant as some vaccinations normally used to prevent serious diseases are not advisable during pregnancy (eg, yellow fever). In addition, some diseases are much more serious for the mother (and may increase the risk of a stillborn child) in pregnancy (eg, malaria).

Most miscarriages occur during the first three months of pregnancy. Miscarriage is not uncommon and can occasionally lead to severe bleeding. The last three months should also be spent within reasonable distance of good medical care. A baby born as early as 24 weeks stands a chance of survival, but only in a good modern hospital. Pregnant women should avoid all unnecessary medication, although vaccinations and malarial prophylactics should still be taken where needed.

Additional care should be taken to prevent illness and particular attention should be paid to diet and nutrition. Alcohol and nicotine, for example, should be avoided.

Less Common Diseases

The following diseases pose a small risk to travellers, and so are only mentioned in passing. Seek medical advice if you think you may have any of these diseases.

Cholera This is the worst of the watery diarrhoeas and medical help should be sought. Outbreaks of cholera are generally widely reported, so you can avoid such problem areas. *Fluid replacement is the most vital treatment* – the risk of dehydration is severe as you may lose up to 20L a day. If there is a delay in getting to hospital, then begin taking tetracycline. The adult dose is 250mg four times daily. It is not recommended for children under nine years nor for pregnant women. Tetracycline may help shorten the illness, but adequate fluids are required to save lives.

Filariasis This is a mosquito-transmitted parasitic infection found in many parts of Asia and the Pacific. Possible symptoms include fever, pain and swelling of the lymph glands; inflammation of lymph drainage areas; swelling of a limb or the scrotum; skin rashes; and blindness. Treatment is available to eliminate the parasites from the body, but some of the damage already caused may not be reversible. Medical advice should be obtained promptly if the infection is suspected.

Lyme Disease This is a tick-transmitted infection that may be acquired throughout Asia. The illness usually begins with a spreading rash at the site of the tick bite and is accompanied by fever, headache, extreme fatigue, aching joints and muscles and mild neck stiffness. If untreated, these symptoms usually resolve over several weeks but over subsequent weeks or months disorders of the nervous system, heart and joints may develop. Treatment works best early in the illness. Medical help should be sought.

Rabies This fatal viral infection is found in many countries. Many animals can be infected (such as dogs, cats, bats and monkeys) and it is their saliva that is infectious. Any bite, scratch or even lick from an animal should be cleaned immediately and thoroughly. Scrub with soap and running water, and then apply alcohol or iodine solution. Medical help should be sought promptly to receive a course of injections to prevent the onset of symptoms and possible death.

Tetanus This disease is caused by a germ that lives in soil and in the faeces of horses and other animals. It enters the body via breaks in the skin. The first symptom may be discomfort in swallowing, or stiffening of the jaw and neck; this is followed by painful convulsions of the jaw and whole body. The disease can be fatal. It can be prevented by vaccination.

Tuberculosis (TB) There is a world-wide resurgence of TB, and in Thailand it's the seventh leading cause of death. TB is a bacterial infection usually transmitted from person to person by coughing but which may be transmitted through consumption of unpasteurised milk. Milk that has been boiled is safe to drink, and the souring of milk to make yoghurt or cheese also kills the bacilli. Travellers are usually not at great risk as close household contact with the infected person is usually required before the disease is passed on. You may need to have a TB test before you travel as this can help diagnose the disease later if you become ill.

Typhus This disease is spread by ticks, mites or lice. It begins with fever, chills, headache and muscle pains followed a few days later by a body rash. There is often a large painful sore at the site of the bite and nearby lymph nodes are swollen and painful. Typhus can be treated under medical supervision. Seek local advice on areas where ticks pose a danger and always check your skin carefully for ticks after walking in a danger area such as a tropical forest. An insect repellent can help, and walkers in tick-infested areas should consider having their boots and trousers impregnated with benzyl benzoate and dibutylphthalate.

Hospitals & Clinics

Thailand's most technically advanced hospitals are in Bangkok. In the south, Phuket and Hat Yai have the best medical care. Elsewhere in the country, every provincial capital has at least one hospital of varying quality as well as several public and private clinics. The best emergency health care, however, can usually be found at military hospitals *(rohng phayaabaan tha-hăan)*; they will usually treat foreigners in an emergency. See the respective destination chapters for information on specific health-care facilities.

WOMEN TRAVELLERS
Attitudes Towards Women

Chinese trader Ma Huan noted in 1433 that among the Thais 'All affairs are managed by their wives, all trading transactions large or small'. In rural areas females typically inherit land and throughout the country they tend to control family finances.

A recent UNDP Human Development Report noted that on the Gender-Related Development Index (GDI) Thailand ranked 31st of 130 countries, thus falling into the 'progressive' category. The nation's GDI increase over the past 20 years was greater than any other country's. According to the report, Thailand 'has succeeded in building the basic human capabilities of both women and men, without substantial gender imparity'. Noted Thai feminist and Thammasat University professor Dr Chatsumarn Kabilsingh has written that 'In economics, academia and health services, women hold a majority of the administrative positions and manifest a strong sense of self-confidence in dealing independently with the challenges presented by their careers.'

Thailand's work force is 44% female, ranking it 27th on a world scale, just ahead of China and the USA. So much for the good news. The bad news is that although women generally fare well in the labour force and in rural land inheritance, their cultural standing is a bit further from parity.

An oft-repeated Thai saying reminds us that men form the front legs of the elephant, women the hind legs (at least they're pulling equal weight).

Thai Buddhism commonly holds that women must be reborn as men before they can attain nirvana, though many Thai *dharma* teachers point out that this presumption isn't supported by the *suttas* (discourses of the Buddha) or by the commentaries. But it is a common belief, supported by the availability of a fully ordained Buddhist monastic status for men and a less prestigious eight-precept ordination for women.

On a legal level, men enjoy more privilege. Men may divorce their wives for committing adultery, but not vice versa, for example. Men who take a foreign spouse continue to have the right to purchase and own land, while Thai women who marry foreign men lose this right. However, the 1997 Thai constitution states 'Men and women hold equal rights'. Few so-called 'developed' countries in the Western world have charters containing such equal-rights clauses; we can expect to see a reformation of such discriminatory laws as 'organic' legislation is put in place.

Safety Precautions

According to the latest TAT statistics, around 40% of all foreign visitors to Thailand are women, a ratio higher than the worldwide average and ahead of all other Asian countries (for which the proportion of female visitors runs lower than 35% with the possible exception of Singapore and Hong Kong. This ratio is growing from year to year and the overall increase for women visitors has climbed faster than that for men for every year since 1993.

Everyday incidents of sexual harassment are much less common in Thailand than in India, Indonesia, Malaysia or Nepal, and this may lull women who have recently travelled in these countries into thinking that Thailand travel is safer than it is. Over the past decade, several foreign women have been attacked while travelling alone in remote areas.

Solo women travellers should take special care on arrival at Bangkok international airport, particularly at night. Don't take one of Bangkok's very-unofficial taxis (black-and-white licence tags) by yourself. A licensed taxi (yellow-and-black tags) or even the public bus are better options. If you're a woman travelling alone, try to pair up with other travellers when travelling at night or in remote areas. Urban areas seem relatively safe; one exception is Ko Pha-Ngan, where there have been several reports of harassment. This is no doubt due to what many Thai men perceive as the 'anything goes' atmosphere at the full-moon parties. Make sure hotel and guesthouse rooms are secure at night – if they're not, demand another room or move to another hotel/guesthouse.

In social situations, especially in bars or at beach resorts, it's also good to bear in mind that Thai women are very modest in their behaviour. This makes it that much easier for Thai men to misinterpret even Platonic friendly gestures from Western women. There are Thai males who already view Western women as 'easy': exercising discreet behaviour is the best way not to encourage such attitudes. The following comment is from a reader:

Thailand is easy to travel alone in as a woman. Virtually no slimy approaches or whistling by males. It's a real joy compared with Kuta Beach in Bali (bad) or India (horror!).

What to Wear Unlike in neighbouring countries to the south, women travelling in Thailand can dress pretty much the way they do back home without raising too much of a fuss. The exceptions include places of worship – whether Buddhist, Hindu, Muslim or Taoist/Confucianist – and government offices. For any place of worship, including all wát, sleeveless tops (capped sleeves are acceptable), shorts of any kind or short skirts are taboo. The same goes for government offices; it's not unusual to see English signs in Thai immigration offices admonishing visitors to 'Please Dress Politely'. In general people dress more conservatively in rural areas of Thailand, so if you want to be treated with respect in these areas, don't wear clothing that reveals your breasts or thighs.

For more on dress, including what to wear at the beach, see Society & Conduct in the Facts about Thailand chapter.

In cases of rape or other assault, the Thai police will investigate and prosecute the crime, but offer little in the way of counselling. If you need to talk with someone, try Community Services of Bangkok (☎ 022 584 998), 15 Soi 33, Th Sukhumvit, which offers a range of counselling services to foreign residents and newcomers to Thailand.

Tampons

Most Thai women don't use tampons, and thus they can be difficult to find in Thailand. In general only the o.b. brand is available, usually in middle-class pharmacies or minimarts that carry toiletries. In Bangkok, more upmarket pharmacies may also carry Tampax brand tampons. If you're staying for a relatively short interval, it's best to bring your own. Sanitary napkins are widely available from minimarts and supermarkets throughout Thailand.

Many women have found that the Keeper menstrual cap – a reusable natural rubber device that may be vaginally inserted to catch menstrual flow – is a very good alternative to disposable tampons or pads. For information on this product, contact Health Keeper (☎ 519-896 8032, 800-663 0427, fax 519-896 8031, e orderinfo@keeper.com, w www.keeper.com), 83 Stonegate Drive, Kitchener, Ontario, Canada N2A 2Y8.

GAY & LESBIAN TRAVELLERS

While Thai culture may seem very tolerant of homosexuality, both male and female, Thailand is not quite the gay 'nirvana' that the foreign media has made it out to be. The Thai aversion to confrontation means that foreign gays need not worry about being physically or verbally bashed. However, gay visitors need to keep in mind that there is a difference between tolerance and acceptance. Thai culture is quite conservative and family-oriented. Many Thais tend to view gays as immature and selfish, as gays seem unwilling to do what most Thais consider to be one of life's principal duties: getting married and having children. Because this belief is especially strong in rural Thailand, many Thai gays from the provinces head for Bangkok once they are old enough to do so. While the nation has no laws that discriminate against homosexuals, Thai society has ways of ensuring that most gays conform to Thai social norms. The importance of living up to society's expectations means that the majority of Thai gays who find themselves in positions of prominence, such as entertainers and politicians, rarely admit to their homosexuality in public. The exception to this rule is comedians – Thai gays with flamboyant mannerisms are often the butt of jokes.

Over the last decade there has been an explosion of entertainment venues – go-go bars, massage parlours and karaoke bars – catering to gay men, both Thai and foreign. The vast majority of these establishments are nothing more than brothels, and studies have shown that a significant number of the commercial sex workers (CSWs) who are employed at such establishments are not even gay. Most of these young men are from poor or broken families and many are addicted to drugs such as methamphetamine. None of this is lost on the Thai. Western gays – especially older men – who come to Thailand to use the services of CSWs, publicly walking hand in hand with their new 'boyfriends' and confident in their belief that tolerant Thailand won't take notice, are sorely mistaken.

While Thai lesbians are subject to the same social pressures to conform, get married and have kids, they are given a bit more leeway than gay Thai men. This is because many Thais believe that young lesbians are simply going through some kind of phase that will pass as soon as the right man comes along.

Organisations & Publications
Utopia (☎ 022 591 619, fax 022 583 250, ⓔ utopia@best.com), 116/1 Soi 23, Th Sukhumvit, is an American-run gay-and-lesbian multipurpose Bangkok centre comprising a guesthouse, bar, cafe, gallery and gift shop. Utopia maintains a very well-organised Web site called Southeast Asia Gay and Lesbian Resources (Ⓦ www.utopia-asia.com/tipsthai.htm).

Other good pages for information on gay-and-lesbian venues in Bangkok are Information Thailand (Ⓦ www.ithailand.com/living/entertainment/bangkok/gay/) and Pink Ink (Ⓦ www.khsnet.com/pinkink).

Anjaree Group (☎/fax 024 771 776), PO Box 322, Ratchadamnoen, Bangkok 10200, is Thailand's premier (and only) lesbian society. Anjaree sponsors various group activities and produces a Thai-only newsletter.

Gay men may be interested in the services of the Long Yang Club (☎/fax 022 867 311, ext125, Ⓦ www.longyangclub.org) at PO Box 1077, Silom Post Office, Bangkok 10504 – a 'multicultural social group for male-oriented men who want to meet outside the gay scene', with branches in London, Amsterdam, Toronto, Canberra, Ottawa and Vancouver.

DISABLED TRAVELLERS
Thailand presents one large, ongoing obstacle course for the mobility-impaired. With its high curbs, uneven sidewalks and non-stop traffic, Bangkok can be particularly difficult – many streets must be crossed via pedestrian bridges flanked by steep stairways, while buses and boats don't stop long enough for even the mildly handicapped. Rarely are there any ramps or other access points for wheelchairs.

Hyatt International (Bangkok, Pattaya), Novotel (Bangkok, Phuket), Sheraton (Bangkok, Phuket), Holiday Inn (Bangkok, Phuket) and Westin (Bangkok) are the only hotel chains in coastal Thailand that make consistent design efforts to provide handicapped access for each of their properties. Because of their high employee-to-guest ratios, home-grown luxury hotel chains such as those managed by Dusit, Amari and Royal Garden Resorts are usually very good in accommodating the mobility-impaired by providing staff help where architecture fails. For the rest, you're pretty much left to your own resources.

For wheelchair travellers, any trip to Thailand will require a good deal of advance planning; fortunately a growing network of information sources can put you in touch with those who have wheeled through Thailand before. There is no better source of information than someone who's already done it.

A reader recently wrote with the following tips:

- The difficulties you mention in your book are all there. However, travel in the streets is still possible, and enjoyable, providing you have a strong, ambulatory companion. Some obstacles may require two carriers; Thais are by nature helpful and could generally be counted on for assistance.
- Don't feel you have to rely on organised tours to see the sights – these often leave early in the morning at times inconvenient to disabled people. It is far more convenient (and often cheaper) to take a taxi or hired car. It's also far more enjoyable as there is no feeling of holding others up.
- Many taxis have an LPG tank in the boot (trunk) that may make it impossible to get a wheelchair in and close it. You might do better to hire a private car and driver (this usually costs no more – and sometimes less – than a taxi).
- A túk-túk is far easier to get in and out of and to carry two people and a wheelchair than a taxi. Even the pedicabs can hang a wheelchair on the back of the carriage.
- Be ready to try anything – in spite of my worries, riding an elephant proved quite easy.

Organisations

Three international organisations that act as clearing houses for information on world travel for the mobility-impaired are:

Access Foundation (☎ 516-887 5798) PO Box 356, Malverne, NY 11565 USA
Mobility International USA (☎ 541-343 1284, e info@miusa.org) PO Box 10767, Eugene, OR 97440, USA
Society for the Advancement of Travel for the Handicapped (SATH; ☎ 212-447 7284, w www.sath.org) Suite 610, 347 Fifth Ave, NY 11242, USA

The book *Exotic Destinations for Wheelchair Travelers* by Ed Hansen & Bruce Gordon contains a useful chapter on seven locations in Thailand. Other books of value include *Holidays and Travel Abroad – A Guide for Disabled People* and Rough Guides' *Able to Travel*.

Accessible Journeys (☎ 610-521 0339, w www.disabilitytravel.com), 35 West Sellers Ave, Ridley Park, Pennsylvania, USA, specialises in organising group travel for the mobility-impaired. Occasionally the agency offers Thailand trips.

SENIOR TRAVELLERS

Senior discounts aren't generally available in Thailand, but the Thais more than make up for this in the respect they typically show for the elderly. In traditional Thai culture, status comes with age; there isn't as heavy an emphasis on youth as in the Western world. Deference for age manifests itself in the way Thais go out of their way to help older persons in and out of taxis or with luggage, and – usually but not always – in waiting on them first in shops and post offices.

Nonetheless, some cultural spheres are reserved for youth. Cross-generational entertainment in particular is less common than in Western countries. There is strict stratification among discos and nightclubs, for example, according to age group. One place will cater to teenagers, another to people in their early 20s, one for late 20s and 30s, yet another for those in their 40s and 50s, and once you've reached 60 you're considered too old to go clubbing! Exceptions to this rule include the more traditional entertainment venues, such as rural temple fairs and other wát-centred events, where young and old will dance and eat together. For men, brothels are another place where old and young clientele mix.

TRAVEL WITH CHILDREN

Like many places in South-East Asia, travelling with children in Thailand can be a lot of fun as long as you are prepared with the right attitudes, physical requirements and the usual parental patience. Lonely Planet's *Travel with Children* by Cathy Lanigan et al contains useful advice on how to cope with kids on the road and what to bring along to make things go more smoothly, with special attention paid to travel in developing countries.

Thais love children and in many instances will shower attention on your offspring, who will find ready playmates among their Thai counterparts and a temporary nanny service at practically every stop.

For the most part parents needn't worry too much about health concerns, though it pays to lay down a few ground rules – such as regular hand-washing – to head off potential problems. All the usual health precautions apply (see the Health section earlier in this chapter); children should especially be warned not to play with animals as rabies is relatively common in Thailand.

DANGERS & ANNOYANCES
Precautions
Although Thailand is in no way a dangerous country to visit, it's wise to be a little cautious, particularly if you're travelling alone. Both men and women should ensure their rooms are securely locked and bolted at night. Inspect cheap rooms with thin walls for strategic peepholes. Take caution when leaving your valuables in hotel safes.

Many travellers have reported unpleasant experiences at Ko Samui guesthouses (particularly on Chaweng beach). Make sure you obtain an itemised receipt for property left with hotels or guesthouses – note the exact quantity of travellers cheques and all other valuables. On the road, keep zippered luggage secured with small locks, especially while travelling on buses and trains. Several readers' letters have recounted tales of theft from their bags or backpacks during overnight bus trips, particularly on routes between Bangkok and Surat Thani and Ko Samui.

Credit Cards
After returning home, some visitors have received huge credit-card bills for purchases (usually jewellery) charged to their cards while the cards had, supposedly, been secure in the hotel or guesthouse safe. It's said that over the two peak months that this was first noticed, credit-card companies lost over US$20 million in Thailand – one major company had 40% of their worldwide losses here! You might consider taking your credit cards with you if you go trekking – if they're stolen on the trail at least the bandits won't be able to use them. Organised gangs in Bangkok specialise in arranging stolen credit card purchases – in some cases they pay 'down and out' foreigners to fake the signatures.

When making credit-card purchases, don't let vendors take your credit card out of your sight to run it through the machine. Unscrupulous merchants have been known to rub off multiple receipts with one credit card purchase; after the customer leaves the shop, they use the one legitimate receipt as a model to forge your signature on the blanks, then fill in astronomical 'purchases'. Sometimes they wait several weeks – even months – between submitting each charge receipt to the bank, so that you can't remember whether you'd been billed at the same vendor more than once.

Druggings
On trains and buses beware of friendly strangers offering cigarettes, drinks or sweets (candy). Several travellers have reported waking up with a headache sometime later to find that their valuables have disappeared. One traveller was offered what looked like a machine-wrapped, made-in-England Cadbury's chocolate. His girlfriend spat it out immediately, while he woke up nine hours later in hospital having required emergency resuscitation after his breathing nearly stopped. This happened on the Surat Thani to Phuket bus. We have not had any reports of bus druggings for some time, so apparently it's a practice that is thankfully on the wane.

Travellers have also encountered drugged food or drink from friendly strangers in bars and from prostitutes in their own hotel rooms. Thais are also occasional victims, especially at the Northern (Moh Chit) bus terminal and Chatuchak Park in Bangkok, where young girls are sometimes drugged and sold to brothels. Conclusion – don't accept gifts from strangers.

Assault

Robbery of travellers by force is very rare in Thailand, but it does happen. Isolated incidents of armed robbery have tended to occur along the Thai-Myanmar and Thai-Cambodian borders and on remote islands.

The safest practice in remote areas is not to go out alone at night and, if trekking, always walk in groups.

Touts

Touting – grabbing newcomers in the street or in train stations, bus terminals or airports to sell them a service – is a long-time tradition in Asia, and while Thailand doesn't have as many touts as, say, India, it has its share. In the popular tourist spots it seems like everyone – young boys waving flyers, túk-túk drivers, sǎamláw drivers, schoolgirls – is touting something, usually hotels or guesthouses.

For the most part they're completely harmless and sometimes they can be very informative. But take anything a tout says with two large grains of salt. Since touts work on commission and get paid just for delivering you to a guesthouse or hotel (whether you check in or not), they'll say anything to get you to the door.

Often the best (most honest and reliable) hotels and guesthouses refuse to pay tout commissions – so the average tout will try to steer you away from such places. Hence don't believe them if they tell you the hotel or guesthouse you're looking for is 'closed', 'full', 'dirty' or 'bad'.

Sometimes (rarely) they're right, but most times it's just a ruse to get you to a place that pays more commission. Always have a careful look yourself before checking into a place recommended by a tout. Túk-túk and sǎamláw drivers often offer free or low-cost rides to the place they're touting; if you have another place you're interested in, you might agree to go with a driver only if he or she promises to deliver you to your first choice after you've had a look at the place being touted. If drivers refuse your request, chances are it's because they know your first choice is a better one.

This type of commission work isn't limited to low-budget guesthouses. Taxi drivers and even airline employees at Thailand's major airports – including Bangkok and Ko Samui – reap commissions from the big hotels as well. At either end of the budget spectrum, the customer ends up paying the commission indirectly through raised room rates. Bangkok international airport employees are notorious for talking newly arrived tourists into staying at badly located, overpriced hotels.

Bus Touts Watch out for touts wearing (presumably fake) TAT badges at Hualamphong train station. They have been known to coerce travellers into buying tickets for private bus rides, saying the train is 'full' or 'takes too long'. Often the promised bus service turns out to be sub-standard and may take longer that the equivalent train ride due to the frequent changing of vehicles. You may be offered a 24-seat VIP 'sleeper' bus to Penang, for example, and end up stuffed into a minivan all the way. Such touts are 'bounty hunters' who receive a set fee for every tourist they deliver to the bus companies. But, as a reader noted:

After reading your book's general chapters I was expecting a much worse situation. Compared to travelling in countries like Morocco, Tunisia, Turkey etc I think travelling in Thailand is relatively easy and hassle-free. When people in Thailand tout something, usually saying 'No' once – or rarely twice – persuades them that you are not interested. In some countries you have to invest much more energy to get rid of people trying to sell.

Insurgent Activity

PULO One continuing thorn in the side of the Thai government is the very small but militant Malay-Muslim movement in the South. The Pattani United Liberation Organisation (PULO) was formed in 1957, trained in Libya and reached its peak in 1981 with a guerrilla strength of around 1800. PULO refers to Thailand's three predominantly Muslim, Malay-speaking provinces of Pattani, Yala and Narathiwat collectively as 'Pattani'; their objective is to create a separate, sovereign state or, at the very least, to obtain annexation to Malaysia. Intelligence sources claim the rebels have been supported by PAS, Malaysia's main opposition party, which is dedicated to making Malaysia a more Islamic state than it already is. UMNO, Malaysia's current ruling party, is clearly against supporting PULO in any way, and has recently extradited several captured members back to Thailand for trial.

PULO's former Muslim separatist allies, Barisan Revolusi Nasional (BRN, or National Revolutionary Front) and Barisan Nasional Pembebasan Pattani (BNPP, or National Front for the Freedom of Pattani), surrendered in late 1991, along with a number of PULO members. PULO remnants persist in Southern Thailand's villages and jungles, but only a few dozen guerrillas are still active, mainly involved in propaganda and extortion activities, plus the occasional attack on Thai government vehicles. PULO members collect regular 'protection' payments, for example, from rubber plantations. Occasional PULO bombings rock the deep south, the most heinous of which killed three people and injured 73 at the Hat Yai train station in 1992. In August 1993 a coordinated terrorist effort set fire to 35 government schools in Pattani, Yala and Narathiwat. Since the fire incident, law enforcement efforts in the South have intensified and the area has stayed relatively quiet, save for one bombing of a railway bridge between Hat Yai and Chana in 1994, which injured no-one.

The Betong area of Yala Province on the Thai-Malaysian border was once the tactical headquarters for the armed Communist Party of Malaya (CPM). But this area is now safe for travel following an agreement by the CPM in December 1989 'to terminate all armed activities' and to respect the laws of Thailand and Malaysia in exchange for an amnesty. The former headquarters, a series of tunnels in the jungle, has recently been opened to visitors.

Drugs

Opium, heroin and marijuana are widely used in Thailand, but it is illegal to buy, sell or possess these drugs in any quantity. A lesser known narcotic, *kràthâwm* (a leaf of the *Mitragyna speciosa* tree), is used by workers and students as a stimulant . A hundred kràthâwm leaves sell for around 100B, and are sold for 5B to 15B each; the leaf is illegal and is said to be addictive.

In the South, especially on the rainy Gulf islands, hallucinogenic mushrooms (*hèt khîi khwai*, 'buffalo-shit mushrooms', or *hèt mao*, 'drunk mushrooms'), containing psilocybin, are sometimes sold to or gathered by foreigners. Using or possessing such mushrooms is now illegal and a risky proposition as well, as the dosage is always uncertain: We've heard confirmed stories of a foreigner who swam to his death off Ko Pha-Ngan after a 'special' mushroom omelette; and there have been other confirmed casualties as well. If you must indulge, watch the dosage carefully.

Also on Ko Pha-Ngan, a hallucinogenic plant called *tôn lamphong* has landed a number of travellers in Surat Thani's psychiatric hospital. Possibly related to datura, a member of the highly toxic nightshade family, ingesting the plant causes some people to be oblivious to anything but their own hallucinations – which they try to follow and grasp – for two or three days. Apparently some guesthouses/restaurants are offering the plant to travellers who ask for magic mushrooms, because the tôn lamphong has not yet been made illegal.

Although in certain areas of the country drugs seem to be used with some impunity, enforcement is arbitrary – the only way not to risk getting caught is to avoid the scene entirely. Every year dozens of visiting foreigners are arrested in Thailand for drug use or trafficking and end up doing hard time. A smaller but significant number die of a heroin overdose. Th Khao San has become the target of cyclic drug enforcement sweeps

Ko Pha-Ngan is also one of Thailand's leading centres for recreational drug use, and the Thai police take notice there as well. On days leading up to Hat Rin's famous monthly full-moon rave, police often set up inspection points on the road between Thong Sala and Hat Rin. Every vehicle, including bicycles and motorcycles, is stopped and the passengers thoroughly searched.

The legal penalties for drug offences are stiff; if you're caught using marijuana, you face a fine (the going rate for escaping a small pot bust – or 'fine' if you wish – is 50,000B) and/or up to five years in prison, while for heroin the penalty for use can be anywhere from six months to 10 years imprisonment. Smuggling – defined as attempting to cross a border – carries higher penalties.

LEGAL MATTERS

In general Thai police don't hassle foreigners, especially tourists. If anything they generally go out of their way not to arrest a foreigner breaking minor traffic laws, rather taking the approach that a friendly warning will suffice.

One major exception is with drugs (see the previous Dangers & Annoyances section for a general discussion of this topic), which most Thai police view as either a social scourge about which it's their duty to enforce the letter of the law, or an opportunity to make untaxed income via bribes. The approach they take often depends on dope quantities; small-time offenders are sometimes offered the chance to pay their way out of an arrest, while traffickers usually go to jail.

Be extra vigilant about where you dispose of cigarette butts and other refuse when in Bangkok. A strong anti-littering law was passed in Bangkok in 1997, and police won't hesitate to cite foreigners and collect fines of 2000B.

If you are arrested for any offence, the police will allow you the opportunity to make a phone call to your embassy or consulate in Thailand if you have one, or to a friend or relative if not. There's a whole set of legal codes governing the length of time and manner in which you can be detained by the police before being charged or put on trial, but a lot of discretion is left to the police. With foreigners the police are more likely to bend these codes in your favour than the reverse. However, as with police worldwide if you don't show respect you will only make matters worse.

Thai law does not presume an indicted detainee to be either 'guilty' or 'innocent' but rather a 'suspect' whose guilt or innocence will be decided in court. Trials are usually speedy.

Thailand has its share of attorneys, and if you think you're a high arrest risk for whatever reason, it might be a good idea to get out the Bangkok *Yellow Pages*, copy down a few phone numbers and carry them with you.

Tourist Police Hotline

The best way to deal with most serious hassles regarding rip-offs or thefts is to contact the Tourist Police, who are used to dealing with foreigners, rather than the regular Thai police. The Tourist Police maintain a hotline – dial ☎ 1155 from any phone in Thailand, and then press 1.

The Tourist Police can also be very helpful in cases of arrest. Although they typically have no jurisdiction over the kinds of cases handled by regular cops, they may be able to help with translation or with contacting your embassy.

BUSINESS HOURS

Most government offices are open from 8.30am to 4.30pm Monday to Friday, but close from noon to 1pm for lunch. Banks are open from 9.30am to 3.30pm Monday to Friday, but in Bangkok in particular several banks have special foreign-exchange offices that are open longer hours (generally until 8pm) and every day of the week. Note that all government offices and banks are closed on public holidays (see Public Holidays & Special Events for details).

Businesses usually operate between 9am and 5pm Monday to Friday, and sometimes Saturday morning as well. Larger shops usually open from 10am to 6.30pm or 7pm but smaller shops may open earlier and close later.

Buddhist monasteries don't post visiting hours, unless there's some attraction or service that might interest travellers. However, it's best to restrict your wát excursions to daylight hours, so as not to disturb the monks.

PUBLIC HOLIDAYS & SPECIAL EVENTS

The number and frequency of festivals and fairs in Thailand is incredible – there always seems to be something going on, especially during the cool season between November and February. Exact dates for festivals vary from year to year, either because of the lunar calendar – which isn't quite in sync with the solar calendar – or because local authorities decide to change festival dates.

The TAT publishes an up-to-date *Major Events & Festivals* calendar each year.

January

New Year's Day A relatively recent public holiday in deference to the Western calendar.

February

Magha Puja *(maakhá buuchaa)* This national public holiday is held on the full moon of the third lunar month to commemorate the preaching of the Buddha to 1250 enlightened monks who came to hear him 'without prior summons'. It culminates in a candle-lit walk around the main chapel at every wát.

Chinese New Year Chinese populations all over Thailand celebrate their lunar new year *(trùt jiin)* with a week of house-cleaning, lion dances and fireworks. The date shifts from year to year between late February and early March.

March

Asean Barred Ground Dove Fair This large dove-singing contest in Yala attracts dove-lovers from all over Thailand, Malaysia, Singapore and Indonesia.

Bangkok International Jewellery Fair During the third week of March in several large Bangkok hotels, this is Thailand's most important annual gem and jewellery trade show. Runs concurrently with the Department of Export Promotion's Bangkok Gems & Jewellery Fair.

April

Chakri Day A public holiday on 6 April commemorates the founder of the Chakri dynasty, Rama I.

Songkran Festival The celebration of the Lunar New Year in Thailand is celebrated from 13 to 15 April. Buddha images are 'bathed', monks and elders receive the respect of younger Thais who sprinkle water over their hands, and a lot of water is tossed about for fun. Songkran generally gives everyone a chance to release their frustrations and literally cool off during the peak of the hot season. Hide out in your room or expect to be soaked; the latter is a lot more fun.

May

Visakha Puja *(wísǎakhà buuchaa)* This public holiday, which falls on the 15th day of the waxing moon in the 6th lunar month, commemorates the Buddha's birth, enlightenment and *parinibbana* (passing away). Activities are centred around the wát, with candle-lit processions, much chanting and sermonising.

Coronation Day The king and queen preside at a ceremony at Wat Phra Kaew in Bangkok on this public holiday on 5 May, commemorating their 1946 coronation.

Royal Ploughing Ceremony The king participates in this ancient Brahman ritual – the kick off for the official rice-planting season – at Sanam Luang (the large field across from Wat Phra Kaew) in Bangkok in the second week of the month. Thousands of Thais gather to watch, and traffic in this part of the city comes to a standstill.

July

Asalha Puja *(àsǎanhà buuchaa)* Commemorates the first sermon preached by the Buddha.

Khao Phansa *(khâo phansǎa)* A public holiday and the beginning of Buddhist 'lent' in mid to late July, this is the traditional time of year for young men to enter the monkhood for the rainy season and for monks to station themselves in a single monastery for three months. It's a good time to observe a Buddhist ordination.

August

Queen's Birthday This public holiday is celebrated on 12 August. In Bangkok, Th Ratchadamnoen Klang and the Grand Palace are festooned with coloured lights.

September

Thailand International Swan-Boat Races These take place in the middle of the month on Mae Nam Chao Phraya (Chao Phraya River) in Bangkok, near the Rama IX Bridge.

Narathiwat Fair This annual festival celebrates local culture with boat races, dove-singing contests, handicraft displays, traditional Southern Thai music and dance. The king and queen almost always attend.

Vegetarian Festival During this nine-day celebration, at the beginning of the ninth lunar month of the Chinese calendar (usually late September or early October), in Trang and Phuket devout Chinese Buddhists eat only vegetarian food. There are also various ceremonies at Chinese temples and merit-making processions that bring to mind Hindu Thaipusam in its exhibition of self-mortification. Smaller towns in the South such as Krabi and Phang-Nga also celebrate on a smaller scale.

October

Chulalongkorn Day A public holiday in commemoration of King Chulalongkorn (Rama V). It is celebrated on 23 October.

Kathin *(thâwt kàthǐn)* A month at the end of the Buddhist lent – usually starting around mid October – during which new monastic robes and requisites are offered to the Sangha (monastic community).

November

Loi Krathong On the proper full-moon night small lotus-shaped baskets or boats made of banana leaves containing flowers, incense, candles and a coin are floated on Thai rivers, lakes and canals. This is a peculiarly Thai festival that probably originated in Sukhothai and is best celebrated in the North.

December

King's Birthday A public holiday (5 December) celebrated with some fervour in Bangkok. As with the queen's birthday, it features lots of lights along Th Ratchadamnoen Klang. Some people erect temporary shrines to the king outside their homes or businesses.

Constitution Day Celebrated 10 December – public holiday.

ACTIVITIES
Diving & Snorkelling

Thailand's two coastlines and countless islands are popular among divers from all over the globe for their mild waters and colourful marine life. Sandy coves, coral reefs, limestone outcrops, rock reefs, seamounts and pinnacles, undersea caverns and tunnels, and sunken ships provide a wide variety of dive sites. Water temperature hovers at 27°C to 29°C year-round, ideal for recreational divers, not to mention coral and tropical fish.

Guided dives and diving instruction have become sizeable industries in Thailand, especially during the high tourist season, No-

vember to April. The biggest diving centre – in terms of the number of participants, – is still Pattaya, simply because it's less than two hours drive from Bangkok and has a year-round dive season. There are several islands with reefs within a short boat ride from Pattaya and the little town is packed with dive shops.

Phuket is the second-biggest jumping-off point, or largest if you count dive operations. It has the advantage of offering the largest variety of dive sites to choose from, including small offshore islands less than an hour away, Ao Phang-Nga (a one- to two-hour boat ride) with its unusual rock formations and clear green waters, and the world-famous Similan and Surin Islands in the Andaman Sea (about four hours away by fast boat). Reef dives in the Andaman are particularly rewarding – some 210 hard corals and 108 reef fish have so far been catalogued in this under-studied marine zone, where probably thousands more species of reef organisms live.

In recent years dive operations have proliferated on the palmy islands of Ko Samui, Ko Pha-Ngan and Ko Tao in the Gulf of Thailand off Surat Thani. Chumphon Province, just north of Surat Thani, is another up-and-coming area where there are a dozen or so islands with undisturbed reefs. Newer frontiers include the so-called Burma Banks (north-west of the Surin archipelago), Hat Khao Lak (on the mainland north of Phuket), Ko Chang and islands off the coast of Krabi and Trang Provinces. All of these places, with the possible exception of the Burma Banks, have areas that are suitable for snorkelling as well as scuba diving, since many reefs are no deeper than 2m.

Dive Centres Most dive shops rent equipment at reasonable rates and offer instruction and NAUI or PADI qualification for first-timers – PADI is by far the most prevalent. The average four-day, full-certification course costs around 8000B to 11,000B (up to 15,000B at luxury resorts), including instruction, equipment and several open-water dives. Shorter, less-

Trouble Underfoot

Irresponsible diving practises have long been blamed for contributing to the destruction of coral reefs and other underwater habitats. But at least divers, before they can become certified, are required to take a course that will teach ways of lessening their impact on the marine environment. Then along came 'seawalking'. Since at least 1997, tour companies in Phuket and other parts of Thailand have been promoting this activity to visitors. To the uninformed it might seem like a great idea. No need for the time-consuming instruction that divers must go through, simply put on some weighted boots, don a special 'bubble helmet' with an air hose connected to a shipboard source (similar in theory to those old-fashioned brass diving helmets), and then go for a leisurely stroll through the undersea gardens. Of course, it doesn't take much thought to imagine what kind of damage this activity, were it to became popular, could soon lead to.

Not long after seawalking came to the attention of environmentalists, it came under fire, and the issue has been kicked around by Thai politicians, environmentalists and entrepreneurs ever since. Meetings have been held, studies have been implemented, and, in the meantime, the coral continues to be trampled on by environmentally clueless (or thoughtless) tourists. On Phuket, the favoured area for seawalking is Ko Hae (also known as Coral Island) off Phuket's southern coast. The area is designated a marine reserve of the Fisheries Department, but that has not stopped local companies from exploiting its coral reefs. These unscrupulous businesses are aided by the fact that damage done to coral is not easily discerned - if a jungle-clad hillside were deforested in the name of tourism, the outcry would be loud and immediate, but unless you don a mask and fins and go down and have look for yourself, it's hard to picture the destruction being wrought on the coral reefs.

Recently, the governor of Phuket, arguing for the legalisation of seawalking, claimed that seawalking companies in Thailand had raked in 96 million baht in 2000. As is often the case in Thailand and most everywhere else, the more money a questionable activity generates, the more difficult it is to enact laws countering that activity.

---

expensive 'resort' courses are also available, including half-day 'introductory' dives. Speciality courses may include dive-master certification and underwater photography. It's a good idea to shop around for courses, not just to compare prices but to suss out the types of instruction, the condition of the equipment and the personalities of the instructors.

The minimum age for PADI or NAUI certification is 12 years; children aged between 12 and 15 are classified 'junior divers' and must be accompanied by an adult. There are no maximum age limits. Beginners should note that courses are usually only available at the larger centres: for example, you can't take an open-water course at the remote Similan Islands.

German and English are the most common languages of instruction, but French and Italian courses are also available at a few places. See the relevant destination sections of this book for names and locations of established diving centres.

Equipment Virtually every dive operation rents gear and air compressors. The better ones provide high-quality equipment, while cheaper places may offer substandard gear – inspect carefully before renting. Tanks, regulators and buoyancy compensation devices (BCDs) are especially critical.

Masks, fins and snorkels are readily available not only at dive centres but also at guesthouses in beach areas. If you're fussy about the quality and condition of the equipment you use, you might be better off bringing your own mask and snorkel – some of the stuff for rent is second-rate. And people with large heads may have difficulty finding masks that fit, since most of

Considerations for Responsible Diving

The popularity of diving is placing immense pressure on many sites. Please consider the following tips when diving and help preserve the ecology and beauty of reefs:

Do not use anchors on the reef, and take care not to ground boats on coral. Encourage dive operators and regulatory bodies to establish permanent moorings at popular dive sites.

Avoid touching living marine organisms with your body, or dragging equipment across the reef. Coral polyps can be damaged by even the gentlest contact. Never stand on coral, even if they look solid and robust. If you must secure yourself to the reef, only hold fast to exposed rock or dead coral.

Be conscious of your fins. Even without contact the surge from heavy fin strokes near the reef can damage delicate organisms. When treading water in shallow reef areas, take care not to kick up clouds of sand. Settling sand can easily smother the delicate organisms of the reef.

Practise and maintain proper buoyancy control. Major damage can be done by divers descending too fast and colliding with the reef. Make sure you are correctly weighted and that your weight belt is positioned so that you stay horizontal. If you have not dived for a while, have a practice dive in a pool before taking to the reef. Be aware that buoyancy can change over the period of an extended trip; initially you may breathe harder and need more weighting, a few days later you may breathe more easily and need less weight.

Take great care in underwater caves. Spend as little time in them as possible as your air bubbles may be caught within the roof and thereby leave previously submerged organisms high and dry. Taking turns to inspect the interior of a small cave will lessen the chances of damaging contact.

Respect the integrity of marine archaeological sites (mainly shipwrecks); they may even be protected by law from looting.

Ensure that you take home all your rubbish, and any litter you may find as well. Plastics are a particularly serious threat to marine life. Turtles often mistake plastic bags for jellyfish and eat them.

Resist the temptation to feed fish. You may disturb their normal eating habits, encourage aggressive behaviour or feed them food that is detrimental to their health.

Minimise your disturbance of marine animals. In particular, do not ride on the backs of turtles as this causes them great anxiety.

---

the masks are made or imported for Thai heads.

Wetsuits are not usually required except for deeper Andaman Sea dives where cold water upwellings and/or thermoclines occur, but a Lycra suit or 'skin' does serve as protection against scrapes and jellyfish. These are available from most dive shops, but if you're particularly tall or large they may have trouble fitting you – in which case bring your own.

Because divers and anglers occasionally frequent the same areas, a good diving knife is essential for dealing with a wayward fish-ing line or net. Bring two knives so you'll have a spare. You may also consider bringing extra O-rings, CO_2 cartridges for flotation vests and a wetsuit patching kit if you plan to dive away from resort areas.

Dependable air for scuba tanks is available in Pattaya, Ko Chang, Ko Samui, Ko Tao, Hat Khao Lak and Phuket. Always check the compressor first to make sure it's well maintained and running clean. Divers with extensive experience usually carry a portable compressor, not only to avoid contaminated air but to use in areas where tank refills aren't available.

Dive Seasons Generally speaking, the Gulf of Thailand has a year-round dive season, although tropical storms sometimes blow out visibility temporarily. The south-western monsoon seems to affect the Ko Chang archipelago more than other eastern Gulf Coast dive sites, hence November to May is the ideal season for these islands.

On the Andaman Coast the best diving conditions – calm surf and good visibility – fall between December and April; from May to November monsoon conditions prevail. However, there are still many calm days even during the south-western monsoon season – it's largely a matter of luck. Whale sharks and manta rays in the offshore Andaman Sea (eg, Similan and Surin Islands) can be spotted during the March and April planktonic blooms.

Dive Medicine Due to the overall lack of medical facilities oriented toward diving injuries, great caution should be exercised when diving anywhere in Thailand. Recompression chambers are located at three permanent facilities:

Bangkok Somdej Phra Pinklao Naval Hospital, Department of Underwater & Aviation Medicine (☎ 024 600 000, 024 600 019, ext 341, 024 601 105), Th Taksin, Thonburi; open 24 hours
Chonburi Apakorn Kiatiwong Naval Hospital (☎ 038 601 185), Sattahip; Chonburi, 26km east of Pattaya; urgent care available 24 hours
Phuket Sub-aquatic Safety Service (SSS; ☎ 076 342 518, 016 061 869, fax 076 342 519), Hat Patong, Phuket

Guidebooks Lonely Planet's richly illustrated *Diving & Snorkeling Thailand* is full of vital diving information written by resident diving instructors.

Environmental Issues To preserve Thailand's impressive marine environment for the future, it is imperative that divers take care not to disrupt the fragile ecosystems beneath the seas. This means, first and foremost, not touching corals, fish or other marine life. It includes refraining from hitching rides on fish, dolphins or turtles by grabbing onto their fins or shells, practices that are thought to frighten them and cause undue stress. Such contact can also adversely affect the health of marine life by scraping away mucous coverings that protect the creatures against infection.

Spear-fishing is not appropriate on a recreational dive as it reduces the number of larger fish necessary to the marine ecosystem. Errant spears also often damage coral. It is also absolutely illegal in national marine parks.

Resist the temptation to collect or buy corals or shells. Aside from the ecological damage, taking home marine souvenirs depletes the beauty of a site and spoils it for others.

See Tourism & the Environment under Ecology & Environment in the Facts about Thailand chapter for important recommendations on boat anchoring and waste disposal. See the boxed text 'Considerations for Responsible Diving' earlier in this chapter for more tips.

Windsurfing

The best combination of rental facilities and wind conditions are found on Pattaya and Jomtien beaches in Chonburi Province, on Ko Samet, on the west coast of Phuket and on Chaweng beach on Ko Samui. To a lesser extent you'll also find rental equipment on Hat Khao Lak (north of Phuket), Ko Pha-Ngan, Ko Tao and Ko Chang.

Windsurfing gear rented at Thai resorts is generally not the most complete and up-to-date. Original parts may be missing, or may have been replaced by improvised Thai-made parts. For the novice windsurfer this probably won't matter, but hot-doggers may be disappointed by the selection – bring your own if you're really fussy. In Thailand's year-round tropical climate, wetsuits aren't necessary.

If you have your own equipment you can set out anywhere you find a coastal breeze. If you're looking for something 'undiscovered', you might check out the cape running north from Narathiwat's provincial capital in Southern Thailand. In general, the windier months on the Gulf of Thailand are mid-February to April. On the Andaman Sea side of the Malay peninsula, winds are strongest from September to December.

Paddling

Touring the islands and coastal limestone formations around Phuket and Ao Phang-Nga by inflatable canoe or kayak has become an increasingly popular activity. The typical sea-canoe tour seeks out half-submerged caves called 'hongs' (*hâwng*, Thai for 'room'), timing the trips so they can paddle into and out of caverns at low tide. Several outfits in Phuket and Krabi hire equipment and guides – see the relevant destination chapters for details. *Faràng* outfitters claim to have 'discovered' the hongs, but local fishermen have known about them for hundreds of years. Several islands with partially submerged caves in Ao Phang-Nga have carried the name Ko Hong (Room Island) for at least the last half century.

You might consider bringing your own craft. Inflatable or folding kayaks make the most sense for travellers, though hard-shell kayaks track better. In Thailand's tropical waters an open-top or open-deck kayak – whether hard-shell, folding or inflatable – is more comfortable and practical than the closed-deck type with spray skirt and other sealing paraphernalia, which only transforms your kayak into a floating sauna. In general, the paddler sits on top of the deck rather than beneath it; the open-top is much easier to exit and thus a bit safer overall. Open-cockpit kayaks are also easier to paddle and more stable than traditional kayaks – almost anyone can paddle one with little or no practice. But they do manoeuvre a bit more slowly due to a wider beam and higher centre of gravity.

Surfing

This sport has never really taken off in Thailand, mainly as there don't seem to be any sizeable, annually dependable breaks (tell us if you find any – yeah, sure!). Phuket's west coast occasionally kicks up some surfable waves during the south-western monsoon from May to November, as does the west coast of Ko Chang. Ko Samet's east

coast gets some waves during the dry season (November to February).

Low-quality boards can be rented in Pattaya and on Phuket's Patong beach (but bigger surf is usually found on nearby Kata Noi, Laem Singh and Hat Surin). Coastal areas of Trang Province are reputed to receive large waves during the south-western monsoon, but there aren't many tales of surfers hitting the breaks out there.

Hiking

You can hike in Southern Thailand's larger national parks – Khao Sam Roi Yot, Khao Sok and Khao Lak – where park rangers may be hired as guides and cooks for a few days. Rates are reasonable; see the respective park descriptions later in this book.

Parks suitable for hiking without a guide – because they contain marked trails – include Khao Sam Roi Yot and Ko Tarutao. Inter-village footpaths on southern Ko Chang can also easily be hiked without a guide, although paths in the island's hilly interior can be challenging due to steep grades and undergrowth.

When hiking without a guide, it is recommended that you always hike with at least one other person and that you let someone in the local community know where you're headed and for how long. Always take plenty of water and insect repellent.

Leeches can be a hindrance during the monsoon seasons, particularly in Khao Sok National Park; see the Health section earlier in this chapter.

Cycling

With the exception of Bangkok, cycling is a great way to get around Thailand: it's cheap, non-polluting and allows you to travel at a speed that permits interaction with your surroundings. It is possible to hire bikes at various places throughout Thailand, especially in centres that attract backpackers, but if you plan to do more than the occasional jaunt it might be advisable to bring your own. See Bicycle in the Getting Around chapter for more information.

The sapping heat and humidity are the main adversities facing cyclists in Southern Thailand but there's often a strong cross wind that cools you down, though it also drains you of fluids because it makes your sweat disappear fast. So drink plenty and try to get on the road early in the day when it's cooler and there are fewer motorists.

Main roads are smooth and wide with plenty of space at the side for cyclists to avoid larger vehicles. Roads near the coast are more variable in quality, and on the islands can be extremely steep and rough, but there are some high-quality roads on the better known and more touristed ones like Phuket. Often these carry little traffic.

Expect to pay for your bike on ferries, even though locals may not be required to.

It is normal for motorists to alert cyclists when approaching from behind, so try not to get too wound up at people hooting at you all the time. They will usually give you a respectfully wide berth, especially if you look sufficiently non-local.

There are plenty of places where cold drinks can be bought and food replenished. Some very good sports-type drinks are available, but water is most essential.

Cycling will often land you in places with little or no accommodation, so try what you can; often wát will provide sleeping space for a small contribution or, occasionally, for free. Police stations are sometimes an option too. At some petrol stations you can wash and possibly even stay the night in fairly modern surroundings. Camping is an option if you feel confident of the safety of the locality, and if there are two or more of you – check for snakes. It's a good idea to carry a mat for those more innovative stops, or for the many occasions when people will take you into their homes.

COURSES
Language

Several language schools in Bangkok and other places where foreigners congregate offer courses in Thai language. Tuition fees average around 250B per hour. Some places will let you trade English lessons for Thai lessons; if not, you can usually teach English on the side to offset tuition costs.

If you have an opportunity to 'shop around' it's best to enrol in programs that offer plenty of opportunity for linguistic interaction rather than rote learning or the passe 'natural method'.

Schools in Bangkok with the best reputations include:

AUA Language Center (☎ 022 528 170) 179 Th Ratchadamri. American University Alumni (AUA) runs one of the largest English-language-teaching institutes in the world, so this is a good place to meet Thai students. AUA-produced books are stodgy and outdated, but many teachers make their own – better – instructional materials. Some foreigners who study Thai here complain that there's not enough interaction in class because of an emphasis on the so-called 'natural method', which focuses on teacher input rather than student practice and has been thoroughly discredited in most Western countries. Others find the approach useful. *Paw hòk* (6th-grade primary school level, essential for anyone wishing to work in the public school system) courses are available. AUA also has branches in Songkhla and Phuket. Not all AUAs offer regularly scheduled Thai classes, but study can usually be arranged on an ad hoc basis.

Nisa Thai Language School (☎ 022 869 323) YMCA Collins House, 27 Th Sathon Tai. This school has a fairly good reputation, though teachers may be less qualified than at Union or AUA language schools. In addition to all the usual levels, Nisa offers a course in preparing for the paw hòk examination.

Siri Pattana Thai Language School (☎ 022 131 206) YWCA, 13 Th Sathon Tai, Bangkok. Offers Thai-language lessons as well as preparation for the paw hòk exam. Siri Pattana has a second branch at 806 Soi 38, Th Sukhumvit.

Union Language School (☎ 022 334 482) CCT Bldg, 109 Th Surawong. Generally recognised as the best and most rigorous course (many missionaries study here). Employs a balance of structure-oriented and communication-oriented methodologies in 80-hour, four-week modules. Private tuition is also available.

Meditation

Thailand has long been a popular place for Western students of Buddhism, particularly those interested in Buddhist meditation. Two basic systems of meditation are taught, *samatha* and *vipassana*. Samatha aims towards the calming of the mind and development of refined states of concentration, and as such is similar to other traditions of meditation or contemplation found in most of the world's religions. Unique to Buddhism, particularly Theravada and to a lesser extent Tibetan Buddhism, is a system of meditation known as vipassana (Thai: *wípàtsànaa*), a Pali word that roughly translates as 'insight'.

Foreigners who come to Thailand to study vipassana can choose among dozens of temples and meditation centres *(sǎmnák wípàtsànaa)* that specialise in these teachings. Teaching methods vary from place to place but the general emphasis is on learning to observe mind-body processes from moment to moment. Thai language is usually the medium of instruction but several places also provide instruction in English. Some centres and monasteries teach both vipassana and samatha, others specialise in one or the other.

Details on some of the more popular meditation-oriented temples and centres are given in the destination chapters. Instruction and accommodation are free of charge at temples, though donations are expected.

The two-month Tourist Visa is ample for most courses of study, but long-term students may want to consider a three- or six-month Non-Immigrant Visa. A few Westerners are ordained as monks or nuns in order to take full advantage of the monastic environment. Monks and nuns are generally (but not always) allowed to stay in Thailand as long as they remain in robes.

Places where English-language instruction is usually available include:

Boonkanjanaram Meditation Centre
(☎ 038 231 865) Hat Jomtien, Pattaya, Chonburi
International Buddhist Meditation Centre
(☎ 026 236 326) Wat Mahathat, Th Maharat, Tha Phra Chan, Bangkok
Thailand Vipassana Centre (☎ 022 164 772, fax 022 153 408) Patumwan, Bangkok
Wat Khao Tham PO Box 8, Ko Pha-Ngan, Surat Thani 84280
Wat Suan Mokkhaphalaram-Chaiya
(fax 076 391 851, attn SMI) Surat Thani

Before visiting one of these centres, it's a good idea to call or write to make sure space and instruction are available. Some places require that lay persons staying overnight wear white clothes. For even a brief visit, wear clean and neat clothing (ie, long trousers or skirt and sleeves that cover the shoulder).

For a detailed look at vipassana study in Thailand, including visa and ordination procedures, read *The Meditation Temples of Thailand: A Guide* (published by Silkworm Books, Chiang Mai); or *A Guide to Buddhist Monasteries & Meditation Centres in Thailand* (available from the World Federation of Buddhists in Bangkok or online at Ⓦ www.dharmanet.org/thai_94.html).

Useful pre-meditation course reading includes Jack Kornfield's *Living Dharma* and *The Path of Purification (Visuddhi Magga)*, available at bookshops in Bangkok (see Shopping later in this chapter).

Martial Arts

Many Westerners have trained in Thailand, but few last more than a week or two in a Thai camp – and fewer still have gone on to compete on Thailand's pro circuit.

Muay Thai (Thai Boxing) Training in
muay thai exists at dozens, perhaps as many as a hundred, camps around the country.

Most are a little reluctant to take on foreign trainees, except in special cases where the applicant can prove a willingness to conform *totally* to the training system, the diet, the rustic accommodations and most of all an ability to learn the Thai language. Newcomers interested in training at a traditional muay thai camp can try the Pattaya International Training School (☎ 038 410 111), 193/15 Th Thepprasit, Pattaya, or Fairtex Muay Thai (☎ 023 855 148), 99/2 Mu 3, Soi Buthamanuson, Th Thaeparak, Bangpli, Samut Prakan. Both of these schools accept foreign students.

Another place that specialises in international training is the Muay Thai Institute (☎ 029 920 095, e khuna@muaythai.th .net), associated with the respected World Muay Thai Council. The Institute is located inside the Rangsit Muay Thai Stadium north of Bangkok international airport.

Be forewarned: muay thai training is gruelling and features full-contact sparring, unlike tae kwon do, kenpo, kung fu and other East Asian martial arts.

In Thailand look for copies of *Muay Thai World*, a biannual periodical published by Bangkok's World Muay Thai Council. Although it's basically a cheap martial arts flick, Jean-Claude Van Damme's *The Kickboxer*, filmed on location in Thailand, gives a more comprehensive, if rather exaggerated, notion of muay thai than most other films on the subject.

The Web site w www.muaythai.com contains loads of information on muay thai in Thailand, including the addresses of training camps.

For more information about muay thai, see Spectator Sports later in this chapter.

Thai Massage

Described by some as a 'brutally pleasant experience', this ancient form of healing was first documented in the West by the French liaison to the Thai Royal Court in Ayuthaya in 1690, who wrote: 'When any person is sick in Siam he causes his whole body to be moulded by one who is skilful herein, who gets upon the body of the sick person and tramples him under his feet'.

Unlike most Western massage methodologies, such as popular Swedish and Californian techniques, Thai massage does not directly seek to relax the body through kneading with palms and fingers. Instead a multipronged approach, using hands, thumbs, fingers, elbows, forearms, knees and feet is applied to traditional pressure points along various *sên* or meridians (the human body is thought to have 72,000 of these, of which 10 are crucial).

The client's body is also pulled, twisted and manipulated in ways that have been compared to a 'passive yoga'. The objective is to distribute energies evenly throughout the nervous system so as to create a harmony of physical energy flows. The muscular-skeletal system is also manipulated in ways that can be compared to modern physiotherapy and chiropractic.

Thailand offers ample opportunities to study its unique tradition of massage therapy. Wat Pho in Bangkok is considered the master source for all Thai massage pedagogy. For details see the Wat Pho section in the Bangkok chapter.

Cooking

More and more travellers are coming to Thailand just to learn how to cook. It's not unusual to meet foreign chefs in Thailand seeking out recipe inspirations for the East-West fusion cuisine that seems to be taking the world by storm. You too can amaze your friends back home after attending a course in Thai cuisine at one of the following places:

The Boathouse (☎ 076 330 557, fax 076 330 561, ☎ 024 381 123 in Bangkok) Hat Kata Yai, Phuket. The chefs at this outstanding Phuket beach restaurant offer occasional weekend workshops.

Modern Housewife Centre (☎ 022 792 834) 45/6–7 Th Sethsiri, Bangkok

Oriental Hotel Cooking School (☎ 022 360 400–39) Soi Oriental, Th Charoen Krung, Bangkok. This school features a plush (and expensive) five-day course under the direction of well-known star chef Chali (Charlie) Amatyakul.

Pat's Home (☎ 076 213 765) 26/4 Th Khwang, Phuket town. Classes are taught by a Thai chef who worked in California for six years.

Samui Institute of Thai Culinary Arts (☎/fax 077 413 172) Chaweng, Ko Samui. SITCA offers daily Thai cooking classes – including vegetarian – as well as courses in the aristocratic Thai art of carving fruits and vegetables into intricate floral designs.

UFM Food Centre (☎ 022 590 620, 022 590 633) 593/29–39 Soi 33/1, Th Sukhumvit, Bangkok. Considered the most serious and thorough cooking school in Thailand, UFM has a multi-layered curriculum. Most classes are offered in Thai – you need at least four people for an English-language class.

WORK

Thailand's steady economic growth has provided a variety of work opportunities for foreigners, although in general it's not as easy to find a job as in the more developed countries. The one exception is English teaching; as in the rest of East and South-East Asia, there is a high demand for English speakers to provide instruction to Thai citizens. This is not due to a shortage of qualified Thai teachers with a good grasp of English grammar, but rather to the desire to have native speaker models in the classroom.

Work Permits

All work in Thailand requires a Thai work permit. Thai law defines work as 'exerting one's physical energy or employing one's knowledge, whether or not for wages or other benefits', hence theoretically even voluntary work requires a permit. A 1979 royal decree closed 39 occupations to foreigners, including civil engineering, architecture, legal services and clerical or secretarial services. However, in 1998 several jobs on this list were re-opened to foreigners.

Work permits should be obtained through an employer, who may file for the permit before the foreigner enters Thailand. The permit itself is not issued until the employee enters Thailand on a valid Non-Immigrant Visa.

For information on obtaining work permits, check out the Web site Ⓦ www .thaiembdc.org/consular/con_info/restpmit/ extvisa.html.

Teaching English

Those with academic credentials such as teaching certificates or degrees in English as a second language get first crack at the better-paying jobs, ie, at universities and international schools. But there are hundreds of private language-teaching establishments that hire non-credentialed teachers by the hour throughout the country. Private tutoring is also a possibility in the larger, wealthier cities such as Bangkok, Phuket, Hat Yai and Songkhla. International oil companies pay the highest salaries for English instructors but are also quite picky.

If you're interested in looking for such teaching work, start with the English-language *Yellow Pages of the Greater Bangkok Metropolitan Telephone Directory*. Check all the usual headings – Schools, Universities, Language Schools and so on. Organisations such as Teachers of English to Speakers of Other Languages (Tesol, suite 300, 1600 Cameron St, Alexandria, Virginia 22314, USA) and International Association of Teachers of English as a Foreign Language (IATEFL; 3 Kingsdown Chamber, Kingsdown Park, Whitstable, Kent CT52DJ, UK) publish newsletters with lists of jobs in foreign countries, including Thailand.

Other Jobs & Volunteer Positions

Voluntary and paid positions with organisations that provide charitable services in education, development or public health are available for those with the right educational backgrounds and/or experience. Contact the usual prospects such as:

Food & Agriculture Organisation
   (☎ 022 817 844) Bangkok
Overseas Service Bureau (OSB; ☎ 03-9279 1788) Melbourne, Australia
UN World Food Programme (☎ 022 800 427) Bangkok
Unesco (☎ 023 910 577) Bangkok
Unicef (☎ 022 805 931) Bangkok
United Nations Development Programme (UNDP; ☎ 022 829 619) Bangkok
US Peace Corps (☎ 800-424 8580) Washington DC, USA
Voluntary Service Overseas (VSO; ☎ 020-8780 7200) London, UK
Volunteer Service Abroad (VSA; ☎ 04-472 5759) Wellington, New Zealand

VSO Canada (☎ 613-234 1364) Ottawa,
  Canada
World Health Organisation (☎ 022 829 700)
  Bangkok

ACCOMMODATION

Places to stay are abundant, varied and reasonably priced in coastal Thailand.

A word of warning though: don't believe touts who say a place is closed, full, dirty or crooked. Sometimes they're right, but most times they just want to get you to a place that pays them more commission. (See Touts under Dangers & Annoyances, earlier in this chapter.)

National Park Accommodation/Camping

All but 10 of Thailand's national parks have bungalows for rent that sleep as many as 10 people for 500B to 1500B, depending on the park and the size of the bungalow. During the low season you can often get a room in one of these park bungalows for 100B per person.

Camping is allowed in all but four of the national parks (Chanthaburi Province's Nam Tok Phliu; Doi Suthep-Pui in Chiang Mai Province; Hat Chao Mai in Trang Province; and Thap Laan in Prachinburi Province) for only 5B to 20B per person per night if you bring your own tent. Some parks have tents for rent at 50B to 100B a night, but always check the condition of the tents before agreeing to rent one. It's a good idea to take your own sleeping bag or mat and other basic camping gear. You should also take a torch (flashlight), rain gear, insect repellent, a water container and a small medical kit.

On weekends and holidays, reservations for bungalows are recommended. In Bangkok the reservations office is at the National Parks Division of the Forestry Department (☎ 025 614 292), Th Phahonyothin, Bangkhen (north Bangkok). Bookings from Bangkok must be paid in advance. Most parks charge an entrance fee of 20B for Thais, 200B for non-Thais (children under 14 half price). Be sure to hang on to your receipt – rangers randomly check

visitors and you may be charged again if you have no proof that you already paid.

Beach Bungalows

Simple palm-thatch and bamboo beach bungalows are generally the cheapest beach and island accommodation in Thailand, although with each passing year they become more and more scarce. The owners of such accommodation now prefer to build with bricks, concrete and other more permanent materials; they vary quite a bit in facilities.

Nightly rates vary according to the popularity of the beach, from a low of 80B per night for a primitive bamboo hut with shared bathroom on the north-western beaches of Ko Pha-Ngan to around 2500B for a high-season beach bungalow with private facilities on Ko Samui's Hat Chaweng.

Some bungalow operations are especially good value, while others are dank, mosquito-filled cells. Many serve food, although there tends to be a bland sameness to meals at beach huts wherever you are in Thailand.

Guesthouses

Cheap urban guesthouses are scarce in coastal areas. Beach huts replace guesthouses, while cheap Chinese-Thai hotels for the most part fill the bill in the inland cities. Exceptions include the provincial capitals of Trat, where there are three or four guesthouses; Krabi, which has over a dozen guesthouses; and the beach resorts of Hua Hin and Pattaya, which have guesthouses in neighbourhoods back from the beach.

The typical Thai guesthouse features simple rooms with very little furniture – at their most basic no more than a mattress on the floor. The cheaper places have shared bathrooms for 80B to 100B per night; some places have private facilities for 150B to 300B a night.

Chinese-Thai Hotels

In inland cities such as Hat Yai, Trat or Surat Thani, standard Thai hotels – often run by Chinese-Thai families – are the most economical accommodation and generally have very reasonable rates (average 150B for rooms without bath or air-con, 180B to 250B with fan and bath, 300B to 500B with air-con). They may be located on the main street of town and/or near bus and train stations.

The cheapest hotels are those without air-con; typical rooms are clean and include a double bed and a ceiling fan. Some have Thai-style bathrooms attached (this will cost a little more). Rates may or may not be posted; if not, they may be increased for faràng, so it is worth bargaining. It's best to have a look around before agreeing to check in, to make sure the room is clean, the fan and lights work and so on. If there is a problem, request another room or a good discount. If possible, always choose a room off the street and away from the front lounge to cut down on noise.

For a room without air-con, ask for a *hâwng thamádaa* (ordinary room) or *hâwng phát lom* (room with fan). A room with air-con is *hâwng ae*. Sometimes travellers asking for air-con are automatically offered a 'VIP' room, which usually comes with air-con, hot water, fridge and TV and is about twice the price of a regular air-con room. The cheapest hotels may have their names posted in Thai and Chinese only, but you will learn how to find and identify them with experience. Many of these hotels have restaurants downstairs; if they don't, there are usually restaurants and noodle shops nearby.

Some Chinese-Thai hotels may double as brothels; the perpetual traffic in and out can be a bit noisy but is generally bearable. Unaccompanied males are often asked if they want female companionship when checking into inexpensive hotels. Even certain middle-class (by Thai standards) hotels are reserved for the 'salesman' crowd, meaning travelling Thai businessmen who frequently expect extra night-time services. Foreign women are usually left alone.

Tourist-Class, Business & Luxury Hotels

These are found only in the main tourist and business destinations: Bangkok, Pattaya, Cha-am, Hua Hin, Ko Pha-Ngan, Ko Samui, Phuket, Songkhla, Hat Yai, and a sprinkling of large provincial capitals such as Chumphon and Surat Thani. Prices start

at around 600B outside Bangkok and proceed to 2000B or more – genuine tourist-class hotels in Bangkok start at 1000B or so and go to 2500B for standard rooms, and up to 5000B or 10,000B for a suite. These will all have air-con, TV, Western-style toilets and restaurants.

Hotels in the provinces tend to cost around 30% less than Bangkok hotels, even in Pattaya and Phuket. Tariffs of around 800B to 1500B usually buy the above-mentioned amenities, plus a pool, while anything over 1500B might include additional restaurants and recreational facilities. The most exclusive places, such as Phuket's Amanpuri, charge as much as 15,000B for their more luxurious quarters. Virtually all beach and island destinations apply high season surcharges – anywhere from 15% to 50% – from around mid-December to mid-March. Added to this is a 7% government tax on hotels, and most establishments will include an extra service charge of 10%.

In addition to the reputable international hotel chains of Hyatt, Sheraton, Accor, Hilton and Westin, Thailand has several respectable home-grown chains, including Dusit, Amari and Royal Garden.

Resorts

In most countries 'resort' refers to hotels that offer substantial recreational facilities (eg, tennis, golf, swimming, sailing etc) in addition to high-class accommodation and dining. In Thai hotel lingo, however, the term simply refers to any hotel that isn't located in an urban area. Hence a few thatched beach huts or a cluster of bungalows in a forest may be called a resort. Several places in Thailand fully deserve the name under any definition – but it pays to look into the facilities before making a reservation.

Discounts Discounts of 30% to 50% for hotels costing 1000B or more per night can easily be obtained through many Thai travel agencies. At Bangkok international airport, in the arrival halls of both the international and domestic terminals, the Thai Hotels Association (THA) desk can also arrange discounts. If you are holding Thai International

Airways tickets (THAI), the airline can also arrange a substantial discount.

Temple Lodgings

If you are a Buddhist or can behave like one, you may be able to stay overnight in some temples for a small donation. Facilities are very basic, though, and early rising is expected. Temple lodgings are usually for men only, unless the wát has a place for lay women to stay. Neat, clean dress and a basic knowledge of Thai etiquette are mandatory.

FOOD

In a survey that polled 1450 travel agencies in 26 countries, Thailand ranked fourth (after France, Italy and Hong Kong) in the excellence of cuisine. Still, some people take to the food in Thailand immediately while others don't; Thai dishes can be pungent and spicy. Lots of garlic and chillies are used, especially *phrík khîi nuu* (literally, mouse-shit peppers – these are the small torpedo-shaped devils that can be pushed aside if you are timid about red-hot curries). Almost all Thai food is cooked with fresh ingredients, including vegetables, fish, poultry, pork and some beef. Of course, in coastal Thailand seafood predominates. Plenty of lime juice, lemon grass and fresh coriander are added to give the food its characteristic tang, and fish sauce *(náam plaa,* generally made from anchovies) or shrimp paste *(kà-pì)* to make it salty.

Other common seasonings include galanga root *(khàa),* black pepper, three kinds of basil, ground peanuts (more often a condiment), tamarind juice *(náam mákhǎam),* ginger *(khǐng)* and coconut milk *(kà-thí).* The Thais eat a lot of what could be called Chinese food, which is generally, but not always, less spicy.

Rice *(khâo)* is eaten with most meals; 'to eat' in Thai is literally 'eat rice' *(kin khâo).* Thais can be very picky about their rice, insisting on the right temperature and cooking times. Ordinary white rice is called *khâo jâo* and there are many varieties and grades. The finest quality Thai rice is known as *khâo hǎwm máli* (jasmine fragrant rice) for its sweet, inviting smell when cooked. 'Sticky'

Fresh from the Sea

Thailand has a well-deserved reputation for fine seafood cuisine, which many gourmets rank among the world's best. The Thais consume more protein via fish than from any other source. With two lengthy seacoasts from which to harvest marine food products, plus an intricate spice pantry that draws from indigenous Indian and Chinese cooking traditions, the menu possibilities are virtually limitless.

Thai chefs are masters at employing quick-cooking techniques to maintain the delicate flavours of fresh seafood. Shrimp and crab are year-round favourites no matter how far inland one wanders; spiny lobster is abundant along the Andaman Coast. Other common fruits of the sea include cuttlefish, oysters, cockles, sea perch, kingfish, shark and pompano.

Thais seem to have a particular genius for preparing molluscs such as shrimp, lobster, mussels and squid so that they remain tender and succulent – no easy task when the difference between undercooking and overcooking is often only a matter of seconds. The liberal use of lime juice, fresh coriander leaf and preserved Chinese plums eliminates or tempers the 'fishy' taste many Westerners object to.

Dipping sauces *(náam jîm)* served in small saucers with Thai seafood can be very simple or very intricate. One of the most typical sauces combines salty *náam plaa* (a thin sauce made from anchovies), tangy *náam mánao* (lime juice), plenty of fresh minced *kràtiam* (garlic), a little *náam-taan* (sugar) and a healthy portion of fresh sliced *phrík* (chillies).

See the Language chapter at the end of this book for a glossary of seafood terms.

Joe Cummings

or glutinous rice *(khâo nǐaw),* a staple in Northern and North-Eastern Thailand, is sometimes found in other regions. A few vegetarian or health-oriented restaurants will also offer *khâo kâwng,* semi-polished brown rice.

What to Eat

Thai food is served with a variety of condiments and sauces, including ground red pepper *(phrík pòn)*, ground peanuts *(thùa pòn)*, vinegar with sliced chillies *(náam sôm phrík)*, fish sauce with chillies *(náam plaa phrík)*, a spicy orange-red sauce called *náam phrík sǐi raachaa* (from coastal Si Racha, of course) and any number of dipping sauces *(náam jîm)* for particular dishes. Soy sauce *(náam sii-íu)* can be requested, though this is normally used as a condiment for Chinese food only.

Except for 'rice plates' and noodle dishes, Thai meals are usually ordered family style, ie, two or more people order together and share the different dishes. Traditionally, the party orders one of each kind of dish, eg, one chicken, one fish, one soup etc. One dish is generally large enough for two people. One or two extras may be ordered for a large party. If you eat at a Thai restaurant alone and order one of these 'entrees', you had better be hungry or know enough Thai to order a small portion. This latter alternative is not really acceptable socially; Thais generally consider eating alone in a restaurant unusual – but then as a faràng you're an exception anyway.

A cheaper alternative is to order dishes 'over rice' *(râat khâo)*. Curry *(kaeng)* over rice is called *khâo kaeng*; in a standard curry shop khâo kaeng is only 10B to 20B a plate.

Another category of Thai food is called *kàp klâem* – dishes meant to be eaten while drinking alcoholic beverages. On some menus these are translated as 'snacks' or 'appetisers'. Typical kàp klâem include *thùa thâwt* (fried peanuts), *kài sǎam yàang* (literally, three kinds of chicken; a plate of chopped ginger, peanuts, mouse-shit peppers and bits of lime – to be mixed and eaten by hand) and various kinds of *yam*, Thai-style salads made with lots of chillies and lime juice.

To end a meal with something sweet, the Thais overwhelmingly prefer to nibble from the country's seemingly infinite variety of tropical fruits. Thai pineapples, available year-round, are among the world's sweetest and juiciest. Bananas come in over 20 varieties, from the tiny, slender 'princess fingernail' bananas (eaten by the bunch) to the

pendulous 'fragrant' bananas more familiar in the West. Rambutan – a succulent grape-like orb surrounded by a thick, soft hull with bright red tendrils poking in all directions – quickly becomes a favourite with many visitors. Definitely an acquired taste is the large, spiky durian fruit that is in season only a couple of months a year. Protected by a formidable, mace-like exterior, the slippery yellow segments inside the fruit exude a musky odour that has been described as a cross between peaches and onions. Aficionados claim that if you can get past the smell, you're more than amply rewarded by a rich, toothsome flavour that has earned the durian its 'king of fruits' reputation in Asia.

Where to Eat

Many smaller restaurants and food stalls do not have menus, so it is worthwhile memorising a standard repertoire of dishes. Most provinces have their own local specialities in addition to the standards, and you might try asking for 'whatever is good', allowing the proprietors to choose for you. Of course, you might get stuck with a large bill this way, but with a little practice in Thai social relations you may get some very pleasing results.

The most economical places to eat – and the most dependable – are noodle shops (ráan kǔaytǐaw), curry-and-rice shops (ráan khâo kaeng) and night markets (tàlàat tôh rûng). Most towns and villages have at least one night market and a few noodle and/or curry shops. Curry shops are generally open for breakfast and lunch only, and are a cheap source of nutritious food.

Another common eatery in larger cities is the ráan khâo tôm (literally, boiled-rice shop), a type of Chinese-Thai restaurant that offers not just boiled-rice soups (khâo tôm) but an assortment of aahǎan taam sàng (food made to order). In the better places, cooks pride themselves in being able to fix any Thai or Chinese dish you name. One attraction of the ráan khâo tôm is that they tend to stay open late – some are even open 24 hours.

In larger cities you may also come across 'food centres' where hawkers serve their specialities from rented stalls in a large room. These are often attached to department stores. You typically purchase a meal via a coupon system – you buy, say, 50B worth of paper coupons printed in denominations of 5B, 10B, 20B etc, and then exchange these coupons for dishes you select.

The Green Bowl

Sponsored by Shell, the famous oil company, Thai food critic Thanad Sri bestows his favourite dishes at restaurants around the country with the 'Shell Chuan Chim' (Shell's Invitation to Taste) designation. Look for a sign bearing the outline of a green bowl next to the familiar Shell symbol posted somewhere on the outside of the restaurant. Though such a designation usually means the food is good at such places, it's not a foolproof guarantee; some restaurants hang onto their Chuan Chim signs long after the kitchen has lowered its standards.

Joe Cummings

Vegetarian

Visitors who wish to avoid eating meat while in Thailand can be accommodated with some effort. Vegetarian restaurants are increasing in number throughout the country, thanks largely to Bangkok's ex-Governor Chamlong Srimuang, whose strict vegetarianism has inspired a nonprofit chain of vegetarian restaurants (ráan aahǎan mangsàwírát) in Bangkok and several provincial capitals. Many of these are sponsored by the Asoke Foundation, an ascetic (some would say heretic) Theravada Buddhist sect that finds justification for vegetarianism in the Buddhist sutras. Look for the green sign out the front featuring large Thai numerals – each restaurant is numbered according to the order in which it was established. The food at these restaurants is usually served buffet style and is very inexpensive – typically 10B to 15B per dish. Most are only open from 7am or 8am until noon.

Other easy, though less widespread, sources of vegetarian meals are Indian restaurants, which usually feature a vegetarian section on the menu. Currently Indian restaurants are most prevalent in Bangkok, Pattaya and Phuket's Patong beach. Chinese restaurants are also a good bet since many Chinese Buddhists eat vegetarian food during Buddhist festivals, especially in Southern Thailand.

More often than not, however, vegetarians are left to their own devices at the average Thai restaurant. In Thai the magic words are phǒm kin jeh (for men) or dì-chǎn kin jeh (women). Like other Thai phrases, getting the tones right makes all the difference – the key word, jeh, should rhyme with the English 'jay'. Loosely translated this phrase means 'I eat only vegetarian food'. It might also be necessary to follow with the explanation phǒm/dì-chǎn kin tàe phàk, 'I eat only vegetables'. Don't worry – this won't be interpreted to mean no rice, herbs or fruit. For other useful food phrases, see the Food Glossary in the Language chapter.

In Thai culture, 'brown' (unpolished) rice (khâo kâwng) is said to be reserved for pigs and prisoners! Look for it at the local feed store or in the less common natural-food shops.

Those interested in tapping into the Thai vegetarian movement can phone the Vegetarian Society of Bangkok (☎ 022 724 282) for information. The society usually meets monthly to share a vegetarian feast, swap recipes and discuss the whys and wherefores of vegetarianism.

DRINKS
Nonalcoholic Drinks

Fruit Juices & Shakes The incredible variety of fruits in Thailand means an abundance of nutritious juices and shakes. The all-purpose term for fruit juice is *náam phŏn-lá-mái*. Put *náam* ('water' or 'juice') together with the name of any fruit and you can get anything from *náam sôm* (orange juice) to *náam taeng moh* (watermelon juice). When an extractor is used, fruit juices may be called *náam khán* ('squeezed juice', eg, *náam sàppàrót khán*, 'pineapple juice'). When mixed in a blender with ice the result is *nàam pon* (literally, mixed juice) as in *nàam málákaw pon*, a papaya smoothie or shake. Night markets will often have vendors specialising in juices and shakes.

Thais prefer to drink most fruit juices with a little salt mixed in. Unless a vendor is used to serving faràng, your fruit juice or shake will come slightly salted. If you prefer unsalted fruit juices, specify *mâi sài kleua* (without salt).

Sugar-cane juice *(náam âwy)* is a Thai favourite and a very refreshing accompaniment to curry and rice plates. Many small restaurants or food stalls that don't offer any other juices will have a supply of freshly squeezed náam âwy on hand.

Coffee Over the last 15 years or so, Nescafe and other instant coffee producers have sadly made deep inroads into Thai coffee culture at the expense of freshly ground coffee. The typical Thai restaurant – especially those in hotels, guesthouses and other tourist-oriented establishments – serves instant coffee with packets of artificial, non-dairy creamer on the side. Upmarket hotels and coffee shops sometimes also offer filtered and espresso coffees at premium prices.

Traditionally, coffee in Thailand is locally grown (mostly in hilly areas of Northern and Southern Thailand), roasted by wholesalers, ground by vendors and filtered just before serving. Thai-grown coffee may not be as full and rich-tasting as gourmet Sumatran, Jamaican or Kona beans but it's still considerably tastier than Nescafe or other instant coffees. To get real Thai coffee ask for *kaafae thăng* (literally, bag coffee), which refers to the traditional method of preparing a cup of coffee by filtering hot water through a bag-shaped cloth filter. Thailand's best coffee of this sort is served in Hokkien-style cafes in the southern provinces. Elsewhere in Thailand, outdoor morning markets are the best place to find kaafae thăng. The usual kaafae thăng is served mixed with sugar and sweetened condensed milk – if you don't want either, ask for *kaafae dam* (black coffee) *mâi sài náam-taan* (without sugar). Kaafae thăng is often served in a glass instead of a ceramic cup – to pick up a glass of hot coffee, grasp it along the top rim.

Tea Both Indian-style (black) and Chinese-style (green or semi-cured) teas are commonly served in Thailand. The latter predominates in Chinese restaurants and is the usual ingredient in *náam chaa*, the weak, often lukewarm tea-water traditionally served free in Thai restaurants. The aluminium teapots seen on every table in the average restaurant are filled with náam chaa; ask for an empty glass *(kâew plào)* and you can drink as much as you like at no charge. For iced náam chaa ask for a glass of ice (usually 1B) and pour your own; for fresh, undiluted Chinese tea request *chaa jiin*.

Black tea, both imported and Thai-grown, is usually available in the same restaurants or food stalls that serve real coffee. An order of *chaa ráwn* (hot tea) almost always results in a cup (or glass) of black tea with sugar and condensed milk. As with coffee you must specify as you order if you want tea without milk and/or sugar.

A favourite thirst quencher, especially for those adventuring among the more chilli-laden dishes, is Thai iced tea. This frothy orange potion – a blend of Thai-grown tea seasoned with ground tamarind seed and mixed with a healthy dollop of palm sugar and condensed milk over ice – is extremely refreshing.

Water Purified water is simply called *náam dèum* (drinking water), whether boiled or filtered. *All* water offered to customers in restaurants or to guests in an office or home will be purified, so you needn't fret about the safety of taking a sip (for more information on water safety, see the Health section earlier in this chapter). In restaurants you can ask for *náam plào* (plain water), which is always either boiled or taken from a purified source; it's served by the glass at no charge or you can order by the bottle. A bottle of carbonated water (soda) costs about the same as a bottle of plain purified water, but the bottles are smaller.

Alcoholic Drinks

Drinking in Thailand can be expensive in relation to the cost of other consumer activities. The Thai government has placed increasingly heavy taxes on liquor and beer, so that it accounts for about 30B out of the 60B to 90B that you pay for a large beer. One large bottle (630ml) of Singha beer costs more than half the minimum daily wage of a Bangkok worker.

Beer Three brands of beer are brewed in Thailand by Thai-owned breweries: Singha, Kloster and Leo. Singha (pronounced 'sing' by the Thais) is by far the most common beer in Thailand. Singha is a strong, hoppy-tasting brew thought by some to be the best beer produced in South or South-East Asia. Singha is sometimes available on tap in pubs and restaurants.

Kloster is quite a bit smoother and lighter than Singha and costs about 5B more per bottle, but it is a good-tasting brew often favoured by Western visitors and expats.

Boon Rawd Breweries, makers of Singha, also produce a lighter beer called Singha

Gold that comes only in small bottles; most people seem to prefer either Kloster or regular Singha to Singha Gold, which is a little on the bland side. Singha's canned 'draft beer' is better – if you like cans.

Carlsberg, jointly owned by Danish and Thai interests, has used an aggressive promotion campaign (backed by the makers of Mekong whisky) to grab around 25% of the Thai market in only a few years. The company adjusted its recipe to come closer to Singha's 6% alcohol content. It has a smoother finish than Singha, and is preferred by some drinkers during spells of hot weather.

Singha retaliated with advertisements suggesting that drinking Carlsberg was unpatriotic. Carlsberg responded by creating 'Beer Chang' (Elephant Beer), which matches the hoppy taste of Singha but ratchets the alcohol content up to 7%. Beer Chang has managed to gain an impressive market share – mainly because it costs significantly less than Singha. Predictably, the next skirmish in the beer war has been set off by the arrival of Boon Rawd's cheaper brand, Leo. Sporting a leopard label, Leo costs only slightly more than Chang but is similarly high in alcohol, with a slightly sweet, malty flavour.

Dutch giant Heineken opened a plant in Nonthaburi in 1995, which is popular with upwardly-mobile Thais. Other beers brewed in Thailand are Black Tiger, Mittweida and Amstel lager.

The Thai word for beer is *bia*. Draught beer is *bia sòt* (literally, 'fresh beer').

Spirits The more adventurous can tipple the Thai workingman's drink, Mekong brand whisky. Distilled from rice at a strength of around 70 proof (35% alcohol), Mekong goes well mixed with any number of fruit juices, with Coke or served in the manner preferred by traditionally minded Thai whisky drinkers – swirled with soda water (one measure of Mekong to two measures of soda) and a wedge of lime over ice. Mekong (pronounced *Mâe-khǒng*) costs around 120B for a large bottle *(klom)* or 60B for the flask-sized bottle *(baen)*.

SODA WATER
ICE
WHISKY
MW

More expensive Thai spirits appealing to wannabe Johnnie Walker drinkers include Blue Eagle whisky, Black Cat whisky and Spey Royal whisky, scotch-style whiskies with 40% alcohol. One company in Thailand produces a true rum, that is, a distilled liquor made from sugar cane, called Sang Thip (formerly Sang Som). Alcohol content is 40% and the stock is supposedly aged. Sang Thip costs several baht more than the rice whiskies, but for those who find Mekong and the like unpalatable, it is an alternative worth trying.

Other Liquor A cheaper alternative to whisky is *lâo khǎo* (white liquor) of which there are two broad categories: legal and contraband. The legal kind is generally made from sticky rice and is produced for regional consumption. Like Mekong and its competitors, it is 35% alcohol, but sells for 50B to 60B per klom, or roughly half the price. It tastes sweet and raw and is much more aromatic than the amber stuff – no amount of mixer will disguise the distinctive taste.

The illegal kinds are made from various agricultural products including sugar palm sap, coconut milk, sugar cane, taro and rice. Alcohol content may vary from as little as 10% or 12% to as much as 95%. Generally this *lâo thèuan* (jungle liquor) is weaker in

the South and stronger in the North and North-East. This is the drink of choice for the many Thais who can't afford to pay the government's heavy liquor taxes; prices vary but 20B worth of the stronger concoctions will intoxicate three or four people. These types of home-brew or moonshine are generally taken straight with water as a chaser. In smaller towns, almost every garage-type restaurant (except, of course, Muslim restaurants) keeps some under the counter for sale. Sometimes roots and herbs are added to jungle liquor to enhance the flavour and colour.

Herbal liquors are somewhat fashionable throughout the country and can be found at roadside vendors, small pubs and in a few guesthouses. These liquors are made by soaking various herbs, roots, seeds, fruit and bark in lâo khǎo to produce a range of concoctions called *lâo yaa dawng*. Many of the yaa dawng preparations are purported to have specific health-enhancing or aphrodisiac qualities. Some of them taste fabulous while others are rank.

Wine Thais are becoming increasingly interested in wine-drinking, but still manage to average a minuscule consumption of one glass per capita per year. Various enterprises have attempted to produce wine in Thailand, most often with disastrous results. However, a winery called Chateau de Loei, near Phu Reua in Loei Province is producing a decent Thai wine. Dr Chaiyut Karnasuta, the owner, spent a lot of money and time studying Western wine-making methods, and his first vintage, a Chenin Blanc, is a quite drinkable wine. It's available at many of the finer restaurants in Bangkok and Phuket.

Imported wines from France, Italy, California, Australia and Chile are also widely available in Western restaurants and supermarkets. If you're a wine connoisseur, note that Thailand's best restaurant wine collection can be found at The Boathouse Wine & Grill on Phuket (see Hat Kata in the Phuket Beaches & Nearby Islands section of the Northern Andaman Coast chapter for details).

ENTERTAINMENT
Bars & Member Clubs

Urban Thais are night people and every town of any size has a selection of nightspots. For the most part they are male-dominated, though the situation is changing rapidly in the larger cities, where young couples are increasingly seen in bars. Of the many types of bars, one of the most popular continues to be the 'old West' style, patterned after Thai fantasies of the 19th-century American West – lots of wood and cowboy paraphernalia.

Another favoured style is the 'Thai classic' pub, which is typically decorated with old black-and-white photos of Thai kings Rama VI and Rama VII, along with Thai antiques from Northern and Central Thailand. The old-West and Thai-classic nightspots are cosy, friendly and popular with couples as well as singles. In beach areas, 'reggae bars', with lots of recorded Marley and Tosh, continue to multiply.

The go-go bars seen in lurid photos published by the Western media are limited to a few areas in Bangkok, Pattaya and Phuket's Patong beach. These are bars in which girls (or guys) typically wear swimsuits or other scant apparel with a number pinned to them. In some bars they dance to recorded music on a narrow raised stage. To some visitors it's pathetic, to others paradise. 'Member clubs,' similar to old-style Playboy clubs, provide a slinky, James Bond atmosphere of feigned elegance and savoir-faire in which women clad in long gowns or tight skirts entertain suited men in softly lit sofa groups. Private rooms are also available. A couple of drinks and a chat with the hostesses typically costs around US$50, including membership. These clubs are thinly scattered across the Soi Lang Suan and Th Sukhumvit areas in Bangkok.

All bars and clubs that don't feature live music or dancing are required to close by 1am. Many get around the law by bribing local police.

Discos

Discos are popular in larger cities; outside Bangkok they're mostly attached to tourist or luxury hotels. The main disco clientele is Thai, though foreigners are welcome. Some provincial discos retain female staff as professional dance partners for men, but for the most part discos are considered fairly respectable nightspots for couples. Ko Samui's Chaweng and Phuket's Patong have the most varied discos and dance venues of all the beaches.

Thai law permits discos and dance clubs to stay open till 2am but in some places like Patong, this is only intermittently enforced. During the full-moon parties on Hat Rin, Ko Pha-Ngan, beach clubs stay open all night and till around 11am the following day.

Cinemas

Movie theatres are found in towns and cities across the country. Typical programs include Hong Kong and US shoot-em-ups mixed with Thai comedies and romances geared toward teenagers. Violent action pictures are always a big draw; as a rule of thumb, the smaller the town, the more violent the film offerings. English-language films are only shown with their original soundtracks in a handful of theatres in Bangkok, Phuket and Hat Yai; elsewhere all foreign films are dubbed in Thai. Tickets range from 70B to 200B. Every film in Thailand begins with the playing of the royal anthem, accompanied by projected pictures of the royal family. Viewers are expected to stand during the anthem.

Coffee Houses

Aside from the Western-style cafe, which is increasingly popular in Bangkok, there are two other kinds of cafes or coffee shops in Thailand. One is the traditional Hokkien-style coffee shop (ráan kaa-fae), where thick, black, filtered coffee is served in simple, casual surroundings. These coffee shops are mostly found in the Chinese quarters of Southern Thai provincial capitals. Frequented mostly by older Thai and Chinese men, they offer a place to read the newspaper, sip coffee and gossip about neighbours and politics. The other type, called kaa-feh (cafe) or 'coffee house', is more akin to a nightclub, where Thai men consort with a variety of Thai female hostesses. This is the Thai counterpart to faràng go-go bars, except girls wear dresses instead of swimsuits.

A variation on this theme is the 'singsong' cafe in which a succession of female singers front a live band. Small groups of men sit at tables ogling the girls while putting away prodigious amounts of whisky. For the price of a few house drinks, the men can invite one of the singers to sit at their table for a while. Some of the singers work double shifts as part-time mistresses, others limit their services to singing and pouring drinks.

Cafes that feature live music are permitted to stay open till 2am.

SPECTATOR SPORTS
Muay Thai (Thai Boxing)

Almost anything goes in this martial sport, both in the ring and in the stands. If you don't mind the violence (in the ring), a *muay thai* match is worth attending for the pure spectacle – the wild musical accompaniment, the ceremonial beginning of each match and the frenzied betting around the stadium. Thai boxing is also telecast on Thai TV every Saturday afternoon; if you're wondering where everyone is, they're probably inside watching the national sport.

History Most of what is known about the history of muay thai comes from Burmese accounts of warfare between Myanmar and Thailand during the 15th and 16th centuries. The earliest reference (AD 1411) mentions a ferocious style of unarmed combat that decided the fate of Thai kings. A later description tells how Nai Khanom Tom, Thailand's first famous boxer and a prisoner of war in Myanmar, gained his freedom by roundly defeating a dozen Burmese warriors before the Burmese court.

To this day, many martial-art aficionados consider Thai boxing the ultimate in hand-to-hand fighting. Hong Kong, China, Singapore, Taiwan, Korea, Japan, the USA, Netherlands, Germany and France have all sent their best challengers and none have

Thai boxing is an extremely popular spectator sport; especially on Sundays when you may find the streets deserted due to the weekly telecast on Channel 7.

been able to defeat top-ranked Thai boxers. On one famous occasion, Hong Kong's top five Kung Fu masters were all dispatched in less than 6½ minutes, all knock outs.

Modern Muay Thai The high incidence of death and physical injury led the Thai government to institute a ban on muay thai in the 1920s, but in the 1930s the sport was revived under a modern set of regulations based on the international Queensberry rules. Bouts were limited to five three-minute rounds separated by two-minute breaks. Contestants had to wear international-style gloves and trunks (always either red or blue), and their feet were taped – to this day no shoes are worn.

In spite of these concessions to safety, today all surfaces of the body are still considered fair targets and any part of the body, except the head, may be used to strike an opponent. Common blows include high kicks to the neck, elbow thrusts to the face and head, knee hooks to the ribs and low crescent kicks to the calf. A contestant may even grasp an opponent's head between his hands and pull it down to meet an upward knee thrust. Punching is considered the weakest of all blows and kicking merely a way to 'soften up' one's opponent; knee and elbow strikes are decisive in most matches.

The woven headbands and armbands worn into the ring by fighters are sacred ornaments that bestow blessings and divine protection; the headband is removed but the armband, which actually contains a small Buddha image, is worn throughout the match.

Musicians play throughout the match and the volume and tempo of the music rises and falls with the events in the ring. As muay thai has become more popular among Westerners (both spectators and participants), an increasing number of bouts are staged for tourists in places like Pattaya, Phuket, Ko Samui and Ko Phi-Phi. In these matches, the action may be genuine but the judging below par. Dozens of authentic matches are held every day of the year at the major Bangkok stadiums and in the provinces.

Meanwhile in some areas of the country a pre-1920s version of muay thai still exists. In pockets of Southern Thailand, fighters practising *muay kàtchii* still bind their hands in hemp, and a more localised southern style in Chaiya known as *muay chaiya* uses the elbows and forearms to good advantage.

International Muay Thai The World Muay Thai Council (WMTC), a relatively new organisation sanctioned by Thailand's Sports Authority and headquartered at the Thai Army Officers Club in Bangkok, organises international muay thai bouts in Bangkok stadiums and elsewhere. The WMTC tracks training facilities as well as ranked fighters, and is the first entity to match champs from all muay thai camps. So far the largest number of WMTC-affiliated muay thai training facilities is found in the USA, followed by Australia, the Netherlands, Canada, Japan, France and the UK.

International participation portends a new era for muay thai; some observers think it will upgrade the martial art by shifting the emphasis from ringside betting to fighting techniques.

Takraw

Takraw *(tàkrâw)* sometimes called Siamese football in old English texts, refers to a game in which a woven rattan (or sometimes plastic) ball about 12cm in diameter is kicked around. The rattan ball is called a *lûuk tàkrâw*. Takraw is also popular in several neighbouring countries; it was originally introduced to the South-East Asian Games by Thailand, and international championships tend to alternate between the Thais and Malays. The traditional way to play tàkrâw in Thailand is for players to stand in a circle (the size of the circle depends on the number of players) and simply try to keep the ball airborne by kicking it soccer style. Points are scored for style, difficulty and variety of kicking manoeuvres.

A popular variation on tàkrâw – and the one used in intramural or international competitions – is played with a volleyball net, using all the same rules as volleyball except only the feet and head are permitted to touch the ball. It's amazing to see the players perform aerial pirouettes, and spike the ball over the net with their feet. Another variation has players kicking the ball into a hoop 4.5m above the ground – basketball with feet, but without a backboard! It can be seen in smaller towns and rural areas.

Buffalo Fighting

Thais have always had a penchant for getting animals to do battle – cocks, fish, even rhinoceros beetles – in order to satisfy their desire to gamble. Buffaloes are no exception. Despite the modernisation that tourism has brought to Ko Samui, locals have yet to lose their enthusiasm for this rustic spectacle.

Water buffaloes are chosen for the ring at a young age. Any animal displaying a temper is a good candidate, as buffaloes are normally quite docile. Matches are held monthly at any one of half a dozen crude rings – usually no more than a level, treeless field. On the scheduled afternoon a crowd gathers early to appraise the six buffaloes that will pair off in one of three matches. The muscles in the buffaloes' legs and chest are examined, and close attention is paid to the thickness and curvature of the horns. Opposing buffaloes always come from different villages to foil attempts to rig matches.

The match begins when two buffaloes are released into the ring. The Thai term for buffalo fighting is *chon wua* (literally, crash cows) and it usually takes little time for the enraged animals to charge each other and collide head to head with a loud wallop. Often the buffaloes then lock horns and try to push each other around the ring, but it's usually only a few minutes before one of the bruised bovines turns tail and runs. The winning buffalo is cheered loudly by those punters that it's unwittingly enriched.

SHOPPING

Many bargains await you in Thailand if you can carry them home. Always haggle to get the best price, except in department stores. And don't go shopping in the company of touts, tour guides or friendly strangers as they will inevitably – no matter what they say – take a commission on anything you buy, thus driving prices up.

Antiques

Real antiques cannot be taken out of Thailand without a permit from the Fine Arts Department. No Buddha image, new or old, may be exported without permission – again refer to the Fine Arts Department, or in some cases, the Department of Religious Affairs, under the Ministry of Education. Too many private collectors smuggling and hoarding Siamese art (Buddhas in particular) around the world have led to strict controls. See the Customs section earlier in this chapter for more information on the export of art objects and antiques.

Chinese and Thai antiques were traditionally sold in two areas of Bangkok's Chinatown: Wang Burapha and Nakhon Kasem. However, the past few years have seen most of the antique shops replaced by motorcycle and auto parts stores. Some antiques (and many fakes) are sold at the Weekend Market in Chatuchak Park. The River City Shopping Complex near Tha Si Praya is filled with high-end antiques shops. Not such a great place to shop but a fascinating glimpse at what's on the Asian antiquities market. More

than a few of the Buddha images here have been pilfered from temples in Myanmar, Laos and Cambodia – but the best pieces of ill-gotten art are said to be kept in warehouses in nearby Chinatown.

Books

Bangkok probably has the largest selection of English-language books and bookshops in South-East Asia. The principal chains are Asia Books (headquarters on Th Sukhumvit near Soi 15) and DK Book House (Siam Square); each has branches in half a dozen locations around Bangkok as well as in Hat Yai and Phuket. Asia and DK offer a wide variety of fiction and periodicals as well as books on Asia. The bookshops in Phuket, Krabi and Phang-Nga also stock English-language reading material. See the Bookshop entries under the relevant cities for further details.

Some of Thailand's larger tourist hotels also have bookshops with English-language books and periodicals.

Ceramics

Many kinds of hand-thrown pottery, old and new, are available throughout the kingdom. Most well known are the greenish Sangkhalok or Thai celadon products from the Sukhothai-Si Satchanalai area and Central Thailand's *bencharong* (five-colour) style. The latter is based on Chinese patterns, while the former is a Thai original that has been imitated throughout China and South-East Asia. Rough, unglazed pottery from the North and North-East can also be very appealing.

Clothing

Tailor-made and ready-made clothes are relatively inexpensive. If you're not particular about style you could pick up an entire wardrobe of clothes at one of Bangkok's many street markets.

You're more likely to get a good fit if you resort to a tailor but be wary of the quickie 24-hour tailor shops; the clothing is often made of inferior fabric or the poor tailoring means the arms start falling off after three weeks wear. It's best to ask Thai or long-time foreign residents for a tailor recommendation and then go for two or three fittings.

Hill-Tribe Crafts

Interesting embroidery, clothing, bags and jewellery from the North can be bought in Bangkok at Narayan Phand, Th Lan Luang, at branches of the Queen's Hillcrafts Foundation, at Chatuchak Weekend Market and at various tourist shops around town. See the Shopping section in the Bangkok chapter for more suggestions. Hill-tribe crafts are almost impossible to find in the South.

Jewellery

Thailand is the world's largest exporter of gems and ornaments, rivalled only by India and Sri Lanka. The International Colorstones Association (ICA) relocated from Los Angeles to Bangkok's Charn Issara Tower several years ago, and the World Federation of Diamond Bourses (WFDB) has established a bourse in Bangkok – both events recognise that Thailand has become the world trade and production centre for precious stones. The biggest importers of Thai jewellery are the USA, Japan and Switzerland. Although rough-stone sources in Thailand have decreased dramatically, stones are now imported from Australia, Sri Lanka, Myanmar, Laos and other countries to be cut, polished and traded here.

There are over 30 diamond-cutting houses in Bangkok alone. One of the results of this remarkable growth of the gem industry – in Thailand the gem trade has increased nearly 10% every year for the last 20 years – is that the prices are rising rapidly. If you know what you are doing you can make some really good buys in both unset gems and finished jewellery. Gold ornaments are sold at a good rate as labour costs are low. The best bargains in gems are jade, rubies and sapphires. Buy from reputable dealers only, unless you're a gemologist.

Warning Be wary of special 'deals' that are offered for one day only or that set you up as a 'courier' in which you're promised big money. Many travellers end up losing big. Shop around and don't be hasty. Remember: there's no such thing as a 'government sale' or a 'factory price' at a gem or jewellery shop; the Thai government does not own or manage any gem or jewellery shops.

Information on gem scams can be found on the Thai Tourist Police Web site **W** www.police.go.th/touristpolice/. If you think you have been scammed, contact the local branch of the Tourist Police or call their country-wide number ☎ 1155.

Lacquerware

Thailand produces some good lacquerware, much of it made and sold along the northern Burmese border. It's available in Bangkok at the shops named in the earlier Hill-Tribe Crafts entry, and at some tourist shops in Phuket.

Styles available today originated in 11th-century Chiang Mai; in 1558 Myanmar's King Bayinnaung captured a number of Chiang Mai lacquer artisans and brought them to Bago in central Myanmar to establish the incised lacquerware tradition. Lacquer comes from the *Melanorrhea usitata* tree (not to be confused with *lac*, which comes from an insect), and in its most basic form is mixed with paddy-husk ash to form a light, flexible, waterproof coating over bamboo frames.

From start to finish it can take five or six months to produce a high-quality piece of lacquerware, which may have as many as five colours. Flexibility is one characteristic of good lacquerware. A top-quality bowl can have its rim squeezed together until the sides meet without suffering damage. The quality and precision of the engraving is another thing to look for.

Nielloware

This art came from Europe via Nakhon Si Thammarat and has been cultivated in Thailand for more than 700 years. Engraved silver is inlaid with niello – an alloy of lead, silver, copper and sulphur – to form striking black-and-silver jewellery designs. Nielloware is one of Thailand's best buys.

Textiles

Fabric is possibly the best all-round buy in Thailand. Thai silk is considered the best in the world – its coarse weave and soft texture means it is more easily dyed than harder, smoother silks, resulting in brighter colours and a unique lustre. Silk can be purchased in Bangkok and in provincial capitals throughout Thailand. Excellent and reasonably priced tailor shops can make your choice of fabric into almost any garment. A Thai silk suit should cost around 4500B to 6500B. Chinese silk is about half the price – 'washed' Chinese silk makes inexpensive, comfortable shirts or blouses. Cottons are also a good deal – common items like the phâakhamáa (short Thai-style sarong for men – reputed in Thailand to have over a hundred uses) and the phâasîn (the slightly larger female equivalent) make great tablecloths and curtains. Good ready-made cotton shirts are available, such as the *mâw hâwm* (Thai work shirt) and the *kúay hâeng* (Chinese-style shirt) – see Ko Yo in the South-Western Gulf Coast chapter for places to see cotton weaving.

Hat Yai is a big centre for trade in Thai cotton fabrics. Fairly nice batik *(paa-té)* is available in the South in patterns that are similar to batik found in Malaysia and Indonesia. Textiles from Northern and North-Eastern Thailand, including *mát-mìi* cloth, a thick cotton or silk fabric woven from tie-dyed threads, can often be found in larger markets throughout Thailand, including the South.

Other Crafts

Under Queen Sirikit's Supplementary Occupations & Related Techniques (Support) foundation, a number of regional crafts from around Thailand have been successfully revived. *Málaeng tháp* collages and sculptures are made by the artful cutting and assembling of the metallic, multi-coloured wings and carapaces of female wood-boring beetles *(Sternocera aequisignata)*, harvested after they die at the end of their reproductive cycle between July and September each year. Hailing mostly from the North and North-East, they can nonetheless be found in craft shops all over Thailand. For 'Damascene ware' *(Kraam)*, gold and silver wire is hammered into a cross-hatched steel surface to create exquisitely patterned bowls and boxes. Look

for them in more-upmarket Bangkok department stores and craft shops.

Yaan líphao is a type of intricately woven basket made from a hardy grass in Southern Thailand. Ever since the queen and other female members of the royal family began carrying delicate yaan líphao purses, they've been a Thai fashion staple. Basketry of this type is most easily found in the Southern provincial capitals, or in Bangkok shops specialising in regional handicrafts.

Fake or Pirated Goods

In Bangkok, Phuket and other tourist centres, there is black-market street trade in fake designer goods; particularly Benetton pants and sweaters, Lacoste (crocodile-logo) and Ralph Lauren polo shirts, Levi's jeans, and Rolex, Dunhill and Cartier watches. Tin-Tin T-shirts are also big. No-one pretends they're the real thing, at least not the vendors themselves. The European and American manufacturers are applying heavy pressure on the Asian governments involved to get this stuff off the street, but so far have met with little success. Members of the International Trademark Association claim that 24% of trademarked goods sold in Thailand are counterfeited or pirated.

In some cases foreign name brands are legally produced under licence in Thailand and are still good value. A pair of legally produced Levi's 501s, for example, typically costs US$10 from a Thai street vendor, and US$35 to US$45 in Levi's home town of San Francisco! Careful examination of the product usually reveals telltale characteristics that confirm or deny the item's authenticity.

Pre-recorded cassette tapes are another illegal bargain in Thailand. The tapes are 'pirated', that is, no royalties are paid to the copyright owners. Prices average 40B per cassette for amazingly up-to-date music.

At the time of writing it was becoming quite difficult to find pirated tapes anywhere in the country except on Bangkok's Th Khao San. Licensed Western-music tapes, when available, cost 90B to 110B each (average price 99B); Thai music tapes cost the same.

Getting There & Away

AIR

The expense of getting to Thailand per air kilometre varies quite a bit depending on your point of departure. However, you can take heart in the fact that Bangkok is one of the cheapest cities in the world to fly out of, due to the Thai government's loose restrictions on airfares and the close competition between airlines and travel agencies. The result is that with a little shopping around you can come up with some real bargains. If you can find a cheap one-way ticket to Bangkok, take it, because you are virtually guaranteed to find one of equal or lesser cost for the return trip once you get there.

From most places around the world your best bet will be budget, excursion or promotional fares – when speaking to airlines ask for the various fares in that order. Each carries its own set of restrictions and it's up to you to decide which works best in your case. Fares fluctuate, but in general they are cheaper from September to April (northern hemisphere) and from March to November (southern hemisphere).

Fares listed in this section should serve as a guideline – don't count on them staying this way (they may go down).

Airports & Airlines

Thailand has four international airports – in Bangkok, Chiang Mai, Phuket and Hat Yai. Chiang Rai and Sukhothai are both designated 'international', but at the time of writing they did not actually field any international flights. Krabi also fielded flights from Singapore and Medan, Malaysia, in the recent past, but at the time of writing the routes had been suspended.

Don Muang, directly north of Bangkok, is home to Bangkok International Airport, the busiest airport in South-East Asia in terms of scheduled arrivals and departures. A second, larger airport is intended to replace Don Muang at Nong Ngu Hao, 20km east of Bangkok in 2004.

Thai Airways International (THAI) dominates air traffic, but 80 other international airlines also fly in and out of Bangkok. Bangkok Airways flies to Phnom Penh from Bangkok and Pattaya, to Siem Reap (in Cambodia's Angkor region) from Bangkok, Sukhothai and Phuket, and to Singapore from Ko Samui.

See the Getting Around chapter for the locations of Thai and domestic airline offices and the Getting There & Away section of the Bangkok chapter for the Bangkok offices of all the international airlines.

For information on getting to/from the airport, see the Air section of the Getting Around chapter. THAI operates a free shuttle bus between the international and domestic terminals every 15 minutes between 6am and 11.20pm.

Buying Tickets

With a bit of research – ringing around travel agents, checking Internet sites, perusing the travel ads in newspapers – you can often get yourself a good travel deal. Start early as some of the cheapest tickets need to be bought well in advance and popular flights can sell out.

Full-time students and people under 26 years (under 30 in some countries) have access to better deals than other travellers. You have to show a document proving your date of birth or a valid International Student Identity Card (ISIC) when buying your ticket and boarding the plane.

Generally, there is nothing to be gained by buying a ticket direct from the airline. Discounted tickets are released to selected travel agents and specialist discount agencies, and these are usually the cheapest deals going.

One exception to this rule is the expanding number of 'no-frills' carriers, which mostly sell direct to travellers only. Unlike the 'full-service' airlines, no-frills carriers often make one-way tickets available at around half the return fare, meaning that it is

Air Travel Glossary

Alliances Many of the world's leading airlines are now intimately involved with each other, sharing everything from reservations systems and check-in to aircraft and frequent-flyer schemes. Opponents say that alliances restrict competition. Whatever the arguments, there is no doubt that big alliances are the way of the future.

Courier Fares Businesses often need to send urgent documents or freight securely and quickly. Courier companies hire people to accompany the package through customs and, in return, offer a discount ticket which is sometimes a bargain. However, you may have to surrender all your baggage allowance and take only carry-on luggage.

Fares Airlines traditionally offer 1st class (coded F), business class (coded J) and economy class (coded Y) tickets. These days there are so many promotional and discounted fares available that few passengers pay full fare.

Lost Tickets If you lose your airline ticket, an airline will usually treat it like a travellers cheque and, after inquiries, issue you with another one. Legally, however, an airline is entitled to treat it like cash and if you lose it then it's gone forever. Take very good care of your tickets.

Onward Tickets An entry requirement for many countries is that you have a ticket out of the country. If you're unsure of your next move, the easiest solution is to buy the cheapest onward ticket to a neighbouring country or a ticket from a reliable airline that can later be refunded if you do not use it.

Open-Jaw Tickets These are return tickets where you fly out to one place but return from another. If available, this can save you backtracking to your arrival point.

Overbooking Since every flight has some passengers who fail to show up, airlines often book more passengers than they have seats. Usually excess passengers make up for the no-shows, but occasionally somebody gets 'bumped' onto the next available flight. Guess who it is most likely to be? The passengers who check in late. If you do get 'bumped', you are normally offered some form of compensation.

Reconfirmation Some airlines require you to reconfirm your flight at least 72 hours prior to departure. Check your travel documents to see if this is the case.

Restrictions Discounted tickets often have various restrictions on them – such as needing to be paid for in advance and incurring a penalty to be altered or cancelled. Others are restrictions on the minimum and maximum period you must be away.

Round-the-World Tickets RTW tickets give you a limited period (usually a year) in which to circumnavigate the globe. You can go anywhere the carrying airlines go, as long as you don't backtrack. The number of stopovers or total number of separate flights is decided before you set off and they usually cost a bit more than a basic return flight.

Ticketless Travel Airlines are gradually waking up to the realisation that paper tickets are unnecessary encumbrances. On simple one-way or return trips, reservations details can be held on computer and the passenger merely shows ID to claim their seat.

Transferred Tickets Airline tickets cannot be transferred from one person to another. Travellers sometimes try to sell the return half of their ticket, but officials can ask you to prove that you are the person named on the ticket. On an international flight, tickets are compared with passports.

easy to put together an open-jaw ticket when you fly to one place but leave from another.

The other exception is booking on the Internet. Many airlines – full-service and no-frills – offer some excellent fares to Web surfers. They may sell seats by auction or simply cut prices to reflect the reduced cost of electronic selling.

Many travel agencies around the world have Web sites, which can make the Internet a quick and easy way to compare prices. There is also an increasing number of on-line agents that operate only on the Internet.

On-line ticket sales work well if you are doing a simple one-way or return trip on specified dates. However, on-line super-fast fare generators are no substitute for a travel agent who knows all about special deals, has strategies for avoiding stopovers, and can offer advice on everything from which airline has the best vegetarian food to the best travel insurance to bundle with your ticket.

You may find the cheapest flights are advertised by obscure agencies. Most of which are honest and solvent, but there are some rogue fly-by-night outfits around. Paying by credit card generally offers protection, as most card issuers provide refunds if you can prove you didn't get what you paid for. Similar protection can be obtained by buying a ticket from a bonded agent, such as one covered by the Air Travel Organiser's Licence (ATOL) scheme in the UK (more details available at **W** www.atol.org.uk). Agents who accept only cash should hand over the tickets straight away and not tell you to 'come back tomorrow'. After you've made a booking or paid your deposit, call the airline and confirm that the booking was made. It's generally not advisable to send money (even cheques) through the post unless the agent is very well established – some travellers have reported being ripped off by fly-by-night mail-order ticket agents.

If you purchase a ticket and later want to make changes to your route or get a refund, you need to contact the original travel agent. Airlines issue refunds only to the purchaser of a ticket – usually the travel agent who bought the ticket on your behalf.

Many travellers change their routes during their trips, so think carefully before you buy a ticket that is not easily refunded.

Although other Asian centres are competitive with Bangkok for buying discounted airline tickets, it's still a good place for shopping around, especially with the baht in its weakened state vis à vis most hard currencies. Phuket flights are less flexible, but in general fares also run lower than average for international travel in Asia.

Travellers should note that some Bangkok travel agencies have a shocking reputation. Taking money and then delaying or not coming through with the tickets, or providing tickets with limited validity periods or severe restrictions are all part of the racket. There are a large number of perfectly honest agents, but beware of the rogues. Travel agents on Phuket are generally more reliable.

Travellers with Specific Needs

If warned early, airlines can often make special arrangements for travellers, such as wheelchair assistance at airports or vegetarian meals on the flight. Children under two years travel for 10% of the standard fare (or free on some airlines) as long as they don't occupy a seat. They don't get a baggage allowance. 'Skycots', baby food and nappies should be provided by the airline if requested in advance. Children aged between two and 12 can usually occupy a seat from 50% to 70% of the full fare, and do get a baggage allowance.

The disability-friendly Web site **W** www .everybody.co.uk has an airline directory that provides information on the facilities offered by various airlines.

Booking Problems

Bookings for flights to/from Bangkok during the high season (December to March) can be difficult. For travel during this time you should book as early as possible. Be sure to reconfirm return or on-going tickets when you arrive in Thailand (though THAI claims this isn't necessary with their tickets). Failure to reconfirm can mean losing your reservation.

Departure Tax

All passengers departing from Thailand on international flights are charged an international departure tax (officially called 'airport service charge') of 500B. The tax is not included in the price of the ticket, but is paid before going through immigration procedures. Only baht are accepted. Be sure to have enough baht left over at the end of your trip to pay this tax – otherwise you'll have to revisit one of the currency exchange booths.

The USA

It is cheapest to fly to Bangkok via West Coast cities rather than from the East Coast. Discount travel agents in the USA are known as consolidators (although you won't see a sign on the door saying Consolidator). San Francisco is the ticket consolidator capital of the USA, although some good deals can be found in Los Angeles, New York and other big cities. Through agencies such as these a return round-trip airfare to Bangkok from any of 10 different West Coast cities starts at around US$750, with occasional specials (especially in May and September) of just US$525. If you're flying from the East Coast, add US$150 to US$200 to these fares.

One of the most reliable discounters is Avia Travel (☎ 800-950 AVIA toll-free, 510-558 2150, fax 558 2158, W www.avia travel.com) at Suite E, 1029 Solano Ave, Albany, CA 94706. Avia specialises in customised around-the-world fares, and 'Circle Pacific' fares such as New York-Bangkok-Bali-Sydney-Auckland-New York for US$1850. The agency sets aside a portion of its profits for Volunteers in Asia, a nonprofit organisation that sends grassroots volunteers to work in South-East Asia.

Another agency that works hard to get the cheapest deals is Ticket Planet (☎ 800-799 8888 toll-free, 415-288 9999, fax 288 9839, W www.ticketplanet.com).

Council Travel, America's largest student travel organisation, has around 60 offices in the USA. Contact it for the office nearest you (☎ 800-226 8624, W www .counciltravel.com).

While the airlines themselves can rarely match the prices of the discounters, they are worth checking if only to get benchmark prices to use for comparison. Tickets bought directly from the airlines may have fewer restrictions and/or less strict cancellation policies than those bought from discounters.

Cheapest airlines departing from the USA are: Korean Air, China Airlines, THAI, EVA Airways and CP Air.

Direct to Phuket If you want to fly straight through to Phuket without staying overnight in Bangkok, expect discount fares of US$850 to US$900 (China Airlines) and US$950 to US$1150 (Singapore Airlines). Singapore Airlines requires a stopover of a few hours in Singapore on the way; for China Airlines it's in Bangkok. If you don't mind overnighting in Bangkok, you have the option of many different daily connections the day after your international flight.

Canada

Travel Cuts (☎ 800-667-2887, W www .travelcuts.com) is Canada's national student travel agency and has offices in all major cities.

Like the USA, Canadian discount airticket sellers are also known as consolidators but their air fares tend to be about 10% higher than those sold in the USA.

Canadian Pacific flies from Vancouver to Bangkok for between C$950 and C$1100 return for advance-purchase excursion fares. Travellers living in eastern Canada will usually find the best deals out of New York or San Francisco, adding fares from Toronto or Montreal (see the USA section earlier).

Australia

Quite a few travel offices specialise in discount air tickets. Some travel agents, particularly smaller ones, advertise cheap air fares in the travel sections of weekend newspapers.

Two well-known agents for cheap fares are STA Travel and Flight Centre. STA Travel (☎ 03-9349 2411) has its main office at 224 Faraday St, Carlton, Vic 3053, and offices in all major cities and on many university campuses. Call ☎ 131 776 Australia wide for the location of your nearest branch or visit its Web site at ⓦ www.statravel.com.au. Flight Centre (☎ 133 600 Australia wide, ⓦ www.flight centre.com.au) has a central office at 82 Elizabeth St, Sydney, and there are dozens of offices throughout Australia.

From the east coast of Australia, Qantas Airways and THAI have direct flights to Bangkok from around A$1000 in the low season to A$1350 in the high season. Garuda Indonesia, Singapore Airlines, Philippine Airlines and Malaysia Airlines also have good fare deals, with stopovers, to Bangkok.

New Zealand

Flight Centre (☎ 09-309 6171) has a large central office in Auckland at National Bank Towers (corner of Queen and Darby Sts) and many branches throughout the country. STA Travel (☎ 09-309 0458, ⓦ www.sta travel.com.nz) has its headquarters at 10 High St, Auckland, and has offices in many other parts of the country.

Air New Zealand and THAI fly direct from Auckland to Bangkok. Low season return fares start at around NZ$1250, high season return fares are around NZ$1500.

The UK & Continental Europe

Discount air travel is big business in London, and London to Bangkok is arguably the most competitive air route in the world. At least two dozen airlines will transport you between the two capitals, though only three of them – British Airways, Qantas Airways and THAI – fly nonstop. If you insist on a non-stop flight, you will probably have to pay between UK£500 and UK£800 return for the privilege (or around UK£100 less if you are a student or under 26). A one-way ticket is only slightly cheaper than a return ticket.

For student and youth fares in the UK, the best bets are STA Travel (☎ 020 7361 6262, ⓦ www.statravel.co.uk) at 86 Old Brompton Rd, London SW7, and Usit Campus (☎ 0870 240 1010, ⓦ www.usitcam pus.co.uk) at 52 Grosvenor Gardens, London SW1 OAG.

In the Netherlands recommended agencies include NBBS Reizen (☎ 020-620 5071, ⓦ www.nbbs.nl), 66 Rokin, Amsterdam, plus branches in most cities, and Budget Air (☎ 020-627 1251, ⓦ www .nbbs.nl), 34 Rokin, Amsterdam. Another agency, Holland International (☎ 070-307 6307), has offices in most cities.

Recommended agencies in Germany include STA Travel (☎ 030-311 0950), 73 Goethestrasse, 10625 Berlin, plus branches in major cities across the country. Usit Campus (Call Centre ☎ 01805 788336, Cologne ☎ 0221 923990, ⓦ www.usitcampus.de) has several offices in Germany (you'll find the details on the Web site), including one at 2a Zuelpicher Strasse, 50674 Cologne.

In France recommended travel agencies include Usit Connect Voyages (☎ 01 42 44 14 00), 14 rue de Vaugirard, 75006 Paris, with branches across the country; and OTU Voyages (☎ 01 40 29 12 12, ⓦ www.otu.fr), 39 ave Georges-Bernanos, 75005 Paris, with branches across the country. Both companies are student and youth specialist agencies. Other recommendations include Voyageurs du Monde (☎ 01 42 86 16 00), 55 rue Ste-Anne, 75002 Paris, and Nouvelles Frontires (nationwide number ☎ 08 25 00 08 25, Paris ☎ 01 45 68 70 00, ⓦ www.nouvelles-front ieres.fr), 87 blvd de Grenelle, 75015 Paris, with branches across the country.

Recommended travel agents in Italy include CTS Viaggi (☎ 06-462 0431), 16 Via Genova, Rome, a student and youth specialist with branches in major cities, and Passagi (☎ 06-474 0923), Stazione Termini FS, Galleria Di Tesla, Rome.

In Spain recommended agencies include Usit Unlimited (☎ 91-225 25 75, ⓦ www .unlimited.es), 3 Plaza de Callao, 28013 Madrid, with branches in major cities; and Barcelo Viajes (☎ 91-559 1819), Princesa 3, 28008 Madrid, plus branches in major cities. Nouvelles Frontires (☎ 91-547 42 00, ⓦ www.nouvelles-frontieres.es) has an office at Plaza de España 18, 28008 Madrid, plus branches in major cities.

In Switzerland recommended agencies include SSR (☎ 022-818 02 02, ⓦ www .ssr.ch), 8 rue de la Rive, Geneva, plus branches throughout the country; and Nouvelles Frontires (☎ 022-906 80 80), 10 rue Chante Poulet, Geneva.

Asia

Bangkok Thanon Khao San (Khao San Rd) in Bangkok is the budget travellers headquarters. Bangkok has a number of excellent travel agents, but there are also some suspect ones; ask the advice of other travellers before handing over your cash. STA Travel (☎ 022 360 262), 33 Surawong Rd, is a good and reliable place to start.

There are regular flights to Bangkok International Airport from every major city in Asia and, conveniently, most airlines offer about the same fares for intra-Asia flights. Immediately following is a list of common one-way fares from Bangkok. Return tickets are usually double the one-way fare, although occasionally airlines run special discounts of up to 25% for such tickets. For fares in the reverse direction, convert to local currency.

from	approx one-way fare
Calcutta	6500B
Colombo	8000B
Hong Kong	8300B
Kathmandu	9700B
Kuala Lumpur	4500B
Kunming	6500B
Manila	9000B
New Delhi	13,000B
Phnom Penh	5000B
Siem Reap	7000B
Singapore	6600B
Taipei	9000B
Vientiane	4000B
Yangon	4000B

Travellers heading for Southern Thailand can skip Bangkok altogether by flying directly to several cities. THAI has regular flights to Phuket from Hong Kong, Singapore, Taipei, Tokyo, Perth and Frankfurt, as well as flights to Hat Yai from Singapore and Kuala Lumpur. During their winter, German carrier LTU offers direct flights to Phuket from Düsseldorf and Munich.

Bangkok Airways offers daily flights between Singapore and Ko Samui.

You can also arrange same-day connections via Bangkok to Phuket from other departure points, depending on your Bangkok arrival time – only international flights arriving during the day will leave you enough time to make afternoon or evening connections to Phuket.

Regional Carriers Thailand allows several international carriers to provide regional air services from Myanmar (Burma), Vietnam, Laos and Cambodia. Routes to/from Thailand include China Yunnan Airlines flights from Kunming to Bangkok; SilkAir between Singapore and Phuket; Dragonair between Hong Kong and Phuket; Malaysia Airlines between Kuala Lumpur and Hat Yai, and between Kuala Lumpur and Phuket; Royal Air Cambodge between Bangkok and Phnom Penh; Biman Bangladesh Airlines between Yangon and Bangkok; Lao Aviation between Bangkok and Vientiane; and Vietnam Airlines between Bangkok and Ho Chi Minh City.

LAND
Malaysia

Hat Yai is the major transport hub in Southern Thailand. See the Getting There & Away – International section of the South-Western Gulf Coast chapter for more details on land transport to Malaysia.

You can cross the west-coast border between Malaysia and Thailand by taking a bus to one side and another bus from the other side, the most obvious direct route being between Hat Yai and Alor Setar. This is the route used by taxis and buses, but there's a 1km-long stretch of no-man's land between the Thai border control at Sadao (also known as Dan Nok) and the Malaysian one at Changlun.

It's much easier to go to Padang Besar, where the train line crosses the border. Here you can get a bus right to the border, walk across and take another bus or taxi on the other side. On either side you'll most likely be mobbed by taxi and motorcycle drivers wanting to take you to immigration. It's better to walk over the railway bridge into Thailand, and ignore the touts until you get

Thailand's International Border Crossings

These are border crossings where all nationalities are permitted to cross, and where there are Thai customs and immigration posts.

Thailand	Malaysia
Betong	Keroh
Padang Besar	Kaki Bukit
Sadao	Changlun
Sungai Kolok	Pasir Mas

Thailand	Laos
Chiang Khong	Huay Xai
Chong Mek	Pakse
Mukdahan	Savannakhet
Nakhon Phanom	Tha Khaek
Nong Khai	Vientiane

Thailand	Cambodia
Aranya Prathet	Poi Pet

Thailand	Myanmar
Mae Sai	Tachilek
Three Pagodas Pass	Payathonzu*
Ranong	Kawthaung (Victoria Point)

*Entry to Payathonzu permitted for day trips only.

to 'official' Thai taxis that will take you all the way to Hat Yai, with a stop at the immigration office (2.5km from the border), for 50B or so.

A daily bus runs between Alor Setar, Hat Yai and Kota Baru and back.

There's also a border crossing at Keroh (Betong on the Thai side), mid-way between the east and west coasts. Few people other than Thais and Malaysians use this crossing as it puts you in the middle of nowhere along the Penang to Kota Bharu road.

See the Sungai Kolok and Ban Taba entries in the South-Western Gulf Coast chapter for information about crossing the border on the east coast.

Riding the rails between Singapore and Bangkok via Butterworth, Malaysia, is a great way to travel to Thailand – as long as you don't count on making a smooth change between the Kereta Api Tanah Melayu (KTM) and State Railway of Thailand (SRT) trains. The Malaysian train rarely arrives on time, and the Thai train almost always leaves Padang Besar on time, even if the Malaysian express from Kuala Lumpur (or the 2nd-class connection from Butterworth) is late. It's best to purchase the Malaysian and Thai portions of your ticket with departures on consecutive days and plan a Butterworth/Penang stopover.

Laos

Lonely Planet's *Laos* and *Thailand* guides contain complete details on how and where to cross the border between these two countries by land or river. Following is a summary of the possibilities.

Road A 1174m Australian-financed bridge across the Mekong River near Nong Khai, the Thai-Lao Friendship Bridge (Saphan Mittaphap Thai-Lao), spans the river between Ban Jommani on the Thai side and Tha Na Leng on the Lao side. The next step in the plan is to build a parallel rail bridge in order to extend the Bangkok–Nong Khai railway into Vientiane. A similar plan for Nakhon Phanom is currently under consideration.

A land crossing from Pakse (Champasak Province) in Laos to Chong Mek in Thailand's Ubon Ratchathani Province is open to foreign visitors. You only need a normal Lao visa if crossing from Thailand to Laos, and in the opposite direction you can obtain a Thai visa on arrival.

Train A joint venture agreement between the Lao government and a new company, Lao Railways Transportation, was signed in 1998 to establish a railway line along the middle of the Friendship Bridge. After a two-year feasibility study is completed, the line, which will reportedly extend to Vientiane and Luang Prabang, is supposed to become operational within four years. Like most other transport projects in Laos, however, it will probably take much longer – if it ever happens at all.

Another rail link under consideration is a spur eastward from Udon Thani, and across Laos to connect with the Ho Chi Minh City–Hanoi railway in Vietnam.

Myanmar
Several land border crossings between Thailand and Myanmar are open to daytrippers for short excursions in the vicinity. As yet, none of these link up with routes to Yangon or Mandalay or other cities of any size. The only place you are permitted to enter Thailand from Myanmar is via boat from Kawthoung (Myanmar) to Ranong (Thailand); see the following Sea section. For more detail, see Lonely Planet's *Thailand* and *Myanmar* guides.

Cambodia
As of early 1998, there has been a legal bordercrossing between Cambodia and Thailand at Aranya Prathet, opposite the Cambodian town of Poipet. If you're coming from Cambodia by rail or road, you don't need a Thai visa (or rather you will be granted a free 30-day tourist visa on arrival), but in the reverse direction you will need a Cambodian visa, which is available from the Cambodian embassy in Bangkok.

Other areas along the border won't be safe for land crossings until mines and booby traps left over from the conflict between the Khmer Rouge and the Vietnamese are removed or detonated.

Travellers can cross to Cambodia by sea from Hat Lek to Koh Kong. From there you can catch a ferry to Sihanoukville and onward transportation to Phnom Penh. See the Hat Lek to Cambodia section in the Eastern Gulf Coast chapter for details.

SEA
Malaysia
There are several ways of travelling between Thailand's southern peninsula and Malaysia by sea. Simplest is to take a long-tail boat between Satun, in the south-west corner of Thailand, and Kuala Perlis. The cost is about M$5, or 50B, and boats cross over fairly regularly.

You can also take a ferry to the Malaysian island of Langkawi from Satun. There are immigration posts at both ports.

From Satun you can take a bus to Hat Yai and then arrange transport to other points in the south or farther north. It's possible to bypass Hat Yai altogether by heading directly for Phuket or Krabi via Trang.

You can also take a ferry to Ban Taba on the east coast of Thailand from near Kota Bharu – see the Sungai Kolok and Ban Taba sections in the South-Western Gulf chapter.

Passenger ferry services also sometimes run between Pulau Langkawi and Phuket. Such services never seem to last longer than nine months or so; your best bet is to make inquiries through local travel agents to find out the latest on sea transport to/from Langkawi.

See the Yachting entry in the Phuket Province section of the Northern Andaman

Coast chapter for information on yachts to Penang and other places.

Laos

It's legal for non-Thai foreigners to cross the Mekong River by ferry between Thailand and Laos at: Nakhon Phanom (opposite Tha Khaek), Chiang Khong (opposite Huay Xai) and Mukdahan (opposite Savannakhet).

Thais may cross at all of the above checkpoints and a half-dozen or so others in Thailand's Loei and Nong Khai provinces. In the future one or more of these may open to foreign visitors as well.

Myanmar

You can travel by boat between Kawthoung ('Ko Song' in Thai) in Myanmar's Tanintharyi Division and the port of Ranong in Thailand's Ranong Province via the Gulf of Martaban/Pakchan Estuary. Leaving Myanmar from Kawthoung is now legal, and you don't need a visa to enter Thailand for 30 days or less. In the reverse direction you won't need a Myanmar visa for a day trip, but if you plan to stay overnight or to continue farther north, you'll need to arrive

with a valid Myanmar visa in your passport. At the time of writing this border crossing was open to foreigners but, given the rocky state of Thai-Myanmar relations, there's always the possibility that the crossing will be closed again by the time you read this – check with TAT to get the latest info. For further details see the Ranong section in the North Andaman Coast chapter.

Warning

The information in this chapter is particularly vulnerable to change: Prices for international travel are volatile, routes are introduced and cancelled, schedules change, special deals come and go, and rules and visa requirements are amended. You should check directly with the airline or a travel agent to make sure you understand how a fare (and ticket you may buy) works and be aware of the security requirements for international travel.

The upshot of this is that you should get opinions, quotes and advice from as many airlines and travel agents as possible before you part with your hard-earned cash. The details given in this chapter should be regarded as pointers and are not a substitute.

Getting Around

AIR
Domestic Air Services

Five domestic carriers, Thai Airways International (THAI), Bangkok Airways, PB Air, Angel Airlines and Air Andaman, make use of domestic airports in 28 cities around the country.

Most domestic air services in Thailand are operated by THAI, which covers 23 airports throughout the kingdom. THAI operates Boeing 737 or Airbus 300 series aircraft on its main domestic routes. Service on THAI's domestic routes doesn't quite live up to the reputation that the airline has built on its international routes – Prime Minister Thaksin Shinawatra even went so far as to complain that the national carrier 'sucks'. Still, it's not bad compared to some national carriers in neighbouring countries.

The Air Fares & Railways map in this section shows some of the fares on routes to coastal Thailand. Note that through fares generally cost less than combination fares. This does not always apply to international fares, however. It's much cheaper to fly from Bangkok to Penang via Phuket or Hat Yai than direct, for example.

Bangkok Airways Bangkok Airways flies four routes: Bangkok-Ko Samui-Phuket; Bangkok-Ranong; Bangkok-Sukhothai-Chiang Mai; and U Taphao (Pattaya)-Ko Samui. There are also international flights between Bangkok and Siem Reap (in Cambodia) and between Pattaya and Phnom Penh. The mainstay of the Bangkok Airways fleet is the Franco-Italian ATR72-200, as well as Boeing 717-200 jets on some of the international flights. The most popular route, by far, is the one between Bangkok and Ko Samui.

The airline's head office (☎ 022 293 434, fax 022 293 456, W www.bangkokair.com) is at Queen Sirikit National Convention Center, Thanon (Th) Ratchadaphisek Mai, Khlong Toey, Bangkok 10110. There are also offices in Ranong, Pattaya, Phuket and Ko Samui.

Angel Airlines This domestic airline began operations in 1998, floundered briefly and then was resurrected after agreements with China Northern Airlines. At present the only route is Bangkok to Phuket but the company has plans to begin flying internationally from Hong Kong and Osaka to Phuket via Bangkok by the time this book is published.

Angel Airlines (☎ 029 532 263) is headquartered at UCOM Building, Th Vibhavadi (Wiphaawadii), Rangsit Hwy, with branch offices in Chiang Mai, Phuket, Udon Thani and Singapore.

Air Andaman The newest domestic airline to fly Thai skies, Air Andaman utilises tiny British Aerospace Jetstream 31s. Apart from a Bangkok to Chumphon route, all of Air Andaman's other routes are short hops between Phuket and either Chumphon, Krabi or Nakhon Si Thammarat.

The main office (☎ 022 514 905, fax 026 552 378, e mkt@airandaman.com) is located on the 4th floor of the Nailert Bldg on Th Sukhumvit.

THAI Offices Offices for THAI's domestic services can be found throughout coastal Thailand. To hear recorded information in Thai and English about routes and fares, call ☎ 02 1566.

Bangkok (Head Office; ☎ 025 130 121, reservations ☎ 026 282 000) 89 Th Vibhavadi, Rangsit Hwy;
(☎ 022 343 100–19) 485 Th Silom;
(☎ 022 800 110) 6 Th Lan Luang;
(☎ 022 152 020–1) Asia Hotel, 296 Th Phayathai;
(☎ 022 239 746–50) 3rd floor, Grand China Tower, 215 Th Yaowarat;
(☎ 025 352 081–2, 025 236 121) Bangkok International Airport, Don Muang
Hat Yai (☎ 074 230 445, 074 246 165, reservations ☎ 074 244 282) 190/6 Th Niphat Uthit 2
Nakhon Si Thammarat (☎ 075 342 491) 1612 Th Ratchadamnoen

Narathiwat (☎ 073 511 161) Narathiwat airport;
(☎ 073 511 595) 322-4 Th Phuphaphakdi
Pattani (☎ 073 335 939) 9 Th Prida
Pattaya (☎ 038 420 995–7) Dusit Resort Hotel,
Th Hat Pattaya Neua
Phuket (☎ 076 258 236, reservations ☎ 076 258
237) Phuket International Airport;
(☎ 076 327 194) 78/1 Th Ranong
Songkhla (☎ 074 311 012) 2 Soi 4, Th Saiburi
Surat Thani (☎ 077 273 710, 237355) 3/27-8
Th Karunarat
Trang (☎ 075 218 066) 199/2 Th Visetkul

Air Passes

THAI occasionally offers special four-coupon passes – available only outside Thailand for foreign currency – in which you can book any four domestic flights for one fare of around US$199 (half-price for children under 12) as long as you don't repeat the same leg. Unless you plan carefully this isn't much of a saving, since it's hard to avoid repeating the same leg in and out of Bangkok. Also, the baht is so low these days it's often cheaper to make arrangements for domestic flights in Thailand rather than from abroad.

For information on the four-coupon deal, known as the 'Amazing Thailand fare', inquire at any THAI office outside Thailand.

Domestic Departure Tax

A departure tax of 30B is now included in all domestic fares, ie, it is no longer collected separately at airline check-in counters. The exception is the privately owned airport at Ko Samui, which collects a 400B departure tax at the check-in counter.

BUS
Government Bus

The cheapest and slowest of the Thai buses are the ordinary government-run buses (*rót thamádaa*) that stop in every little town and for every waving hand along the highway. For some destinations – such as smaller towns – these orange-painted buses are your only choice, but at least they leave frequently. The government also runs faster, more comfortable, but less frequent, air-conditioned buses called *rót ae*, *rót pràp aakàat* or *rót thua*; these are painted with

blue markings. If these are available to your destination, they are your best choice since they don't cost that much more than the ordinary stop-in-every-town buses. The government bus company is called Baw Khaw Saw, an abbreviation of Borisat Khon Song (The Transportation Company). Every city and town in Thailand linked by bus has a Baw Khaw Saw terminal, even if it's just a patch of dirt by the roadside.

The service on the government air-con buses is usually not bad, and includes a complimentary soft drink and (don your earplugs) a video. On longer routes (eg, Bangkok–Ko Samui, Bangkok-Phuket), the air-con buses even distribute claim checks (receipt dockets) for your baggage. Longer routes may also offer two classes of air-con buses, 2nd class and 1st class; the latter have toilets. 'VIP' buses have fewer seats (30 to 34 instead of 44; some routes have Super VIP, with only 24 seats) so that each seat reclines more. Sometimes these are called *rót nawn* (sleepers). For small to medium-sized people the seats are usually comfortable, but if you're big in girth and decide to catch a 34-seater you may find yourself squashed when the person in front of you leans back.

Occasionally you'll get a government air-con bus in which the air-con is broken or the seats are not up to standard, but in general they are more reliable than the private tour buses.

Private Bus

Private buses are available between major tourist and business destinations: Surat Thani, Ko Samui, Phuket, Hat Yai, Pattaya, Hua Hin and others. To Phuket, for example, several companies run daily buses from Bangkok. These can be booked through most hotels or any travel agency, although it's best to book directly through a bus office to ensure you get what you pay for.

Fares may vary between companies, but usually not by more than a few baht. However, fare differences between the government and private bus companies can be substantial. Using Surat Thani as an example, the state-run buses from Bangkok's

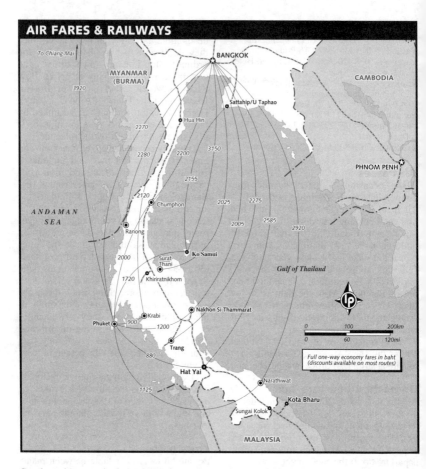

AIR FARES & RAILWAYS

Full one-way economy fares in baht (discounts available on most routes)

Southern bus terminal are 180B for ordinary bus, 346B (1st class) air-con, while the private companies charge up to 550B. On the other hand, to Phuket the private buses often cost less than the government buses, although those that charge less offer inferior service. Departures from some private companies are more frequent than for the equivalent Baw Khaw Saw route.

There are also private buses running between major destinations within the various regions, eg, Nakhon Si Thammarat to Hat Yai in the South. New companies are cropping up all the time. Their numbers seem to

have stabilised due to a crackdown on licensing. Minibuses, vans or share taxis are also used on many routes in the South.

The private air-con buses are usually no more comfortable than the government air-con buses and feature similarly narrow seats and a hair-raising ride. On overnight journeys the buses usually stop somewhere en route and passengers are woken to get off the bus for a free meal of fried rice or rice soup. A few companies even treat you to a meal before an overnight trip.

Like their state-run equivalents, the private bus companies offer VIP (sleeper) buses on long hauls. In general, private bus companies that deal mostly with Thais are good, while tourist-oriented ones – especially those connected with Th Khao San (Khao San Rd) – are the worst. Agents know they don't need to deliver good service because very few customers will be returning. In recent years, the service on many private lines has in fact declined, especially on the Bangkok–Ko Samui, Surat Thani–Phuket and Surat Thani–Krabi routes.

Sometimes the cheaper lines – especially those booked on Th Khao San in Bangkok – will switch vehicles at the last moment so that instead of the roomy air-con bus advertised, you're stuck with a cramped van with broken air-con. Another problem with the private companies is that they generally spend more time cruising the city for passengers before getting under way, meaning that they rarely leave at the advertised departure time. To avoid situations like this, it's always better to book bus tickets directly at a bus office – or at the government Baw Khaw Saw station – rather than through a travel agency.

Out of Bangkok, the safest, most reliable private bus services are the ones that operate from the three official Baw Khaw Saw terminals rather than from hotels or guesthouses. Picking up passengers from any points except these official terminals is actually illegal, and services promised by companies who flout the law are often not delivered. Although it can be a hassle getting out to the Baw Khaw Saw terminals, you're generally rewarded with safer, more reliable and punctual service.

Safety

Statistically, private buses have more accidents than government air-con buses. Turnovers on tight corners and head-on collisions with trucks are probably due to the inexperience of the drivers on a particular route.

Keep an eye on your bags when riding buses – stealth is still the most popular tactic for robbery in Thailand (it's eminently preferable to the forceful variety). While the risks are not that great it is wise to be

aware. Most pilfering seems to take place on the private bus runs between Bangkok and Ko Samui, especially on buses booked on Th Khao San. Keep zippered bags locked and well secured. If the bus makes a late-night snack or toilet stop, be sure not to leave any valuables on the bus no matter how briefly you plan to disembark.

TRAIN

The railway network in Thailand, run by the government-subsidised State Railway of Thailand (SRT), is surprisingly good. In fact, in many ways it's the best form of public transport in the kingdom. If you travel 3rd class, it is often the cheapest way to cover a long distance; by 2nd class it's about the same as a private tour bus but much safer and more comfortable. Trains take a bit longer than chartered buses on the same journey but, on overnight trips especially, are worth the extra travel time.

The trains have many advantages: there is more space with more room to move and stretch out (even in 3rd class) than there is on the best buses. If you're hungry or in the mood for a beer, you can take a stroll down to the dining car – train food is good and reasonably priced. Toilets are generally cleaner and less claustrophobic than those on buses. The windows are big and usually open, so that there is no glass between you and the scenery (good for taking photos) and more to see. The scenery itself is always better along the train routes than the scenery along Thai highways – the trains regularly pass small villages, farmland, old temples etc. The pitch-and-roll of the railway cars is much easier on the bones, muscles and nervous system than the quick stops and starts, the harrowing turns and the pothole jolts endured on buses. The train is safer in terms of both accidents and robberies. Last, but certainly not least, you meet a lot more interesting people on the train, or so it seems to us.

Rail Routes

Four main rail lines cover 4500km along the northern, southern, north-eastern and eastern routes. There are several side routes, notably between Nakhon Pathom and Nam Tok (stopping in Kanchanaburi) in the west central region, and between Tung Song and Kantang (stopping in Trang) in the South. The southern line splits at Hat Yai, one route going to Sungai Kolok on the Malaysian east-coast border, via Yala, and the other route going to Padang Besar in the west, also on the Malaysian border.

A Bangkok to Pattaya spur has not been as popular as expected. Within the next few years, a southern spur may be extended from Khiriratnikhom to Phuket, establishing a rail link between Surat Thani and Phuket.

Bangkok Terminals Most long-distance trains originate from Bangkok's Hualamphong train station. Before a railway bridge was constructed across the Chao Phraya River in 1932, all southbound trains left from Thonburi's Bangkok Noi station. Today Bangkok Noi station services commuter and short-line trains to Kanchanaburi/Nam Tok, Suphanburi, Ratchaburi and Nakhon Pathom (Ratchaburi and Nakhon Pathom can also be reached by train from Hualamphong). A slow night-train to Chumphon and Lang Suan, both in Southern Thailand, leaves nightly from the Bangkok Noi station but it's rarely used by long-distance travellers.

Train Passes
The SRT issues a couple of rail passes that may save on fares if you plan to ride Thai trains extensively within a relatively short interval. These passes are available in Thailand only, and may be purchased at Hualamphong train station.

The cost for 20 days of unlimited 2nd-class rail travel (blue pass) is 1100B, or 2000B for 1st class. These passes include all rapid or express surcharges but do not include sleeping berths or air-con charges, which cost extra according to the standard SRT schedule. Passes must be validated at a local station before boarding the first train. The price of the pass includes seat reservations that, if required, can be made at any SRT ticket office. The pass is valid until midnight on the last day of the pass. However, if the journey is commenced be-

fore midnight on the last day of validity, the passenger can use the pass until that train reaches its destination.

The passes are more economical than buying individual train tickets only if you can average over 110km by rail per day for 20 days. If you travel at these levels (or less), then you'll be paying the same amount (or more) as you would if you bought ordinary train tickets directly. On less crowded routes where there are plenty of available 2nd-class seats the passes save time that might otherwise be spent at ticket windows, but for high-demand routes (eg, from Bangkok to Hat Yai) you'll still need to make reservations.

Classes
The SRT operates passenger trains in 1st, 2nd and 3rd class – but each varies considerably depending on whether you're on an ordinary, rapid or express train.

Third Class A typical 3rd-class car consists of two rows of bench seats divided into facing pairs. Each bench seat is designed to seat two or three passengers, but on a crowded upcountry line nobody seems to care about design considerations. On a rapid train, 3rd-class seats are padded and reasonably comfortable for shorter trips. On ordinary, 3rd-class-only trains in the east and North-East, seats are sometimes made of hard wooden slats, and are not recommended for more than a couple of hours at a time. Express trains do not carry 3rd-class cars at all. Commuter trains in the Bangkok area are all 3rd class and the cars resemble modern subway or rapid transit trains, with plastic seats and ceiling hand straps for standing passengers.

Second Class In a 2nd-class car, seating is similar to that on a bus, with pairs of padded seats all facing towards the front of the train. Usually the seats can be adjusted to recline, and for some people this is good enough for overnight trips. In a 2nd-class sleeper, you'll find rows of facing pairs of seats; each pair is separated from the next by a dividing wall. A table can be set up between each pair and at night the seats convert into two fold-down berths, one over the other. Curtains provide a modicum of privacy and the berths are fairly comfortable, with fresh linen for every trip. The lower berths cost a little more as they're roomier and a few degrees cooler. A toilet stall is located at one end of the car and washbasins at the other. Second-class cars are found only on rapid and express trains; some routes offer air-con 2nd class as well as ordinary 2nd class.

First Class First-class cars provide private double cabins with individually controlled air-conditioning, an electric fan, a washbasin and mirror, a small table and a long bench seat that converts into two beds. Drinking water and towels are provided free of charge. First-class cars are available only on express and special express trains.

Reservations

The disadvantage of travelling by rail, in addition to the time factor mentioned earlier, is that trains can be difficult to book. This is especially true around holiday time, eg, the middle of April approaching the Songkran Festival, since many Thais prefer the train. Trains out of Bangkok should be booked as far in advance as possible – a minimum of a week for a popular route such as the southern line to Hat Yai, especially if you want a sleeper. For the north-eastern and eastern lines a few days will suffice.

Advance bookings may be made at any major station one to 60 days before your intended date of departure. At Bangkok's Hualamphong train station advance bookings are made at the same windows as same-day purchases. Look for the windows with screens above them saying 'All Trains' – these are straight ahead if you enter through the main entrance of the station. Ticket sales are now computerised and take much less time than before the system was installed. Note that only cash baht is accepted here.

Note also that buying a return ticket does not necessarily guarantee you a seat on the way back, it only means you do not have to buy a ticket for the return. If you want a guaranteed seat reservation it's best to make that reservation for the return immediately upon arrival at your destination.

Booking trains back to Bangkok is generally not as difficult as booking trains out of Bangkok; however, at some stations this can be quite difficult (eg, buying a ticket from Surat Thani to Bangkok).

Tickets between any stations in Thailand can be purchased at Hualamphong train station (☎ 022 233 762, 022 256 964, 022 247 788). You can also make advance bookings at Don Muang train station (across from Bangkok International Airport) and at the Advance Booking offices at train stations in the larger cities. Advance reservations can be made by phone from anywhere in Thailand (☎ 022 250 300 ext 5204). Throughout Thailand SRT ticket offices are *generally* open from 8.30am to 6pm on weekdays and until noon on weekends and public holidays. Train tickets can also be purchased at certain travel agencies in Bangkok (see the Travel Agencies entry in the Information section of the Bangkok chapter). It is much simpler to book trains through these agencies than to book them at the station; however, many add a surcharge of 50B to 100B to the ticket price.

Costs

The cost of travelling by train is determined by two factors: distance and any number of surcharges that may apply – depending on the amenities you require. Distance-wise, count on paying roughly 100B, 200B and 400B for every 500km travelled in 3rd, 2nd and 1st class respectively. On top of this, there is a 60B surcharge for express trains *(rót dùan)* and 40B for rapid trains *(rót rahw)*. These trains are faster than ordinary trains, as they make fewer stops. For special express trains *(rót dùan phísèt)* there is an 80B surcharge. The special express trains are faster again and some use newer, quieter passenger cars.

The surcharge for 2nd-class sleeping berths is 100B for an upper berth and 150B for a lower berth (or 130B and 200B respectively on a special express). The difference between upper and lower is that there is a window next to the lower berth and a little more headroom. The upper berth is still quite comfortable. For 2nd-class sleepers with air-con add 250/320B per upper/lower ticket. No sleepers are available in 3rd class.

All 1st-class cabins have individually controlled air-conditioning and a long sofa that folds into two beds, carrying a surcharge of 400B per person. If you're travelling alone and don't want to share your cabin with a stranger, you can pay an extra 300B and have the cabin to yourself.

Eating Facilities

Meals are available in dining cars and at your seat in 2nd- and 1st-class cars. The food is usually not bad, and reasonably priced (about 100B for one dish with rice and a soft drink). Though if you're really concerned with saving baht, bring your own – or take a chance on the iffy offerings of roving vendors who mob the train at major stations.

A small bottle of drinking water is provided on 1st-class and sometimes 2nd-class sleepers. If you forget to buy water on the platform, there are usually vendors walking the length of the train with a bucket of lukewarm beverages for sale. Faràng are invariably offered beer.

Train staff sometimes hand out face wipes, then come by later to collect 10B each for them – a racket since there's no indication to passengers that they're not complimentary.

Several readers have written to complain about being overcharged by meal servers on trains. If you do purchase food on board, be sure to check prices on the menu rather than trusting server quotes. Also, check the bill carefully to make sure you haven't been overcharged.

Station Services

Accurate, up-to-date information on train travel is available at the Rail Travel Aids counter at Hualamphong train station. From here you can pick up timetables or ask about fares and scheduling – one person behind the counter usually speaks a little English. There are two types of timetable available: four condensed English timetables with fares, schedules and routes for rapid, express and special express trains on the four trunk lines; and four Thai timetables for each trunk line, with side lines as well. These latter timetables give fares and schedules for all trains – ordinary, rapid and express. The English timetables only display a couple of the ordinary routes.

All train stations in Thailand have baggage storage services (sometimes called the 'cloak room'). The rates and hours of operation vary from station to station. At Hualamphong train station the hours are from 4.30am to 10.30pm daily, and left luggage costs 10B per day. Hualamphong station also has a 10B shower service in the rest rooms – a great way to freshen up if you're taking a long train trip, say from Chiang Mai to Hat Yai.

All stations in provincial capitals have restaurants or cafeterias as well as various snack vendors. These stations also offer an advance-booking service for rail travel anywhere in Thailand. There are usually hotels within walking distance of major stations.

Bangkok's Hualamphong train station was recently renovated and now boasts a cafeteria (with an excellent Muslim food vendor), a KFC, Dunkin' Donuts and a Coffeebucks (a Starbucks knock-off with a great selection of coffee), as well as a mezzanine overlooking the waiting area – a great place to people-watch if you have some time to kill.

Hualamphong station also has a travel agency where other kinds of transport can be booked, but beware of touts who try and drag you there saying the trains are fully booked when they aren't. This station also has a Mail Boxes Etc (MBE) that provides mailing and packing services from 7.30am to 7.30pm Monday to Friday, 9am to 4pm Saturday and 9am to 8pm Sunday.

CAR & MOTORCYCLE
Roads

Thailand has more than 170,000km of roads. Around 16,000km are classified 'national highways' (both two lane and four lane), which means they're generally well maintained. Route numbering is fairly consistent; some of the major highways have two numbers, one under the national system and another under the optimistic 'Asia Highway' system that indicates highway links with neighbouring countries. Route 105 to Mae Sot on the Myanmar border, for example, is also called 'Asia 1', while Hwy 2 from Bangkok to Nong Khai is 'Asia 12'. For the time being, the only border regularly crossed by non-commercial vehicles is the Thai-Malaysian border.

Kilometre markers are placed at regular intervals along most larger roads, but place names are usually printed on them in Thai script only. Highway signs in both Thai and roman script showing destinations and distances are becoming increasingly common.

Road Rules

Thais drive on the left-hand side of the road – most of the time. Other than that just about anything goes, in spite of road signs and speed limits – Thais are notorious scofflaws when it comes to driving. Like many places in Asia, every two-lane road has an invisible third lane in the middle that all drivers feel free to use at any time. Passing on hills and curves is common – as long as you've got the proper Buddhist altar on the dashboard, what could happen?

The main rule to be aware of is that the right of way belongs to the bigger vehicle; this is not what it says in the Thai traffic law, but it's the reality. Maximum speed limits are 50km/h within city limits, 100km/h on most highways – but on any given stretch of highway you'll see vehicles travelling as slowly as 30km/h or as fast as 150km/h. Speed traps are becoming more common, especially along Hwy 4 in the South and Hwy 2 in the North-East.

Turn signals are often used to warn passing drivers about oncoming traffic. A left-turn signal means it's OK to pass, while a

Road Distances (km)

	Aranya Prathet	Ayuthaya	Bangkok	Chumphon	Hat Yai	Hua Hin	Krabi	Nakhon Si Thammarat	Narathiwat	Pattani	Phuket	Prachinburi	Ranong	Rayong	Sungai Kolok	Surat Thani	Trang	Trat
Aranya Prathet	---																	
Ayuthaya	246	---																
Bangkok	275	79	---															
Chumphon	727	531	452	---														
Hat Yai	1268	1072	993	555	---													
Hua Hin	458	262	183	269	810	---												
Krabi	1278	1082	1003	551	287	820	---											
Nakhon Si Thammarat	971	775	696	244	192	513	209	---										
Narathiwat	1495	1299	1220	782	227	1037	514	580	---									
Pattani	1402	1206	1127	689	134	944	421	487	93	---								
Phuket	1125	929	862	412	474	667	185	394	701	608	---							
Prachinburi	161	124	155	607	1148	338	1158	851	1375	1282	1017	---						
Ranong	855	659	580	128	368	397	368	372	882	789	287	735	---					
Rayong	321	279	200	652	1193	383	1203	1008	1420	1327	1062	248	780	---				
Sungai Kolok	1555	1359	1280	842	287	1097	576	640	60	153	761	1435	944	1480	---			
Surat Thani	927	731	652	214	401	469	318	151	731	638	286	807	315	852	791	---		
Trang	1417	1221	1142	690	147	959	139	142	374	281	324	1297	507	1342	437	234	---	
Trat	285	392	313	765	1306	496	1316	1009	1533	1440	1175	334	893	180	1593	965	1455	---

right-turn signal means someone's approaching from the other direction.

The principal hazard of driving in Thailand, besides the general disregard for traffic laws, is having to contend with so many different types of vehicles on the same road – bullock carts, 18-wheelers, bicycles, túk-túk and customised racing bikes. In village areas the vehicular traffic is lighter but you have to contend with stray chickens, dogs, water buffaloes, pigs, cats and goats. Once you get used to the challenge, driving in Thailand is very entertaining, but first-timers tend to get a bit unnerved.

Checkpoints Military checkpoints are common along highways throughout Northern and North-Eastern Thailand, especially in border areas. Always slow down for a checkpoint – often the sentries will wave you through without an inspection, but occasionally you'll be stopped and briefly questioned. Use common sense and don't be belligerent or you're likely to be detained longer than you'd like.

Rental

Cars, jeeps and vans can be rented in Bangkok, Pattaya, Phuket, Ko Samui and Hat Yai. A Japanese sedan (eg, Toyota Corolla) typically costs from 1000B to 1500B per day; minivans (eg, Toyota Hi-Ace, Nissan Urvan) go for around 1800B to 2500B a day. International rental companies tend to charge a bit more; Avis, for example, rents Nissan 1.4 Sentras for 1500B a day (9000B weekly), slightly larger Mitsubishi 1.5 Lancers for 2000B a day (10,200B weekly) and Mitsubishi 4WD Pajeros for 2200B per day (13,200B weekly).

The best deals are usually on 4WD Suzuki Caribians or Daihatsu Miras, which can be rented for as low as 800B per day with no per-km fees for long-term rentals and during low seasons. Unless you absolutely want the cheapest vehicle, you might be better off with a larger vehicle (eg, the Mitsubishi 4WD Strada, if you absolutely need 4WD); Caribians are notoriously hard to handle at speeds above 90km/h and tend to crumple dangerously in collisions. Cars

with automatic transmissions are uncommon. Drivers can usually be hired with a rental for an additional 300B to 400B per day.

Check with travel agencies or large hotels for rental locations. It is advisable to always verify that a vehicle is insured for liability before signing a rental contract; you should also ask to see the dated insurance documents. If you have an accident while driving an uninsured vehicle you're in for some major hassles.

Motorcycles can be rented in major towns as well as many smaller tourist centres like Krabi, Ko Samui, Ko Pha-Ngan, Ko Chang etc (see Motorcycle Touring in this section). Rental rates vary considerably from one agency to another and from city to city. Since there is a glut of motorcycles for rent on Ko Samui and Phuket, they can be rented on these islands for as little as 150B per day. A substantial deposit is usually required to rent a car; motorcycle rental usually requires that you leave your passport.

Driving Permits

Foreigners who wish to drive motor vehicles (including motorcycles) in Thailand need a valid International Driving Permit. If you don't have one, you can apply for a Thai driver's licence at the Police Registration Division (PRD; ☎ 025 130 051–5) on Th Phahonyothin in Bangkok. Provincial capitals also have PRDs. If you present a valid foreign driver's licence at the PRD you'll probably only have to take a written test; other requirements include a medical certificate and two passport-sized colour photos. The forms are in Thai only, so you may also need an interpreter. Some PRDs request an affidavit of residence, obtainable from your country's embassy in Thailand upon presentation of proof that you reside in Thailand (eg, a utility bill in your name).

Fuel & Oil

Modern petrol (gasoline) stations with electric pumps are in plentiful supply in Thailand where there are paved roads. In more remote off-road areas, petrol *(ben-sin* or *náam-man rót yon)* is usually available at small roadside or village stands – typically just a couple of ancient hand-operated pumps fastened to petrol barrels.

At the time of writing, regular (*thamádaa*, usually 91 octane) petrol cost about 15B per litre, super (*phísèt*, 94 to 95 octane) a bit more. Diesel (*dii-sôen*) fuel is available at most pumps for around 12B.

The Thai phrase for motor oil is *náam-man khrêuang*.

Motorcycle Touring

Motorcycle travel has become a popular way to get around Thailand, especially in the North. In the South there is more round-island touring and less long-distance motorcycling. Dozens of places in tourist areas, including many bungalows and guesthouses, have set up shop with no more than a couple of motorbikes for rent. Think twice about renting a motorcycle in places like Phuket, Ko Samui and Ko Pha-Ngan. Statistics are hard to come by but locals will tell you that visitors are killed or maimed in motorcycle accidents with alarming frequency.

It is also possible to buy a new or used motorbike and sell it before you leave the country – a good, used 125cc bike costs around 20,000B to 25,000B (up to 60,000B for a reconditioned Honda AX-1).

Daily rental ranges from 150B to 200B a day for a 100cc step-through (eg, Honda Dream, Suzuki Crystal) to 500B to 600B a day for a good 250cc dirt bike. The motorcycle industry in Thailand has stopped assembling dirt bikes, so many of those for rent are getting on in years; when they're well maintained they're fine, when they're not they can leave you stranded if not worse. The latest trend in Thailand is for small, heavy racing bikes that couldn't be less suitable for the typical faràng body.

The legal maximum size for motorcycle manufacture in Thailand is 150cc, though in reality few bikes on the road exceed 125cc. Anything over 150cc must be imported, which means an extra 600% in import duties. The odd rental shop specialises in bigger motorbikes (average 200cc to 500cc) – some were imported by foreign residents

and later sold on the local market, but most came into the country as 'parts' and were discreetly assembled, and licensed under the table.

While motorcycle touring is undoubtedly one of the best ways to see Thailand, it is also undoubtedly one of the easiest ways to cut your travels short, permanently. You can also run up very large repair and/or hospital bills in the blink of an eye. However, with proper safety precautions and driving conduct adapted to local conditions, you can see parts of Thailand inaccessible by other modes of transport and still make it home in one piece. Some guidelines to keep in mind:

- If you've never driven a motorcycle before, stick to the smaller 100cc step-through bikes with automatic clutches. If you're an experienced rider but have never done off-the-road driving, take it slowly the first few days.
- Always check a machine over thoroughly before you take it out. Look at the tyres to see if they still have tread, look for oil leaks, test the brakes. You may be held liable for any problems that weren't duly noted before your departure. Newer bikes cost more than clunkers, but are generally safer and more reliable. Street bikes are more comfortable and ride more smoothly on paved roads than dirt bikes; it's silly to rent an expensive dirt bike if most of your riding is going to be along decent roads. A two-stroke bike suitable for off-road riding generally uses twice the fuel of a four-stroke bike with the same size engine, thus lowering your cruising range in areas where roadside pumps are scarce.
- Wear protective clothing and a helmet, which is required by law in 17 provinces – most rental places will provide them. Without a helmet, a minor slide on gravel can leave you with concussion, cuts or bruises. Long pants, long-sleeved shirts and shoes are highly recommended as protection against sunburn and as a second skin if you fall. If your helmet doesn't have a visor, then wear goggles, glasses or sunglasses to keep bugs, dust and other debris out of your eyes. Gloves are also a good idea to prevent blisters caused by holding on to the twist-grips for long periods of time. It is practically suicidal to ride on Thailand's highways without taking these minimum precautions.
- For distances of over 100km or so, take along an extra supply of motor oil, and if riding a two-stroke machine carry two-stroke engine oil. On long trips, oil burns fast.

- You should never ride alone in remote areas, especially at night. There have been incidents where faràng bikers have been shot or harassed while riding alone, mostly in remote rural areas. When riding in pairs or groups, spread out so you'll have room to manoeuvre or brake suddenly if necessary.
- In Thailand, the de facto right of way is determined by the size of the vehicle, which puts the motorcycle pretty low in the pecking order. Don't fight it and keep clear of trucks and buses.
- Distribute whatever weight you're carrying on the bike as evenly as possible across the frame. Too much weight at the back of the bike makes the front end less easy to control and prone to rising up suddenly on bumps and inclines.
- Get insurance with the motorcycle if possible. The more reputable motorcycle rental places insure all their bikes; some will do it for an extra charge. Without insurance you're responsible for anything that happens to the bike. If an accident results in the bike being 'totalled', or if the bike is lost or stolen, you can be up for 25,000B plus. To be absolutely clear about your liability, ask for a written estimate of the replacement cost for a similar bike – take photos as a guarantee. Some agencies will only accept the replacement cost of a new bike. Health insurance is also a good idea – get it before you leave home and check the conditions in regard to motorcycle riding.

BICYCLE

Bicycles can be hired in many locations; guesthouses often have a few for rent at only 50B to 80B per day. Just about anywhere outside Bangkok, bikes are the ideal form of local transport because they're cheap, non-polluting and keep you moving slowly enough to see everything. Carefully note the condition of the bike before hiring; if it breaks down you are responsible and parts can be very expensive.

Many visitors are bringing their own touring bikes to Thailand these days. For the most part, drivers are courteous and move over for bicycles. Most roads are sealed, with roomy shoulders. Grades in most parts of the country are moderate; exceptions include the far north. There is plenty of opportunity for dirt-road and off-road pedalling, so a sturdy mountain bike would make a good alternative to a touring rig. Good potential touring routes include the back roads of Yala, Pattani and Narathiwat provinces in the deep south – the terrain is mostly flat and the village scenery is inspiring.

One note of caution: before you leave home, go over your bike with a fine-toothed comb and fill your repair kit with every imaginable spare part. As with cars and motorbikes, you won't necessarily be able to buy that crucial gizmo for your machine when it breaks down somewhere in the back of beyond as the sun sets.

No special permits are needed for bringing a bicycle into the country, although bikes may be registered by customs – which means if you don't leave the country with your bike you'll have to pay a huge customs duty. Most larger cities have bike shops – there are several in Bangkok and Chiang Mai – but they often stock only a few Japanese or locally made parts. All the usual bike trip precautions apply – bring a repair kit and helmet, reflective clothing and plenty of insurance.

You can take bicycles on the train for a little less than the equivalent of one 3rd-class fare. Buses often don't charge (if they do it will be something nominal); on the ordinary buses they'll place your bike on the roof, and on air-con buses it will be put in the cargo hold.

Thailand Cycling Club (☎ 022 435 139, in Bangkok ☎ 022 412 023), established in 1959, serves as an information clearing house on biking tours and cycle clubs around the country. One of the best shops for cycling gear in Thailand is the centrally located Probike (☎ 022 533 384, fax 022 541 077), 237/1 Soi Sarasin, opposite Bangkok's Lumphini Park.

HITCHING

Hitching is never entirely safe in any country in the world, and we don't recommend it. Travellers who decide to hitch should understand that they are taking a small but serious risk. You may not be able to identify the local rapist/murderer before you get into his vehicle. However, many people do choose to hitch, and the advice that follows should help to make the journeys as fast and safe as possible.

It's safer to hitch in pairs and let someone know where you are planning to go.

People have mixed success with hitch-hiking in Thailand; sometimes it's great and other times no one will pick you up. It seems easiest in the more touristed areas of the North and South, most difficult in the Central and North-Eastern regions where foreigners are a relatively rare sight. To stand on a road and try to flag every vehicle that passes by is, to the Thais, something only a village idiot would do.

If you're prepared to face this perception, the first step is to use the correct gesture used for flagging a ride – the thumb-out gesture isn't recognised by the average Thai. When Thais want a ride they stretch one arm out with the hand open, palm facing down, and move the hand up and down. This is the same gesture used to flag a taxi or bus, which is why some drivers will stop and point to a bus stop if one is nearby.

In general, hitching isn't worth the hassle as ordinary non-air-con buses are frequent and fares are cheap. There's no need to stand at a bus terminal – all you have to do is stand on any road going in your direction and flag down a passing bus or sǎwngthǎew (see the Sǎwngthǎew entry later in this chapter).

The exception is in areas where there isn't any bus service, though in such places there's not likely to be very much private vehicle traffic either. If you do manage to get a ride it's customary to offer food or cigarettes to the driver if you have any.

BOAT

As any flight over Thailand will reveal, there is plenty of water to get out on during your trip. The true Thai river and bay transport is the long-tail boat (reua hǎang yao), so called because the propeller is mounted at the end of a long drive shaft extending from the engine. The engine, which varies from a small marine engine to a large car engine, is mounted on gimbals and the whole unit is swivelled to steer the boat. Long-tail boats can travel at phenomenal speeds.

Between the mainland and islands in the Gulf of Thailand or Andaman Sea, all sorts of larger ocean-going craft are used. The standard is an all-purpose wooden boat, 8m to 10m long with a large inboard engine, a wheelhouse and a simple roof to shelter passengers and cargo. Faster, more expensive hovercraft or jetfoils are sometimes available in tourist areas.

LOCAL TRANSPORT

The Getting Around section in the Bangkok chapter has more information on various forms of local transport.

Bus

In most larger provincial capitals, there are extensive local bus services, generally operating with very low fares (4B to 8B). For the rest, you must rely on sǎwngthǎew, túk-túk or sǎamláw (three-wheeled pedicabs).

Taxi

Many regional centres have taxi services, but while there may well be meters, they're never used. Establishing the fare before departure is essential. Try to get an idea of the fare from a third party and be prepared to bargain. In general, fares are reasonably low.

Sǎamláw/Túk-Túk

Sǎamláw means 'three wheels', and that's just what they are – three-wheeled vehicles. There are two types of sǎamláw: motorised and non-motorised. You'll find motorised sǎamláw throughout the country. They're small utility vehicles, powered by a horrendously noisy two-stroke engine (usually LPG-powered) – if the noise and vibration doesn't get you, the fumes will. These sǎamláw are more commonly known as túk-túk from the noise they make. On the other hand, the non-motorised versions are bicycle rickshaws, similar to those seen all over Asia. There are no bicycle sǎamláw in Bangkok but you will find them elsewhere in the country. For both types of sǎamláw the fare must be established, by bargaining if necessary, before departure.

Sǎwngthǎew

A sǎwngthǎew (literally, two rows) is a small pick-up truck with two rows of bench

SB

These small utility vehicles are called túk-túk from the noise they make.

seats down the sides, very similar to an Indonesian *bemo* or a Filipino *jeepney*. Săwngthăew sometimes operate fixed routes, just like buses, but they may also run a share-taxi type of service or even be booked individually like a regular taxi.

Motorcycle Taxi
Motorcycle taxis are most useful in Bangkok during times of heavy traffic when you want to get across town in a hurry. You'll see groups of them parked on street corners or in front of malls or any other such place that gets a lot of pedestrian traffic – look for the group of guys wearing brightly coloured vests loitering around their parked motorbikes. Outside Bangkok, motorcycle taxis are used for longer rides, such as from a provincial town to its airport. Always negotiate the price of the ride before getting on a motorcycle taxi.

ORGANISED TOURS
Many tour operators around the world can arrange guided tours of Thailand. Most of them simply serve as brokers for tour companies based in Thailand; they buy their trips from a wholesaler and resell them under various names in travel markets overseas. Hence, one is much like another and you might as well arrange a tour in Thailand at a lower cost. Two of Thailand's largest tour wholesalers in Bangkok are: World Travel Service (☎ 022 335 900, fax 022 367 169) at 1053 Th Charoen Krung and Deithelm Travel (☎ 022 559 150, fax 022 560 248) at Kian Gwan Building II, 140/1 Th Withayu.

Bangkok-based Khiri Travel (☎ 026 290 491, fax 026 290 493, [e] info@khiri.com) specialises in ecologically oriented tours. It's located opposite the Viengtai Hotel on Soi Rambutri off Thanon Chakrapong.

Overseas Companies
The better overseas tour companies build their own Thailand itineraries from scratch and choose their local suppliers based on which ones best serve these itineraries. Of these, several specialise in adventure and/or ecological tours, including those in the following list. Asia Transpacific Journeys, for example, offers trips across a broad spectrum of Thai destinations and activities, from trekking in Northern Thailand to sea canoeing in the Phuket Sea. The average trip duration is around 14 to 17 days.

Asia Transpacific Journeys (☎ 800-642 2742, 303-443 6789, fax 303-443 7078, [w] www .southeastasia.com) 3055 Center Green Dr, Boulder, CO 80301 USA
Club Aventure (☎ 514-272 0999, fax 527 3999, [w] www.clubaventure.com) 759 ave du Mont-Royal Est, Montreal, QUE H2J, Canada
Exodus (☎ 020-8673 5550, fax 8673 0779, [w] www.exodustravels.co.uk) 9 Weir Rd, London SW12 OLT, UK
Intrepid Travel (☎ 03-9473 2626, fax 9419 4426, [w] www.intrepidtravel.com) 11-13 Spring St, Fitzroy, VIC 3065, Australia
Mountain Travel Sobek (☎ 800-227 2384, 510-527 8100, fax 510-525 7710, [w] www .mstobek.com) 6420 Fairmount Ave, Berkeley, CA 94530, USA
Ms Kasma Loha-Unchit (☎ 510-655 8900, [w] www.thaifoodandtravel.com) PO Box 21165, Oakland, California 94620, USA. A Thai native living in California, offers highly personalised, 19- to 28-day 'cultural immersion' tours of Thailand.

Bangkok

The very epitome of the modern, steamy Asian metropolis, Bangkok (560 sq km; population six million – perhaps as many as 10 million) has a wealth of attractions if you can tolerate the traffic, noise, heat (in the hot season), floods (in the rainy season) and polluted air. The city is incredibly urbanised, but beneath its modern veneer lies an unmistakable Thai-ness.

The capital of Thailand was established at Bangkok in 1782 by the first king of the Chakri Dynasty, Rama I. The name Bangkok comes from Bang Makok, meaning 'place of olive plums' and refers to the original site, which is only a very small part of what is today commonly known as Bangkok. The official Thai name is quite a tongue twister:

Krungthep mahanakhon amon rattanakosin mahintara ayuthaya mahadilok popnopparat ratchathani burirom udomratchaniwet mahasathan amonpiman avatansathit sakkathattiya visnukamprasit.

A surprising number of Thais can recite the entire name – but only because a clever local rock band set the words to a catchy tune. Fortunately for *faràng* (Westerners), the official name is shortened to Krung Thep (City of Angels) in everyday usage. Metropolitan Krung Thep includes Thonburi, the older part of the city (and predecessor to Bangkok as the capital), which is across Mae Nam Chao Phraya (Chao Phraya River) to the west.

Those anxious to get to Thailand's sand and surf may want to skip this massive urban sprawl and head directly south or east. But there is plenty to see in Bangkok should you decide to stop over for a few days. Even if you're just in town for the afternoon, say waiting for the overnight train to Surat Thani, it's worth taking in a few sights and absorbing the frenetic energy that makes this one of Asia's most fascinating cities.

Highlights

- Wat Phra Kaew, home of the Emerald Buddha, is spectacular with its colourful mosaics, gold leaf and breathtaking spires.

- Jim Thompson's House is a beautifully maintained example of authentic Thai residential architecture, displaying the American silk entrepreneur's extensive Asian art collection.

- Vimanmek Teak Mansion is one of the world's largest golden teak buildings.

- River or canal trips on a Mae Nam Chao Phraya express boat provide an opportunity to observe Thai river life, or you could go for a dinner cruise or see the bustling floating markets.

- Dine in Bangkok's incredible restaurants; try at least one riverside place to soak up the languid ambience of old Bangkok.

- Wat Pho houses Thailand's largest reclining Buddha and traditional massage school.

- Traditional dance-drama at the National Theatre and shrine dancing at various wát are highly recommended.

Bangkok caters to diverse interests. It has many temples, museums and other historic sites for those interested in traditional Thai culture. There's an impressive variety of good restaurants, clubs, international cultural and social events, movies screened in several languages, discos, heavy-metal pubs, folk cafes, even modern art galleries for those seeking contemporary Krung Thep. As the dean of expat authors in Thailand, William Warren, has said, 'The gift Bangkok offers me is the assurance I will never be bored'.

Following is a fairly selective guide to Bangkok's sights, accommodation, eateries and entertainment. For a more detailed look at the city, see Lonely Planet's *Bangkok* and/or *Thailand* guides.

ORIENTATION

The eastern side of Mae Nam Chao Phraya, Bangkok proper, can be divided in two by the main north-south train line. The portion between the river and the railway is old Bangkok (often called Ko Ratanakosin), where most of the older temples and the original palace are located, as well as the Chinese and Indian districts. The part of the city east of the railway, which covers many times more area than the old districts, is new Bangkok. It can be divided again into the business and tourist district wedged between Thanon (Th) Charoen Krung (New Rd) and Th Rama IV, and the sprawling business, residential and tourist district stretching along Th Sukhumvit and Th Phetchaburi Tat Mai.

This leaves the hard-to-classify areas below Th Sathon Tai (South Sathon Rd), which includes Khlong Toey – Bangkok's main port – and the area above Th Rama IV between the train line and Th Withayu (Wireless Rd), where there are scores of office blocks, several cinemas, civil service buildings, the shopping area of Siam Square, Chulalongkorn University and the National Stadium. The areas along the eastern bank of Mae Nam Chao Phraya are undergoing a surge of redevelopment and many new buildings, particularly apartments, are going up.

On the opposite (western) side of Mae Nam Chao Phraya is Thonburi, which was Thailand's capital for 15 years before Bangkok was founded. Few tourists ever set foot on the Thonburi side except to visit Wat Arun, the Temple of Dawn. Fang Thon (Thon Bank), as it's often called by Thais, seems an age away from the glittering high-rises on the river's eastern bank, although it is an up-and-coming area for condo development.

Maps

A map is essential for finding your way around Bangkok, and there are lots of maps competing for your attention. Apart from Lonely Planet's *Bangkok* city map, there are also detailed locally produced maps.

A bus map is necessary if you intend to spend a lot of time in Bangkok and want to use the economical bus system. One of the most popular, because it clearly shows all the bus routes (and some walking tours), and is cheap, is the *Tour 'n Guide Map to Bangkok Thailand*, often referred to by travellers as the 'blue map' because of its monotonous aqua colour. The map costs 40B and although it's regularly updated, some bus routes will inevitably be wrong, so take care. The coated paper, which resists stains, is a plus.

The Tourism Authority of Thailand (TAT) publishes and distributes the free *City Map of Bangkok*, a folded sheet map on coated stock with bus routes, all major hotels, the latest expressways, sightseeing, hospitals, embassies and more – very useful if a bit hard to read due to small print. Separate inset maps of significant areas of the city are also helpful. You can pick it up at the airport TAT desk or at any Bangkok TAT office.

The long-running, oft-imitated and never equalled *Nancy Chandler's Map of Bangkok* costs 140B and contains a whole host of information on out-of-the-way places, including lots of stuff on where to buy unusual things around the city. The six different water-coloured panels (Greater Bangkok, Sampeng Lane, Th Sukhumvit, Chatuchak Weekend Market, Central Shopping Area and Markets of Central Bangkok) are all hand-drawn, hand-lettered and laid out by hand. The 21st edition, published in 2001, has a handy categorised index.

Groovy Map's *Bangkok by Night Map 'n' Guide* combines the usual sightseeing features with restaurant, bar and night-time entertainment recommendations, all on decent coated stock. It is not a map to Bangkok sleaze, but rather a well-rounded survey of many different entertainment venues. The same company puts out a *Bangkok by Day Map 'n' Guide*.

Very detailed and covering a large portion of the city is *Bangkok Map*, a 188-page hardcover street atlas put out by the Agency for Real Estate Affairs, a private company specialising in real estate surveys of the city.

INFORMATION
Tourist Offices

The Tourism Authority of Thailand (TAT) produces useful, informative and well-produced brochures, and many of the staff speak English. The TAT has a desk in the arrivals area of both Terminal 1 (☎ 025 238 972) and Terminal 2 (☎ 025 352 669) at Bangkok International Airport, both open from 8am to midnight. The TAT's main office (☎ 026 941 222, fax 026 941 220, ℮ info1@tat.or.th) occupies 10 floors of Le Concorde Building, 202 Th Ratchadaphisek. It's open from 8.30am to 4.30pm daily. The TAT's information office (☎ 022 829 773, fax 022 829 775) on Th Ratchadamnoen Nok near the Ratchadamnoen Stadium (see Central Bangkok map) is more conveniently located. It's open daily from 8am to 4.30pm. A smaller TAT office with fewer materials can be found at Chatuchak Market, open daily from 9am to 5pm.

The TAT also maintains a 24-hour Tourist Assistance Centre (TAC; ☎ 1155) for matters relating to theft and other mishaps. The paramilitary arm of the TAT, the Tourist Police, can be quite effective in dealing with such matters, particularly 'unethical' business practices – which sometimes turn out to be cultural misunderstandings. Note that if you think you've been overcharged for gems (or any other purchase), there's little the TAC can do.

Immigration Department

For visa extensions or applications, you'll need to visit the Immigration Department office (☎ 022 873 103) on Soi Suan Phlu, off Th Sathon Tai. It's open Monday to Friday from 8.30am to 4.30pm (with limited staff from noon to 1pm), and Saturday until noon. Most applications and extensions require two photos and a photocopy of the photo page and visa page of your passport.

Money

Regular bank hours in Bangkok are from 10am to 4pm and ATMs are common in all areas of the city. Many Thai banks also have currency exchange offices in tourist-oriented areas of Bangkok, which are open from 8.30am to 8pm (some even later) daily. You'll find them in several places along the following roads: Sukhumvit, Nana Neua, Khao San, Patpong, Surawong, Ratchadamri, Rama IV, Rama I, Silom and Charoen Krung. If you're after currency for other countries in Asia, check with the moneychangers along Th Charoen Krung (New Rd) near the main post office.

Post

The main post office is on Th Charoen Krung. The easiest way to get there is via the Chao Phraya express boats to Tha Muang Khae (Muang Khae pier) at the river end of Soi Charoen Krung 34, next to Wat Muang Khae. The main post office is just north of the wát.

The poste restante counter is open Monday to Friday from 8am to 8pm, and on weekends and holidays until 1pm. Each letter you collect costs 1B, parcels 2B. The staff are very efficient.

There's also a packaging service that's open Monday to Friday from 8am to 4.30pm, and Saturday from 9am to noon. When the parcel counter is closed (weekday evenings and Sunday mornings) an informal packing service (using recycled materials) is opened behind the service windows at the centre rear of the building.

Branch post offices throughout the city also offer poste restante and parcel services.

BANGKOK

GREATER BANGKOK

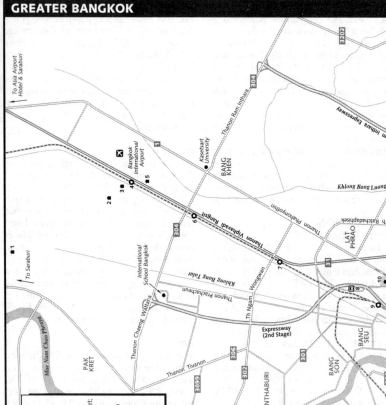

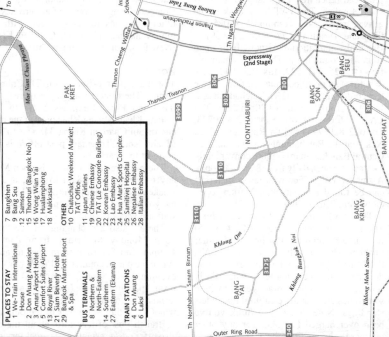

PLACES TO STAY
1 We-Train International
   House
2 Don Muang Mansion
3 Amari Airport Hotel
5 Comfort Suites Airport
13 Royal River
21 Siam Beverly Hotel
29 Bangkok Marriott Resort
   & Spa

BUS TERMINALS
8 Northern &
   North-Eastern
14 Southern
27 Eastern (Ekamai)

TRAIN STATIONS
4 Don Muang
6 Laksi

7 Bangkhen
9 Bang Seu
12 Samsen
15 Thonburi (Bangkok Noi)
16 Wong Wian Yai
17 Hualamphong
18 Makkasan

OTHER
10 Chatuchak Weekend Market;
   TAT Office
11 Japan Airlines
19 Chinese Embassy
20 TAT (Le Concorde Building)
22 Korean Embassy
23 Lao Embassy
24 Hua Mark Sports Complex
25 Samitivej Hospital
26 Nepalese Embassy
28 Italian Embassy

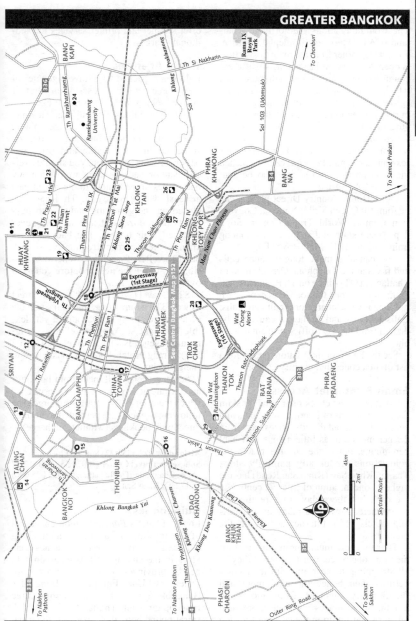

Telephone & Fax

The Communications Authority of Thailand (CAT) international telephone office, around the corner from the main post office, is open 24 hours. At last count, 40 different countries had Home Country Direct service, which means you can simply enter a vacant Home Country Direct booth and get one-button connection to an international operator in any of these countries (see the Telephone section in the Facts for the Visitor chapter for a list). Other countries (except Laos and Malaysia) can be reached via IDD phones. Faxes can also be sent from the CAT office.

Other Home Country Direct phones can be found at Queen Sirikit National Convention Center, World Trade Center, Sogo department store and at the Hualamphong train station MBE (Mail Boxes Etc).

You can also make long-distance calls and faxes at the Telephone Organisation of Thailand (TOT) office on Th Ploenchit near Siam Square, but this office accepts cash only, no reverse charge or credit card calls. Calls to Laos and Malaysia can only be dialled from the TOT office or from private phones.

See the Facts for the Visitor chapter for a list of area codes and country codes.

Email & Internet Access

Internet users can check their email or skim the Net at dozens of Internet cafes, bars and centres throughout the city. Rates vary from 2B per minute to as little as one half-baht per minute, but at the cheaper places the connections are usually painfully slow. Thanon Khao San (Khao San Road) has the highest concentration of Internet centres in the city, but these days they're literally everywhere. Nowadays many guesthouses and hotels offer Internet access on the premises as well.

There's not much point in recommending one place over another as they're all struggling to keep up with their competitors, and hence the equipment and functionality changes from month to month. Some places are little more than one terminal set up in the corner of a *ráan*

cham (sundries shop), while better spots offer scanner and printer services for additional charges.

Travel Agencies

Bangkok is packed with travel agencies of every manner and description, but if you're looking for cheap airline tickets it's wise to be cautious. On and near Th Khao San alone, there are over a dozen places where you can book bus and air tickets; some are highly reliable and offer unbelievably low prices, but you should exercise caution because there are often a few bad apples in the bunch. In the recent past at least two agencies on Th Khao San closed up shop and absconded with payments from dozens of tourists who never received their tickets. The bad agencies change their names frequently, so ask other travellers for advice. Wherever possible, try to see the tickets before you hand over the money.

STA Travel (☎ 022 332 582), Wall Street Tower, 33 Th Surawong, maintains reliable offices specialising in discounted yet flexible air tickets. Another reliable, long-running agency is Viang Travel (☎ 022 803 537), Trang Hotel, 99/8 Th Wisut Kasat, Banglamphu.

Some agencies will make train bookings and pick up tickets by courier – a service for which there's usually a 100B surcharge. The following agencies are permitted to arrange direct train bookings (without surcharge):

Airland (☎ 022 555 432) 866 Th Ploenchit
Songserm Travel Center (☎ 022 558 790) 121/7 Soi Chalermla, Th Phayathai; (☎ 022 828 080) 172 Th Khao San

Guidebooks

Lonely Planet's *Bangkok* guide covers all of the information in this chapter along with extra details concerning business services in the city as well as excursions to nearby provinces. *Vivre à Bangkok*, published by Une Équipe de Bénévoles Bangkok Accueil for La Commuanutée Francophone en Thaïlande, is a thick spiral-bound book that covers all the usual territory with special attention to French speakers – including, for example, a list of French-speaking travel agents. It's available in Bangkok bookshops where foreign-language books are sold, such as Asia Books (see Bookshops following).

Magazines & Newspapers

Several ad-laden giveaways contain tourist information, but the best source for no-frills info is the *Bangkok Metro* magazine. A lifestyle monthly, it is packed with listings on health, entertainment, events, social services, travel tips and consumer-oriented articles. The *Nation* and *Bangkok Post* also contain useful articles and event listings, especially the Friday editions, which contain entertainment supplements.

Bookshops

Bangkok has many good bookshops, possibly the best selection in South-East Asia.

For new books and magazines the two best chains are Asia Books and Duang Kamol (DK) Book House. Asia Books (☎ 022 527 277), 221 Th Sukhumvit, Soi 15, lives up to its name by having one of the largest selections of English-language titles on Asia in Bangkok. Branch stores are scattered around the city in the larger shopping centres. Smaller Asia Books stalls can be found in several larger hotels and at Thai airports.

DK Book House (☎ 022 516 335), 244–6 Soi 2, Th Rama I, Siam Square, is good for textbooks. There's also a branch on Th Sukhumvit across from the Ambassador Hotel (excellent for fiction titles), and branches in other large shopping centres. There are two other bookshops with English-language books in the Siam Square complex: the Book Chest (Soi 2) and Odeon Store (Soi 1). Kinokuniya in The Emporium shopping centre, Soi 24, Th Sukhumvit, is also quite good for Japanese and English-language materials.

Teck Heng Bookstore (☎ 022 341 836), 1326 Th Charoen Krung, between the Shangri-La and Oriental Hotels, is one of the better independent bookshops in this neighbourhood.

Suksit Siam (☎ 022 259 531), opposite Wat Ratchabophit on Th Fuang Nakhon, specialises in books on Thai politics. This shop also has a number of mainstream titles on Thailand and Asia, both in English and Thai.

Used and rare books are available at a few shops, including Shaman Books (☎ 026 290 418), 71 Th Khao San, and Merman Books (☎ 022 313 155), Silom Complex, 191 Th Silom. The Chatuchak Weekend Market in Chatuchak Park is also a source of used, often out-of-print books in several languages. On Th Khao San in Banglamphu, several street-side vendors specialise in used paperback novels and guidebooks, including many Lonely Planet titles.

Medical Services

Bangkok is Thailand's leading health care centre, with three university research hospitals, 12 public and private hospitals, and hundreds of medical clinics. Australian, US and UK embassies usually keep up-to-date lists of doctors who speak English; for doctors who speak other languages, contact the relevant embassy or consulate.

Several shop-front clinics in the Th Ploenchit area specialise in lab tests for sexually transmitted diseases. According to *Bangkok Metro* magazine, Bangkok General Hospital has the most sophisticated HIV blood testing program. Bangkok's better hospitals include:

Bangkok Adventist (Mission) Hospital (☎ 022 811 422, 022 821 100) 430 Th Phitsanulok
Bangkok Christian Hospital (☎ 022 336 981–9, 022 351 000) 124 Th Silom
Bangkok General Hospital (☎ 023 180 066) Soi 47, Th Phetchaburi Tat Mai
Bangkok Nursing Home (☎ 022 332 610–9) 9 Th Convent
Bumrumgrad Hospital (☎ 026 671 000) 33 Soi 3, Th Sukhumvit
Samitivej Hospital (☎ 023 816 728) 133 Soi 49, Th Sukhumvit
St Louis Hospital (☎ 022 120 033–48) 215 Th Sathon Tai

Emergency

All hospitals listed offer 24-hour service. Bangkok does not have an emergency phone system staffed by English-speaking operators. Between 8am and midnight, your best bet for English-speaking assistance is the Tourist Assistance Centre (☎ 022 815 051, 022 828 129), or the Tourist Police (☎ 1155) who can be reached 24 hours a day.

If you speak Thai, or can find a Thai to call on your behalf, here are the city's main emergency numbers:

Ambulance	☎ 022 551 133–6
Police	☎ 191 or 123
Fire	☎ 199

Dangers & Annoyances

Bangkok's most heavily touristed areas, especially around Wat Phra Kaew and Th Khao San, are favourite hunting grounds for Thai con artists of every ilk. There are also some who prowl the areas near Soi Kasem San 1 and Soi Kasem San 2, opposite Mahboonkrong shopping centre and near Jim Thompson's House, and typically dress in business suits and carry mobile phones.

The Chao Phraya express boat piers between Tha Tien and Tha Phra Athit also attract cons who may try to intercept tourists as they get off the boats – the favourite line is 'Wat Pho (or Wat Phra Kaew, Wat Arun or Wat Traimit) is closed today for repairs, government holiday etc'. Don't believe anyone on the street who tells you Wat Pho, Jim Thompson's House or some other attraction is closed for a holiday; check for yourself.

More obvious are the túk-túk drivers who are out to make a commission by dragging you to a local silk or jewellery shop – even though you've requested an entirely different destination. In either case if you accept an invitation for 'free' sightseeing or shopping, you're quite likely to end up wasting an afternoon or – as happens all too often – losing a lot of money. Lonely Planet has also received letters from female travellers who have been scammed by Thai women con artists.

For details on common scams, see the Dangers & Annoyances section in the Facts for the Visitor chapter.

Tourist Police

The head Tourist Police office (☎ 026 786 800) at TPI Tower, Th Chan, deals with tourism-related crime, particularly gem fraud, and can be reached by dialling ☎ 1155. The Tourist Police also have a branch at the TAT compound on Th Ratchadamnoen Nok.

The Tourist Police are a separate force established to deal with tourist problems under the Crime Suppression Division of the National Police Department. In Bangkok, some 500 English-speaking officers are stationed in tourist areas – their kiosks, cars and uniforms are clearly marked. If you have any problems relating to criminal activity, contact the Tourist Police. If they can't solve the problem, or if it's out of their jurisdiction, they can act as a bilingual liaison with the regular police.

WAT PHRA KAEW & GRAND PALACE
วัดพระแก้ว/พระบรมมหาราชวัง

Wat Phra Kaew *(Wat Phra Si Ratana Satsadaram or Temple of the Emerald Buddha; admission 200B; open 8.30am-11.30am & 1pm-3.30pm)* adjoins the Grand Palace *(Phra Borom Maharatchawong)* on common ground that was consecrated in 1782, the first year of Bangkok rule. The grounds encompass more than 100 buildings that represent over 200 years of royal history and architectural experimentation. See the Emerald Buddha boxed text later in this chapter.

The wát structures are extremely colourful, being comprised of gleaming, gilded *chedi* (stupas), polished orange and green roof tiles, mosaic-encrusted pillars and rich marble pediments. Extensive murals depicting scenes from the *Ramakian* (the Thai version of the Indian epic, the *Ramayana*) line the inside walls of the compound.

Except for an anteroom here and there, the Grand Palace is closed to the public. The exteriors of the four buildings are worth a swift perusal, however, for their royal bombast.

The admission fee includes entry to the Royal Thai Decorations & Coins Pavilion (on the same grounds) and to both Viman-mek and Abhisek Dusit Throne Hall (near the Dusit Zoo).

Since wát are sacred to Thai Buddhists – this one particularly so because of its royal associations – visitors should dress and behave decently. If you wear shorts or a sleeveless shirt you may be refused admission; a sarong or baggy pants are sometimes available on loan at the entry area. For walking in the courtyard areas you must wear shoes with closed heels and toes – thongs aren't permitted. As in any temple compound, shoes should be removed before entering the main chapel *(bòt)* or sanctuaries *(wíhǎan)* of Wat Phra Kaew.

The most economical way to reach Wat Phra Kaew and the Grand Palace is by aircon bus No 8 or 12. You can also take a Chao Phraya express boat, disembarking at Tha Chang.

WAT PHO
วัดโพธิ์

Wat Pho *(Wat Phra Chetuphon; admission 20B; open 8am-5pm, ticket booth closed noon-1pm)* is the oldest and largest wát in Bangkok. It features the longest reclining Buddha and the largest collection of Buddha images in Thailand, and was the earliest centre for public education. As a temple site Wat Pho dates back to the 16th century, but its current history really begins in 1781 with the complete rebuilding of the original monastery.

Narrow Th Chetuphon divides the grounds in two, with each section surrounded by huge whitewashed walls. The most interesting part is the northern compound. It includes a large bòt enclosed by a gallery of Buddha images and four wíhǎan (the counterpart to the bòt), four large chedis commemorating the first three Chakri kings (Rama III has two chedis), 91 smaller chedis, an old *Tripitaka* (Buddhist scriptures) library, a sermon hall, a large wíhǎan housing the **reclining Buddha**, and a school building for classes in Abhidhamma (Buddhist philosophy), plus several less important structures.

Emerald Buddha

The so-called Emerald Buddha (Phra Kaew) is not emerald but probably made of jasper quartz or perhaps nephrite jade. It stands 60cm to 75cm high, depending on how it is measured. It is not known for certain where the image originated or who sculpted it, but it first appeared on record in 15th-century Chiang Rai. It is said to have been covered with plaster and gold leaf and placed in Chiang Rai's own Wat Phra Kaew (literally, Temple of the Jewel Image). It is supposed that the image lost its plaster covering in a fall. It next appeared in Lampang where it enjoyed a 32-year stay (again at Wat Phra Kaew) until it was brought to Wat Chedi Luang in Chiang Mai.

In the mid-16th century Laotian invaders took the image from Chiang Mai to Luang Prabang in Laos. Later it was moved to Wiang Chan (Vientiane). When Thailand's King Taksin waged war against Laos 200 years later, the image was taken back to the Thai capital of Thonburi by General Chakri, who later succeeded Taksin as Rama I, the founder of the Chakri dynasty.

Rama I had the Emerald Buddha moved to the new Thai capital in Bangkok and had two royal robes made for it, one to be worn in the hot season and one for the rainy season. Rama III added another to the wardrobe, to be worn in the cool season. The three robes are still solemnly changed at the beginning of each season by the king himself. The huge bòt (central sanctuary) at Wat Phra Kaew in which it is displayed was built expressly for the purpose of housing the diminutive image.

Joe Cummings

Wat Pho is the national headquarters for the teaching and preservation of traditional Thai medicine, including Thai massage. A **massage school** convenes in the afternoons at the eastern end of the compound; a massage costs 200B per hour, 120B for a half-hour. You can also study massage here in seven- to 10-day courses.

You can hire English-, French-, German-and Japanese-speaking guides for 150B for one visitor, 200B for two, 300B for three. Also on the premises are a few astrologers and palmists.

Air-con bus Nos 6, 8 and 12 stop near Wat Pho. The nearest Chao Phraya express pier is Tha Tien.

WAT MAHATHAT
วัดมหาธาตุ

Wat Mahathat *(admission free; open 9am-5pm)*, founded in the late 18th century, is a national centre for the Mahanikai monastic sect and houses one of Bangkok's two Buddhist universities, Mahathat Rajavidyalaya. The university is the most important place of Buddhist learning in mainland South-East Asia; the Lao, Vietnamese and Cambodian governments send selected monks to further their studies here.

Wat Mahathat and the surrounding area have developed into an informal Thai cultural centre of sorts, though this may not be obvious at first glance. A daily **open-air market** features traditional Thai herbal medicine, and out on the street you'll find a string of shops selling herbal cures and offering Thai massage. On weekends, a large produce market held on the temple grounds attracts people from all over Bangkok and beyond.

The temple complex is also open on *wan phrá* – Buddhist holy days (the full and new moons every fortnight).

The wát is located right across the street from Wat Phra Kaew, on the western side of Sanam Luang (Royal Field). Air-con bus Nos 8 and 12 both pass by it, and the nearest Chao Phraya express pier is Tha Maharat.

OTHER WATS
Wat Traimit
(Temple of the Golden Buddha; ☎ 026 231 226; admission 20B; open 9am-5pm) The main attraction here is, of course, the impressively gleaming, solid-gold Buddha image. It pays to arrive in the early morning if you want to avoid the tour groups.

Wat Traimit is near the intersection of Th Yaowarat and Th Charoen Krung, near Hualamphong train station.

Wat Arun
(Temple of Dawn; ☎ 024 663 167; admission 10B; open 8.30am-5.30pm) Named after the Indian god of dawn, Aruna, this striking wát appears in all the tourist brochures and is on the Thonburi side of Mae Nam Chao Phraya. The unique design of the 82m *prang* (Khmer-style tower) elongates the typical Khmer prang into a distinctly Thai shape. To reach Wat Arun from the Bangkok side, catch a cross-river ferry from Tha Tien at Th Thai Wang. Crossings are frequent and cost 2B.

Wat Benchamabophit
(Marble Temple; admission 20B; open 8.30am-5.30pm) This wát is made of white Carrara marble and was built at the end of the 19th century under King Chulalongkorn (Rama V). It is on the corner of Th Si Ayuthaya and Th Rama V, diagonally opposite the south-western corner of Chitlada Palace. Bus Nos 3 (air-con), 5 and 72 (non air-con) stop nearby.

Wat Bowonniwet
(Wat Bovornives; Th Phra Sumen, Banglamphu; admission free) This wát is the national headquarters for the Thammayut monastic sect, a minority in Thai Buddhism. King Mongkut lived here as a monk – in fact, he was the abbot of Wat Bowonniwet for several years. King Bhumibol, Crown Prince Vajiralongkorn and several other males in the royal family have been temporarily ordained here as monks. Bangkok's second Buddhist university, Mahamakut University, is housed here. India, Nepal and Sri Lanka all send monks to study here. Across the street from the main entrance to the wát are an English-language Buddhist bookshop and a Thai herbal clinic.

Because of its royal status, be particularly careful to dress properly when visiting this wát – no shorts or sleeveless shirts.

NATIONAL MUSEUM
พิพิธภัณฑสถานแห่งชาติ

The National Museum (☎ 022 241 370, 022 158 173, Th Na Phra That, Banglamphu; admission 40B; open 9am-4pm Wed-Sun) is the largest in South-East Asia and an excellent place to learn about Thai art.

Excellent, free English-language tours of the museum are given on Wednesday (Buddhism) and Thursday (Thai art, religion and culture), starting from the ticket pavilion at 9.30am. The tours are also conducted in French (Wednesday), German (Thursday) and Japanese (Wednesday). For more information on the tours, contact the museum.

JIM THOMPSON'S HOUSE
บ้านจิมทอมป์สัน

Jim Thompson's House (☎ 022 150 122, Soi Kasem San 2; adult/student/child 100/50/50B; open 9am-5pm Mon-Sat) is a great spot to see authentic Thai residential architecture and South-East Asian art. Located at the end of an undistinguished soi next to Khlong Saen Saep, the premises once belonged to American silk entrepreneur Jim Thompson, who deserves most of the credit for the worldwide popularity of Thai silk.

Thompson was a New York architect who briefly served in the Office of Strategic Services (OSS; the forerunner of the CIA) in Thailand during WWII. After the war he moved to Bangkok and developed an export market for Thai silk.

Thompson, who disappeared mysteriously in the Cameron Highlands of west Malaysia in 1967, collected parts of various derelict Thai homes in central Thailand and reassembled them in the current location in 1959. On display in the main house is his small but splendid Asian art collection as well as his personal belongings.

Admission proceeds go to Bangkok's School for the Blind; you can also wander around the grounds for free. The khlawng (canal) at the end of the soi is one of Bangkok's most lively. Beware of well-dressed touts in the soi who will tell you Thompson's house is closed – it's just a ruse to take you on a buying spree.

VIMANMEK TEAK MANSION (PHRA THII NANG WIMANMEK)
พระที่นั่งวิมานเมฆ

Vimanmek Teak Mansion (Phra Thii Nang Wimanmek; ☎ 026 286 300; adult/child 50/20B; open 9.30am-4pm) was originally built on Ko Si Chang in 1868 and moved to its present site in the Chitlada Palace grounds in 1910. It is a beautiful L-shaped, three-storey mansion said to be the world's largest golden teak building.

English-language tours leave every half-hour between 9.30am and 3pm. The tour covers around 30 rooms and lasts an hour. Smaller adjacent buildings display historic photography, documenting the Chakri Dynasty, and a good collection of antique Thai textiles. Thai classical and folk dances are performed at 10.30am and 2pm in a pavilion on the canal side of the mansion.

Admission is free if you've already been to the Grand Palace or Wat Phra Kaew and still have the entry ticket for Vimanmek or Abhisek. As this is royal property, visitors wearing shorts or sleeveless shirts will be refused entry.

ABHISEK DUSIT THRONE HALL
พระที่นั่งอภิเศกดุสิต

Abhisek Dusit Throne Hall (Phra Thii Nang Aphisek Dusit; admission 50B; open 10am-4pm), also in Chitlada Palace grounds, is a smaller wood, brick and stucco structure completed in 1904 for Rama V. Typical of the fine architecture of this era, the Victorian-influenced gingerbread- and Moorish-style porticoes blend to create a striking and distinctly Thai exterior. The hall houses an excellent display of regional handiwork crafted by members of the Promotion of Supplementary Occupations & Related Techniques (Support) foundation, an organisation sponsored by the queen.

As at Wat Phra Kaew and Vimanmek, visitors must be properly dressed – no sleeveless shirts or shorts.

BANGKOK

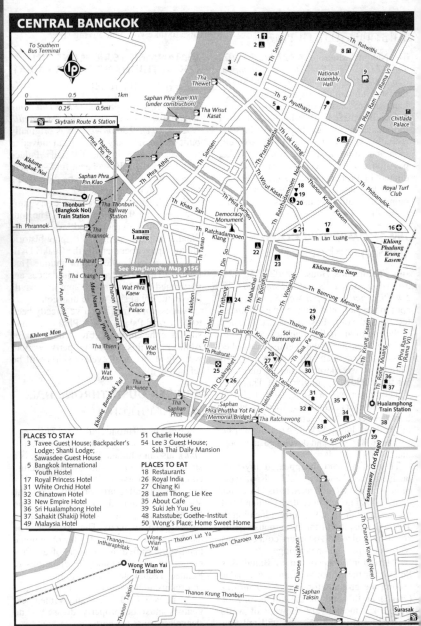

CENTRAL BANGKOK

To Southern
Bus Terminal

Skytrain Route & Station

0   0.5   1km
0   0.25   0.5mi

Saphan Phra Ram XIII
(under construction)

Tha
Thewet

Tha Wisut
Kasat

National
Assembly
Hall

Chitlada
Palace

Royal Turf
Club

Khlong
Bangkok Noi

Saphan Phra
Pin Klao

Thonburi
(Bangkok Noi)
Train Station

Tha Thonburi
Railway
Station

Tha
Phrannok

Th Phrannok

Th Phra Athit

Th Khao San

Democracy
Monument

Sanam
Luang

See Banglamphu Map p156

Tha Maharat

Tha Chang

Wat Phra
Kaew

Grand
Palace

Wat
Pho

Tha Thien

Wat
Arun

Tha
Rachinee

Tha
Saphan
Phut

Saphan
Phra Phuttha Yot Fa
(Memorial Bridge)

Tha Ratchawong

Khlong
Phadung
Krung
Kasem

Khlong Saen Saep

Th Bamrung Meuang

Thanon Luang

Soi
Bamrungrat

Hualamphong
Train Station

Wong
Wian
Yai

Thanon Lat Ya   Thanon Charoen Rat

Thanon
Intharaphitak

Wong Wian Yai
Train Station

Thanon Krung Thonburi

Thanon Taksin

Saphan
Taksin

Surasak

PLACES TO STAY
3 Tavee Guest House; Backpacker's
   Lodge; Shanti Lodge;
   Sawasdee Guest House
5 Bangkok International
   Youth Hostel
17 Royal Princess Hotel
31 White Orchid Hotel
32 Chinatown Hotel
33 New Empire Hotel
36 Sri Hualamphong Hotel
37 Sahakit (Shakij) Hotel
49 Malaysia Hotel

51 Charlie House
54 Lee 3 Guest House;
   Sala Thai Daily Mansion

PLACES TO EAT
18 Restaurants
26 Royal India
27 Chiang Ki
28 Laem Thong; Lie Kee
35 About Cafe
39 Suki Jeh Yuu Seu
48 Ratsstube; Goethe-Institut
50 Wong's Place; Home Sweet Home

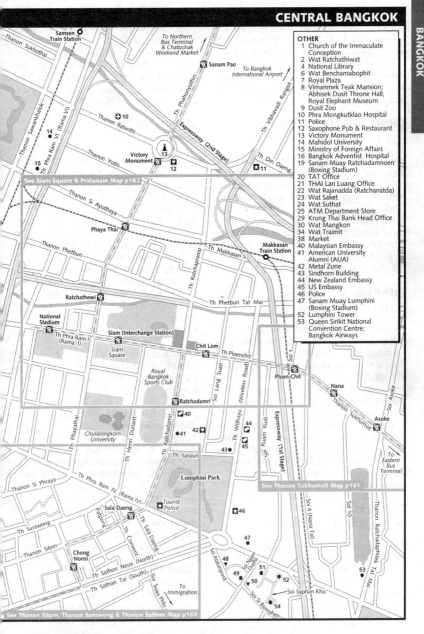

CENTRAL BANGKOK

OTHER
1 Church of the Immaculate Conception
2 Wat Ratchathiwat
4 National Library
6 Wat Benchamabophit
7 Royal Plaza
8 Vimanmek Teak Mansion; Abhisek Dusit Throne Hall; Royal Elephant Museum
9 Dusit Zoo
10 Phra Mongkutklao Hospital
11 Police
12 Saxophone Pub & Restaurant
13 Victory Monument
14 Mahidol University
15 Ministry of Foreign Affairs
16 Bangkok Adventist Hospital
19 Sanam Muay Ratchadamnoen (Boxing Stadium)
20 TAT Office
21 THAI Lan Luang Office
22 Wat Rajanadda (Ratchanatda)
23 Wat Saket
24 Wat Suthat
25 ATM Department Store
29 Krung Thai Bank Head Office
30 Wat Mangkon
34 Wat Traimit
38 Market
40 Malaysian Embassy
41 American University Alumni (AUA)
42 Metal Zone
43 Sindhorn Building
44 New Zealand Embassy
45 US Embassy
46 Police
47 Sanam Muay Lumphini (Boxing Stadium)
52 Lumphini Tower
53 Queen Sirikit National Convention Centre; Bangkok Airways

Thanon Sukhothai
Samsen Train Station
To Northern Bus Terminal & Chatuchak Weekend Market
Sanam Pao
To Bangkok International Airport
Th Phahonyothin
Th Vibhavadi Rangsit
Thanon Ratwithi
10
14
Thanon Sawankhalok
Thanon Phra Ram VI (Rama VI)
Thanon Yothi
Victory Monument
13
12
Th Phra Ram VI (Rama VI)
15
Th Din Daeng
11
Expressway (2nd Stage)

See Siam Square & Pratunam Map p162
Thanon Si Ayuthaya
Phaya Thai
Th Makkasan
Makkasan Train Station
Thanon Phetburi
Th Ratchaprarop
Ratchathewi
Th Phetburi Tat Mai
National Stadium
Th Phra Ram I (Rama I)
Siam (Interchange Station)
Chit Lom
Th Ploenchit
Siam Square
Royal Bangkok Sports Club
Soi Lang Suan
(Wireless Road)
Ploen Chit
Nana
Soi 1
Thanon Sukhumvit
Asoke
Soi Asoke
Ratchadamri
40
Th Ratchadamri
Th Withayu
44
Soi Ruam Rudi
Chulalongkorn University
42
41
43
45
Expressway (1st Stage)
Th Henri Dunant
Th Sarasin
To Eastern Bus Terminal
See Thanon Sukhumvit Map p161
Th Phra Ram IV (Rama IV)
Thanon Si Phraya
Lumphini Park
Soi 4 (Nana Tai)
Soi 10
Thanon Ratchadaphisek, Tat Mai
Sala Daeng
Tourist Police
Th Surawong
Patpong
Pan
Thanon Silom
Th Convent
Th Sala Daeng
46
47
Chong Nonsi
Th Sathon Neua (North)
48
Soi Ngam Duphli
51
Soi 53
49
50
52
Th Sathon Tai (South)
Soi Suan Phlu
To Immigration
Soi S Bamphen
54
Soi Saphan Khu

See Thanon Silom, Thanon Surawong & Thanon Sathon Map p164

Vimanmek and Abhisek lie towards the northern end of the Chitlada Palace grounds, off Th U-Thong Nai (between Th Si Ayuthaya and Th Ratwithi), across from the western side of the Dusit Zoo. Air-con bus No 3 (Th Si Ayuthaya) and air-con bus No 10 (Th Ratwithi) will drop you nearby.

CHINATOWN (SAMPENG)
เยาวราช(สำเพ็ง)

Bangkok's Chinatown (Sampeng), off Th Yaowarat and Th Ratchawong, comprises a confusing and crowded array of jewellery, hardware, wholesale food, automotive and fabric shops, as well as dozens of other small businesses. It's a good place to shop since goods here are cheaper than almost anywhere else in Bangkok, and the Chinese proprietors like to bargain, especially along Soi Wanit 1 (Sampeng Lane).

PHAHURAT
พาหุรัด

At the edge of Chinatown, around the intersection of Th Phahurat and Th Chakraphet (Chakkaphet), is a small but thriving Indian district, generally called Phahurat, where dozens of Indian vendors sell all kinds of fabric and clothes. This is the best place in the city to bargain for such items, especially silk.

Behind the more obvious shopfronts along these streets is a seemingly endless Indian bazaar selling not only fabric, but household items, food and other necessities. There are also some good, reasonably priced Indian restaurants in this area.

DUSIT ZOO
สวนสัตว์ดุสิต(เขาดิน)

The collection of animals at Bangkok's 19-hectare Dusit Zoo (Suan Sat Dusit; ☎ 022 812 000; adult/senior/child 20/10/5B; open 9am-6pm) includes relatively rare indigenous species, such as banteng, gaur, serow and rhinoceros, and is one of the best zoological facilities in South-East Asia.

A couple of lakeside restaurants serve good, inexpensive Thai food. Sunday can be a bit crowded.

The zoo is in the Dusit district between Chitlada Palace and the National Assembly Hall; the main entrance is off Th Ratwithi. Buses that pass the entrance include the ordinary Nos 18 and 28 and the air-con No 10.

LUMPHINI PARK
สวนลุมพินี

Named after Buddha's birthplace in Nepal, this is Bangkok's largest and most popular park. It is bordered by Th Rama IV to the south, Th Sarasin to the north, Th Withayu to the east and Th Ratchadamri to the west, with entrance gates on all sides. A large artificial lake (with boats for rent) in the centre is surrounded by broad, well-tended lawns, wooded areas and walking paths.

In the early morning before 7am legions of Chinese practise t'ai chi here. Also in the morning, vendors set up tables to dispense fresh snake blood and bile, considered health tonics by many Thais and Chinese. The park closes and the gates are locked at 9pm.

From mid-February to April, Lumphini is a favoured kite-flying zone; kites (wâo) can be purchased in the park during these months.

RIVER & CANAL TRIPS

The wheeled motor vehicle has long been Bangkok's conveyance of choice, but fortunately it hasn't yet become universal. A vast network of canals and river tributaries surrounding Bangkok still carry a motley fleet of watercraft, from canoes to rice barges. In these areas many homes, trading houses and temples remain oriented towards water life and provide a fascinating glimpse into the past, when Thais still considered themselves jâo náam (water lords).

Chao Phraya Express Boats

You can observe urban river life for 1½ to three hours for only 10B to 15B by climbing aboard a Chao Phraya express boat at Tha Wat Ratchasingkhon, just north of

Krungthep Bridge. If you want to ride the entire length of the express route all the way to Nonthaburi, this is where you begin. Ordinary bus Nos 1, 17 and 75 and air-con bus No 4 pass Tha Ratchasingkhon. Or you could board at any other express boat pier in Bangkok for a shorter ride to Nonthaburi. Express boats run about every 15 minutes from 6am to 6pm daily.

Other Canal Taxis

The Bangkok Noi canal taxi route leaves from Tha Chang. The fare is reasonable, and the farther up Khlong Bangkok Noi you go, the better the scenery becomes, with teak houses on stilts, old wát and plenty of greenery.

From Tha Tien pier near Wat Pho, you can get a canal taxi along **Khlong Mon** (leaving every half-hour from 6.30am to 6pm, 5B) for more typical canal scenery, including orchid farms. A longer excursion could be made by making a loop along the *khlongs* (canals) Bangkok Noi, Chak Phra and then Mon, an all-day trip. An outfit called Chao Phraya Chartered Company (☎ 026 227 657 ext 111) runs a tour boat to Khlong Mon from Tha River City daily from 2.30pm to 4.30pm for 450B per person, including refreshments.

Boat Charters

If you want to see the canals at your own pace, the best thing to do is charter a long-tail boat – it needn't be expensive if you can get a small group together to share the costs. The usual price is 400B per hour and you can choose from among eight canals in Thonburi alone. Beware of 'agents' who try to put you on the boat and rake off an extra commission. Before travelling by boat, establish the price – you can't bargain when you're in the middle of the river!

The best piers for hiring a boat are **Tha Chang**, **Tha Saphaan Phut** and **Tha Si Phraya**. Close to the latter, to the rear of the River City complex, the Boat Tour Centre charges the same basic hourly price (400B) and there are no hassles with touts. Of these three piers, Tha Chang usually has the largest selection of boats.

Dinner Cruises

A dozen or more companies run regular cruises along Mae Nam Chao Phraya from 70B to 1400B per person, depending on how far they go and what food is included. Most require advance bookings.

The less expensive, more casual cruise operators allow you to order as little or as much as you want from moderately priced menus; a modest charge of 70B per person is added to the bill for the cruise. It's a fine way to dine outdoors when the weather is hot, away from city traffic and cooled by a river breeze. Some of the larger cruise boats are more like floating nightclubs with live bands and a dance floor. Those dinner cruises offering the à la carte menu plus surcharge include:

Khanap Nam Restaurant (☎ 024 248 453) Krungthon Bridge to Sathon Bridge; twice daily
Loy Nava Co (☎ 024 374 932) From Krungthon Bridge to Rama IX Bridge, offers a more swanky weekend dinner cruise with a set price of 880B for the cruise and dinner; extra for alcohol.
Riverside Company (☎ 024 340 090) Krungthon Bridge to Rama IX Bridge; daily

Sunset Cruise

Before its regular three-hour 7.30pm dinner cruise, the *Manohra* sails from the Marriott Royal Garden Riverside Hotel for an hour-long sunset cocktail cruise. The cruise costs about 500B, which includes one drink and one cocktail snack. A free river taxi operates between the River City pier and the Royal Garden pier at 4pm, just in time for the 5pm cruise departure. Call ☎ 024 760 021 for more information.

FLOATING MARKETS

Among the most heavily published photo images of Thailand are those of wooden canoes laden with multicoloured fruits and vegetables, paddled by Thai women wearing indigo-hued clothes and wide-brimmed straw hats. Such floating markets *(talàat náam)* exist scattered throughout the huge canal system surrounding Bangkok – but if you don't know where to go you may end up at an unauthentic tourist-show scene.

There is a large if somewhat commercial floating market on **Khlong Damnoen Saduak** in Ratchaburi Province, 104km southwest of Bangkok, between Nakhon Pathom and Samut Songkhram. You can catch a bus from the Southern bus terminal, starting at 6am, on Th Charan Sanitwong in Thonburi to Damnoen Saduak. Get there as early in the morning as possible to avoid the hordes.

PLACES TO STAY – BUDGET

Bangkok has perhaps the best variety and quality of budget places to stay of any Asian capital, which is one of the reasons it's such a popular destination for roving world travellers. Because of the wide distribution of places, you might first narrow your choices by deciding what part of the city you want to be in – the backpackers' ghetto of Banglamphu, the centrally located Siam Square area, boisterous Chinatown or the old travellers' centre around Soi Ngam Duphli, off Th Rama IV.

Chinatown (around Hualamphong train station) and Banglamphu are the best all-round areas for seeing the real Bangkok, and are the cheapest districts for eating and sleeping. The Siam Square area is also well

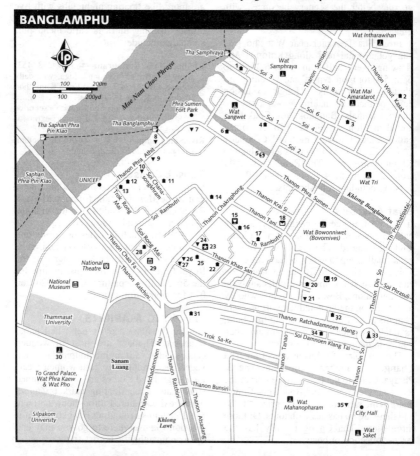

BANGLAMPHU

BANGLAMPHU

PLACES TO STAY
1	River House
2	Trang Hotel; Viang Travel
3	AP Guest House
4	Villa Guest House
6	PS Guest House
11	New Siam Guest House
12	Phra Athit Mansion
13	Peachy Guest House
14	Sawasdee House
16	Viengtai Hotel
17	Orchid House
20	Central Guest House
22	Sawasdee Bangkok Inn
25	Prakorp's House & Food
28	Chai's House
31	Royal Hotel
32	Sweety Guest House
34	Rajdamnoen Hotel

PLACES TO EAT
7	Roti-Mataba
8	Ton Pho Restaurant
9	Hemlock
10	Saffron Bakery; Raan Kin Deum
21	Vegetarian Restaurant
24	Chochana
26	No-Name Food Shop; Padung Chiip Mask Shop
27	Chinese Noodle & Wonton Shop
35	Alloy

OTHER
5	Siam Commercial Bank
15	Dali
18	Post Office
19	Mosque
23	Chana Songkhram Police Station
29	National Gallery; National Film Archives
30	Wat Mahathat
33	Democracy Monument

located, in that it's more or less in the centre of Bangkok and near the Skytrain interchange station. There is also a good selection of city buses that pass through the Rama I and Th Phayathai intersection, making more of the city accessible.

In Bangkok, budget accommodation will be taken to mean places costing 80B to 600B per night.

Banglamphu

If you're really on a tight budget, head for the Th Khao San area, near the Democracy Monument, parallel to Th Ratchadamnoen

Klang – ordinary bus Nos 3, 15, 30, 39, 44, 53, 59 and 79, and air-con bus Nos 11 and 12 will get you there. The Airport Bus (route A-2) also makes a stop nearby.

Banglamphu is very much the main travellers' centre and new guesthouses are continually springing up. Rates here are the lowest in Bangkok and although some of the places are barely adequate (bedbugs are sometimes a problem), a few are excellent value if you can afford just a bit more. At the budget end, rooms are quite small and the walls dividing them are thin. Some places have small cafes attached with limited menus. Bathrooms are usually down the hall or out the back somewhere; mattresses may be on the floor.

The least expensive rooms are 80/120B for singles/doubles, though these are hard to come by due to the hordes of people seeking them out. More common are the 120/160B rooms. Occasionally, triple rooms are available for as low as 180B and dorm beds for 70B. During most of the year, it pays to visit several guesthouses before making a decision, but in the high season (December to February, when Th Khao San is bursting with life), you'd better take the first vacant bed you come across. The best time of day to find a vacancy is from around 9am to 10am.

There are now close to 100 guesthouses in the immediate vicinity of Th Khao San, too many to list here. If you haven't already arrived with a recommendation in hand, you might best use the Banglamphu and Th Khao San area maps and simply pick a place at random for your first night. If you're not satisfied you can stow your gear and explore the area until something better turns up. The guesthouses along Th Khao San tend to be cubicles in modern shophouses, while those in Banglamphu's quieter lanes and alleys are often housed in old homes, some of them with a lot of character.

At the cheaper places it's not worth calling ahead, since the staff usually won't hold a room for you unless you pay in advance.

There are innumerable simple, adequate places on or just off Th Khao San.

Prakorp's House & Food (☎ *022 811 345, fax 026 290 714, 52 Th Khao San)* Singles/doubles 90/200B. Set in a teak house, Prakorp's serves good coffee and is highly recommended.

Sawasdee Bangkok Inn (☎ *022 801 251, fax 022 817 818, 126/2 Th Khao San)* Rooms with bath & fan/air-con 340/440B. Sawasdee has three floors around a court-yard designed to look like early Ratanakosin but somehow coming off more like Creole New Orleans. All rooms have cable TV, hot showers and towels.

Two narrow alleys between Th Khao San and Th Rambutri feature a string of cramped places that nonetheless manage to fill up. All feature small, luggage-crammed lobbies with staircases leading to rooms layered on several floors that cost around 100B to 150B.

Orchid House (☎ *022 802 691, 323/2-3 Th Rambutri)* Singles with fan & hot water 350B, singles/doubles with air-con 450/550B. The friendly Orchid, near the Vieng-tai Hotel north of Th Khao San, offers quiet, clean apartment-style rooms.

There are several guesthouses clustered in the alleys east of Th Tanao. In general, rooms are bigger and quieter here than at places around Th Khao San.

Central Guest House (☎ *022 820 667, 14 Trok Bowonrangsi)* Singles 80B, doubles 130-150B. Situated just off Th Tanao – look for the rather inconspicuous signs – rooms are clean and simple.

Sweety Guest House (☎ *022 802 191, 49 Th Ratchadamnoen)* Singles 80-120B, doubles 140-160B, rooms with air-con 350B. On a small road parallel to Th Ratchadamnoen Klang, the singles are small and windowless rooms. There is a roof ter-race for lounging and for hanging laundry.

On the other side of Th Ratchadamnoen Klang, south of the Th Khao San area, are a couple of independent hotels worth investigating.

Rajdamnoen Hotel (Hotel 90; ☎ *022 241 012, 90 Th Ratchadamnoen Klang)* Singles/doubles with bath & fan 350/550B, with air-con & TV 700B. If you walk south along Th Tanao from Th Ratchadamnoen Klang, then left at the first soi, you'll come

to Rajdamnoen; a respectable hotel with 64 large, clean rooms.

Several long-running guesthouses are on sois between Th Chakraphong and Mae Nam Chao Phraya, putting them within walking distance of Tha Banglamphu, where you can catch express boats. This area is also close to the Thonburi (Bangkok Noi) train station across the river, the National Museum and the National Theatre.

Sawasdee House (☎ *022 818 138, fax 026 290 994, 147 Th Chakraphong)* Singles with fan 160-260B, doubles with fan 320-360B, with bath & fan 460B, with air-con 560B. Sawasdee House follows the trend towards hotel-style accommodation in the Th Khao San area, with a large restaurant downstairs and small to medium-sized rooms on several floors upstairs.

New Siam Guest House (☎ *022 801 465, fax 022 817 461 Soi Chanasongkhram, Th Phra Athit)* Doubles with fan & shared bath/bath 250/395B, with air-con & bath 550B. This guesthouse, with an efficient staff, has an equally popular restaurant in a garden setting – the perfect place for a mango shake and a good book. It's located on the soi that runs between Wat Chana-songkrham and Th Phra Athit.

Chai's House (☎ *022 814 901, fax 022 818 686, 49/4–8 Soi Rong Mai, Th Chao Fa)* Singles/doubles 150/250B, doubles with air-con 350B. The family-run Chai's House offers clean rooms, all with shared bathroom. It's a quiet, security-conscious place with a sitting area out the front. The food is cheap and good, as it's a favourite gathering spot for local Thai college students on weekends.

PS Guest House (☎ *022 823 932, 9 Th Phra Sumen)* Singles/doubles 140/210B. A Peace Corps favourite, PS is near the river-end of Th Phra Sumen, off the south side of Khlong Banglamphu. It has well-kept rooms and friendly staff.

Peachy Guest House (☎ *022 816 471, 10 Th Phra Athit)* Rooms with fan & shared bath 160B, with air-con & bath but shared toilet 250B. This recently renovated place is within easy walking distance from the National Museum and Sanam Luang.

Off Th Samsen, north of Khlong Banglamphu, is a small cluster of guesthouses in convenient proximity to the Tha Samphraya river express landing.

Villa Guest House (☎ 022 817 009, Soi 1, Th Samsen) Rooms 200-450B. This quiet, private old teak house with 10 rooms is often full.

River House (☎ 022 800 876, Soi 3/ Soi Wat Samphraya, Th Samsen) Rooms 150-280B. River House has small but clean rooms with shared bathroom. There are two other similar places here, but this is the best one. Note that Soi 3 zigs left, then zags right before reaching these three guesthouses, a good 10-minute walk from Th Samsen.

AP Guest House (☎ 022 825 530, 118 Soi 6, Th Samsen) Rooms 60-100B. Near Wat Mai Amaratarot, this is probably the cheapest guesthouse in Banglamphu. Though the rooms are predictably spartan, the surrounding neighbourhood has plenty of diversions and feels miles away from Th Khao San.

Thewet & National Library Area

The district north of Banglamphu near the National Library is another little travellers' enclave. It's easiest reached by a Chao Phraya express boat from Tha Thewet, or take a bus (Nos 19 and 53) and get off at the intersection of Th Samsen and Th Si Ayuthaya.

On two parallel sois that run off Th Si Ayuthaya towards the river (west from Samsen) are four guesthouses all run by various members of the same extended family: *Tavee Guest House* (☎ 022 825 983, 83 Soi 14, Th Si Ayuthaya), *Sawasdee Guest House* (☎ 022 810 757, 71 Soi 14, Th Si Ayuthaya) and *Backpacker's Lodge* (☎ 022 823 231, 85 Soi 14, Th Si Ayuthaya). All are clean, well kept and fairly quiet. Room prices at all of them range between 150B and 400B. The Sawasdee also offers dorm beds for just 50B. *Shanti Lodge* (☎ 022 812 497, 37 Soi 16, Th Si Ayuthaya) on the corner of a nearby soi costs a bit more – singles/doubles 200/250B for fan rooms, 400/450B with air-con, or 100B for a dorm bed. It also has a good restaurant and sitting area.

Bangkok International Youth Hostel (☎ 022 820 950, fax 026 287 416, ⓔ bangkok@tyha.org, 25/2 Th Phitsanulok) Bed in 16-bed dorm without/with air-con 70/120B, doubles with fan & hot bath 250B. Singles/doubles with air-con & hot bath 280/350B. There's a cafeteria downstairs. The hostel won't accept guests who are not members; annual Hostelling International (HI; formerly IYHF) membership costs 300B, or you can purchase a temporary membership for 50B.

Chinatown & Hualamphong

This area is central and colourful although rather noisy. There are numerous cheap hotels but it's not a travellers' centre like Soi Ngam Duphli or Banglamphu. Watch your pockets and bags around the Hualamphong train station area, both on the street and on the bus. The cream of the razor artists operate here as the train passengers make good pickings.

New Empire Hotel (☎ 022 346 990–6, fax 022 346 997, 572 Th Yaowarat) Rooms with air-con & hot water 450-800B. This is near the intersection of Th Charoen Krung, a short walk from Wat Traimit. It's a bit noisy but a great location if you like Chinatown. In the evening there are literally hundreds of places to eat on the sidewalks of Th Yaowarat.

Other Chinatown hotels of this calibre, most without English signs, can be found along Th Yaowarat, Th Chakraphet and Th Ratchawong.

River View Guest House (☎ 022 345 429, 022 358 501, fax 022 375 428, 768 Soi Phanurangsi, Th Songwat) Rooms with bath & fan/air-con 490/690B. Straddling the budget and mid-range is this place in the Talaat Noi area south of Chinatown – wedged between Bangrak (Silom) and Chinatown. The building is behind the Jao Seu Kong Chinese shrine, about 500m upriver from the Royal Orchid Sheraton, in a neighbourhood filled with automotive junk shops. To get there, take a Chao Phraya express boat to the Harbour Department (Krom Jao Tha in Thai), turn left after exiting the Harbour Department compound, take the third left, then the first right. As the name suggests, many rooms have a Mae Nam Chao Phraya view; the view from the 8th-floor restaurant is superb, even if you have to wake up the staff to get a meal. If you call from the Harbour Department compound, someone from the guesthouse will pick you up.

Soi Ngam Duphli

This area off Th Rama IV is where most budget travellers used to come in the 1970s and early 1980s. With a couple of notable exceptions, most places here are not especially cheap or even good value any more, and the area has become quite sleazy – it's just a brisk walk away from Patpong.

The entrance to the soi is on Th Rama IV, near the Th Sathon Tai intersection, and within walking distance of verdant Lumphini Park and the Th Silom business district. Ordinary bus Nos 13, 14, 74, 109, 115 and 116, and air-con bus No 7, all pass by the entrance to Soi Ngam Duphli along Th Rama IV.

If you continue east along Soi Si Bamphen and turn left at the next soi, then take the first right, you'll end up in a cul-de-sac with four guesthouses of varying quality.

Lee 3 Guest House (23/13 Soi Si Bamphen) Singles/doubles with fan 140/160B, doubles with private bath 200B. The clean, secure and well-managed Lee 3 is the best of the three Lees.

Sala Thai Daily Mansion (☎ 022 871 436, 15 Soi Si Bamphen) Rooms 250-350B. A stand out in this area, this friendly place is at the end of the alley and has large, very clean rooms, all with shared bathroom. A sitting area with TV on the 3rd floor makes for a pleasant gathering place, and there is a breezy rooftop terrace. The owner speaks English and her design background is evident in the tasteful furnishings. Many repeat or long-term guests fill the rooms here.

Th Sukhumvit

Staying in this area puts you in the newest part of Bangkok and the farthest from old Bangkok near the river, but getting to and from this area is no longer a hassle with the

introduction of the Skytrain service. The majority of the hotels in this area are priced in the mid-range.

Atlanta Hotel (☎ 022 521 650, fax 026 568 123, 78 Soi 2, Th Sukhumvit) Rooms 330-1200B. This is the oldest and most centrally located hostelry in the area. Owned since its construction in the 1950s by Dr Max Henn, a former secretary to the maharajah of Bikaner and owner of Bangkok's first international pharmacy, the Atlanta is a simple but reliable stand-by with clean, comfortable rooms in several price categories. Tax isn't included, but monthly stays paid in advance receive a 10% discount. The Atlanta also has a swimming pool and coffee shop with a selection of international newspapers and evening videos. A map room and letter-writing lounge round out the offerings.

Golden Palace Hotel (☎ 022 525 115, fax 022 541 538, 15 Soi 1, Th Sukhumvit) Doubles with bath & air-con 500-550B. The L-shaped, aquamarine-coloured Golden Palace has a swimming pool and is well situated. The clientele is mostly middle-class tourists 'on a budget'.

Miami Hotel (☎ 022 535 611–3, 022 530 369, fax 022 531 266, 2 Soi 13, Th Sukhumvit) Singles/doubles with air-con, hot water & TV 400/500B. This dates back to the 1960s and 1970s R&R period. The room and service quality seems to seesaw every three years or so but by all accounts it's decent value with clean rooms, plus a small swimming pool and coffee shop; discounts are available for long-term stays.

Siam Square

Several good places can be found in this central area, which has the additional advantage of being on the Khlong Saen Saep canal taxi route and the Skytrain interchange station.

There are several lower- to mid-range places on or near Soi Kasem San 1, off Th Rama I near Jim Thompson's House and the National Stadium.

Muangphol Mansion (Muangphon Mansion; ☎ 022 150 033, fax 022 168 053, 931/8 Th Rama I) Rooms with air-con &

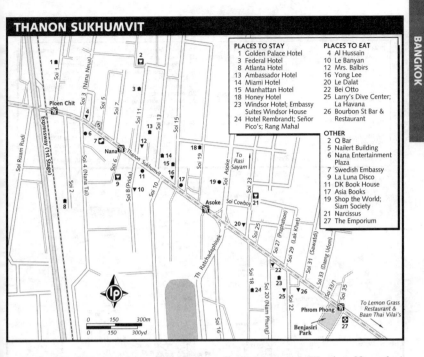

THANON SUKHUMVIT

PLACES TO STAY
1 Golden Palace Hotel
3 Federal Hotel
8 Atlanta Hotel
13 Ambassador Hotel
14 Miami Hotel
15 Manhattan Hotel
18 Honey Hotel
23 Windsor Hotel; Embassy
   Suites Windsor House
24 Hotel Rembrandt; Señor
   Pico's; Rang Mahal

PLACES TO EAT
4 Al Hussain
10 Le Banyan
12 Mrs. Balbirs
16 Yong Lee
20 Le Dalat
22 Bei Otto
25 Larry's Dive Center;
   La Havana
26 Bourbon St Bar &
   Restaurant

OTHER
2 Q Bar
5 Nailert Building
6 Nana Entertainment
   Plaza
7 Swedish Embassy
9 La Luna Disco
11 DK Book House
17 Asia Books
19 Shop the World;
   Siam Society
21 Narcissus
27 The Emporium

hot water 400-450B. This has good-value rooms for the area, even if they are a tad shabby.

Wendy House (☎ 022 162 436, fax 022 168 053, Soi Kasem San 1) Singles/doubles with air-con, hot shower & TV 350/550B. Wendy House has small but clean rooms. If you're carrying unusually heavy bags, note there's no lift. A small restaurant is on the ground floor.

A-One Inn (☎ 022 153 029, fax 022 164 771, 25/13–15 Soi Kasem San 1) Doubles with bath, hot water, air-con & TV 450B, triples 650B. This is a friendly and pleasant place that gets a lot of return business.

PLACES TO STAY – MID-RANGE

Bangkok is saturated with small and medium-sized hotels in this category (from roughly 600B to 1800B per night). Not quite 'international class', these places often offer guests a better sense of being in Thailand than the luxury hotels.

In the low-season (March to November) you may be able to get a reduced-occupancy discount at these places.

Banglamphu

Viengtai Hotel (☎ 022 805 434–45, fax 022 818 153, ℮ info@viengtai.co.th, W www. viengtai.co.th, 42 Th Rambutri) Singles 1225-1575B, doubles 1575-1750B, triples 1750-2275B. Before Th Khao San was 'discovered', this was the most popular place in Banglamphu. Over the last decade or so the Viengtai has continually raised its prices (not always concomitant with an upgrading of facilities) until it now sits solidly in the middle-price range of Bangkok hotels. Price depends on whether the room is in the six-storey old wing or the nine-storey new wing, and includes breakfast. A swimming pool is on the 3rd floor.

Phra Athit Mansion (☎ 022 800 744, fax 022 800 742, 22 Th Phra Athit) Singles & doubles with air-con, TV, hot showers &

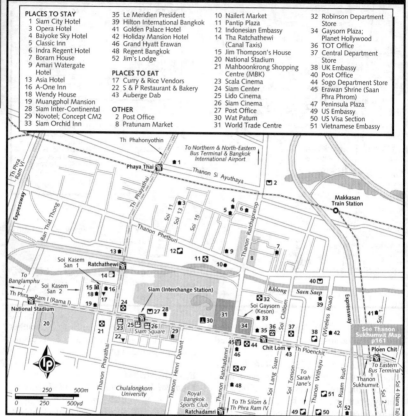

SIAM SQUARE & PRATUNAM

PLACES TO STAY
1 Siam City Hotel
3 Opera Hotel
4 Baiyoke Sky Hotel
5 Classic Inn
6 Indra Regent Hotel
7 Borarn House
9 Amari Watergate Hotel
13 Asia Hotel
16 A-One Inn
18 Wendy House
19 Muangphol Mansion
28 Siam Inter-Continental
29 Novotel; Concept CM2
33 Siam Orchid Inn
35 Le Meridien President
39 Hilton International Bangkok
41 Golden Palace Hotel
42 Holiday Mansion Hotel
46 Grand Hyatt Erawan
48 Regent Bangkok
52 Jim's Lodge

PLACES TO EAT
17 Curry & Rice Vendors
22 S & P Restaurant & Bakery
43 Auberge Dab

OTHER
2 Post Office
8 Pratunam Market
10 Nailert Market
11 Pantip Plaza
12 Indonesian Embassy
14 Tha Ratchathewi (Canal Taxis)
15 Jim Thompson's House
20 National Stadium
21 Mahboonkrong Shopping Centre (MBK)
23 Scala Cinema
24 Siam Center
25 Lido Cinema
26 Siam Cinema
27 Post Office
30 Wat Patum
31 World Trade Centre
32 Robinson Department Store
34 Gaysorn Plaza; Planet Hollywood
36 TOT Office
37 Central Department Store
38 UK Embassy
40 Post Office
44 Sogo Department Store
45 Erawan Shrine (Saan Phra Phrom)
47 Peninsula Plaza
49 US Embassy
50 US Visa Section
51 Vietnamese Embassy

fridge 850B, triples 1050B. The apartment-style Phra Athit offers modern, clean rooms. Try to get a room as far from the street as possible to avoid traffic noise. Discounts are offered for long-term stays.

Royal Hotel (Ratanakosin; ☎ 022 229 111–26, fax 022 242 083, 2 Th Ratchadamnoen Klang) Singles/doubles 960/1300B. Besides the Oriental and the Atlanta, this is the oldest continually operating hotel in the city, still going strong on the corner of Th Ratchadamnoen Klang and Th Atsadang about 500m from the Democracy Monument. The Royal's 24-hour coffee shop is a favourite local rendezvous. One wing is currently being renovated, which may result in a price increase when finished.

Chinatown

Mid-range hotels in Chinatown are tough to find.

Chinatown Hotel (☎ 022 250 230, fax 022 261 295, 526 Th Yaowarat) Rooms 700-1700B. Clean rooms and friendly staff, this hotel is in a great location if you want to be near Th Yaowarat's many gold shops (during the day) and sidewalk seafood restaurants (at night). It also has a roomy lobby where you can watch the Chinatown chaos in air-conditioned comfort.

White Orchid Hotel (☎ 022 260 026, fax 022 556 403, 409–421 Th Yaowarat) Rooms 850B. White Orchid, diagonally opposite the Chinatown Hotel, offers nicer accommodation.

Th Silom & Th Surawong

This area is packed with upper mid-range places; discounts are often available between April and October. Bangkok's YMCA and YWCA are both in this area.

YMCA Collins International House (☎ 022 871 900, 026 376 991, fax 022 871 996, [e] bkkymca@asiaaccess.net.th, [w] www.ymca-hotels.com, 27 Th Sathon Tai) Rooms with air-con, TV, fridge, phone, safe & bath 1300-2300B, suites 2700B. This was temporarily closed at the time of writing but was expected to re-open in the near future.

YWCA Hostel (☎ 026 791 280, fax 022 873 016, 13 Th Sathon Tai) Singles/doubles with air-con, TV, fridge, phone, safe & bath 750/1000B.

Bangkok Christian Guest House (☎ 022 336 303, fax 022 371 742, [e] bcgh@loxinfo.co.th, 123 Sala Daeng Soi 2, Th Convent) Singles/doubles/triples with air-con 1000/1300/1650B. Bangkok Christian, off Th Silom, has very nice rooms, and the price includes breakfast. Lunch and dinner are also available at low prices. Christian missionaries get discounted rates.

New Trocadero Hotel (☎ 022 348 920–8, fax 022 348 929, 343 Th Surawong) Singles & doubles with breakfast 750-2500B. Once a favourite haunt of Western journalists, the New Trocadero Hotel now mostly caters to Africans and South Asians. The rooms are shabby and the staff brusque but the atmosphere is unique in Bangkok.

Orchid Inn (☎ 022 669 310, fax 022 344 159, 719/1–3 Th Si Phraya) Singles/doubles with air-con, fridge & TV 500/600B. Near the Royal Orchid Sheraton, the River City complex and the river (Tha Si Phraya landing), this provides decent value for tidy rooms. Another advantage is that the ordinary No 36 bus terminates almost directly

opposite the hotel. The downside is the high number of touts due to the big-spending tourists in the neighbourhood.

Soi Ngam Duphli & Th Sathon

Malaysia Hotel (☎ 026 797 127–36, fax 022 871 457, [e] malaysia@ksc15.th.com, 54 Soi Ngam Duphli) Singles/doubles with hot water, air-con, fridge & TV 618/718B. Near the southern end of Soi Ngam Duphli, this was once Bangkok's most famous budget travellers' hotel. The Malaysia has a small swimming pool that may be used by visitors for 50B per day (it's free for guests). There's a small desk in the lobby where you can hook up your computer to check emails, or use the house terminals. The hotel coffee shop has also been renovated and is less of an after-hours hooker hang out than it used to be.

Charlie House (☎ 026 798 330, fax 026 797 308, 1034/36–37 Soi Saphan Khu) Rooms with air-con, phone & TV 750-950B. On a soi running north off Soi Si Bamphen, this aims for a slightly more up-scale market with carpeted rooms (lower rates can be negotiated in off-season months like June and September). Smoking is prohibited; a sign in the reception area reads 'Decently dressed ladies, gentlemen and their children are welcome'.

Th Sukhumvit

This area is choked with hotels costing 800-1500B. Stick to the lower numbered sois to save cross-town travel time. Many of the Sukhumvit hotels in this price class were built as R&R hotels for soldiers on leave from Vietnam during the Indochina War era, 1962–74. Some made the transition from the soldiers-on-leave clientele to a traditional tourist base with style and grace, while others continue to have a slightly rough image.

Honey Hotel (☎ 022 530 646, fax 022 544 716, 31 Soi 19, Th Sukhumvit) Recently renovated, this is a former R&R place with a loyal clientele. There's a small soi next door with cheap food stalls during the day.

Federal Hotel (☎ 022 530 175, fax 022 535 332, 27 Soi 11, Th Sukhumvit) Rooms

THANON SILOM, THANON SURAWONG & THANON SATHON

PLACES TO STAY
5 Royal Orchid Sheraton
10 Orchid Inn
11 Tawana Ramada Hotel
12 Montien Hotel
17 Dusit Thani Hotel
22 Bangkok Christian
    Guest House
23 Swiss Lodge
43 Manohra Hotel
45 New Trocadero Hotel
47 Oriental Hotel
50 Shangri-La Hotel
64 Westin Banyan Tree
65 YMCA Collins
    International House
66 Beaufort Sukhothai
67 YWCA Hostel

PLACES TO EAT
1 Pet Tun Jao Tha
7 Harmonique
9 The Cholas
26 Café de Paris
27 Bobby's Arms
29 Mizu's Kitchen
32 Mango Tree
34 Goro
36 Somboon Seafood
37 Rabianthong Restaurant;
    Narai
39 Night Market
44 India Hut
48 Muslim Restaurant
49 Thon Krueng
52 Tiensin
53 Ban Chiang
54 Thanying
56 Madras Cafe;
    Madras Lodge
57 Sun Far Myanmar
    Food Centre

OTHER
2 Holy Rosary Church
3 River City
    Shopping Complex
4 Siam Bronze Factory
6 CAT Office
8 Main Post Office
13 Queen Saovabha
    Memorial Institute
    (Snake Farm);
    Red Cross
14 Bangkok Christian Hospital
15 Chulalongkorn University
16 Tourist Police
18 Silom Centre; Robinson
    Department Store
19 DJ Station
20 O'Reilly's Irish Pub
21 Silom Complex
24 Thaniya Plaza
25 The Balcony; Telephone
28 Marble House; Arima Onsen
30 CP Tower
31 Bangkok Christian Hospital
33 Thai Office
35 Malaysia Embassy
38 Neilson Hays Library
40 Mirasuddeen Mosque
41 Central Department Store
42 Mahesak Hospital
46 Oriental Plaza
51 Wat Suan Phlu
55 Sri Mariamman
    Temple
58 Myanmar Embassy
59 St Louis Hospital
60 Singaporean Embassy
61 Australian Embassy
62 Malaysia Embassy
63 Alliance Française
    & French Consulate
68 German Embassy

700-1700B. Federal Hotel is a favourite among Vietnam War and Peace Corps vets. The added-on rooms at ground level, which occasionally flood in the rainy season, aren't worth the price, so be sure to get one of the larger, older upstairs rooms. The small pool and large, plain coffee shop are the main attractions. It's a short walk to the Asoke Skytrain station.

Manhattan (☎ 022 550 166, fax 022 553 481, 13 Soi 15, Th Sukhumvit) Rooms 1400-7000B. Dating back to the Indochina War era, this has good-sized, well-kept rooms.

Siam Square, Th Ploenchit & Hualamphong
This area tends to offer either upper-end budget or top-end luxury hotels, with little in the middle.

Jim's Lodge (☎ 022 553 100, fax 022 550 190, 125/7 Soi Ruam Rudi) Rooms 950B. These are clean rooms with TV, fridge, air-con & carpeting in a six-storey building.

Siam Orchid Inn (☎ 022 553 140–3, fax 022 553 144, 109 Soi Ratchadamri) Rooms 1200B. Off Ratchadamri, this offers well-appointed rooms with all the amenities. Breakfast is included.

Holiday Mansion Hotel (☎ 022 538 016, fax 022 530 130, 53 Th Withayu) Singles & doubles 1500B. Opposite the UK embassy, this is a simple but well-run mid-range place where good-sized rooms come with air-con, IDD phone, fridge & TV, breakfast included. Other amenities include a pool, business centre and 24-hour coffee shop.

Pratunam
Opera Hotel (☎ 022 524 031, fax 022 535 360, 16 Soi Somprasong 1, Th Phetchaburi) Doubles with hot water & air-con 600-800B. Very near the heart of Pratunam, the Opera has a swimming pool and coffee shop.

Borarn House (☎ 022 532 252, fax 022 533 639, 487/48 Soi Wattanasin) Singles/doubles with air-con & TV 850/950B. A long walk east from the Classic Inn along the soi opposite the Indra Hotel (off Ratchaprarop) leads eventually to here, a Thai-style apartment building.

Airport Area
Finding decent, moderately priced accommodation in the airport area is difficult. Most of the hotels charge nearly twice as much as comparable hotels in the city.

Don Muang Mansion (☎ 025 663 064, 118/7 Th Soranakom, Don Muang) Rooms 1000-1500B. This looks classy on the outside, but asks a lot for a small, stuffy room that in Bangkok would cost half as much. It's possible to negotiate a lower rate with some discussion.

Comfort Suites Airport (☎ 025 528 921–9, fax 025 528 920, W www.comfort suites.com, 88/117 Vibhavadi Rangsit Hwy) Walk-in rates 2500-2800B, booking rates 1500-1800B. About five minutes south of the airport by car, this has large rooms with all the amenities: satellite TV, air-con, private hot bath/shower. Best of all, the hotel provides a free shuttle to and from the airport every hour. Other facilities include a coffee shop, pool, sauna and health club. About the only drawback is that you can hear planes landing and taking off until around midnight.

We-Train International House (☎ 029 292 222, 029 292 301, fax 029 292 300, W www.we-train.linethai.co.th, 501/1 Muu 3, Th Dechatungkha, Sikan, Don Muang) Dorm beds with fan 165B, singles & doubles with 2 beds, fan, bath & fridge 550B, with air-con 770B, extra beds 150B. This has simple but very clean rooms. Add the usual 10% service charge to the rates but no tax since it's operated by the nonprofit Association for the Promotion of the Status of Women (but male guests are welcome). Facilities include a pool, Thai massage, laundry service, coffee shop and beauty salon. One major drawback is its distance from the airport – you must get a taxi to cross the highway and railway, then go about 3km west along Dechatungkha to the Thung Sikan school (*rohng rian thûng sǐi-kan*). If you don't have much luggage, walk across the airport pedestrian bridge to reach Don Muang, then get a taxi – it's cheaper that way because you avoid the high taxi-desk fees. From the guesthouse there are usually no taxis in the area when you're ready to return to the airport or continue on to Bangkok, but transportation to or from the airport can be arranged on request for 200B one way, or 70B one way to/from the Amari Airport Hotel.

PLACES TO STAY – TOP END

Bangkok has all sorts of international-class tourist hotels, from the straightforward package places to some of Asia's classics. Three of Bangkok's luxury hotels, in fact, consistently make *Condé Nast Traveler*'s annual worldwide top 25 list: the Oriental, the Regent and the Shangri-La.

Although there's no single area for top-end hotels you'll find quite a few around the Siam Square area, along the parallel Th Surawong and Th Silom, and along the river, while many of the slightly less expensive 'international standard' places are scattered along Th Sukhumvit.

You should still be able to negotiate discounts of up to 40% on the rates listed during the low season (April to June and July to August). Booking through a travel agency almost always means lower rates, or try asking for a hotel's 'corporate' discount. THAI can also arrange substantial discounts if you hold THAI air tickets.

A welcome trend in Bangkok hotels in the past few years has been the appearance of several European-style 'boutique' hotels – small, business-oriented places of around 100 rooms or less with rates in the 2000B to 3000B range, eg, the Swiss Lodge (see the Th Silom, Th Surawong & Th Sathon entry later in this section for details).

All hotels in this category will add a 10% service charge plus 7% tax to hotel bills.

Central Bangkok

Although there are as yet no top-end hotels in the Banglamphu area itself, a little bit east of the district are a couple of highly recommended places in this general price category.

Royal Princess Hotel (☎ 022 813 088, fax 022 801 314, W *www.royalprincess .com, 269 Th Lan Luang*) Rooms from 3500B. The Royal Princess often has discounts down to about half the listed rates

available through travel agents. It's close to the main central THAI office and a short taxi ride from Banglamphu and the river.

Siam City Hotel (☎ 022 470 130, fax 022 470 178, e *reservations@siamhotels.com,* W *www.siamhotels.com, 477 Th Si Ayuthaya*) Rooms from 4272B. Independently owned and operated, this has large, well-maintained rooms with all the amenities, but again, good discounts are often available through Thai travel agencies. The restaurants at the Siam City are highly regarded by Thai business-people.

On the River

Oriental Hotel (☎ 026 599 000, fax 026 590 000, e *bscorbkk@loxinfo.co.th,* W *www.mandarinoriental.com, 48 Soi Oriental, Th Charoen Krung*) Rooms from US$250, suites US$900. The 122-year-old Oriental, on Mae Nam Chao Phraya, is one of the most famous hotels in Asia, right up there with the Raffles in Singapore or the Peninsula in Hong Kong. What's more it's also rated as one of the best hotels in the world, as well as being just about the most expensive in Bangkok. The hotel management prides itself on providing highly personalised service but the staff can be quite snobby to non-guests. Nowadays the Oriental is looking more modern and less classic – the original Author's Wing is dwarfed by the Tower (built in 1958) and River (1976) wings. Ten restaurants and bars offer a variety of cuisines; the legendary Bamboo Bar is one of the city's best jazz venues, and there's a sports centre and cooking school.

Shangri-La Hotel (☎ 022 367 777, fax 022 368 579, e *slbk@shangri-la.com,* W *www.shangri-la.com, 89 Soi Wat Suan Phlu, Th Charoen Krung*) Rooms US$150-870. The Shangri-La has rooms with minibar, hairdryer, coffeemaker and security box. Facilities and services include helicopter transport from the airport (at extra cost), swimming pools, tennis courts, squash courts, a fully equipped gymnasium overlooking the river, sauna, steam bath, hydropool, outdoor Jacuzzis and nine restaurants (including Angelini's, one of the best Italian eateries in the city). Service is of a very high standard. The capacious lounge areas off the main lobby have a more relaxed feel than those at the Oriental, and are a favourite rendezvous spot even for non-guests.

Bangkok Marriott Resort and Spa (☎ *024 760 022, fax 024 761 120,* e *bangkokmar riott@minornet.com,* W *www.royal-garden .com, 257/1–3 Th Charoen Nakhon)* Rooms US$99, with river view US$110. On the Thonburi bank of Mae Nam Chao Phraya, a bit south of central Bangkok, this tastefully appointed resort, near Krungthep Bridge, is highly valued for its serene atmosphere and expansive, airy public areas. The grounds encompass a large swimming pool, lush gardens, tennis courts, and a health club and spa. There are six restaurants and the *Manohra*, a luxury rice-barge dinner cruiser, is also moored here. A free water taxi service shuttles guests back and forth to the Oriental and River City piers every hour from 7am to 11pm.

Th Silom, Th Surawong & Th Sathon

Beaufort Sukhothai (☎ *022 870 222, fax 022 874 980,* e *info@sukhothai.com,* W *www.sukhothai.com, 13/3 Th Sathon Tai).* Superior/deluxe rooms US$250/290, suites US$390. The Sukhothai features a decor inspired by classical Khmer style, including an inner courtyard with lily ponds; the same architect created Phuket's landmark Amanpuri. Upon request the staff will provide a fax machine for your room at no charge.

Westin Banyan Tree (☎ *026 791 200, fax 026 791 199,* e *westinbangkok@westin bangkok.com,* W *www.westin-bangkok.com, 21/100 Th Sathon Tai)* Rooms US$250. This ultra-modern hotel towers above the street with 216 business suites. The hotel is ensconced on the lower two and top 28 floors of the 60-storey Thai Wah Tower II; its huge rooms feature separate work and sleep areas, two-line speaker phones with data ports and two TV sets along with all the other amenities expected of this standard of lodgings. The spa/fitness centre – the biggest such hotel facility in Bangkok – spans four floors.

Dusit Thani Hotel (☎ *022 360 450, fax 022 366 400,* e *dusitbkk@dusit.com,* W *www.dusit.com, 946 Th Rama IV)* Rooms US$190-260. One of the top hotels in the busy financial and shopping district of Th Silom and Th Surawong.

There are many hotels with similar amenities that are a step down in price because of their smaller staff-to-guest ratios or location.

Swiss Lodge (☎ *022 335 345, fax 022 369 425,* e *info@swisslodge.com,* W *www. swisslodge.com, 3 Th Convent)* Rooms 2800-3700B. With only 57 rooms, the management here is able to pay close attention to service details, such as cold towels whenever you enter the lobby from outside. Data-ports and soundproof windows further enhance the attraction for people doing business in Bangkok. Facilities include a restaurant, pool and business centre.

Th Sukhumvit

Hotel Rembrandt (☎ *022 617 100, fax 022 617 017,* W *www.rembrandtbkk.com, 19 Soi 18, Th Sukhumvit)* Rooms 4200-8500B. This tastefully decorated hotel has 407 large rooms and is close to the Queen Sirikit National Convention Center, off Soi 16. Facilities include a swimming pool and the best Mexican restaurant in Bangkok, Señor Pico's of Los Angeles.

Windsor Hotel (☎ *022 580 160, fax 022 581 491, 8–10 Soi 20/Soi Nam Phung, Th Sukhumvit)* Singles/doubles 1200/1400B. Each of the deluxe 116 rooms and suites have air-con, phone, TV, video & fridge, and come with a cooked-to-order breakfast. On the premises is a 24-hour coffee shop. Guests of the Windsor have use of all amenities at the Windsor Suites Hotel next door.

Windsor Suites Hotel (☎ *022 621 234, fax 022 621 212,* e *info@windsorsuites hotel.com,* W *www.windsorsuiteshotel .com, 8–10 Soi 20/Soi Nam Phung, Th Sukhumvit)* Singles/doubles 6000/7000B. This features spacious suites (each with two TVs). Amenities include a bakery, cafe, restaurant, fitness club, shopping arcade, swimming pool & Jacuzzi. A complimentary buffet breakfast is included.

Siam Square, Th Ploenchit & Pratunam

Regent Bangkok (☎ 022 516 127, fax 022 539 195, ⓦ www.regenthotels.com, 155 Th Ratchadamri) Rooms US$210-410. People accustomed to heady hotels claim the plush Regent Bangkok tops the Oriental in overall quality for the price. This is particularly true for business travellers because of the Regent's efficient business centre and central location (and local calls are free at the Regent, probably the only luxury hotel in the city to offer this courtesy). The hotel also offers (for around 2000B an hour) an 'office on wheels', a high-tech van equipped with computers, mobile phones, fax machines, TVs/VCRs and swivelling leather seats.

Grand Hyatt Erawan (☎ 022 541 234, fax 022 536 308, ⓦ www.hyatt.com, 494 Th Ratchadamri) Rooms US$175-365. At the intersection of Ratchadamri and Ploenchit, this was raised on the site of the original Erawan Hotel (built at the same time as the Royal Hotel) with obvious ambitions to become one of the city's top-ranked hotels. The neo-Thai architecture has been well executed; inside is the largest collection of contemporary Thai art in the world. Adding to the elite atmosphere, rooms in the rear of the hotel overlook the prestigious Bangkok Royal Sports Club racetrack. For most visitors – whether for business or leisure – it vies with the Regent or the Novotel Bangkok on Siam Square for having the best location of all the city's luxury hotels vis-à-vis transport and proximity to shopping.

Amari Watergate (☎ 026 539 000, fax 026 539 045, ⓔ watergate@amari.com, ⓦ www.amari.com, 874 Th Phetchaburi) Rooms US$109-186. Right in the centre of Bangkok's busiest district, Pratunam, this boasts large rooms and impressive sports and entertainment facilities. Tour groups check in via a separate floor and lobby while individually booked guests use the main lobby. The top three floors contain more luxuriously appointed executive rooms. Amari also has other hotels in central Bangkok and at the airport – see the Airport Area section following.

Baiyoke Sky Hotel (☎ 026 563 000, fax 026 563 555, ⓔ baiyoke-sky@baiyoke hotels.co.th, ⓦ www.baiyokehotels.co.th, 130 Th Ratchaparop) Singles/doubles 2600B, suites 5500B. The tallest hotel in the world, the 93-storey Baiyoke, stands right behind the Indra Hotel off Th Ratchaprarop in Pratunam. Spacious rooms and suites with all the amenities – though not quite as luxurious as one might expect – are not a bad deal considering the altitude.

Ratchada

This newish entertainment and business district in the Huay Khwang neighbourhood of north-east Bangkok features several flash hotels along Th Ratchadaphisek.

Siam Beverly Hotel (☎ 022 754 046-8, fax 022 900 170, 188 Th Ratchadaphisek) Singles/doubles 1800/2200B including breakfast. One of the least expensive places in the area, right next to Le Concorde building (home to TAT) and a stone's throw from several upscale 'entertainment centres', is the Siam Beverly Hotel. It's nothing spectacular but service is friendly and the rooms have all the amenities; the 3rd-floor coffee shop is well priced.

Airport Area

Amari Airport Hotel (☎ 025 661 020, fax 025 661 941, ⓦ www.amari.com, 333 Th Choet Wutthakat) Singles/doubles US$202/214. Directly across from the airport, this hotel has undergone recent renovations and is quite well appointed. The executive floor features huge suites and 24-hour butler service.

Asia Airport Hotel (☎ 029 926 999, fax 029 926 828, ⓦ www.asiahotel.co.th, 99 Mu 8, Th Phahonyothin) Rooms from 2000B. A top-end hotel that seems not to have attracted the droves it was hoping to; it's 3km north of the airport and has a free shuttle to/from the airport if you advise them ahead of arrival. Try bargaining – discounts are readily available.

PLACES TO EAT

Wherever you go in Bangkok, you're almost never more than 50m away from a restaurant or sidewalk food vendor. The variety of places to eat is simply astounding. You can find food in every price range in most districts – with a few obvious exceptions. Chinatown is naturally a good area for Chinese food, while Bangrak and Phahurat are good for Indian and Muslim cuisine. Some parts of the city tend to have higher priced restaurants (eg, Siam Square, Silom, Surawong and Sukhumvit) while other areas are full of cheap eats (eg, Banglamphu and the river area around Tha Maharat).

As transport can be such a hassle in Bangkok, most visitors choose to eat in a district most convenient to reach (rather than seeking out a specific restaurant); this section has therefore been organised by area, rather than cuisine.

Banglamphu & Thewet

This area near the river and old part of the city is one of the best for cheap food. Many of the guesthouses on Th Khao San have open-air cafes, which are packed with travellers from November to March and July to August. The typical cafe menu has a few Thai and Chinese standards, plus traveller favourites like fruit salad, muesli and yoghurt. But once you tire of banana pancakes and fried rice, there are a few excellent Thai restaurants in this area where authentic local flavours can be sampled.

Along Th Phra Athit there are several small Thai places with chic but casual decor and good food at prices local university students can afford.

Raan Kin Deum (24 Th Phra Athit) Meals 30-60B. A few doors down from New Merry V, this is a nice two-storey cafe with wooden tables and chairs, traditional Thai food and live folk music nightly; the laid-back atmosphere reaches its acme in the evenings when Thais and faràng crowd the place. There is no roman-script sign.

Saffron Bakery (Th Phra Athit) Pastries 10-15B. Bright and cheery, opposite the Food & Agriculture Organization on Th Phra Athit, this has good pastries but only a few tables.

Hemlock (☎ 022 827 507, 56 Th Phra Athit) Dishes 60-90B. Open 3pm to midnight. Sublime Thai dishes at very reason-

able prices, this place is popular with students from nearby Thammasat University. Try the sweet and tangy angle bean salad (*yam thùa phuu*). If you're in the mood for wine, this is the place to come. Also offers a wide selection of teas.

Ton Pho (☎ 022 800 452, Th Phra Athit) Dishes 60-150B. Next to the Chao Phraya express boats' Banglamphu pier, Ton Pho is in an old wooden house and offers views of the river. The food can be quite spicy – the locals seem to wash it down with endless bottles of beer. Try the no-holds-barred *tôm yam kûng* (spicy prawn soup). This is also a chill place to watch the sunset.

For even more authentic (and cheaper) Thai food check out the places on Soi Rambutri. At the western end are several open-air restaurants serving excellent Thai food at low prices.

Chochana (☎ 022 829 948, 86 Th Chakraphong) Meals 30-50B. Cheap felafel and hummus can be found here, surely the most popular Israeli food in Bangkok. It's down a *trok* (lane) off Th Chakraphong around the corner from Th Khao San, and stays open until 11pm or so.

There is a *no-name food shop (8–10 Th Chakraphong),* which has dishes for 30B to 40B. This is a good spot for Southern Thai food, south of Th Khao San and two doors south of the Padung Chiip mask shop. In the mornings it serves *khâo mòk kài* (Thai chicken biryani) as well as *khâo yam*, a kind of rice salad that is a traditional breakfast in Southern Thailand. Further along this street is a cheap and efficient *Chinese noodle & wonton shop (22 Th Chakraphong)* with dishes for 15B to 25B.

Roti-Mataba (Th Phra Athit) Dishes 30-60B. On the corner of Phra Athit and Phra Sumen, near the river, this offers delicious *kaeng mátsàman* (Thai Muslim curry), chicken korma, chicken or vegetable *mátàbà* (a sort of stuffed crepe) and a bilingual menu; look for a white sign with red letters. There is no roman-script sign. Great food, but count your change before you leave.

Vegetarian Restaurant (117/1 Soi Wat Bowon) Dishes 25-40B. Open 8am-10pm. For an all-vegie menu at low prices, seek

BANGKOK

out this place, south of the wát. To find this out-of-the-way spot, turn left on Tanao at the eastern end of Th Khao San, then cross the street and turn right down the first narrow alley, then left at Soi Wat Bowon – an English sign reads 'Vegetarian'. The fare is basically Western vegie, with wholemeal breads, salads and sandwiches.

Alloy (152 Th Din So) Thai vegie meals 30-50B. Open 7am-7pm. A good place, south of Th Khao San, across Th Ratchadamnoen Klang (opposite the Municipal Hall) near a 7-Eleven store. This was one of Bangkok's first Thai vegetarian restaurants, inspired by ex-Bangkok Governor Chamlong Srimuang.

Chinatown, Hualamphong & Phahurat

Some of Bangkok's best Chinese and Indian food is found in these adjacent districts, but because few tourists stay in this part of town (for good reason – it's simply too congested) they rarely make any eating forays into the area.

A few established Chinese restaurants have moved from Chinatown to locations with less traffic. But many places are still hanging on to their venerable Chinatown addresses, where the atmosphere is still part of the eating experience.

Most specialise in southern Chinese cuisine, particularly that of coastal Guangdong and Fujian provinces. This means seafood, rice noodles and dumplings are often the best choices. The large, banquet-style Chinese places are mostly found along Th Yaowarat and Th Charoen Krung.

Laem Thong (38 Soi Bamrungrat) Mains 80-120B. This is a large, banquet-style Chinese place, just off Th Charoen Krung. It has an extensive menu, including dim sum before lunchtime.

Lie Kee (☎ 022 243 587, 360–362 Th Charoen Krung) Lunch 30-50B. This is an excellent and inexpensive Chinese food centre on the 3rd floor of a building on the corner of Charoen Krung and Bamrungrat, a block west of Th Ratchawong. It's air-conditioned.

The best noodle and dumpling shops are hidden away on smaller sois and alleys.

Chiang Ki (54 Soi Bamrungrat) 60-100B. The *khâo tôm plaa* (rice soup with fish; 100B) belies the casual surroundings – no place does it better.

All-night *food hawkers* set up along Th Yaowarat and along Th Ratchawong near where the two streets intersect; this is the least expensive place to dine in Chinatown. On weekends parts of these two streets are closed to vehicular traffic, turning the area into a pedestrian mall. The seafood is especially good here. A plate of *kûng phão* (grilled prawns) goes for about 300B per kilo. Thais who dine here are fond of washing down their seafood with freshly squeezed orange juice.

Over in Phahurat, the Indian fabric district, most places serve north Indian cuisine, which is heavily influenced by Mogul or Persian flavours and spices.

Royal India (☎ 022 216 565, 92/1 Th Chakraphet, Phahurat) Lunches 40-60B. For many people, this is the best north Indian restaurant in town. It can be very crowded at lunchtime. The place has good food at quite reasonable prices. Royal India also has a branch on Th Khao San but it's not as good.

The ATM department store on Th Chakraphet near the pedestrian bridge has a *food centre* on the top floor that features several Indian vendors – the food is cheap and tasty and there's quite a good selection. Running alongside the ATM building on Soi ATM are several small *tea houses* with inexpensive Indian and Nepali food, including lots of fresh chapatis and strong milk-tea. In the afternoons a Sikh man sets up a pushcart on the corner of Soi ATM and Th Chakraphet and sells *vegetarian samosas* often cited as the best in Bangkok.

During the annual Vegetarian Festival (centred around Soi Songwat, down Soi 20, Th Charoen Krung in September or October), Bangkok's Chinatown becomes a virtual orgy of vegetarian Thai and Chinese food. Restaurants and noodle shops in the area offer hundreds of different dishes. Try seeking out the divine crushed-peanut pastry known as *túp-táp* – just listen for the pounding sound the vendors make as they pulverise the peanuts with cartoon-sized wooden mallets.

Th Silom, Th Surawong & Th Sathon

This area is in the heart of the financial district so it features a lot of pricey restaurants, along with cheaper ones that attract both office workers and the more flush. Many restaurants are found along the main avenues, but there's an even greater number tucked away in sois and alleys. The river end of Silom and Surawong towards Charoen Krung (the Bangrak district) is a good hunting ground for Indian food.

Pet Tun Jao Tha (*Soi Songwat*) Meals 40-60B. Just upriver from the Harbour Department pier (Krom Jao Tha), this place almost certainly serves Bangkok's best stewed duck over rice *(khâo nâa pèt)*. There are also some outstanding stir-fry dishes to be had here: try the *puu phàt phŏng kàrìi* (crab curry).

Soi Pradit Night Market (*Soi 20 Pracheun, Th Silom*) Dishes 25-40B. This assembles each evening in front of the municipal market pavilion and is good for cheap eats. There's a mosque, Masjid Mirasuddeen, so Muslim *food vendors* (dishes 20-30B) are also common during the day.

At lunchtime and early evening a batch of *food vendors* – everything from noodles to raw oysters – set up on Soi 5 next to Bangkok Bank's main branch.

The area to the east of Silom off Th Convent and Soi Sala Daeng is a Thai gourmets' enclave. Most of the restaurants tucked away here are very good, but a meal for two will cost 600B to 800B.

Ban Chiang (☎ 022 367 045, *14 Soi Si Wiang, Th Pramuan*) Meals 80-160B. A restored wooden house in a verdant setting off Silom, this is a great place for traditional Thai and Isan cuisine at moderate prices.

Thanying (☎ 022 364 361, 022 350 371, *10 Soi Pramuan, Th Silom*) Open 11am-11pm. Owned by a Thai movie star, this features elegant decor and very good, moderately expensive royal Thai cuisine, ie,

recipes that were created for the royal court in days past. There's another branch (☎ 022 559 838, *World Trade Center, Th Ploenchit*) open from 11.30am until 10.30pm.

Mango Tree (☎ 022 362 820, *37 Soi Anuman Ratchathon*) Mains 150-200B. Open 11am-11pm. Down Soi Tantawan opposite the Tawana Ramada Hotel on Th Surawong, this offers classic Thai cuisine and live traditional Thai music amid a decor of historical photos and antiques.

Suki Jeh Yuu Seu (*Th Rama IV*) Mains 30-50B. A Chinese vegetarian restaurant just 70m down Th Rama IV from Hualamphong train station, this serves excellent, if a bit pricey, food in a clean, air-con atmosphere. The fruit shakes are particularly refreshing; this is a great place to fortify yourself with food and drink while waiting for a train.

Thon Krueng (*Ton Khreuang;* ☎ 024 379 671, *723 Th Charoen Nakhon*) Dishes 60-120B. Try this pauper's version of dining amid the bright hotel lights of Bangkok. Go to the end of the soi in front of the Shangri-La Hotel and take a ferry (2B) across the river to the wooden pier immediately opposite on the Thonburi shore. Wind your way through the narrow lanes opposite until you come to a main road (Th Charoen Nakhon), then turn left. The large, open-air Thon Krueng is about 200m down on the left, back towards the river. Here you can enjoy a moderately priced Thai seafood meal outdoors with impressive night-time views of the Shangri-La and Oriental hotels opposite. The ferry runs until around 2am.

Somboon Seafood (☎ 022 333 104, *Th Surawong*) Mains 100-180B. Open 4pm-midnight. Towards the eastern end of Th Surawong, about a 10-minute walk west of Montien Hotel, is the famous Somboon, a good, reasonably priced seafood restaurant known for having the best crab curry in town. Soy-steamed seabass *(plaa kràphong nêung sii-yíu)* is also a speciality.

Mizu's Kitchen (*Soi Patpong 1*) Dishes 100-400B. Mizu's Kitchen has a loyal Japanese and Thai following for its inexpensive but good Japanese food, including Japanese-style steak.

Goro (399/1 Soi Siri Chulasewok, Th Silom) Mains 200-600B This is another very good Japanese place, especially for sushi and sashimi. Prices are reasonable.

Towards the western end of Silom and Surawong, Indian eateries begin making an appearance. Unlike at Indian restaurants elsewhere in Bangkok, the menus in Bangrak don't necessarily exhibit the usual, boring predilection towards north Indian Mogul-style cuisine.

Madras Cafe (☎ 022 356 761, 31/10–11 Trok Vaithi/Trok 13, Th Silom) Open 9am-10pm. For authentic South Indian food (*dosa, idli, vada* etc), try here in the Madras Lodge near the Narai Hotel.

Across from the Narai Hotel, near the Sri Mariamman Temple, *street vendors* sometimes sell various Indian snacks.

India Hut (☎ 022 378 812, Th Surawong) Dishes 80-150B. Opposite the Manohra Hotel, this specialises in Nawabi (Lucknow) cuisine; it's quite good and friendly. The vegetarian samosas and fresh prawns cooked with ginger are particularly good. It's three flights of steps off the street, with a modern Indian decor.

The Cholas (Soi Charoen Krung 32) Dishes 50-80B. A small air-con place downstairs in the Woodlands Inn just north of the main post office, this serves decent, no-fuss north Indian food.

Muslim Restaurant (1356 Th Charoen Krung) Meals 40-60B. This place has been here for decades. While the open-front restaurant is noisy, the *khâo mòk kài* (chicken biryani) is quite good and done in the same style as in Yangon – with three kinds of saffron rice.

There are several other Arab/Indian restaurants in this area.

Sun Far Myanmar Food Centre (☎ 022 668 787, 107/1 Th Pan) Dishes 30-50B. Open 8am-10pm. Between Silom and Sathon near the Myanmar embassy, this is a rare and inexpensive place to sample authentic Burmese curries and *thok* (spicy Burmese-style salads).

Rabianthong Restaurant (☎ 022 370 100, Th Silom) Lunches 80-260B. In the Narai Hotel, this offers a very good vege-tarian section in its luncheon buffet, on *wan phrá* (full moon days).

Tiensin (1345 Th Charoen Krung) Open 7am-9pm. Opposite the entrance of the soi that leads to the Shangri-La Hotel, this serves very good Chinese vegetarian food, including many mock meat dishes.

If you crave European or Japanese food, there are plenty of outlets on and around Th Patpong.

Bobby's Arms (Soi Patpong 2) Dishes 80-120B. An Aussie-British pub on the 1st floor of a multi-storey car park off Patpong 2, this has good fish and chips.

Café de Paris (☎ 022 372 776, Soi Patpong 2) Mains 120-260B. Open 11am-1am. Probably the best Patpong find is the Café de Paris, an air-con spot popular with French expats for its decent approximations of Parisian-style bistro fare. The tables outside are an unparalleled place to people watch.

In the CP Tower building on Silom are a cluster of air-con American- and Japanese-style fast-food places.

Harmonique (☎ 022 378 175, Soi Charoen Krung 34) Dishes 80-150B. Open 11am-10pm. This is a refreshing oasis in an extremely busy, smog-filled section of the street. Harmonique is a favourite with Westerners living in Bangkok – the food is authentic Thai without the sting. The shop discreetly sells silk, silverware and antiques.

Soi Ngam Duphli
Home Sweet Home (Soi Si Bamphan) Dishes 35-50B. This serves excellent Pakistani food and has very cold beer.

Ratsstube (☎ 022 864 258, 18 Soi Atakanprasit) Meals 80-120B. Open 11am-2pm, 5pm-10pm. In the Thai-German Cultural Centre (Goethe Institut) this restaurant's home-made sausages and set meals attract a large and steady clientele.

Th Sukhumvit
This avenue stretching east all the way to the city limits has hundreds of Thai, Chinese and Western restaurants to choose from.

Yong Lee Restaurant (Soi 15) Dishes 40-60B. Near Asia Books, this has excellent Thai and Chinese food at reasonable prices, and is a long-time favourite among residents. There is a second Yong Lee between sois 35 and 37.

Lemongrass (☎ 022 588 637, 5/1 Soi 24, Th Sukhumvit) Meals 120-140B. Open 11am-2pm, 6pm-11pm. For nouvelle Thai cuisine, in an atmospheric setting of an old Thai house decorated with antiques. The food is exceptional; try the *yam pèt* (Thai-style duck salad).

There are many restaurants around the major hotels on Th Sukhumvit with mixed Thai, Chinese, European and American menus – most of average quality and slightly above-average prices.

Le Dalat (☎ 022 584 192, 022 601 849, 47/1 Soi 23, Th Sukhumvit) Dishes 120-280B. Open daily 11am-2.30pm, 5.30pm-10pm. The upscale Le Dalat has the most celebrated Vietnamese cuisine in the city. There is another branch at 14 Soi 23, Th Sukhumvit (same hours).

The Emporium shopping centre, Soi 24, Th Sukhumvit, has several *restaurants* on its 4th, 5th and 6th floors, including a wood-panelled *food centre* with upmarket Thai vendors.

Mrs Balbir's (☎ 026 510 498, 155/18 Soi 11) Dishes 40-80B. Closed Monday. This is a restaurant with a good variety of moderately priced vegetarian and meaty Indian food (mostly northern Indian), close to the Ambassador Hotel. A buffet lunch (150B) is served daily. Mrs Balbir has been teaching Indian cooking for many years and has her own Indian grocery shop as well.

Rang Mahal (☎ 022 617 100, Soi 18) Mains 150-300B. A rooftop restaurant in the Rembrandt Hotel, this offers very good northern and southern Indian 'royal cuisine' with cityscape views. On Sunday the restaurant puts on a sumptuous Indian buffet (11.30am to 3pm).

A few medium to expensive restaurants serving Pakistani and Middle Eastern food can be found in the 'Little Arabia' area of Soi 3 (Soi Nana Neua).

Al Hussain (Soi 3/5) Dishes 20-40B. This roofed outdoor cafe (with an air-con dining room behind it) is the best value in the area. Besides the usual mutton and chicken dishes, there are some vegetarian dishes on offer as well.

Several rather expensive European restaurants (Swiss, French, German etc) are also found on Th Sukhumvit.

Bei Otto (☎ 022 600 869, 1 Soi 20/Soi Nam Phung, Th Sukhumvit) Dishes 140-200B. Bei Otto is one of the most popular German restaurants in town and has a comfortable bar. Attached are a bakery, deli and butcher shop.

Bourbon St Bar & Restaurant (☎ 022 590 328, Soi 22) Dinner for 2 people 400B. Open 8am-11pm. Nostalgic visitors from the USA, especially those from the Deep South, will appreciate the well-run Bourbon St, behind the Washington Theatre. Its menu emphasises Cajun and creole cooking, but there are also some Mexican dishes on the menu; some nights there is free live music. It's open for breakfast.

Le Banyan (☎ 022 535 556, 59 Soi 8/Soi Prida, Th Sukhumvit) Dinner for 2 people 600B. One of the top French restaurants in the city, and probably the best outside the luxury hotels, this is in a charming early Ratanakosin-style house. This is definitely a splurge experience, although the prices are moderate when compared with other elegant French restaurants in the city.

Señor Pico's of Los Angeles (☎ 022 617 100, 2nd floor, Rembrandt Hotel, Soi 18, Th Sukhumvit) Dinner for 2 people 500B. This brightly decorated, festive restaurant has the city's best Mexican food. It offers reasonably authentic Tex-Mex cuisine, including *fajitas, carnitas, nachos* and combination platters.

Siam Square, Th Ploenchit & Th Withayu

This shopping area is interspersed with several low- and medium-priced restaurants as well as American fast-food franchises. Chinese food seems to predominate, probably because it's the well-off Chinese Thais who most frequent Siam Square.

S&P Restaurant & Bakery (Soi 11) Breakfast 35-65B, dishes 45-75B. This popular chain has an extensive menu featuring mostly Thai specialities, with a few Chinese, Japanese, European and vegetarian dishes – all high-quality fare at low to moderate prices. It also has a bakery.

Just to the west of Siam Square's Scala Cinema, plunge into the alley that curves behind the Th Phayathai shops to find a row of cheap, good *food stalls*. A shorter alley with food stalls also leads off the northern end of Siam Square's Soi 2.

On both sides of Th Rama I in Siam Square and Siam Center you'll find a battery of American fast-food franchises. Prices are less than what you would pay in the USA. Siam Center contains a bevy of good *Thai coffee shops* on its upper floors.

If you're staying on or near Soi Kasem San 1, there are two very good, inexpensive *curry-and-rice vendors* with tables along the eastern side of the soi. No need to be fluent in Thai – they're used to the point-and-serve system. Two outdoor *cafes* on either side of the White Lodge serve more expensive Thai and European food, burgers, pastries, coffees and breakfast.

Auberge Dab (☎ 026 586 222, One Place Bldg, 540 Th Ploenchit) Meals 250-450B. Open daily 11.30am-11pm. French cuisine with an emphasis on Atlantic seafood – of all things! Relatively new but already one of the best French restaurants in Bangkok.

Sarah-Jane's (☎ 026 509 992, Sindhorn Bldg, 130–132 Th Withayu) Dishes 60-120B. Despite its faràng name, this serves very good Isan food in an air-con dining room.

Mahboonkrong Shopping Centre (MBK), another building studded with restaurants, is directly across from Siam Square at the intersection of Phayathai and Rama I. Among other amenities there are two *food centres* with vendors serving tasty dishes from all over Thailand, including vegetarian, at prices averaging 25B to 40B per plate. Hours are 10am to 10pm, but the more popular vendors run out of food as early as 8.30pm or 9pm – come earlier for the best selection.

East of Siam Square and off Th Ploenchit, Soi Lang Suan offers a number of popular medium-price eateries.

Other Vegetarian Options
Thai vegetarian restaurants (Th Kamphaeng Phet) Dishes 7-12B. Open 8am-noon Sat-Sun. One of the óldest such restaurants is operated by the Buddhist ascetic Asoke Foundation at Chatuchak Weekend Market off Th Kamphaeng Phet (near the main local bus stop, a pedestrian bridge and a Chinese shrine – look for a sign reading 'Vegetarian' in green letters).

The *cafeteria* (☎ 022 811 422, Bangkok Adventist Hospital, 430 Th Phitsanulok) here also serves inexpensive vegetarian fare. All the Indian restaurants in town also have vegetarian selections on their menus.

Dinner Cruises
There are a number of companies that run cruises during which you eat dinner. Prices range from 70B to 1400B per person depending on how far they go and whether dinner is included in the fare. For more information, see Dinner Cruises under River & Canal Trips earlier in this chapter.

ENTERTAINMENT
In their round-the-clock search for *khwaam sanùk* (fun), Bangkokians have made their metropolis one that literally never sleeps. To get an idea of what's available, check out the entertainment listings in the daily *Bangkok Post* and the *Nation* or the monthly *Bangkok Metro*. The latter maintains a good Web page (Ⓦ www.bkkmetro .com) listing current happenings in the city. Possibilities include classical music performances, rock concerts, pubs, videotheque dancing, Asian music/theatre ensembles on tour, art shows and dinner theatre. Boredom should not be a problem in Bangkok, at least not for a short-term visit. But save some energy and money for your islands and beaches trip!

While Bangkok may have the reputation for being Asia's wickedest city – a mantle inherited from Saigon in the 1960s and Shanghai in the 1920s – Bangkok's evening entertainment scene goes way beyond its over-publicised naughty nightlife image. On offer is a heady assortment of entertainment venues, nightclubs, bars, cafes and discos appealing to every proclivity. Many specialise in live music – rock, country and western, Thai pop music and jazz – while you'll hear the latest recorded music in the mega-discos as well as in the smaller neighbourhood bars. Hotels catering to tourists and businesspeople often contain up-to-date discos as well.

All bars and clubs are supposed to close at 1am or 2am (the latter closing time is for places with dance floors and/or live music), but in reality few do.

Bars

Bangkok has long outgrown the days when the only bars around catered to male go-go oglers. Trendy among Bangkok Thais these days are bars that strive for a sophisticated but casual atmosphere, with good service, drinks and music. The Thais often call them pubs but they bear little resemblance to any traditional English pub. Some are theme bars, conceived around a particular aesthetic. All the city's major hotels feature Western-style bars as well.

Dali (☎ 026 291 173, 227 Th Rambutri) A block north of Th Khao San and tucked away amid a row of noodle stands, this is a comfortable, two-storey air-con bar with a casual feel and a long, long cocktail list.

O'Reilly's Irish Pub (☎ 026 327 515, 62/1–2 Th Silom) On the corner of Soi Thaniya, just few blocks away from Patpong, this is one of only two places in Bangkok that serves Guinness on tap. A good place to duck into if you need to escape the crowds on Silom's sidewalks. Bands play on some nights, and the place is often packed from 9pm until closing.

Wong's Place (27/3 Soi Si Bamphen) Wong's is a low-key hang out with Thailand's largest collection of music videos of artists from the 1960s and 1970s. It sometimes stays open very late and is popular with local residents. Actually, Wong's may be a good reason to consider staying in the Soi Ngam Duphli area.

About Cafe (☎ 026 231 742, 402–408 Th Maitrichit) This air-con haven with retro sofas and eclectic tunes sits right smack in the sleaziest section of Chinatown, and its high glass walls and low lighting give you a great view of the action outside.

Q Bar (☎ 022 523 274, 34 Soi Sukhumvit 11) Hosting what are probably Bangkok's trendiest DJs (at the time of writing anyway), it's worth checking out even if you're staying on the other side of town. There is a 300B cover charge (includes two drinks) on weekends.

Discos & Dance Clubs

All the major hotels have international-style discos but only a small number – those at the Dusit Thani, the Shangri-La, the Grand Hyatt and the Regent – can really be recommended as attractions in themselves. Cover charges are pretty uniform: around 300B on weekday nights and around 400B on weekends, including two drinks. Most places don't begin filling up until after 11pm.

Bangkok is famous for its huge high-tech discos that hold up to 5000 people and feature mega-watt sound systems, a giant-screen video and the latest in light-show technology. The clientele for these dance palaces is mostly young moneyed Thais experimenting with lifestyles of conspicuous affluence, plus the occasional Bangkok celebrity and a sprinkling of bloodshot-eyed expats. Cover charges typically run from 400B to 500B per person and include three drinks on weeknights, two drinks on weekends.

Narcissus (☎ 022 584 805, 112 Sukhumvit Soi 23) Open 9pm to 2am. There is a 500B cover (includes three drinks) on weekends. A long-running dance club that continues to attract Bangkok's young, rich and beautiful crowd. Killer light and sound system complement a cavernous and opulent interior. DJs spin the latest trance, house and techno.

La Luna (☎ 022 613 993, Th Sukhumvit Soi 6) An upscale nightclub with lights, lasers and fog, it features both DJs and live bands, La Luna also has a sushi bar and restaurant. As with Narcissus, there is a dress code – don't even think of showing up in Khao San road attire.

Go-Go Bars

By and large these throwbacks are seedy, expensive and cater to men only, whether straight or gay. Unlike go-go bars in the West, virtually everyone working in these establishments is for sale. Number tags are attached to the dancers' bikinis so that potential customers can discreetly pick and choose without having to point at anybody (pointing at people is considered rude in Thailand). Go-go bars are concentrated along Th Sukhumvit (between sois 21 and 23), off Th Sukhumvit on Soi Nana Tai and in the world-famous Patpong area, between Th Silom and Th Surawong.

Patpong has calmed down a lot over the years and become a general tourist attraction in itself. These days it has more of an open-air market feel as several of the newer bars are literally on the street, and vendors set up shop in the evening hawking everything from roast squid to fake designer watches. On Patpong's two parallel lanes there are around 35 to 40 go-go bars, plus a sprinkling of restaurants, cocktail bars, discos and live music venues. The downstairs clubs feature go-go dancing while upstairs the real raunch is kept behind closed doors. Women and couples are welcome. Avoid bars touting free sex shows as there are usually hidden charges and when you try to ditch the outrageous bill the doors are suddenly blocked by muscled bouncers. The 1am closing law is strictly enforced on Patpong 1 and 2.

The gay men's equivalent can be found on nearby Soi Twilight on Th Surawong, opposite the entrance to the Surawong Hotel.

A more direct legacy of the R&R days is Soi Cowboy, a single lane strip of 25 to 30 bars off Th Sukhumvit between sois 21 and 23. By and large it's seedier than Patpong, and you will see far fewer women and couples in the crowd.

Nana Entertainment Plaza (off Soi 4/Soi Nana Tai, Th Sukhumvit) This three-storey complex has surged in popularity among resident and visiting oglers. Nana Plaza comes complete with its own guesthouses in the same complex, used almost exclusively by Nana Plaza's female bar workers for illicit assignations. One bar consists entirely of Thai transvestites and transsexuals – this is a favourite stop for people visiting Bangkok for sex re-assignment surgery. There are 18 bars in the whole complex.

Gay & Lesbian Venues

If you're looking for gay venues without the element of overt prostitution, head to Th Silom. In general the Soi 2 clubs are more gay than the bars on Soi 4 – though Soi 4's *Telephone (☎ 022 343 279 114/11–13 Th Silom Soi 4)* and *The Balcony (☎ 022 355 891, 86–88 Th Silom Soi 4)* are more exclusively gay than other bars on this street.

DJ Station (☎ 022 664 029, 8/6–8 Th Silom Soi 2) This still boasts Soi 2's hottest gay dance scene, plus *kàthoey* (transvestite) cabaret at midnight. There's a 200B cover charge (good for two drinks) on Friday and Saturday.

Kàthoey Cabaret

Transvestite cabarets are big in Bangkok.

Calypso Cabaret (☎ 022 616 355, 022 168 937, 296 Th Phayathai) Admission 600B. Shows 8.15pm & 9.45pm. In the Asia Hotel, has the largest regularly performing transvestite troupe in town. Although the audience is almost 100% tourists, the show is very good and includes plenty of Thai and Asian themes as well as the usual Broadway camp.

Live Music

Bangkok's live music scene has expanded rapidly over the past decade or so, with a multiplicity of new, extremely competent bands and recently opened clubs.

Saxophone Pub Restaurant (☎ 022 465 472, 3/8 Victory Monument, Th Phayathai) Admission free. The three-storey Saxophone, south-east of the Victory Monument circle, has become a Bangkok institution for musicians of several genres. On the ground floor is a bar/restaurant featuring jazz (9pm–1.30am); the next floor has a billiards

RICHARD I'ANSON

BILL WASSMAN

MICK ELMORE

RICHARD I'ANSON

JOE CUMMINGS

JULIET COOMBE

The many faces of Southern Thailand

GREG ELMS

A Grand Palace guardian

JOHN HAY

Meals on wheels

PAUL PIAIA

Everything needed to worship at a nearby Hindu temple.

PAUL BEINSSEN

Tempted by tentacles?

RICHARD I'ANSON

Stacks of snacks

hall with recorded music playing in the background; the top floor has live bands playing reggae, R&B, jazz or blues (10.30pm–4am), and on Sundays there's an open jam session. You don't need to dress up.

La Havana (☎ 022 041 166, 65/6 Soi 22, Th Sukhumvit) Intimate but with a festive decor, this place has acoustic Latin sounds on Friday and Saturday nights. On Sunday things get bluesy. The rest of the week there are scads of Latin CDs to choose from.

Concept CM2 (☎ 022 556 888, Siam Square Soi 6) A multi-themed complex in the basement of the Novotel on Siam Square, this hosts a rotation of live Western bands and Thai recording artists – generally focussing on what passes for alternative these days – interspersed with DJ dance music. Look for V4, a locally based outfit that plays good reggae, funk and acid jazz covers.

Metal Zone (☎ 022 551 913, 82/3 Soi Lang Suan) Around the corner from Th Sarasin, just north of Lumphini Park, this is the best of the city's heavy metal clubs. A regular line-up of bands perform everything from thrash to Gothic to speed metal, Ozzie squeal to Axel rasp, even a few Helmet tunes, in a dungeons-and-dragons setting.

Bamboo Bar (☎ 022 360 400, Soi Oriental, Th Charoen Krung) The Oriental's famous Bamboo Bar has good live jazz nightly in an elegant but relaxed atmosphere.

Thai Dance-Drama

National Theatre (☎ 022 241 342, Th Chao Fa, Banglamphu) Admission 20-200B. Thailand's most traditional *lákhon* and *khŏhn* performances (masked dance-drama based on stories from the *Ramayana*) are held here, near Phra Pinklao Bridge. The theatre's regular public roster schedules six or seven performances per month, usually on weekends. Attending a khŏhn performance is highly recommended.

Shrine Dancing

Free performances of traditional *lákhon kae bon* may be seen daily at the *Lak Muang* and *Erawan* shrines if you happen to arrive

when a performance troupe has been commissioned by a worshipper. Although many of the dance movements are the same as those seen in classical lákhon, these relatively crude performances are specially choreographed for ritual purposes and don't represent true classical dance forms. But the dancing is colourful – the dancers wear full costume and are accompanied by live music – so it's worth stopping by to watch a performance if you're in the vicinity.

Dinner Theatres

Most tourists view performances put on solely for their benefit at one of the several Thai classical dance/dinner theatres in the city. Admission prices at these evening venues average 200B to 500B per person and include a 'typical' Thai dinner (often toned down for faràng palates), a couple of selected dance performances and a martial arts display.

Sala Rim Nam (☎ 024 372 918, 024 373 080, Soi Oriental, Th Charoen Krung) The historic Oriental Hotel has its own dinner theatre, on the Thonburi side of Mae Nam Chao Phraya opposite the hotel. The admission is well above average (about 1500B) but so is the food, the performance and the Thai pavilion decor (teak, marble and bronze); the river ferry between the hotel and restaurant is free. Dinner begins at 7pm, the dance performance at 8.30pm.

Baan Thai (☎ 022 585 403, Soi 32, Th Sukhumvit) In an old Thai house with a leafy garden, the food has been toned-down but the show and setting make up for it. The set menu (500B) does not include drinks and the show begins at 8.30pm. Arrive early to ensure getting a table with a good view of the performance.

Massage Parlours

Massage parlours have been a Bangkok attraction for many years now, though the TAT tries to play down the city's reputation in this respect.

Massage as a healing art is a centuries-old tradition in Thailand, and it is easy to find a legitimate massage in Bangkok, despite the commercialisation of recent years (see the following Traditional Massage entry). That many of the city's modern massage parlours (*àap òp nûat* or bathe-steam-massage, sometimes referred to as Turkish bath) also deal in prostitution is well known; less well known is the fact that many (but by no means all) of the girls working in the parlours are bonded labour – they are not necessarily there by choice. There is a definite AIDS presence in Thailand (see the information on this and other sexually transmitted diseases under Health in the Facts for the Visitor chapter).

All but the most insensitive males will be saddened by the sight of 50 girls/women behind a glass wall with numbers pinned to their dresses. Often the bank of masseuses is divided into sections according to skill and/or appearance. Most expensive is the 'superstar' section, in which the women try to approximate the look of fashion models or actresses. A smaller section is reserved for women who are actually good at giving massages, and who offer nothing extra.

The last several years has seen an increasing number of gay-oriented 'saunas' sprouting up around the capital. Most of these have a contingent of 'masseurs' who, like their female counterparts, are rarely versed in any conventional type of massage. See the Prostitution entry in the Society & Conduct section of the Facts about Thailand chapter for further information.

Traditional Massage

Traditional Thai massage, also called ancient massage, is widely available in Bangkok. Fees for traditional Thai massage should be no more than 300B per hour, though some places have a 1½ hour minimum. Be aware that not every place advertising traditional or ancient massage offers a really good one; sometimes the only thing 'ancient' about the pummelling is the age of the masseuse or masseur. Thai massage aficionados say that the best massages are given by blind masseurs (available at Marble House; see its entry in this section).

Wat Pho (Th Chetuphon) Massage 200B per hour, 120B per half-hour. Wat Pho, Bangkok's oldest temple, was once one of the best places to experience a traditional massage. Unfortunately it may have fallen victim to its own popularity. Many of the *măw nûat* (massage therapists) now watch TV or talk on their cell phones while giving a massage – hardly the most soothing atmosphere. For those interested in studying massage, the temple also offers two 30-hour courses – on general Thai massage, massage therapy and foot massage. For further information call the Wat Pho Thai Traditional Medical & Massage School, (☎ 022 212 974, *Th Sanamchai*), located opposite Wat Pho's western wall.

Next door to Wat Mahathat (towards Thammasat University at the south-east corner of Th Maharat and Th Phra Chan) is a strip of Thai herbal medicine shops offering good massage for a mere 80B to 100B an hour.

A more commercial area for traditional Thai massage, as well as Thai herbal saunas, is Th Surawong near Patpong.

Marble House (☎ 022 353 519, 37/18–19 Soi Surawong Plaza, Th Surawong) Massage 200-300B per hour. Thai herbal sauna is offered here as well as massage.

Arima Onsen (☎ 022 352 142, 37/10–11 Soi Surawong Plaza) Has a predominantly Asian clientele, but is good for groups of four to six, as you can rent a private Japanese-style room and enjoy a kind of room service – ordering drinks from the bar downstairs.

Most upscale hotels also provide a legitimate massage service either through their health clubs or as part of room service.

SPECTATOR SPORTS
Muay Thai (Thai Boxing)

Muay thai can be seen at two boxing stadiums. Admission fees vary according to seating (outer circle to ringside), for eight fights of five rounds each. The outer circle seats are quite OK. Aficionados say the best-matched bouts are reserved for Tuesday nights at Lumphini, and Thursday nights at Ratchadamnoen.

Sanam Muay Lumphini (☎ 022 528 765, Th Rama IV) Admission 220-1000B. Held 6.30pm Tues & Fri, 5pm Sat. Near Lumphini park, the Tuesday night bouts are said to be the best matched. There's an equipment shop at the stadium, open on fight nights, where you can buy authentic muay thai gear.

Sanam Muay Ratchadamnoen (☎ *022 814 205, 1 Th Ratchadamnoen Nok)* Admission 220-1000B. Held 6pm Mon, Wed & Thur, 5pm Sun. The best-matched bouts are held here on Thursday nights. This stadium also has an equipment outlet that's open on fight nights.

Warning At some programs a ticket Mafia tries to steer every tourist into buying an expensive ringside seat, often claiming all other seats are sold out. It's a pretence; you should be able to find a window selling seats as cheap as 220B. Don't believe anyone who says seats are sold out unless you hear it directly from a window ticket vendor.

Takraw

This peculiarly Thai ball sport (see Spectator Sports in the Facts for the Visitor chapter) can be seen at schools and universities around Bangkok, and occasionally at the National Stadium.

SHOPPING

Regular visitors to Asia know that, in many ways, Bangkok beats Hong Kong and Singapore for deals on handicrafts, textiles, gems, jewellery, art and antiques – nowhere else will you find the same combination of range, quality and prices. The trouble is finding the good spots, as the city's intense urban tangle makes orientation sometimes difficult. *Nancy Chandler's Map of Bangkok* makes a very good buying companion, with annotations on all sorts of small, out-of-the-way shopping venues and markets (called *tàlàat* in Thai).

Be sure to read the Shopping section in the Facts for the Visitor chapter before setting out on a buying spree. Amid all the bargains are a number of cleverly disguised rip-off schemes – caveat emptor!

Chatuchak Weekend Market

Chatuchak Weekend Market (Talat Jatujak) is the Disneyland of Thai markets; on weekends 8672 vendor stalls cater to an estimated 200,000 visitors a day. Everything is sold here from live chickens and snakes to opium pipes and herbal remedies. Thai clothing such as the *phâa khăo máa* (sarong for males) and the *phâasîn* (sarong for females), *kaang keng jiin* (Chinese pants) and *sêua mâw hâwm* (blue cotton farmer's shirt) are good buys. You'll also find musical instruments, hill-tribe crafts, religious amulets, antiques, flowers, clothes imported from India and Nepal, camping gear and military surplus. The best bargains of all are household goods like pots and pans, dishes, drinking glasses etc. Don't forget to try out your bargaining skills.

As with any place where large numbers of Thais congregate, there's also some very good food to be had at the Weekend Market, as well as a couple of trendy drink shops where you can cool off with a beer.

The main part of the Weekend Market is open on Saturday and Sunday from around 8am to 6pm, though some places may stay open as late as 8pm, most begin shutting down around 5pm. There are a few vendors out on weekday mornings, and there's a daily market for vegetables, plants and flowers opposite the market's southern side. One section of the latter, known as the Aw Taw Kaw Market, sells organically grown (no chemical sprays or fertilisers) fruit and vegetables.

The Weekend Market lies at the southern end of Chatuchak Park, off Th Phahonyothin, south of the Northern and North-Eastern bus terminal. Air-con bus Nos 2, 3, 9, 10 and 13, and a dozen other ordinary city buses, will get you there. The air-con bus No 12 and ordinary bus No 77 conveniently terminate right next to the market. The Skytrain runs direct to Moh Chit station, which is about 500m past the market. Better yet, get off at Saphan Khwai station, about 1km before the market and browse the wares of the many sidewalk vendors who line the way to the market proper. Prices at these stalls are generally much cheaper than they are inside the market itself.

Other Markets

Th Khao San has itself become a shopping bazaar offering cheap audio tapes, used books, jewellery, beads, clothing, Thai axe pillows, T-shirts, tattoos, body piercing and just about any other product or service you might wish for.

At night Patong Soi 1 and nearby Th Silom fill up with vendors selling cheap tourist junk, inexpensive clothing, fake watches, you name it. Along both sides of Th Sukhumvit between Soi 1 and Soi 5 there are also lots of street vendors selling similar items.

Two other markets set up during the evening near Saphan Phut pier. One, at the foot of Saphan Phut (Memorial Bridge), is mostly clothing and jewellery geared towards Thai teenagers. The more interesting of the two markets – for foreigners anyway – is the cut-flower market known as Pak Khlong Talat. Here you can get a look at the many types of orchids grown in Thailand, as well as some intricate examples of *phuang málai* – garlands of jasmine, marigolds and other flowers used as religious offerings. Pak Khlong Talat is best in the early evening between 5pm and 7pm.

Antiques & Decorative Items
Real Thai antiques are rare and costly. Most Bangkok antique shops keep a few antiques around for collectors, along with lots of pseudo-antiques or traditionally crafted items that look like antiques. The majority of shop operators are quite candid about what's genuinely old and what isn't. As Thai design becomes more popular abroad, many shops are now specialising in Thai home decorative items.

River City Shopping Complex, (☎ 022 370 077, Th Yotha) On the river and attached by a pedestrian bridge to the Royal Orchid Sheraton Hotel off Th Yotha, this complex contains a number of high quality art and antique shops on the 3rd and 4th floors. While great for browsing, many of these shops are something of a grab bag as far as the merchandise goes. There are some genuinely rare pieces with astronomical price tags mixed in with quite ordinary items also with lofty price tags. It helps if you know a little about what you're shop-

ping for. Located on the 3rd floor, *World Art* (☎ 022 370 777 ext 341) has an excellent selection of Chinese snuff bottles and other collectibles at reasonable prices, and the owner is quite straightforward about what is and isn't rare. *Acala*, shop No 312, specialises in intricately painted antique Tibetan trunks – worth a look even if you're not in the market for one.

The *Oriental Plaza* shopping complex, adjacent to the Oriental Hotel, also has several good, if very pricey, antique shops. To give you an idea of just how pricey – some of the owners of the Oriental Plaza shops actually buy their stock from nearby River City!

Shop the World (☎ 026 616 480, 131 Soi Asoke/Soi 31, Th Sukhumvit) This shop is in the compound of the Siam Society and the items for sale belong to members who donate a percentage of every sale to this scholarly organisation. There's a good selection of handicrafts here as well.

Gems & Jewellery
Recommending specific shops is tricky, since to the average eye one coloured stone looks as good as another, so the risk of a rip-off is much greater than for most other popular shopping items. A list of gem dealers who have agreed to comply with TAT guidelines can be found at **W** www .tat.or.th .do/gems.htm.

Johnny's Gems (☎ 022 244 065, 199 Th Fuang Nakhon) This is one shop that's been a long-time favourite with Bangkok expats for service and value in set jewellery.

Lambert Holding (☎ 022 364 343, 807 Th Silom) This is a dependable dealer that specialises in unset stones.

Bronzeware
Thailand has the oldest bronze-working tradition in the world and there are several factories in Bangkok producing bronze sculpture and cutlery.

Buddha Casting Foundry (*Th Phrannok, Thonburi*) Visit here to see the casting process for Buddha images. It's next to Wat Wiset Khan (take a river ferry from Tha Phra Chan or Tha Maharat on the Bangkok side to reach the foot of Th Phrannok).

Many *vendors* at Wat Mahathat's Sunday market sell old and new bronzeware – haggling is imperative.

Handicrafts

Bangkok has excellent buys in Thai handicrafts, though for northern hill-tribe materials you might be able to do better in Chiang Mai. Try the Weekend Market first, where you'll find handicrafts from all over Thailand as well as South-East Asia – even as far afield as Nepal. There are also quite a few shops in town that specialise in handicrafts.

Shop the World (☎ 026 616 480, 131 Soi Asoke/Soi 31, Th Sukhumvit) This shop is in the compound of the Siam Society and the items for sale belong to members who donate a percentage of every sale to this scholarly organisation. There's a good selection of antiques here as well.

Rasi Sayam (☎ 022 584 195, 32 Soi 23, Th Sukhumvit) Quality is high here; many of the items stocked, including wall-hangings and pottery, are made specifically for this shop.

Vilai's (☎ 023 916 106, 731/1 Soi 55/Thong Lor, Th Sukhumvit) This is another good one for pottery as well as lacquerware and especially fabrics.

Thai Celadon (☎ 022 294 383, 8/6–8 Th Ratchadaphisek Tat Mai) For quality Thai celadon (a type of green- or blue-glazed porcelain), this place has a wide selection.

Inexpensive places to pick up new Thai pottery of all shapes and sizes at wholesale prices include two shops on Soi On Nut, off Soi 77, Th Sukhumvit: **United Siam Overseas** *(☎ 027 216 320)* and **Siamese Merchandise** *(☎ 023 330 680)*. Overseas shipping can be arranged.

Tailor Shops

Bangkok abounds in places where you can have shirts, trousers, suits and just about any other article of clothing designed, cut and sewn by hand. Workmanship ranges from shoddy to excellent, so it pays to ask around before committing yourself. Shirts and trousers can be turned around in 48 hours or less with only one fitting. But no matter what a tailor may tell you, it takes more than one or two fittings to create a good suit, and most reputable tailors will ask to fit you two to five times. A custom-made suit, no matter what the material is, should cost less than US$250. An all-cashmere suit can be made for as little as US$175 with a little bargaining; bring your own fabric and it will cost even less.

Bangkok tailors can be particularly good at copying your favourite piece of clothing. If possible, bring your own fabric from home or abroad, especially if it's 100% cotton you want. Most of the so-called 'cotton' offered by Bangkok tailors is actually a blend of cotton and a synthetic; more than a few tailors will actually try to pass off full polyester or dacron as cotton. Good quality silk, on the other hand, is plentiful. Tailor-made silk shirts should cost no more than US$20, depending on the type of silk (Chinese silk is cheaper than Thai).

Generally speaking, the best shops are those found along the outer reaches of Th Sukhumvit (out beyond Soi 20 or so) and on or off Th Charoen Krung. Th Silom also has some good tailors. The worst tailor shops tend to be those in tourist-oriented shopping areas in inner Th Sukhumvit, Th Khao San, the River City Shopping Complex and other shopping malls. 'Great deals' like four shirts, two suits, a kimono and a safari suit all in one package almost always turn out to be made with inferior materials and less care.

Recommended tailor shops include: *Marco Tailor (☎ 022 520 689, Soi 7, Siam Square);* and *Macway's Exporters (☎ 022 352 407, Th Silom),* opposite the Narai Hotel.

As with every other kind of merchandise in Thailand, avoid the suggestions of strangers who may approach you with a good deal on tailoring. Also avoid any tailor shop that posts an employee at the door to try and lure passers-by into the shop. Quality tailors don't have to resort to this tactic.

Camera Supplies, Film & Processing

For a selection of camera supplies across a wide range of models and brand names, one of the best shops is *Sunny Camera* with three branches (☎ *022 338 378, 1267/1 Th Charoen Krung;* ☎ *022 368 627, 144/23 Th Silom;* ☎ *022 179 293, 3rd floor, Mahboonkrong Shopping Centre).* **Niks** *(*☎ *022 352 929, 166 Th Silom)* is also recommended. It sells professional equipment and services Nikon and other brands.

Film prices in Bangkok are generally lower than anywhere else in Asia, including Hong Kong. The highest concentration of photo shops can be found along Th Silom and Th Surawong.

Quick, professional-quality processing of most film types is available at: *Image Quality Lab* (IQ Lab; ☎ *022 384 001, 60 Th Silom)* or (☎ *027 140 644, 9/33 Thana Arcade, Soi 63, Th Sukhumvit);* and **Hollywood Film** *(*☎ *026 922 330, 026 920 690, fax 026 920 689, 5009/4 Soi 23, Th Prachasongkhroh),* where the staff offer a pick-up and delivery service (ask for John).

Scuba Supplies

Larry's Dive Center, Bar & Grill (☎ *026 634 563,* W *www.larrysdive.com,* e *larry bkk@larrysdive.com, 8/3 Soi 22, Th Sukhumvit)* This stocks all manner of diving and snorkelling gear. There's a restaurant and bar attached, so you can fill both your air tanks and your stomach.

GETTING THERE & AWAY
Air

Bangkok is a major centre for international flights throughout Asia, and its international airport is a busy one. Bangkok is also a major centre for buying discounted airline tickets (see the Getting There & Away chapter for details), but be warned that the Bangkok travel agency business has more than a few crooked operators. Domestic flights operated by THAI, Bangkok Airways and other domestic airlines also fan out from Bangkok all over the country (see the Getting Around chapter). Airline offices in Bangkok are:

Air Andaman (☎ 022 514 905) 4th floor, Nailert Bldg, Th Sukhumvit
Air India (☎ 022 350 557) 12th floor, One Pacific Place, 140 Th Sukhumvit
Air New Zealand (☎ 022 548 440) 14th floor, Sindhorn Bldg, 130–32 Th Withayu

Angel Airlines (☎ 029 532 263) UCOM Bldg, Th Vibhavadi Rangsit Hwy
Bangkok Airways (☎ 022 293 434, 022 534 014) 60 Queen Sirikit National Convention Center, Th Ratchadaphisek Tat Mai, Khlong Toey
British Airways (☎ 026 361 700) 14th floor, 990 Th Rama IV
Cathay Pacific Airways (☎ 022 630 606) 11th floor, Ploenchit Tower, 898 Th Ploenchit
Garuda Indonesia (☎ 022 856 470–3) 27th floor, Lumphini Tower, 1168/77 Th Rama IV
Japan Airlines (☎ 026 925 151) JAL Bldg, 254/1 Th Ratchadaphisek
Lao Aviation (☎ 022 369 822) 1st floor, Silom Plaza, 491/17 Th Silom
Lufthansa (☎ 022 642 400) Asoke Bldg, 66 Soi 21, Th Sukhumvit
Malaysia Airlines (☎ 022 630 565) 20th floor, Ploenchit Tower, 898 Th Ploenchit
Myanmar Airways International (☎ 026 300 334) 23rd floor, Jewelry Trade Center Bldg, 919/298 Th Silom
Qantas Airways (☎ 026 361 770) 14th floor, 990 Th Rama IV
Royal Air Cambodge (☎ 026 532 261) 17th floor, Pacific Place Bldg, 142 Th Sukhumvit
Singapore Airlines (☎ 022 360 440) 12th floor, Silom Centre Bldg, 2 Th Silom
Thai Airways International (THAI; head office ☎ 025 130 121) 89 Th Vibhavadi Rangsit; (☎ 022 343 100–19) 485 Th Silom; (☎ 022 880 060) 6 Th Lan Luang; (☎ 022 152 020–1) Asia Hotel, 296 Th Phayathai; (☎ 025 352 081–2) Bangkok International Airport, Don Muang
United Airlines (☎ 022 530 558) 14th floor, Sindhorn Bldg, 130–32 Th Withayu
Vietnam Airlines (☎ 026 569 056–8) 7th floor, Ploenchit Center Bldg, Soi 2, Th Sukhumvit

Airport Facilities During the past decade, the airport facilities at Bangkok International Airport have undergone a US$200 million redevelopment, including the construction of an international terminal that is one of the most modern and convenient in Asia. However, the slow-moving Immigration queues are still a problem – waits of 45 minutes to an hour are not unusual during peak arrival times. On the other hand, baggage claim is usually quick and efficient (of course, they have lots of time to get it right while you're inching along through Immigration).

The customs area has a green lane for passengers with nothing to declare – just walk through if you're one of these and hand your customs form to one of the clerks by the exit. Baggage trolleys are free for use inside the terminal.

Foreign currency booths on the ground floor of the arrival hall and in the departure lounge of both terminals give a good rate of exchange, so there's no need to wait until you're in the city centre to change money. There are also ATMs in the arrival and departure halls.

There is a 24-hour post/telephone office with a Home Country Direct phone service in the departure hall (3rd floor) of Terminal 1. Another 24-hour post office is located in the departure lounge; a third one in the arrival hall is open Monday to Friday from 9am to 5pm.

Left-luggage facilities (70B per piece for 24 hours or less, then a charge of 35B for each additional half-hour) are available in the departure halls in both terminals. In the transit lounge of Terminal 1, clean day rooms with washing and toilet facilities can be rented for US$86 per eight hours.

On the 4th floor of Terminal 1 is a small, reasonably priced 24-hour cafeteria area, a larger THAI restaurant with more expensive fare and, on the 2nd level above the arrival area, there's a coffee shop that is open from 6am to 11pm. There is also a small snack bar in the waiting area on the ground floor. The departure lounge has two snack bars that serve alcohol.

On the 4th floor of Terminal 2 is a cluster of new fast-food–style places including Burger King and Swensen's. Opposite these is a pricey Chinese restaurant and on the arrival floor of this terminal is a KFC.

There are several newsstands and souvenir shops in the arrival and departure areas of Terminal 1. Duty-free shopping is available in the departure lounge as well.

If you leave the airport building area and cross the expressway on the pedestrian bridge (just north of the passenger terminal), you'll find yourself in Don Muang town where there are all sorts of shops, a market, lots of small restaurants and food stalls, even a wát, all within 100m or so of the airport.

The modern and luxurious Amari Airport Hotel (☎ 025 661 020–1) has its own air-conditioned, enclosed footbridge from Terminal 1 and 'special mini-stay' daytime rates (8am to 6pm) for stays of up to a maximum of three hours for US$20 for singles/doubles, including tax and service. Longer daytime rates are available on request. Reservations are not accepted.

Bus

Bangkok is the centre for bus services that fan out all over the kingdom. There are basically three types of long-distance bus. First there is the ordinary public bus, then the air-con public bus. The third choice is the many private air-con services that leave from various offices and hotels all over the city.

Public Bus There are three main public bus (Baw Khaw Saw) terminals. The Northern & North-Eastern bus terminal (☎ 029 363 660 for Northern routes, ☎ 029 360 667 for North-Eastern routes) is on Th Phahonyothin just north of Chatuchak Park (and the Weekend Market). It's also commonly called the Moh Chit station (sathǎanii mǎw chít), or, since it moved to a brand new air-con building on the other side of the highway a little farther north, it's sometimes referred to as 'New' Moh Chit (mǎw chít mài). Air-con city bus Nos 4, 10, 29 and 29, along with a dozen or more ordinary city buses, will take you there. Easier and faster is the Skytrain – the Moh Chit Skytrain station is within walking distance of the bus terminal.

The Eastern bus terminal (☎ 023 912 504), the departure point for buses to Pattaya, Rayong, Chanthaburi and other points east, is a long way out along Th Sukhumvit, at Soi 40 (Soi Ekamai) opposite Soi 63. Most folks call it Ekamai station (sathǎanii èk-amai). Air-con bus Nos 1, 8, 11 and 13 all pass this station. The Skytrain has a station here as well, also called Ekamai Station.

The Southern bus terminal (☎ 024 351 200) for buses south to Phuket, Surat Thani and closer centres to the west like Nakhon Pathom and Kanchanaburi, has one Thonburi location for both ordinary and air-con buses at the intersection of Hwy 338 (Th Nakhon Chaisi) and Th Phra Pinklao. You can reach the station by ordinary city bus Nos 124 and 127.

When travelling on night buses take care of your belongings. Some long-distance buses that leave from Bangkok now issue claim checks for luggage stored under the bus, but valuables are still best kept on your person or within reach.

Allow an hour to reach the Northern and North-Eastern bus terminal from Banglamphu or anywhere along the river, and over an hour to reach the Southern bus terminal. The Eastern bus terminal takes 30 to 45 minutes under most traffic conditions. During occasional gridlock, eg, Friday afternoons before a holiday, it can take up to three hours to get across town to the terminals by public transport. The Skytrain is hands down the fastest way to get to both the Northern and North-Eastern terminal and the Eastern bus terminal.

Private Bus The more reputable and licensed private tour buses leave from the public terminals listed previously. Some private bus companies arrange pick-ups at Th Khao San and other guesthouse areas – these pick ups are illegal since it's against municipal law to carry passengers within the city limits except en route to or from an official terminal. This is why the curtains on these buses are sometimes closed when picking up passengers.

Although fares can be lower on private buses, the incidence of reported theft is far greater than on the Baw Khaw Saw buses. They are also generally – but not always – less reliable, promising services (such as air-con or VIP seats) that they don't deliver. For safer, more reliable, and more punctual service, stick to buses that leave from the official Baw Khaw Saw terminals.

See the Getting Around chapter for more information about bus travel in Thailand. Also, for details on bus fares to/from other towns and cities in Thailand, see the Getting There & Away sections under each destination.

Train

Bangkok is the terminus for main trunk rail services to the South, North, North-East and east. There are two principal train stations. The big Hualamphong train station on Th Rama IV handles services to the North, North-East and some of the Southern services. The Thonburi (Bangkok Noi) train station handles a few services to the South. If you're heading down to Southern Thailand, make sure you know which station your train departs from. See the Train section in the Getting Around chapter for further details.

GETTING AROUND

Getting around Bangkok may be difficult for the uninitiated but once you're familiar with the transport system the whole city is accessible. The main obstacle is traffic, which moves at a snail's pace during much of the day. This means advance planning is a must when you are attending scheduled events or making appointments.

If possible, try travelling by river or Skytrain from one point to another – avoiding roads saves time.

To/From the Airport

There is a choice of transport from the international airport, in Don Muang district, 25km north of Bangkok, to the city; prices range from 3.50B to 300B.

Airport Bus The airport express bus service operates from Bangkok International Airport to four different Bangkok districts for 100B per person. Buses run every 15 minutes from 6am to midnight. A map showing the designated stops is available at the airport; each route has approximately six stops in each direction. A great boon to travellers on a budget, these buses mean that you can avoid hassling with taxi drivers to get a reasonable fare as well as forgo the slow pace of the regular bus routes.

The Airport Bus counter is around 200m to the left (with your back to Terminal 1) of the left-most terminal exit. The routes follow:

A-1 – To the Silom business district via Pratunam and Th Ratchadamri, stopping at big hotels like the Indra, Grand Hyatt Erawan, Regent Bangkok and Dusit Thani.

A-2 – To Sanam Luang via Th Phayathai, Th Lan Luang, Th Ratchadamnoen Klang and Th Tanao; this is the one you want if you're going to the Victory Monument, Siam Square or Banglamphu areas. In Banglamphu, it stops opposite the Food & Agriculture Organization (FAO) headquarters on Th Phra Athit.

A-3 – To the Phrakhanong district via Th Sukhumvit, including Eastern (Ekamai) bus terminal (for buses east to Si Racha – for Ko Samet, Pattaya and Trat) and Soi 55 (Soi Thong Lor).

A-4 – To Hualamphong train station via Th Rama IV and Th Phayathai, with stops at Mahboonkrong shopping centre and Siam Inter-Continental Hotel.

To catch an Airport bus to the airport, just wait at one of the stops listed above and buy a ticket on board the bus.

Public Bus Cheapest of all are the public buses to Bangkok that stop on the highway in front of the airport. There are two non–air-con (ordinary) bus routes and four air-con routes. However, public buses are usually crowded and there is no room to stow luggage. If you're carrying a large backpack, you won't be allowed to board.

Air-con bus No 29 costs 16B and plies one of the most useful, all-purpose routes from the airport into the city as it goes to the Siam Square and Hualamphong areas. After entering the city limits via Th Phahonyothin (which turns into Th Phayathai), the bus passes Th Phetchaburi (where you'll want to get off to change buses for Banglamphu), then Th Rama I at the Siam Square/ Mahboonkrong intersection (for buses out to Th Sukhumvit, or to walk to Soi Kasem San 1 for various lodgings) and finally turns right on Th Rama IV to go to the Hualamphong district (where the main train station is located). You'll want to go the opposite way on Th Rama IV for the Soi Ngam Duphli lodging area. No 29 runs only from 5.45am to 8.30pm, so if you're arriving on a late-night flight you'll miss it.

Air-con bus No 13 (16B; 4.30am to 9pm) also goes to Bangkok from the airport, coming down Th Phahonyothin (like No 29),

turning left at the Victory Monument to Th Ratchaprarop, then south to Th Ploenchit, where it goes east along Th Sukhumvit all the way to Bang Na. This is the one to catch if you're heading for the Th Sukhumvit area.

Air-con bus No 4 (16B; 5.45am to 8pm) begins with a route parallel to that of the No 29 bus – down Th Vibhavadi Rangsit to Th Ratchaprarop and Th Ratchadamri (Pratunam district), crossing Phetchaburi, Rama I, Ploenchit and Rama IV, then down Silom, left on Charoen Krung, and across the river to Thonburi.

Ordinary bus No 59 costs 3.50B (5B between 10pm to 6am) and operates 24 hours – it zigzags through the city to Banglamphu (the Democracy Monument area) from the airport and can take up to two hours or more in heavy traffic.

Ordinary bus No 29 (3.50B or 5B; from 11pm to 5am; 24 hours) plies much the same route as air-con bus No 29.

To catch a bus to the airport, just wait at one of the circular bus stop signs along these routes.

It's worth spending the extra few baht for the air-con and almost guaranteed seating, especially in the hot season, since the trip to central Bangkok usually takes an hour or more. The 100B Airport Bus is really the best choice.

Train You can also get into Bangkok from the airport by train. Just after leaving Terminal 1, turn right (north), cross the highway via the pedestrian bridge, turn left and walk about 100m towards Bangkok. Opposite the big Amari Airport Hotel is the small Don Muang station from where trains depart regularly to Bangkok. The 3rd-class fare from Don Muang is only 5B on the ordinary and commuter trains if you buy your ticket on the platform, 10B if purchased on the train. Tickets for rapid and express trains are 45B and 65B respectively.

There are trains every 15 to 30 minutes between 5am and 8pm and it takes about 50 minutes to reach Hualamphong, the main station in central Bangkok. In the opposite direction trains run frequently between 8am and 10pm. Note that the train can take over an hour to reach the airport when traffic is heavy – there are many busy streets to be crossed at a very slow pace. From Hualamphong station you can walk to the bus stop almost opposite Wat Traimit for bus No 53 to Banglamphu, if that's your destination.

Taxi The Department of Land Transport has stepped in to police the airport taxi service and there are fewer hassles with airport taxi drivers than in previous years. We've had no problems at all during the last couple of years getting regular metered taxis from the airport. In the past, savvy travellers would catch an incoming cab that had just discharged its passengers at the departure area. It's no longer necessary or cheaper to do this.

Taxis waiting near the arrival area of the airport are supposed to be airport-regulated. Ignore all the touts waiting in the arrival hall and buy a taxi ticket from the public taxi booth at the kerb-side outside the hall. Fares differ according to distance; most destinations in central Bangkok are around 200B to 250B by the meter.

On top of the meter fare, airport taxis collect a 50B airport surcharge. You must also reimburse drivers for any toll charges paid if they take the tollway into the city (30B to 70B) depending on where you get off the tollway. Taking the tollway almost always saves time. During heavy traffic you can save money by staying on the surface (non-tollway) streets – which are just as speedy as the expressway during heavy commuter hours, if not speedier. Drivers will usually ask if you want to take the tollway and you'll know which is best by the number of cars on the road; if it's heavy you might as well save the toll and take the surface streets.

If you end up taking a flat-rate taxi, the driver should pay all toll charges. Two, three, or even four passengers (if they don't have much luggage) can split the fare.

Sometimes unscrupulous drivers will approach you before you reach the kerb-side and try to sell you a ticket for 350B or 400B – ignore them and head straight for the kerb queue. A few touts from the old taxi Mafia that used to prowl the arrival area are still around and may approach you

with fares of about 200B. Their taxis have white-and-black plates and are not licensed to carry passengers, hence you have less legal recourse in the event of an incident than if you take a licensed taxi (yellow-and-black plates). Passengers have been robbed at gunpoint in non-licensed taxis in the past.

A few drivers still try to renegotiate the fare once you're inside a metered cab. Occasionally the driver will refuse to use the meter and quote a flat rate of 300B to 400B – though this is a less frequent occurrence than it used to be. Passengers now receive a bilingual Taxi-Meter Information sheet, issued by the Department of Land Transport, on which is written the name of the driver, the cab licence number, the date and the time. A phone number for registering complaints against the driver is listed on this sheet.

Metered taxis flagged down on the highway in front of the airport (turn left from the arrival hall) are even cheaper since they don't have to pay the 50B airport surcharge. When the queue at the public taxi desk is particularly long, it's sometimes faster to go upstairs or walk out to the highway and flag one down.

THAI Services THAI offers an airport limousine (☎ 025 352 801), which is really just a glorified air-con taxi service. Fares are between 500B and 650B to central Bangkok destinations. There are direct air-con buses to Pattaya from the airport thrice daily at 9am, noon and 7pm; the fare is 200B one way. Private sedans cost 1500B to 2500B per trip.

THAI also operates a free shuttle bus between the international and domestic terminals every 20 minutes between 5.30am and 11pm.

City Bus

You can save a lot of money travelling in Bangkok by sticking to the public buses, which are 3.50B for any journey under 10km on the ordinary red or smaller green buses, 5B on the blue buses. Blue air-con buses cost between 6B and 16B, depending on the distance travelled. Orange air-con buses cost 12B regardless of the distance travelled. The air-con buses are not only cooler, but are usually less crowded – except during rush hours.

Bus Maps See the Maps section earlier in this chapter for a list of maps of Bangkok, including bus maps, or have a look at Bangkok Metropolitan Transportation Authority's (BMTA) Web site ([W] www.bmta .motc.go.th) to check the latest on routes and fares.

Safety Be careful with your belongings while riding Bangkok buses. The place you are most likely to be 'razored' is on the crowded ordinary buses. Razor artists are common, particularly on buses in the Hualamphong train station area. These dexterous thieves specialise in slashing your backpack, shoulder bag or even your trouser pockets with a sharp razor and slipping your valuables out unnoticed. Hold your bag in front of you, under close attention, and carry money in a front shirt pocket, preferably (as the Thais do) maintaining a tactile and visual sensitivity to these areas if the bus is packed shoulder to shoulder. Seasoned travellers don't need this advice, as the same precautions are useful all over the world – the trick is to be relaxed but aware.

Skytrain
The Skytrain (*rót fai fáa*) has been in service since December 1999 and is the best way to avoid Bangkok's legendary traffic jams.

There are two lines. The first line, informally known as the Sukhumvit Line, starts at Moh Chit station, near the Northern and North-Eastern bus terminal, and terminates at On Nut station, near Soi 81, Th Sukhumvit. The second line, informally known as the Silom Line, runs from the National Stadium to Saphan Taksin, on the Bangkok side of Mae Nam Chao Phraya. These two lines intersect at Siam station (also called the Interchange Station), near Siam Square and Siam Center.

The Skytrain runs daily from 6am to midnight. Fares are between 10B and 40B, depending on the distance travelled. The system utilises magnetic-stripe cards purchased from ticket machines that accept 5B and 10B coins only. There is a change booth at each station where you can exchange banknotes for coins. The ticket machines have instructions in English and there are maps of the Skytrain routes (also in English) posted nearby, so it's all fairly straightforward. If you have any questions, the friendly security guards will help you figure things out. The Bangkok Mass Transit System (BTS) maintains a Web site at [W] www.bts.co.th where you can see a map of the routes, or call ☎ 026 177 300.

Car & Motorcycle
Cars and motorbikes are easily rented in Bangkok, if you can afford it and have steel nerves. Rates start at around 1500B per day for a small car, much less for a motorcycle, excluding insurance. For long-term rentals you can usually arrange a discount of up to 35% off the daily rate. An International Driving Permit and passport are required for all rentals.

For long, cross-country trips you might consider buying a new or used motorcycle and reselling it when you leave – this can end up being cheaper than renting, especially if you buy a good used bike. See the Getting Around chapter for more details.

A few car-rental companies are:

Avis Rent-A-Car (☎ 022 555 300–4, fax 022 533 734) 2/12 Th Withayu; (☎ 025 354 052) Bangkok International Airport; (☎ 022 541 234) Grand Hyatt Erawan Hotel; (☎ 022 530 444) Le Meridian President Hotel
Budget Car Rental (☎ 022 020 250, fax 022 030 249) 19/23 Bldg A, Royal City Avenue, Th Phatchaburi Tat Mai
National Car Rental (☎ 029 281 525) Amari Airport Hotel, 727 Th Si Nakharin

There are more car-rental agencies along Th Withayu and Th Phetchaburi Tat Mai. Some also rent motorcycles, but you're better off renting or leasing a bike at a place that specialises in motorcycles, such as:

Chusak Yont Shop (☎ 022 519 225) 1400 Th Phetchaburi Tat Mai

SSK Co (☎ 025 141 290) 35/33 Th Lat Phrao
Visit Laochaiwat (☎ 022 781 348) 1 Soi Prom-
mit, Th Suthisan

Taxi

Metered taxis *(tháeksii miitôe)* were finally
introduced in Bangkok in 1993 and now
have almost completely replaced the old
non-meter taxis. Taxis with meters have
signs on top reading Taxi Meter, those
without simply read Taxi. Fares for metered
taxis are always lower than for non-metered
taxis and they're cheaper than riding túk-
túk as well, unless you're only going a
block or so. The only problem is that they
can be a little harder to flag down during
peak commuter hours. Demand often out-
strips supply from 8am to 9am and 6pm to
7pm, also late at night when the bars are
closing (1am to 2am). It can also be difficult
to find a vacant taxi when it's raining. Because metered-taxi drivers use rented vehicles and must return them at the end of their
shifts, they sometimes won't take long-
distance fares as quitting time nears.

Metered taxis charge 35B at flag fall for
the first 2km, then 4.50B for the next 10km,
5B for 13km to 20km and 5.50B for any
distance over 20km, but only when the cab
travels at 6km/h or more; at speeds under
6km/h, a surcharge of 1.25B per minute
kicks in. Freeway tolls – 20B to 40B
depending where you start – must be paid
by the passenger. A 24-hour 'phone-a-cab'
service (Siam Taxi ☎ 023 771 771) is available for an extra 20B over the regular
metered fare. This is only really necessary
if you're in an area where there aren't a lot
of taxis; residents who live down long sois
are the main clientele.

For certain routes it can be very difficult
to find a taxi driver who's willing to use the
meter. One such instance is going from the
Southern bus terminal across the river to
Bangkok proper – most drivers will ask for
a flat 350B but settle for 250B. In the
reverse direction you can usually get them
to use the meter.

Taxis that park in front of expensive
hotels or around nightlife venues – especially at the 2am closing time – often refuse

to use the meter. The best thing to do in this
instance is walk a block or two away and
hail a taxi from there.

You can hire a taxi all day for 1000B to
1500B depending on how much driving is
involved.

A useful *Taxi Guide* brochure distributed
by TAT to both tourists and taxi drivers
lists Thai and English addresses of hotels,
guesthouses, embassies, airlines, shopping
centres, temples and various tourist attractions. The guide can be of considerable help
in communication between non-English-
speaking drivers and non-Thai-speaking
passengers.

Túk-Túk

Since the introduction of air-con metered
taxis, there is really no reason to ride around
in a túk-túk. Quaint and exotic they may be,
but unless you're set on breathing lung-fulls
of exhaust fumes or enjoy the brain-rattling
sound of unmuffled engines, it's best to let
the túk-túk drive on past. The typical túk-
túk fare nowadays offers no savings over a
metered taxi – around 60B for a short hop
(eg, the main post office to Chinatown).

Túk-túk drivers tend to speak less English than taxi drivers, so many new arrivals
have a hard time communicating their
destination. Although some travellers have
complained about drivers deliberately
taking them to the wrong destination (to
collect commissions from certain restaurants, gem or silk shops), others never seem
to have a problem with them. Beware of
túk-túk drivers who offer to take you on a
sightseeing or factory tour for 10B or 20B
– it's a touting scheme designed to pressure
you into purchasing overpriced goods.

When in doubt, use a metered taxi rather
than a túk-túk.

Motorcycle Taxi

As passengers become more desperate in
their attempts to beat rush-hour gridlocks,
motorcycle taxis have moved from the sois
to the main avenues. Fares for a motorcycle
taxi are about the same as those for a túk-túk
except during heavy traffic, when they may
cost a bit more. Motorcycle taxis are able to

weave in and out between cars and trucks, as well as go the wrong direction down one-way roads. If the street is blocked, some motorcycle taxi drivers won't hesitate to use the sidewalk!

Riding on the back of a speeding motorcycle taxi is even more of a Kamikaze experience than riding in a túk-túk. Keep your legs tucked in – the drivers are used to carrying passengers with shorter legs than those of the average faràng and they pass perilously close to other vehicles while weaving in and out of traffic.

Boat

Although many of Bangkok's khlongs (canals) have been paved over, there is still plenty of transport along and across Mae Nam Chao Phraya and up adjoining canals. River transport is one of the best ways of getting around Bangkok as well as quite often being much faster than any road-based alternatives. For a start you get quite a different view of the city; also, it's much less of a hassle than tangling with the polluted, noisy, traffic-congested streets. Just try getting from Banglamphu to the main post office as quickly by road.

Along Mae Nam Chao Phraya the main transport consists of Chao Phraya express boats (☎ 022 225 330), which run between the Wat Ratchasingkhon pier in south central Bangkok and Nonthaburi Province from 6am to 6.30pm daily. Fares are 6B to 10B, except for a special express boat (denoted by a yellow flag, or a red and orange striped flag) which runs only between the hours of 6am to 9am and 3pm to 7pm, and costs 10B stopping at fewer piers along the way.

Over the last decade the Bangkok Metropolitan Transportation Authority (BMTA) has revived four lengthy and useful canal routes: Khlong Saen Saep (Banglamphu to Bang Kapi); Khlong Phrakhanong (Sukhumvit to Sinakarin campus); Khlong Bang Luang/Khlong Lat Phrao (Th Phetchaburi Tat Mai to Phahonyothin Bridge); and Khlong Phasi Charoen in Thonburi (Kaset Bang Khae port to Rama I Bridge). These boats are relatively cramped and are mostly used by daily commuters who are accustomed to the fast pace of embarking and disembarking. Be warned – the boat crews have little patience for head-scratching tourists. Hesitate and they'll leave you behind.

Eastern Gulf Coast

To the south-east of Bangkok, along the fast-developing east coast of the Gulf of Thailand, is a broken string of beaches and islands that range from the country's most heavily touristed to some of its quietest. A major plus for this section of the Gulf is that the waters tend to be calmer – during both monsoon seasons – than anywhere else in coastal Thailand, hence most of it can be considered a year-round destination. Another is that scuba divers and would-be divers will find some of Thailand's highest quality dive operations in Pattaya. And despite the effects of overcrowding and over-commercialisation of Ao Pattaya (Pattaya Bay) itself, there are some decent dive sites nearby. The eastern Gulf Coast's third asset is its close proximity to Bangkok – the farthest coastal capital, Trat (the jumping-off point for Ko Chang National Marine Park), is only five to six hours away by bus. Ban Phe, where boats depart for the beautiful island of Ko Samet, is only a three-hour ride away.

The downside is that this section of coastline – often termed the 'eastern seaboard' by the English-language press – is the country's most industrialised and developed. Some stretches of the coast, especially in Chonburi and Rayong provinces, are lined with factories, condo developments and fishing or shipping ports. But it's also a region of fruit plantations, saltwater estuaries and beaches hardly anyone outside Thailand has heard of.

SI RACHA
ศรีราชา

postcode 20110 • pop 23,700
About 105km from Bangkok on the east coast of the Gulf of Thailand is the small town of Si Racha, home of the famous spicy sauce *náam phrík sǐi raachaa*. Some of Thailand's best seafood, especially the local oysters, is served here accompanied by this sauce.

Highlights

- Ko Chang archipelago is a remote national marine park with forest tracts, waterfalls, coastal walks, diving and coral reefs.

- Ko Samet boasts some of the whitest, squeakiest sand in the kingdom, delectable seafood and boat trips to uninhabited islands.

- Popular Pattaya is Thailand's busiest beach resort, with palm-fringed beaches, diving at nearby islets, water-skiing, go-karting and exciting nightlife.

- Stroll in the peaceful and meticulously restored grounds of King Rama V's 19th-century summer palace on Ko Si Chang.

- Watch the money change hands in gem trading markets in Chanthaburi, Trat and on the Cambodian border.

Si Racha itself is not that interesting, but it's the departure point for boats to nearby Ko Si Chang, a small island flanked by two smaller islands – Kham Yai to the north and Khang Kao to the south. As this provides a natural shelter from the wind and sea, the lee of the island is used as a harbour by large incoming freighters. Smaller boats

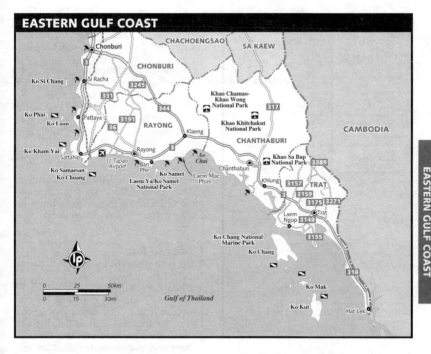

EASTERN GULF COAST

transport goods to Mae Nam Chao Phraya some 50km away.

If you're looking for an easy overnight trip from Bangkok that mixes a bit of classical Thai culture and island scenery, try little-visited Ko Si Chang. There you'll find the recently restored grounds of a century-old royal palace – quite a pleasant place for an afternoon of lazy strolling.

On **Ko Loi**, a small rocky island connected to the mainland by a long jetty, there is a Thai-Chinese Buddhist temple.

Si Racha Tiger Farm
สวนเสือศรีราชา

This zoo-like attraction (☎ *038 296 556, Hwy 26, 20km marker; adult/child 250/150B, for the circus 30/20B; open 9am-6pm, performances 11am, 1.30pm & 4pm)* covers 250 *râi* (40 hectares) off Rte 3241 about 9km south-east of town. The zoo combines a world famous tiger breeding facility with a crocodile farm, 'herbivores zone', scorpion farm and circus-like performances.

The tiger farm – said to be the largest and most successful such facility in the world – contains over 130 Bengal tigers. At the unusual 'kinship to the different families complex' you'll see tiger cubs, pigs and dogs living together; don't be too surprised to see sows nursing tiger cubs. The complex is very popular with Asian package tourists who pay to be photographed posing with tiger cubs, iguanas etc.

There are a number of shows on offer, including a crocodile wrestling show, chimpanzee show, even a 'Scorpion Queen' show. These take place throughout the day but cost extra. Of course, if you're not into watching animals perform for humans, you should give this place a miss.

Places to Stay

For most people, Si Racha is more of a transit point than an overnight stop. The best

EASTERN GULF COAST

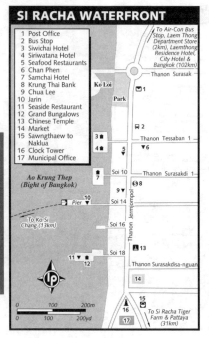

SI RACHA WATERFRONT

1 Post Office
2 Bus Stop
3 Siwichai Hotel
4 Siriwatana Hotel
5 Seafood Restaurants
6 Chan Phen
7 Samchai Hotel
8 Krung Thai Bank
9 Chua Lee
10 Jarin
11 Seaside Restaurant
12 Grand Bungalows
13 Chinese Temple
14 Market
15 Sawngthaew to Naklua
16 Clock Tower
17 Municipal Office

Ao Krung Thep (Bight of Bangkok)

To Ko Si Chang (13km)

To Air-Con Bus Stop, Laem Thong Department Store (2km), Laemthong Residence Hotel, City Hotel & Bangkok (102km)

Thanon Surasak
Ko Loi
Park
Thanon Tessaban 1
Thanon Surasakdi 1
Soi 10
Soi 14
Soi 16
Soi 18
Thanon Surasakdisa-nguan
Pier
Thanon Jermjompol

To Si Racha Tiger Farm & Pattaya (31km)

0   100   200m
0   100   200yd

places to stay in Si Racha are the rambling wooden hotels built on piers over the waterfront.

Siriwatana Hotel (☎ *038 311 037, 35 Thanon (Th) Jermjompol*) Rooms with fan & shower 180B. Siriwatana, opposite Th Tessaban 1, has clean rooms and the service is good. There are rustic sitting areas with tables outside each of the 31 rooms along the piers. Simple, inexpensive meals can be prepared on request, or you're free to bring your own food and use the tables provided.

Siwichai Hotel (☎ *038 311 212, 38 Th Jermjompol*) Rooms with fan & bath 200B, air-con 350-400B. Next to the Siriwatana, this has similar rooms, plus a pier restaurant.

Samchai Hotel (☎ *038 311 234, 3 Th Jermjompol*) Rooms with fan & bath 200B. This has reasonable rooms. It's open and breezy, with outdoor tables where you can bring food in the evening from nearby markets.

Grand Bungalows (☎ *038 311 079, 9 Th Jermjompol*) Bungalows 400-600B. Built off the pier and of various sizes, each bungalow sleeps several people. They are very popular among holidaying Thais and Chinese.

Laemthong Residence Hotel (☎/fax *038 322 886, 135/9 Th Sukhumvit*) Rooms 900-1000B. This 20-storey hotel is in the centre of town and has comfortable rooms with all the amenities; there's also a swimming pool and tennis courts.

City Hotel (☎ *038 322 700, fax 038 322 739, 6/126 Th Sukhumvit*) Rooms 2300-8000B. The classy City offers capacious rooms. An escalator leads from the pavement to 2nd-floor reception; facilities include a pub, coffee shop, fitness and business centres.

Places to Eat

There is plenty of good seafood in Si Racha, but you have to watch the prices.

Chua Lee (☎ *038 311 244, 46/22 Th Jermjompol*) Dishes 150-250B. Across from the Krung Thai Bank, this is best known for its great seafood, but it's also probably the most expensive in town.

Next door and across the street are several seafood places with similar fare at much more reasonable prices, such as ***Chan Phen*** (☎ *038 311 025, 30 Th Tessaban 1*).

Jarin (*Soi 14 pier*) Dishes 50-80B. Jarin has very good one-plate seafood dishes, especially *khâo hàw mòk tha-leh* (seafood curry steamed with rice) and *kŭaytĭaw phàt thai kûng sòt* (Thai-style rice noodles with fresh shrimp). It's a great place to kill time while waiting for the next boat to Ko Si Chang.

Seaside Restaurant (☎ *038 312 537, 9 Soi 18, Th Jermjompol*) Meals 80-180B. At the end of the pier is this large restaurant – just about the best all-round seafood place in town for atmosphere, service and value. Try the tasty grilled seafood platter stacked with squid, mussels, shrimp and cockles. Häagen-Dazs ice cream is also available.

The cheapest place to eat is in the ***market*** near the clock tower at the southern end of town. In the evening the market offers everything from noodles to fresh seafood, while in the daytime it's mostly an ordinary food and clothing market with some noodle and snack stands.

Outside town, off Th Sukhumvit (Hwy 3) on the way to Pattaya, there are a couple of cheap, but good, fresh *seafood places*. Closer to town is Ao Udom, a small fishing bay where there are several open-air seafood places.

Getting There & Around

Buses to Si Racha leave the Eastern bus terminal in Bangkok every half-hour or so from 5am to 7pm. The ordinary bus is 35B, air-con bus is 81B; travel time is around 1¾ hours. Ordinary direct buses stop near the pier for Ko Si Chang, but through buses and air-con buses stop on Th Sukhumvit (Hwy 3), near the Laemthong Department Store, from where there are túk-túk to the pier.

You can also reach Si Racha by 3rd-class train, though not many people come by this method. Train No 365 leaves Hualamphong train station at 6.55am and arrives at Si Racha at 10.11am (about an hour slower – but a good deal more scenic – than the bus). The fare is 28B.

White săwngthăew bound for Naklua (North Pattaya) leave from near the clock tower in Si Racha frequently throughout the day. The fare is 15B per person and the ride takes about half an hour. Once you're in Naklua you can easily catch another săwngthăew on to central Pattaya.

Boats to Ko Si Chang leave from Tha Soi 14.

In Si Racha and on Ko Si Chang there are fleets of huge motorcycle taxis, many powered by Nissan engines, that will take you anywhere in town or on the island for 20B to 30B.

KO SI CHANG
เกาะสีชัง

postcode 20120 • pop 4100

Ko Si Chang makes a nifty one- or two-day getaway from Bangkok. There is only one town on the island, facing the mainland; the rest of the island is practically deserted and fun to explore. Don't come here looking for perfect white sand and turquoise waters

though: the island's proximity to shipping lanes and fishing grounds means its shores are less than tidy. Depending on sea currents and the time of year, the shoreline can be relatively clean, or cluttered with flotsam. If you're going mainly for beaches, you're better off heading farther south-east to Ko Samet.

Ko Si Chang's small population is made up of fisherfolk, mariners and government workers stationed with the customs office or with one of the aquaculture projects on the island. Tourism fills a relatively small portion of local coffers, and the island has a very real, working-class feel to it. Like most islands along Thailand's eastern seaboard, Ko Si Chang is best visited on weekdays; on weekends and holidays the island can get crowded.

Information

A branch of Thai Farmer's Bank in town – on the main road to the right as you walk up from the pier – offers a foreign exchange service on weekdays.

Things to See & Do

A meditation hermitage, **Yai Phrik Vipassana Centre**, is ensconced in limestone caves and palm huts along the island's centre ridge. The hermit caves make an interesting visit but should be approached with respect – monks and nuns from all over Thailand come here to take advantage of the peaceful environment for meditation. Be careful that you don't fall down a limestone shaft; some are almost completely covered with vines.

On the opposite side of the island, facing out to sea, are some beaches with decent swimming – take care with the tide and the sea urchins.

Secluded **Hat Tham** (also called Hat Sai) can be reached by following a branch of the ring road on foot to the back of the island. During low tide there's a strip of sand here; when the tide comes in it disappears. A partially submerged cave can be visited at the eastern end of the little bay. There is also a more public – and generally less clean – beach at the western end of the island (about 2km from the pier) near the old palace grounds called **Hat Tha Wang**. Thai locals and visitors from the mainland come here for picnics.

The **palace** was once used by King Chulalongkorn (Rama V) over the summer months, but was abandoned when the French briefly occupied the island in 1893. The main throne hall – a magnificent golden teak structure called Vimanmek – was moved to Bangkok in 1910. Recently the Fine Arts Department began restoring the remaining palace buildings, which were named after the king's consorts, Pongsri, Wattana and Apirom. As with most royal architecture built during this period, most of the buildings here are a mixture of Thai and European styles. The palace gardens have also been renovated and you can easily spend a couple of hours strolling here. Keep an eye out for Ko Si Chang's protected species of white squirrel, which is making a steady come-back after being hunted to endangered status.

On the crest of the hill overlooking Tha Wang is a large white chedi that contains Wat Atsadangnimit, a small consecrated chamber where King Chulalongkorn used to meditate. The unique Buddha image inside was fashioned 50 years ago by a local monk who now lives in the cave hermitage. Nearby you'll come to a stone outcropping wrapped in holy cloth. The locals call it 'Bell Rock' because if struck with a rock or heavy stick it rings like a bell.

Not far from Wat Atsadangnimit is a large limestone cave called **Tham Saowapha**, which appears to plunge deep into the island – over 1km according to the locals. If you have a torch (flashlight), the cave might be worth exploring.

To the east of town, high on a hill overlooking the sea, is a large Chinese temple called **San Jao Phaw Khao Yai**. During Chinese New Year in late-January to February, the island is overrun with Chinese visitors from the mainland. This is one of Thailand's most interesting Chinese temples, with shrine-caves, several different temple levels and a good view of Si Chang and the ocean. It's a long and steep climb from the road below.

Places to Stay

Tiewpai Guest House (Thiu Phai; ☎ 038 216 084) Rooms with shared bath 150-250B, with bath, air-con & TV 500-600B. The rather bland Tiewpai is the cheapest place to stay in town, not far from the main piers. It has one basic room; and nine more comfortable rooms arranged around a courtyard behind the restaurant. Perhaps because it has the lowest prices on the island and sends touts to the pier to meet visitors, the place is often full and the staff can be rather cold.

Benz Bungalow (☎ 038 216 091, 80 Th Atsadang) Rooms with fan & bath 500B, with air-con 700-800B. Out near the gate to Hat Tha Wang, this offers clean rooms facing the sea in either a basic hotel-style building, or in one of its unique stone bungalows.

Si Phitsanu Bungalow (☎ 038 216 034) Rooms in a row-building cost from 600B; you can also get a 1-bedroom bungalow overlooking the small bay for 800B or a 2-bedroom bungalow for 1200-1500B. To reach this area from town, take the first right past the Tiewpai Guest House, then follow the road straight past the Yai Phrik Vipassana Centre, or take a săamláw for 30B one way.

Green House Bungalow (☎ 038 216 024) Singles/doubles 150/300B. Off the ring road towards the Chinese temple, this has somewhat dark and dingy rooms in a 10-room row-building.

Sichang View Resort (☎ 038 216 210) Bungalows in high season 800-1100B, in low season 600B. Also in the vicinity of the Chinese temple, this has 10 tidy apartment-style bungalows on nicely landscaped grounds.

Sichang Palace (☎ 038 216 276, 81 Th Atsadang) Singles/doubles 900B, with sea view 1000B. In the middle of town, this has clean, comfortable rooms facing the swimming pool. During the week the staff may knock 100B to 200B off these prices.

Places to Eat

There are several small restaurants, but nothing special, all with the Thai and Chinese standard dishes. Along the road that leads to the public beach are a couple of rustic *seafood places*.

Sichang Palace and *Sichang View Resort* each have their own restaurants serving good seafood at medium-high prices. *Tiewpai Guest House* offers reasonably priced Thai and Western food. See Places to Stay previously for locations.

Getting There & Around

Boats to Ko Si Chang leave hourly from a pier in Si Racha at the end of Soi 14, Th Jermjompol. The fare is 30B one way; the first boat leaves at about 6am and the last at 8pm. The last boat back to Si Racha from Ko Si Chang is at 7pm.

As you approach Ko Si Chang, check out the dozens of barges anchored in the island's lee. Their numbers have multiplied from year to year as shipping demand from Thailand's booming import and export business has increased.

There are fleets of motorcycle taxis that will take you anywhere in town for 30B. You can also get a complete tour of the island for 200B per hour. Asking prices for any ride tend to be outrageous; the supply of taxis is plentiful, however, and you can usually get a cheaper price after talking to several drivers.

PATTAYA
พัทยา

postcode 20260 • pop 56,700

Pattaya, 147km south-east of Bangkok, is Thailand's busiest beach resort with over 12,000 rooms available in hotels, bungalows and guesthouses spread along Hat Pattaya and adjoining Naklua and Jomtien beaches. Pattaya is the most active of the three, a crowded crescent of sand where jet skis and powerboats slice the surf and parasails billow over the palms all day long. Sunburned visitors jam the beachfront road in rented jeeps and motorbikes.

According to TAT statistics, an average one-third of foreign tourists to Thailand visit Pattaya; in a typical November to March season it receives around a million visitors. Most of them are package tourists from Europe, Russia, Taiwan and the Middle East. Depending on your tastes, some visitors will find Pattaya lacking in culture as well as good taste, since much of the place seems designed to attract tourists interested in a pre-fabricated, Western-style beach vacation with almost no Thai ingredients.

Hat Pattaya is also not that great (although it must have been at one time) and the town's biggest businesses – water sports and street sex – have driven prices for food and accommodation beyond Bangkok levels. And compared with many other Thai resort areas, it's more money-oriented and less friendly.

Pattaya still continues to attract a loyal following of Bangkok oil company expats, convention goers and package tourists. Local authorities and travel suppliers have been trying to upgrade Pattaya's image as well as clean the place up in general. Lately it has begun attracting family groups again, as the South Pattaya sex industry has been diminishing slightly.

American GIs, from a base in Nakhon Ratchasima, began visiting Pattaya in 1959. This is how this one-time fishing village got its start as a resort. US navy men from nearby Sattahip added to the military influx during the Vietnam War years. Nowadays there are still plenty of sailors around, but of many nationalities. National and international convention-goers make up another large segment of the current market, along with Asian golfers seeking out the 12 local golf courses, including courses designed by names such as Robert Trent Jones and Jack Nicklaus.

Pattaya is acclaimed for its seafood, although it's generally way overpriced by national (but not international) standards. Pattaya's lingering notoriety for sex tourism revolves around a collection of discos, outdoor bars and transvestite cabarets comprising Pattaya's red-light district at the southern end of the beach. The part of South Pattaya known as 'the village' attracts a large number of *kàthoey* (transvestites or transsexuals) – who pose as hookers and ply their trade among the droves of sex tourists – as well as a prominent gay scene.

The one thing the Pattaya area has going for it is diving centres. There are over a dozen nice islands off Pattaya's shore, although they can be expensive (compared

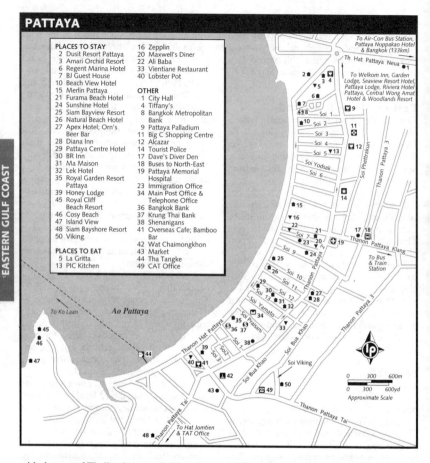

PATTAYA

PLACES TO STAY
2 Dusit Resort Pattaya
3 Amari Orchid Resort
6 Regent Marina Hotel
7 BJ Guest House
10 Beach View Hotel
15 Merlin Pattaya
21 Furama Beach Hotel
24 Sunshine Hotel
25 Siam Bayview Resort
26 Natural Beach Hotel
27 Apex Hotel; Orn's
     Beer Bar
28 Diana Inn
29 Pattaya Centre Hotel
30 BR Inn
31 Ma Maison
32 Lek Hotel
35 Royal Garden Resort
     Pattaya
39 Honey Lodge
45 Royal Cliff
     Beach Resort
46 Cosy Beach
47 Island View
48 Siam Bayshore Resort
50 Viking

PLACES TO EAT
5 La Gritta
13 PIC Kitchen

16 Zepplin
20 Maxwell's Diner
22 Ali Baba
33 Vientiane Restaurant
40 Lobster Pot

OTHER
1 City Hall
8 Tiffany's
8 Bangkok Metropolitan
     Bank
9 Pattaya Palladium
11 Big C Shopping Centre
12 Alcazar
14 Tourist Police
17 Dave's Diver Den
18 Buses to North-East
19 Pattaya Memorial
     Hospital
23 Immigration Office
34 Main Post Office &
     Telephone Office
36 Bangkok Bank
37 Krung Thai Bank
38 Shenanigans
41 Overseas Cafe; Bamboo
     Bar
42 Wat Chaimongkhon
43 Market
44 Tha Tangke
49 CAT Office

with the rest of Thailand) to reach. If you're a snorkelling or scuba enthusiast, equipment can be booked at any of the several diving shops or diving schools at Hat Pattaya. Ko Laan, the most popular of the islands, even has places to stay.

Information

Tourist Offices The TAT office (☎ 038 427 667, ✉ tatpty@chonburi.ksc.co.th), at the north-western edge of King Rama IX Park, keeps an up-to-date list of accommodation in the Pattaya area, and the staff are very helpful. Hours are from 8.30am to

7.30pm. The tourist police office (☎ 038 429 371, 1155) is on Th Pattaya 2.

Immigration The Pattaya immigration office is open Monday to Friday from 8.30am to 4.30pm.

Money The Krung Thai Bank on Soi Praisani is open from 10am to 9pm. There are currency exchange booths and ATMs all over Pattaya.

Post & Communications The main post office is found in South Pattaya on Soi

Praisani. It's open 8.30am to 4.30pm Monday to Friday, and 9am to noon on holidays.

The international telephone office is located at the main post office. There are also several private long-distance phone offices in town: the best one is the Overseas Cafe, near the intersection of Th Hat Pattaya and Th Pattaya Tai. Rates are among the lowest in town, and it's open from 9am to 4am, allowing you to take advantage of night-time discounts.

Pattaya's Internet access centres tend to come and go rather quickly. Try looking around Soi Praisani and Soi Yamato.

Radio Pattaya has an English-language radio station that broadcasts at FM 107.7 MHz. American and British DJs offer a mix of local news and music.

Magazines & Newspapers A free monthly magazine, *Explore Pattaya*, distributed around town contains information on current events, sightseeing and advertisements for hotel and restaurant specials. *What's On Pattaya* is a similar publication. *Pattaya Mail,* a weekly newspaper, publishes articles on political, economic and environmental developments in the area as well as the usual ads. This is also where you'll read lots of articles about *faràng* (Westerner) who get into trouble in Pattaya – stories that don't make it into Bangkok's English-language dailies.

Medical Services Pattaya Memorial Hospital (☎ 038 429 422–4, 038 422 741) on Th Pattaya Klang offers 24-hour service.

For dive medicine, try Apakorn Kiatiwong Naval Hospital (☎ 038 601 185), 26km south-east of Pattaya in Sattahip. This hospital has a fully operative recompression chamber; urgent care is available 24 hours.

Beaches

Curving around Ao Pattaya (Pattaya Bay), **Hat Pattaya** is a relatively scenic crescent of sand backed by a narrow thread of palms and a very dense layer of hotels, restaurants, dive shops, car and motorbike rental agencies, and other commercial establishments.

Changing the Image

In many ways Pattaya serves as the prime example of what can happen to a beach resort area if no controls are applied to the quality and quantity of tourism development. After garnering a long streak of bad press in both the domestic and international media, Pattaya began experiencing a steady decline in tourism in the early 1990s. In 1992 Pattaya lost the privilege of hosting the annual Siam World Cup – one of Asia's biggest windsurfing competitions – to Phuket. The two principal complaints have been the sidewalk sex scene and Pattaya Bay's water quality. Powerboats zooming in and out of the swimming areas have been a nuisance and a hazard.

Local authorities and travel-industry related suppliers continue to struggle to upgrade Pattaya's image as well as clean the place up. You can actually begin to feel sorry for Pattaya in spite of the fact that local developers and authorities have only themselves to blame for creating the reality on which the image is based. It's too late to turn Pattaya back into the fishing village it once was, but it's not too late to re-create a clean, safe tourist destination if all concerned cooperate.

Positive signs that things are changing for the better include a waste-water treatment plant and a pier where powerboats must moor.

A better beach in the immediate Pattaya area is 6km-long **Hat Jomtien** (Jawmthian), about 2km south of Pattaya, where the water is cleaner and you're well away from the noisy Pattaya bar scene. The hotels and restaurants are more spread out here as well, so there's a better sense of space and relaxation.

Hat Naklua, a smaller beach north of Pattaya, is also quiet and fairly tastefully developed. As Pattaya/South Pattaya is pretty much given over to single male tourists or couples on package tours, Jomtien and Naklua are where families tend to stay. **Hat Cliff** is a small cove just south of Hat Pattaya, over which looms a set of cliffs that are home to Pattaya's glitziest hotels.

Water Sports

Pattaya and Jomtien have some of the best water sports facilities in Thailand. Water-skiing costs around 1000B per hour including equipment, boat and driver. Parasailing is 200B to 300B a shot (about 10 to 15 minutes) and windsurfing 500B an hour. Game-fishing is also a possibility; rental rates for boats, fishing guides and tackle are quite reasonable.

Hat Jomtien is the best spot for wind-surfing, not least because you're a little less likely to run into parasailors or jet-skiers.

Diving & Snorkelling Pattaya is the most convenient diving location to Bangkok, but it is far from being the best Thailand has to offer. In recent years the fish population has dwindled considerably and visibility is often poor due to heavy boat traffic. Although nearby Ko Laan, Ko Sak and Ko Krok are fine for beginners, accomplished divers may prefer the 'outer islands' of Ko Man Wichai and Ko Rin, which have more visibility. In most places expect 3m to 9m of visibility under good conditions, or in more remote sites 5m to 12m. Farther south-east, ship-wrecks *Petchburi Bremen* and *Hardeep* off Sattahip and Samae have created artificial reefs and are interesting dive sites.

Diving costs are quite reasonable: a two-dive excursion averages from 1300B to 1800B for boat, equipment, underwater guide and lunch. Snorkellers may join such day trips for 500B to 800B. For shipwrecks, the price goes up to 2500B to 2900B (depending on the season), and for an overnight trip with five to seven dives, figure up to 6000B per person. Full NAUI or PADI certification, which takes three to four days, costs 9000B to 12,000B for all instruction and equipment.

Some shops do half-day group trips to nearby islands for as low as 500B to 800B per person, and to islands a bit farther out for 650B; these prices include lunch, beverages, transport and dive master but not equipment rental beyond mask, fins and snorkel.

Average rental rates are: mask, fins and snorkel 200B to 250B; regulator w/SPG 300B to 400B; buoyancy compensation device 250B to 400B; weight-belt 150B; tank 150B; wetsuit 300B; or full scuba out-fit 1500B. Air-fills typically cost 100B to 150B. To protect themselves from steep baht fluctuations, some diving operators quote only in US dollars – a reasonable strategy considering virtually all equipment must be imported, not to mention the rising cost of fuel to power the boats.

Shops along Th Hat Pattaya advertise trips, and several Pattaya hotels also arrange excursions and equipment.

Aquanauts Diving (☎ 038 361 724, fax 038 412 097, **e** aquanaut@loxinfo.co.th, **w** www.aquanautsdive.com) Soi Yodsak, Th Hat Pattaya

Dave's Diver Den (☎ 038 420 411, fax 038 360 095, **w** www.thaioil.com/pattayadiving) 190/11 Mu 9, Th Pattaya Klang

Larry's Dive (☎ 038 710 999, **w** www .larrysdive.com) Th Pattaya Tai, South Pattaya

Mermaid's Dive Center (☎ 038 232 219, fax 038 232 221, **w** www.mermaiddive.com) Soi White House, Hat Jomtien

Millennium Divers (☎ 038 427 185) Soi Pattayaland 1, South Pattaya

Paradise Scuba Divers (☎ 038 710 567, fax 038 423 879, **e** lscuba@loxinfo.co.th) Siam Bayview Resort

Scuba Professionals (☎ 038 221 860, fax 038 221 618) 3 Th Pattaya-Naklua

Scuba Tek Dive Center (☎ 038 361 616, fax 038 429 461, **e** rickr@loxinfo.co.th) Week-ender Hotel, Th Pattaya 2

Seafari Sports Center (☎ 038 429 253, fax 038 424 708, **w** www.seafari.net) Soi 5, North Pattaya

Karting

One of the legacies left behind by American GIs in Pattaya is karting, the racing of miniature cars (go-karts) powered by 5HP to 15HP engines. Karting has since turned into an international sport often described as the closest approximation to Formula One racing available to the average driver.

Pattaya Kart Speedway (☎ 038 422 044, 248/2 Th Thepprasit; 150B for 10min in 5HP kart, 250B in 10–15HP kart; open 9.30am-6.30pm), boasts Asia's only track sanctioned by the Commission Inter-nationale de Karting (CIK). It's a 1080m loop that meets all CIK safety and sporting standards, plus a beginners' track and an off-road (unpaved) track.

Other Sports

Other recreational activities available in the area include golf, bowling, snooker, archery, target-shooting, horse riding and tennis. Among the several gyms and fitness centres is Gold's Gym in South Pattaya's Julie Complex. Gold's has a second branch in North Pattaya just past Soi 1 on Th Naklua-Pattaya.

Places to Stay – Budget

The number of places to stay in Naklua, Pattaya and Jomtien is mind-boggling, with close to 200 hotels, guesthouses and bungalows. Because of low occupancy rates, some hotels offer special deals, especially mid-week; bargaining for a room may also get a lower rate. On weekends and holidays the cheaper rooms tend to book out.

In Pattaya itself, North Pattaya and Naklua are quieter and better places to stay if you want to avoid the full-on nightlife of South Pattaya. Overall, Hat Jomtien is much better, with clean water and beach, and no obvious sex scene. No place in the area is entirely immune from sex tourism; however, almost every place from Naklua to Jomtien comes with a significant clientele of fat faràng men and their tiny rent-by-the-day-or-week Thai girlfriends.

The average hotel price ranges from 400B to 2000B, and for guesthouses 300B to 450B.

North Pattaya & Hat Naklua Wedged between North and Central Pattaya is *BJ Guest House* (☎ *038 421 147, Th Hat Pattaya Neua*). Rooms with air-con 400B. Three-storey BJ sits right across from the beach. BJ's restaurant serves Thai and German dishes.

Welkom Inn (☎ *038 424 765, fax 038 424 657, 103/1 Th Hat Pattaya Neua*) Doubles with air-con 450-700B. This is a German-oriented place with a large pool, Thai garden-restaurant and Franco-Belgian restaurant.

Central & South Pattaya You'll find the cheapest places in town are the guesthouses

in South Pattaya along Th Pattaya 2, the street parallel to Th Hat Pattaya. Most are clustered near sois 6, 10, 11 and 12.

Apex Hotel (☎ *038 428 281, fax 038 421 184, 216/1 Th Pattaya 2*) Rooms 350-450B. This modern four-storey hotel has rooms with air-con, hot water, TV, fully stocked mini-bar & fridge in the front of the building – great value. There's also a pool on the premises.

Diana Inn (☎ *038 429 675, fax 038 424 566, 216/6–9 Th Pattaya 2*) Rooms with air-con & hot bath 650B. This has large rooms, plus a restaurant and a pool with bar service. A drawback is the noisy nightclub next door.

Honey Lodge (☎ *038 429 133, fax 038 710 185, 597/8 Muu 10, Th Pattaya Tai*) Rooms with air-con, hot water, fridge & phone 500-650B. Honey also has a restaurant and pool.

BR Inn (☎ *038 426 449, 224/26 Muu 10, Soi 12, Th Pattaya Tai*) Rooms with fan/air-con 350/400B. In a lane south of Soi 12, this offers reasonably clean rooms. Many Japanese budget travellers stay here.

Ma Maison (☎ *038 429 318, fax 038 426 060, 386/9 Soi 13, Th Pattaya Tai*) Rooms with air-con 850B. This offers chalet-style rooms around a swimming pool; as the name suggests, it's French-managed and there's a French restaurant on the premises. Advance reservations are highly recommended as it's often booked out.

The rest of the many guesthouses on Soi 13 are in the 200B to 350B range, but rooms are usually cramped and without windows.

Viking (☎ *038 423 164, fax 038 425 964, 43/5 Soi Viking, Th Pattaya Tai*) Rooms 350-450B. Down in South Pattaya, this has been a long-time favourite for its quiet rooms and pool.

Hat Jomtien At Hat Jomtien, the budget category consists of several places around the mid-range Surf House International Hotel towards the northern end of the beach.

Moonshine Place Guest House (☎ *038 231 956, fax 038 232 162, 75/56 Th Hat Jomtien*) Rooms 500B. Friendly staff but

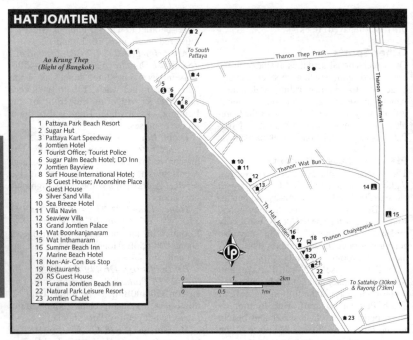

HAT JOMTIEN

Ao Krung Thep
(Bight of Bangkok)

To South
Pattaya

Thanon Thep Prasit

Thanon Sukhumvit

Thanon Wat Bun

Thanon Chaiyapreuk

Th Hat Jomtien

To Sattahip (30km)
& Rayong (73km)

1 Pattaya Park Beach Resort
2 Sugar Hut
3 Pattaya Kart Speedway
4 Jomtien Hotel
5 Tourist Office; Tourist Police
6 Sugar Palm Beach Hotel; DD Inn
7 Jomtien Bayview
8 Surf House International Hotel;
   JB Guest House; Moonshine Place
   Guest House
9 Silver Sand Villa
10 Sea Breeze Hotel
11 Villa Navin
12 Seaview Villa
13 Grand Jomtien Palace
14 Wat Boonkanjanaram
15 Wat Inthamaram
16 Summer Beach Inn
17 Marine Beach Hotel
18 Non-Air-Con Bus Stop
19 Restaurants
20 RS Guest House
21 Furama Jomtien Beach Inn
22 Natural Park Leisure Resort
23 Jomtien Chalet

0   1   2km
0   0.5   1mi

smallish rooms. There is a popular old-West-style bar/restaurant downstairs, which could make it noisy at night.

DD Inn (☎ 038 232 995, 410/50 Th Hat Jomtien) Rooms with air-con 500B. DD is at the northern end of the beach (sometimes referred to as Hat Dong Tan or Sugar Palm Beach), where the road turns towards Pattaya. It has very clean air-con rooms, and discounts are given for long-term stays.

Sugar Palm Beach Hotel (☎ 038 231 386, fax 038 231 713, 45/16 Th Hat Jomtien) Rooms with air-con, TV & fridge 650B, with sea view 800B. This is a small but well-kept beachfront property.

JB Guest House (☎ 038 231 581, 75/14 Th Hat Jomtien) Rooms with fan & cold bath 250B, with air-con 350B, with air-con & sea view 450-600B. JB takes the prize with very decent rooms.

Seaview Villa (Chom Thaleh; ☎ 038 231 070, 321/6 Th Hat Jomtien) Bungalows 1800-2400B. This has nicely appointed

bungalows with all the amenities – though not all have a view of the sea.

Villa Navin (☎ 038 231 066, fax 038 231 318, 350 Muu 12, Th Hat Jomtien) Doubles 500B, bungalows with 3 bedrooms & air-con 3000B. At the friendly four-storey Villa Navin there is an outdoor restaurant that specialises in seafood.

RS Guest House (☎ 038 231 867) Rooms with cold shower & fan/air-con 300/400B. This is one of the cheapest places to stay at the southern end of the beach, near Th Chaiyapreuk. The rooms are reasonable but smallish.

You can also find unnamed ***rooms for rent*** in 'condotels' along Hat Jomtien for about 200B to 400B a night with fan, 400B to 600B with air-con. Most are little more than concrete cubes with box-like rooms, often lacking in ventilation and plumbing efficiency.

Jomtien Hotel (☎ 038 251 606, fax 038 251 097, 403/74 Muu 12, Th Hat Jomtien)

Rooms with fan 350B, air-con & TV 700-1200B. At the northern end of Jomtien off the road leading to South Pattaya, this stands well away from the beach. It's basically a low-end tourist hotel with clean rooms. There is a small rectangular pool on the roof. It's OK value if you don't mind staying in a cement box.

Pattaya Noppakao Hotel (☎/fax 038 370 582, 10/17 Mu 6, Th Hat Pattaya Neua) Clean rooms with air-con, hot-water shower & satellite TV from 450B. Next to the terminal for air-con buses to Bangkok, this is good value for Pattaya.

Places to Stay – Mid-Range

Good mid-range places can be found in Naklua, North Pattaya and Jomtien.

Pattaya Tucked away on a quiet soi is *Sunshine Hotel* (☎ 038 429 247, fax 038 421 302, 217/1 Soi 8, Th Pattaya 2). Rooms with air-con, TV & fridge 550B. This hotel has two pools and a restaurant that stays open until midnight.

Natural Beach Hotel (☎ 038 710 121, fax 038 429 650, 216 Muu 10, Soi 11) Rooms with air-con 800-1000B. This modern breezy two-storey hotel overlooks the beach. It has good rooms. and also contains a small restaurant.

Lek Hotel (☎ 038 425 550–2, fax 038 426 629, 284/5 Th Pattaya 2) Rooms with air-con & TV 550B. On the corner of Th Pattaya 2 and Soi 13, this high-rise has decent rooms.

Regent Marina Hotel (☎ 038 428 015, fax 038 423 296, in Bangkok ☎ 023 902 511, 463/31 Th Pattaya Neua) Rooms with air-con, fridge, phone & TV 800-1500B. In North Pattaya, this bridges the mid-range to top-end gap.

Furama Beach Hotel (☎ 038 428 580, fax 038 428 580, 164 Muu 9, Th Pattaya Klang) Rooms 700B. A couple of blocks back from the beach, this is a worn but clean hotel with all the basic resort amenities. On the premises are a coffee shop, seafood restaurant and pool.

Hat Naklua The two-storey *Garden Lodge* (☎ 038 429 109, fax 038 421 221, 131/8 Soi 12, Th Naklua)* has rooms with air-con for 700B. Built around a circular drive just off Th Naklua, it offers good service and features a clean pool.

Seaview Resort Hotel (☎ 038 429 317, fax 038 423 668, 500/19 Soi 18, Th Pattaya-Naklua) Rooms with air-con 800B. On a quiet soi off of Th Naklua, this is a L-shaped four-storey hotel with decent rooms.

Pattaya Lodge (☎ 038 225 464, in Bangkok ☎ 022 380 230, Th Naklua) Bungalows for 6 people with 2 bedrooms & air-con 2700B, for 9 people with 3 bedrooms 3300B, for 12 people with 4 bedrooms 3800B. Families and small groups may like this place, which is farther off Th Naklua, right on the beach and far from the pollution and bars.

Riviera Hotel Pattaya (☎ 038 225 230, fax 038 225 764, in Bangkok ☎ 022 525 068, 157/1 Soi Wat Pa Samphan, Th Naklua) Rooms with air-con, fridge & TV 400B. Standing between the road and the beach, this has cosy, quiet rooms. The Riviera also boasts a large garden and pool.

Hat Jomtien Peaceful Hat Jomtien has mostly mid-range condotel places costing 500B to 800B.

Silver Sand Villa (☎ 038 231 288–9, fax 038 232 491, Th Hat Jomtien) Doubles with air-con, old wing/new wing 800/1500B. Set back from the main drag, all prices include breakfast. It has a large swimming pool.

Jomtien Bayview (☎ 038 251 889, fax 038 251 890, 192 Muu 12, Th Hat Jomtien) Rooms with air-con 400-700B. OK rooms but try to get one near the back – the karaoke lounge downstairs can be deafening.

Surf House International Hotel (☎ 038 231 025–6, 44/45 Th Hat Jomtien) Rooms with air-con, fridge & TV 400B, with sea view 500-600B. This friendly hotel is next to the Thai Farmer's Bank. The Surf House restaurant serves fresh seafood and offers a good wine selection.

Marine Beach Hotel (☎ 038 231 129–31, 131/62 Th Hat Jomtien) Rooms with air-con 600-1200B. A total of 60 rooms that vary widely as far as cleanliness and comfort goes – check first.

EASTERN GULF COAST

Sea Breeze Hotel (☎ *038 231 056–8, fax 038 231 059, Th Hat Jomtien)* Rooms with air-con 800-1200B. This is well run but not as good value as it used to be.

Summer Beach Inn (☎ *038 231 777, fax 038 231 778, Th Hat Jomtien)* Rooms with air-con, satellite TV & fridge 750B. This good-value, friendly place is near the Marine Beach Hotel.

Furama Jomtien Beach Inn (☎ *038 231 545, fax 038 231 869, 125/16–17 Th Hat Jomtien)* Rooms with air-con & TV 500-800B. The pink-walled Furama is a good deal. It caters especially to Japanese, Chinese and Korean package tourists.

Jomtien Chalet (☎ *038 231 205, fax 038 231 208, 57/1 Muu 1, Th Hat Jomtien)* Bungalows with air-con 700-1900B. This offers simple, clean bungalows. There are also two rooms in an old refurbished railway car; a restaurant on the property serves Thai and Western food.

Jomtien also has several more expensive places that rent bungalows in the 2000B to 3000B range (see Places to Stay – Top End following). The high-rise development of Pattaya and Hat Cliff has already spread to Jomtien.

Places to Stay – Top End

Pattaya is really a resort for package tourists and convention-goers so the vast majority of its accommodation is in this bracket. All of the hotels mentioned in this section have air-con rooms and swimming pools (unless otherwise noted). In most cases the higher prices quoted are for suites, while the lower ones are for standard doubles. Many of the top-end hotels have lowered rates on standard singles and doubles so it's worth asking if anything cheaper is available when requesting a rate quote. Rooms are also often cheaper when booked through a Bangkok travel agency.

Luxury Among the reigning monarchs of Pattaya luxury hotels is *Dusit Resort Pattaya* (☎ *038 425 611, fax 038 428 239, in Bangkok ☎ 022 360 450,* e *booking@dusit.com,* w *www.dusit.com, 240/2 Th Hat Pattaya)*. Rooms 4360-12,098B. At the northern end of

Hat Pattaya, this has two pools, tennis and squash courts, a health centre, a semi-private beachfront and exceptional dim sum in the rooftop restaurant.

Amari Orchid Resort (☎ *038 428 161, fax 038 428 165, in Bangkok ☎ 022 679 708,* e *amorchid@loxinfo.co.th,* w *www .amari.com)* Rooms US$59-191. Set on four lush hectares in North Pattaya, with an Olympic-size swimming pool, two illuminated tennis courts, children's playground, minigolf, garden chess and one of the best Italian restaurants in Pattaya.

Royal Garden Resort Pattaya (☎ *038 412 120, fax 038 429 926, in Bangkok ☎ 024 760 021,* w *www.royal-garden.com, 218/2–4 Th Hat Pattaya)* Rooms 4200-8600B. One of Pattaya's most well-established resorts, this sits on 3.5 hectares of palms in Central Pattaya and has lotus ponds and Thai-style pavilions. It's attached to a four-storey shopping centre as well as a Ripley's Believe It or Not Museum; also on the premises are a fitness centre, two tennis courts, two cinemas and a pool.

Royal Cliff Beach Resort (☎ *038 250 421–30, fax 038 250 522, in Bangkok ☎ 022 820 999,* w *www.royalcliff.co.th, 353 Th Phra Tamnak)* Rooms 5300-12,400B. An older luxury property, this resort is at the southern end of Pattaya. It's really three hotels in one: a central section for package tours and conventions, a family wing and the very up-market Royal Wing.

Hat Naklua & North Pattaya On Hat Naklua is *Central Wong Amat Hotel* (☎ *038 426 990, fax 038 428 599, in Bangkok ☎ 025 471 234,* w *www.central hotelsresorts.com, 277–228 Muu 5, Th Naklua)*. Rooms 2200-2600B. This is a very quiet 25-acre resort.

Woodlands Resort (☎ *038 421 707, fax 038 425 663, in Bangkok ☎ 023 922 159, 164/1 Th Pattaya-Naklua)* Rooms 1350-1550B. This is a smaller place oriented towards families – with a children's pool, playground, babysitting services and lots of bear logos to make the little ones feel at home.

Beach View Hotel (☎ 038 422 660, fax 038 422 664, 389 Soi 2, Th Hat Pattaya) Rooms at booking rate 590-850B, walk-in rate 850-1200B. Recently renovated and good value, as long as you book through a travel agent.

Merlin Pattaya (☎ 038 428 755–9, fax 038 421 673, in Bangkok ☎ 022 532 140, 429 Th Hat Pattaya) Rooms 1700-2500B. Once one of Pattaya's finest hotels, this now seems rather plain beside more elegant properties. It caters to the growing wave of Russian tourists.

Central & South Pattaya Moving south, the top-enders drop in price a bit. Several offer comfortable rooms with phone, TV and mini-fridge, plus other amenities on the premises such as a coffee shop or restaurant and travel agent.

Pattaya Centre Hotel (☎ 038 425 877, fax 038 420 491, W www.pattaya .freeservers.com, 240 Soi 12, Th Hat Pattaya) Singles/doubles with breakfast 1400/2400B. This place has lots of amenities and is very central.

Siam Bayview Resort (☎ 038 423 871, fax 038 423 879, e siamcity@siamhotels .com, W www.siamhotels.com, 310/2 Th Hat Pattaya) Rooms 2600-3200B. Right in the thick of Central Pattaya, this features a lovely pool, garden and terrace cafe. The Bali Hai restaurant is recommended.

Siam Bayshore Resort (☎ 038 428 678–81, fax 038 428 730, in Bangkok ☎ 022 211 004, W www.siamhotels.com, Th Pattaya Tai) Rooms 2990B. Set at South Pattaya's quieter edge, this place is spread out and feels secluded.

Hat Cliff or Cliff Beach, named for the Royal Cliff Resort, bears a few other places.

Cosy Beach (☎ 038 428 818, fax 038 422 818, 400 Th Phra Tamnak) Rooms 850-1600B. This place has two wings, old and new. Rooms in the old wing are quite OK and good value for the view and seclusion.

Island View (☎ 038 250 813, fax 038 250 818, in Bangkok ☎ 022 498 941, Th Phra Tamnak) Rooms 750-1550B. One of the better cliff-side places, there's also a restaurant with a pleasant view.

Hat Jomtien This beach, around the corner from South Pattaya, is lined with hotels, resorts and guesthouses, several qualifying as top end.

Sugar Hut (☎ 038 251 686, fax 038 251 689, W www.sugarhut.co.th, 391/18 Th Pattaya) Single/double bungalows 3350/8120B. One of the best places to stay in the entire Pattaya area, this is not on the beach, but off the road that runs between Pattaya and Hat Jomtien. There are 33 Thai-style bungalows on stilts thoughtfully scattered among 15 râi (approximately 2.4 hectares) of tropical gardens, complete with rabbits and birds, three swimming pools, a restaurant, a modern fitness centre and jogging track. The bungalows feature partially open bathrooms perhaps inspired by upscale Balinese resorts.

Pattaya Park Beach Resort (☎ 038 251 201, fax 038 251 209, in Bangkok ☎ 025 110 717, 345 Th Hat Jomtien) Rooms 2800-4800B. This is a huge cement entertainment/hotel complex oriented towards package tourists or families, with such attractions as a tailor shop, huge 'fun complex', beer garden, dive shop and water park. If you're in need of a thrill, you can slide down a cable that stretches from the top of the resort's 55-storey tower to the ground.

Grand Jomtien Palace (☎ 038 231 405, fax 038 231 404, in Bangkok ☎ 022 713 613, 356 Th Hat Jomtien) Rooms 1200-5800B. This 14-storey place is central but has not much else going for it. It relies on German and Russian package tourists.

Natural Park Leisure Resort (☎ 038 231 561, fax 038 231 567, in Bangkok ☎ 022 472 825, fax 022 471 676, 412 Th Hat Jomtien) Rooms 950-2950B. This is a low-rise hotel with an attractive free-form swimming pool.

Places to Eat

Most food in Pattaya is expensive. The signs outside the many snack bars and restaurants in town reveal the cosmopolitan nature of Pattaya's visitors. Arabs and South Asians have been coming to Pattaya for many years now, so there are also plenty of Indian, Pakistani and Middle Eastern restaurants in town, some with fairly moderate prices. The recent influx of Russians has inspired several restaurants to add Russian translations to their menus; more recently a few Russian cafes have been added to the scene.

Decent Thai food is available along Pattaya's back street (Th Pattaya 2), away from the beach. The best seafood restaurants are in South Pattaya, where you pick out the sea creatures yourself and are charged by weight. Prices tend to be sky-high by Thai standards.

Savoey Seafood (☎ *038 428 580–1, 164 Th Pattaya Klang*) Mains 60-120B. Part of the Furama Beach Hotel in Central Pattaya, this is one of the better places for fresh seafood that doesn't break the bank.

PIC Kitchen (☎ *038 422 773, 10 Soi 5, Th Pattaya 2*) Dishes 70-140B. Open 8am-midnight. A moderately priced yet well-appointed Pattaya restaurant (second entrance on Soi 4), its Thai-style *salas* (open sided rooms) have low wooden tables and cushions for dining, and the emphasis is on Thai food with a limited selection of Western dishes. The upstairs bar area features live jazz nightly.

Vientiane Restaurant (☎ *038 411 298, 485/18 Th Pattaya 2*) Dishes 60-120B. Open 11am-midnight. This is an interesting place to eat, opposite Soi Yamato. The 503-item menu includes mostly Thai and Laotian dishes, plus lunch specials (30-50B).

Maxwell's Diner (☎ *038 361 247, 217/14 Th Pattaya 2*) Dishes 60-140B. Excellent hamburgers, sandwiches, french fries and other Western favourites served in huge, American-sized portions.

Ali Baba (☎ *038 429 262, 1/13–14 Th Pattaya Klang*) Dishes 80-160B. Opposite the Nova Hotel, this place does good vegetarian and non-vegetarian Punjabi cuisine.

La Gritta (☎ *038 428 161, Th Hat Pattaya*) Dishes 120-240B. Open 6am-11pm. Near the Amari Orchid, La Gritta does Italian-style seafood with some flair. Prices are moderate to expensive, but there's a pianist to keep you entertained.

Moonshine Place (☎ *038 231 956, 75/56 Th Hat Jomtien*) Dishes 40-120B. Moonshine Place specialises in Mexican and southern-Thai food; you can also buy takeaway here.

Zeppelin (☎ *038 420 016, 273 Th Hat Pattaya*) Mains 200-500B. Open 9am-2am. In the Nova Hotel, this is one of the more popular German restaurants.

Lobster Pot (☎ *038 426 083, 228 Th Hat Pattaya Tai*) Dishes 120-300B. Opposite Soi 14, this is one of Pattaya's better value seafood restaurants. It's also popular with locals.

The Royal Garden Plaza shopping centre, attached to Royal Garden Resort, contains several fast-food franchise restaurants. The Big C shopping centre on Th Pattaya 2 contains **KFC**, **Burger King**, **Baskin Robbins** and **Mister Donut**.

Opposite the bus station on the corner of Th Hat Jomtien and Th Chaiyapreuk are a few basic and cheap **restaurants** serving the usual Thai and Chinese dishes.

Entertainment

Eating, drinking and making merry are the big pastimes once the sun goes down. Making merry in Pattaya, aside from the professional sex scene, means everything from hanging out in a video bar to dancing all night at one of the discos in South Pattaya.

Two transvestite places, **Alcazar** (☎ *038 428 746, 78/14 Th Pattaya 2*) and **Tiffany's** (☎ *038 421 700, 464 Th Pattaya 2*, Ⓦ *www.tiffany-show.co.th*), offer complete drag-queen shows; the Alcazar is the most well known and puts on three shows nightly at 6.30pm, 8pm & 9.30pm. Tickets for the shows cost 400B to 600B.

Pattaya Palladium (☎ *038 424 922, 78/33–35 Th Pattaya 2*) Open 9.30pm-2am. Among the several discos in town, the very glitzy Pattaya Palladium is a large entertainment complex featuring 12 snooker tables, a 200-bed massage parlour, a Chinese restaurant, karaoke bar, cocktail lounge and a 360° Panorama Cinema. The disco has a capacity of 6000 customers.

Actually, one of the best things to do in the evening is just to stroll down Th Hat Pattaya and check out the amazing variety of bars – there's one for every proclivity, including a couple of outdoor *muay thai* (Thai boxing) bars featuring local talent. Truly the Garden of Earthly Delights, in the most Boschean sense. 'Pattaya Land', encompassing sois 1, 2 and 3 in South Pattaya, is one of the most concentrated bar areas. The many gay bars on Soi 3 are announced by a sign reading 'Boys Town'.

Pattaya's civic leaders have been attempting to clean up the town's seamy nightlife image for years. Although the bars and clubs that are fronts for prostitution are still tolerated, streetwalkers are discouraged outside that part of South Pattaya known as 'the village'. This area attracts a large number of kàthoey. There is also a prominent gay scene. Incidentally, the easiest way to tell a kàthoey is by the Adam's apple – a scarf covering the neck is a dead giveaway. Nowadays, though, some kàthoey have their Adam's apples surgically removed.

After the collapse of the Soviet Union and its satellite states a decade ago, significant numbers of Russian and Eastern European women began coming to Pattaya on tourist visas in order to sell their services to moneyed tourists from Taiwan, Hong Kong and Singapore. Their numbers have since dwindled due to a swift crackdown by Thai police, who were horrified at the thought of having to compete for kickbacks with Russian pimps and mobsters.

With so much emphasis on girlie bars, there's precious little in the way of live music in Pattaya.

Bamboo Bar *(Th Pattaya Tai)* One of the few places you can find live music is at one of the town's original nightspots, the Bamboo Bar, near the intersection with Th Hat Pattaya. There are two bands each night (the second act, starting around midnight, is usually better). There are, of course, plenty of hostesses happy to keep you company, but no-one minds if you just want to knock back a few drinks and take in the music.

Orn's Beer Bar *(Th Pattaya 2)* Next to the Apex Hotel, the quality of the musicians varies, but the place has a good vibe. If you feel you can do justice to a song, you might be able to take to the stage yourself.

Shenanigans *(☎ 038 710 641, Th Pattaya 2)* Shenanigans brings Bangkok's

popular Irish pub to Pattaya with all the usual trimmings, including Guinness on tap. Though be warned – it's not cheap.

Getting There & Away
Air Bangkok Airways (☎ 038 412 382) has daily flights between Ko Samui and U-Taphao airfield (about 30km south of Pattaya) four times weekly. The fare is 2155B one way to Ko Samui. Bangkok Airways also operates flights between Pattaya and Phnom Penh, Cambodia, for 3940B. Its office is at PIC Plaza, Soi 4, Th Pattaya 2.

To/From Bangkok International Airport
If you've just flown into Bangkok and need to get to Pattaya right away, there are airport minibuses that go directly to Pattaya at 9am, noon and 7pm daily for 200B one way. In the reverse direction, the THAI minibus leaves from next to the Gulf Siam Hotel in Pattaya at 6.30am, 2pm and 6.30pm. It takes around 2½ hours to reach the airport; the fare is 200B. Some hotels in Pattaya also run their own buses to Bangkok for fares from 160B to 300B one way.

Bus Air-con buses from Bangkok's Eastern bus terminal leave every half-hour between 4.30am and 7.30pm for 79B. Air-con buses to Pattaya are also available from Bangkok's Northern bus terminal for the same fare. In Pattaya the air-con bus stop is on Th Pattaya Neua, near the intersection with Th Sukhumvit. The air-con route takes around 2½ hours. Several hotels and travel agencies in Bangkok also run thrice-daily air-con tour buses to Pattaya for around 100B to 150B. Cramped minivans from Th Khao San typically cost 170B per person. These buses take around two hours in either direction. Once you reach the main Pattaya bus terminal, waiting red săwngthăew will take you to the main beach road for 20B per person.

From Si Racha you can grab a public bus on Th Sukhumvit to Pattaya for 15B.

There are also buses between Pattaya and several North-Eastern towns, including Khorat (178B air-con), Khon Kaen (125B ordinary, 225B air-con), Nong Khai (165B ordinary, 297B air-con) and Ubon Ratcha-thani (150B ordinary, 275B air-con).

Pattaya has a separate bus stop for buses to the North-East near the intersection of Th Pattaya Klang and Th Pattaya 3.

Train The No 283 train goes from Hualam-phong train station in Bangkok to Pattaya via Chachoengsao daily at 6.55am, arriving at 10.37am. In the opposite direction train No 240 departs from Pattaya at 2.15pm and arrives at Hualamphong station at 6.35pm. The trip costs 31B one way. Although this is an hour longer than the typical bus ride from Bangkok, it beats biting your nails in traffic jams along the highway from Bang Na to Trat. The Pattaya train station is just north of the T-junction of Th Pattaya Klang and Th Sukhumvit.

Getting Around

Săwngthăew (Songthaew) Săwngthăew cruise up and down Hat Pattaya and Th Pat-taya 2 frequently – just hop on and when you get out pay 10B anywhere between Naklua and South Pattaya, 20B as far as Jomtien. Don't ask the fare first as the driver may interpret this to mean you want to charter the vehicle. A chartered săwngthăew to Jomtien should be no more than 40B. It's usually easier to get a share săwngthăew from Jom-tien to Central Pattaya rather than vice versa.

Many readers have complained about riding the 10B săwngthăew with local passengers and then being charged a higher 'charter' price of 20B to 50B or more when they get off. In some instances drivers have threatened to beat faràng passengers when they wouldn't pay the exorbitant fares. It's little use complaining to the tourist police unless you can give them the licence plate number of the offending driver's vehicle. A refund is highly unlikely, but perhaps if the tourist police receive enough complaints they'll take some action to reduce or elimin-ate the rip-offs.

Car & Jeep Jeeps can be hired for around 2000B per day, and cars generally start at 1200B (although sometimes as low as 800B for a 4WD Suzuki in the low season)

depending on size and model; insurance and tax cost up to 160B more. All vehicle rentals in Pattaya are hired on a 24-hour basis.

Avis Rent-A-Car (☎ 038 361 627–8, 038 425 611) has an office at the Dusit Resort, and is by far the most expensive option. Of course, if something goes wrong you don't have to worry about any hassles (like a for-merly unseen disclaimer popping up in your insurance policy). Avis also offers a pickup and drop off service at your hotel.

SIE (☎ 038 410 629), near the Diana Inn on Th Pattaya 2, is pretty good and has com-petitive rates. Although SIE has signs claim-ing it's 'European managed' don't expect smooth sailing if anything goes wrong with the car, or you decide to return it early. There are no refunds, no matter what.

Motorcycle Motorcycles cost 150B to 200B per day for an 80cc or 100cc; a 125cc to 150cc will cost 300B, and you'll even see a few 750cc to 1000cc machines for hire for 500B to 1000B. There are motorcycle-rental places along Th Hat Pattaya and Th Pattaya 2. Pattaya is a good place to purchase a used motorcycle – check the rental shops.

Boat The ferry to Ko Laan leaves from Tha Tangke in South Pattaya, takes 40 minutes and costs 100B. The boat departs in the morning around 9am and returns at 4pm. Boat charters cost around 1000B to 1500B per day depending on the size of the boat.

AROUND PATTAYA

There are plenty of tourist attractions around Pattaya – tacky zoos and crocodile farms – mostly geared for Asian package tourists.

Wat Yansangwararam (☎ 038 237 642, *Th Sukhumvit, 160km marker*) is an ex-ception. Located about 12km south of Pat-taya near Nong Nooch Tropical Garden & Resort, the temple was recently completed on vast grounds and offers meditation courses for laymen (and men only) daily.

Wihan Sian (*admission 30B; open 9am-4.30pm*) is near Wat Yansangwararam and worth a look. This Chinese-style building, lavishly decorated, houses an astounding collection of antique art from China.

Farther south and east from Pattaya are more beaches and more resorts.

Khum Det (☎ *038 437 304, 472 Th Ban Na)* Rooms with cold shower 150B to 400B. In quiet Bang Saray, this offers simple but cheap rooms within walking distance of a decent beach.

Bang Saray Fishing Lodge (☎ *038 436 757, 42 Muu 5)* Rooms with air-con 500-850B. This is a small hotel, but fishing trips can be arranged through the agency in the lobby to the islands of Ko Khrok and Ko Saak.

Sea Sand Sun Resort (☎ *038 435 163, fax 038 435 166, 78/4 Th Sukhumvit, 163km marker)* Bungalows with air-con 900B, with TV 1000B. Well-spaced bungalows that are nicely appointed. A restaurant on the premises does good but expensive seafood.

Nong Nooch Tropical Garden & Resort (☎ *038 709 358, Th Sukhumvit, 163km marker)* Rooms from 300B, bungalows from 1600B. This is a bungalow operation that is transforming itself into a theme park, including a formal garden laid out in the French manner with sculpted shrubs and fountains. There are also elephant shows and demonstrations of classical Thai dance that are popular with Thais and other Asians.

These options have many competitors of similar style, quality and price. Still farther south is Sattahip, a vacation spot for the Thai military – some of the best beaches in the area are reserved for their use. There are several Thai navy and air force bases in the vicinity.

Ko Laan

This is the only nearby island with tourist accommodation and regular transport. The beach becomes quite crowded during the day in the high season (November to April) and is crowded on weekends year-round. At night, though, you and the other guests at the resort will have it all to yourselves. Deep-sea fishing is an activity easily arranged from Ko Laan. Trips can be booked through one of the local agencies (most of whom have offices in Pattaya) to the nearby islands of Ko Khrok and Ko

Saak. You can also charter a boat to Ko Phai (2500-4000B), a small island under the care of the Thai navy. Camping is not permitted and there's no formal accommodation – but if you're looking for a day of sunning yourself on a nearly-deserted island, this is the place.

Ko Laan Resort (☎ *038 429 372, fax 038 426 229, Hat Nuan)* Rooms with fan or air-con 600-1500B. Nicely laid-out and quiet – a great escape from Pattaya. The only drawback is the high prices at the resort's restaurant – try the other seafood restaurants on the island.

RAYONG
อ.เมืองระยอง

postcode 21000 • pop 46,400

Rayong lies on the Gulf of Thailand coast 220km from Bangkok by the old highway (Hwy 3) or 185km on Hwy 36. The general topography surrounding the provincial capital consists of a series of mountains interspersed with plains, large tracts of forest, and rubber and fruit plantations. The province produces fine fruit (especially durian, rambutan and mangosteen) and *náam plaa* (fish sauce). Rayong itself is not really worth visiting, but nearby beaches are fair and Ko Samet is a favourite island getaway for Bangkok residents. Except for Ko Samet, this area does not receive many foreign visitors, although it has been popular with Thai tourists for years.

Estuarial beaches at **Laem Charoen** (see Things to See & Do in this section), about 2km south of the provincial capital of Rayong, aren't that great, but there are some reasonable seafood restaurants. Better are the beaches near **Ban Phe**, a seaside town around 25km south-east of Rayong (this is also the departure point for Ko Samet). If sun and sand are what you're coming for, head straight for Ban Phe. Then pick out a beach or board a boat bound for Samet.

Another much smaller island near Rayong is **Ko Saket**, which is a 20-minute boat ride from the beach of Hat Sai Thong, south-west of Rayong (turn south off Hwy 3 at 208km marker).

Reclining Buddha at Wat Pa Pratu, Rayong

Suan Son (Pine Park), 5km farther down the highway from Ban Phe, is a popular place with Thai picnickers and has white-sand beaches as well.

Suan Wang Kaew is 11km east of Ban Phe and has more beaches and rather expensive bungalows. **Ko Thalu**, across from Suan Wang Kaew, is said to be a good diving area – the proprietors of Suan Wang Kaew, a private park, can arrange boats and gear. A few kilometres north-east of Wang Kaew, the white-sand beach of **Hat Ban Sang** is an area of residential and resort development. Other resort areas along the Rayong coast include **Laem Mae Phim**, to the east, and **Hat Sai Thong**, to the west. **Hat Mae Rampheung**, a 10km strip of sand between Ban Taphong and Ban Kon Ao (11km east of Rayong), is part of Laem Ya-Ko Samet National Park. See the Ko Samet section further in this chapter for more information.

Khao Chamao-Khao Wong National Park (*Bangkok ☎ 025 614 292–3, ext 724; adult/child 200/100B*) is inland, about 17km north of the 274km marker off Hwy 3. Although less than 85 sq km, the park is famous for limestone mountains, caves, high cliffs, dense forest, waterfalls and freshwater swimming and fishing. The park service rents bungalows, longhouses and tents. To get here from Ban Phe take a săwngthăew to the 274km marker for 25B, and another săwngthăew to the park.

Many more resort-type places are popping up along Rayong's coastline. Bangkok developers envisage a string of Thai resorts all the way to Trat along the eastern seaboard, banking on the increasing income and leisure time of Bangkok Thais.

One nonresort development is the new deep-water port at **Maptaphut**, west of Rayong, which, along with Chonburi's Laem Chabang Port, catches the large shipping overflow from Bangkok's Khlong Toey Port.

Information

Tourist Offices TAT (☎ 038 655 420), 153/4 Th Sukhumvit, has a rather inconveniently located office 7km east of Rayong town on the north side of Hwy 3. The staff can provide maps and fairly up-to-date lists of accommodation and sights in Rayong and Chanthaburi provinces.

Money Several banks along Rayong's main drag, Th Sukhumvit, have exchange services, including Bangkok Bank, Thai Farmers Bank and Bank of Ayudhuya. Opening hours are 8.30am to 3.30pm weekdays, 8.30am to noon on Saturday.

Things to See & Do

The **King Taksin Shrine**, on the grounds of Wat Lum Mahachaichumpon, commemorates King Taksin's brief sojourn in Rayong. According to legend, Taksin tethered his

View from a jetty at Ao Cho, Ko Samet, Eastern Gulf Coast

Náam tòk (waterfall), Ko Chang

White Sands Beach Resort, Ko Chang, Eastern Gulf Coast

Beach huts, Ko Chang

Laying low outside the bungalow

Decked out on Ko Chang, Eastern Gulf Coast

Cars, bars & accommodation abound in Pattaya

Gorgeous isn't it?

Delivery of supplies and tourists to Ko Chang

A Hindu shrine, Trat, Eastern Gulf Coast

elephant to the large tree – said to be 300 years old – in front of the shrine, which is highly revered by Thais of Chinese ancestry who flock to the shrine during Chinese New Year.

Wat Pa Pratu, constructed during the Ayuthaya period, boasts a highly stylised Buddha measuring 11.95m long by 3.60m high. Unlike most reclining Buddhas throughout Asia, this one is lying on its left side rather than its right. No one today seems to know whether this was intentional (a Tantric explanation is possible) or an artisan error. A large *wíhǎan* (chapel) was built in 1981 to enshrine the Buddha, which was previously uncovered. There's also a large European-posed Buddha in a wíhǎan nearby, as well as an exquisite 500-year-old whin that's kept locked most of the time.

A very old, 10m-tall stupa known as **Phra Chedi Klang Nam** stands about 2km from the town centre on an islet at the mouth of the Rayong River. An annual festival at the islet every November features boat races in the estuarial bay.

Laem Charoen is a long, narrow cape lined with the homes of local fisherfolk and seafarers. On the inside of the cape facing an estuary are numerous *rohng ngaan náam plaa*, small factory warehouses where Rayong's famous fish sauce is produced and stored. The aromas in this neighbourhood, as might be expected, can be overwhelming. A small garden at the end of Laem Charoen contains sculpted figures of Phra Aphaimani, one of Thailand's most famous heroes of classical myth, along with a pond and a Chinese shrine where locals often bring picnics.

Places to Stay

Should you somehow get caught overnight in Rayong, there are a few inexpensive hotels near the bus station off Th Sukhumvit.

Rayong Otani (☎ 038 611 112, 69 Th Sukhumvit) Rooms with fan/air-con 200/650B. The relatively old Rayong Otani has OK rooms. To reach it, walk south from the bus station out to Th Sukhumvit, turn left and proceed past Rayong hospital, soon after which you'll see the hotel sign.

Rayong President Hotel (☎ 038 611 307, fax 038 612 570, 16/8 Th Phochanakon) Rooms with air-con 440-490B. This is a more upmarket hotel down a small side street, so it's quiet at night. From the bus station, cross to the other side of Th Sukhumvit, turn right and after about three minutes you'll see a sign pointing down the side street.

Rayong Palace (☎ 038 616 438, fax 038 617 204, 109 Th Ratbamrung) Rooms with air-con 350-500B. Rooms are comfortable but the hotel is popular with travelling businesspeople and can be noisy at night.

There are plenty of other places strung out along Th Sukhumvit with accommodation from 150B for simple fan rooms to around 700B for air-con & hot water.

Rayong Orchid (☎ 038 614 340, fax 038 614 780, in Bangkok ☎ 023 920 143, fax 023 813 984, 011 Th Sukhumvit) Rooms 800-2500B. Top-end lodgings include this place, which has large rooms, a coffee shop and a karaoke lounge.

PMY Beach Resort (☎ 038 614 855, fax 038 614 877, 89 Th Liapchaifang) Doubles 2300B, suite with 2 bedrooms 6800B. At the western end of Laem Charoen, this is a huge place. The narrow strip of beach here isn't very good, however, so it's really only visitors with business at the Maptaphut industrial estate who stay.

Places to Eat

For cheap food, check out the *market* near the Thetsabanteung cinema, or there's a string of *restaurants* and *noodle shops* on Th Taksin Maharat just south of Wat Lum Mahachaichumphon.

Samakhom Pramong (Fishing Cooperative; Th Liapchaifang) Dishes 40-180B. On the harbour in Laem Charoen, this has reopened in a clean new *sala* (open-sided room) and does fantastic Thai seafood.

If you have plenty of time, take a sǎwngthǎew (5B) south from Th Sukhumvit to the mouth of the Rayong River at Laem Charoen, where the well-established indoor-outdoor *Laem Charoen (☎ 038 616 357, 001 Th Liapchaifang)*, *Saeng Chan (6/6 Th Liapchaifang)* and *Ocharos (Ocha*

Rot; Th Liapchaifang) serve very good, moderately priced seafood. Săwngthăew (10B) from the bus station take you to a small wooden bridge that crosses the Rayong River onto a long spit of land. After crossing the bridge you can catch a motorcycle taxi (10B) to the restaurants.

Getting There & Away

Regular buses (87B) to Rayong leave about every half-hour between 4.30am and 10pm from Bangkok's Eastern (Ekamai) bus terminal. The trip usually takes more than four hours. First-class air-con buses leave hourly from 5am to 10pm, cost 101B and take about three hours. Săwngthăew from Rayong bus station to Ban Phe cost 15B.

Ordinary buses to Chanthaburi from Rayong cost 42B and take about 2½ hours in either direction. This bus, as well as buses to Pattaya and Bangkok, depart from near the central market and Rayong Otani Hotel, just off Th Sukhumvit (Hwy 3).

COASTAL RAYONG

Though none can rival the beauty of Ko Samet, there are numerous good beaches and islands along Rayong's 100km coast.

The tourists here are almost all Thai. Even the stretches of beach with strips of hotels have a sleepy feel that, for some, may make a nice change from doing the standard Thailand foreign tourist circuit. The few foreigners here are likely to be local residents, mostly employees from one of Rayong's major joint-venture industrial operations, like the enormous petrochemical-refinery complex at Maptaphut west of Rayong town.

Though not outstanding, some of the beaches, such as Mae Rampheung, Ban Sang and Laem Mae Phim, are quite nice. One downside to this area for budget travellers is that it's often difficult to find accommodation for under 500B per night. Unlike foreign travellers, vacationing Thais are usually out to spend cash, and want air-con, a swimming pool and TV, not simple thatched bungalows with bugs and no bath. Beaches tend to be lined not with palm trees but with *sŏn tháleh* or sea pines (casuarina).

The best way to visit most of these places is to rent a car from Pattaya and then go exploring. Nearly all the Thai tourists drive here themselves, so public transport is spotty.

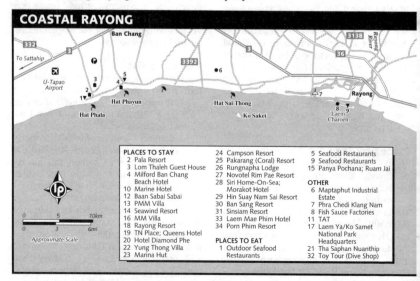

COASTAL RAYONG

PLACES TO STAY	24 Campson Resort	5 Seafood Restaurants
2 Pala Resort	25 Pakarang (Coral) Resort	9 Seafood Restaurants
3 Lom Thaleh Guest House	26 Rungnapha Lodge	15 Panya Pochana; Ruam Jai
4 Milford Ban Chang	27 Novotel Rim Pae Resort	
Beach Hotel	28 Siri Home-On-Sea;	OTHER
10 Marine Hotel	Morakot Hotel	6 Maptaphut Industrial
12 Baan Sabai Sabai	29 Hin Suay Nam Sai Resort	Estate
13 PMM Villa	30 Ban Sang Resort	7 Phra Chedi Klang Nam
14 Seawind Resort	31 Sinsiam Resort	8 Fish Sauce Factories
16 MM Villa	33 Laem Mae Phim Hotel	11 TAT
18 Rayong Resort	34 Porn Phim Resort	17 Laem Ya/Ko Samet
19 TN Place; Queens Hotel		National Park
20 Hotel Diamond Phe	PLACES TO EAT	Headquarters
22 Yung Thong Villa	1 Outdoor Seafood	21 Tha Saphan Nuanthip
23 Marina Hut	Restaurants	32 Toy Tour (Dive Shop)

Hat Phala & Hat Phayun
หาดพลาและหาดพยูน

These two beaches actually link together, making a 5km strip of yellow sand, casuarina trees and slightly cloudy surf. There's not a lot going on around here, even in the heat of the high season. Most of the accommodation is aimed at long-term visitors, with numerous apartment buildings and homes going for 15,000B to 25,000B per month.

Of the shorter-term options, none of them are cheap.

Pala Resort (☎/fax 038 630 358, 78/1 Muu 2, Th Sukhumvit) Bungalows with air-con 650-1500B. This is about five minutes' walk from Hat Phala, and has a small complex of bungalows.

Lom Thaleh Guest House (☎ 038 630 088, 109 Muu 5) Rooms with air-con 500-1100B. Within walking distance of Hat Phala, these small bungalows are clean and well kept.

Milford Ban Chang Beach Hotel (☎ 038 630 019, fax 038 630 024, in Bangkok ☎ 022 614 271, 169–171 Th Hat Phayun) Rooms 1200-5400B. On the beach side of the road, this is a palatial resort hotel. It has a nice stretch of beach in front of it and it's quiet: the only sound you're likely to hear will be your own steps echoing down the vast hallways.

Purimas Beach Hotel (☎ 038 630 382, fax 038 630 380, in Bangkok ☎ 023 926 900, 34 Th Phayun-Nam Rim) Rooms 2400-4500B. Towards the end of Hat Phayun is this luxurious and elegantly designed resort complex with pool, health club and business centre.

Aside from the hotels, there are numerous open-air *seafood restaurants* along the beaches, particularly at Hat Phala and at Hat Phayun where the road from Ban Chang ends.

Getting There & Away To get here by public transport, take a bus to Rayong and get off at the town of Ban Chang. From there you can catch a săwngthăew to Phayun (10B). Most buses stop where the road from Ban Chang meets the beach, so you may have to pay a bit extra if you want them to take you to your hotel, (although the more expensive places should have a pick-up service). There is no regular

EASTERN GULF COAST

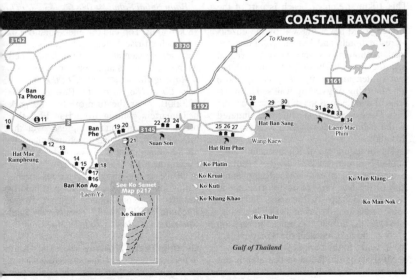

COASTAL RAYONG

săwngthăew service to Hat Phala: a charter should cost around 50B.

If you're driving, just after entering Ban Chang, look for a sign indicating the turn-off for Hat Phala, soon after the 194km marker and opposite Rte 3376. The beach is 6km south along this road. When you get to the intersection before the beach, turn right for Hat Phala and left for Hat Phayun.

Hat Sai Thong & Ko Saket
หาดทรายทองและเกาะสะเก็ด

Forget what the TAT brochures tell you, there's no reason to come to these places. The beach of Hat Sai Thong has been replaced with a concrete breakwater, and the entire area is in spitting distance of the Maptaphut industrial park, home to massive petrochemical plants. Tiny Ko Saket, a 15-minute boat ride from Hat Sai Thong, used to have accommodation, but it has been razed as the island is now being adapted for industrial purposes.

Hat Mae Rampheung
หาดแม่รำพึง

This 10km stretch of beach is part of the Khao Laem Ya/Ko Samet National Park, though you'd never know it by the dozens of resort hotels and bungalows lining the road. Although it's very narrow, even at low tide, it has fairly soft, whitish sand, not much litter, and plenty of space for those long morning or evening walks. The western and middle sections of the beach are the best. The eastern part is a bit more cluttered as the fishing village of Ban Kon Ao is at this end.

The headquarters of Khao Laem Ya/Ko Samet National Park is on the headland behind the eastern end of Mae Rampheung. The office has very basic information in English and maps of the park. There are some trails to hike around the headland; however, the military occupies the very top portion and thus has kept the best views for itself. Entry to the park is 200B.

Most accommodation in this area is up-market.

Marine Hotel (☎ 038 655 101, 79/1 Muu 4) Rooms and bungalows 400-600B. Budget travellers could try this place. Although a bit run-down, it is off the beach, and has the unique feature of several fruit-shaped concrete bungalows, including an apple, a melon and a durian!

MM Villa (☎ 038 651 559, 78/58 Th Hat Mae Rampheung) Rooms with air-con 700-3200B. Concrete bungalows with verandas and comfortable rooms. The restaurant is said to be one of the better ones on this beach.

Along the beach there are at least a dozen places to choose from.

Seawind Resort (☎ 038 651 562, fax 038 652 735, 82/16 Th Hat Mae Rampheung) Rooms with air-con 700-1500B. In terms of value for money, this is one of the better places. You may be able to bargain a bit if it's not full. The hotel has a pleasant courtyard around a large swimming pool (even though the beach is just across the road).

PMM Villa (☎/fax 038 664 647, 78/72 Th Hat Mae Rampheung) Bungalows 1000-4500B. A collection of well-spaced bungalows in a landscaped yard. During the week prices are discounted by 40%.

Baan Sabai Sabai (☎ 038 655 435, 60 Th Hat Mae Rampheung) Doubles/suites 4800/6300B. Top-end travellers should skip all the high-rise hotels and head straight here, an immaculate, tastefully landscaped warren of cottages and small homes.

Rayong Resort (☎ 038 651 000, fax 038 651 007, 186 Muu 1) Rooms 4000-12,000B. Near the turn-off for the park headquarters coming from Ban Phe, this offers rooms in cottages spread over the hills of Laem Ya. It has spacious units with all the amenities and views of the bay between Laem Ya and Ko Samet.

Of the several simple seaside restaurants strung out along the beach (particularly towards Ban Kon Ao), the best are *Panya Pochana* (☎ 038 614 557, Th Sukhumvit) and *Ruam Jai* (☎ 038 655 166, Th Sukhumvit).

Getting There & Away The easiest way to get here by public transport is to get a bus to Rayong, and then from the bus station catch a săwngthăew (15B) to Mae Ram-pheung. The latter run erratically, and you may have to wait for a while if you're going later in the afternoon. If you're driving, take Hwy 3 about 5km west past Rayong to the small town of Ban Ta Phong where you'll see a sign indicating the turn-off for the road to Mae Rampheung. Rayong-bound săwngthăew can be flagged down anywhere along the road to Mae Rampheung.

Ban Phe
บ้านเพ

After Hat Mae Rampheung, the coastal road passes through Ban Phe, the jumping-off point for Ko Samet. If you miss the last boat to Ko Samet, there are several hotels near the pier.

Thai Farmers Bank and Bangkok Bank both have branches with ATMs on the main waterfront street in Ban Phe.

Places to Stay & Eat There are several hotels in Ban Phe near the central market and within walking distance of the Seri pier.

TN Place (☎ *038 825 638, 286/4–5 Th Phe-Klaeng-Kram*) Rooms with fan 250B, with air-con 300-500B. About 100m from the pier, this has decent rooms. The owners are friendly and provide plenty of information, but the hotel can get a bit noisy. There are a couple of computer terminals for Internet use.

Queens Hotel (☎ *038 651 018, 281/1–4 Th Phe-Klaeng-Kram*) Rooms without/with bath 200/250B, singles/doubles with air-con 350/400B. Queen Hotel is across and up the road from the pier, on a soi next to a 7-Eleven store (near the central market); painted ladies on hand testify to its mainly short-time clientele though it's basically an OK place.

Hotel Diamond Phe (☎ *038 651 826, fax 038 651 757, 286/12 Th Phe-Klaeng-Kram*) Rooms with air-con 400-580B. This mid-range, six-storey hotel is close to the pier. Check the rooms out before paying, some are much worse than others.

The *restaurant* in front of where the tour bus from Bangkok stops, opposite Nuan-thip pier, has OK Thai food. The *market* next to the pier is a good place to stock up

on food, mosquito coils and the like to take to Ko Samet. You'll probably spend some time in this spot, waiting either for the boat to leave the nearby pier for Ko Samet or for the bus to arrive from Bangkok.

Getting There & Away Air-con buses to Ban Phe leave Bangkok's Eastern bus ter-minal 12 times per day between 4am and 6.30pm. The fare is 108B and the trip takes about four hours, more if traffic between Si Racha and Bangkok is bad. Cheaper still is the 87B ordinary bus with eight departures per day. Buses from Bangkok stop in Ban Phe in front of the restaurant opposite Tha Saphaan Nuanthip.

Minivans to Pattaya leave from Tha Saphaan Nuanthip thrice daily for 150B per person, or you can take a taxi for about 800B. During the high season there is usu-ally one daily minivan departure from the pier to Ko Chang (or rather to the pier at Laem Ngop, sailing point for Ko Chang) for 250B per person.

For information on boat travel between Ban Phe and Ko Samet, see the Ko Samet section later in this chapter.

Suan Son & Hat Rim Phae
สวนสนและหาดริมแพ

East of Ban Phe, the road is enveloped by a grove of casuarina trees that stretches along the beach for 4km. This area is known as Suan Son, and while the beach is not great, the overall atmosphere is pleasant. It's also a popular spot for Thai picnickers, and you'll find dozens of food vendors servic-ing people in sling chairs and under um-brellas along the beach.

Suan Son is also one of the few places where you can find more reasonably priced accommodation.

Yung Thong Villa (☎ *038 648 463, fax 038 648 465, 162/11–12 Th Phe-Klaeng-Kram*) Bungalows 500-2000B. As the trees thin out, one of the first places you'll come to is Yung Thong.

Marina Hut (☎ *038 648 468, in Bangkok ☎ 024 240 668, 162/8–9 Th Phe-Klaeng-Kram*) Bungalows with fan & bath

500-1200B. There are good bungalows here, and it's conveniently located near a row of beachfront restaurants and Thai-style beach bars.

Campson Resort (☎ 038 648 313, in Bangkok ☎ 024 334 739, 146/1 Muu, 1 Th Phe-Klaeng-Kram) Rooms 400-4000B. East of a gleaming white condo resort, this offers rooms in tidy cottages and leafy grounds.

After turning inland and crossing a small river, the coastal road leads back towards the seashore and Hat Rim Phae. The beach is quite nice around here.

Pakarang Resort (Coral Resort; ☎ 038 648 412, in Bangkok ☎ 022 248 901, fax 022 217 207, 155 Muu 3). Cottages with air-con 600-2960B. This resort looks over a beautiful stretch of clean beach and has plenty of casuarina trees for shade. These well-kept red-tile roofed cottages are among the best for value.

Rungnapha Lodge (☎ 038 648 297, in Bangkok ☎ 022 770 288, fax 022 756 471, 154 Th Suan Son-Wang Kaew) Rooms and bungalows 1200-6000B. The upscale, at least in price, Rungnapha Lodge, is on a fine beach.

Novotel Rim Pae Resort (☎ 038 648 008, fax 038 648 002, in Bangkok ☎ 022 371 305, fax 022 364 353, ⓔ novotel@loxinfo .co.th, 4/5 Muu 3, Th Phe-Klaeng-Kram) Doubles 4120-6599B. For top-of-the-line luxury, you probably won't do better than here. This place is sheer elegance, with graceful architecture, five-star facilities, including two restaurants, two swimming pools, two children's pools, a playground, lit tennis courts, a fitness centre, Thai massage, sailing and canoeing, and a complimentary túk-túk to Ban Phe.

Beyond Hat Rim Pae lies the headland of **Wang Kaew**. Though trumpeted in tourist literature as one of coastal Rayong's most scenic spots, this place is fairly run-down, and the beach is definitely shabbier than others in the area. **Ko Thalu**, across from Wang Kaew, is said to be a good diving and snorkelling area, with beautiful, relatively intact coral. You can arrange trips there at The Toy Tour, in Laem Mae Phim (see later in this section).

Getting There & Away Sǎwngthǎew from Rayong and Ban Phe run past Suan Son and Hat Rim Phae on their way to Laem Mae Phim. The fare should cost 15B to 20B depending on how far you're going.

Laem Mae Phim
แหลมแม่พิมพ์

This long stretch of beach outdoes Mae Rampheung for beauty and cleanliness, and also benefits from shade trees along the entire beachfront. Unfortunately, this idyllic scene evaporates at the eastern end of the beach where all the accommodation is concentrated. This may explain why the rest of Laem Mae Phim – especially Hat Ban Sang – is so pleasant; in any event you need only walk west about 10 minutes to get away from the ugly buildings, jet-skis and speedboats.

Laem Mae Phim village has the area's only dive operation, **Toy Tour** *(☎ 038 638 146, 236/4 Th Mae Phim; 50/950B for snorkelling/scuba gear; open 9am-6pm).* The shop has a fleet of speedboats. Boat charters cost 2000B to 3000B per day, and trips can be made to **Ko Man Nai** or **Ko Thalu**. All-day fishing charters are 3000B.

More low-key activities similar to those found at Suan Son include picnicking and lounging about under beach umbrellas, or floating on the calm seas using large inner tubes available for rent from beach vendors. All in all, the water is much cleaner here than at Suan Son, though the beach can become just as crowded on weekends.

Porn Phim Resort (☎ 038 638 027, 17 Mu 3) Rooms 500-3300B. At the eastern end, one of the few places to stay actually on the beach is Porn Phim, which has 12 bungalows divided up into 54 small rooms – some rooms are a tad shabby while others are OK. This place also doubles as a karaoke parlour at night.

Laem Mae Phim Hotel (☎ 038 638 147, 236/8 Th Phe-Klaeng-Kram) Rooms with air-con 700-1400B. A white hulk with pseudo Greco-Italian columns and balconies. The plumbing on the ground floor works best.

Sinsiam Resort (☎ *038 638 114, fax 038 638 153, in Bangkok* ☎ *024 391 385–6, fax 024 391 388, 235 Th Phe-Klaeng-Kram)* Rooms with air-con cost 1200-1400B. The pseudo-Thai style Sinsiam is decaying and a bit pricey.

Much better options are the newer and quieter accommodations along Hat Bang San to the west toward Rayong town.

Ban Sang Resort (☎ *038 638 118, Th Phe-Klaeng-Kram)* Bungalows 1250-2200B. This place, which features two-room bungalows, is the best of the bunch. The restaurant is one of the best in the area, and the beach is very clean.

Hin Suay Nam Sai Resort (☎ *038 638 260, fax 038 638 034, in Bangkok* ☎ *022 430 095, fax 022 435 188, 250 Muu 2)* Units with 2 rooms 2600-14,000B. Set amid some picturesque boulders, this resort occupies the best stretch of beach.

Less expensive places on or near Hat Bang San include *Siri Home-On-Sea* (☎ *038 648 549, 151 Muu 3)* and *Morakot Hotel* (☎ *038 638 005, 236 Muu 3)*, both off the highway near the 17km marker.

The long string of *seafood restaurants* along the eastern end of Laem Mae Phim all have aquariums where you can pick out live *kâng kràdaan* (rock lobster), *kûng mangkon* (spiny lobster), *puu máa laai* (zebra crab) and more.

Sinsiam Seafood (☎ *038 638 114, fax 038 638 153, in Bangkok* ☎ *024 391 385–6, fax 024 391 388, 231 Th Phe-Klaeng-Kram)* Dishes 140-180B. Across from the resort of the same name, this was one of the first restaurants to open here and is still one of the best.

Getting There & Away Săwngthăew from Rayong and Ban Phe occasionally make their way down to Laem Mae Phim. Expect to pay around 15B to Ban Phe and up to 30B to get to Rayong.

By car there are two options. You can either take Hwy 3 to the intersection with Rte 3192, which heads south to the coastal road, or drive to Ban Phe and then follow the pleasant route east along the coast for about 15km.

Ko Man Klang & Ko Man Nok
เกาะมันกลางและเกาะมันนอก

Ko Man Klang and Ko Man Nok, lying 7km to 10km off Laem Mae Phim, along with Ko Man Nai to their immediate west, are part of Khao Laem Ya/Ko Samet National Park. As with Ko Samet, this official designation has not prevented development, only moderated it. The islands are in fair ecological condition, the main threat to the surrounding corals being the arrival of jet-skis and banana boats.

Sea Turtle Preservation Sanctuary (☎ *038 616 096, open daily, 9am-4pm)*, on Ko Man Nai, is an island that has been set aside as a sanctuary for sea turtles by Queen Sirikit and can be visited by hiring a boat at Laem Mae Phim. It's quite expensive to hire a boat though, figure on at least 4000B. Easier and cheaper is to book a tour through Raya Island Resort (see later in this entry).

Resorts on Ko Man Klang and Ko Man Nok offer accommodation packages that include boat transport from the nearest pier as well as three meals a day. These are best arranged by phone in advance through Bangkok reservation numbers. Just showing up isn't really practical: chartering a boat could easily cost several thousand baht, and the resorts may not have the food and other supplies needed to accommodate you. But book, and the resort operators should help arrange transport to the pier departure points, which can change depending on the season.

Ko Nok Island Resort (☎ *038 661 136, in Bangkok* ☎ *028 603 025–7, fax 028 603 028)* Two-day, one-night package 2600B, three-day, two-night package 4400B. Rather pricey bungalows with a mostly Thai clientele.

Raya Island Resort (Bangkok ☎ *023 166 717, fax 027 402 647)* Two-day, one-night package 1500B, three-day, two-night package 2500B. On Ko Man Klang, this resort offers boat transport and meals. Trips to the Sea Turtle Preservation Sanctuary on Ko Man Nai are also available. See entry earlier for more information on the Sanctuary.

KO SAMET
เกาะเสม็ด

The island of Ko Samet has some of Thailand's best beaches and it's cheaply and conveniently reached from Bangkok – less than half a day's travelling distance away. Ko Samet is also a relatively dry island – which makes it an excellent place to visit during the rainy season. Of course, all of this makes Ko Samet a favourite with foreign visitors but in the past few years the island has become very popular with Thais as well. A massive advertising campaign launched by the TAT after the economic crash of 1997 convinced many Thais that vacationing on Thailand's own beaches was a suitable substitute for travelling abroad. Young urban Thais especially have taken to the beach like never before and so Ko Samet gets more than its share of local visitors, particularly during weekends and the Thai summer vacation months of March, April and May. This can make for very crowded conditions at Ko Samet during these and other public holidays: early November (Loi Krathong Festival); 5 December (King's Birthday); 31 December to 1 January (New Year); mid-January to late February (Chinese New Year); and mid-April (Songkran Festival). Despite this, if you're stuck in Bangkok and looking for a cheap and easy beach getaway, Ko Samet is your best bet. There is even a little surf occasionally (best months are December to January).

The T-shaped island earned a permanent place in Thai literature when classical Thai poet Sunthorn Phu set part of his epic *Phra Aphaimani* on its shores. The story follows the travails of a prince exiled to an undersea kingdom ruled by a lovesick female giant. A mermaid aids the prince in his escape to Samet where he defeats the giant by playing a magic flute. Formerly Ko Kaew Phitsadan or Vast Jewel Isle – a reference to the abundant white sand – this island became known as Ko Samet (Cajeput Isle) after the cajeput tree that grows in abundance here and is very highly valued as firewood throughout South-East Asia. Locally, the cajeput tree has also been used in boat building.

The 13.1-sq-km Ko Samet, along with Laem Ya and other nearby islands, has been a national marine park since 1981, but that didn't keep developers from buying land and building accommodation once it was noticed that visitors had begun making day trips to the island in the early 1980s. The National Parks Division stepped in and built a visitors office on the island, ordered that all bungalows be moved back behind the tree line and started charging a 5B admission into the park.

The admission fee was recently raised to 200B (as it was at all national parks) and there are separate park units at each beach in charge of fees collection. There are plenty of vehicles on the island, more frequent boat services from Ban Phe and a much improved water situation. The northern end of the island is where most of the development is located. Though there's nowhere near the kind of bar and entertainment scene you'd find on Ko Samui, there are some opportunities for more social travellers with a few late night bars and restaurants. As you move south, things get progressively quieter, with the exception of the heavily built-up Ao Wong Deuan. Below there, it really tones down: those seeking solitude will find several beaches and bungalows that should fit the bill.

It should also be pointed out that Ko Samet has what is probably Thailand's largest and most loathsome collection of stray dogs, many of them with advanced cases of mange. They can be especially disturbing during meal times when, hopeful for a handout, the crusty curs park themselves nearby and stare longingly at your food. And if that weren't enough, once night falls the dogs sometimes raise such an astounding din that some visitors find that only by drinking large quantities of alcohol are they able to sleep.

While Ko Samet's dry weather makes it a good place to visit during the rainy season, it also means that fresh water can sometimes be scarce. Please try to conserve water and help ease the strain on an already overtaxed ecosystem. A very new reservoir has been constructed next to the main cross-island

KO SAMET

To Ban Phe

Laem Noi Na

To Ban Phe

To Ban Phe

Ao Wiang Wan

Laem Phra

Ao Kham

Na Dan

1
2
3
4

Ao Phrao

5
6

7

8

Hat Laem Yai

9
10

Laem Ya/Ko Samet National Park

13

16
14
12
11

18
19
15
Hat Sai Kaew

20
17

Laem Yai

Ao Hin Khok

21
22
23
24

Ao Phai

25

Ao Phutsa

26

Laem Rua Taek

27

Ao Nuan

28
29

Ao Cho

30
31
32
33

Ao Wong Deuan

34

Hat Saeng Thian

35

Ao Thian

Gulf of Thailand

36

Ao Wai

Ao Kiu Na Nai

37

Ao Kiu Na Nok

Laem Khut

Ao Karang

0   0.5   1km
0   0.25   0.5mi

EASTERN GULF COAST *(side tab)*

PLACES TO STAY & EAT
1 Samed Hut
2 SK Bungalows
4 Samed Cliff Resort
5 Ao Prao Resort
6 Dome Bungalows
9 Pineapple Bungalow
10 Banana Hut
11 Diamond Beach; Samet Beach Restaurant
12 Coconut Bungalow
14 Saikaew Villa; Toy Restaurant
15 Laem Yai Seaview
16 Ploy Talay
17 White Sand Bungalow & Restaurant
18 Naga Bungalows; Post Office
19 Little Hut
20 Jep's Inn
21 Ao Phai Hut
22 Sea Breeze
23 Silver Sand
24 Samed Villa
25 Ao Pudsa Bungalow
26 Tub Tim
27 Ao Nuan Bangalow
28 Wonderland Resort
29 Tarn Tawan; Bamboo Restaurant
30 Malibu Garden Resort
31 Seahorse Bungalow
32 Vongdeuan Resort
33 Vongdeurn Villa
34 Saeng Thian Beach
35 Lung Dam Bungalow
36 Sametville Resort
37 Ao Kiu Coral Beach

OTHER
3 Tha Na Dan
7 Ko Samet Health Centre; Police Substation
8 Buddhist Temple
13 National Park Office

Ko Samet: Environment or Economics?

Beneath all the resorts, restaurants and jet-skis, Ko Samet is actually part of Khao Laem Ya/Mu Ko Samet Marine National Park. For years the National Parks Division of the Royal Forestry Department has been trying to keep developers at bay, obviously with little success. But now there is a chance the tourist industry may be booted off the island in favour of the flora and fauna.

The park was established in 1981, around the same time that the 13.1-sq-km island began receiving its first tourists – young Thais in search of a retreat from city life. They arrived to find only about 40 houses on the island, built by fisherfolk and Ban Phe locals. But Rayong and Bangkok speculators saw the sudden interest in Ko Samet as a chance to cash in on an 'up-and-coming Phuket' and began buying land along the beaches. No-one bothered about Ko Samet's national park status. When the flow of tourists started picking up, the National Parks Division stepped in and built a visitors office on the island, ordered that all bungalows be moved back behind the tree line and started charging admission to the park. In later years, the Royal Forestry Department temporarily closed the park to all visitors a couple of times in an effort to halt encroachment, but always reopened the island within a month or less in response to protests by resort operators. However, in late 1996, the Thai courts sided with the Royal Forestry Department and, on a case by case basis, began ordering bungalow operations on Ko Samet to shut down. Resort owners say that no-one will have to really do anything until the court has waded through all the bungalow outfits. Even then they should have one year to pack up and move out. And of course there's always the chance of a 'political solution'. So, although the judicial die has been cast, resort owners are still confident they'll be on Ko Samet long into the future. At the same time, some are looking into business opportunities on the mainland or other islands. 'The closure may not happen, but I'm not investing any more here. This time there's really a chance we'll all have to leave', said one Ko Samet bungalow operator. Though it's doubtful this will happen anytime soon – too much money is being made for there to be a simple solution.

Court hearings continue; until a decision is reached, a permanent moratorium on new developments remains in place in order to preserve the island's forested interior.

Joe Cummings

road, which may alleviate the traditional water shortage. See the 'Ko Samet: Environment or Economics' boxed text for more information.

Information

Ko Samet is part of a marine national park, and there is an entry fee of 200B for adults, 100B for children aged from three to 14 years. The park has a main office near Hat Sai Kaew, and a smaller one at Ao Wong Deuan.

An excellent guide to the history, flora and fauna of Ko Samet is Alan A Alan's 94-page *Samet*, published by Asia Books. Instead of writing a straightforward guidebook, Alan has woven the information into an amusing fictional travelogue involving a pair of Swedish twins on their first trip to the island.

Post & Communications A small post office next to Naga Bungalows offers a poste restante service. It's open from 8.30am to noon and 1pm to 4.30pm weekdays, and 8.30am to noon Saturday.

An international satellite phone can be found outside the visitors centre at the main park office; cards cost 1500B and are available at the park office. There's also an ordinary phone booth for domestic calls within Thailand. There is Internet access at a shop next to the post office.

Travel Agencies Near Na Dan and on Hat Sai Kaew and Ao Wong Deuan are several small travel agencies that can arrange long-distance phone calls, as well as bus and train reservations – they even do air ticketing.

Medical Services The Ko Samet Health Centre, a small public clinic, is located midway between the village harbour and Hat Sai Kaew. English-speaking doctors are on hand to help with problems like heat rash, or bites from poisonous sea creatures or snakes.

Malaria A few years ago, if you entered the park from the northern end near the village, you'd have seen a large English-language sign warning visitors that Ko Samet was highly malarial. The sign is gone now, but the island still has a bit of malaria. If you're taking malarial prophylactics you have little to worry about. If not, take a little extra care to avoid being bitten by mosquitoes at night. Malaria is not that easy to contract, even in malarial areas, unless you allow the mosquitoes open season on your flesh. It's largely a numbers game – you're not likely to get malaria from just a couple of bites (that's what the experts say anyway), so make sure you use repellent and mosquito nets at night. See the Health section in the Facts for the Visitor chapter for information about precautions against malaria.

Activities

Several bungalows on the island can arrange boat trips to nearby reefs and uninhabited islands. Ao Phutsa, Naga Beach (Ao Hin Khok), Hat Sai Kaew and Ao Wong Deuan each have sailboard rental places that do boat trips as well. Typical day trips to Ko Thalu, Ko Kuti etc cost about 500B per person, including food and beverages (minimum of 10 people). Sailboards, boogie boards and inner tubes can be rented from a number of guesthouses.

Ao Prao Divers at Ao Prao Resort (see the following Places to Stay section) on the western side of the island offers a full range of dive options, including entry-level open water PADI certification (four days, 10,000B) and advanced open water course (five dives, two to three days, 10,000B).

Places to Stay

The two most developed areas are Hat Sai Kaew and Ao Wong Deuan. All of the other spots are still rather peaceful. Every bungalow operation on the island has at least one restaurant and most now have running water and electricity. Most places have electric power from 5pm or 6pm until 6am; the more upmarket places have 24-hour power.

On less popular beaches you may come across abandoned bungalow sites, and even during the high season some of the most expensive places offer discounts for accommodation to attract customers. Very basic small huts cost 100B to 120B, similar huts with fan and bath cost 150B to 200B. Bungalows with furniture and air-con start at 600B. Many places offer discounts for stays of four or more days, while on weekends and public holidays most will raise their rates to meet the demand – sometimes dramatically.

Some resorts, mainly around the Hat Sai Kaew area, have also been known to boot out foreigners without warning to make room for free-spending Thais during holidays or long weekends. You won't need to worry about this at the more reputable spots, but even so, if possible avoid Ko Samet during the peak times.

Since this is a national park, camping is allowed on any of the beaches. In fact, this is a great island to camp on because it hardly ever rains. There is plenty of room; most of the island is uninhabited and, so far, tourism is pretty much restricted to the north-eastern and north-western beaches.

East Coast The following bays and beaches have various accommodation options.

Samet's prettiest beach, **Hat Sai Kaew** (Diamond Sand), is 800m long and 25m to 30m wide. The bungalows here are the most commercial on the island, with video in the restaurants at night and lots of lights. They're all very similar and offer a range of accommodation from 120B (in the low season) for simple huts without fan or bath, to 200B to 600B for one with fan, mosquito net and private bath, or as high as 2500B with air-con. All face the beach and most have outdoor restaurants serving a variety of seafood. Like elsewhere in Thailand, the daily rate for accommodation can soar suddenly with demand. The more scrupulous places don't hike rates by much, though.

Coconut Bungalow (☎ 038 651 661) Bungalows with fan 350B, with air-con, TV & fridge 1400B. Sturdy and clean bungalows with veranda and chairs.

Diamond Beach (☎ 038 652 514) Bungalows with fan 350B, with air-con 550-900B. Newish wood and concrete bungalows right on the beach.

Ploy Talay Rooms with private bath 400-1500B. The more expensive bungalows were recently built and have good bathrooms. The cheaper ones are a little shabby but passable.

Laem Yai Seaview Rooms 350-1000B. Just beyond Ploy Talay, this features well-spaced wooden huts, all with decks, set in a quiet location among trees.

White Sand Bungalow (☎ 038 617 195) Rooms 500-1500B. Mostly concrete bungalows with a couple of original wooden ones holding out for the time being. The latter are a bit dank, the former a bit rustic. White Sand has a good restaurant that does a reasonably priced seafood barbecue on some evenings – check the chalkboard out front.

Saikaew Villa (☎/fax 038 651 852) Rooms with fan 500-800B, with air-con 1600-4500B. This is a huge, top-end place near the prettiest part of the beach. Breakfast is included and the establishment boasts

24-hour power – try to get a room away from the noisy generators. Discounts for long-term stays are available.

Ao Hin Khok The beach here is about half the size of Sai Kaew but just as pretty – the rocks that give the beach its name add a certain character. Hin Khok is separated from Sai Kaew by a rocky point surmounted by a mermaid statue, a representation of the mermaid that carried the mythical Phra Aphaimani to Ko Samet in the Thai epic of the same name. Ao Hin Khok and Ao Phai, the next inlet south, offer the advantage of having among the least expensive huts on the island along with reasonably priced restaurants serving good food.

Little Hut Bungalows 250-300B. One of the island's first bungalow operations, Little Hut has sturdy and semi-clean bungalows, all with a small porch. The price depends on proximity to the generator.

Naga Bungalow Bungalows 150-250B. Naga offers simple bungalows set on a hill overlooking the sea, and more expensive ones with a good mattress and fan. Its restaurant sells great bread (it is distributed to several other bungalows on the island), cookies, cakes, pizzas and other pastries. There are billiards, darts, various board games and Internet access on offer. Only the latter gets much use.

Jep's Inn Bungalows with bath & fan 350B. This has 14 nicely designed, clean bungalows. Its restaurant (no videos) is also quite good, and there's a nice shaded dining area right at the edge of the beach. Jep's is probably the most pleasant accommodation in the area.

Ao Phai Around the next headland is another shallow bay with a nice wide beach, though it can get fairly crowded.

Ao Phai Hut Doubles with bath & fan 500-1000B, bath & air-con 700-2000B. The friendly Ao Phai is at the northern end, with screened bungalows; weekends and holidays add 200B. Electricity is available from 5pm to 6am. It organises tours around the island, and has an international telephone service and basic postal services.

Sea Breeze Bungalows 250-1500B. Sea Breeze has 40 rather closely spaced bungalows. Price depends on the number each bungalow sleeps and proximity to the beach, as well as how long the generator runs. Adjacent is a small shop and a bookshop and library that also has international phone and fax service.

Silver Sand Bungalows with fan 250-350B, air-con 500-1500B. This has 35 comfortable bungalows with verandas; fan bungalows have 24-hour electricity. Air-con bungalows have electricity from 5pm to 8am.

Samed Villa Bungalows with bath 600-1100B. This has very clean, screened, well-maintained, tree-shaded bungalows with large verandas. It offers 24-hour electricity. The food is quite good, and some of the bungalows have great sea views. This is also one of the few places in the area that doesn't screen videos at night.

Near Sea Breeze, the main road south to Ao Wong Deuan turns inland and heads down the middle of the island. A little farther along the road from here is where the cross-island road to Ao Phrao on the west coast starts.

Ao Phutsa At Ao Phutsa, also known as Ao Thapthim, you'll find a few places to stay.

Ao Pudsa Bungalow Bungalows 300-1200B. Pudsa has both basic well-worn huts and newer ones with air-con. Some of the smaller huts are quite close to the water, making them pretty good value for money.

Tub Tim Bungalows 500-1500B. At the southern end of the beach Tub Tim has older, smaller bungalows on a shady hillside, and newer, more spacious wooden bungalows with sea views and air-con.

After Ao Phutsa, the remaining beaches south are separated from one another by fairly steep headlands. To get from one to the next, you have a choice of negotiating rocky paths over the hilly points or walking west to the main road, which goes along the centre of the island, then cutting back on side roads to each beach.

Ao Nuan If you blink, you'll miss this beach. It's one of the quieter, more secluded places to stay without having to go to the far south of the island.

Ao Nuan Bungalow Huts 200-400B. The nine rustic huts have shared bath and intermittent electricity, and vary in size. Some are little more than bamboo huts. The food is quite good and the eating area is set in an imaginatively arranged garden. It's a five-minute walk over the headland from Ao Phutsa.

Ao Cho (Chaw) A five-minute walk across the next headland from Ao Nuan, this bay has its own pier and can be reached directly from Ban Phe on the boat *White Shark* or aboard the supply boat. Though just north of crowded Ao Wong Deuan, it's fairly quiet here, although the beach is not among Samet's best.

Wonderland Resort (Lung Wang) Bungalows with fan, shower & toilet 150-800B. At the northern end of the beach, this has basic, rather unkempt bungalows. The place looks a bit like a decaying fishing village.

Tarn Tawan Huts 400-600B. There are both tin-roofed cement and bamboo-thatch huts here – the latter have more charm. Its kitchen specialises in Isan food.

Ao Wong Deuan This once gorgeous bay is now filled with speedboats and jet skis, and there's a lot of accommodation packed into a small area making things a bit cramped. The crescent-shaped beach is still nice, but it is noisy and often crowded – imagine a crowd sitting on deck chairs lined up and facing the bay as if it were a cinema screen.

Vongdeuan Resort (☎/fax 038 651 819, ☎ 038 651 777) Bungalows with running water, flush toilet & fan 600-800B, with air-con 1000-1200B. This is the best of the lot, although it's quite a scene by Samet standards.

Vongduern Villa (☎ 038 651 777, fax 038 651 819) Bungalows 800-2500B. This is similar in amenities to the Vongdeuan Resort, but all rooms have air-con.

Malibu Garden Resort (☎ 038 651 292, ⓔ *samet@loxinfo.co.th*) Bungalows with fan 800-1100B, with air-con 1500-2200B.

Malibu Garden has well-built brick or wooden bungalows; the more expensive rooms have a fridge & TV. There's a swimming pool and breakfast is included. The resort has its own boat to Ban Phe that leaves two to three times a day and costs 50B.

Seahorse Bungalow Rooms & bungalows with fan 500B, air-con 800-1200B. Seahorse has practically taken over the beachfront with two restaurants and a travel agency.

Three boats – the *Malibu, Seahorse* and *Vongduern* – go back and forth between Ao Wong Deuan and Ban Phe.

Ao Thian From this point south things start to get much quieter. Better known by its English name, Candlelight Beach, the bay is quite scenic, and rocky outcrops break up the beach, though there's plenty of sand to stretch out upon.

Saeng Thian Beach (Candlelight Beach; ☎ 038 651 223) Bungalows with fan & bath 300-700B. On the bay's northern end, this has wooden bungalows stretched out on the beach and cheaper ones on a hillside. Electricity is on from 6pm to 6am.

Lung Dum Bungalow (☎ 038 651 810) Bungalows with bath 300-400B, treehouse 250B. At the southern end of the beach, this has quite roughly built huts. Good if you're looking for something out of the ordinary – the huts are built of all manner of scrap and junk, both organic and otherwise. It all looks as if it belonged to some settlement of castaways marooned on a deserted island. The treehouse is interesting also.

Keep in mind that you're a captive of guesthouse kitchen choices here; you may want to bring some of your own food from the village on the northern tip of the island.

Other Bays You really have to be determined to get away from it all to go farther south on the east coast of Ko Samet, but it can be well worth the effort. Lovely **Ao Wai** is about 1km from Ao Thian but can be reached by the boat *Phra Aphai* from Ban Phe, which sails once a day and charges 50B per person. There's only one bungalow operation here.

Sametville Resort (☎ 038 651 681, in Bangkok ☎ 022 463 196) Bungalows with 2 beds, fan & bath 800-900B, with air-con 1300B. The very private Sametville offers a fine combination of upscale accommodation and isolation. Most bookings are done by phone, but you could try your luck by contacting someone on the *Phra Aphai* at the Ban Phe pier.

A 20-minute walk over the rocky shore from Ao Wai, **Ao Kiu Na Nok** also still had only one place to stay at the time of writing.

Ao Kiu Coral Beach (☎ 038 652 561) Tents 100B, bungalows with air-con 600-3000B. The friendly and clean Ao Kiu Coral Beach has well-equipped concrete bungalows. The beach here is gorgeous, one of the nicest on the island. Another plus is that it's a mere five-minute walk to the western side of the island and a view of the sunset.

West Coast The only beach on the west side of the island is **Hat Ao Phrao** and it has nice sunset views. In Thai the name means Coconut Bay Beach but for marketing reasons bungalow operators tend to use the cliched Paradise Beach moniker. Local bungalow operators do a good job of keeping the beach clean.

Ao Prao Resort (☎ 038 651 377, fax 038 652 600, ☎/fax 012 785 977, 012 133 533, in Bangkok ☎ 024 389 771, fax 024 390 352, 367 Th Krung Thonburi) Bungalows 2000-6500B. At the northern end of the beach is Ao Prao Resort, where attractive air-con bungalows with large verandas are surrounded by lush landscaping. Amenities include cable TV, private hot showers and perhaps the best restaurant on the island. There is also a free boat service to/from Saphaan Seree in Ban Phe for all guests. Ao Prao Divers at the resort offers diving, windsurfing, kayaking and boat trips.

Dome Bungalows (☎ 038 651 377) Bungalows with fan & bathroom 700-900B, air-con 1000-1400B. In the middle of the beach, friendly Dome Bungalows has 22 bungalows built on the hillside. Breakfast is included. A pleasant restaurant on the premises features a menu of Thai and Western dishes.

There is a daily boat between Ban Phe and Ao Phrao (100B).

North Coast To the north-west of Ko Samet's main pier in Na Dan is a long beach called **Ao Wiang Wan**, where several rather characterless bungalows are set up in straight lines facing the mainland. Here you get neither sunrise (maybe a little) nor sunset.

SK Bungalows Rooms 200-300B. This is the cheapest place, but it only seems to open during Thai holidays when every other place is full, which is just as well since the rooms are very shabby.

Samed Cliff Resort Bungalows 1000-2500B. This offers 24 white-painted, well-maintained masonry cottages built on a hillside opposite the beach. There's a small pool on the nicely landscaped grounds.

South-east of Na Dan toward Hat Sai Kaew, along the north-east corner of the island, are a couple of small beach bays with bungalow operations. Hardly anyone seems to stay here.

Pineapple Bungalow (☎ 038 651 508) Bungalows 400-600B. At Hat Laem Yai (also known as Ao Yon), the bungalows don't look bad but the area is neglected with piles of construction materials and rubbish, and it's rather difficult to find out just who's running the show here.

Banana Hut (☎ 038 612 231) Rooms/bungalows 250/500B. This has rooms in a big brick duplex unit or individual small cement bungalows.

Places to Eat

Nearly all bungalows have restaurants offering mixed menus of Thai and traveller food; prices are typically 30B to 50B per dish. Fresh seafood is almost always available and costs around 60B to 150B per dish.

Bamboo Restaurant Dishes 30-60B. The pleasant Bamboo at Ao Cho, behind Tarn Tawan, offers inexpensive but tasty food and good service. It's open for breakfast, lunch and dinner.

Naga Dishes 30-50B. On Ao Hin Khok, this has a very good bakery with all kinds of breads and cakes.

Ao Wong Deuan has a cluster of restaurants serving Western and Thai food: *Tom's*, *Oasis* and *Nice & Easy*.

Vongduern Villa (☎ 038 651 777, fax 038 651 819) Dishes 50-80B. At the southern tip of the beach, this restaurant is a bit more expensive, but both the food and the location are quite nice.

White Sand Restaurant (☎ 038 617 195) Dishes 100-160B. On Hat Sai Kaew, this has good seafood.

Toy Restaurant Dishes 30-50B. For cheaper fare on this beach, try the popular Toy, next to Saikaew Villa.

Samet Beach Restaurant Meals 40-80B. Next to Diamond Beach, this has been recommended for good food at reasonable prices, and has friendly staff.

Ao Prao Resort (☎ 038 651 377, fax 038 652 600, ☎/fax 012 785 977, 012 133 533, in Bangkok ☎ 024 389 771, fax 024 390 352, 367 Th Krung Thonburi) Mains 80-120B. This fancy open-air terrace restaurant is probably the best eatery on the island.

Getting There & Away

Bus Many Th Khao San agencies in Bangkok offer return transport to Ko Samet, including the boat trip, for 170B (300B return). This is more expensive than doing it on your own, but it's convenient for travellers who don't plan to go anywhere else on the east coast. For information on getting to/from Ban Phe by bus, see the Ban Phe section earlier.

Boat There are various ways to get to/from the island by boat.

To Ko Samet There are three piers: Saphan Nuanthip for the regularly scheduled passenger boats; Saphan Mai for supply boats; and Saphan Sri Ban Phe for tour groups. Nuan Tip is usually the only one you'll need, but if you arrive between passenger boat departure times you can try for a ride aboard one of the cargo boats from Saphan Mai (you must still pay the regular passenger fare).

Passenger boats to Ko Samet leave at regular intervals throughout the day starting at around 8am and ending around 5pm.

How frequently the boats depart mostly depends on whether they have enough passengers or cargo to make the trip profitable; obviously there will be more boats making frequent trips in the high season (December to March). Whatever the season, there are always at least three or four boats a day going to Na Dan and Ao Wong Deuan.

It can be difficult to find the boat you need, as agents and boat owners want you to go with them rather than with their competitors. In most cases they'll be reluctant to tell you about another boat if they won't be making any money from you.

Some travellers have reported being hassled by 'agents' who show them photo albums of bungalows on Ko Samet, claiming that they must book a bungalow for several days in order to get onto the island. This is false; ignore these touts and head straight for the boats. Report any problems with touts to the TAT office in Rayong.

Probably the best place to head is the Saphan Nuan Tip ticket office, behind all the food and souvenir stalls. The staff sell tickets for a number of different boat operators, and are also willing to tell you about private resort boats.

For Hat Sai Kaew, Ao Hin Khok, Ao Phai and Ao Phutsa, catch a boat to Na Dan. These generally leave as soon as there are at least 20 passengers: the return fare is 100B. Ignore touts or ticket agents who claim the fare is more; simply buy a ticket from Saphan Nuan Tip ticket office. From Na Dan you can either walk to these beaches (10 to 15 minutes) or take one of the trucks that go round the island. See the Getting Around section for standard fares.

The Saphan Nuan Tip ticket office also has boats to Ao Wong Deuan (70B one way), Ao Phrao (100B) and Ao Wai (100B). All boats need at least seven people before they'll depart.

The Saphan Sri Ban Phe ticket office also sells tickets for Na Dan (100B), Ao Wong Deuan (70B), Ao Wai (100B), Ao Kiu Na Nok (100B), Ao Phrao (100B), Ao Nuan and Ao Thian (120B). Again, go directly to the ticket office and ignore what touts tell you.

If you arrive in Ban Phe at night and need a boat to Ko Samet, you can usually charter a one-way trip at the Ban Phe pier but prices are steep: plan on about 1500B to 2000B, depending on where you land.

From Ko Samet Samet Tour seems to run a monopoly on return trips from Na Dan and the boats leave only when full. Some boats require a minimum of 18 people, while for others it's as high as 25 people. If the boat is under-loaded anyone wanting to leave immediately may want to contribute more to the passage. The usual fare is 40B.

These days it is so easy to get boats back from the main beaches to Ban Phe that few tourists go to Na Dan to get a boat. There are four daily boats each from Ao Wong Deuan and Ao Cho, plus at least one daily boat from Ao Wai, Ao Kiu Na Nok and Ao Phrao.

While waiting for a boat back to the mainland from Na Dan, you may notice a shrine not far from the pier. This *săan jâo phâw* is a spirit shrine to Pu Dam (Grandfather Black), a sage who once lived on the island. Worshippers offer statues of *reusĭi* (hermit sages), flowers, incense and fruit.

Getting Around

If you take the boat from Ban Phe to the village harbour (Na Dan), you can easily walk the distance to Hat Sai Kaew, Ao Phai or Ao Phutsa. Don't believe the taxi operators who say that these beaches are a long distance away. If you're going farther down the island, or have a lot of luggage, you can take the taxi (which is either a truck or a three-wheeled affair with a trailer) as far as Ao Wong Deuan.

Set fares for transport around the island from Na Dan are posted on a tree in the middle of a square in front of the Na Dan harbour: 20B per person to Hat Sai Kaew (or 150B charter); 30B to Ao Phai or Ao Phutsa (200B charter); 40B to Ao Wong Deuan or Ao Phrao (250B charter); 50B to Ao Thian or Ao Wai (350B and 400B charter); and 60B to Ao Kiu Na Nok (500B charter). Exactly how many people it takes to constitute public service rather than a charter is not a hard and fast number. Figure on 30B per person for six to eight people to anywhere between Na Dan and Ao Cho. If they don't have enough people to fill the vehicle, they either won't go, or passengers will have to pay up to 200B to charter the vehicle.

There are trails from Ao Wong Deuan all the way to the southern tip of the island, and a few cross-island trails as well. Taxis will make trips to Ao Phrao when the road isn't too muddy.

Motorbikes can be rented from a number of bungalow operations on Hat Sai Kaew, Ao Phai and Ao Phrao. Figure on about 500B per day or an hourly rate of 150B.

COASTAL CHANTHABURI

Pickings are a bit more sparse here than in Rayong, with the best beaches pretty much confined to the western section of the province. While not spectacular, they feel even more remote than the beach areas of coastal Rayong. Adding to the sense of isolation is the fact that getting to these places can be quite difficult and time-consuming unless you have your own vehicle. Even then, unless you speak Thai, finding your destination could still prove to be a bit of an adventure.

Chanthaburi's most promising beaches are located about 25km south of Hwy 3, and about 14km west of the border with Rayong Province. Probably the quietest spot around the area is **Hat Khung Wiman**, a 500m strip of golden sand interspersed with rocky outcrops. There is one bungalow operation here.

Khung Wiman Resort Bungalows for 2/4 people 1200/1500B. This has well-constructed slate and plaster bungalows. Discounts should be no problem for longer-term stays and during the low season.

Along the beach are about a dozen small thatched-roof open-air ***restaurant/bars***. There's a scenic, undeveloped bay along the road following the shore to the south-east.

A bit farther east are the beaches of **Laem Sadet** and **Hat Chao Lao**. Together they form an 8km stretch of uninterrupted sand and surf. As with many other Thai resorts, litter is allowed to pile up on some parts of the beach, but it's not enough to ruin the scenery.

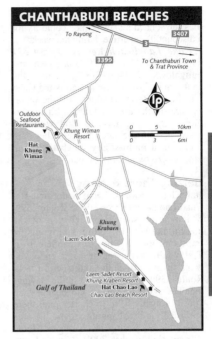

Laem Sadet ends in a small peninsula. There's no accommodation at this end, aside from some corporate and long-term facilities. But there are plenty of open-air ***restaurants***, and scores of casuarina trees provide good shade.

Hat Chao Lao is a bit more developed, with several bungalow outfits and a few faded resort hotels. The beach seems to get a bit whiter as you move south, and even with the hotels nearby, a short walk either north or south will soon reward you with your own private patch of sand.

Laem Sadet Resort (☎ 039 369 194, 18/1 Muu 5) Bungalows 1200-1500B. Despite its name, this actually overlooks Hat Chao Lao. It's one of the nicest bungalow outfits in the area, with nine spacious cottages, a grassy yard and scattered palm trees. But it's not cheap, though discounts may be available.

Khung Kraben Resort (☎ 039 321 035, Muu 4) Rooms 1500B, bungalows 2000-3500B. This has 13 rooms in a hotel building as well as five bungalows with all the amenities surrounded by lawns. You could try for a discount if you arrive during the week.

Chao Lao Beach Resort (☎ *039 321 630, fax 039 321 959, 99 Muu 6*) Rooms/ bungalows 1700/4500B. Down near the southern end of Hat Chao Lao is the Chao Lao Beach Resort. Though still the fanciest spot in the area, it looks a bit like its glory days have passed. You wouldn't know it from the rates though: there are rooms in a multi-storey hotel block and family-size two-storey bungalows.

Getting There & Away

Hat Khung Wiman, Laem Sadet and Hat Chao Lao are all accessed via Route 3399, which heads south from Hwy 3 at the 302km marker. If you're taking public transport, hop on a bus to Chanthaburi or Trat; you'll have to let the driver know you want to get off at the intersection with Route 3399. There is no regular săwng-thăew service to any of the beaches, so you'll probably have to charter one: there are usually a few hanging around the area where the buses stop. A charter to Khung Wiman should cost 200B, one to Laem Sadet or Hat Chao Lao around 250B.

If you're driving, about 12km south along Route 3399 you'll reach a sharp curve, with a road leading off it to the left. (The road is between the third and fourth black and yellow curve signs, and is also bracketed by a few small billboards.) Taking this road to the left is the quickest way to the beaches, and as you follow it you'll see signs for Khung Wiman and Laem Sadet. If you miss the left turn, you'll almost immediately see a sign saying 'Laem Sadet 15km': ignore this sign, look behind you and you'll see the road leading off to the left.

Heading to Laem Sadet you'll eventually reach a T-intersection that's near the beach. The turn on the right takes you to Laem Sadet, the turn on the left to Hat Chao Lao and accommodation. Laem Sadet Resort is 1.4km from the intersection, Had Suay 1.7km and Chao Lao Beach Resort 4.5km.

TRAT
อ.เมืองตราด

postcode 23000 • pop 14,400

About 400km from Bangkok, Trat Province borders Cambodia and, as in Chanthaburi, gem mining and gem trading are important occupations. Gem markets *(talàat phloi)* are open intermittently at the **Hua Thung** and **Khlong Yaw** markets in the Bo Rai district, about 40km north of Trat on Rte 3389. A smaller market is sometimes open all day in **Khao Saming** district only 20km north-west of Trat. There has been a drop in activity in the gem markets due to the dwindling supply of local gem stock. A sad by-product of gem mining has been the destruction of vast tracts of land – the topsoil is stripped away, leaving acres of red-orange mud.

If the gem business doesn't interest you, another attraction Bo Rai district offers is **Salak Tai Falls**, 15km north-west of Bo Rai. The other big industry in Trat is the smuggling of consumer goods between Cambodia and Trat. For this reason, travelling alone along the border, or around the offshore islands that serve as conduits for sea smuggling, requires caution. More and more people have discovered the beaches and islands of Trat, however, and as the nearby Khmer Rouge conflict dissipated with the demise of Pol Pot, security has greatly improved. A good spot for observing the border trade is at the Thai-Cambodian market in **Khlong Yai**, near the end of Rte 318/Hwy 3 south of Trat. As much as 10 million baht changes hands in these markets daily.

South-east of Trat along Rte 318 towards Khlong Yai district, the province thins to a narrow sliver between the Gulf of Thailand and Cambodia. Along this sliver are a number of little-known beaches, including **Hat Sai Si Ngoen**, **Hat Sai Kaew**, **Hat Thap Thim** and **Hat Ban Cheun**. Ban Cheun has a few bungalows, but there is still no accommodation at the other beaches.

At the 70km marker, off Rte 318, is **Jut Chom Wiw** (View-Admiring Point), where you can get a panorama of the surrounding area, including Cambodia. Trat Province's south-easternmost point is at **Hat Lek**,

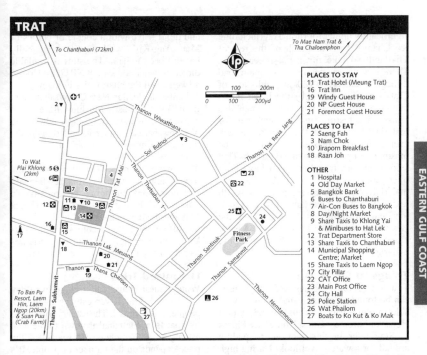

TRAT

To Chanthaburi (72km)

To Mae Nam Trat & Tha Chaloemphon

Thanon Wiwatthana

Soi Bufnoi

Thanon Tat Mai

Thanon Thetsabun 1

Thanon Tha Reua Jang

Thanon Tha Reua Jang

To Wat Plai Khlong (2km)

Thanon Lak Meuang

Thanon Thana Charoen

Thanon Sukhumvit

Thanon Santisuk

Thanon Samanmit

Thanon Nemtameuw

Fitness Park

To Ban Pu Resort, Laem Hin, Laem Ngop (20km) & Suan Puu (Crab Farm)

0   100   200m
0   100   200yd

PLACES TO STAY
11 Trat Hotel (Meung Trat)
16 Trat Inn
19 Windy Guest House
20 NP Guest House
21 Foremost Guest House

PLACES TO EAT
 2 Saeng Fah
 3 Nam Chok
10 Jiraporn Breakfast
18 Raan Joh

OTHER
 1 Hospital
 4 Old Day Market
 5 Bangkok Bank
 6 Buses to Chanthaburi
 7 Air-Con Buses to Bangkok
 8 Day/Night Market
 9 Share Taxis to Khlong Yai & Minibuses to Hat Lek
12 Trat Department Store
13 Share Taxis to Chanthaburi
14 Municipal Shopping Centre; Market
15 Share Taxis to Laem Ngop
17 City Pillar
22 CAT Office
23 Main Post Office
24 City Hall
25 Police Station
26 Wat Phailom
27 Boats to Ko Kut & Ko Mak

which is also a legal jumping-off point for boat trips to the Cambodian coast. Although there are Thai military checkpoints between Trat and Hat Lek (one at last count), there are no problems with Westerners being allowed through. It's now possible to cross between Thailand's Hat Lek and Cambodia's Ko Kong and then catch a ferry to Sihanoukville and explore the surrounding beaches.

Information

The TAT (☎ 039 597 255, 039 597 259) maintains an office at 100 Muu 1, Th Trat-Laem Ngop, in Laem Ngop district.

Information on Ko Chang National Marine Park is available at the park headquarters in Laem Ngop, a small town 20km south-west of Trat town. This is also where you get boats to Ko Chang.

Immigration There is no immigration office in Trat – you must go to the provincial offices in Khlong Yai or Laem Ngop for visa extensions or other immigration matters. Khlong Yai is where you have to go to have your passport stamped upon return from Cambodia.

Money Bangkok Bank and Krung Thai Bank on Th Sukhumvit have foreign exchange windows open daily from 8.30am to 5pm. In Laem Ngop, a Thai Farmers Bank (between Chut Kaew Guest House and the pier) has an exchange counter open Monday to Friday from 8.30am to 3.30pm.

Post & Communications The main post office is a long walk from the town centre on Th Tha Reua Jang. It's open from 8.30am to 4.30pm weekdays, 9am to noon weekends. The telephone office is located on the corner a few doors down from the post office and offers international phone and fax service daily from 7am until 10pm.

Malaria Rates of infection for malaria are significantly higher for rural Trat (including Ko Chang) than for much of the rest of Thailand, so take the usual precautions. There is a malaria centre on the main road through Laem Ngop (20km south-west of Trat) where you can get the latest information on the disease. This office can also assist with testing and/or treatment for malaria. Malaria is not that easy to contract, even in malarial areas, unless you allow the mosquitoes open season on your flesh. That said, there are travellers who have contracted the disease while on Ko Chang, so malarial prophylactics are probably worth taking. But more important is use of a repellent and mosquito nets at night. See the Health section in the Facts for the Visitor chapter for information about avoiding malaria.

Things to See & Do

Trat town's older homes and shophouses can be found along the canal. You may be able to rent a canoe through Windy Guest House or Foremost Guest House (see Places to Stay later in this section) to paddle around for a water-level look. During high tide it's possible to boat from the canal to the Trat estuary on the Gulf. This can also be done from the Trat River, north of the city; inquire at Tha Chaloemphon (also known simply as *thâa reua* or Boat Pier).

Wat Plai Khlong (Wat Bupharam), 2km west of the town centre, is over 200 years old and worth a visit if you want to kill an hour or so. Several of the wooden buildings date to the late Ayuthaya period, including the wíhǎan, bell tower and *kutis* (monk quarters). The wíhǎan contains a variety of sacred relics and Buddha images dating from the Ayuthaya period and earlier.

Trat is famous for **yellow oil** *(náam-man lěuang)*, a herb-infused liquid touted as a remedy for everything from arthritis to stomach upsets. It's produced by local resident Mae Ang-Kii *(Somthawin Pasananon; ☎ 039 511 935, No 5 Th Rat Uthit; open 10am-4pm)* using a secret pharmaceutical recipe that has been handed down through her Chinese-Thai family for generations.

Among Thais it is said that if you visit Trat and don't leave with a couple of bottles of Mae Ang-Kii's yellow oil, you really haven't been to Trat. The stuff is available direct from her house or at NP Guest House, as well as all the pharmacies in town.

Farther afield, **Ban Nam Chiaw**, about 8km from Trat, is a mostly Muslim village where one of the main industries is the handweaving of hemispherical straw hats called *ngôp*, the traditional Khmer rice farmer's hat.

Markets Of Trat's several markets, the largest are the new day market beneath the municipal shopping centre off Th Sukhumvit, the old day market off Th Tat Mai and the day market next to the air-con bus office; the latter becomes a night market in the evening. Look for eccentricities like deep-fried lizards.

Organised Trips

Windy Guest House can arrange local day trips to the Trat River estuary if enough people are interested. The estuary trips leave by boat from the canal in town to the Trat estuary to gather clams (in season) – the price depends on the number of people. It's not clear how long this will last, however, as locals claim that the number of clams has dropped sharply in the last few years.

Places to Stay

Trat The town has a small but reliable guesthouse scene.

Windy Guest House (☎ 039 523 644, 64 Th Thana Charoen) Singles/doubles 80/100B. The friendly Windy consists of a traditional Thai wooden house with a porch built on stilts over the canal and a cosy outdoor lounge area with a small library, travel information and games. Ask about borrowing canoes for exploring the canal; there's no charge for guests, depending on availability and who's managing the guesthouse at the time.

Foremost Guest House (☎ 039 511 923, 19/51 Th Thana Charoen) Dorm beds/singles/doubles 50/80/120B. Near the canal, this offers rooms upstairs in an old shophouse; bathrooms are shared but clean, and a hot shower is available. The staff are a good source of current info on travel to Cambodia from Trat.

Kudos goes to both Windy and Foremost for encouraging guests to tap drinking water from refillable, recyclable containers for a charge of only 1B per litre – a considerable saving over the cost of a typical plastic bottle of drinking water, not to mention the environmental merit.

NP Guest House (☎ *039 512 270, 8/10 Trok Yai Awn*) Bed in 3-bed dorm 60B, singles/doubles 150/200B. NP is down a quiet lane (a soi that is a south-west continuation of Th Tat Mai), Th Lak Meuang; it's a short walk from the main day and night markets as well as local bus stops. It's basically an old wooden shophouse with the downstairs level glassed-in. Thai and Western food is available.

Most of the hotels in Trat are along or just off Th Sukhumvit.

Trat Inn (☎ *039 511 028, 1–5 Th Sukhumvit*) Rooms 110-190B. Though housed in a run-down concrete shell, this place is noted for its friendly staff.

Sukhumvit Inn (☎ *039 512 151, 234 Th Sukhumvit*) Rooms 140-180B. Small and friendly, the Sukhumvit Inn's cheapest air-con rooms are good value.

Trat Hotel (*Meuang Trat;* ☎ *039 511 091, 40 Th Vichit Chanya*) Rooms with fan 220-500B, with air-con 400B. More comfortable than any of the previous options, and the only hotel in town with a lift, the renovated Trat Hotel, off Th Sukhumvit next to the main market, has standard rooms.

Ban Pu Resort (☎/*fax 039 512 355, 199 Th Trat-Laem Sok*) Bungalow with 1-bedroom unit 1200B, with 6 beds 2600B, with 2 bedrooms 3400B. Eleven kilometres south-east of town at Laem Sok, the Ban Pu Resort stands adjacent to Suan Puu, a famous seafood restaurant and crab farm. It has large, well-appointed wooden bungalows connected by a boardwalk surrounding a large crab pond. All bungalows come with air-con, TV and a fridge. There are also deluxe VIP two-bedroom bungalows with TV, VCR and private karaoke room, and there's a health club on the premises. It's a 20B, 15-minute săwngthăew ride from town. Ban Pu can arrange speedboat transport to Ko Chang and other Trat islands for 6000B to 8000B, including life-jackets and snorkelling gear.

Laem Ngop There's usually no reason to stay here because most boats to Ko Chang leave in the morning and early afternoon and it's only 20km from Trat. However, there are a couple of good accommodation choices.

Chut Kaew Guest House (☎ *039 597 088, 29 Muu 1*) Beds 80B. A five-minute walk from the harbour on the right is this guesthouse, with somewhat dated information (including hiking info for Ko Chang) available in thick notebooks compiled by guests. Rooms with bamboo-thatch walls are relatively clean; facilities are shared. Food and laundry services are available.

PI Guest House (*19/5 Muu 1*) Singles/doubles 70/120B. About 100m from the road, this is a clean place with large rooms in a Thai house; it's usually closed during the June to November rainy season. All rooms have one double bed.

Laem Ngop Inn (☎ *039 597 044, fax 039 597 144, 19/14 Muu 1*) Bungalows with fan, phone & TV 300B, with air-con 450B, with fridge, bathtub & hot water 600B. This has clean, concrete bungalows, each with a separate garage.

Paradise Inn (☎ *039 597 131, 9/5 Muu 1*) Bungalows 400-650B. Bungalows of wood and concrete are laid out in a garden-like compound.

Places to Eat

With all the markets in Trat, you're hardly ever more than 50m away from something good to eat. The *indoor municipal market* beneath the shopping centre has a food section with cheap, good noodle and rice dishes from early morning to early evening. A good spot for a cheap breakfast is the ancient *coffee stand* in the old day market on Th Tat Mai.

In the evenings, there's a good *night market* next to the air-con bus station. On the Trat River in the northern part of town is a small but atmospheric *night market* – a good choice for long, leisurely meals. Trat is a good town for seafood, which is cheaper here than in Bangkok or in more touristed cities around the country (it's not the international tourists who drive up the seafood prices but the Thais, who spend huge sums of money eating out).

Jiraporn Breakfast (☎ *039 511 335, 36 Th Vichit Chanya*) Dishes 20-40B. One of the longest-running Thai-Chinese restaurants in town is this small cafe-style place a few doors from the Trat Hotel, where a small crowd of older regulars hang out over tea and coffee every morning. As it's mostly a breakfast place, the main menu offerings are toast and eggs with ham, *jók* and *khâo tôm* but it can also do fried rice or noodles.

Nam Chok (☎ *039 512 389, 3/1 Th Wiwatthana*) Dishes 30-50B. Nam Chok, a tin-roofed, Christmas light-trimmed open-air restaurant on the corner of Soi Butnoi and Th Wiwatthana is another local institution.

Raan Joh (*90 Th Lak Meuang*) Lunch 20-30B. Open lunchtime only, this place is worth finding. There is no roman-script sign and the number is near impossible to see, so look for the only place making *khànŏm beûang,* a Khmer vegie crepe prepared in a wok. It also does other local specialities and is very inexpensive.

Saeng Fah (☎ *039 511 222, 157–9 Th Sukhumvit*) Dishes 30-100B. A good mid-range restaurant, the air-con Saeng Fah has a large menu with Thai specialities. The food is good, and there are plenty of seafood dishes. Try the 'jally fish soup' or 'bloody clam salad'. It also serves breakfast, when you might (or might not) want to try the house speciality – 'rice with curdled pig's blood'.

Suan Puu (*Crab Farm; Ban Laem Hin*) The best place in the whole province for seafood is Suan Puu, on the way to Laem Sok, 11km south-east of town (a 20B sǎwngthǎew ride each way). Tables are atmospherically arranged on wooden piers over Ao Meuang Trat (Trat Bay). All seafood is served fresh; crab, raised on the premises, is of course the house speciality and prices are moderate to medium-high (but still considerably cheaper than

Bangkok). The menu is in Thai only, so bring along a Thai friend to translate.

Laem Ngop At the Laem Ngop pier there are two good seafood restaurants.

Saengchan Restaurant (☎ *039 597 198, 99/3 Muu 1*) Dishes 30-60B. Saengchan, on the right in front of the pier, doesn't have great food but many travellers wait here for minibuses to Trat, which connect with air-con buses to Bangkok.

Nearby are several rustic seafood places with views of the sea and islands.

Ruan Talay (☎ *039 597 092, 148/2 Soi Sukhaphiban 2*) Dishes 30-80B. One of the more popular spots with local Thais and Thai tourists is the inexpensive Ruan Talay, a wooden place on stilts over the water.

Also good are *Kung Luang Seafood* (☎ *039 597 025, 133/1 Soi Sukhaphiban 2*), *Tamnak Chang* (*133/3 Soi Sukhaphiban 2*) and *Krua Rim Thaleh* (*199/9 Soi Krom Luang*), all moderately priced.

Getting There & Away

Bangkok Buses between Trat and Bangkok cost 180B air-con (132B 2nd class, without toilet) or 113B ordinary and use Bangkok's Eastern bus terminal. The trip takes five to six hours one way by air-con bus, or about eight hours by ordinary bus. Three bus companies operate a Trat to Bangkok service; Sahamit-Cherdchai, on Th Sukhumvit near the Trat Hotel and night market, has the best and most frequent (12 a day) air-con buses to Bangkok.

Chanthaburi Ordinary buses between Chanthaburi and Trat cost 32B and leave every half-hour between 6am and 2.30pm and at 3.45pm, 4.20pm and 5.30pm. The 66km trip takes about 1½ hours.

You can also take the quicker share taxis between Trat and Chanthaburi for 60B per person – these take around 45 minutes. During the middle of the day, however, it may take up to an hour to gather the seven passengers necessary for a departure; try to schedule your departure from Trat between 7am and 9am or 4pm and 6pm for the shortest wait.

Laem Ngop Share taxis to Laem Ngop leave Trat from a stand along Th Sukhumvit next to the municipal market; these cost 20B per person shared or 150B to charter. They depart regularly throughout the day, but after dark you will have to charter. Travel agents at the Laem Ngop pier arrange daily minibuses to Th Khao San in Bangkok (11am departure, 350B, five to six hours); Pattaya (1pm departure, 350B, three hours); and Ban Pae (11am departure, 200B, two hours).

Khlong Yai, Hat Lek & Bo Rai Săwng-thăew and share taxis to Khlong Yai cost 35B per person (400B charter) and take about 45 minutes. The săwngthăew fare from Khlong Yai to Hat Lek is 30B (200B charter) for the 16km trip; these taxis leave from the back of the municipal market. Motorcycle taxis are also available between Hat Lek and Khlong Yai for 50B. A door-to-door minibus to Bo Rai is 50B.

Getting Around

Săamláw around town should cost 10B per person. Small săwngthăew cost 5B per person on a share basis or 30B to 40B for the whole vehicle.

KO CHANG NATIONAL MARINE PARK

อุทยานแห่งชาติเกาะช้าง

Forty-seven of the islands off Trat's coastline belong to a national park named after **Ko Chang** (Elephant Island), which at 492 sq km is Thailand's second largest island after Phuket. The entire park officially encompasses 192 sq km of land surface, and 458 sq km of sea. Ko Chang itself is about 70% undisturbed island rainforest – the best preserved in Thailand, perhaps in all South-East Asia – with steep hills and cliffs rising to the 744m Khao Jom Prasat. Beach forest and mangrove are also found in abundance. Many repeat visitors to Thailand who have been to all the islands reckon that Ko Chang is probably the most beautiful. The jungle-covered mountains – wispy with mist at some times of the year – remind many of

Maui. Ko Chang also attracts an authentic Bohemian/Rasta-type of crowd of Thais that are quite unlike the poser variety found at islands in the South.

Notable wildlife includes the stump-tailed macaque, small Indian civet, Javan mongoose, monitor lizard, water monitor, Burmese and reticulated pythons, king cobra, barking deer and wild pig. Avian species include Pacific reef egret, nightjar, green imperial pigeon, white-winged tern, blue-winged pitta, hooded pitta and three hornbill species. An endemic amphibian, the Ko Chang frog *(Rana kohchang)* is also found here.

Other major islands in the park include Ko Kut and Ko Mak. Ko Chang is ringed with small bays and beaches, among them Ao Khlong Son, Hat Sai Khao, Ao Khlong Phrao, Hat Kaibae, Ao Bang Bao and Ao Salak Phet. Near each of these bays are small villages.

Until rather recently there wasn't a single paved road on Ko Chang, only red dirt roads between Khlong Son and Hat Kaibae on the west coast of the island, and between Khlong Son and Ban Salak Phet on the eastern side, plus walking trails passable by motorcycle from Kaibae to Bang Bao and Salak Kok to Salak Phet. A paved section now exists between Ban Dan Mai, north to Khlong Son and along the western side of the island to Ban Bang Bao. Trat authorities say the island will have a paved ring road within the next few years. Electricity now comes from the mainland to the northern part of the island via a cable beneath the sea, and power lines will probably continue to follow the sealing of the roads around the island.

A combination of steep terrain and permanent streams creates several scenic waterfalls. A series of three falls along the stream of Khlong Mayom in the interior of the island, **Than Mayom Falls**, can be reached via Tha Than Mayom on the eastern coast. The waterfall closest to the shore can be climbed in about 45 minutes via a well-marked footpath. The view from the top is quite good and there are two inscribed stones bearing the initials of Rama VI and Rama VII nearby. The second waterfall is about 500m farther

EASTERN GULF COAST

east along Khlong Mayom and the third is about 3km from the first. At the third waterfall is another inscribed stone, this one with the initials of Rama V. At the lower levels are public picnic areas.

A smaller waterfall on the west coast, **Khlong Phu Falls**, can be visited from Ao Khlong Phrao (45 minutes on foot) or from Hat Kaibae (one hour) by following Khlong Phrao 2km inland. Or pedal a bicycle along the main dirt road until you see the sign on the eastern side of the road. Ride up to the restaurant near the falls, from where it is only a 15-minute walk to the falls themselves. A pool beneath the falls is a good spot for a refreshing swim, and it is possible to stay in the bungalows or camp here.

On **Ko Kut** you'll find beaches mostly along the western side, at Hat Khlong Chao, Hat Khlong Yai Kii and Hat Tapho. A dirt road runs between Ban Khlong Hin Dam, the island's main village on the west coast, and Ao Salat along the north-east shore. Other villages on the island include Ban Ta Poi, Bang Ao Salat, Ban Laem Kluai, Bang Khlong Phrao and Ban Lak Uan. Tan Sanuk Falls and Khlong Chao offer inland water diversions. The nearby small islands of Ko Rang and Ko Rayang have good coral in spots. Ko Kut can be reached from Khlong Yai on the mainland or from Ko Mak.

Ko Mak, the smallest of the three main islands, has a beach along the north-west bay and possibly others as yet undiscovered. Monsoon forest covers 30% of the island while coconut plantations take up another 60%. A few tractors or jeeps travel along the single paved road, which leads from the pier to the main village. It is possible to rent motorbikes and organise diving trips from the resorts on the island.

Ko Wai has some of the best coral and is excellent for snorkelling and diving. The island has one bungalow operation. **Ko Kham** is also recommended for underwater explorations; accommodation is available. **Ko Laoya** has natural attributes similar to those at Ko Wai, with one rather expensive place to stay. The tiny **Ko Rang** archipelago, south-west of Ko Chang, is a primary nesting ground for the endangered hawksbill sea turtle.

As with other national marine parks in Thailand, park status versus resort development is a hot issue. On Ko Chang, so far, everyone seems to be in agreement about what is park land and what isn't. Any land that was planted before the conferral of park status in 1982 can be privately deeded, bought, sold and developed – this includes many beach areas used for coconut plantations, or about 15% of the island. The Royal Forestry Department makes regular flights over the island to check for encroachment on the 85% belonging to the national park – mostly in the interior – and they are said to be very strict with interlopers.

Information

The park headquarters are divided into four units, found at Than Mayom, Khlong Son, Tha Khlong Phlu and Salak Phet. All offer roughly the equivalent information, but the Than Mayom visitors centre features informative displays on park flora and fauna.

Entry fees (adult/child 200/100B) are collected at any one of the four park headquarters. Be sure to keep your receipt as rangers may demand payment from visitors who don't have one.

Money There is no bank on Ko Chang, but moneychangers will change US dollars and travellers cheques at very unfavourable rates. The only post office is near the pier at Khlong Son, where there is a telegram and international telephone service. On Hat Sai Khao and Hat Kaibae, a few places offer international phone service at very high rates.

Medical Services Ko Chang Hospital is located at Ban Don Mai and can handle most minor emergencies. Another choice is the hospital at Laem Ngop on the mainland. There are health clinics at Khlong Son, Hat Sai Khao and Hat Kaibae.

Dangers & Annoyances The beaches along the western side of the island are often posted with warnings about dangerous riptides and undercurrents during the monsoon season (June to October). If a beach is posted, you shouldn't go in deeper than your knees.

The local police headquarters is located in Ban Dan Mai and every few months the police do a round of raids on the island's accommodation. Get caught and you'll have to cough up a lot of money to stay out of jail.

Nudity and topless sunbathing are forbidden by law in Ko Chang National Marine Park; this includes all beaches on Ko Chang, Ko Kut, Ko Mak, Ko Kradat etc.

Hiking

In general the more interesting hikes can be found in the southern half of the island where there are fewer roads. At the northern end you can walk from Khlong Son to Hat Sai Khao in about 1½ to two hours; from Hat Sai Khao to Hat Khlong Phrao in about two hours; and from Hat Khlong Phrao to Hat Kaibae in about two hours. All three are straightforward walks along the main road.

If you're looking for more of a grunt, just head for the interior – the steep, forested hills will have you sweating in no time. A footpath connects Khlong Phrao on the west coast with Khlong Mayom on the east, but this all-day cross-island route shouldn't be undertaken without a local guide. The White House Bakery at Hat Sai Khao has information on guides.

Don't try Bang Bao to Salak Phet unless you're an experienced tropical hiker with moderate orienteering skills – there's a lot of up-and-down and many interconnecting trails. A Swede who hiked the entire perimeter of the island suggested that for this part of the island you carry a note in Thai reading 'I would like to go to Salak Phet. I like very much to walk in the jungle and have done it before. Please show me the start of this trail'.

If you don't get lost, this hike will take four to six hours; should you decide to attempt it, carry enough food and water for an overnight, just in case.

If you do get lost, climb the nearest hilltop and try to locate the sea or a stream to get a bearing on where you are. Following any stream will usually take you either to a village or to the sea. Then you can either follow the coast or ask directions. This advice is also good for hiking anywhere across the island, as it is very easy to get lost on the many intersecting, unmarked trails.

At the south-eastern end of Ao Bang Bao, around a headland that leads to Ao Salak Phet, is a beautiful and secluded beach, **Hat Wai Chek**.

On the eastern side of the island it's a one-hour walk between Dan Mai and Than Mayom, two hours between Dan Mai and Sai Thong (or Khlong Son and Sai Thong). Salak Kok to Salak Phet is straightforward and takes around three hours. The **estuary** at Ao Salak Kok's western end boasts one of the best mangrove systems in Thailand, though like other coastal wetlands it's threatened by increased shrimp farming.

A hike around the entire island can be done at a comfortable pace in a week to 10 days. Remember to carry plenty of water and watch out for snakes – a few poisonous varieties live on the island.

Diving & Snorkelling

Ko Chang and its vicinity is a new frontier relative to other marine locales in Thailand. With regard to climate and visibility, November to April is the main diving season. The better dive sites are at islets and seamounts off the south-western tip of the island. **Hin Luuk Bat** and **Hin Laap** are both coral-encrusted seamounts with depths of around 18m to 20m. Nearby **Ko Rang Yai** gets scenic at 10m to 25m, while **Hin Phrai Nam** has whitetip and reef sharks to around 20m. A small islet near Ko Rang Yai's northern tip, **Ko Kra**, has good snorkelling in depths of 4m or 5m near the islet's southern end. The islets around Ko Rang are favoured nesting grounds for sea turtles – this is one of your better opportunities to see them in Thailand.

South-west of Ao Salak Phet, reef-fringed **Ko Wai** features a good variety of colourful hard and soft corals at depths of 6m to 15m.

Near the mouth of Ao Salak Phet, at the south-eastern tip of the island, lies the wreck of a Thai warship at a depth of 15m; the ship was supposedly sunk by the French in 1941 during a dispute over whether these islands belonged to Thailand or to French-colonised Cambodia. According to Thai history there should be a second wreck nearby but divers have yet to report on it. This site should not be dived without a guide.

Dive Services Ko Chang Divers has two branches, one next to Bamboo Bungalows and another near Aranee's Resort, both at Hat Sai Khao. Each specialises in PADI certification for novice divers. Prices for instruction in beginning and advanced diving are US$70 to US$250 per person. Instruction material is available in English, French, German, Italian and Japanese. Dive trips typically include two dives with all guiding, transport, equipment and food, and cost US$50. SeaHorse Dive Centre, located at the Kaibae Hut Resort at Kaibae, has similar instruction from 6500B to 8000B. All-inclusive dive trips cost 1200B to 1500B per person. Eco-Divers, located in the Banpu Koh Chang Resort at Hat Sai Khao, offers diving instruction for US$70 to US$280 and dive trips for US$45 to US$60.

Other Activities

Some of the guesthouses at Hat Sai Khao and to a lesser extent at Hat Kaibae rent kayaks, sailboards, masks and snorkels, and boogie boards. Mountain bikes can be rented for 150B per day at several places on the island, including Muk Hut Restaurant and Ban Nuna's Restaurant at Hat Sai Khao and Coral Resort at Hat Kaibae.

Several bungalow operations along Ko Chang's west coast beaches offer day trips to nearby islands: eg, 150B per person to Ko Yuak or Ko Man; 300B to Ko Rang, Ko Wai, Ko Khlam or Ko Mak; and 1000B to Ko Kut. Overnight trips can also be arranged and cost 1500B to 2000B per person.

Places to Stay – Ko Chang

Many beach huts on the island have only been open about eight years and standards vary quite a bit. Some of the older, simpler bungalow complexes are in the process of being upgraded. A few close down during the rainy season (June to October), but as the island has become more popular most places stay open and offer low season prices, sometimes as low as 40% of the normal rate. Dur-

ing the rainy season, boats usually only go as far as Ao Sapparot (Pineapple Bay), Dan Mai and Than Mayom – the surf farther south along the west coast can be impassable during heavy rains.

Even during dry months, the trend now is for all boats to drop off at Ao Sapparot so that visitors can continue on to the beaches by săwngthăew.

West Coast As the island's better beaches are along the west coast, this is where most of the beach accommodation is located. Most huts and bungalows consist of one double bed plus a mosquito net. In recent years many places have screened-in their windows and taken down the mosquito nets – a problem if doors are left open while the bungalows are being cleaned. If you want to avoid mosquito bites, it's best to bring your own net and lots of repellent. If you are staying longer than a few days all places will discount their rates, even in high season. Most of the island now has electricity; if your bungalow isn't on the grid yet, kerosene or gas lanterns are usually provided. Only a few places have music and, blessedly, even fewer have TVs and videos.

At the northern tip of the island is the largest village, Khlong Son, which has a network of piers at the mouth of the khlong, a wát, a school, several noodle shops and a health clinic.

Manee Guest House Rooms 80-200B. On the northern cape of Ao Khlong Son, Manee offers three bungalows divided into 12 rooms, some with private bath.

Premvadee Resort (☎ 039 597 032) Bungalows 500-800B, houses with bath & fan 1500B. This has 18 rustic bungalows with electricity, as well as one large hall that sleeps 30 people for 6000B (in case you're bringing along a boy-scout troop).

It's 5km from Khlong Son to Hat Sai Khao (White Sand Beach).

White Sand Beach Resort Huts 150B, bungalows with bath 250-600B. At the lower end of the beach, well off the road and separated from other Hat Sai Khao bungalow developments by a couple of small rocky points, is this nicely landscaped

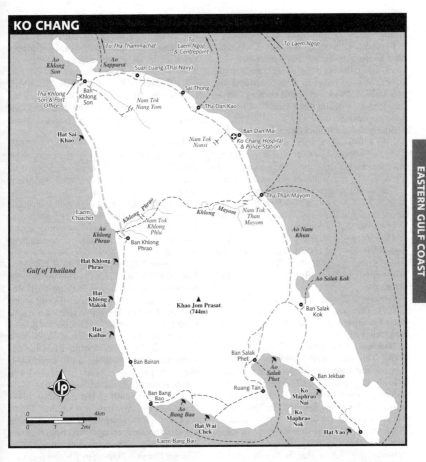

KO CHANG

Gulf of Thailand

EASTERN GULF COAST

resort where there is a long row of simple thatched huts along the beach (no fan, shared bath). Behind these are wooden bungalows (shared bath) and more upmarket tiled-roof bungalows.

Rock Sand Bungalow Bungalows with shared bath 150-200B, with fan & bath 300-500B, with air-con 1000B. This has a few wooden bungalows on a rocky outcrop surrounded by beach on both sides. There's a nice two-storey restaurant/bar with hammocks on the premises.

KC Sand Beach Bungalows 250B. Bamboo-thatch huts are located behind a

row of palms. KC's Pyramid Herbal Sauna costs 200B per person. The herbal sauna is looking rather forlorn these days, but at night its beachside bar blasts techno music onto the beach until 2am – avoid it if you've come for peace and quiet.

Yakah Bungalows Bungalows 180-400B. This has clean bamboo huts with spacious verandas. A swing set for children and a well-stocked library are available to guests.

Arunee's Resort Rooms with bath & fan 250-300B. Across the road from Yakah, this place offers rooms in a wooden hotel-style building. Arunee's offers international call service, currency exchange, and can arrange visas for Cambodia and Vietnam.

Farther south along Hat Sai Khao was once a string of cheap and popular huts that have gradually gone upscale (and up in price) over the past few years. Around the originals a host of new-comers have sprouted up, making this beach Ko Chang's most populated.

Saeng Tawan Resort Bungalows with fan & bath 400-600B. Sturdy bungalows with a choice of wooden or concrete models. There is a minimart in the compound and a couple of motorbike rental places across the road.

Cookie Bungalow Bungalows with fan & bath 500-700B, air-con 800-1000B. Cookie has friendly staff, as well as a large and popular beachside restaurant.

Mac Bungalow Bungalows with bath 600-700B, air-con 1500B. This place has a friendly and efficient staff. There's also a minimart conveniently located on the premises.

Tantawan Cottages with bath & fan 500-1500B. This place has pink-coloured brick cottages where there were once bamboo huts. Ah, progress.

Bamboo (☎/fax 039 552 780) Huts 250-300B. This place has simple but well-built bamboo and thatch huts with shared facilities. There's a branch of Ko Chang Divers here.

Sabay Beach Bungalow Cottages in high season 500-1000B, low season 250-450B. South of Cookie on the beach, this features three rows of cottages that descend in price as you back away from the sand. The accompanying Sabay Bar is the local full moon party headquarters.

Koh Chang Lagoon Resort Bungalows with fan & bath 900B, units with air-con 1600-2000B. This place is more upmarket than the rest. Sensibly, the cheaper fan bungalows are actually closer to the beach than the air-con units.

Apple Huts with fan & bath 250-450B. Apple finishes off this stretch of beach. Upscale wooden huts have roomy verandas furnished with chairs and tables. Apple's something of a Thai-Rasta hang out – expect to listen to Bob Marley tunes at bong-rattling volume.

Cross a stream and continue south, moving away from the more densely packed huts, and you'll come to a couple of places favoured by those into a quieter scene.

Best Garden Beach Resort (☎ 039 529 632) Rooms with fan & bath 150-300B, cabins with air-con 1000B. This has rooms in a wooden complex. The semi-outdoor restaurant does seafood barbecues in the evenings.

Alena Resort Huts with fan 150-250B, with bath 600-800B, with air-con 1500-2000B. Set above a rocky area with no beach, Sunsai has friendly staff and well-kept, well-separated huts.

Moonlight Resort (☎ 039 597 198) Bungalows 150-1500B. Moonlight prices its tidy bungalows of wood or concrete by row. There's a pleasant sala on the beach to relax in.

Ploaloma Cliff Resort (☎ 039 597 060) Bungalows with bath & fan 700-900B, with air-con 1500-1800B. The Plaloma Cliff Resort is spread over a rocky cliff a bit south of Moonlight on the other side of a rocky headland. It has quiet and spacious tile and cement bungalows – shades of Ko Samui. On the cliff's highest point, Plaloma has some very nice bamboo-and-thatch huts; the interspersed coconut palms and sea views are additional pluses.

About 4km south of Hat Sai Khao (9km from Khlong Son) is Ao Khlong Phrao (Coconut Bay). It stretches south of Laem Chaichet and encompasses the canal Khlong Phrao as well as its namesake village, Ban Khlong Phrao (12km from Khlong Son).

Coconut Beach Bungalows Bungalows with fan 200B, with bath 500B, air-con 2000-2500B. Near Ban Chaichet south of Ao Khlong Phrao is Coconut Beach, where there are wooden or concrete bungalows. The bungalows are well kept, though somewhat close together.

Chaichet Bungalows Huts 200B, with fan & bath 500B, air-con 900-1200B. On the northern side of the canal is Chaichet, which has A-frame wooden huts and concrete bungalows. The bungalows are strung out along Laem Chaichet, a gently curving cape, though there's no beach here.

Klong Plow (Phrao) Resort (☎ *039 597 216, 039 597 106*) 'Standard' bungalows with air-con 1400-1600, 'deluxe' with air-con 1600B. Also on the north bank of Khlong Phrao, this place has gone upscale since the last edition. If you can't afford the bungalows, you can rent a tent for 200B, or pitch your own for 50B.

Ko Chang Resort (☎ *039 538 055*) Bungalows 1900-2800B. About a 10-minute walk farther south along the beach from Coconut Beach is the pricey Ko Chang Resort. Upmarket bungalows include all the usual comforts with air-con, hot water and satellite TV. The majority of guests are Thai businesspeople on vacation, many on incentive travel packages. There's a 20% discount on weekdays. The resort owns the Centrepoint pier in Laem Ngop; private boats between that pier and the resort are available for 200B per person.

It is possible to cross the river in a long-tail boat, but you need to call for one on the southern bank. If you are staying at the PSS Thaleh huts the service is only 10B; if you're staying anywhere else it's 20B.

Thaleh Bungalow (*PSS Bungalow*) Huts 150-200B. This place has yet more simple wooden huts with thatched roofs and shared facilities, and price depends on the size. There's a good little restaurant on the premises.

KP Bungalows Huts without bath 150-200B, with fan & bath 600-800B. About a 10-minute walk farther south from PSS, near Wat Ban Khlong Phrao, KP has well-spaced basic thatched huts, and a large wooden bungalow. It rents motorcycles, boats and snorkelling equipment, and can organise trips to nearby islands.

Hobby Hut Huts 150-200B. About 700m past the turn-off for Khlong Phu Falls, off the main road in Ban Khlong Phrao, is the secluded Hobby Hut. A favourite with Thais associated with the music and art business, Hobby Hut has only three simple huts. Rates depend on length of stay and number of guests. It's 300m to the nearest beach; a small inland lagoon offers canoeing. There's live music on some evenings.

Around another headland to the south are two beach areas separated by a canal – Hat Khlong Makok and Hat Kaibae (15km south of Khlong Son). These beaches tend to disappear during high tide but they're OK – lots of coconut palms.

Magic (☎ *039 597 242*) Bungalows with fan 300B, with bath 600B, air-con 1200-1600B. Magic has a pier, telephone service and offers scuba diving tours. The owner has a private boat service from Laem Ngop so is able to funnel many passengers directly to this beach. Magic's best feature is its restaurant built over the bay.

Chokdee Bungalow Huts with shared facilities 100-200B, with fan & bath 800-1500B. Set amid coconut palms but with no beach to speak of, this has clean, nice thatched huts or concrete bungalows.

Next south on Hat Kaibae proper is an area that has become quite developed, with a pier and bungalows with generator-powered electricity.

Coral Resort Bungalows with bath & fan 500-600B. This is set amid a bumper crop of coconut palms. It also has an international telephone service.

Nang Nual Bungalow Bungalows 250-350B. Nang Nual has new natural-looking bungalows. The resort restaurant serves Thai and French dishes. Canoes are available for rent. This area is a bit trashed out in places but otherwise OK.

Kaibae Hut Bungalows with bath 500-1500B, air-con, TV & fridge 2500B. Kaibae, on the southern side of the khlong, has a nicely laid-out restaurant and fair bungalows, plus a bit of a beach even at high tide; bungalows are nice and clean. It's quiet, too, and has a security gate that's locked at night. SeaHorse Dive Centre has an office here and offers dive trips and instruction during the dry season. Conveniently, there's an Internet access centre next door.

There is more of a beach down towards the southern end of Hat Kaibae.

KaiBae Beach Bungalow Huts with shared facilities 150-300B, with bath 500B. This has clean, well-separated huts and the grounds are tidy and well kept.

Porn Bungalow Huts with shared facilities 150-200B, with fan & bath 300-350B. Porn is for party-goers. Bungalows are nothing special, but there's a nightclub on the premises that's quite popular.

Sea View Resort (☎ 039 529 022) Bungalows with fan & bath 900-1200B, with air-con 1700B, bungalow for 10 people 3700B. Comfortable A-frame bungalows on grounds that are leafy and nicely landscaped. There are also hotel rooms with a wide range of amenities including TV.

Siam Bay Resort Bungalows with fan & bath 300-800B. The last place on the beach is the secluded and friendly Siam Bay. At low tide you can walk out to Ko Man Nai opposite (not to be confused with the Ko Man Nai off the Rayong Coast).

Tree House Lodge Huts with shared facilities 150-200B, with bath 220B. A 30-minute walk along the path to Ao Bang Bao, behind the Siam Bay Resort, will take you to Tree House Lodge in a rocky area near a secluded white-sand beach. It has simple thatched huts on stilts in a coconut grove. There is a very good restaurant and a small library. During the high season the Lodge operates a taxi boat from Laem Ngop that costs 50B per person.

Along the coast south to Laem Bai Laan there are a number of newish cheapies offering rustic huts and solitude, including *Sunset Hut* (80-150B), *Happy Hut* (150-250B) and *Jungle Hut* (100-150B).

South Coast This is the place to go if you want to get a feel for the life of Thai fisherfolk or to explore beautiful jungle paths and nearby islets.

Bang Bao Blue Wave Bungalows with bath 180-200B. With thatched huts and a contingent of local hipsters. Electricity is on from 6pm to 10pm. The owner also has a boat for hire.

You can walk between Bang Bao and Hat Kaibae, but since the road has been completed it's also possible to bike it or take a săwngthăew. The walk takes a couple of hours.

The next bay along the coast, Ao Salak Phet, features several possibilities.

Salakpet Seafood Restaurant & Resort (☎ 039 521 751) Rooms with air-con & bath 1200-1400B. At the head of the road near the pier, this has clean rooms built over the water. It's really oriented to people on package tours, though you could book a room by calling ahead.

Haad Sai Yao Resort (*Long Beach Resort*; ☎ 039 511 145) Huts 150B. Closed July to December. This is very secluded near the end of the long cape to the south-east of Ao Salak Phet; it has well-made huts with electricity.

Tantawan House Huts 100-200B. Right at the tip of the cape, the friendly Tantawan is on a rocky outcrop with 12 huts. The beach is only a two-minute swim away. To get here take a boat from Ao Salak Phet for 30B or hike for 20 minutes from Haad Sai Yao Resort.

A partially sealed road leads from Ao Sapparot all the way to Ban Salak Phet; săwngthăew meet the Ao Sapparot and Than Mayom boats. The village itself is very spread out; the main road terminates at the Salakpet Seafood Restaurant, from where there are smaller paths along the southern coast. Power lines also terminate in Ban Salak Phet.

East Coast There are a couple of places to stay near the nicely landscaped national park headquarters at Than Mayom.

Than Mayom Bungalows Houses 500-2200B. Privately managed, opposite the park offices, accommodation ranges from a large, white two-room house to a house that can accommodate 30 people. It has no sign.

Thanmayom Resort Huts 150B. A couple of kilometres north, this rents A-frame huts; there is a pier but no beach to speak of, and since the huts are on the other side of a dusty road from the sea, it's not very inviting.

Koh Chang Cabana Rooms with fan 600B, bungalows with air-con 1500B. This has rooms in a long row-building or separate bungalows. Tour groups are its main clientele.

If you have camping gear, it might be better to hike up and camp near Than Mayom Falls.

The visitors centre contains photo displays with English labels and useful information. At the end of a small pier is a casual *restaurant* with rice and noodle dishes.

Places to Stay – Other Islands

Ko Kut, Ko Mak, Ko Kradat and Ko Kham all feature beach bungalow accommodation. In general these places are quieter and obviously more secluded than their Ko Chang counterparts. The drawbacks are that transport can be a little tricky – though during months of high visitation (December to April) there are daily boats – and the fact that you can't just pack up and walk down the beach to another bungalow if you don't like the one you landed at. Except at the package places, room rates overall are less expensive than on Ko Chang.

From May to November, it's a good idea to call in advance to make sure boat transportation is available. Most close down completely from June to September.

Ko Kut As on Ko Chang, the best beaches are along the west coast, particularly at Hat Tapho. The five bungalow operations on this island are open only from November to May. Three cater to visitors coming on pre-arranged packages that include boat transport, accommodation and meals: *Ko Kut Sai Khao Resort (☎ 039 511 429)*, 1500B; *Kut Island Resort (Bangkok ☎ 023 743 004, 023 756 188)*, 2000-4000B; and *Khlong Hin Hut (☎ 039 530 236)*, 2000-3000B.

Two others, *Ko Kut Cabana (☎ 039 522 955)* and *Khlong Jaow Resort (☎ 039 520 337)*, offer a range of accommodation from 600B for basic huts to nicer bungalows up to 4200B.

Ko Mak On the western bay is *Ko Mak Resort & Cabana (Bangkok ☎ 023 196 714–5)*. Bungalows with fan & bath 350-1400B. This friendly place is amid a coconut and rubber plantation.

TK Huts (☎ 039 521 133) Bungalows 300-1000B. This has bungalows with 'natural air' (no fans).

Ao Khao Resort (☎ 039 538 217) Bun-galows with shared facilities 150B, with fan 350-850B. This resort offers comfortable bungalows with small verandas. Diving equipment and instruction are available. Electricity is on from 6pm to 6am.

Ko Mak Guest House Huts 100-300B. This rents basic huts with verandas near the boat pier to Laem Ngop.

Ko Mak Fantasia Huts with bath 250B. A scuba centre operates here in the high season. Fantasia also rents bikes for exploring the plantations and fishing villages around the island.

Sunshine Resort Bungalows 650B. Over on the eastern side of Ko Mak, this offers nine solid bungalows.

As on Ko Kut, all of the accommodation tends to close during the rainy season.

Ko Kradat The only place for accommodation on the island is *Ko Kradat (Bangkok ☎ 023 682 675)*. Bungalows with air-con 1800B. This can only be booked as a package for two days and one night.

Ko Kham Offering bamboo huts and more upscale bungalows is *Ko Kham Resort*. Huts 100-120B, bungalows 700B. Run by a friendly ex-cop, this resort sponsors a boat that leaves the main Laem Ngop pier daily at 3pm, November to April only.

Ko Wai Accommodation on Ko Wai shuts down during the monsoon and reopens for the high (and dry) season between October and April.

Ko Wai Paradise (☎ 039 597 131) Bungalows with shared facilities 150-300B, with bath 450B. On the western end of the island, this place has sturdy bungalows and a good restaurant.

Ko Wai Pakarang Resort (☎ 039 512 581) Bungalows with bath 500B. On the eastern end of the island, this place has bamboo and thatch huts, and offers discounts on long-term stays.

Places to Eat

Menus at all the bungalows on Ko Chang are pretty similar. On Hat Sai Khao, highest marks this time go to the kitchens at

Apple and *Bamboo* (☎/fax 039 552 780). Several small eateries offer ex-bungalow options along the eastern side of the main road in Hat Sai Khao.

Ban Nuna Restaurant-Cafe Dishes 80-160B. An upstairs place where you sit on cushions, this is good for Thai lunches and dinners, pizza and Western breakfasts.

White House Bakery Dishes 20-40B. Across the road from Sabay Beach Bungalow, this offers a variety of baked goods, fruit shakes and plenty of info on island activities.

Salakpet Seafood Restaurant Mains 60-140B. In the southern part of Ko Chang, at Ao Salak Phet, this serves the very best seafood on the island; prices are moderate.

Getting There & Away

Ko Chang Take a săwngthăew (20B, 25 minutes) from Trat to Laem Ngop on the coast, then a ferry to Ko Chang. In Laem Ngop there are now three piers serving Ko Chang – the main one at the end of the road from Trat, called Tha Laem Ngop; another 4km north-west of Laem Ngop called Tha Ko Chang Centrepoint (operated by Ko Chang Resort); and a newer one called Tha Thammachat at Ao Thammachat, farther west of Laem Ngop.

Tha Laem Ngop (look for the sign that reads Eastern Apex) is the best jumping-off point as there are boats to all the islands from here. Boats go to Tha Dan Kao on Ko Chang year-round; this is the boat most people take. During the high season – roughly December to April – boats depart hourly from 7am to 5pm. For the remainder of the year the schedule is reduced to about every two hours, although departures ultimately depend on weather, number of passengers and any number of other factors. The trip takes one hour and costs 50B per person. You should check on fares in advance – sometimes the boat crews overcharge faràng. At Tha Dan Kao, săwngthăew will be waiting to take you to any of the various beaches along the west coast or to Ao Salak Phet.

One boat leaves Tha Laem Ngop at 3pm daily for the two-hour trip to Hat Sai Khao on Ko Chang's west coast. In the return direction it departs from Hat Sai Khao at 9.30am. The fare is 80B per person.

From the gleaming Tha Ko Chang Centrepoint, there are three or four daily boat departures between 7am and 4pm. The trip takes 45 minutes and costs 30B per person.

The newest way to get to Ko Chang is via a vehicle ferry service from Ao Thammachat. It leaves four times daily; because of the pier's position in relation to the island, and the craft's more powerful engines, the car ferry reaches Ao Sapparot in half an hour. It costs 400B for a vehicle and driver, plus 30B per passenger or pedestrian, to ride the Thammachat ferry. So far custom is for the most part restricted to people doing business on the island but in the future this service could very well supplant the Laem Ngop tourist ferry as well.

There are direct minivans from Th Khao San in Bangkok to Laem Ngop for 250B per person. Although it's no longer the case that the minivans necessarily miss the last boat to Ko Chang, it's better to take a regular bus, spend the night in Trat or Laem Ngop and take your time choosing a boat the next day. Or start out earlier in the day by government tour bus to Trat from Bangkok's Eastern bus terminal, then in Trat catch a săwngthăew to Laem Ngop in time for the afternoon boats.

Ko Mak During the November to May dry season, boats to Ko Mak leave daily from the Laem Ngop pier at 3pm (8am in the reverse direction); the fare is 180B per person and the trip takes around 3½ hours. During the rainy season the departure schedule is cut back to every other day – except in high surf when boats may be cancelled altogether for several days.

Ko Kut Most people get to Ko Kut from Ko Mak, a 100B per person boat ride. There are no direct boats from Laem Ngop to Ko Kut, but the 10am boat to Ko Mak (leaves Monday, Thursday and Saturday) carries on to Ko Kut after making a stop at Ko Mak and departing at 1pm. The cost is 170B and the trip takes three hours. Return boats from

Ko Kut to Laem Ngop via Ko Mak leave on Friday and Saturday at noon.

Although it's a less dependable way to get there (but more adventurous for sure), two or three fishing boats a week go to Ko Kut from the Tha Chaloemphon on the Trat River towards the eastern side of Trat. They'll take passengers for around 100B to 150B per person. Similar boats leave slightly less frequently (six to eight times a month) from Ban Nam Chiaw, a village about halfway between Trat and Laem Ngop. Departure frequency and times from either pier depend on the weather and the fishing season – it's best to inquire ahead of time. The boats take around six hours to reach Ko Kut.

Coconut boats go to Ko Kut once or twice a month from a pier next to the slaughterhouse in town – same fare and trip duration as the fishing boats.

If you want to charter a boat to Ko Kut from the mainland, the best place to do so is from Ban Ta Neuk, near the 68km marker south-east of Trat, about 6km before Khlong Yai off Rte 318. A long-tail boat, capable of carrying up to 10 people, can be chartered here for 1500B. Travel time is about one hour. During the rainy season these boats may suspend service.

Other Islands Daily boats to Ko Kham depart from Laem Ngop around 3pm (arriving at 6pm) for 180B. A boat to Ko Wai leaves at 3pm and arrives at 5.30pm, costing 130B. Both boats return the next day at around 8am.

Getting Around

To get from one part of Ko Chang to another you have a choice of săwngthăew, motorbike, mountain bike, boat and walking (see the Hiking entry earlier in this section).

Săwngthăew Săwngthăew meeting the boats at Tha Dan Kao charge 30B per person to Hat Sai Khao, 40B to Hat Kaibae. One săwngthăew per day goes to Ban Bang Bao at 4pm and costs 80B. Between Than Mayom and Ban Salak Phet, the price is around 20B per person.

Motorcycle Bungalow operations along the west coast charge 60B per hour or 400B per day for motorbike hire; elsewhere on the island rental bikes are scarce. The owners claim they have to charge these rates because the island roads are so hard on the bikes.

Boat Charter trips to nearby islands cost 500B to 800B for a half-day, 1000B to 2000B all day, depending on the boat and distance covered. Make sure that the charter includes all 'user fees' for the islands – sometimes the boatmen demand 200B on top of the charter fee for 'using' the beach.

On the southern end of the island, you can charter a long-tail or fishing boat between Hat Kaibae and Ao Bang Bao for 1000B or around 150B per person shared by a boatful of passengers. Similar charters are available between Ao Bang Bao and Ao Salak Phet and Long Beach Bungalows for around 150B.

Boat rides up Khlong Phrao to the falls cost 50B per person and can be arranged through most bungalows.

AROUND TRAT PROVINCE
Trat Beaches

The sliver of Trat Province that extends south-eastward along the Cambodia border is fringed by several Gulf of Thailand beaches. **Hat Sai Ngoen** (Silver Sand Beach) lies just north of the 41km marker off Hwy 3; a billboard says a resort will be constructed here, but so far there's no sign of development. Nearby at the 42km marker is **Hat Sai Kaew** (Crystal Sand Beach) and at the 48km marker **Hat Thap Thim** (Sapphire Beach); neither quite lives up to its fanciful name, though they're OK places to walk along the water's edge or picnic in the shade of casuarina and eucalyptus trees.

The most promising beach is **Hat Ban Cheun**, a long stretch of clean sand near the 63km marker. The 6km road that leads to the beach passes the leftover foundation pillars from a defunct Cambodian refugee camp. There are casuarina and eucalyptus trees, a small restaurant and basic bungalows (200B) set on swampy land behind the beach. Travellers have reported the friendly family that runs the operation to be accommodating.

EASTERN GULF COAST

AROUND TRAT

Khlong Yai
คลองใหญ่

Khlong Yai consists of a cluster of older wooden buildings west of the highway, surrounded by modern structures on both sides of the highway. There's a large market in the centre of town, as well as the moderately priced Suksamlan Hotel and two banks with foreign exchange services. Just south of town is a large shrimp farm.

Suksamlan Hotel (☎ *039 581 109, fax 039 581 311, 623/1 Th Mungkhiri*) Rooms with fan 150B, singles/doubles with air-con 350B. This is an old-fashioned Thai-Chinese-style place, on a street between the market and the highway.

Bang In Villa (☎ *039 581 401, fax 039 581 403, 47 Muu 7, Th Trat-Khlong Yai*) Rooms 150-250B. Out of town a bit off Hwy 3, this has nice but characterless rooms.

See the Trat Getting There & Away section for information on public transport to Khlong Yai and Hat Lek.

Hat Lek to Cambodia
The small Thai border outpost of Hat Lek is the southernmost part on the Trat mainland. Untaxed goods travel back and forth between Cambodia and Thailand at this point; at the small market just before the border crossing, next to the pier for boats travelling to Cambodia, American Budweiser beer and other untaxed contraband is often available.

Opposite Hat Lek on Cambodian turf (Sao Thong) there's a cockfighting arena and casino popular with residents from both sides of the border.

There are two military checkpoints along Hwy 3 between Trat town and Hat Lek. These are serious checkpoints where searches by the military are common, especially since this area between Khlong Yai and Hat Lek was discovered to harbour a clandestine paramilitary force allegedly training to overthrow Vietnam's communist government.

Motorcycle and automobile taxis are available from Hat Lek across the border into Cambodia for 30B and 50B. There is very basic accommodation on the island of Ko Kong in Cambodia. If you plan to continue farther, you can embark on a 4½-hour boat ride (600B) to Sihanoukville. There is only one boat per day to Sihanoukville and it leaves at 8am, so if you don't get across the border early, you'll have to spend a night on Ko Kong. If you want to get from Trat to Sihanoukville in one day, you should be on the 6am minibus to Hat Lek and at the border with passport in hand as soon as it opens at 7am. This border crossing closes at 5pm.

A Cambodian visa is necessary, and obtainable in Bangkok, not at the border. If you are going into Cambodia for a day trip, you might need to have a valid Thai visa on which you can return to Thailand. Nowadays Thailand grants most nationalities a one-month visa on arrival. If you're nationality is not on the instant visa list, you will find yourself stuck in Cambodia.

North-Western Gulf Coast (Phetchaburi to Chumphon)

Heading south from Bangkok, the Gulf of Thailand's western coast undulates along the edges of four provinces (Samut Sakhon, Samut Songkhram, Phetchaburi and Prachuap Khiri Khan) in a south-westerly direction until it makes an abrupt turn to the north-east at the southern end of Chumphon Province, near Surat Thani. Just north of this point lies the Isthmus of Kra, the narrowest point, and official beginning of the Thai-Malay peninsula.

This coastal section has seen little exploration by foreign tourists. There isn't much in the way of beaches until you pass south of Phetchaburi to the low-key seaside resorts of Cha-am, Hua Hin and Chumphon. Away from these small but slowly growing areas, most of the countryside is agricultural and rural; pineapple-growing and fishing are the mainstays of the local population. In terms of everyday costs for food, lodging and public transport, this is one of Thailand's least expensive coastal areas to visit. But in many ways this stretch requires more initiative, since the most interesting shorelines aren't necessarily signposted. Nor do any guided tours or easy-to-book Bangkok minivans reach the majority of them.

PHETCHABURI (PHETBURI)
อ.เมืองเพชรบุรี

postcode 76000 • pop 36,000

Phetchaburi (more commonly known by its short name Phetburi, and sometimes Meuang Phet), 160km south of Bangkok, is worth a visit for its many old temples spanning several centuries; it's a nice cultural stopover on the way to beaches at Cha-am or Hua Hin a bit farther south. Many temples can be seen while taking a circular walk of two or three hours through the city, including: Wat Yai Suwannaram, Wat

Trailok, Wat Kamphaeng Laeng, Wat Phra Suang, Wat Ko Kaew Sutharam and Wat Mahathat. These temples have made very

NORTH-WESTERN GULF COAST

few concessions to the 20th century, let alone the 21st, and thus provide a glimpse of the traditional Siamese urban wát.

Also noteworthy is Khao Wang, just west of the city, which has the remains of a King Mongkut palace and several wát, plus a good view of the city. Phra Ratchawang Ban Peun, a European-style palace built for King Chulalongkorn, as well as the underground Buddhist shrine at the Khao Luang Caves is also worth seeing.

Orientation

If you arrive at the train station, follow the road south-east of the tracks until you come to Thanon (Th) Ratchadamnoen, then turn right. Follow Th Ratchadamnoen south to the second major intersection and turn left towards central Phetchaburi to begin the walking tour. Or take a săamláw (three-wheeled vehicle) from the train station to Chomrut Bridge (Saphan Chomrut) for 20B. If you've come by bus, you'll be getting off very near Khao Wang, and will have to take a săamláw into the centre of town.

Information

Money The Siam Commercial Bank has an exchange office at 2 Th Damnoen Kasem, just south of the post office. Several other banks in the vicinity have foreign exchange and ATMs.

Post & Communications The post office, on the corner of Th Ratwithi and Th Damnoen Kasem, is open from 8.30am to 4.30pm. Upstairs in the same building, an international telephone office is open daily from 7am to 10pm.

Khao Wang & Phra Nakhon Khiri Historical Park
เขาวัง/อุทยานประวัติศาสตร์
พระนครคีรี

Just west of the city, a short walk or săamláw ride from the bus station, is Khao Wang. Cobblestone paths lead up and around the hill, which is studded with wát and various components of King Mongkut's palace on

PHETCHABURI (PHETBURI)

PLACES TO STAY
11 Nam Chai Hotel
12 Chom Klao Hotel
13 Rabieng Rim Nam Guest House & Restaurant
18 Khao Wang Hotel

PLACES TO EAT
15 Dawarn Bakery
20 Egg Custard Places
28 Mae Lamiet Restaurant
32 Night Market

OTHER
1 Night Market
2 Air-Con Buses to Bangkok
3 Main Post Office; International Telephone Office
4 Wat Trailok
5 Wat Borom
6 Wat Yai Suwannaram
7 Wat Potaram
8 Buses to Cha-am & Hua Hin
9 Day Market
10 Department Store
14 Siam Commercial Bank
16 Wat Chi Sa In
17 Anglican Church
19 Phra Nakhon Khiri Palace
21 Wat Kom Lositaram
22 Wat Sa Bua
23 Wat Phra Phuttaya Saiyat
24 Buses to Southern Provinces
25 Wat Chang
26 Wat Kuti Dao
27 Wat Mahathat
29 Wat Uthai
30 Wat Kamphaeng Laeng
31 Wat Phra Suang
33 Digital Clock Tower
34 Wat Tho
35 Wat Yang
36 Wat Lat
37 Wat Chi Phra Keut
38 Clock Tower
39 Wat Ko Kaew Sutharam
40 Wat Chan
41 Ban Peun Palace

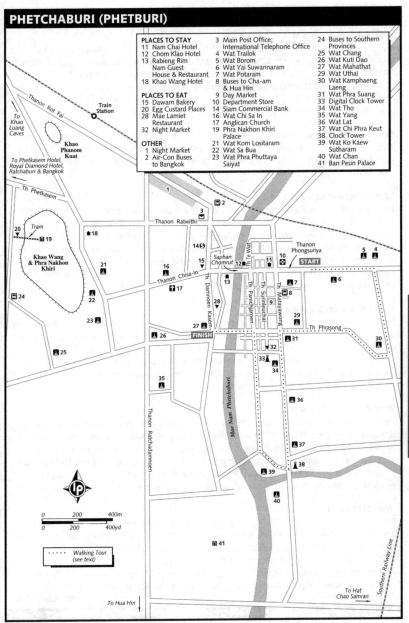

NORTH-WESTERN GULF COAST

Walking Tour – Phetchaburi Temples

Wat Yai Suwannaram

If you walk east from Chomrut Bridge along Th Phongsuriya about 300m past the Nam Chai Hotel on the left, you will see a large temple on the right. This is Wat Yai Suwannaram, originally built in the 17th century and renovated during the reign of King Chulalongkorn (1868–1910).

The main *bòt* (central sanctuary) is surrounded by a cloister filled with sober Buddha images. The murals inside the *bòt* date to the 1730s and are in good condition. Next to the *bòt*, in the middle of a pond, is a beautifully designed old *hǎw trai* (Tripitaka library).

Wat Borom & Wat Trailok

These two *wát* are next to one another on the opposite side of Th Phongsuriya from Wat Yai Suwannaram, a little to the east. They are distinctive for their monastic halls and long, graceful, wooden 'dormitories' on stilts.

Wat Kamphaeng Laeng

Turn right onto the road heading south from Wat Trailok and follow it down, past a bamboo fence on the right, to the entrance of Wat Kamphaeng Laeng. This is a very old (13th century) Khmer site with five *prangs* (towers) and part of the original laterite wall (the literal meaning of *kamphaeng laeng*) still standing. The prang at the front contains a Buddha footprint. Of the other four, two contain images dedicated to famous *lǔang phâw* (venerable elderly monks), one was in ruins (but is being restored) and the last has recently been uncovered from a mound of dirt. The Khmers built these as Hindu monuments, so the Buddhist symbols are late additions.

Wat Phra Suang & Wat Lat

Follow the road (Th Phrasong) beside Wat Kamphaeng Laeng, heading west back towards the river until you pass Wat Phra Suang on the left, undistinguished except for one very nice Ayuthaya-style *prasat*.

Turn left immediately after this *wát*, heading south again until you come to the clock tower at the southern edge of town. You'll have passed Wat Lat on the left side of the street along the way, but it's not worth breaking your momentum for; this is a long walk.

Wat Ko Kaew Sutharam

Turn right at the clock tower and look for signs leading to the Ayuthaya-period Wat Ko. Two different sois on the left lead to the *wát*, which is behind the shops along the curving street. The *bòt* features early 18th-century murals that are among the best conceived in Thailand.

One mural panel depicts what appears to be a Jesuit priest wearing the robes of a Buddhist monk, while another shows other foreigners undergoing Buddhist conversions. There is also a large wooden monastic hall on stilts similar to the ones at Wat Borom and Wat Trailok, but in much better condition.

Wat Mahathat

Follow the street in front of Wat Ko north (back towards central Phetchaburi) and walk over the first bridge you come to on the left, which leads to Wat Mahathat. Alternatively, you can cross the river at Wat Ko, near the clock tower, and take the street on the other side of the river around to Wat Mahathat. The large white prang of this *wát* can be seen from a distance – a typical late Ayuthaya/early Ratanakosin adaptation of the Khmer prangs of Lopburi and Phimai. This is obviously an important temple in Phetchaburi, judging from all the activity here.

Joe Cummings

Phra Nakhon Khiri (Holy City Hill). The views are great, especially at sunset. The walk up looks easy but is fairly strenuous. Fat monkeys loll about in the trees and on top of the walls along the main paths.

In 1988 Phra Nakhon Khiri (☎ 032 425 600; admission 40B; open 8.30am-4.30pm Mon-Fri) was declared a national historical park and later a museum was added. A tram has been installed to save you walking up to the peak (20B per person one way).

Phra Ratchawang Ban Peun
พระราชวังบ้านปืน

Located just over 1km south of the city centre is Phra Ratchawang Ban Peun; (Ban Peun Palace, ☎ 032 428 083, Th Ratchadamnoen; admission free; open 8.30am-4.30pm). Construction was begun in 1910 at the behest of King Rama V who passed away not long after the project was started. Completed in 1916, the German architects who were hired to do the job used it as an opportunity to showcase contemporary German innovations in construction and interior design. The structure is typical of the early 20th century, a period that saw a Thai craze for erecting European-style buildings – seemingly in an effort to keep up with the 'modern' architecture of its colonised neighbours. While the exterior of this two-storey palace promises little excitement, the exquisite glazed tile work in the interior, particularly the columns in the domed foyer, is a must see. Ban Peun Palace is situated on a Thai military base, but is open to the general public on weekdays during civil service hours.

Khao Luang Caves
ถ้ำเขาหลวง

Five kilometres north of Phetchaburi is the cave sanctuary of Khao Luang (Great Hill; admission free/by donation; open 8am-6pm). Concrete steps lead down into an anteroom, then into the main cavern, which is filled with old Buddha images, many of them placed by King Mongkut (Rama IV). Two holes in the chamber ceiling spray

Phetchaburi Festival

The Phra Nakhon Khiri Fair takes place in early February and lasts about eight days. Centred around Khao Wang and the city's historic temples, the festivities include a sound-and-light show at the Phra Nakhon Khiri Palace, temples festooned with lights and performances of Thai classical dance-drama, lákhon chaatrii, lí-keh and modern-style historical dramas. A twist on the usual beauty contest provides a showcase for Phetchaburi widows.

Joe Cummings

sunlight on the images, which are a favourite subject for photographers. To the rear of the main cavern is an entrance to a third, smaller chamber. On the right of the entrance is Wat Bunthawi, with a sala (open-sided shelter) designed by the abbot and a bòt with impressively carved wooden door panels.

A săamláw from the city centre to Khao Luang costs 50B, a motorcycle taxi 30B.

Places to Stay

Chom Klao Hotel (☎ 032 425 398, 1/3 Th Phongsuriya) Rooms 120B, with bath & fan 160B. On the eastern side of Chomrut Bridge, on the right bank of Mae Nam Phetchaburi (Phetchaburi River), is this ordinary, fairly clean Chinese hotel with friendly staff.

Nam Chai Hotel (☎ 032 425 550, 49 Th Phongsuriya) Rooms without/with bath 120/150B. Nam Chai is a block farther east from the Chom Klao Hotel, but is not as good value. There's no roman-script sign.

Rabieng Rim Nam Guest House (☎/fax 032 425 707, 1 Th Chisa-In) Singles/doubles with fan & bath per person 120/250B. Attached to the restaurant of the same name, this has clean rooms and friendly staff.

Khao Wang Hotel (☎ 032 425 167, 174/1-3 Th Ratwithi) Rooms with 1 bed/2 beds, fan & bath 220B, with air-con 320B. Opposite Khao Wang, this used to be a

NORTH-WESTERN GULF COAST

favourite in Phetchaburi, but the rooms have gone downhill a bit in recent years. It's fairly clean and most rooms have TV.

Phetkasem Hotel (☎ 032 425 581, 86/1 Th Phetkasem) Rooms with bath & fan 150-250B, bath & air-con 450B. The best value hotel in town is the friendly and clean Phetkasem, which is on Highway (Hwy) 4, on the western edge of town near the highway bus stop.

Royal Diamond (☎ 032 428 272, fax 032 424 310, 555 Muu1, Th Phetkasem) Rooms 800-1200B. This is quite upscale with 60 air-con rooms. There's a coffee shop and restaurant on the premises.

Places to Eat

Local dishes for which Phetchaburi is famous include *khanǒm jiin thawt man* (thin noodles with fried spicy fish cake), *khâo châe phêtburii* (moist chilled rice served with sweetmeats, a hot season speciality) and *khanǒm mâw kaeng* (egg custard). You'll find these dishes, along with a range of standard Thai and Chinese dishes, at several good restaurants in the Khao Wang area. A variety of cheap eats is available at the *night market* at the southern end of Th Surinleuchai, under the digital clock tower. Another very good *night market* sets up along Th Rot Fai between the train station and the town centre.

Other good eating places can be found in the town centre along the main street to the clock tower.

Mae Lamiet (☎ 032 426 090, 3-5 Th Phetkasem Kao) Dishes 20-30B Across from Wat Mahathat, this sells really good *khanǒm mâw kaeng* and *fǎwy thawng* (sweet shredded egg yolk) – the recipe that is supposedly a relic of Portuguese influence. This shop also has a branch near Khao Wang, where a whole group of *egg custard places* serve tourists.

Rabieng Rim Nam (☎ 032 425 707, 1 Th Chisa-In) Dishes 30-80B. Near Chomrut Bridge, this features a Thai and English menu of over 100 items, including seafood and 30 kinds of *yam*.

Dawarn Bakery (☎ 032 425 830, 28 Th Chisa-In) Dishes 10-20B. At the corner of Th Chisa-In and Th Damnoen Kasem, this offers a decent assortment of baked goods.

Getting There & Away

Bus From Bangkok, buses leave regularly from the Southern bus terminal in Thonburi for 50B (ordinary) on the new road, 46B on the old road (via Ratchaburi and Nakhon Pathom), 60B for 2nd class air-con and 75B for 1st class air-con. The trip takes about 2½ hours.

Buses to Phetchaburi from Cha-am and Hua Hin are 18B (20B air-con) and 22B (30B air-con), and take 60 and 90 minutes respectively. The distance is actually not that great but buses make an obligatory 20-minute stop just north of Cha-am so Thai tourists can load up on local sweets. Other ordinary bus fares are: Ratchaburi 18B (45 minutes); Nakhon Pathom 29B (two hours); Prachuap Khiri Khan 40B (three hours); and Phuket 210B (304B air-con; 12 hours). The main bus terminal in Phetchaburi is just south-west of Khao Wang.

Train Trains leave Bangkok's Hualamphong train station at 12.25pm (rapid), 2.20pm and 2.45pm (special express), 3.50pm, 5.35pm and 6.20pm (rapid), 7.15pm (express) and 10.50pm (express diesel railcar). All of these trains offer seating on 1st, 2nd and 3rd class, except for the 2.45pm special express (1st and 2nd class only) and the 10.50pm (2nd class only). The journey to Phetchaburi takes about three hours. Fares are 34B, 78B and 153B, not including rapid or express surcharges. The bus is faster, unless you count getting out to Bangkok's Southern bus terminal.

There is no ordinary train between Hualamphong and Phetchaburi, but there is one ordinary 3rd-class train daily from Thonburi (Bangkok Noi) station at 1.05pm (34B, no surcharges).

Getting Around

Sǎamláw and motorcycle taxis go anywhere in the town centre for 20B; you can charter one for the whole day for 150B. Share *sǎwngthǎew* (passenger trucks) cost 8B around town, including to or from the train station.

CHA-AM
อำเภอชะอำ

postcode 76120 • pop 22,700

A growing town 178km from Bangkok, 38km from Phetchaburi and 25km from Hua Hin, Cha-am is known for its casuarina-lined beach, a favourite getaway for provincial Thai families. Every weekend and holiday they arrive by the score in multi-hued buses that are seemingly powered by groups of inebriated young men who dance in the aisles while pounding drums and clapping cymbals (Thais call these junkets 'ching chap tours', after the rhythmic noise the musicians produce: ching-chap-ching-chap).

Once on the beach, the families plant themselves comfortably in the shade and spend the day snacking while a few brave souls risk exposure to the sun's rays in order to ride jet skis and banana boats. It's really a Thai scene though and, while some Westerners will find it diverting for an afternoon, eventually most will be driven off by the public address system. Strung along the shore to blare announcements with a ding-dong prelude, it gives the beach all the ambience of an airport departure lounge. Of course it should also be said that if you come during a weekday, you're likely to have the deserted beach all to yourself.

Beach umbrellas and sling chairs are available for hire, and there are public bathhouses where you can bathe in fresh water for 5B to 7B.

The old town centre is on the opposite side of Phetkasem Hwy, where you'll find the main post office, market, train station and government offices. The road that fronts the beach, Th Ruamjit, is a long line of hotels, restaurants and souvenir stalls catering mostly to Thai tourists.

Inland from the beach (follow the signs) at **Wat Neranchararama** is a fat, white, six-armed Buddha statue; the six hands cover the nine bodily orifices in a symbolic gesture denying the senses.

Information
Tourist Offices A TAT office (☎ 032 471 005, ✉ tatphet@tat.or.th) has been established on Phetkasem Hwy just 500m south of town. The staff are very helpful; they distribute information on Cha-am, Phetchaburi, Hua Hin, Prachuap Khiri Khan and Ratchaburi. It's open 8.30am to 4.30pm weekdays, 9am to 4.30pm weekends and holidays. A smaller tourist information office is located on the beach near the intersection of Th Ruamjit and Th Narathip.

Money Several banks maintain foreign exchange booths along the beach strip, typically open 10am to 8pm. In the town centre, west of Hwy 4, are a number of banks with foreign exchange services and ATMs.

Post & Communications There is a post office on the main beach strip. It's open Monday to Friday from 8.30am to 4.30pm and on Saturday from 9am to noon.

International telephone services are available at the post office.

Peggy's Pub (see Places to Eat in this section) offers pay-as-you-go email and Internet services. Jolly & Jumper Guest House and Restaurant offers free email to its guests.

Places to Stay – Budget & Mid-Range
Hat Cha-am (Cha-am Beach) has two basic types of accommodation: tacky apartment-style hotels along the beach road (Th Ruamjit) – built of cheap materials with faulty plumbing, and more expensive 'condotel' developments. New places go up all the time at the northern and southern ends of the beach. Bungalow operations, once common, are now quite rare. Expect a 20% to 50% discount on posted rates for weekday stays.

Th Narathip is the main road leading to the beach area from the highway.

South of Th Narathip Near the air-con bus terminal a couple of *guesthouses,* which change name from time to time, can be found in a row of modern shophouses similar to the scourge of Pattaya, Hua Hin and Phuket's Hat Patong – they all look the same. Rooms cost 300B with fan and shared bathroom to 500B with air-con.

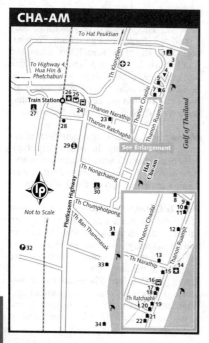

CHA-AM

PLACE TO STAY & EAT
3 Top House
4 Peggy's Pub
5 Cha-am Methavalai Hotel
6 Happy Home; Mark-Land Hotel
7 Kaen-Chan Hotel
8 Gems Cha-am
9 Rua Makam Villa; Poom Restaurant
10 Jolly & Jumper
11 Thiptari Place
12 Jitravee Resort; Khan Had Restaurant
13 Somkheat Villa
15 Nirandorn Resort
17 Savitree Resort
18 Anantachai Guest House
19 Sea Pearl Hotel; Naluman Bungalows
20 Viwathana Bungalows
21 Santisuk Bungalows & Beach Resort
22 Nipon Resort
23 Inthira Plaza
31 Springfield Beach Resort
33 Regent Cha-am Beach Resort
34 Dusit Resort & Polo Club

OTHER
1 Wat Neranchararama
2 Hospital
14 Tourist Police; Tourist Information Booth
16 Air-con Bus Terminal
24 Bus Station
25 Post Office
26 Police Station
27 Wat Cha-am Khiri
28 Market
29 TAT Office
30 Wat Nong Chaeng
32 Springfield Beach Resort Golf Course

Anantachai Guest House (☎ 032 471 980, Th Ruamjit) Rooms 400-600B. South of the air-con bus terminal, this has nice rooms with a beach view, air-con, TV, private shower & toilet. It also provides information about the area and has a cheap Thai restaurant.

Savitree Resort (☎ 032 434 088, 019 313 638, Th Ruamjit) Rooms 500B. The Savitree Resort offers rooms with air-con & TV situated in semi-detached brick bungalows.

Santisuk Bungalows & Beach Resort (☎ 032 471 212, in Bangkok ☎ 022 980 532, 263/3 Th Ruamjit) Room with fan/air-con & bath 800B, cottages with 2 bedrooms, fan/air-con, bath & sitting area 1500/2000B, with 3 bedrooms & 2 baths 3000B. A long-time favourite, with both early Cha-am–style wooden cottages and a newer, equally tasteful section.

Nirandorn Resort (☎ 032 471 893, 247/7 Th Ruamjit) Cottages with fan/air-con, TV & hot water 300/500B. This has similar cottages to the Santisuk.

Sea Pearl Hotel (White Hotel; ☎ 032 471 118, 263/32 Th Ruamjit) Rooms with fan & bath 400B, with air-con 500-600B, with carpet, tub & TV 700B. This is an apartment-style place that's popular with Thais from Bangkok. Long-term discounts are given during the low season.

Somkheat Villa (☎ 032 471 834, fax 032 471 229, 277/3-12 Th Ruamjit) Rooms 400-700B. This is yet another apartment-style hotel, 60 rooms with a largely middle-class Thai clientele. As with most accommodation of this type, long-term residents can get substantial (up to 40%) discounts.

Naluman Bungalows (Lucky House; ☎ *032 471 440, 263/38 Th Ruamjit)* Bungalows with fan/air-con 1200/1700B. Naluman is an old-style place with large bungalows that can sleep 10 to 12 people in three bedrooms. None have a sea view, but all have a big sink and shower outside, as well as a toilet inside, TV, and a large porch and carport. Even if you only have a small group (say two couples), it offers much more peace and privacy than Cha-am's apartment-style accommodation.

Nipon Resort (☎ *032 471 826, Th Ruamjit)* Rooms with TV, air-con & hot water 800B, bungalows with fan/air-con 400/800B. Nipon offers rooms in a hotel-like building as well as bungalows. The air-con bungalows can sleep up to four people.

Viwathana Bungalows (☎ *032 471 289, 263/21 Th Ruamjit)* Bungalows with fan 400B, air-con 800-1200B. These are old style and recently renovated. Fan rooms are simple and a bit neglected. Air-con rooms show more promise and receive less traffic noise.

North of Th Narathip There are a lot of choices here.

Thiptari Place (☎*/fax 032 471 879, Th Ruamjit)* Rooms with air-con 800-1200B. Thiptari is fairly reasonable if you come on a weekday when there is a 40% discount in effect.

Rua Makam Villa (☎ *032 471 073, 236 Th Ruamjit)* Singles/doubles with fan 500/1000B, with air-con 1200/2400B. This has old-style wood and concrete cottages, spacious and off the road – preferable to accommodation in a row-building.

Kaen-Chan Hotel (☎ *032 471 314, 664 Th Ruamjit)* Bungalows with fan/air-con 200/300B, rooms with air-con 600-800B. This friendly place has a variety of accommodation. There was a pool on the 6th floor but it was drained after leaking into the floors below. If you bring a skateboard you might convince the management to let you put the dry pool to some use.

Jitravee Resort (☎ *032 471 382, 241/20 Th Ruamjit)* Rooms 300-600B. Functional but forgettable rooms in a row-building.

Try to get a room at the back – these buildings seem to act as a funnel for traffic noise.

Top House (☎ *032 433 307, Th Ruamjit)* Rooms with fan & bath 400-600B, with air-con, TV & hot water 800-1200B. Top House is a big place with a sign downstairs that says 'International Beverage Mix Bar'. Discounts of up to 50% are available during the week.

Jolly & Jumper (☎*/fax 032 433 887, 274/3 Th Ruamjit)* Rooms with fan 150-250B, with air-con 400-500B. This good-value place has festively painted rooms and is very clean. The friendly proprietors have bicycles that guests can use for free. There is an interestingly decorated restaurant downstairs (check out the tooled-leather saddles from Mexico and the USA) with a mostly Western-food menu. Jolly & Jumper also has a couple of computer terminals in the restaurant and offers free Internet time to guests.

Happy Home (Ban Sabai Dee, ☎ *032 471 393, 271/34 Th Ruamjit)* Cottages with fan/air-con 300/400B. The aptly named Happy Home has older-style cement cottages and the management are friendly. This place has some atmosphere and is quite popular with long-termers.

Inthira Plaza Apartment-style rooms upstairs at a couple of the bars are 250-300B with fan & private bath, 350-400B with air-con. Rooms could be noisy at night. This complex off Th Narathip is striving to become a Pattaya-style bar centre ('entertainment centre' in the local jargon).

Places to Stay – Top End
Many places in Cha-am call themselves resorts but only a handful of places come close to living up to the term.

Cha-am Methavalai Hotel (☎ *032 433 250, fax 032 471 590, Th Ruamjit)* Walk-in rates 2000-4000B. This has well-kept, modern rooms with flowers spilling from every balcony, plus a pool (available to non-guests from 7am to 7pm for 50B) and a small private beach area. During the week an automatic 50% discount applies and you can sometimes get a 30% discount even on weekends, unless it's a major holiday.

Mark-Land Hotel (☎ *032 433 833, fax 032 433 834, Th Ruamjit*) Large luxurious rooms 2500-6000B. Facilities include pool, sauna, fitness room & various food outlets.

Gems Cha-am (☎ *032 434 060, fax 032 434 002, Th Ruamjit*) Rooms 2500-4500B. This resort-style hotel has rooms with ocean views and all the amenities, from satellite TV to IDD phones. There's also a business centre on the premises. Rates do not include tax and service, but are discounted 50% on weekdays; even on weekends you can usually get a 25% discount.

Regent Cha-am Beach Resort (☎ *032 451 240–9, fax 032 471 491–2, in Bangkok* ☎ *022 552 818, fax 022 535 143,* **W** *www .regent-chaam.com, 849/21 Th Phetkasem*) Rooms 4120-11,128B. South of town a bit, facilities include a swimming pool, squash and tennis courts, and a fitness centre.

Dusit Resort & Polo Club (☎ *032 520 009, fax 032 520 296,* **W** *www.dusit.com,* **e** *polo@dusit.com, 1349 Th Phetkasem*) Rooms 5884-18,832B. On the beach, south of town, the posh Dusit Resort has a fitness centre, mini-golf course, horse riding, pool, tennis and squash courts and, of course, polo.

Springfield Beach Resort (☎ *032 451 181–5, fax 032 451 194, in Bangkok* ☎ *022 312 244, fax 022 312 249,* **W** *www.spring fieldresort.com* **e** *info@springfieldresort .com, 193 Th Phetkasem*) Rooms 3000-6000B. South of town at the 210km marker, off Phetkasem Hwy, this is a relatively new luxury hotel. All rooms and suites have sea views, balconies, phones, air-con, fridges, electronic safe boxes, long bathtubs & hairdryers. On the premises are a terrace coffee shop overlooking the ocean, swimming pool & Jacuzzi, tennis court, putting green, exercise room, sauna, steam room and karaoke. Across the highway the resort has a 10-hole Jack Nicklaus-designed golf course.

Places to Eat

The luxury hotels have generally fine Thai, seafood and Western cuisine at the standard hotel prices.

Opposite the beach are several good seafood restaurants, which, unlike the bun-galows, are reasonably priced. Vendors on the beach sell all manner of barbecued and fried seafood.

Khan Had Restaurant (☎ *032 471 312, 246/64 Th Ruamjit*) Dishes 40-80B. Moderately priced, this has an extensive menu of Thai, Chinese and seafood dishes.

Poom Restaurant (☎ *032 471 036, 274/1 Th Ruamjit*) Dishes 60-120B. Near the entrance to Gems Cha-am Hotel, this is an outdoor seafood place that is hugely popular among visiting Thais.

Anantachai Guest House (☎ *032 471 980, Th Ruamjit*) Dishes 40-60B. Anantachai is a good place for inexpensive to moderately priced Thai and seafood dishes.

Jolly & Jumper (☎/*fax 032 433 887, 274/3 Th Ruamjit*) Dishes 40-60B. This does good Thai and Western food, including breakfasts.

Peggy's Pub (*Th Ruamjit*) Dishes 40-100B. On the same soi leading down to the Long Beach Cha-am Hotel, this serves Thai and Scandinavian dishes.

Getting There & Away

Buses from Phetchaburi cost 20B air-con, 18B ordinary. From Hua Hin, take a Phetchaburi-bound bus and ask to be let off at Hat Cha-am; the fare is 10B.

Ordinary buses from Bangkok's Southern bus terminal to Cha-am cost 55B (101B air-con). In Cha-am, ordinary buses stop on Phetkasem Hwy, from where you can take a motorbike taxi (20B) or a share taxi (5B) out to the beach. A few hundred metres south of the corner of Th Narathip and Th Ruamjit, a private bus company operates six daily air-con buses to Bangkok for 97B.

The train station is on Th Narathip, west of Phetkasem Hwy and a 20B motorcycle ride to/from the beach. There's only one train from Hualamphong station, the No 169 Rapid at 3.50pm. There is also one departure from the Sam Sen station in Bangkok at 9.28am, and one from Thonburi's Bangkok Noi station at 1.05pm. The train is slower than the bus by one hour (taking about four hours) and costs 40B 3rd class. First- and 2nd- class seats are also available on the No 169 for 183B and 91B respectively. Cha-am isn't listed on the English-language train schedule.

Getting Around

Standard prices for motorbike taxi and public săwngthăew are 20B and 10B (40B to charter) respectively. You can rent motorcycles for 200B to 300B a day.

Avis Rent-A-Car (☎ 032 520 009) has an office at the Dusit Resort & Polo Club (see Places to Stay, earlier in this section).

AROUND CHA-AM
Hat Peuktian
หาดปึกเตียน

This beach between Cha-am and Phetchaburi has the usual casuarina trees and food vendors favoured by Thai beach-goers, and hardly a *faràng* (Westerner) in sight. Three rocky islets are within wading distance of shore, one with a sala for shade. Standing knee-deep just offshore is a 6m-high statue of Phi Seua Samut, the undersea female deity that terrorised the protagonist of the Thai classical epic *Phra Aphaimani*. A statue of the prince playing a flute sits on a nearby rock.

A tasteless two-storey townhouse-style development has been built off the beach. Designed in the pseudo-classical style prevalent in modern city blocks all over Thailand, it looks rather incongruous with the natural beach surroundings.

Just before the border between Phetchaburi and Prachuap Khiri Khan Provinces is reached – 9km south of Cha-am – stands **Phra Ratchaniwet Marukhathayawan** (☎ 032 472 482, Th Phetkasem; admission free; 8.30am-4.30pm daily), a summer palace built during the reign of King Rama VI. The collection of one- and two-storey buildings are constructed of prime golden teak and interlinked by covered boardwalks, all raised high above the ground on stilts. Along with the high, tiled roofs and tall, shuttered windows, this design allows for maximum air circulation – a tropical building technique sorely missing in most modern Thai architecture. Unlike the current summer palace situated farther south at Hua Hin, this one is open daily to the public. It's now surrounded by the grounds of Camp Rama VI, a military post, but with proper check-in at the gate you should have no trouble receiving permission to tour the palace during opening hours.

HUA HIN
อำเภอหัวหิน

postcode 77110 • pop 35,500

The beaches of Hua Hin first came to the country's attention in 1922, when King Rama VI's royal architect, MJ Ithithepsan Kreudakon, constructed Phra Ratchawong Klai Kangwon, a seafront summer palace of golden teak just north of what was then a small fishing village. Rama VII learned of Thailand's first coup d'état in 1932 while playing golf at the Royal Hua Hin Golf Course. Once endorsed by the royal family, Hua Hin remained a traditional favourite among the Thais long after the beaches of Pattaya and Phuket had been taken over by foreign tourists. The palace is still used by the royal family.

Hua Hin's 5km-long sand beach is studded with large, smooth boulders, enough to give the beach a scenic appeal but not enough to hinder swimming. The surf is safe for swimming year-round, although jellyfish are an occasional problem during the rainy season (May to October). Water sports are limited to sailing and jet-skiing. Overall Hua Hin is still a fairly quiet, economical place to get away from it all, and is less than four hours by train from Bangkok.

Hua Hin, like Cha-am, has traditionally been the domain of domestic beach tourism. The renovation of the colonial-style, 1923-vintage Hua Hin Railway Beach Hotel (now the Hotel Sofitel Central Hua Hin) by a major French hotel group in the late 1980s attracted overseas attention. Now a number of cafes and bistros offer Spanish, French, Italian and German cuisine to an older polyglot bunch enjoying two-week Thai beach holidays at bargain rates.

The first thing you notice when arriving at Hua Hin are the high-rise luxury apartments. For upper-class Bangkok Thais it's

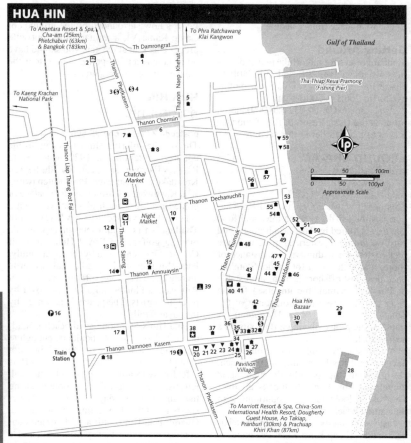

HUA HIN

To Anantara Resort & Spa,
Cha-am (25km),
Phetchaburi (63km)
& Bangkok (183km)

To Phra Ratchawang
Klai Kangwon

Gulf of Thailand

Th Damrongrat

Thanon Phetkasem

To Kaeng Krachan
National Park

Tha Thiap Reua Pramong
(Fishing Pier)

Thanon Naep Khehat

Thanon Chomsin

Thanon Liap Thang Rot Fai

Chatchai
Market

Thanon Dechanuchit

Night
Market

Thanon Sasong

Thanon Amnuaysin

Thanon Phursuk

Thanon Naretdamri

Hua Hin
Bazaar

Train
Station

Thanon Damnoen Kasem

Pavilion
Village

Thanon Phetkasem

To Marriott Resort & Spa, Chiva-Som
International Health Resort, Dougherty
Guest House, Ao Takiap,
Pranburi (30km) & Prachuap
Khiri Khan (87km)

0   50   100m
0   50   100yd
Approximate Scale

something of a status symbol to own a unit in one of these buildings. Despite the glitzy look from a distance, there is accommodation for every budget in Hua Hin. There's also a small community of faràng living here year round – note the predominance of British-style pubs with quaint British names and the number of restaurants offering Scandinavian fare.

Unfortunately, Hua Hin hasn't been totally spared Pattaya-style development. You'll see a lot of the same kind of cheap, unsightly shophouse-apartment buildings with bad plumbing as in Pattaya and

Phuket's Hat Patong, as well as the relatively recent invasion of go-go bars. Hua Hin has for the most part lost its fishing-village atmosphere – the fishing fleet is being moved out and the town's infamous squid-drying piers have been replaced by hotels.

On the bright side, a sewage treatment plant and municipal sewer system are functioning and the beach is cleaner than ever. The main swimming beach still has thatched umbrellas and chairs; vendors from the nearby food stalls will bring loungers steamed crab, mussels, beer etc and there are pony rides for the kids.

HUA HIN

PLACES TO STAY
1 Thananchai Hotel
5 Phananchai Hotel
7 Damrong Hotel
8 Chaat Chai Hotel
12 Siripetchkasem (Siri Phetkasem) Hotel
15 Subhamitra (Suphamit) Hotel
17 Srichan Hua Hin (Top Boss) Hotel
18 Golf Inn
24 Jed Pee Nong Hotel
25 Ban Somboon
26 Patchara House
27 Puangpen Villa Hotel; PP Villa Guest House
28 Hotel Sofitel Central Hua Hin
29 Central Village Resort Hua Hin
32 Thai Thae Guest House
33 Sirin Hotel
36 Ban Boosarin
37 City Beach Resort
41 Ban Pak Hua Hin

42 Usaah Guesthouse
43 Phuen Guest House
44 Fresh Inn
46 Hua Hin Hilton Hotel
48 Sand Inn
50 Bird
52 Mod Guest House; Sirima Guest House
54 Fulay Guest House
55 Memory Guest House
56 All Nations
57 Pattana Guest House

PLACES TO EAT
6 Night Market
10 Chinese-Thai Seafood Restaurants
21 Italian Ice Cream
22 Capo's; Al Fresco
23 Buffalo Bill's Steak & Grill
30 Berny's Inn; Baan Farang; The Strawberry Pig
34 Gee Cuisine; Stone Town
35 La Villa
45 Lo Stivale

47 Sunshine Restaurant & Bakery
49 Luciano Pizza House; Taxi Jack's
51 Taj Mahal
53 Piaf
58 Le Chablis
59 Seafood Restaurants

OTHER
2 Cinema
3 Thai Farmers Bank
4 Bank of Ayudhya
9 Bus Terminal
11 Sawngthaew to Ao Takiap
13 Pran Tour; Air-Con Buses
14 Top Center Supermarket
16 Royal Hua Hin Golf Course
19 Tourist Information
20 Main Post Office; CAT Office
31 Bank of Ayudhya Exchange Booth
38 Police
39 Wat Hua Hin
40 Rockestra Cafe

With golfing in its venerable past, Hua Hin has long been a favourite golf-holiday destination for Thais, and has recently begun receiving attention from international golfers. There are several companies in town that rent golfing equipment and arrange golf tours.

The Hua Hin Web site (**W** www.frangipani.com) has further information on golfing tours and more.

Information

Tourist Offices Tourist information on Hua Hin and the surrounding area is available at the municipal office (☎ 032 511 047, 032 532 433) on the corner of Th Phetkasem and Th Damnoen Kasem, about 200m east of the train station. The *Welcome to Hua Hin* brochure contains a lot of useful information on hotels, restaurants and transport. The office is open 8.30am to 4.30pm daily.

The home-grown *Hua Hin Observer*, an expat-published newsletter with short features in English (and a few in German), contains snippets on eating out, culture and entertainment.

Money There are several banks around town. Most convenient to the beach is the Bank of Ayudhya's exchange booth on Th Naretdamri, which is near the corner of Th Damnoen Kasem.

Post & Communications The post office is on Th Damnoen Kasem near the corner of Th Phetkasem.

The CAT office attached to the post office offers Home Country Direct international phone service daily from 8am to midnight.

Cyber Lounge, off Th Naretdamri in the Pavilion Village shopping centre opposite the Sofitel, offers Internet phone calls as well as access to email.

Beaches

Th Damnoen Kasem leads east directly from the train station to the main beach, which runs about 2km along the southern half of town. The nicest stretch of sand lies in front of the Sofitel. Smooth granite boulders – source of the town's name, which means Stone Head – pierce the surfline.

Eight to 13km south of Hua Hin along Ao Takiap (Chopsticks Bay) are the beaches of **Hat Khao Takiap**, **Hat Suan Son** and **Hat Khao Tao**, all of which are undergoing resort development. Two hilltop temples can be visited here. Wat Khao Thairalat is well off the beach on a rocky hill and is nothing special. At the end of the bay is the more well-endowed **Wat Khao Takiap** – climb the steps for a good bay view.

The southern end of Ao Takiap now has an arsenal of high-rises, blocking the sea view from all points inland. North along the bay, however, are several quiet, wooded spots with cabins and beach houses.

If you're driving, the turn-off for Ao Takiap is 4km south of Hua Hin. Regular sǎwngthǎew go back and forth from town.

Places to Stay – Budget

Not surprisingly, prices are a bit higher for places near the beach. Hotels in town are still reasonably priced and it's only a five- or 10-minute walk to the beach from most of them.

Guesthouses Near – but not on – the beach, the cheapest places are found along or just off Th Naretdamri. A room glut has kept rates low. Several small hotels and guesthouses in this area have rooms with fan & bath from 150B to 200B, with air-con 300B to 500B.

Thai Thae Guest House (*Thae Guest House;* ☎ *032 511 906, 6 Th Damnoen Kasem*) Rooms with fan/air-con & bath 200/400B. Next to the more top-end Sirin Hotel, this place has only eight rooms and is well-managed and personable.

Usaah Guesthouse (☎ *032 532 062, Soi Kanchanamai*) Rooms 100-200B. Opposite the City Beach Resort, the Usaah has only ten rooms and is well run. There's a restaurant that does good breakfasts, as well as a bar (The Amsterdam) downstairs.

Along a soi off Th Naretdamri are a string of guesthouses in old wooden buildings with some charm. Unfortunately the soi has become something of a bar scene, complete with freelance Thai hookers, so can no longer be recommended for anyone wanting a good night's sleep.

Ban Pak Hua Hin (*Hua Hin Guest House;* ☎ *032 511 653, fax 032 533 649, 5/1 Soi Binthabat, Th Phunsuk*) Rooms with fan/air-con & bath 200/350B. This modern, apartment-style guesthouse is quiet and exceptionally clean.

Phuen Guest House (☎ *032 512 344, 4 Soi Binthabat, Th Phunsuk*) Fan rooms 200B, air-con 450B. The rooms at this place are small but clean. There's a bar downstairs, so you're never far from a cold beer.

At the northern end of the beach, along Th Naretdamri, where the old squid piers used to be, are a string of wooden motel-like places built on piers in the sea.

Mod Guest House (*Mot Guest House;* ☎ *032 512 296, 116 Th Naretdamri*) Rooms 200-650B, with air-con and TV 550B, with 3 beds, TV & fridge 1500B. This has rather small but otherwise OK rooms. There's one room with a sea view for 650B.

Sirima (☎ *032 511 060, 33/3 Th Naretdamri*) Rooms with fan 200B, with air-con 550-750B. The fan rooms are a little larger than at neighbouring places but otherwise there is little to distinguish this place.

Bird (☎ *032 511 630, Th Naretdamri*) Doubles with fan 350B, air-con 500B. This is the best of the seaside guesthouses; it's friendly, well kept and well designed.

Pattana Guest House (☎ *032 513 393, fax 032 530 081, 52 Th Naretdamri*) Rooms 200-350B. Farther north along an alley off Naretdamri, this has comfortable fan rooms in two wooden houses. A bar and restaurant are also on the premises.

Memory Guest House (☎ *032 511 816, Th Naretdamri*) Rooms 550-850B. In a long two-storey white building, Memory is super-clean and has a locked entrance gate.

Fulay Guest House (☎ *032 513 670, 110/1 Th Naretdamri*) Rooms 750B. This offers large, comfortable rooms with air-con, cable TV, fridge & balcony.

All Nations (☎ *032 512 747, fax 032 530 474, 10/10 Th Dechanuchit*) Rooms 130-150B. West off Th Naretdamri on Th Dechanuchit (east of Th Phunsuk), is the friendly and clean All Nations. Each room in the tall, narrow building comes with its own balcony and fan; each floor has a bath-

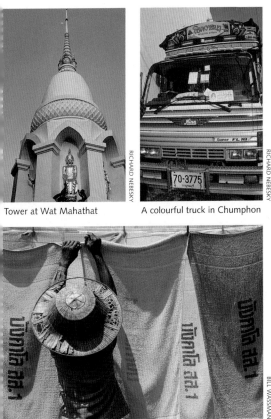
Tower at Wat Mahathat

A colourful truck in Chumphon

Stone carving at Wat Lat

Towels hung out to dry, Prachuap Kiri Khan

Fisherman repairing nets, Hua Hin, North-Western Gulf Coast

Windows into Wat Hua Hin

Buddha statue, Hua Hin

Decorative panel on a truck

The true 'Fisherman's Basket'

Spicing it up at Chatchai Market, Hua Hin

room shared by two or three rooms. There's also a nice sitting area on the roof.

Dougherty Guest House (☎ *032 532 715,* **e** *jtd@prachuab.net, 236/72 Th Jamjuri*) Doubles 600-800B. Located off Th Phetkasem in a quiet neighbourhood south of the city centre is the newly opened Dougherty Guest House. It's good value for families with kids, and there's a pool and restaurant on the premises.

Hotels To find hotels around 300B, go to Th Phetkasem, the main north-south road through town.

Chaat Chai Hotel (☎ *032 511 034, 59/1–3 Th Phetkasem*) Rooms with fan & bath 150-200B. Starting at rock bottom is this decaying Thai–Chinese-style hotel. The rooms actually aren't too bad, but try to get one at the back to avoid traffic noise.

Damrong Hotel (☎ *032 511 574, 46 Th Phetkasem*) Rooms with fan & bath 150B, with air-con 350B. Just past the Chatchai Market, this place has seen better days.

Subhamitra Hotel (*Suphamit Hotel;* ☎ *032 511 208, fax 032 511 508, 19 Th Amnuaysin*) Singles/doubles with fan & bath 250/300B, with air-con 450B, triple with air-con 800B. Just off Phetkasem, behind the bank, the nice Subhamitra has very clean rooms and a pool on the premises.

Siripetchkasem Hotel (*Siri Phetkasem;* ☎ *032 511 394, fax 032 511 464, 7/5-8 Th Sasong*) Rooms with fan/air-con 300/400B. Behind the Chatchai Night Market area, this is similar to the hotels along Th Phetkasem.

Srichan Hua Hin Hotel (*Top Boss;* ☎ *032 513 130, 1/6 Th Sasong*) Rooms with carpet & air-con 500-600B. This place was renovated a couple of years ago but the cracks are already starting to show. Overall it's a bit overpriced.

Sand Inn (☎ *032 533 667, fax 032 533 669, 38-38/4 Th Phunsuk*) Rooms with fan/air-con, TV, phone & hot water 400/500B. Sand Inn is situated between Th Damnoen Kasem and Th Dechanuchit – look for lush plants hanging over the front wall. Attached are a restaurant and coffee shop.

Thanachai Hotel (☎ *032 511 755, 11 Th Damrongrat*) Room with fan/air-con

350/650B. An upper-budget place, it's a bit far from the town centre if you're on foot – but for this very reason it's not a bad place if you want peace and quiet.

Places to Stay – Mid-Range

Hua Hin's mid-range places are typically small, sedate, modern hotels with air-con rooms and such luxuries as telephones.

Ban Boosarin (☎ *032 512 076, 8/8 Th Phunsuk*) Rooms in low/high season 800/950B. This self-proclaimed 'mini-deluxe hotel' has rooms with air-con, hot water, telephone, TV, fridge & private terrace. It's super-clean and rates don't rise on weekends. There's a 10% discount for stays of a week or more.

Patchara House (☎ *032 511 787, Soi Kasem Samphan*) Rooms with air-con, TV, video, phone, hot water & fridge 700B. Well-kept and good-value rooms, especially during the low season when prices drop to 500B.

Ban Somboon (☎ *032 511 538, 13/4 Soi Kasem Samphan, Th Damnoen Kasem*) Rooms with fan/air-con, TV & hot shower 550/750B. This has nicely decorated rooms; all rates include breakfast and there is a pleasant garden on the premises.

Puangpen Villa Hotel (☎ *032 511 216, 11 Th Damnoen Kasem*) Rooms with air-con, hot water, TV & fridge 750B. On the corner of Soi Kasem Samphan and Th Damnoen Kasem, this is only 200m from the beach.

PP Villa Guest House (☎ *032 511 216, 11 Th Damnoen Kasem*) Rooms with air-con, hot water, TV & fridge 650B. This shares a garden, pool and reception area with Paungpen Villa Hotel.

Jed Pee Nong (☎ *032 512 381, fax 032 532 063, 17 Th Damnoen Kasem*) Rooms with fan 600B, air-con, TV & hot bath 800-1200B. This popular place is modern and clean but its rooms are otherwise unimpressive. There's a swimming pool behind the hotel.

Fresh Inn (☎ *032 511 389, fax 032 532 166, 132 Th Naretdamri*) Rooms with air-con 750-850B. This pleasant tourist-class hotel would have had a sea view if not for

Hua Hin Railway Hotel

In 1922 the State Railway of Thailand (then the Royal Thai Railway) extended the national rail network to Hua Hin to allow easier access to the Hua Hin summer palace. The area proved to be a popular vacation spot among the general population too, so in the following year the Hua Hin Railway Hotel was built, a graceful colonial-style inn by the sea, with sweeping teak stairways and high-ceilinged rooms. When I researched the first edition of this guide in 1981, a double room was still only 90B and the service was just as unhurried as it had been when I first stayed here in 1977. It probably hadn't changed much since 1923, except for the addition of electric lighting and screened doors and windows. Big-bladed ceiling fans stirred the humid sea air, and in the dining room one ate using weighty State Railway silverware and thick china from the 1920s. Unfortunately, when Bangkok's Central Department Store took over the management of the hotel it floundered in its attempt to upgrade the facilities, failing to take advantage of the hotel's original ambience.

In 1986 the French hotel chain Accor became part of a joint venture with Central and together they restored the hotel to most of its former glory. It now bears the awkward name *Hotel Sofitel Central Hua Hin Resort*, but if you've been looking for a historic South-East Asian hotel to spend some money on, this might be it. All of the wood panelling and brass fixtures throughout the rooms and hallways have been restored. While the old railway silverware and china have been retired to antique cabinet displays, the spacious, lazy ambience of a previous age remains. Even if you don't want to spend the money to stay here, it's worth a stroll through the grounds and open sitting areas. It's more interesting in terms of atmosphere than either the Raffles in Singapore or the Oriental in Bangkok (neither of which have eight-hectare grounds), and somewhere in between in terms of luxury. Standards are said to have slipped since the lay-off of all European management.

Incidentally, in 1983 this hotel was used as Hotel Le Phnom for the filming of *The Killing Fields*. Also, the State Railway of Thailand still owns the hotel; Accor/Central are just leasing it.

Joe Cummings

the high-rise Hua Hin Hilton between it and the sea. Downstairs is an Italian restaurant called Lo Stivale.

Running north from Th Chomsin (the road leading to the main pier) is Th Naep Khehat.

Phananchai Hotel (☎ 032 511 707, fax 032 530 157, 73/5-7 Th Naep Khehat) Rooms with fan 400B, with air-con & carpet 550-600B. It's a bit of a walk from the swimming beaches, but all rooms come with hot water, TV and telephone. The hotel also has an attached restaurant.

Places to Stay – Top End

Sirin Hotel (☎ 032 511 150, fax 032 513 571, 6 Th Damnoen Kasem) Doubles with breakfast 890-1500B. Towards the beach, rooms here are well kept and come with hot water and a fridge. The semi-outdoor restaurant area is pleasant.

City Beach Resort (☎ 032 512 870–5, 16 Th Damnoen Kasem) Rooms 1300-2600B. This offers quiet, semi-luxurious rooms with the usual service and extras.

Golf Inn (☎ 032 512 473, fax 032 512 474, 29 Th Damnoen Kasem) Rooms with air-con 720-840B. Near the train station and the Royal Hua Hin Golf Course, the Golf Inn is a popular place with Thai golfers – there's a pro-shop on the premises.

Hua Hin also has several super-luxury hotels.

Hotel Sofitel Central Hua Hin Resort (Hua Hin Railway Hotel; ☎ 032 512 036–8, fax 032 511 014, in Bangkok ☎ 025 411 463, W www.centralhotelsresorts.com, 1 Th Damnoen Kasem) Rooms 7062-13,000B. This is a magnificent two-storey colonial-style place on the beach (see the boxed text 'Hua Hin Railway Hotel', in this section). It has rooms in the original L-shaped colonial wing, or in the new wing. Discounts of up to 40% may be possible during the week and in the low season.

Central Hua Hin Village (☎ *032 512 021–38, fax 032 511 014,* W *www.central hotelsresorts.com, Th Damnoen Kasem)* Bungalows 4600-6800B. Opposite is the old Railway Hotel's former Villa Wing, and until recently the Mercure, a collection of charming one- and two-bedroom wooden beach bungalows. Discounts of up to 40% are sometimes given during the low season.

Hua Hin Hilton Hotel (☎ *032 512 888, fax 032 511 135, in Bangkok* ☎ *022 713 435, fax 022 713 689,* W *www.hilton.com, 33/3 Th Naretdamri)* Rooms 7062-41,195B. The plush Hilton, off Th Naretdamri, was once the Meliá Hotel and was the first to rise above the Hua Hin skyline. There's not much of a beach in front of the hotel at high tide, but the adjacent free-form pool area is well designed to encompass sea views. Other facilities include two tennis courts, two air-con squash courts, a fitness centre, sauna and massage service.

Marriott Resort and Spa (☎ *032 511 881, fax 032 512 422,* W *www.marriott .com, 107/1 Th Hat Phetkasem)* Rooms with breakfast 2700-4900B, penthouse suites with Jacuzzi & rooftop garden 15,000B. Formerly the Royal Garden Resort, this is located along Hua Hin's southern beach and has rooms and suites with sea views in a modern high-rise complex. It offers tennis courts and swimming pools, nearby golf-course privileges, Thai massage services and water sport activities; the Royal Garden Resort also has a golf driving range.

Anantara Resort and Spa (☎ *032 520 250, fax 032 520 259, in Bangkok* ☎ *024 760 021, fax 024 761 120,* W *www.anan tara.com,* e *info@anantara.com, 43/1 Th Hat Phetkasem)* Villas 6100-7100B, suites 17,000B. Formerly the Royal Garden Village, this place north of town features Thai-style villas on 14 landscaped acres. Besides the spa and Thai massage services, the hotel offers tennis courts and swimming pools, nearby golf course privileges and water sport activities.

Chiva-Som International Health Resort (☎ *032 536 536, fax 032 511 154, 74/4 Phetkasem Hwy)* Rooms/pavilions US$315/ 399. Life membership US$6,666 (down from US$15,000 last edition). The US$26 million Chiva-Som features ocean-view rooms and Thai-style pavilions on seven beachside acres south of town (before Nong Khae and Ao Takiap). The name means Haven of Life in Thai-Sanskrit. The staff of 200 fuse Eastern and Western approaches to health with planned nutrition, step and aqua aerobics, Thai, Swedish or underwater massage, t'ai chi, dance, and the usual round of mudpacks, saunas (including a multi-level steam room), Jacuzzis and hydrotherapy. Flotation tanks containing tepid salt water are on hand for sensory deprivation sessions. Rates include three meals (with wine at dinner) along with health and fitness consultations, massage and all other activities. One-week, 10-day and two-week packages are also available.

There are a few more top-end places on beaches just north and south of town. Some of these add high-season supplements in December and January.

Places to Stay – Out of Town

Around Hat Takiap and Nong Khae south of Hua Hin you'll find a mixture of high-rise condo-style hotels and low-rise cottages.

Ta-kiab Beach Resort (☎ *032 512 639, fax 032 515 899)* Rooms with air-con & hot water 1200B. South of Khao Takiap village, this has clean rooms and is well managed. The seafood restaurant is quite good, but it's only open in the evening. The complex has a pool and is about 30m from the beach.

Nern Chalet (☎ *032 513 528)* Doubles with air-con, TV, hot water & phone 2000B. In a forested area called Nong Khae at the northern end of Ao Takiap is this quiet and comfortable low-rise hotel. Each room has its own balcony and breakfast is included in the price. Discounts of 20% to 40% are given on weekdays.

Hua Hin Bluewave Beach Resort (☎ *032 511 036, Th Nong Kae-Takiap)* Rooms 1900-2200B including breakfast. Between Nong Khae and Takiap, this is a condotel-style place with 149 rooms; on the grounds are a pool and fitness centre.

Suan Son Padiphat (☎ *032 511 239, Th Phetkasem, 240km marker)* Rooms with fan 400-600B, with air-con 500-1000B. In Hat Suan Son, this place offers tidy bungalows and rooms in a row-building. The compound is shaded by casuarina trees.

In low-key Pranburi, the **Pransiri Hotel** (☎ *032 621 061, 283 Th Phetkasem)* and **Pranburi Hotel** (☎ *032 622 042, 30/9-10 Th Phetkasem)* each have rooms from 150B.

Club Aldiana Siam (☎ *032 631 235, fax 032 631 236, in Bangkok ☎ 022 030 601)* Singles/doubles 2400/4800B. At water sports–oriented Club Aldiana there is resort-style accommodation, and rates include three buffet meals, all sports activities and entertainment. Among the amenities on the grounds are eight quartz-sand tennis courts.

Places to Eat

One of Hua Hin's major attractions has always been the colourful and inexpensive **Chatchai Market** in the centre of town off Th Phetkasem on Th Dechanuchit, where vendors gather nightly to fry, steam, grill, parboil or bake fresh Gulf seafood for hordes of hungry Thais. It is also excellent for Thai breakfast – it sells very good *jók* and *khâo tôm* (rice soups). Fresh-fried *paa-thâwng-kŏ* (Chinese doughnuts in the Hua Hin–style – small and crispy, not oily), are 2B for three. A few vendors also serve hot soy milk in bowls (5B) – break a few paa-thâwng-kŏ into the soy milk. During the day many of these same vendors prepare seafood snacks on the beach; cracked crab and cold Singha beer can be ordered without leaving one's sling chair.

The best seafood to eat in Hua Hin is *plaa sămlii* (cotton fish or kingfish), *plaa kapŏng* (perch), *plaa mèuk* (squid), *hăwy malaeng phûu* (mussels) and *puu* (crab). Fresh seafood is found in three main areas. First, there are some medium-priced restaurants along Th Damnoen Kasem near the Jed Pee Nong and City Beach hotels, and off Th Damnoen Kasem, on Th Phunsuk and Th Naretdamri. Second, there's excellent and inexpensive food in nearby Chinese-Thai restaurants and in the Chatchai Market described earlier. The third area is next to Tha Thiap Reua Pramong, the big fishing pier at the end of Th Chomsin. The fish is, of course, fresh off the boats but not necessarily the cheapest in town.

Saeng Thai (☎ *032 512 144, Th Naret-damri)* Mains 120-220B. Near the pier, this is the oldest seafood restaurant in Hua Hin and quite reliable if you know how to order.

The best value for money can be found in the smaller eating places on and off Th Chomsin, and in the Chatchai night market. There is also a **night market** on Th Chomsin.

Two Chinese-Thai seafood places on Th Phekkasem (neither of them bearing Roman-script signs) are both fairly good value.

Gee Cuisine *(Th Damnoen Kasem)* Dishes 40-80B. Next to the Jed Pee Nong, this caters mostly to faràng but the Thai food is generally good.

Taj Mahal *(Th Naretdamri)* Dishes 60-140B. This serves very good Indian food and is next to Bird guesthouse – almost reason enough to stay at the Bird.

Th Phunsuk and Th Naretdamri are becoming centres for faràng-oriented eateries. There must be more Italian restaurants here per capita than anywhere else in Thailand – except perhaps Chaweng on Ko Samui.

Lo Stivale (☎ *032 513 800, 132 Th Naretdamri)* Mains 120-180B. Lo Stivale serves the usual Italian dishes, including pizza, and claims to import most of its ingredients from the Old Country.

Luciano Pizza House (☎ *032 530 709, 7 Soi Selakam)* Dishes 140-180B. Located just off Th Naretdamri in a cosy wooden house, this features wood-fired pizza and other Italian favourites.

Piaf *(23 Th Naretdamri)* Dishes 80-120B. Piaf is a German/Austrian restaurant that also offers Thai cuisine.

Le Chablis (☎ *032 531 499, 88 Th Naret-damri)* Mains 200-280B. This serves French food and wine (along with live piano music in the evenings).

La Villa (☎ *032 513 435, Th Phunsuk)* Dishes 100-150B. The Italian La Villa has pizza, spaghetti, lasagne etc.

Sunshine Restaurant & Bakery (Th Naretdamri) Dishes 20-80B. This serves German food and fresh baked goods.

Al Fresco (☎ 032 532 678, Th Damnoen Kasem) and *Italian Ice Cream (☎ 032 533 753, 19/4 Th Damnoen Kasem)* offer homemade Italian-style ice cream.

Capo's (Th Damnoen Kasem) Mains 120-180B. In the same building as Al Fresco, this specialises in steak and spare ribs.

Buffalo Bill's Steak & Grill (☎ 032 532 727, Th Damnoen Kasem) Dishes 80-140B. Meat lovers can get their fill here, near the post office.

Berny's Inn (The Golfer's 19th Hole; ☎ 032 532 601, Hua Hin Bazaar) Dishes 60-100B. Open 2pm-2am. This British-style place at the Hua Hin Bazaar, a small shopping centre off Th Damnoen Kasem, specialises in steaks, pork chops, burgers, sandwiches and other hearty Western fare. Berny also freely gives out information about golfing in Hua Hin.

Other British-style pubs with footy on the telly include *Baan Farang (☎ 032 532 692, Hua Hin Bazaar)*, *Taxi Jack's (23 Soi Selakam, Th Naretdamri)* and *The Strawberry Pig (Hua Hin Bazaar)*.

Entertainment

Several faràng bars under European management can be found at the Hua Hin Bazaar, off Th Naretdamri and Th Damnoen Kasem. Many of these offer the familiar Thai hostess atmosphere, but a few bill themselves as sports bars and have a wide-screen TV tuned to sporting events.

Rockestra Cafe (☎ 032 512 175, 26/1 Th Phunsuk) This open-air cafe behind Wat Hua Hin is a lively place with a house band on weekdays and guest bands on weekends.

Stone Town (Th Damnoen Kaseman) This old-West-style pub next to Jed Pee Nong Hotel features live folk and country music nightly. There's no cover charge and drink prices are reasonable.

Getting There & Away

Bus Buses from Bangkok's Southern bus terminal cost 190B (1st class air-con) and 135B (2nd class air-con). The trip takes 3½ to four hours. Various agencies on Th Khao San (Khao San Rd) in Bangkok operate minivans to Hua Hin for 200B per person – but why pay more for less leg and head room than you'd get on a 1st-class air-con bus?

Ordinary buses for Hua Hin leave Phetchaburi regularly for 25B (30B air-con). The same bus can be picked up in Cha-am for 10B (20B air-con). Other ordinary buses from the main terminal in Hua Hin go to/from Prachuap Khiri Khan (30B, 42B air-con), Chumphon (77B, 110B air-con), Surat Thani (136B, 190B air-con), Phuket (198B, 277B air-con), Krabi (177B, 248B air-con) and Hat Yai (251B, 392B air-con).

Pran Tour (☎ 032 511 654) on Th Sasong near the Siripetchkasem Hotel in Hua Hin runs air-con buses to Bangkok about every hour from 3am to 9pm, for 128B 1st class air-con.

Train In 1922 the Royal Railway of Siam (now the State Railway of Thailand) extended a rail link to Hua Hin and today the restored, dollhouse-like train station is a minor attraction in itself. The southern trains described under Phetchaburi's Getting There & Away section also stop here. The train takes 3¾ hours from Bangkok; 1st-class fare is 202B (express only), 2nd class 102B (rapid and express only), 3rd class is 44B. Rapid and express surcharges apply.

You can also come by train from any other station on the southern railway line, including Phetchaburi (3rd class 10B), Nakhon Pathom (2nd/3rd class 71/30B), Prachuap Khiri Khan (3rd class 14B), Surat Thani (2nd/3rd class 146/63B) and Hat Yai (2nd/3rd class 243/105B). The 1st- and 2nd-class fares do not include rapid or express surcharges.

Getting Around

Local buses and sǎwngthǎew from Hua Hin to the beaches of Khao Takiap, Khao Tao and Suan Son cost 10B per person. These buses run from around 6am until 6pm; the ones to Hat Takiap leave from opposite the main bus terminal on Th Sasong; the latter two leave from Th Chomsin opposite the wát. Buses to Pranburi are 12B and leave from the same area on Th Chomsin.

Săamláw fares in Hua Hin have been set by the municipal authorities so there shouldn't be any haggling. Some sample fares are: the train station to the beach, 20B; the bus terminal to Th Naretdamri, 30B to 40B (depending on size of your bags); Chatchai Market to the fishing pier, 20B; the train station to the Marriot Resort and Spa, 40B. Most drivers will ask for twice this much.

Motorcycles and bicycles can be rented from a couple of places on Th Damnoen Kasem near the Jed Pee Nong Hotel. Motorcycle rates are reasonable: 200B per day for 100cc, 250B to 300B for 125cc. Occasionally larger bikes – 400 to 750cc – are available for 500B to 600B a day. Bicycles are 60B to 80B per day. Avis Rent-A-Car (☎ 032 512 021–38) has an office at Hotel Sofitel Central Hua Hin. There are also cheaper places renting sedans for 1300B to 1500B a day, or Suzuki Caribians for 800B to 1000B, but of course there's more chance of something going wrong if you rent from one of these – the vehicles aren't always in the best shape.

You can hire boats out to Ko Singtoh for 1000B to 1500B a day at the fishing pier in Hua Hin, or on Hat Takiap if you haggle.

KHAO SAM ROI YOT NATIONAL PARK
อุทยานแห่งชาติเขาสามร้อยยอด

This 98-sq-km park's name means Three Hundred Peaks. It has magnificent views of the Gulf coastline if you can handle a little climbing. Khao Daeng is only about a half-hour's walk from the park headquarters, and from here you can see the ocean as well as some brackish lagoons. If you have the time and energy, climb the 605m Khao Krachom for even better views. If you're lucky, you may come across a serow (Asian goat-antelope) while hiking. The lagoons and coastal marshes are great places for bird watching. Along the coast you may see an occasional pod of Irrawaddy dolphins (plaa lohmaa hǔa bàat).

Be sure to bring insect repellent for any park visits. King Rama IV (King Mongkut) and a large entourage of Thai and European guests convened here on 18 August 1868 to observe a total solar eclipse – predicted, so the story goes, by the monarch himself – and enjoy an elaborate feast prepared by a French chef. Two months later the king expired from malaria, contracted via mosquito bites inflicted here (see the boxed text 'The Wrath of Rahu' in this section). The risk of malaria in the park is relatively low, but mosquitoes can be pesky.

There is an entrance fee of 200B per adult and 100B for kids under 14 years old.

Fauna
Notable wildlife around Khao Sam Roi Yot includes the crab-eating macaque, dusky langur, barking deer, slow loris, Malayan pangolin, fishing cat, palm civet, otter, serow, Javan mongoose and monitor lizard. However, park officials admit that it's fairly uncommon to actually spot any wild animals, possibly due to the rise of tourism!

Because the park lies at the intersection of the East Asian and Australian fly ways, as many as 300 migratory and resident bird species have been recorded, including the yellow bittern, cinnamon bittern, purple swamp hen, water rail, ruddy-breasted crake, bronze-winged jacana, grey heron, painted stork, whistling duck, spotted eagle and black-headed ibis. The park has Thailand's largest fresh water marsh (along with mangroves and mudflats), and is one of only three places in the country where the purple heron breeds.

Waterfowl are most commonly seen in the cool season. Encroachment by shrimp farmers in the vicinity has sadly destroyed a substantial portion of mangroves and other wetlands, thus depriving the birds of an important habitat.

Beaches & Canals
A sandy beach flanked on three sides by dry limestone hills and casuarinas, **Hat Laem Sala** has a small visitors centre, restaurant, bungalows and camping area. Boats, which take up to 10 people, can be hired from

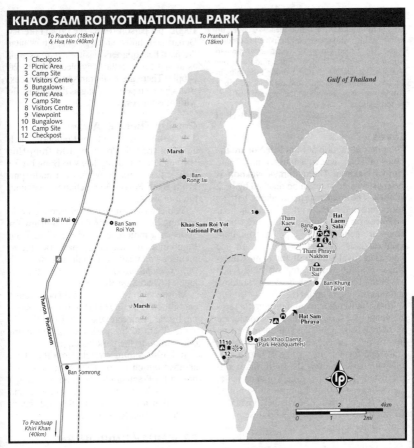

KHAO SAM ROI YOT NATIONAL PARK

1 Checkpost
2 Picnic Area
3 Camp Site
4 Visitors Centre
5 Bungalows
6 Picnic Area
7 Camp Site
8 Visitors Centre
9 Viewpoint
10 Bungalows
11 Camp Site
12 Checkpost

To Pranburi (18km) & Hua Hin (40km)

To Pranburi (18km)

Gulf of Thailand

Marsh

Ban Rong Jai

Ban Rai Mai

Ban Sam Roi Yot

Khao Sam Roi Yot National Park

Tham Kaew

Bang Pu

Hat Laem Sala

Tham Phraya Nakhon

Tham Sai

Ban Khung Tanot

Thanon Phetkasem

Marsh

Hat Sam Phraya

Ban Khao Daeng (Park Headquarters)

Ban Somrong

To Prachuap Khiri Khan (40km)

NORTH-WESTERN GULF COAST

Bang Pu to the beach for 200B return. You can also reach the beach from Bang Pu via a steep trail, about 20 minute's walk.

Hat Sam Phraya, 5km south of Hat Laem Sala, is a 1km-long beach with a restaurant and washrooms. The park headquarters is just past the village of Khao Daeng, about 4km south-west of Hat Sam Phraya. A larger visitor centre at the headquarters features well-curated exhibits; there are also nature trails nearby. Binoculars or telescopes can be rented for bird watching; there are several bird blinds nearby. September to March are the best months to see waterfowl.

A 4km canal trip in a 10-person boat along **Khlong Khao Daeng** can be arranged in Ban Khao Daeng for 400B. The trip lasts about two hours and passes mangrove remnants and waterfowl habitats. The birds are most active in the early morning or late afternoon. You might also spot monitor lizards and monkeys. Before heading out, however, you may want to have a chat with your prospective guide to see how well s/he speaks English. Better guides will know the English names of common waterfowl and will point them out to you. One reader wrote in to relate the following:

After being offered a guide for a 20km canoe trip, I failed to inquire further. Bad idea. We ended up with a 'guide' who spoke no English and couldn't canoe. He turned out to be just a local man to whom we paid 300B to sit in the middle of our boat – safely oarless – so he wouldn't dump us in the river, as he repeatedly did early in the trip. I now advocate asking about the expertise of purported 'guides'.

Brad Berthal

Caves

The other attraction at Sam Roi Yot are the caves of Tham Kaew, Tham Sai and Tham Phraya Nakhon. **Tham Phraya Nakhon** is the most visited and can be reached by boat or foot. The boat trip takes about half an hour there and back, while it's half an hour each way on foot along a steep, rocky trail. There are actually two large caverns, both with sinkholes that allow light in. In one cave is a royal sala built for King Chulalongkorn, who would stop off here when travelling back and forth between Bangkok and Nakhon Si Thammarat.

Tham Kaew, 2km from the Bang Pu turn-off, features a series of chambers connected by narrow passageways; you enter the first cavern by a ladder. Stalactites and other limestone formations – some of which glitter with calcite crystals as if diamond-encrusted (hence the cave's name, Jewel Cave) – are plentiful. Lamps can be rented for 100B, but Tham Kaew is best visited in the company of a park guide because of the dangerous footing.

Tham Sai is in a hill near Ban Khrun Tanot, about 2.5km from the main road between Ale Sala and Sam Phraya beaches. You can rent lamps for 50B from a shelter near the cave mouth. A 280m trail leads up the hillside to the cave, which features a large single cavern. Be careful of steep drop-offs in the cave.

Guides can be hired at the park office for 100B for two people, 50B for each additional person in the group (up to five). Not much English is spoken but they're accustomed to leading non-Thai as well as Thai visitors.

Places to Stay & Eat

Bungalows *(Royal Forestry Department; in Bangkok* ☎ *025 614 292 ext 747)* Camp sites 10B, tents for 3 people 40B, bungalows 400-1000B, per person 100B. The Royal Forestry Department hires out large bungalows near the park headquarters' visitor centre as well as at Hat Laem Sala; they sleep four to 20 people. There are restaurants at both places. Bring insect repellent along as the park is rife with mosquitoes.

Getting There & Away

The park is 37km south of Pranburi. Catch a bus or train to Pranburi (10B from Hua Hin) and then a săwngthăew to Bang Pu for 20B – these run between 6am and 4pm. From Bang Pu you must charter a vehicle, hitch or walk.

You can save the hassle of finding a ride in Bang Pu by chartering a săwngthăew for 300B or a motorcycle taxi for 150B from Pranburi all the way to the park. Be sure to mention you want to go to the national park *(ùthayaan hàeng châat)* rather than the village of Khao Sam Roi Yot.

Most convenient of all would be to rent a car or motorbike in Hua Hin. If you're coming by car or motorcycle from Hua Hin, it's about 25km to the park turn-off, then another 38km to the park headquarters.

If you're coming straight from Bangkok, another option is to catch an air-con bus bound for Prachuap Khiri Khan. Ask to get off at Ban Somrong (286.5km marker) and then hitch a ride 13km to the park headquarters at Ban Khao Daeng.

PRACHUAP KHIRI KHAN
อ.เมืองประจวบคีรีขันธ์

postcode 77000 • pop 14,900
Roughly 80km south of Hua Hin (though somewhat smaller), Prachuap Khiri Khan serves as the capital of the province of the same name. There are no swimming beaches in town, but the 8km-long bay of Ao Prachuap is pretty enough. Better beaches can be found north and south of town. The seafood here is fantastic, however, and cheaper than in Hua Hin. Fishing is still the mainstay of the local economy.

Prachuap (specifically Ao Manao) was one of seven points on the Gulf of Thailand

The Wrath of Rahu?

Despite many years as a highly disciplined Buddhist monk in the austere Thammayut sect, prior to the death of his brother (Rama III) and his own ascension to the throne, King Mongkut (Rama IV) had a keen interest in science. He felt that one of his duties as Siam's monarch was to replace Thai superstition with logic and reason wherever possible.

One of the king's scientific passions was the study of astronomy, and in early 1868 His Majesty calculated the timing of the upcoming 18 August solar eclipse, as well as its exact path over Siam. The king decided to make the event a public lesson in astronomy by organising a large expedition to a spot on the Thai coast where the eclipse could be viewed in totality. According to *Katya and the Prince of Siam* by Eileen Hunter & Narisa Chakrabongse, Rama IV chose 'a wild and uninhabitable spot about 140 miles south of Bangkok'. That translates to 228.4km, almost exactly where Khao Sam Roi Yot shows up in today's atlases, although other chronicles claim the spot was 50km to 60km farther south at Wa Kaw, near Prachuap Khiri Khan.

At the king's invitation, a French expedition travelled all the way overland (the Suez Canal hadn't yet been dug) to Siam to join Rama IV in convincing his subjects that 'contrary to their belief, the eclipse would not be caused by the dragon Rahu making a meal of the sun and disgorging it only when frightened by beating gongs and letting off fireworks, but could be predicted beforehand and explained by rather more rational methods'. According to the French expedition leader, 'The King of Siam with all his court, part of his army and a crowd of Europeans, arrived by sea on 8th August in 12 steamboats of the Royal Navy, while by land came troops of oxen, horses and 50 elephants'. Also in attendance were Mongkut's sons Damrong and Chulalongkorn, along with the court astrologers, who could hardly be blamed if they concealed a certain lack of enthusiasm.

Although a thick layer of cloud threatened to spoil the event – much to the chagrin of the French who had travelled 10,000 miles and spent a fortune to support this royal endeavour – the sky cleared 20 minutes before totality and the event became a grand success.

Unaccounted for in the king's calculations was the fact that the chosen viewing spot was a low-lying swamp. Both Rama IV and 15-year-old Prince Chulalongkorn contracted malaria during their 10-day astronomical sojourn; the king died shortly after his return to Bangkok, on his 64th birthday.

Joe Cummings

coast where Japanese troops landed on 8 December 1941 during their invasion of Thailand. Several street names around town commemorate the ensuing skirmish: Phithak Chat – Defend Country, Salachip – Sacrifice Life, Suseuk – Fight Battle.

Information

Prachuap has its own city-run tourist office next to the Thaed Saban Bungalows. The staff are very friendly, and they have maps and photos of all the attractions in the area.

Things to See & Do

At the northern end of Ao Prachuap is **Khao Chong Krajok** (Mirror Tunnel Mountain – named after the hole through the side of the mountain that appears to reflect the sky). At the top is **Wat Thammikaram**, established by Rama VI. A metal ladder leads into the tunnel from the wát grounds. You can also climb the hill for a view of the town and bay – and entertain the hordes of monkeys who live here.

If you continue north from Prachuap Khiri Khan around Ao Prachuap to the headland you'll come to a small boat-building village on **Ao Bang Nang Lom**, where they still make wooden fishing vessels using traditional Thai methods. It takes about two months to finish a 12m boat, which will sell for around 400,000B without an engine. The industrious folks at Bang Nang Lom also catch fish called *plaa ching*

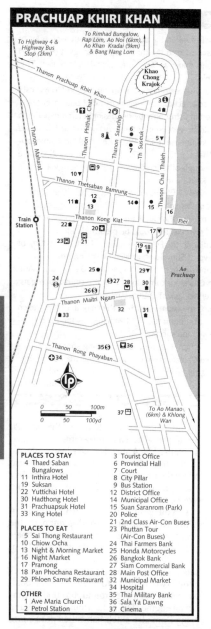

PRACHUAP KHIRI KHAN

To Highway 4 &
Highway Bus
Stop (2km)

To Rimhad Bungalow,
Rap Lom, Ao Noi (6km),
Ao Khan Kradai (9km)
& Bang Nang Lom

Thanon Prachuap Khiri Khan

Khao
Chong
Krajok

Thanon Mahrat

Thanon Phithak Chat

Thanon Sarachip

Th Suseuk

Thanon Chai Thaleh

Thanon Thetsaban Bamrung

Thanon Kong Kiat

Train
Station

Pier

Ao
Prachuap

Thanon Maitri Ngam

Thanon Rong Phayaban

0   50   100m
0   50   100yd

To Ao Manao
(6km) & Khlong
Wan

PLACES TO STAY	3 Tourist Office
4 Thaed Saban	6 Provincial Hall
Bungalows	7 Court
11 Inthira Hotel	8 City Pillar
19 Suksan	9 Bus Station
22 Yuttichai Hotel	12 District Office
30 Hadthong Hotel	14 Municipal Office
31 Prachuapsuk Hotel	15 Suan Saranrom (Park)
33 King Hotel	20 Police
	21 2nd Class Air-Con Buses
PLACES TO EAT	23 Phuttan Tour
5 Sai Thong Restaurant	(Air-Con Buses)
10 Chiow Ocha	24 Thai Farmers Bank
13 Night & Morning Market	25 Honda Motorcycles
16 Night Market	26 Bangkok Bank
17 Pramong	27 Siam Commercial Bank
18 Pan Phochana Restaurant	28 Main Post Office
29 Phloen Samut Restaurant	32 Municipal Market
	34 Hospital
OTHER	35 Thai Military Bank
1 Ave Maria Church	36 Sala Ya Dawng
2 Petrol Station	37 Cinema

chang, which they dry along the roadsides and then store for Sri Lankan traders who arrive by ship at certain times of the year specifically to buy up the catch.

West of the beach at Ao Bang Nang Lom is a canal, **Khlong Bang Nang Lom**, lined with picturesque mangroves. A few kilometres north of Ao Prachuap is another bay, **Ao Noi**, the site of a small fishing village with a few rooms to let.

Beaches South of Ao Prachuap, around a small headland, is the scenic **Ao Manao**, a bay ringed by a clean white-sand beach with small islands offshore. A Thai air force base guards access to the bay (a possible legacy of the 1941 Japanese invasion), and the beach was closed to the public until 1990, when the local authorities decided to open the area to day visitors. The beach is about 2.5km from the base entrance and is very clean due to the military policy of giving the sand a weekly clean-up. There are several salas along the beach, a hotel, restaurant, toilets and a shower. Beach vendors offer chairs, umbrellas and inner tubes for rent at 10B each, plus seafood, North-Eastern Thai dishes and beverages. You must show your passport at the gate and sign in; the beach closes at 8pm except for military personnel and guests at the hotel (see the Ao Manao entry under Places to Stay later in this section).

Each year in September, on the air force base at Ao Manao, the Thai air force sponsors an impressive sound-and-light show commemorating Thai WWII heroes; it's open to the public and entry is free.

Eight kilometres south of Ao Manao, **Hat Wa Kaw** is a pleasant, casuarina-lined beach that is even quieter and cleaner than Ao Manao. A small, recently built museum of astronomy (no English labels) and a Rama IV monument commemorate the 1868 solar eclipse, which the king and his 15-year-old son Prince Chulalongkorn came south to witness. Both contracted malaria during their visit and Rama IV died soon after returning to Bangkok. (Whether the eclipse viewing event really happened here, or at Khao Sam Roi Yot as other chronicles say, is a matter of debate. See also the boxed text 'The Wrath of Rahu?' earlier in this chapter.) Also on display on the museum grounds is an American-built steam locomotive from Baldwin Locomotive Works, 1925.

Organised Tours

Local resident Pinit Ounope arranges popular day tours to Khao Sam Roi Yot National Park, Dan Singkhon and to nearby beaches, other national parks and waterfalls. He lives at 144 Th Chai Thaleh near the beach in town and invites travellers to visit him. His house is rather difficult to find, so take a *túk túk* (motorised pedicab) or a motorcycle taxi. The typical day tour is 500B for person (on the back of a motorcycle) or 1000B for two people (in a pickup truck).

Places to Stay

Prachuap Khiri Khan There are a number of options here.

Yuttichai Hotel (☎ 032 611 055, 115 Th Kong Kiat) Rooms with 1 bed/2 beds & fan 120/180B, with bath 200/240B. Rooms are fair; those at the back of the hotel are quieter. The proprietors lock the front door at 11pm, after which you'll have to ring a doorbell to get in.

Inthira Hotel (☎/fax 032 611 418, 118-120 Th Phithak Chat) Singles/doubles with bath 200-240B. The eight-room Inthira is quite near the night market and tourist office. It's a bit noisy but the location makes up for it.

Prachuapsuk Hotel (☎ 032 601 019, fax 032 601 711, 63-5 Th Suseuk) Rooms with fan/air-con & bath 150/350B. In a two-storey shophouse near the market, this is a friendly, family-run place. There is no English sign.

King Hotel (☎ 032 611 170, 800/3 Th Phithak Chat) Rooms with fan 200B. The three-storey King has largeish rooms, but no English sign.

Suksan (☎ 032 611 145, 11 Th Suseuk) Rooms with fan 270-320B, bungalows with air-con 400-450B. Facing Ao Prachuap is the Suksan, which, because of its location on the bay, is better than the average Thai-Chinese hotel. Also a huge plus is its proximity to the Pan Phochana Restaurant.

Thaed Saban Bungalows (Thetsaban Bungalows, Municipal Bungalows or Mirror Mountain Bungalows; ☎ 032 611 204, Th Suseuk) Bungalows with 1 room, fan/air-con & bath for 2 people 300/500B, with 2 rooms for 4 people 600B, with 3 rooms for 6 people 1200B, with 4 rooms for 8 people 1500B, extra persons 50B. Also facing the bay are these plain but well-kept bungalows, which are now privately owned.

Hadthong Hotel (☎ 032 601 050, fax 032 601 057, Bangkok ☎ 024 113 044, 7 Th Suseuk) Singles/doubles with air-con, TV, fridge & phone 450/700B, with mountain/sea view 700/900B, suites 1300B. The slightly upmarket Hadthong, next to the bay, has modern rooms. There is a pool and restaurant/coffee shop on the premises. The suites sleep up to four people.

Rimhad Bungalow (Rimbad Rest; ☎ 032 601 626, 35 Th Suanson) Doubles with air-con & TV 400-600B, with fridge & ocean view 650B. North of the city, on the road to Ao Noi, this offers tiny bungalows or larger rooms in a hotel building. The bungalows face scenic Khlong Bang Nang Lom and mangroves.

Ao Manao There are three choices here.

Ahkan Sawadii Khan Wing 53 (Manow Bay Beach Hotel; ☎ 032 611 087) Rooms with TV, phone & shower 500B, town houses with bathtubs & hot water 1000B. This sits near the centre of the beach and is operated by the Thai air force. Rooms are supposedly reserved for Thai air force officers and their guests, and only open to foreigners who make reservations through a Wing 53 officer – no walk-ins accepted. All units have sea views. There is no English sign.

Seasand House Resort (☎ 032 661 483, fax 032 661 250, 409/1 Th Prachuap-Khlong Wan) Rooms with TV, fridge, air-con & hot water 700B. A few kilometres south of Ao Manao at Khlong Wan, this offers small, concrete bungalows.

Ban Forty (☎ 032 661 437, 555 Th Prachuap-Khlong Wan) Four-person bungalows 800B, six-person rooms 1000B, two-storey 15-person house 1500B, 25-person house 3500B. In the same area as

Seasand, this offers a number of concrete houses and bungalows located on 8 sq *rai* (hectares) of land with a private coconut palm-lined beach. Owned by a friendly retired Thai air force officer of Thai/English descent, it has simple but clean units. Meals can be arranged ahead of time and served in a sala near the beach.

Ao Noi In Ao Noi there are several rooms and small 'weekend inns', most catering to Thais.

Aow Noi Beach Resort (☎ 032 601 354, 206 Tambon Ao Noi) Doubles with bath & fan 600B, air-con 800B. This offers rustic cottages that have seen better days, but are not too bad. Facilities include a small bar and restaurant with Thai food, plus a clean, secluded beach. The owners of this establishment seem to have plans to renovate or expand every time we swing through, but so far, nothing has changed.

Places to Eat

Because of its well-deserved reputation for fine seafood, Prachuap has many restaurants. One of the seafood specialities of Prachuap Khiri Khan that you shouldn't miss is whole cottonfish that's sliced lengthways and left to dry in the sun for half a day, then fried quickly in a wok, called *plaa sǎmlii tàet dìaw*. It's often served with mango salad on the side.

The least expensive place to dine in the evening is the **night market** that convenes near the government offices in the middle of town. On Th Chai Thaleh, north of the pier, is a smaller **night market** with around 10 vendors selling good seafood at affordable prices; tables set up along the sea wall sometimes get a good breeze. Both night markets are open late; the first until midnight, the second until 2am.

Pan Phochana Restaurant (☎ 032 611 195, 11 Th Suseuk) Dishes 60-100B. Behind Suksan Hotel, this is one of the best seafood restaurants. It's famous for its *hàw mòk hǎwy* (ground fish curry steamed in mussels on the half-shell).

Just north of the Pan Phochana is a good **night market** with many seafood stalls.

Sai Thong Restaurant (Chiow Ocha 2; ☎ 032 611 293, Th Chai Thaleh) Near the Thaed Saban Bungalows, this is one of the best seafood restaurants. It serves Carlsberg draught beer and imported wine, and is a popular stop for tour buses.

Other good restaurants include the *Chiow Ocha* (☎ 032 611 118, 88/1 Th Phithak Chat) and the *Pramong* (☎ 032 611 168, 36 Th Chai Thaleh).

Phloen Samut Restaurant (☎ 032 611 115, 44 Th Chai Thaleh) Dishes 60-180B. Adjacent to Hadthong Hotel, this is a good outdoor seafood place, though it doesn't always have everything that's listed on the menu.

Across from the Inthira Hotel is a small *morning market* with tea stalls that serve cheap curries and noodles.

Duck noodle restaurant (☎ 032 611 055, 115 Th Kong Kiat) Dishes 20-35B. Open 11am-3.30pm. A small, no-name restaurant in the same building as the Yuttichai Hotel, it has excellent *bàmìi pèt* (duck noodle soup).

Several good seafood restaurants can be found along the road north of Ao Prachuap on the way to Ao Noi.

Rap Lom (☎ 032 601 677, Th Suseuk) Dishes 80-200B. Rap Lom is a popular choice along this road. A house speciality is *kaeng sôm yâwt mákhǎam* (prawns in sour tamarind-leaf soup) – look for the Carlsberg Beer sign.

Entertainment

Sala Ya Dawng (Soi Phun Samakhi) Opposite the Thai Military Bank, this is a low-key, open-air, old-West–style bar with live *phleng phêua chiwít* (Thai folk music). Although the place touts its namesake *yaa dawng* (herbal liquor), which can be bought by the bottle or by the shot, beer is also available. There is no roman-script sign. A food stall next door supplies the bar with eats.

Getting There & Away

Bus From Bangkok, ordinary buses cost 93B and leave the Southern bus terminal frequently between 3am and 9.20pm. Second-class air-con buses cost 122B from the same terminal, operating between 7am and 1am. Phuttan Tour operates 15 first-class air-con buses a day in both directions between 6.15am and 1am for 180B. In the opposite direction, Phuttan Tour air-con buses to Bangkok leave from 182 Th Phithak Chat at similar intervals. In either direction the trip takes four to five hours.

From Hua Hin buses are 25B and leave from the bus station on Th Sasong every 20 minutes from 7am to 3pm, taking 1½ to two hours.

From Prachuap you can catch ordinary buses or 2nd-class air-con buses to Chumphon (55/77B), Surat Thani (110/240B), Nakhon Si Thammarat (150/210B), Krabi (170/240B), Phang-Nga (150/210B), Don Sak (for Ko Samui, 128/193B) and Phuket (173/242B).

The air-con bus from Bangkok to Ko Samui stops on the highway in Prachuap between midnight and 1am – if seats are available you can buy a through ticket to Ko Samui for 240B. It's a five-minute, 30B motorcycle-taxi ride from the town centre to the highway bus stop. Though you'd have to be desperately wanting to leave Prachuap for Ko Samui to go to all this trouble with no guarantee of getting a seat.

Train For departure details from Bangkok, see the earlier Phetchaburi Getting There & Away section: the same services apply. Fares from Bangkok are 272B for 1st class, 135B for 2nd class and 58B for 3rd class; to these add the appropriate rapid or express charges. The ordinary train between Hua Hin and Prachuap costs 14B; from Hua Hin it leaves at 5.50pm, arriving in Prachuap at 7.10pm. There are also several rapid and express trains between the two towns, but the time saved is negligible. A 3rd-class ticket on to Chumphon is 24B.

Getting Around

Prachuap is small enough to get around on foot, or you can hop on a túk-túk – actually more akin to the Isan-style *sakailaep*, here called *săaleng* – for 10B anywhere on the main roads.

A săaleng to Ao Noi costs 30B to 40B.

The Honda dealer on Th Sarachip rents 100cc motorcycles for 250B a day, including a helmet.

A motorbike taxi to Ao Manao costs 20B to 25B. They aren't permitted past the gate unless both driver and passenger are wearing helmets. If you are without a helmet you'll have to walk the 3km to the beach.

AROUND PRACHUAP KHIRI KHAN
Wat Khao Tham Khan Kradai
วัดเขาถ้ำคานกระไ ด

About 8km north of town, following the same road beyond Ao Noi, is this small cave wát at one end of **Ao Khan Kradai** (also known as Ao Khan Bandai – a long, beautiful bay).

A trail at the base of the limestone hill leads up and around the side to a small cavern and then to a larger one, which contains a reclining Buddha. If you have a torch you can proceed to a larger second chamber also containing Buddha images. From this trail you get a good view of Ao Khan Kradai. The beach here is suitable for swimming and is virtually deserted. It's not far from Ao Noi, so you could stay in Ao Noi and walk to the beach. Or you could stay in town, rent a motorcycle and make a day trip to Ao Khan Kradai.

Dan Singkhon
ด่านสิงขร

Just south of Prachuap is a road leading west to Dan Singkhon on the Myanmar border. This is the narrowest point in Thailand between the Gulf of Thailand and Myanmar – only 12km across. The Myanmar side changed from Karen to Yangon control following skirmishes in 1988–89. The border is open to Thai and Burmese citizens only. On the Thai side is a small frontier village and a Thai police camp with wooden semi-underground bunkers built in a circle.

Off the road on the way to Dan Singkhon are a couple of small cave hermitages. The more famous one at **Khao Hin Thoen**, surrounded by a park of the same name, has some interesting rock formations and sculptures – but watch out for the dogs. The road to Khao Hin Thoen starts where the paved road to Dan Singkhon breaks left. **Khao Khan Hawk** (also known as Phutthakan Bang Kao) is a less well-known cave nearby where an elderly monk, Luang Phaw Buaphan Chatimetho, lives. Devotees from a local village bring him food each morning.

THAP SAKAE & BANG SAPHAN
ทับสะแก/บางสะพาน

These two districts lie south of Prachuap Khiri Khan and together they offer a string of fairly good beaches that receive hardly any tourists.

The town of Thap Sakae is set back from the coast and isn't much, but along the seashore there are a few places to stay (see the following Places to Stay & Eat section). The beach opposite Thap Sakae isn't anything special either, but north and south of town are the white-sand beaches of **Hat Wanakon** and **Hat Laem Kum**. There is no private accommodation at these beaches at the moment, but you could ask permission to camp at Wat Laem Kum, which is on a prime spot right in the middle of Hat Laem Kum. Laem Kum is only 3.5km from Thap Sakae and at the northern end is the fishing village of Ban Don Sai, where you can buy food. Hat Wanakon is part of Hat Wanakon National Marine Park, which covers 22.6 sq km of coastline and 15.4 sq km of marine resources; it's primary use is as a training centre for park division staff.

Bang Saphan (Bang Saphan Yai) is no great shakes as a town either, but its long beaches are beginning to attract some speculative development. In the vicinity of Bang Saphan you'll find the beaches of **Hat Sai Kaew**, **Hat Ban Krut**, **Hat Khiriwong**, **Hat Ban Nong Mongkon**, **Hat (Ao) Baw Thawng Lang**, **Hat Pha Daeng** and **Hat Bang Boet**. All are worth visiting. Getting around can be a problem; there isn't much public transport between these beaches.

There are also islands off the coast, including **Ko Thalu** and **Ko Sing**, where there is good snorkelling and diving from the end of January to mid-May. The Coral and Suan Luang resorts in Bang Saphan can arrange half-day diving excursions to these islands for 500B to 700B.

Places to Stay & Eat
Thap Sakae There are three places to choose from here.

Chaowarit (Chawalit; ☎ *032 671 010, 38 Th Phetkasem)* Rooms with fan & bath 200-300B. Right off the highway near the southern end of town, this has simple but clean rooms – good value overall.

Sukkasem (☎ *032 671 598, 39/15 Th Sukhaphiban)* Rooms 150-180B. Around the corner, less than 100m away from Chaowarit, this has basic rooms. It's a bit of a dive but friendly, and not as buggy as it might first appear.

On the coast opposite Thap Sakae are a couple of concrete block-style bungalows for 200B to 450B.

Chan Reuan Hotel (☎ *032 671 890, 032 671 930, fax 032 671 401, 37 Th Liap Chai Thaleh)* Rooms with fan 200-300B, air-con 400-1000B. Recently renovated, this place has clean rooms, some with ocean views, and a good restaurant.

Hat Ban Krut There are a number of options here.

Reun Chun Seaview (☎*/fax 032 695 061)* Bungalows with 1 bedroom, air-con, TV & fridge 800B, with 2 bedrooms & bath 1800B. Sturdy bungalows with verandas, some with views. A seafood restaurant is on the premises.

Ban Rim Haad (☎ *032 695 205)* Triples with air-con, TV & fridge 800B, for 10 people 1500B. This offers bungalows in a nicely landscaped garden adjacent to a large coconut grove. The restaurant serves seafood.

Ban Klang Aow Beach Resort (☎*/fax 032 695 086)* Bungalows with air-con, TV & fridge 1000-2000B. This is an upmarket place on the beach with a clean pool. The clientele is mostly Thai.

Suan Ban Krut Resort (☎ *032 695 103, fax 032 695 217)* Bungalows 1500-3500B.

This has 21 bungalows (a bit smaller than the ones at Ban Klang Aow Beach Resort), as well as a number of beach homes for sale or rent. Facilities include a pool, fitness centre and putting green.

Hat Khiriwong To get here, take a train or bus to the nearby town of Ban Krut, then a motorcycle taxi (40-50B) to Hat Khiriwong.

Sai-Eak Beach Resort Bungalows with satellite TV & fridge 2000-4000B. Sai-Eak opened in 1996 and is the nicest resort in the area. It's right on the beach, and features a swimming pool and a variety of bungalows – price depends on whether they face the pool or sea. Low-season discounts of up to 50% are available from May to November.

Bang Saphan Along the bay of Ao Bang Saphan are several beach hotels and bungalows.

Hat Somboon Sea View (☎ 032 543 344, fax 032 543 345) Singles with fan 250B, singles/doubles with hot bath, TV, fridge & air-con 330/440B, bungalows 400B. This is sometimes booked solid with Bangkok-based civil servants on a holiday junket – it can be chaotic and noisy.

Boonsom Guest House (☎ 032 291 273) Bungalows with fan in low/high season 200/300B. This has passable wooden bungalows set on a grassy piece of land – not the fanciest on this beach but certainly one of the cheapest. There's an excellent restaurant opposite.

Van Veena Hotel (Wanwiinaa, ☎ 032 691 251) Rooms with fan/air-con, TV & fridge 250/550B. Not a bad place for the price. Have a look at the fan rooms before laying down your money – some are much better than others.

Bangsaphan Resort (☎ 032 691 152–3) Rooms with fan/air-con 250/550B, 'VIP' rooms 750B. The same management as at the Van Veena also handles the slightly run-down Bangsaphan.

Karol L's Bungalows without bath/with bath 100/150B. Operated by a Thai family, this has bungalows in the old Samui-style 6km south of Bang Saphan Yai. Meals here

are very reasonably priced as well, and it provides free maps for exploring the area.

Suan Luang Resort Bungalows with fans 300B, with air-con, hot water & TV 500B. Suan Luang is 600m from the beach, just up from Karol L's. The resort is friendly and has spacious wooden or concrete bungalows. There are discounts for longer stays.

Bang Saphan Coral Hotel Doubles/triples with air-con, TV, fridge & hot water 995/1350B, with 2 bedrooms for 4 people 1735B. The Bang Saphan Coral Hotel offers beautiful bungalows with terracotta-tiled roofs in a garden setting. The hotel restaurant serves pricey American and continental breakfasts. It also has a swimming pool, and offers sailing, sailboarding, canoeing, diving and fishing equipment for rent, as well as 750B day trips to Ko Thalu.

Hat Bo Kaew Eight kilometres south of Hat Bang Saphan Yai (15km south of Bang Saphan town), this up-and-comer now boasts a handful of places to stay. The beach isn't fantastic but the sheer isolation of the place makes up for it.

Suan Annan Resort (☎ 032 699 118) Bungalows with air-con, TV & fridge 400B. This was one of the first and has bungalows around 300m from the beach.

Getting There & Away
Buses from Prachuap Khiri Khan to Thap Sakae are 12B and from Thap Sakae to Bang Saphan Yai 8B. If you're coming from farther south, buses from Chumphon to Bang Saphan Yai cost 35B.

You can also get 3rd-class trains between Hua Hin, Prachuap Khiri Khan, Thap Sakae, Ban Koktahom, Ban Krut and Bang Saphan Yai for a few baht each leg, as all of them have train stations, (the rapid and express trains do not stop in Thap Sakae, Ban Krut or Bang Saphan). Each of these train stations is around 4km from the beach.

Motorcycle taxis are the only form of public transport available from the stations.

It's possible to rent 100cc motorbikes in Bang Saphan for 200B per day.

CHUMPHON
อ.เมืองชุมพร

postcode 86000 • pop 15,500

About 500km south of Bangkok and 184km from Prachuap Khiri Khan, Chumphon is the junction town where you turn west to Ranong and Phuket or continue south on the newer road to Surat Thani, Nakhon Si Thammarat and Songkhla. In reference to its function as a crossroads, the name de-

rives from the Thai *chumnumphon*, which means meeting place. This busy provincial capital is of no particular interest, except that this is where Southern Thailand really begins in terms of ethnic markers like dialect and religion.

Pak Nam, Chumphon's port, is 10km from Chumphon, and in this area there are a few beaches and a handful of islands with good reefs for diving. The best local beach is 4km-long **Hat Thung Wua Laen** (12km north of town), also known locally as Hat Cabana because the long-running Chumphon Cabana Resort & Diving Center is here.

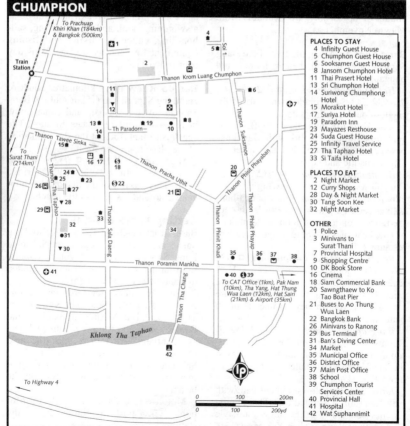

CHUMPHON

PLACES TO STAY
4 Infinity Guest House
5 Chumphon Guest House
6 Sooksamer Guest House
8 Jansom Chumphon Hotel
11 Thai Prasert Hotel
13 Sri Chumphon Hotel
14 Suriwong Chumphong Hotel
15 Morakot Hotel
17 Suriya Hotel
19 Paradorn Inn
23 Mayazes Resthouse
24 Suda Guest House
25 Infinity Travel Service
27 Tha Taphao Hotel
33 Si Taifa Hotel

PLACES TO EAT
2 Night Market
12 Curry Shops
28 Day & Night Market
30 Tang Soon Kee
32 Night Market

OTHER
1 Police
3 Minivans to Surat Thani
7 Provincial Hospital
9 Shopping Centre
10 DK Book Store
16 Cinema
18 Siam Commercial Bank
20 Sawngthaew to Ko Tao Boat Pier
21 Buses to Ao Thung Wua Laen
22 Bangkok Bank
26 Minivans to Ranong
29 Bus Terminal
31 Ban's Diving Center
34 Market
35 Municipal Office
36 District Office
37 Main Post Office
38 School
39 Chumphon Tourist Services Center
40 Provincial Hall
41 Hospital
42 Wat Suphannimit

Sometime in March or April the city hosts the Chumphon Marine Festival, which features cultural and folk art exhibits, a sailboarding competition at Hat Thung Wua Laen and a marathon. In October, the five-day Lang Suan Buddha Image Parade & Boat Race Festival includes a procession of temple boats and a boat race on the Lang Suan River, about 60km south of the capital.

Pak Nam is a major departure point for boats to Ko Tao, a popular island north of Ko Samui and Ko Pha-Ngan. Hence many travellers bound for Ko Tao stop over for a night or two in Chumphon.

Nearer islands include Ko Samet (not to be confused with the island of the same name off the coast near Rayong), Ko Mattara, Ko Maphrao, Ko Rang Kachiu, Ko Ngam Yai and Ko Raet. Landing on Ko Rang Kachiu is restricted as this is where the precious swiftlet's nest is collected for the gourmet market. The other islands in the vicinity are uninhabited; the reefs around Ko Raet and Ko Mattara are the most colourful.

There are many other islands a bit farther out that are also suitable for diving – see Diving & Snorkelling under Around Chumphon later in this chapter for details. Fishing is also popular around the islands – inquire at any of the hotels or guesthouses in town for information on organised fishing trips.

Information

Tourist Offices Chumphon Tourist Services Center, in the provincial offices at the intersection of Th Poramin Mankha and Th Phisit Phayap, has some information on the area including brochures and maps.

Money Several banks in town offer foreign exchange services and ATMs; most are located along Th Sala Daeng and are open weekdays from 8.30am to 3.30pm.

Post & Communications The main post office on Th Poramin Mankha is open weekdays from 8.30am to 4.30pm, weekends 9am to noon. The CAT office, about 1km south-east on the same road, is open for international telephone services daily from 8.30am to 9pm.

Books & Maps A DK Book Store has been established opposite the Jansom Chumphon Hotel, but it's predominantly Thai-oriented and carries only a few titles in English. Maps of Chumphon may be purchased here, however.

Organised Tours

Several travel agencies and guesthouses organise outdoor tours to the surrounding areas. Infinity Travel Service (see Places to Stay following) is one of the best. Tri Star Adventure Tours offers a series of interesting jungle treks, local cave trips and island tours lasting from two to five days and starting at 1250B per person. A one-day cave exploration costs 400B or more, depending on the number of people. Tri Star can be contacted through any travel service or guesthouse.

Club Paradise (☎ 077 503 331, 077 570 114, 014 767 760) at 120 Th Tawee Sinka offers all-day boat trips around the islands for 450B, and camping and fishing tours for 600B to 700B. Any guesthouse or travel agency can hook you up with Club Paradise.

Places to Stay – Budget

Places continue to spring up as more people use Chumphon as a gateway to Ko Tao.

Infinity Travel Service (☎/fax 077 501 937, 68/2 Th Tha Taphao) Singles/doubles 100/150B. North of the bus terminal, on the opposite side of the street, this has four basic but clean rooms upstairs over its travel agency/restaurant. It provides plenty of information on boats to Ko Tao and things to do in the area, and staff will allow travellers to shower while waiting for boat or bus transfers.

Infinity Guest House (224/37 Soi 1, Thanon Krom Luang Chumphon) Fan rooms with shared facilities 100-150B. Under the same ownership as Infinity Travel Service, this place has six basic fan rooms in a two-storey wooden house.

Sooksamer Guest House (☎ 077 502 430, 118/4 Th Suksamoe) Rooms 120B. This has small rooms in a home-like atmosphere. The proprietors will allow you to use the shower on your way to Pak Nam for a Ko Tao boat.

Chumphon Guest House (Miow House; ☎ *077 502 900, Soi 1, Th Krom Luang Chumphon)* Rooms 100-150B. This has basic, clean rooms in an old teak house, as well as a row of simple cubicles out the front. The friendly proprietors can arrange car and motorcycle rental as well as local tours.

Mayazes Resthouse (Mayaset; ☎ *077 504 452, fax 077 502 217, Soi Thanakhan Krung Thep)* Singles/doubles with fan 200/250B, with air-con 350B. Down a soi connecting Th Sala Daeng and Th Tha Taphao, this offers five immaculate rooms.

Suda Guest House (☎ *077 504 366, 8 Soi Thanakhan Krung Thep)* Singles/doubles 250/350B. This newly opened place rents two rooms in the upstairs of a row-building. Add 100B to the prices if you turn on the air-con. Not great value – really only a last resort if the more established guesthouses are full.

Other cheaper hotels can be found along Th Sala Daeng in the centre of town.

Si Taifa Hotel (☎ *077 501 690, Th Sala Daeng)* Singles/doubles 140/180B, doubles with shower & toilet 260B, with air-con 300/350B. This is a clean, old Chinese hotel built over a restaurant, with large rooms. Each floor has a terrace from which you can watch the sun set over the city.

Thai Prasert (☎ *077 511 250, 202-204 Th Sala Daeng)* Rooms 130-150B. This is something of a short-time place and so is a bit noisy and grubby, but it's cheap if that's what counts. There is no roman-script sign.

Suriya (☎ *077 511 144, 125/24-26 Th Sala Daeng)* Singles/doubles with fan & bath 150/250B. This place is rather drab but is a notch up from the Thai Prasert.

Sri Chumphon Hotel (☎ *077 511 280, fax 077 504 616, 127/22-24 Th Sala Daeng)* Rooms with fan & bath 300-400B, with air-con 500-600B. This is a clean and efficient Chinese hotel.

Suriwong Chumphon Hotel (☎ *077 511 203, fax 077 502 699, 125/27-29 Th Sala Daeng)* Singles/doubles with fan & bath 220/280B, with air-con 360/390B. The Suriwong is almost identical to the Sri Chumphon but is slightly cleaner and brighter. Test the air-con before agreeing to an air-con room – some of them are quite loud.

Morakot Hotel (☎ *077 503 628, fax 077 570 196, Th Tawee Sinka)* Rooms with fan/air-con, shower, TV & phone 300/450B. Morakot has very clean, spacious rooms. Parking is available.

Tha Yang & Pak Nam There are two options here.

Tha Yang Hotel (☎ *077 521 953, Th Chumphon-Pak Nam)* Rooms with air-con 400-500B. Near the piers for boats to/from Ko Tao, this has clean rooms but there's really no reason to stay here unless you miss the boat.

Siriphet Hotel (☎ *077 521 304, Th Chumphon-Pak Nam)* Rooms with fan 150B. A typical Chinese hotel, this place is noisier, dirtier and cheaper than the nearby Tha Yang Hotel.

Places to Stay – Mid-Range
Tha Taphao Hotel (☎ *077 511 479, fax 077 502 479, 66/1 Th Tha Taphao)* Rooms with fan 300B, air-con, TV, phone & balcony 450B. Near the bus terminal, this has worn but comfortable rooms.

Paradorn Inn (☎ *077 511 500, fax 077 501 112, 180/12 Th Paradorn)* Rooms with air-con & TV 350B, with TV & fridge 450-550B. The cheapest rooms are good value.

Jansom Chumphon Hotel (☎ *077 502 502, fax 077 502 503, 118/138 Th Sala Daeng)* Rooms with air-con 551B, deluxe with breakfast 708B. This is a bit run-down; it's mostly a short-time place for the neighbouring disco. If you don't mind the noise, there are discounts to be had during the week.

Places to Eat
Food vendors line the south side of Th Krom Luang Chumphon between Th Sala Daeng and Th Suksamoe nightly from around 6pm to 10pm or 11pm.

The several *curry shops* along Th Sala Daeng are proof that you are now in Southern Thailand. Over on Th Tha Taphao is a small *night market*.

Tang Soon Kee (Th Tha Taphao) Dishes 30-50B. This Chinese place is very popular and does stir-fry over rice dishes as well as *phàt thai*.

Several **Isan-style places** can be found along Th Krom Luang Chumphon.

Reun Thai Restaurant (Th Chumphon-Pak Nam) Dishes 50-80B. In Tha Yang, this indoor/outdoor place, next door to the Tha Yang Hotel and near the pier for boats to/from Ko Tao, has good seafood.

Chumphon Province is famous for *klûay lép meu naang* (literally, princess fingernail bananas). Very tasty and cheap – they're available in any fresh market in town.

Getting There & Away

Chumphon can be difficult to get away from, especially if you want to head north to Bangkok during the high season (December to April). If you're planning to use this place as a transport junction, you may need to spend the night here: if you arrive in town late, trains and overnight buses to Bangkok may all be booked out.

Bus Ordinary buses depart from the Southern bus terminal in Bangkok and cost 136B. They only depart once daily, at 6.30am. First-class air-con buses are 245B and leave three times in the afternoon and evening; 2nd class costs 190B and leaves nightly at 9pm. There are no government VIP departures for Chumphon, but Songserm Travel (☎ 077 506 205) next to the Tha Taphao Hotel, does one at 10.30pm and another at 11.30pm each evening for 350B. From Chumphon three different companies run air-con buses to Bangkok, the most reliable being Chok Anan Tour.

Minivans run every two hours between Surat Thani and Chumphon for 120B air-con (hourly departures, 3½ hours). The last van departs at 5pm. To/from Bang Saphan is 35B (80B air-con), Prachuap Khiri Khan is 55B (2nd class air-con 77B). In Chumphon the main terminal for these buses is on the western side of Th Tha Taphao.

Air-con minivans run to/from Ranong daily every hour between 8am and 5.30pm for 80B from opposite Infinity Travel Service; other places do the same trip for 90B to 100B. There is also a minivan to Bangkok that meets the Ko Tao boat at the Pak Nam pier, and leaves from Infinity Travel Service at noon and 5pm, costing 350B.

Train The rapid and express trains from Bangkok take about 7½ hours to reach Chumphon (2nd/1st class 190/394B); this does not include rapid or express surcharges. There are no longer any ordinary trains running between Bangkok and Chumphon.

There are four local 3rd-class trains daily to Prachuap Khiri Khan (24B), and one to Surat Thani (25B) that also continues on to Hat Yai (67B). Southbound rapid and express trains – the only trains with 1st and 2nd class – are much less frequent and can be difficult to book out of Chumphon.

Boat The small island of Ko Tao, north of Ko Samui and Ko Pha-Ngan (all covered in the South-Western Gulf Coast chapter), can be reached by boat from Tha Reua Ko Tao (Ko Tao boat pier), 10km south-east of town in Pak Nam. The regular daily boat leaves at midnight, costs 200B and the journey takes about six hours to reach Ko Tao. From Ko Tao the boat usually leaves at 10am and arrives at Tha Reua Ko Tao around 3.30pm. The ride can be very rough if seas are high – November is the worst month for stormy weather.

More expensive but faster is the Songserm express boat from the Tha Yang, which takes only 2½ hours and costs 400B. Depending on the weather, it usually departs at 7.30am eastbound, 3pm westbound. Faster still are speedboats that take about two hours to make the trip. These depart from Tha Yang (Chumphon) at 7.30am, or in the opposite direction at 10.30am. The fare is 300B to 400B and transfer to/from the pier is usually included in the fare.

Săwngthăew run to both piers frequently between 6am and 6pm for 10B. After 6pm, Infinity and most other travel services and guesthouses can send a van to the pier around 10pm for 50B per person. Going by van means you won't have to wait at the pier for six hours before the boat departs. The only other alternative is an 80B motorcycle-taxi ride to the pier.

Regular air-con minibuses to/from Bangkok's Th Khao San (Khao San Rd) guesthouses and travel agencies also connect with the slow boat for 350B. Be extremely cautious about these though, especially if they are offering the ride for only 50B to 100B. Basically there is no way a transport company can make any kind of profit on such low fares – unless they plan to steal from their passengers.

You can also charter a speedboat to Ko Tao from Pak Nam for 4000B to 5000B.

Getting Around

Motorcycle taxis around town cost a flat 10B per trip.

Săwngthăew to the port of Chumphon (Pak Nam Chumphon) are 13B per person, motorcycle taxis 80B to 100B. To Hat Sairi and Hat Thung Wua Laen they cost 20B (motorcycle 150B). Buses to Tako Estuary (for Hat Arunothai) are 40B.

Infinity Travel Service can arrange rental of motorcycles (200B per day) and cars (1000B per day).

AROUND CHUMPHON
Meditation Temple

Around 48km south of town in Sawi district, Wat Tham Phan Meuang is a Thammayut monastery offering instruction in *vipassana* (Buddhist insight meditation). There is one Thai monk who can speak English and translate.

Beaches

The best beaches in Chumphon Province are north of Chumphon at **Ao Phanang Tak, Ao Thung Wua Laem** and **Ao Baw Mao.** Nearer to town, in the vicinity of Pak Nam Chumphon, are the lesser beaches of **Hat Pharadon Phap** and **Hat Sairi**. About 40km south of Chumphon, past the town of Sawi, is the Tako Estuary and the fair beach of **Hat Arunothai.** Most of these beaches have at least one set of resort bungalows.

Diving & Snorkelling

At Chumphon the Gulf of Thailand begins opening up more to the oceanic influences of the South China Sea and is less affected

by fresh river water drainage than the upper Gulf. This means more coral growth than at Pattaya, Ko Chang and other northern Gulf dive sites. Because there is no operational airport nearby, only the more determined foreign divers seem to make it to Chumphon, which is an all-day bus ride from Bangkok, or 3½ hours from Surat Thani.

There are at least half a dozen small islands and seamounts off the Chumphon coast that are worth diving, most of them 15km to 35km east of the mainland. Among the best are **Ko Ngam Yai** and **Ko Ngam Noi**, where there is abundant coral at depths of 5m to 20m and visibility of up to 15m or more in good conditions. Just off the northern end of Ko Ngam Yai, **Hin Lak Ngam** (also known as Hin Phae) is also very good. All three spots are suitable for snorkelling in good weather.

Diving conditions in this area tend to be best between May and November.

Ban's Diving has an office in town on Th Tha Taphao near the Tha Taphao Hotel. It offers dive trips, instruction and certification, equipment rental and repair, and airfills. Ban's also provides a taxi service to the harbour, speedboat tickets to Ko Tao and minivans to Bangkok (see Getting There & Away in the Chumphon section).

Chumphon's original dive shop, at Chumphon Cabana Resort & Diving Center on Hat Thung Wua Laen (see Places to Stay & Eat following) has rental diving equipment and offers instruction and air-fills. It also has an office in town, next to Infinity Travel. Chumphon Cabana can organise dive trips to Ko Tao, an island that is technically located in Chumphon Province, although it's geographically closer to Surat Thani's Ko Samui archipelago (it's covered in the following South-Western Gulf Coast chapter). For Ko Tao diving, however, you're better off staying on Ko Tao itself as the island is three hours away from Chumphon by the fastest boats.

Places to Stay & Eat

Hat Sairi At Hat Sairi, 21km from Chumphon, options include:

Sai Ree Lodge (☎ 077 521 212) Bungalows with air-con 1000B. This has concrete bungalows with corrugated roofs – not the most exciting of accommodation but it's comfortable. In the low season you can get discounts of nearly 50%.

Sweet Guest House (☎ 077 521 324) Rooms with air-con 400-500B. This family-run place has small but clean rooms and is very friendly.

Nong Mai Resort (☎ 077 558 002) Bungalows 300-500B. This place has tidy concrete bungalows done in a vaguely Mediterranean style. There's also a restaurant on the premises.

MT Resort (*Mother House Resort*) Bungalows with fan & bath 300B. Located just around the cape to the south on Hat Thung Makham Noi, a small, crescent-shaped beach, is MT Resort, a popular cheapie with wood and bamboo A-frame bungalows. There's a beachside restaurant on the premises and air-con rooms were being built at the time of writing. Rides to or from MT Resort can be arranged through Infinity Travel Service (see Chumphon Places to Stay section).

Ao Thung Wua Laen There are a number of choices to stay and eat here.

Chumphon Cabana Resort & Diving Center (☎ 077 560 245–9, W www.cabana .co.th, e info@cabana.co.th) Rooms with fan 600B, air-con 1200-1400B. Twelve kilometres north of Chumphon on Hat Thung Wua Laen – also known as Hat Cabana – this resort has well-appointed and energy-efficient bungalows plus 36 rooms in a three-storey building. It operates the oldest, best and priciest dive operation in the area.

Cleanwave (☎ 077 560 151) Rooms with fan 300B, bungalows with air-con 600-700B. Near the town centre, this is one of the cheapest places on the beach, with clean, wood and bamboo A-frame bungalows. There are even cheaper rooms available in a newly built concrete row-building.

View Seafood Resort (☎ 077 560 214) Singles/doubles with fan & bath 400B, with air-con & TV 700-900B. This place consists of a collection of solid concrete A-frame bungalows with views and, of course, a seafood restaurant. The latter is reasonably priced and quite good.

Seabeach Bungalow (☎ 077 560 115) Rooms with fan 300-400B, air-con 600B. Seabeach has clean and comfortable rooms and a restaurant but it shuts down in the low season.

Khun Rim Lay (☎ 077 560 119) Rooms with air-con 600-800B. This place offers concrete bungalows with small verandas on a tidy compound. There's also a restaurant, but it was closed for renovations on last visit.

Miow House Rooms with fan 200-350B. Newly opened and under the same ownership as the guesthouse of the same name in town, this place has basic but comfortable rooms. There's also a large bungalow with two bedrooms, living room and kitchen area for 4000B per month.

There are several other casual seafood restaurants along Hat Thung Wua Laen where you can dine on the beach.

Hat Sapli A couple of kilometres north of Hat Thung Wua Laem is this newly developing beach area.

Si Sanyalak Rooms with fan 300B, bungalows with air-con, TV & fridge 650B. The friendly, well-situated Si Sanyalak features four small rooms in a longhouse-style building as well as one large bungalow.

Hat Arunothai This is at the Tako Estuary, about 50km south of Chumphon.

Chumphon Sunny Beach (☎ 077 579 148) Bungalows with fan/air-con 500/750B. While the sand here isn't the whitest, it's a wide beach and almost totally empty. This place has both wood and concrete bungalows, and a good restaurant.

South-Western Gulf Coast (Surat Thani to Narathiwat)

South of Chumphon, the Thai-Malay peninsula – the second longest peninsula in the world after the Kamchatka Peninsula in Russia – swells to its widest girth in Thailand. Beyond the well-known islands of Ko Samui, Ko Pha-Ngan and Ko Tao, few tourists are seen along this extensive coastline. With relatively little agribusiness, aquaculture or manufacturing, there's less development here than anywhere else along either the Gulf or the Andaman Sea shores.

The overall lack of tourism south of the Samui archipelago can only be explained by the fact that climatically the South-Western Gulf's best season runs from April to October – the exact opposite of Thailand's typical tourist season (which coincides with the European and North American winter). Ko Samui's natural assets as a beautiful, remote island – coupled with the fact that the original Hainanese inhabitants of the island were quite open to foreign visitation and tourism development – counter this seasonal aspect. The mostly Muslim residents of the coastal provinces farther south have historically been more indifferent to tourism, so they haven't built beach huts, guesthouses or restaurants catering to the foreign tourist trade. This is all the better for those global wanderers seeking less-trodden sands.

SURAT THANI
อ.เมืองสุราษฎร์ธานี

postcode 84000 • pop 43,100
There is little of particular historical interest at Surat Thani, a busy commercial centre and port dealing in rubber and coconut, but the town's busy waterfront lends character nonetheless. It's 651km from Bangkok and the first point in a southbound journey towards Malaysia that really feels and looks like Southern Thailand. For

Highlights

- Chaiya is one of Thailand's oldest cities, featuring 9th-century wàt ruins, a famous Buddhist meditation centre and rainforest.

- Khao Sok National Park's native rainforests, waterfalls, limestone cliffs, streams and lakes are home to a plethora of wildlife and flora, including the Rafflesia, the largest flower in the world.

- Ko Samui's easy accessibility and wide range of accommodation make it Thailand's most convenient beach destination.

- Ko Pha-Ngan has diving, hiking, day-trips to Ang Thong National Marine Park and uncrowded beaches.

- Diving enthusiasts will find Ko Tao the perfect place to explore the Gulf of Thailand's underwater wonders.

- Nakhon Si Thammarat is one of the only places where traditional life-size, buffalo-hide shadow puppets are still made.

- Soak up the traditional southern way of life in Pattani, Narathiwat, Songkhla and Hat Yai, where Buddhism and Islam meet.

SOUTH-WESTERN GULF COAST

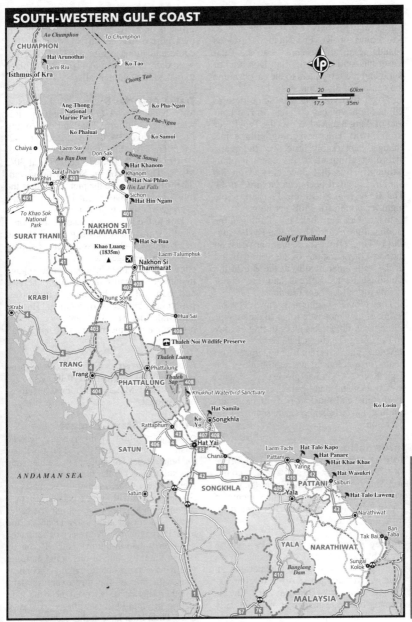

0   20   60km
0   17.5   35mi

CHUMPHON
Ao Chumphon
To Chumphon
Hat Arunothai
Laem Riu
Isthmus of Kra
Ko Tao
Chong Tao

Ang Thong
National
Marine Park
Ko Pha-Ngan
Chong Pha-Ngan
Ko Phaluai
Ko Samui
Chaiya
Laem Sui
Don Sak
Chong Samui
Ao Ban Don
Hat Khanom
Phun Phin
Surat Thani
Khanom
Hat Nai Phlao
SURAT THANI
Hin Lat Falls
Sichon
Hat Hin Ngam
To Khao Sok
National
Park
NAKHON SI
THAMMARAT
Khao Luang
(1835m)
Hat Sa Bua
Laem Talumphuk
Nakhon Si
Thammarat
KRABI
Thung Song
Krabi
Hua Sai

Thaleh Noi Wildlife Preserve
TRANG
Thaleh Luang
Trang
Phattalung
PHATTALUNG
Thaleh
Sap
Khukhut Waterbird Sanctuary
Ko Losin
Hat Samila
Ko
Yo
Songkhla
Rattaphum
Hat Yai
Chana
Laem Tachi
Hat Talo Kapo
Pattani
Hat Panare
Yaring
Hat Khae Khae
PATTANI
Hat Wasukri
Saiburi
SATUN
SONGKHLA
Yala
Hat Talo Laweng
Satun
ANDAMAN SEA
Narathiwat
Ban
Taba
Tak Bai
YALA
NARATHIWAT
Banglang
Dam
Sungai
Kolok
MALAYSIA

Gulf of Thailand

most people Surat Thani (often simply called Surat) is only a stop on the way to Ko Samui or Ko Pha-Ngan – luscious islands 32km off the coast – so the Talat Kaset bus stations in the Ban Don area of Surat and the ferry piers to the east become the centres of attention.

If you find yourself with some time to kill in Surat, you can do a one- or two-hour tour of **Bang Ban Mai**, across the Tapi River from town. This easygoing village has changed remarkably little over the years, affording glimpses of the coconut plantation lifestyle that once existed on Ko Samui. Long-tail boats can be hired at the Tha Reua Klang (Middle Pier), near the night ferry pier, for 250B per hour.

In mid-October Chak Phra (Pulling of the Buddha Image) and Thawt Pha Pa (Laying-Out of Forest Robes) celebrations occur on the same day (first day of the waning moon in the 11th lunar month) at the end of the Buddhist Rains Retreat and are major events for Surat Thani Province.

Thawt Pha Pa begins at dawn with the offering of new monastic robes to the monks, while Chak Phra takes place during the day and evening. During Chak Phra, local lay devotees place sacred Buddha images on boats for a colourful procession along the Tapi River. A similar procession on land uses trucks and hand-pulled carts. Lots of food stalls and musical performances, including *lí-keh* (folk plays), are set up for the occasion.

Information
Tourist Offices The friendly TAT office (☎ 077 288 819, ℮ tatsurat@samart.co.th), at 5 Thanon (Th) Talat Mai near the south-western end of town, distributes plenty of useful brochures and maps. It's open daily from 8.30am to 4.30pm.

Money There's a string of banks – one on every block for five blocks – along Th Na Meuang south-west of Th Chonkasem; all have ATMs and most offer foreign exchange. Bangkok Bank at 193 Th Na Meuang has an exchange booth open daily from 8.30am to 5pm.

Post & Communications The main post office is on Th Talat Mai; Ban Don has its own post office on Th Na Meuang. The communications centre on Th Don Nok, open daily from 7am to 11pm, is the place to make international calls.

Travel Agencies Several travel agents in town handle travel to the islands or elsewhere in Southern Thailand, including Phantip Travel (☎ 077 272 230) at 442/24–5 Th Talat Mai and Songserm Travel (☎ 077 285 124, fax 077 285 127) at 30/2 Mu 3, Th Bangkoong. Songserm has another office opposite the pier. Phantip is the most reliable travel agent in town for the average transport transaction.

Due to the lucrative transport situation – shuttling travellers between Bangkok and nearby islands – Surat has attracted its share of shady travel agencies. At least one company in the area has been known to engage in outrageous scams, including poor service and bait-and-switch tactics with buses, particularly between Ko Samui and Hat Yai and Malaysia. The TAT are aware of the problem but some companies have high connections.

Medical Services Surat has three hospitals, but Taksin Hospital (☎ 077 273 239) on Th Talat Mai is considered the most professional.

Places to Stay – Budget
At some of Surat Thani's cheaper hotels, business consists largely of 'short-time' (by the hour) trade. This doesn't make them any less suitable as regular hotels – it's just that there's likely to be more noise as guests arrive and depart with some frequency. In fact, if you're on a tight budget, it may be better to zip straight through Surat Thani via the night ferry; you may even sleep better on the night ferry than in a noisy hotel. If you arrive in Surat by train or bus in the morning you'll have no problem making a connection with one of the day express boats. Another alternative is to stay near the train station in Phun Phin (see Places to Stay & Eat – Phun Phin later in this section).

All of the following places are within walking or *sǎamláw* (three-wheeled pedicab) distance of the Ban Don boat piers.

Ban Don Hotel (☎ *077 272 167, 219 Th Na Meuang*) Clean singles/doubles with fan & bath 200B, rooms with small bathroom & squat toilet 180B. This continues to be the best budget value in Surat. The entrance is through a Chinese restaurant – quite a good one for inexpensive rice and noodle dishes.

Surat Hotel (☎ *077 272 243, 496 Th Na Meuang*) Spacious rooms with fan & bath 180-350B, with air-con 380-480B. This is between the Grand City Hotel and the bus station. At the rear are some quiet rooms.

Phanfa Hotel (☎ *077 272 287, 247/2–5 Th Na Meuang*) Rooms with fan & bath 180B. Across the street from the Surat Hotel, this has similar rooms.

Grand City Hotel (☎ *077 272 960, fax 077 284 951, 428 Th Na Meuang*) Rooms with 1 bed/2 beds, fan & bath 230/280B, with air-con 400/550B. Grand City has been recently renovated and has plain but clean rooms.

Seree Hotel (*Seri Hotel;* ☎ *077 272 279, Th Ton Pho*) Singles/doubles with fan & bath 250/300B, with air-con 320/400B. On a fairly quiet street off Th Si Chaiya, Seree has adequate but somewhat airless rooms. There's a coffee shop on the premises.

Thai Hotel (☎ *077 272 932, Th Si Chaiya*) Rooms with fan & bath 220-250B. One block from the night ferry pier, this has rooms that are dingy but fairly quiet.

Ratchathani Hotel (*Rajthani Hotel;* ☎ *077 287 638, fax 077 272 972, Th Na Meuang*) Rooms with fan/air-con & bath 260/400B. This scruffy, not-too-clean hotel is near the Talat Kaset 1 bus terminal.

Places to Stay – Mid-Range

Although these hotels don't cost much more than the budget places mentioned, the facilities are considerably better. They're also less likely to attract short-time clientele.

Tapi Hotel (☎ *077 272 575, 100 Th Chonkasem*) Rooms with fan 280-300B, with air-con 400-500B. This is popular with travelling Thai businesspeople – it gets noisy after the karaoke bars close.

Muang Tai (☎ *077 272 367, 390–392 Th Talat Mai*) Rooms with fan/air-con 250/400B. Muang Tai has received good reviews from travellers.

Thai Rung Ruang Hotel (☎ *077 273 249, fax 077 286 353, 191/199 Th Mitkasem*) Rooms with 1 bed/2 beds & fan 280/300B, with air-con, TV & phone 400/420B. This recently renovated hotel, off Th Na Meuang near Talat Kaset 1 bus terminal, is good value.

Places to Stay – Top End

Surat Thani also has a number of more upscale hotels priced slightly lower than those in other large provincial capitals.

Wang Tai (☎ *077 283 020–39, fax 077 281 077, 1 Th Talat Mai*) Rooms 850-2000B. This is a big place with over 200 rooms and a swimming pool.

Siam Thani (☎ *077 273 081, fax 077 282 169, 180 Th Surat Thani-Phun Phin*) Rooms 680-1700B. Siam Thani has a swimming pool, coffee shop and a good restaurant.

Siam Thara (☎ *077 273 740, fax 077 282 169, 67 Th Don Nok*) Rooms with air-con 595-625B. Near the Th Talat Mai intersection, Siam Thara is a bit overpriced for the condition of rooms, an American breakfast is included.

Southern Star Hotel (☎ *077 216 414, fax 077 216 427, 253 Th Chonkasem*) Singles & doubles 1110-2690B. All 150 rooms feature sitting areas that have inspired the hotel proprietors to call them 'suites'. Other facilities include a coffee shop, restaurant, sky lounge and karaoke pub. This is home to the biggest disco in Southern Thailand, the Star Theque.

Saowaluk Thani Hotel (☎ *077 213 700, fax 077 213 735, 99/99 Th Kanjanawithi*) Rooms 850-2100B. A newish top-end place, this 11-storey hotel stands on the north-eastern city limits, on the road to Don Sak. It has a coffee shop, lobby bar, Chinese restaurant and several function rooms.

Places to Eat

The **Talat Kaset market** area next to the Talat Kaset 1 bus terminal and the **morning market** (between Th Na Meuang and

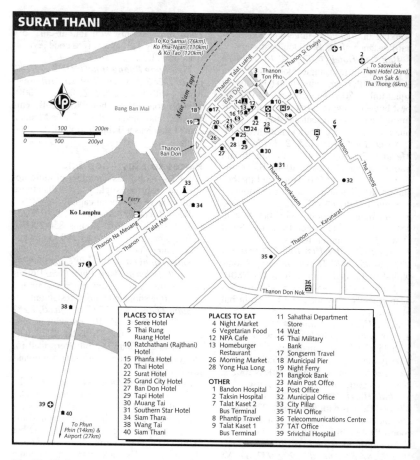

SURAT THANI

PLACES TO STAY
3 Seree Hotel
5 Thai Rung
   Ruang Hotel
10 Ratchathani (Rajthani)
   Hotel
15 Phanfa Hotel
20 Thai Hotel
22 Surat Hotel
25 Grand City Hotel
27 Ban Don Hotel
29 Tapi Hotel
30 Muang Tai
31 Southern Star Hotel
34 Siam Thara
38 Wang Tai
40 Siam Thani

PLACES TO EAT
4 Night Market
6 Vegetarian Food
12 NPA Cafe
13 Homeburger
   Restaurant
26 Morning Market
28 Yong Hua Long

OTHER
1 Bandon Hospital
2 Taksin Hospital
7 Talat Kaset 2
   Bus Terminal
8 Phantip Travel
9 Talat Kaset 1
   Bus Terminal

11 Sahathai Department
   Store
14 Wat
16 Thai Military
   Bank
17 Songserm Travel
18 Municipal Pier
19 Night Ferry
21 Bangkok Bank
23 Main Post Offce
24 Post Office
32 Municipal Office
33 City Pillar
35 THAI Office
36 Telecommunications Centre
37 TAT Office
39 Srivichai Hospital

Th Si Chaiya) are good food-hunting places. Many stalls near the bus terminal specialise in *khâo kài òp* (marinated baked chicken on rice), which is very tasty. During mango season, a lot of street vendors sell incredible *khâo nǐaw mámûang* (coconut-sweetened sticky rice with sliced ripe mango).

The best of Surat's several **night markets** is one that runs along both sides of Th Ton Pho, near the Seree Hotel.

There is an exemplary southern-style **khanǒm jiin place** (curry noodles served with vegies) in an old wooden building, just around the corner, south-west from Bangkok Bank, off Th Na Meuang.

NPA Cafe (Th Na Meuang) Dishes 60-120B. An air-con cafe between the Thai Military Bank and the Phanfa Hotel, this has Western breakfasts, pizzas, burgers, salads, pastas (including macaroni and spaghetti), sandwiches, Thai and Chinese food – plus Corona beer, ice cream and an extensive list of appetisers.

Homeburger Restaurant (Th Na Meuang) Dishes 60-200B. Next to the Phanfa Hotel, this does hamburgers, pizza, steak and some Thai dishes.

Yong Hua Long (Th Na Meuang) Dishes 30-50B. Around the corner from the Grand City Hotel is this inexpensive, popular Chinese restaurant, with roast duck and a large buffet table.

Vegetarian Food (Soi 33, Th Talat Mai) Dishes 25-40B. This serves good vegetarian *kŭaytĭaw* (rice noodles) and some very hot Thai curries. It's a little more expensive than the average for Thai vegetarian.

Places to Stay & Eat – Phun Phin

You may find yourself needing accommodation in Phun Phin (where the Surat Thani train station is actually located), either because you're stranded due to booked-out trains or because you've come in from Ko Samui during the evening and plan to get an early morning train out of Surat Thani before the Surat Thani–Phun Phin bus service starts. If so, there are a couple of cheap, dilapidated hotels just across from the train station – though at least one of them, the *Tai Fah*, seems to be ready to shut down any day. If that's the case, try the *Si Meuang Thani* on the corner, which has a similar setup and rates (100-150B).

Queen (☎ 077 311 033, fax 077 311 381, 12 Th Phun Phin-Surat Thani) Rooms with fan 180-400B, with air-con 400B. If you can afford a few baht more, the good-value Queen is on the road to Surat but still quite close to the train station.

Across from the Queen is a good *night market* with cheap eats.

Oum's Restaurant (Th Rim Thang Rot Fai) Dishes 30-60B. Opposite the northern end of the train station, this has an English-language menu and serves good Thai coffee, Western breakfasts and simple Thai dishes.

Wut (☎ 077 311 532, 2/2 Th Rim Thang Rot Fai) Dishes 30-60B. This place is not quite as good as nearby Oum's, but it does offer email and Internet services.

Getting There & Away

Air THAI flies to Surat Thani from Bangkok twice daily (2055B, 70 minutes). The THAI office (☎ 077 272 610, 077 273 710) in Surat is at 3/27–28 Th Karunarat.

A THAI shuttle van/limo between Surat Thani and the airport costs 80/150B per person.

Bus, Share Taxi & Minivan First-class air-con buses leave Bangkok's Southern bus terminal in Thonburi three times in the morning, arriving in Surat 10 hours later; the fare is 346B. There is also one VIP departure at 7pm (535B).

Ordinary buses leave the Southern bus terminal once in the morning and once in the evening (180B).

Take care when booking private air-con and VIP buses out of Surat. Some companies have been known to sell tickets for VIP buses to Bangkok, then pile hapless travellers onto an ordinary air-con bus and refuse to refund the fare difference. If possible, get a recommendation from another traveller or inquire at the TAT office for reputable companies to make reservations with. See the Information section earlier in this chapter under Travel Agencies for more.

Other fares to/from Surat are:

destination	fare (B)	hours
Hat Yai	100	5
(air-con)	160	4
(share taxi or van)	180	3½
Krabi	70	4
(air-con)	110	3
(share taxi or van)	150	2
Nakhon Si Thammarat	45	2½
(air-con)	70	2
(share taxi)	80	2
Narathiwat	160	6
Phang-Nga	55	4
(air-con)	110	3
(share taxi)	90	2½
Phuket	90	6
(air-con)	150	5
(share taxi or van)	160	4
Ranong	80	5
(air-con)	120	4
(share taxi or van)	130	3½
Satun	85	4
Trang	60	3
(van)	120	3
Yala	120	6
(van)	160	6

Buses From Phun Phin If you're taking the train to Surat Thani, but going on to the Andaman Coast rather than Ko Samui or Ko Pha-Ngan, there are bus services operating out of Phun Phin (where the Surat Thani train station is actually located). This saves you having to go into Surat Thani proper.

The main destinations served are Takua Pa (where you can get buses north to Ranong), Phuket, and Phang-Nga on the Andaman Coast. Nearly all services are by ordinary bus, except for two air-con services to Phuket, which leave at 7.30am and 10.30am. Other buses leave every one to two hours from 6am to 4pm. The ordinary buses to Phuket run past Khao Sok National Park, Takua Pa and Hat Khao Lak; Takua Pa buses also pass Khao Sok. Buses leave from next to a white building, south of the train station; look for the bus schedule painted on the wall.

Train Trains for Surat Thani (which don't really stop in Surat but in Phun Phin, 14km west of town) leave Bangkok's Hualamphong train station at 12.25pm (rapid), 2.20pm and 2.45pm (special express), 3.50pm (rapid), 5.05pm (express), 5.35pm and 6.20pm (rapid), 7.15pm (express), and 10.30pm and 10.50pm (express diesel railcar), arriving 10½ to 12 hours later. The 6.20pm train (rapid No 167) is the most convenient, arriving at 6.25am and giving you plenty of time to catch a boat to Ko Samui, if that's your planned destination. Fares are 519B in 1st class, 248B in 2nd class and 107B in 3rd class, not including the rapid/express/special express surcharges or berths.

The all-2nd-class express diesel railcars Nos 39 and 41 leave Bangkok nightly at 10.30pm and 10.50pm and arrive in Phun Phin at 7.35am and 8.01am. Tickets cost 368B. There are no sleeping berths available on these trains.

The Phun Phin train station has a 24-hour left-luggage room that charges 10B a day for the first five days, 20B a day thereafter. The advance ticket office is open 6am to 6pm daily.

It can be difficult to book long-distance trains out of Phun Phin; it may be easier to take a bus, especially if heading south. The trains are very often full and it's a drag to take the bus 14km from town to the Phun Phin train station and be turned away. You could buy a 'standing room only' 3rd-class ticket and stand for an hour or two until someone vacates a seat down the line. Advance train reservations can be made at Phantip Travel on Th Talat Mai in Ban Don, near the market /bus terminal. You might try making an onward reservation *before* boarding a boat for Ko Samui. On Samui, both Travel Solutions in Chaweng and Songserm Travel Service in Na Thon can assist with reservations.

Train/Bus/Boat Combinations It's possible to buy tickets from the State Railway of Thailand (SRT) that allow you to go straight through to Ko Samui or Ko Pha-Ngan from Bangkok on a train, bus and boat combination. See the Getting There & Away sections under each island for more details.

Getting Around

Air-con vans from Surat Thani airport to town cost 80B per person. THAI runs a more expensive 'limo' service for 150B.

Buses to Ban Don from Phun Phin train station leave every 10 minutes or so from 6am to 8pm for 10B per person. Some of the buses drive straight to the pier (if they have enough tourists), while others terminate at the Talat Kaset 1 bus terminal, from where you must get another bus to Tha Thong (or to Ban Don if you're taking the night ferry).

If you arrive in Phun Phin on one of the night trains, you can get a free bus from the train station to the pier, courtesy of Songserm, Phanthip or Samui Travel Services before the morning boat departures. If your train arrives in Phun Phin and the buses aren't running, you'll have to hire a taxi to Ban Don for 80B to 100B, or hang out in one of the Phun Phin street cafes until buses start running around 5am.

Orange buses run from Talat Kaset 1 bus terminal to Phun Phin train station every 10 minutes from 5am to 7.30pm for 8B per person. Empty buses also wait at the Tha

Thong pier for passengers arriving from Ko Samui on the express boat, ready to drive them directly to the train station or destinations farther afield. There are also share taxis to the Phun Phin train station from Surat for 15B, but these leave only when full, otherwise you'll have to hire the vehicle for 80B to 100B.

Around town, share *săwngthăew* (passenger trucks) cost 6B to 10B depending on the distance travelled. Săamláw rides cost 20B.

AROUND SURAT THANI

Two inland places near Surat are worth visiting if you're looking for a break from sea and sand. Chaiya is an important footnote in Thai history, and boasts one of Thailand's most famous Buddhist meditation centres, while Khao Sok National Park preserves a large chunk of peninsular rainforest.

Chaiya
ไชยา

Just north of Surat Thani and best visited as a day trip from there, Chaiya is one of the oldest cities in Thailand, dating back to the Srivijaya empire. In fact, the name may be a contraction of Siwichaiya, the Thai pronunciation of the city that was a regional capital between the 8th and 10th centuries. Before this time the area was a stop on the Indian trade route through South-East Asia. Many Srivijaya artefacts in the National Museum in Bangkok were found in Chaiya, including a famous *Avalokitesvara Bodhisattva* bronze that's considered a masterpiece of Buddhist art.

Wat Phra Boromathat, Wat Kaew & Chaiya National Museum The restored Borom That Chaiya stupa at Wat Phra Boromathat, just outside of town, is a fine example of Srivijaya architecture. In the courtyard surrounding the revered *chedi* (stupa) are several pieces of sculpture from the region, including an unusual two-sided *yoni* (the uterus-shaped pedestal that holds the Shivalingam), *rishis* (hermit sages) performing yoga, and several Buddha images.

A ruined stupa at nearby Wat Kaew (also known as Wat Long), again from the Srivijaya period, shows the influence of central Javanese architecture (or perhaps vice versa) as well as Cham (9th-century south Vietnam) characteristics.

The Chaiya National Museum (☎ 077 431 066; admission 30B; open 9am-4pm Wed-Sun) near the entrance to Wat Phra Boromathat displays prehistoric and historic artefacts of local provenance, as well as local handicrafts and a shadow puppet exhibit.

You can catch any săwngthăew heading west from the main intersection south of the train station to Wat Phra Boromathat for 8B. This same săwngthăew route passes the turn-off for Wat Kaew, which is about 500m before the turn-off for Boromathat. Wat Kaew is less than 500m from this junction, on the left, almost directly opposite Chaiya Witthaya School.

Wat Suan Mokkhaphalaram This is a modern forest wát *(Wat Suanmok; ☎ 077 431 522, fax 077 431 597)* to the west of Wat Kaew founded by Ajaan Buddhadasa Bhikku (Phutthathat), Thailand's most famous monk. Born in Chaiya in 1906, Buddhadasa was ordained as a monk when he was 21 years old, spent many years studying the Pali scriptures; and then retired to the forest for six years of solitary meditation. Returning to ecclesiastical society, he was made abbot of Wat Phra Boromathat, a high distinction, but conceived of Suanmok as an alternative to orthodox Thai temples. His philosophy was ecumenical in nature, comprising Zen, Taoist and Christian elements as well as the traditional Theravada schemata. During Thailand's turbulent 1970s, he was branded a communist because of his critiques of capitalism, which he saw as a catalyst for greed. Buddhadasa died in July 1993 after a long illness.

Wat Suanmok (literally, Garden of Liberation) is spread over 120 hectares of wooded hillside and features huts for up to 70 monks, a museum/library and a 'spiritual theatre'. This latter building has bas-reliefs on the outer walls that are facsimiles of sculptures at Sanchi, Bharhut and Amaravati in India. The interior walls feature modern Buddhist painting – eclectic to say the least – executed by the resident monks.

At the affiliated **International Dhamma Hermitage** (IDH), across the highway 1.5km from Wat Suanmok, resident monks hold meditation retreats during the first 10 days of every month. Anyone is welcome to participate; the cost is 1200B (120B per day for 10 days) and there is no advance registration or reservation required. Simply arrive in time to register on the final day of the month preceding the retreat. Registration takes place at the main monastery.

Places to Stay Travellers could stay in Surat Thani for visits to Chaiya or request permission from the monks to stay in the guest quarters at Wat Suanmok.

Udomlap Hotel (☎ 077 431 123, Th Mothapheuk) Rooms 150B, with air-con 250-450B. A Chinese-Thai hotel in Chaiya, this has clean rooms in an old wooden building or in a new modern multi-storey wing.

Getting There & Away If you're going to Surat Thani by train from Bangkok, you can get off at the small Chaiya train station, then catch another train to Phun Phin, Surat's train station.

From Surat you can either take a săwngthăew from Talat Kaset 2 in Ban Don (18B to Wat Suanmok or 25B to Chaiya) or get a train going north from Phun Phin. The trains between Phun Phin and Chaiya may be full but you can always stand or squat in a 3rd-class car for the short trip. The ordinary train costs 10B in 3rd class to Chaiya and takes about an hour. The săwngthăew takes around 45 minutes. Or you can take a share taxi to Chaiya from Surat for 30B per person; in Chaiya, Surat-bound taxis leave from opposite the Chaiya train station.

Suanmok is about 7km outside Chaiya on the highway that runs to Surat and Chumphon. Until late afternoon there are săwngthăew from the Chaiya train station to Wat Suanmok for 10B per passenger. From Chaiya you can also catch a Surat-bound bus from the front of the cinema on Chaiya's main street and ask to be let off at Wat Suanmok. (Turn right on the road in front of the train station.) The fare to Wat Suanmok is 5B. If buses aren't running you can hire a motorcycle taxi for 20B anywhere along Chaiya's main street.

Khao Sok National Park
อุทยานแห่งชาติเขาสก

Established in 1980, this 646-sq-km park (*adult/child under 14 years 200/100B*) lies in the western part of Surat Thani Province, off Route (Rte) 401, about a third of the way from Takua Pa to Surat Thani. The park has thick native rainforest with waterfalls, limestone cliffs, numerous streams, an island-studded lake, and many trails, mostly along rivers. According to Thom Henley, author of the highly informative *Waterfalls and Gibbon Calls,* the Khao Sok rainforest is a remnant of a 160-million-year-old forest ecosystem that is much older and richer than the forests of the Amazon and Central Africa.

Connected to two other national parks, Kaeng Krung and Phang-Nga, Khao Sok National Park and the Khlong Saen and Khlong Nakha wildlife sanctuaries form the largest contiguous nature preserve – around 4000 sq km – on the Thai peninsula. Khao Sok shelters a plethora of wildlife, including wild elephant, leopard, serow, banteng, gaur, dusky langur, tiger and Malayan sun bear, as well as over 180 bird species. The tiger population – currently estimated by park staff at less than 10 individuals – is extremely threatened due to the high demand for tiger parts utilised in Chinese aphrodisiacs.

A major watershed for the South, the park is filled with lianas, bamboo, ferns and rattan, including the giant rattan (*wăai tào phráw*), with a stem over 10cm in diameter. One floral rarity found in the park is *Rafflesia kerri meyer,* known to the Thais as *bua phut* (wild lotus), the largest flower in the world. Found only in Khao Sok and an adjacent wildlife sanctuary (different varieties of the same species are found in Malaysia and Indonesia), mature specimens reach 80cm in diameter. The flower has no roots or leaves of its own; instead it lives parasitically inside the roots of the liana, a jungle vine. From October to December, buds burst forth from the liana root and swell to football size. When the bud blooms in January and February it emits a potent stench (said to resemble that of a rotting corpse) that attracts insects responsible for pollination.

A map of **hiking trails** within Khao Sok is available from park headquarters near the park entrance. Various trails lead to the waterfalls of **Mae Yai** (5.5km from park headquarters), **Than Sawan** (9km), **Sip-Et Chan** (4km) and **Than Kloy** (9km). Guesthouses near the park entrance can arrange guided hikes that include waterfalls, caves and river-running. Leeches are quite common in certain areas of Khao Sok, so take the usual precautions – wear closed shoes when hiking and apply plenty of repellent.

The 95m-high, 700m-long, shale-clay Ratchaprapha Dam (also referred to as Chiaw Lan Dam), erected across the Pasaeng River in 1982, creates the vast 165km-long **Chiaw Lan Lake**. Limestone outcrops protruding from the lake reach as high as 960m, over three times the height of similar formations in Ao Phang-Nga. A limestone cave known as **Tham Nam Thalu** contains striking cavern formations and subterranean streams, while **Tham Si Ru** features four converging passageways used as a hide-out by communist insurgents between 1975 and 1982. **Tham Khang Dao**, high on a limestone cliff face, is home to many bat species. All three caves can be reached on foot from the southwestern shore of the lake. The dam is 65km from the visitors centre via a well-marked side road off Route 401 (back towards Surat Thani). You can rent boats from local fishermen to explore the coves, canals, caves and cul-de-sacs along the lakeshore. Two floating lodges belonging to the national park provide overnight accommodation.

The best overall time of year to visit Khao Sok is December to May, when trails are less slippery, river crossings are easier and riverbank camping is safer due to the lower risk of flash flooding. During the June to November wet season, on the other hand, you're more likely to see Malayan and Asiatic black bears, civets, slow loris, wild boar, gaur, deer and wild elephants – and a tiger if you're very, very lucky – along the trail system. During dry months the larger mammals tend to stay near the reservoir in areas without trails.

At the visitors centre, as well as various bookshops in Southern Thailand, you can purchase a copy of Henley's inspirational *Waterfalls and Gibbon Calls,* a wildlife guide to Khao Sok.

Places to Stay & Eat There are several places to stay at *Khao Sok National Park* (☎ *077 299 150–1),* including a camping area. The park no longer offers tents for rent, but you can pitch your own for 30B. Two bungalows near the visitors centre are available for 350B, and there's a longhouse that sleeps up to 12 people on rice mats, available for just 300B. A small co-operative restaurant near the entrance serves inexpensive meals but it's necessary to tell them a day in advance that you will be eating there.

Private 'tree house' style accommodation and food are also available at several places just outside the park. All places offer guides for jungle trips.

Treetop River Huts (☎ 077 421 155, 077 421 613 ext 107) Thatched-roof singles/doubles with bath 250/350B, tree house with bath 500B, plus meals for 50-70B. Next to the park entrance, 1.9km from the highway. Khun Arun, the English-speaking owner, has lots of information about the surrounding area. He offers inner tyre tubes for tubing, and many of the bungalows are lined up along a stream.

Bamboo House Singles/doubles with bath 200/250B. Off the main road to the park, this has seven rustic but clean rooms.

Several other establishments offering thatched-roof huts for 200B to 300B, include *Jampha House*, *Freedom Resort*, *Mountain Jungle View* and *Lotus Bungalows*, all near the park entrance or on the road leading past Bamboo House.

Art's Riverview Jungle Lodge Rooms 200-300B, with bath & deck 600B, treehouses 400B. Meals per day 250B. Beyond the Bamboo House, about 1km from the park, this has seven rooms, plus treehouses and two large houses. Some of the newer treehouses are right on the Sok River and boast good views of nearby mountains. Art's seems to be well run, but success may be tempting the owner to overbuild, especially along the river. Despite the operation's obvious success, however, the owner still prefers a lamp-lit night-time ambience and has no plans to install electricity.

Our Jungle House Treehouses with bath 400-600B. This is run by a friendly Irishman and has nicely designed treehouses with private bath, set along the river facing a huge limestone cliff (good for gibbon-viewing). Overnight lake trips are available with lots of animal-viewing on the jungle's edge for 3100B per person (minimum two people), and full-day rainforest hikes with a guide are also offered for 400B per person. As with Art's, there are no noisy electricity generators to drown out the sounds of the jungle.

Mountain Jungle View (☎ 077 299 088) Treehouses 200B, bungalows with bath 400B. This new family-run place has received rave reviews from readers. Bungalows are sturdy and comfortable, and there are well-designed rooms in a treehouse. The restaurant is also said to be quite good.

Khao Sok Rainforest Resort Cottages with fan, shower & toilet 400-600B. Under the same management as the ecologically oriented Dawn of Happiness in Krabi, this offers sturdy cottages raised on stilts with large verandas overlooking the forest. All cottages have electricity.

Chiaw Lan Lake At Substation 3 near the dam, two large *floating raft houses* contain screened rooms with two to three beds each and good toilet/shower facilities. Another *raft house* at Substation 4 offers seven small bamboo huts with mattresses on the floor and communal facilities outside. The price at both places is 500B per person per night, including meals.

Getting There & Away From Phun Phin or Surat Thani catch a bus bound for Takua Pa and get off at the 109km marker (the park's entrance) on Rte 401. If you're having trouble seeing the kilometre markers, just tell the driver or ticket attendant 'Khao

Sok' and they'll let you off at the right place. The bus fare is 82B air-con, 33B ordinary. You can also come from the Phuket side of the peninsula by bus, but you'll have to go to Takua Pa first; Surat-bound buses from Phuket don't use Rte 401 any more.

To reach Chiaw Lan Lake and the park's floating raft houses, park rangers can arrange transportation from the park headquarters for 1200B to 1700B for the return trip (depending on which Substation you go to). If you have your own vehicle, take the turn-off between the 52 and 53km markers on Rte 401, at Ban Takum. From here it's 14km north-west to Substation 2.

KO SAMUI
เกาะสมุย

postcode 84140 • pop 36,100
Ko Samui is part of an island group that used to be called Muu Ko Samui (Samui Archipelago), though you rarely hear that term these days. The archipelago sits well off the coast of Surat Thani Province and consists of around 80 islands, of which seven – Samui, Pha-Ngan, Tao, Ta Loy, Taen, Ma Ko and Ta Pao – are inhabited. So far the bulk of the tourist interest has focussed on the three largest islands: Ko Samui, Ko Pha-Ngan and Ko Tao.

At 247 sq km, Ko Samui is Thailand's third-largest island. Samui's first settlers were seafaring islanders from Hainan Island (now part of the People's Republic of China) who took up coconut farming here around 150 years ago. You can still see a map of Hainan on the *săan jâo* (Chinese spirit shrine) near Siam City Bank in Na Thon, the oldest town on the island. Muslim families of Thai-Malay descent live in a few of the villages scattered around the island as well.

Beginning around 20 years ago, the island attained a somewhat legendary status among travellers in Asia, but it wasn't until the late 1980s that its popularity escalated to the proportions of other similar getaways found between Goa and Bali. Since the advent of the bus and ferry system and the opening of the airport, things have changed rapidly. During the high seasons – late

A child of the sea gypsies (Moken people)

PAUL BENSSEN

RICHARD NEBESKY

A Pattani movie theatre, South-Western Gulf Coast

RICHARD NEBESKY

Paradise Bungalows, Hat Lamai

RICHARD NEBESKY

Food vendor on a Surat Thani street, South-Western Gulf Coast

DENNIS JOHNSON

The idyllic inlet on Ko Nang Yuan, South-Western Gulf Coast

The Big Buddha, Ko Samui

Gone fishing, Ko Samui

A grand entrance, Songkhla

Coloured streamers placate sea spirits

Another perfect day on Ko Pha-Ngan

December to February and July to August – it can be difficult to find a place to stay, even though most beaches are crowded with bungalows and resorts. The port town of Na Thon teems with foreign travellers getting on and off the ferry boats, booking tickets onward and collecting mail at the post office. With nearly a dozen daily flights to Samui from Bangkok, the island has rushed headlong into top-end development.

Nevertheless, Samui is still an enjoyable place to spend some time, and more than a few people have been making regular visits for nearly 20 years. It has some of the best-value accommodation in Thailand and a casual, do-as-you-please atmosphere that makes it quite attractive. And even with an airport, it still has the advantage of being off the mainland and far away from Bangkok. Coconuts remain an important part of the local economy – up to two million are shipped to Bangkok each month.

But there's no going back to 1971, when the first two tourists arrived on a coconut boat from Bangkok, much to the surprise of a friend who had been living on the island for four years as a Peace Corps volunteer. The main difference is that there are now many more places to stay, most of them in the mid to high range by Thai standards. And of course, with this 'something for everyone' climate, there's more people, more traffic, more noise and more rubbish, but so far not in intolerable proportions. Samui residents and businesspeople have formulated policies to deal with these social and environmental challenges. For example, on Chaweng, Ko Samui's most developed beach, the building code has kept hotels from rising much higher than tree-level, and seaside accommodation places supply the labour that keeps Chaweng's beaches almost litter-free.

Perhaps due to the Hainanese influence, Samui culture differs from that of other islands in Southern Thailand. Its inhabitants refer to themselves as *chao samŭi* (Samui folk) rather than Thais. They can be even friendlier than the average rural Thai and have a great sense of humour, although those who are in constant contact with tourists can be a bit jaded. Nowadays most of the larger resorts, restaurants, bars and other tourist enterprises are owned or operated by Bangkok Thais or Europeans, and most of the hotel and restaurant staff are ethnic-Lao from Thailand's North-East. If you want to meet true chao samŭi, you'll have to stand on the road and flag down a taxi (many work as drivers); don't be surprised if the driver acts as if he's just won the lottery – bargain hard!

The island has a distinctive cuisine, influenced by the omnipresent coconut, still the main source of income for chao samŭi, who have disproportionately less ownership in beach property than outsiders. Coconut palms blanket the island, from the hillocks right up to the beaches. The durian, rambutan and langsat fruits are also cultivated.

The population of Ko Samui is for the most part concentrated in the port town of Na Thon, on the western side of the island facing the mainland, and in 10 or 11 small villages scattered around the island. One main road, which is now paved all the way around, encircles the island with several side roads poking into the interior. About 90% of the island is still uninhabited, though you wouldn't know it from looking at the coastline.

Ecology & Environment

Samui's visitors and inhabitants produce over 50 tonnes of rubbish a day, much of it plastic. Not all is properly disposed of, and quite a few plastic bottles end up in the sea, where they wreak havoc on marine life. Remember to request glass water bottles instead of plastic, or try to fill your own water bottle from the guesthouse or hotel restaurant's large, reusable canisters.

Information

When to Go The best time to visit the Samui group of islands is during the hot and dry season from February to late June. From July to October (south-west monsoon) it can rain on and off, and from October to January (north-east monsoon) there are sometimes strong winds. However, many travellers have reported fine weather

The Face of Peninsula Thailand

Although under Thai political domination for several centuries, the narrow pendant of land dangling between the Andaman Sea and Gulf of Thailand has always remained culturally apart from the other regions of Thailand. Historically, the peninsula has been linked to cultures in ancient Indonesia, particularly the Srivijaya empire, which ruled a string of principalities in what is today Southern Thailand, Malaysia and Indonesia. The Srivijaya dynasty is thought to have been based in Sumatra, with a major satellite in Chaiya. Srivijaya – Siwichai to the Thais – lasted nearly 500 years from the 8th to 13th centuries. The influence of Malay-Indonesian culture is still apparent in the ethnicity, religion, art and language of the *Thai pàk tâi* (Southern Thais).

Geography & Economy

Bounded by water on two sides, the people of Southern Thailand are by and large a seafaring lot. One consequence of this natural affinity with the ocean is the abundance of delectable seafood. Brightly painted fishing boats, hanging nets and neat thatched huts add to the pàk tâi setting; travellers in Southern Thailand are likely to encounter more than a few visions of 'tropical paradise', whatever their expectations might be.

Three of Thailand's most important exports – rubber, tin and coconut – are produced in the South so that the standard of living is a bit higher than in other provincial regions. However, Southern Thais claim that most of the wealth is in the hands of ethnic Chinese. Throughout the peninsula – in Malaysia as well as Thailand – the Chinese are concentrated in the urban provincial capitals while the poorer Muslims live in the rural areas. This urban concentration of Chinese is a fact of life throughout South-East Asia, becoming more noticeable in Southern Thailand and the Islamic state of Malaysia because of religious-cultural differences.

As in Malaysia, higher concentrations of Muslims live on the eastern side of the peninsula than on the western side – a legacy of non-Muslim immigration patterns during the 19th and early-20th century British colonial period when Phuket and Penang were important international trading centres. Although most Thais will vehemently deny that Britain ever ruled any part of the Thai half of the peninsula, the reality is that the British did claim dominion over Narathiwat, Satun and Yala provinces before the Anglo-Siamese Treaty of 1909.

(and fewer crowds) in September and October. November tends to get some of the rain that also affects the east coast of Malaysia at this time. Prices tend to soar from December to July, whatever the weather.

Maps In Surat Thani or on Ko Samui, you can pick up the TAT's helpful Surat Thani map, which has maps of Surat Thani Province, Ang Thong National Marine Park and Ko Samui, along with travel information. A couple of private companies also do good maps of Ko Samui, Pha-Ngan and Tao, which are available in tourist areas of Surat and on the islands for 70B. The most accurate is V Hongsombud's *Guide Map of Koh Samui, Koh Pha-Ngan & Koh Tao*, though it's been a while since it was last updated.

If you fly into Samui airport, look around for the *Green Map*, which is quite good for a freebie.

Tourist Offices The friendly, helpful TAT office (☎ 077 420 504) at the northern end of Na Thon, past the post office on the western side of the road, dispenses handy brochures and maps. TAT claims this is a temporary office (though it has been there over five years now) and that it is looking for a new location elsewhere in town. The office is open daily from 8.30am to 4.30pm.

The Face of Peninsula Thailand

Culture & Language

Officially, as well as ethnolinguistically, Southern Thailand is made up of 14 provinces: Chumphon, Krabi, Nakhon Si Thammarat, Narathiwat, Pattani, Phang-Nga, Phattalung, Phuket, Ranong, Satun, Songkhla, Surat Thani, Trang and Yala. The Thai pàk tâi dress differently, build their houses differently and eat differently from Thais in the North. Due to a common history with Malaysia, many Southern Thais are followers of Islam, and in many areas mosques outnumber Buddhist wát. Local men often cover their heads with white-lace *haji* caps or black Nehru-style *topis* and in rural areas they may favour the long sarong over Western-style trousers worn in the Northern, Central and North-Eastern regions of Thailand. Muslim Thai women sport brightly coloured batik dresses and may wrap their hair in gauzy scarves.

These regional differences will become most visible to those who leave the coastal resort areas and explore inland towns and cities. In the larger southern cities a strong Chinese presence adds another element to the cultural mosaic, so that one can wander from Buddhist wát to Malay tea shop to Chinese joss house in the space of a few blocks. The Chinese influence can also be seen in old urban architecture and in the baggy Chinese pants worn by rural non-Muslims.

All pàk tâi speak a dialect common among southern Thais that confounds even visitors from other Thai regions. Diction is short and fast and the clipped tones fly into the outer regions of intelligibility, giving the aural impression of a tape played at the wrong speed. In the provinces nearest Malaysia – Yala, Pattani, Narathiwat and Satun – many Thai Muslims speak Yawi, an old Malay dialect with similarities to modern Bahasa Malaysia and Bahasa Indonesia. You'll notice that 'Ao' 'Hat' and 'Ko' sometimes precede place names; ao means bay, hàt is beach and ko is island.

Southern Thais are stereotypically regarded as rebellious folk, considering themselves reluctant subjects of Bangkok rule and Thai (Central Thai) custom. Indeed, Thai Muslims (ethnic Malays) living in the provinces bordering Malaysia complain of persecution by the Thai government troops who police the area for insurgent activity. There has even been talk in some quarters of these provinces seceding from Thailand, an event that is unlikely to occur in the near future.

Joe Cummings

Immigration Travellers have been able to extend their tourist visas for 500B at the Ko Samui immigration office (☎ 077 421 069), about 3km south of Na Thon at the intersection of the round island road (Rte 4169) and the road that leads to the hospital (Rte 4172). Opening hours are 8.30am to noon and 1pm to 4.30pm weekdays (closed public holidays).

Money Changing money isn't a problem in Na Thon, Chaweng or Lamai, where several banks and exchange booths offer daily exchange services.

Post The island's main post office is in Na Thon, near the TAT office, but in other parts of the island there are privately run branches. The main office is open from 8.30am to 4.30pm Monday to Friday and 9am to noon on Saturday. Many bungalow operations also sell stamps and mail letters, but most charge a commission.

Telephone An international telephone service is available daily from 7am to 10pm on the 2nd floor of the CAT office, attached to the main post office. Many private phone offices around the island will make a connection for a surcharge over the usual TOT or CAT rates.

Email & Internet Access There are several places in Na Thon, Chaweng and Lamai

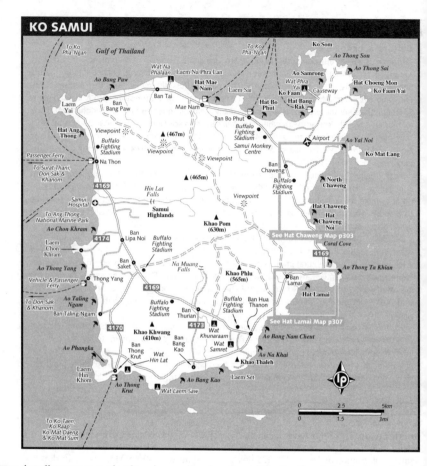

that allow you to send and receive email and surf the Web. In Chaweng, Travel Solutions, on the beach, and La Dolce Vita, next to Swensen's, are helpful and have some atmosphere. The latter has good coffee and fruit shakes.

Internet Resources The Web sites Koh Samui Thailand at W www.sawadee.com, the Samui Business Centre at W www .gosamui.com and the Tourism Association of Koh Samui at W www.samuitoursim .com contain lists of information on dive centres, accommodation and tours, plus timetables for Bangkok Airways, ferries, trains and VIP buses.

Travel Agencies Efficient and reliable Travel Solutions (☎/fax 077 230 706, e ttsolutions@hotmail.com), on Chaweng beach next to Ark Bar, can help with international travel, accommodation and visa arrangements, as well as helping with all national and local travel decisions, such as choosing between the many diving operations on Samui. Surat Thani travel agents Phantip (☎ 077 212 212) and Songserm (☎ 077 421 316) have offices in Na Thon.

Newspapers & Magazines A free home-grown, tourist-oriented newspaper with articles in German, English and Thai, *Samui Welcome* comes out monthly. *What's on Samui*, *Samui Guide* and the pocket-sized *Accommodation Samui* are free and contain listings of hotels, restaurants and suggestions of things to do, buried beneath scads of ads.

Medical Services Samui International Hospital (aka Chaweng Hospital; ☎ 077 422 272, 077 230 781) is your best bet for just about any medical or dental problem. Emergency ambulance service is available 24 hours and credit cards are accepted for treatment fees. It's located opposite the Muang Kulaypan Hotel. Muang Thai Clinic (☎ 077 424 219) on Hat Lamai is open from 9am to 11am and 5pm to 7pm daily. House calls can be arranged if necessary.

Samui International Clinic (☎ 077 230 186), on the main ring road in Chaweng, is open from 11am to 7pm daily. House calls are available from 9am to 9pm. English and German are spoken at the clinic.

Dangers & Annoyances Several travellers have written to warn others to take care when making train and bus bookings. Bookings sometimes aren't made at all, the bus turns out to be far inferior to the one expected or other hassles develop. In another scam involving air tickets, agents say economy class is fully booked and that only business class is available; the agent then sells the customer an air ticket – at business-class prices of course – that turns out to be economy class.

As on Phuket, the rate of road accident fatalities on Samui is quite high. This is due mainly to the large number of tourists who rent motorcycles only to find out that Samui's winding roads, stray dogs and coconut trucks can be lethal to those who have never dealt with them. If you feel you must rent a motorcycle, protect yourself by wearing a helmet, shoes and appropriate clothing when driving.

Snatch thieves have become a problem in the recent past. A bag or purse left in the basket of a motorcycle is a prime target for bag snatchers. Likewise, the nightlife venues of Chaweng have also become hunting grounds for thieves. Keep bags containing valuables on your person at all times.

Diving & Snorkelling
The waters around Ko Tao are much more scenic than Samui's, but if you're only interested in getting certified, doing it on Samui is cheaper. Many dive operations have opened around the island. The franchised operations such as Easy Divers and Samui International Diving School (SIDS) get a large share of the business, but the smaller dive companies are often more flexible than their larger competitors.

Beach dives cost around 900B per day. Dives from boats start from 2000B, and a four-day certification course starts at 6500B and rises to 14,000B for the beach and boat option. An overnight dive trip to Ko Tao, including food and accommodation, can be done for as low as 4500B, plus 900B for each additional day.

The highest concentration of dive shops is on Hat Chaweng. Among the more established are:

Big Blue Diving Center (☎/fax 077 422 617, W www.bigbluediving.com) Hat Chaweng
Easy Divers (☎ 077 231 190, fax 077 230 486, W www.thaidive.com) Hat Chaweng
The Dive Shop (☎/fax 077 230 232, e diveshop@samart.co.th) Hat Chaweng
Samui International Diving School (SIDS; ☎ 077 422 386, fax 077 231 242, e info@planet-scuba.net) Hat Chaweng
Samui Sports Divers (☎ 077 427 203, W www.samuisportsdivers.com) Hat Bo Phut

Paddling
Located in Gallery Lafayette, Chaweng, Blue Stars (☎ 077 413 231, fax 077 230 497, W www.gallerylafayette.com/bluestars) offers guided kayak trips in Ang Thong National Marine Park, to the west of Ko Samui, along with cave exploring, snorkelling and speedboat transfer.

Cooking
The Samui Institute of Thai Culinary Arts (Sitca; ☎/fax 077 413 172, W www.sitca.net) offers daily Thai cooking classes – including

vegetarian dishes – as well as courses in the aristocratic Thai art of carving fruits and vegetables into intricate floral designs. One-day cooking classes cost 1650B and include a five-course group dinner for students and a companion of their choice. Sitca is located down the soi opposite the Central Samui Beach Resort.

Muay Thai

Na Thon and Chaweng have *muay thai* (Thai boxing) rings with regularly scheduled matches. Admission to most fights is around 100B. The quality of the mostly local contestants isn't exactly top-notch.

Buffalo Fighting

Local villagers love to bet on duelling water buffaloes. Events are arranged on a rotating basis at seven rustic fighting rings around the island in Na Thon, Saket, Na Muang, Hua Thanon, Chaweng, Mae Nam and Bo Phut. In these events two buffaloes face off and, at their owners' urging, lock horns and/or butt one another until one of the animals backs down. The typical encounter lasts only a few seconds, and rarely are the animals injured. As such events go, it's fairly tame – certainly far more humane than dog fighting, cockfighting or Spanish bullfighting. Tourists are charged 150B to 200B entry.

Samui Monkey Centre

ศูนย์ลิงสมุย

The Samui Monkey Centre (☎ 077 245 140, *adult/child 150/50B; open 9am-5pm*) is located about 500m south of Ban Bo Phut. Coconut plantation owners have been using trained macaques to climb coconut trees and harvest coconuts for decades. Despite the sign out the front that reads 'Monkey Theatre', the Samui Monkey Centre is not a venue for *lákhon ling* (Thai drama that utilises monkeys as actors). Instead it's more like the 'working elephant' shows in Chiang Mai, with monkeys (and dogs) going through their work routines for the tourists. Not a bad diversion if you're travelling with kids. Show times are at 10.30am, 2pm and 4pm daily.

Waterfalls

Besides the beaches and rustic, thatched-roof bungalows, Samui has a couple of waterfalls. **Hin Lat Falls** is a worthwhile visit if you're waiting in town for a boat back to the mainland. If you're up for a long walk, you can get there on foot – walk 3km or so south of Na Thon on the main road, turning left at the road by the hospital. Go straight along this road for about 2km to arrive at the entrance to the waterfall. From here, it's about a half-hour walk along a trail to the top of the waterfall.

Na Muang Falls, in the centre of the island about 12km from Na Thon, is more scenic and somewhat less frequented. A sǎwngthǎew from Na Thon should cost about 50B per person; get off at the marked turn-off, then walk 2km to the falls. Sǎwngthǎew can also be hired at Chaweng and Lamai beaches.

Temples

For temple enthusiasts, at the southern end of the island, near the village of Bang Kao, **Wat Laem Saw** features an interesting and highly venerated old Srivijaya-style stupa. At Samui's northern end, on a small rocky island joined to Samui by a causeway, is the so-called **Temple of the Big Buddha** (Wat Phra Yai). Erected in 1972, the modern image stands 15m high and makes a nice silhouette against the tropical sky and sea behind it. A sign in English requests that proper attire (no shorts or sleeveless shirts) be worn on temple premises.

Near the south-western tip of Samui near Ban Phangka is **Wat Hin Lat** (☎ 077 423 146), a meditation temple that teaches daily Vipassana courses. Another attraction is the ghostly **Mummified Monk** at Wat Khunaram, which is south of Rte 4169 between Ban Thurian and Ban Hua Thanon. The monk, Luang Phaw Daeng, has been dead for over two decades but his corpse is preserved sitting in a meditative pose and sporting a pair of sunglasses.

At **Wat Samret** near Ban Hua Thanon you can see a typical Mandalay sitting Buddha carved from solid marble – a common sight in Northern Thailand but not so common in the South.

Ang Thong National Marine Park
อุทยานแห่งชาติหมู่เกาะอ่างทอง

The national park *(adult/child 200/100B)* is made up of an archipelago of around 40 small islands combining sheer limestone cliffs, hidden lagoons, white-sand beaches and dense vegetation to provide a nearly postcard-perfect opportunity to enjoy Gulf islands. The park encompasses 18 sq km of islands, plus 84 sq km of marine environments.

From Ko Samui, a couple of tour operators run day trips to the Ang Thong archipelago, 31km north-west of the island. A typical tour leaves Na Thon at 8.30am and returns at 5.30pm. Lunch is included, along with a climb to the top of a 240m hill to view the whole island group, and **snorkelling** in a sort of lagoon formed by the island from which Ang Thong (Golden Jar) gets its name. Some tours also visit **Tham Bua Bok**, a cavern containing lotus-shaped cave formations. Tours depart daily in the high season, less frequently in the rainy season. At least once a month there's also an overnight tour. The tours are still getting mostly good reviews, though one reader complained that the tour was 'not informative'. Bring hiking shoes (the 400m climb on Ko Wua demands some kind of reasonable footwear), snorkelling gear, a hat, and plenty of sunscreen and drinking water. You may be able to book a passage alone to the Ang Thong islands; inquire at Travel Solutions in Chaweng (☎ 077 230 202).

The park headquarters (☎ 077 286 025) on Ko Wat Ta Lap will take reservations for eight- to 10-person bungalows for 800B a night, large tents 200B.

You can also arrange to join a more active but more expensive Ang Thong **kayak trip** through Blue Stars at Gallery Lafayette (☎ 077 413 231) in Hat Chaweng. The cost of 1990B per person includes several hours of paddling on stable open-top kayaks, light breakfast, lunch, nonalcoholic beverages, pickup anywhere on Samui, as well as insurance.

Yet another alternative would be to get a group together, charter a boat and design your own Ang Thong itinerary. This is what the fictional crew in the novel/movie *The Beach* did.

Na Thon
หน้าทอน

On the north-western side of Ko Samui, Na Thon (pronounced *nâa thâwn*) is the arrival point for express and night passenger ferries from the piers in Surat Thani. Car ferries from Don Sak and Khanom land at Thong Yang, about 10km south of Na Thon. If you're not travelling on a combination ticket you'll probably end up spending some time in Na Thon on your way in and/or out, waiting for the next ferry.

Although it's basically a tourist town, Na Thon still sports a few old teak Chinese cafes along Th Ang Thong where descendants of the island's original Hainanese immigrants gather.

Places to Stay If you want or need to stay in Ko Samui's largest settlement there are seven places to choose from.

Seaview Guest House (☎ 077 420 052, *Th Thawi Ratchaphakdi)* Singles/doubles with fan 300/350B, with fan/air-con & bath 450/480B. Check this out if you're looking for something inexpensive. It has good-sized rooms, none of which actually have a sea view.

Palace Hotel (Chai Thaleh; ☎ 077 421 079, fax 077 421 080, Th Chonwithi) Rooms with fan 400B, with air-con 550B. Clean and spacious rooms with a good location right on the waterfront.

Win Hotel (☎ 077 421 500, Th Chonwithi) Rooms with air-con, TV & hot water 500B. Rooms are well kept and staff are helpful. There is a nice coffee shop downstairs.

Seaview Hotel (☎ 077 421 481) Rooms with fan 300B, with air-con, TV, phone & fridge 500B. Around the corner from the Win Hotel, this four-storey hotel has clean rooms and pleasant staff.

Dumrong Town Hotel (☎ 077 420 359, *Th Thawi Ratchaphakdi)* Rooms with air-con & bath 550B. A drawback is the hotel's location on a main street two blocks from the waterfront.

Notes on *The Beach*

'There's no way you can keep it out of Lonely Planet, and once that happens it's countdown to doomsday'; so says one of the backpacker characters in *The Beach*. Set in Thailand, UK author Alex Garland's controversial novel was published in 1997 and is the tale of a failed beach utopia. The story slowly caught fire in the Gen X book market and in 1999 was transformed into a $40 million motion picture.

The story traces the fate of a small, loose-knit group of world travellers who decide to establish their own beach paradise on an island in Thailand's Ang Thong National Marine Park, not far from Ko Samui and Ko Pha-Ngan. The novel's selfish, Vietnam war-obsessed protagonist makes the mistake of passing on a map showing the beach's secret location to a pair of uninvited backpackers, whose intrusion on the island and subsequent confrontation with Thai dope growers brings the novel to its violent climax.

Although the consensus seems to be that the book makes a good beach or airport read, one could quibble about Garland's depiction of Thailand and the roving backpacker scene. In interviews Garland has defended this criticism by pointing out that his portrayals were not intended to be realistic but were merely the perceptions of his characters. As Garland told *Asiaweek* magazine: 'I think it's fairly obvious this novel isn't about Thailand. It's about backpackers'.

The novel's strengths include good faràng dialogue and well-narrated settings and observations. For example, noting the resemblance between a dipterocarp's buttressed root system and a rocket's stabilising fins, Garland coins the delightful term 'rocketship trees'. Intriguing video game references and a realistic travellers' conversation on Hat Rin regarding the use of 'Kampuchea' vs. 'Cambodia' also stand out. Although the novel's dip into backpacker culture and the Khao San Road scene hold up well enough (quote: 'You know, Richard, one of these days I'm going to find one of those Lonely Planet writers and I'm going to ask him, what's so fucking lonely about Khao San Road?'), the novel really hits its stride once the story confines itself to the secret beach and lagoon.

For more discussion of the book's literary merits, check out the lengthy reader reviews on W amazon.com and the lively debate on Lonely Planet's Thorn Tree Web page.

Chao Koh Bungalow (☎ *077 421 157, Th Chonwithi*) Rooms with fan & bath 300B. On the northern fringes of town, the Chao Koh is close to the restaurants of Na Thon but without the urban noise.

Jinta Residence (☎ *077 420 630, fax 077 420 632,* e *tapee@samart.co.th, Th Chonwithi*) Rooms with air-con & bath 350-650B. On the southern edge of town, some rooms have a sea view. There is an Internet cafe attached to this establishment.

Places to Eat There are several good restaurants and watering holes in Na Thon, many of which fill up at night in the high season with travellers waiting for the night ferry.

Chao Koh Restaurant (☎ *077 421 039, Th Chonwithi*) Dishes 40-120B. On the road facing the harbour, this restaurant is still serving good seafood and Thai standards at reasonable prices.

Ko Kaew (☎ *077 421 061, Th Chonwithi*) Mains 40-100B. Ko Kaew is similar to Chao Koh.

Ruang Thong Bakery (☎ *077 422 522, Th Chonwithi*) Dishes 40-60B. This is a good place for breakfast, with home-made pastries and coffee.

Raan Khao Tom Toh Rung (*Th Chonwithi*) Dishes 20-30B. Open 24 hours. Towards the Palace Hotel this Thai rice and noodle place is the cheapest place to eat on this strip. There is no roman-script sign.

Krua Savoiey (☎ *077 420 380, Th Chonwithi*) Mains 80-150B. This Thai/European restaurant has a photo menu to help you

Notes on *The Beach*

Hollywood Invasion

Director Danny Boyle (of *Trainspotting* fame), teen idol Leonardo DiCaprio and a healthy 20th Century Fox crew turned up in Thailand in January 1999 to begin filming *The Beach* on the island of Ko Phi-Phi Leh. Almost immediately the film became embroiled in controversy when Bangkok protestors charged that the production's use of national park lands – with the express permission of the forestry department – was going to turn pristine Ao Maya (Maya Cove) into a wasteland.

The reality is that Ao Maya – like much of the Phi-Phi archipelago – has been under intense environmental pressure for many years. First there were the dynamite and cyanide fishers, then came greedy resort developers and tour operators who over-ran Phi-Phi years ago and turned much of neighbouring Ko Phi-Phi Don into a rubbish heap. Ao Maya itself has received hundreds, perhaps thousands of group-snorkelling tours over the last 10 years. Although some concession to the bay's park status has been observed – there are no bungalows or other permanent developments at Ao Maya (most likely because the licensed birdnest collectors on the island won't allow it) – improper anchoring and the dumping of rubbish toppled this beach from any 'pristine' status it may once have enjoyed years before 20th Century Fox arrived on the scene.

Many local and international observers who visit Ao Maya on a regular basis and who visited the production set here argue that Fox left the bay in better condition than it found it. During the crew's first week on Phi-Phi Leh, for example, they removed an estimated three to four tons of rubbish. Bangkok protestors, on the other hand, offered precious little evidence to support their claims of devastation.

Reef-World, an independent non-profit project that educates tourists and local tropical communities about coral reef ecology and conservation methods, has been supporting snorkelling programs and UN-endorsed Reef Check surveys at Ao Maya and other areas in the Phi-Phi islands for several years. When Reef-World's Thailand coordinators, Robert Cogen and Anne Miller, visited the production site after filming was under way, they published their own observations. You can read them at **w** www.thaistudents.com/thebeach/release5.html. For further information on reef ecology issues, contact Reef-World via email **e** thailand@reef-world.com or check out its Web site **w** www.reef-world.com.

Joe Cummings

---

choose, and a great view of the harbour – especially around sunset.

On Th Ang Thong, the next street back from the harbour, are a few old Chinese *coffee shops*. A small *vegetarian restaurant* opens at night at the southern end of this street.

The third street back from the harbour, Th Thawi Ratchaphakdi, has mostly travel agencies, photo shops and other small businesses. Two small supermarkets, Samui Mart and Giant Supermarket, are also back here.

Charoen Lap day market (*Th Thawi Ratchaphakdi*) This is a good place to buy fruit or Thai snacks before boarding a boat back to the mainland.

Will Wait Bakery (*Th Thawi Ratchaphakdi*) Dishes 80-120B. This is diagonally across from Giant Supermarket and has the same appetising menu as the branch in Chaweng.

Jit Phochana Khao Tom (*Th Thawi Ratchaphakdi*) Dishes 30-80B. This is one of the few places in town still serving Thai (and Chinese) food on a large scale.

Ko Samui Beaches

Samui has plenty of beaches to choose from, although the proliferation of new accommodation is still growing – at last count the TAT had registered over 300 places to stay on the island with a total of 8923 rooms! The most crowded beaches for accommodation are Hat Chaweng and Hat Lamai, both on the eastern side of the island. Both beaches have clear blue-green

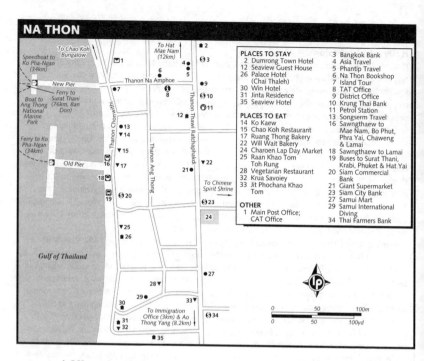

NA THON

To Chao Koh
Bungalow
Speedboat to
Ko Pha-Ngan
(34km)

New Pier

Ferry to
Boat to
Ang Thong
National
Marine
Park

Ferry to Ko
Pha-Ngan
(34km)

Old Pier

To Hat
Mae Nam
(12km)

Thanon Na Amphoe

Thanon Chonwithi

Thanon Thawi Ratchaphakdi

Thanon Ang Thong

To Chinese
Spirit Shrine

Gulf of Thailand

To Immigration
Office (3km) & Ao
Thong Yang (8.2km)

PLACES TO STAY
2 Dumrong Town Hotel
12 Seaview Guest House
26 Palace Hotel
   (Chai Thaleh)
30 Win Hotel
31 Jinta Residence
35 Seaview Hotel

PLACES TO EAT
14 Ko Kaew
15 Chao Koh Restaurant
17 Ruang Thong Bakery
22 Will Wait Bakery
24 Charoen Lap Day Market
25 Raan Khao Tom
   Toh Rung
28 Vegetarian Restaurant
32 Krua Savoiey
33 Jit Phochana Khao
   Tom

OTHER
1 Main Post Office;
   CAT Office

3 Bangkok Bank
4 Asia Travel
5 Phantip Travel
6 Na Thon Bookshop
7 Island Tour
8 TAT Office
9 District Office
10 Krung Thai Bank
11 Petrol Station
13 Songserm Travel
16 Sawngthaew to
   Mae Nam, Bo Phut,
   Phra Yai, Chaweng
   & Lamai
18 Sawngthaew to Lamai
19 Buses to Surat Thani,
   Krabi, Phuket & Hat Yai
20 Siam Commercial
   Bank
21 Giant Supermarket
23 Siam City Bank
27 Samui Mart
29 Samui International
   Diving
34 Thai Farmers Bank

0   50   100m
0   50   100yd

---

waters and OK coral reefs for snorkelling and underwater sightseeing.

Chaweng has more bungalow 'villages' plus several flashy tourist hotels. It is the longest beach – over twice the size of Lamai – and has the island of **Mat Lang** nearby.

There's a bit more to do around Lamai because of its proximity to two villages – Ban Lamai and Ban Hua Thanon. At the wát in Ban Lamai is the **Wat Lamai Cultural Hall** (☎ 077 424 345; open 8am-5pm), a sort of folk museum displaying local ceramics, household utensils, hunting weapons and musical instruments. The drawback to Lamai is the rather sleazy atmosphere of the strip of beer bars behind the beach; Chaweng's bar-and-disco strip is decidedly more sophisticated and more congenial for couples or single women. Both have open-air discos.

Chaweng is the target of upmarket development because of its long beach. Another factor is that only Chaweng (and the northern part of Lamai) has water deep enough for swimming from October to April; most other beaches on the island become very shallow during these months.

For more peace and quiet, try the beaches along the north, south and west coasts. **Mae Nam**, **Bo Phut** and **Bang Rak** (Phra Yai or Big Buddha) are along the northern end; Bo Phut and Bang Rak are part of a bay that holds Ko Faan (the island with the Big Buddha), separated by a small headland. The water here is not quite as clear as at Chaweng or Lamai, but the feeling of seclusion is greater, and accommodation is cheaper.

Hat Thong Yang on the western side of the island is even more secluded (only a few sets of bungalows), but the beach isn't very good by Samui standards. There is also **Hat Ang Thong**, just north of Na Thon, which is very rocky but with more local colour (eg, fishing boats) than the others. The southern end of the island now has many bungalows as well, set in little out-of-the-way coves that are worth seeking out. And then there's everywhere in-between right around the island – every bay, cove or cape with a strip of sand has a bungalow nowadays.

Places to Stay & Eat Prices vary considerably according to the time of year and occupancy rates. Some of the bungalow operators on Samui have a nasty habit of tripling room rates when rooms are scarce, so a hut that's 200B in June could be 600B in August. Rates given in this section can only serve as a guide – they could go lower if you bargain or higher if space is tight.

Everyone has his or her own idea of the perfect beach bungalow. At Ko Samui, the search could take a month or two, with more than 300 licensed places to choose from. Most offer roughly the same service and accommodation for 300B to 500B, though some cost quite a bit more. The best thing to do is go to the beach you think you want to stay at and pick a place you like – look inside the huts, check out the restaurant, the menu, the guests. You can always move if you're not satisfied.

Beach accommodation around Samui now falls into four basic categories chronicling the evolution of places to stay on the island. The first phase consisted of simple bungalows with thatched roofs and walls of local, easily replaceable materials – really quite rare nowadays; the next phase brought concrete bathrooms attached to the old-style huts; then came a transition to the third phase of cement walls and tile roofs – the predominant style now – with more advanced facilities like fans and sometimes air-con. The latest wave is luxury rooms and bungalows indistinguishable from mainland inns and hotels.

For a very basic bungalow with private bath, 150B is the minimum on Ko Samui. Generally anything that costs less than 150B a night will mean a shared bath.

The number of eating establishments on Samui has mushroomed in the past few years. Fans of Italian food will not be disappointed, especially on Chaweng where it seems Italian-owned restaurants outnumber everything else combined. Nearly all bungalow operations have their own restaurant, but because the ownership and management of various lodgings around the island changes so frequently it's difficult to name favourites. Cooks come and go, bungalows flourish and go bankrupt, owners are assassinated by competitors – you never can tell from season to season. It's easy to get from one beach to another, so you can always change bungalows. With the establishment of several places charging well over 5000B per night, the jet set has discovered Samui. Finally, if Samui isn't to your liking, move islands! Think about Ko Pha-Ngan or Ko Tao.

Following are some general comments on staying at Samui's various beaches, moving clockwise around the island from Na Thon.

Warning For years now we have continued to receive reports of theft on Ko Samui. If you're staying in a beach bungalow, consider depositing your valuables with the management while on excursions around the island or while you're swimming at the beach. Most of the theft reports have come from Chaweng, Lamai and Mae Nam beaches.

Ban Tai (Ao Bang Paw) Ban Tai is the first beach area north of Na Thon with accommodation; so far there are just a handful of places to stay here. The beach has fair snorkelling and swimming.

Axolotl Village (☎/fax 077 420 017, e axolotl@loxinfo.co.th, w www.axolotl village.com) Rooms 350-450B, bungalows 550-1550B. This caters to New Age *faràng* (Westerners) who want to spend their holiday cleansing their colons. Tarot reading and 'channelling' (receiving guidance from the spirit world) are on offer. A pleasant restaurant area overlooking the beach has an inventive menu featuring vegetarian, Italian and Thai dishes.

Blue River (☎ 077 421 357) Bungalows 300-500B. Next door to Axolotl is the similar-looking Blue River, under Thai management. Rooms are tastefully designed and decorated. The restaurant does good barbecued seafood.

Sunbeam (☎ 077 420 600) Bungalows with bath 500B. These bungalows are in a very nice setting.

Health Oasis Resort (☎ 077 420 124, fax 077 420 125, e contactus@healthoasis resort.com) Rooms in low season 150-250B, in high season 400-600B. The Health Oasis Resort, formerly the Healing Child Resort, offers many services including 'brain hemisphere tuning and balancing' and 'vortex destiny astrology', along with pyramid-scheming invitations to become 'overseas reps, agents, distributors or business partners'.

Hat Mae Nam Hat Mae Nam, 14km from Na Thon, is expanding rapidly in terms of bungalow development; there are still a few cheapies left but prices are rising steadily.

Home Bay Resort (☎ 077 247 214, fax 077 247 215) Fan/air-con bungalows 300/800B. Spread out on the headland (Laem Na Phra Lan), where Ban Tai ends and Mae Nam begins, you can hear chanting from the nearby wát when the wind is right.

Phalarn Inn 33 Resort (☎ 077 247 111) Bungalows 200-500B. Simple but sturdy fan bungalows made of wood and concrete. A slightly larger bungalow has been rigged up with air-con.

Harry's (☎/fax 077 425 447) Rooms 350-550B. Well run and clean, Harry's is laid out in a peaceful garden setting. Long-term rentals with kitchen and satellite TV are also available.

Sea Fan Resort (☎ 077 425 204, fax 077 422 412) Rooms 3700-4500B. A total of 36 bungalows with all the amenities in a lush garden.

The beach in front of Wat Na Phalaan is undeveloped and the locals hope it will stay that way – topless bathing is strongly discouraged here.

The next group of places east range from 300B to 600B and include *Anong Villa* (☎ 077 247 256), *Shangrilah Bungalows* (☎ 077 425 189), though we don't recommend this one, *Palm Point Village* (☎ 077 425 095), with a nice ambience, and *Shady Shack Bungalows* (☎ 077 425 392).

Maenam Resort (☎ 077 425 116) Spacious bungalows 700-1000B. This is an upper-budget place.

New Sunrise Village (☎ 077 247 219) Rooms 150-500B. New Sunrise has a wide assortment of fan accommodation depending on size and proximity to the beach.

Cleopatra's Place (☎ 077 425 486) Fan bungalows 200-350B, air-con 800B. In the middle of Hat Mae Nam, this has been recommended for its good seafood and bungalows right on the beach.

Friendly (☎ 077 425 484) Bungalows with bath 200-500B. Right on the beach in Hat Mae Nam, Friendly has clean, well-kept bungalows.

New La Paz Villa (☎ 077 425 296, fax 077 425 402) Rooms with fan 500B, with air-con 700-1800B. La Paz is trying for a Latin feel – discounts for the fan rooms are sometimes possible.

Paradise Beach Resort (☎ 077 247 227, fax 077 425 290) Singles in low/high season 3800/4800B, villas 4800/5800B. This has a beachfront restaurant and two pools – perhaps to make up for the beach, which is very narrow in this area.

Santiburi Dusit Resort (☎ 077 425 038, fax 077 425 040, in Bangkok ☎ 022 384 790) Rooms in low/high season US$238/340. This huge resort is the most ritzy on Hat Mae Nam, and comes complete with tennis courts, waterways, ponds, bakery and sports facilities.

There are at least 10 or 15 other bungalow operations between Laem Na Phra Lan and Laem Sai, where Ao Mae Nam ends.

Hat Bo Phut This beach tends to be a little on the muddy side and the water can be too shallow for swimming during the dry season – a blessing in disguise that keeps development rather low-key and has preserved Bo Phut's village atmosphere.

Near Bo Phut village there's a string of bungalows in all price ranges.

Sunny (☎ 077 427 031) Bungalows 200-350B. Farthest north on this beach, this place is budget-friendly though the bungalows are basic.

Starfish & Coffee Bungalows (☎ 077 425 085) Rooms with fan 450-650B, air-con 1000B. This has pleasant glass-fronted bungalows on the beach and duplexes farther inland.

Peace Bungalow (☎ *077 425 357*) Bungalows 600-2500B. Well managed and long-running, Peace Bungalow's rates depend on amenities and proximity to the shore.

Samui Palm Beach Resort (☎ *077 425 494, fax 077 425 358*) Bungalows 3500-6500B. An upscale place with lots of amenities and landscaped grounds.

Proceeding east, a road off the main round-island road runs to the left and along the bay towards the village, where you'll find the following places.

Ziggy Stardust (☎ *077 425 173*) Huts 300B, bungalows with air-con, hot water & fridge 1000B. One of the golden oldies of Samui, this place is clean and popular.

Rasta Baby (☎ *077 245 295*) Rooms with fan & hot water 200-300B. The brightly coloured Rasta Baby is a stoner's paradise. A bohemian crowd of Thais usually hang out here.

Smile House (☎ *077 425 361*) Fan rooms 400-500B, air-con 1500B. On the inland side, this has no sea view, but offers a large swimming pool instead.

The Lodge (☎ *077 425 337, fax 077 425 336*) Rooms with air-con & TV 1200-1400B. The Lodge is built so that it faces the ocean, and features an interesting three-storey design.

Gecko Village Resort (☎ *077 245 554, fax 077 245 553*) Rooms with air-con 600B. Newish Gecko Village has only eight sturdy bungalows and is well-run and friendly.

Sand View (☎ *077 425 438*) Huts 200-450B. If you continue through the village along the water, you'll find the isolated Sand View. This area is sometimes called Hat Bang Rak.

Summer Night Resort (☎ *077 425 199*) Rooms with fan/air-con 400/650B. This stretches over a fairly large area.

The village has a couple of cheap local-style restaurants, as well as French, German and Italian restaurants.

Cafe del Mar Dishes 80-180B. Near the pier, this serves good, reasonably priced Thai and European food.

Ubon Wan Som Tam Dishes 20-30B. On Bo Phut's main street, this serves cheap and tasty Isan food.

Hat Bang Rak (Hat Phra Yai or Big Buddha Beach)
This has around 15 bungalow operations.

Nara Garden Resort (☎ *077 425 364, fax 077 425 292*) Rooms with air-con 1200-2200B. This well-kept resort, with nicely landscaped grounds, a seaside restaurant and a small swimming pool, is just a 10-minute, 50B ride from the airport and is hence a favourite with Bangkok Airways flight crews.

LA Resort (☎ *077 425 330*) Bungalows with fan 200-600B. This is about the most economical place here. Small bungalows close to the road are cheapest.

Pongpetch Servotel (☎ *077 245 100, fax 077 425 148*) Rooms 500-1200B. This has a strangely castle-like decor. Rooms here or in the attached 'guestotel' are clean and comfortable.

Secret Garden Bungalows (☎ *077 425 419, fax 077 245 253*) Bungalows 400B, with air-con 1000-1500B. The pleasant Secret Garden is a good choice, with A-frame bungalows, all with nice sitting areas at the front. It also has a beach pub and restaurant.

Como's (☎ *077 425 210*) Bungalows 300-600B. Well run and comfortable, the air-con bungalow that sleeps three for 600B is good value.

Bo Phud Guest House (☎ *077 425 085*) and ***Number One*** (☎ *077 425 446*) are in the 150B to 300B range.

Beach House (☎ *077 245 124, fax 077 245 123*) Bungalows 300-500B. This has a nice outdoor eating area where you can get Thai and Western dishes. It also has concrete bungalows with attractive roofs.

Chez Ban Ban Resort (☎/fax *077 245 135*) is also the site of a bar/creperie, and the ***Blue Banana Restaurant*** (☎ *077 245 080*), across the road, has dishes for 80B to 120B and does good breakfasts.

Ao Samrong to Ao Thong Sai
The big cape between Bang Rak and Chaweng is actually a series of four capes and coves, the

first of which is Ao Samrong. These small bays are fairly isolated and keeps the area quiet and peaceful.

Bay View Village (☎ 077 427 500, fax 077 413 045) Bungalows 2500-3000B. This is the place if you want moderately priced accommodation with its own beach. There's also a swimming pool and Jacuzzi.

The next cove along is Ao Thong Son, which like Ao Samrong is also isolated but with a larger beach.

Samui Thongson Resort (☎ 077 230 799) Bungalows with air-con 800-1200B. This was recently renovated and has comfortable bungalows above a clean stretch of beach.

Thongson Bay Bungalows Bungalows with fan 250-500B, air-con 1000B. Sharing the beach with the Samui Thongson, this has old-style wooden bungalows.

The next cove along is Ao Thong Sai, with one very expensive option.

The Tongsai Bay Cottages & Hotel (☎ 077 425 015, fax 077 425 462, 🅦 www .tongsaibay.com) Rooms 10,000-50,000B. This is a heavily guarded resort with 72 suites (most with a Jacuzzi) and a swimming pool and tennis courts.

Hat Choeng Mon & Ao Yai Noi The largest cove following Ao Thong Sai has several names, but the beach is generally known as Hat Choeng Mon. It's clean, quiet and recommended for families or for those who don't need night life and a variety of restaurants (these can be found at nearby Chaweng). Opposite the beach is **Ko Faan Yai**, an island that can be reached on foot in low tide.

PS Villa (☎ 077 425 160, fax 077 425 403) Fan rooms 500B, air-con 700-1500B. The well-run PS Villa is friendly and popular with families.

O Soleil Bungalow (☎ 077 425 232) Rooms 200-550B. This has the cheapest accommodation on this stretch of beach, though the fan rooms are basic.

Choeng Mon Bungalow (☎ 077 425 372) Bungalows with fan 250B, with air-con 650-850B. The concrete bungalows with fan are just passable.

Between Choeng Mon Bungalow Village and PS Villa are two top-end places.

Imperial Boat House Hotel (☎ 077 425 041, fax 077 425 460) Rooms/bungalows 5445/9025B. The 216-room Imperial has a three-storey hotel with rooms, and separate two-storey bungalows made from teak rice barges. There's also a boat-shaped swimming pool.

The White House (☎ 077 245 315, fax 077 425 233, 🅔 whitehouse@sawadee .com) Bungalows in high season 3900-4500B, in low season 3200-3800B. This is a collection of deluxe bungalows with all the amenities. The hotel motto is 'Where each guest is a president!'.

Next is a smaller bay called Ao Yai Noi, just before north Chaweng. This little bay is quite picturesque, with large boulders framing the white-sand beach.

IKK Bay Resort (☎ 077 422 482) Bungalows 300-500B. This resort is quite secluded and the bungalows are made of stone instead of the usual concrete.

Coral Bay Resort (☎ 077 422 223, fax 077 422 392, 🅔 info@coralbay.net) Bungalows with air-con in high season 2500-4500B, in low season 2000-4000B. The long-running Coral Bay has large, well-spaced bungalows, set on grassy grounds with a pool. There is also a good Thai restaurant.

Hat Chaweng Hat Chaweng, Samui's longest beach, also has the island's highest concentration of bungalows and tourist hotels. Prices have moved upmarket, and there is a commercial strip behind the central beach that is jam-packed with restaurants, souvenir shops, bars and discos. There are so many, in fact, that once you're on the strip you may have difficulty finding a path back down to the beach. It's perfectly acceptable to cut through any bungalow establishment to make your way to the beach.

Chaweng has kilometre after kilometre of beach bungalows, so look around before deciding on a place. There are basically three sections: North Chaweng, Hat Chaweng proper and Hat Chaweng Noi.

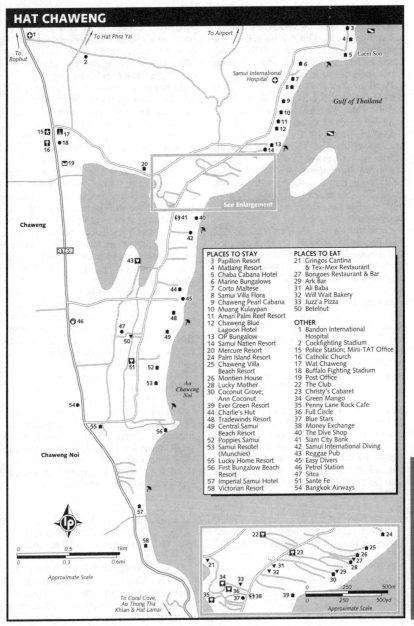

HAT CHAWENG

PLACES TO STAY
3 Papillon Resort
4 Matlang Resort
5 Chaba Cabana Hotel
6 Marine Bungalows
7 Corto Maltese
8 Samui Villa Flora
9 Chaweng Pearl Cabana
10 Muang Kulaypan
11 Amari Palm Reef Resort
12 Chaweng Blue
   Lagoon Hotel
13 OP Bungalow
14 Samui Natien Resort
20 Mercure Resort
24 Palm Island Resort
25 Chaweng Villa
   Beach Resort
26 Montien House
28 Lucky Mother
30 Coconut Grove;
   Ann Coconut
39 Ever Green Resort
44 Charlie's Hut
48 Tradewinds Resort
49 Central Samui
   Beach Resort
52 Poppies Samui
53 Samui Resotel
   (Munchies)
55 Lucky Home Resort
56 First Bungalow Beach
   Resort
57 Imperial Samui Hotel
58 Victorian Resort

PLACES TO EAT
21 Gringos Cantina
   & Tex-Mex Restaurant
27 Bongoes Restaurant & Bar
29 Ark Bar
31 Ali Baba
33 Will Wait Bakery
50 Betelnut

OTHER
1 Bandon International
   Hospital
2 Cockfighting Stadium
15 Police Station; Mini-TAT Office
16 Catholic Church
17 Wat Chaweng
18 Buffalo Fighting Stadium
19 Post Office
22 The Club
23 Christy's Cabaret
34 Green Mango
35 Penny Lane Rock Cafe
36 Full Circle
37 Blue Stars
38 Money Exchange
40 The Dive Shop
41 Siam City Bank
42 Samui International Diving
43 Reggae Pub
45 Easy Divers
46 Petrol Station
47 Sitca
51 Sante Fe
54 Bangkok Airways

North Chaweng Places here have climbed into the upper range, but there are still a few simple bungalows with private bath at the northern end going for 400-500B. North Chaweng has the advantage of lower noise levels and less traffic than farther south.

Papillon Resort (☎/fax 077 231 169) Bungalows 500B, units with air-con 800-1250B. This place has passable concrete bungalows around a garden.

Matlang Resort (☎ 077 422 172) Bungalows 400-650B. This friendly place is a bit overgrown but otherwise OK.

Marine Bungalows (☎ 077 422 416) Units with fan 200-400B, with air-con 800B. This is the least expensive place in this area. Fan bungalows are a bit worn but fairly clean.

Corto Maltese (☎ 077 230 041, fax 077 422 535) Rooms 2990-6990B. The well-designed and decorated, vaguely Mediterranean-style Corto Maltese is an upscale place that seems very popular with the French. It has a pool and bar area.

Muang Kulaypan (☎ 077 230 850, fax 077 230 034, W www.kulaypan.com) Rooms in low season 2000-3285B, high season 2350-4450B. A 'boutique hotel' with Thai accents – all rooms have a balcony or private garden. There's also a swimming pool and Thai classical dance performances on Tuesday, Thursday and Saturday.

There are also a few mid-range places in the area: the *Samui Villa Flora* (☎ 077 422 273, fax 077 422 272), with rooms for 900B to 1500B, *Palm Island Resort* (☎ 077 230 654, fax 077 413 140), with rooms for 1000B to 2400B, and *Chaweng Pearl Cabana* (☎ 077 422 116), which has rooms with fan for 500B to 800B, air-con 1200B.

This area also has a small group of up-market places from 3000B or more: *Chaba Cabana Hotel* (☎ 077 231 350, fax 077 230 771), with rooms for 3200B to 4600B, and *Chaweng Blue Lagoon Hotel* (☎ 077 422 037, fax 077 422 401), with rooms for 3700B to 6200B.

Amari Palm Reef Resort (☎ 077 422 015, fax 077 422 394, in Bangkok ☎ 022 679 708) Singles/doubles US$136/145, suites US$203. The Amari is the nicest of the top-end choices, with individual two-storey Thai-style cottages and two swimming pools; it's also the most environmentally conscious luxury resort on the island, using filtered sea water for most first uses and re-cycled grey water for landscaping.

Mercure Resort (☎ 077 230 864, fax 077 230 866) Doubles/suites 2900/4400B. Off the road that leads away from the beach towards the interior is this resort built in stepped, two-storey hotel wings on a slight slope with sea and lagoon views.

Chaweng Central The central area, Hat Chaweng proper, is the longest section and has the most bungalows and hotels. This is also where the strip behind the hotels and bungalows is at its most urban, with plenty of restaurants, bars, discos, minimarts, one-hour film processing labs, tailors, souvenir shops and currency exchange booths. There is also a Tourist Police office, a TAT mini-office and a post office.

Water sports are big here, so you can hire sailboards, go diving, sail a catamaran, charter a junk and so on. Parasailing costs around 400B and water-skiing is 300B per hour. This area also has the island's highest average prices, not only because accommodation is more upmarket but simply because this is (or was) the prettiest beach on the island.

Samui Natien Resort (☎ 077 422 405, fax 077 422 309) Bungalows with air-con 1200-1400B. At the northern end of central Chaweng, Samui Nation has bungalows set among coconut palms and a swimming pool.

OP Bungalow (☎ 077 422 424) Bungalows with fan 500B, with air-con 700-1000B. At the northern end of central Chaweng, this has clean and comfortable cement bungalows; the more expensive are on the edge of the beach.

Chaweng Villa Beach Resort (☎ 077 231 123, fax 077 230 139) Bungalows with air-con 1800B. This has an excellent location and good service.

Montien House (☎ 077 422 169, fax 077 421 221) Cottages with fan/air-con & breakfast 900/1600B. This has a loyal following for its well-equipped cottages on landscaped grounds.

Lucky Mother (☎ 077 230 931) Basic hut with shared bath 150B, bungalow with fan 300-600B. Discounts for long-term stays are given during the low season. If you're on a budget, this is among the least expensive places along this strip. Cheap Thai massage is also offered.

If you're getting the idea that this isn't the beach for strict budget backpackers, you're right, but surprisingly a couple of popular cheapies have survived; in this high season these places fill early, so it may be easier to go to another beach (or try North Chaweng). The most popular and least expensive budget place is *Charlie's Hut* (☎ 077 422 343), with huts from 200B to 300B. *Coconut Grove* and *Ann Coconut* are central Chaweng bargains at 250B to 400B for fan, 700B and up for air-con. A rather large drawback for some is that these sit smack in the middle of Bangkok Airways' flight path.

Ever Green Resort (☎ 077 230 051, fax 077 413 018) Rooms with fan 300B, with air-con 600-1200B. These simple but comfortable bungalows are almost lost in a lush garden of tropical plants and trees.

Tradewinds Resort (☎/fax 077 231 247) Bungalows with air-con, hot water, fridges & large balconies facing a pleasant garden area 1500-2600B, including breakfast. Something of a yachtie hang-out, the resort offers dive trips, kayaking and snorkelling.

Central Samui Beach Resort (☎ 077 230 500, fax 077 422 385) Rooms 5500-24,000B. This huge neo-colonial-style place is the queen of the central Chaweng properties, with two bars, a restaurant, a pool, tennis courts and health centre.

Poppies Samui (☎ 077 422 419, fax 077 422 420, W www.kohsamui.net/poppies) Cottages US$133. Inspired by the original Poppies on Bali's Kuta Beach, this offers Thai-style cottages with everything from IDD phones to atrium baths.

Samui Resotel (Munchies; ☎ 077 422 374, fax 077 422 421, W www.samuiresotel.com) Bungalows 1500-2500B. An upper mid-range place with lots of amenities and soothing surroundings. Its classy beachfront restaurant serves Thai and international fare.

Most bungalows and all the hotels on the beach provide food service of some kind. Back on the 'strip' are dozens of restaurants and cafes serving Western cuisine, with Italian places outnumbering the rest.

Juzz'a Pizza (☎ 077 422 571) Dishes 150-350B. Serving pasta and pizza, this is near the Green Mango and delivers until 1am.

Ali Baba (☎ 077 230 253) Dishes 80-180B. In north-Central Chaweng, this serves northern Indian cuisine.

Betelnut (☎ 077 413 370) Mains 150-400B. Near the Central Hotel, Betelnut serves innovative Californian cuisine, a refreshing change from Chaweng's ubiquitous pasta parlours.

Will Wait Bakery (☎ 077 230 590) Dishes 80-120B. This bakery serves decent Western breakfasts at two locations, in south and central Chaweng.

Ark Bar Dishes 80-150B. On the beach, this has good Western breakfasts for 99B.

Bongoes Restaurant & Bar (☎ 077 230 931) Dishes 60-150B. On the beach, this serves everything from pseudo-Thai to burgers.

Poppies (☎ 077 422 419) Mains 250-400B. Attached to the hotel of the same name, this is a great place for a splurge on barbecued seafood.

Gringos Cantina & Tex-Mex Restaurant (☎ 077 413 267) Dishes 120-180B. Next to Treasure Island Mini Golf, this serves hearty Mexican and Texan fare.

There are a range of entertainment options in Chaweng central.

Reggae Pub (☎ 077 422 331) This huge zoo-like complex sports an open-air dance floor with music provided by foreign DJs. The club hosts a 'rasta full-moon party' and frequent beer-drinking contests.

Green Mango A popular dance place that's managed to keep going for years and usually stays open until very late.

Full Circle A techno dance club with a stark, modern decor, Full Circle starts going around midnight.

Santa Fe (☎ 077 230 570) Santa Fe is a huge place with an American South-West theme that is popular with young Thais.

The Club (☎ *077 422 341*) This is a mellow alternative to the raging dance clubs.

Penny Lane Rock Cafe (☎ *077 413 014*) This plays classic rock tracks from the 1960s to the 1990s, and also supplies satellite TV, darts, snooker, backgammon and other pub diversions.

Christy's Cabaret This offers free transvestite cabaret nightly from 11pm.

Hat Chaweng Noi Off by itself around a headland at the southern end of central Hat Chaweng, this is a pretty little area that is fairly insulated from the commercialism and clatter of central Chaweng.

First Bungalow Beach Resort (☎ *077 422 327, fax 077 422 243*) Rooms/bungalows 3500/4000B. Straddling the headland on both bays is this aptly named resort that was built in 1970, but has now gone way upscale.

Lucky Home Resort Air-con rooms 450-600B. Just inland from First Bungalow, this has clean, good value-rooms with satellite TV, fridge & hot-water bath. Monthly rates start at 2300B.

Imperial Samui Hotel (☎ *077 422 020, fax 077 422 396,* e *samui@imperial hotels.com*) Rooms with air-con, phone & TV 6050-10,050B. The plush, multi-storey Imperial is built on a slope in the middle of Hat Chaweng Noi proper. The cottages and hotel are built in a pseudo-Mediterranean style with two swimming pools and a terrace restaurant with a view. Its cultural shows on Monday and Friday evenings are available to non-guests.

Victorian Resort (☎ *077 422 011, fax 077 422 111*) Rooms with air-con 2400-4400B. This hotel-style resort is set on a lushly landscaped parcel of beach and has a restaurant, swimming pool & sauna.

Coral Cove (Ao Thong Yang) Another series of capes and coves starts at the end of Hat Chaweng Noi, beginning with scenic Coral Cove. (The Thai name of this cove – Ao Thong Yang – is the same as another bay on the west coast of Samui; this one is more commonly known by its Western name, Coral Cove, and that's how we refer to it.)

Samui Bayview Villa (☎ *077 423 320, fax 077 413 321*) Rooms 2000-4000B. High on a hill overlooking the coast, this place has great views but no beach access.

Coral Cove Resort (☎ *077 422 126, fax 077 422 496*) Bungalows with fan 600B, with air-con 1000-1200B. This is the only place in this area with immediate beach access.

Blue Horizon Bungalows (☎ *077 422 426, fax 077 230 293,* e *montien@samart. co.th*) Rooms with fan/air-con 400/700B, bungalows with air-con 1000B.

Coral Cove Chalet (☎ *077 422 173, fax 077 422 496*) Singles/doubles with air-con & TV 2000/2200B. This has nicely furnished rooms. A restaurant on the property serves Thai, Chinese and Western dishes. Other amenities include a pub, conference room and swimming pool.

Hi Coral Cove (☎ *077 422 495*) Rooms 300-1000B, breakfast included. On a lovely, remote spot above the bay, this place is good value if you don't mind walking to the beach.

Beverly Hills Resort & Restaurant (☎/fax *077 422 232*) Bungalows 600-1000B. The 12 bungalows here sit atop a cliff overlooking Hat Chaweng. Even if you don't stay here, you should consider having a meal in the restaurant, if only for the incredible view.

On the lofty headlands between Coral Cove and Ao Thong Ta Khian are a few more places taking advantage of the relative seclusion and views.

Bird's Eye View Bungalow (☎ *077 422 278*) Rooms with fan 400-500B, with air-con 1000B. This place is the best of the bunch, with white wooden bungalows with little balconies overlooking Hat Chaweng.

Ao Thong Ta Khian This is another small, steep-sided cove, similar to Coral Cove and banked by huge boulders.

Samui Silver Beach Resort (☎ *077 422 478*) Bungalows with fan 400-700B, with air-con 800-1000B. This place has bungalows overlooking the bay, and a pleasant restaurant with a beach view.

Thong Takian Villa (☎ *077 230 978*) Bungalows with fan/air-con 350/600B, with

TV & fridge 900B. This has 10 tidy white-cement bungalows with red tin roofs.

Samui Yacht Club *(☎ 077 422 225, fax 077 422 400)* Bungalows 1500-2000B. At the southern end of the cove, this has luxurious Thai-style bungalows. If you like to fish, this is a good area for shore-casting.

Besides the 'resort restaurants', there are a few good ***seafood restaurants*** on the bay.

Hat Lamai After Chaweng became built-up, budget travellers discovered Lamai. It's still popular – just look at the crowds – but those looking for solitude have moved on to Hat Mae Nam and other more secluded beaches. Hat Lamai accommodation rate, are mostly a bit lower than at Chaweng – there are fewer 1000B-plus places. Following is just a cross section of some of the many places to stay.

There continue to be reports of burglaries and muggings at Lamai. Take care with valuables – have them locked away in a guesthouse or hotel office if possible. Mug-gings mostly occur in dark lanes and along unlit parts of the beach at night.

Northern Hat Lamai Accommodation at the north-eastern end of the beach is quieter and moderately priced, though the beach is a bit thin on sand.

Royal Blue Lagoon Beach Resort *(☎ 077 424 086, fax 077 424 195)* Rooms 2100-2500B. The semi-secluded Royal Blue Lagoon has garden-view rooms and sea-view rooms, as well as a pool and a good open-air seafood restaurant.

Considerably less expensive are the simpler ***Bay View Bungalow*** *(☎ 077 230 769)*, with rooms from 500B to 600B, ***Island Resort*** *(☎/fax 077 424 202)*, with rooms from 500B to 1000B, and ***Rose Garden*** *(☎ 077 424 115, fax 077 424 110)*, which has rooms for 350B to 650B.

Tamarind Retreat *(☎ 077 424 436,* Ⓦ *www.tamarindretreat.com)* Cottages US$68-98. Set on a forested hillside,

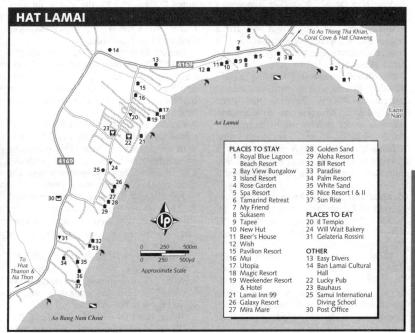

HAT LAMAI

To Ao Thong Tha Khian, Coral Cove & Hat Chaweng

Ao Lamai

Laem Nan

Ao Bang Nam Cheut

To Hua Thanon & Na Thon

PLACES TO STAY	
1	Royal Blue Lagoon Beach Resort
2	Bay View Bungalow
3	Island Resort
4	Rose Garden
5	Spa Resort
6	Tamarind Retreat
7	My Friend
8	Sukasem
9	Tapee
10	New Hut
11	Beer's House
12	Wish
15	Pavilion Resort
16	Mui
17	Utopia
18	Magic Resort
19	Weekender Resort & Hotel
21	Lamai Inn 99
26	Galaxy Resort
27	Mira Mare
28	Golden Sand
29	Aloha Resort
32	Bill Resort
33	Paradise
34	Palm Resort
35	White Sand
36	Nice Resort I & II
37	Sun Rise

PLACES TO EAT	
20	Il Tempio
24	Will Wait Bakery
31	Gelateria Rossini

OTHER	
13	Easy Divers
14	Ban Lamai Cultural Hall
22	Lucky Pub
23	Bauhaus
25	Samui International Diving School
30	Post Office

0   250   500m
0   250   500yd
Approximate Scale

Tamarind Retreat blends well into its surroundings. Cottages are spacious and well appointed. A day spa operates on the premises – the price of the room includes breakfast and access to the spa.

Spa Resort (☎ *077 230 855, fax 077 424 126,* W *www.spasamui.com*) Bungalows with fan & bath 250-550B. This is a New-Agey place that offers herbal sauna, massage, clay facials, natural foods, meditation and, yes, even fasting and colon cleansing. The restaurant serves quite good vegetarian dishes. Other activities include t'ai chi, qi gong, yoga and mountain biking. Fees for health services are extra.

Several cheaper, more easy-going places in the 200B to 400B range include ***My Friend*** (☎ *077 425 187*) and ***Tapee*** (☎ *077 424 096*), as well as ***Sukasem*** (☎ *077 424 119*), with rooms for 300B to 700B. Also worth checking out are ***Beer's House*** (☎ *077 231 088*) and ***Wish***, with simple rooms for 200B to 300B.

New Hut (☎ *077 230 473*) Bungalows 200-500B. You may encounter problems if you stay here and don't eat at New Hut's restaurant. We have received a number of reader's letters complaining about the atmosphere here.

Pavilion Resort (☎ *077 424 420, fax 077 424 029*) Rooms with air-con 3400-3800B, bungalows 4800B. Pavilion has some thatched-roof Thai-style charm. All rooms, whether in the hotel wing or bungalows, come with porches, personal safe, hairdryer, minibar, TV & phone. There is also a Jacuzzi and a swimming pool. Discounts of up to 40% are sometimes given.

Central Hat Lamai Down into the main section of Lamai is a string of places for 300B to 800B, including ***Mui*** (☎ *077 232 400*), ***Utopia*** (☎ *077 233 113*) and ***Magic Resort*** (☎ *077 424 229*).

Weekender Resort & Hotel (☎ *077 424 429, fax 077 424 011, in Bangkok* ☎ *024 662 083*) Rooms/bungalows/Thai-style houses 1450/1330/2220B. The 76-room Weekender offers a wide variety of activities to choose from, including miniature golf, swimming and a bit of nightlife.

Lamai Inn 99 (☎ *077 424 427, fax 077 424 211*) Bungalows with fan 500B, air-con 700-900B. This place has clean and comfortable bungalows of wood and concrete, as well as a decent restaurant.

This is the part of the bay closest to Ban Lamai and the beginning of the Lamai 'scene'. Just about every kind of service is available here, including exchange offices, medical service units, supermarkets, one-hour photo labs, clothing shops, bike and jeep rental places, travel agencies with postal and international telephone services, restaurants (many with videos), discos, bars and food stalls.

Mira Mare (☎ *077 424 262, fax 077 433 378*) Rooms 300-600B. This has good-value budget rooms in an area that has gone upscale. There's also a restaurant with Thai and Italian food.

Aloha Resort (☎ *077 424 014–6, fax 077 424 419,* e *aloha@loxinfo.co.th*) Doubles/suites 1700/4000B. Aloha is a two-storey upmarket resort. As the name implies, there's a bit of a Hawaiian theme to the place. It has a good restaurant with seafood, Thai and European food.

Galaxy Resort (☎ *077 424 441, fax 077 424 137*) Bungalows 1500-2200B. Galaxy has fully equipped bungalows right on the beach as well as cheaper rooms in a hotel building. There's also a restaurant and a beachside bar.

Golden Sand (☎ *077 424 031–2, fax 077 424 430*) Bungalows with fan 500-600B, with air-con 1000-1700B. This place features comfortable bungalows with verandas and is surrounded by banana trees. The restaurant is good but rather slow.

Paradise (☎ *077 424 290*) Rooms with fan 300-600B, with air-con 800-1000B. Paradise has been here for over 20 years and is the second longest-running place on the beach.

Bill Resort (☎ *077 233 054, fax 077 424 286*) Bungalows with fan & bath 500B, with air-con, hot shower and fridge 1000-1200B. This place has bungalows that are close together, but spacious inside.

White Sand (☎ *077 424 298*) Huts 200-400B. This is a Lamai original with passable huts but sparse amenities. The staff are quite friendly.

Palm Resort (☎ *077 424 297*) Bungalows 250-400B. Palm is still keeping it simple and affordable with basic bungalows and a no-nonsense restaurant. The only downside is that it's often booked out.

Nice Resort 1 (☎ *077 424 432, fax 077 424 027*) Bungalows with fan 500-800B, with air-con 1500B. The bungalows are really too close together, but otherwise they're comfortable.

Nice Resort 2 (☎ *077 424 034*) Singles & doubles with fan 300B, with air-con 600-800B. This has cement huts that feel slightly less crowded than at Nice Resort 1.

Sun Rise (☎ *077 424 435*) Huts 250B, bungalows with air-con 500-900B. The huts here are basic but quite good for the price. Less memorable are the concrete bungalows that are priced according to amenities.

Lamai doesn't have as wide a variety of places to eat as Chaweng. Most visitors appear to dine wherever they're staying. Once again, Italian is nearly ubiquitous.

Il Tempio (☎ *077 232 307*) Mains 60-200B. Il Tempio does pizza, Italian and some Thai dishes.

Will Wait Bakery (☎ *077 424 263*) Dishes 30-120B. Behind the Galaxy Resort, Will Wait does good breakfasts and has a large selection of baked goods.

Gelateria Rossini Dishes 40-80B. Gelateria Rossini specialises in homemade Italian ice cream and cakes.

There are also several Thai *food stalls* in the central beach area.

Bauhaus (☎ *077 233 147*) Lamai has one large dance club, the long-running Bauhaus, where music presented by DJs is interspersed with short drag shows and Thai boxing demos.

Lucky Pub Opposite Bauhaus, Lucky Pub offers German beer, snacks and all the typical pub games. Several lanes are lined with Pattaya-style outdoor bars. By and large it's a faràng male-dominated scene.

Ao Bang Nam Cheut At this point a headland interrupts Ao Lamai and the bay beyond is known as Ao Bang Nam Cheut,

named after the fresh water stream that runs into the bay here. During the dry months the sea is too shallow for swimming, but in the late rainy season when the surf is too high elsewhere on the island's beaches this can be a good area for swimming. Look for the well-known, phallus-like 'Grandmother' and 'Grandfather' rock formations.

Samui Park (☎ *077 424 435, Bangkok* ☎ *022 459 238*) Rooms 1900-2400B. Closer to the road than the coast is Samui Park, a concrete block with rooms and a few bungalows.

Swiss Chalet (☎ *077 424 321, fax 077 232 205*) Bungalows with fan 600B, with air-con 900-1200B. Swiss Chalet has large bungalows overlooking the sea. The restaurant does German as well as Thai food.

Rocky (☎ *077 424 326*) Bungalows with fan/air-con 500/1500B. This old-timer has gone upscale with 29 concrete bungalows featuring lots of amenities.

Ao Na Khai & Laem Set Just beyond the village of Ban Hua Thanon at the southern end of Ao Na Khai is an area sometimes called Hat Na Thian. As at Lamai, the places along the southern end of the island are pretty rocky, which means good snorkelling – there's also a long reef here – but perhaps not such good swimming. The inexpensive, natural bungalows that were still found here until recently have disappeared, replaced by the usual air-con architecture. It seems developers never stop and ask themselves, 'Who needs air-con on a tropical beach?' and as long as they keep making money, they probably never will.

Maria Resort (☎ *077 233 395, fax 077 424 024*) Bungalows with air-con, TV, phone & mini-bar 1000-1200B. Nicely landscaped and with sturdy bungalows, this resort is good value for the location and amenities. Discounts of 20% are given with a bit of prompting.

Samui Orchid Resort (☎ *077 424 017, fax 077 424 019*) Rooms 950B, with breakfast 1100B. The drab concrete Samui Orchid has overpriced bungalows and hotel-like rooms, and a swimming pool. It makes an unsuccessful attempt at being upmarket.

Laem Set Inn (☎ *077 424 393, fax 077 424 394*) Bungalows with veranda, hot shower, fan & sea view US$50-75, rooms with air-con US$100-370; more contemporary air-con rooms facing the sea US$120-400. This secluded place commands a pretty corner of the sand-and-boulder beach. On the premises are a minor art gallery and a good Thai restaurant (pricey, small portions according to one reader).

At Laem Set you pay for atmosphere and ecological sensitivity more than for amenities; some people will find this just what they're looking for, while others may feel they can find better value on the more popular beaches.

Central Samui Village (*formerly Samui Butterfly Garden;* ☎ *077 424 020, fax 077 424 022*) Cottages 3200-3800B. Beside Laem Set Inn, this features stylish modern wooden cottages linked by wooden walkways over a rocky landscape. Good landscaping, a pool, and a mixed Thai and foreign clientele are pluses. Cottages have either a garden or sea view.

Ao Bang Kao This bay at the southernmost end of the island, between Laem Set and Laem Saw, has several inexpensive places to stay from 150B to 300B. You'll need to get off the round-island road onto winding sand roads for a couple of kilometres to find these places: *River Garden* (☎ *077 424 035*) and *Diamond Villa* (☎ *077 424 442*).

Ao Thong Krut & Ko Taen From Ban Thong Krut you can arrange boat trips to four offshore islands: **Ko Taen, Ko Raap, Ko Mat Daeng** (which has the best coral) and **Ko Mat Sum**.

Thong Krut Bungalow (*TK Bungalow;* ☎ *077 423 117, fax 077 423 255*) Huts with bath 300-500B, with air-con 800B. Next to the village of Ban Thong Krut on Ao Thong Krut is, what else, Thong Krut Bungalow. The beach here is not very private as it's a jumping-off point for boats to nearby islands as well as a mooring for local fishing boats.

Coconut Villa (☎/fax *077 423 151*) Bungalows with fan & shower 300-400B, with air-con & hot shower 600-900B. Towards the south-western end of the bay, almost on Laem Hin Khom, the new and friendly Coconut Villa occupies a choice piece of property on its own small but clean and quiet beach with views of Ko Taen offshore. Its bungalows are well spaced and facilities include a pool on the beach, restaurant, motorcycle rental, money exchange, laundry service and mini-shop.

Ko Taen has two bungalow villages along the east coast beach at Ao Awk: *Tan Village* and *Coral Beach Bungalows,* both in the range of 250B to 400B. *Dam Bungalows* and *BS Cove,* in a sharply curving bay on the western side, are similar. Ko Mat Sum has good beaches where travellers sometimes camp. Rubbish can be a problem, especially during the rainy season.

Regular boats to Ko Taen cost 50B each way. If you want to have a good look at the islands, fishing boats carrying up to 10 people can be chartered in Thong Krut for 1000B to 1500B; try at one of the seafood restaurants *Gingpagarang* or *Thong Krut Fishing Lodge* (☎ *077 423 257*) along the main beach.

Seagull Coral Tour (☎ *077 423 303*) offers an 8am to 3.30pm boat tour to Ko Taen and Ko Mat Sum for 600B, including lunch, nonalcoholic beverages, snorkelling gear, boat transport and pickup anywhere on Samui.

West Coast Several bays along Samui's western side have places to stay, including Thong Yang, where the Don Sak and Khanom ferries dock. The beaches here turn to mudflats during low tide, however, so they're more or less for people wanting to get away from the east coast scene, not for beach fanatics.

Ao Phangkha Around Laem Hin Khom on the southern end of Samui's west is this little bay, sometimes called Emerald Cove. During the low season there are so few guests on this cove that the bungalow proprietors tend to let the rubbish pile up.

Pearl Bay (☎ *077 423 110*) Rooms 200-500B. Pearl Bay is set in nice surrounds and is very quiet. This is probably the best of the lot.

Gem Cove (☎ *077 423 082*) has rooms for 150B to 300B and *Sea Gull* (☎ *077 423 091*) has rooms for 200B to 500B, which aren't bad. These places offer half-day snorkelling trips to nearby islands for about 500B per person (four-person minimum).

Ao Taling Ngam Ao Taling Ngam is a 20B săwngthăew ride from Na Thon or the vehicle ferry pier.

Le Royal Meridien Baan Taling Ngam (☎ *077 423 019, fax 077 423 220, in Bangkok ☎ 022 360 400)* Rooms US$250-500. Dominating the northern end of this shallow curving bay from its aerial perch atop a steep hill, this is Samui's most ultra-exclusive resort. It boasts tennis courts, two swimming pools, a fitness centre, and a full complement of equipment and instructors for kayaking, sailboarding and diving. Luxuriously appointed guest accommodation contains custom-made Thai-style furnishings. As it's not right on the beach, a shuttle service transports guests back and forth; airport and ferry transfers are also provided.

Ao Thong Yang The vehicle ferry jetty here may be moved to another location in the near future, or this one might remain and a second one built elsewhere along the coast. Either way, the local accommodation will be affected by the change, possibly winding down and eventually closing.

Near the pier are several places from 300B to 900B. *Cococabana Beach Club* (☎ *077 423 174)* has rooms with fan for 500B and is the best pick.

Ao Chon Khram On the way to Na Thon is sweeping Ao Chon Khram. All four places to stay here will provide free transport to/from the Thong Yang pier for guests.

Lipa Lodge (☎ *077 423 028)* Huts 300-850B. This is especially nice, with a good site on the bay. It has a good restaurant and bar.

International Bungalows & Big John Seafood Restaurant (☎ *077 423 025)* Bungalows with fan 500B, with air-con, hot water and sea view 800B. The restaurant is

quite good, but the bungalows seem a bit overpriced.

Rajapruek Resort (☎ *077 423 115)* Rooms with fan/air-con 500/800B. This place is popular with Thai visitors and the restaurant is very good.

Siam Residence (☎ *077 420 008)* Rooms US$132-172. This is isolated but slightly more expensive than other options in the area.

Getting There & Away

Air Bangkok Airways flies 12 times daily to Ko Samui from Bangkok. There is an office in Chaweng (☎ 077 420 133) and another at the airport (☎ 077 422 513). The fare is 3180B one way (or 3510B from Ko Samui to Bangkok, including airport tax). Fares for children are half the adult fare. The flight duration is one hour and 20 minutes.

Bangkok Airways also offers twice-daily flights between Samui and Phuket, as well as daily flights to Krabi, Pattaya and Singapore. During the high season flights may be completely booked out as far as six weeks in advance, so be sure to plan accordingly. If Samui flights are full, you might try flying to Surat Thani from Bangkok aboard THAI (see the Surat Thani Getting There & Away section for details).

The attractive Samui airport is all open-air and has a nice bar, restaurant, money exchange and hotel reservations counter. The airport departure tax is 400B for domestic and international flights.

Bus/Ferry Combination The government bus/ferry combination fare from Bangkok's Northern bus terminal costs 427B. Most private buses from Bangkok charge around 400B for the same journey. From Thanon Khao San (Khao San Rd) in Bangkok it's possible to get bus/ferry combination tickets for as low as 300B, but service is substandard and theft is more frequent than on the more expensive buses. If an agency on Th Khao San claims to be able to get you to Samui for less, it is almost certainly a scam as no profit can be made at such low prices.

Surat Thani bus companies Phantip (☎ 077 421 221–2) and Songserm (☎ 077 421 316) have offices in Na Thon. From Na

Thon, Phantip Travel runs air-con buses to Surat Thani (100B), Krabi (210B), Phuket (230B) and Hat Yai (240B), leaving the waterfront road in Na Thon daily at 7.30am. These fares include the ferry ride. To Surat Thani a bus/ferry combination ticket costs 70B ordinary (six times daily), 90B air-con (three times daily).

Train The State Railway of Thailand does train/bus/ferry combination tickets straight through to Samui from Bangkok. These save you only 10B or 20B on 2nd-class tickets; for all other routes a combination ticket costs around 50B more than separate train, bus (from the train station to piers) and boat tickets – which may be worth it to avoid the hassles of separate bookings/connections.

See the Surat Thani Getting There & Away section for details on train travel.

Boat There are four ferry piers on the Surat Thani coast and two on Ko Samui (four if you count the two piers on the north coast that serve Ko Pha-Ngan). Songserm Travel runs express ferries from Tha Thong, 6km north-east of central Surat, and slow night boats from the Ban Don pier in town. These take passengers only. The express boats used to leave from the same pier in Ban Don as the night ferry – when the river is unusually high they use this pier again.

Vehicle ferries run from Don Sak, or from Khanom around 15km south-east of central Surat at certain times of year. These are the lines that get most of the bus/boat and some of the train/bus/boat combination business.

Which boat you take will depend on what's next available when you arrive at the bus terminal in Surat or train station in Phun Phin – touts working for the ferry companies will lead you to one or the other.

During the low season (any time except December to February or August), young Thais may throng the piers around departure time for the Ko Samui boats, inviting faràng to stay at this or that bungalow. This same tactic is employed at Tha Na Thon and Tha Thong Yang upon arrival at Ko Samui. During the high season, this isn't necessary as almost every place is booked out. Some of the out-of-the-way places to stay put touts on the boats to pass around photo albums advertising their establishments.

Tha Thong – Express Boat Two express boats go to Samui (Na Thon) daily from Tha Thong and each takes around two hours to reach the island. Departure times are usually 7.30am and 2pm, though these change from time to time.

The express ferry boats have two decks: one with seats below, and an upper deck that is really just a big luggage rack – good for sunbathing. The fare is 150B each way, but this seesaws from season to season; if any rivals to Songserm appear on the scene (as has happened twice in the last few years), Songserm tends to drop its fares immediately to as low as 50B one way in order to drive the competition out of business.

From Na Thon back to Surat, there are departures at 7.15am, noon and 2.30pm from November to May, or 7.30am and 2.30pm from June to October. The 7.15am boat includes a bus ride to the train station in Phun Phin; the afternoon boats include a bus to the train station and to the Talat Kaset bus terminal in Ban Don.

Ban Don – Night Ferry There is also a slow boat for Samui that leaves Tha Ban Don in Surat Thani each night at 11pm, reaching Na Thon around 5am. This costs 100B for the upper deck (including pillow and mattress), or 80B down below (straw mats only).

The locals use this boat extensively and the craft is in better shape than some of the express boats. It's particularly recommended if you arrive in Surat Thani too late for the fast boat and don't want to stay in Surat Thani overnight.

The night ferry back to Samui leaves Na Thon at 9pm, arriving at 3am; you can stay on the boat to catch some more sleep until 8am. Ignore the touts trying to herd passengers onto buses to Bangkok, as these won't leave until 8am or later anyway.

Don't leave your bags unattended on the night ferry as thefts can be a problem. The thefts usually occur after you drop your bags on the ferry well before departure and then go for a walk around the pier area. Most victims don't notice anything's missing until they unpack after arrival on Samui.

Vehicle Ferry Tour buses run directly from Bangkok to Ko Samui, via the vehicle ferry from Don Sak in Surat Thani Province, for around 400B and take around 14 hours; check with the big tour bus companies or any travel agency. A pier at nearby Khanom is also used by Songserm, which is now competing with the Raja company whose pier is at Don Sak.

From Th Talat Mai in Surat Thani you can also get bus/ferry-combination tickets straight through to Na Thon. These cost 80B for an ordinary bus, 100B for an aircon bus and take around 2½ hours.

Pedestrians or people in private vehicles can also take the ferry directly from Don Sak, which leaves roughly every two hours between 8am and 5pm, and takes 1½ hours to reach Tha Thong Yang on Samui. The straight fare for pedestrians is 50B, for a motorcycle and driver 80B, and for a car and driver 200B. Passengers in private vehicles pay the pedestrian fare. In the opposite direction, ferries leave Tha Thong Yang between 7am and 4pm. During the rainy season the number of daily departures may decrease to as few as three, particularly in September.

Buses between the Surat Thani bus terminal and Don Sak cost 17B and take 45 minutes to an hour to arrive at the ferry terminal. If you're coming north from Nakhon Si Thammarat, this might be the ferry to take, though from Surat Thani the Tha Thong ferry is definitely more convenient.

From Ko Samui, air-con buses to Bangkok leave from near the old pier in Na Thon at 1.30pm daily, arriving in Bangkok around 6am after a stopover in Surat. Other through-bus services from Na Thon include Hat Yai, Krabi and Phuket; all of these buses leave Na Thon around 7.30am, arriving at their destinations around eight hours later and cost around 250B each. Check with the several travel agencies in Na Thon for the latest routes.

Ko Pha-Ngan Two piers – one each in Bo Phut and Bang Rak – have boats to Hat Rin Nai on Ko Pha-Ngan's south coast. There are usually three departures daily for 100B (150B on full moon nights); these take only 30 minutes. See Laem Hat Rin in the Ko Pha-Ngan section later in this chapter for more details.

Getting Around
To/From the Airport Samui Limousine operates an air-con van service between Samui airport and Hat Phra Yai (Big Buddha Beach, 30B), Chaweng (120B), Lamai (100B), Na Thon (100B) and Mae Nam (100B). For other beaches you'll have to rely on săwngthăew or taxis. Chartered taxis from the airport cost 250B to anywhere on the island. A chartered taxi to the pier at Hat Bang Rak should be no more than 100B.

Public Transport Săwngthăew fares are 15B from Na Thon to Mae Nam, 20B to Bo Phut, Hat Bang Rak and Lamai, and 30B to Chaweng or Choeng Mon. From the carferry landing in Thong Yang, rates are 10B for Na Thon, 30B for Lamai, Mae Nam and Bo Phut/Hat Bang Rak, 40B for Chaweng and Choeng Mon. A few years ago official fares were posted for these routes, but nowadays săwngthăew drivers insist on overcharging newcomers, so take care.

Săwngthăew run regularly during daylight hours only. A regular bus between Thong Yang and Na Thon costs 10B. Note that if you're arriving in Thong Yang on a bus (via the vehicle ferry), your bus/boat fare includes a ride into Na Thon, but not elsewhere.

Car & Motorcycle You can rent motorcycles from several places in Na Thon as well as at various bungalows around the island. The going rate is 150B per day for a 100cc bike, but for longer periods you can bargain the price down (280B for two days, 400B for three days etc). Rates are generally lower in Na Thon and it makes more sense to rent from there if you're going back that way. Take it easy on the bikes; every year several faràng die or are seriously injured in motorcycle accidents on Samui, and besides, the locals don't like seeing their roads become race tracks. A helmet law is enforced with some vigour. Besides avoiding a steep fine (500B at time of writing), wearing a helmet may save your life.

Suzuki Caribian jeeps can be hired for around 800B per day from various Na Thon agencies as well as at Chaweng and Lamai. Aside from all the small independents doing rentals, Avis Rent-A-Car has a branch at the Santiburi Dusit Resort (☎ 077 425 031), and Budget has a desk at Samui airport (☎ 077 427 188).

KO PHA-NGAN
เกาะพงัน

postcode 84280 • pop 10,300

Ko Pha-Ngan, about a half-hour boat ride north of Ko Samui, has become the island of choice for those who find Samui too crowded or too expensive. It started out as a sort of 'back-door escape' from Samui but is well established now, with a regular boat service and over 156 places to stay around the 190-sq-km island. It's definitely worth a visit for its remaining deserted beaches (they haven't all been developed)

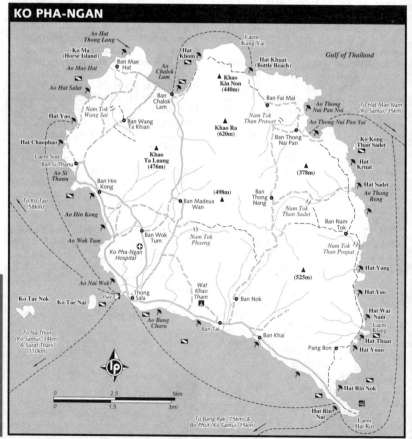

KO PHA-NGAN

and, if you like snorkelling, for its coral formations.

Although hordes of backpackers have discovered Ko Pha-Ngan, the lack of an airport and relative lack of paved roads has so far spared it from tourist-hotel and package-tour development. Compared with Samui, Ko Pha-Ngan has a lower concentration of bungalows, less-crowded beaches and coves, and an overall less-modern atmosphere. Pha-Ngan aficionados say the seafood is fresher and cheaper than on Samui's beaches, but it really varies from place to place.

Hat Rin, the venue for the now world-famous full moon parties, has prospered immensely as a result of the monthly injection of cash. Locals point out that before their beach was 'discovered' by rave-seeking travellers, the village wasn't even important enough to have its own school. On the downside, many residents say they have come to dread the noise and disorder created by the full moon parties.

Dangers & Annoyances

While many travellers may like to sample some of the local herb, it's wise to think twice. There are constant reports of travellers being offered and sold marijuana and other drugs by restaurant or bungalow owners, and then being promptly busted by police officers who *somehow* know exactly who, when and where to check.

Police roadblocks between Thong Sala and Hat Rin are becoming more common, especially in the week leading up to the full moon party on Hat Rin. These aren't cursory checks either; if you're on a motorcycle the police look in the fuel tank, check the tyres and search all your gear. One traveller reported 'the cops played a sort of pocket billiards' with his testicles looking for dope – not just pot, but ecstasy, acid, amphetamines and anything else an enterprising dealer might be shipping in for the big party. The result is often a steep fine (50,000B) and, in some cases, deportation. Not exactly the makings of a laid-back vacation.

Those who come specifically seeking an organic buzz should take note: A hallucinogenic plant, newly exploited on the island,

has caused a number of travellers to pay an unscheduled visit to the local psychiatric hospital. Called *tôn lamphong* in Thai, the plant is possibly related to datura, a member of the highly toxic nightshade family. Eating any part of the plant causes some people to be completely whacked for a couple of days. Locals say it's becoming a problem because people who are on it act pretty much like wandering zombies – stumbling down streets and clawing at thin air – oblivious to anything but their own hallucinations, which they try to follow and grasp. Some guesthouses and restaurants are reportedly offering the plant to travellers who ask for magic mushrooms, apparently because the tôn lamphong has not yet been made illegal.

Diving & Snorkelling

As at Ko Samui, coral reefs can be found intermittently at various points around the island. The better bay-reef spots are at the island's north-western tip and are suitable for snorkelling. There are also some rock reefs of interest on the eastern side of the island.

An outstanding site for scuba divers, a pinnacle called **Hin Bai**, lies about 13.5km north of the island. An abundance of corals and tropical fish can be seen at depths of 10m to 30m; conditions are best from April to October, when divers sometimes enjoy visibility up to 20m or more. Hin Bai can also be reached from Ko Tao, although the boating distance from the latter adds 4km to 5km to the trip.

Phangan Divers (☎ 077 375 117, @ info@ phangandivers.com), near the pier at Hat Rin Nai, charges 700B for beach dive trips, 2000B for a dive trip to Sail Rock or Ang Thong National Marine Park, and 8000B for full certification including lunch and two dives. A snorkelling set can be rented for 100B to 150B. There is also a branch at Hat Yao.

Waterfalls

In the interior of this island are four year-round waterfalls and a number of more seasonal ones. Boulders carved with the royal insignia of Rama V, Rama VII and Rama

Full Mooning

Ravers from around the globe have been gathering for the monthly party for at least 10 years now, and the crowd shows no sign of retreat. When Joe jumped ashore in 1990 for his first Hat Rin mooner it was a relatively small affair of perhaps 800 people. 'Shroom shakes, massive spliffs and glistening capsules of E were sold like sticks of barbecued lûuk chin plaa at a ngaan wát. The heart of the party pulsated in front of Paradise Bungalows, where Thai DJs long-tailed over from Samui to do the knob-twisting.

MW

Nowadays around 5000 ravers – as many as 8000 during the December to February high season – turn up for the party, which has split among several beachfront venues: Paradise Bungalows, Bongo Club, Drop In, Vinyl Club, Cactus Club and Tommy's. On a recent FM party the Cactus drew the steadiest crowd with a concoction of techno, house, drum 'n' bass, reggae, ambient and R&B. But Hat Rin's visiting DJs – who may hail from Belgium, the UK, Israel, Singapore and Thailand among others – are notoriously fickle, so by the time you reach Hat Rin somewhere else will probably be the 'in' house.

Dancers and groovers spill out of the open-air dance halls onto the beach and right up to the water's edge. Some people do their thing standing in the shallow breakers, but watch out where you plant yourself – by 2am there's a chorus line of lads – well, mostly lads – releasing excess bodily fluids into the Gulf Coast. In terms of party goers, the numbers peak at around 5am or 6am. The last of the DJs don't shut down until around 11am. Some ravers take cat naps for an hour or three some time between midnight and 5am, just so they can be up and at it for sunrise.

Drugs are still available, but these days the more hardcore partakers have moved on to other beaches due to a pumped-up police presence (both uniformed and undercover) at Hat Rin's now-legendary full moon raves. Still, sober observers can amuse themselves by trying to guess what's energising the folks hip-hopping in day-glo paint beneath black light tubes rigged to overhead nets. Mushrooms? Ecstasy? Diet pills? Red Bull?

Although the TAT once announced intentions to turn the Hat Rin FM into a family occasion complete with sporting events and beauty contests, authorities have yet to stop or co-opt the party and it's still very much in the original spirit of 'let's paint up and shake it'. The whole event is well organised by Thai residents who run the bungalows and bars along Hat Rin. Public pay toilets are even available at Anant (Anan) Hotel. The proprietors also clean the beach of substantial morning-after litter when the party is over.

Full Moon Party Tips

Safety Be watchful of your belongings and personal safety. Keep in mind that this is one night you can expect people who never otherwise take drugs or drink to excess to be on something and acting a little weird. Don't keep valuables in your bungalow – it's a big night for break-ins, especially at the cheaper bungalows. Buy a padlock and take advantage of the many places that offer lockers for rent. Ravers playing with fireworks add to the potential mayhem. If you're staying alone on the western side of the peninsula, think about having friends escort you home after dark.

IX, all of whom have visited the falls, can be found at **Than Sadet Falls**, which cascades along Khlong Than Sadet in the eastern part of the island. Rama V liked this island so much that he made 18 trips here

between 1888 and 1909. A pleasant way to get to the falls is on one of Cactus Club's 'Reggae Magic Boat Trips', which leave from Hat Rin Nok at 10.30am and return at 6pm and include stops at Hat Khuat and

Full Mooning

Local police report that there is a fatality about every other full moon party. Most are drowning victims who break off their partying for a refreshing swim and are never again seen alive. Others die as a result of accidents that probably wouldn't have happened had the victims been in full control of their faculties.

Accommodation If you arrive on full moon day or even the day before, you can forget about finding a vacant room or bungalow on either Hat Rin Nok (called Sunrise Beach by tourists) or Hat Rin Nai (aka Sunset Beach). Your best bet is to head over the rocky hills to the southern end of the cape to places like Hua Laem Resort, Seaview Resort, Sun Cliff Resort, and especially Lighthouse Bungalows and Leela Beach Bungalows, which are the farthest from the action and may have something available.

Many ravers travel to Hat Rin four or five days in advance to nail down a room, meet friends and 'warm up' for the party. Hat Rin and environs can house, at most, around 2000 people, while the rave attracts 5000 or more on a good full moon. Loads of party goers, especially Thais, boat over from Samui during the afternoon, party all night, then boat back the next morning, thereby sidestepping the accommodation dilemma.

Food Beachfront barbecues offer fresh grilled seafood until around 11pm, after which the pickings are slim. Several beach bungalows shut down their restaurants the morning after so that staff can get some sleep. If you wake before noon you may have to wander into the village between inner and outer Hat Rin to find something to feed your abused stomach.

Transport If you're coming over from Ko Samui for the party, take one of the thrice-daily ferries from Big Buddha Pier or Bo Phut Pier on Samui for 80B per person, or hop on one of the frequent speedboats in operation on the day and night of the full moon for 200B one way, 300B return. The speedboats continue to depart from Big Buddha and Bo Phut until around 1am, reaching a peak number of trips between 8pm and midnight.

What to Bring If you're just a night tripper, all you'll need is a change of clothes, swimsuit, sarong (for sitting or sleeping on the beach), ID (just in case) and money.

Drugs Thai police often set up inspection points on the road between Thong Sala and Hat Rin on days leading up to the full moon party. Every vehicle, including bicycles and motorcycles, is stopped and the passengers searched thoroughly. People go to jail, or pay through the nose. The going rate for escaping a small pot bust – or 'fine' if you wish – is 50,000B. See also Dangers & Annoyances in this section for more information on drugs.

Log onto **w** www.googol.com/moon or check your lunar calendar for upcoming full moon party dates.

Joe Cummings with much inspiration from Nima Chandler

Hat Khom. The cruise costs 350B per person and includes food and refreshments. Contact Cactus Club or Outback Bar (Hat Rin Nai) for information about when the next cruise will get under way.

Phaeng Falls is off the main road between Thong Sala and Ban Chalok Lam, almost in the centre of the island. A third falls, **Than Prapat Falls**, is situated near the eastern shore in an area that can be reached by road or boat, while **Than Prawet Falls** is in the north-east near Ao Thong Nai Pan.

Wat Khao Tham
วัดเขาถ้ำ

This cave temple is beautifully situated on top of a hill near the little village of Ban Tai. An American monk lived in this temple for over a decade and his ashes are interred on a cliff overlooking a palm field below.

It's not a true wát since there are only a couple of monks and a nun in residence (among other requirements, a quorum of five monks is necessary for a temple to reach wát status).

Ten-day meditation retreats taught by an American-Australian couple run during the latter half of most months. The cost is 2900B; write in advance to Wat Khao Tham, PO Box 8, Ko Pha-Ngan, Surat Thani 84280 for information, or pre-register in person.

Anyone under 25 years of age must talk with the teachers before being accepted for the retreat. A bulletin board at the temple also has information.

Massage
Chakra Traditional Thai Massage (☎ 077 375 244), located on Hat Rin Nok between Paradise Bungalows and Drop Inn Bar, offers expert massage for 200B for one hour or 300B for two hours. Yan, the proprietor, studied massage as a monk and is adept at traditional Thai as well as deep tissue techniques.

Gyms
Jungle Gym, on the road between the two sides of the cape, near the pier on Hat Rin Nai, offers muay thai and other martial arts training, Thai and Western massage, sauna, aerobics, yoga, and a full range of weight machines and free weights. Daily and monthly user fees are available, plus separate charges for instruction, massage or sauna.

Thong Sala
ท้องศาลา

About half of Ko Pha-Ngan's population of 10,000 live in and around the small port of Thong Sala. This is where the ferry boats from Surat and Samui (Na Thon) dock, although there are also smaller boats from Mae Nam and Bo Phut on Samui that moor at Hat Rin.

The town sports several restaurants, travel agencies, banks, clothing shops and general stores.

Information Bovy Supermarket, on the main street leading from the pier, sells just about anything you might need – sunglasses, sunscreen, liquor, snorkelling gear, cereal, cosmetics, even Frisbees.

Money If you're continuing on to other areas of the island and need to do some banking, Thong Sala is the place to do it. Krung Thai Bank, Siam City Bank and Siam Commercial Bank buy and sell travellers cheques and can arrange money transfers and credit card cash advances; Siam Commercial generally has the best service. Foreign exchange services at Hat Rin are comparable to those in Thong Sala, though you can't wire money there. Siam City Bank has a foreign exchange kiosk near the Pha-Ngan Bayshore Resort.

Post & Communications The post office is at the southern end of town, in the direction of Hat Rin; it's open Monday to Friday from 8.30am to noon and 1pm to 4.30pm, and on Saturday from 9am to noon. There's also a 'licensed' private post office on the road between Hat Rin Nok and Hat Rin Nai.

Since the arrival of new telephone lines in 1999, the number of places offering long distance telephone and fax services has grown tremendously. Just look for the signs in front of shops offering these services.

Most of these are also hooked onto the Internet. A large Internet access place near the Pha-Ngan Bayshore has several computer terminals and no long queues.

Medical Services The new Ko Pha-Ngan Hospital (☎ 077 377 034), about 2.5km north of Thong Sala off the road to Chalok Lam, offers 24-hour emergency services. Anything that can wait until Bangkok should wait, where medical facilities are better.

For medical emergencies or first aid after hours in Hat Rin, try Sang's clinic (the sign reads 'Nursing Home') near the Hat Rin pier.

Places to Stay & Eat – Thong Sala

There are a few options here.

Pha-Ngan Chai Hotel (☎ *077 377 068, fax 077 377 032*) Rooms with air-con, phone & TV 900-1200B. On the bay about 150m south of the pier, you have a choice of a garden or sea view.

Bua Kao Inn (☎ *077 377 226*) Singles/doubles 300/400B, with air-con 500B. This is about 100m straight ahead from the pier, and is a guesthouse-like place. There's a very popular restaurant downstairs.

Kao Guest House (☎ *077 238 061, 210/9–10 Th Thong Sala-Chalok Lam*) Rooms with fan 250-350B, with air-con 450B. This is a guesthouse-like place with a coffee shop.

Several *cafes* near the pier cater to faràng tastes and sell boat tickets. There are also a couple of *karaoke bars* in Thong Sala.

Places to Stay & Eat – Ao Nai Wok

There are a few beach bungalows within a couple of kilometres north of the pier. Although the beach here isn't spectacular, it's a fairly nice area to while away a few days if you should need to be near Thong Sala. People waiting for an early boat back to Surat or on to Ko Tao may choose to stay here (or south of Thong Sala at Ao Bang Charu) since transport times from other parts of the island can be unpredictable. Swimming at this beach is best from December to April when water levels are high. A reef offshore offers OK snorkelling.

All of the following places to stay are within about 2km of each other.

Phangan Bungalow (☎ *077 377 191*) Rooms without/with bath 150/250B. Turn left at the first main crossing from the pier, then walk straight north until the road crosses a concrete bridge, and then turn left again where the road ends at a T-junction. Soon you'll come to Phangan. This place has passable wooden bungalows and a fine

little restaurant that does whole roast pig on a spit.

Charn (☎ *077 377 411*) Rooms with bath 150-200B. Run by a friendly local family, Charn has simple but sturdy bungalows of wood and concrete.

Siriphun (☎ *077 377 140*) Rooms with bath 200-500B. Siriphun seems particularly good value; it still has the best kitchen, and some larger houses for long-term rentals.

Tranquil Resort Rooms without bath 100B, with bath 300-500B. While this place is the cheapest on the beach, the huts without baths are a bit on the rough side.

Ko Pha-Ngan Beaches

Beach bungalow operations are still concentrated north and south-east of Thong Sala and especially on the southern end of the island at Hat Rin, but there are many other places to stay around the island. Because there are few paved roads on Pha-Ngan, transport can be a bit of a problem, though the situation is constantly improving as enterprising Thais set up taxi and boat services between beaches.

Many of the huts on Pha-Ngan have been established by entrepreneurs from Ko Samui with several years' experience in the bungalow business. Huts with shared bathing facilities generally go for 100B to 150B a night and as low as 80B between May and October. Many of the huts do not have electricity or running water, some have generators that are only on for limited hours in the evening (and the lights dim when they make a fruit shake). For many people, of course, this adds to Pha-Ngan's appeal.

Other places are moving into the 200B to 400B range, which almost always includes a private bath, and there are a few scattered spots on the west and south-east coasts with resort-like amenities for 500B and up. As travel to Pha-Ngan seems particularly seasonal, you should be able to talk bungalow rates down 30% to 40% when occupancy is low. During the peak months (December to February and July and August), there can be a shortage of rooms at the most popular beaches and even the boats coming to the island can be dangerously overcrowded.

Since many of the cheaper bungalows make the bulk of their profits from their restaurants rather than from renting huts, bungalow owners have been known to eject guests who don't take meals where they're staying after a few days. The only way to avoid this, besides forgoing your own choice of restaurants, is to get a clear agreement beforehand on how many days you can stay. This seems to be a problem only at the cheaper (80B to 100B) places.

The following beach accommodation areas are listed in an anticlockwise direction starting south from Thong Sala.

Ao Bang Charu The shallow beach here is not one of the island's best, but it's close to town and so is popular with people waiting for boats or with bank business.

Sundance (☎ 077 238 103), Pha-Ngan Villa (☎ 077 377 083) and *Moonlight (☎ 077 238 398)* have similar basic thatched huts in the 150-200B range, with a few wooden or concrete huts from 300B.

Vieng Thai (☎ 077 377 247) Bungalows with bath 200-300B. Vieng Thai has recently renovated bungalows of wood and concrete. It has a restaurant.

Charm Beach Resort (☎ 077 377 165) Doubles/triples with toilet 300/500B. After a coconut grove to the south are the distinctive high-pitched roofs of Charm Beach Resort, a nicely landscaped place. It has a decent restaurant as well.

Chokana Resort (☎ 077 238 085) Rooms with fan/air-con 150/1000B. Chokana has big, solidly built hexagonal cottages in addition to more traditional huts. Its restaurant does a seafood barbecue on Friday evening.

First Villa (☎ 077 377 225) Cottages with fan/air-con 400/800B. Towards Ban Tai, past a school, this offers cement-block, tiled-roof cottages, but lacks atmosphere.

Ban Tai & Ban Khai Between the villages of Ban Tai and Ban Khai is a series of beaches with well-spaced bungalow operations. Many have replaced their thatched huts with accommodation made of less-perishable materials that typically go for 150B to 300B. Some establishments still

have a few cheap huts on hand (80B to 100B), but these are likely to be relegated to a corner of the lot far from the beach. Not all bungalows here are signed from the paved road; to really survey the area you must walk along the beach.

Dewshore (☎ 077 238 128) Bungalows with fan 350-500B, with air-con 800-1200B. These well-constructed huts in nicely landscaped grounds can be reached from a road in the centre of Ban Tai.

Starting at the southern outskirts of Ban Tai you'll find a cluster of places all around 300B to 600B.

Mac Bay Resort (☎ 077 238 443) Bungalows without bath 150B, with bath 300-450B. This stands out as one of the better choices. The huts with shared facilities are gradually being replaced with sturdier bungalows with bath and veranda. Its restaurant is said to be excellent.

Long-tail boats to other parts of the island can be chartered from Ban Khai. At one time there was a regular boat service to/from Hat Rin, but with the paving of the road all the way to Hat Rin it has been discontinued.

Thong Sala to Ban Tai săwngthăew cost 20B per person, 30B to Ban Khai. A motorbike taxi is 30B to Ban Tai, 40B to Ban Khai.

Laem Hat Rin This long cape juts southeast and has beaches along both its western and eastern sides. The eastern side has the best beach, **Hat Rin Nok**, a long sandy strip lined with coconut palms. The snorkelling here is pretty good, but between October and March the surf can be a little hairy. The western side more or less acts as an overflow for people who can't find a place to stay on the eastern side, as the beach is often too shallow for swimming. Together these beaches have become the most popular on the island.

The eastern beach, or Hat Rin Nok (Outer Rin Beach, often referred to as Sunrise Beach), has gradually become a more or less self-contained town, complete with travel agencies, moneychangers, minimarts, restaurants, bars, tattoo shops and outdoor discos. A pier on **Hat Rin Nai** (Inner Rin Beach, often referred to as Sunset Beach) serves boats from the north-east coast of Ko Samui, half an hour away.

Hat Rin Nok is famous for its monthly full moon parties (see Dangers & Annoyances and the boxed text 'Full Mooning' earlier in this section), featuring all-night beach dancing and the ingestion of various illicit substances – forget about sleeping on these nights unless you get a place off the beach. Even when the moon isn't full, several establishments blast dance music all night long – head for the western side if you prefer a quieter atmosphere.

Warning Suan Saranrom (Garden of Joys) psychiatric hospital in Surat Thani has to take on extra staff during full moon periods to handle the number of faràng who freak out on magic mushrooms, acid or other abundantly available hallucinogens. There are plenty of other drugs available from the local drug Mafia and drug-dependent visitors, and the police occasionally conduct raids. Women travellers in particular should be watchful of their personal safety at these parties; assaults have occasionally been reported.

Information Siam City Bank has a foreign exchange kiosk near the Pha-Ngan Bayshore Resort.

There's a licensed post office on the road between the two sides of the peninsula. There are numerous places offering long distance telephone and fax services in the village between Hat Rin Nai and Hat Rin Nok.

Places to Stay For the most part, bungalows around Hat Rin are expensive and stacked rather close together – the better to take advantage of full moon party goers. There are, however, a few places where you can escape the scene – but if you're not here to take part in the monthly 'gong show', then there's really no reason to stay on Hat Rin. Even when the moon is less than full, clubs on the beach blast their music until late. Needless to say, the prices listed below are meaningless during periods of maximum lunar orbicularity.

Paradise Bungalows (☎ 077 375 244) Rooms 350-750B. This is one of the oldest establishments and offers a variety of cottages both near the beach and inland on the rocks, plus rooms in a motel-like structure perpendicular to the beach.

Beach Blue (☎ 077 375 270) Rooms 150-250B. The trend of renting motel-like rows of rooms extending away from the beach continues here. These are somewhat grubby, but the long-termers seem to like it that way.

Behind this main row of beach lodgings a second row of basic bungalows has mushroomed, including *Bumblebee Huts*, *Haad Rin Hill*, and *Bongo*. All are in the 100B to 300B range.

Back on the beach are the slightly more upmarket *Anant Bungalows* (☎ 077 375 299) and *Haadrin Resort* (☎ 077 375 259), with rooms in the 200B to 600B range.

Phangan Orchid Resort (☎ 077 375 156) Rooms with fan/air-con 400/1200B. This is on the more expensive side and not particularly good value – rooms are clean but cramped. It's proximity to the action makes it prime accommodation during the full moon raves.

Sunrise Bungalows (☎ 077 375 145) Huts with fan 400-600B, with air-con 1200B. This is more or less in the middle of the beach and is well established; it has huts made of local materials. Prices depend on position relative to the beach and the current occupancy rate.

Pha-Ngan Bayshore Resort (☎ 077 375 227) Rooms with 1 bed/2 beds 600/800B, bungalows with air-con 1500B. A semi-upscale establishment, this occupies the middle section of the beach and has a few coconut trees to shade its bungalows.

Tommy Resort (☎ 077 375 215) Bungalows 300B, with bath 700B. This is a popular old-timer, although it doesn't seem to have all that much going for it except location. The Pha-Ngan Bayshore next door acts as a buffer zone between this and most of the action during full moon parties – hence it's close without being in the thick of things.

Palita Lodge (☎ 077 377 132) Bungalows 300-700B. This is a large group of 30 wooden bungalows.

Seaview Haadrin Resort (☎ *077 375 160*) Bungalows with bath 250-600B. Towards the northern end of the beach, this is relatively quiet, with well-spaced bungalows.

Mountain Sea Bungalows (☎ *077 375 274*) Huts with bath 200-500B. Built into the rocky headland at the northern end of Hat Rin. An advantage of staying here is that it's quieter at night than at places right on the beach.

Sun Cliff Resort (☎ *077 375 134*) Bungalows with fan, shower and toilet 200-1000B. Perched on the slopes of the hills in the centre of Hat Rin's southernmost point, overlooking the sea and catching sunset rays amid huge boulders and lots of vegetation, this offers 28 nicely appointed bungalows on stilts. Most have balconies with hammocks facing the sea. Follow signs posted along the cross-cape road.

Leela Beach Bungalows Huts 80-100B. A trail forks off the cross-cape road to the south-east and leads up and over the highlands to Leela Beach (a 20-minute walk from Hat Rin), a set of widely spaced bamboo thatch huts with beds and mosquito nets in a flat coconut grove. There's a thin strip of sand at the front, and good breezes. Leela Beach once belonged to the Rajneesh cult and a board bearing a large photo of 'Osho' has been turned into a sign board.

Lighthouse Bungalow Bungalows 80-150B. If you continue along the path through Leela until it meets a 100m raised walkway around a rocky headland, you'll find Lighthouse. At night, or when the surf is high, walking along this walkway could be tricky. Lighthouse's 18 simple bungalows, perched dramatically on boulders, cost 150B with outside bath and 200B with inside facilities. The best bungalows seem to be occupied by long-termers. The bungalows have their own generator, with power from 6pm to 11pm only. It's a 30-minute walk here without luggage; you can hire a long-tail at Hat Rin to shuttle you to Lighthouse's own pier for 100B. During monsoons the wind can be particularly strong at this spot.

Across the ridge on the western side is Hat Rin Nai (Inner Rin Beach), which overall is much quieter than Hat Rin Nok. Here you'll find long-timers *Palm Beach* (☎ *077 375 340)*, with bungalows for 100B to 200B, and *Sunset Bay Resort,* which has bungalows for 150B to 250B.

Charung (☎ *077 375 168*) Bungalows 200-1250B. This is the best of the pack – quiet and well maintained.

Family House (☎ *077 375 173*) Bungalows with air-con 500-600B. Family House is quite good – friendly and well maintained.

Rin Beach Resort (☎ *077 375 112*) Huts with fan/air-con & bath 400/800B. Rin Beach has a few larger huts as well as concrete bungalows with air-con. There are also rooms available in a new but unspeakably ugly row-building.

At the northern end of Hat Rin Nai, around a small headland, is a bunch of places all in the 100B to 150B range.

Blue Hill Bungalows with bath 150B. Situated on a hill above the beach, these are the nicest thatched bungalows in the area.

Pooltrub Resort (*Phuntrap Resort*) Bungalows in high season 100-300B, in low season 100-150B. Along the road that joins Hat Rin Nok and Hat Rin Nai, in the centre of the cape, this has solidly built bungalows on landscaped grounds. It's a short walk to Hat Rin Nai.

Places to Eat Restaurants here are still less expensive than on Samui, though prices are creeping well beyond 'local'. The seafood is good and fresh.

Outback Bar Mains 60-150B. This is the place to come for a hearty meal of steak and chips – without the high-volume video noise that blares forth from many of Hat Rin's other eating establishments. Outback Bar is also a great place to have a few drinks before heading down to the late-night clubs on Hat Rin Nok.

Rin Beach Kitchen & Bakery Dishes 10-30B. In the commercial zone, this offers a wide variety of cakes, rolls and other baked goods. The bakery stays open until 11pm.

Chicken Corner Dishes 20-40B. This grills Thai-style chicken, then chops it up and makes tasty sandwiches. To find it, just look for the line of hungry people near the Hat Rin Nok crossroads.

Old Lamp Dishes 45-120B. On the road immediately parallel to Hat Rin Nok, this has become very popular for its stuffed baked potatoes, Thai food, sandwiches, salads and fruit shakes served in a rustic, dimly-lit atmosphere.

Oi's Kitchen On the same road as Old Lamp, this is one of the more traditional Thai places in Hat Rin, and is inexpensive.

Orchid Restaurant & Bar Dishes 60-100B. On the cross-cape road towards Hat Rin Nai, this is popular for video dining. To find it, just walk towards the sounds of gunshots and screeching tyres.

Om Ganesh Dishes 50-100B. Near the pier, the relatively new Om Ganesh has good Indian food – try a combination of chicken malai tikka and garlic naan.

Namaste Chai Shop Dishes 50-90B. Off the road between the two beaches, this long-running place serves decent Indian, but seems to be forgotten on the fringe of the village.

Getting There & Away Săwngthăew taxis go to/from Hat Rin and Thong Sala for 50B. The steeper, windier passages of this paved road are quite dangerous as everyone seems to drive fast and the smooth surface doesn't afford much braking traction.

Motorcycles can be rented in Hat Rin Nok. Take extra care when riding on this road as lots of people wipe out on the steep downhill slopes; there's no shoulder on the road either, so watch out for passing vehicles.

There are also regular ferries at least three times a day from two piers on northern Ko Samui, Bo Phut and Hat Bang Rak. Departures are around 10.30am, 1pm and 4pm, and cost 100B per person. During the monthly Hat Rin full moon party the number of departures increases (as does the price of passage) and by midnight speedboats are leaving these piers every 15 or 30 minutes until around 3am or 4am. We recommend you take one of the day boats as they're safer and less crowded.

East Coast Beaches Between Hat Rin and the village of Ban Nam Tok are several little coves. There you'll find the white-sand beaches of Hat Yuan (2.5km north of Hat Rin) and Hat Wai Nam (3.5km).

There are a handful of places with huts on **Hat Yuan**, which is connected by an inland trail with Hat Rin. These include *Good Hope*, *Bamboo Hut* and *Lazy Fish*, which cost 100B to 200B a night. Much cheaper long-term stays can be arranged.

Around a smaller headland at the north-eastern end of Hat Yuan, there is accommodation at **Hat Thian**.

The Sanctuary Bungalows with shared facilities 100-120B, with attached bath up to 1000B. This is a New Age-oriented spot built into boulders overlooking the beach. Instruction in yoga, tai chi, meditation and massage is available. The Sanctuary can be reached on foot or by boat (February to November only) from Hat Rin.

Haad Tien Resort Bungalows with bath 150-200B. Haad Tien has 30 wood and bamboo bungalows with mosquito nets. To get a boat here from Hat Rin contact Yogurt Home 3 in Hat Rin's village. Haad Tien runs regular boat trips from Hat Rin Nok during high season.

Over the next headland at **Hat Wai Nam** is *Why Nam Hut,* which is only open from December to April.

Another 2km (5km north of Hat Rin) walk along the trail north will bring you to the decidedly short **Hat Yao** – not to be confused with the Hat Yao on the western side of the island. There are a couple of on-again-off-again bungalow operations here that are nothing more than rickety bamboo huts on a lonely beach. If you're looking to approximate a *Gilligan's Island* experience, this is the place. The only thing missing are the tiki-torches.

A dirt track (traversable on foot but only partially by motorcycle) runs along the coast from Hat Rin before heading inland to Ban Nam Tok and **Than Sadet Falls**.

Hat Yang (6km north of Hat Rin) is virtually deserted. A farther 2.5km north of Ban Nam Tok is the pretty double bay of **Ao Thong Reng**, where *Thong Reng Resort* bungalows are 150B to 300B.

Than Sadet Resort Huts 150-250B. This is above the beach on the headland and has quite a nice view over the boulder-strewn beach.

North of the headland, a pretty cove ringed by **Hat Sadet** features a string of places in the 80B to 200B range, including at last pass *Silver Cliff Bungalows, Mai Pen Rai, JS Hut* and *Nid's*.

The rough dirt track from Thong Sala to Hat Sadet is usable, subject to weather.

Ao Thong Nai Pan This bay is really made up of two bays, **Ao Thong Nai Pan Yai** and **Ao Thong Nai Pan Noi**. The latter is the best all-round swimming beach, although Thong Nai Pan Yai is quieter and has a good set of rocks for advanced climbers at its eastern end.

On the beach at Thong Nai Pan Yai, south-east of Ban Thong Nai Pan, are the *White Sand, AD View, Nice Beach* and *Central* (☎ *077 299 059*), all with huts from 150B to 200B with shared bath, 300B to 800B for nicer ones with attached bath. The other end of the beach features the similarly priced *Pen's, Pingjun Resort* (☎ *077 299 004*), *Candle Hut* (☎ *077 377 073*) and *Chanchit Dreamland*.

Panviman Resort (☎/*fax 077 377 048, in Bangkok* ☎ *029 108 660*) Rooms with fan/air-con & bath 1000/1800B. Up on Thong Nai Pan Noi, Panviman sits on a cliff between two beaches and offers rooms in wooden bungalows or a two-storey building. It runs its own taxi service from Thong Sala pier.

Thong Ta Pan Resort Rooms 200-400B. This basic but clean place is at the northern end of the smaller bay.

Star Hut I & II Huts 120-180B, with toilet and shower 180-300B. The combined Star Hut is the biggest operation in the area, though Star Hut I at the southern end of the beach seems better kept. Huts and bungalows come in a number of sizes.

Honey Bungalow Huts 150-250B. Behind Star Huts, away from the beach, is Honey offers somewhat primitive huts with shared facilities.

Bio's Huts with shared facilities 100-150B. Near the Honey and Star Huts, this has basic huts as well as a laid-back restaurant with several vegie dishes and a popular bar at night.

Săwngthăew from Thong Sala to Thong Nai Pan cost 100B. During the low season it can be difficult to find enough people to convince a săwngthăew driver to go at that price, so you may have to charter a vehicle. If travelling light it's possible to take a motorcycle taxi for 150B. Take care if you're riding a motorcycle here, as this is probably the most dangerous road on the island – very steep in places, and mostly unsealed.

Hat Khuat & Hat Khom These are two pretty bays with beaches on the northern end of Pha-Ngan, still largely undeveloped because of the distances involved from major transport points to Samui and the mainland. Some of the island's least expensive accommodation is found here – hence it's popular with long-termers – but that means more likelihood of being evicted from your hut if you don't buy meals from the bungalow kitchens. Be sure to establish whether you'll be required to buy meals before taking a hut.

Hat Khuat (Bottle Beach) is the slightly larger of the two and has a handful of bungalows stretched across the beach, all in the 100B to 350B range – *Bottle Beach I*, *Bottle Beach II*, *Bottle Beach III* and *Smile Bungalow*. All are very similar, offering basic huts with shared facilities as well as more permanent-looking bungalows with private bath. Boats leave twice a day during the dry season from Ban Chalok Lam for the 40B ride to Hat Khuat.

West of Hat Khuat, 2.5km across Laem Kung Yai, is Hat Khom, where *Coral Bay* rents standard huts for 100B, with bath 200B to 400B.

Ocean Bay (☎ *077 377 231*) Huts 100B, with bath 300B. The advantage of staying here is that it has a jeep and will pick up guests in Thong Sala if you call in advance.

You can walk to Hat Khuat from Ban Chalok Lam via a steep trail, or get there on a dirt-bike or 4WD.

The fishing village of **Ban Chalok Lam**, at the centre of Ao Chalok Lam, features several small family-run grocery stores, laundry services and lots of fish drying at the side of the main street. You can also rent bikes and diving equipment. Chaloklum Diving School offers **scuba courses** in English and German. Of the several restaurants, the best are *Seaside* and *Porn*. There are also a few inexpensive *noodle stands* around.

There are some places to stay along Hat Chalok Lam at the eastern and western edges of the bay.

Fanta Huts 150B. This has several rows of huts and a fair chunk of beach frontage.

Try Tong Resort (☎ 077 374 115) Bungalows 80-200B. Across Khlong Ok via a rickety footbridge, this offers largish wooden bungalows facing the bay and canal (closed during the rainy season). There's no beach here save for a small chunk with boulders at the surf line.

Thai Life Huts/bungalows 80/200B. Towards Hat Khom, Thai Life has decaying huts and better bungalows.

Wattana (☎ 077 374 022) Huts 100B, bungalows with fan 250B. At the western end of the beach Wattana is on a good piece of beach. We've received mixed reports on this place; some people loved it, others not.

The road between Thong Sala and Ban Chalok Lam is sealed all the way, and săwngthăew do the route regularly for 40B per person, or you can do the same trip by motorcycle for 60B.

Ao Chalok Lam is a good place to hire boats for explorations of the northern coast as many fishermen dock here (particularly from February to September). During this season boats run regularly from here to Hat Khuat twice a day for 40B per person. On some days the service may be cancelled due to high surf, so anyone electing to stay at Hat Khuat should leave a couple of extra days for planned departure from the island just in case.

Ao Hat Thong Lang & Ao Mae Hat
As you move west on Pha-Ngan, as on Samui, the sand gets browner and coarser. The secluded beach and cove at Ao Hat Thong Lang has no accommodation at the moment.

An all-weather road leads west from Ban Chalok Lam to Ban Mae Hat, a small fish-ing village with a few bungalow resorts. The beach at Ao Mae Hat isn't fantastic, but there is a bit of coral offshore. Close by, a little inland via a well-marked dirt track (200m off the road from Chalok Lam near the 9km marker), is **Wang Sai Falls**, also know as Paradise Falls.

At Ban Mae Hat you'll find the following accommodation.

Maehaad Bungalow Huts 80B, with bath 150B. Towards the north-east end of the bay, this has good, simple thatched huts or wood and thatch huts.

Crystal Island Garden Huts 80-150B. Although not on the beach, these small wooden huts have a good beach view.

Island View Cabana Huts 150-250B. This has good weatherboard (clapboard) huts. It also has a restaurant, which we recommend.

Wang Sai Resort (☎ 077 374 025) Bungalows 100-250B. At the south-western end of Mae Hat, this offers nice-sized bungalows built among boulders on a hillside; all have views of beach and bay. Rates depend on position on the slope. An open-air restaurant is situated well away from the huts, down on the beach. A dive operation here offers instruction and guided trips.

On Ko Ma (Horse Island), opposite the beach, *Ko Ma Dive Resort* (☎ 077 374 097) has a few bungalows for 200B to 300B.

Hat Salat & Hat Yao
These coral-fringed beaches are fairly difficult to reach – the road from Ban Si Thanu to the south is very bad in spots, even for experienced dirt-bikers, so you should come by boat if possible. Hat Yao (not to be confused with its namesake on the east coast) is a very long, pretty beach with a reasonable drop-off that makes it one of the island's best swimming beaches. It's also good for snorkelling. Equipment can be rented at the Phangan Divers branch located at Haad Yao Bungalows.

Hat Salat has *My Way,* with huts for 80B to 150B, and *Salad Hut,* with newish bungalows for 200B to 300B. Down at Hat Yao are the basic *Benjawan, Dream Hill, Graceland, Blue Coral Beach, Sandy Bay, Silver Beach, Ibiza, Seaboard, Bayview* and **Hat Thian**; the latter two are isolated on a beach north of Hat Yao around the headland, and the road is very steep and rocky. Most of these places offer basic huts from 60B to 100B, and more luxurious bungalows for up to 800B.

Haad Yao Bungalows Bungalows 200-800B. This place is along the best section of beach; it charges extra for basic accommodation if you don't eat there.

Hat Chaophao & Ao Si Thanu Hat Chaophao is a rounded beach two headlands south of Hat Yao; then around a larger headland at the southern end of Ao Chaophao is Ao Si Thanu. In these areas you begin to see the occasional mangrove along the coast; inland there's a pretty lagoon at the southern end of Hat Chaophao near Laem Son.

There are several places to stay along the beach at Hat Chaophao. The popular **Jungle Huts**, **Sea Flower**, **Sri Thanu** and **Great Bay** all have bungalows with bath for 100B to 300B.

Laem Son I & II Huts 100-300B, bungalows 350-500B. On the rounded, pine-studded cape of Laem Son, at the northern end of Ao Si Thanu proper, this has simple, quiet, shaded huts and sturdier bungalows. Prices fluctuate from low to high season.

Seaview Rainbow and **Lada** (☎ 077 238 095) Huts with fan & bath 200-400B. Under the same ownership, both of these places offer basic bungalows. Lada is down towards the southern end of the bay.

Loy Fah (☎ 077 377 319) Bungalows with fan, mosquito net, toilet & shower 150-500B. Sitting high on a point at the southern end of the bay on Laem Si Thanu, these sturdy huts have good views. It's nicely landscaped and well run, and has both wooden and cement cottages, with two large ones at the bottom of the cliff on a private cove.

Ao Hin Kong & Ao Wok Tum This long bay – sometimes divided in two by a stream that feeds into the sea – is just a few kilometres north of Thong Sala, but has hardly any development so far.

Lipstick Cabana (☎ 077 377 294) Rooms 80-250B. At the centre of Ao Hin Kong, not far from Ban Hin Kong, the accommodation is basic, but its restaurant is excellent.

A little farther down around the same cape are **OK** (☎ 077 377 141), **Darin**, **Sea Scene**, **Porn Sawan** and **Cookies**, most with simple 60B to 80B huts – Darin and Sea Scene also have bungalows with bath in the 150B to 250B range.

Săwngthăew to this area cost 30B per person but you'll only see them at ferry departure and arrival times.

See the Thong Sala entry earlier in this chapter for accommodation just north of Thong Sala at Ao Nai Wok.

Getting There & Away
Ko Samui – Express Boat Songserm (☎ 077 377 046) operates express boats between the Na Thon pier on Ko Samui and the Thong Sala pier on Ko Pha-Ngan two or three times daily, depending on the season. The trip takes 50 minutes and costs 100B each way.

Ko Samui – Other Boats Boats go direct from the pier at Samui's Hat Bang Rak to Hat Rin Nai on Ko Pha-Ngan for 100B (150B on full moon nights). The boat sometimes leaves from the pier at Bo Phut instead. This boat departs from Bang Rak/Bo Phut just about every day at 10.30am, 1pm and 3.30pm, depending on the weather and number of prospective passengers, and takes about 45 minutes to reach the bay at Hat Rin. In the reverse direction it usually leaves at 9.30am, 11.30am, and 2.30pm and takes 30 to 40 minutes.

From January to September there is also one boat a day from Hat Mae Nam on Samui to Ao Thong Nai Pan on Pha-Ngan, with a stop at Hat Rin. The fares are 150B and 100B respectively and the boat usually leaves Mae Nam around 1pm. In the reverse direction the boat starts from Ao Thong Nai Pan around 8am.

Faster, more powerful speedboats carrying 35 passengers go between Samui's Hat Mae Nam and Thong Sala for 200B; this boat only takes about half-an-hour to reach Thong Sala.

Surat Thani – Night Ferry You can also take a slow night ferry direct to Pha-Ngan from Tha Ban Don in Surat. It leaves nightly at 10pm, takes 6½ hours to arrive at Thong Sala, and costs 200B on the upper deck, 150B on the lower.

The night ferry can be a rough ride when seas are high – November is the worst month. As with the night ferry to Samui, don't leave your bags unattended on the boat – there have been several reports of theft.

Ko Tao Subject to weather conditions, there are a total of four daily boats between Thong Sala and Ko Tao, 45km north. The trip takes from 1½ hours to 2½ hours, depending on the boat, and costs 150B to 200B one way. Departures are at 7am, 11.30am and 1pm.

A speedboat operates between Thong Sala and Ko Tao once a day for 350B per person; it leaves at 12.30pm and the crossing takes less than an hour.

Train/Bus/Boat Combination At Bangkok's Hualamphong train station you can purchase train tickets that include a bus from the Surat Thani train station (Phun Phin) to the Ban Don pier and then a ferry to Ko Pha-Ngan. These generally cost around 30B to 50B more than buying each ticket separately yourself.

See the Ko Samui Getting There & Away section for sample joint fares; add 45B for through travel to Thong Sala.

Getting Around

A couple of roads branch out from Thong Sala, primarily to the north and the southeast. One road goes north-west a few kilometres along the shoreline to the villages of Ban Hin Kong and Ban Si Thanu. From Ban Si Thanu the road travels north-east across the island to Ban Chalok Lam. Another road goes straight north from Thong Sala to Chalok Lam. There is also a very poor dirt track along the west coast from Ban Si Thanu to Ao Hat Yao and Ao Hat Salat.

Hat Khuat can be reached on foot from Ban Fai Mai (2km) or Ban Chalok Lam (4km) or by boat.

The road south-east from Thong Sala to Ban Khai passes an intersection with a road north to Ban Thong Nang and Ban Thong Nai Pan. The paved road to Hat Rin is now passable year-round, so there's regular transport between Thong Sala and Hat Rin. Even with the paving, only experienced motorbike riders should attempt the section between Ban Khai and Hat Rin. Steep grades, blind turns and a slippery road surface make it the second most dangerous piece of road on the island after the road to Thong Nai Pan (although there are more fatalities along the Hat Rin stretch due to greater speeds).

Sǎwngthǎew and motorcycle taxis handle all the public transport along island roads. Some places can only be reached by motorcycle, some places only by boat or on foot.

You can rent motorcycles in Thong Sala for 200B to 250B a day.

Sǎwngthǎew & Motorcycle Taxi From Thong Sala, sǎwngthǎew to Hat Chaophao and Hat Yao (in the west) are 40B and 50B per person respectively, while motorcycle taxis cost 50B and 80B. To Ban Khai it's 30B by sǎwngthǎew, or 40B by motorcycle; if you're only going as far as Wat Khao Tham or Ban Tai the fare is 30B for motorcycles and drops to 20B for a sǎwngthǎew.

A sǎwngthǎew from Thong Sala to Ban Chalok Lam is 40B, a motorcycle taxi 50B. To get to Hat Rin from Thong Sala, a sǎwngthǎew costs 50B one way, while a motorcycle is 70B.

Thong Nai Pan can be reached from Thong Sala by sǎwngthǎew (100B) or motorcycle (150B).

Boat There are daily boats from Ao Chalok Lam to Hat Khuat at 8am, 1pm and 5pm (returning at 9.30am, 3pm and 6pm) for 40B per person. Boats run between Thong Sala and Hat Yao (west) daily at noon for 40B per person. The service operates from January to September, depending on the weather. Boats can also be chartered from beach to beach, price negotiable.

KO TAO

เกาะเต่า

Ko Tao translates as Turtle Island, named for its shape. It's only about 21 sq km, and the population of 750 are mostly involved in fishing, growing coconuts and catering to tourism. Snorkelling and diving are particularly good here due to the relative abundance of coral, though most of the beaches, except Ao Leuk (Deep Bay), are too shallow for swimming.

Because it takes three to five hours to get here from the mainland (from either Chumphon or Surat Thani via Ko Pha-Ngan), Ko Tao doesn't get people coming over for day trips or for quick overnighters. Still, the island can become quite crowded during high season, when Mae Hat, Hat Sai Ri and Ao Chalok Ban Kao have people sleeping on the beach waiting for huts to vacate.

Ban Mae Hat, on the western side of the island, is where inter-island boats land. The only other villages on the island are **Ban Hat Sai Ri** in the centre of the northern section and **Ban Chalok Ban Kao** to the south. Just 1km off the north-west shore of the island is **Ko Nang Yuan**, which is really three islands joined by a sand bar.

The granite promontory of **Laem Tato** at the southern tip of Ko Tao makes a nice hike from Ban Chalok Ban Kao. About the only thing of historic interest on the island is a large boulder where King Rama V had his initials carved to commemorate a royal visit in 1900. The boulder, located at the southern end of Hat Sai Ri, has become something of a local shrine and is the focus of a small ceremony every October.

As with Ko Tarutao in Satun Province, Ko Tao is said to have once been a dumping ground for political prisoners.

Information

Ban Mae Hat, a one-street town with a busy pier, is the only commercial centre on the island. Here you'll find a police station, post and telephone office, travel agents, dive shops, restaurants and general stores. Boat tickets can be purchased at a booking

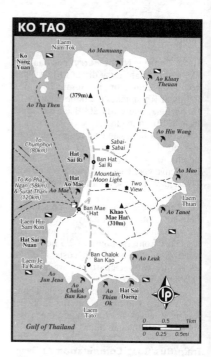

KO TAO

office by the harbour as well as from travel agents. At Mr J's store near the school between Hat Ao Mae and Hat Sai Ri, you'll find information on accommodation and transportation as well as the island's only real selection of books. Mr J also offers a Thai visa extension service.

Krung Thai Bank has a money exchange window near the pier, and several money-changers can also be found around town.

The post and phone office in Ban Mae Hat is open daily from 8.30am to 4pm. Watch out for private phone offices, which charge exorbitant rates.

Diving & Snorkelling

Relative to its size, Ko Tao has a large number of dive centres, with some of Thailand's lowest prices for training and/or excursions. Underwater visibility is high and the water is cleaner than around most other inhabited islands in the Gulf. Due to the faràng presence, the best spots have English

For Divers Only?

In the last five years or so diving has come to dominate Ko Tao. If diving instruction is of interest, Ko Tao is one of the best places to learn in Thailand, as there are many good dive sites close by and prices are reasonable. In a very short time you may find yourself becoming a 'divemaster' (or as many who have gone through the procedure call it, 'dive slave'), a status that allows you to help teach diving courses without pay. It's a great system for the dive centre owners who recruit instructors from their students and then get away with paying them little or nothing as they move through the instructor hierarchy.

On the other hand, if you don't intend to don scuba gear on Ko Tao you may be annoyed by the constant come-ons from dive staff in residence at the various bungalows. You may also find it very difficult to find a bungalow that will accept guests who don't sign up for dive instruction or for some sort of dive trip. Almost all the bungalows on the island have some sort of partnership with a dive operation and during high season few will allow non-divers to spend the night.

Joe Cummings

names such as White Rock, Shark Island, Chumphon Pinnacle, Green Rock and South-West Pinnacles.

At the time of writing there were more than 20 dive operations on the island, most charging basically the same rates. To support so many dive instructors, dive operations have to solicit nearly every tourist who visits Ko Tao; most are directly affiliated with accommodation on the island just for this purpose. During the high season you may have to sign up for diving or be refused accommodation.

Rates are typically 800B per dive to 5400B for a 10-dive package (including gear, boat, guide, food and beverages) or 550B per dive if you bring your own gear. An all-inclusive introductory dive lesson costs 1500B, while a four-day, open-water PADI certificate course costs around 8000B – these rates include gear, boat, instructor, food and beverages. A snorkel, mask and fins are typically hired as a set for 100B per day.

Massage & T'ai Chi

Here & Now (e hereandnow_tao@hot mail.com), just off the inland road directly behind Ban's Diving Resort, offers classes in t'ai chi and qi gong (Chinese breathing exercises) taught by a German expat. Early morning or evening courses lasting nine sessions cost 1800B. His wife and daughter also offer traditional Thai massage for 550B for 2½ hours.

Places to Stay

With the steady transformation of Ko Tao into a diving resort, accommodation has moved upmarket. Especially along Hat Ao Mae and Hat Sai Ri, the days of the thatched hut are over. Most of the bungalow operations along these beaches are quite eye-catching and set on nicely landscaped grounds. The telling difference between bungalow operations here and those on Ko Pha-Ngan's Hat Rin or Ko Samui's Hat Chaweng is that the reception desk is usually a dive shop. Walk in prepared to sign up for a dive course and you will find that prices for accommodation are quite reasonable for the amenities provided – as low as 150B to 300B – or sometimes free! Of course, if you're not interested in diving it's likely that you'll be directed to some vague place farther up the beach. Keep in mind that even if you do sign up for a dive course at one of these places, your welcome will wear out soon after the course is finished. If business is slow you may get away with not taking a diving course, but you'll find the price of accommodation is about three times higher than if you had. Also, be sure to note the check-out time where you're staying. Many places on Ko Tao want you gone by 11am, but some will have you up and out as early as 10am.

Some of the cheaper bungalow operations – especially those at the northern end of Hat Sai Ri and at Ao Tha Then – will give you the boot if you don't buy food at their restaurants; we still receive reports of visitors being locked out of their bungalows or violently ejected.

During the high season from December to March it can be difficult to find accommodation anywhere on the island. On arrival at Ban Mae Hat it may be best to follow a tout who can find vacant bungalows, otherwise your chances of finding a place on your own might be very slim.

Ao Mae At Hat Ao Mae, just north of Ban Mae Hat, the shallow bay has plenty of coral but the southern end receives a lot of rubbish from the pier area at Ban Mae Hat.

Crystal (☎ 077 456 106, fax 077 456 105) Bungalows with bath 200-500B. Crystal offers small, basic plywood huts and more spacious concrete and wood bungalows. If you're not prepared to take a dive course, don't bother here.

Beach Club (☎ 077 456 222) Bungalows with air-con 800-1500B. This has comfortable and modern duplexes right on the beach – quite different from anything else on the island.

Queen Resort (☎ 077 456 002) Bungalows 150-350B. This is on the headland overlooking the bay and is the first non-dive oriented place you'll come to walking north from the pier. Bungalows are rustic but with some character and have verandas. The proprietor is very friendly and there is a restaurant on the premises.

Tommy's (☎ 077 456 039) Bungalows with fan 500B, with air-con 850B. On the headland overlooking the bay, this place is only for those wishing to take a dive course.

View Cliff Restaurant & Bungalows Huts with fan 250B, with air-con 1000-1900B. Just beyond Tommy's, this offers basic huts and more substantial bungalows. The nightly video blaring from the restaurant is a definite minus.

Hat Sai Ri Around the headland to the north is the longest beach on the island, with a string of bungalow and dive operations.

In Touch Bungalows with bath 350-450B. This place has creatively decorated bungalows but that's about all it has going for it. The staff is less than friendly.

AC Resort II (☎ 077 456 195) Bungalows with bath 300-500B. This has sturdy bungalows with nice landscaping.

AC Resort I (☎ 077 456 033) and *Haad Sai Ree Resort* are both affiliated with Ban's Diving Resort, and will only rent rooms to people who agree in advance to sign up for their dives. Rooms at AC I with bath & fan are 250B to 800B, while those at Haad Sai Ree are 300B to 800B.

Ko Tao Marina Resort (☎ 077 456 173) Bungalows with fan 300-500B, with air-con 800-900B. This place has sturdy and, in the case of the air-con units, nicely furnished bungalows.

SB Cabana (☎ 077 456 005) Bungalows with fan & bath 300B. This has good-value, clean wooden bungalows.

Bing Bungalow (☎ 077 456 172) Huts with bath 150-250B. On the other side of the road to SB Cabana, this has cheaper huts, although they aren't in as good shape.

Ban's Diving Resort (☎ 077 456 061) Rooms/bungalows with fan 300B, with air-con 800B. Ban's offers sturdy bungalows and rooms in a hotel building, but only to those who agree to sign up for a dive course. There's even a swimming pool here, one of the two biggest diving schools on the island.

Sunset Buri Resort (☎ 077 456 266) Rooms with fan 800-1000B, air-con 1200B. The air-con stucco cottages here have a Mediterranean look, and there's a swimming pool on the premises.

Also along Hat Sai Ri are some places in the 200B to 400B range: *Sai Ree Cottage (☎ 077 456 126)*, *New Way (☎ 077 456 208)*, *Sai Ree Hut*, *O-Chai*, *Simple Life Villa (☎ 077 456 142)* and *Blue Resort (☎ 077 456 179)*.

Seashell Resort and *Lotus Resort (☎ 077 456 271)* Bungalows with fan 400-1000B, with air-con 1500-1600B. Both of these places are owned by a friendly English-speaking Thai woman from Ko Samui; this is one of the only places along this beach not directly affiliated with a dive operation. Prices are a little high for this beach but cheaper than taking a dive course. The only drawback is the lack of shade – looks like somebody got carried away cutting down the coconut trees.

Pranee's (☎ *077 456 080)* Bungalows with fan & bath 300B. Pranee's is on a large property and boasts electric power all night; the bungalows are good for families with kids.

Sabai-Sabai About 500m up the road behind Ban Hat Sai Ri, this has comfortable and tasteful bungalows that are used exclusively as accommodation for dive students. If you want to stay here you can sign up for a course at Crystal on Hat Ao Mae and request accommodation at Sabai-Sabai. The attached ***Orchid Restaurant*** is said to be good.

North of the beach, in an area sometimes called Ao Ta Then, there are several inexpensive bungalow operations with very basic huts, most off the beach and built high on the rocks, in the 200B to 300B range.

Silver Cliff Huts 200-350B. This is the best choice in the area – some huts have great bay views.

CFT Huts 200B, bungalows with bath 500B. Farther north from Silver Cliff, the lone CFT has basic huts and bungalows – a tranquil place with an edge-of-the-world feel.

Ao Mamuang & Ao Kluay Theuan On
the northern and north-eastern tip of the island, accessible only by boat or on foot, are two coral-fringed coves that are, so far, without bungalow accommodation; however, they are popular dive destinations.

Ao Hin Wong
South of Ao Kluay Theuan by sea, or 2km north-east of Ban Hat Sai Ri by trail, tranquil Ao Hin Wong has a handful of huts named ***Hin Wong Bungalows*** and ***Green Tree,*** which has rooms for 100B to 200B with shared bathroom, or 250B to 300B with attached bath.

Ao Mao, Laem Thian & Ao Tanot
Continuing clockwise around the island, Ao Mao, connected by a 2km dirt trail with Ban Hat Sai Ri, is another cove with no beach accommodation so far.

Laem Thian Bungalows with shared facilities 200B, bungalows with bath 400-

600B. On the cape, which juts out over the northern end of Ao Tanot, this has huts built among the rocks.

Ao Tanot proper, to the south, is one of the island's best spots for snorkelling, and features a good set of bungalow operations and a clean beach.

Tanote Bay Resort Bungalows with bath 300-500B. These well-maintained bungalows are set on landscaped grounds.

Poseidon Huts 100-120B, bungalows with bath 300-400B. Poseidon has very simple huts and much more comfortable bungalows. Its restaurant is quite good.

Bamboo Hut Bungalows 200-500B. Bamboo Hut has 15 decked bungalows; the kitchen specialises in spicy Southern Thai-style food.

From May to August it is difficult to get to Ao Tanot by boat as the water is very shallow and the taxi boats may become stranded and/or damage coral if they attempt it. Some years are better than others depending on tidal cycles.

Khao Mae Hat
On the way to Ao Tanot from Ban Mae Hat, a path forks off the main track and leads up the slopes of 310m Khao Mae Hat in the centre of the island to ***Two View,*** which has bungalows for 80B to 100B. Two View is so named because it affords sunrise and sunset views of both sides of the island. It's a 60-minute walk up the path from Ao Tanot. There are only six bungalows and no electricity or generator: kerosene lamps and candles provide light at night. Organically grown vegetarian food and herbal teas are available in the restaurant. Two View advertises three-day meditation retreats, as well as courses in massage, yoga, chakra-balancing, re-birthing, natural colon-cleansing and sessions to help you recall past lives. Prices for courses cost 600B to US$220. Two View closes in October and November.

Mountain and ***Moonlight*** are in the 50B to 100B range farther along the same trail as Two View atop the ridge in the centre of the island. They're more easily accessed from a trail that leads from near Tommy's on Hat Ao Mae.

Ao Leuk & Hat Sai Daeng Ao Leuk is connected by a 2.2km track with Ban Mae Hat and has three places to stay.

Ao Leuk Resort Huts 200B, with bath 400B. Leuk Resort has eight huts.

Nice Moon Bungalows 200-300B. This has only six simple bungalows and is quite isolated – making for a very tranquil setting.

Coral View Resort (☎ 019 700 378) Bungalows with bath 350B. This has 10 bungalows. If you call in advance and make a reservation, Coral View will send a taxi boat to pick you up at Ban Mae Hat pier.

Ao Thian Ok & Laem Tato Farther west on the side of the impressive Laem Tato is pretty Ao Thian Ok.

Rocky (☎ 077 456 035) Rooms 350-550B. This is a friendly place where rooms are discounted by 100B in the low season.

Ao Chalok Ban Kao This nicely situated coral beach, about 1.7km south of Ban Mae Hat by road, has become quite crowded. In high season it can be very difficult to find a vacant hut here, and travellers end up sleeping on the floor of a restaurant for a night or two until something becomes available.

Laem Khlong (☎ 077 456 083) Rooms 400B. On the hill overlooking the western part of the bay you'll find this place with no beach – making the rooms seem a tad overpriced.

Sunshine (☎ 077 456 219) Bungalows with fan & bath 200-400B. This place has basic, clean bungalows set out on wide and lush grounds.

Buddha View Dive Resort (☎ 077 456 074-5, e buddha@samart.co.th) Bungalows for divers 100B. This is the other big dive school on the island and its getting even bigger. The restaurant is one of the better ones outside of Hat Sai Ri. It also has a swimming pool.

Big Fish Dive Resort (☎ 077 456 132) Huts 50-200B. This is another bungalow-cum-dive-centre with huts; price depends on proximity to the beach. Normally all huts are reserved for divers.

Ko Tao Cottages (☎/fax 077 456 198, e divektc@samart.co.th) Bungalows 550-

850B. The friendly Ko Tao Cottages, towards the eastern end of the bay, has some of the island's most luxurious bungalows; naturally there's a dive centre here, and you get 30% off the room rates when you sign up for a course.

Around a couple of small points to the south along Laem Tato is a beach that can only be reached on foot and at low tide. Here you can find the following places.

Taa Toh Lagoon Dive Resort (☎ 077 456 092) Bungalows with bath 250-500B. This dive-oriented place offers 25 screened bungalows with small verandas. Look elsewhere if you don't want to dive.

Freedom Beach Bungalows with bath 100-500B. Freedom from what, we're not sure, but this place has a few basic bungalows and one nicely furnished wooden bungalow with a view.

Pond Resort (☎ 077 456 044) Bungalows 300-500B. Connected by a network of bridges and walkways, bungalows are perched on rocks overlooking the bay.

South-West of Mae Hat As might be expected, beaches just south of town get better the farther south you go.

Sensi Paradise Resort (☎/fax 077 456 244) Bungalows with fan 800B, with air-con 2500-3500B. A few hundred metres south-west of Mae Hat, across a stream and down a footpath, the upmarket Sensi Paradise has solid bungalows made from local materials, as well as a few larger places with sleeping lofts suitable for families.

Ko Tao Royal Resort (☎ 077 456 157) Bungalows with fan 600-800B, with air-con 1500-2000B. This is a semi-upscale place with landscaping and a good seafood restaurant.

A couple of kilometres farther south is a series of small beaches collectively known as Hat Sai Nuan, where you'll find the popular *Siam Cookie* and *Char Bungalows*, both with rooms for 100B to 150B.

Tao Thong Villa Rooms 100-400B. At Laem Je Ta Kang (about 1.2km west of Ao Chalok Ban Kao), on a difficult-to-reach rocky area between two beaches, you'll find

Tao Thong. It seems popular with long-termers attracted to the isolation of the place.

Sunset (☎ 077 456 268) Rooms 100-150B. South of Laem Je Ta Kang, by itself on Ao Jun Jeua, this commands a beautiful point that juts out into the sea. The only way to get here is to walk along the dirt track from Mae Hat or take a long-tail boat.

Ko Nang Yuan This pretty little tripartite island has one resort.

Ko Nangyuan Dive Resort (☎ 077 456 091-2, fax 077 456 093) Bungalows 1200B, villas with air-con 2400B. As the name suggests, the emphasis here is on diving. Most people come here on package tours that include transportation to the island. Unless business is particularly slow, walk-ins are not likely to be given much attention. Note that management does not allow any plastic bottles on the island – these will be confiscated on arrival.

Boats from Tha Ban Mae Hat to Nang Yuan leave at 10.30am and 5.30pm daily. In the opposite direction boats leave at 8.30am and 4pm. The return trip costs 60B. You can easily charter a ride for 100B at any time of day.

Places to Eat

In Ban Mae Hat there's a string of simple seafood restaurants with dining platforms built over the water's edge. *Baan Yaay* and *Liab Thale* are two of the better ones. The *Swiss Bakery*, next to the post office, sells very good breads and pastries; it's open from 7am to 6pm. There are also several *restaurants* on Hat Sai Ri, most associated with bungalows, as well as a few *eateries* in Ban Hat Sai Ri.

Getting There & Away

Bangkok Bus/boat combination tickets from Bangkok cost 750B to 850B and are available from travel agents on Th Khao San. Promotional bus/boat combination tickets in the opposite direction are sometimes offered for as little as 500B.

Beware of travel agents on Ko Tao selling boat/train combinations. Usually this involves receiving a 'voucher' that you are supposed to be able to exchange for a train ticket in Surat Thani or Chumphon; more than a few travellers have found the vouchers worthless. If you book train reservations a few days (or more) in advance, any legitimate agency on Ko Tao should be able to deliver the train tickets themselves. It's same-day or day-before reservations that usually have voucher problems.

Chumphon At least three boats from the mainland run daily from Chumphon to Ko Tao. There may be fewer departures if the swells are high. The slow boat leaves Chumphon at midnight, takes five or six hours to reach Ko Tao (200B one way). In the opposite direction it departs from Ko Tao at 10am. See the Chumphon section in the North-Western Gulf chapter for more details.

A speedboat departs from Chumphon at 7.30am (from Ban Mae Hat at 10.30am) and takes about one hour and 40 minutes (400B).

Surat Thani Every night, depending on the weather, a boat runs between Surat Thani (Tha Thong) and Ko Tao, a seven- to eight-hour trip (350B one way). From Surat, boats depart at 11pm. From Ban Mae Hat the departure time is 8.30pm.

Ko Pha-Ngan Depending on weather conditions, boats run daily between the Thong Sala pier on Ko Pha-Ngan and Ban Mae Hat on Ko Tao. The trip takes 2½ to three hours (150B). Boats leave Thong Sala at 11.30am and return from Ko Tao at 9.30am the next day.

Songserm also runs an express boat to Thong Sala at 10.30am and 2.30pm that takes 1½ hours (250B). Need even faster service? Once a day – again depending on marine conditions – a speed boat does the trip in an hour, leaving at 9.30am (350B).

Ko Samui A slow boat leaves Ko Tao daily at 9.30am and arrives at Hat Mae Nam at 1pm (250B). Speedboats leave at 9.30am and 3pm, arriving an hour and 20 minutes later at Na Thon and Hat Mae Nam respectively (450B).

Getting Around

Săwngthăew cost 30B per person from the pier to Hat Sai Ri and Ao Chalok Ban Kao. To bays on the other side of the island, such as Ao Tanot, expect to pay about 50B (less if the săwngthăew is full). At night it may take up to 100B to motivate a driver. Long-tail boats can also be chartered for up to 2000B a day depending on the number of passengers carried.

Between 9am and 10am (weather permitting), a round-island boat leaves from Hat Sai Ri and stops off in four or five places, including Ko Nang Yuan, while people snorkel and swim, returning to Hat Sai Ri around 4pm. The cost is 250B per person.

Walking is an easy way to get around the island, but some trails aren't clearly marked and can be difficult to follow. You can walk around the whole island in a day, though the undulating, rocky paths make it a challenging walk.

NAKHON SI THAMMARAT
อ.เมืองนครศรีธรรมราช

postcode 80000 • pop 73,600

Hundreds of years before the 8th-century Srivijaya empire subjugated the peninsula, there was a city-state here called Ligor (or Lagor), capital of the Tambralinga kingdom, which was well known throughout Oceania. Later, when Sri Lankan-ordained Buddhist monks established a cloister at the city, the name was changed to the Pali-Sanskrit Nagara Sri Dhammaraja (City of the Sacred Dharma-King), rendered in Thai phonetics as Nakhon Si Thammarat. An overland route between the western port of Trang and eastern port of Nakhon Si Thammarat functioned as a major trade link between Thailand and the rest of the world, and between the Western and Eastern worlds.

During the early development of the various Thai kingdoms, Nakhon Si Thammarat also became an important centre of religion and culture. Thai *năng thalung* (shadow play) and *lákhon* (classical dance-drama) – Thai pronunciation of 'Lagor' –

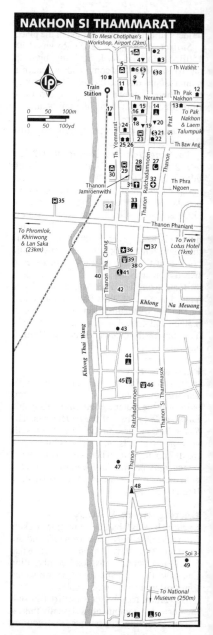

NAKHON SI THAMMARAT

PLACES TO STAY
3   Taksin Hotel
6   Thai Fa Hotel
10 Phetpailin Hotel
11 Si Thong Hotel
12 Nakorn Garden Inn
13 Grand Park Hotel
15 Thai Hotel
16 Siam Hotel
17 Montien Hotel
22 Thai Lee Hotel
24 Muang Thong Hotel
25 Nakhon Hotel
26 Bue Loung (Bua Luang) Hotel

PLACES TO EAT
4   Dam Kan Aeng
9   Yong Seng Restaurant
19 Kuang Meng
20 Bovorn Bazaar; Hao Coffee;
    Khrua Nakhon; Ban Lakhon;
    Ligor Home Bakery; Rock
    99% Bar & Grill

OTHER
1   Share Taxis to Surat Thani,
    Chumphon & Ranong
2   THAI Office
5   Share Taxis to Sichon &
    Khanom
7   Bangkok Bank
8   Thai Farmers Bank
14 Wat Buranaram
18 Muang Thai Tours
21 Siam Commercial
    Bank
23 Minivans to Surat
    Thani
27 Matsayit Yamia (Friday
    Mosque)
28 Minivans to Phuket
    & Krabi
29 Minivan to Hat Yai
30 Share-Taxi Terminal
31 Bethlehem Church
32 Christian Hospital
33 Wat Maheyong

34 Market
35 Bus Station
36 Police Station
37 Main Post Office; Telephone
    Office
38 Traffic Circle/Roundabout
39 Lak Meuang (City Pillar)
40 Handicraft Shops
41 TAT Office
42 Sanaam Na Meuang
    (City Park)
43 Prison
44 Wat Sema Meuang
45 Shiva Shrine
46 Vishnu Shrine
47 Phra Phuttha Sihing Chapel;
    Provincial Offices
48 Clock Tower
49 Suchart's Workshop
50 Wat Na Phra
    Boromathat
51 Wat Phra Mahathat;
    Den Nakhon

were developed in Nakhon Si Thammarat; buffalo-hide shadow puppets and dance masks are still made here.

Today Nakhon Si Thammarat is also known for its *khrêuang thŏm* (nielloware), a silver and black alloy/enamel jewellery technique borrowed from China many centuries ago. Another indigenous handicraft is *yaan lipao*, basketry woven from a hardy local grass into intricate contrasting designs. Yaan lipao handbags are a fashion staple among aristocratic Thai women, so you should see lots for sale around town.

Much of the surrounding province is covered with rugged mountains and forests, which were, until relatively recently, the last refuge of Thailand's communist insurgents. The province's eastern border is formed by the Gulf of Thailand, and much of the provincial economy is dependent on fishing and shrimp farming. Besides fishing, rural Nakhon residents earn a living by growing coffee, rice, rubber and fruit (especially *mongkhút*, or mangosteen).

Along the north coast are several nice beaches: **Ao Khanom, Nai Phlao, Sichon, Thong Yi** and **Hin Ngam** – see the following

Around Nakhon Si Thammarat section for details.

Orientation

Nakhon Si Thammarat can be divided into two sections: the historic section, south of the clock tower, and the new city centre, north of the clock tower and Khlong Na Meuang. The newer part of the city has all the hotels and most of the restaurants, as well as more movie theatres per square kilometre than any other city in Thailand.

Information

The TAT office (☎ 075 346 515–6) is housed in a 1926-vintage building (formerly a club for Thai government officers, restored in 1993) in the north-western corner of the Sanam Na Meuang (City Park) off Th Ratchadamnoen, near the police station. It distributes the usual helpful information printed in English, and can also assist with any tourism-related problems.

The main post office is also on Th Ratchadamnoen and is open from 8.30am to 4.30pm Monday to Friday. An upstairs telephone office with international service is open daily from 8am to 11pm.

Nakhon Si Thammarat National Museum
พิพิธภัณฑสถานแห่งชาตินครศรีธรรมราช

Since the Tampaling (or Tambralinga) kingdom traded with Indian, Arabic, Dvaravati and Champa states, much art from these places found its way to the Nakhon Si Thammarat area, and some is now on display in the national museum *(Th Ratchadamnoen; admission 30B; open 9am-4pm Wed-Sun)*. Notable are Dong-Son bronze drums, Dvaravati Buddha images and Pallava (south Indian) Hindu sculpture. Locally produced art is also on display.

If you've already had your fill of the usual Thai art history surveys from Ban Chiang to Ayuthaya, go straight to the 'Art of Southern Thailand' exhibit in a room to the left of the foyer. Here you'll find many fine images of Nakhon Si Thammarat provenance, including Phutthasihing, U Thong and late-Ayuthaya styles.

The museum is well south of the principal wát on Th Ratchadamnoen, and is located across from Wat Thao Khot and Wat Phet Jarik – 5B by săwngthăew.

Wat Phra Mahathat
วัดพระมหาธาตุ

This is the biggest wát *(Wat Phra Mahathat Woramahawihaan or Wat Phra Boromathat)* in the South and is comparable to Wat Pho in Bangkok. If you like wát, this one is well worth a trip. Reputed to have been founded by Queen Hem Chala over a thousand years ago, and reconstructed in the mid-13th century, the huge complex features a 78m chedi, crowned by a solid gold spire weighing several hundred kilograms. Numerous smaller grey-black chedis surround the main one.

Besides the distinctive *bòt* (central sanctuary) and chedi there are many intricately designed *wíhăan* (large halls) surrounding the chedi, several of which contain crowned Nakhon Si Thammarat/Ayuthaya-style Buddhas in glass cabinets. One wíhăan houses a funky museum, exhibits include:

The garuda, or krut, is used as a royal insignia.

carved wooden *kruts* (garudas, Vishnu's mythical bird-mount), old Siwichai votive tablets, Buddha figures of every description (including a standing Dvaravati figure and a Siwichai Naga Buddha), inlaid-pearl alms bowls and other oddities. A 12m whale skeleton lies in the back of the complex under the northern cloister.

It's about 2km from the new town centre – hop on any bus or săwngthăew going down Th Ratchadamnoen.

Wat Na Phra Boromathat
วัดหน้าพระบรมธาตุ

Across the road from Wat Phra Mahathat, Wat Na Phra Boromathat is the residence for monks serving at Mahathat. There is a nice Gandhara-style fasting Buddha in front of the bòt here.

Phra Phuttha Sihing Chapel (Haw Phra Phuttha Sihing)
หอพระพุทธสิหิงค์

This hall next to the provincial offices contains one of Thailand's three identical Phra Singh Buddhas, one of which is supposed to have been originally cast in Sri Lanka before being brought to Sukhothai (through Nakhon Si Thammarat), Chiang Mai and later, Ayuthaya. The other images are at Wat Phra Singh in Chiang Mai and the National Museum in Bangkok – each is claimed to be the original.

Shadow Puppet Workshops

Traditionally, there are two styles of shadow puppets, *năng thalung* and *năng yài*; the former are similar in size to the typical Malay–Indonesian-style puppets, while the latter are nearly life-size and unique to Thailand. Both are intricately carved from buffalo-hide. Performances of Thai shadow theatre are rare nowadays (usually only during festivals), but there are two places in town where you can see the puppets being made.

The acknowledged master of shadow puppet craft – both manufacture and performance – is **Suchart Subsin** (*Suchaat Sapsin; ☎ 075 346 394, 110/18 Soi 3, Th Si Thammasok; open 9am-4pm*), a Nakhon resident with a workshop not far from Wat Phra Mahathat. Suchart has received several awards for his mastery and preservation of the craft and has performed for the king. His workshop is open to the public; if enough people are assembled he may even be talked into providing a performance at his small outdoor studio. Puppets can be purchased here at reasonable prices – and here only, as he refuses to sell them through distributors. On some puppets the fur is left on the hide for additional effect – these cost a bit more as special care must be taken when tanning them.

Another craftsperson, **Mesa Chotiphan** (*☎ 075 343 979, 558/4 Soi Rong Jeh, Th Ratchadamnoen; open 9am-4pm*), has a workshop in the northern part of the city where visitors are welcome. Call if you would like to be picked up from anywhere in Nakhon Si Thammarat. To get there on your own, go north from the city centre on Th Ratchadamnoen and about 500m north of the sports field, take the soi opposite the Chinese cemetery (before reaching the golf course and military base).

Places to Stay

Most of Nakhon Si Thammarat's hotels are near the train and bus stations.

Thai Lee Hotel (*☎ 075 356 948, 1130 Th Ratchadamnoen*) Rooms with 1/2 beds, fan, shower & toilet 160/220B. The best budget-value hotel in town is the friendly Thai Lee, which has spacious clean rooms. This hotel enforces a midnight curfew, so find another one if you're in town for the nightlife.

Si Thong Hotel (*☎ 075 356 357, Th Yommarat*) Rooms with fan & bath 140-200B. Almost across from the train station, this has adequate rooms.

Nakhon Hotel (*☎ 075 356 318, 1477/5 Th Yommarat*) Rooms with fan & bath 140-200B, with 2 beds and air-con 350B. This has similar rates and facilities to the Si Thong.

Siam Hotel (*☎ 075 356 090, 1403/17 Th Jamroenwithi*) Rooms with fan & bath 150B. This hotel is basically a short-time place, but is fairly clean and quiet.

Muang Thong Hotel (*☎ 075 356 177, 1459/7-9 Th Jamroenwithi*) Singles/doubles with fan & bath 150/200B, with air-con 350B. Farther south on this street from the Siam, Muang Thong has clean rooms but is a bit noisy.

Thai Fa Hotel (*☎ 075 356 727, 1751/5 Th Jamroenwithi*) Rooms 120-180B. A block north of the Siam, on the same side of the street, is this small, two-storey place with adequate rooms.

Thai Hotel (*☎ 075 341 509, fax 075 344 858, 1373 Th Ratchadamnoen*) Singles/doubles with fan 200/300B, with air-con 400-550B. Once Nakhon Si Thammarat's flashiest hotel, two blocks from the train station, this now seems rather ordinary. All rooms have cable TV.

Taksin Hotel (*☎ 075 342 790, fax 075 342 794, 1548/23 Th Si Prat*) Rooms with air-con, hot shower & TV 400B, with phone 500B. The six-storey Taksin stands off Th Si Prat amid a string of massage places. It's popular with travelling Thai businesspeople and can be noisy.

Bue Loung Hotel (*Bua Luang Hotel; ☎ 075 341 518, fax 075 343 418, 1487/19 Soi Luang Meuang, Th Jamroenwithi*) Rooms with fan 180-240B, with air-con 280-340B. This hotel has large, clean rooms and is very friendly. Internet facilities are next door.

Montien Hotel (*☎/fax 075 341 908, 1509/40 Th Yommarat*) Rooms with fan/air-con & bath 240/440B. The fading, eight-storey Montien, next to the train station, has large rooms – a bit overpriced considering the low upkeep.

Phetpailin *(☎ 075 341 896, fax 075 343 943, 1835/38-39 Th Yommarat)* Rooms with fan 160-220B, with air-con 360B. A block north of Montien, this is similar but a bit cheaper.

Nakorn Garden Inn *(☎ 075 344 831, fax 075 342 926, 1/4 Th Pak Nakhon)* Rooms with air-con & TV 450-550B. This quiet mid-range place is east of the city centre.

Grand Park Hotel *(☎ 075 317 666–73, fax 075 317 674, 1204/79 Th Pak Nakhon)* Rooms with fridge & TV 750B, suites 1400B. Grand Park offers nicely furnished, spacious carpeted rooms. Prices come down 20% in the low season. Parking is available.

Twin Lotus Hotel *(☎ 075 323 777, fax 075 323 821, in Bangkok ☎ 027 110 360, fax 023 810 930, 97/8 Th Pattanakan Kukwang)* Rooms 1000-1500B, suites 2500-5000B. The 16-storey, 413-room Twin Lotus has all the amenities expected by Bangkok business travellers, such as IDD phones, mini-bars, satellite TV, restaurants, cocktail lounge, coffee shop, karaoke, massage, swimming pool, saunas and a fully equipped gym. Non-smoking rooms are available. Discounts are easily obtained.

Places to Eat

There are lots of funky old Chinese restaurants along Th Yommarat and Th Jamroenwithi. The latter street is the city's main culinary centre. At night the entire block running south from the Siam Hotel is lined with cheap *food vendors* – Muslim stands opposite the hotel sell delicious *roti klûay* (banana pancakes), *khâo mók* (chicken biryani) and *mátàbà* (pancakes stuffed with chicken or vegetables) in the evening, and by day there are plenty of rice and noodle shops.

Yong Seng *(Th Jamroenwithi)* is a good, inexpensive Chinese restaurant, with no roman-script sign.

Hao Coffee *(☎ 075 317 197, Th Ratchadamnoen)* Dishes 20-40B. To try some of Nakhon's excellent Thai coffee, stop by here at Bovorn Bazaar. Basically an updated version of an original Hokkien-style coffee shop once run by the owner's family in Nakhon, Hao Coffee serves international coffees as well as southern-Thai Hokkien-style coffee (listed as 'Hao coffee' on the menu) served with a tea chaser. Ask for fresh milk *(nom sòt)* if you abhor powdered non-dairy creamer.

Bovorn Bazaar offers several other culinary delights.

Khrua Nakhon *(☎ 075 317 197, 89/6 Th Ratchadamnoen)* Dishes 60-120B. Open 7am-3pm. Adjacent to Hao Coffee this large open-air restaurant serves real Nakhon cuisine. Menu items include *khâo yam* (southern-style rice salad), *kaeng tai plaa* (spicy fish curry), *khanǒm jiin* (curry noodles served with a huge tray of vegies) and seafood. The restaurant also has egg-and-toast breakfasts and you can order Hao coffee from next door if you'd like. With a banyan tree at the front and a modest display of southern-Thai folk art, the atmosphere is hard to beat.

Ban Lakhon *(☎ 075 345 910, 1132 Th Ratchadamnoen)* Mains 40-120B. In Bovorn Bazaar, behind Khrua Nakhon, this old house is very good for Thai food and is open for dinner.

Ligor Home Bakery *(☎ 075 346 563, Th Ratchadamnoen)* Dishes 20-40B. On the corner of the alley leading into Bovorn Bazaar, this bakes fresh European-style pastries daily.

At night the bakery closes and Nakhon's most famous *roti vendors* set up along the alley. In Nakhon, *roti klûay* is a tradition – the vendors here use only fresh mashed bananas. Other offerings include *roti kaeng* (roti with curry), *roti khài* (with egg) or as mátàbà (stuffed with meat and vegetables). They also do great *khanǒm jìip* (dumplings), stuffed with a chicken-shrimp mixture, along with Nakhon coffee and better-than-average milk tea.

Dam Kan Aeng *(☎ 075 344 343, 1979 Th Ratchadamnoen)* Dishes 30-50B. On the north-western corner of Th Ratchadamnoen and Th Watkhit, this popular Thai-Chinese place is packed with hungry customers every night.

Kuang Meng *(343/12 Th Ratchadamnoen)* Dishes 30-50B. Opposite the Siam

Commercial Bank, this is a very small Hokkien coffee shop with marble-top tables and very nice pastries. There is no roman-script sign.

Entertainment
Beyond the cinemas in town, there's not a lot of night life.

Rock 99% Bar & Grill (☎ 075 317 999, Th Ratchadamnoen) Open 6pm-2am. An American roadhouse-style pub inside the Bovorn Bazaar, this offers draught beer, cocktails and Western pop music, as well as pizza, baked potatoes, sandwiches and a few Thai dishes; this is where the few expats hang out.

Shopping
Several shops along Th Tha Chang, just behind the TAT office and Sanaam Naa Meuang (City Park), sell Nakhon's famous line of *thŏm* (nielloware), silver and basketry.

Den Nakhon (Th Ratchadamnoen) On the grounds of Wat Phra Mahathat, this sells thŏm, silver and other local crafts at good prices.

Getting There & Away
Air THAI has daily flights to/from Bangkok (two hours, 2035B). The THAI office (☎ 075 343 874) in Nakhon is at 1612 Th Ratchadamnoen. The airport is a few kilometres north of town on Rte 408. THAI runs vans between its office and the airport (80B).

Bus & Minivan Air-con buses bound for Nakhon Si Thammarat leave Bangkok's Southern bus terminal every 30 minutes or so from 5pm to 8pm daily, arriving 12 hours later (414B). Air-con buses from Nakhon Si Thammarat leave for Bangkok at about the same times. There are also five 2nd-class air-con departures (322B) and one VIP departure (640B) nightly.

Ordinary buses from Surat Thani cost 45B and leave four times a day, while air-con departures are slightly less frequent and cost around 70B. Direct buses run from Songkhla via a bridge over the entrance to Thaleh Noi (the inland sea). There are a

couple of private bus companies on Th Jamroenwithi near the Siam Hotel.

Hourly buses between Nakhon Si Thammarat and Krabi cost 64B (70B air-con) and take about three hours. Other routes include Trang (36B ordinary, 50B air-con), Phattalung (35B ordinary, 63B air-con), Phuket (115B ordinary, 155B air-con) and Hat Yai (64B ordinary, 90B air-con, 100B minivan). The buses leave from the terminal on Th Phaniant.

Minivans to Krabi leave from in front of the municipality office every half-hour from 7am to 3pm (100B, 2½ hours). Minivans to Surat Thani (80B) leave from the same block as the Thai Lee Hotel. You can also catch minivans to Phuket (150B, five hours).

To Ko Samui there is one air-con bus a day from the main terminal at 11.30am (130B, three hours).

Share Taxi This seems to be the most popular form of inter-city travel out of Nakhon. The huge share-taxi terminal on Th Yommarat has taxis to Yala (130B), Thung Song (30B), Khanom (50B), Sichon (30B), Krabi (90B), Hat Yai (80B), Trang (70B) and Phattalung (60B). A second smaller stand on Th Thewarat has taxis to Surat Thani (80B), Chumphon (140B) and Ranong (180B).

Train Most southbound trains stop at the junction of Thung Song, about 40km west of Nakhon Si Thammarat, from where you must take a bus or taxi to the coast. However, two trains actually go all the way to Nakhon Si Thammarat (there is a branch line from Khao Chum Thong to Nakhon Si Thammarat): the rapid No 173, which leaves Bangkok's Hualamphong train station at 5.35pm, arriving in Nakhon Si Thammarat at 9.25am, and the express No 85, which leaves Bangkok at 7.15pm and arrives in Nakhon Si Thammarat at 10.50am.

Most travellers won't be booking a train directly to Nakhon Si Thammarat, but if you want to, 1st class costs 652B, 2nd class 308B and 3rd class 133B, excluding surcharges for rapid/express service or sleeping berths.

Getting Around

Blue sǎwngthǎew run north-south along Th Ratchadamnoen and Th Si Thammasok for 5B (a bit more at night). Motorbike taxi rides start at 10B and cost up to 50B for longer distances.

AROUND NAKHON SI THAMMARAT
Khao Luang National Park
อุทยานแห่งชาติเขาหลวง

Known for its beautiful mountain and forest walks, cool streams, waterfalls and fruit orchards, this 570-sq-km park (☎ 075 309 047; adult/child under 14 years 200/100B) in the centre of the province surrounds **Khao Luang**. At 1835m this is the highest peak in peninsular Thailand. Along with other forested igneous peaks to the west, Khao Luang provides a watershed that feeds the Rapi River. Locals practise a unique form of agriculture called *sǔan rom* (shade garden or shade farm). Instead of clear-cutting the forest, they leave many indigenous trees intact, randomly interspersing them with betel, mangosteen, rambutan, langsat, papaya, durian and banana trees. Cleverly placed bamboo and PVC pipes irrigate the mixed orchards without the use of pumps.

Wildlife includes clouded leopard, tiger, elephant, banteng, gaur, tapir, serow, musk deer, macaque, civet, binturon and Javan mongoose, plus over 200 bird species and more than 300 orchid varieties (including several indigenous species).

Park bungalows can be rented for 600B to 1000B per night and sleep six to twelve persons. Camping is permitted along the trail to the summit of Khao Luang (see the following Hiking Trails entry). There are a few private **bungalows** and **cafes** on the road to the park offices where simple accommodation and food are available.

Hiking Trails Although park facilities are scant, there are several nature trails. You can hike 2.5km through dense tropical forest to the top of **Karom Falls** from the national park unit near Lan Saka (25km from Nakhon Si Thammarat), off Rte 4015.

Every 500m or so there are shelters and seats. To reach seven-tiered **Krung Ching Falls** take the Krung Ching nature trail from Nopphitam at the north-eastern border of the park, off Rte 4140, a half-day walk. Along the way you'll pass the world's largest tree fern, an old communist insurgent camp, Tham Pratuchai (a cave also used by the communists) and a mangosteen forest. This trail is also lined with seats and shelters. The falls are most impressive just after the rainy season has ended in November or December.

A more challenging trail leads from a car park near Khiriwong to the **summit** of Khao Luang, a 14-hour walk best divided into two or more days. Night-time temperatures at the summit can drop to 5°C, so come prepared with plenty of warm clothing and sleeping bags if you have them. At 600m Kratom Suan Sainai offers a simple roofed shelter and also marks the upper limit of the fruit plantations. In the dry season you can camp next to a riverbed at Lan Sai, about six hours' walk from the car park. After a five-hour walk farther on, along a section of very steep trail, you'll enter a cloud forest full of rattan, orchids, rhododendron, ferns and stunted oaks. From here it's another three hours to the summit where, if the weather is clear, you'll be rewarded with stunning views of layer after layer of mountains rolling into the distance.

The best and safest way to appreciate the Khao Luang trek is to go with a guide from the Kiriwong Village Ecotourism Club in Khiriwong (☎ 075 309 010). For about 1300B per person the villagers can arrange a two- or three-night trek along with all meals and guide services. The guides can point out local flora and fauna that you might otherwise miss. The only time to do this hike is January to June when the trails are dry and leeches are less prevalent. During heavy rains the trail can be impassable for days.

Getting There & Away To reach the park, take a sǎwngthǎew (25B) from Nakhon Si Thammarat to the village of Khiriwong at the base of Khao Luang. The entrance to the park and the offices of the Royal Forestry Department are 33km from the centre of Nakhon on Rte 4015, an asphalt road that climbs almost 400m in 2.5km to the office and a farther 450m to the car park.

Laem Talumphuk
แหลมตะลุมพุก

This is a small scenic cape about 50km north-east from Nakhon Si Thammarat. Take a bus from Th Neramit going east to Pak Nakhon for 15B, then cross the inlet by ferry to Laem Talumphuk for 20B.

Hat Sa Bua
หาดสระบัว

Twenty-five kilometres north of Nakhon Si Thammarat in the Tha Sala district, off Rte 401 (at the 12km marker) to Surat and about 15B by săwngthăew, this somewhat muddy beach, lined with casuarinas (a type of sea pine), a few coco palms and a bit of dune vegetation, is a favourite local picnic spot on weekends but virtually deserted during the week. There are some reasonably priced *restaurants* here.

Hat Sichon & Hat Hin Ngam
หาดสิชล/หาดหินงาม

Even the locals have a difficult time separating Hat Sichon from Hat Hin Ngam, two beaches side-by-side along a small curving bay about 65km north of Nakhon Si Thammarat in Sichon district. Hat Sichon ends at a pier in the small fishing hamlet of Sichon, while Hin Ngam to the immediate south is marked by a cluster of boulders at its northern end. Hat Sichon has the advantage of a ban on beach vendors, though you can rent sling chairs and beach umbrellas at one end of the beach. Coconut is a major local product, so there are plenty of palms to set the tone. Very few foreigners seem to turn up here. Anyone who likes a low-key, local scene will like this beach and the fact that you can easily walk to the town of Sichon for a meal or to peruse the market. The harbour in front of the picturesque town is often filled with large, colourful fishing boats lined up along spindly wooden piers – it looks very much the way Hua Hin once did. Near the waterfront are a lot of old one-storey wooden shophouses.

South of Hin Ngam and Sichon are the lesser known beaches of **Hat Piti** and **Hat Saophao**. Hat Piti is quite a pretty stretch of white sand with one medium-scale resort. Hat Saophao stretches for 5km and could be the most beautiful beach in the area if it weren't for the disastrous shrimp farms just inland, which use the most environmentally unfriendly techniques for raising the pink crustaceans the world loves to nibble on. There are some nice sand dunes in the area, but it can be hard to reach them because there are so many artificial shrimp breeding lagoons dug into the beach.

Places to Stay & Eat A good place is **Prasarnsuk Villa** (☎ 075 536 299) Bungalows 350-1200B. It's right at the end of the sandy part of Hat Sichon, so you have easy beach access while also being near the rocky headland (with fair snorkelling) that starts Hat Hin Ngam. It has 30 solid-looking bungalows and there's a simple open-air seafood restaurant out the front.

Hin Ngam Bungalow (☎ 075 536 204) Bungalows 220B. On Hat Hin Ngam, this has six wood-and-thatch bungalows with metal roofs, rather close together, and a restaurant that overlooks the bay. The clientele is almost entirely Thai.

Hat Piti Beach Resort (☎ 075 335 303) Bungalows 1200-2000B. On lengthy, unspoiled Hat Piti, this almost looks lost here with its American South-Western designs. This well-run place has a good open-air restaurant and large, fully equipped bungalows. A single-building, hotel-style unit is going up on the property and may offer less expensive rooms. Discounts of up to 40% are sometimes given.

Hat Sichon Seafood Dishes 40-120B. Open 7am-10pm. This is the best of the local restaurants. It's clean, simple and overlooks the beach.

Phloi Seafood and **Khrua Poi** near Hat Sichon are also quite good. Don't look for

English signs, you won't find any, though the staff at Hat Sichon Seafood can speak a little English and these places are easy to find.

Getting There & Away Get a bus for Sichon from the Nakhon Si Thammarat bus terminal for 20B or take a share taxi for 50B. From Sichon, you can take a motorcycle taxi to Hat Sichon, Hat Hin Ngam or Hat Piti for around 20B per person.

If you have your own vehicle, it's easy to find Sichon district via Rte 401 from Nakhon Si Thammarat (or from Surat Thani, 73km to the north). From Sichon you have to take either Rte 4161 (through town) or Rte 4105, 4km south of town at Ban Chom Phibun, then start heading for the coast. Just remember that the beaches are all south of Sichon; you may have to stop and ask directions. If you're coming north along Rte 401 and turn right onto Rte 4105, you'll end up almost immediately at Hat Saophao. Turn left on the road parallel to the beach and you'll get to the other three beaches mentioned earlier.

Ao Khanom
อ่าวขนอม

About 25km from Sichon, 70km from Surat Thani and 80km from Nakhon Si Thammarat is the bay of Ao Khanom. Not far from the vehicle-ferry landing for Ko Samui in Khanom is a string of four white-sand beaches – **Hat Nai Praet**, **Hat Nai Phlao**, **Hat Na Dan** and **Hat Pak Nam**. In some areas they're starting to develop shrimp farms, which threaten to damage the environment and local tourism, but so far the farms haven't multiplied too much. At the northern end of Ao Khanom is a major quarry site – also a worry.

In Nai Phlao, the best beach (8.4km south of the town of Khanom), the thousands of coconut palms give the impression that a chunk of Ko Samui somehow cut loose and drifted ashore. Two kilometres south of Nai Phlao is scenic **Hin Lat Falls** – another Samui echo. Around a tall headland south of Hat Nai Phlao is the deserted **Hat Thong Yi**. A road was recently built around the headland to the beach, but at the time of

writing it was barricaded off for no apparent reason, so the best way to get here may still be by boat.

Most places to stay are concentrated along the southern half of Hat Nai Phlao, the prettiest part, and offer five to 10 solid, plain bungalows with bath for 500B to 800B a night; the lower end of this range may have fan only, while the upper end offers air-con.

Khanom Hill Resort (☎ 075 529 403) Bungalows 900-1900B. Among the better places to stay along Hat Nai Phlao is the friendly Khanom Hill, which features red-roofed bungalows on stilts overlooking the sea, with large areas of decking for sitting outside and enjoying the view.

Supa Villa (☎ 075 528 522, fax 075 528 553) Bungalows 850B. This offers solid-looking brick bungalows with tile roofs, right on the beach.

Supar Royal Beach (☎ 075 529 237, fax 075 528 553) Rooms with air-con 900-2900B. Opposite Supa Villa (and with the same owners) this is not on the beach, but does have a swimming pool.

Nai Phlao Bay Resort (☎ 075 539 039, fax 075 529 425) Bungalows 450-1500B. This has stone and cement bungalows set on spacious grounds towards the southern end of the bay.

GB Resort (☎ 075 529 253) Bungalows 500-700B. To reach GB, you have to take a narrow sand road off the main road just south of Nai Phlao Resort. There are A-frame bungalows with sloping red roofs and small terraces. Casuarina, pandanus and mango trees provide shade on the property, and there are lots of tables on the beach.

Khanab Nam Diamond Cliff Resort (☎ 075 529 444, fax 075 529 111) Bungalows 900-2200B. High on a rocky cliff at the southern end of the bay, this handles the top end of the market, with octagonal bamboo and thatch bungalows. A free-form pool overlooks the sea, as does the resort's *Khanap Nam restaurant* – a nice place to eat even if you're not staying there.

Up towards Khanom are four or five more places, none of them especially recommended unless everything else is full.

Getting There & Away You can get a share taxi from Nakhon Si Thammarat's share taxi terminal to Khanom for 50B. From Khanom you can hire motorcycle taxis out to the beaches for about 50B. If you're driving, pedalling or riding, get off Rte 401 at the junction marked for Rte 4014, and follow the latter to Rte 4232, which runs parallel to the coast all along Ao Khanom (and as far south as Sichon).

Because one of the terminals for the vehicle ferry to Ko Samui is in Khanom, there are also frequent buses from Surat Thani.

Thaleh Noi Wildlife Preserve
อุทยานนกน้ำทะเลน้อย

Thaleh Noi, a small inland sea or lake 32km north-east of Phattalung, is protected by the Royal Forestry Department – no fishing or hunting is permitted anywhere on or along its shores, islands or waters. Among the 182 species of resident and migratory waterfowl found here, the most prominent is the *nók i kong*, with its long, funny feet that quiver like malfunctioning landing gear as the bird takes flight; and the *nók pèt daeng*, a small red-headed 'duck bird', related to the whistling teal, that skitters along the water. This is also the last natural habitat in Asia for the beautiful painted stork *(nók kàap bua)*, and an important sanctuary for the great egret, purple heron, spot-billed pelican and bronze-winged jacana. The best time for bird sightings is November and December; the least number of birds are seen from May to August.

The sea itself is a sort of large swamp similar to the Everglades in southern USA. The major forms of vegetation are water vines and *dôn kòk*, a reed that the nók i kong uses to build large platforms over the water for nesting purposes. After drying these reeds in the sun, the local Thais also use them to make woven floor mats that are sold throughout Phattalung Province. The village near the park entrance to Thaleh Noi is a good place to observe the reed-weaving methods.

The Royal Forestry Department has a few wooden bungalows built over the lake

available for 250B. These afford good views not only of the bird sanctuary but also of the brilliant sunsets over Thaleh Noi. Long-tail boats can be hired at the pier to take passengers out and around Thaleh Noi for 200B per hour.

Getting There & Away To get there, take a Thaleh Noi bus from the local bus stop on Th Poh Saat in Phattalung. The bus stops at the sanctuary after about an hour's journey and costs 20B. The last bus back to Phattalung leaves around 5pm.

SONGKHLA
สงขลา

postcode 90000 • pop 87,600

Songkhla, 950km from Bangkok, is another former Srivijaya satellite on the east coast. Not much is known about the pre-8th-century history of Songkhla, a name derived from the Yawi 'Singora' – a mutilated Sanskrit reference to a lion-shaped mountain (today called Khao Daeng) opposite the harbour. Originally the settlement lay at the foot of Khao Daeng, on the other side of Thaleh Sap Songkhla, where two cemeteries and the ruins of a fort are among the oldest structural remains.

About 3km north of Khao Daeng village, off the road to Nakhon Si Thammarat, is the tomb of Suleiman (1592–1668), a Muslim trader who was largely responsible for Songkhla's commercial eminence during the 17th century. Just south of Suleiman's tomb, a Dutch graveyard testifies to a 17th-century Dutch presence as well (look for large granite slabs in an overgrown area next to a Total warehouse). Suleiman's son Mustapha subsequently fell out of grace with Ayuthaya's King Narai, who burned the settlement to the ground in the following century.

Songkhla later moved across the harbour to its present site on a peninsula between the Thaleh Sap Songkhla (an inland sea) and the South China Sea (or Gulf of Thailand, depending on how you look at it). Today's inhabitants are a colourful mixture of Thais, Chinese and ethnic Malays, and the local architecture and cuisine reflect the

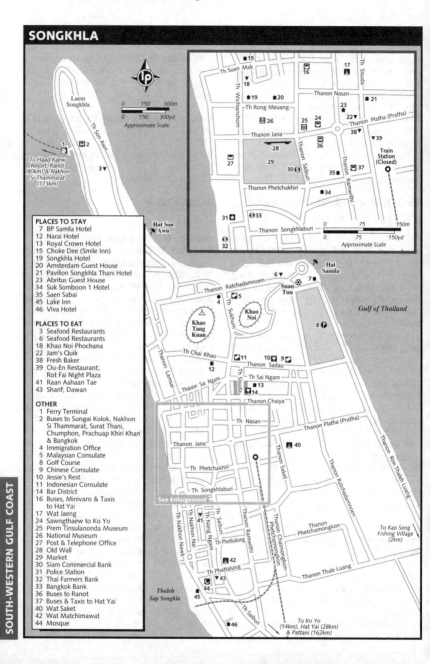

SONGKHLA

PLACES TO STAY
7 BP Samila Hotel
12 Narai Hotel
13 Royal Crown Hotel
15 Choke Dee (Smile Inn)
19 Songkhla Hotel
20 Amsterdam Guest House
21 Pavilion Songkhla Thani Hotel
23 Abritus Guest House
34 Suk Somboon 1 Hotel
35 Saen Sabai
45 Lake Inn
46 Viva Hotel

PLACES TO EAT
3 Seafood Restaurants
6 Seafood Restaurants
18 Khao Noi Phochana
22 Jam's Quik
38 Fresh Baker
39 Ou-En Restaurant;
   Rot Fai Night Plaza
41 Raan Aahaan Tae
43 Sharif; Dawan

OTHER
1 Ferry Terminal
2 Buses to Sungai Kolok, Nakhon
   Si Thammarat, Surat Thani,
   Chumphon, Prachuap Khiri Khan
   & Bangkok
4 Immigration Office
5 Malaysian Consulate
8 Golf Course
9 Chinese Consulate
10 Jessie's Rest
11 Indonesian Consulate
14 Bar District
16 Buses, Minivans & Taxis
   to Hat Yai
17 Wat Jaeng
24 Sawngthaew to Ko Yo
25 Prem Tinsulanonda Museum
26 National Museum
27 Post & Telephone Office
28 Old Wall
29 Market
30 Siam Commercial Bank
31 Police Station
32 Thai Farmers Bank
33 Bangkok Bank
36 Buses to Ranot
37 Buses & Taxis to Hat Yai
40 Wat Saket
42 Wat Matchimawat
44 Mosque

combination. Older Southern Thais still refer to the city as Singora or Singkhon.

The seafood served along Hat Samila is excellent, though the white beach is itself not that great for swimming (especially if you've just come from the Ko Samui archipelago). Beaches are not Songkhla's main attraction, even if the TAT promotes them as such, though the sand-and-casuarina scenery along Hat Samila can be visually striking and the city is keeping the quiet, low-key beach cleaner than ever before.

Offshore petroleum exploration projects commissioned through Unocal and Total – and the resultant influx of multinational oil company employees (particularly British and American) – have created a strong Western presence in Songkhla. This, along with a considerable Thai naval presence, has created a relatively wealthy city.

Orientation
The city has a split personality, with the charming older section west of Th Ramwithi towards the waterfront, and the new section – a modern mix of business and suburbia – to the east.

Information
Foreign Consulates A Malaysian consulate (☎ 074 311 062, 074 311 104) is at 4 Th Sukhum, near Hat Samila. Other foreign missions include a Chinese consulate (☎ 074 311 494) on Th Sadao, not far from the Royal Crown Hotel, and an Indonesian consulate (☎ 074 311 544) on the western end of Th Sadao, near the Th Ramwithi junction.

Money Songkhla is well supplied with banks, and you'll find ATMs at Bangkok Bank (Th Nakhon Nai), Thai Farmers Bank (Th Nakhon Nawk) and Siam Commercial Bank (Th Saiburi), all in the older area of the city.

Post & Communications The post office is opposite the department store/market on Th Wichianchom, open Monday to Friday from 8.30am to 3.30pm; international calls can be made upstairs daily from 8am to 6pm.

Thaleh Sap Songkhla
ทะเลสาบสงขลา

Stretching north-west of the city is the huge brackish lake or 'inland sea' of Thaleh Sap Songkhla. Parts of the Thaleh Sap are heavily fished, the most sought-after catch being the famous black tiger prawn. Illegal gill-net trawling for the prawn is now threatening the whole fish population; legal fishermen have begun organising against gill-net use and the situation has improved slightly in recent years.

The city's waterfront on the inland sea buzzes with activity: ice is loaded onto fishing boats on their way out to sea, baskets of fish are unloaded onto the pier, fish markets are set up and disassembled, and long-tail boats doing taxi business between the islands and mainland tool about. The fish smell along the piers is pretty powerful.

National Museum
พิพิธภัณฑสถานแห่งชาติ

Contained in a 100-year-old building of southern Sino-Portuguese architecture, between Th Rong Meuang and Th Jana (off Th Wichianchom), this museum (☎ 074 311 728, Th Wichianchom; admission 30B; open 9am-4pm Wed-Sun, closed public holidays) is easily the most picturesque national museum in Thailand. Along with the innate architectural charms of its curved rooflines and thick walls, it's a quiet, shady building with a tranquil garden at the front. The museum contains exhibits from all national art-style periods, particularly the Srivijaya, including a 7th- to 9th-century Shivalingam found in Pattani. Also on display are Thai and Chinese ceramics and sumptuous Chinese furniture owned by the local Chinese aristocracy.

Prem Tinsulanonda Museum
พิพิธภัณฑ์พะธำมะรงค์

Dwarfed by the Queen Hotel next door, the Prem Tinsulanonda Museum (☎ 074 312 679, Th Jana; admission free; open 8.30am-4pm Tue-Sun) is touted as the birthplace of

Thailand's 16th prime minister, who served from 1980 to 1988. The 'museum' is a wooden house that was actually recently built upon the site of Prem's birthplace, and contains some of the furniture and personal effects that graced the original home. While something of a shrine to Prem, the museum is still worth a visit even if you have little interest in Thai politics – the wooden structure is a charming example of the combination of breezy verandas and cosy interiors that constitute the traditional Thai house.

Temples & Chedi
Towards Hat Yai, **Wat Matchimawat** typifies the Sino-Thai temple architecture of 17th-century Songkhla. One wíhăan contains an old marble Buddha image and a small museum. Another temple with similar characteristics, **Wat Jaeng** was recently renovated.

There is a Sinhalese-style chedi and royal pavilion atop **Khao Tang Kuan**, a hill at the northern end of the peninsula; to reach the top you'll have to climb 305 steps.

Beaches
The residents have begun taking better care of the strip of white sand along **Hat Samila**, and it is now quite a pleasant beach for strolling or for an early morning read on one of the benches placed in the shade of the casuarina trees. At one end of the beach, a **bronze mermaid sculpture** depicted squeezing water from her long hair in a tribute to Mae Thorani, the Hindu-Buddhist earth goddess, sits atop some rocks. Locals treat the figure like a shrine, tying the waist with coloured cloth and rubbing the breasts for good luck. The rustic seafood restaurants at the back of the beach supply food and cold beverages.

The less frequented **Hat Son Awn** extends along the eastern shore of the slender cape jutting out between the Gulf of Thailand and Thaleh Sap, immediately north-west of Hat Samila. There are also a few restaurants along this stretch but they are on the opposite side of the road from the beach and tend to be slightly more expensive than those at Hat Samila.

Other Attractions
If you are interested in seeing some traditional **Songkhla architecture**, walk along the back streets parallel to the inland sea waterfront – Th Nang Ngam, Th Nakhon Nai and Th Nakhon Nawk all have some older Songkhla architecture showing Chinese, Portuguese and Malay influence. Much of it disappeared during Thailand's economic boom, but a few have been restored and one hopes the city will support some sort of historical architectural legacy.

A few kilometres south of Hat Samila is **Kao Seng**, a quaint Muslim fishing village, where the tourist photos of gaily painted fishing vessels are taken. Săwngthăew run regularly between Songkhla and Kao Seng for 8B per person.

Places to Stay – Budget
Amsterdam Guest House (☎ 074 314 890, 15/3 Th Rong Meuang) Rooms 200B. This homey place is popular and clean, with plenty of cushions, wandering pet dogs and cats, as well as a caged macaque that is said to bite the unwary.

Abritus Guest House (☎ 074 326 047, 28/16 Th Ramwithi, e abritus_th@yahoo .com) Rooms with shared facilities 200B. Recently opened, Abritus has clean fan rooms with shared bath. Downstairs is a restaurant in which guests get a 10% discount on food and drinks. English, German and Russian are spoken here.

Narai Hotel (☎ 074 311 078, 14 Th Chai Khao) Singles/doubles with fan 200/250B, doubles with bath 300B. One of the best deals in Songkhla is the friendly Narai, near the foot of Khao Tang Kuan. It's an older wooden hotel with clean, quiet rooms (each room has a washbasin).

Songkhla Hotel (☎ 074 313 505, 68/70 Th Wichianchom) Rooms 170B, with shower 200B. This refurbished hotel, across from the fishing station, has well-scrubbed rooms.

Choke Dee (Smile Inn; ☎ 074 311 258, 14/19 Th Wichianchom) Rooms with fan/aircon & cold shower 280/380B, with TV 400B. Just up from the Songkhla Hotel, this is a clean place with medium-size rooms. The attached restaurant opens at 5am.

Suk Somboon 1 Hotel (☎/fax 074 311 049, 40 Th Phetchakhiri) Singles/doubles 200/250B, with air-con 350B. These wooden rooms off a large central area are not bad.

Saen Sabai (☎/fax 074 311 090, 1 Th Phetchakhiri) Rooms without/with bath & fan 150/220B, with air-con 300B. Saen Sabai is well located and has clean, small rooms in an early Bangkok-style building that has been remodelled beyond recognition.

Places to Stay – Mid-Range

Viva Hotel (☎ 074 321 033–7, fax 074 312 608, 547/2 Th Nakhon Nawk) Singles/doubles with air-con 550/650B. This is a modern five-storey hotel where the staff speak English and are friendly and helpful. The attached coffee shop has live music nightly.

Royal Crown Hotel (☎ 074 312 174, fax 074 321 027, 38 Th Sai Ngam) Rooms with air-con, TV & fridge 450B. Catering mostly to visiting oil company employees and their families is the five-storey Royal Crown. Rooms are carpeted and everything works – great value at this price.

Lake Inn (☎ 074 314 240, 301-3 Th Nakhon Nawk) Rooms with air-con, carpet, hot water, TV & fridge 400B, with bathtub 500B, with balcony 600B. Popular with Thais, this is a rambling multi-storey place with great views over the Thaleh Sap.

Places to Stay – Top End

Pavilion Songkhla Thani Hotel (☎ 074 441 850, fax 074 323 716, 17 Th Platha) Singles/doubles with air-con from 1020-2400B. The nine-storey Pavilion is one block east of Th Ramwithi at the intersection of Th Nasan and Th Sisuda. It has large, luxurious rooms with wood panelling, IDD phones, satellite TV and carpeting.

BP Samila Hotel (☎ 074 440 222, fax 074 440 442, 106 Th Ratchadamnoen) Rooms 1250-7500B. On the beachfront, this is Songkhla's swankiest accommodation and has all the amenities including air-con, IDD phone, fridge, satellite TV, and sea or mountain views.

Places to Eat

There are a lot of good restaurants in Songkhla but some have a tendency of overcharging travellers.

Raan Aahaan Tae (☎ 074 311 505, 85 Th Nang Ngam) This is the best seafood place according to locals. Look for a brightly lit place just south of the cinema, off Th Songkhlaburi and parallel to Th Saiburi.

Seafood restaurants Open 11.30am-2pm, 5pm-8pm. The restaurants on Hat Samila are pretty good – try the curried crab claws or spicy fried squid. Prices are low to moderate.

Fancier seafood places are found along Th Son Awn near the beach – but these also tend to have hordes of young Thai hostesses to satisfy the Thai male penchant for chatting up *áw-áw* (young girls). Cheaper and better are another string of seafood places on the beach close to where Th Ratchadamnoen and Th Son Awm intersect.

Along Th Nang Ngam north of Th Phattalung in the Chinese section are several cheap *Chinese noodle and congee shops*.

At the end of Th Nang Ngam along Th Phattalung (near the mosque) are some modest Thai Muslim restaurants, including *Sharif*, and *Dawan;* both open 8am until 9pm.

Khao Noi Phochana (Th Wichianchom) Dishes 30-60B. Open 8am-10pm. Near the Songkhla Hotel, this has a very good lunchtime selection of Thai and Chinese rice dishes.

There are several fast-food spots at the intersection of Th Sisuda and Th Platha, including *Jam's Quik* (☎ 074 324 515, 23/3 Th Platha) and *Fresh Baker* (☎ 074 322 007, 32-34 Th Platha), both with burgers, ice cream and Western breakfasts; there are also a few popular Thai and Chinese restaurants. The *kíaw náam* (wonton soup) place next to Fresh Baker is cheap and quite good.

Rot Fai Night Plaza (Th Sisuda) Dishes 20-40B. Near the Chalerm Thong cinema and the old train station is this hawkers' centre and night market.

Ou-en Restaurant Dishes 30-40B. Open 4pm-3am. Also in the Plaza, this is a very popular Chinese place with outdoor tables; the house speciality is Peking duck.

Abritus Guest House (☎ 074 326 047, 28/16 Th Ramwithi, e abritus_th@yahoo.com) has an extensive breakfast menu, including several kinds of omelettes. It is also known for its delicious potato salad.

Entertainment

The string of bars along Th Sadao, between the Chinese and Indonesian embassies, is jokingly referred to among local expats as The Dark Side. Not as ominous as it sounds, this mini bar-district mainly caters to oil company employees and other Westerners living in Songkhla. *Jessie's Rest,* the bar nearest Soi 5, is run by an Englishman and his Thai wife. Besides the ice chest full of beer and the good hamburgers, reliable information about Songkhla's sights is readily obtained here.

On nearby Th Sisuda are a few other bars worth checking out, including *Uncle Sam's*, *The Boozer* and *Corner Bier*. The latter is the hang-out for Songkhla's Canadian community.

Thais tend to congregate at bars with live music on Th Sisuda, of which *Lucky Bar* is a current favourite.

Getting There & Away

Air THAI operates several daily flights to/from nearby Hat Yai; see the Hat Yai section for details further in this chapter. A taxi from Hat Yai airport to Songkhla costs 340B. In the reverse direction you should be able to find a car or săwngthăew to the airport for 200B.

Bus, Minivan & Share Taxi Three aircon public buses leave Bangkok's Southern bus terminal daily between 5pm and 7.30pm, arriving in Songkhla 13 hours later, for 514B. One ordinary bus leaves from Bangkok at 2pm (286B). In the reverse direction the air-con buses leave between 4.45pm and 6.20pm.

Air-con buses from Surat Thani to Songkhla and Hat Yai cost 135B one way. From Songkhla to Hat Yai, big green buses leave every 15 minutes (12B) from Th Saiburi, around the corner from the Songkhla Hotel, or they can be flagged down anywhere along Th Wichianchom or Th Saiburi towards Hat Yai. Directly opposite the ferry terminal on Laem Songkhla is a small Baw Khaw Saw (government) terminal for buses going to Sungai Kolok, Nakhon Si Thammarat, Surat Thani, Chumphon, Prachuap Khiri Khan and Bangkok.

Air-con minivans to Hat Yai are 20B; these arrive and depart from a parking area in front of Wat Jaeng. Share taxis are 20B to Hat Yai if there are five other passengers, 100B if chartered; after 8pm the rates go up to 25B and 125B respectively. Share taxis cost 55B to Pattani and 50B to Yala.

See the Hat Yai Getting There & Away section later in this chapter for more options, as Hat Yai is the main transport hub for Songkhla Province.

Train The old train spur to Songkhla no longer has a passenger service. See the Hat Yai Getting There & Away section later in this chapter for trains to/from nearby Hat Yai.

Ferry At the head of Laem Songkhla, a government-run car ferry plies the short distance across the channel where the Thaleh Sap meets the Gulf of Thailand. The barge-like ferry holds about 15 cars, plus assorted motorcycles and pedestrians. The fare for the seven-minute ride is 12B per car, plus 3B per person; it operates from 6am to dusk daily. The ferry stop on the other side is a semi-floating village called Ban Hua Khao. From this point Sathing Phra is 36km north via Rte 408, which terminates in Nakhon Si Thammarat.

Getting Around

For getting around in town, small red săwngthăew circulate Songkhla and take passengers to any point on their route for 7B. Motorcycle taxis to/from anywhere in town cost 10B per kilometre; rates double after 10pm or so.

KO YO

เกาะยอ

An island on the inland sea, Ko Yo (pronounced kaw yaw) is worth visiting just to see the cotton-weaving cottage industry there. The good-quality, distinctive *phâa kàw yaw* is hand-woven on rustic looms and available on the spot at 'wholesale' prices – meaning you still have to bargain but have a chance of undercutting the usual city price.

Cotton-weaving is a major household activity around this forested, sultry island, and there is a central market off the highway so you don't have to go from place to place comparing prices and fabric quality. At the market, prices for cloth and ready-made clothes are excellent if you bargain, and especially if you speak Thai. If you're more interested in observing the weaving process, take a walk down the road behind the market where virtually every other house has a hand-operated loom or two – listen for the clacking sound. As condo and vacation home developments gradually take over the island, the weaving villages may fade away.

There are also a couple of wát – **Khao Bo** and **Thai Yaw** – that are semi-interesting to visit. Along the main road through Ko Yo are several large seafood restaurants overlooking Thaleh Sap. *Pornthip (☎ 074 331 864, 47/1 Th Ko Yo),* about 500m before the market, is reputedly the best.

Folklore Museum
สถาบันทักษิณคดีศึกษา

At the northern end of the island at Ban Ao Sai, about 2km past the Ko Yo cloth market, is a large folklore museum *(☎ 074 331 185; admission 50B; open 8.30am-5.30pm)* run by the Institute of Southern Thai Studies, a division of Si Nakharinwirot University. Opened in 1991, the complex of Thai-style pavilions overlooking the Thaleh Sap Songkhla contain well-curated collections of folk art (about 75% with English labels), as well as a library and souvenir shop. Displays include pottery, beads, shadow puppets, basketry, textiles, musical instruments, boats, religious art, weapons, and various household, agricultural and fishing implements. Among these is a superb collection of coconut-grater seats carved into various animal and human shapes.

On the institute grounds are a series of small gardens, including one occasionally used for traditional shadow theatre performances, a medicinal herb garden and a bamboo culture garden.

Getting There & Away
From Hat Yai, direct Ko Yo buses – large wooden sǎwngthǎew – leave from near the clock tower on Th Jana throughout the day. The fare is 10B. Although the bus terminates farther on, it will stop in front of the cloth market on Ko Yo (ask for *nâa talàat,* 'in front of the market'). To get off at the museum, about 2km past the market, ask for *phíphíthaphan*. It takes about 30 minutes to reach the museum from Songkhla. Buses to Ranot pass through Ko Yo for the same fare.

Nakhon Si Thammarat- or Ranot-bound buses from Hat Yai also pass through Ko Yo via the new bridge system (part of Rte 4146) and will stop at the market or museum. Another way to get there is to take a Hat Yai–Songkhla bus to the junction for Ko Yo (7B), then catch the Songkhla-Ranot bus for 5B to the market or museum.

KO LOSIN
This dive site on a rocky islet around 80km east of Songkhla boasts more marine species than any other island in the Gulf of Thailand. Because of the island's distance from the mainland and relative isolation from major shipping lanes, the surrounding waters also feature superior visibility – up to 25m in May.

The reef surrounding the islet varies in depth from just below the water's surface to 40m; most of the coral garden (containing around 60 species of hard and soft corals) can be viewed within a range of 5m to 20m. Although trap fishing has had an adverse effect on the coral at Ko Losin, there are plans to make it a marine sanctuary. Whether or not such protection will be enforced is, of course, another story altogether, but if the Thai navy takes a serious interest in enforcement – as it has in the Similan and Surin islands, for example – then Ko Losin may benefit immensely.

In addition to myriad reef shark and smaller tropical fish varieties, divers may commonly encounter manta rays, hammerhead sharks and whale sharks.

Unless you have your own boat, the only feasible way to visit Ko Losin is by joining a live-aboard dive excursion. It takes around five hours to reach the island from Songkhla, so at least one night's stay is necessary. Starfish Scuba (☎ 074 442 170, e starfishscuba@starfishscuba.com), 166 Th Phattalung, offers charters to Ko Losin between June and September.

HAT YAI
หาดใหญ่

postcode 90110 • pop 143,600
Hat Yai, 933km from Bangkok, is Southern Thailand's commercial centre and one of the kingdom's largest cities, much larger in fact than the namesake capital of Songkhla Province. A steady stream of Malaysian customers keeps Hat Yai's central business district booming, but South-East Asia's current economic doldrums and the Malaysian government's ban on the exchange of Malaysian currency anywhere outside Malaysia, have slowed things down considerably. Still it's very much an international market town, and everything from dried fruit to stereos are sold in the shops along Th Niphat Uthit Nos 1, 2 and 3, near the train station.

Hat Yai is also a major transport hub for travel around Southern Thailand and between Thailand and Malaysia. Many travellers stop over in the city on their way to and from Malaysia.

Culturally, Hat Yai is very much a Chinese town at its centre, with loads of gold shops and Chinese restaurants. A substantial Muslim minority is concentrated in certain sections of the city, eg, near the mosque off Th Niphat Songkhrao.

Information
Tourist Offices The TAT office (☎ 074 243 747, e tathatyai@hatyai.inet.co.th), 1/1 Soi 2, Th Niphat Uthit 3, is open daily from 8.30am to 4.30pm. The tourist police

(☎ 074 246 733, ☎ 1155) is opposite the Florida Hotel.

Immigration The Hat Yai immigration office (☎ 074 243 019, 074 233 760) is on Th Phetkasem near the railway bridge, in the same complex as a police station. The nearest Malaysian consulate is in Songkhla.

Money Hat Yai is loaded with banks. Several after-hours exchange windows are along Th Niphat Uthit 2 and 3 near the Th Thamnoonvithi (pronounced Thammanun Withi) intersection. If you have Malaysian ringgit the banks won't take them but many mid-range and top-end hotels have exchange windows that will.

Post & Communications Hat Yai's main post office is on Th Niphat Songkhrao 1, and is open 8.30am to 4.30pm weekdays and 9am to noon weekends. The adjacent telephone office is open 7am to 11pm daily. There is also a more convenient branch post office on Th Na Sathani, just north of the Hat Yai train station. A private packing service is conveniently available next door.

Dentnet, a dental service near the corner of Th Pratchathipat and Th Niphat Uthit 2, has quick terminals and can fill teeth as well.

Bullfighting
Bullfighting (*TAT office* ☎ *074 243 747, 500-800B per day, 100-200B per round; open 9am-4pm*), involving two bulls in opposition rather than a person and a bull, takes place as a spectator sport twice monthly in Hat Yai. Fights take place on the first Saturday of each month, or on the second Saturday if the first Saturday is a *wan phrá* (Buddhist worship day; full or new moon). The venue changes from time to time, but lately they've been held at Noen Khum Thong Stadium, west of the city on the way to airport (50B by túk-túk). On the first Sunday of each month another round is held in Klonggit district (between Hat Yai and Sadao).

Because the times and venues for these bullfights tend to change, check with the TAT office.

HAT YAI

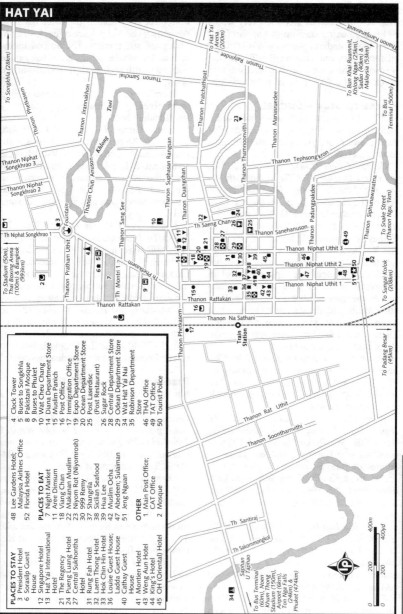

PLACES TO STAY
3 President Hotel
6 Sorasilp Guest House
12 Singapore Hotel
13 Hat Yai International Hotel
21 The Regency
24 Pueng Luang Hotel
27 Central Sukhontha Hotel
31 Rung Fah Hotel
32 Laem Thong Hotel
33 Hok Chin Hin Hotel
36 Louise Guest House; Ladda Guest House
40 Cathay Guest House
41 Montien Hotel
43 Weng Aun Hotel
44 King's Hotel
45 OH (Oriental) Hotel

48 Lee Gardens Hotel; Malaysia Airlines Office
52 Florida Hotel

PLACES TO EAT
7 Night Market
11 Aree Dimsum
18 Viang Chan
22 Makanan Muslim
23 Niyom Rot (Niyomrosh)
30 999 Remy
37 Shangrila
38 Sicilian Seafood
39 Hua Lee
42 Muslim Ocha
47 Abedeen; Sulaiman
51 Jeng Nguan

OTHER
1 Main Post Office; CAT Office
2 Mosque

4 Clock Tower
5 Buses to Songkhla
8 Pakistani Mosque
9 Buses to Phuket
10 Wat Cheu Chang
14 Diana Department Store
15 Muslim Panich
16 Post Office
17 Immigration Office
19 Expo Department Store
20 Ocean Department Store
25 Post Laserdisc (Post Restaurant)
26 Sugar Rock
28 Central Department Store
29 Odean Department Store
34 Wat Hat Yai Nai
35 Robinson Department Store
46 THAI Office
49 TAT Office
50 Tourist Police

Muay Thai

Thai boxing matches are held every weekend in the boxing stadium just north of Hat Yai's sports stadium. Admission is 180B for all foreigners and Thai men, 50B for Thai women. Times vary so it's necessary to check with the TAT to confirm the schedule.

Places to Stay – Budget

Hat Yai has dozens of hotels within walking distance of the train station. During Chinese New Year, prices double for most lower-end rooms.

Cathay Guest House (☎ *074 243 815, fax 074 235 044, 93/1 Th Niphat Uthit 2)* Dorm beds 90B, rooms 160-250B. This is one of the cheaper places, on the corner of Th Thamnoonvithi and Th Niphat Uthit 2 three blocks from the train station. The Cathay has become a travellers centre in Hat Yai because of its good location, helpful staff and plentiful information about onward travel, including tips on travel in Malaysia. It has a laundry service and serves inexpensive breakfasts as well as other meals (and the staff don't mind if you bring in take-aways to eat in the lounge). There is a reliable bus ticket agency downstairs with irregular hours.

Cheaper still are some of the older Chinese hotels in the central area. Rooms are very basic but they're usually secure and service is quite OK – you can get towels and soap on request.

Weng Aun (☎ *074 245 488, 127 Th Niphat Uthit 1)* Singles with shared facilities 120B. Weng Aun is an old Chinese hotel – one of Hat Yai's last remaining examples of Sino-Portuguese architecture – across from King's Hotel and four doors down from the Muslim Ocha restaurant. Rooms in this charmingly decrepit building are very basic.

Hok Chin Hin Hotel (☎ *074 243 258, Th Niphat Uthit 1)* Singles/doubles with fan, bath & TV 150/240B. A couple of blocks from the train station, this is a good deal. It has small but very clean rooms and a good coffee shop downstairs.

Rung Fah Hotel (☎ *074 244 808, 117/5–6 Th Niphat Uthit 3)* Rooms with fan/air-con 250/350B. Rung Fah is a renovated old Chinese place – typical of the older hotels in downtown Hat Yai that are trying to cater to Malaysian sex tourists. The air-con rooms here and at similar places are usually quite adequate, although the fan rooms can be noisy.

There's a rash of places in town calling themselves 'guesthouses' that are really small budget hotels.

Louise Guest House (☎ *074 220 966, 21-23 Th Thamnoonvithi)* Rooms with fan/air-con & hot water 320/400B. This apartment-style guesthouse has clean but small rooms. The advantage of staying in this kind of place is that they rely less on the short-time trade and are hence cleaner and less noisy.

Ladda Guest House (☎ *074 220 233, 13–15 Th Thamnoonvithi)* Rooms with fan 200-250B, air-con 300-350B. At Ladda, next to the Robinson department store near the train station, narrow stairs lead to tiny rooms; this is good value for air-con if the lack of fire exits doesn't frighten you away.

Sorasilp Guest House (☎ *074 232 635, 251/7-8 Th Phetkasem)* Singles/doubles with fan & cold bath 150/200B, with air-con 250/350B. Near the Songkhla bus stop off Th Phetkasem, this has clean rooms.

Places to Stay – Mid-Range

For some reason hotels in Hat Yai take a disproportionate leap upward in quality once you pay another 100B to 200B a night.

King's Hotel (☎ *074 234 140, fax 074 236 103, 126 Th Niphat Uthit 1)* Rooms with air-con, satellite TV & hot water 500-700B. This is a popular spot.

Laem Thong Hotel (☎ *074 352 301, fax 074 237 574, 46 Th Thamnoonvithi)* Rooms with fan & cold bath 250B, with air-con 400-600B. Not far from the train station, the rooms here are fairly noisy but comfortable. The hotel restaurant serves imported coffee, faràng breakfast and Thai dishes.

OH Hotel (Oriental Hotel; ☎ *074 230 142, fax 074 354 824, 135 Th Niphat Uthit 3)* Rooms with fan 250B, singles/doubles with air-con, TV, phone & hot water 450B. This has very good rooms in the new wing, cheaper and slightly grubbier rooms in the old wing.

Singapore Hotel *(☎ 074 237 478, fax 074 244 535, 62-66 Th Suphasan Rangsan)* Rooms with fan & bath 300B, doubles with air-con, satellite TV & hot water 400B. The rooms are comfortable and clean at the friendly, security-conscious Singapore.

Pueng Luang Hotel *(Pheung Luang; ☎ 074 244 548, 241-5 Th Saeng Chan)* Rooms with fan & bath 200-250B. This friendly place has spacious rooms.

Montien Hotel *(☎ 074 234 386, fax 074 230 043, 120-124 Th Niphat Uthit 1)* Rooms with fan 350B, with air-con 550B. The Montien is a large place that caters mostly to mainland Chinese visitors on package tours, and is hence a bit manic and boisterous.

Places to Stay – Top End

The top end in Hat Yai is mainly geared towards Malaysian-Chinese weekenders, which keeps rates considerably lower than in Bangkok or Chiang Mai.

Hat Yai International Hotel *(☎ 074 231 022, fax 074 232 539, 42-44 Th Niphat Uthit 3)* Rooms 550-1250B. This offers a variety of comfortable rooms with all the amenities. The hotel features a coffee house and restaurant with Thai, Chinese and European food, a disco and a traditional massage centre.

Lee Gardens Hotel *(☎ 074 234 422, fax 074 231 888, 1 Th Lee Pattana)* Rooms with satellite TV, phone, bath & fridge 690B. This is at the lower end of the top-enders – the clientele is mostly Malaysian families. On the downside, it's a few blocks away from most of Hat Yai's restaurants.

President Hotel *(☎ 074 349 500, fax 074 230 609, 420 Th Phetkasam)* Rooms 600B, including breakfast. This modern, new cement monolith, near the Songkhla share-taxi stand, has 110 rooms. This one's a bargain while the paint is fresh – though give it a few years and it'll be indistinguishable from the rest.

Florida Hotel *(☎ 074 234 555, fax 074 234 553, 8 Th Siphunawat)* Rooms 520B. Standing alone at the southern edge of the city centre, this tall white hotel has modern but well-worn rooms, along with the usual Chinese restaurant and massage centre.

The Regency *(☎ 074 353 333, fax 074 234 102, 23 Th Prachathipat)* Doubles 798-1872B. The 28-storey Regency has 438 rooms and suites stuffed with modern amenities. Facilities include a lobby lounge, coffee shop, dim sum restaurant, huge swimming pool with bar and a gym.

Central Sukhontha Hotel *(☎ 074 352 222, fax 074 352 223, 3 Th Sanehanuson)* Rooms 3000-17,000B. This is the nicest hotel in town, with spacious, fully outfitted rooms and suites; facilities include a swimming pool with snack bar, sauna, Chinese restaurant, 24-hour cafe, lobby lounge, fitness centre, business centre and shopping mall (with a branch of Central department store).

Places to Eat

Hat Yai is Southern Thailand's gourmet Mecca, offering fresh seafood from both the Gulf of Thailand and the Andaman Sea, bird's nest soup, shark fin soup, Muslim roti and curries, Chinese noodles and dim sum. Lots of good, cheap restaurants can be found along the three Niphat Uthit roads, in the markets off side streets between them, and near the train station.

Chinese Many Hat Yai restaurants, particularly the Chinese ones, close in the afternoon between 2pm and 6pm – unusual for Thailand.

Shangrila *(Th Thamnoonvithi)* Dishes 20-90B. Open 5am-3pm. Start the day with inexpensive dim sum at Shangrila. Specialities include khanŏm jìip (Chinese dumplings), *salabao* (Chinese buns) and *khâo nâa pèt* (roast duck on rice).

Hua Lee *(Th Thamnoonvithi)* Dishes 20-60B. On the corner of Th Niphat Uthit 3 and Th Thamnoonvithi, this is popular in the evenings and open until late.

Aree Dimsum *(116-118 Th Saeng Chan)* Dishes 10-15B. Open 6am-11am, 6.30pm-10pm. This is an excellent dim sum place.

Jeng Nguan *(☎ 074 246 031, 1/4-1/5 Th Niphat Uthit 1)* Dishes 30-40B. Open 11am-2pm, 5pm-9pm. This is an old feasting stand-by. Try the *tâo hûu thâwt kràwp* (fried bean curd), *hŭu chalăam* (shark-fin soup), *bàmìi plaa phàt* (fried noodles with fish) or *kíaw plaa* (fish wonton).

Several hotels in town also have good splurge-style Chinese restaurants, including JB Hotel's well regarded *Dynasty* (☎ 074 234 300-8, fax 074 243 499, 99 Th Chuti Anuson).

Malay & Indian There are a number of options for Malay and Indian food.

Muslim-O-Cha (Muslim Ocha; ☎ 074 244 009, 117 Th Niphat Uthit 1) Dishes 20-40B. Opposite King's Hotel, this is still going strong, with roti kaeng (roti chanai in Malay) in the mornings and curries all day. This is one of the few Muslim cafes in town where women – even non-Muslim – seem welcome. There are a couple of other Muslim restaurants nearby.

Makanan Muslim (Th Saeng Chan) Dishes 20-40B. On the corner of Th Saeng Chan and Th Prachathipat, this is a clean open-air place with roti and *mátàbà*.

Abedeen (☎ 074 231 865, Th Niphat Uthit 1) Dishes 20-40B. This is good for *tôm yam kûng* (spicy shrimp lemon-grass soup), a Thai speciality rendered in a slightly different way.

Sulaiman (Th Niyomrat) Dishes 20-40B. This has the best selection of dishes, including Indian paratha, dahl, chapatti, biryani, and various mutton, chicken, fish and vegie dishes.

Sicilian Seafood (Th Thamnoonvithi) Dishes 40-90B. Opposite the Laem Thong Hotel, this new place advertises 'Muslim seafood' as well as halal Indian specialities.

Thai Although Chinese and Malay food dominates in Hat Yai, there are a few Thai places as well.

Niyom Rot (Niyomrosh; 219-21 Th Thamnoonvithi) Dishes 40-120B. Open 10.30am-2pm, 5pm-9.30pm. The *plaa krabàwk thâwt* (whole sea mullet fried with eggs intact) is particularly prized here.

Viang Chan (12 Th Niphat Uthit 2) Dishes 20-60B. Open 5pm-1am. Although the name is Laotian, this serves Thai and

north-eastern Thai dishes along with Chinese fare. There is no roman-script sign.

999 Remy (12 Th Niphat Uthit 2) Just around the corner from the Laem Thong Hotel, this has a huge selection of curries and closes around 6pm.

Other Cuisine Adjacent to the Robinson department store on Th Thamnoonvithi are *KFC* and *Mister Donut*. A *McDonald's* restaurant can be found at the Lee Gardens Hotel.

Or for something very different, cruise down Th Ngu (Snake Street – Soi 1, Th Thung Sao), Hat Yai's most popular spot for snake fetishists. After a live snake is slit lengthwise with a scalpel, the blood is drained and drunk with honey, Chinese rice wine or herbal liquor. Besides the blood, also highly regarded are the heart, gall bladder and penis. Skins are sold as wallets, belts and other accessories, while the meat is boiled for soup. Rates for a snake-blood cocktail go for thousands of baht, but you can sample a bowl of snake soup for 150B. Snake Street is a 30B túk-túk ride south of the city centre.

Night Markets The extensive night market along Th Montri 1 specialises in fresh seafood, where you can dine on two seafood dishes and one vegetable dish for around 200B. There are smaller night markets along Th Suphasan Rangsan and Th Siphunawanat.

Entertainment

Post Laserdisc (Post Restaurant; ☎ 074 232 027, 82-83 Th Thamnoonvithi) Admission to movies 30B. Open noon-midnight. This is a music video/laserdisc restaurant/bar with an excellent sound system and well-placed monitors. It shows mostly Western movies, and programs change nightly – the fairly up-to-date music videos are fillers between the films. Drink prices are only a little higher than at the average bar. Meals, including breakfast, are served as well.

Sugar Rock (114 Th Thamnoonvithi) Open 8am-12am. Opposite the Post Laserdisc, this is one of the more durable

Hat Yai pubs, with good food, reasonable prices and a low-key atmosphere.

Shopping

Shopping is Hat Yai's No 1 draw, with most of the market action taking place along Th Niphat Uthit 2 and 3. Here you'll find Thai and Malaysian batik *(paa-té)*, cheap electronics and inexpensive clothing.

Muslim Panich *(17 Niphat Uthit 1)* This has an excellent selection of south Indian sarongs, plus Thai, Malay and Indonesian batiks; although the markets are cheaper they don't compare in terms of quality and selection.

Hat Yai has three major department stores on Th Niphat Uthit 3 (Diana, Ocean and Expo) and two on Th Thamnoonvithi (Odean and Robinson), plus the newer Central department store next to the Central Sukhontha Hotel.

Getting There & Away – Within Thailand

Air THAI operates flights between Hat Yai and Bangkok six times daily. The flights take 90 minutes and the fare is 2615B one way. There is also a daily THAI flight to Hat Yai from Phuket for 910B. THAI's office (☎ 074 233 433) in Hat Yai is at 166/4 Th Niphat Uthit 2.

Bus The green buses to Songkhla leave from outside the small clock tower on Th Phetkasem. Share taxis leave from around the corner near the President Hotel.

Air-con buses from Bangkok cost 520B (VIP 760B) and leave the Southern bus terminal at 7am, 4pm, 5.30pm, 6pm, 6.15pm, 6.30pm, 7pm, 8pm and 8.20pm. The journey takes 14 hours. Private companies sometimes have fares as low as 400B. Ordinary government buses cost 289B and leave Bangkok twice daily at 5.30pm and 9.45pm.

There are lots of buses running between Phuket and Hat Yai; ordinary buses cost 135B (eight hours) and air-con are 233B to 243B (six hours). Three daily buses go to Pak Bara (for Ko Tarutao) for 35B (three hours).

Cathay Tour (☎ 074 235 044), 93/1 Th Niphat Uthit 2, a travel agency downstairs from the Cathay Guest House, runs express air-con buses and minivans to Phuket (200B), Krabi (130B), Ko Samui (250B) and Surat Thani (130B). Other buses from Hat Yai include:

destination	fare (B)	hours
Ko Samui		
(air-con only)	240	7
Krabi		
(air-con only)	153	4
Narathiwat	55	3
(air-con)	72	3
Padang Besar	21	1½
Pattani	38	2
(air-con)	55	1½
Phattalung	35	2
Satun	32	2
(air-con)	45	1
Sungai Kolok		
(air-con only)	148	4
Surat Thani	103	6½
(air-con)	180	5½
Trang	50	2
Yala	50	2½
(air-con)	60	2

Travel agencies that arrange private buses include:

Cathay Tour (☎ 074 235 044) Ground floor, Cathay Guest House
Golden Way Travel (☎ 074 233 917) 132 Th Niphat Uthit 3
Hat Yai Swanthai Tours (☎ 074 239 621) 108 Th Thamnoonvithi
Pan Siam (☎ 074 237 440) 99 Th Niphat Uthit 2
Sunny Tour (☎ 074 353 060) Th Niphat Uthit 2
Universal On-Time Co (☎ 074 231 609) 147 Th Niphat Uthit 1

At least one company in the area has been known to engage in outrageous scams, including poor service and bait-and-switch tactics with buses, particularly on Ko Samui–Hat Yai and Hat Yai–Malaysia routes. The TAT are aware of the problem but some companies have high connections.

Share Taxi Share taxis are a good way of quickly getting from one southern province to another. There are several share-taxi stands in Hat Yai, each specialising in certain destinations.

In general, share-taxi fares cost about the same as for an air-con bus, but the taxis are about 30% faster. Share taxis also offer door-to-door drop-offs. The downside is that the drivers wait around for enough passengers (usually five) for a departure. If you hit it right the taxi may leave immediately; otherwise you may have to wait for half an hour or more. The drivers also drive at hair-raising speeds – not a pleasant experience for highly strung passengers.

There is one other small drawback associated with share taxis: the location of the taxi stands tends to change with annoying frequency. According to TAT, share taxis are semi-legal and therefore the locations of the taxi stands are somewhat fluid. When police inevitably crack down on one queue location, the share taxis move to another, usually just around the corner. TAT explains that locals all know where to look when the usual taxi stand has been abandoned. Unfortunately, visitors will be less than clued in. Therefore TAT suggests dropping by its office and asking about the current set up. You may also get this information from Cathay Tour, below the Cathay Guest House.

Train Trains from Bangkok to Hat Yai leave Hualamphong train station daily at 12.25pm (rapid No 171), 2.20pm (special express No 35, 1st and 2nd class only), 2.45pm (special express No 37), 3.50pm (rapid No 169) and 10.50pm (express diesel railcar No 41, 2nd class only), arriving in Hat Yai at 6.30pm, 7.05pm, 7.25pm, 9.45pm and 12.17pm respectively. The basic fare is 734B 1st class (express only), 345B 2nd class and 149B 3rd class. In the reverse direction to Bangkok you can take the 2.45pm (rapid No 172), 3.15pm (rapid No 170), 4.20pm (express diesel railcar No 42), 5.40pm (special express No 38) and 6.10pm (special express No 36), arriving in Bangkok at 8.35pm, 9.45pm, 6.35am, 10.35am and 11am respectively.

There are four ordinary 3rd-class trains per day between Hat Yai and Sungai Kolok (31B) and one daily to Padang Besar (10B).

The advance booking office at Hat Yai train station is open from 7am to 5pm daily. A left-luggage office (the sign reads 'Cloak Room') is open from 6am to noon and 1pm to 5pm daily.

Getting There & Away – International

Hat Yai is an important travel junction – almost any Thailand-Malaysia overland trip involves a stop here.

Air THAI flies from Hat Yai to Kuala Lumpur and Singapore. Malaysia Airlines flies from Penang; there are also Silk Air flights from Singapore.

THAI (☎ 074 233 433) has an office in the centre of town at 166/4 Th Niphat Uthit 2. Malaysia Airlines (☎ 074 245 443) has its office in the Lee Gardens Hotel, with a separate entrance on Th Niphat Uthit 1.

Hat Yai international airport has a post office with an IDD telephone in the arrival area; it's open from 8.30am to 4.30pm weekdays, 9am to noon Saturday. Other airport facilities include the Sky Lounge Cafe & Restaurant on the ground floor near the domestic check-in, a less expensive coffee shop on the 2nd floor departure level and foreign-exchange kiosks.

Bus From Padang Besar at the Malaysian border, buses cost 18B and take 90 minutes to reach Hat Yai. Buses run every 10 minutes between 6am and 7.20pm.

Cathay Tour (☎ 074 235 044), a travel agency downstairs from the Cathay Guest House, books express air-con buses and minivans to Penang (230B, four hours), Kuala Lumpur, Singapore and places in Thailand. Golden Way Travel (☎ 074 233 917, fax 074 235 083), 132 Th Niphat Uthit 3, runs VIP buses with reclining seats to Singapore for 450B including all meals; super VIP costs 550B.

Warning Care should be taken in selecting travel agencies for bus trips into Malaysia.

There are still reports of bus companies demanding 'visa fees' before crossing the border – since visas aren't required for most nationalities, this is a blatant rip-off. The offending company collects your passport on the bus and then asks for the fee – holding your passport hostage. Refuse all requests for visa or border-crossing fees – all services are supposed to be included in the ticket price.

Private Car Several travel agencies in town specialise in arranging a private car and driver for a quick trip to the border and back for those who need to cross the border to have their visas renewed automatically. The going rate for this service is 500B to 600B.

Share Taxi Share taxis are a popular way of travelling between Hat Yai and Penang in Malaysia. They're faster than the tour buses, although less comfortable and more expensive.

Big old Thai-registered Chevys or Mercedes depart from Hat Yai around 9am daily. You'll find them at the train station or along Th Niphat Uthit 1, near King's Hotel.

In Penang you can find them around the cheap travellers hotels in Georgetown. The cost is about 250B/24 Malaysian Ringgit – this is probably the fastest way of travelling between the two countries and you cross the border with a minimum of fuss.

From Hat Yai the fare to Padang Besar is 100B for the one-hour trip; taxis are on Th Duangchan.

Getting Around
To/From the Airport The THAI van costs 50B per person for transport to the city and there's also a private THAI limo service (☎ 074 238 452) that costs 200B.

A regular taxi costs 150B from the airport to the city and about 100B in the reverse direction.

Car Avis Rent-A-Car (☎ 074 352 222) maintains an office at the Central Sukhontha Hotel. You may also be able to arrange car rental through travel agencies in town.

Local Transport The innumerable săwngthăew around Hat Yai cost 10B per person. Watch out when you cross the street or they'll mow you down.

AROUND HAT YAI
Ton Nga Chang Falls
น้ำตกโตนงาช้าง

Also referred to as Elephant Tusk Falls, 24km south-west of Hat Yai via Hwy 4 in Rattaphum district, is a 1200m, seven-tier cascade that falls in two streams (thus resembling two tusks). If you're staying in Hat Yai, the falls make a nice break from the hustle and bustle of the city. The waterfall looks its best at the end of the rainy season, October to December.

To get to the falls take a Rattaphumbound săwngthăew (25B) from anywhere along Th Phetkasem and ask to get off at the *náam tòk* (waterfall).

Khao Nam Khang Tunnels
อุโมงค์ประวัติศาสตร์เขาน้ำค้าง

Located in the Khao Nam Khang National Park, this tunnel complex *(adult/child under 14 years 200/100B; open 9am-4pm daily)* was used by Communist Party of Malaysia (CPM) guerrillas as a base camp until they finally gave up the struggle in 1989. At least 1km of tunnels on three levels has been preserved and a portion of these have been widened to accommodate visitors. The underground base boasted conference rooms, a radio room, an operating room and, oddly, three long, straight passageways where the tunnel-bound communists could practice riding their motorbikes! The whole complex is said to have taken two years to build.

Park officials say that bungalows to accommodate visitors are planned for the future. In the meantime there is a small restaurant on the premises. To get here it is necessary to have a private vehicle as there are no public buses plying the route. From Hat Yai take Hwy 4 south toward Sadao, turning left at the Sadao district office and driving for another 26km. The tunnels are located about 4km beyond the park headquarters.

PATTANI
อ.เมืองปัตตานี

postcode 94000 • pop 42,200

Unlike most provincial capitals in the deep south, which tend to function as trading posts operated by the Chinese for the benefit (or exploitation, depending on your perspective) of the surrounding Muslim villages, Pattani has more of a Muslim character. In the streets, you are more likely to hear Yawi, the traditional language of Java, Sumatra and the Malay peninsula (the written form uses classic Arabic script plus five more letters), than any Thai dialect. The markets are visually similar to those in Kota Bharu in Malaysia.

Until the start of the 20th century, Pattani was the centre of an independent principality that included Yala and Narathiwat. It was also one of the earliest kingdoms in Thailand to host international trade; the Portuguese established a trading post here in 1516, the Japanese in 1605, the Dutch in 1609 and the British in 1612. A cosmopolitan collection of antique cannons unearthed at Pattani and now on display at the national museum in Songkhla attests to the competitive nature of trade in early Pattani. During WWII, Japanese troops landed in Pattani to launch attacks on Malaya and Singapore.

Although they can be somewhat difficult to reach, Pattani's beaches are among the most pristine in Thailand.

Orientation & Information

The centre of this mostly concrete town is at the intersection of Th Naklua Yarang, the road that runs north-south between Yala and Pattani harbour, and Th Ramkomud, which runs east-west between Songkhla and Narathiwat provinces. Intercity buses and taxis stop at this intersection. Th Ramkomud

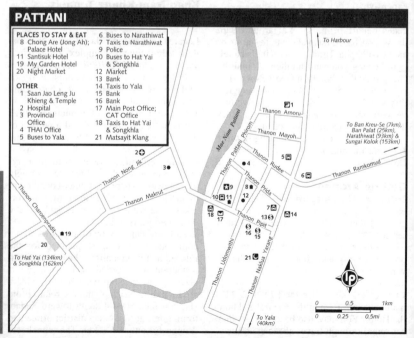

PATTANI

PLACES TO STAY & EAT	
8	Chong Are (Jong Ah); Palace Hotel
11	Santisuk Hotel
19	My Garden Hotel
20	Night Market

OTHER	
1	Saan Jao Leng Ju Khieng & Temple
2	Hospital
3	Provincial Office
4	THAI Office
5	Buses to Yala
6	Buses to Narathiwat
7	Taxis to Narathiwat
9	Police
10	Buses to Hat Yai & Songkhla
12	Market
13	Bank
14	Taxis to Yala
15	Bank
16	Bank
17	Main Post Office; CAT Office
18	Taxis to Hat Yai & Songkhla
21	Matsayit Klang

To Harbour

Thanon Arnoru

To Ban Kreu-Se (7km), Ban Palat (25km), Narathiwat (93km) & Sungai Kolok (153km)

Thanon Mayoh

Mae Nam Pattani

Thanon Pattani Phrom

Thanon Rudee

Thanon Ramkomud

Thanon Nong Jik

Thanon Prida

Thanon Makrut

Thanon Pipit

Thanon Charoempradit

Thanon Udomwithi

Thanon Naklua Yarang

To Hat Yai (134km) & Songkhla (162km)

To Hat Yai (134km) & Songkhla (162km)

To Yala (40km)

0   0.5   1km
0   0.25   0.5mi

crosses Th Yarang and then becomes Th Rudee, and it is along Th Rudee that you can see what is left of old Pattani architecture – the Sino-Portuguese style that was once so prevalent in this part of Southern Thailand.

Pattani's main post office is on Th Pipit, near the bridge. The attached CAT office provides an overseas telephone service daily between 7am and 10pm.

Several banks are found along the south-eastern end of Th Pipit, near the intersection with Th Naklua Yarang.

Mosques & Shrines

Thailand's second-largest mosque is the **Matsayit Klang**, a traditional structure with a green hue, probably still the South's most important mosque. It was built in the early 1960s.

The oldest mosque in Pattani Province is the **Matsayit Kreu-Se**, built in 1578 by an immigrant Chinese named Lim To Khieng who had married a Pattani woman and con-verted to Islam. Actually, neither To Khieng, nor anyone else, ever completed the structure.

The story goes that To Khieng's sister, Lim Ko Niaw, sailed from China on a sam-pan to try and persuade her brother to aban-don Islam and return to his homeland. To demonstrate the strength of his faith, he began building the Matsayit Kreu-Se. His sister then put a Chinese curse on the mosque, saying it would never be com-pleted. In a final attempt to dissuade To Khieng, she hanged herself from a nearby cashew-nut tree. In his grief, Khieng was unable to complete the mosque, and to this day it remains unfinished – supposedly every time someone tries to work on it, lightning strikes.

The brick, Arab-style building has been left in its original semi-completed form, but the faithful keep up the surrounding grounds. The mosque is in the village of Ban Kreu-Se, about 7km east of Pattani next to Hwy 42 at the 10km marker; a gaudy Tiger Balm Gardens-style Chinese temple has been built next to it.

The tree that Lim Ko Niaw hanged herself from has been enshrined at the **San Jao Leng Ju Kieng** (San Jao Lim Ko Niaw), the site of an important Chinese-Muslim festival in late February or early March. During the festival a wooden image of Lim Ko Niaw is carried through the streets; additional rites include fire-walking and seven days of vegetarianism. The shrine is in the northern part of Pattani towards the harbour.

Another festival fervently celebrated in Pattani is Hari Rayo, the Muslim month of fasting during the 10th lunar month.

Beaches

Pattani has some of the prettiest beaches in peninsular Southern Thailand. Because of the local Muslim culture, women visitors should wear T-shirts over their swimsuits when at the beach or swimming.

The only beach near town is at **Laem Tachi**, a cape that juts out over the northern end of Ao Pattani. You must take a boat taxi from the Pattani pier or Yaring district to get there. This white-sand beach is about 11km long, but is sometimes marred by refuse from Ao Pattani, depending on the time of year and the tides.

About 15km west of Pattani, **Hat Ratchadaphisek** (Hat Sai Maw) is a relaxing spot, with lots of casuarinas for shade, but the water is a bit on the murky side. Then there's **Hat Talo Kapo**, 14km east of Pattani, near Yaring district, a pretty beach that's also a harbour for *kaw-lae*, the traditional fishing boats of Southern Thailand. A string of vendors at Talo Kapo sell fresh seafood; during the week it's practically deserted.

About 50km north-west of Pattani is **Hat Thepha**, near Khlong Pratu village at the 96km marker near the junction of Hwy 43 and Rte 4085. Hwy 43 has replaced Rte 4086 along this stretch and parallels the beach. Vendors with beach umbrellas set up here on weekends. Places to stay at Hat Thepha are oriented towards middle-class Thais and almost no English is spoken here.

Sakom Bay Resort (☎ 073 238 966) Rooms with fan 300B, air-con 400-600B. The presence of a couple of English-speakers on the staff make this place the best choice for travellers. Rooms in a hotel-style building are cheapest and there are also comfortable air-con bungalows. An open-air restaurant that does seafood rounds out the offerings here.

Other places in the area include *Sakom Cabana*, *Club Pacific* and *Leela Resort*.

Any Songkhla-bound bus from Pattani can drop you off at the 96km marker for around 24B. From here it's less than 1km to the beach.

Other beaches can be found south-east of Pattani on the way to Narathiwat, especially in the Panare and Saiburi districts, where there are kilometres of virtually deserted beach. **Hat Chala Lai** is a broad white-sand beach 43km south-east of Pattani, near Panare. Eight kilometres farther towards Narathiwat is **Hat Khae Khae**, a pretty beach studded with boulders. Three kilometres north of Panare is **Hat Panare**, which is another colourful kaw-lae harbour.

If you have your own wheels, follow Rte 4136 along the coast south of where the broad Saiburi River empties into the Gulf.

Near Saiburi is **Hat Wasukri**, also called Chaihat Ban Patatimaw, a beautiful white-sand beach with shade. It's 53km from Pattani. You'll find long stretches of deserted beach starting around the 22km marker, a few kilometres before you reach the Narathiwat provincial border. The cleanest and prettiest stretch, **Hat Talo Laweng**, is found near a Muslim cemetery just south of the tidy Muslim village of Laweng, where you could probably rent rooms from local villagers. The people here make their living from fishing and coconuts. If you're heading north to Pattani, Rte 4136 veers off to Mai Kaen just before Laweng. None of these beaches are signposted but you can't miss them if you're on Rte 4136.

A good place to watch the building of kaw-lae is in the village of Pase Yawo (Ya-Waw), near the mouth of the Saiburi River. It's a tradition that is slowly dying out as the kaw-lae is replaced by flat-sterned boats painted in the same style.

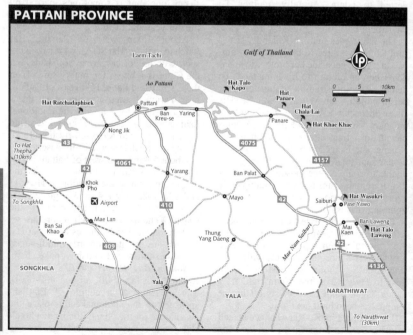

SOUTH-WESTERN GULF COAST

Places to Stay & Eat

Palace Hotel (☎ *073 349 171, fax 073 349 711, 38 Soi Talaat Tetiwat)* Rooms with cold bath & fan 140B, with 2 beds and air-con 340B. Off Th Prida, this is a decent place with fairly clean rooms.

Santisuk (☎ *073 349 122, 29 Th Pipit)* Rooms with fan/air-con & bath 200/350B. Santisuk has OK rooms but is something of a short-time hotel.

My Garden Hotel (☎ *073 331 055–8, fax 073 336 217, 8/28 Th Chareonpradit)* Rooms with 2 beds, fan & bath 300B, with air-con, hot shower, phone, cable TV & fridge 600-800B. A favourite with travelling businesspeople, the four-storey My Garden, about 1km outside town, is good mid-range value. The disco is very popular on weekends. Săamláw or săwngthăew drivers may know it by its former name, the Dina.

Chong Are *(Jong Ah; Th Prida)* Dishes 30-50B. Next to the Palace Hotel, this serves decent Thai and Chinese food.

A *night market* with plenty of food vendors convenes opposite My Garden Hotel nightly.

Shopping

Thai Muslims in Southern Thailand have their own traditional batik methods that are similar but not identical to the batik of north-east Malaysia. The best place to shop for local batik is at the *Palat Market* *(talàat nát paalát),* which is off Hwy 42 south-east of Pattani on the way to Saiburi in Ban Palat. The market is held all day Wednesday and Sunday only. If you can't make it to this market, the shops of Muslim Phanit and Nadi Brothers on Th Rudee in Pattani sell local and Malaysian batik at slightly higher prices.

Getting There & Away

Air Pattani has an airport, but since mid-1994 no flights have been available. However, Pattani's THAI office (☎ 073 349 149) at 9 Th Prida will check you in and take you to Hat Yai airport (110km away) as part of its service for no additional charge.

Bus & Share Taxi Pattani is only 40km from Yala. Share taxis cost 30B and take about 30 minutes; buses cost only 20B but take around an hour. From Narathiwat, a share taxi is 50B, minivan 60B and bus 30B. From Hat Yai ordinary buses cost 38B and air-con 55B.

From Bangkok there is only one ordinary bus departure at 6.30pm; the fare for the 17-hour trip is 285B. A 1st-class air-con bus departs at 10am and 6pm for 563B. In the reverse direction these buses leave Pattani at 2pm and 2.30pm.

Boat Certain boats between Songkhla and Pattani will reputedly take paying passengers – the fare depends on boat size.

Getting Around

Săwngthăew go anywhere in town for 8B per person.

NARATHIWAT
อ.เมืองนราธิวาส

postcode 96000 • pop 41,700
Narathiwat is a pleasant, even-tempered little town, one of Thailand's smallest provincial capitals, with a character all of its own. Many of the wooden buildings are a hundred years old or more. The local businesses seem to be owned by both Muslims and Chinese, and nights are particularly peaceful because of the relative absence of male drinking sessions typical of most provincial towns in Thailand.

Narathiwat is right on the sea, and some of the prettiest beaches on Southern Thailand's east coast are just outside town. A new promenade has been built along the waterfront at the southern end of town.

Local radio stations broadcast in a mix of the Yawi, Thai and Malay languages, with musical selections to match – everything from North-Eastern *lûuk thûng* to Arabic-melodied *dangdut*. Many signs around town appear in Yawi as well as Thai, Chinese and English.

Information

The main post office is at the southern end of Th Pichitbamrung. An attached international phone office is open daily from 7am to 10pm.

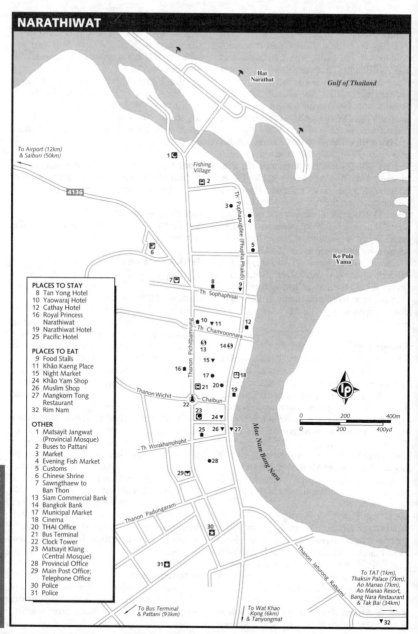

NARATHIWAT

To Airport (12km) & Saiburi (50km)

4136

Hat Narathat

Gulf of Thailand

Fishing Village

Ko Pula Yama

Th Puphapugdee (Phupha Plakdi)

Th Sophaphisai

Th Chamroonnara

Thanon Pichitbamrung

Thanon Wichit

Chaibun

Mae Nam Bang Nara

Thanon Padungaram

Th Worakhamphiphit

Thanon Jaturong Ratsami

0   200   400m
0   200   400yd

To Bus Terminal & Pattani (93km)

To Wat Khao Kong (6km) & Tanyongmat

To TAT (1km), Thaksin Palace (7km), Ao Manao (7km), Ao Manao Resort, Bang Nara Restaurant & Tak Bai (34km)

PLACES TO STAY
8 Tan Yong Hotel
10 Yaowaraj Hotel
12 Cathay Hotel
16 Royal Princess Narathiwat
19 Narathiwat Hotel
25 Pacific Hotel

PLACES TO EAT
9 Food Stalls
11 Khâo Kaeng Place
15 Night Market
24 Khâo Yam Shop
26 Muslim Shop
27 Mangkorn Tong Restaurant
32 Rim Nam

OTHER
1 Matsayit Jangwat (Provincial Mosque)
2 Buses to Pattani
3 Market
4 Evening Fish Market
5 Customs
6 Chinese Shrine
7 Sawngthaew to Ban Thon
13 Siam Commercial Bank
14 Bangkok Bank
17 Municipal Market
18 Cinema
20 THAI Office
21 Bus Terminal
22 Clock Tower
23 Matsayit Klang (Central Mosque)
28 Provincial Office
29 Main Post Office; Telephone Office
30 Police
31 Police

Beaches

Just north of town is a small Thai-Muslim fishing village at the mouth of the Bang Nara River, lined with the large painted fishing boats called *reua kaw-lae*, which are peculiar to Narathiwat and Pattani. Near the fishing village is **Hat Narathat**, a 5km-long sandy beach, which serves as a kind of public park for locals, with outdoor seafood restaurants, tables and umbrellas etc. The constant breeze here is excellent for sailboarding, though only the occasional visiting Malaysian seems to take advantage of this. Shade is provided by a mixture of casuarinas and coconut palms.

The beach is only 2km north of the town centre – you can easily walk there or take a săamláw. This beach extends all the way north to Pattani, interrupted only by the occasional stream or river mouth; the farther north you go, the cleaner and prettier the beach becomes.

Seven kilometres south of town, **Ao Manao**, is a pretty, curved bay lined with casuarinas. Vendors on the beach offer food and drinks, along with umbrellas and sling chairs. The locals believe Ao Manao to be the province's prettiest bay, but it's not as nice as some stretches of sand farther north or south.

Almost the entire coastal stretch between Narathiwat and Malaysia, 40km south, is sandy beach as well – so remote that the beaches don't even have names yet. Unfortunately there is no direct public transport to any of them. Either you must have your own transport or you'll have to try your luck getting off along the highway on the way to Sungai Kolok, then walk to the coast – which is often no more than a couple of kilometres away.

Matsayit Klang (Central Mosque)
มัสยิดกลาง

Towards the southern end of Th Pichitbamrung stands this old wooden mosque built in the Sumatran style. It was reputedly built by a prince of the former kingdom of Pattani, over a hundred years ago. Today it's of secondary importance relative to the newer Arabian modernist-style provincial mosque, at the northern end of town, but is architecturally more interesting.

Thaksin Palace
พระตำหนักทักษิณราชนิเวศน์

About 7km south of town, at the end of Ao Manao, is Tanyongmat Hill, where Thaksin Palace *(Phra Taksin Ratchaniwet; Th Narathiwat-Tak Bai; open 8.30am-4.30pm)* is located. The royal couple stay here for about two months between August and October every year. When they're not in residence, the palace is open to the public. The buildings themselves are not that special, but there are gardens with the Bangsuriya palm, a rare fan-like palm named after the embroidered sunshades used by monks and royalty as a sign of rank. There is also a small zoo and a ceramics workshop on the grounds.

A săwngthăew from town to the palace area is 5B. Săwngthăew services stop at sunset.

Wat Khao Kong
วัดเขากง

The tallest seated-Buddha image in Thailand is at Wat Khao Kong, 6km south-west on the way to the train station in Tanyongmat. Called Phra Phuttha Taksin Mingmongkon, the image is 25m high and made of reinforced concrete covered with tiny gold-coloured mosaic tiles that glint magically in the sun. The wát itself isn't much to see. A săwngthăew to Wat Khao Kong costs 5B from Narathiwat Hotel.

Golden-tiled Buddha on Khao Kong, Narathiwat

Narathiwat Fair

Every year during the third week of September, the Narathiwat Fair features *kawlae* boat racing, a singing dove contest judged by the queen, handicraft displays and *silat* martial arts exhibitions. Other highlights include per-formances of the local dance forms, *ram sam pen* and *ram ngeng*.

Places to Stay

The cheapest places to stay are all on Th Phupha Phakdi (signposted as 'Pupha-pugdee') along the Bang Nara River.

Narathiwat Hotel (☎ 073 511 063, 341 Th Phupha Phakdi) Rooms 100B. The best deal is this place, a funky wooden building that's quiet, breezy, clean and comfortable. The downstairs rooms can sometimes get a bit noisy due to the night trade – try to get an upstairs room. Mosquitos could be a problem – don't forget your repellent or mosquito coils.

Cathay Hotel (☎ 073 511 014, 275 Th Phupha Phakdi) Rooms with bath & fan 120B. An OK place, the quiet Cathay – signed in Yawi, English, Thai and Chinese – has spacious, clean, if somewhat cheerless, rooms. The elderly Chinese owner speaks good English. There's a view of the river from the roof.

Yaowaraj Hotel (☎ 073 511 320, 131 Th Pichitbamrung) Rooms with fan 160-220B, with air-con 360-400B. This hotel is on a busy corner and it's quite noisy.

Pacific Hotel (☎ 073 511 076, 41/1-2 Th Worakhamphiphit) Rooms with fan & bath 350B, with air-con 400B. The renovated Pacific has large, clean rooms.

Tan Yong Hotel (☎ 073 511 477, 16/1 Th Sophaphisai) Rooms with air-con 350-450B. Formerly Narathiwat's top-end accommodation, standards at this place have slipped in the last year or so. Then again so have the prices.

Royal Princess Narathiwat (☎ 073 515 041–50, 228 Th Pichitbamrung). Rooms 1900-21,000B, including breakfast. A new eight-storey place with all the amenities, in-cluding swimming pool, conference room and karaoke lounge.

Ao Manao Resort (☎ 073 513 640) Cot-tages with fan & bath 350-500B. Seven kilometres south of town at Ao Manao, this features large but closely spaced cement cottages in a small compound. It's about 400m from the beach.

Places to Eat

The *night market* off Th Chamroonnara be-hind the Bang Nara Hotel is good. There are also several inexpensive places along Th Chamroonnara, especially the *khâo kaeng place* next to the Yaowaraj Hotel, for cur-ries. A cluster of *food stalls* on Th Sophaphisai at Th Phupha Phakdi serve in-expensive noodle dishes.

On Th Phupha Phakdi at the north-west corner of a soi leading to the back of the Central Mosque, an elderly couple operate a *small shop* (in a wooden building with a tile roof) selling delicious and inexpensive *khâo yam* (rice salad with coconut, shrimp and lime leaves). Malay-style fried rice noodles are served on the side with each order. Curries and rice are also available at this shop. Other places in town have khâo yam in the morning, but this one's best so go early before they run out. Farther south on the same side of the street is a *Muslim shop* with *khâo mók* (chicken biryani) and duck over rice. Along Th Wichit Chaibun west of Th Phupha Phakdi are several inexpensive Muslim food shops.

Mangkorn Tong Restaurant (☎ 073 511 835, 433 Th Phupha Phakdi) Dishes 40-180B. This is a small seafood place that has a floating dining section out the back. The food's quite good and prices are reasonable.

Rim Nam (☎ 073 511 559, 45/6 Th Narathiwat-Tak Bai) Dishes 80-180B. This outdoor restaurant, 2km south of town, has good medium-priced seafood and curries.

Bang Nara (☎ 073 513 108, 61/7 Th Narathiwat-Tak Bai) Dishes 80-140B. South of Rim Nam is the similar but larger Bang Nara.

Shopping

Several batik factories near town will sell batik direct to visitors at decent prices. *JK Batik* (☎ 073 512 452, 96/3 Muu 8 Tambon Lamphu*)*, on the way to Wat Khao Kong, has good prices.

Getting There & Away

Air THAI has daily flights between Narathiwat and Bangkok, via Phuket. The fare to Phuket is 990B, to Bangkok it's

2575B. The THAI office (☎ 073 511 161, 073 513 090–2) is at 322-324 Th Phupha Phakdi. A THAI van between the office and the airport, 12km north via Rte 4136, costs 30B per person.

Bus & Share Taxi Share taxis between Yala and Narathiwat are 50B, buses 40B (with a change in Pattani).

Buses cost 30B from Pattani. From Sungai Kolok, buses are 25B, share taxis and minivans 40B. To Hat Yai it's 55B by bus (72B air-con), 130B by share taxi or 120B by air-con minivan; the latter leave several times a day from near the Yaowaraj Hotel.

To/from Tak Bai, a border crossing, it's 15B by săwngthăew (catch one in front of the Narathiwat Hotel) or 25B by taxi.

Train The train from Yala costs 13B for 3rd-class seats to Tanyongmat, 20km west of Narathiwat, then it's either a taxi (15B) or săwngthăew (13B) to Narathiwat.

Getting Around
Motorcycle taxis around town cost 10B to 20B. Wicker-chair săamláw from Malaysia are mainly used for carrying goods back and forth to the market; these cost 10B to 25B depending on the distance and load.

AROUND NARATHIWAT
Wadi Al Husen Mosque
มัสยิดวาดีอัลฮูเซ็น

The Matsayit Wadi Al Husen (Wadi Al Husen Mosque) is also known locally as Matsayit Song Roi Pi (200-year-old mosque), and is one of the most interesting in Thailand. Constructed in 1769 of Malabar ironwood, it mixes Thai, Chinese and Malay architectural styles to good effect. It's in the village of Lubosawo in Bajo (Ba-Jaw) district, about 15km north-west of Narathiwat off Hwy 42, about 10B by săwngthăew.

Wat Chonthara Sing-He
วัดชลธาราสิงเห

During the British colonisation of Malaysia (then called Malaya), the British tried to claim Narathiwat as part of their Malayan empire. The Thais constructed Wat Chonthara Sing-He (Wat Phitak Phaendin Thai) in Tak Bai district near the border to prove that Narathiwat was indeed part of Siam. As a result the British relinquished their claim.

Today it's most notable because of the genuine Southern-Thai architecture that's rarely seen in a Buddhist temple – the Thai-Buddhist equivalent of the Wadi Al Husen Mosque. A wooden wíhăan here resembles a Sumatran-style mosque. An 1873 wíhăan on the grounds contains a reclining Buddha decorated with Chinese ceramics from the Song dynasty. Another wíhăan contains murals painted by a famous Songkhla monk during the reign of King Mongkut (1910–1925). The murals are religious in message but also depict traditional southern-Thai life. There is also a larger, typical Thai wíhăan.

Wat Chon is 34km south-east of Narathiwat in Tak Bai. It's probably not worth a trip from Narathiwat just to see this 100-year-old temple unless you're a real temple freak, but if you're killing time in Tak Bai or Sungai Kolok this is one of the prime local sights. It's next to the river and the quiet, expansive grounds provide a retreat from the busy border atmosphere.

To get there from Narathiwat, take a bus or săwngthăew bound for Ban Taba and get off in Tak Bai. The wát is on the river about 500m from the main Tak Bai intersection.

SUNGAI KOLOK & BAN TABA
สุไหงโกลก, บ้านตาบา

These small towns in the south-east of Narathiwat Province are departure points for the east coast of Malaysia. There is a fair batik cottage industry in this district.

Be prepared for linguistic shock if you're coming from Malaysia. Not only are most signs in Thai script, but fewer people speak English in Thailand than in Malaysia.

Sungai Kolok
The Thai government once planned to move the border crossing from Sungai Kolok to Ban Taba in Tak Bai district, on the coast 32km

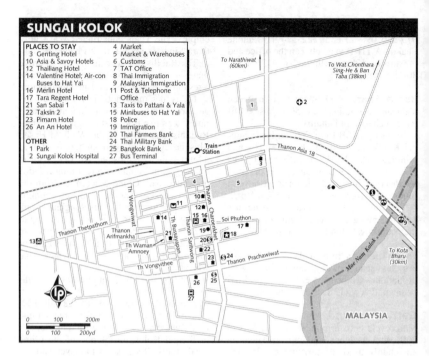

SUNGAI KOLOK

PLACES TO STAY
3 Genting Hotel
10 Asia & Savoy Hotels
12 Thailiang Hotel
14 Valentine Hotel; Air-con Buses to Hat Yai
16 Merlin Hotel
17 Tara Regent Hotel
21 San Sabai 1
22 Taksin 2
23 Pimarn Hotel
26 An An Hotel

OTHER
1 Park
2 Sungai Kolok Hospital

4 Market
5 Market & Warehouses
6 Customs
7 TAT Office
8 Thai Immigration
9 Malaysian Immigration
11 Post & Telephone Office
13 Taxis to Pattani & Yala
15 Minibuses to Hat Yai
18 Police
19 Immigration
20 Thai Farmers Bank
24 Thai Military Bank
25 Bangkok Bank
27 Bus Terminal

north-east. The Taba crossing is now open and is a shorter, quicker route to Kota Bharu, the first Malaysian town of any size, but it looks like Sungai Kolok will remain open as well for a long time. The Thais even maintain a TAT office next to the immigration post.

As a town it's a bit of a mess; prostitution is the second biggest industry. The rest of the economy is dedicated to Thai-Malaysia shipping; in the north-eastern part of town there's an entire district of warehouses that store goods moving between the countries.

The Thailand-Malaysia border is open from 5am to 5pm (6am to 6pm Malaysian time). On slow days officials may close the border as early as 4.30pm.

Information The TAT office (☎ 073 612 126), next to the immigration post, is open daily from 8.30am to 5pm.

The post and telephone office is on Th Thetpathom, while immigration is near the Merlin Hotel on Th Charoenkhet.

Places to Stay & Eat According to the TAT there are over 45 hotels in Sungai Kolok, most in operation to accommodate the weekend trips of Malaysian males, and bearing names like *Come In*, *Honey* and *My Love*. Of the cheaper hotels, only a handful are under 200B and they're mainly for those crossing for a couple of hours. So if you have to spend the night here it's best to pay a little more and get away from the short-time trade.

Most places in Sungai Kolok will take Malaysian ringgit as well as Thai baht for food or accommodation.

The cheapest places are along Th Charoenkhet.

Thailiang Hotel (☎ 073 611 132, 12 Th Charoenkhet) Rooms 220B. Thailiang is clean but noisy.

Pimarn Hotel (☎ 073 611 464, 76-4 Th Charoenkhet) Rooms with fan & bath 150B, with TV 200B. This is good value.

Valentine Hotel (☎ 073 611 229, 2/1 Th Waman Amnoey) Rooms with fan 180B, with air-con 280-350B. On the corner of Th Thetpathom and Th Waman Amnoey is the pleasant Valentine. There's a coffee shop downstairs.

Other reasonably decent hotels in the 150B to 200B range include *An An Hotel* (☎ 073 611 058, 183/1-2 Th Prachawiwat), *Taksin 2* (☎ 073 611 088, 4 Th Prachasamran) and the cheaper *San Sabai 1* (☎ 073 612 157, 32/34 Th Bussayapan). Some of these offer air-con rooms for 300B to 400B.

Mid-range and top-end hotels in Sungai Kolok include *Genting Hotel* (☎ 073 613 231, fax 073 611 259, Asia Hwy 18), from 500B; *Merlin Hotel* (☎ 073 611 003, fax 073 611 431, 40 Th Charoenkhet), from 350B; and *Tara Regent Hotel* (☎ 073 611 401, fax 073 611 801, Soi Phuthon, Th Charoenkhet), from 400B.

The town has plenty of food stalls selling Thai, Chinese and Malaysian food. There's a good Chinese *vegetarian restaurant* between the Asia and Savoy hotels that's open daily from 7am to 6pm. A cluster of reliable *Malay food vendors* can be found at the market and in front of the train station.

Getting There & Away Air-con buses to/from Bangkok cost 646B, take 18 hours and depart from Bangkok at 6.30pm (from Sungai Kolok at 1.30pm). At 9pm a 2nd-class bus departs from Bangkok (503B). A VIP bus from Bangkok leaves at 5.30pm (1005B). In the reverse direction the bus leaves at 12.30pm.

To Surat Thani, standard buses cost 155B (taking 10 hours), air-con 285B (nine hours).

Share taxis from Yala to Sungai Kolok cost 70B, from Narathiwat 40B; in Sungai Kolok the taxi stand is at the western end of Th Thetpathom. There are also buses from Narathiwat for 25B (35B air-con). From Sungai Kolok taxis to Narathiwat leave from near the train station.

Air-con buses to Hat Yai leave from the Valentine Hotel twice in the morning and twice in the afternoon (148B). From Hat Yai, departure times are similar. The trip takes about four hours. Share taxis to Hat Yai leave from next to the Thailiang Hotel (130B).

The rapid No 171 train leaves Bangkok at 12.25pm and arrives at 10am the next day. The daily special express No 37 to Sungai Kolok departs from Bangkok at 2.45pm and arrives at 10.55am the next day. These trains have 1st/2nd/3rd-class fares for 893/417/180B, excluding the special express or rapid surcharges of 80B or 40B (and 1st- or 2nd-class sleeping berths).

You can also get trains to Sungai Kolok from Yala and Tanyongmat (for Narathiwat), but buses are much faster and more convenient along these routes.

From Sungai Kolok to points farther north (via Yala), however, the train is a reasonable alternative. A train to Hat Yai takes about 4½ hours and costs 31B for a 3rd-class seat, 75B for 2nd class.

Local train Nos 448 and 452 leave Sungai Kolok at 6.30am and 8.55am, arriving in Hat Yai at 11.30am and 1.45pm. You won't find these trains listed on your English train timetable.

From Sungai Kolok special express No 38 leaves at 2.05pm and arrives in Bangkok at 10.35am the next day, with stops in Hat Yai (5.40pm), Surat Thani (10.38pm) and Hua Hin (6.08am), among other towns along the way.

Getting Around The border is about 1km from the centre of Sungai Kolok or the train station. Transport around town is by motorcycle taxi – it's 20B for a ride to the border. Coming from Malaysia, just follow the old train tracks to your right, or, for the town, turn left at the first junction and head for the high-rises. From Rantau Panjang (Malaysian side), a share taxi to Kota Bharu will cost about 5 Malaysian ringgit per person (or 20 ringgit to charter the whole car) and takes around an hour. To Kota Bharu it costs 3.50 ringgit on the regular yellow and orange bus.

Ban Taba

Ban Taba, 5km south of bustling Tak Bai, is a blip of a town with a large market and a few hotels. Takbai Border House, a large customs complex built in the hope of diverting traffic from Sungai Kolok, is underused and neglected. From the customs and market area you can see Malaysia across Sungai Kolok.

A few hundred metres north of the complex, **Hat Taba** is a beach park of sorts planted with casuarinas and bearing a few open-air shelters. You can change money at street vendors by the ferry on the Thai side.

A ferry across the river into Malaysia is 10B. The border crossing here is open the same hours as in Sungai Kolok. From the Malaysian side you can get buses direct to Kota for 2.50 ringgit.

Places to Stay *Masaya Resort (☎ 073 581 125, 58/7 Th Meuang Mai)* Rooms with fan & bath 150-250B, with air-con 350B, with air-con & TV 400B. This is set back off the road leading to the Malaysian border and is a bit difficult to find (a motorcycle taxi for 10B will get you there). It has comfortable rooms.

Pornphet (☎ 073 581 331) Rooms with fan 150B, air-con 350B. A motel-like place near the beach north of Taba, this isn't bad for the price.

Takbai Lagoon Resort (☎ 073 581 478) Bungalows with air-con 500B. Newly opened, this is the best choice in this area due to the clean and comfortable rooms and excellent restaurant.

Northern Andaman Coast (Ranong to Phuket)

Stretching from the Isthmus of Kra south to Ko Phuket and Ao Phang-Nga, Thailand's Northern Andaman Coast probably offers more geographic variety than any other coastal stretch in the country. Pristine, little-visited mangrove forests in Ranong Province, the remote oceanic island groups of Surin and Similan, the quiet beaches around Khao Lak and the international jet-set destination of Phuket are all encompassed within this relatively compact area.

RANONG
อ.เมืองระนอง

postcode 85000 • pop 18,500

The small capital and port of Ranong is only separated from Myanmar (Burma) by Pak Chan, the estuary of the Chan River. Burmese residents from nearby Kawthoung (Ko Song) hop across to trade in Thailand or to work on fishing boats. Many Burmese now reside in Ranong as well, and you'll see lots of men wearing the Burmese *longyi*, a long plaid cotton sarong. Although there are no great cultural attractions in town, the buildings are architecturally interesting since this area was originally settled by Hokkien Chinese. Ranong also has a lively, friendly appeal that makes it easy to while away a day or two just strolling about, poking around the market and visiting a Hokkien coffee shop or two.

Beaches with tourist facilities include nearby Hat Chandamri and the coastal islands of Ko Chang and Ko Phayam; see the Around Ranong and Laem Son National Park sections for details.

Tourists, mostly of Asian origin, are beginning to use Ranong as a gateway to Kawthoung and Thahtay Island. Several Phuket-based dive tour operators arrange live-aboard dive excursions to various islands and reefs off the southern tip of Myanmar, using Ranong as a launching point.

Highlights

- The Similan and Surin Islands National Marine Parks have Thailand's best coral colonies and are world-famous for their magnificent diving and snorkelling.

- The sea cliffs, beaches, estuaries and forested valleys of Khao Lak/Lam Ru National Park contain an exotic array of wildlife, including the Asiatic black bear, drongos and tapirs.

- Rent a canoe and take a guided tour through the caves and grottoes of Ao Phang Nga's myriad jungle-clad islands.

- Phuket, one of Thailand's most popular beach destinations, has world-class diving and yachting, a unique cuisine, lively markets and cosmopolitan nightlife.

- Ko Yao Yai and Ko Yao Noi are covered with rubber and palm plantations, and offer a taste of the unhurried island lifestyle that's all but disappeared from more developed islands.

- Friendly Ranong town boasts hot springs at Wat Tapotaram, where you can bathe in rustic rooms Thai style, as well as being a gateway to Myanmar.

Information

Ranong is about 600km south of Bangkok and 300km north of Phuket. Most of Ranong's banks are on Thanon (Th) Tha Meuang (the road to the fishing pier), near the intersection with Th Ruangrat. The main post office is on Th Dap Khadi, while the Communications Authority of Thailand (CAT) telephone office is off Th Phoem Phon in the south of town. There is also a Telephone Organization of Thailand (TOT) office in Th Ruangrat at the northern end of town.

Chaon Thong Food & Drinks, 8–10 Th Ruangrat, dispenses good travel information. The proprietor, Khun Thongsook, is quite knowledgeable and speaks English.

The proprietors of JT Food & Ice, also on Th Ruangrat, opposite the old post office, are also flush with information about accommodation possibilities on Ko Chang and Ko Phayam.

Kay-Kai (☎ 077 812 967), a restaurant near the cinema on Th Ruangrat, has Ranong's fastest computers for email and Internet access.

Immigration The main Thai immigration office can be found on the road to Saphaan Plaa, about halfway between town and the main piers, across from a branch of Thai Farmer's Bank. There is also a smaller immigration post in the vicinity of the Saphaan Plaa pier. If you're just going in and out of Kawthoung, Myanmar, for the day, a visit to the small post will suffice. However if you're entering Thailand from Myanmar via Kawthoung, you'll have to visit the larger office to get your passport stamped with a visa on arrival.

Nai Khai Ranong
ในค่ายระนอง

During the reign of King Rama V, a Hokkien named Koh Su Chiang became governor of Ranong (thus gaining the new name Phraya Damrong Na Ranong). His former residence, Nai Khai Ranong *(Th Ruangrat; open 9am-4.30pm),* has become a combination clan house (clubhouse for Chinese who share the

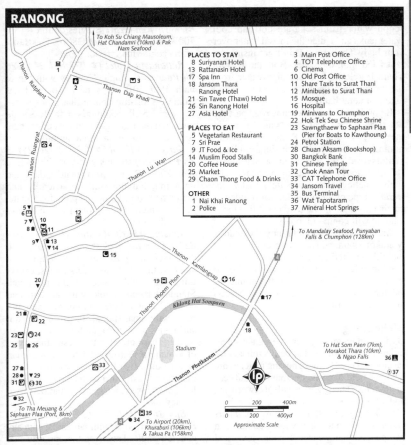

RANONG

To Koh Su Chiang Mausoleum,
Hat Chandamri (10km) & Pak
Nam Seafood

PLACES TO STAY
8 Suriyanan Hotel
13 Rattanasin Hotel
17 Spa Inn
18 Jansom Thara
Ranong Hotel
21 Sin Tavee (Thawi) Hotel
26 Sin Ranong Hotel
27 Asia Hotel

PLACES TO EAT
5 Vegetarian Restaurant
7 Sri Prae
9 JT Food & Ice
14 Muslim Food Stalls
20 Coffee House
25 Market
29 Chaon Thong Food & Drinks

OTHER
1 Nai Khai Ranong
2 Police

3 Main Post Office
4 TOT Telephone Office
6 Cinema
10 Old Post Office
11 Share Taxis to Surat Thani
12 Minibuses to Surat Thani
15 Mosque
16 Hospital
19 Minivans to Chumphon
22 Hok Tek Seu Chinese Shrine
23 Sawngthaew to Saphaan Plaa
(Pier for Boats to Kawthoung)
24 Petrol Station
28 Chuan Aksam (Bookshop)
30 Bangkok Bank
31 Chinese Temple
32 Chok Anan Tour
33 CAT Telephone Office
34 Jansom Travel
35 Bus Terminal
36 Wat Tapotaram
37 Mineral Hot Springs

same surname) and shrine. It's on the northern edge of town and is worth a visit.

Of the three original buildings, one still stands and is filled with mementoes of the Koh family glory days. The main gate and part of the original wall also remain. Koh Su Chiang's great-grandson Koh Sim Kong is the caretaker; he speaks some English.

Several shophouses on Th Ruangrat preserve this old Hokkien style. Koh Su Chiang's mausoleum (Susăan Jâo Meuang Ranong) is set into the side of a hill a few hundred metres north, on the road to Hat Chandamri.

Hot Springs & Wat Hat Som Paen
บ่อน้ำร้อน/วัดหาดส้มแป้น

About 1km east of the Jansom Thara Ranong Hotel is the Ranong Mineral Hot Springs at Wat Tapotaram *(Th Kamlangsap; open 8am-5pm)*. The water temperature hovers around 65°C, hot enough to boil eggs. The names of the three springs translate to Father Spring, Mother Spring and Baby Spring and each spring is said to have a distinct flavour. The spring water is thought to be sacred as well as having miraculous healing powers.

You can bathe in rustic rooms where you scoop water from separate hot and cool water tanks and sluice the mixed water over your body Thai style. Don't get inside the tanks and spoil the water. Both the Jansom Thara Hotel and Spa Inn pipe water from the springs into the hotels, where you can take a mineral bath.

If you continue on the same road past the hot springs for about 7km, you'll come to the village of Hat Som Paen, a former tin-mining community. At Wat Hat Som Paen, visitors feed fruit to the huge black carp (*plaa phluang*) in the temple stream. The faithful believe these carp are actually *the-wada*, a type of angel, and it's forbidden to catch and eat them. Legend has it that those who do will contract leprosy.

Another 3km down a bumpy dirt road is **Morakot Thara**, an emerald-green reservoir that fills an old tin quarry. Although tin production in Ranong has slackened off due to the depressed global market, the mining of calcium compounds, used to make porcelain, is still profitable.

Kickboxing

During certain festivals, eg, the annual Vegetarian Festival in September/October, old-fashioned Thai-Burmese boxing matches are held in a field opposite the municipal offices in Ranong. There are usually between six and 12 bouts on any given evening's schedule. This fighting style is known as *muay khàat che ak*; contestants wrap their hands in hemp rather than wearing boxing gloves and follow pre-Queensbury rules.

Places to Stay

Asia Hotel (☎ 077 811 113, 39/9 Th Ruangrat) Rooms with fan & bath 250-300B, with air-con 580B. Near the market, this has spacious clean rooms. Information on local islands is posted in the lobby.

Sin Ranong Hotel (☎ 077 811 454, 24/24 Th Ruangrat) Singles/doubles with fan 180/200B, with air-con 350/400B. This is across from the market with adequate rooms. It's a short-time place, but doesn't get too much traffic except on weekends.

Sin Tavee Hotel (*Thawi*, ☎ 077 811 213, 81/1 Th Ruangrat) Singles/doubles 180/200B, with air-con 360/380B. This hotel offers somewhat inferior rooms.

Rattanasin Hotel (☎ 077 811 242, 226 Th Ruangrat) Singles/doubles with fan & bath 100/150B. This is a typical Thai-Chinese short-time place that looks worse for wear. Still, Ranong's a fairly sedate town and the Rattanasin reflects this. There is no sign; look for a green building.

Suriyanan Hotel (☎ 077 811 420, 281–3 Th Ruangrat) Rooms without/with bath & fan 120/140B. The Suriyanan is dark and decaying, but the staff are friendly and claim they don't allow any prostitutes in the hotel – which would explain why it always seems deserted.

Jansom Thara Ranong Hotel (☎ 077 823 350, in Bangkok ☎ 029 463 639, 2/10 Th Phetkasem) Rooms 660-1998B. Just south of the river this offers almost everything you could possibly want in a hotel. Standard rooms come with air-con and colour TV and there's in-house video, hot bath with spa (piped in from the hot springs), and a refrigerator stocked with booze. There are also two restaurants, one of which specialises in Chinese *dim sum* and noodles, two large mineral spas, a fitness centre, a disco, a coffee house/cocktail lounge, a swimming pool and a travel agency.

Spa Inn (☎ 077 811 715, 25/11 Th Phetkasem) Rooms with fan 250B, with air-con 450-550B. This is on the opposite side of the river from Jansom Thara Hotel, on Hwy 4. While the Jansom Thara seems to overshadow this place – Spa Inn's low-key atmosphere, friendly staff and access to the famed spring water makes it a favourite with visiting Thais.

Places to Eat

For inexpensive Thai and Burmese breakfasts, try the *market* on Th Ruangrat. Also along Th Ruangrat are several traditional *Hokkien coffee shops* with marble-topped tables and enamelled metal teapots.

Between the Rattanasin and Sin Tavee hotels (same side of Th Ruangrat as the Rat-

Regional Food Differences

For the most part, people living along the eastern and northern coasts of the Gulf of Thailand eat standard, central Thai cuisine as found in Bangkok and the surrounding Chao Phraya River Valley. From Chumphon Province south, on both sides of the Thai-Malay peninsula, you'll find yourself in the domain of southern Thai cuisine – *aahǎan pàktâi*. One of the major hallmarks of this style of cooking is that curries are generally hotter – sometimes much hotter, sometimes only marginally – than their counterparts elsewhere in the country. One of the most notorious is *kaeng tai plaa*, a thick, yellow fish curry that, when prepared in the typical style, will leave all but the most chilli-habituated *faràng* weeping.

Another southern Thai speciality – particularly in Trang and Phuket – is *khǎnom jiin náam yaa*, a thin, yellowish fish curry served over white wheat noodles. Several Malay- and Indian-style curries are also available in the South, and these tend to be milder than most Thai curries. In the four southernmost, Muslim-dominated provinces you may come across *roti kaeng*, a breakfast dish that consists of *roti* – a fried flatbread similar to India's paratha – dipped in a mild curry gravy (*kaeng*). Served with jam, chocolate or fruit fillings, roti is also a common street vendor food throughout the South – Nakhon Si Thammarat is known to have the best sweet roti.

For breakfast the most typical southern Thai dish is *khâo yam*, a delicious concoction of room-temperature rice, chopped lemon grass and lime leaves, bean sprouts, dried shrimp, toasted coconut and powdered red chilli served with a salty-sour-sweet tamarind sauce – sort of a southern-style rice salad.

Joe Cummings

tanasin) are three modest **Muslim food stalls** where you can get Malaysian-style curry, rice and *roti*.

Coffee House *(Th Ruangrat)* Dishes 30-60B. This is a tiny place that serves Western-style breakfasts and light meals.

Just north of the cinema on Th Ruangrat is a small *vegetarian restaurant* serving inexpensive Thai vegie dishes; it's open Monday to Saturday from around 7am to 6pm.

Sri Prae *(☎ 077 833 141, 313/2 Th Ruangrat)* Dishes 60-150B. The moderately priced Sri Prae is very popular with locals for its stuffed crab and other seafood.

Chaon Thong Food & Drinks *(☎ 077 834 150, 8–10 Th Ruangrat)* Dishes 30-60B. Open 6am–9.30pm. This clean, aircon place serves inexpensive Thai food and Western breakfasts.

JT Food & Ice *(Th Ruangrat)* Dishes 20-80B. Opposite the old post office, this aircon place serves ice cream and Thai versions of Western food. The restaurant fills up with Thai families on Sunday afternoons.

Mandalay Seafood *(☎ 077 822 340, Th Phetkasem)* A couple of kilometres north of town on Highway (Hwy) 4, between Caltex and PT petrol stations, this place specialises in Burmese and Thai-style seafood.

Pak Nam Seafood *(☎ 077 812 497, Th Pak Nam)* Main meals 80-160B. On the road to Hat Chandamri, this serves delicious and relatively inexpensive Thai seafood in a terraced dining area overlooking the seaside.

Getting There & Away

Air Ranong airport is 20km south of town off Hwy 4. Bangkok Airways is the only carrier, with four flights weekly. The two-hour flight from Bangkok costs 2280B one way (half that for children). Bangkok Airways' Ranong office (☎ 077 835 096–7) is at 50/18 Mu 1, Th Phetkasem, about 5km south of town on Hwy 4, near the 616km marker. You can also purchase Bangkok Airways tickets inside Chaon Thong Food & Drinks in town.

Bus You can get to Ranong via Chumphon (40B, 60B air-con), Surat Thani (80B, 120B air-con), Takua Pa (54B, 80B air-con) and Phuket (91B, 170B air-con). The bus terminal is on Hwy 4 near the Jansom Thara Hotel, but buses stop in town on Th Ruangrat (passengers flag them anywhere along Th Ruangrat) before proceeding on to the terminal. *Sǎwngthǎew* No 2 passes the terminal.

To/from Bangkok, ordinary buses cost 160B, 2nd-class air-con 230B, 1st-class air-con 302B, VIP 470B. Air-con buses depart usually once in the morning and three or four times in the afternoon or evening. From Ranong, Chok Anan Tour (☎ 077 811 337) on Th Phoem Phon, operates 1st-class air-con buses to Bangkok at 8am and 8pm daily for 302B, as well as a VIP bus at 8pm for 350B.

Air-con minibuses run between Ranong and Surat Thani for 130B. Departure from Ranong's Th Lu Wan (near the Rattanasin Hotel) is at about 8am, arriving in Surat Thani at about noon. From Surat Thani the bus leaves at about 1pm and returns to Ranong at 4pm. You can also catch share taxis to Surat Thani for the same fare at the north-east corner of the intersection of Th Lu Wan and Th Ruangrat.

Daily air-con minibuses to Chumphon cost 80B and depart hourly between 7am and 5.30pm from Th Phoem Phon near the hospital. Buses to Chumphon have the letters 'CTR' printed on the back.

Buses to Khuraburi from Ranong cost 37B and take one hour and 20 minutes. Other routes include Khao Lak (35B ordinary, 60B air-con) and Phang-Nga (70B ordinary, 120B air-con).

Getting Around

Săwngthăew ply the roads around Ranong and out to the hot springs and Hat Som Paen (No 2), Hat Chandamri (No 3) and Saphaan Plaa (No 2). The fare is 8B to any of these places. See the Around Ranong section for details. Motorcycle taxis (look for the orange vests) will take you anywhere in town for 15B, or to the area around Jansom Thara Hotel for 20B.

Both Chaon Thong Food & Drinks and JT Food & Ice can assist with motorcycle and car rentals.

AROUND RANONG
Hat Chandamri
หาดชาญดำริ

Touted as the nearest beach to Ranong, Hat Chandamri is really more of a mud flat.

Jansom Thara Resort (☎ 077 821 611, fax 077 821 821) Bungalows 945-1200B. A sister hotel to the Jansom Thara in Ranong, this has similarly equipped bungalows (but no spas). From the dining terrace overlooking the bay you can eat seafood and watch the sun set over Kawthoung.

Hat Chandamri is 10km north-west of Ranong, about 50B by motorcycle taxi or 10B by săwngthăew.

Saphaan Plaa (Fishermen's Pier)
สะพานปลา

The provincial fishing port, Tha Thiap Reua Pramong, is 8km south-west of Ranong. It's called **Saphaan Plaa** for short and is always bustling with activity as fishing boats are loaded and unloaded with great cargoes of flapping fish. The fish traders buy from anyone who lands fish here, and about half the boats are Burmese. Boats can be chartered here for day trips to nearby islands. Unless you want to see heaps of fish or charter a fishing boat (or visit Kawthoung, see the following section), there's really no reason to go out to the port. Săwngthăew (No 2) ply the route between central Ranong and the port frequently during daylight hours for 8B per person.

Kawthoung (Ko Song)
วิคตอเรียพอยท์(เกาะสอง)

This lively, dusty port at the southern-most tip of mainland Myanmar is only separated from Thailand by a broad estuary of the Chan River. To the British it was Victoria Point and to the Thais it's Ko Song, which means Second Island. The Burmese name, Kawthoung, is probably a corruption of the latter.

The main business here is trade with Thailand, followed by fishing. Among the Burmese, Kawthoung is perhaps best known for producing some of the country's best kickboxers. Most residents are bilingual, speaking Thai and Burmese. Many people born and raised around Kawthoung, especially Muslims, also speak Pashu, a dialect that mixes Thai, Malay and Burmese.

Nearby islands are inhabited by bands of nomadic Moken (*chao náam*; sea gypsies).

At the moment Kawthoung is only accessible by boat from Ranong. It's probably not worth making a special trip to Ranong just to visit Kawthoung, but if you're in the area and decide to cross over, you'll find it's similar to Southern Thailand except that many more men wear the longyi. It is now legal to travel from Kawthoung into the interior of Myanmar – eg, Dawei (Tavoy), Myeik (Mergui) or Yangon – by plane or ship. Road travel north of Kawthoung, however, is forbidden by the Myanmar government due to security concerns – this is an area plagued by insurgents or bandits (sometimes one and the same).

Boats to Kawthoung leave the Saphaan Plaa pier in Ranong regularly from around 7am till 6pm for 50B. Take the No 2 săwngthăew from Ranong and when the vehicle stops to pay a toll at the entrance to the pier area, get off and walk down a *soi* to the right (you'll see a petrol station on your left). At the end of the soi are boats to Kawthoung, you can charter a boat holding six to seven people for 500B return.

Once the boat is under way, there's an initial stop at Thai immigration, where your passport is stamped. Then upon arrival at the Kawthoung jetty, again before leaving the boat, there's a stop at Myanmar immigration. At this point you must inform immigration authorities whether you're a day visitor – in which case you must pay a fee of US$5 or 300B for a day permit. If you have a valid Myanmar visa in your passport, you'll be permitted to stay for up to 28 days, but are required to buy US$200 worth of foreign exchange certificates (FECs).

Yangon Airways sometimes flies to Yangon for US$120. Their Kawthoung office is located at 1/1 Bogyoke Lan. By ship it's two nights (one night each is spent in Dawei and Myeik) – 36 hours total.

Organised Tours Jansom Travel (☎ 077 821 576, 077 835 317–8) on Th Phetkasem in Ranong offers Kawthoung and island tours aboard four boats with capacities ranging from 15 to 200 people. A half-day tour costing 750B per person (minimum of 10) sails from Ranong, visits a couple of pagodas in Kawthoung and returns to Ranong around 11am.

Places to Stay So far there are two places in Kawthoung itself that are approved to accept foreigners.

Honey Bear Hotel Rooms with satellite TV & cold shower 700B. Closest to the pier is the modern-and-friendly Honey Bear, which offers 24-hour power and clean rooms: not a great deal by Thai standards but it's a comfortable hotel.

Kawthoung Motel Doubles with cold bath US$25 or 1000B. Located about 300m beyond the main immigration office and about 500m from the pier, this is looking a bit shabby.

Andaman Club Resort (in Ranong ☎ 077 830 463) Rooms 1800-3200B, but if you happen to be a regular high roller, the casino will pick up your room tab. On nearby Thahtay Island (Thahtay Kyun in Burmese, also spelt Thahte or Thade – literally, Rich Man's Island), well-heeled Thai and Singaporean gamblers stay at this resort, a huge five-star hotel complex sporting a casino and a Jack Nicklaus-designed, 18-hole golf course. All rooms have sea views. Guests with bookings are able to take a boat direct from Jansom Thara Resort on Hat Chandamri, about 10km north-west of Ranong. If you're already in Kawthoung, you can catch a five-minute boat ride out to the island from the Kawthoung jetty for 100B.

Waterfalls

Of the several well-known waterfalls in Ranong Province, **Ngao Falls** and **Punyaban Falls** are within walking distance of Hwy 4. Ngao is 13km south of Ranong while Punyaban is 15km north. Just take a săwngthăew in either direction and ask to be let off at the *náam tòk* (waterfall).

Isthmus of Kra

คอคอดกระ

About 60km north of Ranong, in Kraburi district, is the Isthmus of Kra, the narrowest strip of land in Thailand, where barely 50km separates the Gulf of Thailand from the Andaman Sea. Just off Hwy 4 is a monument commemorating this geographical wonder. At one time the Thai government had plans to construct the so-called Kra Canal here, but the latest word is that the canal – if it's built – will run east from Satun Province through Songkhla, about 500km farther south.

Ko Chang
เกาะช้าง

Don't confuse this island off the coast of Ranong with the much larger Ko Chang in Trat Province. As with many of the islands in this area, estuarial effluent from the Chan River inhibits clarity in the surrounding Andaman waters, but natural mangrove on the east coast and a hilly, forested interior are attractions enough for some. Birdlife includes hornbills, sea eagles and Andaman kites.

A couple of trails meander around the island and so far there are no motor vehicles. Nor is there electricity – the few resorts on the island either do without or generate their own. Beaches are found along the western shore, and though they're not classic white-sand strands, regular visitors enjoy the laid-back atmosphere.

Bungalow operations on the island can arrange boat trips to Ko Phayam and other nearby islands for around 150B per person (including lunch) for groups of six or more.

Places to Stay & Eat Several beach places have opened up over the last few years, though for the most part they're only open from November to April. Some places that only a couple of years ago were offering bamboo huts are now rebuilding with concrete. Air-con can't be too far ahead in the future.

Ko Chang Contex (Ranong ☎ 077 833 137) Huts 100-200B. This is run by a Thai family and has an a-la-carte restaurant menu.

Eden Bistro Café Bungalows 100B, with shower 150B. This offers a few small bungalows and one large bungalow.

Sunset Bungalow Bungalows 150-250B. Just down the beach from Eden Bistro Café,

this offers nicely built bungalows in a shady, breezy spot.

Cashew Resort (☎ 077 824 741) Bungalows 200-500B. This is the oldest and largest place on the island. Recently renovated, the bungalows are now sturdy A-frames.

Eden, Cashew and Sunset will pick prospective guests up at JT Food & Ice in Ranong.

Chang Thong Bungalows (☎ 077 833 820) and *Pheung Thong (☎ 077 833 820)* Huts without/with bath 100/150B. A few hundred metres past the pier for boats from the mainland these friendly places, next door to one another, are run by a brother and sister. The restaurant at Chang Thong serves decent Thai food. Chang Thong often picks visitors up at Chaon Thong Food & Drinks in Ranong.

Ko Chang Resort Huts without/with bath 100/150B. This sits on a section of rocky – but shady – headland.

Sharing a small bay just beyond are newcomers *Lae Tawan* and *Ta Daeng Bay* with wood and concrete bungalows for 100B to 200B, as well as *N & X Bungalows* at the southern end of the island at Ao Lek (Small Bay), which offers wooden bungalows for 100B to 200B.

Getting There & Away From Ranong take a săwngthăew (red No 2, 6B) to Saphaan Plaa, getting off by the petrol station towards the main pier. Look for signs advertising Ko Chang bungalows and follow them down a zigzagging soi for a couple of hundred metres, where you'll find long-tail boats that run to Ko Chang. If you have a heavy bag a motorcycle taxi can bring you to this landing for 20B. Depending on the tides, two or three boats leave every morning from November to April; turn up around 9am to see when they're going; they don't usually leave before then. During the high season – December to March – there's a consistent 12pm departure daily. Boats return to Ranong at 8am the next day.

The cost is negotiable depending on how many passengers board; if you book a bungalow through Ranong Travel in town, you may get a free boat ride along with a ride down to Saphaan Plaa. Otherwise count on paying up to 100B per person.

LAEM SON NATIONAL PARK
อุทยานแห่งชาติแหลมสน

The Laem Son (Pine Cape) Wildlife & Forest Preserve *(admission 200B)* covers 315 sq km of the Kapoe district of Ranong and Khuraburi district in Phang-Nga. This area includes about 100km of Andaman Sea coastline – the longest protected shore in the country – as well as over 20 islands. Much of the coast here is covered with mangrove swamps, home to various species of birds, fish, deer and monkeys, including crab-eating macaques, often seen while driving along the road to the park headquarters. Sea turtles lay eggs on Hat Praphat.

The best-known and most-accessible beach is **Hat Bang Ben**, where the main park offices, restaurant and bungalows are. This is a long, sandy beach backed by shady casuarina trees and is said to be safe for swimming year-round. From Hat Bang Ben you can see several islands, including the nearby Ko Kam Yai, Ko Kam Noi, Mu Ko Yipun, Ko Khang Khao and, to the north, Ko Phayam. The park staff can arrange boat trips out to any of these islands for 800B per boat per day. During low tide you can walk to an island just a couple of hundred metres away from Hat Bang Ben.

Ko Phayam is inhabited by around 100 Thais, who mostly make their living fishing or growing cashews. There are good swimming beaches on Phayam and on the western side of some of the Kam islands, as well as some live coral. Ko Khang Khao is known for a beach on the northern end of the island that is covered with colourful pebbles. Although underwater visibility isn't great, it's a little better here than on Ko Chang as it's farther from the mouth of the Chan River. The beach on **Ko Kam Noi** has relatively clear water for swimming and snorkelling (April is the best month) plus the added bonus of fresh water year-round and plenty of grassy areas for camping. One island on the other side of Ko Kam Yai that

can't be seen from the beach is **Ko Kam Tok** (also called Ko Ao Khao Khwai). It's only about 200m from Ko Kam Yai, and, like Ko Kam Noi, has a good beach, coral, fresh water and a camping area. **Ko Kam Yai** is 14km south-west of Hat Bang Ben.

About 3km north of Hat Bang Ben, across the canal, is another beach, **Hat Laem Son**, which is almost always deserted. The only way to get there is to hike from Bang Ben. In the opposite direction, about 50km south of Hat Bang Ben, is **Hat Praphat**, very similar to Bang Ben with casuarina trees and a long beach. There is a second park office here that can be reached by road via the Phetkasem Hwy (Hwy 4).

In the canals you ford coming into the park, you may notice large wooden racks that are used for raising oysters.

Places to Stay & Eat
Camping is allowed anywhere among the casuarina trees for 10B per person (pay at the park unit just inside the park entrance).

National park bungalows (☎ 077 823 255, Bangkok ☎ 025 790 529) Per person 100B, houses with 10/16 beds 700/900B. These are dorm-like wooden houses. Similar park accommodation is also available on Ko Kam Yai and can be arranged in advance by contacting the above numbers.

Wasana Resort Bungalows with fan & bath 300B, with veranda 600B. A few hundred metres before the park entrance (9.5km from the Hwy 4 junction) is the private Wasana Resort. It has clean bamboo bungalows with mosquito nets and larger concrete bungalows with verandas.

Andaman Peace Resort (☎ 077 821 796) Bungalows 500-1000B. This offers five different styles of concrete bungalows. Discounts are given for long-termers.

Komain Villa Bungalows with fan & bath 250B. Just outside the park entrance, this offers small bungalows and not much else.

The food at the *park canteen* is quite reasonable, although *Wasana Resort* is the better choice.

Ko Phayam There are only a few places to stay on Ko Phayam.

Aow Yai Bungalow (☎ 077 821 753) Bungalows 100-150B. This is on the south-western side of the island on a curving beach. Wood and bamboo bungalows (with concrete bathrooms) are spaced rather close together. The kitchen does some wonderful things with fish though.

Bamboo Bungalows Bungalows with bath 100-150B. A stone's throw away from Aow Yai Bungalow, this place offers much the same set up, without the restaurant.

Payam Island Resort (☎ 077 812 297, in Bangkok ☎ 023 902 681) Bungalows with bath 1400-2200B, meals included. On the eastern side is the more expensive Payam Island Resort. Bungalows are of sturdy wood and concrete construction. This place has its own boat to transport guests from Ranong and is open year-round.

On a larger north-west beach, *Vijit Bungalow* (☎ 077 834 082) has wooden bungalows for 150B with private facilities. Sharing the same beach are *JPR Bungalow* and *Mr Gao Bungalow*, which have similar accommodation and prices. Mr Gao also has its own boat that can be hired for trips around the island.

On Ko Chang to the immediate north there are also several places to stay – see the earlier entry under Around Ranong.

Getting There & Away

The turn-off for Laem Son National Park is about 58km down the Phetkasem Hwy (Hwy 4) from Ranong, between the 657km and 658km markers. Any bus heading south from Ranong can drop you off here (ask for Hat Bang Ben). Once you're off the highway, however, you'll have to wait to flag down a pickup truck going towards the park. If you can't get a ride all the way, it's a 10km walk from Hwy 4 to the park entrance. At the police box at the junction you may be able to hire a motorcycle taxi for 30B. The road is paved all the way to the park, so if you're driving, it's a breeze.

Ferries to Ko Phayam leave Ranong's Saphaan Plaa for Ko Phayam at 2pm and arrive on the east coast at 4pm and on the west coast at 4.30pm. In the reverse direction they leave from Phayam's west coast at 7am and the east coast at 8am, arriving in Ranong around 10am. The ferry fare is 100B per person. Long-tail boats also make this route for 200B per person or 2000B for a charter. Sometimes the Ko Chang boats continue to Ko Phayam – inquire at Ranong's Jansom Thara Hotel, Ranong Travel or at Saphaan Plaa. Motorcycle taxis can be hired to cross the island for 100B.

Boats out to the various islands can be chartered from the park's visitors centre; the general cost is 800B per day. You can arrange to go as far as the Similan or Surin Islands (see later in this chapter) for 900B and 1200B per person respectively.

KHURABURI, TAKUA PA & THAI MUANG
กุระบุรี,ตะกั่วป่าและท้ายเหมือง

These districts of Phang-Nga Province are of minor interest in themselves but are departure points for other destinations. From **Khuraburi** you can reach the remote Surin and Similan Islands, or from **Takua Pa** you can head east to Khao Sok National Park and Surat Thani. (See the South-Western Gulf Coast chapter for details.) Takua Pa is also about halfway between Ranong and Phuket so buses often make rest stops here.

Extra Hotel (☎ 076 421 026, fax 076 421 412, 46 Th Senarat) Rooms with fan 180-200B, air-con 320B. The Extra is just off the highway and is really only recommended if you're driving and need to stop for the night – otherwise there's nothing to see or do here.

In the district of **Thai Muang** is Hat Thai Muang National Park, where sea turtles lay eggs between November and February. **Thap Lamu**, about 23km north of Thai Muang, has a pier with boats to the Similan Islands.

SURIN ISLANDS (MUU KO SURIN) NATIONAL MARINE PARK
อุทยานแห่งชาติหมู่เกาะสุรินทร์

A national park since 1981, the Surin Islands *(adult/child under 14 years 200/100B)* are

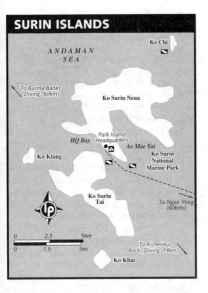

SURIN ISLANDS

ANDAMAN SEA

Ko Chi

To Burma Banks (Diving, 60km)

Ko Surin Neua

Park Island Headquarters

HQ Bay

Ao Mae Yai

Ko Klang

Ko Surin National Marine Park

Ko Surin Tai

To Ngan Yong (60kms)

To Richelieu Rock (Diving, 14km)

Ko Khai

0   2.5   5km
0   1.5   3mi

famous for excellent diving and snorkelling. The two main islands (there are five in all) of Ko Surin Neua and Ko Surin Tai ('North Surin Island' and 'South Surin Island') lie about 70km north-west of Khuraburi and less than 5km from Thailand's marine border with Myanmar. The park office and visitor centre are on the south-western side of the northern island at Ao Mae Yai, where boats anchor. Admission to the park is 200B for adults, 100B for kids under 14. Some of the best diving is said to be in the channel between the two islands.

On the southern island is a village of chao náam (sea gypsies). In April the chao náam hold a major ancestral worship ceremony, called Loi Reua. The island may be off limits during that time, so check first at the park office. Long-tail boats can be hired at Ao Mae Yai to take you to the southern island for about 200B per person for the day.

Compared with the Similan Islands to the south, Surin is more suited to visitors who are interested in hiking and exploring rather than solely diving. There are several hiking trails, especially on the northern island. Also, getting to some of the best reefs doesn't require scuba gear, another plus for non-

divers. Snorkelling gear can be rented at the park office for 150B per day.

Most visitors to the islands are Thai tourists, who tend to arrive in large numbers on national holidays. There also seems to be a fairly steady flow of tour groups, again mostly Thai, visiting from December to March, though most only stay a night or two. The main advantage of going at this time, especially if you're not a diver, is that you can probably catch a ride on one of the tour boats for 1000B return: at other times the only way out to the islands is chartering your own boat (which is costly) or joining a diving trip. The disadvantage of course is that accommodation can easily get booked up.

Surrounding the Surin Islands are the most well-developed coral colonies in Thai seas, according to Piprell & Boyd's *Diving in Thailand*, though the Similans boast a richer variety of fish species. There are seven major dive sites in the immediate vicinity of the Surin Islands, of which the best are found extending south-east from **HQ Bay** on Surin Neua; at **Ko Chi**, a small island off the north-eastern shore of Surin Neua; and at **Richelieu Rock**, a seamount about 14km south-east of Surin Tai. Whale sharks – the largest fish in the world – are reportedly spotted near Richelieu on 50% of dive trips, most commonly during the months of March and April. Snorkelling is excellent in many areas due to relatively shallow reef depths of 5m to 6m.

The so-called **Burma Banks**, a system of submerged seamounts around 60km north-west of the Surin Islands, are so prized by Thai dive operations that the Global Positioning System (GPS) co-ordinates are kept virtually secret. The only way to visit the Burma Banks – unless you have your own boat – is by way of 7- to 10-day live-aboard dive trips out of Phuket. The three major banks – Roe, Silvertip and Rainbow – provide four- to five-star class diving experiences, with fields of psychedelic coral laid over an underwater plateau and loads of large oceanic as well as smaller reef marine species. Sharks – silvertip, reef, nurse, leopard and at least a half dozen other species – abound.

Many of the dive operations in Phuket have live-aboard diving excursions to the Surin Islands. Because of the distances involved, Surin is the most expensive dive destination in Thailand; rates start at around 9000B to 10,000B for a minimum two-night, three-day trip.

Ko Surin National Marine Park closes in early to mid May every year and doesn't re-open till mid November. The exact dates appear to vary from year to year, perhaps influenced by perceived weather patterns.

Places to Stay & Eat

Accommodation at the *park longhouses* (*mainland office* ☎ *076 491 378*) is 100B per person or you can rent six- and eight-person bungalows for 1200B. At the campground, two-person tents cost 300B a night or you can use your own (or camp without a tent) for 20B per night per person. The park also offers three good meals a day (mostly seafood) for 350B or you can order meals separately. Electricity is generated from 6pm to 11pm. It's strongly recommended that you book in advance.

Nangnuan Hotel (☎ *076 491 401, 203/35 Soi Sukhaphiban*) Rooms 250-350B. Should you get stuck in Khuraburi, this place, located near the bus stop, has adequate rooms and a decent restaurant.

Tararain River Hut Resort (*Th Khuraburi-Takua Pa*) Bungalows 300-500B. This is 2km south of town, and has three-person bungalows of wood and concrete. The attached restaurant isn't always open but is great when the cook is in. There are discounts for long-term stays.

At the park office in Ngan Yong is a good *outdoor restaurant* serving Thai seafood daily from 7am to 8pm.

Getting There & Away

The mainland office of Ko Surin National Park is in the messy fishing village of Ngan Yong, from where boats to the islands depart. The road to Ngan Yong turns off Hwy 4 at the 720km marker, 6km north of Khuraburi and 109km south of Ranong. The park office, which is also where the pier is located, is about 2km down the road

on the right-hand side: from Hwy 4 a motorcycle taxi will take you there for 10B.

Buses between Khuraburi and Ranong cost 37B and take about an hour and 20 minutes; ask to be let off at Ngan Yong (saying Ko Surin should also work). To/from Phuket, buses cost 55B and take about three hours. From Khuraburi to Ngan Yong costs 50B by motorcycle taxi.

The cheapest way out to the island is to latch on to one of the tour-group boats heading out there. To do this you'll need to call the Surin mainland office (☎ 076 491 378) to find out if and when any boats are making the trip. If so, park staff will try and book you a seat: the price is usually 1200B per person return. Tour boats run from December to April, and the busiest time is between February and April.

You can charter a boat out to the Surin Islands from Ngan Yong through the park officers, who will serve as brokers/interpreters. A boat that takes up to 30 people can be chartered for 6000B return – it takes four to five hours each way. Ordinarily, boat travel is only considered safe between December and early May, ie, between the two monsoons. The park itself is closed mid May to mid November.

HAT BANG SAK
หาดบางสัก

About 14km south of Takua Pa, this beach stretches for several kilometres, and is mainly a destination for locals out for a picnic or drinks and seafood at one of the little open-air places that line the shore. The beach itself is nice, offers good views of the coast to the south, and is lined with casuarinas. But it's not regularly cleaned, so there's more litter here than farther south at Hat Khao Lak. The areas inland are cluttered with shrimp farms and are not too inviting. Still, if you have time on your hands, it might be fun to do like the locals and come for a sunset meal or drink.

If you do decide it's worth more than that, there are two places to stay:

Bang Sak Resort (☎ *076 421 471*) Bungalows and rooms with fan & bath 600B.

This place has 16 wooden bungalows with verandas and the family that runs it is quite friendly. From the Bang Sak beach turn-off from Hwy 4 (near the 77km marker), it's about 2km north on the road running along the beach.

Bangsak Beach Resort (☎ *076 412 973–5, fax 076 446 520*) Bungalows with air-con 560B. A short walk down the beach from Bang Sak Resort is the similarly named Bangsak Beach Resort that offers newly built and comfortable bungalows of wood – it's good value during the low season when you can sometimes knock 100-150B off the quoted rates. There's a good restaurant on the premises.

Hat Bang Sak has several good, relatively inexpensive seafood restaurants.

Buses running between Takua Pa and Phuket will get you here; just ask to be let off at Hat Bang Sak.

HAT KHAO LAK
หาดเขาหลัก

Though still pretty sleepy, this scenic beach is becoming increasingly popular, mainly with European visitors. It's easy to reach, quiet and, as yet, not overdeveloped: the kind of place you can imagine Phuket to have been 20 years ago. The beach is a pretty stretch of sand studded with smooth granite boulders. You can easily walk northward along the sand for many kilometres, almost as far as Hat Bang Sak. A coral reef suitable for snorkelling lies 45 minutes offshore by long-tail boat, and some of the bungalow resorts here offer dive excursions to this reef, as well as to the Similan and Surin Islands groups.

Hat Khao Lak is located about 25km south of Takua Pa. It's actually located in a town called Ban La-on, but developers decided associating the beach with the nearby national park would sound more appealing.

The area immediately south of Hat Khao Lak is encompassed by the 125-sq-km **Khao Lak/Lam Ru National Park** (*adult/child under 14 years 200/100B*), a beautiful collection of sea cliffs, 1000m hills, beaches, estuaries, forested valleys and mangroves. Wildlife seen in the park includes hornbills, drongos, tapirs, gibbons, monkeys and Asiatic black bears. The visitors centre, just off Hwy 4 between the 56km and 57km markers, has little in the way of maps or printed info, but there's a very nice open-air restaurant perched on a shady slope overlooking the sea.

Activities
Park ranger-guided treks along the coast or inland can be arranged through Poseidon Bungalows (☎/fax 076 443 258), as can long-tail boat trips up the scenic Khlong Thap Liang estuary. The latter afford opportunities to view mangrove communities of crab-eating macaques.

Live coral formations can be found just off Hat Khao Lak and along the western tip of the bay near Poseidon. Sea Dragon Dive Center (☎ 076 420 418, fax 076 420 419), on Hwy 4 opposite Nang Thong Bay Resort, is the main diving operation in the area. In addition to selling and renting diving and snorkelling equipment, it offers PADI-certified scuba instruction and dive trips to the Similan Islands. Sea Dragon's four-day, four-night Similan and Surin excursion costs 15,000B for divers, including

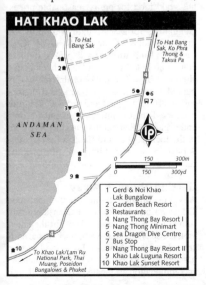

HAT KHAO LAK

To Hat Bang Sak

To Hat Bang Sak, Ko Phra Thong & Takua Pa

ANDAMAN SEA

0   150   300m
0   150   300yd

1 Gerd & Noi Khao Lak Bungalow
2 Garden Beach Resort
3 Restaurants
4 Nang Thong Bay Resort I
5 Nang Thong Minimart
6 Sea Dragon Dive Centre
7 Bus Stop
8 Nang Thong Bay Resort II
9 Khao Lak Luguna Resort
10 Khao Lak Sunset Resort

To Khao Lak/Lam Ru National Park, Thai Muang, Poseidon Bungalows & Phuket

11 dives, food, transport, accommodation and all equipment, or 7000B for nondivers. These are among the lowest rates available for dive excursions to the Similans since most companies work out of Phuket. Local dive trips to nearby coral reefs cost 1200B per day including equipment and two tanks.

Poseidon Bungalows offers three-day, two-night snorkelling-only trips to the Similan Islands for 4900B per person. These trips depart twice a week during November to April. For both Poseidon and Sea Dragon, count on five hours each way to reach the islands. For further information on getting to the Similans, see the Similan Islands National Marine Park section later in this chapter.

Between Khao Lak and Bang Sak is a network of sandy beach trails – some of which lead to deserted beaches – that are fun to explore on foot or by rented motorcycle.

Places to Stay & Eat

Hat Khao Lak There is still some reasonably priced accommodation at Hat Khao Lak, although the area has moved up-market. There are now several 'resorts' fat with amenities, including swimming pools.

Gerd & Noi Khao Lak Bungalow Huts 150B, cottages with bath and fan 600B, with air-con 800B. At the northern end of Hat Khao Lak, this place has basic huts and nicely designed Thai-style bungalows. The entire operation is set in a pleasant landscaped courtyard.

Garden Beach Resort (☎ 076 420 121, fax 076 420 129) Bungalows with bath 300-500B, air-con 900-1000B. This has clean and spacious bungalows – price depends on proximity to the beach. It has a relaxed atmosphere and the restaurant is good. It also rents motorbikes (200B per day).

Nang Thong Bay Resort I (☎ 076 420 088, fax 076 420 090) Bungalows with bath & air-con 700-1000B. This place is towards the centre of Hat Khao and is similar in style to the Garden Beach Resort. Motorbikes and jeeps are also available for rent here. Prices drop by about 40% during slow periods.

Nang Thong Bay Resort II (☎ 076 420 078, fax 076 420 079) Bungalows with bath & air-con 700-1200B. Towards the south-

ern end of the beach, this has larger and attractive cottages.

Khao Lak Laguna Resort (☎ 076 420 200, fax 076 431 297) Bungalows with fan/air-con 3500/3800B. This features 56 Thai-style cottages. It's very popular, commands a nice section of beach and has attractively landscaped grounds with a pond. There are also a beachside swimming pool, minimarket and Internet cafe on the premises.

Khao Lak Sunset Resort (☎ 076 420 075, fax 076 420 147) Rooms with fan/air-con 800/1500B. At the southern end of the beach, along Hwy 4, this has upscale hotel rooms stacked against a cliff with balcony and sea views.

A cluster of simple thatched-roof *beach restaurants* towards the centre of the beach (just north of Nang Thong Bay Resort I) offer reasonably priced Thai dishes and tasty seafood, as well as a fine view of the sea and sunset.

National Park Environs Khao Lak/Lam Ru National Park has four simple *bungalows* for 200B at its headquarters, located 2km south of Hat Khao Lak. The *restaurant* nearby, in addition to its wonderful setting, has good food for pretty reasonable prices.

Poseidon Bungalows (☎ 076 443 258) Bungalows 150B, with bath 400-500B. On the other side of the headland of Khao Lak/Lam Ru National Park, 5.5km south of Hat Khao Lak, Poseidon Bungalows is in a sheltered bay. The huts are discretely dispersed among huge boulders and coastal forest, affording quiet and privacy. The proprietors dispense information on the area and organise boat excursions and dive trips to the local reef and to the Similan Islands. A pleasant restaurant built on stilts over the sea serves Thai and European food.

Getting There & Away

Any bus running along Hwy 4 between Takua Pa and Phuket or Thai Muang will stop at Hat Khao Lak if asked (for the latter, look for Sea Dragon Dive Service on the eastern side of the highway). From the bus stop it's about 400m to the dirt road on which the accommodation is located. Buses will also stop near Hat Chongfa, Khao Lak Laguna and Khao Lak Sunset resorts and the Khao Lak/Lam Ru National Park Headquarters.

If you're headed to Poseidon Bungalows, your best bet is to get off the bus at Thap Lamu and then take a motorcycle taxi from there for 30B to 40B. The turn-off for Poseidon is located between the 53km and 54km markers, but from there it's another 1.2km; a hot and dusty walk if you have bags to carry.

AROUND HAT KHAO LAK & HAT BANG SAK

Along the beach north of the Hat Khao Lak area are a few places to stay that offer still more solitude.

Chongfa Beach Resort (☎ 076 420 056–7, fax 076 420 055) Rooms 500-2000B. This has 33 rooms in two-storey, four-unit blocks – they're not the most architecturally appealing, but are quite clean. Considering the nearly private beach, which doesn't have the boulders of Khao Lak, and the pleasant restaurant overlooking the sea, this is one of the best deals in the area. Turn off Hwy 4 between the 62km and the 63km markers to reach it.

Similana Resort (☎ 076 420 166, fax 076 420 169) Rooms with breakfast 2300B, bungalows with fan/air-con 2500/3600B. If you're looking for a luxurious, aesthetic get-away, this is a good choice. Sitting atop a headland 20km south of Takua Pa, it's a beautifully designed and landscaped group of all-wood Thai-style bungalows with tiled roofs and hotel rooms, artfully hidden among pandanus trees and coco palms. Amenities include a swimming pool, although the beach around here looks so clean and secluded you may never touch the diving board. Food at the restaurant (your only eating option for several kilometres) is good, but quite expensive. Breakfast is included in the rates. Management will usually offer a discount of 25% unless it's a major public holiday; in the low season, rates drop by around 50%.

The resort has pickup and drop-off service (1000B to 1500B) to Surat Thani and Phuket, and jeeps and motorcycles are available for rent. Staff will also pick you up from Takua Pa free of charge if you ring them up.

Bang Sak Beach Resort (☎ 076 412 973, fax 076 446 520) Bungalows 1500-4800B. Of several in the area, this place stands out for its creative use of natural materials in the construction of its bungalows – wood, bamboo and thatch. The grounds are also landscaped in a way to give a tropical village feel – lots of banana trees are used to good effect (uncommon in Thailand as Thais associate banana trees with ghosts!). There's also a swimming pool and restaurant.

Ko Phra Thong
เกาะพระทอง

Golden Buddha Beach Resort (Bangkok ☎ 028 683 180, fax 028 681 301, e reservations@losthorizonsasia.com) Rooms 1200B, full board per person an extra 550B. Set on a sandy peninsula between two pristine beaches, the only resort on the large island of Ko Phra Thong (Golden Buddha Island), Golden Buddha offers 29 rooms, including wooden one-bedroom thatched-roof bungalows and two-bedroom bungalows with mosquito nets. All have open-air bathrooms with views of the sea and surrounding forest. There are also yoga courses on offer here.

Call Golden Buddha Beach Resort in advance to arrange transport. The turn-off for the Golden Buddha pier is near 722km marker on Hwy 4.

SIMILAN ISLANDS (MUU KO SIMILAN) NATIONAL MARINE PARK
อุทยานแห่งชาติหมู่เกาะสิมิลัน

The Similan Islands are world-renowned among diving enthusiasts for incredible underwater sightseeing at depths ranging from 2m to 30m. Besides attractive sandy beaches, there are huge, smooth granite formations that plunge into the sea to form seamounts, rock reefs and dive-throughs. As elsewhere in the Andaman Sea, the best diving months are December to May when the weather is good and the sea is at its clearest (and boat trips are much safer).

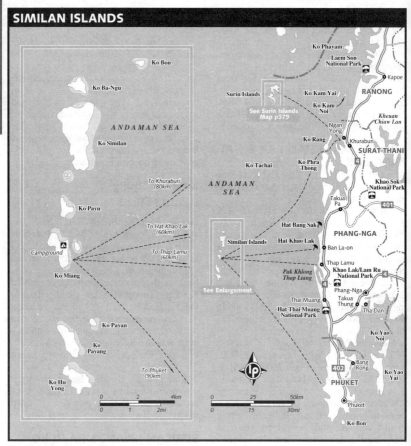

The Thais sometimes refer to the Similans as Ko Kao, or Nine Islands, because there are nine of them – each has a number as well as a name. The word 'Similan' in fact comes from the Malay word *sembilan* meaning 'nine'. Counting in order from the north, they are Ko Bon, Ko Ba-Ngu, Ko Similan, Ko Payu, Ko Miang (which is actually two islands close together), Ko Payan, Ko Payang and Ko Hu Yong. They're relatively small islands and uninhabited except for park officials and occasional tourist groups from Phuket.

Princess Chulabhorn, the present Thai monarch's youngest daughter, has a cottage on **Ko Miang**, a royal association that adds an extra layer of protection to the islands' national park status. The Thai navy operates a sea-turtle preserve on **Ko Ba-Ngu**, yet another bonus for enforcement of park preservation.

Also on **Ko Miang**, which is second in size to Ko Similan, you'll find the park headquarters, a visitors centre and accommodation. Venturing inland from the beach, you should easily be able to catch glimpses of the Nicobar pigeon or the hairy-legged mountain land crab. The beaches on this island are good for snorkelling (as opposed to scuba diving), as is the channel between Ko Miang and Ko Payu.

Ko Similan is also good for hiking and snorkelling. In a small bay on Similan's western side you may be able to see spiny lobsters resting in rock crevices, along with sea fans, plume worms and soft corals swaying in the current. The largest granite outcrop in the Similan archipelago is also found on Ko Similan; scramble to the top to enjoy a sweeping view of the sea.

Thirty-two species of birds can be seen on the nine islands, including resident birds such as the Brahminy kite and the white-breasted waterhen. Migratory species of note include the pintail snipe, grey wagtail, cattle egret, watercock and the roseate tern. Fairly common resident mammals include the bush-tailed porcupine, common palm civet, flying lemur and bottle-nosed dolphin. Species of reptiles and amphibians found in the park include the banded krait, reticulated python, white-lipped pit viper, common pit viper, hawksbill turtle, leather turtle, Bengal monitor lizard, common water monitor lizard and ornate froglet.

Admission to the park – collected on Ko Miang – is 200B per adult, half that for kids under 14.

Ko Bon & Ko Tachai
เกาะบอนและเกาะตาชัย

These small islands lie approximately midway between the Similan and Surin archipelagos. Profuse hard corals appear at depths of 18m to 35m and, in good weather, visibility extends to 25m. Without a doubt these are two of the area's top dive sites and both islands are usually included in longer live-aboard dive trips that run between the Similan and Surin Islands.

Organised Tours
Khao Lak Sea Dragon at Hat Khao Lak does four-day/four-night Similan and Surin trips for 15,800B. Poseidon Bungalows next to Khao Lak/Lam Ru National Park does a Similan snorkelling trip for a bargain 4900B. Their boats depart from Thap Lamu; see the earlier Hat Khao Lak section for more details.

Phuket Overnight diving excursions from Phuket are priced at about 5000B a day including food, accommodation, diving equipment and underwater guides. Non-divers may be able to join these trips for around half the cost – snorkellers are welcome.

Package deals out of Phuket typically start at US$220 per day per person. A trip to Similan costs about US$1500, to the Burma Banks about US$2500. Siam Dive n' Sail (☎ 076 330 967, 076 330 990, W www.siamdivers.com), 121/9 Th Patak, in Kata is a reliable outfit. Whale sharks are sometimes spotted on these trips, but the latest El Niño seems to have affected the migratory patterns of these huge fish and sightings are not as regular as they once were – the months of March through May are best.

Places to Stay & Eat
Accommodation, including camping, is only allowed on Ko Miang. Bookings must be made in advance at the park's mainland office in Thap Lamu (☎ 076 411 913–4).

The park has *bungalows* for 600B and four-bed rooms in a *longhouse* for 400B. If there are only one or two in your party, you may be able to get a per-person rate of 100B for the longhouse, but don't count on it. Tent rental costs 150B, and there's a 20B tent site fee if you bring your own.

The only source of food is a privately run *restaurant* on Ko Miang. Prices here are ridiculously high – everything must be shipped from the mainland. If you want food for several people, you'll need to let the restaurant know in advance. Bringing your own food is strongly recommended, though restrictions on open fires may force you to the restaurant at least a few times.

Getting There & Away
You can get boats to the Similans from the port at Thap Lamu (39km south of Takua Pa off Hwy 4, or 20km north of Thai Muang) and from Phuket. The park mainland office is also in Thap Lamu, about 1km from the pier.

The islands are 60km from Thap Lamu, about three hours by boat. Met Sine Tours (☎ 076 443 276), near the pier, is the place to go for boat bookings. When last checked, boats ran daily, departing Thap Lamu at 8.30am and heading back from Ko Miang at 5pm the same day. The return fare is 2100B. It would be best to call ahead just to check what's going on, as the situation seems rather fluid (there is at least one English speaker at Met Sine). Boats run to the Similans from November to May only; during the remainder of the year the seas are too rough. If the weather looks rough when you arrive give some thought as to how badly you want to go: there have been several incidents in recent years of boats operating out of Thap Lamu having foundered or becoming stranded, though no casualties have resulted.

AO PHANG-NGA & PHANG-NGA
อ่าวพังงา/อ.เมืองพังงา

Over 95km north-east of Phuket, this expansive, turquoise extension of the Andaman Sea is dotted with hundreds of islands; many are mere limestone outcrops that protrude from the sea. At some islands, partially submerged grottoes (called *hâwng*) can be entered by small boats during low tide. Other islands are encircled by sandy coves where the only visible inhabitants are swiftlets that build their nests on high cliffs. Itinerant collectors farm the highly prized nests for use in the Chinese delicacy 'birds'-nest soup', a broth made from the hardened bird saliva holding the nests together. Many of the islands are part of **Ao Phang-Nga National Marine Park** and can be explored by boat or canoe.

Very few of these islands receive overnight visitors. Ko Phi-Phi, the most famous, is a dumbbell-shaped island ringed by coral reefs, caves and white-sand beaches; in this book it is covered in the Southern Andaman Coast chapter under Krabi Province.

Information
The TAT distributes a map of Phang-Nga Province that includes a separate map of Phang-Nga town, as well as pamphlets listing sights, accommodation and restaurants. The most complete information is at the regional office in Phuket town, and you may be able to get some material in Bangkok. The Books, 265/1 Th Phetkasem, carries a small selection of English-language books and magazines.

In the centre of Phang-Nga town along Hwy 4 are several banks open during regular banking hours.

The post-and-telephone office is on Th Phetkasem, opposite the hospital and about 2km south-west of the bus station. Phone booths in front of the telephone office accept coins and Thai phonecards.

Things to See & Do
Along the northern shore of the bay is **Phang-Nga**, a small provincial capital wedged between verdant limestone cliffs. Phang-Nga is the best – and least expensive – place to hire boats for exploring the northern half of the bay. The southern half of the bay is best approached from Phuket or Krabi.

In Phang-Nga itself there's little to see or do that isn't beachy unless you happen to be there during the annual Vegetarian Festival in October (see the boxed text 'Vegetarian Festival' in the Phuket section for informa-

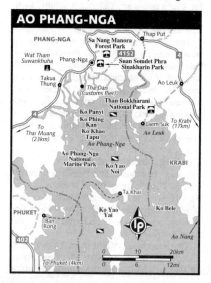

AO PHANG-NGA

PHANG-NGA
Wat Tham Suwankhuha
Takua Thung
Sa Nang Manora Forest Park
Thap Put
4152
Phang-nga
Suan Somdet Phra Sinakharin Park
Tha Dan (Customs Pier)
Ao Leuk
Than Bokkharani National Park
Ko Panyi
Ko Phing Kan
To Thai Muang (23km)
Ko Khao Tapu
Laem Suk
To Krabi (17km)
Ao Leuk
Ao Phang-Nga
Ao Phang-Nga National Marine Park
Ko Yao Noi
KRABI
Ta Khai
PHUKET
Ban Rong
Ko Yao Yai
Ko Bele
Ao Nang
402
To Phuket (4km)
0   10   20km
0   6   12mi

Sustainable Soups?

Birds' Nest Soup is made from swiftlet nests that are woven from the male bird's saliva. There are two species: one uses saliva only, the other saliva and feathers. Considered a delicacy by Chinese for its purported regenerative and aphrodisiacal qualities, the demand for the soup has resulted in a decline in swiftlet numbers. The swiftlet has been considered for inclusion on the Convention on International Trade on Endangered Species (Cites) 'threatened species' list. The practise of collecting nests is regulated; however, as the demand and value for them increases, so do reports of eggs and chicks being discarded to acquire the sought-after nests.

Phang Nga Bay's unique environment supports both species of swiftlet. In the collecting season, villagers use an intricate system of bamboo scaffolding to reach the nests adhered to cave roofs by swiftlet spit. The technique is one steeped in tradition, superstition and danger. Apart from the obvious peril associated with teetering on the end of a pole, there were reportedly 14 deaths in Southern Thailand during the 1990s. These resulted from clashes between licensed collectors and people with other interests in the nests, including tour operators and poachers.

Another Chinese delicacy found in Southern Thailand is Shark Fin Soup. Tens of thousands of sharks are killed in Asian waters solely for their fins. Sometimes hunters cut the fins off the shark before dumping it back into the ocean to die. Thai Airways International, Thailand's national air carrier, recently removed Shark Fin Soup from its 1st-class menu in response to complaints from passengers.

Simone Egger

tion on this unusual event). Nearby Suan Somdet Phra Sinakharin Park and Sa Nang Manora Forest Park are good places for hiking and picnicking (see Around Phang-Nga further on).

On the way to Phang-Nga, turn left off Hwy 4 at the 31km marker. Just 5km past the small town of Takua Thung is **Wat**

Tham Suwankhuha (*Heaven Grotto Temple*), a cave shrine full of Buddha images. The shrine consists of two main caverns: a larger one containing a 15m reclining Buddha and tiled with *laikhram* and *benjarong*, two coloured patterns more common in pottery, and a smaller cavern displaying spirit flags and a *rishi* (hermit-sage) statue. Royal seals of several kings, including Rama V, Rama VII and Rama IX – as well those of lesser royalty – are inscribed on one wall of the latter cave.

Other nearby caves in the province include **Tham Reusisawan** (*Hermit Heaven; 3km south of Phang-nga*) and **Tham Phung Chang** (*Elephant Belly Cave; also 3km south*).

Phang-Nga Province's best beach areas are on the west coast facing the Andaman Sea. Between Thai Muang in the south and Takua Pa in the north are the beaches of Hat Thai Muang and Hat Bang Sak – see the Khuraburi, Takua Pa & Thai Muang and the Hat Bang Sak sections earlier for more details.

Organised Tours

Boat Trips Between Takua Thung and Phang-Nga is the road to **Tha Dan**, where you can find the Phang-Nga customs pier. At an adjacent pier, boats can be hired to tour Ao Phang-Nga National Park, with visits to a Muslim fishing village on stilts, half-submerged caves, and strangely shaped islands, including several that were used in the 1970s James Bond film *The Man with the Golden Gun*.

While it's possible to charter a boat at the pier for a tour of the islands, unless you enjoy haggling with greedy boat drivers, it's much easier to go with a local tour arranged through one of the two small agencies next to the bus terminal in Phang-Nga town. Sayan Tours (☎ 076 430 348) has been doing overnight tours of Ao Phang-Nga for many years now, and these continue to receive good reviews from some travellers. The overnight tour costs 750B per person and includes a boat tour of **Tham Lawt** ('Tunnel Cave', a large water cave), **Ko Phing Kan** ('Leaning Island', aka 'James

Bond Island'), **Ko Khao Tapu** (Nail Mountain Island), **Khao Maju** (Poodle Mountain), **Tham Naak** (Dragon Cave), **Khao Khian** ('Drawing Mountain'; rock wall murals), a former mangrove charcoal factory, plus dinner, breakfast and newly built accommodation in a Muslim fishing village on **Ko Panyi**. Sayan also leads half-day tours for 500B. Both of these prices include the 200B entrance fee to the National Park zone. The overnight trip is recommended over the day trip, which tends to be a bit rushed. Sayan Tours can also arrange trips to nearby sites on land, including Sa Nang Manora Forest Park and the various caves near town.

The other tour agency at the bus terminal, Kean Tours (☎ 076 411 247), charges exactly the same rates for similar half-day, full-day and overnight tours.

These same tours are available out of Phuket, but cost at least 200B to 400B per person more. Whatever you do, try to avoid touring the bay in the middle of the day (10am to 4pm) when hundreds of package tourists crowd the islands.

Alternatively, you could do a canoe tour from Phuket. See the following Paddling entry.

See the Around Phang-Nga section for more extensive descriptions and information about Ao Phang-Nga National Park.

Paddling Several companies based in Phuket offer inflatable-canoe tours of scenic Ao Phang-Nga. Sea Canoe Thailand (☎ 076 212 252, fax 076 212 172, **W** www .seacanoethailand.com), 367/4 Th Yao warat, Phuket, was the first and is still the most famous. The kayaks are able to enter semi-submerged caves (which Thai fishermen have called hâwng or 'room' for centuries) inaccessible by the long-tail boats. A day paddle costs 2970B per person and includes meals, beverages, equipment and transfer, while all-inclusive, three/six-day camping trips are US$550/1050 per person. The three-day trips leave Wednesday and Sunday; six-day trips leave on Sunday. If your group has less than three people, sleeping arrangements are made with Tha Khao Bungalow on Ko Yao Noi. Larger groups

usually camp on the beach in tents provided. The day trips can also be booked from Ao Nang in Krabi for 1700B, but a different area, without semi-submerged caves, is explored.

Several other companies in the area offer similar inflatable-canoe trips for less than half these prices, but Sea Canoe Thailand claims it is still the most ecologically conscious in terms of the way in which it organises and operates tours. Another company with experience navigating the hâwng, and for which we've received good feedback from readers, is Andaman Sea Kayak (☎ 076 235 353, 076 235 098, **W** www .andamanseakayak.com). Almost any travel agency on Phuket can book trips with this outfit.

Places to Stay – Budget

Phang-Nga There are several small hotels in this area.

Thawisuk (☎ *076 412 100, 77–79 Th Phetkasem)* Rooms with 1 bed/2 beds, fan & bath 150/200B. Right in the middle of town, this bright blue building has an English sign reading 'Hotel'. It has simple but usually clean rooms upstairs – the staff provide a towel and soap on request. You can sit and have a beer on the roof while watching the sun set over Phang-Nga's rooftops and the limestone cliffs surrounding the town.

Lak Meuang Hotel (☎ *076 412 486, fax 076 411 512, 1/2 Th Phetkasem)* Rooms with fan/air-con & bath 250/450B. Just outside town towards Krabi, this is well worn but clean. There is a restaurant downstairs that opens at 6am and does a passable Western breakfast of eggs, toast and coffee.

Ratanapong Hotel (☎ *076 411 247, 111 Th Phetkasem)* Rooms with fan & 1 bed/2 beds/3 beds/4 beds 150/250/300/350B, doubles with air-con 450B. This place offers decent rooms but gets a fair amount of short-time trade and can be noisy on weekends.

Muang Thong (☎ *076 412 132, 128 Th Phetkasem)* Singles/doubles with fan 120/180B, with air-con 350B. Down the road towards Phuket, this has grubby rooms and antique air conditioners that grind away through the night.

Places to Stay – Mid-Range

New Lak Meuang II (☎ 076 411 500, fax 076 411 501, 540 Th Phetkasem) Rooms with air-con & TV 450B. Large rooms with fridge & hot-water bath 650B. This is on the outskirts of town in the direction of Phuket and is popular with Thai businesspeople. The cheaper rooms are the best value. It's in a convenient location for exploring the central area.

Sunimit Mansion Inn (☎ 076 440 400, fax 076 411 130, 21/1 Th Sirirat) Rooms with air-con 350B, with fridge & TV 400B, suites 600B. Summit is a 20-room, four-storey hotel off the main drag in the centre of town. Some rooms are much better than others, so have a look before agreeing to anything.

Phang-Nga Valley Resort (☎ 076 412 201, 076 411 353, fax 076 411 393, 5/5 Th Phetkasem) Rooms 1000-2500B. This is on the southern outskirts of town before you reach the highway to Krabi. Rooms are in large tile-roofed bungalows set in a garden. Prices fluctuate wildly between weekdays and weekends – it pays to haggle during the slow periods.

Tha Dan On Route 4144 towards the customs pier is *Phang-Nga Bay Resort Hotel (☎ 076 412 067–70, fax 076 412 057)* Rooms with TV, phone & fridge in low/high season 1100/3500B. This fading hotel has a swampy swimming pool and a restaurant. Given the inferior facilities, only tour groups with no other choice end up staying here.

Places to Eat

Duang Restaurant (☎ 076 411 216, 122 Th Phetkasem) Dishes 60-100B. Next to Bangkok Bank on the main road, this has a bilingual menu and a good selection of Thai and Chinese dishes, including southern Thai specialities. Prices have crept up a little higher than the standard of the food would justify.

Suan Aahaan Islam (Th Phetkasem) Dishes 20-30B On the left just north-east of Soi Langkai, this serves simple Thai Muslim food, including *roti kaeng* (flatbread and curry) in the morning. There is no roman-script sign.

Bismilla (6 Th Phetkasem) Dishes 30-40B. South-west of the market, a little way past the bus terminal, the tidy Bismilla does Thai Muslim food.

Phang-Nga Satay (189 Th Phetkasem) Dishes 10-20B This simple shop specialises in Malay-style satay. The shrimp satay is highly recommended. It's open from early evening till late at night.

Chai Khai (Th Phetkasem) Dishes 10-20B This cafe opens early and specialises in *paa-thawng-kŏh* (Chinese doughnut) and Hokkien-style coffee. There is no roman-script sign.

Several *food stalls* on the main street of Phang-Nga sell cheap and delicious *khanŏm jiin* (thin wheat noodles) with chicken curry, *náam yaa* (spicy ground-fish curry) or *náam phrík* (sweet and spicy peanut sauce). One vendor in front of the market (opposite Bangkok Bank) serves khanŏm jiin with an amazing variety of free vegetable accompaniments – but only from 1pm to 8pm Tuesday to Sunday; an adjacent vendor does *khâo mòk kài* (chicken biryani) from 6am to noon. Roti kaeng is available in the *morning market* from around 5am to 10am. There are also the usual Chinese *khâo man kài* (chicken rice) places around town.

Getting There & Away

Buses for Phang-Nga leave from the Phuket bus terminal on Th Phang-Nga, near the Th Thepkasatri intersection, at 10.10am, noon, 1.40pm, 3.30pm and 4.30pm. The trip to Phang-Nga takes 2½ hours and the one-way fare is 41B, ordinary bus. Alternatively you could rent a motorcycle in Phuket and navigate here on your own.

Buses to/from Krabi leave every half hour, cost 36B and take 1½ hours; air-con buses leave hourly and cost 52B. To and from Surat Thani ordinary buses cost 55B and take 3½ hours. Other air-con departures to/from destinations around Southern Thailand include Ranong (120B, two times per day), Hat Yai (196B, six times), Trang (121B, 11 times) and Satun (198B, two times).

Ordinary buses to/from Bangkok cost 192B and take 14 hours, while air-con is

350B and VIP is 403B, both taking 13 hours. All buses depart from the main bus terminal in the centre of town, but they can also be flagged down along Th Phetkasem (Hwy 4), the main road through Phang-Nga.

Getting Around
Most of the town is easily accessible on foot. Sayan Tour at the bus terminal can assist with motorcycle rental.

Săwngthăew between Phang-Nga and Tha Dan (the Phang-Nga customs pier) cost 15B.

AROUND PHANG-NGA
Suan Somdet Phra Sinakharin Park
สวนสมเด็จพระศรีนครินทร์

This public park *(admission free)* has two entrances. The most dramatic entry is through a huge hole through a limestone cliff near Phang-Nga Bay Resort. A road goes through the cliff, so if you have a vehicle you can drive through into the park. The main entrance is towards the southern end of town, opposite the provincial transport department. Nearly the entire park is surrounded by limestone cliffs and bluffs, into which nature has carved a scenic network of caves and tunnels, some containing ponds. Wooden walkways link the water-filled caverns so that visitors can admire the ponds and amazing limestone formations. One of the larger caves, **Tham Reusi Sawan**, is marked by a gilded statue of a *reu-sĭi* (Hindu sage) – complete with tiger skins and staff – outside the entrance. The other rather large cavern is known locally as **Tham Luk Seua** (Tiger Cub Cave).

Sa Nang Manora Forest Park
สวนป่าสระนางมโนราห์

North of town via Hwy 4 (turn off 3.4km from the Shell station and the New Lak Muang II Hotel, then 4.5km down a winding road through rubber plantations), this park *(admission free)* features lots of dense rainforest and a set of cool, green cascades. The setting is truly impressive, with plenty of rattan vines, moss-encrusted roots and

rocks. The many-levelled waterfall has several pools suitable for swimming. The overall impression is similar to that of Krabi's Than Bokkharani National Park but it receives fewer visitors and as a result is much cleaner. Crude trails follow the falls level after level and beyond – you could easily get a full day's hiking in without backtracking. Bring plenty of drinking water – although the shade and the falls moderate the temperature, the humidity in the park is quite high.

The park's name comes from a local folk belief that the mythical Princess Manora bathes in the pools of the park when no one else is around.

Facilities include some tables and chairs here and there, plus a small restaurant next to the car park.

Ao Phang-Nga National Park
อุทยานแห่งชาติอ่าวพังงา

Established in 1981 and covering an area of 400 sq km, Ao Phang-Nga National Park *(adult/child under 14 years 200/100B)* is noted for its classic karst scenery, created by fault movement on the mainland that pushed massive limestone blocks up to form geometric patterns. Extending southward into Ao Phang-Nga, they form over 40 islands with huge vertical cliffs. Over 80% of the area within the park boundaries is covered by the Andaman Sea. The bay itself is composed of large and small tidal channels that originally connected with the mainland river system. The main tidal channels – Khlong Ko Panyi, Khlong Phang-Nga, Khlong Bang Toi and Khlong Bo Saen – run through vast mangroves in a north-south direction and today are used by fisherfolk and island inhabitants as aquatic highways. This is the largest remaining primary mangrove forest in Thailand.

The biggest tourist destination in the park is so-called 'James Bond Island', known to the Thais as **Ko Phing Kan** (Leaning on Itself Island). Once used as a location for the James Bond flick, *The Man with the Golden Gun*, the island is now given over to souvenir vendors hawking all manner of coral and shells that should have stayed in the sea, along with butterflies, scorpions and spiders encased in plastic – not exactly the stuff to inspire confidence in Thailand's national-park system.

The Thai name for the island refers to a flat limestone cliff that appears to have tumbled sideways to lean on a similar rock face in the centre of the island. Off one side of the island in a shallow bay stands a tall slender limestone formation that looks like a big rock spike that fell from the sky. There are a couple of caves you can walk through on the island, and a couple of small sand beaches.

There are two ways to see the park. The cheapest way is to take an organised boat tour that hits the main visitors' sites of the islands. The more-expensive option is to go on a paddling tour that focuses on lesser-explored corners of the park. Many people reckon that if you can't afford the latter option, it's best not to bother going. See the Organised Tours section earlier in this chapter for more information.

Flora & Fauna Two types of forest, limestone scrub and true evergreen forest, predominate in the park. The marine limestone environment supports a long list of reptiles including the Bengal monitor, flying lizard, banded sea snake, dog-face water snake, shore pit viper and Malayan pit viper. Keep an eye out for the two-banded or water monitor (*Varanus salvator*), which looks like a crocodile when seen swimming in the mangrove swamp and can measure up to 2.2m in length (only slightly smaller than the Komodo dragon, the largest lizard in the Varanidae family). Like its Komodo cousin, the water monitor (called *hĩa* by the Thais, who generally fear or hate the lizard) is a carnivore that prefers to feed on carrion but occasionally preys on live animals. Amphibians in the Ao Phang-Nga area include marsh frog, common bush frog and crab-eating frog. Avian residents of note are the helmeted hornbill (the largest of Thailand's 12 hornbill species, with a body length of up to 127cm), the edible-nest swiftlet (*Aerodramus fuciphagus*), white-bellied sea eagle, osprey and Pacific reef egret.

Over 200 species of mammals reside in the mangrove forests and on some of the larger islands, including the white-handed gibbon, crab-eating macaque, serow and dusky langur.

Rock Art Many of the limestone islands in Ao Phang-Nga feature prehistoric rock art painted or carved onto the walls and ceilings of caves, rock shelters, cliffs and rock massifs. In particular you can see rock art on Khao Khian, Ko Panyi, Ko Raya, Tham Nak and Ko Phra At Thao. The images contain scenes of human figures, fish, crab, shrimp, bats, birds and elephants, as well as boats and fishing equipment – it's obvious this was some sort of communal effort tied to the all-important harvesting of sustenance from the sea. Some drawings also contain rows of lines thought to be some sort of cabbalistic writing. The rock paintings are sometimes right-side up, sometimes upside-down or sideways. Most of them are mono-coloured, while some have been repeatedly traced over in orange-yellow, blue, grey and black.

Places to Stay & Eat National park *bungalows* (☎ 076 412 188) are available for rent next to the visitors centre parking lot. Small four-bed bungalows cost 500B, larger ones that sleep up to ten cost 900B. Camping is permitted in certain areas within park boundaries but you should ask permission at the visitors centre first.

There's a small, clean *restaurant* in front of the visitors centre.

Getting There & Around To reach the park headquarters and pier for Ao Phang-Nga trips, take a sǎwngthǎew going from Phang-Nga to Tha Dan (customs pier). If you're driving yourself, proceed 8km south-east of Phang-Nga on Hwy 4, then turn left onto Route 4144; you'll reach park headquarters after another 2km.

Boats can be hired to explore the bay from the *thâa reua naam thîaw* (tourist pier) opposite the visitors centre in Tha Dan. See Organised Tours earlier for details.

Ko Panyi & Muslim Stilt Villages
เกาะปันหยี

This small island in the north-western part of Ao Phang-Nga is well known for its Muslim fishing village built almost entirely on stilts and nestled against a towering limestone cliff. The village appears very commercialised during the day when hordes of tourist boats invade to eat lunch at one of the village's many overpriced seafood restaurants and buy souvenirs from the many stalls. Many visitors may be disappointed by the hyper-tourist scene, with tourists haggling for lacquered blowfish and tour groups taking photos. If you stay on the island overnight, things quiet down considerably once the tour groups have left and the settlement takes on some charm.

The 200 households here – supporting perhaps a total of 2000 inhabitants – are said to descend from two seafaring Muslim families who arrived here from Java around 200 years ago. Ko Panyi's primary livelihood is fishing, since only during the dry season do a significant number of tourists visit. In addition to a big green mosque, a health clinic and a school, you'll find a market filled with small shops selling clothes, toiletries, medicines and all the other usual staples seen in markets all over Thailand (except for alcoholic beverages). Besides alcohol, two other things forbidden on the island are dogs and pigs. Houses mixed in with the shops vary from grubby little shacks to houses with fancy tile fronts and curtained windows. The people are generally quite friendly, especially if you can speak a little Thai. Village men often gather to gossip and watch the sunset on the western side of the village near the mosque.

If you fancy a look at similar but less well-known Muslim stilt villages in Ao Phang-Nga, take a boat to one of these villages in the huge mangrove forests at the northern end of the bay: **Ban Ling** (Monkey village), **Ban Mai Phai** (Bamboo village) or **Ban Sam Chong** (Three Channels Village). All are smaller and less touristed than Ko Panyi.

Places to Stay & Eat Very basic accommodation with shared toilet and scoop shower is available at a tattered set of *thin-walled rooms* near the village's northern pier for 100B per night. Although the rooms aren't much, they do have windows that catch sea breezes. The overnight tours from Phang-Nga used to book these rooms, but they're usually empty nowadays.

Sayan Tour (☎ 076 430 348) has a group of *bungalows* used exclusively for visitors that book one of its overnight tours of Ao Phang-Nga – see the Organised Tours section earlier in this chapter for more information.

Along with the more expensive seafood restaurants built out over the sea in front of the village (which are generally open for lunch only), there are some smaller *cafes* and *restaurants* along the interior alleys where locals eat. *Khâo yam* (southern Thai rice salad) and roti are available in the morning. The villagers raise grouper in floating cages next to the island, selling them to the island restaurants and on the mainland. A local culinary speciality is *khanŏm pâo lâng*, a dish made with black sticky rice, shrimp, coconut, black pepper and chilli steamed in a banana leaf – a breakfast favourite.

Getting There & Away Most visitors to the island arrive on tour boats, whether for day visits or overnight stays.

You can take a regular ferry from Tha Dan for 50B per person. These leave frequently from dawn to dusk, arriving and departing from the village's northern pier (the southern pier is mostly reserved for tourist boats). Or you can charter a long-tail boat from the pier opposite Phang-Nga National Park headquarters in Tha Dan direct to the island for 500B.

During heavy monsoon weather boat services may be cancelled.

Ko Yao
เกาะยาว

Ko Yao Yai and Ko Yao Noi ('Big Long Island' and 'Little Long Island'), directly south of the provincial capital, in the middle of the bay between the provinces of Phuket and Krabi, together encompass 137 sq km of forest, beaches and rocky headlands with views of surrounding karst formations characteristic of Ao Phang-Nga. These two islands have been steadily gaining a reputation among repeat visitors looking to get off the grid without having to spend hours of transit time in a boat.

In spite of being smaller, **Ko Yao Noi** is the main population centre of the two, although even there fishing, coconuts and tourism sustains a relatively small group of year-rounders. There are several places of accommodation on the island now, one of them a full-scale resort offering rooms with satellite TV (as if watching TV were a reason to come to Ko Yao Noi). **Hat Paa Sai** and **Hat Tha Khao**, both on Yao Noi, are the best beaches. Bring along a mountain bike if you want to explore the island's numerous dirt trails. **Ta Khai**, the largest settlement on Ko Yao Noi, is a subdistrict government seat and the source of minimal supplies. Boat trips to neighbouring islands are possible.

Ko Yao Yai is less developed than Ko Yao Noi. **Hat Lo Paa Raet** and **Hat Tiikut** are the island's best beaches, the former lined with coconut palms, the latter with casuarina trees. A handful of rustic bungalow operations have sprouted up here over the last couple of years – so far none offering more than electric fans in the way of amenities.

Ko Bele, a small island east of the twin Ko Yao, features a large tidal lagoon, three white-sand beaches, and easily accessible caves and coral reefs around the entire island. A long-tail boat from Ko Yao Noi or from Ao Nang in Krabi can be chartered for around 600B to 1000B per day depending on the size of the boat.

Places to Stay One of the first bungalow operations to open here was *Sabai Corner*. Bungalows 350-550B. On Ko Yao Noi's Hat Paa Sai, this has sturdy thatch-and-wood bungalows with small verandas. The restaurant here is excellent and can do great barbequed fish with a day's advance notice.

Long Beach Village Bungalows 500-1500B. The aptly named Long Beach Vil-

lage has over 30 wood-and-thatch bungalows of various sizes – all a bit crowded together and feeling like a tourist village. Staff can arrange boats to nearby islands and rent snorkelling equipment.

Tha Khao Bungalow Bungalows 400-800B. This place is located on Hat Tha Khao and has sturdy bungalows of wood and thatch. There's a small eatery that does surprisingly good food.

Ban Thakao (☎ 076 212 172) Bungalows 500-1000B. This is a very quiet place just up from the beach with decent bungalows and amiable management. Prices drop by about 50% during the low season, and it's worth asking for a discount even during the high season.

Koyao Island Resort (ⓔ info@koyao .com, ⓦ www.koyao.com) Bungalows 1900-4500B. This place heralds the death knell for those who were coming to Ko Yao Noi to get away from the 21st century. Just in case you couldn't find these things on Ko Phi-Phi or Phuket, Koyao Island Resort offers bungalows with satellite TV, minibar and phone. The resort also has its own speedboat so you can hurry back to civilisation after a relaxing night of watching the Home Box Office (HBO) channel.

On Ko Yao Yai there are a couple of places that offer basic wood-and-thatch bungalows for 400B to 500B per night, including *Halawee Bungalow* and *Thiw Son Bungalow*.

Getting There & Away Although both islands fall within the Phang-Nga Province boundaries, the easiest places to find boat transport to Ko Yao Noi are Phuket (Phuket Province), Ao Leuk and Ao Nang (both in Krabi Province).

In Phuket city, catch a săwngthăew from in front of the Th Ranong market to Bang Rong on Ao Paw for 25B. From the public pier at Bang Rong there is usually one mail boat a day to Ko Yao Noi at noon. Some days there is an additional boat in the morning between 8am and 9am. The fare is 50B per passenger and the trip takes about one hour. Between departures or after hours you can charter a long-tail boat out to the island for 600B to 1200B one way. There are also speed boats for hire that will do the one-way trip for around 5000B. Coming back to Phuket from Yao Noi, there's one mail boat that leaves between 6am and 7am.

You can also get boats from Ko Yao Noi north-east across Ao Phang-Nga to Tha Laem Sak at Ao Leuk, Krabi Province. These cost around 50B on regular ferries, or 1000B to charter. From Krabi's Ao Nang you can charter a boat for about 1000B each way. Shared with five or six friends, this doesn't have to dent your budget much.

If you want to take a look around Ko Yao Yai, which is similar to Ko Yao Noi though more sparsely populated, catch a shuttle boat from Ko Yao Noi's Tha Manaw pier (20B each way), or charter a long-tail boat for 200B to 300B.

Phuket Province

Dubbed 'Pearl of the South' by the tourist industry, Phuket (pronounced 'Poo-get') is Thailand's largest, most populous and most visited island, a whirl of colour and cosmopolitanism that's a province unto itself. The coastal terrain of the 810-sq-km island encompasses broad, sandy bays, rocky peninsulas, limestone cliffs, forested hills and tropical vegetation. Phuket's inland area supports rice paddies, rubber, cashew-nut, cacao, pineapple and coconut plantations, as well as the island's last bit of rainforest. Although Phuket is connected to Phang-Nga Province by a causeway, most visitors arrive via the island's international airport located near its northern tip.

Formerly called Ko Thalang and before that Junk Ceylon (an English corruption of the Malay 'Tanjung Salang' or Cape Salang), Phuket has a culture all of its own, combining Chinese and Portuguese influences with that of the Southern Thais, and the chao náam, a seafaring, semi-nomadic group that depend on fishing and boat building. Only about 35% of the island's population is Thai Muslims; even so, mosques slightly outnumber Buddhist *wat*, 38 to 37. This is Thailand's wealthiest

province, and since the late 1980s tourism has eclipsed tin mining as the island's largest source of income.

There is a lot to do in Phuket, and consequently, a lot to spend your money on. There are also more tourists in Phuket than on any other Thai island, though most flock to three beaches on the south-western side – Patong, Karon and Kata. The beach towns are quite built up, and have all the amenities and entertainment one could want for. This is the area to visit if you're looking for a lively, action-filled vacation.

Beaches like Nai Han, near the southern tip, and Kamala, on the western coast, are relatively quiet, in spite of major tourist development at both, while Nai Thon, Nai Yang and Mai Khao to the north remain mostly untouched. In general the northern half of the island, both along the shore and in the interior, has not been swept up in the development wave, and thus offers quiet beach retreats and chances to explore rural inland areas.

Development on Phuket has been influenced by the fact that it is connected to the mainland by a bridge, and hence it receives much more vehicular traffic than any other island in the country. Phuket's high per-capita wealth also means there's plenty of money available for investment. A turning point was reached when a Club Méditerranée (Club Med) was established at Hat Kata, followed by the construction of the more lavish Phuket Yacht Club on Hat Nai Han and Le Meridien on Karon Noi (Relax Bay). This marked an end to the decade-long cheap bungalow era, which started in the early 1970s when a 10B guesthouse was attached to a laundry on Hat Patong. The cheapies have long since been bought out and replaced by all manner of hotel and bungalow developments, some ill-conceived, others quite appealing.

The era of going for quick money regardless of the cost to the environment has, sadly, not passed. Don't assume that just because an activity is on offer, that it won't be harmful to the environment. Most beach resorts however, seem to be looking towards long-term, sustainable practices. For

PHUKET PROVINCE

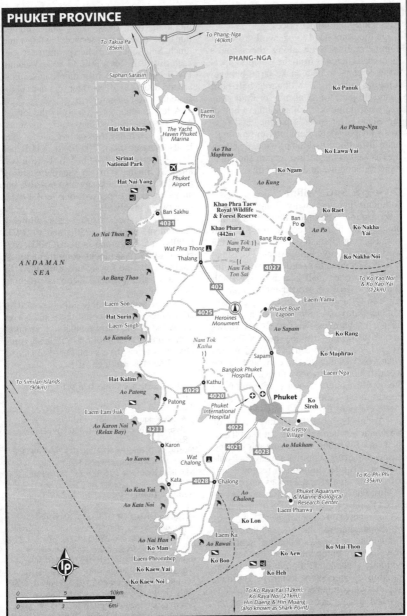

To Takua Pa (85km)

To Phang-Nga (40km)

PHANG-NGA

Saphan Sarasin

Laem Phrao

The Yacht Haven Phuket Marina

Hat Mai Khao

Ao Tha Maphrao

Ko Panuk

Ao Phang-Nga

Ko Lawa Yai

Sirinat National Park

Phuket Airport

Hat Nai Yang

Ko Ngam

Ao Kung

Ban Sakhu

4031

Ao Nai Thon

Khao Phra Taew Royal Wildlife & Forest Reserve

Khao Phara (442m)

Ban Po

Ao Po

Ko Raet

Ko Nakha Yai

Bang Rong

Wat Phra Thong

Nam Tok Bang Pae

Thalang

Nam Tok Ton Sai

4027

Ko Nakha Noi

ANDAMAN SEA

Ao Bang Thao

402

To Ko Yao Noi & Ko Yao Yai (12km)

Laem Son

4025

Hat Surin

Laem Singh

Heroines Monument

Laem Yamu

Phuket Boat Lagoon

Ao Kamala

Nam Tok Kathu

Ao Sapam

Ko Rang

Ko Maphrao

Laem Nga

To Similan Islands (90km)

Hat Kalim

Ao Patong

Sapam

Bangkok Phuket Hospital

4029

Kathu

4020

Laem Lam Jiak

Patong

Phuket International Hospital

4022

Phuket

Ko Sireh

Ao Karon Noi (Relax Bay)

4233

Karon

Sea Gypsy Village

4021

4023

Ao Makham

Wat Chalong

Ao Karon

Kata

4028

Chalong

Ao Kata Yai

Ao Chalong

Phuket Aquarium & Marine Biological Research Center

Ao Kata Noi

Laem Phanwa

Ko Lon

Ao Nai Han

Laem Ka

Ko Man

Ao Rawai

Laem Phromthep

Ko Bon

Ko Aew

Ko Mai Thon

Ko Kaew Yai

Ko Heh

Ko Kaew Noi

To Ko Raya Yai (12km), Ko Raya Noi (21km), Hin Daeng & Hin Muang (also known as Shark Point)

To Ko Phi Phi (35km)

0   5   10km
0   3   6mi

this long-term outlook, the Phuket visitor pays somewhat higher prices.

On the other hand the general growth of commercialism seen along the island's main roads detracts from the island's appeal – there seems to be a snake farm, bungee-jumping operation, billboard, half-built condo project, travel agency or craft shop every half kilometre in the southern half of the island. The island's beaches and relatively unspoiled northern interior remain its main attractions, and the provincial authorities as well as the business sector should do more to recognise and support this.

Diving & Snorkelling

Although there are many, many places to dive around Thailand, Phuket is indisputably the primary centre for the Thai scuba-diving industry and one of the world's top 10 dive destinations. The island is ringed by good to excellent dive sites, including several small islands to the south and east – Ko Heh, Ko Raya (Noi & Yai), Ko Yao (Noi & Yai), Hin Daeng and Hin Muang (known as Shark Point as it is a habitat for harmless leopard sharks, (however Hin Muang literally means 'Purple Rock'). Excursions further afield to Ao Phang-Nga islands to the east, and to the world-famous Surin and Similan Islands to the north-west, are also primarily run from Phuket. Some outfits are now also providing live-aboard trips to islands in the Mergui Archipelago off the southern coast of Myanmar – when relations between Thailand and Myanmar are favourable. When the neighbouring countries are having a political spat (quite common in recent years) trips to the area are sometimes suspended.

Most Phuket diving operations are centred at Hat Patong, with a sprinkling of branch offices in town or on other beaches. Many companies stagger regularly scheduled dives throughout the week so that different dive groups don't bump into one another; for example, Santana might go to Ko Raya Yai on Monday and Shark Point on Tuesday, while Calypso might do Shark Point on Monday and Raya Yai on Tuesday, and so on. Typical one-day dive trips to nearby sites

such as these cost around 1900B to 2600B, including two dives, tanks and weights, transport, dive master service, breakfast and lunch. Snorkellers are often permitted to join such dive trips for a 30% to 50% discount. PADI open-water certification courses cost around 8000B to 11,000B for four days of instruction and all equipment.

A few companies – generally the larger, more well-established ones – offer extended three- to seven-day trips on live-aboard dive boats, ranging from 3000B to 5000B per day per person, to Ko Phi-Phi, Ko Similan and Ko Surin. Trips to the increasingly popular Burma Banks are also possible but are a bit more expensive due to the extra paperwork involved.

Most dive shops also rent the following equipment: regulator (250B a day), BCD (300B), mask, fins and snorkel (250B), wetsuit (200B). Ask about equipment rental packages that go for around 500B to 700B per day with further discounts given to long-term renters.

Phuket boasts a large number of dive companies – at last count there were over 50. A list of the more reputable dive companies on the island follows (of these, Aqua Divers, Marina Divers and Paradise Diving have French-speaking staff):

Andaman Divers (☎/fax 076 341 126) Hat Patong

Aqua Divers (☎ 076 327 006, fax 076 327 338, W www.aquadivers.de) Pearl Village Resort

Calypso Divers (☎/fax 076 330 869) Hat Kata-Karon

Fantasea Divers (☎ 076 340 088, fax 076 340 309, W www.fantasea.net) Hat Patong

Marina Divers (☎ 076 330 272–516) Hat Karon

Neptune Diving (☎/fax 076 340 585) Hat Patong

Paradise Diving (☎ 076 327 420, W www .paradise-diving.com) Crown Nai Yang Hotel

PIDC Divers (☎ 076 280 644, fax 076 381 219, W www.pidcdivers.com) Ao Chalong

Santana (☎ 076 294 220, fax 076 340 360, e diving@santanaphuket.com) Hat Patong

Scuba Cat Diving (☎ 076 293 121, fax 076 293 122, W www.scubacat.com) Hat Patong

Sea Bees Diving (☎/fax 076 381 765, W www .sea-bees.com) Ao Chalong

Sea Hawk Divers (☎ 076 341 179, fax 076 344 151) Hat Patong
South East Asia Divers (☎ 076 344 022, fax 076 342 530, ⓦ www.phuketdive.net) Hat Patong
South East Asia Live Aboard (☎ 076 340 406, fax 076 340 586, ⓦ www.sealiveaboards.com) Hat Patong

There are many others in Phuket that are equally good, but it's a good idea to make sure that the dive shop you pick is affiliated with Sub-aquatic Safety Service (SSS; ☎ 076 342 518, 016 061 869, fax 076 342 519), which operates a hyperbaric (decompression) chamber in Patong. This means the dive shop is insured should one of their customers need to use the chamber in an emergency. If a shop is not a member, then, should you need Dive Safe Asia's services, you may end up footing the bill (around US$3000).

Snorkelling is best along Phuket's west coast, particularly at rock headlands between beaches. Mask, snorkel and fins can be rented for around 250B a day. As with scuba diving, you'll find better snorkelling, with greater visibility and variety of marinelife, along the shores of small outlying islands like Ko Heh, Ko Yao and Ko Raya.

As elsewhere in the Andaman Sea, the best diving months are December to May when the weather is good and the sea is at its clearest (and boat trips are much safer).

There are a number of shops that rent diving supplies:

Dive Supply (☎ 076 342 511, ⓔ dsupply@ loxinfo.co.th) 189 Th Rat Uthit, Hat Patong. Stocks a large variety of dive supplies and equipment.
Phuket Wetsuits (☎ 076 381 818, ⓦ www .phuketwetsuit.com) Offers both custom and ready-made wet suits.
Sea Sports (☎ 076-381065) 1/11–12 Th Chao Fa. Carries all manner of water sport equipment and supplies, along with canoes and kayaks.

Yachting
Phuket is one of South-East Asia's main destinations for yachts and you'll find all manner of craft anchored along its shores, from 80-year-old wooden sloops that look like they can barely stay afloat, to the latest in high-tech world motor cruisers. Marina-style facilities with year-round anchorage

are available at two locations on the protected eastern side of the island: Phuket Boat Lagoon (☎ 076 239 055, fax 076 239 056) at Ao Sapam, about 20km north of Phuket town on the east shore; and The Yacht Haven Phuket Marina (☎ 076 206 022–5, fax 076 206 026) at Laem Phrao on the eastern side of the northern tip.

Phuket Boat Lagoon offers an enclosed marina with tidal channel access, serviced pontoon berths, 60- and 120-tonne travel lifts, hard-stand area, plus a resort hotel, laundry, coffee shop, fuel, water, repairs and maintenance services. The Yacht Haven boasts 130 berths, condominiums, immigration facilities, restaurants and a health spa.

Port clearance is rather complicated; both marinas will take care of the paperwork (for a fee), if notified of your arrival in advance.

You may be able to travel by yacht between Phuket and Penang (Malaysia) as a paying passenger or as crew. Ask around at these marinas or at Hat Patong to see what's available. You may also find yachts going farther afield, particularly to Sri Lanka. December and early January are the best months to look for them. The crossing takes about 10 to 15 days.

Ao Chalong Yacht Club (☎ 076 381 488, fax 076 381 934) sometimes holds races for members. Other Phuket residents and visitors to Phuket are also welcome to participate; call for details.

Jimmy's Lighthouse (☎ 076 381 709) is another yachtie hang-out where you can get yachting information and a cold beer.

Parts & Service The Yacht Haven and Phuket Boat Lagoon offer routine repair and maintenance services, along with limited parts and supplies. In Ao Chalong there are several smaller marine repair and supply shops. If you need sails, Rolly Tasker Sailmakers (☎ 076 280 347, fax 076 280 348, ⓔ rolly@sun.phuket.ksc.co.th) claims to have the lowest sail prices in Asia; riggings, spars and hardware are also available.

Charters For information on yacht charters – both bareboat and crewed – yacht sales and yacht deliveries, contact the following:

Asia Yachting (☎ 076 381 615) Ao Chalong
Big A Yachting Swann 55 (☎ 076 381 934, fax 076 381 934) Ao Chalong
Phuket Boating Association (☎/fax 076 381 322) Phuket Boat Lagoon
South East Asia Liveaboards (☎ 076 340 406, fax 076 340 586) Hat Patong
Sunsail Yacht Charters (☎ 076 239 057, fax 076 238 940, e sunthai@phuket.loxinfo.co .th) Phuket Boat Lagoon
Thai Marine Leisure (☎ 076 239 111, fax 076 238 974, e tml@thaimarine.com) Hat Patong

Charters aboard 32- to 44-foot yachts start at 9000B a day, while 39- to 85-foot yachts start at 18,000B a day. Discounts of around 33% are available June to October. Day trips usually include boat, crew, lunch and soft drinks, plus snorkelling and fishing gear.

Paddling

Several companies based in Phuket offer inflatable canoe tours of scenic Ao Phang-Nga; see section earlier for details.

Island Tours & Elephant Trekking

Siam Safari (☎ 076 280 116) and Adventure Safaris (☎ 076 341 988) combine 4WD tours of the island's interior with brief elephant rides and short hikes for around 1950B a day. Half-day trips are also available, although the difference in price is not that great.

If you're interested in riding an elephant through some spectacular scenery, Kalim Elephant Trekking (☎ 076 290 056, fax 076 342 435), 154 Th Hat Kalim, just north of Patong, has a stable of elephants and experienced mahouts. Hour-long treks cost 900B per person, half-hour treks cost half that. The price includes transfer to and from your hotel.

Fishing

Phuket Sportfishing Centre (☎ 076 341 379 fax 076 236 182, e wahoo@phket.lox info.co.th) has three sport-fishing boats and does charters for individuals and groups. Prices start at 3000B per person for individuals (with a minimum of five), and 15,000B to charter the boat for up to eight persons. The price includes lunch and transfer to and from your hotel. Boats usually depart at 7.30am and return at 6.30pm.

Horse Riding

Phuket Laguna Riding Club (☎ 076 324 199, fax 076 324 099, e lagunariding@phuket dir.com) in Hat Bangtao offers guided rides through hills and along beaches for experts as well as beginners. They have a stable of over 30 horses to choose from. Prices are 660B for one hour of riding, 1100B for 1½ hours and 1600B for 2½ hours.

Cooking

Pat Thienthong, who worked as a chef at a Thai restaurant in California for six years, offers Thai cooking courses at her home, located just outside Phuket town. Pat lets her students choose their own course, either Central Thai or traditional Phuket cuisine. Half-day courses cost 900B, or 1200B. She can be contacted by calling Phuket Reminder (☎ 076 213 765), 85 Th Rasada, a souvenir shop in Phuket town.

Dinner Theatre

Phuket Fantasea (☎ *076 271 222,* w *www .phuket-fantasea.com; admission without/with buffet dinner 1000/1500B; open 5.30pm-11.30pm daily, except Tues),* a US$60 million 'cultural theme park', is located just north of Hat Kamala. Despite the billing, there aren't any rides but there is a truly magical show that manages to capture the colour and pageantry of traditional Thai dance and costumes and combine them with state-of-the-art light and sound techniques that rival anything found in Las Vegas. This takes place on a stage dominated by a full-scale replica of a Khmer temple reminiscent of Angkor Wat. Kids especially would be captivated by the spectacle. There is also quite a good and varied collection of souvenir shops in the park offering Thai-made handicrafts. Tickets for Fantasea can be booked through most hotels and tour agencies.

PHUKET
อ.เมืองภูเก็ต

postcode 83000 • pop 61,800

Centuries before Phuket began attracting sand-and-sea hedonists it was an important trade centre for Arab, Indian, Malay, Chinese

PHUKET

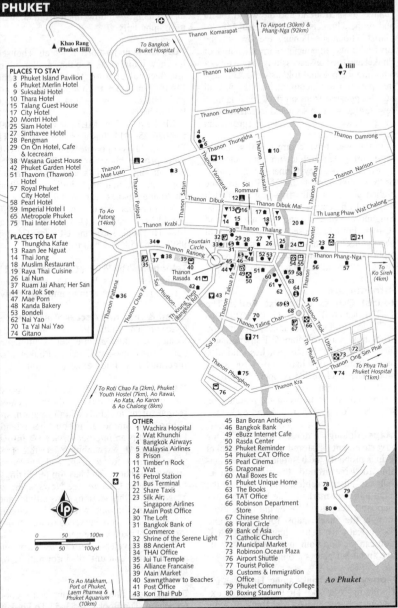

▲ Khao Rang
(Phuket Hill)

To Bangkok
Phuket Hospital

Thanon Komarapat

To Airport (30km) &
Phang-Nga (92km)

Thanon Nakhon

▲ Hill
▼7

Thanon Chumphon

PLACES TO STAY
3 Phuket Island Pavilion
6 Phuket Merlin Hotel
9 Suksabai Hotel
10 Thara Hotel
15 Talang Guest House
17 City Hotel
20 Montri Hotel
25 Siam Hotel
27 Sinthavee Hotel
29 On On Hotel, Cafe
   & Icecream
38 Wasana Guest House
42 Phuket Garden Hotel
51 Thavorn (Thawon)
   Hotel
57 Royal Phuket
   City Hotel
58 Pearl Hotel
59 Imperial Hotel I
65 Metropole Phuket
75 Thai Inter Hotel

PLACES TO EAT
7 Thungkha Kafae
13 Raan Jee Nguat
14 Thai Jong
18 Muslim Restaurant
19 Raya Thai Cuisine
26 Lai Nun
37 Ruam Jai Ahan; Her San
44 Kra Jok See
47 Mae Porn
48 Kanda Bakery
53 Bondeli
62 Nai Yao
70 Ta Yal Nai Yao
74 Gitano

Thanon Thungkha

Thanon Damrong

Thanon Mae Luan

Thanon Palipat

To Ao
Patong
(14km)

Thanon Satun

Thanon Krabi

Thanon Yaowarat

Thanon Thepkasatri

Thanon Suthat

Thanon Narison

Th Luang Phaw Wat Chalong

Soi
Rommani

Thanon Dibuk

Thanon Dibuk Mai

Thanon Thalang

Thanon Ranong

Fountain
Circle

Thanon
Rasada

Thanon Takua Pa

Montri

Thanon Phang-Nga

To
Ko Sireh
(4km)

To Ao
Patong
(14km)

Soi Phuthon

Thanon Chao Fa

Thanon Pattana

Th Krung Thep (Bangkok Rd)

Soi 9

Thanon Taling Chan

Thanon Phunphon

Thanon Kra

Thanon Tilok Uthit

Th Phuket

Thanon Ong Sim Phai

To Phya Thai
Phuket Hospital
(1km)

To Roti Chao Fa (2km), Phuket
Youth Hostel (7km), Ao Rawai,
Ao Kata, Ao Karon
& Ao Chalong (8km)

OTHER
1 Wachira Hospital
2 Wat Khunchi
4 Bangkok Airways
5 Malaysia Airlines
8 Prison
11 Timber'n Rock
12 Wat
16 Petrol Station
21 Bus Terminal
22 Share Taxis
23 Silk Air;
   Singapore Airlines
24 Main Post Office
30 The Loft
31 Bangkok Bank of
   Commerce
32 Shrine of the Serene Light
33 88 Ancient Art
34 THAI Office
35 Jui Tui Temple
36 Alliance Francaise
39 Main Market
40 Sawngthaew to Beaches
41 Post Office
43 Kon Thai Pub

45 Ban Boran Antiques
46 Bangkok Bank
49 eBuzz Internet Cafe
50 Rasda Center
52 Phuket Reminder
54 Phuket CAT Office
55 Pearl Cinema
56 Dragonair
60 Mail Boxes Etc
61 Phuket Unique Home
63 The Books
64 TAT Office
66 Robinson Department
   Store
67 Chinese Shrine
68 Floral Circle
69 Bank of Asia
71 Catholic Church
72 Municipal Market
73 Robinson Ocean Plaza
76 Airport Shuttle
77 Tourist Police
78 Customs & Immigration
   Office
79 Phuket Community College
80 Boxing Stadium

0   50   100m
0   50   100yd

To Ao Makham,
Port of Phuket,
Laem Phanwa &
Phuket Aquarium
(10km)

Ao Phuket

and Portuguese traders who came here to exchange goods from around the world for tin and rubber. Francis Light, the British colonialist who made Penang the first of the British Straits settlements, married a native of Phuket and tried unsuccessfully to pull this island into the colonial fold as well. Although this polyglot, multicultural heritage has all but disappeared from most of the island, a few vestiges can be seen and experienced in the province's *amphoe meuang* (provincial capital), Phuket.

In the older town centre you'll see some Sino-Portuguese architecture, characterised by ornate two-storey Chinese *hâang thâew* or 'row companies' fronted by Romanesque arched porticoes with 'five-foot ways' that were a 19th-century tradition in Malaysia, Singapore, Macau and Hainan Island (China). For a time it seemed this wonderful old architecture was all being torn down and replaced with modern structures but in recent years a preservation ethic has taken hold.

Information

Tourist Offices & Tourist Police The TAT office (☎ 076 212 213, 076 211 036) at 73–75 Th Phuket has maps, information brochures, a list of standard sǎwngthǎew fares out to the various beaches, and also the recommended charter costs for a vehicle. The TAT office is open daily from 8.30am to 4.30pm.

The Tourist Police can be reached on ☎ 1699, 076 355 015 or 076 254 693.

Maps Although it doesn't look like it, the advertisement-plastered A-O-A Phuket Map is probably the best one if you're planning to drive around. It's more accurate than the other freebies, and it has all the route numbers marked. The free Thaiways map isn't very good for island navigation, though the inset maps for Patong and Karon-Kata are better than the A-O-A's. You can pick up both maps at the TAT office and other places around the island.

Money Several banks along Th Takua Pa, Th Phang-Nga and Th Phuket offer exchange services and ATMs. Bank of Asia,

opposite the TAT office on Th Phuket, has an exchange window open from 8.30am until 8pm daily.

Post The main post office, which is housed in a new building next to the smaller, older architectural gem on Th Montri, is open Monday to Friday from 8.30am to 4.30pm, and Saturday, Sunday and holidays from 9am to noon.

Mail Boxes Etc (MBE; ☎ 076 256 409, fax 076 256 411) has a branch at 168/2 Th Phuket, almost opposite The Books. MBE rents private mail boxes, sells packaging and mailing materials and offers photocopying, laminating, binding, passport photo and business-card services.

Two courier services in town are DHL World Wide Express (☎ 076 258 500), at 61/4 Th Thepkasatri; and UPS (☎ 076 263 989), at 64/53 Th Chao Fa.

Telephone The Phuket CAT office, on Th Phang-Nga, offers Home Country Direct service and is open 8am to midnight daily.

Email & Internet Access eBuzz Internet Cafe on Th Takua Pa, is conveniently located near the On On Hotel. A quiet corner of The Books, at 53–55 Th Phuket, also functions as an Internet-access point.

Internet Resources Phuket Island Access (Ⓦ www.phuket.com) is a sophisticated source for many kinds of information, including accommodation on the island. Phuket Net is an Internet service (Ⓔ info@ phuket.net, Ⓦ www.phuket.net) that provides forums for tourism and business-oriented exchange, and has limited listings.

The *Phuket Gazette* (see Newspapers & Magazines in this section) posts articles and updated info along with its searchable *Gazette Guide* on Phuket Gazette Online (Ⓦ www.phuketgazette.net).

Phuket Travelers' Net (Ⓦ www.trv.net) has a small amount of information on Phuket.

Bookshops Phuket has one very good bookshop, The Books, at 53–55 Th Phuket, near the TAT office. The selection includes English-language magazines, guidebooks and novels. There's also a branch at 198/2 Th Rat Uthit in Patong.

Newspapers & Magazines The fortnightly English-language *Phuket Gazette* publishes lots of information on activities, events, dining and entertainment in town as well as around the island. An online version of the newspaper (**W** www.phuketgazette .net) is updated daily.

In 2000 the same publisher issued *Gazette Guide*, a 385-page listing of services and businesses on the island, though it's unclear whether the directory will be updated yearly.

A weekly English-language newspaper called *Siangtai Times* is also available, along with the usual tourist freebies such as *What's On South* and *Phuket Guide*, the latter being the better of the two.

The small-format *Phuket Holiday Guide* (120B) contains lots of solid information and insider's tips on accommodation, transport and other travel practicalities on the island. It also contains the most unbiased sightseeing information of any of the glossies available, probably because it relies less on advertising.

Medical Services Hospitals on the island include:

Bangkok Phuket Hospital (☎ 076 254 421) Th Yongyok Uthit
Patong/Kathu Hospital (☎ 076 340 444) Th Sawatdirak, Patong
Phuket International Hospital (☎ 076 249 400, emergency ☎ 076 210 935) Airport Bypass Rd
Phya Thai Phuket Hospital (☎ 076 252 603) 28/36–37 Th Si Sena, Phuket
Wachira Hospital (☎ 076 211 114) Th Yaowarat, Phuket

International doctors rate the Phuket International Hospital, as the best on the island, while Bangkok Phuket (run by Bangkok General Hospital) is reportedly favourite with the locals. Both Phuket International and Bangkok Phuket hospitals are equipped with modern facilities, emergency rooms and outpatient care clinics. Feedback we've received about these hospitals indicates that, although they're well equipped, better treatment is readily available in Bangkok.

Dangers & Annoyances Every year about 20 people lose their lives in drowning accidents off Phuket's beaches. Red flags are posted on beaches to warn bathers of riptides and other dangerous conditions. If a red flag is flying at a beach, don't go into the water.

Renting and riding a motorcycle on Phuket is a high-risk proposition. The death rate for motorcycle accidents is high, the injury rate is appallingly so – over 10,000 people are injured each year on Phuket's highways alone. Quite a few of those killed or maimed are travellers who thought that they were skilled enough to navigate Phuket's chaotic traffic.

Things to See & Do

If you want to see historic **Sino-Portuguese architecture**, your best bets are along Thalang, Dibuk, Yaowarat, Ranong, Phang-Nga, Rasada and Krabi streets. The most magnificent examples in town are the Standard Chartered Bank – Thailand's oldest foreign bank – on Th Phang-Nga and the THAI office on Th Ranong, but there are lots of more-modest buildings of interest along these streets. The best restored homes are found along Th Dibuk and Th Thalang.

Phuket's main **market** on Th Ranong is fun to wander through and is a good place to buy Thai and Malay sarongs as well baggy Shan (fisherman's) pants. A few old **Chinese temples** can be found in this area. Most are standard issue, but one that's a little bit different is the **Shrine of the Serene Light** (*Saan Jao Sang Tham or Shrine of Dharmic Light; open 8.30am–noon, 1.30pm–5.30pm*), which is tucked away at the end of a 50m alley right next to the Bangkok Bank of Commerce on Th Phang-Nga. There's a little garden in front of the shrine, which is a very calm and peaceful spot with some interesting pieces of temple art. Said to be 100 to 200 years old, the shrine was restored a few years ago.

Walk up **Khao Rang**, sometimes called Phuket Hill, north-west of town, for a nice view of the city, jungle and sea. If, as many people say, Phuket is a corruption of the Malay word *bukit* (hill), then this is probably its namesake.

Vegetarian Festival

The Vegetarian Festival, is Phuket's most important and usually takes place during late September or October.

The TAT office in Phuket prints a helpful schedule of events for the Vegetarian Festival. If you plan to attend the street processions, consider bringing earplugs to make the noise of the firecrackers more tolerable. See the 'Vegetarian Festival' boxed text for more information.

Places to Stay – Budget

On On Hotel (☎ 076 211 154, 19 Th Phang-Nga) Singles with fan 120B, singles/doubles with bath 180/250B, with air-con 360B. This is near the centre of town and close to the săwngthăew terminal for most outlying beaches. It has real character with its old Sino-Portuguese architecture (established 1929), though the rooms are basically just four walls and a bed. It was used as a set for the movie *The Beach*.

Pengman (☎ 076 211 486 ext 169, 69 Th Phang-Nga) Rooms with fan 100B. The simple Pengman, above a Chinese restaurant, has basic but quite clean rooms. As long as you're not put off by having to walk through the restaurant to get to your room, it's the best-value deal going in town.

Talang Guest House (☎ 076 214 225, 37 Th Thalang) Rooms in low/high season 250/300B, with 3 beds or 4 beds & air-con 400B. Three-storey Talang, in a classic, tidy shophouse in the old city centre rents large rooms. If you want a good street view, ask for No 31, a fan room on the third floor with a wide veranda.

Wasana Guest House (☎ 076 211 754, 159 Th Ranong) Rooms with fan/air-con & bath 200/350B. Next to the Th Ranong market, this has clean rooms and is conveniently located near Phuket's vegetarian eateries.

Montri Hotel (☎ 076 212 936, fax 076 232 097, 12/6 Th Montri) Rooms with fan 220B, with air-con 550-650B. Once one of Phuket's nicer hotels, this has descended into a zone somewhere between budget and mid-range, with rather ordinary rooms.

Thai Inter Hotel (☎ 076 220 275, fax 076 225 287, 22 Soi 3, Th Phunphon) Rooms with fan/air-con & bath 300/400B. This is convenient to the airport-shuttle drop-off in town if you've just flown into Phuket or you're catching an early morning flight.

Phuket Youth Hostel (☎ 076 280 806, 73/11 Th Chao Fa, Chalong) Fan rooms with bath 195B. This is located 7km south of the city centre. Those without Hostelling International membership must pay 50B extra per night. The Phuket Youth Hostel is located on the left between Wat Chalong and the five-road intersection.

About the only time it's really necessary to know about the following three hotels is during the Vegetarian Festival when it's very difficult to find vacant rooms in Phuket.

Thara Hotel (☎ 076 216 208, 148/24 Th Thepkasatri) Rooms with fan & bath 120B. The Thara is well-worn and dominated by short-time trade, but it's quite cheap for a room with an attached bath.

Suksabai Hotel (☎ 076 212 287, 82/9 Soi Nam Pheung, Th Thepkasatri) Rooms 150-200B. This is a bit of a short-time place but is fairly clean and, on weekdays anyway, very quiet.

Siam Hotel (☎ 076 224 543, 13–15 Th Phuket) Single/double rooms with fan & bath 150/200B. The dark Siam Hotel is basically a brothel but has adequate rooms.

Places to Stay – Mid-Range

Thavorn Hotel (Thawon Hotel; ☎ 076 211 333, 74 Th Rasada) Singles/doubles with fan & bath 350B, with air-con, TV, hot water & carpet 550B. This huge place consists of an original, less-expensive wing at the back and a flashier place up front. The best thing about the Thavorn is the lobby, which is filled with antiques and historic photos of Phuket.

Vegetarian Festival

The Vegetarian Festival, Phuket's most important festival, takes place during the first nine days of the ninth lunar month of the Chinese calendar – usually late September or October.

Basically, the festival celebrates the beginning of the month of 'Taoist Lent', when devout Chinese abstain from eating all meat and meat products. In Phuket, the festival activities are centred around five Chinese temples, with the Jui Tui temple on Th Ranong the most important, followed by Bang Niaw and Sui Boon Tong temples. Events are also celebrated at temples in the nearby towns of Kathu (where the festival originated) and Ban Tha Reua.

The TAT office in Phuket prints a helpful schedule of events for the Vegetarian Festival each year. The festival also takes place in Trang, Krabi and other Southern Thai towns.

Besides abstention from meat, the Vegetarian Festival involves various processions, temple offerings and cultural performances, and culminates with incredible acts of self-mortification – walking on hot coals, climbing knife-blade ladders, piercing the skin with sharp objects and so on. Shop owners along Phuket's central streets set up altars in front of their shopfronts offering nine tiny cups of tea, incense, fruit, candles and flowers to the nine emperor gods invoked by the festival. Those participating as mediums bring the nine deities to earth for the festival by entering into a trance state and piercing their cheeks with all manner of objects – sharpened tree branches (with leaves still attached), spears, slide trombones, daggers; some even hack their tongues continuously with saw or axe blades. During the street processions these mediums stop at the shopfront altars, where they pick up the offered fruit and either add it to the objects piercing their cheeks or pass it on to bystanders as a blessing. They also drink one of the nine cups of tea and grab some flowers to stick in their waistbands. The shop owners and their families stand by with their hands together in a *wâi* gesture, out of respect for the mediums who are temporarily possessed by the deities.

The entire atmosphere is one of religious frenzy, with deafening firecrackers, ritual dancing, and bloody shirt fronts. Oddly enough, there is no record of this kind of activity associated with Taoist Lent in China. Some historians assume that the Chinese here were somehow influenced by the Hindu festival of Thaipusam in nearby Malaysia, which features similar acts of self-mortification. The local Chinese claim, however, that the festival was started by a theatre troupe from China that stopped off in nearby Kathu around 150 years ago. The story goes that the troupe was struck seriously ill because the members had failed to propitiate the nine emperor gods of Taoism. The nine-day penance they performed included self-piercing, meditation and a strict vegetarian diet.

Joe Cummings

City Hotel (☎ *076 216 910–7, 9/1 Th Thepkasatri*) Singles/doubles with air-con, TV, phone, bath & carpet 1090/1290B, suites 1908B. At the corner of Th Thepkasatri and Th Dibuk, this offers barely decent rooms and is the kind of place that fills its vacant rooms by netting fresh arrivals at the airport.

Imperial Hotel I (☎ *076 212 311, fax 076 212 894, 51 Th Phuket*) Rooms with air-con, TV & hairdryer 650-1250B. The friendly, recently refurbished and well-located Imperial has clean and comfortable rooms.

Sinthavee Hotel (☎ *076 211 186, fax 076 211 400, 85–91 Th Phang-Nga*) Rooms with air-con, hot bath, fridge & carpet in the low/high season 500/700B, deluxe rooms with TV 800/1300B, suites 4500B. Even during the high season it's worth asking about discounts here. Other facilities include a 24-hour coffee shop and business centre.

Places to Stay – Top End

Phuket Garden Hotel (☎ *076 216 900–8, fax 076 216 909, 40/12 Th Krung Thep*) Rooms 850-1200B. This has all the usual amenities, though its location west of the town centre isn't a big recommendation.

Pearl Hotel (☎ *076 211 044, 076 212 911, fax 076 212 911, 42 Th Montri*) Rooms 1883-2119B. Pearl has a rooftop restaurant, fitness centre, swimming pool and so on.

Phuket Merlin Hotel (☎ *076 212 866, fax 076 216 429, 158/1 Th Yaowarat*) Rooms 1452-4598B. Like all the hotels in the Merlin chain, this place has seen better days. There's a swimming pool and fitness centre.

Metropole Phuket (☎ *076 215 050, fax 076 215 990, 1 Soi Surin, Th Montri*) Rooms with breakfast 2000-11,000B. One of the best located top-enders is the plush Metropole, right in the centre of things. Facilities include two Chinese restaurants, a coffee shop, three bars, swimming pool, fitness centre, business centre and airport shuttle service.

Phuket Island Pavilion (☎ *076 210 444, fax 076 210 458, 133 Th Satun*) Rooms 1140-1600B. This well-located place has spacious, well-appointed rooms.

Royal Phuket City Hotel (☎ *076 233 333, fax 076 233 335,* e *royalpktcity@ phuket.com, 154 Th Phang-Nga*) Rooms 2514-5028B. A short walk east of the CAT office is this towering hotel, which has state-of-the-art rooms.

Places to Eat

Town Centre If there's one thing the town of Phuket is known for, it's good food – even if you're staying at the beach it's worth a trip into the city to sample authentic, Phuket-style cooking (a blend of Thai, Malay and Straits Chinese influences). Meals in the city tend to cost 50% less than meals at the beach.

Raan Jee Nguat (*Th Yaowarat*) Dishes 20-40B. Open 7am-2pm. One long-running local institution is Raan Jee Nguat, a very humble, Phuket-style restaurant run by Hokkien Chinese, on the corner of historic Th Yaowarat and Th Dibuk. Raan Jee Nguat serves Phuket's most famous dish, delicious *khanǒm jiin náam yaa phukèt* – Chinese noodles in a pureed fish and curry sauce, Phuket style, with fresh cucumbers, long green beans and other fresh vegetables on the side. Also good are *khài plaa mòk*, a

Phuket version of *hàw mòk* (eggs, fish and curry paste steamed in banana leaves), and the *kari mai fan*, similar to Malaysian laksa, but using rice noodles. The curries are highly esteemed as well.

Thai Jong (*Th Yaowarat*) Dishes 20-40B. A few doors south of Jee Nguat, this is a small Hokkien coffee shop serving southern Thai food until mid-afternoon. There is no roman-script sign.

The inexpensive **coffee shop** below the Pengman Hotel specialises in seafood noodles and is popular at lunchtime.

On On Cafe (*Th Phang-Nga*) Dishes 20-40B. Open 7am-7pm. A tiny place without a sign beside the On On Hotel, this serves all kinds of rice dishes and curries at reasonable prices.

On On Ice Cream (*19 Th Phang-Nga*) 20-60B. Adjacent to the hotel – part of the same building – is an air-con ice-cream parlour that also serves cold beer.

Mae Porn (☎ *076 212 106, 50/52 Th Phang-Nga*) Dishes 30-120B. Very popular with Thais and *faràng* alike, and deservedly so, is this restaurant on the corner of Th Phang-Nga and Soi Pradit, close to the On On and Sinthavee hotels. It sells curries, seafood, fruit shakes – you name it and Mae Porn has it – all at very reasonable prices.

Kanda Bakery (☎ *076 223 410, 31–33 Th Rasada*) Dishes 20-80B. A popular spot in town, Kanda is just south of Bangkok Bank. It's open early in the morning with fresh-baked whole-wheat bread, baguettes, croissants, cakes and real brewed coffee; it also serves a variety of *khâo tôm* specialities any time of day.

Roti Chao Fa (*Muslim; Th Chao Fa*) Dishes 20-30B. Open 6am-noon. A bit out of the city centre but well worth the effort to find is this clean and spacious place run by Thai-Malays. Besides superb *roti kaeng* (curries served with flat bread instead of rice), this restaurant has a wide variety of teas including what is known in Malaysia as *teh tarik* or 'pull tea' (*chaa ráwn maleh* in Thai). This frothy tea gets its Malay name from the process of aerating it, which involves an engaging show of pouring the tea from cup to cup at arm's length.

Muslim restaurant (Th Thepkasatri) This simple restaurant on the corner of Th Thepkasatri and Th Thalang is a good local discovery – look for the star and crescent. This friendly family-run place serves delicious and inexpensive *mátsaman kài* (chicken-potato curry), roti kaeng (flatbread and curry – in the morning only) and khâo mòk kài (usually gone by 1pm).

Lai Nun (Th Thalang) This is a good, friendly Muslim restaurant. There is no roman-script sign, look for the sign with a red star.

Nai Yao (☎ 076 212 719, Th Phuket) Dishes 25-40B. Open evenings only. Venerable Nai Yao is still hanging on in an old wooden building with a tin roof near the Honda dealer on Th Phuket. It features an excellent, inexpensive seafood menu (bilingual), cold beer and tables on the sidewalk. The house speciality is the unique and highly recommended *tôm yam hâeng* (dry *tôm yam*), which can be ordered with chicken, shrimp or squid.

Ta Yai Nai Yao (Nai Yao 2; ☎ 076 256 497 Th Taling Chan) Dishes 25-50B. Open 5.30pm–5.30am. This is a second and larger branch, opposite a Catholic church. Besides fresh seafood, Ta Yai Nai Yao offers Isan dishes and khâo tôm; the place keeps *tôh rûng* (until dawn) hours.

Kra Jok See (☎ 076 217 903, Th Takua Pa) Dishes 60-120B. Open 6pm-midnight Tues-Sun. A Phuket institution, perfect for an intimate night out, is Kra Jok See, in an old shophouse on the western side of Th Takua Pa. It's hard to spot as the front of the restaurant is screened by plants; look for Ban Boran Antiques next door. The kitchen specialises in a faràng-friendly Phuket cuisine, including delicious *hàw mòk tháleh* (steamed seafood curry). On slow nights the kitchen (but not the bar) may close as early as 10pm.

Raya Thai Cuisine (☎ 076 218 155, 48/1 Th Dibuk Mai) Dishes 80-160B. The tourist-oriented Raya Thai, on the corner of Th Thepkasatri, is a place that takes advantage of old Phuket architecture. Housed in a two-storey Sino-Portuguese mansion, the high ceilings and tall windows provide lots of air-flow and offer glimpses of the surrounding garden. The food is good, if a bit expensive by local standards.

A couple of vegetarian eateries *Ruam Jai Ahan Jeh (☎ 076 222 821, Th Ranong)* and *Her San (☎ 076 256 443, Th Ranong)* are located east of the colourful Jui Tui Chinese temple and serve good and cheap Chinese vegetarian food from 7am to 8pm.

Gitano (☎ 076 225 797, 14 Th Ong Sim Phai) Dishes 40-100B. Located near Robinson Ocean Plaza, this is a great place for a change from Phuket fare. Great Latin decor compliments a menu of Mexican, Californian and Thai dishes, as well as fruit shakes. And there's always something remarkable on the sound system.

Bondeli (☎ 076 212 639, 52 Th Rasada) Dishes 40-150B. Situated on the corner of Th Rasada and Th Thepkasatri, the air-conditioned Bondeli does sandwiches and pizza and has a selection of imported wines.

There's a *KFC* in the Robinson Ocean Plaza off Th Ong Sim Phai towards the southern end of town, as well as a *McDonald's* in the same vicinity. Next door to the shopping complex is Phuket's municipal market. Around three sides of this market you'll find an inexpensive *night market*.

Khao Rang (Phuket Hill) An unparalleled spot for an iced coffee at sunset is *Thungkha Kafae (☎ 076 211 500)*. Dishes 40-80B. Open 11am–11pm. This outdoor restaurant is at the top of the hill and has a pleasant atmosphere and good food. Try the *tôm khàa kài* (chicken coconut soup) or *khài jiaw hǎwy naang rom* (oyster omelette).

Ao Chalong Just past Wat Chalong is *Kan Eang 1 (☎ 076 381 661, 9/3 Th Chao Fa)*. Dishes 120-190B. On the left past the five-road intersection this good fresh-seafood place used to sit on a pier over the bay itself. Now housed in an enclosed air-con restaurant (open-air dining is still available as well), it still sets a standard for Phuket seafood, though prices have risen considerably. You order by weight, choosing from squid, oysters, crab, mussels and several kinds of fish, and then specify the method of cooking, whether grilled *(phǎo)*, steamed *(nêung)*, fried *(thâwt)*, parboiled *(lûak* – for squid), or in soup (tôm yam). It also offers a decent wine list.

Kan Eang 2 (☎ *076 381 323)* Dishes 120-190B. This second location is at the other end of Ao Chalong.

Entertainment

Alliance Française (☎ *076 222 988, 3 Soi 1, Th Phattana)* has weekly screenings of French films (subtitled in English). It also has a TV with up-to-date news broadcasts and a library.

Gitano (☎ *076 225 797, 14 Th Ong Sim Phai)* Open 10am-1am. This bar/restaurant has an excellent collection of Latin CDs as well as Tequila and Colombian coffee. There's also live music twice weekly. It's located near Robinson Ocean Plaza.

The major hotels have discos and/or karaoke clubs.

Timber 'n Rock (☎ *076 211 839, Th Yaowarat)* Open 7pm–2am. Just south of Th Thungkha, this is a well-run pub with attractive rustic decor, a variety of Phuket and Thai food and live music after 10pm.

Kon Thai Pub *(Th Krung Thep)* Along the same lines as Timber 'n Rock, this has a Thai band playing rock, folk and Thai pop tunes from 9.30pm nightly.

Eight real bouts of Thai boxing can be viewed every Friday night at 8pm at the ***boxing stadium*** near the pier on the southern edge of town. All seats are 500B and tickets can be purchased at the gate or, more conveniently, through a desk in the lobby of the On On Hotel (which includes transfer to and from the stadium).

Shopping

Although there are loads of souvenir shops and clothing boutiques surrounding the beach resorts of Patong, Kata and Karon, some of the best bargains on the island are found in the provincial capital. There are two main markets, one off the southern side of Th Ranong near the centre of town, and a second off the northern side of Th Ong Sim Phai a bit south-east of the town centre. The Th Ranong market traces its history back to the days when pirates, Indians, Chi-

nese, Malays and Europeans traded in Phuket and offers a wide variety of sarongs and fabrics from Thailand, Malaysia, Indonesia and India. You'll also find inexpensive clothing and crafts here.

At the newer Th Ong Sim Phai market the focus is on fresh produce. Adjacent to the market is the large Robinson Ocean Plaza, which contains a branch of the Robinson department store, as well as smaller shops with moderately priced clothing and housewares. Along Th Yaowarat between Th Phang-Nga and Th Thalang are a number of Indian-run tailor and fabric shops, while Chinese gold shops line Th Ranong opposite the market. Another shopping venue is the small Rasda Center/ Phuket shopping centre on Th Rasada.

The Loft (☎ *076 258 160, 36 Th Thalang)* In a restored shophouse, this sells Asian antiques, Nepalese-Tibetan carpets and ornaments downstairs, contemporary art upstairs.

Other antique shops in central Phuket town include ***88 Ancient Art*** (☎ *076 258 043, Th Yaowarat)* and ***Ban Boran Antiques*** (☎ *076 212 473, 24 Th Takua Pa)* next to Kra Jok See restaurant.

Phuket Unique Home (☎ *076 212 093, 186 Th Phuket)* Opposite The Books and the Imperial Hotel, this carries lots of original designs in silverware, dishware, home decor accessories and furniture, much of it a blend of old and new influences.

Tailors can be found along Th Yaowarat, but be wary of any place that has to post a tout at the door – tailors with a good reputation don't use these methods.

Getting There & Away

Air THAI operates nearly a dozen daily flights from Bangkok for 2270B one way. The direct flight takes an hour and 25 minutes, but some flights stop in Hat Yai for half an hour. There are also regular flights to/from Hat Yai for 880B. The THAI office (☎ 076 258 236) is at 78/1 Th Ranong.

Bangkok Airways (☎ 076 225 033–5) flies between Ko Samui and Phuket twice daily (once a week in June and September) for 1720B one way. The office is at 158/2–3 Th Yaowarat.

THAI flies between Phuket and several international destinations, including Penang, Kuala Lumpur, Singapore, Hong Kong, Taipei and Tokyo.

Angel Airlines flies daily between Bangkok and Phuket. There are also flights between Hong Kong and Phuket on Wednesday and Sunday. Their office on Phuket (☎/fax 076 351 339) is located in the Phuket international airport.

Other international airlines with offices in Phuket are: Malaysia Airlines (☎ 076 216 675), 1/8–9 Th Thungkha; Singapore Airlines (same offices as Silk Air; ☎ 076 213 891), 183/103 Th Phang-Nga; Dragonair (☎ 076 217 300), 37/52 Th Montri; and China Airlines (☎ 076 327 099), at Phuket international airport.

Bus From Bangkok, one government 1st-class air-con bus leaves the Southern bus terminal for Phuket at 7pm for 446B. Buses leave Phuket for the return journey at 5.30pm. Two VIP buses (690B) run daily from Bangkok (Southern bus terminal) at 5.30pm and 6pm. Departure times from Phuket are 4pm and 5pm. The trip takes 14 hours. The ride along winding Hwy 4 between Ranong and Phuket can be hair-raising if you are awake. Only ordinary buses travel during the day; these leave six times a day from 6am until 6.30pm for 254B, and take a gruelling 15 or 16 hours.

A couple of private tour buses run from Bangkok's Southern bus terminal to Phuket in the early evening with fares of 457B one way or 800B return. From Phuket, tour buses to Bangkok leave between 3pm and 6pm. Several agencies have offices on Th Rasada and Th Phang-Nga in the city's centre.

The main bus terminal for government buses is off the north side of Th Phang-Nga, a little to the north of Royal Phuket City Hotel. Fares and durations for bus trips to and from Phuket's government terminal include:

destination	fare (B)	hours
Hat Yai	135	8
(air-con)	233 to 243	7
Krabi	56	4½
(air-con)	101	4
Nakhon Si Thammarat	85 to 93	8
(air-con)	150 to 180	7
Phang-Nga	31	2½
Surat Thani	92	6
(air-con)	150	5½
Takua Pa	45	3
Trang	95	6
(air-con)	132 to 169	5

Taxi & Mini-van There are share taxis between Phuket and other provincial capitals in the south; taxi fares are generally around double the fare of an ordinary bus. The taxi stand for Nakhon Si Thammarat, Surat Thani, Krabi, Trang and Hat Yai is on Th Phang-Nga, near the Pearl Cinema.

Some companies sell air-con minivan (*rót tûu*) tickets to Ko Samui; the fare includes ferry transport. Air-con minivan services to Surat, Krabi and Ranong are also available. As in share taxis, fares are about double the public bus fares.

Getting Around

Phuket is a big island, and while there is public transport, it's only available during the day. In many cases you'll still need to take a taxi or *túk-túk* to get to some of the more out-of-the-way destinations, which will often cost 200B or more. Unless you're happy to stay rooted to one area of the island, you should seriously consider renting either a motorcycle or jeep, especially if there are several of you to share the cost.

To/From the Airport There is a minibus service at the airport that will theoretically take you into town for 80B per person. The minibus also continues to Patong, Kata or Karon beaches for 120B. If there aren't enough passengers to make the minibus run profitable, you may have to shell out the taxi rate: 360B for the trip from the airport to the city, or 480B to 540B to the beaches. In the reverse direction you should be able to negotiate a fare for 300B.

You can also rent cars at the airport; see the Car entry following.

Săwngthăew & Túk-túk Large bus-size săwngthăew run regularly from Th Ranong near the market to the various Phuket beaches for 10B to 30B per person – see the following Phuket Beaches & Nearby Islands section for details. Beware of tales about the tourist office being 5km away, or that the only way to reach the beaches is by taxi, or even that you'll need a taxi to get from the bus station to the town centre (the bus station is more or less *in* the town centre). Officially, beach săwngthăew run from 7am to 5pm; after that time you must charter a túk-túk to the beaches. The latter cost from 150B for Karon, Kata, Nai Han and Patong to 250B for Hat Kamala.

Smaller săwngthăew around town cost a standard 10B, túk-túk cost 20B.

Car Several agencies in town rent Suzuki jeeps for 900B per day, including insurance. If you rent for a week or more you can get the price down to 800B per day.

Avis Rent-A-Car (airport ☎ 076 351 243). Charges a bit more (around 1500B a day) but has outlets around the island at Le Meridien, Dusit Laguna, Novotel Patong, Sheraton Grande Laguna Beach and the airport. Avis is also more reliable than the local rental agencies.

Pure Car Rent (☎ 076 211 002) 75 Th Rasada. In the centre of town, this is your best choice.

Via Rent-A-Car (☎ 076 341 660) 189/6 Th Rat Uthit, Patong. Offers competitive rates and can deliver to anywhere on the island.

In the bigger beach towns there are numerous shops, hotels and bungalows where you can rent jeeps and motorcycles.

Motorcycle Motorcycle taxis around town are 10B. You can hire motorcycles (usually 100cc Japanese bikes) along Th Rasada between Th Phuket and Th Yaowarat or from various places at the beaches. Costs are around 200B to 300B per day. Bigger bikes (over 125cc) can be rented at a couple of shops at Patong and Karon.

Take care when riding a bike, and use common sense. People who ride around in shorts, T-shirt, a pair of thongs and no helmet are asking for trouble – a minor spill while wearing reasonable clothes would leave you bruised and shaken, but for somebody clad in shorts it could result in enough skin loss to end your travels right there. If you do have an accident you're unlikely to find that medical attention is up to international standards.

You should think seriously about whether or not it's worth the convenience to rent a motorcycle on Phuket. Even Thais admit that driving on the island is dangerous. In 2000, 159 people were killed and 10,359 were injured in motorcycle accidents on Phuket. A significant number of these were foreign visitors.

Phuket now has a helmet law that police claim will be enforced without exception: those caught not wearing one will be fined 300B. When we last visited there still seemed to be plenty of 'exceptions', but then again, it's just stupid to ride without a helmet.

AROUND THE ISLAND
Ko Sireh

This tiny island, 4km east of the capital and connected to the main island by a bridge over a canal, is known for its chao náam (sea gypsy) village and a hilltop reclining Buddha. There's a loop road that goes around the island, passing a few residences, shrimp farms, lots of rubber plantations and a bit of untouched forest. On the eastern side of the island is a public beach called **Hat Teum Suk** with a few chairs and thatched-roof shelters; it's nothing special, rather a local hang-out.

This village, the largest settlement of Urak Lawoi sea gypsies in Thailand, is little more than a poverty stricken cluster of tin shacks on stilts, plus one seafood restaurant called *Gypsy World*. The Urak Lawoi, the most sedentary of the three sea gypsy groups, are found only between the Mergui Archipelago and the Tarutao-Langkawi Archipelago and speak a creolised mixture of Malay and Mon-Khmer.

Laem Phanwa
แหลมพันวา

South of Phuket town, Route 4023 splits off Route 4021, then connects with Route 4129 to lead south-east from Phuket town to Laem Phanwa, a large cape that juts out into the Sea of Phuket. Just past the junction of Routes 4023 and 4129 you'll pass **Ao Makham**, a large mudflat bay where the Petroleum Authority of Thailand maintains a large oil depot. Most of the cape is inhabited by Thai Muslims; you'll see lots of goats wandering around and, in the village of **Ban Makham**, facing Route 4129, stands a very large and beautiful mosque. Past the oil facility is the **Port of Phuket**, near the entrance to which are several little roadside restaurants serving khâo mòk kài and other Muslim food.

Rubber, coconut and tamarind are farmed heavily in the interior of the cape. A winding, unnumbered road leads up the western side of the cape through the plantations, should you have your own wheels and care to see them.

At the end of Route 4129, at the tip of the cape, **Phuket Aquarium & Marine Biological Research Center** (☎ *076 391 128; admission 20B; open 8.30am–4pm*) displays a varied collection of tropical fish and other marine life. Some are alive in tanks, others stuffed and displayed. The sea turtle exhibit is the most impressive and informative.

The seafood restaurants along the Laem Phanwa waterfront are a great place to hang out for a while, to check out the pleasure skiffs and painted fishing boats passing by.

Places to Stay & Eat The luxurious *Cape Phanwa Hotel* (☎ *076 391 123–5, fax 076 391 177, in Bangkok* ☎ *022 339 560, 8 Th Sakdet*) has rooms from 3700B to 16,000B. This offers luxury accommodation spread out over a ridge.

Phanwa House, a classic Sino-Portuguese mansion, on the grounds of the hotel, is open to the public. The mansion has a library and a collection of antique furniture and art; tea and cocktails are served daily on the veranda, as well as Thai cuisine in the original dining room. A lighthouse on the grounds has also been turned into a lounge.

Not far from the aquarium are several old-fashioned Thai *seafood restaurants*.

Yam Yen Seafood (☎ *076 391 103*) Dishes 80-200B. This offers excellent and moderately priced outdoor dining under thatched shelters facing the bay.

Khao Phra Taew Royal Wildlife & Forest Reserve
อุทยานสัตว์ป่าเขาพระแทว

This mountain range in the northern interior of the island protects 2333 hectares of virgin island rainforest (evergreen monsoon forest). There are some nice jungle hikes in this reserve, along with a couple of waterfalls, **Ton Sai** and **Bang Pae**. The falls are best seen in the rainy season between June and November; in the dry months they slow to a trickle. Because of its royal status, the reserve is better protected than the average Thai national park.

A German botanist discovered a rare and unique species of palm in Khao Phra Taew about 50 years ago. Called the white-backed palm or langkow palm, the fan-shaped plant stands 3m to 5m tall and is found only here and in Khao Sok National Park. The highest point in the park is the 442m **Khao Phara**.

Tigers, Malayan sun bears, rhinos and elephants once roamed the forest here, but nowadays resident mammals are limited to humans, pigs, monkeys, slow loris, langur, civets, flying foxes, squirrels, mousedeer and other smaller animals. Watch out for cobras and wild pigs.

The **Phuket Gibbon Rehabilitation Centre** (☎ *076 381 065, 076 260 492; admission free; open 10am–4pm*), in the park near Bang Pae Falls (see entry above), is open to the public. Financed by donations (1500B will care for a gibbon for a year), the centre adopts gibbons that have been kept in captivity and re-introduces them to the wild.

Park rangers may act as guides for hikes in the park on request; call ☎ *016 767 864* and ask for Mr Phongchat. Payment for services is by donation.

To get to Khao Phra Taew from Phuket town, take Th Thepkasatri north about 20km to the district of Thalang, and turn right at the intersection for Ton Sai Falls, which is 3km down the road.

Thalang District

A few hundred metres north-east of the famous Heroines Monument in Thalang District on Route 4027, about 11km north of Phuket town or about 4km south-east of Thalang town is **Phuket National Museum** (☎ *076 311 426; admission 30B; open 8.30am–4pm)*, which recently underwent renovations. Altogether the museum contains five exhibit halls that mainly chronicle southern themes such as the history of Thalang-Phuket and the colonisation of the Andaman Coast, as well as descriptions of the various ethnicities found in Southern Thailand. The legend of the 'two heroines' (memorialised on the nearby monument) who supposedly drove off an 18th-century Burmese invasion force by convincing the island's women to dress as men, is also recounted in detail utilising back-lit display panels and touch-screen electronic presentations. The focal point of one hall is the impressive 2.3m-tall statue of Vishnu, which dates to the 9th century and was found in Takua Pa early in the 20th century.

Also in Thalang district, just north of the crossroads near Thalang town, is **Wat Phra Thong**, Phuket's 'Temple of the Gold Buddha'. The image is half buried so that only the head and shoulders are visible above ground. According to local legend, those who have tried to excavate the image have become very ill or encountered serious accidents soon after their failed attempts to move the image. The temple is particularly revered by Thai Chinese, many of whom believe the image hails from China. During Chinese New Year the temple is an important focus for pilgrims from Phang-Nga, Takua Pa and Krabi. In addition to Phra Thong there are several other Buddha images, including seven representing the different days of the week, plus a Phra Praket (an unusual pose in which the Buddha is touching his own head with his right hand) and a Phra Palelai (sitting in 'European pose').

Some parts of the movie *Good Morning Vietnam* were filmed on location in Thalang.

PHUKET BEACHES & NEARBY ISLANDS

Phuket beach accommodation has come a long way since 1977 when we first visited Kata and Nai Han and found thatched-roof huts for 10B a night. Nowadays 500B is rock-bottom. Patong is the most popular beach; its 'village' is now as large and populous as the provincial capital. Patong is worth a night or two, if only to get a dose of the beachside party scene. Keep in mind though that there are plenty of places on the island that, distance-wise, are relatively close to Patong while remaining light years away in attitude. If Patong gives you the creeps, don't flee Phuket, just try another beach.

Warning

Red flags are posted on beaches to warn bathers of riptides and other dangerous conditions. If a red flag is flying at a beach, don't go into the water. Especially during the May to October monsoon, the waves on the west coast of Phuket sometimes make it too dangerous to swim. The east coast is usually tamer at this time of year but, of course, there isn't much in the way of beaches there. Hat Rawai, on the south-eastern edge of the island is usually a safe bet at any time of year.

Keep an eye out for jet skis when you're in the water. Although the Phuket governor declared jet skis illegal in 1997, enforcement of the ban is cyclic.

Hat Patong

หาดป่าตอง

Fifteen kilometres west of Phuket by road, this large curved beach is the epicentre of the tourist earthquake that rattles Phuket throughout the high season (December to March). Over the last 10 years, Hat Patong has been rapidly turning into another Pattaya in all respects. It is now made up by a strip of hotels, upmarket bungalows, German and Italian restaurants, expensive seafood places, beer bars, nightclubs and coffee houses – and lots of locals on the make. It's a major party scene; anyone looking for peace and quiet will be disap-

Local Faràng

Of the gazillions of faràng visitors who have landed in Phuket over the last decade, a significant number of them must have stepped off the plane (or bus, or yacht) and thought: 'This is it. This is where I want to be'. At least, that's the idea you'll get if you hang around the island for a month or so. A huge service industry has grown up around the beaches most favoured by visitors and many of the businesses catering to faràng visitors – from restaurants to dive centres to day spas – are run by faràng.

Examine a few back issues of the *Phuket Gazette* to get an idea of just how extensive the faràng community of Phuket is. Stories in the English-language newspaper also shed some light on how Phuket's faràng community are adapting to life in the kingdom. According to faràng accounts, both the yachting and diving industry on Phuket have suffered because local officials haven't yet figured out what it is that brings faràng visitors to Phuket in the first place. Also commonly heard are faràng charges that greed causes some Thai officials to selfishly grasp for a piece of the tourist pie. A fair number of Phuket's faràng residents seem to think that official corruption is much worse here than anywhere else in Thailand, including Bangkok. Many Thais, on the other hand, feel that a good portion of the tourist dollars that come to the island is promptly being pocketed by faràng, whom they feel, have an unfair advantage. Thai locals believe that faràng visitors would rather patronise the businesses of other faràng due to their irrational fear that all Thais habitually try to rip them off. In their own defence, Phuket's faràng entrepreneurs explain that they provide jobs and training that the locals could never hope to receive without faràng support and guidance. They are not displacing the Thais, claim the faràng, but teaching them valuable skills. Officially however, the Thais aren't convinced, and they demonstrate their scepticism by periodically rounding up faràng without work permits and unceremoniously deporting them.

Despite the friction, there seems to be no shortage of faràng dreamers willing to sink money into opening and managing bars (the English tend to dominate in this category), restaurants (where the Italians are firmly in control) and dive shops (Germans and Scandinavians seem to gravitate in this direction). Should you decide to join their ranks, keep in mind that, along with the restaurateurs, bar-owners and dive instructors, there are also a number of faràng lawyers making a brisk living in Phuket – a fact that should set your alarm bells ringing.

Steven Martin

---

pointed, while those looking for maximum nightlife need look no further. Ironically, although this began as Phuket's most expensive beach, the prices have stabilised as the local accommodation market has become saturated. As it becomes funkier and rowdier, Patong is rapidly becoming the cheapest beach on the island for accommodation.

Information Patong has many foreign-exchange booths, plus a post-and-telephone office on the corner of Soi Phoemphong (Soi Post Office) and Th Thawiwong.

Several places in Patong offer terminals for email and Internet access, including Pizzedelic on Th Thawiwong next to the Banana Disco.

Dive Shops Patong is the diving centre of the island. See Diving & Snorkelling at the beginning of the Phuket Province section for a list of established dive shops.

Surfing Phuket's west-coast beaches get a good pounding during the May to October monsoon. Kata and Nai Han are said to be best for surfing, especially after a storm has blown through from the south-west. There are a few surf shops with boards for rent in Kata and Patong. Aloha Surf Sports Co (☎ 076 344 504), at 124/14 Th Thawiwong in Patong, rents out surfboards and other surfing accessories.

Boat Trips Several companies on Patong do one-day cruises to nearby islands. For

PATONG

PLACES TO STAY
1 Patong Lodge Hotel
2 Diamond Cliff Resort
6 PS Bungalow (PS II)
9 Patong Grand Condotel;
  Sky Inn
10 Club Andaman Beach Resort
11 Casuarina Patong
  Garden Resort
12 Phuket Cabana Resort
13 Patong Beach Bungalow
14 Patong Bay
  Garden Resort
15 Thara Patong
16 Chanathip Guest House
21 999 Peters
  Guest House
22 PS Hotel (PS I)
23 Expat Hotel
25 K Hotel
26 Capricorn Village
29 Safari Beach Hotel
31 Tropica Bungalow
36 Patong Beach Hotel
39 Baan Sukhothai Hotel
41 Andaman Resortel;
  Casa Summer Breeze
42 Sansabai Bungalows
46 Holiday Inn
  Resort Phuket
48 Comfort Resort Patong

49 Duangjit Resort
50 Amari Coral Beach
  Resort

PLACES TO EAT
3 Da Maurizio
4 Otowa
5 Baan Rim Pa
27 Restaurant 4
30 Savoey
32 Pizzedelic
37 Navrang Mahal
38 Le Croissant

OTHER
7 Mosque
8 Wat Suwan Khiri Wong
17 Night Market
18 Pow Wow Pub
19 Hospital
20 Paradise Complex
24 Tai Pan
28 Andaman Queen
33 Shipwreck
34 Banana Disco & Pub
35 Shark Club
40 Shark Club
43 The Hideaway
44 Post & Telephone Office
45 Patong Shopping Centre
47 Buses to Phuket

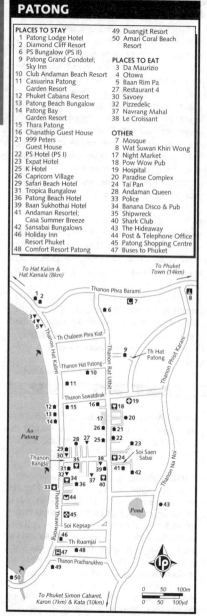

excursions to the Similan and Surin Islands off the Andaman Coast of Phang-Nga Province, see the sections on those islands earlier in this chapter.

Motor yachts, sailboats and catamarans can sometimes be chartered with or without crew. Read the Yachting section at the beginning of the Phuket Province section, or check with dive shops around Patong to find out who has what.

Massage & Herbal Sauna The Hideaway (☎ 076 340 591), on Th Na Nai in the foothills of east Patong, is an excellent sauna and massage centre. A two-hour Thai-herbal-massage-and-sauna package costs 950B. Massage alone is 500B per hour; sauna alone is also 500B per hour. Other treatments are available, including facials and aromatherapy. Open noon to 9pm daily.

Places to Stay – Budget Rates on Patong vary according to season. In the high season (December to March, and August) you'll be doing very well to find something under 400B a night. On the beach there is nothing under 600B, but on and off Th Rat Uthit, especially in the Paradise Complex and along Soi Saen Sabai, there are several nondescript guesthouses with rooms for 300B to 500B.

Budget places usually come with fan and shared bathroom; more expensive rooms in this category will have a private bath and perhaps air-con.

999 Peters Guest House (*☎/fax 076 340 555, 143/8 Soi Paradise*) Fan rooms 300-350B, with bath 450B. The best of the lot to be found in the soi leading to the Paradise Complex is the central but quiet 999 Peters Guest House. It's in a row-building and has a sitting area downstairs. Prices drop 100B in the low season.

Chanathip Guest House (*☎ 076 294 087, fax 076 294 088, 53/7 Th Rat Uthit*) Rooms with fan/air-con, fridge, satellite TV, phone & hot shower 450/700B. This place is friendly and good value. It's located on an unnamed soi off Th Rat Uthit, south of Th Sawatdirak (opposite Pow Wow Pub). Private lockers are available but you must supply your own lock. Try getting a room at the back of the building – the soi can be noisy at night.

PS Bungalow (PS II; ☎ 076 342 207–8, fax 076 290 034, 78/54 Th Rat Uthit) Rooms 400-650B. This place is off Th Rat Uthit and located a few blocks north of the action on Th Bangla, which may be a plus or a minus, depending on what you're here for. Prices are 100B higher during the December peak season.

Capricorn Village (☎/fax 076 340 390, 82/29 Th Rat Uthit) Bungalows 700-1000B. This has good bungalows, though the ones closest to the street catch a lot of traffic noise. Capricorn Village is often fully booked from mid November through January when the prices jump to 1000B to 1500B.

Places to Stay – Mid-Range A large number of places in Patong fall into the 800B-to-2000B range, which always includes air-con and private bath; the more expensive ones will have hot showers, lower priced ones cold water only. Room rates vary widely depending on the time of year. Besides high and low season, some establishments find it necessary to jack up their prices even higher during the peak season, roughly December and January. On the bright side, prices in this category can usually be negotiated down substantially during the rainy season.

Sansabai Bungalows (☎ 076 342 948–9, fax 076 344 888, 171/21 Soi Saen Sabai) Rooms with fan/air-con, hot water, fridge, TV & breakfast 1100/1300B, superior rooms 1450-1550B, bungalows with air-con & kitchen 2000B. At the friendly, quiet and efficient Sansabai, off Th Rat Uthit, there is a restaurant serving Italian and Thai dishes. A 10% service charge is tacked onto the room rates.

Andaman Resortel (☎ 076 341 516, fax 076 340 847, 65/21–25 Soi Saen Sabai), Rooms 900-1200B. This place is larger and less personal than neighbouring establishments.

Casa Summer Breeze (☎ 076 340 464, fax 076 340 493, 171/12 Muu 4, Soi Saen Sabai) Rooms 500-1100B. This small place (only 18 rooms) is clean, friendly and centrally located.

Expat Hotel (☎ 076 342 143, fax 076 340 300, 163/17 Th Rat Uthit) Rooms 750-1100B. Down a soi off Th Rat Uthit, this offers spacious rooms that have a bit of a short-time feel about them. Still, it's located right in the edge of the party zone and boasts a 24-hour coffee shop.

PS Hotel (PS I; ☎ 076 340 184, fax 076 341 097, 157 Th Rat Uthit) Rooms with air-con & satellite TV 1250-1550B. On a soi south of the Paradise Complex, this has decent if characterless rooms and is popular for its location in the heart of Patong.

Safari Beach Hotel (☎ 076 341 170, fax 076 340 231, 136 Th Thawiwong) Rooms in low/high season 900/1900B. Considering its central location facing the beach, rooms at the friendly Safari Beach are a bargain. On the premises are a small but pleasant pool and a good seafood restaurant.

Tropica Bungalow (☎ 076 340 204, fax 076 340 206, 94/4 Th Thawiwong) Rooms 1300-2000B. A good place to stay if you want to be near the action – Th Bangla is on one side and the Banana Disco is on the other. There's a swimming pool on the lush grounds and the rooms are surprisingly quiet given the location. During the low season prices drop by about 30%.

K Hotel (☎ 076 340 833, fax 076 340 124, 82/47 Th Rat Uthit) Rooms 1000-3000B. A one-storey place in a pleasant garden setting with a slick restaurant, this deals mostly with German package tourists, but when there's space you can get a decent room. Prices fluctuate wildly between high and low seasons.

Sky Inn (☎ 076 342 486, fax 076 340 576, 63 Th Rat Uthit) Rooms with fan/air-con 700/1200B. On the 9th floor of the Patong Grand Condotel, this caters to a primarily gay clientele. Prices drop by 20% during the low season.

Patong Lodge Hotel (☎ 076 341 020–4, fax 076 340 287, 284/1 Th Phra Barami) Rooms 1000-2500B. Just north of Hat Patong in a more secluded and rocky area known as Hat Kalim, this has well-kept rooms with all the amenities. This place is recommended if you want to be fairly close to the nightlife of Patong without actually being a part of it. There are also some excellent restaurants within walking distance.

Places to Stay – Top End At the lower end of the top price range, roughly 2000B to 3000B, you'll find a number of all-aircon places with swimming pools, modest room service, phones and most of the other amenities desired by the average mainstream visitor and package tourist.

Duangjit Resort (☎ 076 340 778–9, fax 076 340 288, 18 Th Prachanukhro) Rooms 2000-2800B. Near the intersection of Th Thawiwong and Th Prachanukhro, this has rooms in a solidly built, attractive hotel on landscaped grounds with pool.

Casuarina Patong Garden Resort (☎/fax 076 341 197–8, 188 Th Thawiwong) Rooms 1600-3200B. Towards the northern end of Th Thawiwong facing the beach, this long-established place has transformed itself bit by bit from a small collection of bungalows to a top-ender. There's a restaurant and a swimming pool.

Thara Patong (☎ 076 340 135, fax 076 340 446, 170 Th Thawiwong, ℮ thara@sun.phuket.ksc.co.th) Rooms 1300-2900B. Between Th Sawatdirak and Th Bangla on the beachfront road, this is a similar place to Casuarina but with a tennis court and business centre as well. Balcony rooms overlook the pool and can get noisy at times.

Only a few hotels in central Hat Patong actually sit right on the beach side of Th Thawiwong.

Patong Bay Garden Resort (☎ 076 340 297–8, fax 076 340 560, 33/1 Th Thawiwong) Rooms 2900B. This is a luxury place on the beach with all the amenities including a restaurant and pool.

Patong Beach Bungalow (☎ 076 340 117, fax 076 340 240, 39 Th Thawiwong) Bungalows 2000-3300B. This is a smaller operation than the neighbouring places and has comfortable rooms and friendly staff. There's a restaurant and a pool on the lush landscaped grounds.

Comfort Resort Patong (☎ 076 294 130–4, fax 076 294 143, 18/110 Th Ruamjai) Singles/doubles 2800/3200B. At the recently renovated Comfort Resort rooms have all the amenities and are immaculate. On the premises are a pool and restaurant. Rates drop by about 30% during the low season.

Moving up a couple of notches to places with true world-class standards, rates start at 3000B and reach sky high for large suites with the best bay views. Many top-end places add a 500B to 1000B peak-season surcharge between late December and mid-January.

Phuket Cabana Resort (☎ 076 340 138, fax 076 340 178, 41 Th Thawiwong, ℮ cabana@samart.co.th) Bungalows with breakfast 5500B. Right on the beach, this place has luxuriously appointed bungalows. There's a restaurant with a bar as well as a swimming pool.

Patong Beach Hotel (☎ 076 340 301, fax 076 340 541, 124 Th Thawiwong) Rooms 5200-7500B. Despite the name, Patong Beach isn't actually on the beach, but back off Th Thawiwong south of Th Bangla. It has luxurious rooms on landscaped grounds. There's a restaurant and nightclub as well as a huge swimming pool with islands sprouting coconut trees in the middle of it.

Amari Coral Beach Resort (☎ 076 340 106–14, fax 076 340 115, ℮ coralbea@phuket.loxinfo.co.th, 2 Th Meun Ngoen) Rooms 4387-7412B. The private, five-star Amari is the southernmost property in Hat Patong, on a cliff overlooking the bay.

Baan Sukhothai Hotel (☎ 076 340 155–6, fax 076 340 197, 70 Th Bangla) Rooms 3884-8440B. If you're looking for Thai ambience, this place off Th Bangla may be your best choice. Set on spacious grounds, the hotel uses lots of teak assembled in semi-open, central Thai architectural motifs – a bit out of place in Phuket perhaps, but a favourite with tour groups.

Club Andaman Beach Resort (☎ 076 340 530, 076 340 361, fax 076 340 527, ℮ admin@clubandaman.com, 2 Th Hat Patong) Rooms 4324-9778B. Up towards the northern end of the beach, this resort has a creatively designed building that fits in well with the surrounding tropical gardens. If you get bored with the beach, there are fruit-carving and garland-stringing classes to occupy your time.

Holiday Inn Resort Phuket (☎ *076 340 608, fax 076 340 435,* e *holidayinn@ phuket.com, 52 Th Thawiwong*) Rooms with breakfast in low/high season 3400/4400B. Always a safe bet as far as comfort and security go, the Holiday Inn has a tennis court, fitness room and swimming pool along with the expected amenities.

Diamond Cliff Resort (☎ *076 340 501, fax 076 340 507, 61/9 Hat Kalim*) Cottages 4296-18,000B. Up on Hat Kalim, this place has cottages in spacious grounds with good sea views.

Places to Eat Patong has stacks of restaurants, some of them quite good. The seafood restaurants are concentrated along Th Bangla. Most are expensive; lobster in Patong is going for about 1000B per kilogram these days.

Restaurant 4 (*Th Bangla*) Dishes 80-200B. In a no-nonsense, fluorescent-lit shed, off Th Bangla, this is the best priced of the seafood places.

A couple more bargain *seafood places* can be found on the tiny soi opposite Soi Eric on Th Bangla. Walk a few meters down the soi and look for the push carts on the right.

Savoey (☎ *076 340 230, 136 Th Thawiwong*) Dishes 80-220B. If you can afford to spend a little more, this is a big open-air place in front of the Safari Beach Hotel with good atmosphere and a 'slay 'em and weigh 'em' style setup.

Around the intersection of Th Rat Uthit and Th Bangla are a few inexpensive Thai and faràng *cafes* worth trying.

Le Croissant (☎ *076 342 743, 95/7 Th Bangla*) Dishes 40-180B. This carries French pastries, French wines, sandwiches, salads, baguettes and imported cheeses.

Pizzedelic (☎ *076 341 545, 93/3 Th Thawiwong*) Dishes 40-160B. Located next to the Banana Disco. Besides creative pizza toppings, Pizzedelic also does a killer Caesar salad.

Navrang Mahal (☎ *076 292 280, 94/29 Soi Patong Resort*) Dishes 60-120B. This place offers what is probably Patong's best Indian food.

For inexpensive **noodle and rice vendors**, check Th Sawatdirak or Th Rat Uthit. Cheap eats on the latter can be found in a **night market** opposite the entrance to the Paradise Complex.

Baan Rim Pa (☎ *076 340 789, 223/1 Th Phra Barami*) Dishes 120-300B. Set above a thicket of mangrove trees on the beach, this affords a stunning view of the ocean beyond. The restaurant serves Thai food just slightly toned down for visitors' tastes. There is also a bar and cigar lounge.

Otowa (☎ *076 344 254, 223/3 Th Phra Barami*) Dishes 200-300B. This Japanese restaurant is situated just above the crashing waves and specialises in Japanese barbecue. There's also a sushi bar.

Da Maurizio Bar Ristorante (☎ *076 344 079, 223/2 Th Phra Barami*) Dishes 120-300B. In a town that boasts several excellent Italian restaurants, this one stands out because of its spectacular setting.

Entertainment For its size, Patong probably has the best and most varied nightlife scene in Thailand. Within a few short blocks are clubs, discos, pubs and bars to fit every taste.

Banana Disco (☎ *076 340 301, 96 Th Thawiwong*) Cover charge 100-200B. This is still one of the more popular dance clubs.

Banana Pub (☎ *076 340 301, 94 Th Thawiwong*) This offers a non-threatening coffee house-like atmosphere where most Western women and couples should feel comfortable.

Shipwreck (*Th Bangla*) This is a bar but without the ubiquitous hostesses. Its location opposite Soi Kathoey makes it a great place to sit and people watch.

Two other popular dance clubs are the high-tech *Shark Club* (☎ *076 340 525, Th Bangla*) and the nearby *Tai Pan* (*Th Rat Uthit*). The Tai Pan is more of an after-hours place and doesn't get kicking until about 3am. Some of these big clubs collect cover charges of 100B to 200B, which includes a drink coupon or two.

Pow Wow Pub (☎ *076 340 756, 70/179–180 Th Rat Uthit*) Near the Paradise Complex, this is a typical old-West Thai bar with live country and western mixed with Thai folk rock.

There are dozens of simple *bars* around town, many of them little more than a collection of stools around a rectangular bar and a handful of female touts whose objective is to hook passers-by and keep them drinking long enough to pay the rent. Th Bangla is the main 'zone' but they're also found all along Th Sawatdirak, Th Thawiwong and Th Rat Uthit – anywhere there isn't a hotel, restaurant or souvenir shop.

There's a strip of gay *go-go bars* on the network of soi leading into the Paradise Complex. If you like transvestite shows, check out the well-done *Phuket Simon Cabaret* (☎ 076 342 011), south of town on the way to Karon and Kata. Performances are at 7.30pm and 9.30pm nightly. Sleazier but more of a hoot is the *kàthoey* go-go and cabaret show at *Andaman Queen* at the end of Soi Kathoey off Th Bangla.

Shopping A string of shops and stalls along the central part of Th Thawiwong sell clothing, silk, jewellery and souvenirs from all over Thailand. Prices are higher than average. If you want to find a great selection of handicrafts at reasonable prices, check out Phuket Fantasea (☎ 076 271 222) just north of Hat Kamala. The shopping there is better than anything in Patong.

Getting There & Away Săwngthăew to Patong from Phuket leave from Th Ranong, near the day market and fountain circle; the fare is 30B. The after-hours charter fare is 150B. From Patong you can find săwngthăew to Phuket anywhere along Th Rat Uthit and Th Thawiwong.

Getting Around Túk-túk circulate around Patong for 10B per ride. There are numerous places to rent 125cc motorcycles and jeeps. Patong Big Bike (☎ 076 340 380) on Th Rat Uthit rents 250cc to 750cc bikes. Keep in mind that the helmet law is strictly enforced in Patong.

Hat Karon
กะรน

Karon is a long, gently curving beach with small sand dunes and a few palms and casuarina trees. Sometimes it is referred to as two beaches: Karon Yai and Karon Noi. Karon Noi, also known as Relax Bay, can only be reached from Hat Patong and is almost entirely monopolised by Le Meridien Hotel. The main section of Karon now has a paved promenade with streetlights, and the entire area has blended with Hat Kata to the south to produce a self-contained village inhabited by a mixture of tourists, seasonal residents and year-rounders. It is still a fairly peaceful beach where a few fisherfolk cast nets – you can occasionally buy fresh seafood from their boats. The rice fields between the beach and the surrounding hills have been abandoned or filled with high-rise hotels.

Dino Park (☎ 076 330 625), next to Marina Cottage, features an 18-hole minigolf course with a Fred Flintstone-looking environment, along with a fake waterfall. There is also food (eg, Bronto Burgers) and music in the Rock Garden and drinks at the Dino Bar. It's open all day and late into the night.

Places to Stay Karon is lined with inns and deluxe bungalows, along with a number of places with rooms or huts for under 400B. During the low season – May to November – you can often get a 400B room for as low as 200B to 250B, a 1000B room for 600B and a 2000B room for 1000B.

Most of the places under 700B are located well off the beach, often on small hillocks to the east of the main road.

Lumee & Yai Bungalow (☎/fax 076 396 096, Th Patak) Bungalows 500B. This has the advantage of a hillside location for its 19 bungalows. Another advantage of this place is that beach săwngthăew pass right in front.

Karon Seaview Bungalow (☎ 076 396 798–9, 36/9 Th Patak-west) Rooms 300-500B. In the commercial centre of Karon, near the roundabout, quiet Karon Seaview offers OK concrete duplexes and row-houses.

Crystal Beach Hotel (☎ 076 396 580–5, fax 076 336 584, 36/10 Th Patak-west)

A savoury stall at the Vegetarian Festival

Sweet stall, Vegetarian Festival

The main street, Hat Patong, Phuket Province

Cooking with flair

Zipping around Phuket town, Phuket Province

Sea gypsy village, Surin Islands

Casting a net off Hat Patong, Phuket Province

Villagers assess what's been netted

Touring around Ao Phang-Nga, Northern Andaman Coast

Rooms with air-con in low/high season 450/1000B. On the main road away from the beach, this is good value in the low season.

My Friend Bungalow (☎ *076 396 344, 36/6 Th Patak-west)* Rooms low season 300-400B, high season 600-900B. Near the beach is this popular and friendly place; the cafe out front is a plus.

Fantasy Hill Bungalow (☎ *076 330 106, 112/1 Th Patak)* Bungalows with fan in low season 150-250B, in high season 300-500B. On a small hill off the main road, this has good budget bungalows of a type that has almost disappeared from this beach.

In the mid-range (averaging 500B and up) are the *Karon Village* (☎ *076 396 431, 62/3 Th Patak)*, low season 500B, high season 1000B; *Karon Guest House* (☎ *076 396 860, 29/2 Th Patak)*, fan/air-con 500/600B; *Phuket Ocean Resort* (☎ *076 396 176, fax 076 396 632, 9/1 Th Patak-west)*, 1500B to 1800B; and *Ruam Thep Inn* (☎ *076 330 281, 120/4 Th Patak-west)*, 600B to 900B.

The remaining places on Karon are newer resort-type hotels with rooms starting at 1500B or above, with air-con, swimming pools, multiple restaurants, etc. Prices at most places have come down a bit over the last two years due to competition, though a few places have raised their rates. Bargaining at the larger ones is worthwhile; as a rule of thumb the more rooms they have, the more they'll drop the price, especially during the south-west monsoon season, May to October.

Among the more reliable are vaguely American South-Western-style *Felix Karon View Point* (☎ *076 396 666, fax 076 396 853, 4/8 Th Patak)*, 119 rooms, from 3800B; *The Islandia Travelodge Resort* (☎ *076 396 604, fax 076 396 139, 33/125 Th Patak)*, 128 rooms, 1000B to 3000B; *Phuket Arcadia Hotel* (☎ *076 396 038, fax 076 396 136,* e *arcadia@phuket.ksc.co.th, 78/2 Th Patak)*, 468 rooms, from 4000B; *Thavorn Palm Beach Hotel* (☎ *076 396 090, fax 076 396 555,* e *palm@phuket.com, Th Patak-west)*, 210 rooms, 5400B to 10,000B. These last two are just opposite the beach from Th Patak.

Le Meridien Phuket (☎ *076 340 480, fax 076 340 479,* e *meridien@phuket.ksc .co.th)* Rooms 3500-21,500B. Up at Karon Noi, the small bay around the northern headland of Karon (that some creative genius has attempted to rename Relax Bay), the top-end Le Meridien has 476 well-appointed rooms.

Karon Hill (☎/*fax 076 341 343)* Rooms with bath 500-1000B. Above Le Meridien on a hillside, a bit of a hike from the beach, this place has simple but adequate rooms.

Places to Eat As usual, almost every place to stay provides some food. The cheapest *Thai and seafood places* are off the roundabout near the commercial centre.

The Little Mermaid (☎ *076 396 628, fax 076 330 733, 36/10 Th Patak)* Dishes 50-250B. Open 24 hours. The Little Mermaid, 100m south-east of the traffic circle, has a long, inexpensive, mostly Scandinavian menu written in 12 languages. Get a free salad from the generous salad bar when you order any main dish. Also a great place for a cold draught beer – Skoal!

Red Onion (Hawm Daeng; *Th Patak)* Dishes 30-50B. Located about 200m south-east of the traffic circle, this is a simple, open-air Thai restaurant with good, cheap eats.

Old Siam Restaurant (☎ *076 396 090, Th Patak-west)* Dishes 100-300B. Open 12pm–3pm and 6pm–11pm. Part of Thavorn Palm Beach, this is a large open-air place, designed in central Thai style, and producing Thai dishes for the tourist palate. On Sunday evenings there's a performance of classical Thai dance.

Getting There & Away See the Hat Kata Getting There & Away section for details on transport to Karon.

Hat Kata

หาดกะตะ

Just around a headland south from Karon, Kata is a more interesting beach and is divided into two – Ao Kata Yai (Big Kata Bay) and Ao Kata Noi (Little Kata Bay). The small island of Ko Pu is within swimming distance

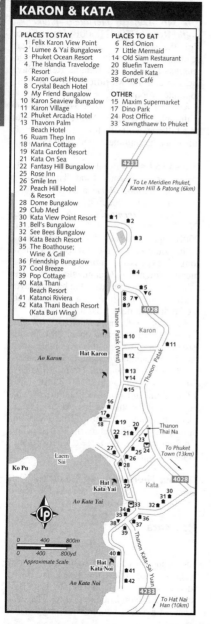

KARON & KATA

PLACES TO STAY
1 Felix Karon View Point
2 Lumee & Yai Bungalows
3 Phuket Ocean Resort
4 The Islandia Travelodge Resort
5 Karon Guest House
8 Crystal Beach Hotel
9 My Friend Bungalow
10 Karon Seaview Bungalow
11 Karon Village
12 Phuket Arcadia Hotel
13 Thavorn Palm Beach Hotel
16 Ruam Thep Inn
18 Marina Cottage
19 Kata Garden Resort
21 Kata On Sea
22 Fantasy Hill Bungalow
25 Rose Inn
26 Smile Inn
27 Peach Hill Hotel & Resort
28 Dome Bungalow
29 Club Med
30 Kata View Point Resort
31 Bell's Bungalow
32 See Bees Bungalow
34 Kata Beach Resort
35 The Boathouse; Wine & Grill
36 Friendship Bungalow
37 Cool Breeze
39 Pop Cottage
40 Kata Thani Beach Resort
41 Katanoi Riviera
42 Kata Thani Beach Resort (Kata Buri Wing)

PLACES TO EAT
6 Red Onion
7 Little Mermaid
14 Old Siam Restaurant
20 Bluefin Tavern
23 Bondeli Kata
38 Gung Café

OTHER
15 Maxim Supermarket
17 Dino Park
24 Post Office
33 Sawngthaew to Phuket

4233

To Le Meridien Phuket, Karon Hill & Patong (6km)

Ao Karon
Hat Karon
Thanon Patak (West)
Karon
Thanon Patak
4028

Thanon Thai Na
To Phuket Town (13km)

Laem Sai
Ko Pu

Hat Kata Yai
Kata
4028
Ao Kata Yai

Thanon Kata-Sai Yuan

0   400   800m
0   400   800yd
Approximate Scale

Hat Kata Noi
Ao Kata Noi
4233
To Hat Nai Han (10km)

---

of the shore and on the way are some OK coral reefs. Snorkelling gear can be rented from several of the bungalow groups.

Although it has around 30 hotels and bungalow resorts and a slightly urban feel – the back alleys and soi have an interesting array of shops and cafes – Kata is much less crowded and more friendly than Patong and without the constant come-ons.

Contrary to persistent rumour, the beach in front of Club Med is open to the public.

Information Along Th Thai Na in Kata Yai, near the Rose Inn, is a Thai Farmers Bank (with exchange services) and a post office.

Activities & Events The Boathouse offers a two-day Thai **cooking class** each Saturday and Sunday from 10am to 2pm for a reasonable 2200B per person including two lunches, Boathouse recipes and a certificate.

Places to Stay – Budget In general the less expensive places tend to be off the beach between Kata Yai (to the north) and Kata Noi (to the south) or well off the beach on the road to the island interior. Over the past couple of years a few guesthouses have opened up in shophouses along Th Patak and Th Thai Na, near the post office. For the most part these places are dodgy at best – they were built in a hurry and now it's beginning to show. If you're on a budget, staying at one of the following bungalow operations is vastly preferable to the substandard rooms found in most apartment-style places.

Bell's Bungalow (☎ 076 330 111, 1/2 Th Patak) Bungalows with fan 100-300B. This is quite a distance back from the beach towards the southern end of Kata Yai. The 14 bungalows are kind of packed together but for this price you can't expect too much.

Kata View Point Resort (☎ 076 330 815, 1/5 Th Patak) Rooms with fan & bath 200-300B. Just north-east of Bell's Bungalow, this has adequate rooms.

Friendship Bungalow (☎ 076 330 499, 6/5 Th Patak) Bungalows 400-700B. This is a popular place off the beach at the headland between Kata Yai and Kata Noi. It's often full even during the low season.

Kata On Sea (☎ *076 330 594, 116/16 Th Patak*) Bungalows with fan & bath 250-300B. On a ridge off Th Thai Na east of Kata Yai, this offers 25 basic but clean bungalows.

Cool Breeze (☎ *076 330 484, fax 076 330 173, 5/5 Th Patak*) Rooms with fan/air-con 350/700B. On the headland between Hat Kata and Hat Kata Noi, this place is within walking distance of both beaches.

A sprinkling of other spots starting under 500B include *Dome Bungalow* (☎ *076 330 620, fax 076 330 269, 116 Th Patak*), 400B to 800B; *Sea Bees Bungalow* (☎/*fax 076 330 090, 13/2 Th Patak*), 250B to 350B; and the hotel-like *Rose Inn* (☎ *076 396 519, fax 076 396 526, 14/24 Th Patak*), 250B to 500B. All will give discounts during the low season from May to October.

Places to Stay – Mid-Range In a nice setting with a pool is *Peach Hill Hotel & Resort* (☎ *076 330 603, fax 076 330 895, 113/16–18 Th Patak*) Rooms with air-con cost from 500B to 3500B. It recently went a bit upscale but there are still a few good-value rooms to be had.

Smile Inn (☎ *076 330 926, fax 076 330 925, 116/10–12 Th Patak*) Rooms with air-con, hot shower, TV & fridge 700B, with breakfast 800B. This is a clean, friendly place with a nice open-air cafe. It's centrally located where Th Thai Na intersects with Th Patak (West).

Pop Cottage (☎ *076 330 181, fax 076 330 794,* e *popcott@loxinfo.co.th, 2/12 Th Patak*) Bungalows 400-1000B. Pop has bungalows high on a hill opposite the southern end of Hat Kata Yai.

Kata Garden Resort (☎ *076 330 627, fax 076 330 446, 121/1 Th Patak*) Bungalows with fan/air-con 500/1500B. Opposite Marina Cottage, this has 52 stilted bungalows among lots of trees.

Katanoi Riviera (☎ *076 330 726, fax 076 330 294, 3/21 Th Hat Kata Noi*) Bungalows 500-1200B. Across the road from the beach at Kata Noi, this is a cluster of row-houses and bungalows on modestly landscaped grounds. Much of its beach view is blocked by other hotels, but the setting is still relaxing.

Places to Stay – Top End Moving up in price, *Marina Cottage* (☎ *076 330 625, fax 076 330 516,* e *info@marina-cottage.com, 120 Th Patak*) has bungalows from US$100 to US$160. One of the more exemplary of the less-extravagant top end places is Marina, an enduring, medium-scale, low-rise, low-density place set on shady, palm-studded grounds near the beach.

The Boathouse (☎ *076 330 015, fax 076 330 561, in Bangkok* ☎ *024 381 123,* e *the .boathouse@phuket.com, 2/2 Th Patak*) Rooms 9743-19,586B. The brainchild of architect and Phuket resident ML Tri Devakul, this is a 36-room boutique resort that manages to stay full year-round. In spite of rather ordinary-looking if capacious rooms, the hotel hosts a steady influx of Thai politicos, pop stars, artists, celebrity authors (the hotel hosts periodic poetry and fiction readings) on the strength of its stellar service and acclaimed restaurant, and because it commands a scenic spot at the southern end of Kata Yai. Room rates drop by about 40% in the low season.

Kata Thani Beach Resort (☎ *076 330 124–6, fax 076 330 426,* e *katathani@ phuket.com, 3/24 Th Hat Kata Noi*) Rooms including breakfast 2953-3724B. The palatial Kata Thani commands most of the beach at Kata Noi and is one of the choicest spots anywhere along Karon or Kata. It has upmarket, well-appointed rooms on nicely landscaped grounds. There are two pools at the main resort, and there's another across the road and south a bit at the Kata Buri Wing (formerly under separate management).

Kata Beach Resort (☎ *076 330 530, fax 076 330 128,* e *katagrp@loxinfo.co.th, 5/2 Th Patak*) Rooms 2900-5200B. Close to Hat Kata Yai and Club Med, this is a three-storey concrete hotel that's on the access road to the beach – not all rooms have beach views.

Club Med (☎ *076 330 455–9, fax 076 330 461, 7/3 Th Patak*) Rooms 3800-5700B. Club Med occupies a large chunk of land near Kata Yai, as well as a fair swathe of beachfront. During the high season rates double.

Places to Eat Most of the restaurants in Kata offer standard tourist food and service. Two of the best restaurants in the entire area, including Karon and Patong to the north, are owned by ML Tri, the architect who has brought high culture, art and cuisine to Phuket.

The Boathouse Wine & Grill (☎ 076 330 015, 2/2 Th Patak) Dishes 250-600B. Open 7am–11.30pm. This started as an indoor/outdoor restaurant only, but now has 36-rooms attached to its original location at the southern end of Kata Yai. It boasts a wine collection that so far is the only one in Thailand to have been cited for excellence by *Wine Spectator* magazine. The nightly seafood buffet is excellent. It's a pricey place but the atmosphere is casual and service is tops.

Gung Café (Kang; ☎ 076 330 015 ext 704, 2/2 Th Patak) Dishes 100-300B. Next to The Boathouse, and under the same ownership, this features good seafood served in a casual atmosphere.

Bondeli Kata (☎ 076 396 482, 33/93 Th Patak) Dishes 40-150B. A branch of the Bondeli in Phuket town, this air-con place serves fresh pastries, four kinds of coffee and nine teas.

Bluefin Tavern (☎ 076 330 856, 111/17 Th Thai Na) Dishes 60-120B. This features Mexican favourites, pizza, burgers and Thai food. It's a great place for a hearty breakfast and there's also a bar with beer on tap.

Getting There & Away The main săwng-thăew stop is in front of Kata Beach Resort. Săwngthăew to both Kata and Karon leave frequently from the Th Ranong market in Phuket from 7am to 5pm for 30B per person. After-hour charters cost 150B to 200B.

Hat Nai Han
ในหาน

A few kilometres south of Kata, this beach set around a picturesque bay is similar to Kata and Karon but, in spite of the Phuket Yacht Club, less developed – thanks to the presence of Samnak Song Nai Han, a monastic centre that claims most of the beachfront land. To make up for the lack of saleable beachfront, developers started cutting away the forests on the hillsides overlooking the beach. Recently, however, the development seems to have come to a halt.

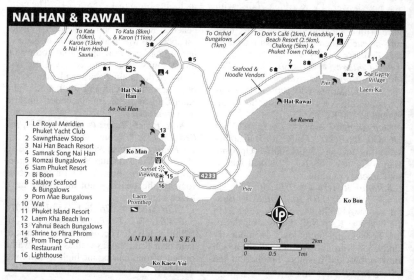

NAI HAN & RAWAI

To Kata (10km), Karon (13km) & Nai Harn Herbal Sauna
To Kata (8km) & Karon (11km)
To Orchid Bungalows (1km)
To Don's Café (2km), Friendship Beach Resort (2.5km), Chalong (5km) & Phuket Town (16km)

Hat Nai Han

Ao Nai Han

Seafood & Noodle Vendors

Hat Rawai

Ao Rawai

Pier

Sea Gypsy Village

Laem Ka

Ko Man

Sunset Viewing

Laem Promthep

Pier

Ko Bon

ANDAMAN SEA

Ko Kaew Yai

1 Le Royal Meridien Phuket Yacht Club
2 Sawngthaew Stop
3 Nai Han Beach Resort
4 Samnak Song Nai Han
5 Romzai Bungalows
6 Siam Phuket Resort
7 Bi Boon
8 Salaloy Seafood & Bungalows
9 Porn Mae Bungalows
10 Wat
11 Phuket Island Resort
12 Laem Kha Beach Inn
13 Yahnui Beach Bungalows
14 Shrine to Phra Phrom
15 Prom Thep Cape Restaurant
16 Lighthouse

0   1   2km
0   0.5   1mi

This means that Nai Han is usually one of the least crowded beaches on the southern part of the island.

The TAT says Nai Han beach is a dangerous place to swim during the monsoon season (May to October), but it really varies depending on the weather – look for the red flag, which means dangerous swimming conditions.

Places to Stay Except for the Phuket Yacht Club, there's really not much accommodation available on or even near the beach. The budget places here seem to cater to bashful faràng sex tourists and their Thai *mia châo* (rental wives).

Romzai Bungalows (Rom Sai; ☎ 076 381 338, 14/7 Th Wiset) Huts in low/high season 300/450B. This has 14 simple concrete bungalows. The small restaurant here is quite good but is open only in the afternoon.

Orchid Bungalows (☎ 076 381 396, 13/2 Th Wiset) Rooms 550-850B. About a kilometre farther along from Romzai there's a road branching north. It leads to Orchid that offers motel-like rooms next to an orchid nursery.

Nai Han Beach Resort (☎ 076 381 810, 14/29 Th Wiset) Rooms with fan/air-con 800/1000B. Well back from the beach, near the road into Nai Han and behind a small lagoon, is the motel-like Nai Han. Prices drop a couple of hundred baht in the low season but, still, this place is overpriced.

Le Royal Meridien Phuket Yacht Club (☎ 076 381 156, fax 076 381 164, ℮ info@ phuket-yachtclub.com, 23/3 Th Wiset) Rooms US$530 to $2000. This sits on the western end of Nai Han. Built at the astronomical cost of 145 million baht, the hotel has given up on the idea of becoming a true yacht club with a mobile pier (apparently the bay currents aren't right for such an endeavour). The pier has gone but luxurious 'state rooms' are still available. Prices come down quite a bit during the low season. A line of bamboo-and-thatch huts housing cheap eateries and bars sits outside the gated entrance to Le Royal Meridian, tempting its guests to stray from their posh digs.

Yahnui Beach Bungalows (☎/fax 076 238 180, 93/1 Soi Yanui, Th Wiset) Bungalows with fan & shower 350-500B. On the other end of the bay from the Yacht Club, off the road to Rawai, the Yahnui features a set of plain cottages opposite the beach. A rustic restaurant enjoys a beautiful location on its own small sandy cove opposite the bungalows. It's a very quiet and peaceful spot among coconut palms, mangroves and casuarina trees; the cape and grassy hills nearby have lots of hiking potential. You'll need your own transport to get here.

Getting There & Away Nai Han is 18km from Phuket and a săwngthăew (leaving from the intersection of Th Krung Thep and the fountain circle) costs 25B per person. Túk-túk charters are 150B to 200B one way.

Hat Rawai & Laem Ka
หาดราไวย์และแหลมกา

Rawai was one of the first coastal areas on Phuket to be developed, simply because it was near Phuket and there was already a rather large fishing community. Once other nicer beach areas like Patong and Karon were 'discovered', Rawai gradually began to lose popularity and today is quite peaceful. If you want to sit on a beach without being distracted every few minutes by wandering vendors trying to sell hammocks, sarongs, seashells or themselves, check out Rawai.

The beach is not great, but there is a lot happening in or near Rawai: there is a local chao náam (sea gypsy) village; Hat Laem Ka (better than Rawai) to the north-east; boats to the nearby islands and good snorkelling off Laem Phromthep at the southern tip of Phuket island. In fact, most of the visitors who stay at Rawai these days are divers who want to be near Phromthep and/or boat facilities for offshore diving trips.

Laem Phromthep is also a popular viewing point at sunset, when bus-loads of tourists come to pose for photos and enjoy the view. On a hill next to the viewpoint is a shrine to Phra Phrom (Brahma) as well as a lighthouse built to commemorate King Rama IX's 50th anniversary on the throne.

On a clear day you can see Ko Phi-Phi from the back of the lighthouse.

The diving around the offshore islands is not bad, especially at Kaew Yai and Kaew Noi, off Phromthep and at Ko Heh. It's a good idea to shop around for boat trips to these islands to find the least expensive passage – the larger the group, the lower the cost per person.

Places to Stay With a restaurant attached, *Salaloy Seafood & Bungalows (Salaloy Resort; ☎ 076 381 370, 52/2 Th Wiset)* has bungalows with fan/air-con 300/800B. They're slightly worn and made out of concrete and wood. The well patronised seafood restaurant here is one of the better – and more moderately priced – ones in the area. The whole operation closes down in the low season.

Porn Mae Bungalows (☎/fax 076 381 300, 58/1 Th Wiset) Fan bungalows 350-450B. This is a tranquil place that seems to be a favourite with long-termers. The sturdy bungalows are of concrete and wood. There's no restaurant here.

Siam Phuket Resort (☎ 076 381 346, fax 076 381 2347, 24/24 Th Wiset) Bungalows 1300-1800B. Near Salaloy Seafood & Bungalows, this upscale place offers comfortable bungalows on landscaped grounds with a pool. Prices drop by about 50% during the low season.

Laem Ka Beach Inn (☎ 076 381 305) Fan rooms 600-900B, air-con 1000-1200B. This has 20 rooms spread out among coconut groves. Laem Ka is named after the cape it sits on, an interesting mix of clean sand and large boulders, and is a favourite local picnic spot. The swimming is good.

Friendship Beach Resort (☎ 076 381 281, fax 076 381 424, 27/1 Th Wiset) Bungalows 300-500B. About 2.5km north of Rawai, about halfway to the Ao Chalong traffic roundabout, this is a little self-contained bungalow complex that seems to cater to long-term visitors.

Places to Eat Aside from the restaurants attached to the *resorts* in Rawai (Salaloy is the best), the only places to eat are the *seafood and noodle vendors* set up along the roadside near the beach.

Prom Thep Cape Restaurant Dishes 60-100B. Just below the viewpoint for Laem Phromthep, this offers simple Thai meals.

Bi Boon Dishes 40-100B. Located between Salaloy and Siam Phuket Resort, this offers an extensive breakfast menu including American, Continental and German breakfasts.

Don's Café (☎ 076 288 229, fax 076 288 413, 53/5 Soi Sai Yuan) Main meals 80-200B. Off Th Wiset between Rawai and Chalong, Don's offers hearty meals of steak and ribs barbecued over a mesquite-wood fire.

Getting There & Away Rawai is about 16km from Phuket and getting there costs 15B by săwngthăew from the circle at Th Krung Thep. Túk-túk charters cost at least 150B from Phuket.

Laem Singh & Hat Kamala
แหลมสิงห์/หาดกมลา

North of Ao Patong, 24km from Phuket, Laem Singh (Cape Singh) is a beautiful little rock-dominated beach. You could camp here and eat at the rustic roadside seafood places at the northern end of Singh or in Ban Kamala, a village farther south. If you're renting a motorbike, this is a nice little trip down Route 4025 and then over dirt roads from Surin to Kamala.

Hat Kamala is a lovely stretch of sand and sea south of Hat Surin and Laem Singh. The north end, the nicest area, is shaded by casuarinas and features a small thatched-roof snack bar with free sling chairs and umbrellas available. The middle of the beach is dominated by resorts and seafood restaurants. Most of the villagers here are Muslim, and there are a couple of mosques towards the southern end of the main village, also known as Bang Wan. Visitors should dress modestly when walking around the village in deference to local mores. Topless or nude beach bathing would be extremely offensive to the locals.

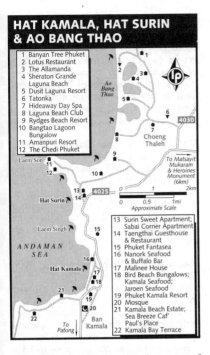

HAT KAMALA, HAT SURIN & AO BANG THAO

1 Banyan Tree Phuket
2 Lotus Restaurant
3 The Allamanda
4 Sheraton Grande Laguna Beach
5 Dusit Laguna Resort
6 Tatonka
7 Hideaway Day Spa
8 Laguna Beach Club
9 Rydges Beach Resort
10 Bangtao Lagoon Bungalow
11 Amanpuri Resort
12 The Chedi Phuket

13 Surin Sweet Apartment; Sabai Corner Apartment
14 Taengthai Guesthouse & Restaurant
15 Phuket Fantasea
16 Nanork Seafood & Buffalo Bar
17 Malinee House
18 Bird Beach Bungalows; Kamala Seafood; Jaroen Seafood
19 Phuket Kamala Resort
20 Mosque
21 Kamala Beach Estate; Sea Breeze Caf'; Paul's Place
22 Kamala Bay Terrace

Ao Bang Thao

Choeng Thaleh

To Matsayit Mukaram & Heroines Monument (6km)

Laem Son

Hat Surin

Laem Singh

ANDAMAN SEA

Hat Kamala

To Patong

Ban Kamala

Approximate Scale

0 — 1 — 2km
0 — 0.5 — 1mi

Places to Stay Dominating the centre of the beach, *Phuket Kamala Resort (☎ 076 324 396, fax 076 324 399, 78/4 Th Hat Kamala)* has bungalows with air-con & TV from 850B to 1950B. All have private balconies and the coffee shop serves Thai and Western food.

Bird Beach Bungalows (☎/fax 076 270 669, 73/3 Th Hat Kamala) Cottages with fan & cold water 500-1100B. Prices for each of the 11 clean cottages. are determined by size and proximity to the beach. In this same area are several laundry services and minimarts, evidence that Kamala is attracting long-termers.

Some of the following places don't take guests from May to October.

Malinee House (☎ 076 271 355, 75/4 Th Hat Kamala) Rooms with fan 350-440B. This place has basic rooms in a family home.

Nanork Seafood & Buffalo Bar (☎ 076 270 668, Th Hat Kamala) Rooms with fan 500B. Towards the northern end of the beach near the police station, this has clean rooms but is in a fairly noisy location.

Kamala Beach Estate (☎ 076 279 756–7, fax 076 324 115, e *kamala.beach@ phuket.com, 33/6 Th Hat Kamala)* Apartments 7400-15,000B. At the southern end of the bay, overlooking but not on the beach, this has fully equipped, high-security, modern time-share apartments.

Kamala Bay Terrace (☎ 076 270 801, fax 076 270 818, e *kamala@samart.co.th, 16/12 Th Hat Kamala)* Apartments 6000-15,000B, depending on size and season. This has luxurious apartments and time-shares. Between 20 December and 5 January there is a five-night minimum stay; peak-season surcharges apply.

Places to Eat The best value for eating is the friendly and moderately priced *thatched-roof restaurant* at the north end of the beach.

Near Bird Beach Bungalows are the decent *Kamala Seafood (Th Hat Kamala)* and *Jaroen Seafood (Th Hat Kamala)*, both family-run Thai seafood places that cater to faràng.

Sea Breeze Caf' (☎ 076 279 580, Th Hat Kamala) Dishes 80-180B. Next to Kamala Beach Estate, this has a good selection of both Thai and Western food; it overlooks the bay and has a casual atmosphere.

Paul's Place (☎ 076 279 756) Dishes 120-200B. Next to Kamala Beach Estate at the southern end of the bay, this is the most up-market place to eat; it offers good views of the bay and reliable Thai and Western food.

For something more local, try one of the several *kop-íi shops* (with strong coffee or *kop-íi*) in the village.

Getting There & Away A regular sǎwng-thǎew to Kamala costs 25B per person 7am to 5pm, while a charter costs 250B.

Hat Surin
หาดสุรินทร์

North of Hat Kamala and a little north of Laem Singh, Hat Surin has a long beach and sometimes fairly heavy surf. When the water is calm, there's fair snorkelling here. The beach has long been a popular place for locals to come and nibble at seafood snacks sold by vendors along the beach. Just before Surin, in Bang Thao Village No 2, is one of Southern Thailand's most beautiful mosques, **Matsayit Mukaram**, a large, whitewashed, immaculate structure with lacquered wooden doors.

Places to Stay Surin's northern end has been dubbed 'Pansea Beach' by developers and is claimed by the exclusive Amanpuri and The Chedi resorts.

The Chedi Phuket (☎ 076 324 017, fax 076 324 252, e info@chedi-phuket.com) Rooms and cottages US$295-480. This offers 89 rooms and 21 two-bedroom cottages with teak floors and private verandas. The Chedi has its own golf course.

Amanpuri Resort (☎ 076 324 333, fax 076 324 100, e amanpuri@phuket.com) Pavilions US$510-945, villas US$1150-5040. This plays host to Thailand's celebrity traffic, each of whom gets a 133-sq-metre pavilion or private two- to six-bedroom villa with personal attendant; the staff to guest ratio is 3½ to one. It's owned by Indonesian, Adrian Zecha, and designed by the architect who designed the former Shah of Iran's Winter Palace. The resort offers about 20 cruisers for sailing, diving and overnight charters, six tennis courts, a gym, and Thai and Italian restaurants.

Towards the southern end of Hat Surin, *Surin Sweet Apartment* (☎ 076 270 863, fax 076 270 865), *Sabai Corner Apartment* (☎ 076 271 146) and *Taengthai Guesthouse & Restaurant* (☎ 076 270 259) offer simple but modern rooms in the 400B to 800B range.

Getting There & Away A regular săwngthăew from Phuket's Th Ranong to Hat Surin costs 25B per person and túk-túk or săwngthăew charters cost 250B to 300B.

Ao Bang Thao

อ่าวบางเทา

North of Surin around Laem Son lies Ao Bang Thao, an 8km sand-rimmed bay and beach with an 18-hole golf course that has attracted much upscale development. A steady breeze makes it a haven for sailboarders; since 1992 the annual Siam World Cup windsurfing championships have been held here (formerly at Pattaya's Hat Jomtien). A system of lagoons inland from the beach has been incorporated into the resorts and golf course, hence this is sometimes referred to as 'Laguna Beach'.

Massage & Herbal Sauna Hideaway Day Spa (☎ 076 271 549) Open 11am–9pm. About 200m east of Tatonka restaurant, this offers half-day programs of traditional Thai massage, herbal sauna and aromatherapy for 2500B to 3000B. The spa is located in a soothingly wooded setting next to one of Bang Thao's lagoons. Reservations are suggested.

Places to Stay With one exception, Bang Thao is strictly for the well-to-do. All the hotels here (except for Rydges Beach Resort) are part of an integrated resort system, so if you stay at one of the hotels you can use any of the facilities of the other hotels. A shuttle operates between all of the properties.

Bangtao Lagoon Bungalow (☎ 076 324 260, fax 076 324 168, Th Sisunthon) Bungalows in high season 500-1600B, low season 400-1300B. Least expensive is this quiet and secluded place at the southern end of the bay, with 50 private bungalows. The restaurant on the premises serves Thai and European dishes.

Dusit Laguna Resort (☎ 076 324 320, fax 076 324 174, in Bangkok ☎ 022 384 790, e dusit@lagunaphuket.com, 390 Th Sisunthon) Rooms and suites US$110–210. The plush Dusit has 226 guest rooms and suites. From 20 December to 20 February peak-season surcharges apply.

Rydges Beach Resort (☎ 076 324 021–2, fax 076 324 243, e rydges_phuket@rydges.com) Rooms in high season 4800-11,000B, low season 2400-5500B. This top-end place towards the centre of the beach was formerly the Royal Park Beach Resort. After completing an US$8 million renovation, it's reopened with a lobby done up in Sino-Portuguese style – something that hasn't been attempted on Phuket in over a century.

Sheraton Grande Laguna Beach (☎ 076 324 101-7, fax 076 324 108, e sheraton@ phuket.com) Rooms US$180–270, villas US$325–545. There are 240 guest rooms sprawled on lushly landscaped grounds. Despite the grand facade, the staff can be rather unhelpful at times.

Banyan Tree Phuket (☎ 076 324 374, fax 076 324 375, e banyanrs@samart .co.th) Villas US$280-1050. Banyan Tree has 98 villas (all with open-air sunken bathtubs, 34 with private pool and Jacuzzi). The hotel boasts a golf course, full-service spa, three tennis courts, a lap pool & free-form swimming pool. It specialises in spiritual and physical spa treatments, including massage, seaweed packs and meditation. In 1998 the spa here was voted the world's best by readers of Condé Nast Traveler.

The Allamanda (☎ 076 324 359, fax 076 324 360, e allamanda@lagunaphuket .com) Suites US$116–140, villas US$80-199. This offers 94 units; all suites come with kitchenette & satellite TV. Prices depend largely on what kind of view the room has – views of the lagoon will cost you more than a view of the golf fairway.

Laguna Beach Club (☎ 076 324 352, fax 076 324 353 or 076 270 993 reservation fax only, e beachclub@lagunaphuket.com, 323 Th Sisunthon) Rooms US$155-625. This rivals the Sheraton and Dusit in providing 252 rooms. Set on 20 acres, the resort features a four-acre water park incorporating waterfalls, water slides, whirlpool swimming pools & a scuba pool.

Places to Eat Despite what local hoteliers would have you believe, there is some good food to be had outside the confines of Bang Thao's luxury hotels.

Tatonka (☎/fax 076 324 349) Dishes 80-220B. Tatonka, near the entrance to the Dusit Laguna Resort, features 'globetrotter' cuisine, which owner-chef Harold Schwarz developed by taking fresh local products and combining them with cooking and presentation techniques from his experience in Europe and with the foods of Hawaii and the

American South-West ('tatonka' is the Sioux word for 'buffalo'). Besides the eclectic regular menu, there are some creative vegetarian dishes to be sampled here and prices are quite reasonable. Tatonka is open daily except Wednesday from 5pm; reservations are suggested in the high season.

Just beyond the entrance to Banyan Tree Phuket, heading south, is a turn-off for the beach. Follow this road into what looks like a shanty town but is actually a group of beachside Thai and seafood restaurants. Of these, the clean and breezy **Lotus Restaurant** stands out.

Getting There & Away A săwngthăew from Phuket's Th Ranong to Bang Thao costs 20B per person. Túk-túk charters are 200B.

Nai Thon
ในทอน

Improved roads to Hat Nai Thon have brought only a small amount of development to this broad expanse of pristine sand backed by casuarina and pandanus trees. Down on the beach, umbrellas and sling chairs are available from vendors. Swimming is quite good here except at the height of the monsoon, and there is some coral near the headlands at either end of the bay. The submerged remains of a wrecked 50m-long tin dredger lie farther off the coast near tiny **Ko Waew** at a depth of 16m. Naithon Beach Resort can arrange dive trips in the vicinity.

North of Naithon Beach Resort on the beach side of the road stands a **spirit shrine** erected by local Muslim fishermen to appease the sea deities of their chao náam forebears. Recently the old wooden shrine lost much of its rustic charm when it was renovated in concrete and ceramic tiles. The road up over the headland of Laem Son (Pine Cape) to the south was completed in 1995 but has already suffered bridge washouts and pot-holing. This road passes two smaller coves, **Nai Thon Noi** and **Hin Khruai** with deserted strips of sand. Hin Khruai usually has a seafood vendor or two during the dry months. The tiny settlement of **Ban Sakhu**, inland to the north-east of

Hat Nai Thon, is awash with flowers and fruit orchards.

Places to Stay & Eat On the opposite side of the access road from the beach is *Naithon Beach Resort* (☎ *076 205 379, fax 076 205 381, 22/2 Th Surin*) Bungalows 1200B, with air-con 1500B. This is large, tastefully designed wooden cottages. A small restaurant serves sandwiches and Thai food. The resort closes down in the rainy season.

Tien Seng Guest House (*Th Surin*) Fan rooms 500B, air-con 700B. Located just south of the Naithon Beach Resort, this has, according to its sign, 'rooms for rant' in a modern shophouse building. There is also a restaurant that serves Thai and Chinese dishes.

Getting There & Away Săwngthăew from Phuket cost 30B per person and run between 7am and 5pm only. A charter costs 300B; if you're coming straight from the airport it would be less trouble, less expensive and quicker to hire a taxi for 200B.

Hat Nai Yang & Hat Mai Khao
ในยาง/ไม้ขาว

Both of these beaches are near Phuket international airport, about 30km from Phuket town. Nai Yang, a fairly secluded beach favoured by Thais, is part of Sirinat National Park, a relatively new protected area that combines former Nai Yang National Park with a wildlife reserve at Mai Khao. The park encompasses 22 sq km of coastal land, plus 68 sq km of sea, from the western Phang-Nga provincial border south to the headland that separates Nai Yang from Nai Thon.

About 5km north of Nai Yang is Hat Mai Khao, Phuket's longest beach. Sea turtles lay their eggs on the beach here between November and February each year. A visitors centre with toilets, showers and picnic tables can be found at Mai Khao, from where there are some short trails through the casuarinas to a steep beach. Take care when swimming at Mai Khao, as there's a strong year-round undertow. Except on

weekends and holidays you'll have this place almost entirely to yourself; even during peak periods, peace and solitude are usually only a few steps away, as there's so much space here.

On the other side of the road from the visitors centre, a network of raised wooden walkways takes visitors on a self-guided tour of natural mangrove forest.

About a kilometre off Nai Yang is a large reef at a depth of 10m to 20m. Snorkelling and scuba equipment can be hired at the Pearl Village Resort. Judging from the lie of the reef, there could be a surfable reef break here during the south-west monsoon.

The area between Nai Yang and Mai Khao is largely given over to shrimp farming. Fortunately shrimp farmers here don't dig artificial lagoons into the beach or mangrove (as at Ko Chang or Khao Sam Roi Yot) but rather they raise the spawn in self-contained concrete tanks, a practice significantly less harmful to the environment.

Places to Stay & Eat Camping is allowed on both Nai Yang and Mai Khao beaches without any permit.

Sirinat National Park (☎ *076 328 662, 076 327 152, 076 328 226*) Tents 60B, bungalows with 6/12 beds 400/800B. Check in at the building opposite the visitors centre. Two-person tents can be rented for the night. There is also an entrance fee of 200B per adult, 100B per child under 14.

Phuket Campground Tents per person 100B. Privately operated, this campground on Ao Mai Khao rents tents very near the beach, each with rice mats, pillows, blankets and a torch (flashlight). A light mangrove thicket separates the campground from the beach, but the proprietors don't mind if you move their tents onto the beach crest. A small outdoor restaurant/bar provides sustenance. Other amenities include a shower and toilet, hammocks, sling chairs and beach umbrellas, and a campfire ring.

Commercial hotel development has been permitted towards the southern end of Hat Nai Yang, well back from the beach itself.

Garden Cottage (☎/fax *076 327 293*) Cottages with fan/air-con, fridge & bath in low season 600/800B, high season 1000/1300B. This is actually on Route 4026, back from the southern end of Hat Nai Yang, 1.5km from the airport, but still within a five-minute walk of the beach. It has tidy cottages.

Pearl Village Resort (☎ *076 327 006, fax 076 327 338,* [e] *pearlvil@loxinfo.co.th*) Rooms 3300-22,000B. The Pearl commands 8.1 hectares at the southern end of Nai Yang. The resort has three pricey restaurants and a dive centre.

Crown Nai Yang Suite Hotel (☎ *076 327 420, fax 076 327 323,* [e] *crown@phuket .com, 117 Th Hat Nai Yang*) Rooms 3800-17,000B. This is a rather unsightly multistorey place that rents modern boxes (some without windows). Airline crews stopping over between flights in and out of Phuket often use this hotel. The walk-in rates are ludicrous for what you get.

Along the dirt road at the very southern end of the beach is a seemingly endless strip of *seafood restaurants* and, oddly enough, tailor shops. There is also a small minimart near the entrance to the Pearl Village Resort.

Getting There & Away A săwngthăew from Phuket to Nai Yang costs 20B, while a túk-túk charter is 250B to 300B. There is no regular săwngthăew stop for Mai Khao but a túk-túk charter costs between 250B and 300B.

Nearby Islands
For information on attractions and accommodation on the island of Ko Yao Noi and Ko Yao Yai, off Phuket's north-eastern shore, see the Around Phang-Nga section earlier in this chapter.

Ko Heh Also referred to as Coral Island, Ko Heh is a few kilometres south-south-east of Ao Chalong. It's a good spot for diving and snorkelling if you don't plan on going farther out to sea, although jet skis and other pleasure craft can be an annoyance. The island gets lots of day-trippers from Phuket, but at night it's pretty quiet. There is one place to stay:

Coral Island Resort (☎ *076 281 060, fax 076 381 957,* [e] *coral@phuket.com*) Bungalows with air-con 1500-3600B. This has 64 bungalows of concrete with tile floors that are clean and rather characterless. Most are arranged around the swimming pool but the more expensive bungalows are seaside. There's a pool and karaoke lounge and cable TV in the lobby just in case you can't live without a daily dose of the tube.

Ko Mai Thon This island, south-east of Laem Phanwa, is similar to Ko Heh, but slightly smaller. There is only one place to stay on the island:

Maiton Resort (☎ *076 214 954, fax 076 214 959,* [e] *maiton@phuket.com*) Bungalows 9416-21,092B. This offers semi-luxurious hillside or beachside bungalows; all rooms have air-con, cable TV, phone & bath tub. There are two pools (indoor and outdoor), a sauna, fitness centre, tennis court and five restaurants, including one serving Japanese food, one Thai and one European. This is the kind of self-contained place that could be anywhere – Bali or the Bahamas, perhaps. If you happen to be staying here in December and January prices are 3500B higher, and if you're lucky enough to be spending Christmas and the New Year here, you'll be treated to 'compulsory gala dinners' on both nights – add another 3500B and 4500B to the bill for each dinner.

Ko Raya Yai & Ko Raya Noi There two islands, about 1½ hours by boat south of Phuket, are also known as Ko Racha Yai/Noi, and are highly favoured by divers and snorkellers for their hard coral reefs. Because the coral is found in both shallow and deep waters, it's a good area for novice scuba divers and snorkellers as well as accomplished divers. Visibility can reach 15m to 30m during dry, post-monsoon months. Most tourist activity focuses on Ao Nam Ta Tok (Falling Teardrops Bay), a broad sandy beach on Ko Raya Yai with very calm surf November to May and several types of accommodation. A footpath leads over a central ridge from Ao Nam Ta Tok to a pretty and as yet undeveloped white sand beach on the other side of the island. Accommodation is available on both islands.

Raya Resort Bungalows 500-700B. This has 20 wooden and palm-thatch bungalows and a decent restaurant.

Ban Raya (☎ 076 354 682, e banraya@phuket.com) Bungalows with fan 1300B, air-con 1900B. This place has comfortable bungalows, and if you're interested in doing a dive, this is the place to come. Prices range from 700B for a beach dive to 25,000B for a two-week divemaster course. All equipment is provided.

Getting There & Away Boats leave Ao Chalong for Ko Heh once daily at 9.30am; the trip takes 30 minutes and costs 60B.

Boats leave Ao Chalong for Ko Heh once daily at 9.30am; they also take 30 minutes and cost 60B.

Songserm Travel (☎ 076 222 570) runs passenger boats to Ko Raya Yai from Phuket town port daily at 9.00am. The trip takes 30 minutes and costs 350B one way or 750B return. Pal Travel Service (☎ 076 344 920) runs a similar service. Both companies suspend service from May to October. You can also charter a long-tail boat or speed boat from Rawai or from Ao Chalong for 1500B.

Southern Andaman Coast (Krabi to Satun)

South-east of Phuket, the southern reach of island-studded Ao Phang-Nga opens into the Andaman Sea, and Thailand's greatest concentration of national marine parks begins to unfold, one after another all the way to the Malaysian border. The coastal provinces of Krabi, Trang and Satun represent the country's new frontier in terms of marine tourism. Aside from intensive developments on Ko Phi-Phi, Ko Lanta and along one small area of the mainland coast near Krabi's provincial capital, most of this stretch remains relatively undiscovered by international visitors.

Krabi Province

The coastal province of Krabi, 60km due east of Phuket, continues the scenic marine karst topography typical of Ao Phang-Nga. More than 200 islands offer excellent recreational opportunities; many of the islands belong to **Hat Nopparat Thara/Ko Phi-Phi National Marine Park** or **Ko Lanta National Marine Park**. Many of Krabi's beaches feature shimmering stretches of sand lapped by calm, clear seas and backed by vine-choked limestone cliffs. Such cliffs have become a world-class rock-climbing mecca, and good reef diving is available at several offshore islets nearby. Intact mangrove forests can be seen in several estuarial areas. Krabi is also a jumping off point for Ko Phi-Phi, Ko Lanta and other islands in the area.

Hundreds of years ago, Krabi's waters were a favourite hide-out for Asian pirates because of the abundance of islands and water caves. Latter-day pirates now steal islands or parts of islands for development: targets thus far include Ko Phi-Phi Don, Ko Poda, Ko Bubu, Ko Jam (Ko Pu), Ko Po, Ko Bilek (Ko Hong), Ko Kamyai and Ko Kluang – despite the fact that these islands are

Highlights

- Krabi Province's Ao Nang has become a rock-climbing mecca because of its high-quality pocketed limestone surfaces and overhangs.

- At Wat Tham Seua, a beautiful forest wàt near Krabi town, monastic cells are built into cliffs and caves.

- Ko Lanta boasts a densly forested interior, a stretch of wide beach on its shoreline, as well as mangrove swamps that flitter with songbirds and giant tropical butterflies.

- Stunning beaches with magnificent scenery can be found at popular Ko Phi-Phi, known to movie-goers around the world as the setting for *The Beach*.

- Trang province's little-visited coves and beaches reward those willing to make the effort to seek them out.

- Satun Province's Ko Tarutao National Marine Park is remote and virtually uninhabited, one of the most pristine coastal areas in the country.

BANGKOK

ANDAMAN SEA

Gulf of Thailand

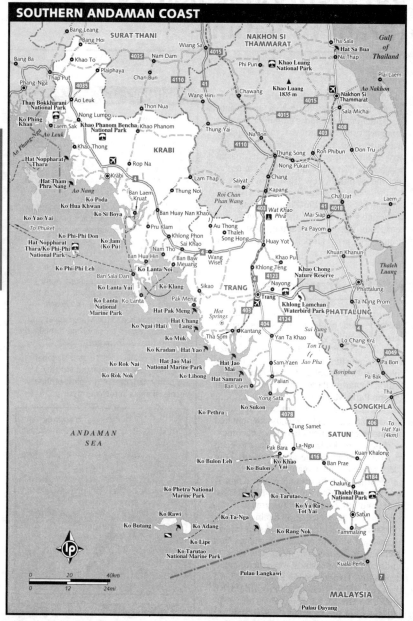

SOUTHERN ANDAMAN COAST

Bang Leang
Bang Hoi
SURAT THANI
Wiang Sa
4015
Nam Dam
NAKHON SI
THAMMARAT
Tha Sala
Hat Sa Bua
Na Thap
Gulf
of
Thailand

Bang Ba
Khao To
4035
Plaiphaya
Chan Buri
4110
Phi Pun
Khao Luang
National Park
Plai Laem

Phang-Nga
Thap Put
4035
Thon Nua
Wang Hin
Chawang
Khao Luang
1835 m
Nakhon Si
Thammarat
Ao Nakhon

Than Bokkharani
National Park
Ao Leuk
Nong Lumpo
Khao Phanom Bencha
National Park
Thung Yai
Na Bon
4015
Sala Michai

Ko Phing
Khan
Laem Sak
Ao Leuk
Khao Phanom
4015
4015
403
408
Don Tru

Ao Phang-Nga
Khao Thong
KRABI
4110
Thung Song
Nong Pukari
Ron Phibun

Hat Noppharat
Thara
Rop Na
Lam Thap
Saiyat
Chang
Kapang
Cha Uat
Laem

Hat Tham
Phra Nang
Krabi
4
Ban Laem
Kruat
Thung Noi
Roi Chan
Phan Wang
403
Wat Khao
Phra
41
4018

Ao Nang
Ko Poda
Ko Hua Khwan
Ko Si Boya
Pru Klam
Ban Huay Nan Khao
Au Thong
Thaleh
Song Hong
Mai Siap
Pa Payom
Khuan Khanun

Ko Yao Yai
To Phuket
Ko Phi-Phi Don
Ko Jam
(Ko Pu)
Khlong Phon
Sai Khao
Huay Yot
Khao Pu
Thaleh
Luang

Hat Noppharat
Thara/Ko Phi-Phi
National Park
Ban Hua Hin
Nam Tho
Ban Baw
Meuang
Wang
Wiset
Khlong Teng
Khao Chong
Nature Reserve
Nayong
Phattalung

Ko Phi-Phi Leh
Ban Sala Dan
Ko Lanta Noi
Sikao
4123
Ta Nang Prom

Ko Lanta Yai
Ko Klang
TRANG
Trang
PHATTALUNG

Ko Lanta
National
Marine Park
Ko Lanta
Pak Meng
403
Khlong Lamchan
Waterbird Park

Hat Pak Meng
Hat Chang
Lang
Hot
Springs
404
4124
Sai Rung
Lo Chang Kra

Ko Ngai (Hai)
Ko Muk
Tha Som
Kantang
Yan Ta Khao
Ton Te
&
Jao Pha
4049
Pa Bon

Ko Kradan
Hat Yao
Sam Yaen
Boriphat
Pa Bak

Ko Rok Nai
Hat Jao Mai
National Marine Park
Hat Jao
Mai
Palian
Tha

Ko Rok Nok
Ko Libong
Hat Samran
Ban Laem
Yong Sata
SONGKHLA

ANDAMAN
SEA
Ko Pethra
Ko Sukon
4078
Tung Samet
SATUN
406
To
Hat Yai
(4km)

Pak Bara
La-Ngu
Kuan Khalong

Ko Bulon Leh
Ko Bulon
Ko Khao
Yai
416
Ban Prae
4184

Ko Phetra National
Marine Park
Ko Tarutao
Chalung
Thaleh Ban
National Park

Ko Rawi
Ko Ta-Nga
Ko Ya Ra
Tot Yai
Satun

Ko Butang
Ko Adang
Ko Rang Nok
Tammalang

Ko Lipe
Ko Tarutao
National Marine Park
Kuala Perlis
7

Pulau Langkawi
MALAYSIA

0   20   40km
0   12   24mi

Pulau Dayang

LP

supposed to be protected by the Thai government. Keep in mind that by visiting and patronising the businesses on these islands, you are contributing to an unfortunate trend.

The interior of the province, noted for its tropical forests and the Phanom Bencha mountain range, has barely been explored. Taking a flight over the area will explain why – the combination of vertical limestone cliffs and thick jungle make many areas uninhabitable. This has kept development to a minimum and much of the province remains pristine. Birdwatchers come from far and wide to view Gurney's pitta (formerly thought to be extinct) and Nordmann's greenshank. About 40% of the provincial population is Muslim.

Beach accommodation is plentiful and there are regular boats to Ko Phi-Phi, 42km south-west. While nearly deserted in the rainy season (a good time to go if you're seeking solitude or low rates – but you'd better be very fond of heavy rain), the hotels and bungalows along Krabi's beaches can fill up from December to March.

KRABI
กระบี่

postcode 81000 • pop 18,500
Nearly 1000km from Bangkok and 180km from Phuket, this fast-developing provincial capital has friendly people, good food and some good beaches nearby. The capital sits on the banks of the Krabi River right before it empties into the Andaman Sea. Across from town you can see Bird, Cat and Mouse islands, limestone isles named for their shapes.

Most travellers breeze through town on their way to Ko Lanta to the south, Ko Phi-Phi to the south-west or the beaches near Ao Nang to the west. But Krabi, with its pleasant riverside setting and good selection of restaurants, is not a bad place to kick back for a day or two.

Although Krabi is more Taoist-Confucianist and Muslim than Theravada Buddhist, **Wat Kaew** contains some older late 19th- and early 20th-century buildings and lots of large old trees.

Orientation
Maps Bangkok Guide publishes the handy *Guide Map of Krabi* (50B), which contains several minimaps of areas of interest throughout the province. If it's kept up to date it should prove to be very useful for travel in the area. Visid Hongsombud's *Guide Map of Krabi* (look for the picture of the bespectacled Mr Visid on the cover) is detailed and up-to-date, as well as being printed on water-proof paper. Frank Tour's *Krabi* (70B) is also quite good and is also printed on waterproof stock.

Information
Tourist Offices Tourism Authority of Thailand (TAT; ☎ 075 612 740) maintains a small office on Thanon (Th) Utarakit near the waterfront. They have lots of useful printed information, including a few maps that depict the province, the capital and the islands of Ko Phi-Phi and Ko Lanta, along with accommodation lists.

Another 'tourist information booth', which is actually a ticket agency for buses and boats run by PP Family Co, can be found near the night market on the waterfront.

Immigration Visas can easily be extended at the immigration office, south of the post and telephone office on Th Chamai Anuson.

Post & Communications The post and telephone office is on Th Utarakit past the turn-off for Saphaan Jao Fah (Saphaan Jao Fah pier); a separate poste-restante entrance is at the side. The Communications Authority of Thailand (CAT) office is located about 1km north of Krabi Hospital on Th Utarakit. Home Country Direct international phone service is available here daily from 7am to midnight.

Vieng Thong Hotel (☎ 075 620 020, fax 075 612 525), 155 Th Utarakit, is one of many places that offers email and Internet services.

Travel Agencies Krabi has dozens of fly-by-night travel agencies that will book

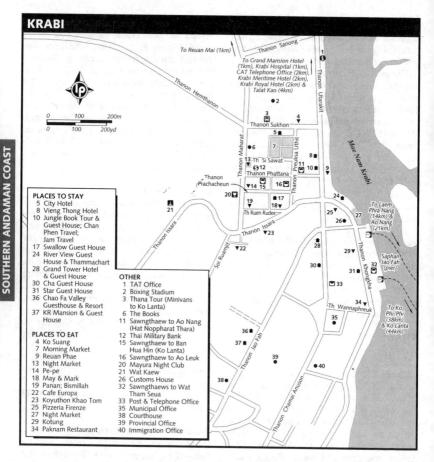

KRABI

PLACES TO STAY
5 City Hotel
8 Vieng Thong Hotel
10 Jungle Book Tour & Guest House; Chan Phen Travel; Jam Travel
17 Swallow Guest House
24 River View Guest House & Thammachart Guest House
28 Grand Tower Hotel & Guest House
30 Cha Guest House
31 Star Guest House
36 Chao Fa Valley Guesthouse & Resort
37 KR Mansion & Guest House

PLACES TO EAT
4 Ko Suang
7 Morning Market
9 Reuan Phae
13 Night Market
14 Pe-pe
18 May & Mark
19 Panan; Bismillah
22 Cafe Europa
23 Koyuthon Khao Tom
25 Pizzeria Firenze
27 Night Market
29 Kotung
34 Paknam Restaurant

OTHER
1 TAT Office
2 Boxing Stadium
3 Thana Tour (Minivans to Ko Lanta)
6 The Books
11 Sawngthaew to Ao Nang (Hat Nopparat Thara)
12 Thai Military Bank
15 Sawngthaew to Ban Hua Hin (Ko Lanta)
16 Sawngthaew to Ao Leuk
20 Mayura Night Club
21 Wat Kaew
26 Customs House
32 Sawngthaews to Wat Tham Seua
33 Post & Telephone Office
35 Municipal Office
38 Courthouse
39 Provincial Office
40 Immigration Office

accommodation at beaches and islands as well as tour-bus and boat tickets. Use these places with caution – few travellers have given any of these places glowing reports. Chan Phen and Jungle Book, both on Th Utarakit, are still the most reliable. Jam Travel, between the two aforementioned places, is also good.

Bookshops Phuket-based The Books has an outlet at 78–80 Th Maharat. The selection of English-language books and magazines is rather slim, although they do carry same-day issues of the *Bangkok Post*.

Medical Services Krabi hospital (☎ 075 611 266, 075 611 210) is 1km north of the city on Th Utarakit.

Eco-Trips

Chan Phen Travel (☎ 075 612 004, fax 075 612 661, 145 Th Utarakit) runs half-day boat tours to nearby estuaries for a look at mangrove ecology (300B to 350B per person – four person minimum), or you can simply hire a boat at Saphaan Jao Fah for 200B to 250B per hour. Chan Phen Travel also offers birdwatching tours that begin at 7am and last four hours. The advantage of taking Chan Phen's birdwatching tour, rather than hiring a boat at the pier, is that Chan Phen's boat drivers can point out birds and name them in English (though they're not quite up to conversational level yet). Bird species that frequent mangrove areas include the sea eagle and ruddy kingfisher. In mud and shallow waters, keep an eye out for fiddler crabs and mudskippers.

At the Khao Nor Chuchi (Naw Juu-Jii) Lowland Forest Project, south-east of the city, visitors can follow trails through lowland rainforest, swim in clear forest pools and observe or participate in local village activities like rubber-tapping.

Chan Phen and other travel agencies in Krabi do day trips to Khao Nor Chuchi for 650B per person with lunch at a hot springs (Sa Thung Tiaw) near Khlong Thom, a rubber plantation and a visit to the recently renovated museum at Wat Khlong Thom. Besides weapons and pottery, the museum has an extensive collection of the ancient beads that are still being unearthed in the surrounding fields. The fee includes air-con transport, lunch and beverages; bring a swimsuit and good walking shoes.

Travel agencies in Krabi (as well as at Ao Nang) can also arrange trips to idyllic uninhabited isles nearby, all with coral reefs and luscious beaches set in tranquil sandy coves. Rates for such trips usually run from 1300B to 1500B for up to eight people.

Sea Canoe Thailand operates sea canoe/kayak trips along the coast and can be contacted on Ao Nang (see the later Ao Nang & Laem Phra Nang section).

Places to Stay

Guesthouses The cheapest places to stay in Krabi are the many guesthouses, which seem to be everywhere. Some stay around only a season or two, others are fairly stable. The ones situated in the business district consist of windowless, closet-like rooms above modern shop buildings, often with faulty plumbing – OK for one night before heading to a nearby beach or island but not great for longer stays.

Star Guest House (☎ 075 630 234, Th Khongkha) Rooms low/high season 100/250B. A rare example of Krabi's traditional wooden shophouse architecture, this guesthouse is located just opposite the pier and has fan rooms with shared bath. Every room has a window and there are spacious common areas, including a wide veranda overlooking the river.

River View Guest House (☎ 075 612 536, 13 Th Khongkha) Rooms 80-150B. The small River View, near Saphaan Jao Fah and Customs House, has decent rooms and a restaurant with good vegetarian food. There's also a terrace on the roof with good views of the river.

Swallow Guest House (☎ 075 611 645, Th Prachacheun) Rooms 150-200B. This is a popular place with fairly clean and comfortable rooms; price depends on whether the room has a window or not.

Grand Tower Hotel & Guest House (☎ 075 621 456–7, fax 075 611 741, 73/1 Th Utarakit) Rooms with fan/air-con 300/450B. The air-con rooms here are OK. However, the fan rooms are on the fourth floor and, as there's no elevator, it's a bit of a climb.

Quieter and more comfortable are a few guesthouses just south-west of town near the courthouse.

Chao Fa Valley Guesthouse & Resort (☎ 075 612 499, 50 Th Jao Fah) Bungalows with fan 150-500B. This place has good-sized bungalows of concrete and wood.

KR Mansion & Guest House (☎ 075 612 761, 52/1 Th Jao Fah) Rooms without/with bath & fan 150/250B. KR offers 40 hotel-style rooms and will rent by the month. The rooftop beer garden provides a 360° view of Krabi – great for sunsets. The staff can arrange motorcycle rentals, local tours and boat tickets as well.

Cha Guest House (☎ 075 611 141, 45 Th Utarakit) Bungalows with shared facilities 80-120B, with bath 220B. Near the post and telephone office, this is a group of concrete bungalows (some windowless) in a compound behind a shophouse.

Jungle Book Tour & Guest House (☎ 075 611 148, ☎/fax 075 621 186, 141 Th Utarakit) Cubicles with fan 50-80B. This has tiny, windowless cubicles, all with good mattresses and surprisingly friendly bedbugs.

Hotels There are several hotels in Krabi.

Vieng Thong Hotel (☎ 075 620 020, fax 075 612 525, 155 Th Utarakit) Rooms with fan 350B, with air-con 500-750B. Vieng Thong has clean rooms with TV and phone. The fan rooms are especially good value. There's a travel agency and several computer terminals, where you can check email, in the lobby.

City Hotel (☎ 075 621 280, fax 075 621 301, 15/2–3 Th Sukhon) Rooms with fan 350B, with air-con 500-550B. In the centre of town, the City Hotel has clean rooms. Parking is available.

Grand Mansion Hotel (☎ 075 620 833, fax 075 611 372, 289/1 Th Utarakit) Rooms with fan & hot shower 350B, with air-con 500-750B. The well-run Grand Mansion offers plain but comfortable rooms.

Krabi Royal Hotel (☎ 075 611 582, fax 075 611 581, 403 Th Utarakit) Rooms with air-con, TV, fridge, phone, hot shower & breakfast 1000B. This is near the more expensive Krabi Meritime at the northern edge of town. Discounts are available for stays of more than one night.

Krabi Meritime Hotel (☎ 075 620 028–46, fax 075 612 992, in Bangkok ☎ 027 190 034, fax 023 187 687) Rooms 2900B to 17,200B. The swanky Krabi Meritime is near the river on the way to Talaat Kao, about 2km from downtown Krabi. It has well-decorated rooms with balconies and impressive views of the river and mountains. Facilities include a nightclub, a great swimming pool, walking path, a lake (with swan-shaped paddleboats!) and canoes, a fitness centre, sauna and convention rooms. The pool is open to the public for a daily fee of 60/40B for adults/children.

Places to Eat

What Krabi lacks in good guesthouses it more than makes up for in good eating places. Along Th Khongkha is a *night market* near Saphaan Jao Fah, with great seafood at low prices and a host of Thai dessert vendors. There's also another *night market* near the intersection of Th Maharat and Th Si Sawat (aka Soi 8, Th Maharat). Quite a few of Krabi's travel agencies double as

traveller-oriented restaurants, but the food leads you to believe that the restaurant was an afterthought – with some exceptions.

May & Mark (☎ 075 612 562, 6 Th Ruen Rudee) Dishes 40-80B. Simple and unpretentious, this place has some of the best food in town. Bread baked fresh on the premises makes for excellent sandwiches and they also do good vegetarian dishes. This is also the place to come for hearty Western breakfasts, as well as Thai food. They're open from 6.30am to 9pm.

Kotung (☎ 075 611 522, 36 Th Khongkha) Dishes 40-80B. One of the better and most reasonably priced restaurants in town for standard Thai dishes and local cuisine is the Kotung, also near Saphaan Jao Fah. The *tôm yam kûng* (spicy shrimp lemon-grass soup) is especially good, as is anything else made with fresh seafood.

Reuan Phae (☎ 075 611 956, 256/1 Th Utarakit) Dishes 40-100B. This is an old floating restaurant on the river in front of town and is fine for a beer or rice whisky while watching the river rise and fall with the tide. Although the food at Reuan Phae is not that great overall, certain dishes, including the *thâwt man kûng* (fried shrimp cakes) and *hàw mòk tháleh* (spicy steamed curried fish), are well worth trying and prices are low to moderate.

Pe-pe (5 Th Maharat) Dishes 20-35B. On the corner of Th Maharat and Th Prachacheun, Pe-pe is a clean place that serves good, inexpensive noodles and *khâo man kài* (Hainanese-style chicken and rice); it's very popular at lunchtime.

Another good area for lunches is the intersection of Th Preuksa Uthit and Th Sukhon (aka Soi 10, Th Maharat), where you'll find several inexpensive *noodle and rice shops*.

Ko Suang (Th Sukhon) Dishes 20-30B. Opposite the northern end of Th Preuksa Uthit, this place serves good, inexpensive khâo man kài, *khâo mǔu dàeng* ('red' pork with rice), *kǔaytǐaw* (wide rice noodles) and *bà-mìi* (wheat noodles). There is no roman-script sign.

Pizzeria Firenze (10 Th Khongkha) Pizzas 80-160B. This does good pizza, pasta, gelato and Italian breads, and serves good wine.

Paknam Restaurant (☎ *075 612 722, 133 Th Khongkha*) Dishes 30-50B. Open 8am-11pm. This small bar/restaurant has limited food service. It offers email and Internet connection downstairs.

Thammachart (☎ *075 612 536, 13 Th Khongkha*) Dishes 40-60B. Below the River View Guest House, this restaurant serves good vegetarian food.

Cafe Europa (☎/*fax 075 620 407, 1/9 Soi Ruamjit*) Main meals 50-100B. More substantial Western meals are available at this place, south of Th Issara. It's a Scandinavian-style restaurant with imported Danish cheeses, steaks, Danish roast pork, baked potatoes, sandwiches and imported wines.

Reuan Mai (☎ *075 631 797 Th Maharat*) Dishes 60-180B. Reuan Mai is a very good Thai-style *sŭan aahǎan* (garden restaurant), near Krabi Hospital about 1.6km north-north-east from the intersection of Th Maharat and Th Sukhon, 400m past the big Chinese temple on the left. It's mostly a locals' place but well worth seeking out for the high-quality Thai food.

Koyuthon Khao Tom (*6/5 Th Issara*) Dishes 20-40B. A great option if you're out late; many restaurants in town close by 9pm, but this *khâo tôm/aahǎan taam sàng* place, near Th Maharat, goes all night. There is no roman-script sign.

Panan (*Th Ruen Rudee*) Dishes 20-40B. On the corner of Th Ruen Rudee and Th Maharat, this has southern Muslim specialities such as *khâo mòk kài* (chicken biryani) in the mornings, and inexpensive curries and *kŭaytǐaw* the rest of day. The roman-script sign reads 'Makanan Islam' (Malay for 'Muslim food').

Next door is another decent Muslim place, **Bismillah** (*Th Ruen Rudee*) with a sign in Thai/Yawi only.

Getting There & Away

Air The airport is 17km north-east of Krabi, on the northern side of Hwy 4. THAI flies between Bangkok and Krabi daily. A one-way fare is 2120B and the flight is 1¼ hours. Bangkok Airways flies between Ko Samui and Krabi during the high season. This flight takes around 40 minutes. Air Andaman flies between Phuket and Krabi daily for 900B one way. Tickets can be booked through Vieng Thong Travel in the lobby of the Vieng Thong Hotel (☎ 075 620 020).

Bus & Minivan Pushy agents at Songserm Travel and PP Family Co (both on Th Khongkha opposite the pier) scoop up much of the naive tourist business in the city centre. It's easy buying tickets here but departure times and bus conditions are unreliable and at times unpredictable. If you use the Baw Khaw Saw (government bus) terminal in nearby Talaat Kao you'll save yourself the trouble of worrying about whether private buses booked in town really turn out to be what was advertised or whether they will leave at the scheduled time. Here, the well-organised Baw Khaw Saw terminal features separate ticket booths for each line (printed in English), a clean little restaurant, snacks and drinks for sale and clean toilets. The Talat Kao terminal is about 4km north of Krabi on the highway between Phang-Nga and Trang. To get to the centre of Krabi, catch a sǎwngthǎew for 10B or motorcycle taxi for 30B.

Government buses to/from Bangkok cost 240B ordinary, 328B to 347B 2nd class air-con (no toilet), 446B 1st class air-con or 550B VIP (655B for super VIP with 24 seats). Air-con buses leave Bangkok's Southern bus terminal between 6pm and 8pm; they leave Krabi between 4pm and 5pm. Songserm and PP Family arrange air-con buses (or vans) to Th Khao San in Bangkok for 350B.

Buses to/from Phuket leave hourly during daylight hours, cost 56B (101B with air-con) and take three to four hours. Air-con minivans from PP Family cost 200B to Phuket airport or Phuket town, 250B to Patong, Karon or Kata beaches.

Buses for Krabi leave Phang-Nga hourly throughout the day for 36B ordinary, 52B air-con. Most of these buses originate in Phuket and have Trang as their final destination. Government buses to/from Hat Yai cost 150B air-con and take five hours; from

Trang it's 43B (77B air-con) and takes 2½ hours. There are also share taxis to/from Trang, Hat Yai and Satun; fares are roughly twice the ordinary bus fare.

Ordinary buses between Surat Thani and Krabi make the four-hour trip 13 times daily between 5am and 2.30pm for 70B. Air-con buses depart three times a day between 7am and 3.30pm for 160B and take around three hours (it's the same price if you get out at Khao Sok National Park). Through various agencies in town you can pay 150B for a private air-con bus or minivan to Surat. These agencies also arrange minivans to Hat Yai, Trang or Phattalung, each for the same fare of 180B. There are no minivans from the Baw Khaw Saw terminal, so if you want to go by this method, you'll have to book through one of the many private agencies in town.

Săwngthăew to Ban Hua Hin (for Ko Lanta) leave from Th Phattana (aka Soi 6, Th Maharat) in town, with a second stop in Talat Kao, for 30B. They leave about every half-hour from 10am to 2pm and take 40 minutes to reach Ban Hua Hin. There are also air-con minivans available from Thana Tour (☎ 075 631 219), 42 Th Sukhon, straight through to Ko Lanta departing at 11am and 1pm. The fare is 150B.

Boat Krabi can be reached by sea from Ko Phi-Phi and Ko Lanta. See the respective Ko Phi-Phi and Ko Lanta sections for details.

Getting Around

Any place in town can easily be reached on foot, but if you plan to do a lot of exploring out of town, renting a motorcycle might be a good idea. Several travel agencies and guesthouses can arrange motorcycle rentals for 150B to 250B a day, with discounts for multi-day rentals. Jeep rentals range from 800B (open-top) to 1200B (air-con) per day.

Most buses into Krabi terminate at Talat Kao, about 4km north of Krabi on the highway between Phang-Nga and Trang. You can catch a săwngthăew between Talat Kao and the centre of Krabi for 10B, or a motorcycle taxi for 30B.

From the airport, 17km from the city centre, you can catch a minivan for 60B, or hire a car for 300B. A car all the way to Ao Nang costs 500B. From town to the airport a taxi is 200B or, if you're travelling light, a motorcycle taxi will take you for 100B.

Săwngthăew to Ao Leuk (for Than Bokkharani National Park) leave from the intersection of Th Phattana and Th Preuksa Uthit for 30B. To Ao Nang (30B) they leave from Th Phattana opposite the New Hotel – departures are about every 15 minutes from 7am to 6pm during the high season (December to March), until 4pm for the remainder of the year. Boats to the islands and beaches mostly leave from Saphaan Jao Fah. See the Getting There & Away entry under Ao Nang & Laem Phra Nang for boat details.

AROUND KRABI

Nineteen kilometres west of Krabi, on Laem Pho, is the so-called **Shell Fossil Cemetery (Su-Saan Hoi)**, a shell 'graveyard' where 75-million-year-old shell fossils have formed giant slabs jutting into the sea.

To get there, take a săwngthăew from the Krabi waterfront for 20B – they're marked 'shell cemetery'.

Wat Tham Seua
วัดถ้ำเสือ

In the other direction, about 5km north and 2km east of town, is Wat Tham Seua (Tiger Cave Temple) one of Southern Thailand's most famous forest *wát* (temples). The main *wíhǎan* is built into a long, shallow limestone cave, on either side of which dozens of *kuti* (monastic cells) are built into the cliffs and caves.

Wat Tham Seua's abbot is Ajaan Jamnien Silasettho, a Thai monk in his 50s who has allowed a rather obvious personality cult to develop around him. In the large, main cave the usual pictures of split cadavers and decaying corpses on the walls (useful meditation objects for countering lust) are interspersed with large portraits of Ajaan Jamnien, who is well known as a teacher of *vipassana* (meditation) and *metta* (loving-kindness). It is said that he was

A Reminder

If you decide to visit Wat Tham Seua, please try to remember the dress protocol for Thai monasteries. On my last visit every single *faràng* visitor I saw here was dressed impolitely in spite of an English sign at the cave entrance asking visitors not to enter wearing shorts, sleeveless tops, tank tops and so on. Every Western visitor – male and female – I encountered over two hours of wandering the grounds was wearing very abbreviated shorts. Two Western male visitors arrived wearing only shorts and no shirts. It is absolutely insulting to dress like this in a Thai temple compound, as was obvious from looking at the faces of all the Thais visiting or residing at the temple. If the Southern Thai climate is too hot for you and you simply can't suffer the pain of wearing long pants/skirts, and shirts with short sleeves, then consider crossing Wat Tham Seua off your itinerary.

Joe Cummings

apprenticed at an early age to a blind lay priest and astrologer who practised folk medicine and that he has been celibate his entire life. On the inside of his outer robe, and on an inner vest, hang scores of talismans presented to him by his followers – altogether they must weigh several kilograms, a weight Ajaan Jamnien bears to take on his followers' karma. Many young women come to Wat Tham Seua to practise as eight-precept nuns.

In the back of the main cave a set of marble stairs behind the altar leads up to a smaller cavern (watch your head when you go up the steps) known as Tiger Cave, behind which a Buddha footprint symbol sits on a gilded platform, locked behind a gate. Near one of the main cave entrances a life-size wax figure of Ajaan Jamnien sits in a glass case. A sign on the case in English and Thai says 'Not real man', though the more you look at the figure the more real it appears.

The best part of the temple grounds can be found in a little valley behind the ridge where the *bòt* (central sanctuary) is located. Follow the path past the main wát buildings, through a little village with nuns' quarters, until you come to a pair of steep stairways on the left. The first stairway leads to an arduous climb of 1272 steps to the top of a karst hill with another Buddha footprint shrine and a magnificent view of the area.

The second stairway, next to a large statue of Kuan Yin, leads over a gap in the ridge and into a valley of tall trees and limestone caves, 10 of which are named. Enter the caves on your left and look for light switches on the walls – the network of caves is wired so that you can light your way chamber by chamber through the labyrinth until you rejoin the path on the other side. There are several kuti in and around the caves, and it's interesting to see the differences in interior decorating – some are very spartan and others are outfitted like oriental bachelor pads.

A path winds through a grove of 1000-year-old dipterocarps surrounded by tall limestone cliffs covered with a patchwork of foliage. If you continue to follow the path you'll eventually end up where you started, at the bottom of the staircase.

Places to Stay The following might be a good place to stay if you wanted to explore Wat Tham Seua thoroughly.

Tiger House (☎ 075 631 625) Rooms with fan/air-con & bath 200/300B. The friendly Tiger, on the access road, is just outside the entrance to the temple grounds and has 13 rooms surrounding a shaded parking area. It is spotlessly clean and nicely landscaped with potted plants.

Getting There & Away To get to Wat Tham Seua, take a săwngthăew from Th Utarakit to the Talat Kao junction for 10B, then catch any bus or săwngthăew east on Highway (Hwy) 4 towards Trang and Hat Yai and get off at the road on the left just after the 108km marker – if you tell the bus driver 'Wat Tham Seua', they'll let you off at the right place. It's a 2km walk straight up this road to the wát.

In the mornings there are a few săwng-thăew from Th Phattana in town that pass the turn-off for Wat Tham Seua (12B) on their way to Ban Hua Hin. Also in the morning there is usually a săwngthăew or two going direct to Wat Tham Seua from Talat Kao for around 20B. If you're in a group it might be easier to hail one of the blue or yellow mini-săwngthăew from anywhere around town and hire it (100B to 150B one-way) for the trip all the way to Wat Tham Seua.

Wat Sai Thai
วัดไสไทย

A 15m reclining Buddha can be seen in a long rock shelter under an immense limestone cliff on the way to Ao Nang, about 7km from Krabi beside Route 4034. Though a wát in name only (there aren't sufficient monks in residence for official wát status), you can see an old bell-less bell tower, some thâat kradùuk (bone reliquaries; small stupas where devotees' ashes are interred) and the foundation for a former cremation hall remaining from the time it was an active monastery.

Hat Noppharat Thara
หาดนพรัตน์ธารา

Eighteen kilometres north-west of Krabi, this beach used to be called Hat Khlong Haeng (Dry Canal Beach) because the canal that flows into the Andaman Sea here is dry except during, and just after, the monsoon season. Field marshal Sarit gave the beach its current Pali-Sanskrit name, which means Beach of the Nine-Gemmed Stream, as a tribute to its beauty. A new royal residence was recently constructed here.

The 2km-long beach, part of Hat Noppharat Thara/Ko Phi-Phi National Marine Park, is a favourite spot for Thai picnickers. There are some government bungalows for rent and a recently upgraded visitors centre with wall maps of the marine park and displays on coral reefs and ecotourism – most labelled in Thai only, a few in English.

Places to Stay & Eat There are plenty of accommodation options on this beach.

Government bungalows (☎ 075 637 200, park headquarters) 3-person/9-person bungalows 400/1200B. These bungalows are quite OK, though on weekends the beach and visitors centre throngs with local visitors. You can also rent tents for 200B (two persons) to 300B (three persons). A row of open-air restaurants and vendors strung out along the parking lot sell snacks and simple meals.

Andaman Inn (☎ 075 612 728) Bungalows with bath 150-350B. The park pier, at the eastern end of Noppharat Thara, has boats across the canal to where the Andaman Inn has well-spaced bungalows and well-maintained grounds. The simple restaurant here is quite good.

Down the beach are the similar but even more secluded *Emerald Bungalows* (300B to 500B with attached bath), *Bamboo Bungalows* (150B with attached bath) and *Sara Cove* (100B with shared bathroom, 250B with private bath). Sara Cove can arrange inexpensive boating or fishing trips.

Farther west, around Laem Hang Naak (where a newly built royal residence crowns a hill on the cape), near the village of Ban Khlong Muang is Hat Khlong Muang, a secluded beach with accommodation. If you have your own vehicle, it can be approached by road via Route 4034. You can also hire a boat from Ao Nang if the weather is good.

Andaman Holiday Resort (☎ 075 644 321–3, fax 075 644 320) Rooms with air-con, TV & fridge 3000-3800B, bungalows 4000-4800B. This has rooms in a hotel building and two sizes of bungalow, some have rooftop sitting areas. There's a restaurant and swimming pool and tours of the surrounding area can be arranged.

Pine Bungalow (☎ 075 644 332) Bungalows with shared facilities 150B, with attached bath 250B. Farther south on Ao Siaw, Pine Bungalow is secluded and has simple but clean bungalows.

Getting There & Away Hat Noppharat Thara can be reached by săwngthăew that leave about every 15 minutes from 7am to 6pm (high season) or 4pm (low season) from Th Phattana in Krabi town.

Boats from Saphaan Jao Fah pier in Krabi also do the one-hour run to Hat Noppharat Thara frequently between 7am and 4pm for 70B per person. There are also occasional boats between Hat Noppharat Thara and Ao Nang, mainly in the high season, during the same hours (10B, 10 minutes).

Ao Nang & Laem Phra Nang
อ่าวนาง/แหลมพระนาง

South of Noppharat Thara is a series of bays where limestone cliffs and caves drop right into the sea. The water is quite clear and there are some coral reefs in the shallows. The longest beach runs along Ao Nang, a lovely but fast-developing strand easily reached by road from Krabi. Judging from the signs in Ao Nang's ubiquitous Indian-owned tailor shops, this beach has become quite popular with Swedish package tourists.

Over the headlands to the south are the beaches of **Hat Phai Phlong**, **Hat Ton Sai** and **Hat Rai Leh West**, and then the cape of Laem Phra Nang, which encompasses **Hat Tham Phra Nang** (Princess Cave Beach) on the western side, a mangrove-rimmed beach facing east usually called **Hat Rai Leh East**, but also known as Hat Ao Nam Mao, and finally **Hat Nam Mao** proper. These beaches have become quite popular in the past few years, so popular in fact that accommodation is often fully booked out during the high season. Since there's really no way of knowing whether there are vacancies or not before arriving, some visitors end up sleeping on the beach for a night or two while waiting for a room.

All these beaches are accessible either by hiking over the headland cliffs or by taking a boat from Ao Nang or Krabi – although for several years now there have been rumours that a tunnel road will be built to Hat Phai Phlong to provide access for a new resort hotel being constructed there. So far nothing has happened, and with local conservation groups growing stronger it's unlikely any such tunnel will be built in the near future.

Highway signs are beginning to refer to Ao Nang as 'Ao Phra Nang', which was its original full name (in typical Southern Thai fashion, the locals shortened it to Ao Nang), but it leads some people to confuse Ao Nang/Ao Phra Nang with Laem Phra Nang,

SOUTHERN ANDAMAN COAST

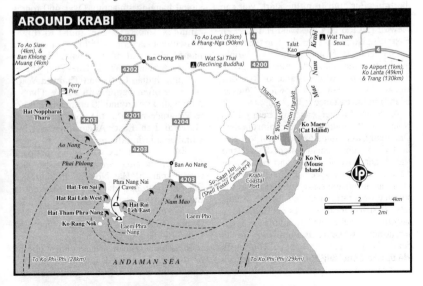

the cape with the famous cave for which the bay was named, or Hat Tham Phra Nang, the beach near this cave.

Hat Tham Phra Nang This is perhaps the most beautiful beach in the area. At one end is a tall limestone cliff that contains **Tham Phra Nang Nok** (Outer Princess Cave), a cave that is said to be the home of a mythical sea princess. Local legend says that during the 3rd century BC a passing royal barque carrying a charismatic Indian princess named Sri Guladevi foundered in a storm. The princess' spirit came to inhabit a large cave near the wreck, using power gained through many past lives to grant favours to all who came to pay respect. Local fisherfolk place carved wooden phalli in the cave as offerings to the Phra Nang (Holy Princess) so that she will provide plenty of fish for them. Inside the cliff is a hidden lagoon called **Sa Phra Nang** (Holy Princess Pool) that can be reached by following a sometimes-slippery cave trail into the side of the mountain. A rope guides hikers along the way and it takes about 45 minutes to reach the pool – guides are available from local guesthouses. If you turn left off the trail after 50m from the start, you can reach a 'window' in the cliff that affords a view of Hat Rai Leh West and Hat Rai Leh East. It's also possible to climb to the top of the mountain from here (some rock climbing is involved) and get an aerial view of the entire cape and the islands of **Ko Poda** and **Ko Hua Khwan** (also known as Chicken Island) in the distance.

A second, larger cave on Laem Phra Nang is in the middle of the peninsula near Diamond Cave Bungalows on Hat Rai Leh East. This one is called **Tham Phra Nang Nai** (Inner Princess Cave) and consists of three caverns. All three contain some of the most beautiful limestone formations in the country, including a golden 'stone waterfall' of sparkling quartz. Local mythology says that this cave is the grand palace of the sea princess while Tham Phra Nang on the beach is her summer palace. The cliffs around Ao Phra Nang have become a mecca for rock climbers from around the world

and it's easy to arrange equipment, maps and instruction from beach bungalows on Hat Rai Leh West and Hat Rai Leh East.

The islands off Laem Phra Nang are good for snorkelling. Besides Ko Poda and Ko Hua Khwan there is the nearer island of **Ko Rang Nok** (Bird Nest Island) and, next to that, a larger, unnamed island (possibly part of the same island at low tide and sometimes referred to as 'Happy Island') with an undersea cave. Some of the bungalows do reasonably priced day trips to these and other islands in the area.

Ao Phai Phlong This peaceful, palm-studded cove is worth boating to for the day. At the moment there is no accommodation here. It's been rumoured for years that a hotel conglomerate had purchased the land, but so far there are no signs of construction.

Rock Climbing Limestone cliffs on the huge headland between Hat Tham Phra Nang and Hat Rai Leh East, and on nearby islands, offer practically endless rock climbing opportunities. Most surfaces provide high-quality limestone with steep, pocketed walls, overhangs, and the occasional hanging stalactite. Over 460 routes have been identified and bolted by zealous climbers, most in the mid- to high-difficulty level (grades 16 to 25). They bear names like Lord of the Thais, The King and I, Andaman Wall, One-Two-Three, Sleeping Indian Cliffs and Thaiwan Wall. Novices often begin with Muay Thai, a 50m wall with around 20 climbs in the 17- to 21-grade range at the southern end of Hat Rai Leh East. According to King Climbers, during the high season as many as 300 visitors a day will climb this rock face. Certain areas are off limits because they're part of Hat Noppharat Thara/Ko Phi-Phi National Marine Park, including the cliff next to the Rayavadee Premier resort and cliffs outside Tham Phra Nang Nai (Inner Princess Cave, called 'Diamond Cave' by the tourist industry).

Most lodgings can arrange guided climbs or rock-climbing instruction. A half-day climb with instruction and guidance costs about 500B, an all-day costs 1000B, three days 3000B; all equipment and insurance is included. Equipment rental rates for a two person lead set are around 500B for a half-day, 800B for a full day.

King Climbers Rock Climbing School (**e** kingclimbers@iname.com) has one branch in Ao Nang (☎ 075 639 125) and another at Hat Rai Leh East (☎ 014 764 035).

Diving & Snorkelling Phra Nang Divers at Hat Rai Leh West, Coral Diving at Krabi Resort and Aqua Vision Dive Center on Ao Nang arrange day dives to local islands and live-aboard trips as far afield as Ko Bida Nawk/Ko Bida Nai, the Maya Wall, Hin Daeng, Hin Muang, and the Surin and Similan archipelagos. Going rates are 1000B to 1800B for a day trip to nearby islands, while three- to four-day certification courses cost 8000B to 9000B. The most convenient local dive spots are Ko Poda Nai and Ko Poda Nawk. At nearby Ko Mae Urai, a kilometre west of Poda Nok, two submarine tunnels lined with soft and hard corals are home to lots of tropical fish and are suitable for all levels of diving experience. Another fairly interesting dive site is the sunken boat just south of Ko Rang Nawk, a favoured fish habitat.

Barracuda's Tour & Travel (☎ 075 637 092) on Ao Nang operates daily four-island trips for 280B, including snorkelling gear and a basic lunch.

You can also negotiate directly with the boat pilots along Ao Nang. To hire a boat that carries up to six people costs 800B for half a day, 1500B for the full day.

Paddling Tours of the coast, islands and semi-submerged caves by inflatable canoe or kayak can be arranged through Sea Canoe Thailand (☎ 075 637 170) near Ao Nang Supermarket, or through Land & Trek (☎ 075 637 364) near Ao Nang Ban Lae on the Ao Nang beach road.

One of the best local paddles is the Tha Lin canyon river cruise, an estuary trip that cuts through 200m-tall foliaged limestone cliffs, mangrove channels and tidal lagoon tunnels (called 'hongs', from the Thai word

for 'room'). Birds frequently sighted in the mangroves include brown-winged kingfishers, Pacific reef egrets, Asian dowitchers and white-bellied sea eagles, while the most commonly seen mammals and reptiles are otters, macaques, gibbons and two-banded monitor lizards. Mudskippers and fiddler crabs abound.

Sea Canoe Thailand charges 1700B for a full-day excursion, 200B less in the low season. It also does an overnight trip to Ko Yao Noi for 7400B, including accommodation. Sea, Land & Trek does cavern explorations for 1500B.

Sailing Look for information about yachts sailing in and out of Ao Nang waters on the bulletin board at Sea World Guest House.

Places to Stay & Eat A large and growing number of bungalows and inns can be found along Ao Nang and nearby beaches. Most of the cheap places are being edged out, but there are still a few to be found in the 200B to 300B range – mostly in the upper floors of shophouses. When picking a place, look around for open-air bars in the area – these often go late and sound carries pretty easily. Light sleepers take heed.

Ao Nang Because it's easily accessible by road, this beach has become fairly developed. The more expensive places usually have booking offices in Krabi town. The cheapest places can be found in a block of unsightly modern shophouses just up from the beach on the left side of Route 4203.

Jinda Guest House (☎ 075 637 524) Rooms with fan 600B, air-con 1000B. This place offers apartment-like rooms upstairs in a shophouse. Prices drop by 50% during the low season.

Sea World Guest House (☎ 075 637 388) Rooms with fan 550B, air-con 1200B. Well run and clean, this place has rooms upstairs from a shophouse. There's a good little eatery downstairs and a few computer terminals, where you can check email, in the reception room.

There are several other similar places in the immediate area that have smaller (sometimes

SOUTHERN ANDAMAN COAST

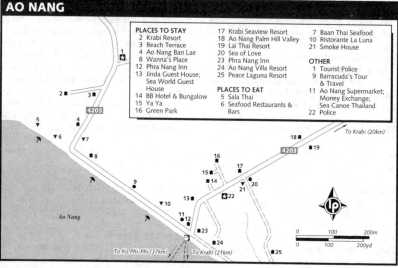

AO NANG

PLACES TO STAY
2 Krabi Resort
3 Beach Terrace
4 Ao Nang Ban Lae
8 Wanna's Place
12 Phra Nang Inn
13 Jinda Guest House;
    Sea World Guest
    House
14 BB Hotel & Bungalow
15 Ya Ya
16 Green Park
17 Krabi Seaview Resort
18 Ao Nang Palm Hill Valley
19 Lai Thai Resort
20 Sea of Love
23 Phra Nang Inn
24 Ao Nang Villa Resort
25 Peace Laguna Resort

PLACES TO EAT
5 Sala Thai
6 Seafood Restaurants &
    Bars
7 Baan Thai Seafood
10 Ristorante La Luna
21 Smoke House

OTHER
1 Tourist Police
9 Barracuda's Tour
    & Travel
11 Ao Nang Supermarket;
    Money Exchange;
    Sea Canoe Thailand
22 Police

To Krabi (20km)

4203

Ao Nang

To Ko Phi Phi (37km)   To Krabi (21km)

0   100   200m
0   100   200yd

windowless) rooms but are very cheap for being so close to the beach (150B to 250B). These include *Angie's*, *Bernie's* and *Sea Beer*.

Krabi Resort (☎ *075 637 030–5, fax 075 637 051, in Bangkok* ☎ *022 089 165)* Bungalows 2376- 5866B. The oldest resort in the area, at the northern end of Ao Nang, this place has luxury bungalows; price depends on proximity to the beach and whether you stay in a bungalow or in the hotel wing. Most of the guests here are with package tours or conferences. There are the usual resort amenities, including a swimming pool, bar and restaurant. Bookings can be made at the Krabi Resort office on Th Phattana in Krabi and guests receive free transport out to the resort. The resort also runs a bungalow operation on the island of Ko Poda, a 30-minute boat ride from Ao Nang. We've received complaints that Krabi Resort bookings are not always honoured, however.

Beach Terrace (☎ *075 637 180, fax 075 637 184)* Rooms with air-con, hot water, TV & fridge 2200B. Off Route 4203, the road leading to the beach's northern end, this is a modern apartment-style hotel with

40 identical rooms to choose from. Prices drop by more than half in the low season.

Ao Nang Ban Lae (☎ *075 637 189)* Bungalows 250-300B. About 150m south-west on the same side of Route 4203 as Beach Terrace, this cluster of simple but well-maintained bungalows isn't too far from the beach.

Wanna's Place (☎ *075 637 322)* Bungalows with fan in low/high season 300/700B, with air-con 600/900B. Down on the beach, heading south you'll come to Wanna's with simple bungalows and a restaurant in front. While it doesn't look like much, this place tends to be full from November to April and is even popular during the low season. They're obviously doing something right.

Phra Nang Inn (☎ *075 637 130, fax 075 637 134)* Rooms with air-con in low/high season 1500/2900B. The beach road intersects Route 4203 to Krabi just before you arrive at Phra Nang Inn, a tastefully designed 'tropical hotel' with partial views of the bay and a small pool. Every room is decorated with whimsy and attention to detail. A refreshingly different place to stay in an area with lots of look-alike bungalow operations and hotels. Phra Nang Inn has a good but pricey restaurant that's enclosed but has picture windows and a view of the bay. A second, similarly designed branch stands just across the road from the original, but it's hardly worth staying in.

Ao Nang Villa Resort (☎ 075 637 270–3, fax 057 637 274) Bungalows with air-con, TV & fridge 1500-2900B. This place has luxury bungalows situated around a pool.

BB Bungalows (☎ 075 637 148, fax 075 637 304) Bungalows with air-con 600-900B, rooms with air-con 1200-1600B. About 100m from the beach, BB has renovated and gone upscale recently – but the bungalows are good enough value.

Ya Ya Bungalow (☎ 075 637 176) Bungalows 500B. Not to be confused with Ya-Ya on Hat Rai Leh East, this has nice bungalows with terraces. This place closes during the low season.

Green Park (☎ 075 637 300) Bungalows without/with bath 300/700B. About 200m from the beach, this is one of the better cheapies with well-maintained bungalows. The price drops to as low as 100/200B in the low season.

Krabi Seaview Resort (☎ 075 637 242, fax 075 637 246) Bungalows with fan 500-700B, air-con 1900-2600B. Moving farther away from the beach along Route 4203 is Krabi Seaview, with modern air-con A-frames.

Peace Laguna Resort (☎ 075 637 345, fax 075 637 347) Bungalows with air-con 800-1200B. Off Route 4203, set well back from the road next to a pond, is the upmarket Peace Laguna. A trail leads directly to the beach so that it's not necessary to walk out to the main road.

Sea of Love (☎ 075 637 204) Fan rooms during the high/low season 700/250B, air-con rooms 1200/400B. This place has just four rooms, but they're creatively done. The fan rooms are set atop spiral staircases and afford a terrific view of the mountains.

Lai Thai Resort (☎ 075 637 281, fax 075 637 283) Rooms with air-con & satellite TV 2500-3500B. This is a collection of upscale northern Thai-style pavilions with marbled bathrooms situated around a pool. They've put a lot of time into the landscaping here – a relaxing place.

Ao Nang Palm Hill Valley (☎ 075 637 207) Bungalows with air-con 500-1100B. This place has comfortable bungalows in a garden setting, but it's a long walk to the beach.

At the northern end of the beach, past where Hwy 4203 turns inland, is Soi Sunset, a string of *seafood restaurants* and *bars* along the waterfront.

Sala Thai Dishes 45-220B. Sala Thai has the best Thai-style seafood, while most of the other restaurants in the area serve ordinary cuisine.

Baan Thai Seafood Dishes 60-140B. A short distance north along Route 4203, around the corner from Wanna's Place, this features a nice outdoor bar and decent barbecued seafood. Out on the Ao Nang 'strip'.

Ristorante La Luna Dishes 60-180B. What would a Thai beach be without the obligatory pizza/pasta joint? Fortunately this place does it with some flair.

Smoke House Dishes 60-120B. Located opposite the Krabi Seaview Resort, the Smoke House does delicious burgers and steaks.

Hat Ton Sai Not to be confused with the Hat Ton Sai on Ko Phi-Phi, this beach also known as Banyan Tree Beach can only be reached by boat from Ao Nang, Ao Nam Mao and Krabi. It's beauty and relative isolation has made it the venue for small but increasingly popular alternative full-moon parties. There are three bungalow operations here so far. *Ton Sai Hut* has basic wooden bungalows, some with attached bath for 200B to 350B. *Andaman Nature Resort* (☎ 075 637 092) has newish bungalows with verandas & attached bath for 300B to 500B. Electricity is only turned on at night. Between them is *Dream Valley*, a newish place with similar rates to the others'.

Hat Rai Leh West Within a relatively short time, Hat Rai Leh – both East and West – has gone from having a few primitive bungalow operations to going upscale in the Thai 'resort' sense. Some places now offer rooms with air-con and satellite TV. Naturally, prices have also gone upscale. Hat Rai

The Black Sheep's Revenge

'In the old days nobody wanted the beach. If a father owned a piece of land that included beach, when he died the least-favourite child would inherit the beach. Back then there was nothing you could do with a beach', muses Wichai Chamna. 'You can't plant rice on a beach'. Wichai sits back and surveys his land while running a hand absently through his greying curly hair. In front of him stretches his livelihood, a tatty collection of old-style huts of wood, bamboo and thatch along a stretch of golden-sand beach. Interspersed among the huts are a few coconut palms and a sickly jackfruit tree that looks as though someone started to chop it down and then had a change of heart. There are piles of scrap wood and tin roofing here and there, and underfoot there is a dog or two.

'That's my older sister's place there,' says Wichai, motioning with a nod of his head towards a tidier set of concrete bungalows situated within a coconut grove just inland. 'She says my huts spoil her view of the beach. She wants to buy my piece of land, but I won't sell. Where would I go?'

The monologue is interrupted by a couple of faràng, sunburnt and leggy, approaching with the cautious stride and downcast eyes peculiar to those carrying heavy loads on their backs. 'The rooms, how much?' one of them asks.

'Hunnet baht no toilet. Hunnet fipty baht toilet insite loom.'

The faràng pair discuss this price in some Nordic tongue but Wichai has already lost interest in them. He can sense that they're prepared to walk another kilometre or two in order to save 20 baht.

'My sister borrowed some money from a relative last year and rebuilt her bungalows with cement. Then she put an air machine in every room. She has to charge 400 baht per room to make a profit – the price of electricity keeps going up. She had to buy a mobile phone too, in case guests want to call and ask the price of a room.'

Wichai watches without curiosity as the faràng pair take turns swigging from a water bottle and prepare for some more exertion. They turn their backs on us without a word and continue down the trail.

'My sister has 12 bungalows but I've never seen more than two or three of them occupied,' Wichai continues, 'she says it's because her view of the beach is spoiled by my huts'.

Wichai smilingly ponders this while using the butt-end of a matchstick to clean his fingernails. After a moment he flicks the matchstick away and it lands in the dirt, causing a scruffy dog to walk over and give it a sniff. The dog looks up at us, its head tilted quizzically, and Wichai and I share an amused chuckle.

Steven Martin

Leh West is also known as Sunset Beach and has the more expensive accommodation of the two beaches.

Railay Bay Bungalows Bungalows with fan & bath in low/high season 500/1000B, with air-con 1100/2800B. At the centre of this pretty bay, this place packs in over a hundred bungalows right across the peninsula to Hat Rai Leh East. The rooms are nice enough but the rates are a bit high.

Sand Sea Railay Beach Bungalows (Bangkok ☎ 026 431 191–2) Bungalows with fan & bath 900-1350B, with air-con 2200-2800B. Sand Sea features concrete bungalows with verandas in a garden-like setting. They're fairly similar to nearby establishments, but much more expensive. The restaurant is quite good however, especially the seafood barbecue.

Railay Village Resort Bungalows with fan 800B, with air-con 1400-2500B. This place has small bungalows with glass fronts in two facing rows. There's a pleasant dining area with good food and a nice atmosphere.

Railei Beach Club (Langkha Daeng or Red Roof; ☎/fax 014 644 338, fax 075 612 914, e rbclub@phuket.ksc.co.th) Houses 3000-7000B. At the northern end of the beach, this is a private home development where it's possible to rent one- to three-bedroom beach houses; a daily light house-keeping service is included. It's necessary to book several months in advance (several years in advance if you want to book for December).

BoBo Bar & Restaurant Dishes 60-120B. The only place to eat not associated with overnight accommodation is BoBo, next to Railay Village going north. Here you'll find a stand selling real coffee and a good assortment of herbal teas, plus a little bar.

Hat Rai Leh West can be reached by long-tail boat from Ao Nang, Ao Nam Mao or Krabi, or on foot from Hat Tham Phra Nang and Hat Rai Leh East (but these must be approached by boat as well).

Hat Rai Leh East Often referred to as Sunrise Beach or sometimes Hat Ao Nam Mao, the beach along here tends towards mud flats during low tide. The north-eastern end of the bay is vegetated with mangroves, and between them and the mudflats there's not much traditional beach scenery. Most people who stay here walk over to Hat Tham Phra Nang for beach activities.

Railay Bay Bungalows has another entrance on this side (see Hat Rai Leh West).

Sunrise Bay Bungalows Bungalows with fan & bath 550-600B. The place has 40 simple but clean bungalows, though they are a bit pricey compared with what you'd get on other beaches. Videos are played at high volume nightly in Sunrise Bay's large restaurant.

Ya-Ya Rooms with bath 450-600B, tents 150B. Ya-Ya has some interesting bungalow designs, mostly two- and three-storey structures with brick downstairs and wood upstairs; the designs are integrated with pre-existing coconut palms and such. There are also a few 'tree house' units remaining. If you can't find any accommodation, Ya-Ya's tents are a good option while waiting for a room to free up. The restaurant here also screens nightly videos. In the mornings there's a good little coffee house nearby serving java and herbal teas.

Coco Bungalows Bungalows in low/high season 250/300B. Coco, north-east towards the mangrove area, is set back from the

shoreline and offers quiet but very tattered thatched or concrete bungalows; it has one of the better restaurants in the area. Because this is one of the cheapest places on the beach it's usually full.

Diamond Cave Bungalows (☎ 075 622 589, 🅔 diamondcave@aonang.com) Bungalows with fan & bath 650B, air-con 1250B. Near the Phra Nang Nai caves, this enjoys a beautiful setting and has large, comfortable bungalows with verandas. If you can afford an extra couple of hundred baht a night, the fan rooms here are far superior to the others on this beach.

Viewpoint Resort Bungalows with fan & bath 500B, with air-con 1000-1200B. On a hill overlooking Hat Rai Leh East and the mangroves, this place offers clean, well-maintained two-storey bungalows. As the name suggests, the view from here is quite stunning.

Hat Tham Phra Nang There's only one place to stay on this beautiful beach.

Rayavadee Premier (☎ 075 620 740, 🅦 www.rayavadee.com) Bungalows in low/high season 16,600/23,000B. Rayavadee Premier is a tastefully designed and fairly unobtrusive resort with 179 luxurious rooms in domed cement-and-stucco or wooden pavilions.

The beach is not Rayavadee Premier's exclusive domain – a wooden walkway has been left around the perimeter of the limestone bluff so that you can walk to Hat Tham Phra Nang from Hat Rai Leh East. From Hat Rai Leh West a footpath leads through the forest around to the beach.

Hat Tham Phra Nang is accessible by boat or foot only.

Ao Nam Mao This large bay, around a headland to the north-east of Hat Rai Leh East, about 1.5km from Su-Saan Hoi (Shell Fossil Cemetery), has a coastal environment similar to that of Hat Rai Leh East – mangroves and shallow, muddy beaches.

Dawn of Happiness Beach Resort Bungalows with bath in low/high season 500/950B. The beach is sandier towards the bay's eastern end, where you'll find the environmentally friendly Dawn of Happiness Beach. Natural, renewable, locally available building materials are used wherever possible and no sewage or rubbish ends up in the bay. The thatched bungalows have mosquito nets, and price ranges depending on whether you have a garden or sea view. The staff can arrange trips to nearby natural attractions. Among many local excursions offered is an overnight camping safari to Khao Phanom Bencha National Park.

Ao Nam Mao is accessible by road via Route 4204. The turn-off for Dawn of Happiness Resort is exactly 4.2km south-east of the 0km marker on Route 4203, the road to Su-Saan Hoi, where it splits from Route 4204 on its way to Ao Nang. It's about 6km from Ao Nang.

Getting There & Away Hat Noppharat Thara and Ao Nang can be reached by săwngthăew that leave about every 15 minutes from 7am to 6pm (high season) or to 4pm (low season) from Th Phattana in Krabi town, near the New Hotel. The fare is 30B and the trip takes 30-40 minutes.

You can get boats to Hat Ton Sai, Hat Rai Leh West and Laem Phra Nang at several places. For Hat Ton Sai, the best thing to do is get a săwngthăew to Ao Nang, then a boat from Ao Nang to Hat Ton Sai. It's 40B per person for two people or more, 100B if you don't want to wait for a second passenger to show up. (You may have to bargain to get this fare.) Boats also go between Ao Nang and Ko Phi-Phi for 250B, October through May.

For Hat Rai Leh West or anywhere on Laem Phra Nang, you can get a boat direct from Krabi's Saphaan Jao Fah pier for 50B. It takes about 45 minutes to reach Phra Nang; however, boats will only go all the way around the cape to Hat Rai Leh West and Hat Tham Phra Nang from October to April when the sea is tame enough. During the other half of the year they only go as far as Hat Rai Leh East, but you can easily walk from here to Hat Rai Leh West or Hat Phra Nang. You can also get boats from Ao Nang for all year round, but in this case they only go as far as Hat Rai Leh West and Hat Phra Nang (you can walk to Hat Rai Leh East from there). From Ao Nang you'll have to pay 40B per person for two or more passengers, 100B for one.

Another alternative is to take a săwngthăew from Krabi as far as Ao Nam Mao, to the small fishing bay near the Su-Saan Hoi, for 15B and then a boat to Laem Phra Nang for 50B (three or more people required).

Some of the beach bungalows have agents in Krabi who can help arrange boats – but there's still a charge.

Than Bokkharani National Park
อุทยานแห่งชาติธารโบกขรณี

In Ao Leuk district in northern Krabi Province, Than Bokkharani National Park *(Than Bok, adult/child under 14 years 200/100B)* encompasses nine caves, as well as the former botanical gardens for which the park was named.

The park is best visited just after the monsoons – when it has been dry a long time the water levels go down and in the midst of the rains it can be a bit murky. In December Than Bokkharani looks like something cooked up by Walt Disney, but it's real and entirely natural. Emerald-green waters flow out of a narrow cave in a tall cliff and into a large lotus pool, which overflows steadily into a wide stream, itself dividing into many smaller streams in several stages. At each stage there's a pool and a little waterfall. Tall trees spread over 40 *rai* (6.4 sq km) provide plenty of cool shade. Thais from Ao Leuk come to bathe here on weekends when it's full of laughing people playing in the streams and pools. During the week there are only a few people about, mostly kids doing a little fishing. Vendors sell noodles, roast chicken, delicious batter-fried squid and *sôm-tam* (green-papaya salad) under a roofed area to one side. Watch out for aggressive monkeys in the park.

Caves Among the protected caves scattered around the Ao Leuk district, one of the most interesting is **Tham Hua Kalok** (Skull

Cave), set in a limestone hill in a seldom-visited bend of mangrove-lined Khlong Baw Thaw. This cave is also known as Tham Phii Hua Toh (Big-Headed Ghost Cave). Besides impressive stalactite formations, the high-ceilinged cave features 2000- to 3000-year-old cave paintings of human and animal figures and geometric designs. As the cave's names imply, the locals have a story about a giant human skull that was found in the cave long ago. The floor of the cave is littered with crushed seashells.

Nearby **Tham Lawt** (literally, Tube Cave) is distinguished by a navigable stream flowing through it – it's longer than Phang-Nga's Tham Lawt but shorter than Mae Hong Son's.

There are seven other similar limestone caves in Ao Leuk district – Tham Chao Leh, Tham Khao Phra Khao Rang, Tham Phet, Tham Sa Yuan Thong, Tham Thalu Fah, Tham To Luang and Tham Waririn. To find them will require the services of a guide; further information is available at the Than Bokkharani visitors centre.

Places to Stay There are a number of accommodation options to choose from.

Ao Leuk Resort (☎ *075 681 133, fax 075 681 135*) Bungalows with fan & bath 250B, air-con 500B. On the highway about 300m north-east of Than Bokkharani, bungalows here are OK.

Al Leuk Bungalow (☎ *075 681 369*) Bungalows with fan & bath 200-300B. Located in Ban Ao Leuk Neua not far from the district hospital, this place has simple but comfortable bungalows.

Bulan Anda Eco-Resort Huts in low/high season 600/700B. This place is located on Laem Sak, at the southernmost terminus of Route 4039, about 15km south of Than Bokkharani. The rustic but comfortable huts are made almost completely of palm thatch and are situated on the edge of an oil palm plantation. There's also a decent restaurant here.

Getting There & Away Than Bokkharani is off Hwy 4 between Krabi and Phang-Nga, 1.3km south-west of the town of Ao Leuk, on Route 4039 towards Laem Sak. To get there, take a săwngthăew from the intersection of Th Phattana and Th Preuksa Uthit in Krabi to Ao Leuk for 30B; get off just before town and it's an easy walk to the park entrance on the left.

To visit Tham Lawt and Tham Hua Kalok you must charter a boat from Tha Baw Thaw, 6.5km west of Than Bokkharani. The tours are run exclusively by Ao Leuk native Uma Kumat and his son Bunmaak. They'll take one or two people for 200B; up to 10 can charter a boat for 500B. The boats run along secluded Khlong Baw Thaw and through Tham Lawt before stopping at Tham Hua Kalok. The pier at Tha Baw Thaw is 4.3km from Than Bokkharani via Route 4039, then 2km by dirt road through an oil palm plantation. You must find your own transport to Tha Baw Thaw. Most people go by rented motorcycle or car (you could also charter a săwngthăew from Ao Leuk for around 200B one way, but you'd have to hitchhike back).

Khao Phanom Bencha National Park
อุทยานแห่งชาติเขาพนมเบ็ญจา

This 50-sq-km park (*adult/child under 14 years 200/100B*) is in the middle of virgin rainforest along the Phanom Bencha mountain range. The main scenic attractions are the three-level **Huay To Falls**, **Tham Khao Pheung** and **Huay Sadeh Falls**, all within 3km of the park office. Other less well-known streams and waterfalls can be discovered as well. Clouded leopards, black panthers, tigers, Asiatic black bears, barking deer, serows, Malayan tapirs, leaf monkeys, gibbons and various tropical birds – including the helmeted hornbill, argus pheasant and extremely rare Gurney's pitta – make their home here. At 1350m, Khao Phanom Bencha is the highest point in Krabi Province. The name means 'Five-Point Prostration Mountain', a reference to the mountain's resemblance, in profile, to a person prostrating so that the knees, hands and head all touch the ground.

The park has a campground where you are welcome to pitch your own tent for 10B per person per night.

Getting There & Away Public transport direct to Khao Phanom Bencha National Park from Krabi or Talat Kao is rare. Two roads run to the park off Hwy 4. One is only about half a kilometre from Talat Kao – you could walk to this junction and hitch, or hire a truck in Talat Kao all the way for 100B or so. The other road is about 10km north of Krabi off Hwy 4. You could get to this junction via a săwngthăew or a bus heading north to Ao Leuk.

It would be cheaper to rent a motorcycle in Krabi for a day trip to Phanom Bencha than to charter a pickup. Try to have someone at the park watch your bike while hiking to nearby falls – motorcycle theft at Phanom Bencha has been a problem in the past.

KO PHI-PHI
เกาะพีพี

Ko Phi-Phi consists of two islands situated about 40km from Krabi, Phi-Phi Leh and Phi-Phi Don. Both are part of Hat Nop-pharat Thara/Ko Phi-Phi National Park, though this means little in the face of the blatant land encroachment taking place on Phi-Phi Don.

Only parts of Phi-Phi Don are actually under the administration of the National Parks Division of the Royal Forestry Department. Phi-Phi Leh and the western cliffs of Phi-Phi Don are left to the nest collectors, and the parts of Phi-Phi Don where the *chao náam* (sea gypsies) live are also not included in the park.

After Phuket this is probably the most popular tourist destination along the Andaman Coast, especially during the peak months from December to March, when hordes descend on the island and snatch up every room and bungalow on Phi-Phi Don. Even so, the island still retains some of its original beauty, though to truly appreciate it usually means a fair hike to escape the crowds.

Ko Phi-Phi Don
เกาะพีพีดอน

Phi-Phi Don is the larger of the two islands, a sort of dumbbell-shaped island with scenic hills, awesome cliffs, long beaches, emerald waters and remarkable bird and sea life. The 'handle' in the middle has long, white-sand beaches on either side, only a few hundred metres apart. The beach on the southern side curves around **Ao Ton Sai** (Banyan Tree Bay), where boats from Phuket and Krabi dock. There is also an untidy Thai-Muslim village here. On the northern side of the handle is **Ao Lo Dalam**.

The uninhabited (except for beach huts) western section of the island is called Ko Nawk (Outer Island), and the eastern section, which is much larger, is Ko Nai (Inner Island). At the north of the eastern end is Laem Tong, where the island's chao náam population lives. The number of chao náam living here varies from time to time, as they are still a somewhat nomadic people, but there are generally about 100. With stones tied to their waists as ballast, chao náam divers can reportedly descend up to 60m while breathing through an air hose held above the water surface.

Hat Yao (Long Beach), facing south at the south-eastern tip of the island, has some of Phi-Phi Don's best coral reefs. Ton Sai, Ao Lo Dalam and Hat Yao all have beach bungalows. Over a ridge north from Hat Yao is another very beautiful beach, **Hat Ranti**, with good surf. For several years the locals wouldn't allow any bungalows to be built here out of respect for the large village mosque in a coconut grove above the beach – but money talked, and the chao náam walked. Farther north is the sizeable bay of **Ao Lo Bakao**, where there is a small resort, and near the tip of Laem Tong are three luxury resorts.

Park administrators have allowed development on Phi-Phi Don to continue unchecked, though it's doubtful they ever had the power or influence to stop the building. Rumour has it that many park officials won't dare even set foot on Ko Phi-Phi for fear of being attacked by village

The approach to Ko Phi-Phi Don, Krabi Province

KAREN TRIST

Long-tail boats moored off Krabi

SARA-JANE CLELAND

A climber takes on the cliffs at Hat Ton Sai.

ANDERS BLOMQVIST

View from one of the many caves that line the shore, Krabi Province

RICHARD NEBESKY

A goalie waits for the ball, Krabi Province

Long-tail boat, Ao Nang, Krabi Province

chiefs and bungalow developers profiting from tourism.

Beautiful Ao Ton Sai is more of a boat basin than a beach, and more and more bungalows have crowded onto this section of the island. A tourist village of sorts has developed in the interior of the island near Ao Ton Sai and Hat Hin Khom. If you've already been to Ko Pha-Ngan's Hat Rin, you may experience a bit of deja vu. For solitude and scenery, this place falls short. On the other hand, those in search of a lively social scene will be rewarded by a wide choice of restaurants, beachfront bars and upmarket accommodation.

Other parts of Phi-Phi Don aren't so bad, though the once-brilliant coral reefs around the island are suffering from anchor drag and run-off from large beach developments. The least-disturbed parts of the island are those still belonging to the few chao náam who haven't cashed in.

Development on Ko Phi-Phi Don has stabilised to a significant degree over the last four years and it seems a near-truce between park authorities and greedy developers has come about. Still, there's much room for improvement in terms of rubbish collection and waste disposal.

A small power plant has been built in the centre of the island, but it doesn't have sufficient capacity to power all the resorts, even those in Ao Lo Dalam and Ton Sai. Many on this part of the island are forced to use generators on certain calendar days (odd or even depending on their location). Likewise, the single brackish reservoir on this island usually can't supply enough water, so some resorts have to turn their water supply off completely during certain hours of the day. In 1997 and 1998 there was an extreme water shortage on the island due to general lack of rain in the south, and all tap water was brackish.

If you want to air your opinion on what's going on here with regard to the environment, please contact one of the organisations listed under Ecology & Environment in the Facts about Thailand chapter with your assessments, whether good or bad.

Ko Phi-Phi Leh
เกาะพีพีเล

Phi-Phi Leh is almost all sheer cliffs, with a few caves and a sea lake formed by a cleft between two cliffs that allows water to enter into a bowl-shaped canyon. The so-called **Viking Cave** (officially called Tham Phaya Naak or Revered Naga Cave) on Phi-Phi Leh's north-east shore contains prehistoric paintings of stylised human and animal figures alongside later paintings of ships (Asian junks) no more than 100 years old.

The cave is also a collection point for swiftlet nests. The swiftlets build their nests high up in the caves in rocky hollows that can be very difficult to reach (see the boxed text further in this section 'White Gold').

Ao Maya and Lo Sama, scenic coves on the island's western and south-eastern shores, are favourite stops for day-tripping snorkellers. Although once pristine, the corals at these coves have been marred by bad anchoring and the beaches littered with rubbish jettisoned by people on tour boats. In 1999 a Hollywood film company spent about two months shooting scenes for the motion picture *The Beach*, based on UK author Alex Garland's novel of the same name. See the boxed text 'Notes on *The Beach*' in the South-Western Gulf chapter for more on the controversy that surrounded filming here.

Information
All the infrastructure is on the larger island, Ko Phi-Phi Don.

Krung Thai Bank has an exchange booth open daily from 8.30am to 3.30pm next to Reggae Bar in the tourist village. Many of the travel agents will also change money, though at predictably poor rates.

Phi-Phi Health Centre, east of the harbour near Ton Sai Village, can handle minor emergencies and is open 24 hours.

Diving & Snorkelling
Several places in Ton Sai village (Ko Phi-Phi Don) – about 15 at last count – can arrange diving and snorkelling trips around the island or to nearby islands. Several dive centres maintain small offices along the

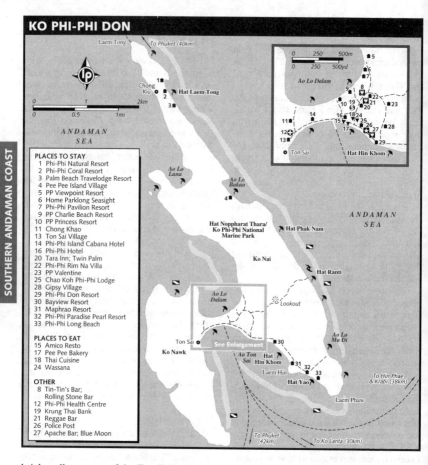

KO PHI-PHI DON

PLACES TO STAY
1 Phi-Phi Natural Resort
2 Phi-Phi Coral Resort
3 Palm Beach Travelodge Resort
4 Pee Pee Island Village
5 PP Viewpoint Resort
6 Home Parklong Seasight
7 Phi-Phi Pavilion Resort
9 PP Charlie Beach Resort
10 PP Princess Resort
11 Chong Khao
13 Ton Sai Village
14 Phi-Phi Island Cabana Hotel
16 Phi-Phi Hotel
20 Tara Inn; Twin Palm
22 Phi-Phi Rim Na Villa
23 PP Valentine
25 Chao Koh Phi-Phi Lodge
28 Gipsy Resort
29 Phi-Phi Don Resort
30 Bayview Resort
31 Maphrao Resort
32 Phi-Phi Paradise Pearl Resort
33 Phi-Phi Long Beach

PLACES TO EAT
15 Amico Resto
17 Pee Pee Bakery
18 Thai Cuisine
24 Wassana

OTHER
8 Tin-Tin's Bar;
    Rolling Stone Bar
12 Phi-Phi Health Centre
19 Krung Thai Bank
21 Reggae Bar
26 Police Post
27 Apache Bar; Blue Moon

brick walkway east of the Ton Sai harbour.
The typical all-day snorkelling trip includes
lunch, water, fruit and equipment for 360B
to 400B. These usually stop at Ko Yung
(Mosquito Island), Ko Mai Phai (Bamboo
Island), Hin Phae (Goat Rock) and Ko Phi-
Phi Leh.

A ferry, *King Cruiser*, sank between Ko
Phi-Phi and Phuket in 1997. The uppermost
deck is only twelve metres below the surface and dive operators from both Ko Phi-
Phi and Phuket do dives at the wreck site.

Prices are more or less uniform at Ko
Phi-Phi Don's dive shops. Guided dive trips
start at 900B for one dive or 1800B for two.
An open-water certification course costs
9900B. Snorkelling trips can be arranged
for 400B to 600B. You can rent masks, fins
and snorkels for 100B a day. The best
months for diving are December to April.
Phi Phi Scuba (☎ 012 284 500,
W www.phiphi-scuba.com), on Hat Ton Sai
near the banyan tree, is a reliable and long-
running outfit.

Paddling

You can rent kayaks on the beach along Ao
Lo Dalam (Ko Phi-Phi Don) for 300B per

White Gold

On either side of the Thai-Malay peninsula – in Ao Phang-Nga, parts of the Andaman Sea near Phuket and the Gulf of Thailand near Chumphon – limestone caves and cliffs are often home to birds whose nests are a highly valued ingredient in 'bird's nest soup'. Sea swallows (*Collocalia esculenta*, also known as 'edible-nest swiftlets') build their nests high up in rocky limestone hollows. Agile collectors build vine-and-bamboo scaffolding to get at the nests but are occasionally injured or killed in falls. Before ascending the scaffolds, the collectors pray and make offerings of tobacco, incense and liquor to the cavern *phĭi* (spirits). The collectors sell the nests to intermediaries who then sell them to Chinese restaurants abroad. Known as 'white gold', premium teacup-sized bird nests sell for US$2000 per kg – Hong Kong alone imports US$25-million worth every year.

MH

The translucent nests are made of the bird's saliva that hardens when exposed to the air. Cooked in chicken broth, the bird's nests soften and separate resembling bean thread noodles. The Chinese value these expensive bird secretions highly, believing them to be a medicinal food that imparts vigour.

Joe Cummings

hour, 600B per half-day (700B for a double seater), or 800B for a full-day (1000B double).

Fishing
All-day (8am to 5pm) fishing trips for marlin, sailfish, barracuda and other game fish in nearby waters are available aboard longtail boats for 1800B per boat, including soft drinks, lunch and fishing tackle. A half-day trip (9am to 1pm or 1pm to 5pm) costs 400B less. Look for signboards along the brick walkway in Ton Sai (Ko Phi-Phi Don). Imperial Travel & Sport Fishing (☎ 018 941 422) is a good bet.

Organised Tours & Boat Charters
From Ko Phi-Phi Don, boats can be chartered for a half/full-day trip to Phi-Phi Leh or Bamboo Island for 600/800B. Fishing trips average 1800B a day.

Places to Stay
During the busy tourist months of December to February, July and August, nearly all the accommodation on Ko Phi-Phi Don is booked out. As elsewhere during these months, it's best to arrive early in the morn-

ing to stake out a room or bungalow. Latecomers sometimes wind up sleeping on the beach. At this time, prices are at their peak, but during the low season rooms free up and rates are negotiable.

During the last couple of years there has been a rash of break-ins at bungalows along Ao Lo Dalam and Ao Ton Sai. These typically occur during the early-morning hours when occupants are asleep. The best way to foil thieves is to make sure your doors are locked at night.

Some bungalow operations provide lockers for guests to keep their valuables (though you must supply your own lock).

All the following places are on Ko Phi-Phi Don. There is no accommodation on Ko Phi-Phi Leh.

Ao Ton Sai The south-facing beach at Ao Ton Sai has several places to stay.

Ton Sai Village (☎ 075 612 434, fax 075 612 196) Bungalows with air-con, hot water, TV, fridge & breakfast 2000B. Towards the western end of the bay, this place offers comfortable wooden bungalows; it's also a little removed from others on this beach and so is a bit quieter. Many Korean and Taiwanese tour groups make a stop at the beach chairs in front of this hotel.

***Phi Phi Island Cabana Hotel** (☎ 075 620 634, fax 075 612 132)* Bungalows with fan 1500B, rooms 3500-8000B. The oldest resort on the island stretches across from the centre of Ton Sai to the beach at Ao Lo Dalam. It has bungalows and standard rooms in a three-storey hotel building. Amenities include a restaurant, coffee shop, snooker club, nightclub, tennis and basketball courts and a swimming pool. The pool overlooks the beach and is surrounded by pseudo-Greek statues and a large fountain that looks like it's been brought in from Las Vegas. Nonguests may use the pool for a steep 300B.

***Phi Phi Hotel** (☎/fax 075 611 233)* Rooms with air-con, hot shower, satellite TV & fridge in low/high season 1500/1800B. Behind the main restaurant-bar-dive shop strip, Phi-Phi has 64 well-appointed rooms in a four-storey building. These rooms are probably the best on the island in terms of amenities.

***Chao Koh Phi-Phi Lodge** (☎ 075 611 313)* Bungalows with air-con 700-900B. This place consists of fairly basic but clean concrete bungalows, a bit off the beach on the way to Hat Hin Khom.

Ao Lo Dalam This beach faces north and has most of the other accommodation places on the island.

***Chong Khao** Bungalows and rooms 300-600B. Inland along a path between Ao Lo Dalam and Ton Sai beaches, Chong Khao has fairly quiet rooms in a row-house or bungalows situated among coconut palms. Even with recent rate hikes, this is still one of the best deals on the island as long as you don't need to be on the beach.

***PP Princess Resort** (☎/fax 075 622 079)* Bungalows 1400-4000B. This has large, well-spaced upscale wooden bungalows with glass doors and windows. The bungalows feature nice deck areas and are connected by wooden walkways.

***PP Charlie Beach Resort** (☎ 075 620 615)* Rooms with fan & bath 350-650B. This has simple, clean, thatched-roof bungalows, a pleasant restaurant and a beach bar. Price depends on size and position on the beach. The 350B rooms are quite far back and near a generator. When the island gets crowded all the room rates jump.

***Phi Phi Pavilion Resort** (☎ 075 620 633)* Bungalows with fan in low/high season 650/900B, with air-con 1000/1400B. This is a thatched-roof place nicely situated in a coconut grove with high-ceilinged bungalows. Security isn't the best however, as it's impossible to lock the door-sized windows.

***Home Parklong Seasight** Rooms with fan & bath in low/high season 550/800B, with 2 beds 800/1200B. Home Parklong consists of five rooms in the home of a local entrepreneur on the beach just before you get to the end of Ao Lo Dalam. It has small but clean rooms, sharing a spacious, covered wooden sitting area in front.

***PP Viewpoint Resort** Rooms with fan in low/high season 300/900B, air-con 700/1500B. PP Viewpoint is situated on a hillside and can be approached via a small bridge over a canal. The newly renovated air-con bungalows in front overlook Ao Lo Dalam while the fan bungalows sit higher on the hill; their verandas are great for cocktails at sunset. During the hot dry season from March to June, this hillside is hotter than most other locations.

Hat Hin Khom This beach, a little east of Hat Ton Sai, has gone way downhill, with lots of rubbish floating on the water and collecting on the land. Although many bungalows have been rebuilt and improved, bungalow operators here don't seem to give a toss about keeping the area clean.

***Phi-Phi Don Resort** Bungalows with air-con 800-1200B. This place has new cement and stucco bungalows but it's overpriced and the staff can be downright surly.

***Gipsy Village** Bungalows with toilet and shower in low/high season 200/400B. Well away from the beach, the well-kept Gipsy is a collection of solid bungalows arranged in a large U shape amid coconut palms. A second group of huts under the same name, farther back towards the interior of the island, costs about the same but is far inferior. Both of these places get very dark and lonely at night, so be careful and bring a flashlight.

Bayview Resort *(☎ 075 621 223)* Bungalows with air-con, fridge & hot water 1200-1600B. Bayview is an upmarket place with modern-looking bungalows geared to the Thai market, though plenty of foreigners stay here as well. Clean, spacious, wood-floored bungalows sit on a hillside and have large decks overlooking the sea. The Thai cuisine at the restaurant is quite good.

Hat Hin Khao This little cove must be reached via a path over a headland to the south of Hin Khom.

Maphrao Resort *(☎ 075 622 485)* Bungalows without/with bath 300-450B/550-600B. Off by itself, Maphrao Resort offers thatched huts in a natural setting.

Hat Yao Bungalows on this beach are practically piled onto one another, with very little space in between. A shortage of fresh water means no showers are salt water. The beach, however, is long and pretty. You can follow a trail over to a secluded beach at Ao Lo Mu Di.

Phi-Phi Paradise Pearl Resort *(☎ 075 622 100)* Bungalows 500-1100B. A little tidier, better spaced and more substantial than others on Hat Yao, this place consists of nearly 80 solid, well-kept bungalows in all shapes and sizes; prices drop by half in the low season. All bungalows come with toilet, shower and fan.

Phi-Phi Long Beach *(☎ 075 612 410)* Bungalows 100-150B, with bath & fan 200-300B. Phi-Phi Long has bungalows either on the hillside, or in better locations.

Hat Ranti A Muslim family living on this beach offers a dozen thatched *huts,* with beds and mosquito nets, on stilts on a hillside overlooking the beach. These cost 150B year-round – no dickering between high and low seasons. The huts are in varying condition so look around before choosing one, but basically it's a clean place. Toilets and showers are in separate huts.

It can be hard to get boat drivers from Ao Ton Sai to bring you to Hat Ranti, since the family here refuses to pay commissions. You can walk via the viewpoint trail, however once you get past the viewpoint the trail becomes overgrown and would be difficult to do with a large pack. Once you're on Hat Ranti the family can arrange boat trips anywhere around the island more cheaply than in Ton Sai. Note that the management at Phi-Phi Paradise Pearl Resort and other places on Hat Yao may tell you there are no bungalows on Hat Ranti, or that they've been torn down; see for yourself.

The family patriarch does a little farming and fishing; one almost gets the impression he builds and rents these bungalows as much for company as for extra income. A nice little rustic restaurant overlooks the bay. The family cooks Thai-Muslim food only and not much English is spoken; if you speak a little Thai you could very well learn a lot more here. There's decent snorkelling right off the beach.

Ao Lo Bakao This secluded stretch of sand on the island's east coast has only one place to stay. Limestone outcrops here add a dramatic background, along with rock climbing and hiking potential.

Pee Pee Island Village *(in Phuket ☎ 076 215 014, Bangkok ☎ 022 766 056, fax 022 773 990)* Rooms in low season 1800-2400B, high season 3000-5000B. This is the only resort on this beautiful bay.

Hat Laem Tong This is another nice beach, with pricey resorts and its own pier.

Palm Beach Travelodge Resort *(in Phuket ☎ 076 214 654, fax 076 215 090)* Singles/doubles with fan, cold water & verandas 6600/12,000B. At the southernmost point of the beach, European-managed Palm Beach consists of large Thai/Malay-style bungalows on 2m stilts spread over spacious, landscaped grounds with lots of coconut palms. There's a medium-sized free-form swimming pool and a well-equipped water sports centre.

Phi-Phi Coral Resort *(☎/fax 075 214 056, in Bangkok ☎ 022 701 520)* Bungalows in low season 1800-2200B, high season 2300-2500B. This place offers octagonal wood and bamboo bungalows on the beach. One major drawback is that the resort caters to huge tour groups that visit the beach daily, and the beach is not very well maintained.

Phi-Phi Natural Resort (*in Phuket* ☎ *076 223 636, fax 076 214 301, in Bangkok* ☎ *029 845 600*) Rooms 1500-2500B. At the northern end of the beach, with views over the rocky cape, this resort has very spacious grounds, a restaurant overlooking the sea, and large split-level rooms with air-con and hot water. Although the rooms are very well maintained, maintenance in the public areas could be better. Rooms have either mountain, garden or sea views.

Between Phi-Phi Coral Resort and the Palm Beach Travelodge Resort is a beach area with sling chairs, a restaurant and small dive centre with inexpensive snorkelling equipment for hire. A chao náam settlement at the end of the beach – signed 'Yipsae Village' in English, 'Muu Baan Thai Mai Phattana' (New Thai Development Village) in Thai – consists of 17 households living in corrugated-metal shacks.

Ko Phi-Phi Don Interior Amid the gift shops, scuba shops and cafes of the tourist village there are a handful of budget-oriented places to stay (though none of these can be recommended as a first choice) as well as an upscale place or two.

Tara Inn (☎ *075 612 402*) Rooms with fan & bath 600-900B, air-con 1500-2000B. Tara has newish rooms on a ridge overlooking the village. Prices drop by almost half in the low season.

Reggae Bar Rooms with fan & bath 250B. If you find you can't get enough of the Reggae Bar, there is a row of rooms available overlooking the boxing ring inside the complex.

The Backpacker (☎ *075 612 402*) Dorm beds 200B, bungalows with fan 800-900B, air-con 1800B. This place is clean and friendly and has rooms at every price level. The dorm room has 16 beds and is only 80B per bed in the low season.

Phi-Phi Rim Na Villa Singles/doubles with fan & bath 350/750B. The view of the reservoir isn't particularly inspiring.

PP Valentine Bungalows with bath 350B. Away from the centre of the village just after the reservoir, PP Valentine is a collection of sturdy, good-value bungalows.

On the trail near PP Valentine are a bunch of cheapies – cubicles with mattresses on the floor – that are really only a last resort, including **Banana House** and **Lek's House**.

Places to Eat

Most of the resorts, hotels and bungalows around Ko Phi-Phi Don have their own restaurants. Cheaper and sometimes better food is available at the restaurants and cafes in the tourist village. However virtually all of it is prepared for faràng, not Thai, palates so the Thai dishes usually aren't very authentic.

Thai Cuisine (*Khrua Thai*) Dishes 40-160B. Located on the brick walkway east of the pier, this place is packed out nightly.

Wasana Dishes 40-180B. One of the better places on Phi-Phi, specialising in seafood, this is located on the brick walkway in the tourist village.

Amico Resto Dishes 60-120B. Opposite the entrance to Phi-Phi Hotel, this is possibly the best Italian food on the island, the seafood calzone being one of many excellent choices.

Pee Pee Bakery Dishes 20-60B. Two branches of this friendly bakery are in operation, one on the brick walkway east of the pier; the other at the back entrance of the Phi-Phi Pavilion Resort. Both offer a wide range of baked goods. The former branch stays open quite late and screens videos nightly.

A row of **noodle shops** and **barbecued chicken stands**, beyond Tin Tin's Bar (down the soi and make a left), awaits those who tire of pasta, schnitzel and banana pancakes. A no-name **khao kaeng shop** set up in front of a wooden house just beyond Twin Palm Resort pulls no punches when it comes to mouth-searing curries. Many locals eat here, but don't expect to get local prices – reckon on paying about 50B for a plate of curry over rice and a warm soft drink.

Entertainment

The most popular late night spots are *Tin-Tin's Bar* and the large *Reggae Bar*, both in the tourist village in the island centre. The latter has a Thai boxing ring set up in the middle of it and fights are staged on some nights.

Rolling Stoned Bar is a laid-back place with occasional live music.

Apache Bar is an open-air place built up the side of a hill just beyond the police post, commands an impressive view of Ao Ton Sai and the mountains – of course you'll have to get there before dusk to enjoy it. Nearby *Blue Moon* has a similar view but a cosier ambience.

Getting There & Away

Ko Phi-Phi is equidistant from Phuket and Krabi, but Krabi is the most economical point of departure. Until recently, boats travelled only during the dry season, from late October to May, as the seas are often too rough during the monsoons for safe navigation. Nowadays the boat operators risk sending boats year-round – we've received several reports of boats losing power and drifting in heavy swells during the monsoons. It all depends on the weather – some rainy-season departures are quite safe, others are risky. If the weather looks chancy, keep in mind that there sometimes aren't enough life jackets to go around on these boats.

On Ko Phi-Phi Don, boats moor at the pier at Ao Ton Sai, except for a few from Phuket that go to the pier at Laem Tong.

Krabi From Krabi's Saphaan Jao Fah pier, there are four departures daily at 10.30am, 11.30am, 2.30pm and 4pm (in the reverse direction the times are 9am, 1.30pm, 2.15pm and 3.30pm). The one-way fare is 160B and the trip takes 1½ hours. These fares are sometimes discounted by agents in town to as low as 120B. Departures are sometimes delayed because boats often wait for buses from Bangkok to arrive at the Krabi pier.

Ao Nang You can also get boats from Ao Nang on the Krabi Province coast for 250B from October to April; there's usually only one departure a day, at around 9am. The trip lasts 80 minutes. In the reverse direction, boats leave from Ko Phi-Phi Don to Ao Nang at 3.30pm.

Phuket A dozen different companies operate boats from various piers on Phuket. Prices start from 250B upwards (the price depends on the speed of the boat; trips take between one hour, 40 minutes and two hours). Any guesthouse or hotel on Phuket can arrange tickets; the more expensive fares include bus or van pickup from your hotel. Boats leave frequently between 8.30am and 1.30pm. Boats from Ko Phi-Phi Don to Phuket leave at 9am and 2.30pm and cost 250B.

Andaman Wave (☎ 076 232 561) runs the 40-minute *Jet Cruise*, which leaves Phuket at 8.30pm (from Laem Tong at 3pm) and costs 400B one way.

Various tour companies in Phuket, including Andaman Wave, offer day-trips to Phi-Phi for 500B to 950B per person, including return transport, lunch and a tour. If you want to stay overnight and catch another tour boat back, you have to pay another 100B. Of course it's cheaper to book one-way passage on the regular ferry service.

Ko Lanta There are boats between Ko Lanta and Ko Phi-Phi from October to April. Boats generally leave from the pier on Lanta Yai around 8am, arriving at Ko Phi-Phi Don around 9.30am (sometimes there is a second boat leaving at 1pm). In the reverse direction the departure is usually at 2pm (sometimes there is also a departure at 11am). Passage is 170B per person. It's also possible to get boats to/from Ko Jam; the same approximate departure time, fare and trip duration applies.

Getting Around

Transport on the island is mostly on foot, although fishing boats can be chartered at Ao Ton Sai for short hops around Phi-Phi Don and Phi-Phi Leh. Touts meet boats from the mainland to load people onto long-tail boats going to Hat Yao (Long Beach) for 40B per person. Other boat charters around the island from the pier at Ton Sai include Laem Tong (400B), Lo Bakao (300B) and Viking Cave (200B).

KO JAM (KO PU) & KO SI BOYA
เกาะจำ(ปู)/เกาะศรีบอยา

These large islands between Krabi and Ko Lanta (see the Ko Lanta map) are inhabited by a small number of fishing families and are good for those seeking escape from the faràng video restaurants, beach bars, ravers and so on – at least they are at the time of writing. Hurry up and see them before they change beyond recognition.

The handful of accommodation places on Ko Jam is concentrated along the island's south-western coast between the villages of Ban Ko Jam and Ban Ting Lai.

Joy Resort Bungalows with bath 350-450B. On the south-western coast of Ko Jam, this offers 28 spacious wooden bungalows arranged on grassy and shady grounds. Joy sensibly uses mosquito nets instead of putting mesh screens on the windows. Of course, there's a restaurant here with Thai and faràng food.

New Bungalows Huts in low season 50-150B, high season 120-400B. Located just south of Joy Resort, this place has huts of bamboo and palm thatch and a couple of tree houses.

Andaman Beach Resort Bungalows with fan & bath 500-750B. Andaman has concrete A-frame bungalows priced according to size and situated on rather shadeless grounds. The electricity is on from 6pm to 6am.

Ko Si Boya's accommodation is limited to one place, which is located on the island's west coast just south of the village Ban Lang Ko:

Siboya Bungalow Bungalows 200-400B. This place has 24 well-designed huts of wood, bamboo and thatch. Each unit has a veranda and hammock. The restaurant is quite good and the prices are reasonable. The bungalows are surrounded by rubber plantations and there are plenty of trails to hike.

Getting There & Away
Boats to both islands leave once or twice a day from Ban Laem Kruat, a village about 30km from Krabi, at the end of Route 4036, off Hwy 4. The cost is 25B to Si Boya, 30B to Ban Ko Jam.

You can also take boats bound for Ko Lanta from Krabi's Saphaan Jao Fah and ask to be let off at Ko Jam. There are usually two boats daily that leave Krabi at 10.30am and 1.30pm; 8.30am and 1.30pm in the opposite direction. The fare is supposed to be 150B as far as Ko Jam, but some boat operators will charge the full Ko Lanta fare of 170B. The Ko Lanta-Ko Jam boats from Krabi only run mid-October through mid-May.

It's also possible to catch the boat from Ko Lanta to Ko Jam during the mid-October through mid-May season. Boats leave Ko Lanta from the pier at Ban Sala Dan at 8am and 1pm; in the opposite direction the boats leave from Ko Jam at 11.30am and 2.30pm. The trip takes less than an hour.

KO LANTA
เกาะลันตา

postcode 81150 • pop 18,540

Ko Lanta is a district of Krabi Province that consists of 52 islands. The geography here is typified by stretches of mangrove interrupted by coral-rimmed beaches, rugged hills and huge umbrella trees. Twelve of the islands are inhabited and, of these, three are easily accessible: **Ko Klang**, **Ko Lanta Noi** and **Ko Lanta Yai**. You can reach the latter by ferry and road from Ban Hua Hin on the mainland across from Ko Lanta Noi, from Ban Baw Meuang, farther south, and by ferry from Ko Phi-Phi, Ko Jam and Krabi.

The archipelago's largest island, Ko Lanta Yai, is long and slender with low, forested hills down the middle and beaches on its west coast. The last few years have seen an explosion of building on this island, and now, except for a few acres of casuarina trees at the island's northern end, almost the entire west coast is lined with bungalows. Still, it's not as crowded as it sounds – the beach along this stretch is fairly wide and most bungalow

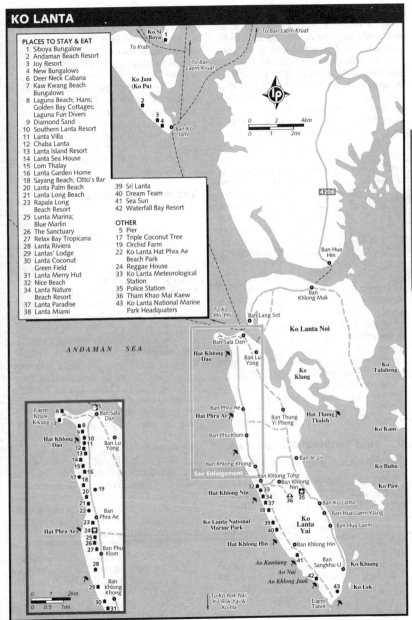

KO LANTA

PLACES TO STAY & EAT
1 Siboya Bungalow
2 Andaman Beach Resort
3 Joy Resort
4 New Bungalows
6 Deer Neck Cabana
7 Kaw Kwang Beach
  Bungalows
8 Laguna Beach; Hans;
  Golden Bay Cottages;
  Laguna Fun Divers
9 Diamond Sand
10 Southern Lanta Resort
11 Lanta Villa
12 Chaba Lanta
13 Lanta Island Resort
14 Lanta Sea House
15 Lom Thalay
16 Lanta Garden Home
18 Sayang Beach; Otto's Bar
20 Lanta Palm Beach
21 Lanta Long Beach
23 Rapala Long
  Beach Resort
25 Lunta Marina;
  Blue Marlin
26 The Sanctuary
27 Relax Bay Tropicana
28 Lanta Riviera
29 Lantas' Lodge
30 Lanta Coconut
  Green Field
31 Lanta Merry Hut
32 Nice Beach
34 Lanta Nature
  Beach Resort
37 Lanta Paradise
38 Lanta Miami

39 Sri Lanta
40 Dream Team
41 Sea Sun
42 Waterfall Bay Resort

OTHER
5 Pier
17 Triple Coconut Tree
19 Orchid Farm
22 Ko Lanta Hat Phra Ae
  Beach Park
24 Reggae House
33 Ko Lanta Meteorological
  Station
35 Police Station
36 Tham Khao Mai Kaew
43 Ko Lanta National Marine
  Park Headquaters

operations are situated within coconut groves along the beach. A tourist village, still in the embryonic stage but along the lines of the ones at Ko Phi-Phi and Ko Pha-Ngan, seems to be sprouting up at Hat Khlong Dao. **Ban Sala Dan**, at the northern tip of the island, is the largest settlement on the island and has a couple of ferry piers, tour outfits, dive shops and a Siam City Bank with exchange services. The district capital **Ban Ko Lanta**, towards the south of the east coast, boasts a post office, long pier and fairly solid-looking buildings. A vehicle ferry service to Ban Ko Lanta was recently discontinued. The village of **Ban Sangkha-U** on Lanta Yai's southern tip is a traditional Muslim fishing village.

The people in this district are a mixture of Thai-Muslims and chao náam who settled here long ago. Their main livelihood was traditionally the cultivation of rubber, cashew nuts and bananas, along with a little fishing.

A road nearly encircles the island – but only about half of its length is sealed. Only the south-eastern tip around Ban Sangkha-U is totally devoid of vehicles. In the centre of the island is **Tham Khao Mai Kaew**, a five- or six-cavern limestone cave complex. A narrow, 1.5km dirt track through a rubber plantation leads to the cave from the more southerly of the two cross-island roads.

During the rainy season – May through October – Ko Lanta Yai gets buckets of rain and the beach becomes covered with all manner of driftwood, rubbish and junk.

Ko Lanta National Marine Park
อุทยานแห่งชาติเกาะลันตา

In 1990, 15 islands in the Lanta group (covering an area of 152 sq km) were declared part of Ko Lanta National Marine Park in an effort to protect the fragile coastal environment. **Ko Rok Nawk** is especially beautiful, with a crescent-shaped bay featuring cliffs and a white-sand beach and a stand of banyan trees in the interior. The intact coral at **Ko Rok Nai** and limestone caves of **Ko Talang** are also worth seeing. Dive shops in Ban Sala Dan can arrange dives to these islands as well as to coral-encrusted **Ko Ha**,

Ko Bida, **Hin Bida** and **Hin Muang**. Camping is permitted on Ko Rok Nawk.

Ko Lanta Yai itself is only partially protected since most of the island belongs to chao náam. As on Ko Phi-Phi, many bungalows have been built on shore-lands under the nominal protection of the Royal Forestry Department. The interior of the island consists of rubber, cashew and fruit plantations, with a few stands of original forest here and there, mostly in the hilly southern section of the island. The park headquarters is situated at the southern tip of Ko Lanta Yai.

Tham Khao Mai Kaew
ถ้ำเขาไม้แก้ว

A great break from the beach is a trip to this complex of caves in the centre of Ko Lanta Yai. Even the hike in, through virgin forest, is quite pleasant. But the real fun begins when you descend through a small, indistinct hole in the rocks and enter the series of diverse caverns. Some sections are as large as church halls, others require you to squeeze through on hands and knees. Sights en route include impressive stalactites and stalagmites, bats and even a cavern pool that you can swim in. The latter is not recommended for the faint-hearted, as access to the pool is via a long, slippery slope and a knotted rope that's almost as slimy – a bit of a challenge on the way back up. Wear appropriate shoes if you want to attempt this – wear flip flops and you'll be on your butt at least once.

A Muslim family that lives near the trailhead to the caves offers a guide service for 100B per person. You really do need a guide to find your way around, particularly inside the caves, and the service is definitely worth it. The family also runs a basic restaurant where you can get snacks and drinks.

The caves are off the more southerly of the two cross-island roads, down a narrow, 1.5km dirt track through a rubber plantation which ends up at the Muslim home. The best way to get there is by renting a motorcycle, though some bungalows will arrange transport.

Beaches

The western sides of all the islands have beaches, though in overall quality Lanta's beaches don't quite measure up to those found in Phuket or along Krabi's Hat Tham Phra Nang. The best are at either end of Lanta Yai's west coast, with middle sections given over more to rocky shores and reefs. There are coral reefs along parts of the western side of Lanta Yai and along Laem Khaw Kwang (Deer Neck Cape) at the north-western tip. A hill atop the cape gives a good aerial view of the island.

There is a nice beach on the little island south-east of Ko Klang called **Hat Thung Thaleh** – hire a boat from Ko Klang to get there. Also worth exploring is Ko Ngai (Hai), south-east of Ko Lanta – see Beaches & Islands in the Trang Province section later in this chapter for more details; Ko Ngai is more accessible from that province.

Diving & Snorkelling

The uninhabited islands of **Ko Rok Nai, Ko Rok Yai** and **Ko Ha**, south of Ko Lanta Yai, offer plenty of coral along their western and south-western shores. According to Ko Lanta Dive Centre in Sala Dan, the undersea pinnacles of **Hin Muang** and **Hin Daeng** farther south-west are even better, with good-weather visibility of up to 30m, hard and soft corals, and plenty of large schooling fish such as shark, tuna and manta ray. Whale sharks have also been spotted in the area.

There are several dive operations on Ko Lanta, some working out of Sala Dan (most can be booked at beach bungalows) and others attached to certain bungalow operations. Atlantis Dive Centre (☎ 075 684 081) in Ban Sala Dan charges 2400B for a one-day dive trip, including equipment hire. Two-day trips with five dives start at 5000B. Laguna Fun Divers (☎ 075 611 572), at the Laguna Beach Club, and Dive Zone (☎ 075 684 056) in Ban Sala Dan also appear to be well equipped. November to April is the best season for diving in these areas.

Elephant Trekking

A small herd of elephants was recently brought to Ko Lanta to give visitors treks through the forested paths inland. If you've never tried it, riding an elephant is a relaxing way to take in some scenery for an hour or so. Most bungalow operations can arrange transport to and from the elephant camp, treating it as a package.

Orchid Farm

Lanta Orchid Nursery (☎ *075 684 258, open 9am-4pm, admission free*) is open to the public, offering a bit of a diversion for flora aficionados. Located near Lanta Long Beach bungalows, here you'll see lots of

Elephant Trekking

When a Thai government ban on logging was enacted in 1989, many saw it as a victory for the environment. Sadly, an unexpected casualty of the ban was soon detected – Thailand's domesticated elephants. Long used in the extraction of teak and other tropical hardwoods, working elephants and their handlers found themselves jobless after the ban. There was a time in the mid- to late 1990s when the outlook was particularly bleak. The elephant, once the majestic symbol of old Siam, had been reduced to begging for bananas in the harsh and polluted streets of Bangkok. Popular outcry after a number of accidents involving elephants has forced Bangkok police to sporadically enforce a law against keeping elephants in urban areas – but this has done nothing to solve the employment situation of the elephants or their handlers.

Recently, someone had the idea to bring the out-of-work elephants to areas in Southern Thailand that are well touristed. As it has been in Northern Thailand for some time now, elephant trekking – riding an elephant through the jungle – is now on offer on some of Thailand's more popular islands. Take an elephant trek on Ko Samui, Ko Lanta or Phuket and you'll help ensure that Thailand's last generation of working elephants lives comfortably to a ripe old age.

Dendrobium pompadour, the delicate mauve orchid that seems to adorn every stewardess and tropical cocktail in Thailand.

Places to Stay

Not surprisingly perhaps, Ko Lanta seems to have wasted its opportunity to become a model for environmentally conscious island tourism. Huts and bungalows made of bamboo or palm thatch have become scarce as bungalow operators – tired of having to make extensive repairs after each rainy season – have rebuilt in concrete. The result is that much of the beach is lined with lookalike bungalow operations that can only be differentiated by the colour of their roofs. As happened elsewhere in Thailand, the national-park system couldn't be relied upon to protect the lands, and the local private sector did as it pleased.

Typically, the row of bungalows closest to the beach is the most expensive. These often have air-con, a fridge and other unnecessary appliances to justify the high price of the room. Bungalows farther inland, with a blocked view and limited airflow, are the cheaper fan rooms. A handful of places retain the simpler huts of natural materials and have taken up the 'ecotourism' mantra.

The prettiest beach areas are found along the north- of the island just south of Ban Sala Dan, and this is where the heaviest development is concentrated. Because it's long, wide and flat, this is a perfect beach for walking and jogging. Few places at this end costs less than 500B a night during high season (November to May). During low season prices drop to 200B a night. A handful of places are still in the 100B to 250B per night range even during the high season, but these tend to close during the low season. At this time proprietors make little effort to clean the beach of accumulating refuse and hence it becomes rather unappealing.

Deer Neck Cabana (☎ 075 684 048) At the northernmost section of the beach near Ban Sala Dan is Deer Neck, one of the oldest operations on Ko Lanta. Facing the western side of the small Laem Khaw Kwang that juts west from the island, it sits on its own shallow beach – a particularly safe one for children. When the tide is in you can see trees seemingly growing out of the sea (rooted in submerged sand banks). At the time of research Deer Neck Cabana was undergoing renovations and it was unclear what prices would be when it reopens.

Kaw Kwang Beach Bungalows (☎ 075 684 083) Bungalows with fan & bath 400-1500B, suites with air-con 1800-2000B. The locally owned Kaw Kwang is the oldest of the beach places and still commands one of the best stretches of beach; it's also close to snorkelling areas on the southeastern side of this tiny cape. The price of each nicely separated concrete bungalow depends on size, time of year and proximity to the beach. Hammocks are strung between casuarina trees along the beach and snorkelling gear is available for rent. The proprietors offer fishing and snorkelling trips to nearby islands.

Starting about 2.5km south of Ban Sala Dan along the western side of the island are a cluster of places at various prices along a wide stretch of sand known as Hat Khlong Dao.

Laguna Beach (☎ 075 611 572) Rooms with fan 600-1000B, air-con 800-3000B. This place is one long building – imagine a row of attached bungalows. Doors between rooms can be opened to create bigger living spaces as visitors require. There's one 'VIP' room right on the beach. A small bar also on the beach has a pool table. Laguna Fun Divers has its dive shop on the premises.

Hans (☎ 075 684 152) Bungalows 350-550B. This place seems to have begun life as a beach bar, but there's a collection of bungalows in different sizes and of different materials, as well as a good restaurant. Hans is popular with German dive instructors working on the island.

Golden Bay Cottages (☎ 075 684 161) Bungalows with fan & bath 650B, air-con 1000-1450B. Golden Bay has recently undergone a facelift, though the new concrete bungalows are fairly typical for this beach. The restaurant screens videos nightly.

Diamond Sand (☎ 075 621 135) Bungalows with air-con & bath 1500B. This has large, overpriced concrete bungalows. The restaurant has very good Thai food, and unlike the bungalows, its prices are fair.

Southern Lanta Resort (☎ 075 684 174) Rooms with air-con, satellite TV & fridge 1600-2200B. This place has a pool with 65 air-con rooms arranged around it. Prices include breakfast.

Lanta Villa (☎ 075 684 129) Bungalows with air-con 1300-2200B. Having recently gone upscale, Lanta Villa offers over 50 bungalows, some with their original distinctive high-pitched roofs, arranged around a swimming pool; it's open year-round. There's an Internet-access place on the main road at its entrance.

Chaba Lanta (☎ 075 684 119) Huts 150B, bungalows with bath 400B. This place is located next to a cluster of open-air bars, known as the Lanta Night Plaza, so it's either convenient or noisy, depending on what you're here to do.

Lanta Island Resort (☎ 075 621 524) Bungalows with fan 350B, air-con 900-1600B. These bungalows, with faux thatch walls and red corrugated roofs, are popular with tour groups.

Lanta Sea House (☎ 075 684 113, fax 075 684 114) Rooms with fan 600-800B, bungalows with fan 900-1300B, with air-con 1500-2500B. The upmarket Lanta Sea has rooms in an apartment-style building and vaguely Malay-style bungalows; open year-round.

Lom Thalay (☎ 075 684 150–1) Units with fan 100-200B. Lom Thalay consists of just a few units, thatched and natural.

Lanta Garden Home, (☎ 075 684 084) Huts without/with bath 150/400B. Next door to the Lom Thalay, this place has similarly basic huts.

Just around a headland famous for a triple-trunked coconut palm, Hat Phra Ae begins where there are a few cheapies and former cheapies going upscale.

Sayang Beach (☎ 075 684 156) Bungalows 600-1500B. This place is trying to look eco-friendly by forgoing the usual concrete bungalows for some sturdy ones made of wood with walls of woven bamboo. Each bungalow has a small veranda.

Lanta Palm Beach Huts 100-150B. This friendly place has both wooden and concrete huts of widely varying quality.

Lanta Long Beach (☎ 075 684 217, fax 075 684 215) Bungalows 200-1000B. Just before Ko Lanta Hat Phra Ae Beach Park, an access road leads 400m to this group of rustic thatched bungalows with attached bathrooms and nice verandas. The open-air restaurant offers good beach views. Rates vary widely between low, high and 'peak' seasons.

Rapala Long Beach Resort (☎ 075 684 250) Bungalows 600-1500B. Just beyond the small village of Ban Phra Ae is the upmarket Rapala, with 22 hexagonal units.

Lunta Marina Bungalows 500-600B. The same access road for Rapala leads also to Lunta, where wood and bamboo bungalows are in an interesting elevated A-frame design with a ladder up to each unit, and a deck underneath with a built-in bench. They're back away from the beach, near the bars, *Reggae House* and *Blue Marlin*, both of which offer basic but cheap (80B to 100B) huts.

The Sanctuary Huts 80-100B. This offers rustic huts and good vegetarian food; it's a nice place but is almost always full (closed during the rainy season).

Relax Bay Tropicana (☎ 075 684 194–5, fax 075 684 195) Bungalows 200-600B. Forty spacious bungalows of wood and bamboo, with large decks, are perched around a rocky hillside overlooking the sea. The beach along this stretch – and for the next 2km – is nothing special, but it looks nice from a distance.

Lanta Riviera Bungalows with bath 300-500B. Very small but well-kept concrete bungalows with wooden cladding on the front walls and corrugated roofs are set in a nice coconut grove. There's also an open-air restaurant.

Lantas' Lodge Huts in low season 200-300B, high season 500-700B. Farther south towards Ban Khlong Khong (the beach here is also sometimes referred to as Hat Khlong Khong), this place has thatched

SOUTHERN ANDAMAN COAST

huts in a coconut grove; it's a little over-priced, but it's quiet and has a pleasant outdoor restaurant.

Lanta Coconut Green Field Bungalows with bath 350-550B. Located down a sandy road that winds through coconut trees, the tidy thatched bungalows here have cement foundations and small verandas. There's a restaurant on the beach in front. The operation closes during the rainy season.

Lanta Merry Hut Huts with bath 300-400B. To reach this place, take a dirt road to the right through a village and past a mosque, then through a wooden gateway past some private homes. It has nine traditional thatch huts, and a simple open-air restaurant. This is a good place to stay if you want to get involved in village life at Ban Khlong Khong.

Another kilometre or so farther south the beach changes name again, to Hat Khlong Nin, and the accommodation becomes cheaper.

Nice Beach (☎ 075 697 276) Bungalows with bath 250-350B. Nice Beach offers what's become the Lanta mid-range bungalow stereotype: cement walls with corrugated roofs and small terraces. If you don't mind the lack of imagination behind this and neighbouring places, the semi-secluded beach here is lovely.

Lanta Nature Beach Resort Bungalows 200-350B. This and the next two are owned by the same local family and have very similar bungalows of concrete.

Lanta Paradise Bungalows 150-400B. This place offers comfortable wood and concrete bungalows with good beach frontage.

Lanta Miami (☎ 075 697 081) Bungalows with bath 300-600B. This family-run place is friendly and flexible with its rates. Bungalows are constructed of concrete and have small verandas.

Sri Lanta (☎ 075 697 288) Bungalows with air-con & fridge 3000-4000B. This newly built place has spacious and comfortable bungalows, all with verandas. There's a swimming pool and restaurant. Breakfast is included in the rates.

Dream Team Bungalows with air-con & TV 1500-2500B. Sitting on a little headland

with a rocky stretch of beach is the well-landscaped Dream Team, which despite rave reviews as a simpler place, recently went up-scale. There are now 36 units, some with satellite TV. A better sand beach at Ao Kantiang is only about 10 minutes away on foot.

Sea Sun Bungalows without/with bath 80/120B. At the northern end of Ao Kantiang is the secluded Sea Sun, with small cement bungalows; one of the huts has a particularly good view.

The next cove down, Ao Nui, is one of the most beautiful on the island and as yet has no bungalows – probably because it's a steep walk down to the beach. At this point the road begins climbing and winding steeply as it approaches the southern tip of the island.

Waterfall Bay Resort (☎ 075 612 806) Bungalows 900-2000B. Near the end of the road, on Ao Khlong Jaak, the well-designed, eco-oriented Waterfall Bay offers 18 well-spaced wooden bungalows with thatched roofs overlooking a secluded bay. Price depends on position relative to the beach. All have two rooms, one below and one above as a loft, making it very suitable for family stays. The restaurant serves Thai and faràng food. Waterfall is open October to mid-June only. The namesake waterfall is a 30- to 40-minute walk away. From the resort a dirt track continues to the park headquarters and Ban Sangkha-U. This is a good spot to stay if you're interested in hiking into the park interior.

Places to Eat

If you get tired of bungalow food there are a few restaurants in Ban Sala Dan at the northern end of Lanta Yai. Better still are the pickings to be had at Hat Khlong Dao. Restaurants here come and go with the seasons but usually offer German or Italian food.

Seaview and ***Seaside*** are two small, moderately priced restaurants located in Ban Sala Dan. Both are built over the water and serve Thai food and seafood.

Catfish Restaurant & Bar (☎ 075 684 185) Located in Ban Sala Dan between the boat pier and the police station, this does Thai and European food as well as English breakfasts. You can eat inside or on the breezy veranda overlooking the water.

Otto's Bar Dishes 50-140B. This serves good, inexpensive to moderately priced Thai and Western dishes. Occasionally during the high season the restaurant hosts a small full moon party with *muay thai*, music, dancing and a seafood barbecue.

The Sanctuary Dishes 30-60B. This makes good vegetarian food, including a few Indian dishes.

Getting There & Away

Krabi Minibuses to Ko Lanta leave from Krabi's Th Sukhon at 11am and 1pm. The ride costs 150B and takes about 1½ hours. There is a vehicle ferry across the narrow channel between Ban Hua Hin on the mainland and Ban Khlong Mak, on Ko Lanta Noi, and another across the even narrower channel to Ban Sala Dan on Ko Lanta Yai. Both ferries cost 3B for pedestrians, 5B for a bicycle and one rider, 10B per motorcycle and 50B in a car or truck. If you take the minibus this is included in the fare. Going from Ko Lanta to Krabi, the minibus leaves from Anut Tour in Ban Sala Dan at 7.30am, 8am and 12.30pm. You can usually arrange for the minibus to pick you up at the bungalows where you're staying by informing the management of the bungalows a day ahead of time.

Not all ferries go directly to/from Ban Sala Dan – a newish, larger ferry leaves a little south of Ban Sala Dan. Both ferries run frequently from 7am to 8pm. There is talk of building a bridge somewhere along here to supplant the ferry services to Ban Sala Dan.

Ban Hua Hin is 26km down Route 4206 from Ban Huay Nam Khao, which is about 44km from Krabi along Hwy 4.

If you're coming from Trang, there's no direct public transport to Ban Hua Hin, but you can take a bus from Trang to Ban Huay Nam Khao (25B), then transfer to a săwngthăew south to the Ban Hua Hin pier.

The quickest way to reach Ko Lanta from Krabi is to take a boat from Krabi's Saphaan Jao Fah pier, only available November to April. Boats usually depart at 10.30am and 1.30pm and take one to 1½ hours to reach Ban Sala Dan; the fare is 170B. In the reverse direction boats leave at 10am and 1pm.

Ko Phi-Phi During the dry season, from October to April, there are boats from Ko Phi-Phi at 2pm (and sometimes 11am) for 170B per person. They take about 80 minutes to reach Ban Sala Dan; in the opposite direction boats leave Ko Lanta around 8am (and sometimes 1pm). There are also occasional boats to Lanta from Ko Jam.

Getting Around

Most of the bungalows on Ko Lanta will provide transport to and from Ban Sala Dan for a fee. A few bungalows offer free rides to their guests when they make the daily grocery run – but this practice seems to be on the wane. Motorcycle taxis are available from Ban Sala Dan to almost anywhere along the beaches for 20B to 50B depending on the distance.

Motorcycles can be rented in Ban Sala Dan at Catfish Restaurant & Bar (☎ 075 684 185) for 200B per day.

Trang Province

The province of Trang, as well as its southern neighbour Satun Province, bears a geography similar to that of Krabi and Phang-Nga, with islands and beaches along the coast and limestone-buttressed mountains inland. The area is much less frequented by tourists though. Caves and waterfalls are the major attractions in the interior.

Twenty kilometres east of Trang's provincial capital is the 5.6-sq-km Khao Chong Nature Reserve, which preserves a tropical forest in its original state. In the park there are three waterfalls and government resthouses.

To the north-west is **Thaleh Song Hong** (Sea of Two Rooms), a large lake surrounded by limestone hills. Hills in the middle of the lake nearly divide it in half, hence the name.

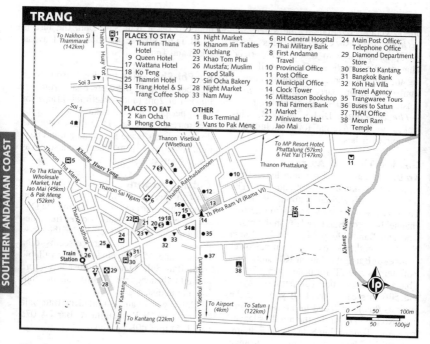

TRANG

PLACES TO STAY	13 Night Market	6 RH General Hospital	24 Main Post Office;
4 Thumrin Thana	15 Khanom Jiin Tables	7 Thai Military Bank	Telephone Office
Hotel	20 Yuchiang	8 First Andaman	29 Diamond Department
9 Queen Hotel	23 Khao Tom Phui	Travel	Store
17 Wattana Hotel	26 Mustafa; Muslim	10 Provincial Office	30 Buses to Kantang
18 Ko Teng	Food Stalls	11 Post Office	31 Bangkok Bank
25 Thamrin Hotel	27 Sin Ocha Bakery	12 Municipal Office	32 Koh Hai Villa
34 Trang Hotel & Si	28 Night Market	14 Clock Tower	Travel Agency
Trang Coffee Shop	33 Nam Muy	16 Mittasason Bookshop	35 Trangwaree Tours
		19 Thai Farmers Bank	36 Buses to Satun
PLACES TO EAT	OTHER	21 Market	37 THAI Office
2 Kan Ocha	1 Bus Terminal	22 Minivans to Hat	38 Meun Ram
3 Phong Ocha	5 Vans to Pak Meng	Jao Mai	Temple

Music & Dance

As in other southern provinces, public holidays and temple fairs feature performances of *Manohra*, the classical Southern Thai dance-drama, and *năng thalung* (shadow play). But because of its early role as a trade centre, Trang has a unique Indian-influenced music-and-dance tradition as well as *lí-keh pàa* (also called *lí-keh bòk* and *lí-keh ram ma-naa*), a local folk opera with a storyline depicting Indian merchants taking their Thai wives back to India for a visit. It's part farce, part drama, with Thais costumed as Indians with long beards and turbans.

Traditional funerals and Buddhist ordinations often feature a musical ensemble called *kaa-law*, which consists of four or five players sitting on a small stage under a temporary coconut-leaf roof or awning. The instruments include two long Indian drums, a *pii haw* (a large oboe similar to the Indian *shahnai*) and two gongs.

TRANG
อ.เมืองตรัง

postcode 92000 • pop 50,900

Historically, Trang has played an important role as a centre of trade since at least the 1st century AD; it was especially important between the 7th and 12th centuries, when it was a seaport for sampans sailing between Trang and the Straits of Malacca. Nakhon Si Thammarat and Surat Thani were major commercial and cultural centres for the Srivijaya empire at this time, and Trang served as a relay point for communications and shipping between the east coast of the Thai peninsula and Palembang, Sumatra. Trang was then known as Krung Thani and later as Trangkhapura (City of Waves) until the name was shortened during the early years of the Ratanakosin period.

During the Ayuthaya period, Trang was a common port of entry for seafaring Western visitors, who continued by land to Nakhon

Si Thammarat or Ayuthaya. The town was then located at the mouth of the Trang River, but King Mongkut later gave orders to move the city to its present location inland because of frequent flooding. Today Trang is still an important point of exit for transporting rubber from the province's many plantations.

Trang's main attractions are the nearby beaches and islands, plus the fact that it can be reached by train. Among Thais, one of Trang's claims to fame is that it often wins awards for 'Cleanest City in Thailand' – its main rival in this regard is Yala. It may not seem that sparkling to the average visitor, but Trang does have a lively, trading town appeal that merits a stroll if you find yourself here overnight.

Orientation

Maps Outdated but useful maps of Trang, as well as English-language newspapers, are available at Mittasason Bookshop near the intersection of Th Visetkul (Wisetkun) and Th Phra Ram VI (Rama VI). Finding a good map that focusses on Trang's islands and beaches is difficult – one of the reasons that these areas are only now beginning to get visitors.

Information

Tourist Offices Trang has no TAT office but if you plan on spending a lot of time

exploring it, it's worth dropping by the TAT office in Nakhon Si Thammarat, which is responsible for dispensing information about Trang.

Money Bangkok Bank, Thai Farmers Bank and Siam Commercial Bank all have branches along Th Phra Ram VI in the centre of town. Bangkok Bank and Thai Farmers Bank have ATMs, as does the Thai Military Bank on Th Visetkul.

Post & Communications The post and telephone office is on the corner of Th Phra Ram VI and Th Kantang.

Bookshops Mittasason Bookshop, right across from the municipal office near the clock tower, carries the *Bangkok Post*, the *Nation* and a few English-language magazines.

Things to See

One odd aspect of Trang is the seeming lack of Thai Buddhist temples. Most of those living in the central business district are Chinese, so you do see a few joss houses but that's about it.

Meun Ram, a Chinese temple between Soi 1 and Soi 2, Th Visetkul, sometimes sponsors performances of Southern Thai shadow theatre.

Places to Stay

A number of hotels are found along the city's two main thoroughfares, Th Phra Ram VI and Th Visetkul, which intersect at the clock tower.

Ko Teng (☎ 075 218 148, 77–79 Th Phra Ram VI) Singles/doubles 200/300B. The long-running Ko Teng has large rooms, and a good restaurant downstairs. The front doors of the hotel are closed at 7pm every day; there's another entrance around the back.

Wattana Hotel (☎ 075 218 184, 127/3–4 Th Phra Ram VI) Rooms with fan & bath 150B, with TV & phone 300B, with air-con 400B. This is one of those hotels with lots of smoking men and painted ladies in the lobby.

Queen Hotel (☎ 075 218 522, 85–89 Th Visetkul) Rooms with fan/air-con 250/400B. This place has large clean rooms though the air-con is rather weak in some rooms.

Trang Hotel (☎ 075 218 944, fax 075 218 157, 134/2–5 Th Visetkul) Rooms with bath, air-con, TV, hot water & phone 500-1500B. The business-like Trang Hotel is near the clock tower. The downstairs coffee shop is quite popular.

Thamrin Hotel (☎ 075 211 011, fax 075 218 057, 99 Th Sathani) Rooms with air-con 570-800B. This 10-storey upmarket place is near the train station. Breakfast is included but a 17% tax and service charge is tacked onto the bill. The Trang Hotel is better value.

Thumrin Thana Hotel (☎ 075 211 211, fax 075 223 288, 69/8 Th Huay Yot) Rooms 1200-1500B. Uppermost on the local scale is the relatively new Thumrin Thana, a big fancy place, not far from the bus terminal, with a gleaming marbled lobby and 289 spacious rooms, each with two beds, IDD voice-mail phones, fridge, TV & smoke detector. Other facilities include a small bakery, three restaurants, coffee shop, shopping centre, business centre, safety-deposit boxes, pool, fitness centre, sauna room and spa bath.

MP Resort Hotel (☎ 075 214 230, fax 075 211 177, 184 Th Trang-Phattalung) Rooms 1200-1500B, suites 2500B. Looking like a beached Titanic on the north-eastern outskirts of town, this is a huge sky-blue building designed to resemble a cruise ship from a distance. Despite the strange, kitsch exterior, the hotel has a classy lobby and the rates are pretty good considering the luxuries: pool, sauna, Jacuzzi, snooker, tennis court, golf driving range, games room, fitness centre, karaoke, restaurants and business centre. However it's a bit far from town compared with the Thumrin Thara and lacks the polish of the latter.

Kantang If you happen to become stranded in nearby Kantang waiting for a boat to the islands, there is one inexpensive place to stay.

JT Hotel (☎ 075 251 755, 181 Th Ratsada Uthit) Rooms with fan 250B, air-con 350-450B. This is near the main market near the waterfront and has less of a short-time presence than its competitors.

Places to Eat

Plenty of good restaurants can be found at or near the hotels.

Ko Teng (☎ 075 218 622, 77–79 Th Phra Ram VI) Dishes 30-80B. The Ko Teng hotel still serves some of the best kaeng kari kài (chicken curry) in the city. The English tourist menu prices it at 60B, which means a bowl of the stuff, while the Thai menu lists 25B – served râat khâo (over rice).

Si Trang Coffee Shop (☎ 075 218 944, 134/2–5 Th Visetkul) Dishes 40-60B. This air-con place in the Trang Hotel (not to be confused with the smaller Si Trang Hotel, which has no restaurant other than guests cooking in the hallway!) serves very good Thai, Chinese and Western food at moderate prices.

Nam Muy (☎ 075 218 504, Th Phra Ram VI) Dishes 40-80B. This large Chinese restaurant opposite the Ko Teng Hotel looks fancy, although the menu is medium-priced.

Khao Tom Phui (☎ 075 210 127, Th Phra Ram VI) Dishes 30-70B. Open 9pm-2am. This serves all manner of Thai and Chinese standards, and has been honoured with the Shell Chuan Chim designation for its tôm yam (available with shrimp, fish or squid), plaa kraphŏng náam daeng (sea bass in red sauce) and yâwt phàk kha-náa pûm pûy (greens stir-fried in red bean sauce with chunks of smoked mackerel). There is no roman-script sign; look for a red sign with chopsticks.

Diamond department store (Th Phra Ram VI) Dishes 20-30B. This has a small hawkers' centre on the 3rd floor.

Around the corner from the department store along Th Sathani, a **night market** convenes in the evening.

Khanŏm Jiin Trang is famous for khanŏm jiin (Chinese noodles with curry). One of the best places to try it is at the **tables** set up at the intersection of Th Visetkul and Th

Phra Ram VI. You have a choice of dousing your noodles in *náam yaa* (a spicy ground fish curry), *náam phrík* (a sweet and slightly spicy peanut sauce) or *kaeng tai plaa* (a very spicy mixture of green beans, fish, bamboo shoots and potato). To this you can add your choice of fresh grated papaya, pickled vegies, cucumber and bean sprouts – all for just 10B per bowl.

Across the street from this vendor, in front of the municipal offices, is a small **night market** that usually includes a couple of khanŏm jiin vendors.

Muslim The Malay culinary influence is strong in Trang.

Mustafa (Th Sathani) Dishes 20-40B. Near the train station, this place serves inexpensive Malay-style curries, *roti kaeng* (roti and curry), *roti khài* (roti with egg) and *màtàbà* (martabak) in relatively clean surroundings. There is no roman-script sign – look for a large, brightly lit tiled place with curries in a glass cabinet at the front.

Nearby are several smaller *food stalls* serving Muslim cuisine.

Ko-píi Shops Trang is even more famous for its coffee and *ráan kaafae* or *ráan ko-píi* (coffee shops), which are easily identified by the charcoal-fired aluminium boilers with stubby smokestacks seen somewhere in the middle or back of the open-sided shops. Usually run by Hokkien Chinese, these shops serve real filtered coffee (called *kaafae thŭng* in the rest of the country) along with a variety of snacks, typically *paa-thông-kŏ* (fried sweet pastry), *salapao* (Chinese buns), *khanŏm jìip* (dumplings), Trang-style sweets, *mǔu yâang* (barbecued pork) and sometimes noodles and *jók* (thick rice soup).

When you order coffee in these places, be sure to use the Hokkien word *ko-píi* rather than the Thai *kaafae*, otherwise you may end up with Nescafe or instant Khao Chong coffee – the proprietors often think this is what faràng want. Coffee is usually served with milk and sugar – ask for *ko-píi dam* for sweetened black coffee or *ko-píi dam, mâi sài náam-taan* for black coffee without sugar.

The most convenient ráan ko-píi for most visitors staying in the town centre is the *Sin Ocha Bakery (Th Sathani)* near the train station. Once the queen of Trang coffee shops (under its old name, Sin Jiaw), it was completely renovated a few years ago and made into a modern cafe. Ko-píi is still available here, along with international pastries and egg-and-toast breakfasts.

Yuchiang (Th Phra Ram VI) Dishes 20-30B. If you're more hard core, try Yuchiang, at the corner of Soi 1 and Soi 6, Th Phra Ram VI (opposite Khao Tom Phui). This is a classic Hokkien coffee house with marble-topped round tables in an old wooden building. It's open early morning to mid afternoon. There is a sign in Thai and Chinese only.

Phong Ocha (☎ 075 219 918, Th Huay Yot) Dishes 20-35B. Open 7am-10pm. Between the Thumrin Thana Hotel and the turn-off for the bus terminal, this place does traditional ko-píi along with jók and *mìi sŭa kài tŭun*, super-thin rice noodles with herb-steamed chicken. It's busiest in the morning.

Kan Ocha (Th Huay Yot) 20-35B. Close to the bus terminal, this catches the evening ko-píi shift.

Shopping

Trang is known for its wickerwork and, especially, mats woven of *bai toei* (pandanus leaves), which are called *sèua paa-nan*, or Panan mats. Panan mats are important bridal gifts in rural Trang, and are a common feature of rural households. The process of softening and drying the pandanus leaves before weaving takes many days. They can be purchased in Trang for about 100B to 200B. Another item to look for are surprisingly pliant pillows made from these mats.

The province also has its own distinctive cotton-weaving styles. The villages of Na Paw and Na Meun Si are the most highly regarded sources for these fabrics, especially the intricate diamond-shaped *lai lûuk kâew* pattern, once reserved for nobility.

The best place in town for good buys is the Tha Klang wholesale market along Th Tha Klang.

SOUTHERN ANDAMAN COAST

Getting There & Away

Air THAI operates daily flights from Bangkok to Trang (2275B). The Trang THAI office (☎ 075 218 066) is at 199/2 Th Visetkul. The airport is 4km south of Trang; THAI runs shuttle vans back and forth for 50B per person.

Bus & Share Taxi Ordinary buses from Satun or Krabi to Trang cost 43B. A share taxi from the same cities is around 80B. Air-con buses from Satun cost 86B and take three hours. From Phattalung it's 20B (two hours) by bus, 40B by share taxi. You can get an air-con minivan to Hat Yai from the Trang bus terminal for 65B (two hours); they leave frequently from 5.30am to 5.30pm. Otherwise an ordinary bus to/from Hat Yai is 50B.

Air-con 1st-class buses to/from Bangkok are 443B (344B for 2nd-class air-con) or 685B for a VIP bus. The air-con buses take about 12 hours.

Trang's open-air bus terminal is on a back street off Th Huay Yot.

If you're coming from Ko Lanta, you can catch any north-bound vehicle and get off at Ban Huay Nam Khao, at the junction of Hwy 4 and the road to Ko Lanta, then catch a bus south to Trang for 30B.

Big orange buses to the harbour at Kantang leave frequently from Th Kantang near the train station for 10B. There are also air-con minivans that do the same trip every hour or so for 35B each; a motorcycle taxi will cost 80B, but this is really too long a jaunt for a comfortable pillion ride.

Train Only two trains go all the way from Bangkok to Trang: the express No 83, which leaves Bangkok's Hualamphong station at 5.05pm and arrives in Trang at 9.40am the next day; and the (painfully slow) rapid No 167, which leaves Hualamphong station at 6.20pm, arriving in Trang at 12.20pm the next day. Both trains offer all three classes of travel. The fare is 660/311/135B 1st/2nd/3rd class, not including rapid or express surcharges. From Thung Song in Nakhon Si Thammarat Province there are two trains daily to Trang,

leaving at 8.13am and 10.39am, arriving an hour and 45 minutes later.

If you want to continue to Kantang on the coast, there is one daily rapid train out of Trang at 12.20pm, which arrives in Kantang at 12.50pm. The fare from Trang to Kantang is 45B in 3rd class (including rapid surcharge).

Boat From the harbour at nearby Kantang, ferries used to operate to/from Pulau Langkawi, just across the border in Malaysia; at times the service has gone as far afield as Medan (Indonesia) and Singapore, but for the moment the only boat option is the ferry across the Trang River estuary to Tha Som for Hat Jao Mai and Ko Libong. See the Trang Beaches & Islands section for details.

Getting Around

Săamláw and *túk-túk* around town cost 10B to 20B per trip.

TRANG BEACHES & ISLANDS

Trang Province has several sandy beaches and coves along the coast, especially in the Sikao and Kantang districts. On Route 403 between Trang and Kantang is a turn-off west onto a paved road that leads down to the coast through some interesting Thai-Muslim villages. At the end, it splits north and south. The road south leads to Hat Yao, Hat Yong Ling and Hat Jao Mai. The road north leads to Hat Chang Lang and Hat Pak Meng. A more direct way to Hat Pak Meng from Trang is to take Route 4046 via Sikao.

Hat Pak Meng
หาดปากเม็ง

Thirty-nine kilometres from Trang in Sikao district, north of Hat Jao Mai, Yao and Chang Lang, is another long, broad, sandy beach near the village of Ban Pak Meng. The waters are usually shallow and calm, even in the rainy season. A couple of hundred metres offshore are several limestone rock formations, including a very large one with caves. Several vendors and a couple of restaurants offer fresh seafood. You can use the sling chairs and umbrellas on the beach as long as you order something. A long promenade/sea wall runs along the middle and southern sections of the beach.

Around the beginning of November, locals flock to Hat Pak Meng to collect *hǎwy taphao*, a delicious type of sea mussel. The tide reaches its lowest this time of year, so it's relatively easy to pick up the shells.

About halfway between Pak Meng and Trang, south of Route 4046, is the 20m-high **Ang Thong Falls**.

Pakmeng Resort (☎ *075 210 321*) Bungalows with air-con & bath 1800-4700B. This resort has sturdy wooden bungalows with verandas; the more expensive of them have views of the ocean. While the grounds are nicely landscaped, the rooms seem overpriced and are geared towards tour groups. The attached restaurant does good seafood. Breakfast is included.

Pakmeng Resort operates one-day boat tours of Ko Cheuak, Ko Muk and Ko Kradan for 450B per person including lunch and beverages.

Getting There & Away Take a van (20B) or sǎwngthǎew (15B) to Sikao from Trang, and then a sǎwngthǎew (12B) to Hat Pak Meng. There are also one or two direct vans daily to Pak Meng from Trang for 30B.

If you're coming by your own transport from Trang, make a left before you get to the clock circle in Sikao, following a blue sign for Route 2021. You'll come to a forked junction after 3.5km, where you should continue straight ahead to get to Pak Meng, 6km farther.

A paved road connects Pak Meng with the other beaches south, so if you have your own wheels there's no need to backtrack through Sikao.

Ko Ngai (Hai)
เกาะไหง(ไห)

This island is actually part of Krabi Province to the north, but is most accessible from Trang's Pak Meng It's a fairly small island, covering about 4.8 sq km, but the beaches are fine white sand, the water is clear and virtually the entire island is ringed by coral. The resorts on the island operate half-day boat tours of nearby islands, including Morakot Cave on Ko Muk, for around 400B per person.

Places to Stay Along the eastern shore of Ko Ngai are three 'resorts' of varying price and comfort.

Koh Hai Villa (in Trang ☎ *075 210 496*) Tents 150B, bungalows with fan 300B, for 4 people 600-800B. Towards the middle of the island is Koh Hai. Once the only accommodation on the island, this place had a bad reputation. It seems to have cleaned up its act somewhat – probably due to the arrival of competition.

Ko Ngai Resort (☎ *075 210 496, 075 210 317, in Bangkok* ☎ *022 464 399*) Tents 150B, bungalows with fan 600-900B, with air-con 1100-2200B. At the southern end of the island this resort has wooden bungalows with huge verandas.

Fantasy Bungalow Bungalows with air-con & fridge 1500-3000B. Fantasy lives up to its name with bizarrely shaped bungalows in festive Caribbean hues that are priced according to view. The restaurant does excellent seafood and breakfast is included in the room rate.

You can book any of these places through Trangwaree Tours in Trang (☎ *075 219 448, fax 075 225 282, 223/3–4 Th Visetkul*). Each resort has its own office in the city, but this one is the most helpful.

Getting There & Away Two kinds of boats leave from the jetty at Pak Meng for Ko Ngai daily at 10.30am. Slow boats cost 80B per person and take about an hour. Fast boats cost 150B per person and do the trip in 20 minutes. From Ko Ngai the boats depart at 8.30am. You can also charter a longtail for 500B.

Hat Chang Lang
หาดฉางหลาง

Hat Chang Lang is part of the Hat Jao Mai National Marine Park, and this is where the park office is located. The beach, about

2km long, is very flat and shallow. At the northern end is a stream, Khlong Chang Lang. On a cliff near the office is a series of ancient rock art sketched in ochre. There's also a fresh-water spring and a grassy campsite beneath casuarinas.

Ko Muk & Ko Kradan
เกาะมุก/เกาะกระดาน

Ko Muk is nearly opposite Hat Chang Lang and can be reached by boat from Kantang or Pak Meng. The coral around Ko Muk is lively, and there are several small beaches on the island suitable for camping and swimming. The best beach, Hat Sai Yao, is on the western side of the island and is nicknamed Hat Farang because it's 'owned' by a faràng from Phuket. It's about a half-hour walk from the pier, or you can take a motorcycle taxi for 50B.

Near the northern end is **Tham Morakot** (Emerald Cave), a beautiful limestone tunnel that can be entered by boat during low tide. The tunnel stretches for 80m to emerge in an open pool of a beautiful emerald hue, hence the cave's name. At the southern end of the island is pretty Phangka Cove and the fishing village of Hua Laem.

Ko Kradan is the most beautiful of the islands that belong to Hat Jao Mai National Park. Actually, only five of six precincts on the island belong to the park – one is devoted to coconut and rubber plantations. At both islands the water is so clear in places that the bottom is clearly visible from the surface. This clear water permits the growth of corals in good healthy reefs along the northern side of the islands, and the water is often shallow enough for snorkelling. There are fewer white-sand beaches on Ko Kradan than on Ko Muk, but the coral reef on the side facing Ko Muk is quite good for diving. **Ko Cheuak** and **Ko Waen** are small islands between Ko Muk, Ko Kradan and the Trang coast. Both feature sand beaches and coral reefs. Ko Cheuak has a small cave that can be entered by boats at low tide.

Places to Stay & Eat There are a number of options here.

Ko Muk Resort (☎ 075 212 613 Trang office, 25/36 Th Sathani) Bungalows with/without bath 300/250B. On the east coast of Ko Muk, near the Muslim fishing village of Hua Laem and about a 10-minute walk north of the pier, this place has simple but nicely designed bungalows. The beach in front tends towards mud flats during low tide; the beach near the village is slightly better but modest dress is called for – no topless sunbathing please. The resort organises boats to nearby islands like Ko Ngai (Hai), Ko Waen, Ko Kradan and Ko Lanta.

Sabai Dee Resort Tents 100B, bungalows with bath 300-350B. On the beach at Hat Farang, this place is popular and has comfortable wooden bungalows. The restaurant does a seafood barbecue on Fridays.

Charlie's Bungalows Tents 200B, bungalows with shared bath 300B. This place has sturdy bungalows and new bathrooms/toilets were being built at the time of research. The restaurant service is painfully slow though the food isn't too bad.

Hat Farang Resort Rooms 100B, bungalow with bath 250B. This place is set in a coconut grove about 100 metres from the beach. Rooms in the main building are basic – mattresses on the floor – but they're clean and the staff are friendly. The attached restaurant does excellent Thai food.

Getting There & Away The easiest place to get a boat to either Ko Muk or Ko Kradan is from Kantang. Sawngthaew from Trang to Kantang leave regularly and cost 20B; air-con minivans (35B) are also available. Once in Kantang you must charter another sawngthaew to the ferry pier for 20-30B, where you can get a regular long-tail boat to Ko Muk for 50B (or charter for 300B), to Ko Kradan for 100B or to Ko Libong for 25B. These boats leave Kantang in the late morning and return to Kantang in the late afternoon.

You can also get to the islands from Hat Pak Meng. There are two piers, one at the northern end of the beach and one at the southern end. Boats are more frequent from the southern pier, especially during the rainy season. Boats cost 30B to 60B per person to Ko Muk (depending on the number of passengers), and 120B to Ko Kradan.

It's also possible to get a boat to Ko Muk from the pier at Ban Khuan Thung Kuu, near the Hat Jao Mai National Park headquarters. This is where you'll depart from if you book a tour through one of Trang's travel agencies. Boats leave for Ko Muk at noon and return at 8am the following day. Săwngthăew between Trang and Ban Khuan Thung Kuu run rather infrequently and cost 40B per person.

Hat Yong Ling & Hat Yao
หาดหยงหลิง/หาดยาว

A few kilometres north of Hat Jao Mai are these two white-sand beaches separated by limestone cliffs pocked with caves. Hat Yong Ling is a short walk from the Hat Yong Ling park unit parking lot. It's a pretty bay lined with casuarina trees and there are snack stands on weekends. There are some tidal pools off the beach at the base of the limestone cliffs, and you can camp nearby if you check in with the park officers first. Another curving beach nearby, **Hat San**, can only be approached via a large cave that connects the two beaches. The striking karst formation that rises to the north of the beach is thought by locals to resemble a shark's dorsal fin. The access road into the Yong Ling unit is 2km long.

Hat Jao Mai & Ko Libong
หาดเข้าไหม/เกาะลิบง

Hat Jao Mai and Ko Libong are in Kantang district, about 35km from Trang. The wide white-sand beach of Hat Jao Mai is 5km long and gets some of Thailand's biggest surf (probably the source of Trang's original unshortened name, City of Waves). Hat Jao Mai is backed by casuarina trees and limestone hills with caves, some of which reputedly contain prehistoric human skeletal remains. Two large caves nearby can be reached by boat. You can charter a fisherman's long-tail for 100B an hour from Ban Jao Mai Hat Yao; two hours is enough. Trangwaree Tours in Trang (☎ 075 219

448, fax 075 225 282), 223/3–4 Th Visetkul, offers kayak trips to the caves, including lunch, for 750B per person.

Tham Jao Mai is big enough to enter by boat, and contains at least three levels and many side caverns with extensive stalactites, stalagmites, crystal curtains and fossils. In a small chamber at the top level is a beautiful small spring.

Hat Jao Mai is part of the 231,000-sq-km **Hat Jao Mai National Park**, which includes Hat Chang Lang farther north and the islands of Ko Muk, Ko Kradan, Ko Jao Mai, Ko Waen, Ko Cheuak, Ko Pling and Ko Meng. In this area, endangered dugong (also called manatees or sea cows) can sometimes be spotted. In their only known appearance on the Thai-Malay peninsula, rare black-necked storks frequent Jao Mai to feed on molluscs and crustaceans. More-common wildlife that visitors may actually spot include sea otters, macaques, langurs, wild pigs, pangolins, little herons, Pacific reef-egrets, white-bellied sea eagles, monitor lizards and water monitors. The park is also rich in evergreen forest, mangrove forest, beach forest and limestone crag forest.

National park admission fees apply to all areas of Hat Jao Mai National Park – 200B for adults, 100B for children under 14.

Ko Libong, Trang's largest island, lies opposite Hat Jao Mai. There are three Muslim fishing villages on the island, so boats from Kantang port are easy to get for the half-hour trip, or from Ban Jao Mai Hat Yao near Hat Jao Mai it's about 15 minutes.

The island has its own wildlife sanctuary, a no-hunting zone located inland from Laem Ju Hoi, a cape that juts out from the island's east coast. Many species of birds from northern Asia and Siberia annually migrate here to pass the winter.

Places to Stay A number of *bungalows* are available for rent at Hat Jao Mai National Marine Park. Some are newly built and quite comfortable. The nicest goes for 2000B per night and sleeps eight people. There are also bungalows for 600B to 800B that sleep six. For reservations call ☎ 075 210 099, or contact the National

Park Division, Royal Forest Department (☎ 025 790 529, 025 794 842, 025 795 269). *Camping* is permitted all through the park, including Hat Jao Mai and the various islands.

Sinchai's Chaomai Resort Tents 50B, bungalows without/with bath 200/300B. Sinchai's offers a few two-room wooden bungalows and two more substantial bungalows. Tents are available for rent during the dry season. Sinchai's wife cooks great Thai food and meals are inexpensive. The family can arrange boat trips to nearby caves and islands and it's a short walk from here to the village of Ban Jao Mai Hat Yao, where there's a local *coffee shop* and a *seafood restaurant* built on one of the village piers. There are also a few wood *bungalows* on the pier for rent for an overpriced 200B.

The turn-off for Sinchai's is 3.6km past the turn-off for the Hat Yong Ling park unit (or 9km from Pak Meng). There's a sign for the resort at the entrance to the access road. After you're on this access road, the road forks; the right fork goes to the resort. It's the only dirt road between Ban Jao Mai Hat Yao and the limestone cliff, which you see about half a kilometre from the village.

The following places are on Ko Libong:

The Botanical Department maintains free *shelters* on Laem Ju Hoi, a cape on the eastern tip of Ko Libong. On the south-western side of the island is a beach where camping is permitted.

Libong Beach Resort (in Trang ☎ 075 214 676) Bungalows 350-500B. This place has A-frame thatched bungalows and is located on the western side of the island. If there are enough guests, the restaurant will cook seafood on request.

Libong Nature Beach Bungalow Bungalows 350B. Located just south of Libong Beach Resort, this place is basic. Bungalows are made of bamboo and thatch and there's a simple restaurant with cheap but good food.

Getting There & Away The quickest way to reach Hat Jao Mai by public transport is via minivans from near the Trang market, which leave every hour in the high season,

less frequently in the low season, for 50B per person. You can also catch a bus, train or taxi from Trang to Kantang harbour, then hop on one of the frequent ferries across to Tha Som on the opposite shore of the Trang River estuary. Tickets cost 2B for pedestrians, 5B for motorcycles, 15B per car and 20B per pickup; the ferry operates daily from 6am to 8pm. From Tha Som there are frequent săwngthăew to Hat Jao Mai.

Boats bound for Ko Libong leave Ban Jao Mai Hat Yao every hour during daylight hours for 20B per person, or you can charter to Ko Libong Resort for 400B.

Hat Samran & Ko Sukon
หาดสำราญ/เกาะสุกร

Hat Samran is a beautiful, shady white-sand beach in Palian district, about 40km south of Trang city. It's rather difficult to get to if you don't have your own transportation though. Hiring a săwngthăew from the market in Trang should cost no more than 500B.

Ko Sukon is the island visible from Hat Samran. Its residents are mostly Thai-Muslims involved in fishing and working on rubber plantations. Ko Sukon can be reached from either Ban Ta Seh, a village at the southern end of Hat Samran or from the Customs pier at Palian. From Ta Seh long-tail boats can be hired for 200B to make the 15-minute passage. When the tide is low, it's sometimes not possible to do the trip in a long-tail boat – if drivers are refusing to go, this is probably the reason. From Palian a daily boat departs at 2.30pm, arriving at Sukon an hour later. In the opposite direction the boat leaves at 7.30am; the fare is 20B.

So far there are just a couple of places to stay on the island, both located on a beach facing southward.

Sukon Island Resort (☎ 075 211 460, Trang ☎ 075 219 679) Bungalows with bath 400-600B. This place has a collection of wood and concrete bungalows and maintains a small kiosk at the Trang bus terminal for advance bookings and transport.

Sukon Beach Bungalows (Trang ☎ 075 211 457) Bungalows with bath & fan 450-750B. This place has 20 bungalows of wood and concrete situated in a coconut grove. The price of bungalows depends on proximity to the beach. Sukon Beach Bungalows also offers Thai massage and has a couple of kayaks that guests can use for free. Snorkelling trips to Ko Lao Liang, a small island about an hour's boat ride away can be arranged here.

WATERFALLS

A lightly trafficked, paved road runs south from Hwy 4 near the Trang-Phattalung border past a number of scenic waterfalls where the Trang and Palian rivers (or their tributaries) meet the Khao Banthat Mountains. **Ton Te Falls**, 46km from Trang, is the loftiest. It's best seen during or just after the rainy season (September to November) when the 320m waterfall is fullest.

Jao Pha Falls in the Palian district, southeast of Trang, near Laem Som, has about 25 stepped falls of 5m to 10m each, with pools at every level. The semi-nomadic Sakai tribe are sometimes seen in this area.

Perhaps the most unusual waterfall in the province is **Roi Chan Phan Wang** (literally, Hundred Levels – Thousand Palaces), about 70km north-west of Trang in Wang Wiset district, a little-explored corner of the province. Surrounded by rubber groves, dozens of thin cascades of water tumble down limestone rock formations into pools below. The entire area is well shaded and a good spot for picnics. There is no public transport to the falls, however, and the road is not too good – motorcycle or jeep would be the best choice of transport.

CAVES

A limestone cave in the north-eastern district of Huay Yot, **Tham Phra Phut**, contains a large Ayuthaya-period reclining Buddha. When the cave was re-discovered early in the 20th century, a cache of royal-class silverwork, nielloware, pottery and lacquerware was found hidden behind the image – probably stashed there during the mid-18th-century Burmese invasion.

Also in this district, near the village of Ban Huay Nang, is **Tham Tra** (Seal Cave), with mysterious red seals carved into the cave walls, which have yet to be explained by archaeologists. Similar symbols have been found in the nearby cave temple of **Wat Khao Phra**.

More easily visited is **Tham Khao Pina**, off Hwy 4 between Krabi and Trang at the 43km marker, which contains a large, multi-level Buddhist shrine popular with Thai tourists. Another famous cave, **Tham Khao Chang Hai** near Na Meun Si village, in Nayong district, contains large caverns with impressive interior formations.

There is no public transport available to any of these.

KHLONG LAMCHAN WATER-BIRD PARK
อุทยานนกน้ำคลองลำชาน

This large swampy area in the Nayong district, east of Trang, is an important habitat for several waterbird species – similar to Thaleh Noi or Khukhut in Songkhla Province. The best time for birdwatching is between January and March. There are no visitors facilities and no accommodation places in the immediate vicinity. Serious birdwatchers can get permission to explore the area by contacting the Royal Forestry Department in Bangkok (☎ 025 614 292, ext 714).

Satun Province

Bordering Malaysia, Satun (or Satul) is the Andaman Coast's southernmost province. Besides offering a convenient crossing to Malaysia by land or sea, Satun is also home to the stunningly beautiful Ko Tarutao National Marine Park.

Before 1813 Satun was a district of the Malay state of Kedah – the name 'Satun' comes from the Malay *setul*, a type of tree common in this area. At the time, Kedah along with Kelantan, Terengganu and Perlis, paid tribute to Siam. The Anglo-Siamese Treaty of 1909 released parts of these states to Britain and they later became part of independent Malaysia. Satun didn't become a province of Siam until 1925.

SOUTHERN ANDAMAN COAST

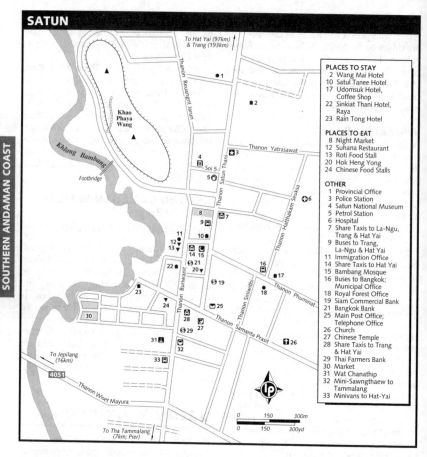

SATUN

To Hat Yai (97km)
& Trang (193km)

Thanon Reuangrit Jarun

Khao
Phaya
Wang

Khlong Bambang

Footbridge

Thanon Yatrasawat

Thanon Satun Thani

Soi 5

Thanon Hatthakam Seuksa

Thanon Buriwani

Thanon Sihwithi

Thanon Samanta Prasit

Thanon Phuminat

To Jepilang
(16km)

4051

Thanon Wiset Mayura

To Tha Tammalang
(7km; Pier)

0   150   300m
0   150   300yd

PLACES TO STAY
2 Wang Mai Hotel
10 Satul Tanee Hotel
17 Udomsuk Hotel,
   Coffee Shop
22 Sinkiat Thani Hotel,
   Raya
23 Rain Tong Hotel

PLACES TO EAT
8 Night Market
12 Suhana Restaurant
13 Roti Food Stall
20 Hok Heng Yong
24 Chinese Food Stalls

OTHER
1 Provincial Office
3 Police Station
4 Satun National Museum
5 Petrol Station
6 Hospital
7 Share Taxis to La-Ngu,
   Trang & Hat Yai
9 Buses to Trang,
   La-Ngu & Hat Yai
11 Immigration Office
14 Share Taxis to Hat Yai
15 Bambang Mosque
16 Buses to Bangkok;
   Municipal Office
18 Royal Forest Office
19 Siam Commercial Bank
21 Bangkok Bank
25 Main Post Office;
   Telephone Office
26 Church
27 Chinese Temple
28 Share Taxis to Trang
   & Hat Yai
29 Thai Farmers Bank
30 Market
31 Wat Chanathip
32 Mini-Sawngthaew to
   Tammalang
33 Minivans to Hat-Yai

Today an estimated 66% of the province's population is Muslim, most of whom speak Yawi or Malay as a first language, and there are 14 mosques to every wát in the province.

SATUN
อ.เมือง สตูล

postcode 91000 • pop 22,700
The provincial capital of Satun itself is not that interesting, but you may enter or leave Thailand here by boat via Kuala Perlis in Malaysia. Sixty kilometres north-west of

Satun is the small port of Pak Bara, the departure point for boats to Ko Tarutao.

As in Pattani and Narathiwat, one hears a lot of Yawi spoken in the streets of Satun. In the not too distant past, the Thai government maintained a loudspeaker system that would broadcast government programs at 6am and 6pm (beginning with a wake-up call to work and ending with the Thai national anthem, for which everyone had to stop and stand in the streets). Whether this was to instil a sense of nationalism in the typically rebellious Southern Thais, or to try to drown out the prayer calls from local

Vanishing Nomads

From southern Myanmar to the southern Philippines, semi-nomadic seafarers collectively known as 'sea gypsies' have plied the coastal waters for as long as anyone can remember. Likewise, in the jungles of southern Thailand, through those of the Malay archipelago and up into the Philippines, dwell groups of semi-nomadic hunter-gatherers commonly known as 'Negritos'. For centuries these two distinct semi-nomadic peoples went about their lives knowing little change, while around them South-East Asian cultures waxed and waned as kingdoms rose and fell. Until relatively recently, both the sea gypsies and Negritos were largely ignored by the Thai government.

Called *chao leh* (sea folk) by most Thai, the sea gypsies who inhabit Thailand's Andaman Coast region belong to two groups that speak languages related to Malay, have no written script, and hold a mixture of animist and Muslim or Buddhist belief systems. The vast majority are fisherfolk. Foreign visitors are most likely to come across sea gypsies at one of the more accessible villages on Phuket or Ko Lanta in Krabi, but there are settlements of sea gypsies to be found in the coastal regions and islands of Ranong, Phang-Nga, Trang and Satun as well. Due mainly to their nomadic past, the culture of the sea gypsies seems simple when compared with other ethnicities in the region – the pursuit of the arts and material wealth is simply not suited to their traditional lifestyle. Instead they possess a rich tradition of storytelling. One custom that many of the sea gypsy groups have in common is the 'boat floating' ceremony, in which an elaborate model boat is set adrift, taking bad luck along with it. The ceremony usually takes place twice a year, in May and November, and is preceded by a procession of drum pounding and dancing revellers.

The Negritos are known to the Thai as *saakai* or, more colloquially as *ngáw* (rambutans), because their frizzy hair is thought to resemble the fuzzy skin of that tropical fruit. The Negritos also have dark complexions and negroid features. The Thai view these forest dwellers in a romanticised fashion, due in part to a play that was written about the Negritos by King Rama VI (and is still regularly performed in Bangkok). An exhibit about Negritos at the National Museum in Satun describes them as 'cheerful, fun-loving, music-loving, ghost-fearing, hearty eaters who are fond of wearing the colour red'. In reality the lives of the Negritos is, of course, rather less idyllic. Nowadays they are found in small jungle settlements in the provinces of Thailand's South, some clinging to a hunter-gatherer lifestyle – building simple huts of bamboo and leaves and hunting with blowguns or slingshots. Once an area is hunted out, they move on. Settlements typically have between 20 and 30 people and the Negritos choose their village leaders by popular vote. There are said to be four distinct groups of Negritos living in Southern Thailand, but their exact numbers are not known.

Unfortunately a number of reasons make it impossible for these peoples – both sea gypsies and Negritos – to keep up their semi-nomadic lifestyles; modern governments seem to feel threatened by minorities that have no regard for international boundaries. Typically, the reaction of South-East Asian governments to these peoples has been to coerce them to settle (using varying degrees of force) in one place so that they can be monitored, educated and, eventually it is hoped, assimilated into the society and culture of the majority. Both groups have also been targets of Christian missionising.

As it is with most semi-nomadic peoples, the transition to stationary living has not been easy for the sea gypsies or Negritos. The older generation of both groups has resisted assimilation to a certain degree, preferring their own ways to those of outsiders. As a result, both groups are much poorer and live shorter lives than the peoples around them. However the younger generation, equipped with language skills and cultural knowledge of the majority, have begun leaving their settlements to look for work elsewhere. As has already happened with other small minority groups in Thailand, it is only a matter of time before both peoples are absorbed into the culture of the majority and become 'Thai'.

Steven Martin

mosques, it was never quite certain. Now a government museum showcasing Thai-Muslim culture has opened in Satun – evidence that Bangkok now views the deep South with much less suspicion.

A very few old Sino-Portuguese shop-houses, some said to date back as far as 1839, can be seen along Th Buriwanit. The modern, parachute-domed Bambang Mosque nearby was constructed n 1979.

Information

Immigration The Wang Prachan customs complex at the Tammalang pier south of town contains an immigration office where anyone travelling to/from Malaysia by boat will have their papers processed. You can also use this office for visa extensions. There's an immigration office in town as well, but compared to the Wang Prachan customs complex it's understaffed and if you try to extend your visa there you will probably be sent to Tammalang.

Money You can change money at Thai Farmers Bank, Bangkok Bank or Siam Commercial Bank, all of which have branches, the latter two with ATMs, in the town centre, either on Th Buriwanit or Th Satun Thani.

Post & Communications The main post and telephone office is on the corner of Th Samanta Prasit and Th Satun Thani.

National Museum

The newly opened Satun National Museum (*Soi 5, Th Satun Thani; admission 30B; open 9am-4pm Wed-Sun*) is actually an early 20th-century 'palace' that was built by a local prince to accommodate King Rama V during a royal visit. Unfortunately the king never stayed here but the handsome two-storey structure served as the provincial office of Satun and later, during WWII, was sequestered by the Japanese and used as a military headquarters.

Built in a pseudo-European style common in nearby Malaysia, the building has been restored and its rooms arranged to give a surprisingly thorough introduction to the traditions and folkways of the Thai-Muslim South. Most of the displays are miniature dioramas (with recorded narration in both Thai and English) that cover everything from Southern mat weaving techniques to the traditional martial art called *silá*. Exhibits labelled in English also explain local marriage rites as well as male and female ritual circumcision. There are also narrated exhibits describing the Sakai, the tribal people who are believed to have inhabited the region long before the arrival of the Thai or Malay.

Khao Phaya Wang
เขาพญาวัง

If you find yourself with time to kill in Satun, you might consider a visit to the park along the western side of Khao Phaya Wang, a limestone outcrop next to Khlong Bambang (sometimes referred to as 'Khlong Mambang'). Steps lead up the vine-choked cliff on the khlong side of Khao Phaya Wang and at the top there are views of the winding green khlong, rice fields and coconut plantations. Pandan mats are available at the cool, bamboo-shaded picnic area next to the canal below. Vendors sell sôm-tam, *khâo niǎw* (sticky rice), *kài thâwt* (fried chicken), *kûng thâwt* (fried prawns) and *mîang kham* (pieces of ginger, onion, dried shrimp, toasted coconut, chilli, peanuts and lime placed into a wild tea leaf with a thick, sweet and salty tamarind sauce).

Places to Stay

Rain Tong Hotel (*Rian Thong Hotel;* ☎ 074 711 036, 4–6, Th Samanta Prasit) Rooms with fan, shower & toilet 100-140B. This is a three-storey cube, next to the Rian Thong pier, an embarkation point for boats to/from Malaysia. It has the cheapest rooms in town but the bugs (mosquitoes and roaches) are running the show here.

Udomsuk Hotel (☎ 074 711 006, 201 Th Hatthakam Seuksa) Singles/doubles with fan & bath 120/130B. Near the municipal offices is the two-storey Udomsuk with reasonably clean rooms.

Satul Tanee Hotel (Satun Thani; ☎ 074 711 010, 90 Th Satun Thani) Singles/ doubles with fan 200/250B, with air-con 350/400B. The four-storey Satul, near the centre of town, is OK but a bit noisy.

Wang Mai Hotel (☎ 074 711 607–8, fax 074 722 162, 43 Th Satun Thani) Singles/ doubles with air-con, carpet, hot water & TV 550/650B, deluxe 700B, VIP 1000B. The Wang Mai, near the northern end of town, is upmarket. Try to get a room at the back if you don't like street noise.

Sinkiat Thani Hotel (☎ 074 721 055, fax 074 721 059, 50 Th Buriwanit) Rooms 600-700B. In the centre of town, this has comfortable rooms similar to those at the Wang Mai but in better condition.

Places to Eat

Suhana Restaurant (☎ 074 711 023, 16/7 Th Buriwanit) Dishes 20-40B. Near the gold-domed Bambang Mosque in the centre of town are several cheap Muslim food shops, including the reliable Suhana, almost opposite the mosque.

Two doors south of Suhana, a *roti food stall* with bright green walls serves light-and-fluffy roti with curry. A cluster of cheap *Chinese food stalls* can be found on Th Samanta Prasit near the intersection with Th Buriwanit. Lots of places serve khâo man kài (Hainanese-style chicken and rice) and kǔaytǐaw (wide rice noodles) around town, though none of them stand out.

Hok Heng Yong (Th Satun Thani) Dishes 10-20B. Across from Siam Commercial Bank, this is a traditional Hokkien coffee shop with round marble-topped tables where older Chinese men sit around and chat.

Raya (Th Yontakan Thawon) Dishes 20-40B. This is the coffee shop behind Sinkiat Thani Hotel, it has more Thai dishes than anywhere else in town.

A no-name *coffee shop* next to the Udomsuk Hotel is a good spot for Thai and Western breakfasts. For Chinese food, wander about the little Chinese district near the Rain Tong Hotel. There's nothing fancy, just a few *noodle shops* and small *seafood places*.

North of the Satul Tanee Hotel, along a short street running west off Th Satun Thani, a very good *night market* convenes every evening beginning around 5pm. Many of the vendors sell Thai-Muslim food and the prices are quite low. Considering the overall quality of food in Satun, this is one of the best places to eat in town.

Getting There & Away

Bus & Share Taxi A share taxi or air-con van to Hat Yai costs 50B per person, while an air-con bus costs 40B. Buses to Trang are 43B (86B air-con), share taxis 80B. Air-con minivans to Hat Yai depart from Th Buriwanit, just south of Wat Chanathip.

Share taxis to Hat Yai park in at least three places in Satun: near the Satul Tanee Hotel, near the mosque, and on the corner of Th Samanta Prasit and Th Buriwanit. The stand near the Satul Tanee Hotel also has taxis to La-Ngu (30B) and to Trang, and the stand at the corner of Th Samanta Prasit and Th Buriwanit also goes to Trang. You can hire a whole taxi straight to Pak Bara for 300B.

An air-con bus leaves Bangkok's Southern bus terminal once a day for Satun around 7pm (2pm in the reverse direction) and costs 480B for the 15-hour trip. Ordinary buses leave around the same time, cost 284B and take 16 to 17 hours. But this is really too long a bus trip for comfort – if you want to get to Satun from Bangkok, it would be better to take a train to Hat Yai and then a bus or taxi to Satun. See the following Train section.

A new highway between Satun and Perlis in Malaysia has been proposed. The highway would cut travel time between the two towns, but it would also cut through some of Southern Thailand's dwindling rainforest – many Thais have organised to protest the proposal. For the moment the empty coffers of both governments preclude the possibility the highway will be completed anytime in the near future.

Buses to Bangkok leave from the terminal near the municipal office on the corner of Th Phuminat and Th Hatthakam Seuksa.

Train If you're set on taking the train, it's best to get off at Hat Yai (Songkhla province) and continue from there to Satun by bus or minivan. Any way you do it, the overland trip from Bangkok to Satun is a long one – about 15 hours if everything goes smoothly. See the Hat Yai Getting There & Away section in the South-Western Gulf chapter for information about trains to Hat Yai from Bangkok and other points north.

Boat From Kuala Perlis in Malaysia, boats are M$5. All boats dock at the Wang Prachan customs complex in Tammalang, the estuary 7.5km south of Satun. In the reverse direction the fare is 50B. Boats leave frequently in either direction between 9am and 1pm, then less frequently to around 4pm, depending on marine conditions. You can charter a boat to Perlis holding up to 20 people for 1000B.

From Pulau Langkawi in Malaysia boats for Tammalang leave daily at 8am and 10am and 3pm and 4pm. The crossing takes 1½ to two hours and costs M$18 one way. Bring Thai money from Langkawi, as there are no money-changing facilities at Tammalang pier. In the reverse direction boats leave Tammalang for Langkawi at 8am, 10am, 1pm and 4pm and cost 200B. Keep in mind that there is one-hour time difference between Thailand and Malaysia. Tickets for the Satun-Langkawi boat are sold at booths outside the immigration building at Wang Prachan.

Getting Around
Small orange săwngthăew to Tammalang pier (for boats to Malaysia) cost 10B from Satun. The săwngthăew run every 20 minutes between 8am and 5pm; catch one from opposite Wat Chanathip on Th Buriwanit. A motorcycle taxi from the same area costs 40B.

PAK BARA
ปากบารา

Pak Bara is the jumping-off point for the Ko Tarutao National Marine Park islands.

There is not much to the town itself but you may find yourself spending the night if you miss the boat to the islands.

Places to Stay & Eat
Bara Guest House Singles/doubles 100/150B, bungalows 250-350B. This place has a travel agency and cafe downstairs, five rooms upstairs and a couple of bungalows out the back. You can walk to the Ko Tarutao pier from the guesthouse.

Just over a kilometre before the pier in Pak Bara, along the shore among the casuarina trees, are the *Diamond Beach Bungalows*, *Saengthien Bungalows (Candle Light Bungalows)* and *Sai Kaew Resort*, all with bungalows for around 250B to 400B a night. None are that special; Diamond Beach is the top pick, only because it's nearest to town.

Paknam Resort (☎ 074 781 129) Bungalows 250-450B. On rocky, palm-fringed Ko Baw Jet Luk (often referred to as 'Ko Kabeng', though that's an adjacent island), a 10-minute drive north of Pak Bara over a new bridge, the quiet Paknam offers thatched A-frame bungalows on shady grounds.

You can also stay in nicely designed *park bungalows* at the mainland headquarters for Ko Phetra National Marine Park (☎ 074 781 582), which is near Ban Talo Sai, about 4km before you reach Pak Bara off Route 4052. The turn-off is between the 5km and 6km markers on this highway; from here it's about 1.5km to the park headquarters.

There are several *food stalls* near the Pak Bara pier that do fruit shakes and seafood.

Getting There & Away
From Hat Yai (Songkhla Province), there are three daily buses to La-Ngu and Pak Bara that cost 43B and take 2½ hours. If you miss one of the direct La-Ngu buses, you can also hop on any Satun-bound bus to the junction town of Chalung (28B, 1½ hours), which is about 15km short of Satun, then get a săwngthăew north-west on Route 416 for the 12B, 45-minute trip to La-Ngu. Or take a share taxi from Hat Yai to La-Ngu for 50B; there is also a minivan service from Hat Yai for 50B, a better deal since it goes all the way to Pak Bara.

To get to Pak Bara from Satun, you must take a share taxi or bus to La-Ngu, then a săwngthăew on to Pak Bara. Taxis to La-Ngu leave from a stand diagonally opposite a petrol station on Th Satun Thani, about a hundred metres north of the Satul Tanee Hotel, when there are enough people to fill a taxi for 30B per person. Buses leave frequently from a spot on the opposite side of the road, a little south towards the hotel, and cost 18B. From La-Ngu, săwngthăew rides to Pak Bara are 10B and terminate right at the harbour; you can take a motorcycle taxi this same distance for 40B. You can also charter a whole taxi to Pak Bara from Satun for 300B.

You can travel to La-Ngu from Trang by săwngthăew for 30B, or by share taxi for 50B.

For getting to the Ko Tarutao National Marine Park see that section's Getting There and Away information.

KO TARUTAO NATIONAL MARINE PARK
อุทยานแห่งชาติหมู่เกาะตะรุเตา

This park (adult/child under 14 years 200/100B) protects a sizeable archipelago of 51 islands, approximately 30km from Pak Bara in La-Ngu district, which is 60km north-west of Satun. Ko Tarutao, the biggest of the group, is only 5km from Langkawi island in Malaysia. Only five of the islands (Ko Tarutao, Ko Adang, Ko Lipe, Ko Rawi and Ko Klang) have any kind of regular boat service to them, and of these, only the first three are generally visited by tourists. Access to the other islands, which offer excellent beaches and coral reefs, can only be arranged by chartering long-tail boats.

This park remains one of the most pristine and beautiful coastal areas in Thailand, in part because it requires a bit more effort to get there. Accommodation is fairly basic and transport slow and sometimes inconvenient.

The Royal Forestry Department has been considering requests from private firms to build hotels and bungalows in Tarutao National Park. This would be a very unfortunate event if it means Ko Tarutao is going

Treading Lightly on Tarutao

A remote location, small population and, more recently, near heroic efforts by Thailand's park service have kept Ko Tarutao National Marine Park one of the country's most pristine and beautiful areas. Not surprisingly it is drawing increasing numbers of tourists, both Thai and foreign, which poses a threat to the park's delicate environment. How you decide to visit it, therefore, may help stop it from going the way of Ko Phi-Phi or Ko Samet.

While the park officials and staff are quite hospitable, they have limited time and resources to cater to tourists. This is particularly true of Ko Adang, which has only basic facilities and accommodation (Ko Tarutao is better equipped and staffed). If the number of visitors demanding modern services grows too quickly, the National Parks Division of the Royal Forestry Department may consider requests from private firms to build bungalows and hotels on park land to handle the load. If recent history is any guide, this could ruin the park.

If you want to stay on Ko Adang, try to be fairly self-sufficient – bring a tent and your own food. Kitchen staff will happily prepare meals using visitors' food: it's a way for the cash-strapped operation to bring in a little extra revenue. But the restaurant's own food stocks are usually inadequate. The more visitors that show up prepared to look after themselves, the more confident park staff will be that the current set up can do the job. And the greater the chance that Ko Tarutao's gorgeous coral formations, pearl-white beach and lush islands will remain intact.

Joe Cummings

to become like Ko Phi-Phi or Ko Samet, both of which are national parks that have permitted private development with disastrous results. So far nothing has transpired.

Ko Tarutao
เกาะตะรุเตา

The park's 151-sq-km namesake island features waterfalls, inland streams, beaches, caves and protected wildlife. Nobody lives on this island except for the employees of the Royal Forestry Department. It was a place of exile for political prisoners between 1939 and 1947, and remains of the prisons can be seen near Ao Talo Udang, on the southern tip of the island, and at Ao Talo Wao, on the middle of the east coast. There is also a graveyard, charcoal furnaces and even fermentation tanks for making fish sauce.

For centuries the islands of the region, including Ko Tarutao, have been a haven for pirates. Even as late as 1964 the British navy had to intervene to pacify the area.

Wildlife on the island includes the dusky langur, mouse deer, wild pig, fishing cat and crab-eating macaque; dolphins and whales may be sighted offshore. Four varieties of sea turtle swim the surrounding waters – Pacific ridley, hawksbill, leatherback and green. All four lay eggs on the beaches between September and April.

Tarutao's largest stream, Khlong Phante Malaka, enters the sea at the north-western tip of the island at Ao Phante Malaka; the brackish waters flow out of **Tham Jara-Khe** (Crocodile Cave – the stream was once inhabited by ferocious crocodiles, which seem to have disappeared) on the eastern side of the island. The cave extends for at least 1km under a limestone mountain – no one has yet followed the stream to the cave's end. The mangrove-lined watercourse should not be navigated at high tide, when the mouth of the cave fills.

The park headquarters, pier and bungalows are also here at Ao Phante Malaka. The park fee is payable on arrival. For a view of the bays, climb Topu Hill, 500m north of the park office.

The best camping is at the beaches of **Ao Jak** and **Ao San**, two bays south of park headquarters on the west coast. There is also camping at Ao Makham (Tamarind Bay), at the south-western end of the island, about 2.5km from another park office at Ao Talo Udang. Except for Ao Jak, these beaches are a long walk from park headquarters so you may want to consider hiring a long-tail to take you there: there are usually one or two boat operators snoozing in the shade near the information booth.

There is a road between Ao Phante Malaka, in the north, and Ao Talo Udang, in the south, of which 11km was constructed by political prisoners in the 1940s and 12km has since been constructed by the park division. The road is, for the most part, overgrown, but park personnel have kept a path open to make it easier to get from north to south without having to climb over rocky headlands along the shore. The entire trek takes about eight hours, and while there are ranger stations to Talo Wao and Talo Udang, you'll need to bring a tent and your own supplies if you want to head down there.

Ko Rang Nok (Bird-Nest Island), off Ao Talo Udang, is another treasure trove of the valuable swiftlet nests craved by Chinese throughout the world. Good coral reefs are at the north-western part of Ko Tarutao at **Pha Papinyong** (Papillon Cliffs), at Ao San and in the channel between Ko Tarutao and Ko Takiang (Ko Lela) off the north-east shore.

At the park headquarters, for 20B, you can pick up *Tarutao National Park: a Travellers Adventure Handbook*, a paper booklet that details the park's facilities, flora and fauna and hiking options. It's quite informative, and the history section in particular makes for interesting reading, complete with tales from the prison camps and accounts of gun battles between early park officials and angry locals opposed to having their home turf turned into protected parkland.

Ko Khai & Ko Klang

เกาะไข่/เกาะกลาง

Between Ko Tarutao and Ko Adang and Rawi is a small cluster of three islands called **Muu Ko Klang** (Middle Island Group), where there is good snorkelling. One of the islands, Ko Khai, also has a good white-sand beach. Boats from Ko Tarutao take about 40 minutes to reach Ko Khai. You can also charter long-tails from Ko Lipe out to here: a full day's hire will cost around 700B.

Ko Adang & Ko Rawi
เกาะอาดัง/เกาะราวี

Ko Adang is 43km west of Tarutao, and about 80km from Pak Bara on the mainland. The 30-sq-km island is covered with forest and fresh-water streams, which fortunately supply water year-round. Green sea turtles lay their eggs here between September and December. At the south-eastern corner of the island where the pier and park office are located, visitors can stay in a thatched longhouse. Camping is also allowed. The restaurant is a little expensive considering the basic fare served – but then considering the transport problems, perhaps not. As on Tarutao, it's a good idea to bring some food from the mainland.

An interesting hike can be undertaken along the island's east coast to a pretty beach 2km from the park station. Inland a little way from the beach is a waterfall once – perhaps still – used by passing pirate ships as a source of fresh water. Around on the west coast, 3km from Laem Son, is another waterfall and the chao náam village of Talo Puya.

Ko Rawi is just west of Ko Adang, and a bit smaller. There are no facilities there at all. Off the west coast of Ko Adang, and the south-east coast of Ko Rawi, are coral reefs with many live species of coral and tropical fish. Other excellent snorkelling spots include the northern side of **Ko Yang** and tiny **Ko Hin Ngam**. The latter is known for its beautiful smooth stones. However, you may not want to take one as a souvenir. Doing so is said to bring bad luck, and the visitors centre on Ko Tarutao has a basket of stones sent back by people who blamed the rocks for their subsequent misfortunes.

Through the efforts of park officials, many of these reefs have been spared degradation caused by dynamite fishing and other human activities. The park service has also set up around 40 mooring buoys in this area (used mainly by long-tails bringing snorkellers to the area) so that boat operators need not drop anchor in this ecologically delicate area. Try to make sure your boat uses one of the moorings. Long-tail boat operators on Ko Lipe generally charge around 800B to 1000B to take groups out for a full day of snorkelling.

Ko Lipe
เกาะหลีเป๊ะ

Ko Lipe is immediately south of Ko Adang and is inhabited by about 500 chao náam who are said to have originated on the Lanta islands in Krabi Province. They subsist on fishing and some cultivation of vegetables and rice on the flatter parts of the island.

For some reason the sea gypsies on this island prefer to be called *chao leh* – a term despised by other sea gypsies on islands to the north, who prefer the term chao náam. In their own tongue, they refer to themselves as *iraklahoi*. They also go by the term Thai Mai (New Thai), nomenclature favoured by the Thai government. The chao leh village is in the island's north-east.

Ko Lipe is not under park control, and has thus become the main place to stay in this part of the park, given the limited facilities on Ko Adang. Several bungalow operations have been set up in the main village along the east coast and on Hat Pattaya, on the southern side of this island. There are also one or two simple restaurants and shops in the main village. You can walk overland between the village and Hat Pattaya in around 20 to 30 minutes, or take a long-tail passenger boat for 20B.

There is a **coral reef** along the southern side of the small island and several small **beach coves**. The chao náam can provide boat hire to nearby islets ringed by coral reefs.

Hat Pattaya is the nicest of the two main beaches, as the one in front of the chao leh village is partially covered with boat moorings and some litter. However, the little island just opposite the village, **Ko Kra**, has some well-preserved coral and makes for fine snorkelling. You can easily swim there from the village beach.

One can camp here, or rent a hut from the chao náam for 200B to 300B a night at any of several bungalow operations in or near the main village along both the east and west coasts.

Places to Stay & Eat

Officially, Ko Tarutao National Park is only open from November to May. Visitors who show up on the islands during the monsoon season can stay in *park accommodation*, but they must bring their own food from the mainland unless staying with the chao náam on Ko Lipe.

Bungalows may be booked at the park office in Pak Bara (☎ 074 711 383), but no English is spoken here, or through the Royal Forestry Department (☎ 025 614 292) in Bangkok. For Ko Tarutao and/or Ko Adang, you may want to bring some food of your own from Satun or Pak Bara – the park restaurants are a bit expensive and nothing to write home about.

Ko Tarutao Park accommodation on Ko Tarutao, near the park headquarters, costs 1000B for a large 'deluxe' two-room bungalow sleeping four. A four-bed room in a longhouse goes for 320B. Full rates for all rooms and bungalows must be paid even if only one person takes a bed. Tents can be rented for 100B. If you have your own, the camping fee is 10B.

Staying at the park is a bit like going back to summer camp: lights off at 10.30pm, running water from 6am to 8am and 6pm to 10pm only. But the buildings are clean and well maintained. One point worth noting: the longhouses have no screens or mosquito nets, so you may want to bring your own net, or at least some effective insect repellent.

Ko Adang Laem Son has *longhouse accommodation* similar to that on Ko Tarutao, and for the same rates. A small *restaurant* provides basic meals and sundries; it's closed in the rainy season. You can pitch your own tent for 10B.

Ko Lipe There are basically five places to stay on the island. Two are in the chao leh village, on the north-east side of the island.

Andaman Resort (in Satun ☎ 074 711 313) Camp site 20B, bungalows with bath 300B. On the northern side of the village, this has sturdy and comfortable bungalows. You can also pitch your own tent here.

Lee Pae Resort Bungalows with bath & shower 500-600B. On Hat Pattaya the biggest operation is Lee Pae, which has spacious thatch bungalows. There's an attached restaurant but, like the rooms, it's overpriced.

Pattaya Song Huts 150B, with bath 250B. Down at the western end of the beach, this place has simple huts right on the beach.

Porn Bungalows Bungalows with bath 200-250B. On the adjacent hillside, overlooking the bay, are slightly fancier bungalows.

Pattaya Seafood Bungalows with bath 200B. At the other end of the beach, this is mainly a restaurant, but the owner also has three decent bungalows. This seems to be the only operation on the island that's actually run by an islander. Even if you don't stay, stop by for dinner – the food is excellent.

See the previous section for places to stay and eat in Pak Bara if you miss the boat.

Getting There & Away

Ko Tarutao The main way to reach the park is via Pak Bara, 60km north-west of Satun and 22km from Ko Tarutao. Boats to Tarutao leave regularly between November and April from the Pak Bara pier. During the rest of the year, boat service is irregular, since the park is supposedly closed. Satun Province officials have discussed constructing a new pier in Tan Yong Po district, nearer Satun, that will serve tourist boats to Tarutao and other islands, possibly on a year-round basis.

Boats leave Pak Bara for Tarutao in season daily at 10.30am and 3pm. The return fare is 240B, one way 120B, and it takes 1½ to two hours, depending on the boat. Food and beverages are available on the boat. Departures back to Pak Bara are at 9am and 2pm.

If possible, it would be best to buy one-way tickets for each leg of your journey, as this would allow a choice of routes back (say direct from Ko Lipe to Pak Bara). Also, if the boat you have a ticket for doesn't make it to the islands due to bad weather or an engine mishap, you won't have to worry about getting a refund for both

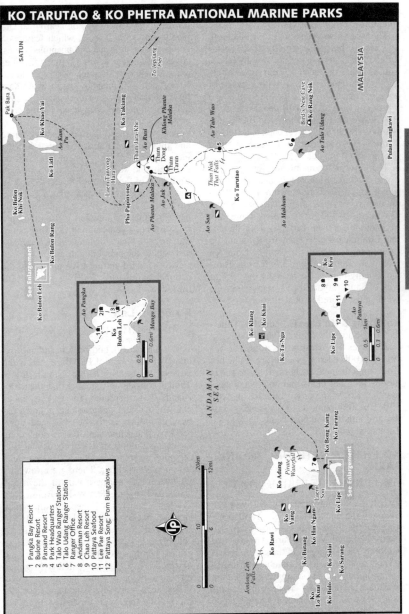

KO TARUTAO & KO PHETRA NATIONAL MARINE PARKS

SATUN

MALAYSIA

Pulau Langkawi

SOUTHERN ANDAMAN COAST

Pak Bara

Ko Khao Yai

Ko Kam Pu

Ao Kam Pu

Ko Lidi

Ko Bulon Khi Nok

Ko Bulon Rang

See Enlargement

Ko Bulon Leh

To Jepilang Pier

Ko Takiang

Tham Jara-Khe

Khlong Phante Malaka

Ao Rusi

Laem Tanyong Hara

Pha Papiyong

Tham Bu-Rusi

Ao Phante Malaka

Tham Dong

Tham Tarun

Ao Jak

Ao Talo Wao

Bird's Nest Cave

Ko Rang Nok

Ao Talo Udang

Ao San

Thun Nak Thai Falls

Ko Tarutao

Ao Makham

Ao Pangka

Ko Bulon Leh

Mango Bay

Ko Kra

Ao Pattaya

Ko Lipe

Ko Klang

Ko Khai

Ko Ta-Nga

ANDAMAN SEA

Ko Bong Kang

Ko Tarang

Pirate's Waterfall

Ko Adang

Laem Son

Ko Lipe

See Enlargement

Jonung Leh Falls

Ko Rawi

Ko Yang

Ko Hin Ngam

Ko Butang

Ko Lo Kuai

Ko Bulo

Ko Salai

Ko Surang

1 Pangka Bay Resort
2 Bulone Resort
3 Pansand Resort
4 Park Headquarters
5 Talo Wao Ranger Station
6 Talo Udang Ranger Station
7 Ranger Office
8 Andaman Resort
9 Chao Leh Resort
10 Pattaya Seafood
11 Lee Pae Resort
12 Pattaya Song; Porn Bungalows

0   10   20km
0   6   12ml

tickets. Some companies will refuse to refund unused return tickets.

There are also occasional tour boats out to Tarutao, but these usually cost several hundred baht per person, as they include a guided tour, meals etc. Your final alternative is to charter a boat with a group of people. The cheapest are the long-tail boats, which can take eight to 10 people out from Pak Bara's commercial pier for 1000B. On holidays, boats may travel back and forth to Tarutao every hour or so to accommodate the increased traffic.

There are other mainland piers you can use to reach the islands. It is also possible to hire boats to Ko Tarutao from three different piers (*thâa reua*) on the coast near Satun. The nearest is the Ko Nok pier, 4km south of Satun (40km from Tarutao). Then there is the Tammalang pier, 9km from Satun, on the opposite side of the estuary from Ko Nok pier. Tammalang is 35km from Tarutao. Finally there's the Jepilang pier, 13km west of Satun (30km from Tarutao); this one seems most geared to boat charters.

Ko Adang & Ko Lipe On Tuesday, Thursday and Saturday (November to May), a boat leaves Ko Tarutao at noon for Ko Adang (100B each way). Before it reaches Ko Adang, the boat anchors off shore and is met by long-tail boats that take passengers to either Ko Adang or Ko Lipe for an extra 30B. The following day (Wednesday, Friday and Sunday) the boat heads back to Ko Tarutao at 9am.

KO PHETRA NATIONAL MARINE PARK
อุทยานแห่งชาติหมู่เกาะเภตรา

Twenty-two islands stretching between Pak Bara and the boundaries of Ko Tarutao belong to the little-visited, 495-sq-km Ko Phetra National Marine Park. Uninhabited **Ko Khao Yai**, the largest in the group, boasts several pristine beaches suitable for swimming, snorkelling and camping. Crab-eating macaques are plentiful here as local Muslims don't hunt them. There's a castle-shaped rock formation on one shore; during low tide

boats can pass beneath a natural arch in the formation. A park unit is on nearby **Ko Lidi** (sometimes spelt 'Lide'), which features a number of picturesque and unspoiled caves, coves, cliffs and beaches. Camping facilities are available here. Between Ko Lidi and Ko Khao Yai is a channel bay known as **Ao Kam Pu**, a tranquil passage with cascading waters during certain tidal changes and some coral at shallow depths.

A new park headquarters, visitors centre and pier for Ko Phetra National Marine Park (☎ 074 781 582) recently opened on the mainland at Ban Talo Sai, about 4km south-east of Pak Bara off Route 4052. You can arrange boat transport to Ko Lidi and Ko Khao Yai here. Trees and plants on the park grounds are labelled in English, and staff are busy constructing a 300m nature trail through intact lowland evergreen forest just behind the park bungalows.

The standard entrance fee applies to the national marine park: 200B for adults, 100B for kids under 14.

Ko Bulon Leh
เกาะบุโหลนเล

This is a beautiful, laid-back island approximately 20km west of Pak Bara, and is the largest of the Ko Bulon island group. Though considerably smaller than the major islands of Ko Tarutao, Bulon Leh shares many of the same geographical characteristics, including sandy beaches and coral reefs. A fine white-sand beach runs along the east and north shores of the island, and offshore are some fine coral sites that make for good snorkelling. There are a few tiny villages in the northern part of the island near Ao Pangka. Nearby Ko Bulon Don sports a chao leh village and some nice beaches, but no accommodation so far. Ko Bulon Mai Phai farther out is uninhabited and pristine. Officially all of the Bulon group belongs to Ko Phetra National Marine Park, a fact conveniently forgotten by people living on these islands.

Boat trips around the island and to nearby snorkelling sites can be easily arranged. The best place to check is at Bulone Resort, which has good contacts with some of the long-tail operators. You can also arrange passage direct between Bulon Leh and Ko Lipe in Ko Tarutao National Marine Park for around 300B to 400B per person if you can get a group of five or six together. Four-to five-day island-hopping trips out to Ko Tarutao are also available. Rates vary depending on the specific itinerary, but range from 2500B to 3000B and include accommodation, snorkelling and fishing gear, lunch and one barbecue dinner.

Places to Stay & Eat Ko Bulon Leh has three accommodation options – all of which shut down between April and October.

Pansand Resort Bungalows with fan & bath 1000-1500B. The most upmarket option is the nicely designed Pansand, which has solid brick and thatch bungalows with deck. Prices depend on the bungalow's proximity to the beach. For more information and reservations you can also contact First Andaman Travel in Trang (☎ 075 218 035, fax 075 211 010), 82–84 Th Visetkul, opposite the Queen Hotel.

Bulone Resort Bungalows with bath 250-300B. On the north-east shore close to Pansand, this place has simple bungalows of wood and bamboo. The bungalows are well spread out, giving guests a sense of privacy. Both Pansand and Bulone enjoy nice locations overlooking the island's best beach.

Pangka Bay Resort (in Satun ☎ 074 711 982) Bungalows 300B. On the north side of the island, set near a rocky cove, this has fairly primitive bungalows. It's not really possible to go swimming around here; you'll need to hike about 15 minutes back to the main beach.

Although Ko Bulon Leh is still a sleepy place, it is getting increasingly popular, and in the high season both Pansand and Bulone resorts are often booked solid, though you can usually get a tent at Pansand. Reservations are highly recommended. You probably won't have trouble finding a vacant bungalow at Pangka Bay Resort due to its more remote location.

Bulone Resort probably has the best food of the three places, though Pansand's fare is good too.

Getting There & Away Long-tail boats to Ko Bulon Leh depart from the Pak Bara pier at 2pm and cost 100B per person one way. The trip takes 1½ to two hours each way. On the return trip, boats usually leave Bulon Leh at 9am.

Other Islands

Ko Kabeng and **Ko Baw Jet Luk**, accessible by boat and bridge from Pak Bara, are of mild interest. The beaches here are often littered and murky, so it's basically just a convenient place to stay in Pak Bara, but if you have time to kill visit the charcoal factory at Khlong La-Ngu or check out the cashew plantations. Paknam Resort on Ko Baw Jet Luk can also arrange boat trips to other, more pristine islands in the area, or if you speak enough Thai you could hire a fishing boat directly from Ko Kabeng's little harbour at the fishing village of Ban Jet Luk.

Language

Learning some Thai is indispensable for travelling in the kingdom; naturally, the more language you pick up, the closer you get to Thailand's culture and people. Foreigners who speak Thai are so rare in Thailand that it doesn't take much to impress most Thais with a few words in their own language.

Your first attempts to speak the language will probably meet with mixed success, but keep trying. When learning new words or phrases, listen closely to the way the Thais themselves use the various tones – you'll catch on quickly. Don't let laughter at your linguistic forays discourage you; this apparent amusement is an expression of appreciation. Thais are among the most supportive people in the world when it comes to foreigners learning their language.

Travellers, both young and old, are particularly urged to make the effort to meet Thai college and university students. Thai students are, by and large, eager to meet visitors from other countries. They will often know some English, so communication is not as difficult as it may be with shop owners, civil servants etc, plus they are generally willing to teach you useful Thai words and phrases.

For a handy pocket-size guide to Thai, get a copy of Lonely Planet's excellent *Thai phrasebook*; it contains a section on basic grammar and a broad selection of useful words and phrases for travel in Thailand.

Many people have reported modest success with *Robertson's Practical English-Thai Dictionary* (Charles E Tuttle Co, Tokyo), which has a phonetic guide to pronunciation with tones and is compact in size. If you have difficulty finding it, write to the publisher at 2-6 Suido 1-chome, Bunkyo-ku, Tokyo, Japan.

More serious learners of the language should get Mary Haas' *Thai-English Student's Dictionary* (Stanford University Press, Stanford, California) and George

McFarland's *Thai-English Dictionary* (also Stanford University Press) – the cream of the crop. Both of these require that you know the Thai script. The US State Department's *Thai Reference Grammar* by RB Noss (Foreign Service Institute, Washington, DC, 1964) is good for an in-depth look at Thai syntax.

Other learning texts worth seeking out include:

AUA Language Center Thai Course: Reading & Writing (two volumes) – AUA Language Center (Bangkok), 1979

AUA Language Center Thai Course (three volumes) – AUA Language Center (Bangkok), 1969

Foundations of Thai (two volumes) – by EM Anthony, University of Michigan Press, 1973

A Programmed Course in Reading Thai Syllables – by EM Anthony, University of Hawaii, 1979

Teaching Grammar of Thai – by William Kuo, University of California at Berkeley, 1982

Thai Basic Reader – by Gething & Bilmes, University of Hawaii, 1977

Thai Cultural Reader (two volumes) – by RB Jones, Cornell University, 1969

Thai Reader – by Mary Haas, American Council of Learned Societies, Program in Oriental Languages, 1954

The Thai System of Writing – by Mary Haas, American Council of Learned Societies, Program in Oriental Languages, 1954

A Workbook for Writing Thai – by William Kuo, University of California at Berkeley, 1979

An interactive CD-ROM called *Learning Thai Script* (Allen & Unwin, 1997) is also an excellent resource for teaching yourself to read and write the Thai script.

For information on language courses, see Language under Courses in the Facts for the Visitor chapter.

Dialects

Thailand's official language is Thai as spoken and written in Central Thailand. This dialect has successfully become the lingua franca of all Thai and non-Thai ethnic groups in the kingdom. Of course, native Thai is spoken with differing tonal accents and with slightly differing vocabularies as you move from one part of the country to the next, especially in a north to south direction. But it is the central Thai dialect that is most widely understood.

All Thai dialects are members of the Thai half of the Thai-Kadai family of languages and are closely related to languages spoken in Laos (Lao, northern Thai, Thai Lü), northern Myanmar (Shan, northern Thai), north-western Vietnam (Nung, Tho), Assam (Ahom) and pockets of south China (Zhuang, Thai Lü). Modern Thai linguists recognise four basic dialects within Thailand: central Thai (spoken as a first dialect through Central Thailand and throughout the country as a second dialect); northern-Thai (spoken from Tak Province north to the Myanmar border); north-eastern Thai (north-eastern provinces towards the Lao and Cambodian borders); and southern Thai (from Chumphon Province south to the Malaysian border). Each of these can be further divided into subdialects; north-eastern Thai, for example, has nine regional variations easily distinguished by those who know Thai well. There are also a number of Thai minority dialects such as those spoken by the Phu Thai, Thai Dam, Thai Daeng, Phu Noi, Phuan and other tribal Thai groups, most of whom reside in the North and North-East.

Vocabulary Differences

Like most languages, Thai distinguishes between 'vulgar' and 'polite' vocabulary, so that *thaan*, for example, is a more polite everyday word for 'eat' than *kin*, and *sĭi-sà* for 'head' is more polite than *hŭa*. When given a choice, foreigners are better off learning and using the polite terms since these are less likely to lead to unconscious offence.

A special set of words, collectively called *kham raachaasàp* (royal vocabulary), is set aside for use with Thai royalty within the semantic fields of kinship, body parts, physical and mental actions, clothing and housing. For example, in everyday language Thais use the word *kin* or *thaan* for 'eat', while with reference to the royal family they say *sà wŏey*. For the most part these terms are used only when speaking to or referring to the king, queen and their children, hence as a foreigner you will have little need to learn them.

Script

The Thai script, a fairly recent development in comparison with the spoken language, consists of 44 consonants (but only 21 separate sounds) and 48 vowel and diphthong possibilities (32 separate signs). Experts disagree as to the exact origins of the script, but it was apparently developed around 800 years ago using Mon and possibly Khmer models, both of which were in turn inspired by south Indian scripts. Like these languages, written Thai proceeds from left to right, though vowel signs may be written before, after, above, below, *or* 'around' (before, after *and* above) consonants, depending on the sign.

Though learning the alphabet is not difficult, the writing system itself is fairly complex, so unless you are planning a lengthy stay in Thailand it should perhaps be foregone in favour of actually learning to speak the language. The names of major places included in this book are given in both Thai and roman script, so that you can at least 'read' the names of destinations at a pinch, or point to them if necessary.

Tones & Pronunciation

In Thai the meaning of a single syllable may be altered by means of different tones – in standard central Thai there are five: low tone, level or mid tone, falling tone, high tone and rising tone. For example, depending on the tone, the syllable *mai* can mean 'new', 'burn', 'wood', 'not?' or 'not'; ponder the phrase *mái mài mâi mâi mǎi* (New wood doesn't burn, does it?) and you begin to appreciate the importance of tones in spoken Thai. This makes it a rather tricky language to learn at first, especially for those of us unaccustomed to the concept of tones. Even when we 'know' what the correct tone in Thai should be, our tendency to denote emotion, verbal stress, the interrogative etc, through tone modulation often interferes with producing the correct tone. Therefore the first rule in learning to speak Thai is to divorce emotions from your speech, at least until you have learned the Thai way to express them without changing essential tone value.

The following is visual representation in chart form to show relative tone values:

Thai Tones

Low	Mid	Falling	High	Rising

The following is a brief attempt to explain the tones. The only way to really understand the differences is by listening to a native or fluent non-native speaker. The range of all five tones is relative to each speaker's vocal range so there is no fixed 'pitch' intrinsic to the language.

1 The low tone is 'flat' like the mid tone, but pronounced at the relative *bottom* of one's vocal range. It is low, level and with no inflection, eg, *bàat* (baht – the Thai currency).

2 The level or mid tone is pronounced 'flat', at the relative middle of the speaker's vocal range, eg, *dii* (good); no tone mark used.

3 The falling tone is pronounced as if you were emphasising a word, or calling someone's name from afar, eg, *mâi* (no/not).

4 The high tone is usually the most difficult for Westerners. It is pronounced near the relative top of the vocal range, as level as possible, eg, *máa* (horse).

5 The rising tone sounds like the inflection used by English speakers to imply a question – 'Yes?', eg, *săam* (three).

Words in Thai that appear to have more than one syllable are usually compounds made up of two or more word units, each with its own tone. They may be words taken directly from Sanskrit, Pali or English, in which case each syllable must still have its own tone.

The following is a guide to the phonetic system that has been used for the words and phrases included in this chapter (and throughout the rest of the book when transcribing directly from Thai). It's based on the Royal Thai General System (RTGS), except that it distinguishes: between short and long vowels (eg, 'i' and 'ii'; 'a' and 'aa'; 'e' and 'eh'; 'o' and 'oh'); between 'o' and 'aw' (both would be 'o' in the RTGS); between 'u' and 'eu' (both would be 'u' in the RTGS); and between 'ch' and 'j' (both would be 'ch' in the RTGS).

Consonants

The majority of consonants correspond closely to their English counterparts. Here are a few exceptions:

k	as the 'k' in 'skin'; similar to 'g' in 'good', but unaspirated (no accompanying puff of air) and unvoiced
p	as the 'p' in 'stopper', unvoiced and unaspirated (not like the 'p' in 'put'); actually sounds closer to an English 'b', its voiced equivalent
t	as the 't' in 'forty', unaspirated; similar to 'd' but unvoiced
kh	as the 'k' in 'kite'
ph	as the 'p' in 'put' (never as the 'ph' in 'phone')
th	as the 't' in 'tea'
ng	as the 'nging' in 'singing'; can occur as an initial consonant (practise by saying 'singing' without the 'si')
r	similar to the 'r' in 'run' but flapped (tongue touches palate); in everyday speech often pronounced like 'l'

Vowels

i	as the 'i' in 'it'
ii	as the 'ee' in 'feet'
ai	as the 'i' in 'pipe'
aa	as the 'a' in 'father'
a	half as long as **aa**, as the 'a' in 'about'

ae	as the 'a' in 'bat' or 'tab'
e	as the 'e' in 'hen'
eh	as the 'a' in 'hate'
oe	as the 'er' in 'fern' (without the 'r' sound)
u	as the 'u' in 'flute'
uu	as the 'oo' in 'food', longer than **u**
eu	as the 'u' in 'fur'
ao	as the 'ow' in 'now'
aw	as the 'aw' in 'jaw' or 'prawn'
o	as the 'o' in 'bone'
oh	as the 'o' in 'toe'
eua	a combination of **eu** and **a**
ia	as 'ee-ya', or as the 'ie' in French *rien*
ua	as the 'ou' in 'tour'
uay	sounds like 'oo-way'
iu	as the 'ew' in 'yew'
iaw	as the 'io' in 'Rio' or Italian *mio*
aew	like a Cockney pronunciation of the 'ow' in 'now'
ehw	as 'air-ooh'
awy	as the 'oi' in 'coin'

Here are a few extra hints to help you with the alphabetic tangle:

- **ph** is never pronounced as the 'ph' in phone but like the 'p' in 'pound' (the 'h' is added to distinguish this consonant sound from the Thai 'p' which is closer to the English 'b'). This can be seen written as **p, ph**, and even **bh**.

- to some people, the Thai **k** sounds closer to the English 'g' than the English 'k'. The standard RTGS chooses to use 'k' to represent this sound to emphasise that it is not a 'voiced' sound, but more a glottal stop.

- there is no 'v' sound in Thai. *Sukhumvit* is pronounced Sukhumwit and *Viang* is really Wiang.

- **l** and **r** are always pronounced as an 'n' when word-final, eg, *Satul* is pronounced as Satun, *Wihar* as Wihan. The exception to this is when 'er' or 'ur' are used to indicate the sound 'oe', as in 'ampher' (*amphoe*). In the same way 'or' is sometimes used for the sound 'aw', as in 'Porn' (*phawn*).

- **l** and **r** are often interchanged in speech and this shows up in some transliterations. For example, *naliga* (clock) may appear as 'nariga' and *râat nâa* (a type of noodle dish) might be rendered 'laat naa' or 'lat na'.

- **u** is often used to represent the short 'a' sound, as in *tam* or *nam*, which may appear as 'tum' and 'num'. It is also used to represent the 'eu' sound, as when *beung* (swamp) is spelt 'bung'.

- phonetically, all Thai words end in a vowel (**a, e, i, o, u**), semi-vowel (**w, y**), nasal (**m, n, ng**) or one of three stops (**p, t, k**). That's it. Words transcribed with 'ch', 'j', 's' or 'd' endings – like Panich, Raj, Chuanpis and Had – should be pronounced as if they end in 't', as in Panit, Rat, Chuanpit and Hat. Likewise 'g' becomes 'k' (Ralug is actually Raluk) and 'b' becomes 'p' (Thab becomes Thap).

- the 'r' in *sri* is always silent, so the word should be pronounced 'sii' (extended 'i' sound, too). Hence 'Sri Racha' really comes out 'Si Racha'.

Transliteration

Writing Thai in roman script is a perennial problem – no wholly satisfactory system has yet been devised to assure both consistency and readability. The Thai government uses the Royal Thai General System of transcription for official government documents in English and for most highway signs. However, local variations crop up on hotel signs, city street signs, menus and so on in such a way that visitors often become confused. Add to this the fact that even the government system has its flaws. For example, 'o' is used for two very different sounds ('o' and the 'aw' in the Vowels section earlier), as is 'u' (for 'u' and 'eu' earlier). Likewise for 'ch', which is used to represent two different consonant sounds ('ch' and 'j'). The government transcription system also does not distinguish between short and long vowel sounds, which affect the tonal value of every word.

To top it off, many Thai words (especially names of people and place) have Sanskrit and Pali spellings but their actual pronunciation bears little relation to that spelling if Romanised strictly according to the original

Sanskrit/Pali. Thus Nakhon Si Thammarat, if transliterated literally, becomes 'Nagara Sri Dhammaraja'. If you tried to pronounce it using this Pali transcription, very few Thais would be able to understand you.

Generally, names in this book follow the most common practice or, in the case of hotels for example, simply copy their roman script name, no matter what devious process was used in its transliteration! When this transliteration is markedly different from actual pronunciation, the pronunciation is included (according to the system outlined in this section) in parentheses after the transliteration. Where no Roman model was available, names have been transliterated phonetically, directly from Thai. Of course, this will only be helpful to readers who bother to acquaint themselves with the language – and it's surprising how many people manage to stay for great lengths of time in Thailand without learning a word of Thai.

Problems often arise when a name is transliterated differently, even at the same location. 'Thawi', for example, can be seen as Tavi, Thawee, Thavi, Tavee or various other versions. Outside the International Phonetic Alphabet, there is no 'proper' way to transliterate Thai – only wrong ways. The Thais themselves are incredibly inconsistent in this matter, often using English letters that have no equivalent sound in Thai: Faisal for Phaisan, Bhumibol for Phumiphon, Vanich for Wanit, Vibhavadi for Wiphawadi. Sometimes they even mix literal Sanskrit transcription with Thai pronunciation, as in King Bhumibol (which is pronounced Phumiphon and if transliterated according to the Sanskrit would be Bhumibala).

Here are a few words that are often spelt in a way that encourages native English speakers to mispronounce them:

Common Spelling	Pronunciation	Meaning
bung	beung	pond or swamp
ko or *koh*	kàw	island
muang	meuang	city
nakhon or *nakorn*	nákhawn	large city

raja	usually râatchá if at the beginning of a word, râat at the end of a word	royal

Greetings & Civilities

When being polite, the speaker ends his or her sentence with *khráp* (for men) or *khâ* (for women). It is the gender of the speaker that is being expressed here; it is also the common way to answer 'yes' to a question or show agreement.

Greetings/Hello.
  sàwàt-dii   สวัสดี
   (khráp/khâ)   (ครับ/ค่ะ)
How are you?
  sàbai dii rěu?   สบายดีหรือ?
I'm fine.
  sàbai dii   สบายดี
Thank you.
  khàwp khun   ขอบคุณ
Excuse me.
  khǎw thôht   ขอโทษ

I/me
  phǒm   ผม
  (for men)
  dì-chǎn   ดิฉัน
  (for women)
you
  khun   คุณ
  (for peers)
  thâan   ท่าน
  (for elders and
  people in authority)

What's your name?
  khun chêu àrai? คุณชื่ออะไร?
My name is ...
  phǒm chêu ...   ผมชื่อ...
  (men)
  dì-chǎn chêu ... ดิฉันชื่อ...
  (women)

Do you have ...?
  mii ... măi?/ มี...ไหม/
  ... mii măi? ...มีไหม?
No.
  mâi châi ไม่ใช่
No?
  măi?/châi măi? ไหม?/ใช่ไหม?
(I) like ...
  châwp ... ชอบ...
(I) don't like ...
  mâi châwp ... ไม่ชอบ...
(I) would like ...
(+ verb)
  yàak jà ... อยากจะ...
(I) would like ...
(+ noun)
  yàak dâi ... อยากได้...
When?
  mêua-rai? เมื่อไร?
It doesn't matter.
  mâi pen rai ไม่เป็นไร
What is this?
  nîi àrai? นี่อะไร?
go
  pai ไป
come
  maa มา

Language Difficulties

I understand.
  khâo jai เข้าใจ
I don't understand.
  mâi khâo jai ไม่เข้าใจ
Do you understand?
  khâo jai măi? เข้าใจไหม?
A little.
  nít nàwy นิดหน่อย
What do you call
this in Thai?
  nîi phaasăa thai นี่ภาษาไทย
  rîak wâa àrai? เรียกว่าอะไร?

Getting Around

I'd like to go ...
  yàak jà pai ... อยากจะไป...
Where is (the) ...?
  ... yùu thîi năi? ...อยู่ที่ไหน?
airport
  sànăam bin สนามบิน
bus station
  sàthăanii khŏn sòng/ สถานีขนส่ง/
  baw khăw săw บขส
bus stop
  pâi rót meh ป้ายรถเมล์
train station
  sàthăanii rót fai สถานีรถไฟ
taxi stand
  thîi jàwt rót ที่จอดรถแท็กซี่
  tháek-sîi
I'd like a ticket.
  yàak séu tŭa อยากซื้อตั๋ว
What time will the ...
leave?
  ... jà àwk kìi ...จะออกกี่
  mohng ? โมง?
bus
  rót meh/rót bát รถเมล์/รถบัส
car
  rót yon รถยนต์
motorcycle
  rót maw-toe-sai รถมอเตอร์ไซค์
train
  rót fai รถไฟ
straight ahead
  trong pai ตรงไป
left
  sái ซ้าย
right
  khwăa ขวา
far/not far/near
  klai/mâi klai/ ไกล/ไม่ไกล/
  klâi ใกล้

Accommodation

hotel
  rohng raem   โรงแรม

guesthouse
  kèt háo   เกสต์เฮาส์

Do you have a
room available?
  mii hâwng wâang   มีห้องว่าง
    măi?   ไหม?

How much is it
per night?
  kheun-lá thâo rai?   คืนละเท่าไร?

bathroom
  hâwng náam   ห้องน้ำ

toilet
  hâwng sûam   ห้องส้วม

room
  hâwng   ห้อง

hot
  ráwn   ร้อน

cold
  yen   เย็น

bath/shower
  àap náam   อาบน้ำ

towel
  phâa chét tua   ผ้าเช็ดตัว

Around Town

Can (I/we) change money here?
  lâek ngoen thîi níi dâi măi?

แลกเงินที่นี้ได้ไหม?

What time does it open?
  ráan pòet mêua rai?

ร้านเปิดเมื่อไร?

What time does it close?
  ráan pìt mêua rai?

ร้านปิดเมื่อไร?

bank
  thánaakhaan   ธนาคาร

beach
  hàat   หาด

market
  tàlàat   ตลาด

museum
  phíphítháphan   พิพิธภัณฑ์

post office
  praisànii   ไปรษณีย์

restaurant
  ráan aahăan   ร้านอาหาร

tourist office
  sămnák ngaan   สำนักงาน
  thâwng thîaw   ท่องเที่ยว

Shopping

How much?
  thâo raí?   เท่าไร?

too expensive
  phaeng pai   แพงไป

How much is this?
  níi thâo rai?/   นี่เท่าไร?/
  kìi bàat?   กี่บาท?

cheap, inexpensive
  thùuk   ถูก

Geographical features

beach
  hàat sai   หาดทราย

countryside
  chonnábòt   ชนบท

island
  kàw   เกาะ

lake
  tháleh sàap   ทะเลสาบ

map
  phăen thîi   แผนที่

mountain/hill
  phuu khăo/khăo   ภูเขา/เขา

paddy (field)
  (thûng) naa   (ทุ่ง) นา

Emergencies

I need a doctor.	
tâwng-kaan măw	ต้องการหมอ
Help!	
chûay dûay!	ช่วยด้วย
Stop!	
yùt!	หยุด
Go away!	
pai sí!	ไปซิ
I'm lost.	
chăn lŏng thaang	ฉันหลงทาง

pond	
năwng/beung	หนอง/บึง
river	
mâe náam	แม่น้ำ
sea	
tháleh	ทะเล
town	
meuang	เมือง
track	
thaang	ทาง
village	
(mùu) bâan	(หมู่) บ้าน
waterfall	
náam tòk	น้ำตก

Health

chemist/pharmacy	
ráan khăi yaa	ร้านขายยา
dentist	
măw fan	หมอฟัน
doctor	
măw	หมอ
hospital	
rohng pháyaabaan	โรงพยาบาล
aspirin (pain killer)	
yaa kâe pùat	ยาแก้ปวด
mosquito repellent	
yaa kan yung	ยากันยุง

Please call a doctor.
> *kàrúnaa rîak măw nàwy*
> กรุณาเรียกหมอหน่อย

I'm allergic to penicillin.
> *pháe yaa phenísinlin*
> แพ้ยาเพนิซิลลิน

I'm pregnant.
> *tâng khan láew/mii tháwng*
> ตั้งครรภ์แล้ว/มีท้อง

It hurts here.
> *jèp trong níi*
> เจ็บตรงนี้

I feel nauseous.
> *rúusèuk khlêun sâi*
> รู้สึกคลื่นไส้

I keep vomiting.
> *aajian bàwy bàwy*
> อาเจียนบ่อยๆ

I feel faint.
> *rúusèuk jà pen lom*
> รู้สึกจะเป็นลม

I have diarrhoea.
> *tháwng rûang*
> ท้องร่วง

I have a fever.
> *pen khâi*
> เป็นไข้

I have a stomachache.
> *pùat tháwng*
> ปวดท้อง

I have a headache.
> *pùat hŭa*
> ปวดหัว

I have a toothache.
> *pùat fan*
> ปวดฟัน

Time, Days & Numbers

What's the time?

kìi mohng láew? กี่โมงแล้ว?

today

wan níi วันนี้

tomorrow

phrûng níi พรุ่งนี้

yesterday

mêua waan เมื่อวาน

Sunday

wan aathít วันอาทิตย์

Monday

wan jan วันจันทร์

Tuesday

wan angkhaan วันอังคาร

Wednesday

wan phút วันพุธ

Thursday

wan phréuhàt วันพฤหัสฯ

Friday

wan sùk วันศุกร์

Saturday

wan săo วันเสาร์

0	*săun*	ศูนย์
1	*nèung*	หนึ่ง
2	*săwng*	สอง
3	*săam*	สาม
4	*sìi*	สี่
5	*hâa*	ห้า
6	*hòk*	หก
7	*jèt*	เจ็ด
8	*pàet*	แปด
9	*kâo*	เก้า
10	*sìp*	สิบ

11	*sìp-èt*	สิบเอ็ด
12	*sìp-săwng*	สิบสอง
13	*sìp-săam*	สิบสาม
20	*yîi-sìp*	ยี่สิบ
21	*yîi-sìp-èt*	ยี่สิบเอ็ด
22	*yîi-sìp-săwng*	ยี่สิบสอง
30	*săam-sìp*	สามสิบ
40	*sìi-sìp*	สี่สิบ
50	*hâa-sìp*	ห้าสิบ
100	*ráwy*	ร้อย
200	*săwng ráwy*	สองร้อย
300	*săam ráwy*	สามร้อย
1000	*phan*	พัน
10,000	*mèun*	หมื่น
100,000	*săen*	แสน
one million	*láan*	ล้าน
one billion	*phan láan*	พันล้าน

FOOD
Ordering

(For 'I' men use *phŏm*; women use *dì-chăn*)

I eat only vegetarian food.

phŏm/dì-chăn kin jeh
ผม/ดิฉันกินเจ

I can't eat pork.

phŏm/dì-chăn mâi kin mŭu
ผม/ดิฉันไม่กินหมู

I can't eat beef.

phŏm/dì-chăn mâi kin néua
ผม/ดิฉันไม่กินเนื้อ

(I) don't like it hot & spicy.

mâi châwp phèt
ไม่ชอบเผ็ด

(I) like it hot & spicy.

châwp phèt
ชอบเผ็ด

(I) can eat Thai food.

kin aahăan thai dâi

กินอาหารไทยได้

What do you have that's special?

mii a-rai phí-sèt?

มีอะไรพิเศษ?

I didn't order this.

nîi phŏm/dì-chăn mâi dâi sàng

นี่ผม/ดิฉันไม่ได้สั่ง

Do you have ...?

mii ... măi?

มี ... ไหม?

Food Glossary

The following list gives standard dishes in Thai script with a transliterated pronunciation guide, using the system outlined at the beginning of this chapter.

Soups *(súp)* ซุป

mild soup with vegetables & pork

kaeng jèut

แกงจืด

mild soup with vegetables, pork & bean curd

kaeng jèut tâo-hûu

แกงจืดเต้าหู้

soup with chicken, galanga root & coconut

tôm khàa kài

ต้มข่าไก่

prawn & lemon grass soup with mushrooms

tôm yam kûng

ต้มยำกุ้ง

fish-ball soup

kaeng jèut lûuk chín

แกงจืดลูกชิ้น

rice soup with fish/chicken/shrimp

khâo tôm plaa/kài/kûng

ข้าวต้มปลา/ไก่/กุ้ง

Egg *(khài)* ไข่

hard-boiled egg

khài tôm

ไข่ต้ม

fried egg

khài dao

ไข่ดาว

plain omelette

khài jiaw

ไข่เจียว

omelette with vegetables & pork

khài yát sâi

ไข่ยัดไส้

scrambled egg

khài kuan

ไข่กวน

Noodles *(kŭaytĭaw/ bà-mìi)* ก๋วยเตี๋ยว/ บะหมี่

rice noodle soup with vegetables & meat

kŭaytĭaw náam

ก๋วยเตี๋ยวน้ำ

rice noodles with vegetables & meat

kŭaytĭaw hâeng

ก๋วยเตี๋ยวแห้ง

rice noodles with gravy

râat nâa

ราดหน้า

thin rice noodles fried with tofu, vegetables egg & peanuts

phàt thai

ผัดไทย

fried noodles with soy sauce

phàt sii-íu

ผัดซีอิ๊ว

wheat noodles in broth with vegetables & meat

bà-mìi náam

บะหมี่น้ำ

wheat noodles with vegetables & meat
 bà-mìi hâeng
 บะหมี่แห้ง

Rice *(khâo)* ข้าว

fried rice with pork/chicken/shrimp
 khâo phàt mǔu/kài/kûng
 ข้าวผัดหมู/ไก่/กุ้ง

boned, sliced Hainan-style chicken with marinated rice
 khâo man kài
 ข้าวมันไก่

chicken with sauce over rice
 khâo nâa kài
 ข้าวหน้าไก่

roast duck over rice
 khâo nâa pèt
 ข้าวหน้าเป็ด

'red' pork with rice
 khâo mǔu daeng
 ข้าวหมูแดง

curry over rice
 khâo kaeng
 ข้าวแกง

Curries *(kaeng)* แกง

hot Thai curry with chicken/beef/ pork
 kaeng phèt kài/néua/mǔu
 แกงเผ็ดไก่/เนื้อ/หมู

rich & spicy, Muslim-style curry with chicken/beef & potatoes
 kaeng mátsàmàn kài/néua
 แกงมัสมั่นไก่/เนื้อ

mild, Indian-style curry with chicken
 kaeng karìi kài
 แกงกะหรี่ไก่

hot & sour, fish & vegetable ragout
 kaeng sôm
 แกงส้ม

'green' curry with fish/chicken/beef
 kaeng khǐaw-wǎan plaa/kài/néua
 แกงเขียวหวานปลา/ไก่/เนื้อ

savoury curry with chicken/beef
 phánaeng kài/néua
 พะแนงไก่/เนื้อ

chicken curry with bamboo shoots
 kaeng kài nàw mái
 แกงไก่หน่อไม้

catfish curry
 kaeng plaa dùk
 แกงปลาดุก

Seafood *(aahǎan tháleh)* อาหารทะเล

steamed crab
 puu nêung
 ปูนึ่ง

steamed crab claws
 kâam puu nêung
 ก้ามปูนึ่ง

shark-fin soup
 hǔu chalǎam
 หูฉลาม

crisp-fried fish
 plaa thâwt
 ปลาทอด

fried prawns
 kûng thâwt
 กุ้งทอด

batter-fried prawns
 kûng chúp pâeng thâwt
 กุ้งชุบแป้งทอด

grilled prawns
 kûng phǎo
 กุ้งเผา

steamed fish
plaa nêung
ปลานี่ง

grilled fish
plaa phǎo
ปลาเผา

whole fish cooked in ginger,
onions & soy sauce
plaa jǐan
ปลาเจี่ยน

sweet & sour fish
plaa prîaw wǎan
ปลาเปรี้ยวหวาน

cellophane noodles baked with crab
puu òp wún-sên
ปูอบวุ้นเส้น

spicy fried squid
plaa mèuk phàt phèt
ปลาหมึกผัดเผ็ด

roast squid
plaa mèuk yâang
ปลาหมึกย่าง

oysters fried in egg batter
hǎwy thâwt
หอยทอด

squid
plaa mèuk
ปลาหมึก

shrimp
kûng
กุ้ง

fish
plaa
ปลา

saltwater eel
plaa lòt
ปลาหลด

spiny lobster
kûng mangkawn
กุ้งมังกร

green mussel
hǎwy malaeng phûu
หอยแมลงภู่

scallop
hǎwy phát
หอยพัด

oyster
hǎwy naang rom
หอยนางรม

Miscellaneous

stir-fried mixed vegetables
phàt phàk ruam
ผัดผักรวม

spring rolls
pàw-pía
เปาะเปี๊ยะ

beef in oyster sauce
néua phàt náam-man hǎwy
เนื้อผัดน้ำมันหอย

duck soup
pèt tǔn
เป็ดตุ๋น

roast duck
pèt yâang
เป็ดย่าง

fried chicken
kài thâwt
ไก่ทอด

chicken fried in holy basil
kài phàt bai kà-phrao
ไก่ผัดใบกะเพรา

grilled chicken
kài yâang
ไก่ย่าง

chicken fried with chillies
kài phàt phrík
ไก่ผัดพริก

chicken fried with cashews
kài phàt mét má-mûang
ไก่ผัดเม็ดมะม่วง

morning-glory vine fried in garlic, chilli & bean sauce
phàk bûng fai daeng
ผักบุ้งไฟแดง

skewers of barbecued meat (satay)
sà-té
สะเต๊ะ

spicy green papaya salad (North-Eastern speciality)
sôm-tam
ส้มตำ

noodles with fish curry
khanŏm jiin náam yaa
ขนมจีนน้ำยา

prawns fried with chillies
kûng phàt phrík phăo
กุ้งผัดพริกเผา

chicken fried with ginger
kài phàt khĭng
ไก่ผัดขิง

fried wonton
kíaw kràwp
เกี๊ยวกรอบ

cellophane noodle salad
yam wún sên
ยำวุ้นเส้น

spicy chicken or beef salad
lâap kài/néua
ลาบไก่/เนื้อ

hot & sour, grilled beef salad
yam néua
ยำเนื้อ

fried chicken with bean sprouts
kài phàt thùa ngâwk
ไก่ผัดถั่วงอก

fried fish cakes with cucumber sauce
thâwt man plaa
ทอดมันปลา

Southern Thailand Specialities

flat bread (roti)
roh-tii
โรตี

roti with bananas
roh-tii klûay
โรตีกล้วย

roti with curry dip
roh-tii kaeng
โรตีแกง

strong Hokkien-style coffee
koh-píi
โกปี้

chicken briyani
khâo mòk kài
ข้าวหมกไก่

rice salad (with toasted coconut, dried shrimp, lime leaves)
khâo yam
ข้าวยำ

southern fish curry (very hot)
kaeng tai plaa
แกงไตปลา

Vegetables *(phàk)* ผัก

bitter melon
márá-jiin
มะระจีน

brinjal (round eggplant)
mákhěua pràw
มะเขือเปราะ

cabbage
kà-làm plii
กะหล่ำปลี

cauliflower
dàwk kà-làm
ดอกกะหล่ำ

Chinese radish
hǔa phàk kàat
หัวผักกาด

corn
khâo phôht
ข้าวโพด

cucumber
taeng kwaa
แตงกวา

eggplant
mákhěua
มะเขือ

garlic
kràthiam
กระเทียม

lettuce
phàk kàat
ผักกาด

long bean
thùa fàk yao
ถั่วฝักยาว

okra ('ladyfingers')
krà-jíap
กระเจี๊ยบ

onion (bulb)
hǔa hǎwm
หัวหอม

onion (green, 'scallions')
tôn hǎwm
ต้นหอม

peanuts (ground nuts)
tùa lísǒng
ถั่วลิสง

potato
man faràng
มันฝรั่ง

pumpkin
fák thawng
ฟักทอง

taro
phèuak
เผือก

tomato
mákhěua thêt
มะเขือเทศ

Fruit *(phǒn-lá-mái)* ผลไม้
banana – over 20 varieties (year-round)
klûay
กล้วย

coconut (year-round)
máphráo
มะพร้าว

custard-apple
náwy nàa
น้อยหน่า

durian
thúrian
ทุเรียน

guava (year-round)
fa-ràng
ฝรั่ง

jackfruit
kha-nǔn
ขนุน

lime (year-round)
má-nao
มะนาว

longan – 'dragon's eyes'; similar to
rambutan (July to October)
lam yai
ลำไย

mandarin orange (year-round)
sôm
ส้ม

mango – several varieties & seasons
má-mûang
มะม่วง

mangosteen
mang-khút
มังคุด

papaya (year-round)
málákaw
มะละกอ

pineapple (year-round)
sàp-pàrót
สับปะรด

pomelo
sôm oh
ส้มโอ

rambeh – small, reddish-brown and apricot-
like (April to May)
máfai
มะไฟ

rambutan
ngáw
เงาะ

rose-apple – apple-like texture; very fragrant
(April to July)
chom-phûu
ชมพู่

sapodilla – small and oval; sweet but
pungent (July to September)
lámút
ละมุด

tamarind – sweet and tart varieties
mákhăam
มะขาม

watermelon (year-round)
taeng moh
แตงโม

Sweets *(khăwng wăan)*   ของหวาน
Thai custard
săngkha-yăa
สังขยา

coconut custard
săngkha-yăa má-phráo
สังขยามะพร้าว

sweet shredded egg yolk
făwy thawng
ฝอยทอง

egg custard
mâw kaeng
หม้อแกง

banana in coconut milk
klûay bùat chii
กล้วยบวชชี

fried, Indian-style banana
klûay khàek
กล้วยแขก

sweet palm kernels
lûuk taan chêuam
ลูกตาลเชื่อม

Thai jelly with coconut cream
ta-kôh
ตะโก้

sticky rice with coconut cream
khâo nĭaw daeng
ข้าวเหนียวแดง

sticky rice in coconut cream with ripe mango
khâo nĭaw má-mûang
ข้าวเหนียวมะม่วง

DRINKS

Beverages *(khrêuang dèum)* เครื่องดื่ม

plain water
náam plào
น้ำเปล่า

hot water
náam ráwn
น้ำร้อน

boiled water
náam tôm
น้ำต้ม

bottled drinking water
náam khùat
น้ำขวด

cold water
náam yen
น้ำเย็น

ice
náam khǎeng
น้ำแข็ง

soda water
náam soh-daa
น้ำโซดา

orange soda
náam sôm
น้ำส้ม

iced lime juice with sugar
(usually with salt too)
náam mánao
น้ำมะนาว

no salt (command)
mâi sài kleua
ไม่ใส่เกลือ

plain milk
nom jèut
นมจืด

Chinese tea
chaa jiin
ชาจีน

weak Chinese tea
náam chaa
น้ำชา

iced Thai tea with milk & sugar
chaa yen
ชาเย็น

iced Thai tea with sugar only
chaa dam yen
ชาดำเย็น

no sugar (command)
mâi sài náam-taan
ไม่ใส่น้ำตาล

hot Thai tea with sugar
chaa dam ráwn
ชาดำร้อน

hot Thai tea with milk & sugar
chaa ráwn
ชาร้อน

hot coffee with milk & sugar
kaafae ráwn
กาแฟร้อน

traditional filtered coffee
with milk & sugar
kaafae thǔng (*ko-píi* in the South)
กาแฟถุง(โกพี้)

iced coffee with sugar, no milk
oh-líang
โอเลี้ยง

Ovaltine
oh-wantin
โอวันติน

bottle
khùat
ขวด

glass
kâew
แก้ว

Glossary

aahăan – food
aahăan jeh – vegetarian food
aahăan pàa – 'jungle food'; usually referring to dishes made with wild game
aahăan pàktâi – Southern Thai food
aahăan taam sàng – 'food according to order'; a type of restaurant where cooks will attempt to prepare any Thai dish you name, including one-plate rice and noodle dishes as well as more complex multi-dish meals
amphoe – also *amphur;* district, the next subdivision down from province
amphoe meuang – provincial capital
ao – bay or gulf

bâan – also *ban;* house or village
bhikkhuni – *(phík-khù)* Pali term for Buddhist monk
bòt – central sanctuary or chapel in a Thai temple; from the Pali *uposatha*

chaa – tea
chao leh – also *chao náam;* sea gypsies
chedi – *(jeh dii) stupa;* monument erected to house a Buddha relic

faràng – foreigner of European descent

hat – also *hàat;* beach, short for *chaihaat*
hâwng phát lom – room with fan
hâwng thamádaa – ordinary room, without fan
hăw trai – a *Tripitaka* (Buddhist scripture) hall
hong – *(hâwng)* room; in Southern Thailand this may also refer to the island caves semi-submerged in the sea

isan – also *isăan;* general term for North-Eastern Thailand; from the Sanksrit name for the medieval kingdom Isana, which encompassed parts of Cambodia and North-Eastern Thailand

jangwàt – province
jataka – stories of the Buddha's previous lives

jiin – Chinese
jók – broken-rice soup

kâew – also keo; crystal, jewel, glass or gem
kàthoey – transvestites and transsexuals; often translated 'lady-boy' in Thai English
kaw-lae – traditional fishing boats of Southern Thailand
khăo – hill or mountain
khâo tôm – boiled rice soup
khlong – *(khlawng)* canal
Khmer – people of a civilisation that flourished between 800AD and 1370AD, remarkable for its architecture
khŏhn – masked dance-drama based on stories from the *Ramakian*
khun – honorific used before first name
ko – *(kàw)* also *koh;* island
ko-píi – southern-style filtered coffee, particularly famous in Trang Province on the Southern Andaman Coast
kúay hâeng – Chinese-style work shirt
kuti – a monk's hut or living quarters

lăem – cape (in the geographical sense)
lákhon – classical Thai dance-drama
lí-keh – Thai folk dance-drama
longyi – Burmese sarong also worn particularly in Ranong

mâe chii – Thai Buddhist nun
mâe náam – river; literally, water mother
maha that – common name for temples that contain Buddha relics; from the Sanskrit-Pali *mahadhatu;* literally, great element
mánohraa – Southern Thailand's most popular traditional dance-drama
masjid – *(mátsàyít)* mosque
mâw hâwn – Thai work shirt
máw-mìi – tie-dyed cotton or silk
meuang/muang – *(meu-ang)* city
muay thai – Thai boxing
muu – short for *mùu bâan;* village

náam – water
náam phrík – chilli sauce
náam plaa – fish sauce

náam tòk – waterfall
naga – *(nâak)* dragon-headed serpent
nákhon – also *nakhorn;* city; from the Sanskrit-Pali *nagara*
năng – Thai shadow play; movies
ngaan wát – temple fair

pàk tâi – Southern Thailand
Pali – language derived from Sanskrit in which the Buddhist scriptures are written
phâakhamáa – cotton cloth worn as a wraparound by men
phâasîn – cotton cloth worn as a wraparound by women
phrá – monk or Buddha image; an honorific term from the Pali *vara* meaning excellent
pii-phâat – classical Thai orchestra
pradesha – country
prang – Khmer-style tower on temples
prasat – *(pràasàat)* small ornate building with a cruciform ground plan and needle-like spire, used for religious purposes, located on *wát* grounds; from the Sanskrit term *prasada*

ráan aahăan mangsàwírát – vegetarian restaurant
rafflesia – parasitic leafless plant that produces flowers that can grow up to 45cm across
râi – an area of land measurement equal to 1600 sq metres
Ramakian – Thai version of India's epic literary piece, the *Ramayana*
reua hăang yao – long-tail taxi boat
reusăi – a Hindu *rishi* or sage
rishi – hermit sage, a popular figure in the Hindu-Buddhist tradition
roti – *(roh tii)* round flatbread; common street food found particularly in the South
rót nawn – transport sleepers
rót thammádaa – ordinary bus (non aircon) or ordinary train (not rapid or express)

Saakai – Negritos; an indigenous people found in small numbers in Southern Thailand and other parts of Southeast Asia; called *orang asli* in Malaysia
săamláw (samlor) – *(săam-láw)* three-wheeled pedicab

săan jâo – Chinese shrine or joss house
sala (săalaa) – an open-sided, covered meeting hall or resting place; from the Portuguese meaning room
samatha – meditation practice aimed at developing refined states of concentration
sanùk – fun
săwngthăew – literally, two rows; common name for small pickup trucks with two benches in the back, used as buses/taxis
Shivalingam – *(sìwá leung)* sculpture representing the phallus of Shiva, an object of veneration in the Hindu-Buddhist world
soi – lane or small street
Songkhran – Thai New Year, held in mid-April
stupa – a domed edifice housing Buddhist relics
sŭan aahăan – garden restaurant
suttas – discourses of the Buddha

talàat náam – floating market
tambon – also *tambol;* precinct, next subdivision below *amphoe*
tha – *(thâa)* pier, landing
thâat kràdùuk – bone reliquary, a small stupa containing remains of a Buddhist devotee
thaleh sàap – inland sea or large lake
thâm – cave
thànŏn – street/road/avenue
thêp – angel or divine being; from the Sanskrit *deva*
tôn lamphong – a hallucinogenic plant
Tripitaka – Theravada Buddhist scriptures
túk-túk – motorised *săamláw*

vipassana – Buddhist insight meditation

wâi – palms-together Thai greeting
wang – palace
wan phrá – Buddhist holy days, falling on the days of the main phases of the moon (full, new and half) each month
wát – temple-monastery; from the Pali *avasa*, meaning monk's dwelling
wíhăan – also *wihan* or *viharn;* counterpart to *bòt* in Thai temple, containing Buddha images but not circumscribed by *sema* stones; from the Sanskrit *vihara*

yam – Thai-style salad; usually made with meat or seafood

yoni – *(yoh nii)* uterus-shaped pedestal that holds the Shivalingam

Acronyms

Asean – Association of South-East Asian Nations

BMA – Bangkok Metropolitan Authority

CAT – Communications Authority of Thailand

NGO – Nongovernment Organisation

SRT – State Railway of Thailand

TAT – Tourism Authority of Thailand

THAI – Thai Airways International

WFT – Wildlife Fund Thailand

LONELY PLANET

You already know that Lonely Planet produces more than this one guidebook, but you might not be aware of the other products we have on this region. Here is a selection of titles that you may want to check out as well:

Bangkok
ISBN 1 86450 285 1

Chiang Mai & Northern Thailand
ISBN 1 74059 064 3

World Food Thailand
ISBN 1 86450 026 3

Chasing Rickshaws
ISBN 0 86442 640 2

Thai phrasebook
ISBN 0 86442 658 5

Hill Tribes phrasebook
ISBN 0 86442 635 6

Bangkok City Map
ISBN 1 86450 004 2

Thailand
ISBN 1 86450 251 7

Bangkok CitySync
www.citysync.com

Buddhist Stupas in Asia: The Shape of Perfection
ISBN 1 86450 120 0

Diving & Snorkeling Thailand
ISBN 1 86450 201 0

South-East Asia on a shoestring
ISBN 1 86450 158 8

South-East Asia phrasebook
ISBN 0 86442 435 3

Read This First: Asia & India
ISBN 1 86450 049 2

Healthy Travel: Asia & India
ISBN 1 86450 051 4

Thailand, Vietnam, Laos & Cambodia Road Atlas
ISBN 1 86450 102 2

Available wherever books are sold

Index

Abbreviations

NP National Park   NMP National Marine Park

Bold indicates maps.

Bold indicates maps.

Boxed Text

MAP LEGEND

CITY ROUTES		REGIONAL ROUTES		BOUNDARIES	
Freeway	Freeway		Freeway		International
Highway	Primary Road		Primary Road		Provincial
Road	Secondary Road		Secondary Road		Disputed
Street	Street		Minor Road		Wall
Lane	Lane				
	On/Off Ramp				

CITY ROUTES (continued)
- Unsealed Road
- One Way Street
- Pedestrian Street
- Stepped Street
- Tunnel
- Footbridge

HYDROGRAPHY
- River, Creek
- Canal
- Lake
- Spring; Waterfalls

TRANSPORT ROUTES & STATIONS
- Train
- Tram/Cable Car
- Skytrain
- Ferry
- Walking Trail
- Walking Tour
- Path
- Pier or Jetty

AREA FEATURES
- Building
- Park, Gardens
- Market
- Sports Ground
- Beach
- Cemetery
- Campus
- Plaza

POPULATION SYMBOLS

✪ CAPITAL	National Capital	● CITY	City	● Village	Village
◉ CAPITAL	Provincial Capital	● Town	Town		Urban Area

MAP SYMBOLS

■	Place to Stay	▼	Place to Eat	●	Point of Interest

✈	Airport	Cinema, Theatre	Mosque, Museum	⟂	Stupa or Chedi
	Archaeological Site	Dive Site, Snorkelling	National Park		Stately Home/Palace
	Bank, Bird Sanctuary	Embassy, Fort	Parking, Picnic Area		Surf Beach
	Border Crossing	Fountain, Golf Course	Petrol Station, Police		Taxi or Tuk-Tuk
	Bus Terminal, Stop	Hospital, Information	Post Office, Pub/Bar		Telephone
	Cafe, Camping	Internet Cafe	Sawngthaew		Temple (Buddhist)
	Cave	Lighthouse, Lookout	Shopping Centre		Temple (Hindu)
	Cathedral, Church	Mountain, Monument	Shrine (Chinese)		Temple (Sikh), Zoo

Note: not all symbols displayed above appear in this book

LONELY PLANET OFFICES

Australia
Locked Bag 1, Footscray, Victoria 3011
☎ 03 8379 8000 fax 03 8379 8111
email: talk2us@lonelyplanet.com.au

USA
150 Linden St, Oakland, CA 94607
☎ 510 893 8555 TOLL-FREE: 800 275 8555
fax 510 893 8572
email: info@lonelyplanet.com

UK
10a Spring Place, London NW5 3BH
☎ 020 7428 4800 fax 020 7428 4828
email: go@lonelyplanet.co.uk

France
1 rue du Dahomey, 75011 Paris
☎ 01 55 25 33 00 fax 01 55 25 33 01
email: bip@lonelyplanet.fr
www.lonelyplanet.fr

World Wide Web: www.lonelyplanet.com *or* AOL keyword: lp
Lonely Planet Images: lpi@lonelyplanet.com.au